M000112349

CORPORATE FINANCE

Ivo Welch

Anderson Graduate School of Management

University of California, Los Angeles

There have been numerous contributors to this book, far too many to mention individually. I appreciate the input of every one of them and apologize for not formally acknowledging their contributions here. However, I have to single out one individual: Without Mary Clare McEwing, the executive development editor in charge of the first edition, this textbook would have not come together. There is no better editor in the business. Moreover, although Prentice Hall (Pearson) no longer publishes this book, their team (led by Donna Battista) were absolutely first-rate in all respects. I appreciate their help along the way.

Website: book.ivo-welch.info
Copyright Ivo Welch, 2011. All Rights Reserved.
ISBN-10: 09840049-5-5
ISBN-13: 978-0984004959
2nd Edition to "Corporate Finance: An Introduction," ISBN-10 0321277996.

Cover Images: scripophily.com.
Software: LaTeX and R.
Fonts: Charter, Bera. Main Font: 11pt.
Paper: Glossy, 60#. Cover, 16pt.
Printer: Printing Source Inc., Marina del Rey, CA 90292.
Date: October 17, 2011

About the Author

Ivo Welch is the J. Fred Weston Professor of Finance and Economics at the Anderson Graduate School of Management at UCLA. He previously held similar positions at the Yale School of Management and the Brown University Economics Department. He received his BA in computer science from Columbia University, and both his MBA and PhD in finance from the University of Chicago. His work has been featured in many academic journals, as well as in the popular press. More information about the author can be found at book.ivo-welch.info.

This book is dedicated to my parents, Arthur and Charlotte Welch, to my wife Lily, and to my children, Arthur, Leonard and Greta.

Preface

Most corporate finance textbooks cover a similar canon of concepts, and my book is no exception. A quick glance at the table of contents will show you that most—though not all—of the topics in this book (formerly titled *Corporate Finance: An Introduction*) overlap with those in traditional finance textbooks and syllabi. That said, this book is intentionally different. It features many innovations in approach and emphasis. After you have used this book once, you will not want to go back.

This book is also an experiment in pricing. All major economics book publishers believe that professors do not care how much their textbooks cost. This book puts this belief to the test: the first edition was priced at $200; this edition is priced at $60, and it is also available for free on the web. (This price is low enough to allow many students to keep this book even after they have completed the course.) Of course, professors should adopt this book not because of its price, but because it is better than all other corporate finance textbooks on the market today.

The author raises some thought-provoking questions beyond those found in most books of this genre.
— Marianne Plunkert
University of Colorado, Denver

Innovations in Approach

Every interested and modestly talented student can understand finance. I believe that our finance concepts are no more difficult than those in standard texts covering the principles of economics and that our mathematics is no more difficult than that in high school. I believe that finance is easiest when explained from basic principles and only gradually ramped up in complexity. I also believe that, although it is important for our students to learn how to solve traditional textbook problems, it is more important for them to learn how to think about and approach new problems that they will inevitably encounter in the real world.

A Logical Progression

The book starts with simple and stylized scenarios in which solutions are easy. It then progresses to more complex and realistic scenarios in which solutions are more difficult. Within this architecture, chapters build organically on concepts learned earlier. This incremental progression allows students to reuse what they have learned and to understand the effect of each new change in and of itself.

One theme that binds the book together is the progression from the perfect-market, law-of-one-price ideal world (on which almost all finance formulas are based) to an imperfect market (in which our formulas may need explicit or implicit adjustments).

I really like the approach starting from an ideal, simple market to more realistic and complex market conditions... [this is] one of the best written and easiest to understand texts I have ever read in finance.
— Kuo Tseng
California State University, Fresno

Numerical Example Leading to Formula

I learn best by following a numerical example, and I believe that students do, too. Whenever I want to understand an idea, I try to construct numerical examples for myself—the simpler, the better. Therefore, this book relies on simple numerical examples as its primary tutorial method. Instead of a "bird's eye" view of the formula first and application second, students start with a "worm's eye" view and work their way up—from simple numbers to progressively more complex examples. (Numbers are

I like this approach very much. This is, in fact, the optimal way to learn.
— Richard Fendler
Georgia State University

often carried in "blue" to make it easier to see the progress of the numerical example.) Each step is easy. At first glance, you may think this may be less "executive" or perhaps not as well-suited to students with only a cursory interest in finance. I assure you that neither of these is the case.

Critical questions such as, "What would this project be worth?" are answered in numerical step-by-step examples, and right under the computations are the corresponding symbolic formulas. I believe that the pairing of numerics with formulas ultimately helps students understand the material both on a higher level and with more ease.

Without a doubt, this is the greatest strength of the text.
— Sharon Garrison
University of Arizona

Problem Solving

A corollary to the numbers-first approach is my belief that formulaic memorization is a last resort. Such a rote approach leaves the house without a foundation. Instead of giving students canned formulas, I try to teach them how to approach and solve problems—often by discovering the methods themselves. My goal is to teach students how to dissect new problems with a set of analytical tools that will stand them in good stead in their future careers.

The use of...simple numerical examples throughout...to explain essential concepts and formulas is outstanding.
— Effi Benmelech
Harvard University

Self-Contained

Many students come into class with a patchwork of background knowledge. Along the way, holes in their backgrounds cause some of them to get lost. Not realizing when this happened, student frustration rises. I have therefore tried to keep this book largely self-contained. For example, all necessary statistical concepts are integrated in Chapter 8 (Investor Choice: Risk and Reward), and all necessary accounting concepts are explained in Chapter 13 (From Financial Statements to Economic Cash Flows).

I think [the] approach of integrating necessary material is perfect. It helps remind students [about] what they need to know and should bolster their confidence.
— Angela Lavin
University of South Dakota

Innovations in Content and Perspective

This book also offers numerous topical and expositional innovations, of which the following is a limited selection.

A Strong Distinction between Expected and Promised Cash Flows

I clearly distinguish between the premium to compensate for default (credit risk), which is introduced in Chapter 6 (Uncertainty, Default, and Risk); and the risk premium, which is introduced in Chapter 9 (The Capital Asset Pricing Model). Students should no longer mistakenly believe that they have taken care of credit risk by discounting a promised cash flow with a CAPM expected rate of return. (If they commit this error, it would have been better if they had never taken a finance course to begin with.)

Robustness

Much more honest than other introductory books.
— Adam Gehr
DePaul University

Throughout, I describe what finance practitioners can know clearly and what they can only guess at (with varying degrees of accuracy). In the application of a number of financial tools, I point out which of the guessed uncertainties are likely to have important repercussions and which are minor in consequence. I also try to be honest about where our academic knowledge is solid and where it is shaky.

A Spotlight on the Pitfalls of Capital Budgeting

A self-contained chapter (Chapter 12: Capital Budgeting Applications and Pitfalls) describes real-world difficulties and issues in applying capital budgeting techniques, ranging from externalities to real options, to agency problems, to behavioral distortions, and so on. The chapter ends with an "NPV Checklist."

I really love the NPV Checklist. This alone makes the book stand high above the competition.

— Joe Walker
University of Alabama, Birmingham

Financials from a Finance Perspective

A self-contained accounting chapter (Chapter 13: From Financial Statements to Economic Cash Flows) explains how earnings and economic cash flows relate. When students understand the logic of corporate financial statements, they avoid a number of common mistakes that have crept into financial cash flow calculations "by tradition." In addition, a synthesizing chapter on pro formas (Chapter 20: Pro Forma Financial Statements) combines all the ingredients from previous chapters—capital budgeting, taxes, cost of capital, capital structure, and so on. Many students will be asked in their future jobs to construct pro formas, and our corporate finance curriculum has not always prepared them well enough to execute such assignments appropriately and thoughtfully.

The best discussion relating accounting to the financial inputs for valuation at this level that I have ever seen.

— Robert Hansen
Tulane University

Comparables

A chapter on comparables (Chapter 14: Valuation from Comparables and Some Financial Ratios), usually not found in other corporate finance textbooks, shows that if used properly, the comparables valuation method is a good cousin to NPV.

An Updated Perspective on Capital Structure

The academic perspective on capital structure has been changing. Here are a few of the more novel points emphasized in this book:

The [capital structure] material is current and practical—much better done than other books I have seen.

— Richard Fendler
Georgia State University

- Corporate claims do not just have cash flow rights but important control rights as well. This fact has many implications—even for one common proof of Modigliani-Miller.

- Unless the firm is close to financial distress, it probably does not matter much how the firm is financed. Project choice is likely to be far more important than the debt-equity choice. (This does not mean that access to financing is not important, just that the exact mix is not.)

- Corporate liabilities are broader than just financial debt. In fact, on average, about two-thirds of firms' liabilities are nonfinancial. The firm value is thus the sum of its financial debt and equity *plus* its nonfinancial debt (often linked to operations). Again, this can be important in a number of applications.

- Adverse selection causes a pecking order, but so do other effects. Thus, the pecking order does not necessarily imply adverse selection.

- The debate about trade-off theory today has moved to how slowly it happens—whether it takes 5 or 50 years for a firm to readjust.

- Historical stock returns are a major determinant of which firms today have high debt ratios and which have low debt ratios. A simple inspection of the evolution of IBM's capital structure from 2001 to 2003 in Chapter 15 makes this plainly obvious.

- Capital structure may not necessarily be a corporate-control device. On the contrary, equity-heavy capital structures could be the result of a breakdown of corporate control.

- Preferred equity and convertibles have become rare among publicly traded corporations over the past decade.

- A novel synthesizing figure (Exhibit 18.7) provides a conceptual basis for thinking about capital structure in imperfect markets. It shows how APV fits with other non-tax-related imperfections.

Basic Organization

Essential Corporate Finance covers all the topics of the usual corporate finance curriculum. However, as noted above, the organizing principle of moving from perfect to imperfect markets unifies the core chapters. This progression from financial "utopia" to the complex real world is especially apparent in the first three parts of the book and is revisited multiple times in Part V on capital structure.

...The transition from perfect to imperfect markets makes a lot of sense... and is consistent with the overall theme of the book, which is starting with simple concepts and gradually introducing more complex, realistic elements. I... like to structure my lectures according to similar logic.

— Evgeny Lyandres
Boston University

Part I: Value and Capital Budgeting shows how to work with rates of return and how to decide whether to take or reject projects in a perfect market under risk neutrality. Five chapters lay out the basics of the time value of money, net present value, valuation of perpetuities and annuities, capital budgeting, interest rates, uncertainty, and debt and equity in the absence of risk aversion.

Part II: Risk and Return introduces risk aversion and shows how it creates a relation between risk and expected returns in a perfect market. It first provides a historical backdrop of rates of return on various asset classes and some institutional background. It then proceeds to the key concepts of risk, reward, and diversification from an investor's perspective, and culminates with a discussion of the Capital Asset Pricing Model.

Part III: Value and Market Efficiency in an Imperfect Market describes what happens if the perfect market assumptions do not hold in our messier real world. Although the perfect market assumptions form the basis of most finance formulas (such as NPV and the CAPM) and have facilitated the development of finance into a modern science, they are not always realistic. Thus, in this part, two chapters examine the reality of information differences, noncompetitive markets, transaction costs, and taxes. The differences between efficient and inefficient markets, and between rational and behavioral finance, are also explained.

Part IV: Real-World Application puts the theory to work in three chapters. It shows that although the financial concepts may be simple, their application can be complex. This part examines a wide range of issues and pitfalls to consider when putting NPV and IRR to work, looks at financial statement analysis from a finance perspective, and considers the valuation technique of comparables.

Part V: Capital Structure and Payout Policy considers the capital structure that firms should choose. It starts again with a perfect-market theme and then shows in five chapters how this should play out in an imperfect world of corporate taxes and other issues. Some market imperfections should push firms toward more equity and others toward more debt.

Part VI: Projecting the Future shows how to think about the construction of pro formas. In a certain sense, it is what much of corporate finance is all about.

The Companion

The second edition of the book is disciplined in keeping only enough content to fit the essential first course in finance. This keeps the book to about 700 pages. Other material—no less important but impossible to cover in a first course—is now layed out into a companion book. This 300-page companion is available at cost. (This means an on-demand book print for $25, and online accessibility for free.) Instructors can also print and distribute individual chapters. Formatting and quality are the same as they are in this primary book. The companion includes such chapters as "International Finance," which are a necessary checkbox for AACSB accreditation—but which no introductory finance course has ever found time to cover.

The companion includes more detailed coverage of capital structure dynamics (Chapter 21), capital structure patterns in the United States (Chapter 22), Investment Banking and Mergers & Acquisitions (Chapter 23), Corporate Governance (Chapter 24), International Finance (Chapter 25), and Options and Risk Management (Chapter 26). It also includes appendices to Chapter 5 (how to extract and lock in forward rates, how to calculate bond durations, how to hedge interest risk, how to compound continuously, and how Treasuries are quoted in the real world); Chapter 8 (more explanations for the efficient frontier); and Chapter 9 (certainty equivalence, two-portfolio separation, the relation between the mean-variance efficient frontier and the CAPM, and available CAPM alternatives, such as the APT); Chapter 11 (an event study); Chapter 12 (more real-option decision trees); Chapter 13 (the Coca-Cola financials); Chapter 16 (how CAPM, WACC, and NPV fit); and Chapter 17 (how to think of the discount factor on tax obligations and on the tax shelter effect of debt). Each chapter appendix is briefly previewed in the main text. Finally, the book's website (book.ivo-welch.info) has a chapter on quantitative real option implementation and a provocative chapter on ethics.

Specific Changes for the Second Edition

- (All:) As just noted, the book has been restructured into this main text and a companion book. The companion contains all chapter appendices (the chapters themselves tell the reader what is in the companion; the companion is of course free on the web, too, just like the book); and chapters that would not fit into a one-semester course.

- (All:) Questions and answers were checked *again*. Some ambiguities in the questions were eliminated. Some questions were deleted because they were too hard. A few other questions were added.

- (All:) The book was updated to explain aspects of the 2008-9 financial crisis.

- (All:) Many figures were updated to 2010.
- (All:) Many small improvements and updates to more recent data throughout.
- (Ch6,16,etc.:) The "house" example was rewritten. The numbers are "nicer" now.
- (Ch6:) The text now mentions that Treasuries were downgraded by S&P in August 2011. The text still treats Treasuries as the risk-free benchmark, a reasonable but not indisputable assumption.
- (Ch8:) The investor choice chapter was rewritten—the example numbers are "nicer" now. The graphical illustrations are clearer. The efficient frontier and "time-changes to risk" were rewritten and integrated.
- (Ch9:) The CAPM figures and descriptions were improved.
- (Ch11:) The full event study (on the Congressional election) migrated into the companion.
- (Ch12:) The "project interactions" were rewritten. Corporate governance was enhanced.
- (Ch13:) The section "what to believe on a balance sheet" was added.
- (Ch14:) Much of the comparables chapter was enhanced. The empirical data was updated.
- (Ch17,Ch18:) The "personal taxes" aspects of capital structure moved from Ch18 to Ch17, where they are described together with corporate taxes.
- (Ch19) The dividend event study was updated.

As the author, my goal for future editions is to converge to the best stable finance textbook. Updates should be necessitated by academic progress and changes in the economy, and not by the need to suppress the resale market. I did not write this textbook to maximize my own finances, but to influence how financial economics is taught. It was a labor of love. I believe that it is the best and most logical way to teach finance today. I hope you will agree.

Ivo Welch
Anderson Graduate School of Management
University of California, Los Angeles
September 2011

Contents

Part V   Capital Structure and Payout Policy   459

Chapter 15   Corporate Claims   461

Chapter 16   Capital Structure in a Perfect Market   491

Chapter 17   Taxes and Capital Structure   523

Chapter 18   More Imperfect-Market Capital Structure   569

Introduction

What Finance is All About

Finance is such an important part of modern life that almost everyone can benefit from understanding it better. What you may find surprising is that the financial problems facing *PepsiCo* or *Microsoft* are not really different from those facing an average investor, small business owner, entrepreneur, or family. On the most basic level, these problems are about how to allocate money. The choices are many: Money can be borrowed, saved, or lent. Money can be invested into projects. Projects can be undertaken with partners or with the aid of lenders. Projects can be avoided altogether if they do not appear to be valuable enough. Finance is about deciding among these and other investment alternatives—and this textbook will explain how.

1.1 The Goal of Finance: Relative Valuation

There is one principal theme that carries through all of finance: *value*. What exactly is a particular object worth? To make smart decisions, you must be able to assess value—and the better you can assess value, the smarter your decisions will be.

Theme number one of this book is *value*! Make decisions based on value.

The main reason why you need to estimate value is that you will want to buy objects whose values are above their costs and avoid those where it is the reverse. Sounds easy? If it were only so. In practice, finding a good value (**valuation**) is often very difficult. But it is not the formulas that are difficult—even the most complex formulas in this book contain just a few symbols, and the overwhelming majority of finance formulas use only the five major operations (addition, subtraction, multiplication, division, and exponentiation). Admittedly, even if the formulas themselves are not sophisticated, there are a lot of them, and they have an intuitive economic meaning that requires experience to grasp. But if you managed to pass high-school algebra, and if you are motivated, you will be able to handle the math. Math is *not* the real difficulty in valuation.

Everyone needs to know how to value objects.

Instead, the big difficulties lie in the real world, beyond finance theory. You often have to decide how you should judge the future—whether your gizmo will be a hit or a bust, whether the economy will enter a recession or not, where you will find product markets, how you can advertise, how interest rates or the stock market will move, and on and on. This book will explain what you should forecast and how you should use your forecasts in the best way, but it mostly remains up to you to make these forecasts. Putting this more positively, if forecasts and valuation were easy, a computer could take

The tough aspect about valuation is the real world, not the theory.

over this job. This will never happen. Valuation will always remain a matter of both art and science, which requires judgment and common sense. The formulas and finance in this book are necessary tools to help you convert your reasoned, informed, and intuitive assessments into good decisions. But they are not enough.

The Law of One Price

The law of one price. Valuing objects is easier in relative terms.

So how do you assess value? Most of finance and thus most of this book is based on the **law of one price**. It states that two identical items at the same venue should cost the same. Otherwise, why would anyone buy the more expensive item? This means that value in finance is defined in *relative* terms. The reason is that it is easier to determine whether an object is worth more or less than equivalent alternatives, than it is to put an absolute value on it.

A car example.

For example, consider the value of a car—say, a 2007 Toyota Camry—that you own. If you can find other cars that are identical to your Camry—at least along all dimensions that matter—then it should be worth the same and sell for the same price. Fortunately, for a 2007 Toyota Camry, this is not too difficult. There are many other 2007 Toyota Camries, as well as 2006 Toyota Camries, 2008 Toyota Camries, and 2007 Honda Accords, that you can readily purchase. If there are 10 other exact equivalents on the same block for sale, your valuation task is outright trivial.

Mistakes, both too low and too high, are costly.

What would happen if you make a mistake in valuing your Camry? If you put too low a value on your car, you would sell it too cheaply. If you put too high a value on your car, you would not be able to sell it. Naturally, you want to get the value right.

Don't forget about "opportunity costs."

A related way of thinking about your Camry versus the alternatives is that your Camry has an "opportunity cost." Your ownership of the Camry is not free. Ignoring transaction costs, your opportunity is to sell your car and purchase another Camry, or Accord, or anything else with this money. Let's say that the Accord is your alternative, and it is equivalent in all dimensions that matter. If someone were to offer to pay $1,000 above the Accord value for your Camry, the price would be above your opportunity cost. You should then sell the Camry, buy the Accord, and gain $1,000.

Approximations: Similar goods that are not perfectly the same.

The law of one price rarely applies perfectly. But it often applies imperfectly. For example, your Camry may have 65,334 miles on it, be green, and be located in Providence, RI. The comparable cars may have between 30,000 and 50,000 miles on them, feature different colors, and be located in other spots on the East Coast. In this case, the law of one price no longer works exactly. Instead, it should hold only approximately. That is, your car may not be worth the same exact amount as your comparables, but it should be worth a similar amount, perhaps using a few sensible price adjustments.

In the absence of similar objects, valuation is more difficult.

The task of valuing objects becomes more difficult when you are unable (or not allowed) to find similar objects for which you know the value. If you had to value your 2007 Camry based on knowledge of the value of plasma televisions, vacations, or pencils, then your valuation task would be much more difficult. Common sense implies that it is easier to value objects relative to close comparable objects than to objects that are very different. In the real world, some objects are intrinsically easy to value; others are not.

Q 1.1. Discuss how easy it is to put a value on the following objects:

1. An envelope containing foreign currency—say, 10,000 euros
2. Paintings
3. The Washington Monument
4. Manhattan
5. The Chrysler Building in New York
6. Foreign stamps
7. Love
8. Yourself
9. The species chimpanzee, or the Yangtze river dolphin

1.2 Investments, Projects, and Firms

The most basic object in finance is the project. As far as finance is concerned, every **project** is a set of flows of money (**cash flows**). Most projects require an up-front cash outflow (an **investment** or **expense** or **cost**) and are followed by a series of later cash inflows (**payoffs** or **revenues** or **returns**). It does not matter whether the cash flows come from hauling garbage or selling Prada handbags. Cash is cash. However, it is important that all costs and benefits are included as cash values. If you have to spend a lot of time hauling trash, which you find distasteful, then you have to translate your dislike into an equivalent cash negative. Similarly, if you want to do a project "for the fun of it," you must translate your "fun" into a cash positive. The discipline of finance takes over after all positives and negatives (inflows and outflows) from the project "black box" have been translated into their appropriate monetary cash values.

To value projects, make sure to use all costs and benefits, including opportunity costs and pleasure benefits.

A N E C D O T E   **The Joy of Cooking: Positive Prestige Flows and Restaurant Failures**

In New York City, two out of every five new restaurants close within one year. Nationwide, the best estimates suggest that about 90% of all restaurants close within two years. If successful, the average restaurant earns a return of about 10% per year. One explanation for why so many entrepreneurs are continuing to open up restaurants, despite seemingly low financial rates of return, is that restaurateurs enjoy owning a restaurant so much that they are willing to buy the prestige of owning one. If this is the case, then to value the restaurant, you must factor in how much the restaurateur is willing to pay for the prestige of owning it, just as you would factor in the revenues that restaurant patrons generate.

This does not mean that the operations of the firm—issues like manufacturing, inventory, sales, marketing, payables, working capital, competition, and so on—are unimportant. On the contrary, these business factors are all of the utmost importance in making the cash flows happen, and a good (financial) manager must understand them. After all, even if all you care about are cash flows, it is impossible to understand them well if you have no idea where they come from and how they could change in the future.

What is in the black box "project" is not trivial, but we won't cover much of it.

Cash flows must
include (quantify)
nonfinancial benefits.

Projects need not be physical. For example, a company may have a project called "customer relations," with real cash outflows today and uncertain future inflows. You (a student) can be viewed as a project: You pay for education (a cash outflow) and will earn a salary in the future (a cash inflow). If you value the prestige that the degree will offer, you should also put a cash value on it. Then, this too will count as another cash inflow. In addition, some of the payoffs from education are metaphysical rather than physical. If you like making friends in school or if knowledge provides you with pleasure, either today or in the future, then education yields a value that should be regarded as a positive cash flow. (The discipline of finance makes it easy on itself by asking *you* to put a hard cash value number on these or any other emotional factors.) Of course, for some students, the distaste of learning should be factored in as a cost (equivalent cash outflow)—but I trust that you are not one of them. All such nonfinancial flows must be appropriately translated into cash equivalents if you want to arrive at a good project valuation.

In finance, firms are
basically collections of
projects.

In finance, a **firm** is viewed as a collection of projects. This book assumes that the value of a firm is the value of all its projects' net cash flows, and nothing else. Actually, the metaphor can also extend to a family. Your family may own a house, a car, have tuition payments, education investments, and so on—a collection of projects.

The firm is the sum of
all its inflows and all
its outflows. Stocks
and bonds are just
projects with inflows
and outflows.

There are two important specific kinds of projects that you may consider investing in—**bonds** and **stocks**, also called **debt** and **equity**. These are financial **claims** that the firm usually sells to investors. As you will learn later, you can mostly think of buying a stock as the equivalent of becoming an owner. You can think of buying a bond as the equivalent of lending money to the issuer. In effect, a bondholder is just a creditor. For example, a firm may sell a lender a $100 bond in exchange for a promised payment of $110 next year. (If the firm were to perform poorly, the bond would have to be paid off first, so it is less risky for an investor than the firm's equity. However, it has limited upside.) In addition, the firm usually has other obligations, such as money that it has to pay to its suppliers (called "payables"). Together, if you own all outstanding claims on the firm, that is, all obligations and all stock, then you own the firm. This logic is not deep—simply speaking, there is nobody else: "You are it."

$$\text{Entire Firm} \; = \; \text{All Outstanding Stocks} + \text{All Outstanding Liabilities}$$

As the 100% owner of a firm, you own all its stocks, bonds, and other obligations. Your entire firm then does its business and hopefully earns money. It does not need to pay out immediately what it earns, though. It can reinvest the money. Regardless of what the firm does, you still own it in its entirety.

A firm is all inflows
and outflows, too.

This means you own all net cash flows that the firm earns, after adjusting for all your necessary investments.

$$\text{Entire Firm} \; = \; \text{All (Current and Future) } \textit{Net} \text{ Earnings}$$

Yet another way to look at the firm is to recognize that you will receive all the net cash flows that the firm will pay out (e.g., interest payments or dividends), adjusting, of course, for all the money that you may put into the firm in the future.

Entire Firm = All (Current and Future Cash) Inflows – Outflows

It follows immediately that all the payments satisfying stocks and liabilities must be equal to all the firm's net cash flows, which must be equal to the firm's net payouts. All of these equalities really just state the same thing: "Value adds up."

Our book will spend a lot of time discussing claims, and especially the debt and equity forms of financing—but for now, you can consider both debt and equity to be just simple investment projects: You put money in, and they pay money out. For many stock and bond investments that you can buy and sell in the financial markets, it is reasonable to assume that most investors enjoy very few, if any, non-cash-based benefits (such as emotional attachment).

We emphasize stocks and bonds.

Q 1.2. In computing the cost of your M.B.A., should you take into account the loss of salary while going to school? Cite a few nonmonetary benefits that you reap as a student, too, and try to attach monetary value to them.

Q 1.3. If you purchase a house and live in it, what are your inflows and outflows?

1.3 Firms versus Individuals

This book is primarily about teaching concepts that apply to firms. In particular, if you are reading this, your goal will be to learn how you should determine projects' values, given appropriate cash flows. What is your best tool? The law of one price, of course.

We use the same principles in corporate finance as in "home economics."

The same logic that applies to your Camry applies to corporate projects in the real world. Many have close comparables that make such relative valuation feasible. For example, say you want to put a value on building a new factory in Rhode Island. You have many alternatives: You could look at the values of similar existing or potential factories in Massachusetts. Or you could look at the values of similar factories in Mexico. Or you could look at how much it would cost just to purchase the net output of the factory from another company. Or you could determine how much money you could earn if you invested your money instead in the bank or the stock market. If you understand how to estimate your factory's value *relative to your other opportunities*, you then know whether you should build it or not. But not all projects are easy to value in relative terms. For example, what would be the value of building a tunnel across the Atlantic, of controlling global warming, or of terraforming Mars to make it habitable for humans? There are no easy alternative objects to compare such projects to, so any valuation would inevitably be haphazard.

Relative valuation often works well in the corporate world.

If a corporation can determine the value of projects, then it can determine whether it should take or pass up on them. In the first part of this book, where we assume that the world is perfect (which will be explained in a moment), you will learn that projects have a unique value and firms should take all projects that add value (in an absolute sense). Later on, the world will become more realistic, and you will recognize that projects can have a value that is different for some firms than it is for others. In this case, you must take your specific firm's position into account when deciding whether you should take or leave projects.

Value in the corporate context can depend on the quality of the market.

Separation of ownership and management (control).

An interesting aspect of corporate decision making is that the owners are often not the managers. Instead, the managers are hired professionals. For a publicly traded corporation that may have millions of shareholder owners, even the decision to hire managers is de facto no longer made by the owners, but by their representatives and by other managers.

Managers should do what owners want—value maximization!?

Unfortunately, it is just not feasible for managers simply to ask all the owners what they want. Therefore, one of the basic premises of finance is that owners expect their managers to maximize the value of the firm. You will learn that, in a perfect world, managers always know how to do this. However, in the world we live in, this can sometimes be difficult. How should a manager act if some owners dislike investing in cigarettes, yet others believe that the firm has great opportunities in selling green tea, yet others believe the firm should build warships, yet others believe the firm should just put all the money into the bank, and yet others believe the firm should return all their money to them? These are among the more intriguing problems that this book covers.

Ethical dilemmas.

The need for managers to decide on appropriate objectives also raises some interesting ethical concerns, most of which are beyond the scope of this book. But let me mention one anyway. As I just noted, the standard view is that corporations are set up to maximize the wealth of their owners. It is the government's job to create rules that constrain corporations to do so only within ethically appropriate boundaries. Thus, some will argue that it is the role of public institutions to pass laws that reduce the sale of products that kill (e.g., cigarettes), not the role of the corporation to abstain from selling them. If nothing else, they argue, if your corporation does not sell them, someone else almost surely will. (You can see this as a framework to help you understand corporations, not a normative opinion on what the moral obligations of companies should be. Nevertheless, it is also a view that many people have adopted as their normative perspective.) As if selling harmful products were not a complex enough dilemma, consider that laws are often passed by legislators who receive donations from tobacco corporations. (Indeed, public institutions are intentionally set up to facilitate such two-way "communications.") What are the moral obligations of tobacco firm owners, their corporations, and their managers now? Fortunately, you first need to learn about value maximization before you are ready to move on to these tougher questions. For the most part, this book sticks with the view that value maximization is the corporation's main objective.

Let's get rolling.

Let's begin looking at how you should estimate project value.

Q 1.4. Can you use the "law of one price" in your decision of whether to take or reject projects?

Q 1.5. What is the main objective of corporate managers that this book assumes?

Keywords

Bond, 12. Cash flow, 3. Claim, 4. Cost, 3. Debt, 134. Equity, 462. Expense, 379. Firm, 4. Investment, 3. Law of one price, 29. Payoff, 3. Project, 3. Return, 13. Revenue, 383. Stock, 462. Valuation, 1.

Answers

Q 1.1 Here are my own judgment calls.

1. Easy. There are many foreign currency transactions, so you can easily figure out how many U.S. dollars you can get for 10,000 euros. You can find this exchange rate on many web sites, e.g., **YAHOO!** FINANCE (http://finance.yahoo.com).

2. Depends. Some paintings are easier to value than others. For example, Warhol painted similar works repeatedly, and the price of one may be a good indication for the price of others. For other paintings, this can be very hard. What is the value of the *Mona Lisa,* for example? There are other da Vincis that may help, but ultimately, the *Mona Lisa* is unique.

3. The Washington Monument is more than just the value of its closest alternative—which would be rebuilding it elsewhere. This may or may not be easy.

4. Many individual buildings in Manhattan have sold, so you have good comparables for the individual components (buildings). However, no one has attempted to purchase a world center like Manhattan, which means that it may be difficult to estimate it accurately.

5. The Chrysler Building would be relatively easy to value. There are many similar buildings that have changed hands in the last few years.

6. Foreign stamps are harder to value than foreign currency, but probably not that much harder. Stamp collectors know and usually publish the prices at which the same stamps have traded in the past years.

7. Love—oh, dear.

8. Valuing yourself is a tough issue. You can look at yourself as a collection of cash flows, similar to other "walking cash flows," but doing so is highly error-prone. Nevertheless, having no other opportunities, this is how insurance companies attach a value to life in court. You may consider yourself more unique and irreplaceable. Still, you can infer your own value for your life by figuring out how willing you are to take the risk of losing it—e.g., by crossing the street, snowboarding, or motorcycling. I have also read that doctors work out what the value of all the proteins in your body are, which comes out to be many million dollars. Physicists, on the other hand, break down the proteins further and come up with an estimate that is less than a dollar.

9. This is a very difficult task. We know that governments have spent a great amount of cash trying to preserve the environment in order to help species. The Yangtze river dolphin, however, just recently became extinct, primarily due to human activity. What is the value of this loss? Unfortunately, we don't have good comparables.

Q 1.2 Definitely yes. Forgone salary is a cost that you are bearing. This can be reasonably estimated, and many economic consulting firms regularly do so. As to (partly) nonmonetary benefits, there is the reputation that the degree bestows on you, the education that betters you, and the pleasure that excessive beer consumption gives you (if applicable).

Q 1.3 Inflows: Value of implicit rent. Capital gain if house appreciates. Outflows: Maintenance costs. Transaction costs. Mortgage costs. Real estate tax. Uninsured potential losses. Capital loss if house depreciates. And so on.

Q 1.4 Often, absolutely yes. Indeed, the law of one price is the foundation upon which all project choice is based.

Q 1.5 Maximizing the value of the firm.

End of Chapter Problems

Q 1.6. What is the law of one price?

Q 1.7. A degree program costs $50,000 in total expenses: $30,000 in tuition and $20,000 in housing and books. The U.S. government provides a $10,000 grant for the tuition. Moreover, the university pays $20,000 of the $30,000 tuition in salary to your instructors. Because being in the program is so much fun, you would be willing to pay a net of $5,000 for the pleasure, relative to your alternatives. What is the net cost of the education to you?

Q 1.8. What is the difference between investing in the stock and investing in the bond of a corporation? Which one is the less risky investment and why?

Q 1.9. What is the difference between the value of the firm and the sum of the values of all outstanding obligations and all outstanding stocks?

Part I

Value and Capital Budgeting

...in a Perfect Market under Risk Neutrality

The two primary goals of this first part of the book (Chapters 2–6) are to explain how to work with rates of return and how to decide whether to accept or reject investment projects. We assume in this part that there are no taxes, no transaction costs, no disagreements, and no limits as to the number of sellers and buyers in the market. This is the so-called perfect market. I will explain later why a perfect market makes your life a lot easier.

What You Want to Learn in this Part

- In Chapter 2, we start with the simplest possible scenario. In addition to the perfect market, we assume that there is no uncertainty: You know everything. And we assume that all rates of return in the economy are the same: A 1-year investment pays the same and perfectly known rate of return per annum as a 10-year investment. Under these assumptions, you learn how 1-year returns translate into multiyear returns and when you should accept or reject a project. The chapter introduces the important concept of "present value."

  Typical questions: If you earn 5% per year, how much will you earn over 10 years? If you earn 100% over 10 years, how much will you earn per year? What is the value of a project that will deliver $1,000,000 in 10 years? Should you buy this project if it cost you $650,000? What inputs do you need to decide this?

- In Chapter 3, you learn how to value particular kinds of projects—perpetuities and annuities—if the economy-wide interest rate remains constant. You then learn how to apply the formulas to the valuation of stocks and bonds. The popular Gordon dividend growth model for valuing stocks assumes that dividends are a simple growing perpetuity cash flow stream, which makes it a perfect application of the perpetuity formula. Mortgages and other bonds are good applications of pricing using the annuities formulas.

  Typical questions: If a firm pays $1/share dividends next year, growing by 3% per year forever, then what should its stock price be? What is the monthly payment for a $300,000 mortgage bond if the interest rate is 4% per year?

- In Chapter 4, you learn more about capital budgeting methods. Although net present value (NPV) is the correct method, at least one other common method often comes to the correct result: the internal rate of return. In the real world, a number of other plainly incorrect methods are also widely used. You should know why you should be wary of them. This chapter also tells you what CFOs actually rely on.

Typical questions: If a project has one investment outflow and two return inflows, how would you compute a "rate of return"? Can you accept projects whose rates of return are above their cost of capital? How bad is it when you use incorrect estimates—as you inevitably will—in your calculations? What are the big problems with a rule that accepts those projects that return money most quickly?

- In Chapter 5, you abandon the assumption that annual rates of return are the same for projects with different durations. For example, 1-year investments may pay 2% per year, while 10-year investments may pay 5% per year. The scenario of time-varying rates of return is more realistic, but the questions that you want to answer still remain the same as those in Chapter 2. (The chapter then also explains more advanced aspects of bonds, such as the Treasury yield curve.)

Typical questions: If you earn 5% in the first year and 10% in the second year, how much will you earn over both years? What is the meaning of a 4% annualized interest rate? What is the meaning of a 4% yield-to-maturity? How can you value projects if appropriate rates of return depend on different time horizons?

- In Chapter 6, you abandon the assumption that you know the future. To be able to study un-

certainty in the real world, you must first learn how to describe it. This is done with statistics, the necessary aspects of which are also explained here. The chapter then introduces risk neutrality, which is an assumption that can make it easier to understand some concepts in finance under uncertainty. Perhaps the two most important concepts are the difference between promised and expected rates of return and the difference between debt and equity. Under uncertainty, a project may not return the promised amount. Because of the possibility of default, the *stated* rate of return must be higher than the *expected* rate of return. Although you are interested in the latter, it is almost always only the former that you are quoted (promised). It is important that you always draw a sharp distinction between promised (stated) rates of return and expected rates of return. The second concept that this chapter explains is the difference between debt and equity—corporate claims that have a meaningful difference only under uncertainty.

Typical questions: If there is a 2% chance that your borrower will not return the money, how much extra interest should you charge? From an investment perspective, what is the difference between debt and equity? What is financing priority? What is a residual claim?

Looking ahead, Part II will continue with uncertainty scenarios in which investors are risk averse. Part III will explain what happens when financial markets or decision rules are not perfect.

Present Value

The Mother of All Finance

We begin with the concept of a rate of return—the cornerstone of finance. You can always earn an interest rate (and interest rates are rates of return) by depositing your money today into the bank. This means that money today is more valuable than the same amount of money next year. This concept is called the *time value of money*—$1 in present value is better than $1 in future value.

Investors make up just one side of the financial markets. They give money today in order to receive money in the future. Firms make up the other side. The process firms use to decide what to do with their money—which projects to take and which projects to pass up—is called *capital budgeting*. You will learn that there is one best method for making this critical decision. The firm should translate all *future* cash flows—both inflows and outflows— into their equivalent *present values* today. Adding in the cash flow today gives the *net present value*, or NPV. The firm should take all projects that have positive net present values and reject all projects that have negative net present values.

This all sounds more complex than it is, so we'd better get started.

2.1 The Basic Scenario

As promised, we begin with the simplest possible scenario. In finance, this means that we assume that we are living in a so-called **perfect market**:

We start with a so-called perfect market.

- There are no taxes.

- There are no transaction costs (costs incurred when buying and selling).

- There are no differences in information or opinions among investors (although there can be risk).

- There are so many buyers and sellers (investors and firms) in the market that the presence or absence of just one (or a few) individuals does not have an influence on the price.

The perfect market allows us to focus on the basic concepts in their purest forms, without messy real-world factors complicating the exposition. We will use these assumptions as our sketch of how financial markets operate, though not necessarily how firms' product markets work. You will learn in Chapter 10 how to operate in a world that is not perfect. (This will be a lot messier.)

In early chapters only,
we add even stronger
assumptions.

In this chapter, we will make three additional assumptions (that are not required for a market to be considered "perfect") to further simplify the world:

- There is no risk or uncertainty. You have perfect foresight.

- There is no inflation.

- The interest rate per period is the same.

Of course, this financial utopia is unrealistic. However, the tools that you will learn in this chapter will also work in later chapters, where the world becomes not only progressively more realistic but also more difficult. Conversely, if any tool does not give the right answer in our simple world, it would surely make no sense in a more realistic one.

Q 2.1. What are the four perfect market assumptions?

2.2 Loans and Bonds

Finance jargon: interest, loan, bond, fixed income, maturity.

The material in this chapter is easiest to explain in the context of bonds and loans. A **loan** is the commitment of a borrower to pay a predetermined amount of cash at one or more predetermined times in the future (the final one called **maturity**), usually in exchange for cash up-front today. Loosely speaking, the difference between the money lent and the money paid back is the **interest** that the lender earns. A **bond** is a particular kind of loan, so named because it "binds" the borrower to pay money. Thus, for an investor, "buying a bond" is the same as "extending a loan." Bond buying is the process of giving cash today and receiving a promise for money in the future. Similarly, from the firm's point of view, it is "giving a bond," "issuing a bond," or "selling a bond." Loans and bonds are also sometimes called **fixed income**, because they "promise" a fixed amount of payments to the holder of the bond.

Why learn bonds first? Because they are easiest.

You should view a bond as just another type of investment project—money goes in, and money comes out. *You could slap the name "corporate project" on the cash flows in the examples in this chapter, and nothing would change.* In Chapter 5, you will learn more about Treasuries, which are bonds issued by the U.S. Treasury. The beauty of such bonds is that you know exactly what your cash flows will be. (Despite Washington's dysfunction, we will assume that Treasuries cannot default.) Besides, much more capital in the economy is tied up in bonds and loans than is tied up in stocks, so understanding bonds well is very useful in itself.

Interest rates: limited upside. Rates of return: arbitrary upside.

You already know that the net return on a loan is called interest, and that the rate of return on a loan is called the **interest rate**—though we will soon firm up your knowledge about interest rates. One difference between an interest payment and a noninterest payment is that the former usually has a maximum payment, whereas the latter can have unlimited upside potential. However, not every rate of return is an interest rate. For example, an investment in a lottery ticket is not a loan, so it does not offer an interest rate, just a rate of return. In real life, its payoff is uncertain—it could be anything from zero to an unlimited amount. The same applies to stocks and many corporate projects. Many of our examples use the phrase "interest rate," even though the examples almost always work for any other rates of return, too.

Is there any difference between buying a bond for $1,000 and putting $1,000 into a bank savings account? Yes, a small one. The bond is defined by its future promised payoffs—say, $1,100 next year—and the bond's value and price today are based on these future payoffs. But as the bond owner, you know exactly how much you will receive next year. An investment in a bank savings account is defined by its investment today. The interest rate can and will change every day, so you do not know what you will end up with next year. The exact amount depends on future interest rates. For example, it could be $1,080 (if interest rates decrease) or $1,120 (if interest rates increase).

If you want, you can think of a savings account as a sequence of consecutive 1-day bonds: When you deposit money, you buy a 1-day bond, for which you know the interest rate this one day in advance, and the money automatically gets reinvested tomorrow into another bond with whatever the interest rate will be tomorrow.

> Bond: defined by payment next year. Savings: defined by deposit this year.

> A bank savings account is like a sequence of 1-day bonds.

Q 2.2. Is a deposit into a savings account more like a long-term bond investment or a series of short-term bond investments?

2.3 Returns, Net Returns, and Rates of Return

The most fundamental financial concept is that of a return. The payoff or (dollar) **return** of an investment is simply the amount of cash (C) it returns. For example, an investment project that returns $12 at time 1 has

> Defining return and our time. Our convention is that 0 means "right now."

$$C_1 = \text{Return at Time 1} = \$12$$

The subscript is an instant in time, usually abbreviated by the letter t. When exactly time 1 occurs is not important: It could be tomorrow, next month, or next year. But if we mean "right now," we use the subscript 0.

The net payoff, or **net return**, is the difference between the return and the initial investment. It is positive if the project is profitable and negative if it is unprofitable. For example, if the investment costs $10 today and returns $12 at time 1 with nothing in between, then it earns a net return of $2. Notation-wise, we need to use two subscripts on returns—the time when the investment starts (0) and when it ends (1).

> Defining net return and rate of return.

$$\text{Net Return from Time 0 to Time 1} = \$12 - \$10 = \$2$$
$$\text{Net Return}_{0,1} = C_1 - C_0$$

The double subscripts are painful. Let's agree that if we omit the first subscript on flows, it means zero. The **rate of return**, usually abbreviated r, is the net return expressed as a percentage of the initial investment.

$$\text{Rate of Return} \atop \text{from Time 0 to Time 1} = \frac{\$2}{\$10} = 20\%$$

$$r_{0,1} = r_1 = \frac{\text{Net Return from Time 0 to Time 1}}{\text{Purchase Price at Time 0}}$$

where I use our new convention and abbreviate $r_{0,1}$ as r_1. Often, it is convenient to calculate the rate of return as

$$r_1 = \frac{\$12 - \$10}{\$10} = \frac{\$12}{\$10} - 1 = 20\%$$

$$r_1 = \frac{C_1 - C_0}{C_0} = \frac{C_1}{C_0} - 1 \tag{2.1}$$

Percent (the symbol %) is a unit of $1/100$. So 20% is the same as 0.20.

A N E C D O T E   **Interest Rates over the Millennia**

Historical interest rates are fascinating, perhaps because they look so similar to today's interest rates. Nowadays, typical interest rates range from 2% to 20% (depending on other factors). For over 2,500 years, from about the thirtieth century B.C.E. to the sixth century B.C.E., normal interest rates in Sumer and Babylonia hovered around 10–25% per annum, though 20% was the legal maximum. In ancient Greece, interest rates in the sixth century B.C.E. were about 16–18%, dropping steadily to about 8% by the turn of the millennium. Interest rates in ancient Egypt tended to be about 10–12%. In ancient Rome, interest rates started at about 8% in the fifth century B.C.E. but began to increase to about 12% by the third century A.C.E. (a time of great upheaval). When lending resumed in the late Middle Ages (twelfth century), personal loans in England fetched about 50% per annum, though they tended to hover between 10–20% in the rest of Europe. By the Renaissance, commercial loan rates had fallen to 5–15% in Italy, the Netherlands, and France. By the seventeenth century, even English interest rates had dropped to 6–10% in the first half, and to 3–6% in the second half. (And mortgage rates were even lower.) Most of the American Revolution was financed with French and Dutch loans at interest rates of 4–5%.

Homer and Sylla, A History of Interest Rates

How to compute returns with interim payments. Capital gains versus returns. Many investments have interim payments. For example, many stocks pay interim cash **dividends**, many bonds pay interim cash **coupons**, and many real estate investments pay interim rent. How would you calculate the rate of return then? One simple method is to just add interim payments to the numerator. Say an investment costs $92, pays a dividend of $5 (at the end of the period), and then is worth $110. Its rate of return is

$$r = \frac{\$110 + \$5 - \$92}{\$92} = \frac{\$110 - \$92}{\$92} + \frac{\$5}{\$92} = 25\%$$

$$r_1 = \frac{C_1 + \text{All Dividends from 0 to 1} - C_0}{C_0} = \underbrace{\frac{C_1 - C_0}{C_0}}_{\text{Capital Gain, in \%}} + \underbrace{\frac{\text{All Dividends}}{C_0}}_{\text{Dividend Yield}}$$

When there are intermittent payments and final payments, then returns are often broken down into two additive parts. The first part, the price change or **capital gain**, is the difference between the purchase price and the final price, *not* counting interim payments.

Here, the capital gain is the difference between $110 and $92, that is, the $18 change in the price of the investment. It is often quoted in percent of the price, which would be $18/$92 or 19.6% here. The second part is the amount received in interim payments. It is the dividend or coupon or rent, here $5. When it is divided by the price, it has names like **dividend yield**, **current yield**, **rental yield**, or **coupon yield**, and these are also usually stated in percentage terms. In our example, the dividend yield is $5/$92 ≈ 5.4%. Of course, if the interim yield is high, you might be experiencing a negative capital gain and still have a positive rate of return. For example, a bond that costs $500, pays a coupon of $50, and then sells for $490, has a **capital loss** of $10 (which comes to a –2% capital yield) but a rate of return of ($490 + $50 – $500)/$500 = +8%. You will almost always work with rates of return, not with capital gains. The only exception is when you have to work with taxes, because the IRS treats capital gains differently from interim payments. (We will cover taxes in Section 10.4.)

➤ *Corporate payouts and dividend yields, Chapter 19, Pg.611.*

➤ *Taxes on capital gains, Sect. 10.4, Pg.261.*

Most of the time, people (incorrectly but harmlessly) abbreviate a rate of return or net return by calling it just a return. For example, if you say that the return on your $10,000 stock purchase was 10%, you obviously do not mean you received a unitless 0.1. You really mean that your rate of return was 10% and you received $1,000. This is usually benign, because your listener will know what you mean. Potentially more harmful is the use of the phrase *yield*, which, strictly speaking, means *rate of return*. However, it is often misused as a shortcut for dividend yield or coupon yield (the percent payout that a stock or a bond provides). If you say that the yield on your stock was 5%, then some listeners may interpret it to mean that you earned a total rate of return of 5%, whereas others may interpret it to mean that your stock paid a dividend yield of 5%.

People often use incorrect terms, but the meaning is usually clear, so this is harmless.

Interest rates should logically always be positive. After all, you can always earn 0% if you keep your money under your mattress—you thereby end up with as much money next period as you have this period. Why give your money to someone today who will give you less than 0% (less money in the future)? Consequently, interest rates are indeed almost always positive—the rare exceptions being both bizarre and usually trivial.

(Nominal) interest rates are usually nonnegative.

Here is another language problem: What does the statement "the interest rate has just increased by 5%" mean? It could mean either that the previous interest rate, say, 10%, has just increased from 10% to 10% · (1 + 5%) = 10.5%, or that it has increased from 10% to 15%. Because this is unclear, the **basis point** unit was invented. A basis point is simply 1/100 of a percent. If you state that your interest rate has increased by 50 basis points, you definitely mean that the interest rate has increased from 10% to 10.5%. If you state that your interest rate has increased by 500 basis points, you definitely mean that the interest rate has increased from 10% to 15%.

Basis points avoid an ambiguity in the English language: 100 basis points equals 1%.

> 100 basis points constitute 1%. Basis points reduce "percentage ambiguities."

IMPORTANT

Q 2.3. An investment costs $1,000 and pays a return of $1,050. What is its rate of return?

Q 2.4. An investment costs $1,000 and pays a net return of $25. What is its rate of return?

Q 2.5. Is 10 the same as 1,000%?

Q 2.6. You purchase a stock for $40 per share today. It will pay a dividend of $1 next month. If you can sell it for $45 right after the dividend is paid, what would be its dividend yield, what would be its capital gain (also quoted as a capital gain yield), and what would be its total holding rate of return?

Q 2.7. By how many basis points does the interest rate change if it increases from 9% to 12%.

Q 2.8. If an interest rate of 10% decreases by 20 basis points, what is the new interest rate?

2.4 Time Value, Future Value, and Compounding

Time Value of Money = Earn Interest.

Because you can earn interest, a given amount of money today is worth more than the same amount of money in the future. After all, you could always deposit your money today into the bank and thereby receive more money in the future. This is an example of the **time value of money**, which says that a dollar today is worth more than a dollar tomorrow. It may well be the most basic and important concept in finance.

The Future Value of Money

Here is how to calculate future payoffs given a rate of return and an initial investment.

➤ Rate of Return, Formula 2.1, Pg.14.

How much money will you receive in the future if the rate of return is 20% and you invest $100 today? Turn around the rate of return formula (Formula 2.1) to determine how money will grow over time given a rate of return:

$$20\% = \frac{\$120 - \$100}{\$100} \iff \$100 \cdot (1 + 20\%) = \$100 \cdot 1.2 = \$120$$

$$r_1 = \frac{C_1 - C_0}{C_0} \iff C_0 \cdot (1 + r_1) = C_1$$

The $120 next year is called the **future value (FV)** of $100 today. Thus, future value is the value of a present cash amount at some point in the future. It is the time value of money that causes the future value, $120, to be higher than its present value (PV), $100. Using the abbreviations FV and PV, you could also have written the above formula as

$$r_1 = \frac{FV - PV}{PV} \iff FV = PV \cdot (1 + r_1)$$

➤ Apples and Oranges, Sect. 5.2, Pg.90.

(If we omit the subscript on the r, it means a 1-period interest rate from now to time 1, i.e., r_1.) Please note that the time value of money is not the fact that the prices of goods may change between today and tomorrow (that would be inflation). Instead, the time value of money is based exclusively on the fact that your money can earn interest. Any amount of cash today is worth more than the same amount of cash tomorrow. Tomorrow, it will be the same amount plus interest.

Q 2.9. A project has a rate of return of 30%. What is the payoff if the initial investment is $250?

Compounding and Future Value

Now, what if you can earn the same 20% year after year and reinvest all your money? What would your two-year rate of return be? Definitely *not* 20% + 20% = 40%! You know that you will have $120 in year 1, which you can reinvest at a 20% rate of return from year 1 to year 2. Thus, you will end up with

Interest on interest (or rate of return on rate of return) means rates cannot be added.

$$C_2 = \$100 \cdot (1 + 20\%)^2 = \$100 \cdot 1.2^2 = \$120 \cdot (1 + 20\%) = \$120 \cdot 1.2 = \$144$$
$$C_0 \cdot (1 + r)^2 \qquad\qquad = \quad C_1 \cdot (1 + r) \qquad\qquad = \quad C_2$$

This $144—which is, of course, again a future value of $100 today—represents a total two-year rate of return of

$$r_2 = \frac{\$144 - \$100}{\$100} = \frac{\$144}{\$100} - 1 = 44\%$$
$$\frac{C_2 - C_0}{C_0} = \frac{C_2}{C_0} - 1 = r_2$$

This is more than 40% because the original net return of $20 in the first year earned an additional $4 in interest in the second year. You earn interest on interest! This is also called **compound interest**. Similarly, what would be your 3-year rate of return? You would invest $144 at 20%, which would provide you with

$$C_3 = \$144 \cdot (1 + 20\%) = \$144 \cdot 1.2 = \$100 \cdot (1 + 20\%)^3 = \$100 \cdot 1.2^3 = \$172.80$$
$$C_2 \cdot (1 + r) \qquad\qquad = \quad C_0 \cdot (1 + r)^3 \qquad\qquad = \quad C_3$$

Your 3-year rate of return from time 0 to time 3, call it r_3, would thus be

The "one-plus" formula.

$$r_3 = \frac{\$172.80 - \$100}{\$100} = \frac{\$172.80}{\$100} - 1 = 72.8\%$$
$$\frac{C_3 - C_0}{C_0} = \frac{C_3}{C_0} - 1 = r_3$$

This formula translates the three sequential 1-year rates of return into one 3-year **holding rate of return**—that is, what you earn if you hold the investment for the entire period. This process is called **compounding**, and the formula that does it is the "one-plus formula":

$$(1 + 72.8\%) = (1 + 20\%) \cdot (1 + 20\%) \cdot (1 + 20\%)$$
$$(1 + r_3) = (1 + r) \cdot (1 + r) \cdot (1 + r)$$

or, if you prefer it shorter,

$$1.728 = 1.2^3$$

Exhibit 2.1 shows how your $100 would grow if you continued investing it at a rate of return of 20% per annum. The function is exponential—that is, it grows faster and faster as interest earns more interest.

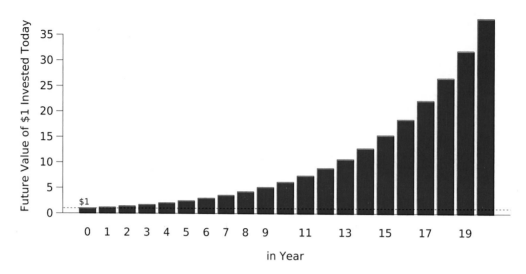

Period	Start value	1 + one-year rate	End value	Total factor from time 0	Total rate of return $r_{0,t} = (1+r)^t - 1$
0 to 1	$100	(1 + 20%)	$120.00	1.2	20.0%
1 to 2	$120	(1 + 20%)	$144.00	$1.2 \cdot 1.2 = 1.44$	44.0%
2 to 3	$144	(1 + 20%)	$172.80	$1.2 \cdot 1.2 \cdot 1.2 = 1.728$	72.8%
⋮					

Exhibit 2.1: *Compounding over 20 Years at 20% per Annum.* Money grows at a constant rate of 20% per annum. If you compute the graphed value at 20 years out, you will find that each dollar invested right now is worth $38.34 in 20 years. The money at first grows in a roughly linear pattern, but as more and more interest accumulates and itself earns more interest, the graph accelerates steeply upward.

IMPORTANT

The compounding formula translates sequential future rates of return into an overall holding rate of return:

$$\underbrace{(1 + r_t)}_{\substack{\text{Multiperiod Holding} \\ \text{Rate of Return}}} = \underbrace{(1 + r)^t}_{\substack{\text{Multiperiod Holding} \\ \text{Rate of Return}}} = \underbrace{(1 + r)}_{\substack{\text{Current 1-Period} \\ \text{Spot Rate of Return}}} \cdot \underbrace{(1 + r)}_{\substack{\text{Next 1-Period} \\ \text{Rate of Return}}} \cdots \underbrace{(1 + r)}_{\substack{\text{Final 1-Period} \\ \text{Rate of Return}}}$$

> The first rate is called the spot rate because it starts now (on the spot).
> **The compounding formula is so common that you must memorize it.**

You can use the compounding formula to compute all sorts of future payoffs. For example, an investment project that costs \$212 today and earns 10% each year for 12 years will yield an overall holding rate of return of

Another example of a payoff computation.

$$r_{12} = (1 + 10\%)^{12} - 1 = (1.1^{12} - 1) \approx 213.8\%$$
$$(1 + r)^t - 1 \qquad\qquad = \quad r_{12}$$

Your \$212 investment today would therefore turn into a future value of

$$C_{12} = \$212 \cdot (1 + 10\%)^{12} = \$212 \cdot 1.1^{12} \approx \$212 \cdot (1 + 213.8\%) \approx \$665.35$$
$$C_0 \cdot (1 + r)^{12} \qquad\qquad\qquad\qquad\qquad = \quad C_{12}$$

Now suppose you wanted to know what constant two 1-year interest rates (r) would give you a two-year rate of return of 50%. It is not 25%, because $(1+25\%)\cdot(1+25\%)-1 = 1.25^2 - 1 = 56.25\%$. Instead, you need to solve

"Uncompounding": Turn around the formula to compute individual holding rates.

$$(1 + r) \cdot (1 + r) = (1 + r)^2 = 1 + 50\% = 1.50$$

The correct answer is

$$r = \sqrt[2]{1.50} - 1 \approx 22.47\%$$
$$= \sqrt[t]{1 + r_t} - 1 = \quad r$$

Check your answer: $(1+22.47\%)\cdot(1+22.47\%) = 1.2247^2 \approx (1+50\%)$. If the 12-month interest rate is 213.8%, what is the 1-month interest rate?

$$(1 + r)^{12} \qquad \approx \qquad 1 + 213.8\%$$
$$\Leftrightarrow r = \sqrt[12]{1 + 213.8\%} - 1 = (1 + 213.8\%)^{1/12} - 1 \approx 10\%$$

➤ *Exponentiation, Book Appendix, Chapter A, Pg.695.*

Interestingly, compounding works even over fractional time periods. Say the overall interest rate is 5% per year, and you want to find out what the rate of return over half a year would be. Because $(1 + r_{0.5})^2 = (1 + r_1)$, you would compute

You can determine fractional time interest rates via compounding, too.

$$(1 + r_{0.5}) = (1 + r_1)^{0.5} = (1 + 5\%)^{0.5} \approx 1 + 2.4695\% = 1.024695$$

Check—compounding 2.4695% over two (6-month) periods indeed yields 5%:

$$(1 + 2.4695\%) \cdot (1 + 2.4695\%) = 1.024695^2 \approx (1 + 5\%)$$
$$(1 + r_{0.5}) \cdot (1 + r_{0.5}) \qquad = (1 + r_{0.5})^2 = (1 + r_1)$$

A N E C D O T E   Life Expectancy and Credit

Your life expectancy may be 80 years, but 30-year bonds existed even in an era when life expectancy was only 25 years—at the time of Hammurabi, around 1700 B.C.E. (Hammurabi established the Kingdom of Babylon and is famous for the Hammurabi Code, the first known legal system.) Moreover, four thousand years ago, Mesopotamians already solved interesting financial problems. A cuneiform clay tablet contains the oldest known interest rate problem for prospective students of the financial arts. The student must figure out how long it takes for 1 mina of silver, growing at 20% interest per year, to reach 64 minae. Because the interest compounds in an odd way (20% of the principal is accumulated until the interest is equal to the principal, and then it is added back to the principal), the answer to this problem is 30 years, rather than 22.81 years. This is not an easy problem to solve—and it even requires knowledge of logarithms!   *William Goetzmann, Yale University*

You need logs to determine the time needed to get x times your money.

If you know how to use logarithms, you can also use the same formula to determine how long it will take at the current interest rate to double or triple your money. For example, at an interest rate of 3% per year, how long would it take you to double your money?

$$(1 + 3\%)^x \;=\; (1 + 100\%) \;\Leftrightarrow\; x \;=\; \frac{\log(1 + 100\%)}{\log(1 + 3\%)} \;=\; \frac{\log(2.00)}{\log(1.03)} \;\approx\; 23.5$$

$$(1 + r)^t \;=\; (1 + r_t) \;\Leftrightarrow\; t \;=\; \frac{\log(1 + r_t)}{\log(1 + r)}$$

How Bad Are Mistakes?

Adding or Compounding Interest Rates?

Unfortunately, when it comes to interest rates in the real world, many users are casual, sometimes to the point where they are outright wrong. Some people mistakenly add interest rates instead of compounding them. When the investments, the interest rates, and the time periods are small, the difference between the correct and incorrect computation can be minor, so this practice can be acceptable, even if it is wrong. For example, when interest rates are 10%, compounding yields

$$(1 + 10\%) \quad\cdot\quad (1 + 10\%) - 1 \;=\; 1.1^2 - 1 \;=\; 21\%$$

$$(1 + r) \quad\cdot\quad (1 + r) \quad - 1 \qquad\qquad =\quad r_2$$

$$=\; 1 + r + r + r \cdot r \quad - \qquad 1$$

which is not exactly the same as the simple sum of two r's, which comes to 20%. The difference between 21% and 20% is the "cross-term" $r \cdot r$. This cross-product is especially unimportant if both rates of return are small. If the interest rate were both 1%, the cross-term would be 0.0001. This is indeed small enough to be ignored in most situations and is therefore a forgivable approximation. However, when you compound over many periods, you will accumulate more and more cross-terms, and eventually the quality of your approximation will deteriorate.

Q 2.10. If the 1-year rate of return is 20% and interest rates are constant, what is the 5-year holding rate of return?

Q 2.11. If you invest $2,000 today and it earns 25% per year, how much will you have in 15 years?

Q 2.12. What is the holding rate of return for a 20-year investment that earns 5%/year each year? What would a $200 investment grow into?

Q 2.13. A project lost one-third of its value each year for 5 years. What was its total holding rate of return? How much is left if the original investment was $20,000?

Q 2.14. If the 5-year holding rate of return is 100% and interest rates are constant, what is the (compounding) annual interest rate?

Q 2.15. What is the quarterly interest rate if the annual interest rate is 50%?

Q 2.16. If the per-year interest rate is 5%, what is the two-year total interest rate?

Q 2.17. If the per-year interest rate is 5%, what is the 10-year total interest rate?

Q 2.18. If the per-year interest rate is 5%, what is the 100-year total interest rate? How does this compare to 100 times 5%?

Q 2.19. At a constant rate of return of 6% per annum, how many years does it take you to triple your money?

IMPORTANT

When you compare your answers to those in the back of the chapter, you will often find that your answers are slightly different. This is usually a matter of rounding precision. It can matter whether you carry intermediate calculation at full precision or whether you round intermediate results (as the solutions sometimes do), too. This is an unavoidable nuisance, but it is *not* a problem. You should check whether your answers are close, not whether they are exact to the x-th digit after the decimal point.

How Banks Quote Interest Rates

Banks add to the
confusion, quoting
interest rates using
strange but traditional
conventions.

Banks and many other financial institutions use a number of conventions for quoting interest rates that may surprise you.

An annual percentage yield (APY) is the simple rate of return. (It is what our book calls an interest rate. Your bank sometimes calls this an **annual equivalent rate (AER)** or an **effective annual rate.**) If you invest $100, and the APY is 10%, you end up with $110 at the end of the year.

The interest rate stated without qualification is not really a rate of return, but just a method of quoting. The true daily interest rate is this annual interest quote divided by 365 (or 360 by another convention). For example, if your bank quotes you an annual interest rate of 10%, it means that the daily interest rate is $10\%/365 \approx 0.0274\%$. This is also why your bank may call this the **annual rate, compounded daily.** Therefore, if you leave your money in the bank for one year, you really earn

$$\text{Actual Rate of Return} = [1 + (10\%/365)]^{365} - 1 \approx 10.52\%$$

In sum, at a quoted bank interest rate of 10%, $100 turns into $110.52 after one year.

An annual percentage rate (APR) is the rate that a bank is required to quote on the loans it extends, according to the Consumer Credit Act of 1980. This act requires lenders to quote an "annual rate, compounded monthly," thus rendering APR as a number similar to a plain interest quote (not an APY). For example, if the quote to you is 10% per annum, then the lender will collect $(1 + 10\%/12)^{12} - 1 \approx 10.47\%$ per year on the money lent to you. For every $100 you borrow, you will have to pay the bank $10.47 every year. However, in contrast to the simple interest quote, APR not only has a different compounding interval, but is also required to reflect other closing costs and fees in order to aid consumers. Yet even though APR is supposedly a standardized measure, there are still enough variations in common use that comparing APRs may not always be comparing apples to apples.

A certificate of deposit (CD) is a longer-term investment vehicle than a savings account deposit. If your bank wants you to deposit your money in a CD, do you think it will put the more traditional interest rate quote or the APY on its sign in the window? Because the APY of 10.52% looks larger and thus more appealing to depositors than the traditional 10% interest rate quote, most banks advertise the APY for deposits. If you want to borrow money from your bank, do you think your loan agreement will similarly emphasize the APY? No. Most of the time, banks leave this number to the fine print and focus on the APR (or the traditional interest rate quote) instead.

Watch out for
ambiguities.

Interest rates are not intrinsically difficult, but they can be tedious, and definitional confusions abound in their world. My best advice when money is at stake: If in doubt, ask how the interest rate is computed! Even better, ask for a simple illustrative calculation.

Q 2.20. If you earn an (effective) interest rate of 12% per annum, how many basis points do you earn in interest on a typical calendar day? (Assume a year has 365.25 days.)

Q 2.21. If the bank quotes an interest rate of 12% per annum (not as an effective interest rate), how many basis points do you earn in interest on a typical day?

Q 2.22. If the bank states an *effective* interest rate of 12% per annum, and there are 52.2 weeks per year, how much interest do you earn on a deposit of $1,000 over 1 week? On a deposit of $100,000?

Q 2.23. If the bank quotes interest of 12% per annum, and there are 52.2 weeks, how much interest do you earn on a deposit of $1,000 over 1 week?

Q 2.24. If the bank quotes interest of 12% per annum, and there are 52.2 weeks, how much interest do you earn on a deposit of $1,000 over 1 year?

Q 2.25. If the bank quotes an interest rate of 6% per annum, what does a deposit of $100 in the bank come to after one year?

Q 2.26. If the bank quotes a loan APR rate of 8% per annum, compounded monthly, and without fees, what do you have to pay back in one year if you borrow $100 from the bank?

2.5 Present Value, Discounting, and Capital Budgeting

Now turn to the flip side of the future value problem: If you know how much money you will have next year, what does this correspond to in value *today*? This is especially important in a corporate context, where the question is, "Given that Project X will return $1 million in 5 years, how much should you be willing to pay to undertake this project today?" The process entailed in answering this question is called **capital budgeting** and is at the heart of corporate decision making. (The origin of the term was the idea that firms have a "capital budget," and that they must allocate capital to their projects within that budget.)

Capital budgeting: Should you budget capital for a project?

Start again with the rate of return formula

$$r_1 = \frac{C_1 - C_0}{C_0} = \frac{C_1}{C_0} - 1$$

You only need to turn this formula around to answer the following question: If you know the prevailing interest rate in the economy (r_1) and the project's future cash flows (C_1), what is the project's value to you *today*? In other words, you are looking for the **present value** (**PV**)—the amount a future sum of money is worth today, given a specific rate of return. For example, if the interest rate is 10%, how much would you have to save (invest) to receive $100 next year? Or, equivalently, if your project will return $100 next year, what is the project worth to you today? The answer lies in the present value formula, which translates future money into today's money. You merely need to rearrange the rate of return formula to solve for the present value:

The "present value formula" is nothing but the rate of return definition—inverted to translate future cash flows into (equivalent) today's dollars.

$$C_0 \;=\; \frac{\$100}{1 + 10\%} \;=\; \frac{\$100}{1.1} \;\approx\; \$90.91$$

$$C_0 \;=\; \frac{C_1}{1 + r_1} \qquad\qquad =\; PV(C_1)$$

Check this—investing \$90.91 at an interest rate of 10% will indeed return \$100 next period:

$$10\% \;\approx\; \frac{\$100 - \$90.91}{\$90.91} \;=\; \frac{\$100}{\$90.91} - 1 \;\Leftrightarrow\; (1 + 10\%) \cdot \$90.91 \;\approx\; \$100$$

$$r_1 \;=\; \frac{C_1 - C_0}{C_0} \;=\; \frac{C_1}{C_0} - 1 \;\Leftrightarrow\; (1 + r_1) \cdot C_0 \;=\; C_1$$

Discounting translates future cash into today's equivalent.

This is the **present value formula**, which uses a division operation known as **discounting**. (The term "discounting" indicates that we are reducing a value, which is exactly what we are doing when we translate future cash into current cash.) If you wish, you can think of discounting—the conversion of a future cash flow amount into its equivalent present value amount—as the *reverse* of compounding.

Present value varies inversely with the cost of capital.

Thus, the present value (PV) of next year's \$100 is \$90.91—the value today of future cash flows. Let's say that this \$90.91 is what the project costs. If you can borrow or lend at the interest rate of 10% elsewhere, then you will be indifferent between receiving \$100 next year and receiving \$90.91 for your project today. In contrast, if the standard rate of return in the economy were 12%, your specific project would not be a good deal. The project's present value would be

$$PV(C_1) \;=\; \frac{\$100}{1 + 12\%} \;=\; \frac{\$100}{1.12} \;\approx\; \$89.29$$

$$C_0 \;=\; \frac{C_1}{1 + r_1} \qquad\qquad =\; PV(C_1)$$

which would be less than its cost of \$90.91. But if the standard economy-wide rate of return were 8%, the project would be a great deal. Today's present value of the project's future payoff would be

$$PV(C_1) \;=\; \frac{\$100}{1 + 8\%} \;=\; \frac{\$100}{1.08} \;\approx\; \$92.59$$

$$C_0 \;=\; \frac{C_1}{1 + r_1} \qquad\qquad =\; PV(C_1)$$

which would exceed the project's cost of \$90.91. It is the present value of the project, weighed against its cost, that should determine whether you should undertake a project today or avoid it. The present value is also the answer to the question, "How much would you have to save at current interest rates today if you wanted to have a specific amount of money next year?"

The PV formula with two periods.

Let's extend the time frame in our example. If the interest rate were 10% per period, what would \$100 in two periods be worth today? The value of the \$100 is then

$$\text{PV}(C_2) = \frac{\$100}{(1+10\%)^2} = \frac{\$100}{1.21} \approx \$82.64$$

$$\text{PV}(C_2) = \frac{C_2}{(1+r)^2} = C_0 \qquad (2.2)$$

Note the 21%. In two periods, you could earn a rate of return of $(1+10\%)\cdot(1+10\%)-1 = 1.1^2-1 = 21\%$ elsewhere, so this is your appropriate comparable rate of return.

This discount rate—the rate of return, r, with which the project can be financed—is often called the **cost of capital**. It is the rate of return at which you can raise money elsewhere. In a perfect market, this cost of capital is also the **opportunity cost** that you bear if you fund your specific investment project instead of the alternative next-best investment elsewhere. Remember—you can invest your money at this opportunity rate in another project instead of this one. The better these alternative projects in the economy are, the higher will be your cost of capital, and the lower will be the value of your specific investment project with its specific cash flows. An investment that promises $1,000 next year is worth less today if you can earn 50% rather than 5% elsewhere. A good rule is to always mentally add the word "opportunity" before "cost of capital"—it is always your **opportunity cost of capital**. (In this part of our book, I will just tell you what the economy-wide rate of return is—here 10%—for borrowing or investing. In later chapters, you will learn how this opportunity cost of capital [ahem "rate of return"] is determined.)

The interest rate can be called the "cost of capital."

> **IMPORTANT**
>
> Always think of the r in the present value denominator as your "opportunity" cost of capital. If you have great opportunities elsewhere, your projects have to be discounted at high discount rates. The discount rate, the cost of capital, and the required rate of return are really all just names for the same factor.

When you multiply a future cash flow by its appropriate **discount factor**, you end up with its present value. Looking at Formula 2.2, you can see that this discount factor is the quantity

The discount factor is a simple function of the cost of capital.

$$\text{discount factor} = \left(\frac{1}{1+21\%}\right) \approx 0.8264$$
$$\left(\frac{1}{1+r_2}\right)$$

In other words, the discount factor translates 1 dollar in the future into the equivalent amount of dollars today. In the example, at a two-year 21% rate of return, a dollar in two years is worth about 83 cents today. Because interest rates are usually positive, discount factors are usually less than 1—a dollar in the future is worth less than a dollar today. (Sometimes, people call this the **discount rate**, but the discount rate is really r_t if you are a stickler for accuracy.)

Exhibit 2.2 shows how the discount factor declines when the cost of capital is 20% per annum. After about a decade, any dollar the project earns is worth less than 20 cents to you today. If you compare Exhibit 2.1 to Exhibit 2.2, you should notice how each is the "flip side" of the other.

The discount rate is higher for years farther out, so the discount factor is lower.

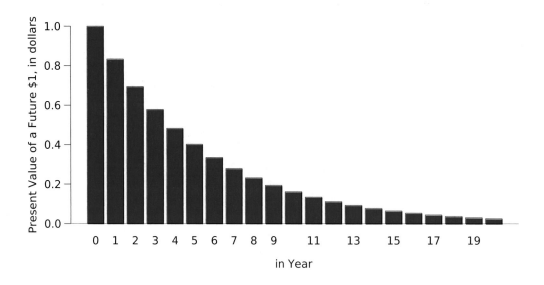

Exhibit 2.2: *Discounting over 20 Years at a Cost of Capital of 20% per Annum.* Each bar is $1/(1+20\%) \approx 83.3\%$ of the size of the bar to its left. After 20 years, the last bar is 0.026 in height. This means that $1 in 20 years is worth 2.6 cents in money today.

IMPORTANT

The cornerstones of finance are the following formulas:

$$\text{Rate of Return:} \quad r_t = \frac{C_t - C_0}{C_0} = \frac{C_t}{C_0} - 1$$

Rearrange the formula to obtain the future value:

$$\text{Future Value:} \quad FV_t = C_t = C_0 \cdot (1 + r_t) = C_0 \cdot (1 + r)^t$$

The process of obtaining r_t is called compounding, and it works through the "one-plus" formula:

$$\text{Compounding:} \quad \underbrace{(1 + r_t)}_{\substack{\text{Total Holding} \\ \text{Rate of Return}}} = \underbrace{(1 + r)}_{\substack{\text{First Period} \\ \text{Rate of Return}}} \cdot \underbrace{(1 + r)}_{\substack{\text{Second Period} \\ \text{Rate of Return}}} \cdots \underbrace{(1 + r)}_{\substack{\text{Third Period} \\ \text{Rate of Return}}}$$

Rearrange the formula again to obtain the present value:

$$\text{Present Value:} \quad PV = C_0 = \frac{C_t}{(1 + r_t)} = \frac{C_t}{(1 + r)^t}$$

The process of translating C_t into C_0—that is, the multiplication of a future cash flow by $1/(1 + r_t)$—is called discounting. The discount factor is:

> **Discount Factor:** $\dfrac{1}{(1 + r_t)} = \dfrac{1}{(1 + r)^t}$
>
> It translates one dollar at time t into its equivalent value today.

Remember how bonds are different from savings accounts? The former is pinned down by its promised fixed future payments, while the latter pays whatever the daily interest rate is. This induces an important relationship between the value of bonds and the prevailing interest rates—*they move in opposite directions*. For example, if you have a bond that promises to pay $1,000 in one year, and the prevailing interest rate is 5%, the bond has a present value of $1,000/1.05 \approx $952.38. If the prevailing interest rate suddenly increases to 6% (and thereby becomes your new opportunity cost of capital), the bond's present value becomes $1,000/1.06 \approx $943.40. You would have lost $8.98, which is about 0.9% of your original $952.38 investment. The value of your fixed-bond payment in the future has gone down, because investors can now do better than your 5% by buying new bonds. They have better opportunities elsewhere in the economy. They can earn a rate of return of 6%, not just 5%, so if you wanted to sell your bond now, you would have to sell it at a discount to leave the next buyer a rate of return of 6%. If you had delayed your investment, the sudden change to 6% would have done nothing to your investment. On the other hand, if the prevailing interest rate suddenly drops to 4%, then your bond will be more valuable. Investors would be willing to pay $1,000/1.04 \approx $961.54, which is an immediate $9.16 gain. The inverse relationship between prevailing interest rates and bond prices is general and worth noting.

Bonds' present values and the prevailing interest rates move in opposite directions.

> **IMPORTANT**
>
> The price and the implied rate of return on a bond with fixed payments move in opposite directions. When the price of the bond goes up, its implied rate of return goes down. When the price of the bond goes down, its implied rate of return goes up.

Q 2.27. A project with a cost of capital of 30% pays off $250. What should it cost today?

Q 2.28. A bond promises to pay $150 in 12 months. The annual true interest rate is 5% per annum. What is the bond's price today?

Q 2.29. A bond promises to pay $150 in 12 months. The bank quotes you an interest rate of 5% per annum, compounded daily. What is the bond's price today?

Q 2.30. If the cost of capital is 5% per annum, what is the discount factor for a cash flow in two years?

Q 2.31. Interpret the meaning of the discount factor.

Q 2.32. What are the units on rates of return, discount factors, future values, and present values?

Q 2.33. Would it be good or bad for you, in terms of the present value of your liabilities, if your opportunity cost of capital increased?

Q 2.34. The price of a bond that offers a safe promise of $100 in one year is $95. What is the implied interest rate? If the bond's interest rate suddenly jumped up by 150 basis points, what would the bond price be? How much would an investor gain/lose if she held the bond while the interest rate jumped up by these 150 basis points?

2.6 Net Present Value

Present values are alike and thus can be added, subtracted, compared, and so on.

An important advantage of present value is that all cash flows are translated into the same unit: cash today. To see this, say that a project generates $10 in one year and $8 in five years. You cannot add up these different future values to come up with $18—it would be like adding apples and oranges. However, if you translate both future cash flows into their present values, you *can* add them. For example, if the interest rate was 5% per annum (so $(1 + 5\%)^5 = (1 + 27.6\%)$ over 5 years), the present value of these two cash flows together would be

$$\text{PV}(\,\$10 \text{ in 1 year}\,) \quad = \quad \frac{\$10}{1.05} \quad \approx \ \$9.52$$

$$\text{PV}(\,\$8 \text{ in 5 years}\,) \quad = \quad \frac{\$8}{1.05^5} \quad \approx \ \$6.27$$

$$\text{PV}(\,C_t\,) \qquad = \quad \frac{C_t}{(1 + r)^t}$$

Therefore, the total value of the project's future cash flows *today* (at time 0) is $15.79.

The definition and use of NPV.

The **net present value** (**NPV**) of an investment is the present value of all its future cash flows minus the present value of its cost. It is really the same as present value, except that the word "net" up-front reminds you to add and subtract *all* cash flows, including the *up-front* investment outlay today. The NPV calculation method is always the same:

1. Translate all future cash flows into today's dollars.

2. Add them all up. This is the present value of all future cash flows.

3. Subtract the initial investment.

NPV is the most important method for determining the value of projects. It is a cornerstone of finance. Let's assume that you have to pay $12 to buy this particular project with its $10 and $8 cash flows. In this case, it is a positive NPV project, because

$$\text{NPV} \quad = \quad -\$12 + \frac{\$10}{1.05} + \frac{\$8}{1.05^5} \quad \approx \ \$3.79$$

$$C_0 \quad + \quad \frac{C_1}{1 + r_1} + \frac{C_5}{(1 + r)^5} \quad = \quad \text{NPV}$$

(For convenience, we omit the 0 subscript for NPV, just as we did for PV.)

There are a number of ways to understand net present value.

Think about what NPV means, and how it can be justified.

- One way is to think of the NPV of $3.79 as the difference between the market value of the future cash flows ($15.79) and the project's cost ($12)—this difference is the "value added."

- Another way to think of your project is to compare its cash flows to an equivalent set of bonds that exactly *replicates* them. In this instance, you would want to purchase a 1-year bond that promises $10 next year. If you save $9.52—at a 5% interest rate—you will receive $10. Similarly, you could buy a 5-year bond that promises $8 in year 5 for $6.27. Together, these two bonds exactly replicate the project cash flows. The **law of one price** tells you that your project should be worth as much as this bond project—the cash flows are identical. You would have had to put away $15.79 today to buy these bonds, but your project can deliver these cash flows at a cost of only $12—much cheaper and thus better than your bond alternative.

- There is yet another way to think of NPV. It tells you how your project compares to the alternative opportunity of investing in the capital markets. These opportunities are expressed in the denominator through the discount factor. What would you get if you took your $12 and invested it in the capital markets instead of in your project? Using the future value formula, you know that you could earn a 5% rate of return from now to next year, and 27.6% from now to 5 years. Your $12 would grow into $12.60 by next year. You could take out the same $10 cash flow that your project gives you and be left with $2.60 for reinvestment. Over the next 4 years, at the 5% interest rate, this $2.60 would grow into $3.16. But your project would do better for you, giving you $8. Thus, your project achieves a higher rate of return than the capital markets alternative.

Yet another way to justify NPV: opportunity cost.

The conclusion of this argument is not only the simplest but also the best capital budgeting rule: If the NPV is positive, as it is for our $3.79 project, you should take the project. If it is negative, you should reject the project. If it is zero, it does not matter.

The correct capital budgeting rule: Take all positive NPV projects.

IMPORTANT

- The NPV formula is

$$\text{NPV} = C_0 + \text{PV}(C_1) + \text{PV}(C_2) + \text{PV}(C_3) + \text{PV}(C_4) + \cdots$$

$$= C_0 + \frac{C_1}{1+r_1} + \frac{C_2}{1+r_2} + \frac{C_3}{1+r_3} + \frac{C_4}{1+r_4} + \cdots$$

$$= C_0 + \frac{C_1}{(1+r)} + \frac{C_2}{(1+r)^2} + \frac{C_3}{(1+r)^3} + \frac{C_4}{(1+r)^4} + \cdots$$

The subscripts are time indexes, C_t is the net cash flow at time t (positive for inflows, negative for outflows), and r_t is the relevant interest rate for investments from now to time t. With constant interest rates, $r_t = (1+r)^t - 1$.

- The **NPV capital budgeting rule** states that you should accept projects with a positive NPV and reject those with a negative NPV.

> - Taking positive NPV projects increases the value of the firm. Taking negative NPV projects decreases the value of the firm.
>
> - NPV is definitively the best method for capital budgeting—the process by which you should accept or reject projects.
>
> **The NPV formula is so important that you must memorize it.**

Let's work a project NPV example.

Let's work another NPV example. A project costs $900 today, yields $200/year for two years, then $400/year for two years, and finally requires a cleanup expense of $100. The prevailing interest rate is 5% per annum. These cash flows are summarized in Exhibit 2.3. Should you take this project?

First, determine your multiyear costs of capital.

1. You need to determine the cost of capital for tying up money for one year, two years, three years, and so on. The compounding formula is

$$(1 + r_t) = (1 + r)^t = (1.05)^t = 1.05^t$$

So for money right now, the cost of capital r_0 is $1.05^0 - 1 = 0$; for money in one year, r_1 is $1.05^1 - 1 = 5\%$; for money in two years, r_2 is $1.05^2 - 1 = 10.25\%$. And so on.

2. You need to translate the cost of capital into discount factors. Recall that these are 1 divided by 1 plus your cost of capital. A dollar in one year is worth $1/(1 + 5\%) = 1/1.05 \approx 0.9524$ dollars today. A dollar in two years is worth $1/(1 + 5\%)^2 = 1/1.05^2 \approx 0.9070$. And so on.

3. You can now translate the future cash flows into their present value equivalents by multiplying the payoffs by their appropriate discount factors. For example, the $200 cash flow at time 1 is worth about $0.9524 \cdot \$200 \approx \$190.48$.

4. Because present values are additive, you then sum up all the terms to compute the overall net present value. Make sure you include the original up-front cost as a negative.

Consequently, the project NPV is $68.16. Because this is a positive value, you should take this project.

If the up-front cost was higher, you should not take the project.

However, if the up-front expense was $1,000 instead of $900, the NPV would be negative (–$31.84), and you would be better off investing the money into the appropriate sequence of bonds from which the discount factors were computed. In this case, you should have rejected the project.

Q 2.35. Work out the present value of your tuition payments for the next two years. Assume that the tuition is $30,000 per year, payable at the start of the year. Your first tuition payment will occur in 6 months, and your second tuition payment will occur in 18 months. You can borrow capital at an effective interest rate of 6% per annum.

Q 2.36. Write down the NPV formula from memory.

Q 2.37. What is the NPV capital budgeting rule?

Time	Project Cash Flow	Interest Rate Annualized	Discount Holding	Present Factor	Value
t	C_t	r	r_t	$\dfrac{1}{(1+r)^t}$	$PV(C_t)$
Today 0	−$900	5.00%	0.00%	1.0000	−$900.00
Year +1	+$200	5.00%	5.00%	0.9524	+$190.48
Year +2	+$200	5.00%	10.25%	0.9070	+$181.41
Year +3	+$400	5.00%	15.76%	0.8638	+$345.54
Year +4	+$400	5.00%	21.55%	0.8227	+$329.08
Year +5	−$100	5.00%	27.63%	0.7835	−$78.35
			Net Present Value (Sum):		$68.16

Exhibit 2.3: *Hypothetical Project Cash Flow Table.* As a manager, you must provide estimates of your project cash flows. The appropriate interest rate (also called cost of capital in this context) is provided to you by the opportunity cost of your investors—determined by the supply and demand for capital in the broader economy, where your investors can invest their capital instead. The "Project Cash Flow" and the left interest rate column are the two input columns. The remaining columns are computed from these inputs. The goal is to calculate the final column.

Q 2.38. Determine the NPV of the project in Exhibit 2.3, if the per-period interest rate were 8% per year, not 5%. Should you take this project?

Q 2.39. You are considering a 3-year lease for a building, where you have to make one payment now, one in a year, and a final one in two years.

1. Would you rather pay $1,000,000 up-front, then $500,000 each in the following two years; or would you rather pay $700,000 each year?

2. If the interest rate is 10%, what equal payment amount (rather than $700,000) would leave you indifferent? (This is also called the equivalent annual cost (EAC).)

➤ *Equivalent (Annual) Cost,* Sect. App.3.A (Companion), Pg.≈3.

Q 2.40. Use a spreadsheet to answer the following question: Car dealer A offers a car for $2,200 up-front (first payment), followed by $200 lease payments over the next 23 months. Car dealer B offers the same lease at a flat $300 per month (i.e., your first up-front payment is $300). Which lease do you prefer if the interest rate is 0.5% per month?

Application: Are Faster-Growing Firms Better Bargains?

The firm's price should incorporate the firm's attributes.

Let's work another NPV problem, applying to companies overall. Does it make more sense to invest in companies that are growing quickly rather than slowly? If you wish, you can think of this question loosely as asking whether you should buy stock of a fast-growing company like Google or stock of a slow-growing company like Procter & Gamble. Actually, you do not even have to calculate anything. In a perfect market, the answer is always that every publicly traded investment comes for a fair price. Thus, the choice does not matter. Whether a company is growing quickly or slowly is already incorporated in the firm's price today, which is just the present value of the firm's cash flows that will accrue to the owners. Therefore, neither is the better deal. Yet, because finance is so much fun, we will ignore this little nuisance and work out the details anyway.

Should you invest in a fast-grower or a slow-grower?

For example, say company "Grow" (G) will produce over the next 3 years

$$G_1 = \$100 \qquad G_2 = \$150 \qquad G_3 = \$250$$

and company "Shrink" (S) will produce

$$S_1 = \$100 \qquad S_2 = \$90 \qquad S_3 = \$80$$

Is G not a better company to buy than S?

Let's find out: Compute the values.

There is no uncertainty involved, and both firms face the same cost of capital of 10% per annum. The price of G today is its present value (PV)

$$\mathrm{PV}(G) = \frac{\$100}{1.1^1} + \frac{\$150}{1.1^2} + \frac{\$250}{1.1^3} \approx \$402.70 \qquad (2.3)$$

and the price of S today is

$$\mathrm{PV}(S) = \frac{\$100}{1.1^1} + \frac{\$90}{1.1^2} + \frac{\$80}{1.1^3} \approx \$225.39$$

Your investment dollar grows at the same 10% rate. Your investment's growth rate is disconnected from the cash flow growth rate.

What is your rate of return from this year to next year? If you invest in G, then next year you will have $100 cash and own a company with $150 and $250 cash flows coming up. G's value at time 1 (so PV now has subscript 1 instead of the usually omitted 0) will thus be

$$\mathrm{PV}_1(G) = \$100 + \frac{\$150}{1.1^1} + \frac{\$250}{1.1^2} \approx \$442.98$$

Your investment will have earned a rate of return of $442.98/$402.70 − 1 ≈ 10%. If you invest instead in S, then next year you will receive $100 cash and own a company with "only" $90 and $80 cash flows coming up. S's value will thus be

$$\mathrm{PV}_1(S) = \$100 + \frac{\$90}{1.1^1} + \frac{\$80}{1.1^2} \approx \$247.93$$

Your investment will have earned a rate of return of $247.93/$225.39 − 1 ≈ 10%. In either case, you will earn the fair rate of return of 10% from this year to next year. Whether cash flows are growing at a rate of +50%, -10%, +237.5%, or -92% is irrelevant: *The firms' market prices today already reflect their future growth rates.* There is no necessary connection between the growth rate of the underlying project cash flows or earnings and the growth rate of your investment money (i.e., your expected rate of return).

Make sure you understand the thought experiment here: This statement that higher-growth firms do not necessarily earn a higher rate of return does not mean that a firm in which managers succeed in increasing the future cash flows at no extra investment cost will not be worth more. Such firms will indeed be worth more, and the current owners will benefit from the rise in future cash flows, but this will also be reflected immediately in the price at which you, an outsider, can purchase this firm. This is an important corollary worth repeating. If General Electric has just won a large defense contract (like the equivalent of a lottery), shouldn't you purchase GE stock to participate in the windfall? Or if Wal-Mart managers do a great job and have put together a great firm, shouldn't you purchase Wal-Mart stock to participate in this windfall? The answer is that you cannot. The old shareholders of Wal-Mart are no dummies. They know the capabilities of Wal-Mart and how it will translate into cash flows. Why should they give you, a potential new shareholder, a special bargain for something to which you contributed nothing? Just providing more investment funds is not a big contribution—after all, there are millions of other investors equally willing to provide funds at the appropriate right price. It is competition—among investors for providing funds and among firms for obtaining funds—that determines the expected rate of return that investors receive and the cost of capital that firms pay. There is actually a more general lesson here. Economics tells you that you must have a scarce resource if you want to earn above-normal profits. Whatever is abundant and/or provided by many competitors will not be a tremendously profitable business.

> Any sudden wealth gains would accrue to existing shareholders, not to new investors.

Q 2.41. Assume that company G pays no interim dividends, so you receive $536 at the end of the project. What is G's market value at time 1, 2, and 3? What is your rate of return in each year? Assume that the cost of capital is still 10%.

Q 2.42. Assume that company G pays out the full cash flows (refer to the text example) in earnings each period. What is G's market value after the payout at time 1, 2, and 3? What is your rate of return in each year?

Q 2.43. One month ago, a firm suffered a large court award against it that will force it to pay compensatory damages of $100 million next January 1. Are shares in this firm a bad buy until January 2?

Summary

This chapter covered the following major points:

- A perfect market assumes no taxes, no transaction costs, no opinion differences, and the presence of many buyers and sellers.

- A bond is a claim that promises to pay an amount of money in the future. Buying a bond is extending a loan. Issuing a bond is borrowing. Bond values are determined by their future payoffs.

- One hundred basis points are equal to 1%.

- The time value of money means that 1 dollar today is worth more than 1 dollar tomorrow because of the interest that it can earn.

- Returns must not be averaged, but compounded over time.

- Interest rate quotes are *not* interest rates. For example, stated annual rates are usually not the effective annual rates that your money will earn in the bank. If in doubt, ask!

- The discounted present value (PV) translates future cash values into present cash values. The net present value (NPV) is the sum of all present values of a project, including the investment cost (usually, a negative up-front cash flow today).

- The values of bonds and interest rates move in opposite directions. A sudden increase in the prevailing economy-wide interest rate decreases the present value of a bond's future payouts and therefore decreases today's price of the bond. Conversely, a sudden decrease in the prevailing economy-wide interest rate increases the present value of a bond's future payouts and therefore increases today's price of the bond.

- The NPV formula can be written as

$$
\begin{aligned}
\text{NPV} &= C_0 + \frac{C_1}{1 + r_1} + \frac{C_2}{1 + r_2} + \cdots \\
&= C_0 + \frac{C_1}{1 + r} + \frac{C_2}{(1 + r)^2} + \cdots
\end{aligned}
$$

In this context, r is called the discount rate or cost of capital, and $1/(1 + r)$ is called the discount factor.

- The net present value capital budgeting rule states that you should accept projects with a positive NPV and reject projects with a negative NPV.

- In a perfect market, firms are worth the present value of their assets. Whether firms grow quickly or slowly does not make them more or less attractive investments in a perfect market, because their prices always already reflect the present value of future cash flows.

- In a perfect market, the gains from sudden surprises accrue to old owners, not new capital providers, because old owners have no reason to want to share the spoils.

Keywords

AER, 22.   APR, 465.   APY, 22.   Annual equivalent rate, 22.   Annual percentage rate, 22.   Annual percentage yield, 22.   Annual rate, compounded daily, 22.   Basis point, 15.   Bond, 12.   CD, 22.   Capital budgeting, 23.   Capital gain, 14.   Capital loss, 15.   Certificate of deposit, 22.   Compound interest, 17. Compounding, 17.   Cost of capital, 505.   Coupon yield, 15.   Coupon, 14.   Current yield, 15.   Discount factor, 25.   Discount rate, 25.   Discounting, 24.   Dividend yield, 623.   Dividend, 612.   Effective annual rate, 22.   FV, 16.   Fixed income, 12.   Future value, 16.   Holding rate of return, 17.   Interest rate, 22. Interest, 12.   Law of one price, 29.   Loan, 134.   Maturity, 465.   NPV capital budgeting rule, 29.   NPV, 28. Net present value, 28.   Net return, 13.   Opportunity cost of capital, 25.   Opportunity cost, 256.   PV, 23. Perfect market, 11.   Present value formula, 24.   Present value, 23.   Rate of return, 13.   Rental yield, 15. Return, 13.   Time value of money, 16.

Answers

Q 2.1 The four perfect market assumptions are no taxes, no transaction costs, no differences in opinions, and no large buyers or sellers.

Q 2.2 A savings deposit is an investment in a series of short-term bonds.

Q 2.3 $r = (\$1,050 - \$1,000)/\$1,000 = 5\%$

Q 2.4 $r = \dfrac{\$25}{\$1,000} = 2.5\%$

Q 2.5 Yes, $10 = 1,000\%$.

Q 2.6 The dividend yield would be $\$1/\$40 = 2.5\%$, the capital gain would be $\$45 - \$40 = \$5$, so that its capital gain yield would be $\$5/\$40 = 12.5\%$, and the total rate of return would be $(\$46 - \$40)/\$40 = 15\%$.

Q 2.7 $1\% = 100$ basis points, so an increase of 3% is 300 basis points.

Q 2.8 20 basis points are 0.2%, so the interest rate declined from 10.0% to 9.8%.

Q 2.9 $r = 30\% = (x - \$250)/\$250 \implies x = 1.3 \cdot \$250 = \$325$

Q 2.10 $1.20^5 - 1 \approx 148.83\%$

Q 2.11 $\$2,000 \cdot 1.25^{15} \approx \$56,843.42$

Q 2.12 The total holding rate of return is $1.05^{20} - 1 \approx 165.33\%$, so you would end up with $\$200 \cdot (1 + 165.33\%) \approx \$530.66$.

Q 2.13 Losing one-third is a rate of return of –33%. To find the holding rate of return, compute $[1 + (-1/3)]^5 - 1 \approx -86.83\%$. About $(1 - 86.83\%) \cdot \$20,000 \approx \$2,633.74$ remains.

Q 2.14 $(1 + 100\%)^{1/5} - 1 \approx 14.87\%$

Q 2.15 $(1 + r_{0.25})^4 = (1 + r_1)$. Thus, $r_{0.25} = \sqrt[4]{1 + r_1} - 1 = 1.5^{1/4} - 1 \approx 10.67\%$.

Q 2.16 $r_2 = (1 + r_{0,1}) \cdot (1 + r_{1,2}) - 1 = 1.05 \cdot 1.05 - 1 = 10.25\%$

Q 2.17 $r_{10} = (1 + r_1)^{10} - 1 = 1.05^{10} - 1 \approx 62.89\%$

Q 2.18 $r_{100} = (1 + r_1)^{100} - 1 = 1.05^{100} - 1 = 130.5 \approx 13,050\%$. In words, this is about 130 times the initial investment, and about 26 times more than the 500% (5 times the initial investment).

Q 2.19 Tripling is equivalent to earning a rate of return of 200%. Therefore, solve $(1 + 6\%)^x = (1 + 200\%)$, or $x \cdot \log(1.06) = \log(3.00)$ or $x = \log(3.00)/\log(1.06) \approx 18.85$ years.

Q 2.20 $(1 + r)^{365.25} = 1.12$. Therefore, $1.12^{(1/365.25)} - 1 \approx 0.000310 = 0.0310\% \approx 3.10\text{bp/day}$.

Q 2.21 The bank means to collect $12\%/365.25 \approx 3.28\text{bp/day}$.

Q 2.22 This question demonstrates a nuisance problem that is pervasive in this book: calculations often have rounding error, especially when intermediate results are shown. The following three routes are logically the same, but the precise number differs based on when and where you round:

- Based on 365.25 days per year (which is incidentally itself rounded from the more exact 365.2422 days), the true daily interest rate is 0.00031032517117.... If you use full precision in your calculations, your weekly interest comes to $1.00031032517117\ldots^7 - 1 \approx 0.002174300\ldots$.
- If you round the true daily interest rate to 0.00031, your weekly interest comes to $1.00031\ldots^7 - 1 \approx 0.002172\ldots$.
- Based on 52.2 weeks per year (itself rounded from 52.177 weeks), you could have computed $r = (1 + 12\%)^{(1/52.2)} - 1 \approx 0.002173406\ldots$.

In the $1,000 case, all three methods give you the same answer of $1,002.17. In the $100,000 case, you would have ended up with slightly different numbers based on your route of calculation. All three methods would have been acceptably correct.

In any case, don't blame this book or yourself for small discrepancies in calculations.

Q 2.23 With 12% in nominal APR interest *quoted*, you earn 12%/365 ≈ 0.032877% per day. Therefore, the weekly rate of return is $(1 + 0.032877\%)^7 - 1 \approx 0.23036\%$. Your \$1,000 will grow into \$1,002.30. Note that you end up with more money when the 12% is the quoted rate than when it is the effective rate.

Q 2.24 With 12% in nominal APR interest *quoted*, you earn 12%/365 ≈ 0.032877% per day. Therefore, the annual rate of return is $(1 + 0.032877\%)^{365} - 1 \approx 12.747462\%$. Your \$1,000 will grow into \$1,127.47.

Q 2.25 The bank quote of 6% means that it will pay an interest rate of 6%/365 ≈ 0.0164384% per day. This earns an actual interest rate of $(1 + 0.0164384\%)^{365} - 1 \approx 6.18\%$ per annum. Therefore, each invested \$100 grows to \$106.18, thus earning \$6.18 over the year.

Q 2.26 The bank quote of 8% means that you will have to pay an interest rate of 8%/12 ≈ 0.667% per month. This earns an actual interest rate of $(1 + 0.667\%)^{12} - 1 \approx 8.30\%$ per annum. You will have to pay \$108.30 in repayment for every \$100 you borrowed.

Q 2.27 r = 30% = (\$250–x)/x. Thus, x = \$250/1.30 ≈ \$192.31.

Q 2.28 \$150/(1.05) ≈ \$142.86

Q 2.29 $\$150/[1 + (5\%/365)]^{365} \approx \$142.68$

Q 2.30 1/[(1.05) · (1.05)] ≈ 0.9070

Q 2.31 It is today's value in dollars for 1 future dollar, that is, at a specific point in time in the future.

Q 2.32 The rate of return and additional factors are unit-less. The latter two are in dollars (though the former is dollars in the future, while the latter is dollars today).

Q 2.33 Good. Your future payments would be worth less in today's money.

Q 2.34 The original interest rate is \$100/\$95 – 1 ≈ 5.26%. Increasing the interest rate by 150 basis points is 6.76%. This means that the price should be \$100/(1.0676) ≈ \$93.67. A price change from \$95 to \$93.67 is a rate of return of \$93.67/\$95 – 1 ≈ –1.40%.

Q 2.35 The first tuition payment is worth $\$30,000/(1.06)^{1/2} \approx$ \$29,139. The second tuition payment is worth $\$30,000/(1.06)^{3/2} \approx$ \$27,489. Thus, the total present value is \$56,628.

Q 2.36 If you cannot write down the NPV formula by heart, do not go on until you have it memorized.

Q 2.37 Accept if NPV is positive. Reject if NPV is negative.

Q 2.38 $-\$900 + \$200/(1.08)^1 + \$200/(1.08)^2 + \$400/(1.08)^3 + \$400/(1.08)^4 - \$100/(1.08)^5 \approx \$0.14$. The NPV is positive. Therefore this is a worthwhile project that you should accept.

Q 2.39 For the 3-year building leases:

1. Your preference depends on the interest rate. If the interest rate is zero, then you would prefer the \$2 million sum-total payment to the \$2.1 million rent. If the prevailing interest rate is less than 21.5%, it is better to lease. If it is more than 21.5%, you prefer the rent. For example, if it is 40%, the net present cost of the lease is \$1.612 million, while the net present cost of the rent is \$1.557 million.

2. At a 10% interest rate, the total net present cost of the lease is $\$1 + \$0.5/1.1 + \$0.5/1.1^2 \approx \$1.868$ million. An equivalent rent contract must solve

$$x + \frac{x}{1.1} + \frac{x}{1.1^2} = \$1.868$$

Multiply by $1.1^2 = 1.21$

$$1.21 \cdot x + 1.1 \cdot x + x = \$1.868 \cdot 1.21$$
$$\Leftrightarrow x \cdot (1.21 + 1.1 + 1) = \$2,260.28$$

Therefore, the equivalent rental cost would be x ≈ \$682.864.

Q 2.40 Lease A has an NPV of –\$6,535. Lease B has an NPV of –\$6,803. Therefore, lease A is cheaper.

Q 2.41 For easier naming, call 2000 your year 0. The firm's present value in 2000 is $\$536/1.10^3 \approx \$402.70$—but you already knew this. If you purchase this company, its value in 2001 depends on a cash flow stream that is \$0 in 2001, \$0 in year 2002, and \$536 in year 2003. It will be worth $\$536/1.10^2 \approx \$442.98$ in 2001. In 2002, your firm will be worth \$536/1.10 ≈ \$487.27. Finally, in 2003, it will be worth \$536. Each year, you expect to earn 10%, which you can compute from the four firm values.

Q 2.42 Again, call 2000 your year 0. The firm's present value in 2000 is based on dividends of \$100, \$150, and \$250 in the next three years. The firm value in 2000 is the \$402.70 from Page 32. The firm value in 2001 was also worked out to be \$442.98, but you immediately receive \$100 in cash, so the firm is worth only \$442.98 – \$100 = \$342.98. As an investor, you would have earned a rate of return of \$442.98/\$402.70 – 1 ≈ 10%. The firm value in 2002 is $PV_2(G) = \$250/1.1 \approx \$227.27$, but you will also receive \$150 in cash, for a total firm-related wealth of \$377.27. In addition, you will have the \$100 from 2001, which would have grown to \$110—for a total wealth of \$487.27. Thus, starting with wealth of \$442.98 and ending up with wealth of \$487.27, you would have earned a rate of return of \$487.27/\$442.98 – 1 ≈ 10%. A similar computation shows that you will earn 10% from 2002 (\$487.27) to 2003 (\$536.00).

Q 2.43 No! The market price will have already taken the compensatory damages into account in the share price a month ago, just after the information became public..

End of Chapter Problems

Q 2.44. What is a perfect market? What were the assumptions made in this chapter that were not part of the perfect market scenario?

Q 2.45. What is the difference between a bond and a loan?

Q 2.46. In the text, I assumed you received the dividend at the end of the period. In the real world, if you received the dividend at the beginning of the period instead of the end of the period, could this change your effective rate of return? Why?

Q 2.47. Your stock costs $100 today, pays $5 in dividends at the end of the period, and then sells for $98. What is your rate of return?

Q 2.48. The interest rate has just increased from 6% to 8%. How many basis points is this?

Q 2.49. Assume an interest rate of 10% per year. How much would you lose over 5 years if you had to give up interest on the interest—that is, if you received 50% instead of compounded interest?

Q 2.50. Over 20 years, would you prefer 10% per annum, with interest compounding, or 15% per annum but without interest compounding? (That is, you receive the interest, but it is put into an account that earns no interest, which is what we call simple interest.)

Q 2.51. A project returned +30%, then –30%. Thus, its arithmetic average rate of return was 0%. If you invested $25,000, how much did you end up with? Is your rate of return positive or negative? How would your overall rate of return have been different if you first earned –30% and then +30%?

Q 2.52. A project returned +50%, then –40%. Thus, its arithmetic average rate of return was +5%. Is your rate of return positive or negative?

Q 2.53. An investment for $50,000 earns a rate of return of 1% in each month of a full year. How much money will you have at the end of the year?

Q 2.54. There is always disagreement about what stocks are good purchases. A typical disagreement is whether a particular stock is likely to offer, say, a 10% (pessimistic) or a 20% (optimistic) annualized rate of return. For a $30 stock today, what does the difference in belief between these two opinions mean for the expected stock price from today to tomorrow? (Assume that there are 365 days in the year. Reflect on your answer for a moment—a $30 stock typically moves about ±$1 on a typical day. This unexplainable up-and-down volatility is often called noise. How big is the average move compared to the noise?)

Q 2.55. If the interest rate is 5% per annum, how long will it take to double your money? How long will it take to triple it?

Q 2.56. If the interest rate is 8% per annum, how long will it take to double your money?

Q 2.57. From Fibonacci's *Liber Abaci*, written in the year 1202: "A certain man gave 1 denaro at interest so that in 5 years he must receive double the denari, and in another 5, he must have double 2 of the denari and thus forever. How many denari from this 1 denaro must he have in 100 years?"

Q 2.58. A bank quotes you an annual loan interest rate of 14%, daily compounding, on your credit card. If you charge $15,000 at the beginning of the year, how much will you have to repay at the end of the year?

Q 2.59. Go to the website of a bank of your choice. What kind of quote does your bank post for a CD, and what kind of quote does your bank post for a mortgage? Why?

Q 2.60. What is the 1-year discount factor if the interest rate is 33.33%?

Q 2.61. You can choose between the following rent payments:

- a A lump sum cash payment of $100,000;
- b 10 annual payments of $12,000 each, the first occurring immediately;
- c 120 monthly payments of $1,200 each, the first occurring immediately. (Friendly suggestion: This is a lot easier to calculate on a computer spreadsheet.)

Now choose among them:

1. Which rental payment scheme would you choose if the interest rate was an effective 5% per year?
2. Spreadsheet question: At what interest rate would you be indifferent between the first and the second choice above? (Hint: Graph the NPV of the second project as a function of the interest rate.)

Q 2.62. A project has cash flows of $15,000, $10,000, and $5,000 in 1, 2, and 3 years, respectively. If the prevailing interest rate is 15%, would you buy the project if it costs $25,000?

Q 2.63. Consider the same project that costs $25,000 with cash flows of $15,000, $10,000, and $5,000. At what prevailing interest rate would this project be profitable? Try different interest rates, and plot the NPV on the y-axis, and the interest rate on the x-axis.

Q 2.64. Assume you are 25 years old. The IAW insurance company is offering you the following retirement contract (called an *annuity*): Contribute $2,000 per year for the next 40 years. When you reach 65 years of age, you will receive $30,000 per year for as long as you live. Assume that you believe that the chance that you will die is 10% per year after you will have reached 65 years of age. In other words, you will receive the first payment with probability 90%, the second payment with probability 81%, and so on. If the prevailing interest rate is 5% per year, all payments occur at year-end, and it is now January 1, is this annuity a good deal? (Use a spreadsheet.)

Q 2.65. A project has the following cash flows in periods 1 through 4: –$200, +$200, –$200, +$200. If the prevailing interest rate is 3%, would you accept this project if you were offered an up-front payment of $10 to do so?

Q 2.66. On April 12, 2006, Microsoft stock traded for $27.11 and claimed to pay an annual dividend of $0.36. Assume that the first dividend will be paid in one year, and that it then grows by 5% each year for the next four years. Further, assume that the prevailing interest rate is 6% per year. At what price would you have to sell Microsoft stock in five years in order to break even?

Q 2.67. Assume that you are a real estate broker with an exclusive contract—the condo association rules state that everyone selling their condominiums must go through you or a broker designated by you. A typical condo costs $500,000 today and sells again every 5 years. Assume the first sale will happen in 5 years. This will last for 50 years, and then all bets are off. Your commission will be 3%. Condos appreciate in value at a rate of 2% per year. The interest rate is 10% per annum.

1. What is the value of this exclusivity rule for one condo? In other words, at what price should you be willing to sell the privilege of being the exclusive representation for one condo to another broker?
2. If free Internet advertising was equally effective and if it could replace all real-estate agents so that buyers' and sellers' agents would no longer earn the traditional 6% (3% each), what would happen to the value gain of the condo?

Q 2.68. If the interest rate is 5% per annum, what would be the equivalent annual cost (see Question 2.39) of a $2,000 lease payment up-front, followed by $800 for three more years?

Q 2.69. The prevailing discount rate is 15% per annum. Firms live for three years. Firm F's cash flows start with $500 in year 1 and grow at 20% per annum for two years. Firm S's cash flows also start with $500 in year 1 but shrink at 20% per annum for two years. What are the prices of these two firms? Which one is the better "buy"?

Stock and Bond Valuation: Annuities and Perpetuities

Important Shortcut Formulas

The present value formula is the main workhorse for valuing investments of all types, including stocks and bonds. But these rarely have just two or three future payments. Stocks may pay dividends forever. The most common mortgage bond has 30 years of monthly payments, i.e., 360 of them. It would be possible but tedious to work with NPV formulas containing 360 terms.

Fortunately, there are some shortcut formulas that can speed up your PV computations if your projects have a particular set of cash flow patterns and the opportunity cost of capital is constant. The two most prominent such formulas are for projects called perpetuities (that have payments lasting forever) and annuities (that have payments lasting for a limited amount of years). Of course, no firm lasts forever, but the perpetuity formula is often a useful "quick-and-dirty" tool for a good approximation. In any case, the formulas you will learn in this chapter are widely used, and they can even help you to understand the economics of corporate growth.

3.1 Perpetuities

A simple **perpetuity** is a project with a stream of constant cash flows that repeats forever. If the cost of capital (i.e., the appropriate discount rate) is constant and the amount of money remains the same or grows at a constant rate, perpetuities lend themselves to fast present value solutions—very useful when you need to come up with quick rule-of-thumb estimates. Though the formulas may seem a bit intimidating at first, using them will quickly become second nature to you.

"Perpetuities" are projects with special kinds of cash flows, which permit the use of shortcut formulas.

The Simple Perpetuity Formula

At a constant interest rate of 10%, how much money do you need to invest today to receive the same dollar amount of interest of $2 each year, starting next year, forever? Exhibit 3.1 shows the present values of all future payments for a perpetuity paying $2 forever, if the interest rate is 10% per annum. Note how there is no payment at time 0, and that the individual payment terms become smaller and smaller the further out we go.

Here is an example of a perpetuity that pays $2 forever.

Time	Cash Flow	Discount Factor	Present Value	Cumul PV
0	Nothing! You have no cash flow here!			
1	$2	$1/(1+10\%)^1 \approx 0.909$	$1.82	$1.82
2	$2	$1/(1+10\%)^2 \approx 0.826$	$1.65	$3.47
3	$2	$1/(1+10\%)^3 \approx 0.751$	$1.50	$4.97
⋮	⋮	⋮	⋮	⋮
50	$2	$1/(1+10\%)^{50} \approx 0.0085$	$0.02	$19.83
⋮	⋮	⋮	⋮	⋮
		Net Present Value (Sum):		$20.00

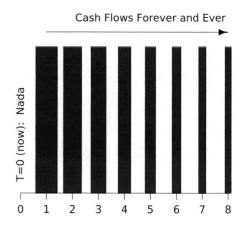

Exhibit 3.1: *Perpetuity Stream of $2 with Interest Rate* r = 10%. The table shows cash flows, discount factors, and cumulated value. The height of the bars in the graph shows that the nominal cash flows are the same in every future period. Their widths (and thus their areas) indicate the present value of these cash flows. Each bar has less area than the preceding one. Otherwise, the cumulative sum could never be a finite number.

The shortcut perpetuity formula.

To confirm the table's last row, which gives the perpetuity's net present value as $20, you can spend from here to eternity to add up the infinite number of terms. But if you use a spreadsheet to compute and add up the first 50 terms, you will get a PV of $19.83. If you add up the first 100 terms, you will get a PV of $19.9986. Mathematically, the sum eventually converges to $20 sharp. This is because there is a nice shortcut to computing the net present value of the perpetuity if the cost of capital is constant:

$$\text{Perpetuity PV} = \frac{\$2}{10\%} = \frac{\$2}{0.1} = \$20$$

$$PV_0 = \frac{C_1}{r}$$

The "1" time subscript in the formula is to remind you that the first cash flow occurs not now, but next year—the cash flows themselves will remain the same amount next year, the year after, and so on.

IMPORTANT

A stream of constant cash flows (C dollars each period and forever) beginning *next* period (i.e., time 1), which is discounted at the same per-period cost of capital r forever, is a special perpetuity worth

$$PV_0 = \frac{C_1}{r}$$

which is a shortcut for

$$PV_0 = \frac{C_1}{1+r} + \frac{C_2}{(1+r)^2} + \frac{C_3}{(1+r)^3} + \cdots + \frac{C_t}{(1+r)^T} + \cdots$$

C_2 and all other C_t are the same as C_1.

ANECDOTE The Oldest Institutions and Perpetuities

Perpetuities assume that projects last forever. But nothing does. The oldest Western institution today may well be the Roman Catholic Church. It is about 2,000 years old. Wikipedia lists the oldest existing company as the Keiunkan hotel in Japan, founded in 705. (A number of existing restaurants, hotels, and breweries in the West are also fairly old, dating from the late ninth century.) The oldest existing corporation in the United States is the Collegiate Reformed Protestant Dutch Church of the City of New York, formed in 1628 and granted a corporate charter by King William in 1696. The Canadian Hudson's Bay Company was founded in 1670 and claims to be the oldest continuously *incorporated* company in the world. The oldest U.S. companies are the Stroh's brewery and the Bowne printing firm, both of which were founded in 1885.

Guantanamo Naval Base was leased from Cuba in 1903 as a perpetuity by the United States in exchange for 2,000 pesos per annum in U.S. gold, equivalent to $4,085. In a speech, Fidel Castro has redefined time as "whatever is indefinite lasts 100 years." In any case, the Cuban government no longer recognizes the agreement and does not accept the annual payments—but it has also wisely not yet tried to expel the Americans. *Wikipedia*

The easiest way for you to get comfortable with perpetuities is to solve some problems. Easier done than said.

Q 3.1. From memory, write down the perpetuity formula. Be explicit on when the first cash flow occurs.

Q 3.2. What is the PV of a perpetuity paying $5 each month, beginning *next* month, if the monthly interest rate is a constant 0.5%/month?

Q 3.3. What is the PV of a perpetuity paying $15 each month, beginning *next* month, if the *effective* annual interest rate is a constant 12.68% per year?

Q 3.4. Under what interest rates would you prefer a perpetuity that pays $2 million per year beginning next year to a one-time payment of $40 million?

Q 3.5. In Britain, there are **Consol** bonds that are perpetuity bonds. (In the United States, the IRS does not allow companies to deduct the interest payments on perpetual bonds, so U.S. corporations do not issue Consol bonds.) What is the value of a Consol bond that promises to pay $2,000 per year if the prevailing interest rate is 4%?

The Growing Perpetuity Formula

Time	Cash Flow	Discount Factor	Present Value	Cumul PV
0	Nothing! You have no cash flow here!			
1	$(1+5\%)^0 \cdot \$2$ $= \$2.000$	$(1+10\%)^1$ ≈ 0.909	$1.818	$1.82
2	$(1+5\%)^1 \cdot \$2$ $= \$2.100$	$(1+10\%)^2$ ≈ 0.826	$1.736	$3.56
3	$(1+5\%)^2 \cdot \$2$ $= \$2.205$	$(1+10\%)^3$ ≈ 0.751	$1.657	$5.22
$\vdots$	$\vdots$	$\vdots$	$\vdots$	$\vdots$
30	$(1+5\%)^{29} \cdot \$2$ $\approx \$8.232$	$(1+10\%)^{30}$ ≈ 0.057	$0.472	$30.09
$\vdots$	$\vdots$	$\vdots$	$\vdots$	$\vdots$
		Net Present Value (Sum):		$40.00

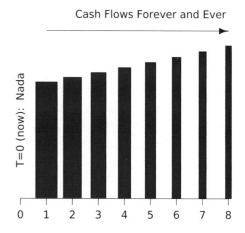

Exhibit 3.2: *Perpetuity Stream with* $C_1 = \$2$, *Growth Rate* $g = 5\%$, *and Interest Rate* $r = 10\%$. The table shows cash flows, discount factors, and cumulated value. The height of the bars in the graph shows that the nominal cash flows are growing over time. However, their widths (and thus their areas) indicate the present value of these cash flows. Each bar has less area than the preceding one, which explains why the cumulative sum can be a finite number.

A growing perpetuity assumes that cash flows grow by a constant rate g forever.

➤ *Growing Perpetuities, Exhibit 3.2, Pg.42.*

What if, instead of the same amount of cash every period, the cash flows increase over time? The **growing perpetuity** formula allows for a constant rate g per period, provided it is less than the interest rate. Exhibit 3.2 shows a growing perpetuity that pays $2 next year, grows at a rate of 5%, and faces a cost of capital of 10%. The present value of the first 30 terms adds up to $30.09. The first 100 terms add up to $39.64. The first 200 terms add up to $39.98. Eventually, the sum approaches the formula

$$\text{PV of Growing Perpetuity} = \frac{\$2}{10\% - 5\%} = \$40$$

$$\text{PV}_0 = \frac{C_1}{r - g} \qquad (3.1)$$

No cash flow at time 0. First growth is from time 1 to time 2.

As before, the "1" subscript indicates that cash flows begin next period, not this period, but here it is necessary because future cash flows will be different. The interest rate is r and it is reduced by g, the growth rate of your cash flows. Note how the table shows that the first application of the growth factor g occurs 1 period after the first application of the discount factor. For example, the cash flow at time 30 is discounted by $(1+r)^{30}$, but its cash flow is C multiplied by a growth factor of $(1+g)^{29}$. You will later encounter many applications of the growing perpetuity formula. For example, it is common to assume that cash flows grow by the rate of inflation. You will also later use this formula to obtain so-called terminal values in a chapter of this book, in which you design so-called pro formas.

➤ *Terminal value,*
Sect. 20.2, Pg.644.

IMPORTANT

A stream of cash flows growing at a rate of g each period and discounted at a constant interest rate r is worth

$$PV_0 = \frac{C_1}{r-g}$$

The first cash flow, C_1, occurs next period (time 1), the second cash flow of $C_2 = C_1 \cdot (1+g)$ occurs in two periods, and so forth, *forever*. For the formula to work, g can be negative, but r must be greater than g.
   You need to memorize the growing perpetuity formula!

Be careful to use the cash flow *next* year in the numerator. The subscript "1" is there to remind you. For example, if you want to use this formula on your firm, and it earned $100 million this year, and you expect it to grow at a 5% rate forever, then the correct cash flow in the numerator is $C_1 = \$105$ million, not $100 million!

Although a subscript on C makes this seem more painful, it is a good reminder here.

What would happen if the cash flows grew faster than the interest rate (g > r)? Wouldn't the formula indicate a negative PV? Yes, but this is because the entire scenario would be nonsense. The present value in the perpetuities formulas is only less than infinity, because *in today's dollars*, each term in the sum is a little less than the term in the previous period. If g were greater than r, however, the cash flow 1 period later would be worth more even in today's dollars. For example, take our earlier example with a discount rate of 10%, but make the growth rate of cash flows g = 15%. The first cash flow would be $2 \cdot 1.15 = \$2.30$, which discounts to $2.09 today. The second cash flow would be $2 \cdot 1.15^2 = \$2.645$, which discounts to $2.186 today. The present value of each cash flow is higher than that preceding it. Taking a sum over an infinite number of such increasing terms would yield infinity as the value. A value of infinity is clearly not sensible, as nothing in this world is worth an infinite amount of money. Therefore, the growing perpetuity formula yields a nonsensical negative value if g ≥ r—as it should!

The formula is nonsensical when r < g.

Q 3.6. From memory, write down the growing perpetuity formula.

Q 3.7. What is the PV of a perpetuity paying $5 each month, beginning *this* month (in 1 second), if the monthly interest rate is a constant 0.5%/ month (6.2%/year) and the cash flows will grow at a rate of 0.1%/month (1.2%/year)?

Q 3.8. What is the PV of a perpetuity paying $8 each month, beginning *this* month (in 1 second), if the monthly interest rate is a constant 0.5%/ month (6.2%/year) and the cash flows will grow at a rate of 0.8%/month (10%/year)?

Q 3.9. Here is an example of the most common use of the growing perpetuity model (called a pro forma). Your firm just finished the year, in which it had cash earnings of $100 million. You forecast your firm to have a quick growth phase for 3 years (from year 0 to year 2), in which it grows at a rate of 20% per annum. Your firm's growth then slows down to 10% per annum for the next 3 years. Finally, beginning in year 7, you expect it to settle into its long-term growth rate of 5% per annum. You also expect your cost of capital to be 10% over the first 3 years, then 9% over the next 3 years, and 8% thereafter. What do you think your firm is worth today?

Q 3.10. An eternal patent contract states that the patentee will pay the patentor a fee of $1.5 million next year. The contract terms state a fee growth with the inflation rate, which runs at 2% per annum. The appropriate cost of capital is 14%. What is the value of this patenting contract?

Q 3.11. How would the patent contract value change if the first payment did not occur next year, but tonight?

Application: Stock Valuation with A Gordon Growth Model

Perpetuities are imperfect approximations, but often give a useful upper bound. With their fixed interest and growth rates and eternal payment requirements, perpetuities are rarely exactly correct. But they can be very helpful for quick back-of-the-envelope estimates. For example, consider a mature and stable business with profits of $1 million next year. Because it is stable, its profits are likely to grow at the inflation rate of, say, 2% per annum. This means that it will earn $1,020,000 in 2 years, $1,040,400 in 3 years, and so on. The firm faces a cost of capital of 8%. The growing perpetuity formula indicates that this firm should probably be worth no more than

$$\text{Business Value} \;=\; \frac{\$1,000,000}{8\% - 2\%} \;\approx\; \$16,666,667$$

$$\text{Business Value} \;=\; \frac{C_1}{r - g}$$

because in reality, the firm will almost surely not exist forever. Of course, in real life, there are often even more significant uncertainties: Next year's profit may be different, the firm may grow at a different rate (or may grow at a different rate for a while) or face a different cost of capital for 1-year loans than it does for 30-year loans. Thus, $16.7 million should be considered a quick-and-dirty useful approximation, perhaps for an upper limit, and not an exact number.

The Gordon growth model: constant eternal dividend growth. The growing perpetuity model is sometimes directly applied to the stock market. For example, if you believe that a stock's dividends will grow by $g = 5\%$ forever, and if you believe that the appropriate rate of return is $r = 10\%$, and you expect the stock to earn and/or pay dividends of $D = \$10$ *next year*, then you would feel that a stock price today of

$$\text{Stock Price P Today} \quad = \quad \frac{\$10}{10\% - 5\%} \quad = \$200$$

$$\text{Stock Price P Today} \quad = \quad \frac{\text{Dividends D Next Year}}{r - g} \qquad (3.2)$$

would be appropriate. In this context, the growing perpetuity model is often called the **Gordon growth model**, after its inventor, Myron Gordon.

Let us explore the Gordon growth model a bit. In October 2004, **YAHOO!** FINANCE listed General Electric (GE) with a dividend yield of 2.43%. This is the analysts' consensus forecast of next year's dividends divided by the stock price, D/P. This is called the **dividend yield**. Rearrange Formula 3.2:

You could estimate the cost of capital for GE, based on its dividend yield and its expected dividend growth rate.

$$\frac{\text{Dividends Next Year}}{\text{Stock Price Today}} = r - g = 2.43\%$$

Therefore, you can infer that the market believes that the appropriate cost of capital (r) for General Electric exceeds its growth rate of dividends (g) by about 2.4%. **YAHOO!** FINANCE further links to a summary of GE's cash flow statement, which indicates that GE paid $7.643 billion in dividends in 2003, and $6.358 billion in 2001. Over these 2 years, the growth rate of dividends was about 9.6% per annum ($6.358 \cdot 1.096^2 \approx \$7.643$). Therefore, if you believe 9.6%/year is also a fair representation of the eternal future growth rate of GE's dividends, then the financial markets valued GE as if it had a per-annum cost of capital of about

$$r = \frac{\text{Dividends Next Year}}{\text{Stock Price Today}} + g \approx 2.4\% + 9.6\% = 12\%$$

Let's play another game that is prominent in the financial world. Earnings are, loosely speaking, cousins of the cash flows that corporate stockholders receive. You can then think of the value of the stock today as the value of the earnings stream that the stock will produce. After all, recall from Chapter 1 that owners receive all dividends and all cash flows (earnings), presumably the former being paid out from the latter. (In Chapter 13, I will explain a lot of this in more detail as well as why earnings are only approximately but not exactly cash flows.)

Let's presume that the formula also applied to earnings.

Furthermore, it is common to assume that stock market values are capitalized as if corporate earnings were eternal cash flows that are growing at a constant rate g applicable to earnings (which is not necessarily the same as the growth rate applicable to dividends). This means that you would assume that the value of the firm is

You could also estimate the cost of capital for GE based on its price/earnings ratio and its earnings growth rate.

$$\text{Stock Price P Today} = \frac{\text{Earnings E Next Year}}{r - g}$$

Thus, to determine the rate of return that investors require (the cost of capital), all you need is a forecast of earnings, the current stock price, and the eternal growth rate of earnings. Again, **YAHOO!** FINANCE gives you all the information you need. In October 2004, it listed GE's "trailing P/E" ratio—calculated as the current stock price divided by historical earnings—as 21. More interestingly, it listed the "forward P/E" ratio—calculated as the price divided by analysts' expectations of *next* year's earnings—as 18.5.

The growing perpetuity formula wants the earnings *next* year, so the latter is closer to what you need. **YAHOO!** FINANCE further tells you that GE's earnings growth rate was 6.3%—the g in the formula if you are willing to assume that the current earnings growth rate is the long-term growth rate. Therefore, all you have to do is rearrange the growing perpetuity formula, and out comes an appropriate rate of return:

$$r = \frac{\text{Earnings Next Year}}{\text{Stock Price Today}} + g = \frac{1}{\text{P/E}} + g \approx \frac{1}{18.5} + 6.3\% \approx 11.7\%$$

Given GE's price/earnings ratio and growth rate of earnings, investors are expecting a rate of return of about 12% per annum.

Keep perspective! The model provides only a quick approximation.

It is important that you recognize these are just approximations that you should not take too seriously in terms of accuracy. GE will not last forever, earnings are not the cash flows you need, the discount rate is not eternally constant, earnings will not grow forever at 6.3%, and so on. However, the numbers are not uninteresting and may not even be too far off, either. GE is a very stable company that is likely to be around for

➤ *Price-earnings ratio, Sect. 14.2, Pg.418.*

a long time, and you could do a lot worse than assuming that the cost of capital (for investing in projects that are similar to GE stock ownership) is somewhere around 12% per annum—say, somewhere between 10% to 14% per annum.

Q 3.12. A stock is paying a quarterly dividend of $5 in 1 month. The dividend is expected to increase every quarter by the inflation rate of 0.5% per quarter—so it will be $5.025 in the next quarter (i.e., paid out in 4 months). The prevailing cost of capital for this kind of stock is 9% per annum. What should this stock be worth?

Q 3.13. If a $100 stock has earnings of $5 per year, and the appropriate cost of capital for this stock is 12% per year, what does the market expect the firm's "as-if-eternal dividends" to grow at?

3.2 Annuities

An annuity pays the same amount for T years.

The second type of cash flow stream that lends itself to a quick formula is an **annuity**, which is a stream of equal cash flows for a given number of periods. Unlike a perpetuity, payments stop after T periods. For example, if the interest rate is 10% per period, what is the value of an annuity that pays $5 per period for 3 periods?

By hand.

Let's first do this the slow way. You can hand-compute the net present value as

$$PV = \frac{\$5}{1.10} + \frac{\$5}{1.10^2} + \frac{\$5}{1.10^3} \approx \$12.4343$$

$$PV = \frac{C_1}{(1 + r_1)} + \frac{C_2}{(1 + r_2)} + \frac{C_3}{(1 + r_3)}$$

$$= \frac{C_1}{(1 + r)} + \frac{C_2}{(1 + r)^2} + \frac{C_3}{(1 + r)^3}$$

The annuity formula makes short work of this NPV calculation,

$$PV = \$5 \cdot \left\{ \frac{1 - [1/(1 + 10\%)]^3}{10\%} \right\} \approx \$12.4343$$

$$PV = C_1 \cdot \left\{ \frac{1 - [1/(1 + r)]^T}{r} \right\} = PV$$

Is this really a shortcut? Maybe not for 3 periods, but try a 360-period annuity—which method do you prefer? Either works.

IMPORTANT

A stream of constant equal cash flows, beginning next period (time 1) and lasting for T periods, and discounted at a constant interest rate r, is worth

$$PV_0 = \frac{C_1}{r} \cdot \left[1 - \frac{1}{(1 + r)^T} \right]$$

Q 3.14. How many years does it take for an annuity to reach three-quarters the value of a perpetuity if the interest rate is 5%? If the interest rate is r? To reach fraction f of the value?

Q 3.15. Recall from memory the annuity formula.

Q 3.16. What is the PV of a 360-month annuity paying \$5 per month, beginning at \$5 next month (time 1), if the monthly interest rate is a constant 0.5%/month (6.2%/year)?

Q 3.17. Solve Fibonacci's annuity problem given in the anecdote on the next page: Compare the PV of a stream of quarterly cash flows of 75 bezants versus the PV of a stream of annual cash flows of 300 bezants. Payments are always at period-end. The interest rate is 2% per month. What is the relative value of the two streams? Compute the difference for a 1-year investment first.

Q 3.18. In *L'Arithmetique*, written in 1558, Jean Trenchant posed the following question: "In the year 1555, King Henry, to conduct the war, took money from bankers at the rate of 4% per fair [quarter]. That is better terms for them than 16% per year. In this same year before the fair of Toussaints, he received by the hands of certain bankers the sum of 3,945,941 ecus and more, which they called 'Le Grand Party' on the condition that he will pay interest at 5% per fair for 41 fairs after which he will be finished. Which of these conditions is better for the bankers?" Translated, the question is whether a perpetuity at 4% per quarter is better or worse than a 41-quarter annuity at 5%.

ANECDOTE   Fibonacci and the Invention of Net Present Value

William Goetzmann argues that Leonardo of Pisa, commonly called Fibonacci, may have invented not only the famous "Fibonacci series" but also the concept of net present value.

Fibonacci's family were merchants in the Mediterranean in the thirteenth century, with trade relations to Arab merchants in Northern Africa. Fibonacci wrote about mathematics primarily as a tool to solve merchants' problems—in effect, to understand the pricing of goods and currencies relative to one another. Imagine how rich you could get if you were the only one who could quickly determine which goods were worth more than others! In fact, you should think of Fibonacci and other Pisan merchants as the "financial engineers" of the thirteenth century.

In 1202, the 30-year-old Fibonacci published his most famous treatise, *Liber Abaci*. We still are using its problems and answers today. One of his puzzles—which you solve in Q3.17—is called "On a Soldier Receiving 300 Bezants for His Fief":

> A soldier is granted an annuity by the king of 300 bezants per year, paid in quarterly installments of 75 bezants. The king alters the payment schedule to an annual year-end payment of 300. The soldier is able to earn 2 bezants on 100 per month (over each quarter) on his investment. How much is his effective compensation after the terms of the annuity changed?

To answer this problem, you must know how to value payments at different points in the future—you must understand the time value of money. What is the value of 75 bezants in one quarter, two quarters, and so forth? What is the value of 300 bezants in one year, two years, and so on? Yes, money sooner is usually worth more than money later—but you need to determine by exactly how much in order to determine how good or bad the change is for the king and the soldier. You must use the interest rate Fibonacci gives and then compare the two different cash flow streams—the original payment schedule and the revised payment schedule—in terms of a common denominator. This common denominator will be the two streams' present values.

William Goetzmann, Yale University

Application: Fixed-Rate Mortgage Payments

Mortgages and other loans are annuities, so the annuity formula is in common use.

Most mortgages are **fixed-rate mortgage loans**, and they are basically annuities. They promise a specified stream of equal cash payments each month to a lender. A 30-year mortgage with monthly payments is really a 360-payment annuity. (The "annu-ity" formula should really be called a "month-ity" formula in this case.) What would be your monthly payment if you took out a 30-year mortgage loan for $500,000 at a quoted interest rate of 7.5% per annum?

Lenders quote interest rates using the same convention as banks.

Before you can proceed further, you need to know one more bit of institutional knowledge here: Mortgage providers—like banks—quote interest by just dividing the mortgage quote by 12, so the true monthly interest rate is $7.5\%/12 = 0.625\%$. (They do not compound; if they did, the monthly interest rate would be $(1 + 7.5\%)^{1/12} - 1 \approx 0.605\%$.)

The mortgage payment can be determined by solving the annuity formula.

A 30-year mortgage is an annuity with 360 equal payments with a discount rate of 0.625% per month. Its PV of $500,000 is the amount that you are borrowing. You want to determine the fixed monthly cash flow that gives the annuity this value:

$$\$500{,}000 \;=\; \frac{C_1}{0.625\%} \cdot \left[1 - \frac{1}{(1 + 0.625\%)^{360}} \right] \;\approx\; C_1 \cdot 143.018$$

$$PV \;=\; \frac{C_1}{r} \cdot \left[1 - \frac{1}{(1 + r)^{T}} \right]$$

Solving for the cash flow tells you that the monthly payment on your $500,000 mortgage will be $500,000/143.018 ≈ $3,496.07 for 360 months, beginning next month (time 1).

Principal and Interest Components

There are two reasons why you may want to determine how much of your $3,496.07 payment should be called interest payment and how much should be called principal repayment. The first reason is that you need to know how much principal you owe if you want to repay your loan early. The second reason is that Uncle Sam allows mortgage borrowers to deduct the interest, but not the principal, from their tax bills.

Repayment and taxes are reasons to determine principal and interest components.

Here is how you can determine the split: In the first month, you pay 0.625% · $500,000 = $3,125 in mortgage interest. Therefore, the principal repayment is $3,496.07 – $3,125 = $371.07 and the remaining principal is $499,628.93. The following month, your interest payment is 0.625% · $499,628.93 ≈ $3,122.68 (note that your interest payment is now on the remaining principal), which leaves $3,496.07 – $3,122.68 = $373.39 as your principal repayment, and $499,255.54 as the remaining principal. And so on.

Principal repayment is the sum left over after the interest payment from your monthly installment.

Q 3.19. Rental agreements are not much different from mortgages. For example, what would your rate of return be if you rented your $500,000 warehouse for 10 years at a monthly lease payment of $5,000? If you can earn 5% per annum elsewhere, would you rent out your warehouse?

Q 3.20. What is the monthly payment on a 15-year mortgage for every $1,000 of mortgage at an effective interest rate of 6.168% per year (here, 0.5% per month)?

Application: A Level-Coupon Bond

Let us exercise your newfound knowledge in a more elaborate example—this time with bonds. Recall that a bond is a financial claim sold by a firm or government. Bonds come in many varieties, but one useful classification is into coupon bonds and zero-bonds (short for **zero coupon bonds**). A **coupon bond** pays its holder cash at many different points in time, whereas a **zero-bond** pays only a single lump sum at the maturity of the bond with no interim coupon. Many coupon bonds promise to pay a regular coupon similar to the interest rate prevailing at the time of the bond's original sale, and then return a "principal amount" plus a final coupon at the end of the bond.

Unlike zero-bonds, coupon bonds pay not only at the final time.

Bond naming
conventions specify
their promised payout
patterns.

For example, think of a coupon bond that will pay $1,500 each half-year (semi-annual payment is very common) for 5 years, plus an additional $100,000 in 5 years. This payment pattern is so common that it has specially named features: A bond with coupon payments that remain the same for the life of the bond is called a **level-coupon bond**. (In fact, these types of bonds are by far the most common among all bonds in the wild.) The $100,000 here would be called the **principal**, in contrast to the $1,500 semiannual coupon. Level bonds are commonly named by just adding up all the coupon payments over 1 year (here, $3,000) and dividing this sum of annual coupon payments by the principal. Thus, this particular bond would be called a "3% semiannual coupon bond" ($3,000 coupon per year divided by the principal of $100,000). Now, the "3% coupon bond" is just a naming convention for the bond with these specific cash flow patterns—it is not the interest rate that you would expect if you bought this bond. In Section 2.4, we called such name designations interest *quotes*, as distinct from interest *rates*. Of course, even if the bond were to cost $100,000 today (and you shall see below that it usually does not), the interest rate would not be 3% per annum, but $1.015^2 - 1 \approx 3.02\%$ per annum.

➤ *Compounding,*
Sect. 2.4, Pg.17.

Step 1: Write down
the bond's payment
stream.

What should this $100,000, 3% semiannual level-coupon bond sell for today? First, you should write down the payment structure for a 3% semiannual coupon bond. This comes from its defined promised payout pattern:

Year	Due Date	Bond Payment	Year	Due Date	Bond Payment
0.5	Nov 2002	$1,500	3.0	May 2005	$1,500
1.0	May 2003	$1,500	3.5	Nov 2005	$1,500
1.5	Nov 2003	$1,500	4.0	May 2006	$1,500
2.0	May 2004	$1,500	4.5	Nov 2006	$1,500
2.5	Nov 2004	$1,500	5.0	May 2007	$101,500

Step 2: Find the
appropriate cost of
capital for each
payment.

Second, you need to determine the appropriate rates of return that apply to these cash flows. In this example, assume that the prevailing interest rate is 5% per annum. This translates into 2.47% for 6 months, 10.25% for 2 years, and so on.

Year	Maturity	Discount Rate	Year	Maturity	Discount Rate
0.5	6 Months	2.47%	3.0	36 Months	15.76%
1.0	12 Months	5.00%	3.5	42 Months	18.62%
1.5	18 Months	7.59%	4.0	48 Months	21.55%
2.0	24 Months	10.25%	4.5	54 Months	24.55%
2.5	30 Months	12.97%	5.0	60 Months	27.63%

Step 3: Compute the
discount factor
$1/(1 + r_t)$.

Third, compute the discount factors, which are just $1/(1 + r_t) = 1/(1 + r)^t$, and multiply each future payment by its discount factor. This will give you the present value (PV) of each bond payment. From there, you can compute the bond's overall value:

Year	Due Date	Bond Payment	Rate of Return	Discount Factor	Present Value
0.5	Nov 2002	$1,500	2.47%	0.9759	$1,463.85
1.0	May 2003	$1,500	5.00%	0.9524	$1,428.57
1.5	Nov 2003	$1,500	7.59%	0.9294	$1,394.14
2.0	May 2004	$1,500	10.25%	0.9070	$1,360.54
2.5	Nov 2004	$1,500	12.97%	0.8852	$1,327.76
3.0	May 2005	$1,500	15.76%	0.8638	$1,295.76
3.5	Nov 2005	$1,500	18.62%	0.8430	$1,264.53
4.0	May 2006	$1,500	21.55%	0.8277	$1,234.05
4.5	Nov 2006	$1,500	24.55%	0.8029	$1,204.31
5.0	May 2007	$101,500	27.63%	0.7835	$79,527.91
				Sum:	$91,501.42

You now know that you would expect this 3% semiannual level-coupon bond to be trading for $91,501.42 today in a perfect market. Because the current price of the bond is below its named final principal payment of $100,000, this bond would be said to trade at a **discount**. (The opposite would be a bond trading at a **premium**.)

Discount and premium bonds.

The bond's value can be calculated more quickly via the annuity formula. Let's work in half-year periods. You have 10 coupon cash flows, each $1,500, at a per-period interest rate of 2.47%. According to the formula, these 10 coupon payments are worth

Using the annuity formula to speed your calculations.

$$PV = C_1 \cdot \left\{ \frac{1 - [1/(1+r)]^T}{r} \right\} = \$1,500 \cdot \left\{ \frac{1 - [1/(1.0247)]^{10}}{2.47\%} \right\} \approx \$13,148.81$$

In addition, you have the $100,000 repayment of principal, which will occur in year 5 and is therefore worth

$$PV = \frac{\$100,000}{(1+5\%)^5} \approx \frac{\$100,000}{1+27.63\%} \approx \$78,352.62$$

$$PV = \frac{C_5}{(1+r)^5} = \frac{C_5}{(1+r_5)}$$

Together, the present values of the bond's cash flows again add up to $91,501.42.

Important Reminder of Quotes versus Returns: Never confuse a bond designation with the interest it pays. The "3% semiannual coupon bond" is just a designation for the bond's payout pattern. The bond will not give you coupon payments equal to 1.5% of your $91,501.42 investment (which would be $1,372.52). The prevailing interest rate (cost of capital) has nothing to do with the quoted interest rate on the coupon bond. You could just as well determine the value of a 0% coupon bond, or a 10% coupon bond, given the prevailing 5% economy-wide interest rate. Having said all this, in the real world, many corporations choose coupon rates similar to the prevailing interest rate, so that at the moment of inception, the bond will be trading at neither a premium nor a discount. At least for this one brief at-issue instant, the coupon rate and the economy-wide interest rate may actually be fairly close. However, soon after issuance, market interest rates will move around, while the bond's payments remain fixed, as designated by the bond's coupon name.

The coupon rate is not the interest rate.

Q 3.21. You already learned that the value of one fixed future payment and the interest rate move in opposite directions (Page 27). What happens to the bond price of $91,501.42 in the level-coupon bond example if the economy-wide interest rates were to suddenly move from 5% per annum to 6% per annum?

Q 3.22. Assume that the 3% level-coupon bond discussed in this chapter has not just 5 years with 10 payments, but 20 years with 40 payments. Also, assume that the interest rate is not 5% per annum, but 10.25% per annum. What are the bond payment patterns and the bond's value?

Q 3.23. Check that the rates of return in the coupon bond valuation example on Page 50 are correct.

3.3 The Four Formulas Summarized

The growing annuity formula—it is used only rarely.

I am not a fan of memorization, but you must remember the growing perpetuity formula. It would likely be useful if you could also remember the annuity formula. These formulas are used in many different contexts. There is also a fourth formula, the **growing annuity formula**, which nobody remembers, but which you should know to look up if you need it. It is

$$ PV = \frac{C_1}{r - g} \cdot \left[1 - \frac{(1 + g)^T}{(1 + r)^T} \right] \tag{3.3} $$

It is sometimes used in the context of pension cash flows, which tend to grow for a fixed number of time periods (T in the formula above) and then stop. However, even then it is not a necessary device. It is often more convenient and flexible to just work with the cash flows themselves within a spreadsheet.

A full summary.

   Exhibit 3.3 summarizes the four special cash flows. The top graph shows the pattern of cash flows. For perpetuities, they go on forever. For annuities, they stop eventually. The bottom graph shows the present value of these cash flows. Naturally, these bars are shorter than those of their cash flows, which just means that there is a time value of money. The applicable formulas are below the graphs.

Q 3.24. In many defined-contribution pension plans, the employer provides a fixed-percentage contribution to the employee's retirement. Assume that you must contribute $4,000 per annum beginning next year (time 1), growing annually with the inflation rate of 2% per year. What is the pension cost of hiring a 25-year-old who will stay with the company for 35 years? Assume a discount rate of 8% per year. Note: Please look up the growing annuity formula to solve this problem.

Simple Perpetuity

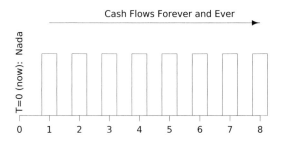

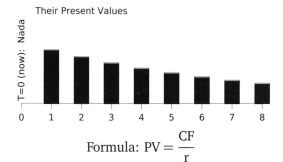

Formula: $PV = \dfrac{CF}{r}$

Growing Perpetuity

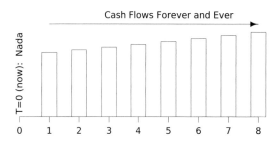

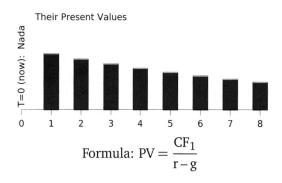

Formula: $PV = \dfrac{CF_1}{r-g}$

Simple Annuity

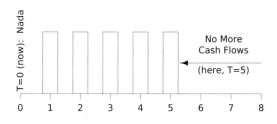

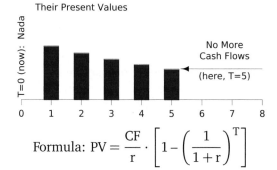

Formula: $PV = \dfrac{CF}{r} \cdot \left[1 - \left(\dfrac{1}{1+r}\right)^{T}\right]$

Growing Annuity

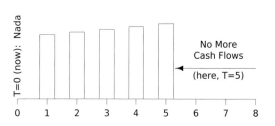

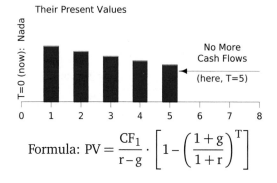

Formula: $PV = \dfrac{CF_1}{r-g} \cdot \left[1 - \left(\dfrac{1+g}{1+r}\right)^{T}\right]$

Exhibit 3.3: *The Four Payoff Streams and Their Present Values.*

Summary

This chapter covered the following major points:

- Exhibit 3.3 summarizes the four special cash flows and their quick valuation formulas.

- The PV of a simple perpetuity, which is a stream of constant cash flows that begin next period and that are to be discounted at the same annual cost of capital forever, is

$$PV = \frac{C_1}{r}$$

- The PV of a growing perpetuity—with constant growth g, cash flows C beginning next year (time 1), and constant per-period interest rate r—is

$$PV = \frac{C_1}{r - g}$$

- Stocks are often valued through an application of the growing perpetuity formula, called the Gordon dividend growth model.

- The PV of an annuity—T periods of constant C cash flows (beginning next year) and constant per-period interest rate r—is

$$PV = C_1 \cdot \left\{ \frac{1 - [1/(1 + r)]^T}{r} \right\}$$

- Fixed-rate mortgages are annuities. Interest rate quoted on such bonds are computed with the annuity formula.

Preview of the Chapter Appendix in the Companion

In the Appendix

The appendix to this chapter

- shows how the annuity and perpetuity formulas can be derived.

- explains "equivalent annual costs" (which you already briefly encountered in Question 2.39). These allow you to compare projects with different rental periods— such as an 8-year lease that charges $1,000 per year and a 10-year lease that charges $900 per year.

➤ *Equivalent Annual Cost, Question 2.39, Pg.31.*

Keywords

Answers

Q 3.1 C_1/r. The first cash flow occurs next period, not this period.

Q 3.2 $PV = C_1/r = \$5/0.005 = \$1,000$

Q 3.3 The interest rate is $1.1268^{(1/12)} - 1 \approx 1\%$ per month. Thus, $PV = C_1/r \approx \$15/0.01 \approx \$1,500$.

Q 3.4 Rearrange $P = C_1/r$ into $r = C_1/P = \$2/\$40 = 5\%$. At a 5% interest rate, you are indifferent. If the interest rate is above 5%, the immediate one-time payment is better, because future cash flows are less valuable. If the interest rate is below 5%, the perpetuity payment is better, because future cash flows are more valuable.

Q 3.5 $PV = \$2,000/4\% = \$50,000$

Q 3.6 $C_1/(r-g)$.

Q 3.7 You get $C_0 = \$5$ today, and next month you will receive a payment of $C_1 = (1+g) \cdot C_0 = 1.001 \cdot \$5 = \$5.005$. The growing perpetuity is worth $PV = C_1/(r-g) = \$5.005/(0.5\% - 0.1\%) = \$1,251.25$. The total value is $\$1,256.25$.

Q 3.8 This is a nonsensical question, because the value would be infinite if $g \geq r$.

Q 3.9 Your earnings will be as follows:

Y	Yearly Dscnt R	Comp. Dscnt R	Growth Rate	Earnings	Present Value
0	10%	10%	20%	($100.0)	
1	10%	21%	20%	$120.0	$109.09
2	10%	33.1%	20%	$144.0	$119.01
3	9%	45.1%	10%	$172.8	$129.83
4	9%	58.1%	10%	$190.1	$131.02
5	9%	72.4%	10%	$209.1	$132.22
6	8%	86.2%	5%	$230.0	$133.43
7	8%	101.1%	5%	$241.5	$129.73
8	⋮	⋮	⋮	$253.6	⋮
⋮	⋮	⋮	⋮	⋮	⋮

Standing in year 7, the growing perpetuity with cash flows of $253.6 (projected for year 8) is worth $253.6/(8% - 5%) ≈ $8,500. (If you are concerned about my rounding too aggressively, you have lost perspective—there is no firm in this world for which you can forecast the value in eight years with more accuracy!) The $8.5 billion is our assumption of what we will be able to sell the firm for at the end of year 7. It is our **terminal value**. All cash flows in year 7 (both the $129.73 that we will still take home, plus the $8,500) are discounted by 101.1%. Therefore, the PV is about $900

million from cash flows that you computed explicitly (years 1 through 7), plus $8,500/(1 + 101.1\%) \approx \$4.2$ billion from the cash flows that is the terminal value stand-in for all cash flows from year 8 to infinity. In sum, the estimate of this firm's present value is around $5.1 billion. (Note: You could also calculate a terminal value in year 6 (for year 7 and beyond), and reach the same answer.)

Q 3.10 $\$1.5$ million/$(14\% - 2\%) = \$12.5$ million.

Q 3.11 The immediate dividend would be worth $1.5 million. In addition, you now have a growing perpetuity that starts with a payment of $1.530 million. Therefore, the PV would be $\$1.500 + \$1.530/12\% = \$14.250$ million. Alternatively, you could multiply the $12.5 million from your answer to Question 3.10 by $(1 + 14\%)$.

Q 3.12 First work out what the value would be if you stood at 1 month. The interest rate is $(1 + 9\%)^{1/12} - 1 \approx 0.7207\%$ per month, and $1.007207^3 - 1 \approx 2.1778\%$ per quarter. Thus, in 1 month, you will be entitled to a dividend stream of $\$5.025/(2.1778\% - 0.5\%) \approx \$299.50$. In addition, you get the $5 for a total of $304.50. Because this is your value in 1 month, discount $304.50 at a 0.7207% interest rate to $302.32 today.

Q 3.13 $g = r - E/P = 12\% - \$5/\$100 = 7\%$ per annum

Q 3.14 Compare the annuity and perpetuity formulas. The difference between them is the $1 - 1/(1 + r)^t$ term. To be three-quarters of the value, this term has to be 3/4. So you must solve $1 - 1/(1 + r)^t = 3/4$, or $1/(1+r)^t = 1 - 3/4 = 1/4$ or $(1+r)^t = 4$. Taking logs, $t = \log(4)/\log(1+r)$. In the main question, r was 5%, so $t = \log(4)/\log(1.05) \approx 28.41$ years. More generally, to reach a given fraction f of value, $t = \log[1/(1-f)]/\log(1+r)$. Think of this number of years as helping you judge the quality of the infinite-period approximation in the real world. If it is more realistic that you have fewer than 30 years of cash flows instead of an infinite stream, then the perpetuity formula may not be a great approximation of value when the interest rate is 5%.

Q 3.15 The annuity formula is $C_1 \cdot \left(\{1 - [1/(1+r)]^T\}/r \right)$.

Q 3.16 Your 360-month annuity is worth

$$C_1 \cdot \left\{ \frac{1 - [1/(1+r)]^T}{r} \right\} = \$5 \cdot \left\{ \frac{1 - [1/(1 + 0.005)]^{360}}{0.005} \right\}$$

$$\approx \$5 \cdot \left\{ \frac{1 - 0.166}{0.005} \right\} \approx \$833.96$$

Q 3.17 For one year, the 300 bezants paid once at year-end are worth $300b/1.02^{12} \approx 236.55$ bezants today. Now for the quarterly payment schedule: The quarterly interest rate is $1.02^3 - 1 \approx 6.12\%$. Therefore, the 4-"quartity" is worth $75b/0.0612 \cdot [1 - 1/1.0612^4] \approx 75b/1.0612^1 + 75b/1.0612^2 + 75b/1.0612^3 + 75b/1.0612^4 \approx 259.17$ bezants. The soldier would have lost 22.62 bezants in present value, which is 8.73% of what he was promised. (The same loss of $236.55/259.17 - 1 \approx 8.73\%$ would apply to longer periods.)

Q 3.18   For each ecu (e), the perpetuity is worth $1e/0.04 = 25e$. The annuity is worth $1e/0.05 \cdot (1 - 1/1.05^{41}) \approx 17.29e$. Therefore, the perpetuity is better.

Q 3.19   To find the implicit cost of capital of the lease, you need to solve

$$\$500,000 = \frac{\$5,000}{r} \cdot \left[1 - \frac{1}{(1+r)^{120}} \right]$$

The solution is $r \approx 0.31142\%$ per month, or 3.8% per annum. This is the implied rate of return if you purchase the warehouse and then rent it out. You would be better off earning 5% elsewhere.

Q 3.20   For \$1,000 of mortgage, solve for C_1 in

$$
\begin{aligned}
PV &= C_1 \cdot \left\{ \frac{1 - [1/(1+r)]^T}{r} \right\} \\
\$1,000 &= C_1 \cdot \left\{ \frac{1 - [1/(1.005)]^{15 \cdot 12 = 180}}{0.005} \right\} \approx C_1 \cdot 118.504 \\
&\Longleftrightarrow \qquad C_1 \approx \$8.44
\end{aligned}
$$

In other words, for every \$1,000 of loan, you have to pay \$8.44 per month. For other loan amounts, just rescale the amounts.

Q 3.21   The semiannual interest rate would now increase from 2.47% to

$$r = \sqrt[2]{1 + 6\%} - 1 = \sqrt{1.06} - 1 \approx 2.9563\%$$

To get the bond's new present value, reuse the annuity formula

$$
\begin{aligned}
PV &= C_1 \cdot \left\{ \frac{1 - [1/(1+r)]^T}{r} \right\} &+& \quad \frac{C_t}{1 + r_t} \\
&\approx \$1,500 \cdot \left\{ \frac{1 - [1/(1 + 2.9563\%)]^{10}}{2.9563\%} \right\} &+& \quad \frac{\$100,000}{(1 + 2.9563\%)^{10}} \\
&\approx \qquad \$12,823.89 &+& \qquad \$74,725.82 \\
&\approx \qquad \$87,549.70
\end{aligned}
$$

This bond would have lost \$3,951.72, or 4.3% of the original investment.

Q 3.22   The interest rate is 5% per half-year. Be my guest if you want to add 40 terms. I prefer the annuity method. The coupons are worth

$$
\begin{aligned}
PV(\text{Coupons}) &= C_1 \cdot \left\{ \frac{1 - [1/(1+r)]^T}{r} \right\} \\
&= \$1,500 \cdot \left\{ \frac{1 - [1/(1.05)]^{40}}{0.05} \right\} \approx \$25,738.63
\end{aligned}
$$

The final payment is worth PV(Principal Repayment) $=$ $\$100,000/(1.05)^{40} \approx \$14,204.57$. Therefore, the bond is worth about \$39,943.20 today.

Q 3.23   For 6 months, $(1 + 2.47\%)^2 - 1 \approx 5\%$. Now, define 6 months to be 1 period. Then, for t 6-month periods, you can simply compute an interest rate of $(1 + 2.47\%)^t - 1$. For example, the 30 months interest rate is $1.0247^5 - 1 \approx 12.97\%$.

Q 3.24   The solution is $\$4,000/(0.08 - 0.02) \cdot \left[1 - \frac{1.02^{35}}{1.08^{35}} \right] \approx$ \$57,649.23.

End of Chapter Problems

Q 3.25. A tall Starbucks coffee costs \$1.65 a day. If the bank's quoted interest rate is 6% per annum, compounded daily, and if the Starbucks price never changed, what would an endless, inheritable free subscription to one Starbucks coffee per day be worth today?

Q 3.26. If you could pay for your mortgage forever, how much would you have to pay per month for a \$1,000,000 mortgage, at a 6.5% annual interest rate? Work out the answer (a) if the 6.5% is a bank APR quote and (b) if the 6.5% is a true effective annual rate of return.

Q 3.27. What is the PV of a perpetuity paying \$30 each month, beginning *next* month, if the annual interest rate is a constant effective 12.68% per year?

Q 3.28. What is the prevailing interest rate if a perpetual bond were to pay \$100,000 per year *beginning next year* and costs \$1,000,000 today?

Q 3.29. What is the prevailing interest rate if a perpetual bond were to pay \$100,000 per year *beginning next year* (time 1) and payments grow with the inflation rate at about 2% per year, assuming the bond costs \$1,000,000 today?

Q 3.30. A tall Starbucks coffee costs \$1.65 a day. If the bank's quoted interest rate is 6% per annum and coffee prices increased at a 3% annual rate of inflation, what would an endless, inheritable free subscription to one Starbucks coffee per day be worth today?

Q 3.31. Economically, why does the growth rate of cash flows have to be less than the discount rate?

Q 3.32. Your firm just finished the year, in which it had cash earnings of $400. You forecast your firm to have a quick growth phase from year 0 to year 5, in which it grows at a rate of 40% per annum. Your firm's growth then slows down to 20% per annum between year 5 to year 10. Finally, beginning in year 11, you expect the firm to settle into its long-term annual growth rate of 2%. You also expect your cost of capital to be 15% over the first 5 years, then 10% over the next 5 years, and 8% thereafter. What do you think your firm is worth today? (Advice: Use a computer spreadsheet program.)

Q 3.33. A stock pays an annual dividend of $2. The dividend is expected to increase by 2% per year (roughly the inflation rate) forever. The price of the stock is $40 per share. At what cost of capital is this stock priced?

Q 3.34. A tall Starbucks coffee costs $1.65 a day. If the bank's quoted interest rate is 6% per annum, compounded daily, and if the Starbucks price never changed, what would a lifetime free subscription to one Starbucks coffee per day be worth today, assuming you will live for 50 more years? What should it be worth to you to be able to bequeath or sell it upon your departure?

Q 3.35. What maximum price would you pay for a standard 8% level-coupon bond (with semiannual payments and a face value of $1,000) that has 10 years to maturity if the prevailing discount rate (your cost of capital) is an effective 10% per annum?

Q 3.36. If you have to pay off an effective 6.5% loan within the standard 30 years, then what are the per-month payments for the $1,000,000 mortgage? As in Question 3.26, consider both an effective 6.5% interest rate per year, and a bank quote of 6.5% (APR) per year.

Q 3.37. Structure a mortgage bond for $150,000 so that its monthly payments are $1,000. The prevailing interest rate is quoted at 6% (APR) per year.

Q 3.38. (Advanced) You are valuing a firm with a "pro forma" (i.e., with your forward projection of what the cash flows will be). The firm just had cash flows of $1,000,000 today. This year, it will be growing by a rate of 20% per annum. That is, at the end of year 1, the firm will have a cash flow of $1.2 million. In each of the following years, the difference between the growth rate and the inflation rate of 2% will (forever) halve. Thus, from year 1 to year 2, the growth rate will be $2\% + (20\% - 2\%)/2 = 11\%$, so the next cash flow will be $\$1,200 \cdot 1.11 = \$1,332$ at the end of year 2. The following year, the growth rate will be $2\% + (11\% - 2\%)/2 = 6.5\%$, and the cash flow will be $1,419 at the end of year 3. The growth will be less every year, but it will never reach the inflation rate of 2% perfectly. Next, assume that the appropriate discount rate for a firm of this riskiness is a constant 12%/year. It is not time-varying. (The discount rate on the $1.2 million cash flow is 12%. The total discount rate for the $1,332 cash flow in year 2 is thus 25.4%, and so on.) What do you believe the value of this firm to be? (Hint: It is common in pro formas to project forward for a given number of years, say, 5 to 10 years, and then to assume that the firm will be sold for a terminal value, assuming that it has steady growth.)

4

A First Encounter with Capital Budgeting Rules

The Internal Rate of Return, and More

This chapter elaborates on the ideas presented in the previous chapter. We still remain in a world of constant interest rates, perfect foresight, and perfect markets. Let's look a little more closely at capital budgeting—the possible decision rules that can tell you whether to accept or reject projects. You already know the answer to the mystery, though: NPV is best. Still, there is one very important alternative to NPV: the internal rate of return, which generalizes the rate of return concept, can often give you good recommendations, too. You will see how these all fit together.

One caveat—although you already know the concept of NPV, and although you will learn more about capital budgeting rules in this chapter, most of the interesting and difficult issues in its application are delayed until Chapter 12 (i.e., after we have covered uncertainty and imperfect markets).

4.1 Net Present Value

Recap: NPV is the most important building block in finance. You must be able to compute it in your sleep.

You have already learned how to use NPV in our perfect world. You first translate cash flows at different points in time into the same units—dollars today—before they can be compared or added. This translation between future values and present values—and its variant, net present value—may well be the most essential concept in finance.

A "free money" interpretation of NPV.

But why is NPV the right rule to use? The reason is that, at least in our perfect world with perfect information, a positive-NPV project is the equivalent of free money. For example, if you can borrow or lend money at 8% anywhere today, and you have an investment opportunity that costs $1 and yields $1.09, you can immediately contract to receive $0.01 next year *for free*. (If you wish, discount it back to today, so you can consume it today.) Rejecting this project would make no sense. Similarly, if you can sell someone an investment opportunity for $1, which yields only $1.07 next year, you can again earn $0.01 *for free*. Again, rejecting this project would make no sense. (Remember that in our perfect world, you can buy or sell projects at will.) Only zero-NPV projects ($1 cost for $1.08 payoff) do not allow you to get free money. Of course, I am using this argument not to show you how to get rich, but to convince you that the NPV rule makes sense and that any rule that comes to a different conclusion does not.

IMPORTANT

> In a perfect world, if you have all the right inputs to NPV, no other rule can make better decisions. Thus, it is the appropriate decision benchmark—and no other rule can beat it. This also means that information other than the NPV is redundant.

Positive-NPV projects are scarce.

In our perfect world with no uncertainty, logic dictates that positive-NPV projects should be scarce. If they were not scarce and you could find them at will, you could get rich too easily. But not just you—everyone with access would want to take on cartloads of them. In real life, the economy would adjust. The "run" on positive-NPV projects would continue until the economy-wide appropriate rate of return (cost of capital) has been bid up to the level where positive-NPV projects are scarce again.

In the real world, NPV is very important, but other measures can provide useful information, too.

As you will find out in later chapters, despite its conceptual simplicity, the application of NPV in the real world is often surprisingly difficult. The primary reason is that you rarely know cash flows and discount factors perfectly. This means that you must estimate them. The secondary reason is that the world is never 100% perfect—that there are absolutely zero taxes, no transaction costs, no disagreements, and infinitely many buyers and sellers. Nevertheless, even in an imperfect market, NPV remains the most important benchmark. Yet, other rules may then provide you with some additional useful information and potentially recommend alternative project choices.

Separating Investment and Consumption Decisions: Does Project Value Depend on When You Need Cash?

Who owns a project is not important in a perfect capital market.

In our perfect world, when you choose between NPV projects, should you let your preferences about the timing of cash flows influence your decisions? Perhaps you don't want to incur an up-front expense; perhaps you want money today; perhaps you want to defer your consumption and save for the future. Aren't these important factors in making your decision as to which project to choose? The answer is no—the value of any project is its net present value, regardless of your preferences.

The capital markets allow you to shift money across time periods—better than your investment projects can.

In a perfect market, how much cash the owner has also does not matter. Let me explain why. You already know about the time value of money, the fact that cash today is worth more than cash tomorrow. If you do not agree—that is, if you value money tomorrow more than you value money today—then just give it to me until you need it back. I can deposit it in my bank account to earn interest in the interim. In a perfect capital market, you can, of course, do better: You can always shift money between time periods at an "exchange rate" that reflects the time value of money.

Example: Even an "eager" consumer should take the positive-NPV project.

It is this shifting-at-will that explains why ownership does not matter. Assume that you have $150 cash on hand and that you have exclusive access to a project that costs $100, and returns $200 next year. The appropriate interest rate (cost of capital) is 10%—but you *really* want to live it up today. How much can you consume? And, would you take the project? Here is the NPV prescription in a perfect market:

- Sell the project in the competitive market for its NPV:

$$- \$100 + \left(\frac{\$200}{1 + 10\%} \right) = -\$100 + \left(\frac{\$200}{1.10} \right) \approx \$81.82$$

- Spend the $150 + ($181.82 − $100) ≈ $231.82 today. You will be better off taking the project than consuming just your $150 cash at hand.

Now, assume that you are Austin Powers, the frozen spy, who cannot consume this year. How much will you be able to consume next year? And, would you take the project? NPV tells you what you should do:

A "sleeper" consumer should also take the positive-NPV project.

- Sell the project in the competitive market for

$$- \$100 + \frac{\$200}{1 + 10\%} \approx \$81.82$$

- Put the $81.82 into the bank for 10% today. Get $90 next year.

- Also put your $150 into the bank at 10% interest to receive $165 next year.

- Next year, consume $90 + $165 = $255.

Of course, an equally simple solution would be to take the project and just put your remaining $50 into a bank account.

The point of this argument is simple: Regardless of when you need or want cash (your consumption decision), you are better off taking all positive-NPV projects (your investment decision), and then using the capital markets to shift consumption to when you want it. It makes no sense to let your *consumption decisions* influence your *investment decisions*. This is called the **separation of decisions**: You can make investment decisions without concern for your consumption preferences. (However, this separation of investment and consumption decisions does not always hold in imperfect markets, in which you can face different borrowing and lending interest rates. You might take more projects if you have more cash.)

The moral of the story: Consumption and investment decisions can be separated in a perfect capital market.

➤ *Imperfect markets, lack of separation, Sect.* 10.1, *Pg.248.*

Here is a simple application of this simplest of insights. After they have lost their clients' money, many brokers like to muddle the truth by claiming that they invested their clients' money for the long term and not for the short term. This excuse presumes that, compared with short-term investments, long-term investments do worse in the short run but better in the long run. However, this makes no sense. See, if your broker had really known that the short-term asset would be better in the short-term, he should have purchased it first, realized its higher rate of return over the short-run for you, and then bought you more of the long-term asset (which would now have been relatively cheaper). The fact is that no matter whether an investor needs money sooner or later, a broker should always purchase the highest NPV investments. In the end, this is what is best for all clients.

Investing for the long-run should be in the same assets as investing for the short-run.

How Bad Are Mistakes?

Errors in Cash Flows versus Errors in the Cost of Capital

Although it would be better to get everything perfect, it is often impossible to come up with perfect cash flow forecasts and appropriate interest rate estimates. Everyone makes errors when outcomes in the world are uncertain. How bad are estimation mistakes? Is it worse to commit an error in estimating cash flows or in estimating the cost of capital? To answer these questions, we will do a simple form of **scenario analysis**, in which we consider a very simple project to learn how changes in our estimates matter to the ultimate present value. Scenario analysis is also essential for managers, who need to learn how sensitive their estimated value is to reasonable alternative possible outcomes. Therefore, this method is also called a **sensitivity analysis**. (It becomes even more important when you work with real options in Chapter 12.)

Short-term projects: Assume that your project will pay off $200 next year, and the proper interest rate for such projects is 8%. Thus, the correct project present value is

$$\text{Correct PV} = \frac{\$200}{1 + 8\%} \approx \$185.19$$

If you make a 10% error in your cash flow, mistakenly believing it to return $220, you will compute the present value to be

$$\text{Cash Flow Error PV} = \frac{\$220}{1 + 8\%} \approx \$203.70$$

The difference between $203.70 and $185.19 is a 10% error in your present value. In contrast, if you make a 10% error in your cost of capital (interest rate), mistakenly believing it to require a cost of capital (expected interest rate) of 8.8% rather than 8%, you will compute the present value to be

$$\text{Discount Rate Error PV} = \frac{\$200}{1 + 8.8\%} \approx \$183.82$$

The difference between $183.82 and $185.19 is less than $2, which is an error of about 1%. In sum, discount rate errors tend to be less harmful than cash flow errors for short-run projects.

Long-term projects: Now take the same example but assume the cash flow will occur in 30 years. The correct present value is now

$$\text{Correct PV} = \frac{\$200}{(1 + 8\%)^{30}} = \frac{\$200}{1.08^{30}} \approx \$19.88$$

The 10% "cash flow error" present value is

$$\text{Cash Flow Error PV} = \frac{\$220}{(1 + 8\%)^{30}} = \frac{\$220}{1.08^{30}} \approx \$21.86$$

and the 10% "interest rate error" present value is

$$\text{Discount Rate Error PV} = \frac{\$200}{(1 + 8.8\%)^{30}} = \frac{\$200}{(1.088\%)^{30}} \approx \$15.93$$

This calculation shows that cash flow estimation errors and interest rate estimation errors are now both important. For longer-term projects, estimating the correct interest rate becomes relatively more important. Yet, though correct, this argument may be misleading. Estimating cash flows 30 years into the future often seems more like voodoo than science. Your uncertainty usually explodes over longer horizons. In contrast, your uncertainty about the long-term cost of capital tends to grow very little with horizon—you might even be able to ask your investors today what they demand as an appropriate cost of capital for a 30-year investment! Of course, as difficult as cash flow estimation may be, you have no alternative. You simply must try to do your best at forecasting.

IMPORTANT

- For short-term projects, errors in estimating correct interest rates are less problematic in computing NPV than are errors in estimating future cash flows.

- For long-term projects, errors in estimating correct interest rates and errors in estimating future cash flows are both problematic in computing NPV. Nevertheless, in reality, you will tend to find it more difficult to estimate far-away future cash flows (and thus you will face more errors) than to estimate the appropriate discount rate demanded by investors today for far-away cash flows.

Q 4.1. What is the main assumption that allows you to consider investment (project) choices without regard to when you need wealth (or how much money you currently have at hand)?

Q 4.2. You have $500 and really, really want to go to the Superbowl tonight (which would consume all your cash). You cannot wait until your project completes: This project would cost $400 and offer a rate of return of 15%, although equivalent interest rates are only 10%. If the market is perfect, what should you do?

4.2 The Internal Rate of Return (IRR)

IRR ≈ NPV.

There is another common capital budgeting method, which often leads to the same recommendations as the NPV rule. This method is useful because it does so through a different route and often provides good intuition about the project.

Our new capital budgeting method compares the project's rate of return to the prevailing rate of return.

Let's assume that you have a project with cash flows that translate into a rate of return of 20% (e.g., $100 investment, $120 payoff), and the prevailing discount rate is 10%. Because your project's rate of return of 20% is greater than the prevailing discount rate of 10%, you should intuitively realize that it is a good one. It is also a positive-NPV project—in the example, $-\$100 + \$120/1.1 \approx \$9.10$.

We need a "sort-of average rate of return" that is implicit in future cash flows.

There is only one problem: How would you compute the rate of return on a project or bond that has many different payments? For example, say the investment costs $100,000 and pays off $5,000 in one year, $10,000 in two years, and $120,000 in three years. What is the rate of return of this project? Think about it. The rate of return formula works only if you have exactly one inflow and one outflow. This is not the case here. What you need now is a "kind of rate of return" (a "statistic") that can take many inflows and outflows and provide something similar to a rate of return. If there is only one of each, it should give the same number as the simple rate of return.

The IRR is this characteristic that describes multiple cash flows.

Such a measure exists. It is called the internal rate of return (IRR). The word "internal" is an indicator that the rate is intrinsic to your project, depending only on its cash flows.

IMPORTANT

> - The **internal rate of return** is the quantity **IRR**, which, given a complete set of cash flows, is the equation that solves the NPV formula set to zero,
>
> $$0 = C_0 + \frac{C_1}{1 + \text{IRR}} + \frac{C_2}{(1 + \text{IRR})^2} + \frac{C_3}{(1 + \text{IRR})^3} + \cdots \qquad (4.1)$$
>
> - If there are only two cash flows, the IRR is the rate of return. Thus, the IRR generalizes the concept of rate of return to multiple cash flows. Every rate of return is an IRR, but the reverse is not the case.
>
> - The IRR itself is best thought of as a characteristic of project cash flows.

YTM is the same as IRR.

The internal rate of return is such a common statistic in the context of bonds that it has acquired a second name: the **yield-to-maturity (YTM)**. There is no difference between the IRR and the YTM.

IRR generalizes rates of return: A simple project's rate of return is its IRR.

Let's illustrate the IRR. First, if there is only one inflow and one outflow, the IRR is the simple rate of return. For example, if a simple project costs $100 today and pays $130 next year, the IRR is obtained by solving

$$-\$100 + \frac{\$130}{1 + \text{IRR}} = 0 \iff \text{IRR} = \frac{\$130 - \$100}{\$100} = 30\%$$

$$C_0 + \frac{C_1}{1 + \text{IRR}} = 0 \iff \text{IRR} = \frac{C_1 - C_0}{C_0}$$

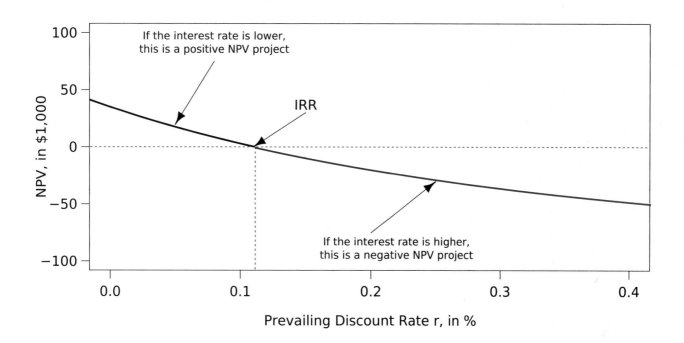

Exhibit 4.1: *NPV as a Function of the Interest Rate.* This figure draws the NPV for a project that costs $100,000 and pays $5,000, $10,000, and $120,000 in consecutive years. The IRR is the x-coordinate where the NPV function intersects the zero-line.

Now consider an example where a simple rate of return won't work: What number would best characterize the implied rate of return for a project that costs $100,000 today and that will yield $5,000, $10,000, and $120,000? You cannot compute a simple rate of return with four cash flows. Exhibit 4.1 shows you the NPV of this project as a function of the prevailing interest rate. If the discount rate is very low, then the NPV is positive. IRR is the interest rate that makes the NPV exactly equal to zero. In this case, this means that you should solve

Here is an iteration method that shows how you can solve the IRR equation yourself.

$$0 = -\$100,000 + \frac{\$5,000}{1 + IRR} + \frac{\$10,000}{(1 + IRR)^2} + \frac{\$120,000}{(1 + IRR)^3}$$

$$0 = C_0 + \frac{C_1}{1 + IRR} + \frac{C_2}{(1 + IRR)^2} + \frac{C_3}{(1 + IRR)^3}$$

What is the discount rate that sets the NPV equation to zero? If you do not want to draw the full figure to find out where your NPV function crosses the zero axis, then you can try to solve such equations by trial and error. Start with two values, say, 5% and 10%.

$$-\$100{,}000 + \frac{\$5{,}000}{1+5\%} + \frac{\$10{,}000}{(1+5\%)^2} + \frac{\$120{,}000}{(1+5\%)^3} \approx \$17{,}493$$

$$-\$100{,}000 + \frac{\$5{,}000}{1+10\%} + \frac{\$10{,}000}{(1+10\%)^2} + \frac{\$120{,}000}{(1+10\%)^3} \approx \$2{,}968$$

To reach zero, you need to slide above 10%. Try 11% and 12%,

$$-\$100{,}000 + \frac{\$5{,}000}{1+11\%} + \frac{\$10{,}000}{(1+11\%)^2} + \frac{\$120{,}000}{(1+11\%)^3} \approx \$364$$

$$-\$100{,}000 + \frac{\$5{,}000}{1+12\%} + \frac{\$10{,}000}{(1+12\%)^2} + \frac{\$120{,}000}{(1+12\%)^3} \approx -\$2{,}150$$

Okay, the solution is closer to 11%. A lucky trial reveals

$$-\$100{,}000 + \frac{\$5{,}000}{1+11.14252\%} + \frac{\$10{,}000}{(1+11.14252\%)^2} + \frac{\$120{,}000}{(1+11.14252\%)^3} \approx 0$$

Therefore, the answer is that this project has an IRR of about 11.14%. You can think of the internal rate of return as a sort-of average rate of return embedded in the project's cash flows.

Spreadsheets make it easy to find the IRR fast.

There is no easy general formula to compute the IRR if you are dealing with more than three cash flows. However, an automated trial-and-error function to compute an IRR is built into modern computer spreadsheets and usually precludes the need to solve algebraic equations. Exhibit 4.2 (row 1) shows how you would find the IRR for this project in a spreadsheet.

	A	B	C	D	E	
1	−100,000	5,000	10,000	120,000	=IRR(A1:D1)	← E1 will become 11.142%
2	100,000	−5,000	−10,000	−120,000	=IRR(A2:D2)	← E2 will become 11.142%
3	−1,000	600	600	=IRR(A3:C3)		← D3 will become 13%

Exhibit 4.2: *IRR Calculations in a Computer Spreadsheet (Excel or OpenOffice).* The first line is the project worked out in the text. The second line shows that the negative of the project has the same IRR. The third line is just another example that you can check for yourself.

Multiplying all cash flows by the same factor does not change the IRR.

Note that the negative cash flow pattern in row 2 of Exhibit 4.2 has the same IRR. That is, receiving an inflow of $100,000 followed by *payments* of $5,000, $10,000, and $120,000 also has an 11.14252% internal rate of return. You can see that this must be the case if you look back at the IRR formula. Any multiplicative factor (like −1) simply cancels out and therefore has no impact on the solution.

$$
\begin{aligned}
0 \;&=\; \text{Factor} \cdot C_0 \;+\; \frac{\text{Factor} \cdot C_1}{1 + \text{IRR}} \;+\; \frac{\text{Factor} \cdot C_2}{(1 + \text{IRR})^2} \;+\; \frac{\text{Factor} \cdot C_3}{(1 + \text{IRR})^3} \;+\; \cdots \\[2ex]
&=\; \text{Factor} \cdot \left[C_0 \;+\; \frac{C_1}{1 + \text{IRR}} \;+\; \frac{C_2}{(1 + \text{IRR})^2} \;+\; \frac{C_3}{(1 + \text{IRR})^3} \;+\; \cdots \right] \\[2ex]
&=\; C_0 \;+\; \frac{C_1}{1 + \text{IRR}} \;+\; \frac{C_2}{(1 + \text{IRR})^2} \;+\; \frac{C_3}{(1 + \text{IRR})^3} \;+\; \cdots
\end{aligned}
$$

Q 4.3. From memory, write down the equation that defines IRR.

Q 4.4. What is the IRR of a project that costs $1,000 now and produces $1,000 next year?

Q 4.5. What is the IRR of a project that costs $1,000 now and produces $500 next year and $500 the year after?

Q 4.6. What is the IRR of a project that costs $1,000 now and produces $600 next year and $600 the year after?

Q 4.7. What is the IRR of a project that costs $1,000 now and produces $900 next year and $900 the year after?

Q 4.8. A project has cash flows of –$100, $55, and $70 in consecutive years. Use a spreadsheet to find the IRR.

Q 4.9. What is the YTM of an x% annual level-coupon bond whose price is equal to the principal paid at maturity? For example, take a 5-year bond that costs $1,000 today, pays 5% coupon ($50 per year) for 4 years, and finally repays $1,050 in principal and interest in year 5.

Q 4.10. What is the YTM of a 5-year zero-bond that costs $1,000 today and promises to pay $1,611?

Q 4.11. Compute the yield-to-maturity of a two-year bond that costs $25,000 today and pays $1,000 at the end of each of the 2 years. At the end of the second year, it also repays $25,000. What is the bond's YTM?

Projects with Multiple or No IRRs

Here is an example of a project with two IRRs.

When projects have many positive and many negative cash flows, they can often have multiple internal rates of return. For example, take a project that costs $100,000, pays $205,000, and has cleanup costs of $102,000. Exhibit 4.3 shows that this project has two internal rates of return: r = −15% and r = 20%. Confirm this:

$$- \$100,000 + \frac{\$205,000}{1 + (-15\%)} + \frac{-\$102,000}{[1 + (-15\%)]^2} = 0$$

$$- \$100,000 + \frac{\$205,000}{1 + 20\%} + \frac{-\$102,000}{(1 + 20\%)^2} = 0$$

Huh? So does this project have an internal rate of return of −15% or an internal rate of return of 20%? The answer is both—the fact is that both IRRs are valid according to the definition. And don't think the number of possible solutions is limited to two—with other cash flows, there could be dozens. What do computer spreadsheets do if there are multiple IRRs? You may never know. They usually just pick one for you. They don't even give you a warning.

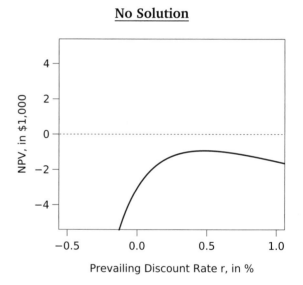

Exhibit 4.3: *Multiple and No IRR Solutions.* The left figure draws the NPV for a project that costs $100,000, pays $205,000, and then has cleanup costs of $102,000. The right figure draws the NPV for a project that costs $10,000, pays $27,000, and then requires a $20,000 cleanup cost.

Projects that have all negative or all positive cash flows have no IRRs—but so do some other projects.

While some projects have multiple IRRs, other projects have none. For example, what is the internal rate of return of a project that yields $10 today and $20 tomorrow (that is, it never demands an investment)? Such a project has no internal rate of return.

The NPV formula is never zero, regardless of what the prevailing interest rate is. This makes sense, and the fact that there is no IRR is pretty obvious from the cash flows. After all, they both have the same sign. But what is the IRR of a project that has cash flows of $10,000, pays $27,000, and then requires a cleanup cost of $20,000? Exhibit 4.3 shows that this project also has no rate of return at which its NPV would turn positive. Therefore, it has no IRR. What do computer spreadsheets do if there are no IRRs? Thankfully, most of the time, they give an error message that will alert you to the problem.

Can you ever be sure that your project has one unique internal rate of return? Yes. It turns out that if you have one negative cash flow followed only by positive cash flows—which happens to be far and away the most common investment pattern—then your project has one and only one IRR. (Projects with cash flows with many different positive and negative signs can still have only one IRR, but it's not guaranteed.) Partly because bonds have such cash flow patterns, YTM is even more popular than IRR. Obviously, you also have a unique IRR if a project has the opposite cash flow pattern—that is, a positive cash inflow followed only by negative cash flows.

The most common types of investment projects have a unique IRR, because they have one outflow followed only by inflows (or vice versa).

Q 4.12. Give an example of a problem that has multiple IRR solutions.

Q 4.13. Give an example of a project that has no IRR.

Q 4.14. For the following projects A through G, plot the NPVs as a function of the prevailing interest rate and determine the appropriate IRRs.

	Y0	Y1	Y2	Y3	Y4
A	+$1,000	−$5,000	+$9,350	−$7,750	+$2,402.4
B	+$50,000	−$250,000	+$467,500	−$387,500	$120,120
C	+$100,000	−$250,000	+$200,000		
D	−$100	+$300	−$400	+$400	
E	+$100	−$300	+$400	−$400	
F	+$200	−$600	+$800	−$800	
G	−$100	+$300	−$200		

IRR as a Capital Budgeting Rule

One important reason why IRR is so useful is that it can often substitute for NPV as an investment criterion.

IRR rule often yields the same result as the NPV rule.

IMPORTANT

- The IRR capital budgeting rule states that if and only if an investment project's IRR (a characteristic of project cash flows) is above the appropriate discount rate (cost of capital) for the project, then the project should be taken. In this context, the cost of capital is often called the **hurdle rate**.

> In many cases, the IRR capital budgeting rule gives the same correct answer as the NPV capital budgeting rule. However, there are some delicate situations in which this is not the case. This will be explained below.

Confirm that the IRR and NPV capital budgeting rules give the same recommendation.

Let me illustrate that you usually get the same answer. Return to our project that costs $100,000 and yields $5,000, $10,000, and $120,000 with its IRR of 11.14%. The IRR capital budgeting rule states that if the prevailing cost of capital in the economy (i.e., the hurdle rate) to finance our project is 11.20%, then you should not take this project. If it is 11.10%, then you should take this project. Does NPV offer the same recommendation? Try it:

$$\text{NPV at } 11.10\% \;=\; -\$100,000 + \frac{\$5,000}{1+11.10\%} + \frac{\$10,000}{(1+11.10\%)^2} + \frac{\$120,000}{(1+11.10\%)^3} \approx +\$108$$

$$\text{NPV at } 11.20\% \;=\; -\$100,000 + \frac{\$5,000}{1+11.20\%} + \frac{\$10,000}{(1+11.20\%)^2} + \frac{\$120,000}{(1+11.20\%)^3} \approx -\$146$$

Indeed, you get the same recommendation.

If the cash flow is negative, the IRR stays the same, but the take-it-or-leave-it rule reverses.

If the cash flows are the exact opposite—that is, if you receive $100,000 up-front and pay out $5,000, $10,000, and $120,000—then this would not really be an investment project, but more like investment financing. You would now want to take this financing alternative if and only if the prevailing interest rate is *above* 11.14%. Be careful about whether you want your IRR to be above or below the hurdle rate! (My advice to avoid such errors is to always work out the NPV, too—it will never mislead you.)

IRR can be computed before the cost of capital is known.

Why use the IRR instead of the NPV investment criterion? The answer is that the former is often quite intuitive and convenient, provided that the project's cash flow stream implies one unique IRR. In this case, IRR is convenient because you can compute it without having looked at financial markets, interest rates, or costs of capital. This is IRR's most important advantage over NPV: *It can be calculated even before you know the appropriate interest rate (cost of capital).* Moreover, IRR can give you useful project information in and of itself. It is also helpful in judging project profitability and thereby allows you to judge the performance of a manager—it is often easier to hold her to her earlier promise of delivering an IRR of 20% than it is to argue with her about what the appropriate cost of capital for her project should be.

IRR is a characteristic of a project's cash flows. (It is not an interest rate.)

Q 4.15. A project has cash flows of –$1,000, –$2,000, +$3,000, and +$4,000 in consecutive years. Your cost of capital is 30% per annum. Use the IRR rule to determine whether you should take this project. Does the NPV rule recommend the same action?

Q 4.16. A project has cash flows of –$1,000, –$2,000, –$3,000, +$4,000, and +$5,000 in consecutive years. Your cost of capital is 20% per annum. Use the IRR rule to determine whether you should take this project. Confirm your recommendation using the NPV rule.

Q 4.17. A project has cash flows of +$200, –$180, –$40 in consecutive years. The prevailing interest rate is 5%. Should you take this project?

Q 4.18. You can invest in a project with diminishing returns. Specifically, the formula relating next year's payoff to your investment today is $C_1 = \sqrt{-C_0}$, where C_0 and C_1 are measured in million dollars. For example, if you invest $100,000 in the project today, it will return $\sqrt{\$0.1} \approx \$0.316$ million next year. The prevailing interest rate is 5% per annum. Use a spreadsheet to answer the following two questions:

1. What is the IRR-maximizing investment choice? What is the NPV at this choice?
2. What is the NPV-maximizing investment choice? What is the IRR at this choice?

Problems with IRR as a Capital Budgeting Rule

If you use IRR *correctly* and in the right circumstances, it can give you the same answer as the NPV rule. (Of course, you cannot do better than doing it correctly, so it is always safer to use the NPV rule than the IRR rule.) When does the IRR capital budgeting rule work well? If there is only one unique IRR, it is often an elegant method. Of course, as just noted, you still have to make sure that you get the sign right. If your project requires an up-front outlay followed by inflows, you want to take the project if its IRR is *above* your cost of capital. If the project is financing (like debt, which has an up-front inflow followed by outflows), you want to take this project if its IRR is *below* your cost of capital. My advice is to use NPV as a check of your IRR calculations in any case.

> IRR is safe to use when there is only one positive or only one negative cash flow.

Unfortunately, if the IRR is not unique (and recall that there are projects with multiple IRRs or no IRR), then the IRR criterion becomes outright painful. For example, if your prevailing cost of capital is 9% and your project has IRRs of 6%, 8%, and 10%, should you take this project or avoid it? The answer is not obvious. In this case, to make an investment decision, you are better off falling back to drawing a part of the NPV graph in one form or another. My advice: just avoid IRR. (Yes, it is possible to figure out how to use IRR, depending on whether the NPV function crosses the 0-axis from above or below, but working with IRR under such circumstances only begs for trouble, i.e., mistakes. There is also a "modified IRR" [the so-called MIRR] measure that can sometimes eliminate multiple solutions. It is not worth the trouble.) If you have a project without any valid IRR, you again have to fall back to NPV, but using NPV will be simple. Just work out whether the NPV function is above or below the 0-axis for any arbitrary discount rate (e.g., $r = 0$), and use this to decide whether to take or to reject your project.

> IRR often fails in nonobvious ways when there are multiple negative or positive cash flows.

There are two more problems when using IRR that you need to be aware of:

> Two more problems: (1) IRR has no concept of scale; (2) there may not be an obvious hurdle rate to compare it to.

1. **Project comparisons and scale:** The IRR criterion can be misleading when projects are mutually exclusive. For example, if you had to choose, would you always prefer a project with a 100% IRR to a project with a 10% IRR? Think about it.

   What if the first project is an investment opportunity of $5 (returning $10), and the second project is an investment opportunity of $1,000 (returning $1,100)? Take the case where the prevailing discount rate is 5% per annum. Then,

	Y0	Y1	IRR	NPV at 5%
A	−$5	+$10	100%	+$4.52
B	−$1,000	+$1,100	10%	+$47.62

If you can only take one project, then you should take project B, even though its IRR is much lower than that of project A.

2. **Cost of capital comparison:** The next chapter explains that long-term interest rates are often higher than short-term interest rates. For example, in mid-2002, a 1-year Treasury bond offered a rate of return of 2%, while a 20-year bond offered a rate of return of 6%. Let's assume that your project is risk-free, too. Should you take a risk-free project that has an IRR of 4%? There is no clear answer.

These two problems may seem obvious when highlighted in isolation. But in the context of complex, real-world, multiple-project analyses, they are surprisingly often overlooked.

Q 4.19. What are the problems with the IRR computation and criterion?

Q 4.20. The prevailing interest rate is 25%. If the following two projects are mutually exclusive, which should you take?

	Y0	Y1	Y2	Y3	Y4
A	+$50,000	−$250,000	+$467,500	−$387,500	+$120,120
B	−$50,000	+$250,000	−$467,500	+$387,500	−$120,120

What does the NPV rule recommend? What does the IRR rule recommend?

Q 4.21. The prevailing interest rate is 25%. If the following two projects are mutually exclusive, which should you take?

	Y0	Y1	Y2	Y3
A	+$500,000	−$200,000	−$200,000	−$200,000
B	+$50,000	+$25,000		

What does the NPV rule recommend? What does the IRR rule recommend?

Q 4.22. The prevailing interest rate is 10%. If the following three projects are mutually exclusive, which should you take?

	Y0	Y1	Y2
A	−$500	+$300	+$300
B	−$50	+$30	+$30
C	−$50	+$35	+$35

What does the NPV rule recommend? What does the IRR rule recommend?

Q 4.23. The prevailing interest rate is 5% over the first year and 10% over the second year. That is, over two years, your compounded interest rate is $(1+5\%) \cdot (1+10\%) - 1 = 15.5\%$. Your project costs $1,000 and will pay $600 in the first year and $500 in the second year. What does the IRR rule recommend? What does the NPV rule recommend?

4.3 The Profitability Index

A less prominent measure sometimes used in capital budgeting is the **profitability index**. It divides the present value of future cash flows by the project cost (the negative of the first cash flow). For example, if you have a project with cash flows

	Y0	Y1	Y2	Y3	PV(Y1 to Y3)
Project A Cash Flow	–$100	$70	$60	$50	$128.94

How the probability index is computed.

and the interest rate is 20% per annum, you would first compute the present value of future cash flows as

$$PV = \frac{\$70}{1.2} + \frac{\$60}{1.2^2} + \frac{\$50}{1.2^3} \approx \$128.94$$

$$= PV(C_1) + PV(C_2) + PV(C_3)$$

Subtract the $100 up-front cost, and the NPV is $28.94. The profitability index is

$$\text{Profitability Index} = \frac{\$128.94}{-(-\$100)} \approx 1.29$$

$$\text{Profitability Index} = \frac{PV(\text{Future Cash Flows})}{\text{Original Cost}}$$

A positive-NPV project usually has a profitability index above 1—"usually" because the profitability index is meaningful only if the first cash flow is a cash outflow. When this is the case, you can use either NPV or the profitability index for a simple "accept/reject" decision: The statements "NPV > 0" and "profitability index > 1" are the same. That is, like IRR, the profitability index can give the correct answer in the most common situation of one negative cash flow up-front followed by all positive cash flows thereafter.

A profitability index–based capital budgeting rule can give the same answer as IRR (and NPV).

Some managers like the fact that the profitability index gives information about relative performance and use of capital. For example,

Here it works nicely, and may even convey some information above and beyond IRR.

	Y0	Y1	Y2	Y3	PV(Y1 to Y3)
Project B Cash Flow	–$10.00	$21.14	$18.12	$15.10	$38.94

has the same NPV of $28.94 as the original project, but B's profitability index is higher than 1.29 because it requires less capital up-front.

$$\text{Profitability Index} = \frac{\$38.94}{-(-\$10)} \approx 3.89$$

$$\text{Profitability Index} = \frac{PV(\text{Future Cash Flows})}{\text{Original Cost}}$$

The reason is that the profitability index values the scale of the project differently. It is intuitively apparent that you would prefer the second project, even though it has the same NPV, because it requires less capital. It may even be less risky, but this can be deceiving, because we have not specified the risk of the future cash flows.

But here is where the profitability index can go wrong: Like IRR, it has no concept of scale.

Unfortunately, this feature that you just considered an advantage can also be a disadvantage. You cannot use the profitability index to choose among different projects. For example, assume that your first project returns twice as much in cash flow in all future periods, so it is clearly the better project now.

	Y0	Y1	Y2	Y3	PV(Y1 to Y3)	NPV	Profitability Index
B	−$10	$21.14	$18.12	$15.10	$38.94	$28.94	$\dfrac{\$38.94}{-(-\$10)} \approx 3.89$
C	−$100	$140	$120	$100	$257.87	$157.87	$\dfrac{\$257.87}{-(-\$100)} \approx 2.58$

Note that the profitability index of project C is less than that of project B. The reason is that, when compared to NPV, the profitability index *really* "likes" lower-up-front investment projects. It can therefore indicate higher index values even when the NPV is lower. This is really the same scale problem that popped up when we tried to use IRR for comparing mutually exclusive projects. Both look at relative "percentage" performance, not at the dollar gain, like NPV does. You should really consider the profitability index in choosing among projects only if the NPVs of the two projects are equal (or at least very similar).

Q 4.24. The prevailing interest rate is 10%. If the following three projects are mutually exclusive, which should you take?

	Y0	Y1	Y2
A	−$500	+$300	+$300
B	−$50	+$30	+$30
C	−$50	+$35	+$35

You have already worked out the recommendations of the NPV and the IRR rule. What does the profitability rule recommend?

4.4   The Payback Capital Budgeting Rule

The most common aberrant capital budgeting rule in the real world is the payback rule.

What if you want something more "practical" than the eggheaded "theoretical" capital budgeting methods? Aren't there easier methods that can help you make investment decisions? Yes, they exist—and they usually result in bad (though practical) choices. Indeed, after IRR and NPV, the most commonly used capital budgeting rule is a "practical" one, the **payback rule**. You need to know why you should not fall for it.

Under the payback rule, projects are assumed to be better if you can recover their original investment faster. For the most part, this is a stupid idea. Consider the following three projects:

Here is why choosing projects based solely on payback speed is dumb.

	Y1	Y2	Y3	Y4	Payback Period
A	−$5	+$8			1 year
B	−$5	+$4	$100		2 years
C	−$5	+$4	$0	$100,000	3 years

Project A has the shortest (best) payback period, but it is the worst of the three projects (assuming common discounting rates). Project B has the next shortest payback period, but it is the second-worst of the three projects (assuming reasonable interest rates). Project C has the longest (worst) payback period, but is the best project. There is also a version of payback in which future paybacks are discounted (**discounted payback**). This measure asks not how long it takes you to get your money back, but how long it takes you to get the present value of your money back. It is still a bad idea.

To be fair, payback can be an interesting number.

In fairness, the speed of payback can be an interesting statistic.

1. There is a beautiful simplicity to payback. Everyone will understand "you will get your money back within five years," but not everyone will understand "the NPV is $50 million." Payback is "finance for dummies."

2. Payback's emphasis on earlier cash flows helps firms set criteria when they don't trust their managers. For instance, if your department manager claims that you will get your money back within one year, and three years have already passed without your having seen a penny, then something is probably wrong and you may need a better manager.

3. Payback can also help if you are an entrepreneur with limited capital, faced with an imperfect capital market. In such cases, your cost of capital can be very high and getting your money back in a short amount of time is paramount. The payback information can help you assess your future "liquidity."

➤ *Entrepreneurial finance, Sect. 10.5, Pg.269.*

4. Finally, in many ordinary situations, in which the choice is a pretty clear-cut yes or no, the results of the payback rule may not lead to severe mistakes (as would a rule that would ignore all time value of money). If you have a project in which you get your money back within one month, chances are that it's not a bad one, even from an NPV perspective. If you have a project in which it takes fifty years to get your money back, chances are that it has a negative NPV.

Having said all this, if you use payback to make decisions, it can easily lead you to take the wrong projects and ruin your company. Why take a chance when you know better capital budgeting methods? My view is that it is not a bad idea to work out the payback period and use it as "interesting supplemental information," but you should never base project choices on it—and you should certainly never compare different projects primarily on the basis of payback.

It is best to avoid payback as a primary decision rule.

4.5 How Do Executives Decide?

Method	CFO Usage	Yields Correct Answer	Main Explanation
Internal Rate of Return (IRR)	▬▬▬▬▬▬ (76%)	Often	Chapter 4
Net Present Value (NPV)	▬▬▬▬▬▬ (75%)	(Almost) Always	Chapter 2
Payback Period	▬▬▬▬ (57%)	Rarely	Chapter 4
Earning Multiples (P/E Ratios)	▬▬▬ (39%)	With Caution	Chapter 14
Discounted Payback	▬▬▬ (30%)	Rarely	Chapter 4
Accounting Rate of Return	▬▬ (20%)	Rarely	Chapter 14
Profitability Index	▬ (12%)	Often	Chapter 4

Exhibit 4.4: *CFO Valuation Techniques.* Rarely means "usually no—often used incorrectly in the real world." NPV works *if correctly applied*, which is why I added the qualifier "almost" to always. Of course, if you are considering an extremely good or an extremely bad project, almost any evaluation criterion is likely to give you the same recommendation. (Even a stopped clock gives you the correct time twice a day.) Source: John Graham and Campbell Harvey, 2001.

A survey asked CFOs what they use. It found the good methods (NPV and IRR) are most important.

So what do managers really use for capital budgeting? In a 2001 survey, Graham and Harvey (from Duke University) asked 392 managers, primarily **chief financial officers (CFOs)**, what techniques they use when deciding on projects or acquisitions. The results are listed in Exhibit 4.4. The two most prominent measures are also the correct ones: They are the "internal rate of return" and the "net present value" methods. Alas, the troublesome "payback period" method and its cousin, the "discounted payback period," still remain surprisingly common.

The two unexplained methods (P/E and accounting rate of return) in the table are based on accounting numbers.

➤ *Financials, Chapter 13, Pg.369.*

➤ *Comparables, Chapter 14, Pg.413.*

➤ *ROE=Accounting rate of return, Formula 14.5, Pg.452.*

➤ *Warning about BV stock numbers, Sect. 13.7, Pg.405.*

Of course, this is your first encounter with capital budgeting rules, and there will be a lot more details and complications to come (especially for NPV). Let me also briefly explain the two methods mentioned in the table that you do not know yet: the "earnings multiples" and the "accounting rate of return" methods. They will be explained in great detail in Chapters 13 and 14. In a nutshell, the "earnings multiples" method tries to compare your project's earnings directly to the earnings of other firms in the market. If your project costs less and earns more than these alternative opportunities, then the multiples approach usually suggests you take it. It can often be useful, but considerable caution is warranted. The "accounting rate of return" method uses an accounting "net income" and divides it by the "book value of equity." This is rarely a good idea—financial accounting is not designed to accurately reflect firm value. (Accounting statements are relatively better in measuring flows [like earnings] than they are in measuring stocks [like book value].)

Graham and Harvey did not allow respondents to select a third measure for project choice: a desire to maximize reported earnings. Managers care about earnings, especially in the short run and just before they are up for a performance evaluation or retirement. Thus, they may sometimes pass up good projects for which the payoff is far in the future.

As you will learn, rules that are based on accounting conventions and not on economics are generally not advisable. I almost always recommend against using them. I have no idea what kind of projects you will end up with if you were to follow their recommendations—except that in many cases, if the measures are huge (e.g., if the accounting rate of return is 190% per annum), then chances are that the project has positive NPV, too.

One view, perhaps cynical, is that all the capital budgeting methods you have now learned give you not only the tools to choose the best projects but also the language to argue intelligently and professionally to get your favorite projects funded. In many corporations, "power" rules. The most influential managers get disproportionally large funding for their projects. This is of course not a good objective, much less a quantitative value-maximization method for choosing projects.

> The survey unfortunately did not ask managers whether they select projects primarily to increase earnings—a pity.
>
> Accounting-based rules are problematic.
>
> In real-life, the best projects are often not taken. Math may just be a weapon to win the fight to convince others to fund projects.

Summary

This chapter covered the following major points:

- If the market is perfect and you have the correct inputs, then net present value is the undisputed correct method to use.

- In a perfect market, projects are worth their net present values. This value does not depend on who the owner is or when the owner needs cash. Any owner can always take the highest NPV projects and use the capital markets to shift cash into periods in which it is needed. Therefore, consumption and investment decisions can be made independently.

- The internal rate of return, IRR, is computed from a project's cash flows by setting the NPV formula equal to zero.

- The internal rate of return does not depend on the prevailing cost of capital. It is a project-specific measure. It can be interpreted as a "sort-of-average" rate of return implicit in many project cash flows. Unlike a simple rate of return, it can be computed when a project has more than one inflow and outflow.

- Projects can have multiple IRR solutions or no IRR solutions.

- Investment projects with IRRs above their costs of capital often, but not always, have positive net present values (NPV), and vice versa. Investment projects with IRRs below their costs of capital often, but not always, have negative net present values (NPV), and vice versa. If the project is a financing method rather than an ordinary investment project, these rules reverse.

- IRR suffers from comparison problems because it does not adjust for project scale. IRR can also be difficult to use if the cost of capital depends on the project cash flow timing.

- The profitability index is often acceptable, too. It rearranges the NPV formula. If used by itself, it often provides the same capital budgeting advice as NPV. But, like IRR, the profitability index can make projects with lower up-front costs and scale appear relatively more desirable.

- The payback measure is commonly used. It suggests taking the projects that return the original investment most quickly. It discriminates against projects providing very large payments in the future. Although it sometimes provides useful information, it is best avoided as a primary decision rule.

- The information that many other capital budgeting measures provide can sometimes be "interesting." However, they often provide results that are not sensible and therefore should generally be avoided—or at least consumed with great caution.

- NPV and IRR are the methods most popular with CFOs. This makes sense. It remains a minor mystery as to why the payback method enjoys the popularity that it does.

Keywords

CFO, 76.   Chief financial officer, 76.   Discounted payback, 75.   Hurdle rate, 69.   IRR, 64.   Internal rate of return, 64.   Payback rule, 74.   Profitability index, 73.   Scenario analysis, 350.   Sensitivity analysis, 62. Separation of decisions, 61.   YTM, 64.   Yield-to-maturity, 64.

Answers

Q 4.1 The fact that you can use capital markets to shift money back and forth without costs allows you to consider investment and consumption choices independently.

Q 4.2 If you invest $400, the project will give $400 \cdot 1.15 = $460 next period. The capital markets will value the project at $460/1.10 \approx $418.18. You should take the project and immediately sell it for $418.18. Thereby, you will end up being able to consume $500 - $400 + $418.18 = $518.18.

Q 4.3 The equation that defines IRR is Formula 4.1 on Page 64.

Q 4.4 $-\$1,000 + \dfrac{\$1,000}{(1+\text{IRR})} = 0 \implies \text{IRR} = 0\%$

Q 4.5 $-\$1,000 + \dfrac{\$500}{(1+\text{IRR})} + \dfrac{\$500}{(1+\text{IRR})^2} = 0 \implies \text{IRR} = 0\%$

Q 4.6 $-\$1,000 + \dfrac{\$600}{(1+\text{IRR})} + \dfrac{\$600}{(1+\text{IRR})^2} = 0 \implies \text{IRR} \approx 13.07\%$

Q 4.7 $-\$1,000 + \dfrac{\$900}{(1+\text{IRR})} + \dfrac{\$900}{(1+\text{IRR})^2} = 0 \implies \text{IRR} = 50\%$

Q 4.8 The spreadsheet function is called IRR(). The answer pops out as 15.5696%. Check: $-\$100 + \$55/1.16 + \$70/1.16^2 \approx 0$.

Q 4.9 The coupon bond's YTM is 5%, because $-\$1,000 + \dfrac{\$50}{1.05} + \dfrac{\$50}{1.05^2} + \dfrac{\$50}{1.05^3} + \dfrac{\$50}{1.05^4} + \dfrac{\$1,050}{1.05^5} = 0$. The YTM of such a bond (annual coupons) is equal to the coupon rate when a bond is selling for its face value.

Q 4.10 The YTM is 10%, because $-\$1,000 + \$1,611/1.10^5 \approx 0$.

Q 4.11 You are seeking the solution to $-\$25,000 + \dfrac{\$1,000}{(1+\text{YTM})^1} + \dfrac{\$1,000}{(1+\text{YTM})^2} + \dfrac{\$25,000}{(1+\text{YTM})^2} = 0$. It is YTM = 4%.

Q 4.12 For example, $C_0 = -\$100, C_1 = +\$120, C_2 = -\$140, C_3 = +\$160, C_4 = -\$20$. (The solutions are IRR $\approx -85.96\%$ and

IRR $\approx$ +$9.96%. The important aspect is that your example has multiple inflows and multiple outflows.)

Q 4.13 For example, $C_0 = -\$100, C_1 = -\$200, C_2 = -\$50$. No interest rate can make their present value equal to zero, because all cash flows are negative. This project should never be taken, regardless of cost of capital.

Q 4.14 For projects A and B, the valid IRRs are 10%, 20%, 30%, and 40%. The plot for A follows. The plot for B has a y-scale that is 50 times larger. For project C, there is no IRR, also shown in the plot below.

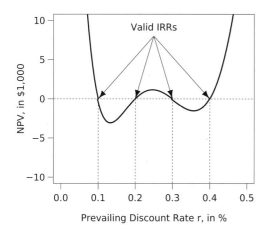

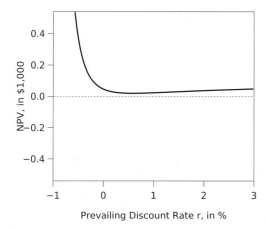

For projects D, E, and F, the IRR is 100%. For project G, the IRRs are 0% and 100%.

Q 4.15 The (unique) IRR is 56.16%. This is higher than your 30% cost of capital, so you should take this project. The NPV is +$1,057.35. Because this is positive, it gives the same recommendation—accept.

Q 4.16 The IRR is 19.73%. This is lower than your 20% cost of capital, so you should not take this project. The NPV is –$23.92. IRR and NPV agree on the reject recommendation.

Q 4.17 The IRR is 8.44%. This is above the prevailing interest rate. However, the cash flows are like that of a financing project. This means that it is a negative NPV project of –$7.71. You should not take it.

Q 4.18 (a) The IRR-maximizing investment choice of C_0 is an epsilon. The IRR is then close to infinity. The NPV is 0. (b) The NPV-maximizing (and best) choice is an investment of $226,757. This also happens to be the project's NPV. The IRR is 110%.

Q 4.19 The problems are (a) you need to get the sign right to determine whether you should accept the project above or below its hurdle rate; (b) you need to make sure you have only one unique IRR (or work with a more complicated version of IRR, which we have not done); (c) you cannot use it to compare different projects that have different scales; and (d) you must know your cost of capital.

Q 4.20 The first project has a positive NPV of

$$\$50,000 + \frac{-\$250,000}{1.25} + \frac{\$467,500}{1.25^2}$$
$$+ \frac{-\$387,500}{1.25^3} + \frac{\$120,120}{1.25^4} \approx \$1.15$$

The second project has an NPV of –$1.15. You should take project A, but not B. If you plot the NPV as a function of the interest, you will see that there are multiple IRRs for these projects, specifically at 10%, 20%, 30%, and 40%. With a cost of capital of 25%, you cannot easily determine which of these two projects you should take. Make your life easy, and just use NPV instead.

Q 4.21 Project A has an NPV of

$$+ \$500,000 + \frac{-\$200,000}{1.25} + \frac{-\$200,000}{(1.25)^2} + \frac{-\$200,000}{(1.25)^3}$$
$$= \$109,600$$

It has an IRR of 9.70%. Project B has an NPV of $70,000, and no IRR (it is always positive). Therefore, even though the second project should be taken for any interest rate—which is not the case for the first—the first project is better. Take project A.

Q 4.22 The first project (A) has an NPV of $20.66 and an IRR of 13.07%. The second project (B) has an NPV of $2.07 and the same IRR of 13.07%. The third project (C) has an NPV of $10.74 and an IRR of 25.69%. Even though project A does not have the highest IRR, you should take it.

Q 4.23 The IRR is 6.81%. This is between the one-year 5% and the two-year 10% interest rates. Therefore, the IRR capital budgeting rule cannot be applied. The NPV rule gives you –$1,000+$600/1.05+$500/1.155 $\approx$ $4.33, so this is a good project that you should take.

Q 4.24 The first project (A) has present values of future cash flows of $520.66; the second (B) of $52.07; the third (C) of $60.74. The profitability indexes are $520.66/$500 $\approx$ 1.04, $52.07/$50 $\approx$ 1.04, and $60.74/$50 $\approx$ 1.21. Nevertheless, you should go with the first project, because it has the highest net present value. The discrepancy between the NPV and the profitability rule recommendations is because the latter does not take project scale into account.

End of Chapter Problems

Q 4.25. Given the same NPV, would you be willing to pay extra for a project that bears fruit during your lifetime rather than after you are gone?

Q 4.26. How bad a mistake is it to misestimate the cost of capital in a short-term project? Please illustrate.

Q 4.27. How bad a mistake is it to misestimate the cost of capital in a long-term project? Please illustrate.

Q 4.28. What is the difference between YTM and IRR?

Q 4.29. A project has cash flows of –$1,000, +$600, and +$300 in consecutive years. What is the IRR?

Q 4.30. What is the YTM of a standard 6% level semi-annual 10-year coupon bond that sells for its principal amount today (i.e., at par = $100)?

Q 4.31. A coupon bond costs $100, then pays $10 interest each year for 10 years, and pays back its $100 principal in 10 years. What is the bond's YTM?

Q 4.32. A project has cash flows –$100 as of now, +$55 next year, and +$60.50 in the year after. How can you characterize the "rate of return" (loosely speaking) embedded in its cash flows?

Q 4.33. Under what circumstances is an IRR a rate of return? Under what circumstances is a rate of return an IRR?

Q 4.34. Give an example of a problem that has multiple IRR solutions.

Q 4.35. Your project has cash flows of –$1,000 in year 0, +$3,550 in year 1, –$4,185 in year 2, and +$1,638 in year 3. What is its IRR?

Q 4.36. Your project has cash flows of –$1,000 in year 0, +$3,550 in year 1, –$4,185 in year 2, and –$1,638 in year 3. What is its IRR?

Q 4.37. A project has cash flows of +$400, –$300, and –$300 in consecutive years. The prevailing interest rate is 5%. Should you take this project?

Q 4.38. A project has cash flows of –$100, +$55, and +$60.50 in consecutive years starting from right now. If the hurdle rate is 10%, should you accept the project?

Q 4.39. If a project has a cash inflow of $1,000 followed by cash outflows of $600 in two consecutive years, then under what discount rate scenario should you accept this project?

Q 4.40. You can invest in a project with returns that depend on the amount of your investment. Specifically, the formula relating next year's payoff (cash flow) to your investment today is $C_1 = \sqrt{-C_0 - \$0.1}$, where C_0 and C_1 are measured in million dollars. For example, if you invest $500,000 in the project today, it will return $\sqrt{\$0.5 - \$0.1} \approx \$0.632$ million next year. The prevailing interest rate is 6% per annum. Use a spreadsheet to answer the following two questions:

1. What is the IRR-maximizing investment choice of C_0? What is the NPV at this level?

2. What is the NPV -maximizing investment choice of C_0? What is the IRR at this level?

Q 4.41. The prevailing interest rate is 10%. If the following three projects are mutually exclusive, which should you take?

	Y0	Y1	Y2
A	+$500	–$300	–$300
B	+$50	–$30	–$30
C	+$50	–$35	–$35

What does the NPV rule recommend? What does the IRR rule recommend?

Q 4.42. What are the profitability indexes and the NPVs of the following two projects: project A that requires an investment of $5 and gives $20 per year for three years, and project B that requires an investment of $9 and gives $25 per year for three years? The interest rate is 10%. If you can invest in only one of the projects, which would you choose?

Q 4.43. Consider the following project:

Year	Y0	Y1	Y2	Y3	Y4	Y5	Y6
Cash Flow	–$10	$5	$8	$3	$3	$3	–$6

1. What is the IRR?
2. What is the payback time?
3. What is the profitability index?

Q 4.44. Consider the following project:

Y0	Y1	Y2	Y3	Y4	Y5	Y6	Y7
CF $0	–$100	$50	$80	$30	$30	$30	–$60

1. What is the IRR?
2. What is the payback time?
3. What is the profitability index?

Q 4.45. The prevailing cost of capital is 9% per annum. What would various capital budgeting rules recommend for the following projects?

	Y0	Y1	Y2	Y3	Y4
A	–$1,000	$300	$400	$500	$600
B	–$1,000	$150	$200	$1,000	$1,200
C	–$2,000	$1,900	$200		
D	–$200	$300			
E	–$200	$300	$0	–$100	

Q 4.46. What are the most prominent methods for capital budgeting in the real world? Which make sense?

Time-Varying Rates of Return and the Yield Curve

When Rates of Return are Different

In this chapter, we will make the world a little more complex and a lot more realistic, although we are still assuming perfect foresight and perfect markets. In the previous chapters, the interest rate was the same every period—if a thirty-year bond offered an interest rate of 5% per annum, so did a one-year bond. But this is not the case in the real world. Rates of return usually vary with the length of time an investment requires. For example, on April 23, 2011, obligations issued by the U.S. Treasury paid an interest rate of 0.21% per annum for promised repayment in one year, but 4.46% per annum for promised repayment in thirty years.

Is this just stuff that bond traders need to know? Not at all. In fact, this stuff matters to you, too. Have you ever walked by your bank and wondered why their one-month CD offered only 0.1%, while their five-year CD offered 1.5% (as Allstate bank did on the same day)? Which should you choose? And have you not wondered what role inflation plays in setting these interest rates?

And it is not only individual investors who need to worry about time-varying interest rates, but also corporate CEOs. If you are a CEO, you must be able to compare short-term and long-term projects and to compare short-term and long-term financing costs. After all, if your investors can earn higher rates of return in long-term Treasury bonds than in short-term Treasury bills, then they will likely also demand higher rates of return if you ask them to finance long-term projects instead of short-term projects. Conversely, if your corporation wants to finance projects by borrowing, you will likely have to pay a higher rate of return if you want to borrow long term.

In this chapter, you will learn how to work with time-dependent rates of return and inflation. In addition, this chapter contains an optional section that explains the U.S. Treasury yield curve.

5.1 Working With Time-Varying Rates of Return

Interest rates can differ based on the length of the commitment.

In the real world, rates of return usually differ depending on when the payments are made. For example, the interest rate next year could be higher or lower than it is this year. Moreover, it is often the case that long-term bonds offer different interest rates than short-term bonds. You must be able to work in such an environment, so let me give you the tools.

Compounding Different Rates of Return

A compounding example with time-dependent rates of return.

Fortunately, when working with time-varying interest rates, all the tools you have learned in previous chapters remain applicable (as promised). In particular, compounding still works exactly the same way. For example, what is the two-year holding rate of return if the rate of return is 20% in the first year and 30% in the second year? (The latter is sometimes called the **reinvestment rate**.) You can determine the two-year holding rate of return from the two one-year rates of return using the same compounding formula as before:

$$(1 + r_{0,2}) = (1 + 20\%) \cdot (1 + 30\%) = (1 + 56\%)$$

$$(1 + r_{0,1}) \cdot (1 + r_{1,2}) = (1 + r_{0,2})$$

Subtract 1, and the answer is a total two-year holding rate of return of 56%. If you prefer it shorter,

$$r_{0,2} = 1.20 \cdot 1.30 - 1 = 1.56 - 1 = 56\%$$

The calculation is not conceptually more difficult, but the notation is. You have to have subscripts not just for interest rates that begin now, but also for interest rates that begin in the future. Therefore, most of the examples in this chapter must use two subscripts: one for the time when the money is deposited, and one for the time when the money is returned. Thus, $r_{1,2}$ describes an interest rate from time 1 to time 2. Aside from this extra notation, the compounding formula is still the very same multiplicative "one-plus formula" for each interest rate (subtracting 1 at the end).

The general formula for compounding over many periods.

You can also compound to determine holding rates of return in the future. For example, if the one-year rate of return is 30% from year 1 to year 2, 40% from year 2 to year 3, and 50% from year 3 to year 4, then what is your holding rate of return for investing beginning next year for three years? It is

$$\text{Given:} \qquad r_{1,2} = 30\% \quad r_{2,3} = 40\% \quad r_{3,4} = 50\%$$

$$(1 + r_{1,4}) = (1 + 30\%) \cdot (1 + 40\%) \cdot (1 + 50\%) = (1 + 173\%)$$

$$(1 + r_{1,2}) \cdot (1 + r_{2,3}) \cdot (1 + r_{3,4}) = (1 + r_{1,4})$$

Subtracting 1, you see that the three-year holding rate of return for an investment that takes money *next* year (not today!) and returns money in 4 years (appropriately called $r_{1,4}$) is 173%. Let's be clear about the timing. For example, say it was midnight of December 31, 2008, right now. This would be time 0. Time 1 would be midnight December 31, 2009, and this is when you would invest your $1. Three years later, on midnight December 31, 2012 (time 4), you would receive your original dollar plus an additional $1.73, for a total return of $2.73. Interest rates that begin right now—where the first subscript would be 0—are usually called **spot rates**. Interest rates that begin in the future are usually called **forward rates**.

Q 5.1. If the first-year interest rate is 2% and the second year interest is 3%, what is the two-year total interest rate?

Q 5.2. Although a two-year project had returned 22% in its first year, overall it lost half of its value. What was the project's rate of return after the first year?

Q 5.3. From December 31, 2000 (when it closed at 1,320.28) to December 31, 2008 (when it closed at 903.25), the S&P 500 returned the following annual rates of returns *with dividends*:

2001	2002	2003	2004	2005	2006	2007	2008
–11.81%	–21.99%	28.21%	10.56%	4.61%	15.40%	5.28%	–36.60%

What was the rate of return over the first 4 years, and what was it over the second 4 years? What was the rate of return over the whole 8 years? Was the realized rate of return time-varying?

Q 5.4. A project lost one-third of its value the first year, then gained fifty percent of its value, then lost two-thirds of its value, and finally doubled in value. What was the overall rate of return?

Annualized Rates of Return

Time-varying rates of return create a new complication that is best explained by an analogy. Is a car that travels 163,680 yards in 93 minutes fast or slow? It is not easy to say, because you are used to thinking in "miles per sixty minutes," not in "yards per ninety-three minutes." It makes sense to translate speeds into miles per hour for the purpose of comparing them. You can even do this for sprinters, who run for only 10 seconds. Speeds are just a standard measure of the rate of accumulation of distance per unit of time.

> Per-unit standard measures are statistics that are conceptual aids.

The same issue applies to rates of return: A rate of return of 58.6% over 8.32 years is not as easy to compare to other rates of return as a rate of return per year. Therefore, most rates of return are quoted as **annualized rates**. The average annualized rate of return is just a convenient unit of measurement for the rate at which money accumulates—a "sort-of-average" measure of performance. Of course, when you compute such an annualized rate of return, you do not mean that the investment earned the same annualized rate of return of, say, 5.7% each year—just as the car need not have traveled at 60 mph (163,680 yards in 93 minutes) each instant.

> A per-unit standard for rates of return: annualized rates.

Return to our example:
You want to annualize
our three-year total
holding rate of return.

If you were earning a total three-year holding rate of return of 173% over the three-year period, what would your *annualized* rate of return be? The answer is not the **average rate of return** of 173%/3 $\approx$ 57.7%, because if you earned 57.7% per year, you would have ended up with $1.577^3 - 1 \approx 292\%$, not 173%. This incorrect answer of 57.7% ignores the *compounded interest on the interest* that you would earn after the first and second years. Instead, to compute the annualized rate of return, you need to find a single hypothetical annual rate of return that, if you received it each and every year, would give you a three-year holding rate of return of 173%.

To find the t-year
annualized interest
rate, take the t-th root
of the total return (t is
number of years).

How can you compute this? Call this hypothetical annual rate that you would have to earn each year for three years $r_{\overline{3}}$ (note the bar above the 3) in order to end up with a holding rate of return of 173%. To find $r_{\overline{3}}$, solve the equation

$$(1 + r_{\overline{3}}) \cdot (1 + r_{\overline{3}}) \cdot (1 + r_{\overline{3}}) \ = \ (1 + 173\%)$$

$$(1 + r_{\overline{3}}) \cdot (1 + r_{\overline{3}}) \cdot (1 + r_{\overline{3}}) \ = \ (1 + r_{0,3})$$

or, for short,

$$(1 + r_{\overline{3}})^3 \ = \ (1 + 173\%)$$

$$(1 + r_{\overline{t}})^t \ = \ (1 + r_{0,t}) \tag{5.1}$$

In our example, the holding rate of return $r_{0,3}$ is known (173%) and the annualized rate of return $r_{\overline{3}}$ is unknown. Earning the same rate $(r_{\overline{3}})$ three years in a row should result in a holding rate of return of 173%. It is a "smoothed-out" rate of return of the three years' rates of return. Think of it as a hypothetical, single, constant-speed rate at which your money would have ended up as quickly at 173% as it did with the 30%, 40%, and 50% individual annual rates of return. The correct solution for $r_{\overline{3}}$ is obtained by computing the third root of 1 plus the total holding rate of return:

➤ *Math Background,*
Chapter A, Pg.695.

$$(1 + r_{\overline{3}}) \ = \ (1 + 173\%)^{(1/3)} \ = \ \sqrt[3]{1 + 173\%} \ \approx \ 1 + 39.76\%$$

$$(1 + r_{0,t})^{(1/t)} \ = \ \sqrt[t]{1 + r_{0,t}} \ = \ (1 + r_{\overline{t}})$$

Confirm with your calculator that $r_{\overline{3}} \approx 39.76\%$,

$$1.3976 \ \cdot \ 1.3976 \ \cdot \ 1.3976 \ \approx \ (1 + 173\%)$$

$$(1 + r_{\overline{3}}) \cdot (1 + r_{\overline{3}}) \cdot (1 + r_{\overline{3}}) \ = \ (1 + r_{0,3})$$

In sum, if you invested money at a rate of 39.76% per annum for 3 years, you would end up with a total three-year holding rate of return of 173%. As is the case here, for very long periods, the order of magnitude of the annualized rate will often be so different from the holding rate that you will intuitively immediately register whether the quantity $r_{0,3}$ or $r_{\overline{3}}$ is meant. In the real world, very few rates of return, especially over long horizons, are quoted as holding rates of return. Almost all rates are quoted in annualized terms instead.

> **IMPORTANT**
>
> The total holding rate of return over t years, called $r_{0,t}$, is translated into an annualized rate of return, called $r_{\bar{t}}$, by taking the t-th root:
>
> $$(1 + r_{\bar{t}}) = \sqrt[t]{1 + r_{0,t}} = (1 + r_{0,t})^{1/t}$$
>
> Compounding the annualized rate of return over t years yields the total holding rate of return.

You also will often need to compute annualized rates of return from payoffs yourself. For example, what annualized rate of return would you expect from a $100 investment today that promises a return of $240 in 30 years? The first step is computing the total holding rate of return. Take the ending value ($240) minus your beginning value ($100), and divide by the beginning value. Thus, the total thirty-year holding rate of return is

Translating long-term dollar returns into annualized rates of return.

$$r_{0,30} = \frac{\$240 - \$100}{\$100} = 140\%$$

$$r_{0,30} = \frac{C_{30} - C_0}{C_0}$$

The annualized rate of return is the rate $r_{\overline{30}}$, which, if compounded for 30 years, offers a 140% rate of return,

$$(1 + r_{\overline{30}})^{30} = (1 + 140\%)$$

$$(1 + r_{\bar{t}})^t = (1 + r_{0,t})$$

Solve this equation by taking the 30th root,

$$(1 + r_{\overline{30}}) = (1 + 140\%)^{1/30} = \sqrt[30]{1 + 140\%} \approx 1 + 2.96\%$$

$$(1 + r_{\bar{t}}) = (1 + r_{0,t})^{1/t} = \sqrt[t]{1 + r_{0,t}}$$

Subtracting 1, you see that a return of $240 in 30 years for an initial $100 investment is equivalent to a 2.96% annualized rate of return.

In the context of rates of return, compounding is similar to adding, while annualizing is similar to averaging. If you earn 1% twice, your compounded rate is 2.01%, similar to the rates themselves added (2%). Your annualized rate of return is 1%, similar to the average rate of return of 2.01%/2 = 1.005%. The difference is the interest on the interest.

Compounding $\approx$ adding. Annualizing $\approx$ averaging.

Now assume that you have an investment that doubles in value in the first year and then falls back to its original value. What would its average rate of return be? Doubling from, say, $100 to $200 is a rate of return of +100%. Falling back to $100 is a rate of return of ($100 – $200)/$200 = –50%. Therefore, the average rate of return would be [+100% + (–50%)]/2 = +25%.

Averaging can lead to surprising results—returns that are much higher than what you earned per year.

But you have not made any money! You started with $100 and ended up with $100. If you compound the returns, you get the answer of 0% that you were intuitively expecting:

Look how deceptive!

$$(1 + 100\%) \cdot (1 - 50\%) \quad = \quad 1 + 0\% \quad \Rightarrow r_{0,2} \ = \ 0\%$$

$$(1 + r_{0,1}) \quad \cdot (1 + r_{1,2}) \quad = \quad (1 + r_{0,2})$$

It follows that the annualized rate of return $r_{\overline{2}}$ is also 0%. Conversely, an investment that produces +20% followed by –20% has an average rate of return of 0% but leaves you with a loss:

$$(1 + 20\%) \cdot (1 - 20\%) \quad = \quad (1 - 4\%) \quad \Rightarrow r_{0,2} \ = \ -4\%$$

$$(1 + r_{0,1}) \quad \cdot (1 + r_{1,2}) \quad = \quad (1 + r_{0,2})$$

For every \$100 of your original investment, you now have only \$96. The average rate of return of 0% does not reflect this loss. Both the compounded and therefore the annualized rates of return do tell you that you had a loss:

$$1 + r_{\overline{2}} = \sqrt{(1 + r_{0,2})} = \sqrt{1 - 4\%} = 1 - 2.02\% \Rightarrow r_{\overline{2}} \approx -2.02\%$$

If you were an investment advisor and quoting your historical performance, would you rather quote your average historical rate of return or your annualized rate of return? (Hint: The industry standard is to quote the average rate of return, not the annualized rate of return!)

Do it!   Make sure to solve the following questions to gain more experience with compounding and annualizing over different time horizons.

Q 5.5. If you earn a rate of return of 5% over 4 months, what is the annualized rate of return?

Q 5.6. Assume that the two-year holding rate of return is 40%. The average (arithmetic) rate of return is therefore 20% per year. What is the annualized (geometric) rate of return? Is the annualized rate the same as the average rate?

Q 5.7. Is the compounded rate of return higher or lower than the sum of the individual rates of return? Is the annualized rate of return higher or lower than the average of the individual rates of return? Why?

Q 5.8. Return to Question 5.3. What was the annualized rate of return on the S&P 500 over the eight years in the table?

Q 5.9. If the total holding interest rate is 50% for a five-year investment, what is the annualized rate of return?

Q 5.10. If the per-year interest rate is 10% for each of the next 5 years, what is the annualized five-year rate of return?

Present Values with Time-Varying Interest Rates

Let's proceed now to net present value with time-varying interest rates. What do you need to learn about the role of time-varying interest rates when computing NPV? The answer is essentially nothing new. You already know everything you need to know here. The net present value formula is still

The PV formula still looks very similar.

$$
\begin{aligned}
\text{NPV} &= \text{PV}(C_0) + \text{PV}(C_1) + \quad \text{PV}(C_2) \quad + \quad\quad \text{PV}(C_3) \quad\quad + \cdots \\[2mm]
&= \quad C_0 \quad + \frac{C_1}{1+r_{0,1}} + \frac{C_2}{1+r_{0,2}} \quad + \quad\quad \frac{C_3}{1+r_{0,3}} \quad\quad + \cdots \\[2mm]
&= \quad C_0 \quad + \frac{C_1}{1+r_{\overline{1}}} + \frac{C_2}{(1+r_{\overline{2}})^2} \quad + \quad\quad \frac{C_3}{(1+r_{\overline{3}})^3} \quad\quad + \cdots \\[2mm]
&= \quad C_0 \quad + \frac{C_1}{1+r_{0,1}} + \frac{C_2}{(1+r_{0,1})\cdot(1+r_{1,2})} + \frac{C_3}{(1+r_{0,1})\cdot(1+r_{1,2})\cdot(1+r_{2,3})} + \cdots
\end{aligned}
$$

The only novelty is that you need to be more careful with your subscripts. You cannot simply assume that the multiyear holding returns (e.g., $1+r_{0,2}$) are the squared one-year rates of return $((1+r_{0,1})^2)$. Instead, you must work with time-dependent costs of capital (interest rates). That's it.

For example, say you have a project with an initial investment of $12 that pays $10 in one year and $8 in five years. Assume that the one-year interest rate is 5% and the five-year annualized interest rate is 6% per annum. In this case,

Present values are still alike and thus can be added, subtracted, compared, and so on.

$$
\text{PV}(\$10 \text{ in 1 year}) = \frac{\$10}{1.05} \approx \$9.52
$$

$$
\text{PV}(\$8 \text{ in 5 years}) = \frac{\$8}{1.06^5} \approx \$5.98
$$

It follows that the project's total value *today* (time 0) is $15.50. If the project costs $12, its net present value is

$$
\text{NPV} = -\$12 + \frac{\$10}{1.05} + \frac{\$8}{1.06^5} \approx \$3.50
$$

$$
\text{NPV} = \quad C_0 \quad + \frac{C_1}{1+r_{0,1}} + \frac{C_5}{1+r_{0,5}} = \text{NPV}
$$

You can also rework a more involved project, similar to that in Exhibit 2.3, But to make it more interesting, let's now use a hypothetical current term structure of interest rates that is upward sloping. Assume this project requires an appropriate discount rate of 5% over one year, and 0.5% more for every subsequent year, so that the cost of capital reaches 7% annualized in the fifth year. The valuation method works the same way as it did in Exhibit 2.3—you only have to be a little more careful with the interest rate subscripts. The project's value is thus

Here is a typical NPV example.

► *Hypothetical Project Cash Flows, Exhibit 2.3, Pg. 31.*

Time	Project Cash Flow	Rate In Year	Com-pounded	Discount Factor	Value
t	C_t	$r_{\bar{t}}$	$r_{0,t}$	$\dfrac{1}{1+r_{0,t}}$	$PV(C_t)$
Today	−$900	any	0.0%	1.0000	−$900.00
Y1	+$200	5.0%	5.0%	0.9524	$190.48
Y2	+$200	5.5%	11.3%	0.8985	$179.69
Y3	+$400	6.0%	19.1%	0.8396	$335.85
Y4	+$400	6.5%	28.6%	0.7773	$311.04
Y5	−$100	7.0%	40.3%	0.7130	−$71.33
			Net Present Value (Sum):		$45.73

Q 5.11. A project costs $200 and will provide cash flows of +$100, +$300, and +$500 in consecutive years. The annualized interest rate is 3% per annum over one year, 4% per annum over two years, and 4.5% per annum over three years. What is this project's NPV?

5.2 Inflation

Inflation is the increase in the price of the same good.

Let's make our world a little more realistic—and complex—by working out the effects of inflation. **Inflation** is the process by which the same goods cost more in the future than they do today. With inflation, the price level is rising and thus money is losing its value. For example, if inflation is 100%, an apple that costs $0.50 today will cost $1 next year, a banana that costs $2 today will cost $4, and bread that costs $1 today will cost $2.

Inflation matters when contracts are not written to adjust for it.

Inflation may or may not matter in a corporate context, depending on how contracts are written. If you ignore inflation and write a contract that promises to deliver bread for the price of $1 next year, it is said to be in **nominal terms**—and you may have made a big mistake. The money you will be paid will be worth only half as much. You will only be able to buy one apple for each loaf of bread that you had agreed to sell for $1, not the two apples that anyone else will enjoy. On the other hand, you could write your contract in **real terms** (or **inflation-indexed terms**) today, in which case the inflationary price change would not matter. That is, you could build into your promised banana delivery price the inflation rate from today to next year. An example would be a contract that promises to deliver bananas at the rate of four apples per banana. If a contract is indexed to inflation, then inflation does not matter. However, in the United States inflation often does matter, because most contracts are in nominal terms and not inflation indexed. Therefore, you have to learn how to work with inflation. What effect, then, does inflation have on returns? On (net) present values? This is our next subject.

Measuring the Inflation Rate

The first important question is how you should define the inflation rate. Is the rate of change of the price of apples the best measure of inflation? What if apples (the fruit) become more expensive, but Apples (the computers) become less expensive? Defining inflation is actually rather tricky. To solve this problem, economists have invented *baskets* or *bundles* of goods and services that are deemed to be representative. Economists then measure an average price change for these items. The official source of most inflation measures is the **Bureau of Labor Statistics (BLS)**, which determines the compositions of a number of prominent bundles (indexes) and publishes the average total price of these bundles on a monthly basis. The most prominent such inflation measure is a hypothetical bundle of average household consumption, called the **Consumer Price Index (CPI)**. (The CPI components are roughly: housing 40%, food 20%, transportation 15%, medical care 10%, clothing 5%, entertainment 5%, others 5%.) The BLS offers inflation data at http://www.bls.gov/cpi/, and the *Wall Street Journal* prints the percent change in the CPI at the end of its regular column "Money Rates." In March 2011, the official inflation rate was 2.68%. (However, since 2000, we have had months with rates as low as –2.1% [July 2009], called deflation instead of inflation, and months with rates are high as +5.60% [July 2008].) A number of other indexes are also commonly used as inflation measures, such as the **Producer Price Index (PPI)** or the broader **GDP Deflator**. They typically move fairly similarly to the CPI. There are also more specialized bundles, such as computer inflation indexes (the price of equivalent computer power does not inflate, but deflate, so the rate is usually negative), or indexes for prices of goods purchased in a particular region.

> The CPI is the most common inflation measure.

ANECDOTE **The German Hyperinflation of 1922**

The most famous episode of **hyperinflation** occurred in Germany from August 1922 to November 1923. Prices more than quadrupled every month. The price for goods was higher in the evening than in the morning! Stamps had to be overprinted by the day, and shoppers went out in the morning with bags of money that were worthless by the end of the day. By the time Germany printed 1,000 billion Mark Bank Notes, no one trusted the currency anymore. This hyperinflation was stopped only by a drastic currency and financial system reform. But high inflation is not just a historic artifact. For example, many Latin American countries experienced annual doubling of prices in the early 1980s.

Many economists now believe that a modest inflation rate between 1% and 3% per year is a healthy number.

The official inflation rate is not just a number—it is important in itself, because many contracts are specifically indexed to a particular inflation definition. For example, even if actual true inflation is zero, if the officially reported CPI rate is positive, the government must pay out more to Social Security recipients. The lower the official inflation rate, the less the government has to pay. You would therefore think that the government has the incentive to understate inflation. But, strangely, this has not been the case. On the contrary, there are strong political interest groups that hinder the BLS from even fixing mistakes that everyone knows overstate the CPI—that is, corrections that would result in *lower* official inflation numbers. In 1996, the Boskin Commission, consisting of a number of eminent economists, found that the CPI overstates inflation by about 74

> The CPI matters—even if it is calculated incorrectly.

basis points per annum—a huge difference. The main reasons were and continue to be that the BLS has been tardy in recognizing the growing importance of such factors as effective price declines in computer and telecommunication and the role of superstores such as Wal-Mart and Target.

Before we get moving, a final warning:

IMPORTANT

> The common statement "in today's dollars" is ambiguous. Some people mean "inflation adjusted." Other people mean present values (i.e., "compared to an investment in risk-free bonds"). When in doubt, ask!

Q 5.12. Read the Bureau of Labor Statistics' website descriptions of the CPI and the PPI. How does the CPI differ conceptually from the PPI? Are the two official rates different right now?

Real and Nominal Interest Rates

Nominal returns are what is normally quoted. *Real* returns are adjusted for inflation. They are what you want to know if you want to consume.

To work with inflation and to learn how you would properly index a contract for inflation, you first need to learn the difference between a **nominal return** and a **real return**. The nominal rate is what is usually quoted—a return that has not been adjusted for inflation. In contrast, the real rate of return "somehow takes out" inflation from the nominal rate in order to calculate a return "as if" there had been no price inflation to begin with. The real return reflects the fact that, in the presence of inflation, dollars in the future will have less purchasing power than dollars today. It measures your trade-off between present and future consumption, taking into account the change in prices.

An extreme 100% inflation rate example: Prices double every year.

Start with a simple exaggerated scenario: Assume that the inflation rate is 100% per year and you can buy a bond that promises a *nominal* interest rate of 700%. What is your *real* rate of return? To find out, assume that $1 buys one apple today. With an inflation rate of 100%, you need $2 next year to buy the same apple. Your investment return will be $1 \cdot (1 + 700\%) = \$8$ for today's $1 of investment. But this $8 now applies to apples costing $2 each. Your $8 will buy 4 apples, not 8 apples. Your real rate of return (1 apple yields 4 apples) is therefore

$$r_{real} = \frac{(4 \text{ Apples for } \$8) - (1 \text{ Apple for } \$2)}{(1 \text{ Apple for } \$2)} = 300\%$$

For each dollar invested today, you will be able to purchase only 300% more apples next year (not 700% more) than you could purchase today. This is because inflation will reduce the purchasing power of your dollar by half.

Here is the correct conversion formula from nominal to real rates.

The correct formula to adjust for the inflation rate (π) is again a "one-plus" type formula. In our example, it is

$$(1 + 700\%) \quad = (1 + 300\%) \cdot (1 + 100\%)$$

$$(1 + r_{nominal}) \quad = \quad (1 + r_{real}) \quad \cdot \quad (1 + \pi)$$

Turning this formula around gives you the real rate of return,

$$(1 + r_{\text{real}}) = \frac{1 + 700\%}{1 + 100\%} = 1 + 300\%$$

$$(1 + r_{\text{real}}) = \frac{(1 + r_{\text{nominal}})}{(1 + \pi)}$$

In plain English, a nominal interest rate of 700% is the same as a real interest rate of 300%, given an inflation rate of 100%.

IMPORTANT

The relation between the nominal rate of return (r_{nominal}), the real rate of return (r_{real}), and the inflation rate (π) is

$$(1 + r_{\text{nominal}}) = (1 + r_{\text{real}}) \cdot (1 + \pi) \qquad (5.2)$$

As with compounding, if the rates are small, the mistake of just subtracting the inflation rate from the nominal interest rate to obtain the real interest rate is not too grave. For example, a ten-year U.S. Treasury note offered a yield of 3.4% in April 2011, when the inflation rate was about 2.5%. If the inflation rate had remained constant, then your real rate of return would have been

For small rates, adding/ subtracting is an okay approximation.

$$(1 + 3.4\%) \approx (1 + 0.9\%) \cdot (1 + 2.5\%) \approx 1 + 0.9\% + 2.5\% + 0.000\ldots$$

➤ *Bills, notes, and bonds, Sect. 5.3, Pg. 95.*

$$(1 + r_{\text{nominal}}) = (1 + r_{\text{real}}) \cdot (1 + \pi) = 1 + r_{\text{real}} + \pi + \underbrace{r_{\text{real}} \cdot \pi}_{\text{cross-term}}$$

The difference between the correct and the approximation, i.e., the cross-term, is about 2 basis points (0.0002). The cross-term difference of 2 basis points is easily swamped by your uncertainty about the ten-year future inflation rate. However, when inflation and interest rates are high—as they were, for example, in the late 1970s—then the cross-term can be important.

➤ *Adding or compounding interest rates, and the cross-term, Pg. 20.*

A positive time value of money—the fact that money tomorrow is worth more than money today—is only necessarily true for nominal quantities, not for real quantities. Only nominal interest rates are never negative. In the presence of inflation, real interest rates not only *can* be negative, but often *are* negative. In fact, this was the case in April 2004 for some other bonds. For example, a one-year U.S. Treasury note offered 0.21% and the inflation rate was 2.5%, which means that your real interest rate was –2.2% per annum. Every dollar you invested in such U.S. Treasuries would be worth *less* in real purchasing power one year later. You would have ended up with more cash—but also with *less* purchasing power. Of course, if there are goods or projects that appreciate with inflation (inflation hedges, such as real estate or gold), and to the extent that these goods are both storable and traded in a perfect market, you would not expect to see negative real rates of return. After all, you could buy these projects today and sell them next year, thereby earning a positive real rate of return. Many investors also reasonably believe that, unlike bonds that promise to pay fixed nominal amounts in the future, stocks are good insurance against inflation. They should appreciate in value when the price level increases because they are claims on real underlying projects, which presumably will similarly experience a price increase.

Real interest rates can be negative.

Q 5.13. From memory, write down the relationship between nominal rates of return ($r_{nominal}$), real rates of return (r_{real}), and the inflation rate (π).

Q 5.14. The nominal interest rate is 20%. Inflation is 5%. What is the real interest rate?

Inflation in Net Present Values

The most fundamental rule: never mix apples and oranges. Nominal cash flows must be discounted with nominal interest rates.

When it comes to inflation and net present value, there is a simple rule: Never mix apples and oranges. The beauty of NPV is that every project's cash flows are translated into the same units: today's dollars. Keep everything in the same units in the presence of inflation, so that this NPV advantage is not lost. When you use the NPV formula, always discount nominal cash flows with nominal discount rates, and real (inflation-adjusted) cash flows with real (inflation-adjusted) discount rates.

Our example discounted both in real and nominal terms.

Let's return to our "apple" example. With 700% nominal interest rates and 100% inflation, the real interest rate is $(1 + 700\%)/(1 + 100\%) - 1 = 300\%$. What is the value of a project that gives 12 apples next year, given that apples cost $1 each today and $2 each next year?

There are two methods you can use:

Discount nominal cash flows with nominal rates. Discount real cash flows with real rates.

1. Discount the nominal cash flow of 12 apples next year ($\$2 \cdot 12 = \$24$) with the nominal interest rate. Thus, the 12 future apples are worth

$$\frac{\text{Nominal Cash Flow}}{1 + \text{Nominal Rate}} = \frac{\$24}{1 + 700\%} = \$3$$

2. Discount the real cash flows of 12 apples next year with the real interest rate. Thus, the 12 future apples are worth

$$\frac{\text{Real Cash Flow}}{1 + \text{Real Rate}} = \frac{12 \text{ Apples}}{1 + 300\%} = 3 \text{ Apples}$$

in today's apples. Because an apple costs $1 today, the 12 apples next year are worth $3 today.

Both the real and the nominal methods arrive at the same NPV result. The opportunity cost of capital is that if you invest one apple today, you can quadruple your apple holdings by next year. Thus, a 12-apple harvest next year is worth 3 apples to you today. The higher nominal interest rates already reflect the fact that nominal cash flows next year are worth less than they are this year. As simple as this may sound, I have seen corporations first work out the real value of their goods in the future, and then discount this with standard nominal interest rates. Just don't!

IMPORTANT

- Discount nominal cash flows with nominal interest rates.

- Discount real cash flows with real interest rates.

Either works. Never discount nominal cash flows with real interest rates, or vice versa.

If you want to see this in algebra, the reason that the two methods come to the same result is that the inflation rate cancels out,

$$PV = \frac{\$24}{1 + 700\%} = \frac{12A}{1 + 300\%} = \frac{12A \cdot (1 + 100\%)}{(1 + 300\%) \cdot (1 + 100\%)}$$

$$= \frac{N}{1 + r_{nominal}} = \frac{r}{1 + r_{real}} = \frac{r \cdot (1 + \pi)}{(1 + r_{real}) \cdot (1 + \pi)}$$

Usually, it is best to work only with nominal quantities.

where N is the nominal cash flow, r is the real cash flow, and π is the inflation rate. Most of the time, it is easier to work in nominal quantities. Nominal interest rates are far more common than real interest rates, and you can simply use published inflation rates to adjust the future price of goods to obtain future expected nominal cash flows.

Q 5.15. If the real interest is 3% per annum and the inflation rate is 8% per annum, then what is the present value of a $500,000 nominal payment next year?

5.3 U.S. Treasuries and the Yield Curve

It is now time to talk in more detail about the most important financial market in the world today: the market for bonds issued by the U.S. government. These bonds are called Treasuries and are perhaps the simplest projects around. This is because, in theory, Treasuries cannot fail to pay. They promise to pay U.S. dollars, and the U.S.-controlled Federal Reserve has the right to print more U.S. dollars if it were ever to run out. Thus, there is no uncertainty about repayment for Treasuries. (In contrast, some European countries or U.S. states that borrow in currencies that they cannot create may well not have the money to pay and therefore default.)

The simplest and most important benchmark bonds nowadays are Treasuries. They have known and certain payouts.

The shorthand "Treasury" comes from the fact that the debt itself is issued by the U.S. Treasury Department. There are three main types:

U.S. Treasury bills, notes, and bonds have different maturities.

1. **Treasury bills** (often abbreviated as **T-bills**) have maturities of up to one year.

2. **Treasury notes** have maturities between one and ten years.

3. **Treasury bonds** have maturities greater than ten years.

The thirty-year bond is often called the **long bond**. Together the three are usually just called **Treasuries**. Conceptually, there is really no difference among them. All are really just obligations issued by the U.S. Treasury. Indeed, there can be Treasury notes today that are due in 3 months—such as a 9-year Treasury note that was issued 8 years and 9 months ago. This is really the same obligation as a three-month Treasury bill that was just issued. Thus, we shall be (very) casual with name distinctions.

The Treasuries market is one of the most important financial markets in the world.

In early 2011, the United States Federal Government owed over $14.19 trillion in Treasury obligations. With a population of 311 million, this is about $45,000 per person—incidentally also approximately the annual GDP of the United States. (The far worse problem, however, is that the United States has already promised benefits to future retirees that far exceed this number.) After Treasuries are sold by the government, they are then actively traded in what is one of the most important financial markets in the world today. It would not be uncommon for a dedicated bond trader to buy $100 million of a Treasury note originally issued 10 years ago that has 5 years remaining, and 10 seconds later sell $120 million of a three-year Treasury note issued 6 years ago. Large buyers and sellers of Treasuries are easily found, and transaction costs are very low. Trading volume is huge: In 2009, it was about $500 billion per trading day. Therefore, the annual trading volume in U.S. Treasuries—about $252 \cdot \$500$ billion $\approx \$130$ trillion— totaled about 10 times the U.S. economy's gross domestic product (GDP) of $\approx\$14$ trillion. Who owns them? Not just the Chinese, although they do own a lot of these bonds (in 2011, about a third). In 2009, the U.S. Federal Reserve estimated that 10.2% of bills, notes and bonds were held by individuals, 11.7% by banks and mutual funds, 6.6% by public and private pension funds, 47.7% by foreign investors, 6.8% by state and local governments, and 16.9% by other investors.

The yield curve shows the annualized interest rate as a function of bond maturity.

It turns out that at any given moment in time, the interest rates on Treasuries usually differ, depending on their maturity terms. Fortunately, you already know how to handle time-varying rates of return, so we can now put your knowledge to the test. The principal tool for working with Treasury bonds is the **yield curve** (or **term structure** of interest rates). It is a graphical representation, where the time to maturity is on the x-axis and the annualized interest rates are on the y-axis. There are also yield curves on non-Treasury bonds, but the Treasury yield curve is so prominent that unless clarified further, the yield curve should be assumed to mean investments in U.S. Treasuries. (A more precise name would be the "U.S. Treasuries yield curve.") This yield curve is so important that most other debts in the financial markets, like mortgage rates or bank lending rates, are "benchmarked" relative to the Treasury yield curve. For example, if your firm wants to issue a five-year bond, your creditors will want to compare your interest rate to that offered by equivalent Treasuries, and often will even describe your bond as offering "x basis points above the equivalent Treasury."

Q 5.16. What are the three types of Treasuries? How do they differ?

Yield Curve Shapes

Yield curves are often, but not always, upward sloping.

Exhibit 5.1 shows some historical yield curves. They are commonly classified into four basic shapes:

1. Flat: There is little or no difference between annualized short-term and long-term rates. A flat yield curve is basically the scenario that was the subject of the previous chapter. It means you can simplify $(1 + r_{0,t}) \approx (1+r)^t$.

2. Upward sloping ("normal"): Short-term rates are lower than long-term rates. This is the most common shape. It means that longer-term interest rates are higher

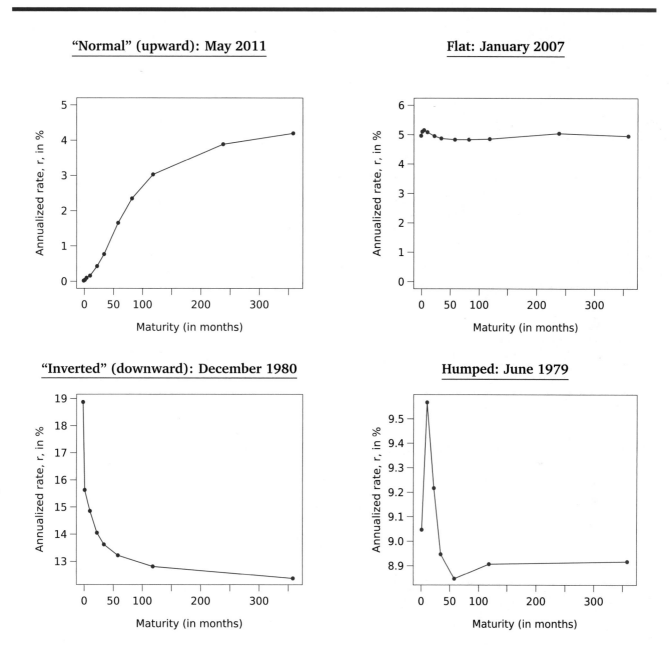

Exhibit 5.1: *Various Historical Yield-Curve Shapes.* The upward slope is so common that it is considered the normal shape. Thus, a downward slope is sometimes called "inverted."

than shorter-term interest rates. Since 1934, the steepest yield curve (the biggest difference between the long-term and the short-term Treasury rates) occurred in October 1992, when the long-term interest rate was 7.3% and the short-term interest rate was 2.9%—just as the economy pulled out of the recession of 1991.

   3. Downward sloping ("inverted"): Short-term rates are higher than long-term rates.

   4. Humped: Short-term rates and long-term rates are lower than medium-term rates.

Inverted and humped yield curves are relatively rare.

A N E C D O T E   **Macroeconomic Implications of Different Yield Curve Shapes**

Economists and pundits have long wondered what they can learn from the shape of the yield curve about the future of the economy. It appears that the yield curve shape is a useful—though unreliable and noisy—signal of where the economy is heading. Steep yield curves often signal emergence from a recession. Inverted yield curves often signal an impending recession. But can't the Federal Reserve Bank control the yield curve and thereby control the economy? It is true that the Fed can influence the yield curve. But ultimately the Fed does not control it—instead, it is the broader demand and supply for savings and credit in the economy. Economic research has shown that the Federal Reserve Bank typically has a good deal of influence on the short end of the Treasury curve—by expanding and contracting the supply of money and short-term loans in the economy—but not much influence on the long end of the Treasury curve. And, in the financial crisis of 2008, the Fed's influence on the short end was severely limited, too—the nominal rate already stood at 0% and there was little the Fed could do to drop it further.

Common data sources for interest rates.

If you want to undertake your own research, you can find historical interest rates at the St. Louis Federal Reserve Bank at http://research.stlouisfed.org/fred. There are also the Treasury Management Pages at http://www.tmpages.com/. Or you can look at SmartMoney.com for historical yield curves. PiperJaffray.com has the current yield curve—as do many other financial sites and newspapers. Finance.yahoo.com/bonds provides not only the Treasury yield curve but also yield curves for many other types of bonds.

An Example: The Yield Curve on December 31, 2004

We will analyze the Treasury yield curve at the end of December 2004.

Let's focus on working with one particular yield curve. Exhibit 5.2 shows the Treasury yields on December 31, 2004. This yield curve had the most common upward slope. The curve tells you that if you had purchased a three-month Treasury at the end of the day on December 31, 2004, your annualized interest rate would have been 1.63% per annum. (A $100 investment would turn into $100 \cdot (1 + 1.63\%)^{1/4} \approx \$100 \cdot 1.0041 = \$100.41$ on March 31, 2004.) If you had purchased a twenty-year bond, your annualized interest rate would have been 4.85% per annum.

Deeper: There are some small inaccuracies in my description of yield curve computations. My main simplification is that U.S. yield curves are based on semi-annually-compounded coupon bonds in real life, whereas our textbook pretends that the yield is on a zero bond. In corporate finance, the yield difference between annual compounding and semi-annual compounding is almost always inconsequential. However, if you want to become a fixed-income trader, you cannot take this approximation literally. Consult a dedicated fixed-income text instead.

Sometimes it is necessary to determine an interest rate for a bond that is not listed. This is usually done by interpolation. For example, if you had wanted to find the yield for a 9-month bond, a good guess would have been an interest rate halfway between the 6-month bond and the 12-month bond. In December 2004, this would have been an annualized yield of $(2.05\% + 2.23\%)/2 \approx 2.14\%$.

You can interpolate annualized interest rates on the yield curve.

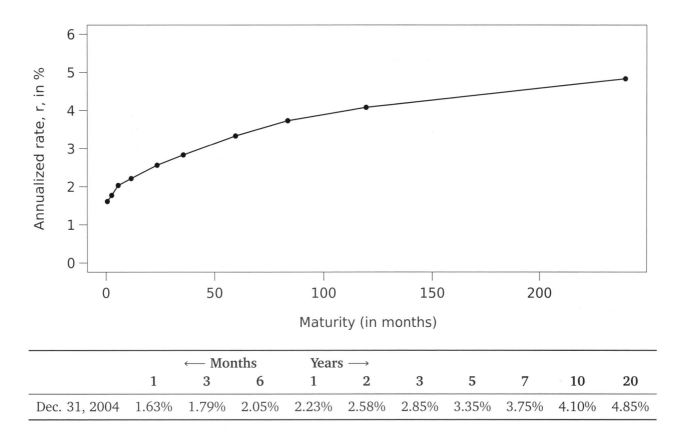

| | ← Months | | | Years → | | | | | |
	1	3	6	1	2	3	5	7	10	20
Dec. 31, 2004	1.63%	1.79%	2.05%	2.23%	2.58%	2.85%	3.35%	3.75%	4.10%	4.85%

Exhibit 5.2: *The Treasury Yield Curve on December 31, 2004.* These rates are calculated from Treasury prices and are their annualized yields-to-maturity (internal rates of return). When using Treasury zero-bonds, they are just the standard discount rates computed from the final payment and today's price. Similar data can be found on the U.S. Treasury website at http://www.ustreas.gov or in the *Wall Street Journal*. The yield curve changes every day—although day-to-day changes are usually small. We shall work only with the December 2004 yield curve. (Note: In 2004, the U.S. Treasury did not issue thirty-year bonds.) Source: Federal Reserve, www.federalreserve.gov/releases/h15/data.htm.

As notation for the annualized horizon-dependent interest rates, we continue using our earlier method. We call the two-year annualized interest rate $r_{\overline{2}}$ (here, 2.58%), the three-year annualized interest rate $r_{\overline{3}}$ (here, 2.85%), and so on. It is always these overlined-subscript yields that are graphed in yield curves. Let's work with this particular

The December 2004 yield curve was upward sloping: Annualized interest rates were higher for longer maturities.

yield curve, assuming it is based exclusively on zero-bonds, so you don't have to worry about interim payments.

Computing the holding rate of return for two-year Treasuries.

Holding rates of return First, let's figure out how much money you will have at maturity. That is, how much did an investment of $500,000 in U.S. two-year notes (i.e., a loan to the U.S. government of $500,000) on December 31, 2004, return on December 31, 2006? Use the data in Exhibit 5.2. Because the yield curve prints annualized rates of return, the total two-year holding rate of return (as in Formula 5.1) is the twice compounded annualized rate of return,

➤ *Annualizing,*
Formula 5.1, Pg. 86.

$$r_{0,2} = 1.0258 \cdot 1.0258 - 1 \approx 5.23\%$$

$$r_{0,2} = (1 + r_{\overline{2}}) \cdot (1 + r_{\overline{2}}) - 1$$

so your $500,000 will turn into

$$C_2 \approx (1 + 5.23\%) \cdot \$500,000 \approx \$526,150$$

$$C_2 = (1 + r_{0,2}) \cdot C_0$$

on December 31, 2006. (In the real world, you might have to pay a commission to arrange this transaction, so you would end up with a little less.) What if you had invested $500,000 into 20-year Treasuries? Your twenty-year holding rate of return would have been

Computing the holding rate of return for 20-year bonds.

$$r_{0,20} = 1.0485^{20} - 1 \approx 2.5785 - 1 \approx 157.85\%$$

$$r_{0,20} = (1 + r_{\overline{20}})^{20} - 1$$

Thus, an investment of $C_0 = \$500,000$ in December 2004 will turn into $C_{20} \approx \$1.29$ million in December 2024.

Let's work out one forward rate implied by the December 2005 yield curve.

Forward rates of return Second, let's figure out what the yield curve in December 31, 2004, implied about the one-year interest rate from December 31, *2005,* to December 31, 2006. This would be best named $r_{1,2}$. It is an interest rate that begins in one year and ends in two years. This is called a **forward rate**.

Our yield curve tells you that the one-year annualized interest rate is $r_{\overline{1}} = 2.23\%$, and that the two-year annualized rate of return is $r_{\overline{2}} = 2.58\%$. You already know that you can work out the two holding rates of return, $r_{0,1} = 2.23\%$ and $r_{0,2} = (1 + r_{\overline{2}})^2 - 1 \approx 5.23\%$. You only need to use the compounding formula to determine $r_{1,2}$:

$$(1 + 5.23\%) = (1 + 2.23\%) \cdot (1 + r_{1,2}) \quad \Rightarrow \quad r_{1,2} \approx 2.93\%$$

$$(1 + r_{0,2}) = (1 + r_{0,1}) \cdot (1 + r_{1,2})$$

This is higher than both $r_{\overline{1}}$ and $r_{\overline{2}}$ from which you computed $r_{1,2}$.

| | | Rates of Return | |
Maturity	Total Holding	Annualized	Compounded Rates
1 Year	$(1 + 2.23\%)$	$= (1 + 2.23\%)^1$	$= (1 + 2.23\%)$
	$(1 + r_{0,1})$	$= (1 + r_{\bar{1}})^1$	$= (1 + r_{0,1})$
2 Years	$(1 + 5.23\%)$	$\approx (1 + 2.58\%)^2$	$\approx (1 + 2.23\%) \cdot (1 + 2.93\%)$
	$(1 + r_{0,2})$	$= (1 + r_{\bar{2}})^2$	$= (1 + r_{0,1}) \cdot (1 + r_{1,2})$
3 Years	$(1 + 8.80\%)$	$\approx (1 + 2.85\%)^3$	$\approx (1 + 2.23\%) \cdot (1 + 2.93\%) \cdot (1 + 3.39\%)$
	$(1 + r_{0,3})$	$= (1 + r_{\bar{3}})^3$	$= (1 + r_{0,1}) \cdot (1 + r_{1,2}) \cdot (1 + r_{2,3})$

Exhibit 5.3: *Relation between Holding Returns, Annualized Returns, and Year-by-Year Returns on December 31, 2004, by Formula.* The individually compounded rates are the future interest rates. They are implied by the annualized rates quoted in the middle column. The text worked out the two-year case. You will work out the three-year case in Question 5.17. This computation will be repeated more slowly in Section App.5.A (Companion).

Exhibit 5.3 summarizes our two-year calculations, and extends them by another year. (This allows you to check your results in an exercise below. It is also worked slowly in Appendix App.5.A (Companion)). One question that you should ask yourself is whether I use so many subscripts in the notation just because I enjoy torturing you. The answer is an emphatic no: The subscripts are there for good reason. When you look at Exhibit 5.3, for example, you have to distinguish between the following:

Is the proliferation of subscripts torture or necessity?

- the three holding rates of return, $r_{0,t}$ (2.23%, 5.23%, and 8.80%)

- the three annualized rates of return, $r_{\bar{t}}$ (2.23%, 2.58%, and 2.85%)

➤ *Step-by-step computation of forward interest rates,* Sect. **App.5.A (Companion)**, *Pg. ≈ 11.*

- the three individual annual rates of return $r_{t-1,t}$ (2.23%, 2.93%, and 3.39%), where the second and third begin at different points in the future.

In real life, you have not just three yearly Treasuries, but many Treasuries between 1 day and 30 years. Anyone dealing with Treasuries (or CDs or any other fixed-income investment) that can have different maturities or start in the future must be prepared to suffer double subscripts.

If Treasuries offer different annualized rates of return over different horizons, do corporate projects have to do so, too? Almost surely yes. If nothing else, they compete with Treasury bonds for investors' money. And just like Treasury bonds, many corporate projects do not begin immediately, but may take a year or more to prepare. Such project rates of return are essentially forward rates of return. Double subscripts—sometimes there is no way out in the real world!

Yes, corporate projects have double subscripts, too!

Q 5.17. Compute the three-year holding rate of return on December 31, 2004. Then, using the two-year holding rate of return on December 31, 2004, of 5.23% and your calculated three-year holding rate of return, compute the forward interest rate for a one-year investment beginning on December 31, *2006*, and ending on December 31, 2007. Are these the numbers in Exhibit 5.3?

Q 5.18. Repeat the calculation with the five-year annualized rate of return of 3.35%. That is, what is the five-year holding rate of return, and how can you compute the forward interest rate for a two-year investment beginning on December 31, *2007*, and ending on December 31, 2009?

Bond Payoffs and Your Investment Horizon

Your investment horizon has no link to the time patterns of bond payoffs you invest in. You can always sell long-term bonds to get money quickly, if need be.

Should there be a link between your personal investment horizon and the kinds of bonds you may be holding? Let's say that you want to purchase a three-year zero-coupon bond because it offers 2.85%, which is more than the 2.23% that a one-year zero-coupon bond offers—but you also want to consume in one year. Can you still buy the longer-term bond? There is good news and bad news. The good news is that the answer is yes: There is no link whatsoever between your desire to get your money back and the point in time when the three-year bond pays off. You can always buy a three-year bond today, and sell it next year when it will have become a two-year bond. The bad news is that in our perfect and certain market, this investment strategy will still only get you the 2.23% that the one-year bond offers. If you purchase $100 of the three-year bond for $P = \$100/1.0285^3 \approx \$91.92$ today, next year it will be a two-year bond with an interest rate of 2.93% in the first year and 3.39% in the second year (both worked out in Exhibit 5.3). You can sell this bond next year for a price of

$$\frac{\$100}{1 + r_{1,3}} = \frac{\$100}{(1 + r_{1,2}) \cdot (1 + r_{2,3})} = \frac{\$100}{1.0293 \cdot 1.0339} \approx \$93.97$$

Your one-year holding rate of return would therefore be only $(\$93.97 - \$91.92)/\$91.92 \approx$ 2.23%—the same rate of return you would have received if you had purchased a one-year bond.

The Effect of Interest Rate Changes on Different-Term Bonds

Treasuries pay what they promise. They have no default risk. They do have the risk of interim interest rate changes.

Are twenty-year bonds riskier than one-year bonds? Of course, recall that repayment is no less certain with twenty-year Treasury bonds than one-year Treasury notes. (This would be an issue of concern if you were to evaluate corporate projects that can go bankrupt. Long-term corporate bonds are often riskier than short-term corporate bonds—most firms are unlikely to go bankrupt this week, but more likely to go bankrupt over a multidecade time horizon.) So, for Treasury bonds, there is no uncertainty as far as payment uncertainty is concerned. But there may still be some interim risk, and even though we have not yet fully covered it, you can still intuitively figure out why this is so. Ask yourself how economy-wide bond prices (interest rates) can change in the interim (before maturity). What are the effects of sudden interest rate changes before maturity on bond values? It turns out that an equal-sized interest rate movement can be much more dramatic for long-term bonds than for short-term bonds. Let me try to illustrate why.

The 20-year bond:

First, the effect of a 10 bp change on the price of a 20-year bond.

Work out the value of a $1,000 twenty-year zero-bond at the 4.85% interest rate prevailing in December 2004. It costs $1,000/1.0485^{20} \approx $387.82. You already know that when prevailing interest rates go up, the prices of outstanding bonds drop and you will lose money. For example, if interest rates increase by 10 basis points to 4.95%, the bond value decreases to $1,000/1.0495^{20} \approx $380.50. If interest rates decrease by 10 basis points to 4.75%, the bond value increases to $1,000/1.0475^{20} \approx $395.29. Thus, the effect of a 10-basis-point change in the prevailing twenty-year yield induces an immediate percent change (an instant rate of return) in the value V of your bond of

$$\text{Up 10 bp:} \quad r = \frac{V(r_{\overline{20}} = 4.95\%) - V(r_{\overline{20}} = 4.85\%)}{V(r_{\overline{20}} = 4.85\%)} = \frac{\$380.50 - \$387.82}{\$387.82} \approx -1.89\%$$

$$\text{Down 10 bp:} \quad r = \frac{V(r_{\overline{20}} = 4.75\%) - V(r_{\overline{20}} = 4.85\%)}{V(r_{\overline{20}} = 4.85\%)} = \frac{\$395.29 - \$387.82}{\$387.82} \approx +1.93\%$$

So for every $1 million you invest in twenty-year bonds, you expose yourself to about $19,000 in instant risk for every 10-basis-point yield change in the economy.

The one-year Note: To keep the example identical, let's now assume that the one-year note also has an interest rate of 4.85% and consider the same 10-basis-point change in the prevailing interest rate. In this case, the equivalent computations for the value of a one-year note are $954.65 at 4.75%, $953.74 at 4.85%, and $952.83 at 4.95%. Therefore, the equivalent instant rates of return are

Second, the effect of a 10 bp point change on the price of a one-year note.

$$\text{Up 10 bp:} \quad r = \frac{V(r_{\overline{1}} = 4.95\%) - V(r_{\overline{1}} = 4.85\%)}{V(r_{\overline{1}} = 4.85\%)} = \frac{\$952.83 - \$953.74}{\$953.74} \approx -0.095\%$$

$$\text{Down 10 bp:} \quad r = \frac{V(r_{\overline{1}} = 4.75\%) - V(r_{\overline{20}} = 4.85\%)}{V(r_{\overline{1}} = 4.85\%)} = \frac{\$954.65 - \$953.74}{\$953.74} \approx +0.095\%$$

For every $1 million you invest in one-year notes, you expose yourself to a $950 risk for a 10-basis-point yield change in the economy.

It follows that the value effect of an *equal-sized* change in prevailing interest rates is more severe for longer-term bonds. In turn, it follows that if the bond is due tomorrow, interest rate changes can usually wreak very little havoc. You will be able to reinvest tomorrow at whatever the new rate will be. A long-term bond, on the other hand, may lose (or gain) a lot of value.

An equal interest rate move affects longer-term bonds more strongly.

In sum, you should always remember that Treasury bonds are risk-free in the sense that they cannot default (fail to return the promised payments), but they are risky in the sense that interim interest changes can alter their values. Only the most short-term Treasury bills (say, due overnight) can truly be considered risk-free—virtually everything else is risky.

Again, in the interim, T-bonds are *not* risk-free!

IMPORTANT

> Though "fixed income," even Treasuries do not guarantee a "fixed rate of return" over horizons shorter than their maturities. Day to day, long-term Treasury bonds are generally riskier investments than short-term Treasury bills.

For the sake of illustration, I have not told you about two issues. The important one is that long-term rates are not as volatile as short-term rates. Nevertheless, in the real world, longer-term Treasuries are riskier.

Confession time: I have pulled two tricks on you. First, in the real world, it could be that short-term, economy-wide interest rates typically experience yield shifts of plus or minus 100 basis points, while long-term, economy-wide interest rates rarely budge. If this were true, long-term bonds could even be safer. The empirical evidence suggests that even though the volatility of prevailing interest rates in twenty-year bonds is smaller than that of one-year notes, it is not *that much* smaller. As a consequence, the typical annual variability in the rate of return of an investment in twenty-year Treasury bonds was higher historically (around 10%) than the typical variability in the rate of return of an investment in one-year Treasury notes (around 5%). Long-term Treasury securities are indeed riskier. Second, when I quoted your value losses of $950 (for the one-year note) and $19,000 (for the twenty-year bond), I ignored that between today and tomorrow, you would also earn 1 day's interest. On a $1,000,000 investment, this would be about $130. If you had invested the money in one-year Treasury notes at 2.23% instead of in twenty-year bonds at 4.85%, you would have only received about $60. Strictly speaking, this favors the long-term bond and thus $70 should be added to the long-term bond investment strategy—but $70 on $1 million is only about 1 basis point, and so for a quick-and-dirty calculation such as ours, ignoring it was reasonable.

Q 5.19. A ten-year and a one-year zero-bond both offer an interest rate of 8% per annum.

1. How does an increase of 1 basis point in the prevailing interest rate change the value of the one-year bond? (Use 5 decimals in your calculation.)

2. How does an increase of 1 basis point in the prevailing interest rate change the value of the ten-year bond?

3. What is the ratio of the value change over the interest change? In calculus, this would be called the derivative of the value with respect to interest rate changes. Which derivative is larger?

How Bad Are Mistakes?

Paper Losses

If you really need cash from a bond investment in 20 years, doesn't a prevailing interest rate increase cause only an interim **paper loss**? This is a capital logical error many investors commit. Say that a 10-basis-point increase happened overnight, and you had invested $1 million yesterday. You would have lost $19,000 of your net worth in 1 day! Put differently, waiting 1 day would have saved you $19,000 or allowed you to buy the same item for $19,000 less. Paper money is actual wealth. Thinking paper losses are any different from actual losses is a common but capital error. (The only exception to this rule is that realized gains and losses have different tax implications than unrealized gains and losses.)

➤ *Tax treatment of realized and unrealized capital gains,* Sect. 10.4, Pg. 261.

"Paper losses" are no less real than realized losses.

IMPORTANT

5.4 Why Does the Yield Curve Usually Slope Up?

Aren't you already wondering *why* the yield curve is not usually flat? Take our example yield curve from December 2004. Why did the twenty-year Treasury bonds in December 2004 pay 4.85% per year, while the three-month Treasury bills paid only 1.63% per year? And why is an upward slope the most common shape?

But why? Why? Why?

Let's work with a simpler two-year example. Let's say that the yield curve tells you that the one-year rate is $r_1 = 5\%$ and the two-year rate is $r_2 = 10\%$. You can work out that the one-year forward rate is then $r_{1,2} \approx 15.24\%$. There are really only two possible explanations:

The two possible explanations are (1) higher future interest rates and/or (2) compensation for risk.

1. The one-year interest rate next year will be higher than the 5% that it is today. Indeed, maybe next year's one-year interest rate will be the 15.24% that it would be in a perfect world with perfect certainty.

2. Investors tend to earn higher rates of return holding long-term bonds than they do holding short-term bonds. For example, if the yield curve were to remain at exactly the same shape next year, then a $100 investment in consecutive one-year bonds would give you interest of only about $10.25, while the same investment in two-year bonds would give you (on average) $21.

In other words, the question is whether higher long-term interest rates today predict higher interest rates in the future, or whether they offer extra compensation for investors willing to hold longer-term bonds. Let's consider two possible variants of each of these two possibilities.

Does It Predict Higher Future Inflation?

In general, when inflation is higher, you would expect investors to demand higher nominal interest rates. Consequently, you would expect nominal rates to go up when inflation rate expectations are going up. Similarly, you would expect nominal rates to go down when inflation rate expectations are going down. Of course, demand and supply do not mean that real rates of return need to be positive—indeed, the real rate of return is often negative, but the alternative of storing money under the mattress is even worse.

If inflation is high, investors (typically) demand higher interest rates.

Are higher future inflation rates the cause of higher future interest rates?

Therefore, our first potential explanation for an upward-sloping yield curve is that investors believe that cash will be worth progressively less in the more distant future. That is, even though you will be able to earn higher interest rates over the long run, you may also believe that the inflation rate will increase from today's rate. Because inflation erodes the value of higher interest rates, interest rates should then be higher in the future just to compensate you for the lesser value of money in the future. Of course, this argument would apply only to a yield curve computed from Treasury debt that pays off in nominal terms. It should not apply to any bond payoffs that are inflation indexed.

A N E C D O T E   **Inflation-Neutral Bonds**

As it turns out, inflation-adjusted bonds had already been invented once before! The world's first known inflation-indexed bonds were issued by the Commonwealth of Massachusetts in 1780 during the Revolutionary War. These bonds were invented to deal with severe wartime inflation and discontent among soldiers in the U.S. Army with the decline in purchasing power of their pay. Although the bonds were successful, the concept of indexed bonds was abandoned after the immediate extreme inflationary environment passed, and largely forgotten. In 1780, the bonds were viewed as an irregular expedient, because there was no formulated economic theory to justify indexation.   *Robert Shiller, "The Invention of Inflation-Indexed Bonds in Early America," October 2003*

TIPS are inflation-indexed Treasury bonds. They are not affected by inflation.

Fortunately, since 1997 the Treasury has been selling bonds that are inflation indexed. These bond contracts are written so that they pay out the promised interest rate plus the CPI inflation rate. They are called Treasury Inflation Protected Securities (**TIPS**), or sometimes just **CPI bonds**). By definition, they should not be affected by inflation in a perfect market. If the nominal yield curve is upward sloping because of higher future inflation rates, then a TIPS-based real yield curve should not be upward sloping.

You can compute an inflation-adjusted yield curve and compare it to the nominal yield curve—in December 2004, future inflation expectations were not the main driver of the upward-sloping yield curve.

In December 2004, the Treasury had issued four kinds of TIPS. Their interest rates (to which the CPI would be added) and the corresponding standard Treasury interest rates were

Maturity	5-year	7-year	10-year	20-year
TIPS Interest Rate	0.97%	1.35%	1.73%	2.13%
Ordinary Treasury Bonds	3.35%	3.75%	4.10%	4.85%

Obviously, the TIPS yield curve is also upward sloping. This suggests that higher future expected inflation rates were not the sole reason for the upward-sloping yield curve. If you work out the implied inflation rates from these real and nominal interest rates using Formula 5.2, you find

➤ *Inflation Adjusting, Formula 5.2, Pg. 93.*

Maturity	5-year	7-year	10-year	20-year
Implied Inflation Rate	2.36%	2.37%	2.33%	2.66%

So, in December 2004, about a 3 basis points slope could be attributed to higher inflation expectations from 2014 to 2024, but that was about it. Most of the 150-basis-point difference between the five-year and the twenty-year Treasury bond must have been due to something else.

Of course, this was the case in December 2004. In the other example we used in this chapter, in April 2011,

Different times, slightly different inference.

Maturity	5-year	7-year	10-year	20-year
TIPS Interest Rate	0.15%	0.79%	1.48%	1.74%
Ordinary Treasury Bonds	2.11%	2.78%	3.39%	4.24%
Implied Inflation Rate	2.0%	2.0%	1.9%	2.5%

Here, there was some evidence that inflation expectations ten to twenty years out were higher than inflation rates over the next ten years.

Q 5.20. On May 31, 2002, the *Wall Street Journal* reported on page C10 that a thirty-year inflation-adjusted bond offered a real yield of about 3.375% per year. The current inflation rate was only 1.6% per year, and a normal thirty-year Treasury bond (not inflation adjusted) offered a nominal yield of 5.600% per year. In what inflation scenario would you have been better off buying one or the other?

Does It Predict Higher Future Interest Rates?

A closely related possibility is that the yield curve is typically upward sloping because short-term interest rates will be higher in the future. This is more generic than the previous explanation—higher future interest rates need not be caused by higher future inflation expectations. Maybe the twenty-year yield of 4.85% was much higher than the one-year yield of 2.23% because investors expected the one-year interest rate in 2024 to be above 5% (the forward rate, $r_{20,21}$). This does not tell you *why* investors would expect interest rates to be so much higher in 2024 than in 2004—maybe capital will be more scarce then and investment opportunities will be better—but the precise reason is not important.

Does a high forward interest rate predict a high future interest rate?

Unfortunately, we do not have a direct estimate of future interest rates the way we had a direct estimate of future inflation rates (from TIPS). Therefore, investigating this hypothesis requires looking at many years of evidence to learn whether future interest rates were well predicted by prevailing forward rates. The details are beyond our scope. However, I can tell you the punchline: Expectations of higher future rates of return are not the reason why the yield curve is typically upward sloping (except maybe at the very short end of the yield curve, say, for interest rates that are for cash investments for less than 1 month).

Alas, the historical data tells us "probably not much."

Does It Mean Bargains on the Long End?

If it is not the case that future interest rates are higher when forward rates are higher, it means that we are dealing with the second possible reason: On average, investors must have earned more in long-term bonds than in rolled-over short-term bonds. The empirical data confirms that you would have ended up with more money if you had purchased twenty-year bonds than if you had purchased one-month bonds every month for 20 years.

It must be either higher future interest rates or higher compensation for long-term bond investors.

Free money? Not in a
perfect market.

But why were long-term bonds better investments than short-term bonds? Maybe the yield curve was upward sloping because investors were stupid. In this case, you might conclude that the twenty-year bond offering 4.85% was a much better deal than the one-year bond offering 2.23%. Alas, investor stupidity seems highly unlikely as a good explanation. The market for Treasury bond investments is close to perfect in the sense that we have used the definition. It is very competitive. If there was a great deal to be had, thousands of traders would have immediately jumped on it. More likely, the interest rate differential does not overthrow the old tried-and-true axiom, *You get what you pay for.* It is just a fact of life that investments for which the interest payments are tied down for 20 years must offer higher interest rates now in order to entice investors—for some good reason yet to be identified. It is important that you recognize that your cash itself is *not* tied down if you invest in a twenty-year bond, because you can, of course, sell your twenty-year bond tomorrow to another investor if you so desire.

Does It Compensate Investors For Risk?

The answer is
probably
compensation for risk.

➤ Bond Risk, _Sect. 5.3,_
_Pg. 102_

If it isn't market stupidity that allows you to earn more money in long-term bonds than in rolled-over short-term bonds, then what else could it be? The empirical evidence suggests that it is most likely the phenomenon explained in Section 5.3: Interim changes in prevailing interest rates have much more impact on long-term bonds than they have on short-term bonds. Recall that rolling over short-term bonds insulates you from the risk that interest rates will change in the future. If you hold a one-day bond and interest rates double by tomorrow, you can just purchase more bonds tomorrow that will offer you twice the interest rate. In contrast, if you hold a long-term bond, you could lose your shirt if interest rates go up in the future. With long-term bonds being riskier than short-term bonds, investors only seem to want to buy them if they get some extra rate of return. Otherwise, they prefer rolling short bonds. Thus, long-term bonds need to offer investors more return on average than short-term bonds.

5.5 Corporate Insights about Time-Varying Costs of Capital

Extend this insight to
corporations:
Longer-term projects,
even if they are not
more likely to default,
often face a higher
cost of capital, and
therefore should have
to deliver higher
returns.

Now that you understand that the yield curve is usually upward sloping for a good reason, you should recognize the family resemblance: Corporate projects are offering cash flows, just like Treasury bonds. Thus, it should not surprise you that longer-term projects usually have to offer higher rates of return than shorter-term projects. And just because a longer-term project offers a higher expected rate of return does not necessarily mean that it has a higher NPV. Conversely, just because shorter-term borrowing allows firms to pay a lower expected rate of return does not necessarily mean that this creates value. (Neither firms nor the U.S. Treasury rely exclusively on short-term borrowing.) Paying a higher expected rate of return for longer-term obligations is (usually) a fact of life.

IMPORTANT

> Even in a perfect market without uncertainty:
>
> - The appropriate cost of capital (rate of return) should usually depend on how long term the project is.
>
> - Short-term corporate projects usually have lower costs of capital than long-term projects.
>
> - Conversely, corporations usually face lower costs of capital (expected rates of return offered to creditors) if they borrow short term rather than long term.

Summary

This chapter covered the following major points:

- Different horizon investments can offer different rates of return. This phenomenon is often called time-varying rates of return.

- The general formula for compounding works just as well for time-varying rates of return as it does for time-constant rates of return. You only lose the ability to exponentiate (one plus the one-year rate of return) when you want to compute multiyear rates of return.

- A holding rate of return can be annualized for easier interpretation.

- The graph of annualized interest rates as a function of maturity is called the "term structure of interest rates" or the "yield curve."

- The yield curve is usually upward sloping. However, no law of finance (i.e., no-arbitrage) is violated if it is downward sloping (inverted), humped, or flat.

- Net present value also works just as well for time-varying interest rates. You merely need to use the appropriate rate of return as the opportunity cost of capital in the denominator.

- An important side observation: "Paper losses" are no different from real losses.

- Inflation is the process by which money will buy fewer goods in the future than it does today. If contracts are inflation indexed in a perfect market, inflation is irrelevant. This is rarely the case.

- The relationship between nominal interest rates, real interest rates, and inflation rates is

$$(1 + r_{nominal}) = (1 + r_{real}) \cdot (1 + \text{Inflation Rate})$$

- Unlike nominal interest rates, real interest rates can—and often have been—negative.

- In NPV, you can either discount real cash flows with real interest rates, or discount nominal cash flows with nominal interest rates. The latter is usually more convenient.

- TIPS are Treasury bonds that protect against future inflation. Short-term bond buyers are also less exposed to inflation rate changes than long-term bond buyers.

- Higher long-term interest rates could be either due to expectations of higher future interest rates or due to extra required compensation for investors willing to hold longer-term bonds. The empirical evidence suggests that historically the latter has been the more important factor.

- Corporations should realize that corporate project cash flows need to be discounted with specific costs of capital that may depend on when the cash flows will come due. It is not unusual that cash flows in the more distant future require higher discount rates.

Preview of the Chapter Appendix in the Companion

In the Appendix

The appendix to this chapter explains

- how you can translate the yield curve (in Exhibit 5.3) step by step into forward and total holding rates of return.

- how shorting works in the real world, and how you can lock in a future interest today with clever bond transactions today.

- how the "duration" of bonds helps you measure when you receive your cash flows on average—a bond paying $100,000 next year and $1 in 20 years is obviously different from one that has the opposite payment pattern, even though both are twenty-year bonds. This can also be useful in measuring the duration of corporate projects.

- continuous compounding, which is a different way of quoting interest rates.

- that Treasury notes and bonds are not really zero bonds (as we pretended in this chapter) but coupon bonds, and why this rarely matters in a corporate context. True Treasury zero bonds are called STRIPS.

Keywords

Answers

Q 5.1 $r_{0,2} = (1 + r_{0,1}) \cdot (1 + r_{1,2}) - 1 = 1.02 \cdot 1.03 - 1 = 5.06\%$

Q 5.2 Solve $(1 + x) \cdot (1 + 22\%) = (1 - 50\%)$, so the project had a rate of return of -59.00%.

Q 5.3 The first four-year compounded rate of return was $r_{2000,2004} \approx (1 - 0.1181) \cdot (1 - 0.2199) \cdot (1 + 0.2821) \cdot (1 + 10.56) - 1 \approx -2.5\%$. The second four-year rate was $r_{2004,2008} \approx -19.4\%$. The full eight-year compounded rate of return was thus $r_{2000,2008} \approx (1 + -2.5\%) \cdot (1 + -19.4\%) - 1 \approx -21.4\%$. Yes, the realized rate was indeed time-varying.

Q 5.4 The returns were $(-33\%, +50\%, -67\%, +100\%)$, so the overall rate of return was -33.33%.

Q 5.5 $1.05^{12/4} \approx 15.76\%$

Q 5.6 The annualized rate of return is $\sqrt{1.4} - 1 \approx 18.32\%$. It is therefore lower than the 20% average rate of return.

Q 5.7 The compounded rate of return is always higher than the sum, because you earn interest on interest. The annualized rate of return is lower than the average rate of return, again because you earn interest on the interest. For example, an investment of \$100 that turns into an investment of \$200 in two years has a total holding rate of return of 100%—which is an average rate of return of $100\%/2 = 50\%$ and an annualized rate of return of $\sqrt{(1 + 100\%)} - 1 \approx 41.42\%$. Investing \$100 at 41% per annum would yield \$200, which is higher than 50% per annum.

Q 5.8 The eight-year rate of return was -21.4%. Thus, the annualized rate of return was $r_{\overline{8}} = \sqrt[8]{1 - 21.4\%} - 1 \approx -3.0\%$.

Q 5.9 $r_{0,5} = 50\%$ $(1 + r_{\overline{5}})^5 = 1.50 \implies r_{\overline{5}} = 1.50^{1/5} - 1 \approx 8.45\%$.

Q 5.10 The annualized five-year rate of return is the same 10%.

Q 5.11 This project is worth

$$- \$200 + \frac{\$100}{1.03} + \frac{\$300}{1.04^2} + \frac{\$500}{1.045^3} \approx \$612.60$$

Q 5.12 The CPI is the average price change to the consumer for a specific basket of goods. The PPI measures the price that producers are paying. Taxes, distribution costs, government subsidies, and basket composition drive a wedge between these two inflation measures.

Q 5.13 $(1 + r_{nominal}) = (1 + r_{real}) \cdot (1 + \pi)$

Q 5.14 $1.20/1.05 \approx 1.1429$. The real interest rate is 14.29%.

Q 5.15 The nominal interest rate is $1.03 \cdot 1.08 - 1 = 11.24\%$. Therefore, the cash flow is worth about $\$500,000/1.1124 \approx \$449,479$.

Q 5.16 Bills, notes, and bonds. T-bills have maturities of less than 1 year. T-notes have maturities from 1 to 10 years. T-bonds have maturities greater than 10 years.

Q 5.17 Yes. The answers are right in the table. The three-year rate of return is $1.0285^3 - 1 \approx 8.80\%$. The forward rate is $1.088/1.0523 - 1 \approx 3.39\%$.

Q 5.18 $r_{0,5} = 1.0335^5 - 1 \approx 17.91\%$. Therefore, $1 + r_{3,5} = 1.0335^5/1.0285^3 - 1 \approx 8.38\%$, which is $\sqrt{1.0838} - 1 \approx 4.10\%$ in annualized terms.

Q 5.19   1. For the one-year bond, the value of a \$100 bond changes from $\$100/1.0800 \approx \$92.59259$ to $\$100/1.0801 \approx \$92.58402$. This is about a -0.009% change.

   2. For the ten-year bond, the value of a \$100 bond changes from $\$100/1.08^{10} \approx \$46.31935$ to $\$100/1.0801^{10} \approx \$46.27648$. This is a -0.09% change—ten times that of the one-year bond.

   3. The derivative of the one-year bond is $-0.009/0.01 \approx -1$. The derivative of the ten-year bond is $-0.09/0.01 \approx -9$. The derivative of the ten-year bond is nine times more negative.

Q 5.20 If inflation were to remain at 1.6% per year, the plain Treasury bond would offer a higher real rate of return because $1.056/1.016 - 1 \approx 3.9\%$ per year. But if inflation were to rise in the future, the inflation-adjusted TIPS bond could end up offering the higher rate of return.

End of Chapter Problems

Q 5.21. Are you better off if a project first returns −10% followed by +30%, or if it first returns +30% followed by −10%?

Q 5.22. Compare two stocks. Both have earned 8% per year on average. However, stock A has oscillated between 6% and 10%. Stock B has oscillated between 3% and 13%. (For simplicity, say that they alternated.) If you had purchased $500 in each stock, how much would you have had 10 years later?

Q 5.23. Stock A alternates between +20% and −10% with equal probability. Stock B earns 4.5% per annum.

1. What is the average rate of return for stock A?

2. What is the average rate of return for stock B?

3. How much would each dollar invested today in stock A earn in 10 years?

4. How much would each dollar invested today in stock B earn in 10 years?

5. What would a risk-neutral investor prefer on a one-shot basis versus on a multiyear basis?

6. What is the main reason for what is going on here?

Q 5.24. Return to Question 5.3. What was the annualized geometric rate of return, and what was the average rate of return on the S&P 500? Would stock brokers prefer to tell their clients the former or the latter?

Q 5.25. The following were the daily values of an investment in January 2001:

2-Jan	3-Jan	4-Jan
$1,283.27	$1,347.56	$1,333.34

5-Jan	8-Jan	9-Jan
$1,298.35	$1,295.86	$1,300.80

If returns had accumulated at the same rate over the entire 252 trading days of 2001, what would a $100 investment in 2001 have turned into? (Use 7 decimal places in this problem.)

Q 5.26. If the annualized five-year rate of return is 10%, what is the total five-year holding rate of return?

Q 5.27. If the annualized five-year rate of return is 10%, and if the first year's rate of return is 15%, and if the returns in all other years are equal, what are they?

Q 5.28. The annual interest rate from year t to year $t+1$ is $r_{t,t+1} = 5\% + 0.3\% \cdot t$ (e.g., the rate of return from year 5 to year 6 is $5\% + 0.3\% \cdot 5 = 6.5\%$).

1. What is the holding rate of return of a ten-year investment today?

2. What is the annualized interest rate of this investment?

Q 5.29. A project has cash flows of +$100 (now at time 0), and −$100, +$100, and −$100 at the end of consecutive years. The interest rate is 6% per annum.

1. What is the project's NPV?

2. How does the value change if all cash flows will occur one year later?

3. Repeat these two questions, but assume that the one-year (annualized) interest rate is 5%, the two-year is 6%, the three-year is 7%, the four-year is 8%, and so on.

Q 5.30. Using information from a current newspaper or a financial website, find out the current inflation rate.

Q 5.31. Using information from a current newspaper or a financial website, find the annualized current nominal interest rate on 30-day U.S. Treasury bills.

Q 5.32. Using the information from Questions 5.30 and 5.31, compute the annualized current real interest rate on 30-day Treasuries.

Q 5.33. If the nominal interest rate is 7% per year and the inflation rate is 2% per year, what is the exact real rate of return?

Q 5.34. The inflation rate is 1.5% per year. The real rate of return is 2.0% per year. A perpetuity project that paid $100 this year will provide income that grows by the inflation rate. Show what this project is truly worth. Do this in both nominal and real terms. (Be clear on what *never* to do.)

Q 5.35. If the annualized rate of return on insured tax-exempt municipal bonds will be 3% per annum and the inflation rate remains at 2% per annum, then what will be their real rate of return over 30 years?

Q 5.36. If the real interest rate is –1% per annum and the inflation rate is 3% per annum, then what is the present value of a $1,000,000 nominal payment next year?

Q 5.37. Inflation is 2% per year; the interest rate is 8% per year. Your perpetuity project has cash flows that grow at 1% faster than inflation forever, starting with $20 next year.

1. What is the real interest rate, both accurate (the "1+" version) and approximate (the subtraction version)?
2. What is the correct project PV ?
3. What would you get if you grew a perpetuity project of $20 by the real growth rate of 1%, and then discounted it at the nominal cost of capital?
4. What would you get if you grew a perpetuity project of $20 by the nominal growth rate of 3%, and then discounted it at the real cost of capital?

Performing either of the latter two calculations is not an uncommon mistake in practice.

Q 5.38. You must value a perpetual lease. It will cost $100,000 each year *in real terms*—that is, its proceeds will not grow in real terms, but just contractually keep pace with inflation. The prevailing interest rate is 8% per year, and the inflation rate is 2% per year forever. The first cash flow of your project *next year* is $100,000 *quoted in today's real dollars*. What is the PV of the project? (Warning: Watch the timing and amount of your first payment.)

Q 5.39. If the real rate of return has been about 1% per month for long-term bonds, what would be the value of an investment that costs $100 today and returned $200 in 10 years?

Q 5.40. At your own personal bank, what is the prevailing savings account interest rate?

Q 5.41. Look up today's yield curve on a financial website. What is the one-year rate of return on a risk-free Treasury? What is the ten-year rate of return on a risk-free Treasury? What is the thirty-year rate of return on a risk-free Treasury?

Q 5.42. The one-year forward interest rates are

Y1	Y2	Y3	Y4	Y5	Y6
3%	4%	5%	6%	6%	6%

Y7	Y8	Y9	Y10	Y11	Y12
7%	7%	7%	6%	5%	4%

1. Compute the 12 n-year compounded holding rates of return from now to year n.
2. Compute the 12 annualized rates of return.
3. Draw the yield curve.
4. Is there anything wrong in this example?

Q 5.43. The *annualized* interest rates are

Y1	Y2	Y3	Y4	Y5	Y6
3%	4%	5%	6%	6%	6%

Y7	Y8	Y9	Y10	Y11	Y12
7%	7%	7%	6%	5%	4%

1. Draw the yield curve.
2. Compute the 12 n-year compounded holding rates of return from now to year n.
3. Compute the 12 1-year forward rates of return.
4. Is there anything wrong in this example?

Q 5.44. At today's prevailing Treasury rates, how much money would you receive from an investment of $100 in 1 year, 10 years, and 30 years? What are their annualized rates of return? What are their total holding rates of return?

Q 5.45. Do long-term bonds pay more than short-term bonds because you only get money after a long time—money that you could need earlier?

Q 5.46. A five-year, zero-coupon bond offers an interest rate of 8% per annum.

1. How does a 1-basis-point increase in the prevailing interest rate change the value of this bond in relative terms?

2. What is the ratio of the relative bond value change over the interest change? In calculus, this would be called the derivative of the value with respect to interest rate changes.

3. How does the derivative of wealth with respect to the interest rate vary with the length of the bond?

Q 5.47. Look at this week's interest rate on ordinary T-bonds and on TIPS. (You should be able to find this information, e.g., in the *Wall Street Journal* or through a fund on the Vanguard website.) What is the implied inflation rate at various time horizons?

Q 5.48. The yield curve is usually upward sloping. Assess whether this means that the following statements are true or false:

1. Investors earn a higher annualized rate of return from long-term T-bonds than short-term T-bills.

2. Long-term T-bonds are better investments than short-term T-bills.

3. Investors are expecting higher inflation in the future than they are today.

4. Investors who are willing to take the risk of investing in long-term bonds on average earn a higher rate of return because they are taking more risk (that in the interim bond prices fall / interest rates rise).

Q 5.49. Evaluate and Discuss: Does the evidence suggest that long-term bonds tend to earn higher average rates of return than short-term bonds? If yes, why is this the case? If no, why is this not possible?

Uncertainty, Default, and Risk

Promised vs Expected Returns and Debt vs Equity in a Risk-Neutral World

You are now entering the world of uncertainty and abandoning the idea that you have perfect foresight. We shall still pretend that you live in a perfect market with no taxes, no transaction costs, no differences of opinion, and infinitely many investors and firms. But the presence of uncertainty adds enough additional complexity and realism for now.

Net present value still rules supreme, but you will now have to face the sad fact that it is no longer easy to use. It is *not* the NPV concept that is difficult. Instead, it is the inputs that are difficult—the expected cash flows and appropriate costs of capital that you now have to guestimate.

In a world of uncertainty, there are scenarios in which you will get more cash than you expected and scenarios in which you will get less. The single most important insight under uncertainty therefore is that you must always draw a sharp distinction between *promised* (or *quoted* or *stated*) returns and *expected* returns. Because firms can default on payments or go bankrupt in the future, expected returns are lower than promised returns.

After some necessary statistical background, this chapter will cover two important finance topics: First, you must determine how much lenders should charge borrowers if there is the possibility of default. Second, you learn how to work with the two building blocks of financing—namely, debt and equity.

6.1 An Introduction to Statistics

Statistics has the reputation of being the most painful of the foundation sciences for finance—but you absolutely need to understand it to describe an uncertain future. Yes, it can be a difficult subject, but if you have ever placed a bet in the past, chances are that you already have a good intuitive grasp of what you need. In fact, I had already sneaked the term "expected" into previous chapters, even though it is only now that this book covers what this precisely means.

Statistics is about characterizing an uncertain world.

Random Variables and Expected Values

The "expected value" is the average outcome if the random draw is repeated infinitely often. It need not be a possible realization.

The most important statistical concept is the **expected value**, which is the probability-weighted average of all possible outcomes. It is very similar to a **mean** or **average**. The difference is that the latter two names are used if you work with *past* outcomes, while the expected value applies if you work with *future* outcomes. For example, say you toss a coin, which can come up either heads or tails with equal probability. You receive $1 if the coin comes up heads and $2 if the coin comes up tails. Because you know that there is a 50% chance of $1 and a 50% chance of $2, the expected value of each coin toss is $1.50. If you repeated this infinitely often, and if you recorded the series of **realizations** (actual outcomes), the mean would converge to exactly $1.50. Of course, in any one throw, $1.50 can never come up—the expected value does not need to be a possible realization of a single coin toss.

IMPORTANT

> The expected value is just a mean (or average) if you could repeat an experiment (the random draws) infinitely often.

A random variable is a number whose realization is not yet known.

To make it easier to work with uncertainty, statisticians have invented the concept of the **random variable**. It is a variable whose outcome has not yet been determined. In the coin toss example, you can define a random variable named c (for "coin toss outcome") that takes the value $1 with 50% probability and the value $2 with 50% probability. (Random variables often have tildes over them, such as č, but we will dispense with this formality.) The expected value of c is $1.50. To denote the expected value, we use the notation $\mathcal{E}$. In this bet,

$$\mathcal{E}(c) \quad = \quad 50\% \cdot \$1 \quad + \quad 50\% \cdot \$2 \quad = \$1.50$$

$$\text{Expected Value(Coin Toss)} \; = \; \mathcal{P}rob(\text{Heads}) \cdot \$1 + \mathcal{P}rob(\text{Tails}) \cdot \$2$$

After the coin has been tossed, the actual outcome c could, for example, be c = $2. After the toss, this c is no longer a random variable. Also, if you are certain about the outcome, perhaps because there is only one possible outcome, then the actual realization and the expected value are the same. The random variable is then the same as an ordinary nonrandom variable. Is the expected outcome of the coin toss a random variable? No: You know the expected outcome is $1.50 even before the toss of the coin. The expected value is known; the uncertain outcome is not. The expected value is an ordinary nonrandom variable; the possible outcome is a random variable. Is the outcome of the coin throw *after* it has come down heads a random variable? No: It is an actual outcome and you know what it is (heads), so it is no longer a random variable.

A random variable is a statistical distribution.

A random variable is defined by the **probability distribution** of its possible outcomes. The coin throw distribution is simple: the value $1 with 50% probability and the value $2 with 50% probability. This is sometimes graphed in a **histogram**, which is a graph that has the possible outcomes on the x-axis and the frequency (or probability) on the y-axis. Exhibit 6.1 shows the histogram for the coin throw. In fact, you can think of a random variable as a placeholder for a histogram.

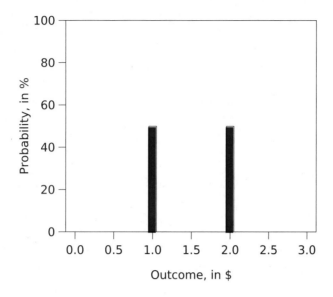

Exhibit 6.1: *A Histogram for a Random Variable with Two Equally Likely Outcomes, $1 and $2.*

One final clarification: In this chapter, we are eliminating our certainty assumption. But we are *not* (yet) eliminating our perfect market assumption. The assumption of no-disagreement means that we all must agree on the probabilities of all possible outcomes. An example of an imperfect market would be if you believed that there was a 51% probability of an outcome of $1, and I believed there was a 50% probability of $1.

A final note—perfect markets.

Fair Bets

A **fair bet** is a bet that costs its expected value. If repeated infinitely often, both the person offering the bet and the person taking the bet would expect to end up even. For example, call D your payoff based on the following structure:

An example with three possible outcomes.

- There is a $1/4$ chance that you will be paid $2;

- a $1/4$ chance that you will be paid $10;

- and a $2/4$ chance that you will be paid $8.

You can simulate this payoff structure by drawing a card from a complete deck. If it is ♣, you get a value V of $2; if it is ♦, you get $10, and if it is ♥ or ♠, you get $8. What would be a fair price for this card bet? The uncertain payoff is a random variable. Let's call it D. First, you must determine $\mathcal{E}(D)$. It is

$$\mathcal{E}(D) = \quad 1/4 \quad \cdot \$2 + \quad 1/4 \quad \cdot \$10 + \quad 2/4 \quad \cdot \quad \$8 \quad = \$7$$
$$\mathcal{E}(D) = \quad \mathcal{P}rob(\clubsuit) \cdot V\clubsuit + \mathcal{P}rob(\diamondsuit) \cdot V\diamondsuit + \mathcal{P}rob(\heartsuit \text{ or } \spadesuit) \cdot V\heartsuit \text{ or } \spadesuit$$

If you repeat this bet a zillion times, you would expect to earn $7 zillion. On average, each bet would earn $7, although some sampling variation in actual trials would make this a little more or a little less. If it costs $7 to buy each single bet, it would be fair.

The expected value is the probability-weighted sum of all possible outcomes.

Generally, the procedure to compute expected values is always the same: Multiply each outcome by its probability and add up all these products.

$$\mathcal{E}(X) = \mathcal{P}rob(\text{First Possible Outcome}) \cdot \text{Value of First Possible Outcome}$$
$$+ \ \mathcal{P}rob(\text{Second Possible Outcome}) \cdot \text{Value of Second Possible Outcome}$$
$$+ \qquad\qquad\qquad\qquad \vdots$$
$$+ \ \mathcal{P}rob(\text{Last Possible Outcome}) \cdot \text{Value of Last Possible Outcome}$$

This is the formula that you used above,

$$\mathcal{E}(D) = \quad 1/4 \cdot \$2 \ + \ 1/4 \cdot \$10 \ + \ 2/4 \cdot \$8 \qquad = \$7$$
$$= \ \text{Sum of } [\mathcal{P}rob(\text{Each Outcome}) \times \text{Each Outcome}]$$

Note that the formula is general. It works even with outcomes that are impossible. You would just assign probabilities of zero to them.

IMPORTANT

> You must understand the following:
> 1. The difference between an ordinary variable and a random variable
> 2. The difference between a realization and an expectation
> 3. How to compute an expected value, given probabilities and outcomes
> 4. What a fair bet is

Q 6.1. Is the expected outcome (value) of a die throw a random variable?

Q 6.2. Could it be that the expected value of a bet is a random variable?

Q 6.3. For an ordinary die, assume that the random variable is the number on the die times two. Say the die throw came up with a "six" yesterday. What was its expected outcome before the throw? What was its realization?

Q 6.4. A stock that has the following probability distribution (outcome P_{+1}) costs $50. Is an investment in this stock a fair bet?

$\mathcal{P}rob$	P_{+1}	$\mathcal{P}rob$	P_{+1}	$\mathcal{P}rob$	P_{+1}	$\mathcal{P}rob$	P_{+1}
5%	$41	20%	$45	20%	$58	5%	$75
10%	$42	30%	$48	10%	$70		

Variance and Standard Deviation

In finance, we often need to measure the (average) **reward** that you expect to receive from making an investment. Usually, we use the expected value of the investment as our measure. We also often need to measure a second characteristic of an investment, namely its **risk**. Thus, we also need summary measures of how spread out the possible outcomes are. These two concepts will play starring roles in the next few chapters, where you will explore them in great detail. For now, if you are curious, think of risk as a measure of the variability of outcomes around your expected mean. The most common measure of risk is the standard deviation, which takes the square root of the sum of squared deviations from the mean—a mouthful. Let's just do it once for our card-draw problem. First, work out each squared deviation from the mean:

We will measure the "reward" as the expected value. Looking ahead, the standard deviation is the most common measure of "risk" (spread).

The first outcome is $2. The mean is $7, so the deviation from the mean is $2 − $7 = −$5. You need the squared deviation from the mean, which is $(−\$5)^2 = +\$\$25$. The units are strange—dollars squared—and impossible to interpret intuitively. Don't even try.

(Computing the variance can be a demeaning task.)

The second outcome is $10, so the deviation from the mean is $10 − $7 = +$3. You need the squared deviation from the mean, which is $(+\$3)^2 = +\$\$9$.

The third outcome is $8, so the deviation from the mean is $8 − $7 = +$1. You need the squared deviation from the mean, which is $(\$1)^2 = +\$\$1$.

Now compute the expected value of these squared deviations, which is called the **variance**:

$$\mathcal{V}ar(\text{Dice}) \;=\; 1/4 \cdot (\$\$25) + 1/4 \cdot (\$\$9) + 2/4 \cdot \$\$1 \;=\; \$\$9$$

The **standard deviation** is therefore

$$\mathcal{S}dv(\text{Dice}) \;=\; \sqrt{\$\$9} \;\approx\; \$3$$

There you have it—our mouthful: The standard deviation is the square root of the average squared deviation from the mean. Unlike the variance, the standard deviation has sensible units. Together, the mean and standard deviation allow you to characterize your bet. It is common phrasing, though a bit loose, to state that you expect to earn $7 (the expected value) from a single card draw, plus or minus $3 (the standard deviation).

Q 6.5. Reconsider the stock investment from Question 6.4. What is its risk—that is, what is the standard deviation of its outcome P_{+1}?

Risk Neutrality (and Preview of Risk Aversion)

Choosing investments
only on the basis of
expected values is
assuming risk
neutrality.

Fortunately, the expected value is all that you need to learn about statistics for this chapter. This is because we are assuming—only for learning purposes—that everyone is **risk neutral**. Essentially, this means that investors are willing to write or take any fair bet. For example, if you are risk neutral, you would be indifferent between getting $1 for sure and getting either $0 or $2, each with 50% probability. And you would be indifferent between earning 10% from a risk-free bond and earning either 0% or 20%, again with fifty-fifty probability, from a risky bond. You have no preference between investments with equal expected values, no matter how safe or uncertain these investments may be.

Risk aversion means
you would prefer the
safe project. Put
differently, you would
demand an extra
"kicker" to take the
riskier project instead.

If, instead, you are risk averse, you would not want to invest in the more risky alternative if both the risky and safe alternatives offered the same expected rate of return. You would prefer the safe $1 to the unsafe $0 or $2 investment. You would prefer a 10% risk-free bond to the unsafe corporate bond that would pay either 0% or 20%. In this case, if I wanted to sell you a risky project or a risky bond, I would have to offer you a higher expected rate of return as risk compensation. I might have to pay you, say, 5 cents to get you to be willing to accept the project that pays off $0 or $2 if you can instead earn $1 elsewhere. Alternatively, I would have to lower the price of my corporate bond so that it offers you a higher expected rate of return, say, 1% or 21% instead of 0% or 20%.

For a given investor,
bigger bets usually
require more
compensation for risk.

It is true that if you are risk averse, you should not accept fair bets. (You can think of this as the definition of risk aversion.) But would you really worry about a bet for either +$1 or –$1? Probably not. For small bets, you are probably close to risk neutral—I may not have to pay you even 1 cent extra to induce you to take this bet. But what about a bet for plus or minus $100? Or for plus or minus $10,000? My guess is that you would be fairly reluctant to accept the latter bet without getting extra compensation for risk bearing. If you are like most investors, you are more risk averse when the bet is larger. To take the plus or minus $10,000 bet, I would probably have to offer you several hundred dollars extra.

Financial markets can
spread risk and
thereby lower the
aggregate risk
aversion.

However, your own personal risk aversion is not what matters in financial markets. Instead, the financial markets price investments in line with the market's aggregate risk aversion. The reason is risk sharing. For example, if you could share the $10,000 bet with 10,000 other students in your class, your own part of the bet would be only plus or minus $1. And some of your colleagues may be willing to accept even more risk for relatively less extra risk compensation—they may have healthier bank accounts or wealthier parents. Therefore, when you can lay bets across many investors, the effective risk aversion of the group will be lower than that of any of its members. And this is exactly how financial markets work: Their aggregate risk absorption capabilities are considerably higher than those of their individual investors. In effect, the financial markets are less risk averse than individual investors.

The tools you learn
now will remain
applicable under risk
aversion.

You will study risk aversion in the next chapters. In this chapter, we will focus on pricing under risk neutrality. But, as always, all tools you learn in this simpler scenario will remain applicable in the more complex scenario in which investors are risk averse. Moreover, in the real world, the differences between promised and expected returns that are discussed in this chapter are often more important (in terms of value) than the extra compensation for risk aversion that is ignored in this chapter.

Q 6.6. Are investors more risk averse for small bets or for large bets? Should "small" be defined relative to investor wealth?

Q 6.7. Are individual investors or investors in the aggregate more risk averse?

6.2 Interest Rates and Credit Risk (Default Risk)

Most loans in the real world are not risk free, because the borrower may not fully pay back what was promised. We will assume that there is one exception, which is that U.S. Treasuries are risk-free loans in nominal terms. In principle, the U.S. can always tax more and print more dollars to satisfy all promised bond payments. Therefore, it is reasonable to assume the U.S. cannot default. (Intelligent people can disagree. Washington politics is so dysfunctional that the U.S. may actually default not for lack of dollars, but by choice.) So, how do you compute appropriate expected rates of return for risky bonds?

Risk-free and risky lending.

ANECDOTE   The Ruin of the First Financial System

The earliest known example of widespread financial default occurred in the year 1788 B.C.E., when King Rim-Sin of Uruk (Mesopotamia) repealed *all* loan repayments. The royal edict effectively destroyed a system of flourishing commerce and finance, which was already many thousands of years old! It is not known why Rim-Sin did so. Interest rates were modest, roughly 4% per annum for five year loans.   *William Goetzmann, Yale University*

Risk-Neutral Investors Demand Higher Promised Rates

Now, put yourself into the position of a banker. Assume that a 1-year Treasury note offers a safe annual rate of return of 10%. Your immediate problem is that you are contemplating making a 1-year loan of $1 million to me. What interest rate should you charge me on the loan? If you are 100% certain that I will fully pay the agreed-upon amount, you can just charge me 10%. You earn just as much from me as from the Treasury note. Both will pay back $1,100,000.

If my repayment is certain, you should be accept the same interest rate that the U.S. Treasury offers.

However, in the real world, there are few borrowers for whom you can be 100% certain that they will fully repay a loan. For example, assume you believe there is only a 50% chance that I will pay back the principal plus interest. (If I do pay it back, I will be called **solvent**). There is also a 50% chance that I will **default** (fail to pay all that I have promised). This is often informally called bankruptcy. In this case, I may only be able to pay back $750,000—all that I have left. If, as the bank, you were to charge me a 10% interest rate, your expected payout would be

If you quote me the same interest rate, you would expect to earn a lower interest rate if there is a chance of default.

$$50\% \quad \cdot \quad \$750{,}000 \quad + \quad 50\% \quad \cdot \quad \$1{,}100{,}000 \quad = \$925{,}000$$

$$\mathscr{P}rob(\,\text{Default}\,) \; \cdot \; (\text{Pay if Default}) \; + \; \mathscr{P}rob(\,\text{Solvent}\,) \; \cdot \; (\text{Pay if Solvent})$$

Your *expected* return would not be $1,100,000, but only $925,000. Your *expected* rate of return would not be +10%, but only $\$925{,}000/\$1{,}000{,}000 - 1 = -7.5\%$. Extending such a loan would not be—pardon the pun—in your best interest: You can do better by investing your $1,000,000 into government Treasury notes.

A N E C D O T E   A Short History of Bankruptcy

The framers of the United States Constitution had the English bankruptcy system in mind when they included the power to enact "uniform laws on the subject of bankruptcies" in Article I (powers of the legislative branch). The first United States bankruptcy law, passed in 1800, virtually copied the existing English law. United States bankruptcy laws thus have their conceptual origins in English bankruptcy law prior to 1800. On both sides of the Atlantic, however, much has changed since then.

Early English law had a distinctly pro-creditor orientation and was noteworthy for its harsh treatment of defaulting debtors. Imprisonment for debt was the order of the day, from the time of the Statute of Merchants in 1285 until Charles Dickens's time in the mid-nineteenth century. (In fact, when Charles was a child, his father spent time in debtor's prison.) The common law *Writs of Capias* authorized "body execution," that is, seizure of the body of the debtor, to be held until payment of the debt.

English law was not unique in its lack of solicitude for debtors. History's annals are replete with tales of harsh treatment of debtors. Punishments inflicted upon debtors included forfeiture of all property, relinquishment of the consortium of a spouse, imprisonment, and death. In Rome, creditors were apparently authorized to carve up the body of the debtor. However, scholars debate the extent to which the letter of that law was actually enforced.

Charles Jordan Tabb, 1995, "The History of the Bankruptcy Laws in the United States."

> You must ask for a higher promised interest—received only in good times—in order to make up for my default risk.

You should conclude that you must demand a higher interest rate from risky borrowers as a banker, even if you just want to "break even" (i.e., expect to earn the same $1,100,000 that you could earn in Treasury notes). If you solve

$$50\% \cdot \quad \$750{,}000 \qquad + 50\% \cdot (\text{Promised Repayment}) \quad = \quad \$1{,}100{,}000$$

$$\mathscr{P}rob \cdot (\text{Payment if Default}) \; + \; \mathscr{P}rob \cdot \quad (\text{Payment if Solvent}) \quad = \text{Treasury Payment}$$

for the desired promised repayment, you will find that you must ask me for $1,450,000. The promised interest rate is therefore $\$1{,}450{,}000/\$1{,}000{,}000 - 1 = 45\%$. Of this 45%, 10% is the **time premium** that the Treasury pays. Therefore, you can call the remaining 35% the **default premium**—the difference between the promised rate and the expected rate that you, the lender, would have to demand just to break even. It is very important that you realize that the default premium is not extra compensation for your taking on more risk, say, relative to holding Treasuries. You don't receive any such extra compensation in a risk-neutral world. The default premium just fills the gap between the expected return and the promised return.

> You are always quoted promised returns, and not expected returns. The risk is called "credit risk."

You rarely observe expected rates of return directly. Newspaper and financial documents almost always provide only the **promised interest rate**, which is therefore also called the **quoted interest rate** or the **stated interest rate**. When you read a published yield-to-maturity, it is also usually only a promised rate, not an expected rate—that is, the published yield is an internal rate of return that is calculated from promised payments, not from expected payments. Of course, you should never make capital budgeting decisions based on promised IRRs. You almost always want to use an expected IRR (YTM). But you usually have easy access only to the promised rate, not the expected rate. On Wall Street, the default premium is often called the **credit premium**, and **default risk** is often called **credit risk**.

➤ *IRR, YTM, Sect.* 4.2, *Pg.64.*

Q 6.8. For what kind of bonds are expected and promised interest rates the same?

A More Elaborate Example With Probability Ranges

This distinction between expected and promised rates is so important that it is worthwhile to work another more involved example. Assume again that I ask you to lend me money. You believe that I will pay you what I promise with 98% probability; that I will repay half of what I borrowed with 1% probability; and that I will repay nothing with 1% probability. I want to borrow $200 from you, which you could alternatively invest into a government bond promising $210 (i.e., a 5% interest rate). What interest rate would you ask of me?

Again, I sometimes may not be able to repay.

If you ask me for a 5% interest rate, next year (time 1), your $200 investment today (time 0) will produce the following:

If you ask me to pay the risk-free interest rate, you will on average earn less than the risk-free interest rate.

Payoff (C_1)	Rate of Return (r)	Frequency ($\mathcal{P}rob$)
$210	+5.0%	98% of the time
$100	−50.0%	1% of the time
$0	−100.0%	1% of the time

Therefore, your expected payoff is

$$\mathcal{E}(C_1) \ = \ 98\% \cdot \ \$210 \ + \ 1\% \cdot \ \$100 \ + \ 1\% \cdot \ \$0 \ = \$206.80$$
$$= \ \mathcal{P}rob \cdot \text{Cash Flow} + \mathcal{P}rob \cdot \text{Cash Flow} + \mathcal{P}rob \cdot \text{Cash Flow}$$

Your expected return of $206.80 is less than the $210 that the government promises. Put differently, if I *promise* you a rate of return of 5%,

$$\text{Promised}(r) \ = \ \frac{\$210 - \$200}{\$200} \ = 5.00\%$$

$$\text{Promised}(r) \ = \ \frac{\text{Promised}(C_1) - C_0}{C_0}$$

then your expected rate of return would only be

$$\mathcal{E}(r) \ = \ \frac{\$206.80 - \$200}{\$200} \ = 3.40\%$$

$$\mathcal{E}(r) \ = \ \frac{\mathcal{E}(C_1) - C_0}{C_0}$$

This is less than the 5% interest rate that Uncle Sam promises—and surely delivers.

Let's determine how much more interest promise you need to break even.

You need to determine how much I have to promise you just to break even. You want to expect to end up with the same $210 that you could receive from Uncle Sam. The expected loan payoff is the probability-weighted average payoff. You want this payoff to be not $206.80 but the $210 that you can earn if you invest your $200 into government bonds. You need to solve for an amount x that you receive if I have money,

$$\mathcal{E}(C_1) \quad = 98\% \cdot x + 1\% \cdot \$100 + 1\% \cdot \$0 \quad = \$210.00$$

The solution is that if I promise you x ≈ $213.27, you will expect to earn the same 5% interest rate that you can earn in Treasury notes. This $213.27 for a cash investment of $200 is a *promised* interest rate of

$$\text{Promised}(r) \quad \approx \quad \frac{\$213.27 - \$200}{\$200} \quad \approx 6.63\%$$

$$\text{Promised}(r) \quad = \quad \frac{\text{Promised}(C_1) - C_0}{C_0}$$

Such a promise provides the following:

Payoff (C_1)	Rate of Return (r)	Frequency ($\mathcal{P}rob$)
$213.27	+6.63%	98% of the time
$100.00	−50.00%	1% of the time
$0.00	−100.00%	1% of the time

This comes to an *expected* interest rate of

$$\mathcal{E}(r) \approx 98\% \cdot (+6.63\%) + 1\% \cdot (-50\%) + 1\% \cdot (-100\%) \approx 5\%$$

Q 6.9. Recompute the example from the text, but assume now that the probability of receiving full payment in one year on a $200 investment of $210 is only 95%, the probability of receiving $100 is 1%, and the probability of receiving absolutely no payment is 4%.

1. At the promised interest rate of 5%, what is the expected interest rate?
2. What interest rate is required as a promise to ensure an expected interest rate of 5%?

Deconstructing Quoted Rates of Return—Time and Default Premiums

The difference between the promised and expected interest rate in a risk-neutral perfect world is the default premium.

The difference of 1.63% between the promised (or quoted) interest rate of 6.63% and the expected interest rate of 5% is the default premium—it is the extra interest rate that is caused by the default risk. Of course, you only receive this 6.63% *if* everything goes perfectly. In our perfect market with risk-neutral investors,

$$6.63\% \quad = \quad 5\% \quad + \quad 1.63\%$$

$$\text{"Promised Interest Rate"} = \text{"Time Premium"} + \text{"Default Premium"}$$

> **IMPORTANT**
>
> Except for 100%-safe bonds, the promised (or quoted) rate of return is higher than the expected rate of return. Never confuse the promised rate with the (lower) expected rate. If you only remember one thing from this book, this should be it!
>
> Financial securities and information providers rarely, if ever, provide information about expected rates of return. They almost always provide only quoted rates of return.

On average, the expected rate of return is the expected time premium plus the expected default premium. Because the *expected* default premium is zero *on average*,

In a perfect risk-neutral world, all securities have the same expected rate of return.

$$\mathcal{E}(\text{Rate of Return}) = \mathcal{E}(\text{Time Premium}) + 0$$
$$= \mathcal{E}(\text{Time Premium}) + \mathcal{E}(\text{Realized Default Premium})$$

If you want to work this out, you can compute the expected realized default premium as follows: You will receive $6.63\% - 5\% = 1.63\%$ in 98% of all cases; $-50\% - 5\% = -55\%$ in 1% of all cases (note that you lose the time premium); and $-100\% - 5\% = -105\%$ in the remaining 1% of all cases (i.e., you lose not only all your money, but also the time premium). Therefore,

$$\mathcal{E}(\text{Realized Default Premium}) \approx 98\% \cdot (+1.63\%) + 1\% \cdot (-55\%) + 1\% \cdot (-105\%) \approx 0\%$$

In addition to the 5% time premium and the 1.63% default premium, in the real world, there are also other premiums that we have not yet covered:

Warning: Additional premiums will follow later.

Risk premiums that compensate you with higher expected rates of return for your willingness to take on risk. They will be the subject of Chapter 9.

Imperfect market premiums (e.g., liquidity premiums) that compensate you for future difficulties in finding buyers for your bonds. They will be the subject of Chapter 10.

In normal times, these premiums are typically much lower than time premiums and default premiums in a bond context.

Q 6.10. Is the expected default premium positive?

Credit Ratings and Default Rates

To make it easier for lenders to judge the probability of default, a number of data vendors for credit ratings have appeared. For individuals, Experian, Transunion, and Equifax provide credit ratings—you should request a free credit report for yourself from the Federal Trade Commission if you have never seen one. For small companies, Dun & Bradstreet provides similar credit scores. For corporations, the two biggest credit rating agencies are **Moody's** and **Standard&Poor's** (**S&P**). (There are also other less influential ones, like *Duff and Phelps* and *Fitch*.) For a fee, these agencies rate the probability that the issuer's bonds will default. This fee depends on a number of factors,

Bond rating agencies: The most important are Moody's and Standard & Poor's.

such as the identity of the issuer, the desired detail in the agencies' investigations and descriptions, and the features of the bond (e.g., a bond that will pay off within one year is usually less likely to default before maturity than a bond that will pay off in thirty years; thus, the former is easier to grade).

Investment Grade

	Best									Barely
Moody's	Aaa	Aa1	Aa2	Aa3	A1	A2	A3	Baa1	Baa2	Baa3
Standard & Poor's	AAA	AA+	AA	AA–	A+	A	A–	BBB+	BBB	BBB–

Non-Investment Grade (Speculative or "Junk")

	Speculative								in Default
Moody's	Ba1	Ba2	Ba3	B1	B2	B3	Caa1, Caa2, Caa3, Ca , C		D
Standard & Poor's	BB+	BB	BB–	B+	B	B–	CCC		D

Exhibit 6.2: *Bond Rating Categories Used by Moody's and Standard & Poor's.*

The most important grade distinction is "junk" versus "investment grade."

The credit rating agencies ultimately do not provide a whole set of default probabilities (e.g., 1% chance of 100% loss, 1.2% chance of 99% loss, etc.), but just an overall rating grade. Exhibit 6.2 shows the categories for Moody's and Standard & Poor's. It is then up to the lender to translate the rating into an appropriate compensation for default risk. The top rating grades are called **investment grade**, while the bottom grades are called **speculative grade** (or **junk grade**).

Conflicted Ratings (and the 2008 crisis).

Ratings have limited usefulness. First, they do not consider systemic risk. Most bond buyers care more about the small risk of all their bond holdings blowing up together at the same time, than they care about an individual bond defaulting. But systematic risk assessments are *not* what rating agencies provide. Second, unlike most other financial market experts, rating agencies are not liable for their ratings or perspectives even if they deliberately deceive investors. (Repealing this exemption, called SEC rule 436(g), is still being debated in Congress in 2011. It is not yet clear what the outcome will be.) Interestingly, the rating agencies make most of their money by rating securities on behalf of investment banks. Not surprisingly, although they need to maintain some independence and reputation, the agencies are also often good game when it comes to being manipulated—some would even call it bribed. A good part of the financial crisis of 2008 falls squarely on the shoulders of the rating agencies, which earned billions providing optimistic ratings for issues explicitly engineered by investment banks to have high ratings. And although some steps have been taken to improve the situation, all the same issues are still present. When the public attention will have moved on to another issue of the day, chances are that we will return back to business as usual.

Empirical Evidence on Default

Ed Altman and his coauthors (from New York University) collected corporate bond statistics from the 1970s to 2010. Exhibit 6.3 gives you a sketch of how likely default (defined as missing at least one coupon payment) was. The average default rate was about 3.6% per year— but the left plot shows that it was much higher in recessions, where defaults typically shot up to over 10%. For example, in the 2009 financial crisis, about 11% of bonds failed to pay. (In 2008, about half of all defaults were Lehman Bros' bankruptcy. In 2010, the worst seemed to have passed.) The typical recovery in a default was about 30-40 cents on the dollar, with 25 cents in recessions and 50 cents in booms being ballpark estimates. Low-rated bonds would pay less. The right plot shows that corporate bonds originally rated A or better rarely defaulted, even 10 years after issue. However, about half of all CCC junk bonds would fail to pay at least one coupon within the first five years of issue.

Here are historical probabilities of bond defaults by credit ratings.

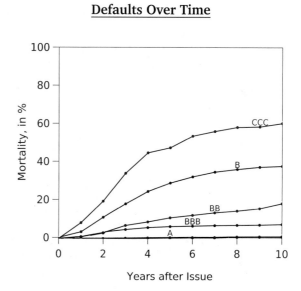

Exhibit 6.3: *Cumulative Probability of Default by Original Bond Rating, 1971–2010.* The left plot shows the rate at which bonds defaulted. For example, in 2009, about 11% of all corporate bonds failed to make at least one payment. The right plot shows the probability of default within x years after issue, given the bond rating at-issue. For example, at some point during the first 7 years of their issue, 34% of all bonds originally issued as B (poor) had not delivered on at least one promised bond payment. Corporate bonds originally rated A and better essentially have not defaulted over the first 10 years of their existence. Source: Edward Altman and Brenda Kuehne, New York University, April 2011.

Bond Contract Option Features

Before I show you real-world quoted returns, I must explain that they can contain contract premiums.

Before I show you how bonds are priced, I need to let you know that bonds in the real world differ from one another not just in credit risk. Most bonds have additional contract features that may also influence their quoted rates of return. For example, many corporate bonds allow the issuer to repay the loan early. (The same applies to almost all domestic mortgages.) If the interest rates in the future fall, this can be a good thing for the borrower and a bad thing for the lender. The borrower would pay off the loan and borrow more cheaply elsewhere. If the interest rates in the future rise, the borrower gets to pay just the earlier low interest rate. For example, assume that the interest rate is 10% today and you are lending me \$90,909 in exchange for my promise to pay you \$100,000 next year. One second after you extend the loan, one of two scenarios can happen:

1. The interest may fall to 5%. I would then simply repay your \$90,909 loan and refinance at this lower interest rate elsewhere.

2. The interest rate may rise to 15%. In this case, I keep my \$100,000 promise to pay next year—I received \$90,909 for a loan that should have given me only \$100,000/1.15 ≈ \$86,957.

This would not be a good arrangement for you—unless you are appropriately compensated for giving me this option to prepay. Borrowers who want the right to repay without penalty therefore have to pay higher interest rates when they issue such bonds. Virtually all mortgage bonds in the United States allow prepayment and therefore carry higher interest rates than they would if they did not have a prepayment feature. Loosely speaking, you can classify these contract option features as default premiums, too, because on average they tend not to add or subtract from your expected rate of return. Sometimes they increase the amount paid, and sometimes they decrease the amount paid by the lender—just as a solvent bond would pay more to the lender and an insolvent bond would pay less to the lender.

Q 6.11. Does the historical evidence show that lower-grade borrowers default more often or that they pay less upon default?

Differences in Quoted Bond Returns in 2011

Historical rates of return: Riskier bonds indeed have higher stated rates of return.

So how do real-world bond credit ratings translate into differences in promised (quoted) bond yields? Exhibit 6.4 lists the borrowing rates of various issuers in April 2011 when the 10-year Treasury paid about 3.4% per annum. (Many current interest rates can be found at http://www.bloomberg.com and http://bonds.yahoo.com.) The data look broadly consistent with the theory—bonds that have higher default risk have to offer higher promised rates of return. Bonds with higher (better) credit ratings can find lenders at lower interest rates (higher bond prices).

Expected rates of return were more similar to one another than Exhibit 6.4 suggests.

Do lenders to creditors with higher risk end up with about the same average rate of return as lenders to creditors with lower risk? This would be the case in a perfect market in which lenders and borrowers are risk neutral. The evidence suggests that this

Security (Bond)	Rating	Quoted Yield	Spread Over U.S. Treasury
Corporate Bond Average	AAA	3.9%	50 bp
Corporate Bond Average	A	4.3%	90 bp
Federal Farm Corp	AAA	3.6%	20 bp
Wal Mart	AA	3.9%	50 bp
Wells Fargo	AA	4.3%	90 bp
Verizon	A	4.2%	180 bp
Jefferies Group (Investment Bank)	BBB	5.4%	200 bp
Limited Brands (Victoria's Secret, etc.)	BB	5.9%	250 bp
AMR (American Airlines)	CCC	10.4%	700 bp

Exhibit 6.4: Promised *Interest Rates for 10-Year Bonds in April 2011.* The first two rows are average interest rates computed from many firms, the seven other bonds are from individual firms. The Federal Farm Corp is a government-sponsored entity. In August 2011, S&P downgraded the U.S. from AAA to AA status, but this did not affect the yields on U.S. Treasuries. Source: http://screen.yahoo.com/bonds.html, April 25, 2011.

is not exactly true, but it is also not too far from reality. The overwhelming majority of the spreads above the Treasury simply make lenders come out even. If I had to guess, I would say that of the roughly 100-basis-point spread between AA and A bonds in Exhibit 6.4, about 80 basis points is due to credit risk; about 10 basis points is due to discrepancies exactly when coupons are paid; and only about 10 basis points is extra compensation that creditors of low-quality bonds will earn *on average* relative to creditors of high-quality bonds.

Credit Default Swaps

The financial world is always changing and innovating. The components of bond returns described above used to be primarily a conceptual curiosity—firms would borrow money from their lenders, paying one interest rate that just contained all premiums. But then, with the introduction of **credit default swaps** (often abbreviated **credit swaps** or **CDS**), some premium components suddenly became themselves tradeable.

A large new market: credit default swaps.

Here is an example of a CDS: A large pension fund that holds a $15 million bond issued by HCA Inc. may decide to purchase a $10 million credit swap from a hedge fund that wants to bet that HCA will not go bankrupt. (The *Wall Street Journal* reported that this CDS contract cost about $130,000 in June 2006, but rose to over $400,000 in July because of a potential buyout deal that would increase the risk of future default.) If HCA goes bankrupt, the hedge fund owes the pension fund $10 million. In this case, purchasing the CDS in June was a lucky deal for the pension fund and an unlucky deal for the hedge fund—HCA indeed went bankrupt. The best way to think of such credit

A CDS example: The swap seller insures the swap buyer.

swaps is as an insurance contract, in which the swap seller (the hedge fund) is the insurance provider. The buyer of the credit swap pays the seller an up-front premium in exchange for a payment if a credit event (e.g., a failed payment or bankruptcy) occurs for a particular bond within a given number of years. The payment itself can be formula-determined, or it can be a guarantee by the CDS seller to buy the bond at a predetermined price. Another way of thinking of the up-front cost (the $130,000 that increased to $400,000) is as the default premium.

In effect, credit swaps allow investors to hold different premium components.

Credit swaps allow different funds to hold different premiums of a bond. In our example, the pension fund decided to earn primarily the time premium component of HCA's bonds, divesting itself of the credit risk and other components. The hedge fund took over the credit premium. It decided to speculate that HCA would not go bankrupt, and it could do so without having to take a large cash position in HCA's bonds. Of course, hedge funds and other investors could also have speculated with CDS's that HCA would go bankrupt.

The CDS market size was huge.

➤ Over-the-counter, Sect. 7.2, Pg.169.

Credit swaps are typically traded in lots of $5 million and last for 5 years (but 3 to 10 years is not unusual, either). This market is **over-the-counter** (**OTC**)—that is, negotiated one-to-one between two parties. This market was also very big: In 1997, there were "only" about $180 billion of credit swaps outstanding, but as of 2006, there were more than $17 trillion! But this is ancient history.

The financial crisis and the CDS collapse. The shifting of risk everywhere.

We do know that the CDS market temporarily collapsed with the financial crisis of 2008, when the insurer AIG (whose financial arm had sold too many CDSs, booking them as profit) was bailed out by the government. (The Treasury feared that too many bond buyers were relying on AIG's insurance, and would themselves have to default if this insurance became worthless.) Unfortunately, after it has come back, the CDS market is still "dark": no one really knows how big or small it is, who is trading, who has exposures, and so on—and this includes the Federal Reserve and the Treasury. In 2007, I also wrote in the first edition of this book that no one knows who is really holding most of the credit risk in the economy nowadays. I gave as an example the German bank IKB which collapsed to everyone's surprise, because it had owned too many financial securities that were tied to U.S. mortgages. I was prescient (or just lucky). During the 2008 crisis, investors did not want to trust even good corporations and banks, simply because they did not know what their actual exposures were. However, CDSs are not intrinsically evil. Like most other financial instruments, they can be used to reduce risk or to increase risk. The problem, even today, is that no one really knows what is going on in this OTC market, and if large institutions speculate too much with them (and pay bonuses based on estimated profitability) and then fail, the government may have no choice but to bail out such institutions *again*.

6.3 Uncertainty in Capital Budgeting

Let's now return to the basic tasks of capital budgeting: selecting projects under uncertainty. Your task is to compute present values with imperfect knowledge about future outcomes. The principal tool in this task will be the **payoff table** (or **state table**), which assigns probabilities to the project value in each possible future value-relevant scenario. For example, the value of a factory producing hard disks may depend on computer sales (say, low, medium, or high), whether hard disks have become obsolete (yes or no), whether the economy is in a recession or expansion, and what the oil price (a major transportation cost factor) turns out to be. It is the manager's task to create the appropriate "state" table, which specifies what variables and scenarios are most value-relevant and how the business will perform in each of them. Clearly, it is not an easy task even to understand what the key factors are, much less to determine the probabilities under which these factors will take on one or another value. Assessing how your own project will respond to them is an even harder task—but it is an inevitable one. If you want to understand the value of your project, you must understand what your project's key value drivers are and how your project will respond to these value drivers. Fortunately, for many projects, it is usually not necessary to describe all possible outcomes in the most minute detail—just a dozen or so scenarios are often enough to cover the most important possibilities.

Next you learn about payoff diagrams, to characterize the main future contingencies.

Present Value with Outcome-Contingent Payoff Tables

We begin with the hypothetical purchase of a building for which the future value is uncertain. Next year, this investment will either be worth $60 thousand (with $1/4$ probability) or $100 thousand (with $3/4$ probability). These values can themselves be the results of future probabilistic outcomes, which is why we are not losing anything by assuming that the firm only lasts until next year. To help us remember states, let's just call the bad outcome "Rain" and the good outcome "Sun."

Our example of this section: A building can end up with one of two possible future values.

The Building's Expected Value

If you own the full building, your payoff table, omitting thousands henceforth, is as follows:

A payoff table.

Event	Probability	Value
Rain	$1/4$	$60
Sun	$3/4$	$100
$\Longrightarrow$ Expected Future Value		$90

The expected future building value of $90 (thousand) was computed as

To obtain the expected future cash value of the building, multiply each possible outcome by its probability.

$$\mathcal{E}(\text{Value at Time 1}) = 1/4 \cdot \$60 + 3/4 \cdot \$100 = \$90$$
$$= \mathscr{P}rob \cdot \text{Value Rain} + \mathscr{P}rob \cdot \text{Value Sun}$$

Then discount back
the expected cash
value using the
appropriate cost of
capital.

Now, assume that the appropriate expected rate of return for a project of type "building" with this type of riskiness and with 1-year maturity is 20%. (This 20% discount rate is provided by demand and supply in the financial markets, and it is assumed to be known by you, the manager.) Your goal is to determine the present value—the appropriate price—for the building *today*.

Under uncertainty,
you can use the net
present value formula
with expected (rather
than actual, known)
cash flows and with
appropriate expected
(rather than actual,
known) rates of return.

There are two methods to arrive at the present value of the building—and they are almost identical to what you have done earlier. You only need to replace the known value with the expected value, and the known future rate of return with an expected rate of return. The first PV method is to compute the expected value of the building next period and to discount it at the cost of capital, here 20%:

$$PV = \frac{\$90}{1 + 20\%} \approx \$75$$

$$= \frac{\mathcal{E}(\text{Value at Time 1})}{1 + \mathcal{E}(r)}$$

Taking expectations
and discounting can
be done in any order.

The second method is to compute the discounted state-contingent value of the building, and then take expected values. To do this, augment the earlier table:

Event	Probability	Value	Discount Factor	⇒	PV
Rain	$1/4$	$60	$1/(1+20\%)$	⇒	$12.5
Sun	$3/4$	$100	$1/(1+20\%)$	⇒	$62.5

If it rains, the present value is $12.5. *If* the sun shines, the present value is $62.5. Thus, the expected value of the building can also be computed as

$$\mathcal{E}(\text{Value at Time 1}) = 1/4 \cdot \$12.5 + 3/4 \cdot \$62.5 = \$75$$

$$= \mathcal{P}rob \cdot \text{Value if Rain} + \mathcal{P}rob \cdot \text{Value if Sun}$$

Both methods lead to the same result: You can either first compute the expected value of the investment next year ($1/4 \cdot \$60 + 3/4 \cdot \$100 = \$90$) and then discount this expected value of $90 to $75; or you can first discount all possible future outcomes ($60 to $12.5, and $100 to $62.5) and then compute the expected value of the discounted values ($1/4 \cdot \$12.5 + 3/4 \cdot \$62.5 = \$75$.)

IMPORTANT

> Under uncertainty, in the NPV formula,
>
> - known future cash flows are replaced by expected discounted cash flows, and
>
> - known appropriate rates of return are replaced by appropriate expected rates of return.
>
> You can first do the discounting and then take expectations, or vice versa. The order does not matter.

The State-Contingent Rates of Return

What would the rates of return be in the two states, and what would your overall expected rate of return be? If you have bought the building for $75 and it will be sunny, your actual rate of return will be

$$\text{If Sun:} \quad r \approx \frac{\$100 - \$75}{\$75} \approx +33\%$$

If it's rainy, your rate of return will be

$$\text{If Rain:} \quad r \approx \frac{\$60 - \$75}{\$75} \approx -20\%$$

The state-contingent *rates* of return can also be probability-weighted to arrive at the average (expected) *rate* of return.

Therefore, your expected rate of return is

$$\mathcal{E}(r) \quad \approx \quad \tfrac{1}{4} \cdot \quad (-20\%) \quad + \quad \tfrac{3}{4} \cdot \quad (+33\%) \quad \approx 20\%$$

$$\mathcal{P}\!rob \; \cdot \; \text{Rain Rate of Return} \qquad \mathcal{P}\!rob \; \cdot \; \text{Sun Rate of Return}$$

The probability state-weighted rates of return add up to the expected overall rate of return. This is as it should be: After all, you derived the proper price of the building today using a 20% expected rate of return.

Q 6.12. What changes have to be made to the NPV formula to handle an uncertain future?

Q 6.13. A factory can be worth $500,000 or $1,000,000 in two years, depending on product demand, each with equal probability. The appropriate cost of capital is 6% per year. What is the present value of the factory?

Q 6.14. A new product may be a dud (20% probability), an average seller (70% probability), or dynamite (10% probability). If it is a dud, the payoff will be $20,000; if it is an average seller, the payoff will be $40,000; and if it is dynamite, the payoff will be $80,000.

1. What is the expected payoff of the project?

2. The appropriate expected rate of return for such payoffs is 8%. What is the PV of the payoff?

3. If the project is purchased for the appropriate present value, what will be the rates of return in each of the three outcomes?

4. Confirm the expected rate of return when computed from the individual outcome-specific rates of return.

6.4 Splitting Uncertain Project Payoffs into Debt and Equity

Most projects are financed with a mix of debt and equity.

The most important reason for you to learn about state payoff tables is that they will help you understand cash flow rights. This leads to one of the most important concepts in finance: the difference between a **loan** (also called **debt** or **leverage**) and **levered ownership** (also called **levered equity** or simply **equity** or **stock**). Almost all companies and projects are financed with both debt and levered equity. You already know in principle what debt is. Levered equity is simply what accrues to the business owner *after* the debt is paid off. We leave it to later chapters to make a distinction between financial debt and other obligations—for example, tax obligations—and to cover the control rights that flow from securities—for example, how debt can force borrowers to pay up and how equity can replace poorly performing managers.

Other projects are financed the same way.

You probably already have an intuitive understanding about the distinction between debt and equity. If you own a house with a mortgage, you really own the house only after you have made all debt payments. If you have student loans, you *yourself* are the levered owner of your future income stream. That is, you get to consume "your" residual income only *after* your liabilities (including your nonfinancial debt) are paid back. But what will the levered owner and the lender get if the company's projects fail, if the house collapses, or if your career takes a turn toward the prison on Rikers Island? What is the appropriate compensation for the lender and the levered owner? The split of net present value streams into loans (debt) and levered equity lies at the heart of finance.

Outcome (or "State")-contingent claims have payoffs that depend on future states of nature.

You now know how to compute the present value of state-contingent payoffs—your building paid off differently in the two states of nature. Thus, your building was a state-contingent claim—its payoff depended on the outcome. But it is just one of many possible state-contingent claims. Another might promise to pay $1 if the sun shines and $25 if rain falls. Using payoff tables, you can work out the value of *any* state-contingent claim and, in particular, the value of our two most important state-contingent claims, debt and equity.

The Loan

Assume that the building is funded by (a) a mortgagor and (b) a residual (the levered building owner).

Let's assume you want to finance the building purchase of $75 with a mortgage of $70. In effect, the single project "building" is being turned into two different projects, each of which can be owned by a different party. The first project is "Mortgage Lending." The second project is "Residual Building Ownership," that is, ownership of the building but bundled with the obligation to repay the mortgage. The "Residual Building Ownership" investor will not receive a dime until *after* the debt has been satisfied. As already explained, such residual ownership is called levered equity, equity (or even stock) in the building, in order to avoid calling it "what's-left-over-after-the-loans-have-been-paid-off."

The first goal is to determine the appropriate promised interest rate on a "$70 value today" mortgage loan on the building.

What sort of interest rate would the creditor demand? To answer this question, you need to know what will happen if the building were to be condemned, because the mortgage value ($70 today) will be larger than the value of the building if rain falls ($60 next year). We are assuming that the owner could walk away from it, and the creditor could repossess the building but not any of the borrower's other assets. Such a mortgage loan is called a **no-recourse loan**. There is no recourse other than taking possession of the asset itself. This arrangement is called **limited liability**. The building owner cannot lose more than the money that he originally puts in. Limited liability is the mainstay of many financial securities: For example, if you purchase stock in a company in the stock market, you cannot be held liable for more than your investment, regardless of how badly the company performs.

To compute the present value for the project "Mortgage Lending," return to the problem of setting an appropriate interest rate, given credit risk (from Section 6.2). Start with the following payoff table:

Start with the payoff table, and write down payoffs to project "Mortgage Lending."

➤ *Credit Risk, Sect. 6.2, Pg.121.*

Event	$\mathcal{P}rob$	Value	Discount Factor
Rain	$1/4$	$60	1/1.20
Sun	$3/4$	Promised	1/1.20

A N E C D O T E   Limited Liability

Limited liability was invented after the Renaissance, but it only became common in the nineteenth and twentieth centuries. Ultimately, it is this legal construction that allowed corporations to evolve into entities distinct from their owners. Thus, in 1911, the President of Columbia University wrote: "The limited liability corporation is the greatest single discovery of modern times.... Even steam and electricity are less important."

William Goetzmann, Yale University

The creditor receives the property worth $60 if it rains, or the full promised amount (to be determined) if the sun shines. To break even, the creditor must solve for the payoff to be received if the sun shines in exchange for lending $70 today. This is the "quoted" or "promised" payoff:

The quoted (or promised) payoff.

$$\$70 \quad = \quad 1/4 \quad \cdot \quad \left(\frac{\$60}{1 + 20\%} \right) + \quad 3/4 \quad \cdot \quad \left(\frac{\text{Promise}}{1 + 20\%} \right)$$

$$\text{Loan Value}_0 \qquad \mathcal{P}rob \cdot \text{Rain Loan PV} \qquad \mathcal{P}rob \cdot \text{Sun Loan PV}$$

You can solve this equation for the necessary promise, which is

$$\text{Promise} \quad = \quad \frac{(1 + 20\%) \cdot \$70 - 1/4 \cdot \$60}{3/4} \qquad = \$92$$

$$= \quad \frac{[1 + \mathcal{E}(r)] \cdot \text{Loan Value}_0 - \mathcal{P}rob(\text{Rain}) \cdot \text{Rain Value}}{\mathcal{P}rob(\text{Sun})}$$

in repayment, paid by the borrower only if the sun shines.

Nerdnote: Special liability and tax rules apply to private residences. Mortgages can have limited liability ("non recourse") or unlimited liability ("full recourse"). The latter can also have further nasty tax consequences, where a capital loss in the home can create a large ordinary income tax obligation, adding insult to injury. (If interested, google for "cancellation-of-debt income.") Moreover, as a home owner, you can deduct interest only on the first $1 million in mortgage; and capital losses on the home do not create a tax credit, but large capital gains can create a tax obligation.

The state-contingent
rates of return in the
rainy ("default") state
and in the sunny
("solvent") state can
be
probability-weighted
to arrive at the
expected rate of
return.

With this promised payoff of $92 (if the sun shines), the lender's rate of return will be the **promised rate of return**:

$$\text{If Sun:} \quad r = \frac{\$92 - \$70}{\$70} \approx +31.4\%$$

The lender would not provide the mortgage at any lower promised interest rate. If it rains, the owner walks away, and the lender's rate of return will be

$$\text{If Rain:} \quad r = \frac{\$60 - \$70}{\$70} \approx -14.3\%$$

Therefore, the lender's *expected* rate of return is

$$\mathcal{E}(r) \;=\; 1/4 \;\cdot\; (-14.3\%) \;+\; 3/4 \;\cdot\; (+31.4\%) \;\approx\; 20\%$$

$$\mathcal{P}rob \;\cdot\; \text{Rain Rate of Return} \qquad \mathcal{P}rob \;\cdot\; \text{Sun Rate of Return}$$

The stated rate of return is 31.4% (and it is not an exorbitant rate!), but the expected rate of return is 20%. After all, in our risk-neutral perfect market, anyone investing for one year expects to earn an expected rate of return of 20%.

The Levered Equity

Now compute the
payoffs of the
post-mortgage (i.e.,
levered) ownership of
the building. The
method is exactly the
same.

As the residual building owner, what rate of return would you expect as proper compensation? You already know the building is worth $75 today. Thus, after the loan of $70, you need to pay in $5—presumably from your personal savings. Of course, you must compensate your lender: To contribute the $70 to the building purchase today, you must promise to pay the lender $92 next year. If it rains, the lender will confiscate your house, and all your invested personal savings will be lost. However, if the sun shines, the building will be worth $100 minus the promised $92, or $8. Your payoff table as the levered equity building owner is as follows:

Event	$\mathcal{P}rob$	Value	Discount Factor
Rain	1/4	$0	1/1.20
Sun	3/4	$8	1/1.20

This allows you to determine that the *expected* future levered building ownership payoff is $1/4 \cdot \$0 + 3/4 \cdot \$8 = \$6$. Therefore, the present value of levered building ownership is

$$\text{PV} \;=\; 1/4 \;\cdot\; \left(\frac{\$0}{1 + 20\%} \right) + 3/4 \;\cdot\; \left(\frac{\$8}{1 + 20\%} \right) \approx \$5$$

$$\mathcal{P}rob \;\cdot\; \text{Rain PV} \qquad \mathcal{P}rob \;\cdot\; \text{Sun PV}$$

Again, knowing the
state-contingent cash
flows permits
computation of
state-contingent rates
of return and the
expected rate of
return.

You rates of return are

$$\text{If Sun:} \quad r \;\approx\; \frac{\$8 - \$5}{\$5} \;=\; +60\%$$

$$\text{If Rain:} \quad r \;\approx\; \frac{\$0 - \$5}{\$5} \;=\; -100.00\%$$

The expected rate of return of levered equity ownership, that is, the building with the bundled mortgage obligation, is

$$\mathcal{E}(r) \quad = \quad \tfrac{1}{4} \quad \cdot \quad (-100.00\%) \quad + \quad \tfrac{3}{4} \quad \cdot \quad (+60\%) \quad = 20\%$$

$$\underbrace{\mathcal{P}rob}_{} \cdot \text{Rain Rate of Return} \qquad \underbrace{\mathcal{P}rob}_{} \cdot \text{Sun Rate of Return}$$

Reflections On The Example: Payoff Tables

Payoff tables are fundamental tools to help you think about projects and financial claims. Admittedly, they can sometimes be tedious, especially if there are many different possible states. (There may even be infinitely many states, as in a bell-shaped, normally-distributed project outcome—but you can usually approximate even the most continuous and complex outcomes fairly well with no more than 10 discrete possible outcomes.)

Payoff tables are great conceptual tools.

Exhibit 6.5 shows how elegant such a table can be. It describes everything you need in a very concise manner: the state-contingent payoffs, expected payoffs, net present value, and expected rates of return for your house scenario. Because owning the mortgage and the levered equity is the same as owning the full building, the last two columns must add up to the values in the "Building Value" column. You could decide to be any kind of investor: a creditor (bank) who is loaning money in exchange for promised payment; a levered building owner who is taking a "piece left over after a loan"; or an unlevered building owner who is investing money into an unlevered project (i.e., taking the whole piece). All three investments are just state-contingent claims.

There are three possible investment opportunities here. The bank is just another investor, with particular payoff patterns.

Event	$\mathcal{P}rob$	Building	$92-Promise Mortgage	Levered Equity
Rain	$\tfrac{1}{4}$	$60	$60	$0
Sun	$\tfrac{3}{4}$	$100	$92	$8
Expected Value at Time 1		$90	$84	$6
Present Value at Time 0		$75	$70	$5
From Time 0 to Time 1, $\mathcal{E}(r)$		20%	20%	20%

Exhibit 6.5: *Payoff Table and Overall Values and Returns.*   In this example, the project is financed with $70 in mortgage promising $92 in payment.

Whenever possible, in the presence of uncertainty, write down a payoff table to describe the probabilities of each possible event ("state") with its state-contingent payoff.

IMPORTANT

Q 6.15. In the example, the building was worth $75, the mortgage was worth $70, and the equity was worth $5. The mortgage thus financed about 93.3% of the cost of the building, and the equity financed 7.7%. Is the arrangement identical to one in which two partners purchase the building together—one puts in $70 and owns 93.3% of the building, and the other puts in $5 and owns 7.7%?

Q 6.16. Buildings are frequently financed with mortgages that cover 80% of the purchase price, not 93.3% ($70 of $75). Produce a table similar to Exhibit 6.5 for this case.

Reflections on The Example: Debt and Equity Risk

Evaluate the risk of the three types of projects, even if riskier projects do not earn higher expected rates of return.

We have only briefly mentioned risk. It was just not necessary to illustrate the main insights. In a risk-neutral world, all that matters is the expected rate of return, not the uncertainty about what you will receive. Of course, you can assess the risk even in our risk-neutral world where risk earns no extra compensation (a risk premium). So, which investment is riskiest: full ownership, loan ownership, or levered ownership?

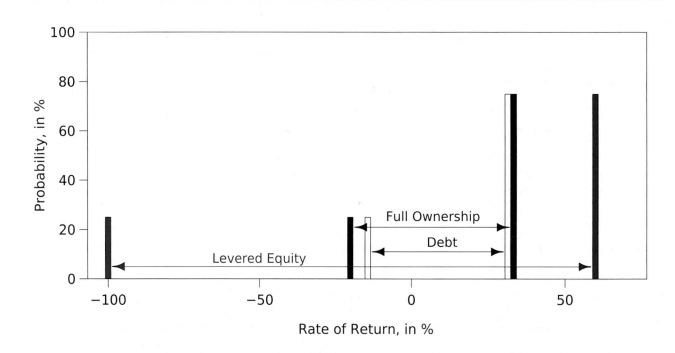

Exhibit 6.6: *Three Probability Histograms for Project Rates of Return.* The solid blue bars are the payoffs to equity, the riskiest investment. The solid black bars are the payoffs to full ownership. The white bars are the payoffs to debt, the least risky investment. You can judge risk by how spread out the two bars are.

Exhibit 6.6 plots the histograms of the rates of return for each of the three types of investments. The equity loses everything (–100%) with a $1/4$ probability but earns 60% with $3/4$ probability. The debt loses about 14.3% with $1/4$ and gains 31.4% with $3/4$ probabilities. The full ownership loses about –20% with $1/4$ and gains 33.3% with $3/4$ probabilities. As the visuals show, the loan is least risky, followed by the full ownership, followed by the levered ownership. There is an interesting intuition here. By taking the mortgage, the medium-risk project "building" has been split into one more risky project "levered building" and one less risky project "mortgage." The combined "full building ownership" project therefore has an average risk.

Leveraging (mortgaging) a project splits it into a safer loan and a riskier levered ownership.

Of course, regardless of leverage, all investment projects in our risk-neutral world expect to earn a 20% rate of return. After all, 20% is the universal time premium here for investing money. (The default premium is a component only of promised interest rates, not of expected interest rates; see Section 6.2.) By assuming that investors are risk neutral, we have assumed that the risk premium is zero. Investors are willing to take any investment that offers an expected rate of return of 20%, regardless of risk. (If investors were risk averse, debt would offer a lower expected rate of return than the project, which would offer a lower expected rate of return than equity.)

If everyone is risk neutral, everyone should expect to earn 20%.

Although our example was a little sterile because we assumed away risk preferences, it is nevertheless very useful. Almost all projects in the real world are financed with loans extended by one party and levered ownership held by another party. Understanding debt and equity is as important to corporations as it is to building owners. After all, stocks in corporations are basically levered ownership claims that provide money only *after* the corporation has paid back its liabilities. The building example has given you the skills to compute state-contingent, promised, and expected payoffs, as well as state-contingent, promised, and expected rates of return. These are the necessary tools to work with debt, equity, or any other state-contingent claim. And really, all that will happen later when we introduce risk aversion is that you will add a few extra basis points of required compensation—more to equity (the riskiest claim), fewer to the project (the medium-risk claim), and still fewer to debt (the safest claim).

Unrealistic, maybe! But ultimately, this is the basis for more realistic examples, and illustrative of the most important concepts.

Q 6.17. Compare a "junk" mortgage (with its requisite junk equity, receiving payments only if the junk mortgage is paid off) that promises to pay off $70 with a "solid" mortgage (with its requisite solid equity) that promises to pay off $60.

1. Does the junk mortgage seem riskier than the solid mortgage?
2. Does the junk equity seem riskier than the solid equity?
3. Does the building seem riskier if financed with a junk mortgage rather than with a solid mortgage?

What "Leverage" Really Means—Financial and Operational Leverage

Leverage "amplifies" the equity stake.

I already mentioned that debt is often called leverage and equity is called "levered equity." Let me now explain why. A lever is a mechanical device that can amplify effects. In finance, a lever is something that allows a smaller equity investment to still control the firm and be more exposed to the underlying firm's gain or loss than unlevered ownership. That is, with leverage, a small change in the underlying project value translates into a larger change in value for levered equity, both up and down. You have seen this in our house example above, and specifically in Exhibit 6.6. Ordinary ownership would have cost you $75. But with leverage, you could take control of the house with cash of only $5. In addition, it also meant that if the sun shone, you would earn 60%, not just 31.4%; but if it rains, you would lose *everything* rather than just –14.3%. Leverage amplified your stake.

Example Assumptions:

- The machine costs $400 and can be resold for $150. The net operating cost is thus $250.
- In a hypothetical lease, the lessee would pay the lessor $250 for use of the machine, and the lessor would own the machine ($150) at the end.
- Labor costs are $75.
- Product produces $200 ("Bad") or $1,000 ("Good").
- Assume prevailing interest rate is 0.

Leverage	Investment	Out of Pocket	Dollars Bad	Dollars Good	Percent Bad	Percent Good	FLR
None	Pay for everything.	$475	$350	$1,150	–26%	+142%	0%
Financial	Borrow $350.	$125	$0	$800	–100%	+540%	74%
Real	Lease machine, Pay $250.	$325	$200	$1,000	–38%	+208%	0%
Real+Financial	Lease machine & Borrow $200.	$125	$0	$800	–100%	+540%	62%
Different Technology—Labor costs $40, different machine costs $400, has residual value of $115.							
Technology	Pay for everything.	$440	$315	$1,115	–28%	+153%	0%

Exhibit 6.7: *Financial and Real Leverage.* FLR is financial leverage, which is defined as the fraction of financial debt divided by the sum of debt and equity.

The leverage concept can encompass more than just financial debt.

➤ *Calculating leverage, Sect. 22.A (Companion), Pg. ≈149.*

Financial debt is a lever, but it is not the only one. Leverage can also be calculated using all corporate liabilities (which may include, e.g., accounts payable and pension obligations). More importantly, because leverage is a general concept rather than an accounting term, you should think of it in even broader terms. The idea of leverage is always that a smaller equity investment can control the firm and is more sensitive to firm value changes. Exhibit 6.7 illustrates some different types of levers. In this table, you can pay $475 for machine and labor, and receive either $200 or $1,000 in product revenues, plus $150 as resale value for the machine. In the bad state, you lose 26%; in the good state, you earn 142%. The next line shows that financial leverage can magnify these rates of return into –100% or +540%. But instead of taking on financial debt, you could also lease the machine, which costs you $250 in leasing fees (with no residual ownership of the machine at the end), and pay for labor of $75. In this case, you have effectively levered up, increasing your risk to –38% and +208% but without taking on any financial leverage. It is the lease that has now become your leverage! And you can also combine real and financial leverage. Finally, there can even be differences in the degree to which the production technologies themselves are levered. The final example shows a different method of production, which is intrinsically more levered.

Working with More Than Two Possible Outcomes

Can you use the same method if you have more than two scenarios? For example, assume that the building could be worth $60, $70, $80, $90, or $100 with equal probability and that the appropriate expected interest rate is 20%. It follows that the building has a PV of $60/1.20 = $50. If a loan promised $60, how much would you expect to receive? The full $60, of course.

$$\mathcal{E}(\text{ Payoff}(\$0 \leq \text{ Loan Promise} = x \leq \$60)) = 100\% \cdot x$$

But if a loan promised $61, how much would you expect to receive? You would expect $60 for sure, plus the extra "marginal" $1 with 80% probability (because there is an 80% chance that $61 is covered; only if the outcome is $60, which happens 20% of the time, would you not receive the full $61). Thus, for the $61 loan promise, you would expect to receive $60.80. In fact, you would expect only 80 cents for each dollar promised between $60 and $70. So, if a loan promised x between $60 and $70, you would expect to receive

$$\mathcal{E}(\text{ Payoff}(\$60 \leq \text{ Loan Promise} = x \leq \$70)) = \$60 + 80\% \cdot (x - \$60)$$

If a loan promised $71, how much would you expect to receive? You would expect $60 for sure, plus $8 for the next promised $10, plus 60 cents on the dollar for anything above $70, i.e., $68.60,

$$\mathcal{E}(\text{ Payoff}(\$70 \leq \text{ Loan Promise} = x \leq \$80)) = \$60 + \$8 + 60\% \cdot (x - \$70)$$

Exhibit 6.8 plots these expected payoffs as a function of the promised payoffs. With this figure, mortgage valuation becomes easy. For example, how much would the loan have to promise to provide $50 today? The expected payoff would have to be $(1 + 20\%) \cdot \$50 = \$60$. This is on the linear segment, so you would have to promise $60. Of course, you cannot offer an expected payoff of more than $80, so forget about borrowing more than $80/1.2 ≈ $66.67 today.

Multiple outcomes will cause multiple breakpoints in the relation from promised to expected payoffs.

You can now read off the appropriate promised value from the graph for any mortgage.

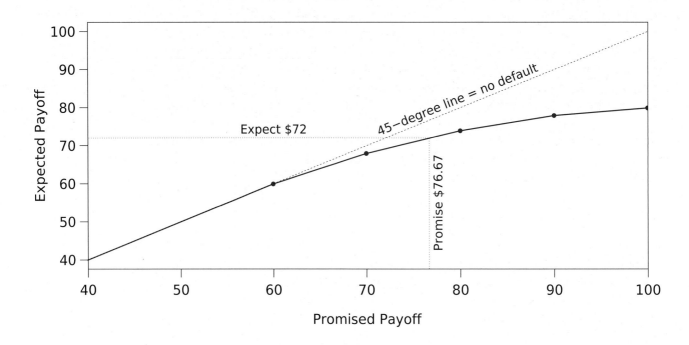

Exhibit 6.8: *Promised versus Expected Payoff for a Loan on the Project with Five Possible Payoffs.* The dotted line is one-to-one, where a promised dollar is an expected dollar (i.e., risk-free). The blue line shows the payoffs to the bond. The firm will be worth $60, $70, $80, $90, or $100, each with equal probability. To borrow $60 today, the bond must offer an expected payoff of $60 · 1.2 = $72 next year. Following the arrow from the y-axis at $72 to the payoff function and then down to the x-axis shows that this high an expected payoff requires a promised payoff of $76.67.

Q 6.18. What is the formula for a promised loan payoff between $80 and $90?

Q 6.19. What is the expected payoff if the promised payoff is $72?

Q 6.20. If you want to borrow $65, what do you have to promise?

Q 6.21. If there were infinitely many possible outcomes (e.g., if the building value followed a statistical normal distribution), what would the graph of expected payoffs of the loan as a function of promised payoffs look like?

Q 6.22. A new product may be a dud (20% probability), an average seller (70% probability), or dynamite (10% probability). If it is a dud, the payoff will be $20,000; if it is an average seller, the payoff will be $40,000; if it is dynamite, the payoff will be $80,000. The appropriate expected rate of return is 6% per year. If a loan promises to pay off $40,000, what are the promised and expected rates of return?

How Bad Are Mistakes?

Discounting Promised Cash Flows with the Promised Cost of Capital

A common mistake is the attempt to avoid the need to estimate expected values by discounting promised cash flows with promised discount rates in the economy. After all, both numbers reflect default risk. The two default issues might cancel out one another, and you might end up with the correct inference. *Or they might not cancel out, in which case you will end up with bad inference!*

To illustrate this, say the appropriate expected rate of return is 20%. A newly available bond investment promises $25 for a $100 investment with fully-insured principal but a 50% probability of default on the interest payment. Say, your other risky bonds in the economy offer 11.4% (for a total interest rate of 31.4%). If you discounted the promised interest payment of $25 with the quoted interest rate on your benchmark bonds, you would get

$$\text{Bad NPV Calculation} = -\$100 + \frac{\$100}{1 + 20\%} + \frac{\$25}{1 + 31.4\%} \approx +\$2.36$$

Wrong! Instead, you must work with expected values:

$$\text{Correct NPV Calculation} = -\$100 + \frac{\$100}{1 + 20\%} + \frac{\$12.50}{1 + 20\%} = -\$6.25$$

This bond would be a bad investment.

Summary

This chapter covered the following major points:

- Uncertainty means that a project may not return its promised amount.

- A random variable is one whose outcome has not yet been determined. It is characterized by its distribution of possible future outcomes.

- The "expected value" is the probability-weighted sum of all possible outcomes. It is the "average" or "mean," but it is applied to the future instead of to a historical data series. It is a measure of "reward."

- Risk neutrality means indifference between a safe bet and a risky bet if their expected rates of return are the same.

- The possibility of future default causes promised (quoted) interest rates to be higher than expected interest rates. Default risk is also often called credit risk.

- Most of the difference between promised and expected interest rates is due to default. Extra compensation for bearing more risk—the risk premium—and other premiums are typically smaller than the default premium for bonds.

- Credit ratings can help judge the probability of potential losses in default. Moody's and S&P are the two most prominent vendors of ratings for corporate bonds.

- The key tool for thinking about uncertainty is the payoff table. Each row represents one possible outcome, which contains the probability that the state will come about, the total project value that can be distributed, and the allocation of this total project value to different state-contingent claims. The state-contingent claims "carve up" the possible project payoffs.

- Most real-world projects are financed with the two most common state-contingent claims—debt and equity. Their payoff rights are best thought of in terms of payoff tables.

- Debt and equity are methods to parcel out total firm risk into one component that is safer than the overall firm (debt) and one that is riskier than the overall firm (equity).

- The presence of debt "levers up" equity investments. That is, a smaller up-front cash investment becomes more exposed to swings in the value of the underlying firm. However, there are also other leverage mechanisms that firms can choose (e.g., leasing or technology).

- If debt promises to pay more than the project can deliver in the worst state of nature, then the debt is risky and requires a promised interest rate in excess of its expected interest rate.

- NPV is robust to modest errors in the expected interest rate (the discount rate) for near-term cash flows. However, NPV is not necessarily robust with respect to modest errors in either expected cash flows or discount rates for distant cash flows.

- NPV is about discounting *expected* cash flows with *expected* rates of return. You cannot discount *promised* cash flows with *promised* rates of return.

Keywords

Average, 116. CDS, 129. Credit default swap, 129. Credit premium, 123. Credit risk, 123. Credit swap, 129. Debt, 134. Default premium, 122. Default risk, 123. Default, 121. Equity, 462. Expected value, 116. Fair bet, 117. Histogram, 116. Investment grade, 126. Junk grade, 126. Leverage, 462. Levered equity, 134. Levered ownership, 134. Limited liability, 172. Loan, 134. Mean, 116. Moody's, 125. No-recourse loan, 134. OTC, 169. Over-the-counter, 169. Payoff table, 131. Probability distribution, 116. Promised interest rate, 122. Promised rate of return, 136. Quoted interest rate, 122. Random variable, 116. Realization, 116. Reward, 179. Risk neutral, 120. Risk, 119. S&P, 125. Solvent, 121. Speculative grade, 126. Standard deviation, 179. Standard&Poor's, 125. State table, 131. Stated interest rate, 122. Stock, 462. Time premium, 122. Variance, 179.

Answers

Q 6.1 No! The expected outcome (value) is assumed to be known—at least for an untampered die throw. The following is almost philosophy and beyond what you are supposed to know or answer here: It might, however, be that the expected value of an investment is not really known. In this case, it, too, could be a random variable in one sense—although you are assumed to be able to form an expectation (opinion) over anything, so in this sense, it would not be a random variable, either.

Q 6.2 If you do not know the exact bet, you may not know the expected value, which means that even the expected value is unknown. This may be the case for stocks, where you are often forced to guess what the expected rate of return will be (unlike for a die, for which you know the underlying physical process, which assures an expected value of 3.5). However, almost all finance theories assume that you know the expected value. Fortunately, even if you do not know the expected value, finance theories hope you still often have a pretty good idea.

Q 6.3 If the random variable is the number of dots on the die times two, then the expected outcome is $1/6 \cdot (2) + 1/6 \cdot (4) + 1/6 \cdot (6) + 1/6 \cdot (8) + 1/6 \cdot (10) + 1/6 \cdot (12) = 7$. The realization was 12.

Q 6.4 The expected value of the stock investment is $5\% \cdot (\$41) + 10\% \cdot (\$42) + 20\% \cdot (\$45) + 30\% \cdot (\$48) + 20\% \cdot (\$58) + 10\% \cdot (\$70) + 5\% \cdot (\$75) = \$52$. Therefore, purchasing the stock at $50 is not a fair bet, but it is a good bet.

Q 6.5 The variance of the P_{+1} stock investment is $Var(P_{+1}) = 5\% \cdot (\$41-\$52)^2 + 10\% \cdot (\$42-\$52)^2 + 20\% \cdot (\$45-\$52)^2 + 30\% \cdot (\$48-\$52)^2 + 20\% \cdot (\$58-\$52)^2 + 10\% \cdot (\$70-\$52)^2 + 5\% \cdot (\$75-\$52)^2 = 5\% \cdot \$\$121 + 10\% \cdot \$\$100 + 20\% \cdot \$\$49 + 30\% \cdot \$\$16 + 20\% \cdot \$\$36 + 10\% \cdot \$\$324 + 5\% \cdot \$\$529 = \$\$96.70$. Therefore, the standard deviation (risk) is $Sdv(P_{+1}) = \sqrt{\$\$96.70} \approx \$9.83$.

Q 6.6 Investors are more risk averse for large bets relative to their wealth.

Q 6.7 Individual investors are more risk averse than investors in the aggregate.

Q 6.8 Expected and promised rates are the same only for government bonds. Most other bonds have some kind of default risk.

Q 6.9 With the revised probabilities:

1. The expected payoff is now $95\% \cdot \$210 + 1\% \cdot \$100 + 4\% \cdot \$0 = \$200.50$. Therefore, the expected rate of return is $\$200.50/\$200 = 0.25\%$.

2. You require an expected payoff of $210 to expect to end up with 5%. Therefore, you must solve for a promised payment $95\% \cdot P + 1\% \cdot \$100 + 4\% \cdot \$0 = \$210 \Rightarrow P = \$209/0.95 = \$220$. On a loan of $200, this is a 10% promised interest rate.

Q 6.10 No, the expected default premium is zero by definition.

Q 6.11 Both. The historical evidence is that lower-grade borrowers both default more often and pay less upon default.

Q 6.12 The actual cash flow is replaced by the expected cash flow, and the actual rate of return is replaced by the expected rate of return.

Q 6.13 The factory's expected value is $\mathcal{E}(\text{Value at Time 2}) = [0.5 \cdot \$500,000 + 0.5 \cdot \$1,000,000] = \$750,000$. Its present value is therefore $\$750,000/1.06^2 \approx \$667,497.33$.

Q 6.14 For the dynamite/dud project:

1. The expected payoff is $\mathcal{E}(P) = 20\% \cdot \$20,000 + 70\% \cdot \$40,000 + 10\% \cdot \$80,000 = \$40,000$.

2. The present value of the expected payoff is $\$40,000/1.08 \approx \$37,037$.

3. The three rate of return outcomes are $\$20,000/\$37,037 - 1 \approx -46\%$, $\$40,000/\$37,037 - 1 \approx +8\%$, $\$80,000/\$37,037 - 1 \approx +116\%$.

4. The expected rate of return is $20\% \cdot (-46\%) + 70\% \cdot (+8\%) + 20\% \cdot (+116\%) \approx 8\%$.

Q 6.15 No! Partners would share payoffs proportionally, not according to "debt comes first." For example, if it rains, the 7.7% partner would still receive $4, and not $0 that the levered equity owner would receive.

Q 6.16 To finance 80% of a $75 building, the mortgage has to provide $60 today. Start with the payoff table that contains what you know:

Event	$Prob$	Building	80% Mortgage	Levered
Rain	$1/4$	$60	$60	$0
Sun	$3/4$	$100	x	$100-x
$\mathcal{E}(V)$, Time 1		$90	y	$90-y
PV, Time 0		$75	$60	$15
$\mathcal{E}(r_{0,1})$		20%	20%	20%

In this interest environment, a mortgage that has a value of $60 today must have an expected value of $y = \$60 \cdot (1 + 20\%) = \$72$. $60 next year are worth $50 today. Thus, $1/4 \cdot \$50 + 3/4 \cdot x = \$60$, which tells you that the promise to pay must be $x = \$76$.

Q 6.17 The text worked out the rates of return in the case of the junk mortgage. The previous question worked out the rates of return in the case of the solid mortgage.

	Rain	Sun	Expected
Junk Mortgage ($70)	–14.3%	+31.4%	20%
Junk Equity ($70)	–100.0%	+60.0%	20%
Solid Mortgage ($60)	0%	+26.7%	20%
Solid Equity ($60)	–100%	+60.0%	20%

The junk mortgage is indeed riskier than the solid mortgage. The junk equity is no riskier than the solid equity (though in a more general example, it would be). The building is the same building, and thus its risk has not changed.

Q 6.18

$$\mathcal{E}(\text{Payoff}(\$80 \le \text{Loan Promise} = x \le \$90))$$
$$= \$60 + \$8 + \$6 + 40\% \cdot (x - \$80)$$

Q 6.19 The relevant line segment is $\mathcal{E} = \$68 + 60\% \cdot (P - \$70)$, so solve $\$72 = \$68 + 60\% \cdot (P - \$70)$. The answer is $P = \$76.67$.

Q 6.20 The \$65 today requires an expected payoff of $1.2 \cdot \$65 = \$78$. This is on the final line segment. The formula is

$$\mathcal{E}\big(\text{ Payoff}(\$90 \leq \text{Loan Promise} = x \leq \$100) \big)$$

$$= \$60 + \$8 + \$6 + \$4 + 20\% \cdot (x - \$90)$$

$$= \$78 + 20\% \cdot (x - \$90)$$

Thus, $x = \$90$.

Q 6.21 With infinitely many possible outcomes, the function of expected payoffs would be a smooth increasing function. For the mathematical nitpickers: [a] We really should not allow a normal distribution, because the value of the building cannot be negative; [b] The function would increase monotonically, but it would asymptote to an upper bound.

Q 6.22 With 20% probability, the loan will pay off \$20,000; with 80% probability, the loan will pay off the full promised \$40,000. Therefore, the loan's expected payoff is $20\% \cdot \$20,000 + 80\% \cdot \$40,000 = \$36,000$. The loan's price is $\$36,000/1.06 \approx \$33,962$. Therefore, the promised rate of return is $\$40,000/\$33,962 - 1 \approx 17.8\%$. The expected rate of return was given: 6%.

End of Chapter Problems

Q 6.23. Is this morning's CNN forecast of tomorrow's temperature a random variable? Is tomorrow's temperature a random variable?

Q 6.24. Does a higher reward (expected rate of return) always come with more risk?

Q 6.25. Would a single individual be effectively more, equally, or less risk averse than a pool of such investors?

Q 6.26. A bond will pay off \$100 with probability 99% and will pay off nothing with probability 1%. The equivalent risk-free rate of return is 5%. What is an appropriate promised yield on this bond?

Q 6.27. An L.A. Lakers bond promises an investment rate of return of 9%. Time-equivalent Treasuries offer 6%. Is this necessarily a good investment? Explain.

Q 6.28. A financial instrument will pay off as follows:

$\mathcal{P}rob$	50%	25%	12.5%	6.25%	3.125%	3.125%
Payoff	\$100	\$110	\$130	\$170	\$250	\$500

Assume that the risk-free interest rate is 0.

1. What price today would make this a fair bet?

2. What is the maximum price that a risk-averse investor would be willing to pay?

Q 6.29. Now assume that the financial instrument from Q 6.28 costs \$100.

1. What is its expected rate of return?

2. If the prevailing interest rate on time-equivalent Treasuries is 10%, and if financial default happens either completely (i.e., no repayment) or not at all (i.e., full promised payment), then what is the probability p that the security will pay off? In other words, assume that full repayment occurs with probability p and that zero repayment occurs with probability $1 - p$. What is the p that makes the expected rate of return equal to 10%?

Q 6.30. Go to the Vanguard website. Look at funds by asset class, and answer this question for bond funds with different durations.

1. What is the current yield-to-maturity of a taxable Vanguard bond fund invested in Treasuries?

2. What is the current yield-to-maturity of a taxable Vanguard bond fund invested in investment-grade bonds?

3. What is the current yield-to-maturity of a taxable Vanguard bond fund invested in high-yield bonds?

Q 6.31. A Disney bond promises an investment rate of return of 7%. Time-equivalent Treasuries offer 7%. Is the Disney bond necessarily a bad investment? Explain.

Q 6.32. Return to the example on Page 124, but assume that the probability of receiving full payment of $210 in one year is only 95%, the probability of receiving $100 is 4%, and the probability of receiving absolutely no payment is 1%. If the bond quotes a rate of return of 12%, what is the time premium, the default premium, and the risk premium?

Q 6.33. Using information from a current newspaper or the WWW, what is the annualized yield on corporate bonds (high-quality, medium-quality, high-yield) today?

Q 6.34. Can you remember the names of the main bond rating agencies and the meanings of their ranking categories? Roughly, what are the 10-year default rate differences between investment-grade and non-investment grade bonds this month?

Q 6.35. How is a credit swap like an insurance contract? Who is the insurer in a credit swap? Why would anyone want to buy such insurance?

Q 6.36. A bond promises to pay $12,000 and costs $10,000. The promised discount on equivalent bonds is 25% per annum. Is this bond a good deal?

Q 6.37. A project costs $19,000 and promises the following cash flows:

	Y1	Y2	Y3
Cash Flows	$12,500	$6,000	$3,000

The appropriate discount rate is 15% per annum. Should you invest in this project?

Q 6.38. Assume that the probability that the Patriots will win the Superbowl is 55%. A souvenir shop outside the stadium will earn net profits of $1.5 million if the Patriots win and $1.0 million if they lose. You are the loan officer of the bank to whom the shop applied for a loan. You can assume that your bank is risk neutral and that the bank can invest in safe projects that offer an expected rate of return of 10%.

1. What interest rate would you quote if the owner asked you for a loan for $900,000 today?

2. What interest rate would you quote if the owner asked you for a loan for $1,000,000 today?

(These questions require that you compute the amount that you would demand for repayment.)

Q 6.39. A new project has the following success probabilities:

	Failure	Success	Buyout
Prob	10%	85%	5%
Payoff (in millions)	$50	$200	$400

Assume risk neutrality. If a bond with $100 face value collateralized by this project promises an interest rate of 8%, then what is the prevailing cost of capital, and what do shareholders receive if the buyout materializes?

Q 6.40. Debt is usually safer than equity. Does the risk of the rate of return on equity go up if the firm takes on more debt, *provided* the debt is low enough to remain risk free? Illustrate with an example that you make up.

Q 6.41. Under risk neutrality, a factory can be worth $500,000 or $1,000,000 in *two* years, depending on product demand, each with equal probability. The appropriate cost of capital is 6% per year. The factory can be financed with proceeds of $500,000 from loans today. What are the promised and expected cash flows and rates of return for the factory (without a loan), the loan, and the levered factory owner?

Q 6.42. Assume that the correct future cash flow is $100 and the correct discount rate is 10%. Consider the value effect of a 5% error in cash flows and the effect of a 5% error in discount rates.

1. Graph the valuation impact (both in absolute values and in percent of the correct up-front present value) as a function of the number of years from one year to twenty years.

2. Is this an accurate real-world representation of how your uncertainty about your own calculations should look? In other words, is it reasonable to assume a 5% error for cash flows in twenty years? For the appropriate discount-rate applicable to twenty-year cash flows?

Part II

Risk and Return

...in a Perfect Market under Risk Aversion

We are now moving on to the next step in complexity. We shall still (cowardly) maintain that financial markets are perfect: no information differences, no transaction costs, no taxes, and many buyers and sellers. But we are now abandoning the assumption that investors are risk neutral—that they are indifferent between receiving $1 million for sure, and receiving $500,000 or $1,500,000 with equal probability. An investor who is risk averse prefers the safe $1 million.

Risk aversion creates one huge novel complication: Under risk aversion, projects can influence one another from an "overall risk" perspective. If one project's return is always high (say, +20%) when the other project's return is low (say, −20%), and vice versa, then it can even be possible that the overall risk cancels out completely! This simple insight means that determining the best investment choices, selected from the large universe of available investment projects, becomes a much more difficult task for corporate investors and consequently, for their corporations' managers. Projects are no longer self-contained islands.

As a corporate manager, it now becomes a question of how your corporate projects work together with your other projects (for internal corporate risk management) or even with your investors' projects elsewhere. This also means that you need to first understand your investors' problems before you can answer what projects they would like you to undertake. So, who are your investors, what do they like and dislike, and how should you evaluate your project relative to what you believe your investors' alternatives are? What exactly *are* your investors' alternatives? How do your projects interact with your investors' other projects? This is a wide and deep subject, which is why we require an unprecedented three chapters: It requires a larger expedition into the world of uncertainty.

Although the details of how to invest now become more difficult, fortunately, all the important questions and tasks still remain the same—and, fortunately, so do many of the answers. As a corporate executive, you must still understand how to work with rates of return and how to decide whether to accept or reject investment projects. You can still use the net present value method. You still need knowledge of projects' expected cash flows, $\mathscr{E}(C)$, and of the cost of capital, $\mathscr{E}(r)$,

$$\text{NPV} = C_0 + \frac{\mathscr{E}(C_1)}{1 + \mathscr{E}(r_1)} + \frac{\mathscr{E}(C_2)}{1 + \mathscr{E}(r_2)} + \cdots$$

The novel complication arises in the denominator. Investors' risk aversion influences the NPV (only) through $\mathscr{E}(r)$. Still, it continues to be best to think of it as the opportunity cost of capital. As a manager, the difficulty is only that you must somehow calculate what it should be on behalf of your corporation's owners (investors). The cost of capital still measures the same thing: whether your investors have better alternatives elsewhere in the economy. If they do, you should return their capital to them and let them invest their money there. The opportunities elsewhere determine your corporation's cost of capital, which in turn determines what projects you should take.

What You Want to Learn in this Part

In sum, we now assume that investors are risk averse—as they truly are in the real world. Then what is the correct $\mathcal{E}(r)$, the opportunity cost of capital, in the NPV formula? As in earlier chapters, great opportunities elsewhere in the economy still manifest themselves as a high cost of capital $\mathcal{E}(r)$ that you should apply to your projects. But in this part of the book, you must judge all opportunities not only by their rewards, but also by their risks.

- Chapter 7 gives you a short tour of historical rates of return on various asset classes to whet your appetite, and explains some of the institutional setups of equity markets.

  Typical questions: Did stocks, bonds, or cash perform better over the last 30 years? How safe were stocks compared to bonds or cash? What are the roles of brokers and exchanges? How do stocks appear and disappear?

- Chapter 8 considers choices if investors like more reward and less risk. It takes the perspective of an investor. It explains how you should measure risk and reward, and how diversification reduces risk. It draws a strong distinction between a security's own risk and a security's contribution to an investor's overall portfolio risk.

  Typical questions: What is the standard deviation of the rate of return on my portfolio? What is IBM's market beta, and what does it mean for my portfolio? What is IBM's own risk, and should I care? What is the average market beta of my portfolio?

- Chapter 9 takes the perspective of a corporate CFO. It explains how you should measure investors' opportunity costs of capital, $\mathcal{E}(r)$, given that your own corporate investment projects can help or hurt your investors in their overall risk-reward trade-off. This is the domain of the "capital asset pricing model" (CAPM).

  Typical questions: What characteristics should influence the appropriate expected rate of return that your investors care about? What should be the appropriate expected rate of return for any one particular project? Where do you find all the necessary inputs to use the CAPM? Can you trust it?

Looking ahead, Part III will explain what happens when financial markets or decision rules are not perfect.

You can find an intuitive explanation of investments, based on the proverb not to put all your eggs into one basket, at the book website, book.ivo-welch.info.

A First Look at Investments

Historical Rates of Return Background and Market Institutions

The subject of investments is so interesting that I first want to give you a quick tour, instead of laying all the foundations first and showing you the evidence later. I will give you a glimpse of the world of historical returns on the three main asset classes of stocks, bonds, and "cash," so that you can visualize the main patterns that matter—patterns of risk, reward, and covariation. This chapter also describes a number of important institutions that allow investors to trade equities.

7.1 Stocks, Bonds, and Cash, 1970-2010

Financial investments are often classified into just a few broad **asset classes**. The three most prominent such classes are cash, bonds, and stocks.

Cash, bonds, and stocks are the most commonly studied asset classes.

Cash: The name *cash* here is actually a misnomer because it does not designate physical dollar bills under your mattress. Instead, it means debt securities that are very liquid, very low-risk, and very short-term. Other investments that are part of this generic asset class may be certificate of deposits (CDs), savings deposits, or commercial paper. (These are briefly explained in Book Appendix A.) Another common designation for cash is **money market**. To make our life easy, we will just join the club and also use the term "cash."

Bonds: These are debt instruments that have longer maturity than cash. You already know much about bonds and their many different varieties. I find it easiest to think of this class as representing primarily long-term Treasury bonds. You could also broaden this class to include bonds of other varieties, such as corporate bonds, municipal bonds, foreign bonds, or even more exotic debt instruments.

Stocks: Stocks are sometimes all lumped together, and sometimes further categorized into different kinds of stocks. The most common such subclassification for U.S. domestic stocks is as follows:

- The asset class containing a few hundred stocks of the largest firms that trade very frequently is often called **large-cap stocks**. (Cap is a common abbreviation for capitalization.) Although not exactly true, you can think of the largest 500 firms as roughly the constituents of the popular **S&P 500** stock market index. (S&P is Standard and Poor's, the company which invented this index in 1923 and continues to maintain it. Stocks continuously change in value, disappear, etc.) Our chapter focuses mostly on these large-cap S&P 500 stocks and often just calls them "stocks."

- There are a few thousand other stocks. They are also sometimes put into multiple categories, such as "mid-cap" or "small-cap." Inevitably, these stocks tend to trade less often, and some seem outright neglected. Small caps can be really small. They may have only $10 million in market cap, and not a single share may be traded for days at a time. In any case, it is so expensive to trade most small-cap stocks that large investors do not bother with them.

There are also other stock-related subclasses, such as industry stock portfolios, or a classification of stocks into "value firms" and "growth firms," and so on. We shall ignore everything except the large-cap stock portfolio.

These asset classes are only broadly representative of similar individual investments. We are omitting many other important asset classes.

Do not take these categories too literally. They may not be representative of all assets that would seem to fit the designation. For example, most long-term bonds in the economy behave like our bond asset class, but some long-term corporate bonds behave more like stocks. Analogously, a particular firm may own a lot of bonds, and its rates of return would look like those on bonds and not like those on stocks. It would also be perfectly reasonable to include more or fewer investments in these three asset classes. (We would hope that such modifications would alter our insights only a little bit.) More importantly, there are also many other important asset classes that we do not even have time to consider, such as real estate, hedge funds, financial derivatives, foreign investments, or art. Nevertheless, cash, bonds, and stocks (or subclasses thereof) are the three most studied financial asset classes, so we will begin our examination of investments by looking at their historical performances.

Graphical Representations of Historical Returns for the S&P 500

All rates of return data are in the time-series diagram.

Start with Exhibit 7.1. It shows the year-by-year rates of return (with dividends) of the S&P 500. Actually, because of how different sources treat dividends (reinvest or not?), the numbers are never exact. Some sources even omit dividends, which is definitely wrong. The series we are using take dividends into account. (All the numbers we are using are posted on the book's website. Obviously, I do not want to write this textbook with 8 decimal points of precision, so please be aware of—and do not worry about—rounding errors in any of the calculations that follow.) The table and the plot illustrate the same data: You would have earned 3.5% in 1970, 14.1% in 1971, 18.7% in 1972, –14.5% in 1973, and so on. The average rate of return over all 41 years was 11.4% per annum—which I marked with a blue triangle on the left side and the dot-dashed line.

The histogram (statistical distribution) shows how spread out returns are.

Exhibits 7.2 and 7.3 take the same data as Exhibit 7.1 but present it differently. Exhibit 7.2 shows a histogram that is based on the number of returns that fall within a range. This makes it easier to see how spread out returns were—how common it was for the S&P 500 to perform really badly, perform just about okay, or perform really well. For example, the table in Exhibit 7.1 shows that 8 years (1971, 1972, 1979, 1982, 1986, 1988, 2004, and 2006) had rates of return between 10% and 20%. In our 41 years, the most frequent return range was between 0% and 10%. Yet there were also many years that had rates of return below 10%—and even three years in which you would have lost more than 20% of your money (1974, 2002, and 2008). Again, the blue triangle indicates that the average rate of return was 11.4%.

Decade	Year									
	0	**1**	**2**	**3**	**4**	**5**	**6**	**7**	**8**	**9**
1970	3.5%	14.1%	18.7%	–14.5%	–26.0%	36.9%	23.6%	–7.2%	6.4%	18.2%
1980	31.5%	–4.8%	20.4%	22.3%	6.0%	31.1%	18.5%	5.7%	16.3%	31.2%
1990	–3.1%	30.0%	7.4%	9.9%	1.3%	37.1%	22.7%	33.1%	28.3%	20.9%
2000	–9.0%	–11.9%	–22.0%	28.4%	10.7%	4.8%	15.6%	5.5%	–36.6%	25.9%
2010	14.8%									

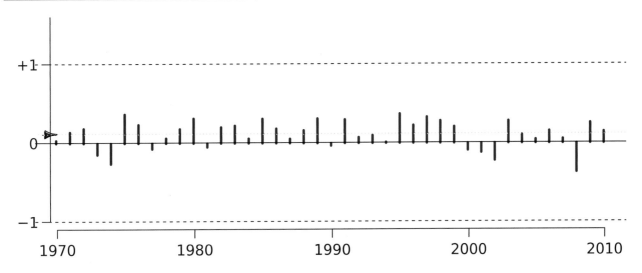

Exhibit 7.1: *The Time Series of Rates of Return on the S&P 500, 1970-2010.* The time-series graph is a representation of the rates of return of the S&P 500 index (including dividends), as shown in the table above. The average rate of return was 11.4% (indicated by the blue triangle and the dot-dashed line); the standard deviation was 17.7%. Original source of data for all applicable figures in this chapter: Ibbotson Stocks, Bonds, Bills and Inflation, SBBI Valuation Yearbook, Morningstar 2011.

Most investors are not interested in statistics as much as they are interested in how much money they would have ended up with. Can you take $1 and the 11.4% average return, and use the compounding formula? Well, this would indicate a payoff of $1 \cdot 1.114^{41} - 1 \approx \$82.62$ in 2010. Unfortunately, you would have been far off the mark.

What would a $1 investment been worth?

Instead, you need a graph of the compound rate of return, which is in Exhibit 7.3. It plots the compounded annual returns (on a logarithmic scale). For example, by the end of 1973, the compound return of $1 invested in 1970 would have been

The compound rate of return graph shows how long-run investments would have fared.

$$\$1 \quad \cdot (1 + 3.5\%) \cdot (1 + 14.1\%) \cdot (1 + 18.7\%) \cdot (1 - 14.5\%) \approx \$1.20$$

$$P_{1/1/70} \cdot (1 + r_{1970}) \cdot (1 + r_{1971}) \cdot (1 + r_{1972}) \cdot (1 + r_{1973}) = P_{12/31/73}$$

If you do this for all 41 years, you end up with $46.80, much less than the naïve $82.62.

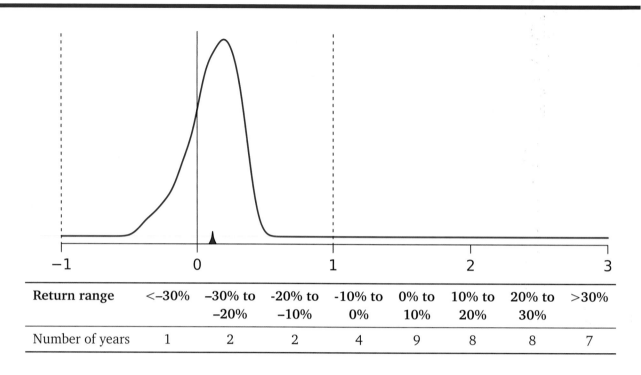

Return range	<–30%	–30% to –20%	-20% to -10%	-10% to 0%	0% to 10%	10% to 20%	20% to 30%	>30%
Number of years	1	2	2	4	9	8	8	7

Exhibit 7.2: *The Statistical Distribution Function of S&P 500 Rates of Return, 1970-2010.* The graph and table are just different representations of the data in Exhibit 7.1. Formally, this type of graph is called a density function. It is really just a smoothed histogram.

Thus, many long-term investors are misled by the more common arithmetic average rate of return—commonly just called the mean or average. What is the intuition? For example, think of a rate of return of –50% (you lose half) followed by +100% (you double). It has the intuitively correct geometric net return of zero. However, the average rate of these two returns is a positive (–50% + 100%)/2 = +25%. Yikes. Unfortunately, there is no simple way to convert an arithmetic rate of return into a geometric rate of return (or an annualized rate of return). You will later even see a real-world example in which the geometric rate of return was –100% and the average rate of return was positive.

> Watch out for whether you are being quoted average or annualized returns. The former is always higher, which is sometimes misleading.

> Geometric returns are more relevant.

The annualized compound rate of return is sometimes called a **geometric average**. To compute the geometric average, you uncompound. The annualized rate of return from 1970-2010 (41 years) was

$$\$1 \cdot (1 + r)^{41} \approx \$46.80 \iff r \approx \sqrt[41]{46.80} - 1 \approx 9.8\%$$

The arithmetic rate of return of 11.4% was 1.6% higher. This is the rate of return that is relevant for a (long-term) buy-and-hold investor. There is one novel aspect to this graph, which is the gray shaded area. It marks the cumulative CPI inflation. The purchasing power of $1 in 1970 was about the same as $5.79 in 2010. Thus, the

➤ Apples, *Sect. 5.2, Pg.90.*

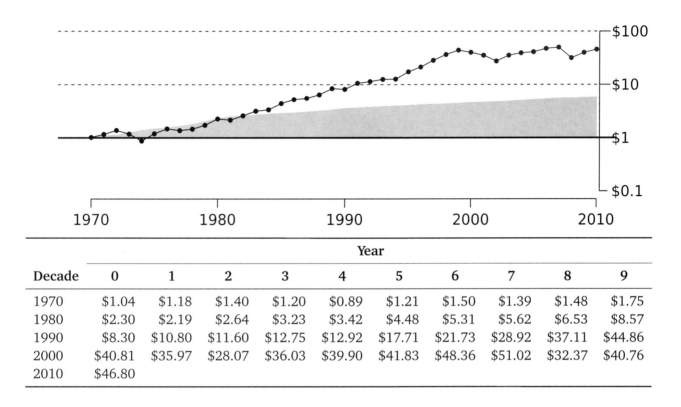

Decade	0	1	2	3	4	5	6	7	8	9
1970	$1.04	$1.18	$1.40	$1.20	$0.89	$1.21	$1.50	$1.39	$1.48	$1.75
1980	$2.30	$2.19	$2.64	$3.23	$3.42	$4.48	$5.31	$5.62	$6.53	$8.57
1990	$8.30	$10.80	$11.60	$12.75	$12.92	$17.71	$21.73	$28.92	$37.11	$44.86
2000	$40.81	$35.97	$28.07	$36.03	$39.90	$41.83	$48.36	$51.02	$32.37	$40.76
2010	$46.80									

Exhibit 7.3: *Compound Rates of Return for the S&P 500, 1970-2010.* This graph and table are again just different representations of the same data in Exhibit 7.1. The gray area underneath the figure is the cumulative inflation-caused loss of purchasing power.

$46.80 nominal value at the end of 2010 was really only worth $46.80/$5.79 ≈ $8.08 in 1970 inflation-adjusted dollars. (And, of course, none of these figures take taxes into account.)

➤ *Tax Basics, Sect.* 10.4, *Pg.261*.

IMPORTANT

The annualized holding rate of return cannot be inferred from the average annual rate of return, and vice versa. The two are identical only if all rates of return are the same (i.e., when there is no risk). Otherwise, the geometric rate of return is always less than the arithmetic rate of return. (And the more risk, the bigger the difference.)

Q 7.1. What can you see in a time-series graph that is not in a histogram?

Q 7.2. What can you see in a histogram that is more difficult to see in the time-series graph?

Q 7.3. What can you see in a compound return graph that is difficult to see in the time-series graph?

Q 7.4. What is the annualized holding rate of return and the average rate of return for each of the following?

1. An asset that returns 5% each year.

2. An asset that returns 0% and 10% in alternate years.

3. An asset that returns –10% and 20% in alternate years.

Is the distance between the two returns larger when there is more risk?

Historical Performance for a Number of Investments

Stocks, Bonds, and Cash

Explore the large comparative Exhibit 7.4.

What does history tell you about rate of return patterns on the three major investment categories—stocks, bonds, and cash? You can find out by plotting exactly the same graphs as those in Exhibits 7.1, 7.2, and 7.3. Exhibit 7.4 repeats them for cash, bonds, and stocks *all on the same scale.* You have already seen the third row, but I have changed the scale to make it easier to make direct comparisons to the other two asset classes. These mini-graphs display a lot of information about the performance of these investments.

The first three rows show historical returns for the three asset classes.

So let's compare the first three rows:

Cash in the first row is the overnight Federal Funds interest rate. Note how tight the distribution of cash returns was around its 5.7% mean. You would never have lost money (in nominal terms), but you would rarely have earned much more than its mean. The value of your total investment portfolio would have steadily marched upward—although pretty slowly. Each dollar invested in January 1970 would have become $9.59 at the end of 2010. Of course, inflation would have eroded the value of each dollar. In purchasing power, your $1 in 1970 was equivalent to $5.79 in 2010. Therefore, the $9.59 investment result in cash would have only been worth about $9.59/$5.79 $\approx$ $1.66 in 1970 inflation-adjusted dollars. Over 41 years, you would not even have doubled your real purchasing power.

How much extra real inflation-adjusted value were these nominal returns really worth?

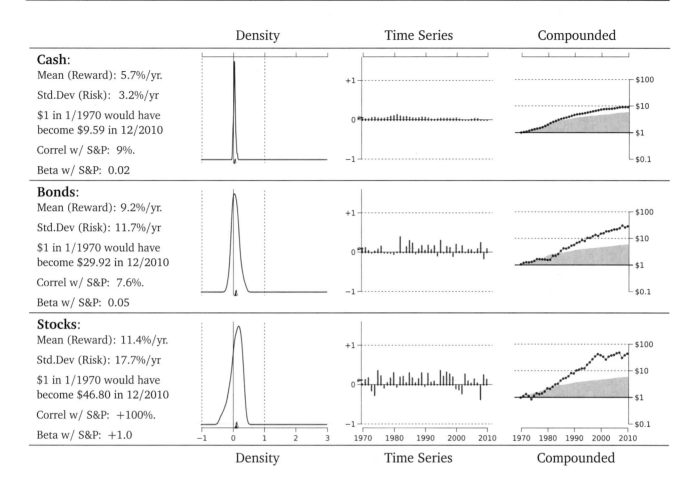

| | Density | Time Series | Compounded |

Exhibit 7.4: *Comparative Investment Performance, 1970-2010.*

Bonds in the second row are long-term Treasury bonds. The middle graph shows that the bars are now sometimes slightly negative (years in which you would have earned a negative rate of return)—but there are now also years in which you would have done *much* better than cash. This is why the histogram is much wider for bonds than it is for cash: Bonds were riskier than cash. The standard deviation tells you that bond risk was 11.7% per year, much higher than the 3.2% cash risk. Fortunately, in exchange for carrying more risk, you would have also enjoyed an average rate of return of 9.2% per year, which is a lot more than the 5.7% of cash. And $1 invested in 1970 would have become not just the $9.59 in 2010 (cash), but $29.92 ($5.17 in real terms).

Long-term bonds offered more reward, but were more variable, too.

➤ *Uncertainty and Variance, Sect. 6.1, Pg. 119.*

Stock Market in the third row is a portfolio of the S&P 500 firms. (Returns are calculated with dividends.) The left graph shows that large stocks would have been even riskier than bonds. The stock histogram is more "spread out" than

Stocks offered even more reward, but were even more variable.

the bond histogram. The middle graph shows that there were years in which the negatives of stocks could be quite a bit worse than those for bonds, but that there were also many years that were outright terrific. And again, the higher risk of stocks also came with more reward. The S&P 500's risk of 17.7% per year was compensated with a mean rate of return of 11.4% per year. Your $1 invested in 1970 would have ended up being worth $46.80 in 2010 ($8.08 in real terms).

Fixed-income investments performed relatively worse for taxable investors than the graphs in Table 7.4 indicate at first glance.

The difference between $46.80 in stocks and $9.59 in cash or $29.92 in bonds is an understatement if you are a common taxable retail investor in a high tax bracket. *Nominal* interest payments would have been taxed each year at your full income tax rate, between 30% and 50% per year. In contrast, the capital gains on stocks would have been taxed only at the end and at the much lower capital gains tax rate, between 15% and 30%. Roughly speaking, taking taxes into account, if you had invested in cash, you would not have ended up with more real purchasing power than you started with. You would have gained a little bit of real purchasing power in bonds (maybe $1.50-$2.00). And you would have roughly quadrupled your purchasing power in stocks. This was a great—and perhaps even unusually great—41 years for stocks! Not every historical 41-year period would have shown as large a difference between cash, bonds, and stocks.

Other Asset Classes

Asset Class	1926-2010			1970-2010		
	"Reward"		Risk	"Reward"		Risk
	Geo	Ari	SDV	Geo	Ari	SDV
Small-Firm Stocks (I)	12.1	16.7	32.6	12.5	15.1	23.4
Large-Firm Stocks (I)	9.9	11.9	20.4	10.0	11.6	17.9
Long-Term Corporate Bonds (I)	5.9	6.2	8.3	8.9	9.3	10.2
Long-Term Government Bonds (I)	5.5	5.9	9.5	8.7	9.3	11.7
Intermediate Government Bonds (I)	5.4	5.5	5.7	8.0	8.2	6.6
30-Day Treasuries (I)	3.6	3.7	3.1	5.6	5.6	3.1
Gold (L)	5.1	6.9	22.7	9.4	12.6	29.8
Housing *Appreciation* (S)	3.7	3.9	6.7	5.0	5.2	6.3
U.S. Inflation (I)	3.0	3.1	4.2	4.4	4.4	3.1

Exhibit 7.5: *Comparative Investment Performance, 1970-2010.* Original data sources: See leftmost column: L= London Gold Exchange. I=Ibbotson Stocks, Bonds, Bills and Inflation, SBBI Valuation Yearbook, Morningstar 2011. S= Robert Shiller, *Irrational Exuberance,* 2nd Ed. Note that housing appreciation ignores the useful housing rental yield, and thus understates the rate of return.

Exhibit 7.5 shows the performance of a few other large asset classes and over a longer time period, too. Small-firm stocks were riskier (and more difficult to trade), but their average rate of return was higher. Corporate bonds sit between government bonds and stocks in terms of reward, although their risk was comparable to the former. Intermediate government bonds (i.e., with about 5-year maturity) were somewhere between cash and long-term bonds. Gold was an extremely risky investment by itself, but it also did well over the sample. (Not shown in this table, it did well in years when stocks did poorly.) Moreover, unlike bonds, gold's gains were taxed at the lower capital-gains rate. Housing is the average price appreciation of residential houses. It probably understates the rate of return by about 3-6% per year, because it omits the value and other costs of living in a house. Owning a house from 1970 to 2010 was a good investment, especially if you take into account that tax rules now shelter most gains from *any* taxes. However, the 6-7% risk may be a bit misleading. Many economists believe that there was a housing bubble in the 2000's, which explains both the fantastic appreciation and the subsequent crash. From 1992 to 2006, there was not a single year in which prices declined. But from 2007 to 2009, residential houses lost about 30% of their values.

Recent asset class performance.

Individual Stocks

Instead of holding entire asset classes, you could also have purchased just an individual stock. How would such holdings have differed from an investment in the broader asset class "stocks"? Exhibit 7.6 keeps the same scale but now shows the rates of return of a few sample stalwart firms: Coca-Cola [KO], PepsiCo [PEP], Sony [SNE], and United Airlines [UAL]. For comparison, the bottom is again the S&P 500. You can see that individual stocks' histograms are really wide: Investing in a single stock would have been a rather risky venture, even for these four household names. Indeed, it is not even possible to plot the final year for UAL in the rightmost compound return graph, because UAL stock investors lost *all* invested money in the 2003 bankruptcy, which on the logarithmic scale would have been minus infinity. And UAL illustrates another important issue: Despite losing all the money, it still had a positive average rate of return. (You already know why: This was the difference between geometric and arithmetic averages explained on Page 154.)

Individual stocks can offer more reward and be even more risky.

Q 7.5. Rank the following asset categories in terms of risk and reward: cash (money market), long-term bonds, the stock market, and a typical individual stock.

Q 7.6. Is the average individual stock safer or riskier than the stock market?

Q 7.7. Is it possible for an investment to have a positive average rate of return, but still lose you every penny?

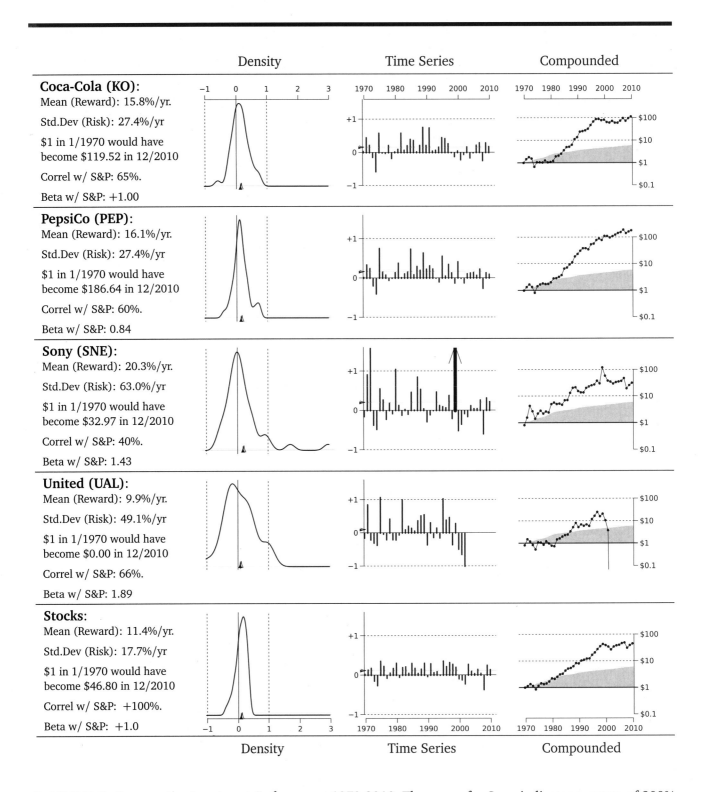

	Density	Time Series	Compounded
Coca-Cola (KO): Mean (Reward): 15.8%/yr. Std.Dev (Risk): 27.4%/yr $1 in 1/1970 would have become $119.52 in 12/2010 Correl w/ S&P: 65%. Beta w/ S&P: +1.00			
PepsiCo (PEP): Mean (Reward): 16.1%/yr. Std.Dev (Risk): 27.4%/yr $1 in 1/1970 would have become $186.64 in 12/2010 Correl w/ S&P: 60%. Beta w/ S&P: 0.84			
Sony (SNE): Mean (Reward): 20.3%/yr. Std.Dev (Risk): 63.0%/yr $1 in 1/1970 would have become $32.97 in 12/2010 Correl w/ S&P: 40%. Beta w/ S&P: 1.43			
United (UAL): Mean (Reward): 9.9%/yr. Std.Dev (Risk): 49.1%/yr $1 in 1/1970 would have become $0.00 in 12/2010 Correl w/ S&P: 66%. Beta w/ S&P: 1.89			
Stocks: Mean (Reward): 11.4%/yr. Std.Dev (Risk): 17.7%/yr $1 in 1/1970 would have become $46.80 in 12/2010 Correl w/ S&P: +100%. Beta w/ S&P: +1.0			

Exhibit 7.6: *Comparative Investment Performance, 1970-2010.* The arrow for Sony indicates a return of 300% in 1999. The original data source for individual stock returns was CRSP.

Comovement, Market Beta, and Correlation

Exhibit 7.7 highlights the rates of return on the S&P 500 and one specific stock, PepsiCo (PEP). The bottom row redraws the time-series graphs for these two investments (history in the top row). Do you notice a correlation between these two series of rates of return? Are the years in which one is positive (or above its mean) more likely also to see the other be positive (or above its mean), and vice versa? It does seem that way. For example, the worst rates of return for both are 1974. Similarly, 1973 and 2002 were bad years for investors in either the S&P 500 or PepsiCo. In contrast, 1975, 1985, 1989, and 1995 were good years for both. The correlation is not perfect: In 1999, the S&P 500 had a good year, but PepsiCo had a bad one; and in 2000, the market had a bad year, but PepsiCo had a good one. It is very common for all sorts of investments in the economy to move together with the stock market: In years of malaise, almost everything tends to be in malaise. In years of exuberance, almost everything tends to be exuberant. This tendency is called **comovement**.

The comovement of investments is very important if you do not like risk. An investment that increases in value whenever the rest of your portfolio decreases in value is practically like "insurance" that pays off when you need it most. You might buy into such an investment even if it offers only a very low expected rate of return. In contrast, you might not like an investment that does very badly whenever the rest of your portfolio also does badly. To be included in your portfolio, such an investment would have to offer a very high expected rate of return.

How can you measure the extent to which securities covary with others? For example, how does PepsiCo covary with the S&P 500 (our stand-in for the market portfolio)? Did PepsiCo also go down when the market did (making a bad situation worse), or did it go up (thereby serving as useful insurance)? How can you quantify such comovement?

You can answer this graphically. Plot the two return series against one another, as is done in the bottom plot in Exhibit 7.7. Then find the line that best fits between the two series. (You will learn later how to compute it.) The slope of this line is called the **market beta** of a stock, and it is a measure of comovement between the rate of return on the stock with the rate of return on the market. It tells an investor whether this stock moved with or against the market. It carries great importance in financial economics.

- If the best-fitting line has a slope that is steeper than the 45° diagonal (well, if the x- and y-axes are drawn with the same scale), then the market beta is greater than 1. Such a line would imply that when the stock market did better (the x-axis), on average your stock did *a lot better* (the y-axis). For example, if a stock has a very steep positive slope—say, +3—then (assuming you hold the market portfolio) if the market dropped by an additional 10%, this stock would have been expected to drop by an additional 30%. If you primarily held the market portfolio, this new stock would have made your bad situation worse.

- If the slope is less than 1 (or even 0, a plain horizontal line), it means that, on average, your stock did not move as much (or not at all) with the stock market.

- If a stock has a very negative slope such as –2, this investment would likely have "rescued" you when the market dropped by 10%. On average, it would have earned a positive 20% rate of return. Adding such a stock to your market portfolio would be like buying insurance.

Now look at the correlation of PEP with the market, mentioned also in the leftmost column of Exhibit 7.6.

Why do you care about comovement? Because you want assets that do well when everything else does poorly.

Quantifying comovement.

Market beta is the slope of the best-fitting line (with the market's rate of return on the x-axis and the firm's rate of return on the y-axis).

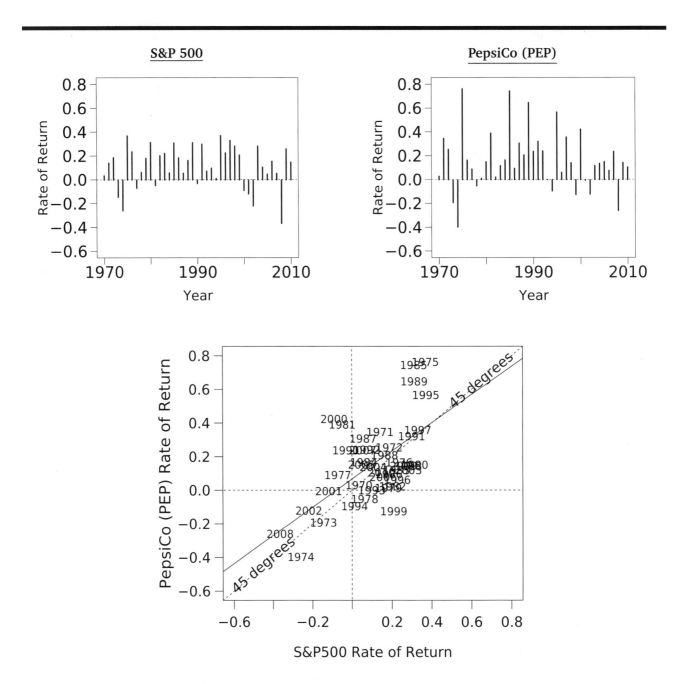

Exhibit 7.7: *Rates of Return on the S&P 500 and PepsiCo (PEP), 1970-2010.* The top left graph plots the annual rate of return on the S&P 500; the top right graph plots the annual rate of return on PepsiCo. The bottom graph combines the information. The stock market rate of return is on the x-axis, the PepsiCo rate of return is on the y-axis. The figure shows that in years when the stock market did well, PepsiCo tended to do well, too, and vice versa. This can be seen in the slope of the best-fitting line, which is called the market beta of PepsiCo. The market beta will play an important role in investments. *Real-world Advice:* In practice, it is better to compute a market beta from the most recent 3 years of *daily* stock return data, and not from 41 years of *annual* stock return data, as I have done in this figure.

PepsiCo's particular line had a slope of 0.84. That is, it was a little less steep than the diagonal line. In effect, this means that if you had held the stock market, PepsiCo would have been neither great insurance nor a great additional hazard for you. A 1% performance above (below) normal for the S&P would have meant you would have expected to earn 0.84% above (below) normal in your PepsiCo holdings.

Instead of beta, you could measure comovement with another statistic that you may already have come across: the so-called **correlation**. Correlation and beta are related. The correlation has a feature that beta does not. A correlation of +100% indicates that two variables always perfectly move together; a correlation of 0% indicates that two variables move about independently; and a correlation of –100% indicates that two variables always perfectly move in opposite directions. (A correlation can never exceed +100% or –100%.) In PepsiCo's case, one can work out that the correlation is +60%. The correlation's limited range from –1 to +1 is both an advantage and a disadvantage. On the positive side, the correlation is a number that is often easier to judge than beta. On the negative side, the correlation has no concept of scale. It can be 100% even if the y variable moves only very, very mildly with x (e.g., if every $y = 0.0001 \cdot x$, the correlation is still a positive 100%). In contrast, beta can be anything from minus infinity to plus infinity.

Market beta is a cousin of correlation.

A positive correlation always implies a positive beta, and vice versa. Of course, beta and correlation are only measures of *average* comovement: Even for investments with positive betas, there are individual years in which the investment and stock market do not move together (look back at 1999 and 2000 for PepsiCo and the S&P 500). Stocks with negative betas, for which a negative market rate of return *on average* associates with a positive stock return (and vice versa), are rare. There are only a very few investment categories that are generally thought to be negatively correlated with the market—principally gold and other precious metals.

The signs of the correlation and the beta are always the same.

Q 7.8. How do you graph a "market beta"? What should be on the x-axis, and what should be on the y-axis? What is an individual data point?

Q 7.9. What is the market beta of the market?

The Big Picture Take-Aways

What can you learn from these graphs? Actually, almost everything there is to learn about investments! I will explain these facts in much more detail soon. In the meantime, here are the most important points that the graphs show:

The main empirical regularities.

- History tells us that stocks offered higher average rates of return than bonds, which in turn offered higher average rates of return than cash. However, keep in mind that this was only *on average*. In any given year, the relationship might have been reversed. For example, stock investors lost 22% of their wealth in 2002, while cash investors gained about 1.7%.

- Although stocks did well (on average), you could have lost your shirt investing in them, especially if you had bet on just one individual stock. For example, if you had invested in United Airlines in 1970, you would have lost all your money.

- Cash was the safest investment—its distribution is tightly centered around its mean, so there were no years with negative returns. Bonds were riskier. And stocks were even riskier. (Sometimes, stocks are said to be "noisy," because it is really difficult to predict how they will perform.)

- There seems to be a relationship between risk and reward: Riskier investments tended to have higher average rates of return. (However, you will learn soon that risk has to be looked at in context. Thus, please do not overread the simple relationship between the mean and the standard deviation here.)

- Large portfolios consisting of many stocks tended to have less risk than individual stocks. The S&P 500 stocks had a risk of around 15-20% per year, which was less than the risk of most individual stocks (e.g., PepsiCo had a risk of about 27%). This is due to the phenomenon of diversification.

➤ *Diversification, Sect. 8.2, Pg. 181.*

- The average rate of return is always larger than the geometric (compound) rate of return. A positive average rate of return usually, but not always, translates into a positive compound holding rate of return. For example, United Airlines had a positive average rate of return, despite having lost all its investors' money.

- Stocks tend to move together. For example, if you look at 2001 and 2002, not only did the S&P 500 go down, but all the individual stocks tended to go down, too. In 1998, on the other hand, most stocks tended to go up (or at least not down much). The mid-1990s were good to all stocks. In contrast, money market returns had little to do with the stock market. Long-term bonds were in between.

- On an annual frequency, the correlation between the stock market and either cash or long-term bonds (the S&P 500) was about 10%. The correlation between individual stocks and the stock market was around 50% to 70%. The fact that investment rates of return tend to move together is important. It is the foundation for the market beta, a measure of risk that we have touched on and that will be explained in detail in Chapter 8.

Will History Repeat Itself?

History is only useful over long horizons, not over just a few years.

As a financier, you are not interested in history for its own sake. Instead, you really want to know more about the future. History is useful only because it is your best available indicator of the future. But which history? One year? Thirty years? One hundred years? I can tell you that if you had drawn the graphs beginning in 1926 instead of 1970, the big conclusions would have remained the same. However, if you had started in 2001, things would have been different. What would you have seen? Four awful years for stock investors. You should know intuitively that this would not have been a representative sample period. To make any sensible inferences about what is going on in the financial markets, you need many years of history, not just one, two, or three—and certainly not the 6-week investment performance touted by some funds or friends (who also often display remarkable selective memory!). The flip side of this argument is that you cannot reliably say what the rate of return will be over your next year. It is easier to forecast the *average* annual rate of return over five to ten years than over one year. Your investment outcome over any single year will be very noisy.

Instead of relying on just one year, relying on statistics computed over many years is much better. However, although twenty to thirty years of performance is the minimum number necessary to learn something about return patterns, this is still not sufficient for you to be very confident. Again, you are really interested in what will happen in the next five to ten years, not what happened in the last five to ten years. Yes, the historical performance can help you judge, but you should not trust it blindly. For example, an investor in UAL in 2000 might have guessed that the average rate of return for UAL would have been positive—and would have been sorely disappointed. Investors in the Japanese stock market in 1986 saw the Nikkei-225 stock market index rise from 10,000 to 40,000 by 1990—a 40% rate of return per year. If they had believed that history was a good guide, they would have expected $40,000 \cdot 1.40^{13} \approx 3.2$million by the end of 2002. Instead, the Nikkei had fallen below 8,000 in April 2003 and has only recently recovered to 15,307 by December 2010. History would have been a terrible guide.

Even over long horizons, history can sometimes be misleading. The Nikkei-225 stock index is a good example.

Nevertheless, despite the intrinsic hazards in using historical information to forecast future returns, having historical data is a great advantage. It is a rich source of forecasting power, so like everyone else, you will have to use historical statistics. But please be careful not to rely too much on them. For example, if you look at an investment that had extremely high or low past historical rates of return, you may not want to believe that this is likely to continue.

But you do not have much choice other than to rely on history.

In relative terms, what historical information can you trust more and what historical information should you trust less?

Historical standard deviations and variances are good estimators of their future equivalents. This is not the case for historical average rates of return.

Historical risk: Standard deviations and correlations (how stock movements tend to be related or unrelated) tend to be fairly stable, especially for large asset classes and diversified portfolios. That is, for 2010 to 2020, you can reasonably expect PepsiCo to have a risk of about 25-30% per year, a correlation of about 50-70% with the market, and a market beta of about 0.7 to 1.1.

Historical mean reward: Historical average rates of return are not very reliable predictors of future expected rates of return. That is, you should not necessarily believe that PepsiCo will continue to earn an expected rate of return of 16% per year.

Realizations: You should definitely not believe that past realizations are good predictors of future realizations. Just because PepsiCo had a rate of return of 10% in 2010 does not make it likely that it will have a rate of return of 10% in 2011.

A lottery analogy may help you understand the last two points better. If you have played the lottery many times, your historical average rate of return is unlikely to be predictive of your future expected rate of return—especially if you have won it big at least once. Yes, you could trust it if you had millions of historical realizations, but you inevitably do not have so many. Consequently, your average historical payoff is only a mediocre predictor of your next week's payoff. And you should definitely not trust your most recent realization to be indicative of the future. Just because "5, 10, 12, 33, 34, 38" won last week does not mean that it will likely win again.

Henceforth, like almost all of finance, we will just assume that we know the statistical distributions from which future investment returns will be drawn. For exposition, this makes our task a lot easier. When you want to use our techniques in the real world, you will usually collect historical data and pretend that the future distribution is the same as the historical distribution. (Some investors in the real world use some more sophisticated techniques, but ultimately these techniques are also just variations on this theme.) However, always remember: historical data is an imperfect guide to the future.

To make life easier, most finance assumes that we know all the statistical distributions describing future *expected* rates of return. But remain mindful of this leap of faith.

7.2 Overview of Equity-Related Market Institutions

Why more info on equities?

Let's look into the institutional arrangements for equity trading. After all, from our corporate perspective, stocks are more interesting than many other financial instruments, such as foreign government bonds, even if there is more money in foreign government bonds than in corporate equity. After all, it is the equity holders who finance most of the risks of corporate projects. Moreover, although there is more money in nonequity financial markets, the subject area of investments often focuses on equities (stocks), too, because retail investors find it easier to buy stocks, and historical data for stocks is relatively easy to come by. So it makes sense to describe a few institutional details as to how investors and stocks "connect"—exchange cash for claims, and vice versa.

Brokers

Retail brokers execute trades and keep track of portfolios. They also arrange shorts.

➤ Market maker, Sect. 7.2, Pg.167.

Most individuals place their orders to buy or sell stocks with a **retail broker**, such as *Ameritrade* (a "deep-discount" broker), *Charles Schwab* (a "discount" broker), or *Merrill Lynch* (a "full-service" broker). Discount brokers may charge only about $10 commission per trade, but they often receive "rebate" payments back from the market maker to which they route your order. This is called "payment for order flow." The market maker in turn recoups this payment to the broker by executing your trade at a price that is less favorable. Although the purpose of such an arrangement seems deceptive, the evidence suggests that discount brokers are still often cheaper in facilitating investor trades—especially small investor trades—even after taking this hidden payment into account. They just are not as (relatively) cheap as they want to make you believe. Investors can place either **market orders**, which ask for execution at the current price, or **limit orders**, which ask for execution if the price is above or below a limit that the investor can specify. (There are also many other modifications of orders, e.g., *stop-loss* orders [which instruct a broker to sell a security if it has lost a certain amount of money], *good-til-canceled* orders, and *fill-or-kill* orders.) The first function of retail brokers then is to handle the execution of trades. They usually do so by routing investors' orders to a centralized trading location (e.g., a particular stock exchange), the choice of which is typically at the retail broker's discretion, as is the particular individual (e.g., floor broker) engaged to execute the trade. The second function of retail brokers is to keep track of investors' holdings, to facilitate purchasing **on margin** (whereby investors can borrow money to purchase stock, allowing them to purchase more securities than they could afford on a pure cash basis), and to facilitate selling securities "short," which allows investors to speculate that a stock will go down.

Prime brokers leave execution to the client investor.

Many large institutional investors separate the two functions: The investor employs its own traders, while the broker takes care only of the bookkeeping of the investor's portfolio, margin provisions, and shorting provisions. Such limited brokers are called **prime brokers**.

How Shorting Stocks Works

If you want to speculate that a stock will go down, you would want to short it. This shorting would be arranged by your broker. Shorting is important enough to deserve an extended explanation:

- You find an investor in the market who is willing to lend you the shares. In a perfect market, this does not cost a penny. In the real world, the broker has to find a willing lender. Both the broker and lender usually earn a few basis points per year for doing you the favor of facilitating your short sale.

- After you have borrowed the shares, you sell them into the market to someone else who wanted to buy the shares. In a perfect market, you would keep the proceeds and earn interest on them. In the real world, your broker may force you to put these proceeds into low-yield safe bonds. If you are a small retail investor, your brokerage firm may even keep the interest proceeds altogether.

- When you want to "unwind" your short, you repurchase the shares and return them to your lender.

For example, if you borrowed the shares when they were trading for $50 (and sold them into the market), and the shares now sell for $30, you can repurchase them for $20 less than what you sold them for into the market. This $20 is your profit. In an ideal world, you can think of your role effectively as the same as that of the company—you can issue shares and use the $50 proceeds to fund your investments (e.g., to earn interest). In the real world, you have to take transaction costs into account. (Shorting has become so common that there are now exchange-traded futures on stocks that make this even easier.)

> Shorting is like borrowing and then issuing securities. The interest on the proceeds may be earned by the broker or by the client (or be shared).
>
> ➤ *Future Interest Rate Speculating,* Sect. App.5.B (Companion), *Pg.*≈*13*.

> ➤ *Forwards and Futures,* Sect. 25.A (Companion), *Pg.*≈*276*.

Q 7.10. What are the two main functions of brokerage firms?

Q 7.11. How does a prime broker differ from a retail broker?

Q 7.12. Is your rate of return higher if you short a stock in the perfect world or in the real world? Why?

Exchanges and Non-Exchanges

A retail broker would route your transaction to a centralized trading location. The most prominent are exchanges. An **exchange** is a centralized trading location where financial securities are traded. The two most important stock exchanges in the United States are the **New York Stock Exchange** (**NYSE**, also nicknamed the Big Board) and **NASDAQ** (originally an acronym for "National Association of Securities Dealers Automated Quotation System"). The NYSE used to be exclusively an **auction market**, in which one designated **specialist** (assigned for each stock) managed the auction process by trading with individual brokers on the floor of the exchange. This specialist was often a monopolist. However, even the NYSE now conducts much of its trading electronically. In contrast to the NYSE's hybrid human-electronic process primarily in one physical location on Wall Street, NASDAQ has always been a purely electronic exchange

> The two big stock exchanges are the NYSE and NASDAQ. The NYSE is a hybrid market. The NASDAQ is only electronic.

without specialists. (For security reasons, its location—well, the location of its many computer systems—is secret.) For each NASDAQ stock, there is at least one **market maker**, a broker-dealer who has agreed to stand by continuously to offer to buy or sell shares, electronically of course, thereby creating a liquid and immediate market for the general public. Moreover, market makers are paid for providing liquidity: They receive additional rebates from the exchange when they post a bid (short for bid price) or an ask (short for ask price) that is executed. Most NASDAQ stocks have multiple market makers, drawn from a pool of about 500 trading firms (such as J.P. Morgan or ETrade), which compete to offer the best price. Market makers have one advantage over the general public: They can see the **limit order book**, which contains as-yet-unexecuted orders from investors to purchase or sell if the stock price changes—giving them a good idea at which price a lot of buying or selling activity will occur. The NYSE is the older exchange, and for historical reasons, is the biggest exchange for trading most "blue chip" stocks. ("Blue chip" now means "well-established and serious." Ironically, the term itself came from poker, where the highest-denomination chips were blue.) In 2006, the NYSE listed just under 3,000 companies worth about $25 trillion. (This is about twice the annual U.S. GDP.) NASDAQ tends to trade smaller and high-technology firms, lists about as many firms, and has more trading activity than the NYSE. Some stocks are traded on both exchanges.

Auction markets, popular in other countries, have lower execution costs, but also slower execution speeds.

Continuous trading—trading at any moment an investor wants to execute—relies on the presence of the standby intermediaries (specialists or market makers), who are willing to absorb shares when no one else is available. This is risky business, and thus any intermediary must earn a good rate of return to be willing to do so. To avoid this cost, some countries have organized their exchanges into noncontinuous auction systems, which match buy and sell orders a couple of times each day. The disadvantage is that you cannot execute orders immediately but have to delay until a whole range of buy and sell orders have accumulated. The advantage is that this eliminates the risk that an (expensive) intermediary would otherwise have to bear. Thus, auctions generally offer lower trading costs but slower execution.

New alternative trading institutions: electronic communication networks (ECNs).

Even in the United States, innovation and change are everywhere. For example, electronic communication networks (ECNs) have recently made big inroads into the trading business, replacing exchanges, especially for large institutional trades. (They can trade the same stocks that exchanges are trading, and thus they compete with exchanges in terms of cost and speed of execution.) An ECN cuts out the specialist, allowing investors to post price-contingent orders themselves. ECNs may specialize in lower execution costs, higher broker kickbacks, or faster execution. The biggest ECNs are Archipelago and Instinet. In 2005, the NYSE merged with Archipelago, and NASDAQ purchased Instinet. (It is hard to keep track of the most recent trading arrangements. For example, in 2006, the NYSE also merged with ArcaEx, yet another electronic trading system, and merged with Euronext, a pan-European stock exchange based in Paris. As of this writing, it is now officially called **NYSE Euronext**—and the Deutsche Boerse is in the process of acquiring it in turn. In addition, the NYSE converted from a mutual company owned by its traders into a publicly traded for-profit company itself.)

Crossing networks and more...

An even more interesting method to buy and trade stocks is that of crossing system, such as ITG's POSIT. ITG focuses primarily on matching large institutional trades with one another in an auction-like manner. If no match on the other side is found, the order may simply not be executed. But if a match is made, by cutting out the specialist or market maker, the execution is a lot cheaper than it would have been on an exchange. Recently, even more novel trading places have sprung up. For example, Liquidnet uses peer-to-peer networking—like the original Napster—to match buyers and sellers in real time. ECNs and electronic limit order books are now the dominant trading systems for equities worldwide, with only the U.S. exchange floors as holdouts. Similar exchanges and computer programs are also used to trade futures, derivatives, currencies, and even some bonds.

There are many other financial markets, too. There are financial exchanges handling stock options, commodities, insurance contracts, and so on. A huge segment is the **over-the-counter** (**OTC**) markets. Over-the-counter means "call around, usually to a set of traders well known to trade in the asset, until you find someone willing to buy or sell at a price you like." Though undergoing rapid institutional change, most bond transactions are still over-the-counter. Although OTC markets handle significantly more bond trading in terms of transaction dollar amounts than bond exchanges, OTC transaction costs are prohibitively high for retail investors. If you call without knowing the market in great detail, the person on the other end of the line will be happy to quote you a shamelessly high price, hoping that you do not know any better. The **NASD** (National Association of Securities Dealers) also operates a semi-OTC market for the stocks of smaller firms, which are listed on the so-called **pink sheets**. Foreign securities trade on their local national exchanges, but the costs for U.S. retail investors are again often too high to make direct participation worthwhile.

There are also informal financial markets, especially OTC (over-the-counter).

Q 7.13. How does a crossing system differ from an electronic exchange?

Q 7.14. What is a specialist? What is a market maker? When trading, what advantage do the two have over you?

Q 7.15. Describe some alternatives to trading on the main stock exchanges.

Investment Companies and Vehicles

In 1933/1934, Congress established the *U.S. Securities and Exchange Commission* (**SEC**) through the *Securities Exchange Acts*. The SEC regulates investment advisors and funds according to the *Investment Advisers Act of 1940*. In practice, this has allowed three different types of regulated **investment companies** to operate in the public markets: open-end funds, closed-end funds, and unit investment trusts (UITs).

The SEC regulates investment funds and advisors.

In the United States, open-end fund is a synonym for mutual fund. (Elsewhere, mutual funds can include other classes.) Being **open end** means that the fund can create shares at will. Investors can also redeem their fund shares at the end of each trading day in exchange for the **net asset value** (**NAV**), which must be posted daily. This gives investors little reason to sell their fund shares to other investors—thus, mutual funds do not trade on any exchanges. The redemption right gives the law of one price a lot of bite—fund shares are almost always worth nearly exactly what their underlying holdings are worth. If an open-end fund's share price were to fall much below the value of its holdings, an arbitrageur could buy up the fund shares, redeem them, and thereby earn

The "open end" feature allows investors to redeem their shares. It forces the fund's shares to trade for close to the value of its holdings.

free money. (One discrepancy is due to some odd tax complications: the fund's capital gains and losses are passed through to the fund investors at the end of every year, but they may not be what every investor experienced.) Interestingly, in the U.S. financial markets, there are now many more stock funds than individual stocks.

In a **closed-end fund**, there is one big initial primary offering of fund shares, and investors cannot redeem their fund shares for the underlying value. The advantage of a closed-end fund is that it can itself invest in assets that are less liquid. After all, it may not be forced to sell its holdings on the whims of its own investors. Many closed-end funds are exchange traded, so that if a closed-end fund investor needs cash, she can resell her shares. The disadvantage of the closed-end scheme is that the law of one price has much less bite. On average, closed-end funds trade persistently below the value of their underlying holdings, roughly in line with the (often high) fees that the managers of many of these closed-end funds are charging.

Both mutual funds and closed-end fund managers are allowed to trade fund holdings quite actively—and many do so. Although some funds specialize in imitating common stock market indexes, many more try to guess the markets or try to be more "boutique." Most funds are classified into a category based on their general trading motivation (such as "market timing," or "growth" or "value," or "income" or "capital appreciation").

A **unit investment trust** (**UIT**) is sort of closed end in its creation (usually through one big primary offering) and sort of open end in its redemption policies (usually accepting investor redemption requests on demand). Moreover, regulatory rules forbid UITs to trade actively (although this is about to change), and UITs must have a fixed termination date (even if it is 50 years in the future). UITs can be listed on a stock exchange, which makes it easy for retail investors to buy and sell them. Some early **exchange-traded funds** (**ETFs**) were structured as UITs, although this required some additional legal contortions that allowed them to create more shares on demand. This is why ETFs are nowadays usually structured as open-end funds.

Some other investment vehicles are regulated by the SEC under different rules. The most prominent may be certain kinds of **American Depositary Receipt** (**ADR**). An ADR is a passive investment vehicle that usually owns the stock of only one foreign security, held in escrow at a U.S. bank (usually the Bank of New York). ADRs make it easier for U.S. retail investors to trade in foreign securities without incurring large transaction costs. ADRs are redeemable, which gives the law of one price great bite.

There are also funds that are structured so that they do not need to register with the SEC. This means that they cannot openly advertise for new investors and are limited to fewer than 100 investors. This includes most **hedge funds**, **venture capital** funds, and other **private equity** funds. Many **offshore funds** are set up to allow foreign investors to hold U.S. stocks not only without SEC regulation, but also without ever having to tread into the domain of the U.S. IRS.

> Closed-end funds do not allow shares to be redeemed. This is useful for funds which are investing in illiquid assets.

> Mutual funds are open-ended, actively traded investment vehicles.

> UITs are passive "basket" investment vehicles.

> ADRs are investment vehicles, too. Many ADRs (though not all) are regulated by the SEC under different rules.

> Other funds are entirely unregulated.

Q 7.16. What should happen if the holdings of an open-end fund are worth much more than what the shares of the fund are trading for? What should happen in a closed-end fund?

Q 7.17. What is the OTC market?

Q 7.18. What are the three main types of investment companies as defined by the SEC? Which is the best deal in a perfect market?

How Securities Appear and Disappear

Inflows

Most publicly traded equities appear on public exchanges, almost always NASDAQ, through **initial public offerings** (**IPOs**). This is an event in which a privately traded company first sells shares to ordinary retail and institutional investors. IPOs are usually executed by **underwriters** (investment bankers such as Goldman Sachs or Merrill Lynch), which are familiar with the complex legal and regulatory process and have easy access to an investor client base to buy the newly issued shares. Shares in IPOs are typically sold at a fixed price—and for about 10% below the price at which they are likely to trade on the first day of after-market open trading. (Many IPO shares are allocated to the brokerage firm's favorite customers, and they can be an important source of profit.)

Firms first sell public shares in IPOs.

➤ *Goldman Sachs, Sect.* 23.A (Companion), *Pg.*≈*186.*

A N E C D O T E **Trading Volume in the Tech Bubble**

During the tech bubble of 1999 and 2000, IPOs appreciated by 65% on their opening day *on average*. Getting an IPO share allocation was like getting free money. Of course, ordinary investors rarely received any such share allocations—only the underwriter's favorite clients did. This later sparked a number of lawsuits, one of which revealed that Credit Suisse First Boston (CSFB) allocated shares of IPOs to more than 100 customers who, in return for IPO allocations, funneled between 33% and 65% of their IPO profits back to CSFB in the form of excessive trading of other stocks (like Compaq and Disney) at inflated trading commissions.

How important was this "kickback" activity? In the aggregate, in 1999 and 2000, underwriters left about $66 billion on the table for their first-day IPO buyers. If investors rebated 20% back to underwriters in the form of extra commissions, this would amount to $13 billion in excessive underwriter profits. At an average commission of 10 cents per share, this would require 130 billion shares to be traded, or an average of 250 million shares per trading day. This figure suggests that kickback portfolio churning may have accounted for as much as 10% of all shares traded!

Ritter and Welch (2002)

Usually, about a third of the company is sold in the IPO, and the typical IPO offers shares worth between $20 million and $100 million, although some are much larger (e.g., privatizations, like British Telecom). About two-thirds of all such IPO companies never amount to much or even die within a couple of years, but the remaining third soon thereafter offer more shares in **seasoned equity offerings** (**SEOs**). These days, however, much expansion in the number of shares in publicly traded companies—especially for large companies—comes not from seasoned equity offerings but from employee stock option plans, which eventually become unrestricted publicly traded shares.

Money also flows into the financial markets through SEOs.

The SEC is also in charge of regulating some behavior of publicly traded companies. This includes how they conduct their IPOs. It also describes how they have to behave thereafter. For example, publicly traded companies must regularly report their financials and some other information. Moreover, Congress has banned **insider trading** on unreleased *specific* information, although more general informed trading by insiders is legal (and seems to be done fairly commonly and profitably). The SEC can only pursue civil fines. If there is fraud involved, then it is up to the states to pursue criminal

The behavior at the IPO and subsequently is also regulated by the SEC.

sanctions, which they often do simultaneously. (Publicly traded firms also have to follow a hodgepodge of other federal and state laws.)

A reverse merger has become another common way to enter the public financial markets.

Because IPOs face unusually complex legal regulations and liability, the alternative of **reverse mergers** has recently become prominent. A larger privately-owned company simply merges with a small company (possibly just a shell) that is already publicly traded. The owners of the big company receive newly issued shares in the combined entity. And, of course, the newly issued shares in effect move private-sector assets into the public markets, where it appears as more market capitalization.

Outflows

Money flows out from the financial markets via dividends and share repurchases.

➤ *Dividend irrelevance, Sect.* 19.2*, Pg.* 614*.*

Capital flows out of the financial markets in a number of ways. The most important venues are capital distributions such as dividends and share repurchases. Many companies pay some of their earnings in **dividends** to investors. Dividends, of course, do not fall like manna from heaven. For example, a firm worth $100,000 may pay $1,000, and would therefore be worth $99,000 after the dividend distribution. If you own a share of $100, you would own (roughly) $99 in stock and $1 in dividends after the payment—still $100 in total, no better or worse. (If you have to pay some taxes on dividend receipts, you might come out for the worse.) Alternatively, firms may reduce their outstanding shares by paying out earnings in **share repurchases**. For example, the firm may dedicate the $1,000 to share repurchases, and you could ask the firm to use $100 thereof to repurchase your share. But even if you hold onto your share, you have not lost anything. Previously, you owned $100/$100,000 = 0.1% of a $100,000 company, for a net of $100. Now, you will own $100/$99,000 ≈ 1.0101% of a $99,000 company—multiply this to find that your share is still worth $100. In either case, the value of outstanding public equity in the firm has shrunk from $100,000 to $99,000. We will discuss dividends and share repurchases in Chapter 19.

Shares can also shrink out of the financial markets in bankruptcies, liquidations, and delistings.

➤ *Bankruptcy and managers, Sect.* 25.C (Companion)*, Pg.* ≈289*.*

Firms can also exit the public financial markets entirely by delisting. Delistings usually occur either when a firm is purchased by another firm or when it runs into financial difficulties so bad that they fail to meet minimum listing requirements. Often, such financial difficulties lead to bankruptcy or liquidation. Some firms even voluntarily liquidate, determining that they can pay their shareholders more if they sell their assets and return the money to them. This is rare because managers usually like to keep their jobs—even if continuation of the company is not in the interest of shareholders. More commonly, firms make bad investments and fall in value to the point where they are delisted from the exchange and/or go into bankruptcy. Fortunately, investors enjoy **limited liability**, which means that they can at most lose their investments and do not have to pay further for any sins of management.

➤ *Limited liability, Sect.* 6.4*, Pg.* 136*.*

Q 7.19. What are the main mechanisms by which money flows from investors into firms?

Q 7.20. What are the institutional mechanisms by which funds disappear from the public financial markets back into the pockets of investors?

Q 7.21. How do shares disappear from the stock exchange?

Summary

This chapter covered the following major points:

- Exhibits 7.4 and 7.6 showed an analysis of historical rate of return patterns of investments in cash, bonds, stock indexes, and individual stocks.

  - Stocks, on average, had higher average rates of return than bonds, which in turn had higher average rates of return than cash investments.

  - Individual stocks were riskiest. Large stock market portfolios had lower risk than individual stock holdings. Bonds had even lower risk, and cash was least risky.

- Stocks (and many other investments) tended to correlate positively: When the stock market overall had a good (bad) year, most stocks also had a good (bad) year.

- Most finance assumes that statistics are known. This is a leap of faith. In real life, historical data can help you in predicting the future, but it is not perfect. Historical risks and correlations are good predictors of their future equivalents; historical means may not be.

- Section 7.2 explained many institutional arrangements governing publicly traded equity securities. This includes the roles of retail and prime brokers, exchanges, and funds. It also described how stocks can be shorted, and how funds flow in and out of the financial markets.

Keywords

ADR, 170. American Depositary Receipt, 170. Asset classes, 151. Auction market, 167. Closed-end fund, 170. Comovement, 161. Correlation, 163. Dividend, 612. ETF, 170. Exchange, 167. Exchange-traded fund, 170. Geometric average, 154. Hedge fund, 170. IPO, 171. Initial public offering, 171. Insider trading, 171. Investment companies, 169. Large-cap stock, 151. Limit order book, 168. Limit order, 166. Limited liability, 172. Market beta, 221. Market maker, 168. Market order, 166. Money market, 151. NASD, 169. NASDAQ, 167. NAV, 169. NYSE Euronext, 168. NYSE, 167. Net asset value, 169. New York Stock Exchange, 167. OTC, 169. Offshore fund, 170. On margin, 166. Open end, 169. Over-the-counter, 169. Pink sheets, 169. Prime broker, 166. Private equity, 583. Retail broker, 166. Reverse merger, 172. SEC, 169. SEO, 171. S&P 500, 151. Seasoned equity offering, 171. Share repurchase, 172. Specialist, 167. UIT, 170. Underwriter, 171. Unit investment trust, 170. Venture capital, 170.

Answers

Q 7.1 A time-series graph shows how individual years matter. This can no longer be seen in a histogram.

Q 7.2 A histogram makes it easier to see how frequent different types of outcomes are—and thus, where the distribution is centered and how spread out it is.

Q 7.3 A compound return graph shows how a time series of rates of return interacts to produce long-run returns. In other words, you can see whether a long-run investment would have made or lost money. This is difficult to see in a time-series graph.

Q 7.4 Note that because the returns in (b) and (c) alternate, you just need to work out the safe two-year returns—thereafter, they will continue in their (unrealistic) patterns.

1. 5% for both.
2. Over two years, you earn $1.00 \cdot 1.10 - 1 = 10.00\%$. This means that the annualized rate of return is $\sqrt{1.1} - 1 \approx 4.88\%$. This is lower than the average rate of return, which is still 5%.
3. Over two years, you earn $0.9 \cdot 1.20 - 1 = 8.00\%$. This means that the annualized rate of return is $\sqrt{1.08} - 1 \approx 3.92\%$. This is lower than the 5% average rate of return.

Yes. The difference between its annualized and its average rate of return is greater for a more volatile investment.

Q 7.5 The risk is usually increasing: lowest for cash, then bonds, then the stock market portfolio, and finally individual stocks. The average reward is increasing for the first three, but this is not necessarily true for an individual stock.

Q 7.6 Usually (but not always), individual stocks are riskier.

Q 7.7 Yes. For example, look at UAL in Exhibit 7.6. It lost everything but still had a positive average arithmetic rate of return.

Q 7.8 To graph the market beta, the rate of return on the market (e.g., the S&P 500) should be on the x-axis, and the rate of return on the investment for which you want to determine the market beta should be on the y-axis. A data point is the two rates of return from the same given time period (e.g., over a year). The market beta is the slope of the best-fitting line.

Q 7.9 The market beta of the market is 1—you are plotting the rate of return on the market on both the x-axis and the y-axis, so the beta is the slope of this 45° diagonal line.

Q 7.10 Brokers execute orders and keep track of investors' portfolios. They also facilitate purchasing on margin.

Q 7.11 Prime brokers are usually used by larger investors. Prime brokers allow investors to employ their own traders to execute trades. (Like retail brokers, prime brokers provide portfolio accounting, margin, and securities borrowing.)

Q 7.12 Your rate of return is higher if you short a stock in the perfect world because you earn interest on the proceeds. In the real world, your broker may help himself to this interest.

Q 7.13 A crossing system does not execute trades unless there is a counterparty. It also tries to cross orders a few times a day.

Q 7.14 The specialist is often a monopolist who makes the market on the NYSE. The specialist buys and sells from his own inventory of a stock, thereby "making a market." Market makers are the equivalent on NASDAQ, but there are usually many and they compete with one another. Unlike ordinary investors, both specialists and market makers can see the limit orders placed by other investors.

Q 7.15 The alternatives are often electronic, and they often rely on matching trades—thus, they may not execute trades that they cannot match. Electronic communication networks are the dominant example of these. Another alternative is to execute the trade in the over-the-counter (OTC) market, which is a network of geographically dispersed dealers who are making markets in various securities.

Q 7.16 In an open-ended fund, you should purchase fund shares and request redemption. (You could short the underlying holdings during the time you wait for the redemption in order not to suffer price risk.) In a closed-ended fund, you would have to oust the management to allow you to redeem your shares.

Q 7.17 It is not really a market, at all. Instead, it simply means that traders handle transactions on a one-on-one basis.

Q 7.18 UITs, open-end funds (mutual funds), and closed-end investment funds. In a perfect market, none is the best deal. You always get what you pay for.

Q 7.19 The main mechanisms by which money flows from investors into firms are first IPOs and SEOs, and second reverse mergers, which are then sold off to investors.

Q 7.20 Funds disappear from the public financial markets back into the pockets of investors through dividends and share repurchases.

Q 7.21 Shares can disappear in a delisting or a repurchase.

End of Chapter Problems

Q 7.22. Using the information in Exhibit 7.4, compute the discrepancy between arithmetic and geometric rates of return for cash and stocks. Which one is lower? Why?

Q 7.23. Broadly speaking, what was the average rate of return on cash, bonds, and stocks? What time period are your numbers from?

Q 7.24. Broadly speaking, what was the average risk of cash, bonds, and stocks? What time period are your numbers from?

Q 7.25. How good are historical statistics as indicators of future statistics? Which kinds of statistics are better? Which kinds are worse?

Q 7.26. Does the market beta of stocks in the market average out to zero?

Q 7.27. Give an example in which a stock had a positive average rate of return, even though it lost its investors' money.

Q 7.28. Looking at the figures in this chapter, did 20-year bonds move with or against the U.S. stock market? Did bonds move more or less with the U.S. stock market than the foreign stock, Sony?

Q 7.29. Do individual stocks tend to move together? How could this be measured?

Q 7.30. Explain the differences between a market order and a limit order.

Q 7.31. What extra function do retail brokers handle that prime brokers do not?

Q 7.32. Describe the differences between the NYSE and NASDAQ.

Q 7.33. Roughly, how many firms are listed on the NYSE? How many are listed on NASDAQ? Then use a financial website to find an estimate of the current number.

Q 7.34. Is NASDAQ a crossing market?

Q 7.35. What are the two main mechanisms by which a privately held company can go public?

Q 7.36. When and under what circumstance was the SEC founded?

Q 7.37. Insider trading is a criminal offense. Does the SEC prosecute these charges?

Q 7.38. What is the OTC market?

Q 7.39. If a firm repurchases 1% of its shares, does this change the capitalization of the stock market on which it lists? If a firm pays 1% of its value in dividends, does this change the capitalization of the stock market on which it lists?

Investor Choice: Risk and Reward

We are still after the same prize: a good estimate of the corporate cost of capital ($\mathcal{E}(r)$) in the NPV formula. But before you can understand the opportunity costs of capital for your firm's own projects, you have to understand your investors' other opportunities. This means that you must understand better what investors like (reward) and what they dislike (risk), how they are likely to measure their risks and rewards, how diversification works, what portfolios smart investors are likely to hold, and why it matters that "market beta" is a good measure of an investment asset's contribution to the market portfolio's risk.

8.1 Measuring Risk and Reward

Put yourself into the shoes of an investor and start with the most basic questions: How should you measure the risk and reward of your portfolio? As always, we first cook up a simple example and then generalize our insights into a broader real-world context. Say you are currently investing in an asset named *M*, short for "My Portfolio," but there are also other assets you could buy, named *A* through *C*, plus a risk-free asset named *F*. These assets could even be portfolios, themselves consisting of many individual assets, or even portfolios. (This is essentially what a mutual fund is.) So, let's just call M, A, B, C, and F themselves portfolios, too.

We work with five assets that have four equally likely outcomes.

We will work with four equally likely scenarios, named S1 through S4, as in Exhibit 8.1. Each gets a card deck suit to remind you that it is a random draw. (If you find it easier to think in terms of historical outcomes, you can pretend that you are analyzing historical data: scenario S1 happened at time 1, S2 at time 2, and so forth. This is not entirely correct, but it is often a helpful metaphor.) Which investment strategies do you deem better or worse, safer or riskier? If you can only buy these portfolios, what trade-offs of risk and reward are you facing?

Historical samples can be viewed as scenarios.

➤ *Why this is not entirely correct, Pg.196.*

If you like visuals, Exhibit 8.1 shows off these returns in graphic form, too. The middle figure is the standard histogram, which you have seen many times elsewhere. However, each scenario is equally likely (the bars are equally tall), so it's more visually obvious to just put the card suit symbols where the bar is. This is the lower figure. It makes it easier to compare many different investments.

Graphics version of the table.

In this plot, you prefer assets that have scenario outcomes farther to the right (they have higher returns), outcomes that are *on average* farther to the right (they have higher

In a histogram, bars to the right mean higher returns. Bars that are more spread out indicate higher risk.

	In S1 (♣)	In S2 (♦)	In S3 (♥)	In S4 (♠)	Reward $\mathcal{E}(r)$	Variance[a] $\mathcal{V}ar(r)$	Risk $\mathcal{S}dv(r)$
Investment M	–3%	3%	5%	11%	4%	25%%	5%
Investment A	3%	11%	–3%	5%	4%	25%%	5%
Investment B	5%	–1%	7%	13%	6%	25%%	5%
Investment C	17%	3%	11%	–7%	6%	81%%	9%
Investment F	1%	1%	1%	1%	1%	0%%	0%

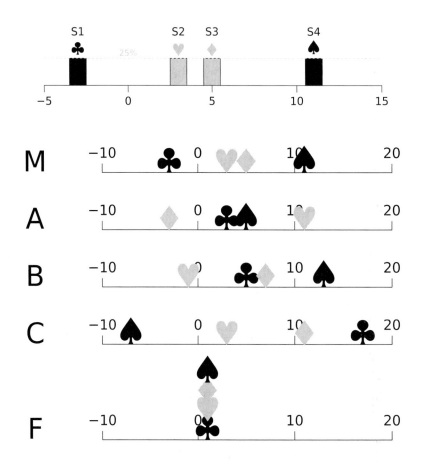

Exhibit 8.1: *Rates of Return on Five Investment Assets.* There are only four possible future scenarios, S1 through S4, each equally likely and indicated with a card suit. There are only 5 available investments (M, A, B, C, and F). (These could themselves be portfolios, of course.) The variance ($\mathcal{V}ar$) and standard deviation ($\mathcal{S}dv$) were explained in Section 6.1. The middle figure is a "traditional" histogram of M. The bottom figure contains the "condensed" histograms for all 5 assets.

Table note [a]: We use the '%%' notation only for variance computations. Just like '%' means 'divide by 100', '%%' means 'divide by 100 and then divide by 100 again', i.e., 'divide by 10,000'. This makes it easy to see that $\sqrt{(5\%)^2 + (5\%)^2 + (5\%)^2 + (5\%)^2}$ is $\sqrt{25\%\% + 25\%\% + 25\%\% + 25\%\%} = \sqrt{100\%\%} = 10\%$. If you find it easier to read $\sqrt{0.0025 + 0.0025 + 0.0025 + 0.0025} = 0.01 = 10\%$, then be my guest and use this notation instead. The answers are always the same.

expected rates of return), and outcomes that are more bunched together (they have less risk). Visual inspection confirms that investment F has outcomes perfectly bunched at the same spot, so it is not only least risky but also risk-free. It is followed by the risky M and A, then B, and finally, the riskiest investment, C.

> *Random variables* are *histograms, Pg. 116.*

Measuring Reward: The Expected Rate of Return

Although graphical measures are helpful, we really need formulas to give us numerical measures. A good measure for the **reward** is easy: You can use the **expected rate of return**, which is the probability-weighted average of all possible returns. For example, the mean rate of return for your portfolio M is

Measure reward with the expected rate of return.

$$\mathscr{E}(r_M) = (1/4) \cdot (-3\%) + (1/4) \cdot (+3\%) + (1/4) \cdot (+5\%) + (1/4) \cdot (+11\%) = +4\%$$

$$= \quad \text{Sum of (each probability times its outcome)}$$

If you invest in M, you would expect to earn a rate of return of 4%. Because each outcome is equally likely, you can compute this faster as a simple average, $\mathscr{E}(r_M) = [(-3\%) + (+3\%) + (+5\%) + (+11\%)]/4 = 4\%$.

Measuring Risk: The Standard Deviation of the Rate of Return

A good measure of risk is less obvious than a good measure of reward, but fortunately you already learned a good measure—the standard deviation—in Section 6.1. Let's compute it in the context of our assets. We first write down how far away each point is from the center (average). The average for M was +4%. An outcome of +3% would be closer to the mean than an outcome of –3%. The former is only 1 unit away from the mean. The latter is 7 units away from the mean.

Measure risk with the standard deviation of the rate of return.

> *The standard deviation (measure of risk), Sect. 6.1, Pg. 119.*

	In S1 (♣)	In S2 (♦)	In S3 (♥)	In S4 (♠)
Asset M Rate of Return	–3%	+3%	+5%	+11%
...in deviation from its 4% mean	–7%	–1%	1%	+7%

Unfortunately, you cannot compute risk as the average deviation from the mean, which is always zero ($[-7 + (-1) + 1 + 7]/4 = 0$). You must first "neutralize" the sign, so that negative deviations count the same as positive deviations. The "fix" is to compute the average *squared* deviation from the mean. This is the **variance**:

The average deviation from the mean is always 0. It cannot measure risk.

$$\mathscr{V}ar(r_M) = 1/4 \cdot (-3\% - 4\%)^2 + 1/4 \cdot (3\% - 4\%)^2 + 1/4 \cdot (5\% - 4\%)^2 + 1/4 \cdot (11\% - 4\%)^2$$

$$= \quad [(-7\%)^2 + (-1\%)^2 + (+1\%)^2 + (+7\%)^2]/4 = 25\%\% \quad (8.1)$$

$$= \quad \text{Sum of (each probability times its squared-deviation-from-the-mean)}$$

The variance has units that are intrinsically impossible to interpret by humans (% *squared* $= 0.01 \cdot 0.01$, written as x%%). Therefore, the variance carries very little intuition, except that more variance means more risk.

The measure that has more humanly-meaningful units is the **standard deviation**, which is just the square root of the variance:

The standard deviation of the portfolio's rate of return is a common measure of risk.

$$\mathcal{S}dv(r_M) = \sqrt{\mathcal{V}ar(r_M)} = \sqrt{25\%\%} = 5\% \qquad (8.2)$$

*The standard deviation of the portfolio's rate of return is the most common measure of overall **portfolio risk**.* Now look at Exhibit 8.1. You can see that this standard deviation of 5% seems like a reasonable measure of how far the typical outcome of M is away from the overall mean of M. (However, 5% is more than the average absolute deviation from the mean, which in this case would be 4%; the standard deviation puts more weight on far-away outcomes than the average absolute deviation.) The last column in Exhibit 8.1 lists the standard deviations of all investments. As the visuals indicate, F is risk-free; M, A, and B are equally risky at 5%; and C is riskiest at a whopping 9%.

IMPORTANT

- You can measure investment portfolio reward by the expected rate of return on the *overall* portfolio.

- You can measure investment portfolio risk by the standard deviation of the rate of return on the *overall* portfolio.

(Warning: You will not measure the investment risk *contributions* of individual assets *inside* a portfolio via their standard deviations. This will be explained in Section 8.3.)

A preview: Smart investors eliminate unnecessary risk. After they have done so, more reward requires taking more risk.

At this point, you should begin to wonder how risk and reward are related in a reasonable world. This will be the subject of much of the next chapter. The brief answer for now is that you can speculate in dumb ways that give you high investment risk with low reward—as anyone who has gambled knows. However, if you are smart, after eliminating all investment mistakes (the low-hanging fruit), you have no choice but to take on more risk if you want to earn higher rewards.

Q 8.1. What happens if you compute the average deviation from the mean, rather than the average squared deviation from the mean?

Q 8.2. Asset M from Exhibit 8.1 offers −3%, +3%, +5%, and +11% with equal probabilities. Now add 5% to each of these returns. This new asset offers +2%, +8%, +10%, and +16%. Compute the expected rate of return, the variance, and the standard deviation of this new asset. How does it compare to the original M?

Q 8.3. Confirm the risk and reward of C in Exhibit 8.1.

8.2 Diversification

In the real world, you are usually not constrained to purchase assets in isolation—you can purchase a little bit of many assets. This ability to purchase many assets has the important consequence of allowing you to reduce your overall portfolio risk. Let's go over this.

Many assets at the same time.

An Example Mixing Portfolio

Start again with your portfolio M. Now let's consider adding some of portfolio A. Why would you? It has the same risk and reward as M. However, although A has the same list of possible returns, it offers them in different scenarios. This will make all the difference. So, let's say you have $100 in M, but you now sell half of these holdings to buy A. You will have $50 in M and $50 in A. Let's call this investment portfolio MA. In this case, your $100 investment would look like this:

Portfolios are bundles of multiple assets. Their returns can be averaged.

	In S1 (♣)	In S2 (♦)	In S3 (♥)	In S4 (♠)	Average
Return on $50 in M:	$48.50	$51.50	$52.50	$55.50	$52.00
Return on $50 in A:	$51.50	$55.50	$48.50	$52.50	$52.00
⇒ Total return in MA:	$100.00	$107.00	$101.00	$108.00	$104.00
Rate of return in MA:	0%	7%	1%	8%	4%

You could have computed this more quickly by using the returns on M and A themselves. Your portfolio MA invests portfolio weight $w_M = 50\%$ into M and $w_A = 50\%$ in A. For example, to obtain the 7% in scenario S2, you could have computed the portfolio rate of return from M's 3% rate of return and A's 11% rate as

$$r_{MA} = r_{MA=50\% \text{ in } M, 50\% \text{ in } A \text{ (all in S2)}} = 50\% \cdot 3\% + 50\% \cdot 11\% = 7\%$$

$$r_{MA=(w_M, w_A) \text{ in S2}} = w_M \cdot r_{M \text{ in S2}} + w_A \cdot r_{A \text{ in S2}}$$

Now let's look at these three portfolios (M, A, and MA) in a histogram. Even better, because our histogram bars are all equally tall, we can omit the bars and plot just the symbols. As Exhibit 8.2 shows, the range of M is from –3% to +11%; the standard deviation is 5%. The range of A is also from –3% to +11%; the standard deviation is also 5%. Yet the average of M and A has a much lower range (0% to 8%) and a much lower standard deviation:

Visually, the M and A combination portfolio called MA has lower variability (risk and range) than either M or A.

$$\mathcal{V}ar_{\substack{50\% \text{ in } M \\ 50\% \text{ in } A}} = \frac{(0\% - 4\%)^2 + (7\% - 4\%)^2 + (1\% - 4\%)^2 + (8 - 4\%)^2}{4} = 12.5\%\%$$

$$= \frac{[r_{S1} - \mathcal{E}(r)]^2 + [r_{S2} - \mathcal{E}(r)]^2 + [r_{S3} - \mathcal{E}(r)]^2 + [r_{S4} - \mathcal{E}(r)]^2}{N}$$

$$\implies \mathcal{S}dv_{50\% \text{ in } M, \, 50\% \text{ in } A} = \sqrt{\mathcal{V}ar} = \sqrt{12.5\%\%} \approx 3.54\%$$

MA is simply less risky than either of its ingredients.

	In S1 (♣)	In S2 (♦)	In S3 (♥)	In S4 (♠)	Reward $\mathcal{E}(r)$	Variance $\mathcal{V}ar(r)$	Risk $\mathcal{S}dv(r)$
Investment M	–3%	3%	5%	11%	4%	25%%	5%
Investment A	3%	11%	–3%	5%	4%	25%%	5%
Portfolio MA	0%	7%	1%	8%	4%	12.5%%	3.54%

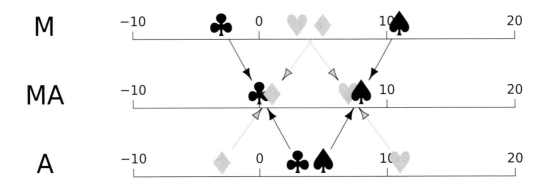

Exhibit 8.2: *Rate of return outcomes for M, A, and the (50%, 50%) combination portfolio MA.* Because each half-M/half-A point is halfway between M and A, MA has lower spread (risk) than either of its components, M and A, by itself.

This is caused by diversification.

The reason for this reduction in risk is **diversification**—the mixing of different investments within a portfolio that reduces the impact of each one on the overall portfolio performance. More simply put, diversification means that not all of your eggs are in the same basket. If one investment component goes down, the other investment component sometimes happens to go up, or vice versa. The imperfect correlation ("non-synchronicity") reduces the overall portfolio risk.

Q 8.4. The combination portfolio named MA invests 90% in M and 10% in A.

1. Compute its risk and reward.

2. In a plot similar to those in Exhibit 8.1, would this new MA portfolio look less spread out than the MA = (50%, 50%) portfolio that was worked out in the table in Exhibit 8.2?

How Risk Grows With Time

Before we continue, I need to cover two aspects that fit more into the subfield of investments than into the subfield of corporate finance. But both are important for a general competence in finance. We will only look at them in passing.

Brief important diversions.

The first diversion is about how risk grows with time. Trust me on the following: If two random draws are independent, then the sum of these two random variables has a variance that is the sum of the two variances.

If two variables are uncorrelated, the variance of the sum is the sum of the variances.

$$\mathcal{V}\!ar\big(X+Y\big) \;=\; \mathcal{V}\!ar\big(X\big) + \mathcal{V}\!ar\big(Y\big) \qquad \text{if X and Y are uncorrelated}$$

(This is not true if the two variables move together!) Why do you care? Well, the rates of return of any one asset in a perfect market should be uncorrelated over time—if not, you could earn an extra rate of return by trading this asset based on its own lagged return. (If the correlation were positive, you would get rich quick by buying the asset *after* it has gone up and selling it *after* it has gone down.)

Now let's use an approximation: Ignore compounding. This means that the total return is approximately the sum of the consecutive returns. Now, if you expect a stock to earn a 10% mean expected rate of return with a standard deviation of 20% over one year ($20\% \cdot 20\% = 400\%\%$ variance), then over two years, you expect the same stock to earn 20% with a variance of $400\%\% + 400\%\% = 800\%\%$. Thus, this stock's risk (standard deviation) is $\sqrt{800\%\%} \approx 28.28\%$. In other words, its mean goes up by a factor of 2, but its risk goes up only by a factor of $\sqrt{2} \approx 1.4$.

Stocks have uncorrelated returns. Thus, with time, the risk grows slower than the reward.

Q 8.5. Ignoring compounding:

1. What is the risk and reward of the "10% mean, 20% risk" investment in the text over 4 years? What is your risk-reward ratio? (This specific one is called the **Sharpe ratio**.)

2. What is the risk and reward of the 10% mean, 20% risk investment in the text over 9 years? What is the Sharpe ratio?

3. Can you guess what the risk and reward of a stock with annual mean $\mathcal{E}$ and risk $\mathcal{S}\!dv$ is over T years? What is the Sharpe ratio?

The Best Mixing Portfolio — The Efficient Frontier

The second diversion is not just about how you calculate the risk and reward of any given portfolio, but how the set of *best* possible portfolios looks like. And how well can your best portfolios do? The details of this question are covered better in this chapter's appendix (in the companion), but this section gives a basic flavor.

The best choice.

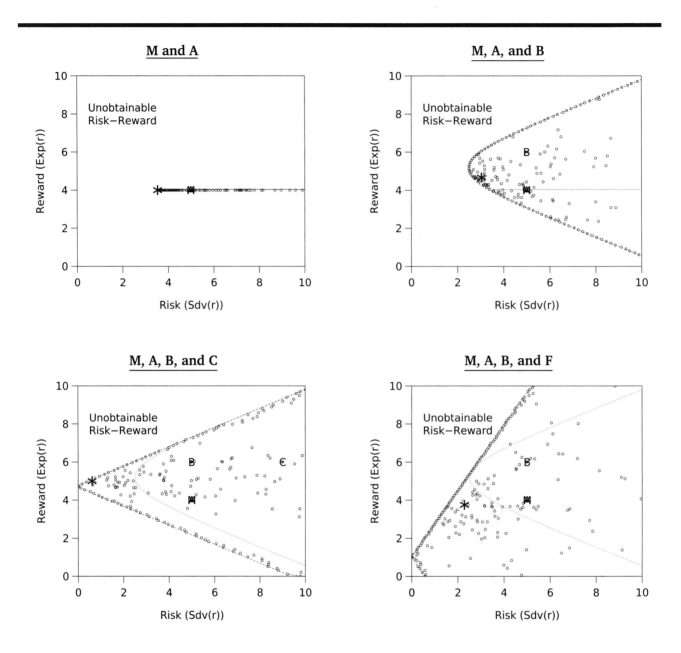

Exhibit 8.3: *The Efficient Frontier.* These plots show the mean and standard deviation of returns of portfolios composed of the stocks that are indicated in the header. (They appeared earlier, e.g., in Exhibit 8.1.) The '*' in the plots is the equal-weighted portfolio. The northwest border (dashed) is the efficient frontier. (Note that the two lower plots even allow you to invest money and earn a risk-free rate.) The dotted line is the frontier from a previous plot.

Exhibit 8.3 plots the investment performance (mean and standard deviation) of various portfolio combinations. In the top-left plot, you can only invest in M and A. They are both at the same spot in the plot. Because both have a 4% mean rate of return, any combination of them does, too. The best portfolio is the left-most one, which happens to be the equal-weighted combination. The top-right plot allows you to invest not only in M and A, but in B, too. You can see that B helps greatly, but not because you would purchase it by itself. In fact, B itself is far inside the northwest boundary—the **efficient frontier**—which is the lowest-risk highest-reward set of portfolios. (Its shape is always a hyperbola.) Presumably, smart investors would purchase only portfolios on this efficient frontier. Anything inside is worse. Anything beyond it is not obtainable. The equal-weighted portfolio is close to, but not on the efficient frontier. This is often the case for large diversified portfolios—the S&P 500 is reasonably close, but not exactly on the efficient frontier. The bottom-left plot allows you to invest in C, too. You can see how this expands the efficient frontier even further. In fact, it is now possible to create a risk-free asset with a rate of return of about 3.6% by cleverly combining investments. (Not that clever—invest about 0.377 in M, 0.261 in A, 0.091 in B, and 0.272 in C.) But even if you do not want to play it safe, you can always do at least as well with more assets than with fewer, so your efficient frontier has been pushed out further. The bottom-right plot shows your possible investments if instead of access to C, you had access to F. In both bottom figures, in which there is a risk-free asset, the efficient frontier is a line.

> More assets expand your opportunity set. The best investment choices are on the "efficient frontier."

Q 8.6. How would the efficient frontier look like if you were allowed to invest in all 5 assets, M, A, B, C, and F?

8.3 Investor Preferences and Risk Contribution

You now understand that diversification can reduce risk. You still need to understand what projects the investors in your corporation—remember, this is *corporate finance*—would like you to invest in on their behalves.

> The main question.

Assume Investors Care Only about Risk and Reward

Your intuition should now tell you that well-diversified portfolios—portfolios that invest in many different assets—tend to have lower risk. As a corporate manager, it would be reasonable for you to assume that your investors are smart. Because diversification helps investors reduce risk, you can also reasonably believe that they are indeed holding well-diversified portfolios. The most well-diversified portfolio may well contain a little bit of every possible asset under the sun. Therefore, like most corporate executives, you would probably assume that your investors' portfolios are typically the overall **market portfolio**, consisting of all available investment opportunities.

> Investors love diversification: the more the better. They could like the market portfolio because it is highly diversified.

Why would you even want to make any assumptions about your investors' portfolios? The answer is that if you are willing to assume that your investors are holding the market (or something very similar to it), your job as a corporate manager becomes much easier.

> If your investors like high reward and low risk and hold the market portfolio, you can work out how your projects affect them.

Instead of asking what each and every one of your investors might possibly like, you can just ask, "When would my investors want to give me their money for investment into my firm's project, given that my investors are currently already holding the broad overall stock market portfolio?" The answer will be as follows:

1. Your investors should like projects that offer more reward—this means higher expected rates of return.

2. Your investors should like projects that help them diversify away some of the risk in the market portfolio, so that their *overall* portfolios end up being less risky. Be careful, though. This does not mean always going for the lowest-risk projects. Instead, you will learn next that this means going for projects that behave very differently from other projects—unusual ones.

In sum, your corporate managerial task is to take those projects that your investors would like to add to their current (market) portfolios. You should therefore search for projects that have high expected rates of return and high diversification benefits with respect to the market. Let's now turn toward measuring this second characteristic: How can your projects aid your investors' diversification, and how should you measure how good this diversification is?

IMPORTANT

> - Diversification is based on imperfect correlation, or "non-synchronicity," among investments. It helps smart investors reduce the overall portfolio risk.
>
> - Therefore, as a corporate manager, in the absence of contradictory intelligence, you should believe that your investors tend to hold diversified portfolios. They could even hold portfolios as heavily diversified as the "entire market portfolio."
>
> - As a corporate manager, your task is to think about how a little of your project can aid your investors in terms of its contribution to the risk and reward of their heavily diversified overall portfolios. (You should not think about how risky your project is in itself.)

Assume that investors hold the overall market. Now what?

If we are willing to assume that our smart investors are holding all assets in the market, then what projects offer them the best diversification?

Asset Own Risk ($\mathscr{S}dv$) and Portfolio Risk Contribution

Comovement determines risk contribution.

Obviously, diversification does *not* help if two investment opportunities always move in the same direction. For example, if you try to diversify one $50 investment in M with another $50 investment in M (which always has the same outcomes), then your risk does not decrease. On the other hand, if two investment opportunities always move in *opposite* directions, then diversification works extremely well: One is a buffer for the other.

Pretend M is not just "My portfolio," but the market.

Let's formalize this intuition. For explanation's sake, assume that "My Portfolio" M is also the market portfolio.

Is B or C a better addition to your M portfolio?

Assume that B and C are two projects that your firm could invest in, but you cannot choose both. Both offer the same expected rate of return (6%), but B has lower risk

(5%) than C (9%). As a manager, would you therefore assume that project B is better for your investors than C?

	In S1 (♣)	In S2 (♦)	In S3 (♥)	In S4 (♠)	Reward $\mathcal{E}(r)$	Variance $\mathcal{V}ar(r)$	Risk $\mathcal{S}dv(r)$
Investment M	−3%	3%	5%	11%	4%	25%%	5%
Investment B	5%	−1%	7%	13%	6%	25%%	5%
Investment C	17%	3%	11%	−7%	6%	81%%	9%
Portfolio MB	1%	1%	6%	12%	5%	20.5%%	4.5%
Portfolio MC	7%	3%	8%	2%	5%	6.5%%	2.6%

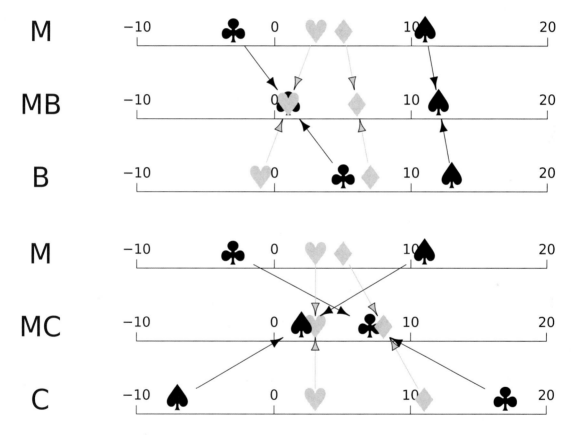

Exhibit 8.4: *Combining the Market M with Either B or C.* Although C is riskier than B by itself (look at C's one disaster outcome!), C is much better than B in reducing risk when it is added to the market portfolio M. This is because C tends to move opposite to M, especially if M turns in its worst outcome (−3%).

The combination MC has almost the same risk as M.

The answer is no. Let's assume that your investors start out with the market portfolio, M. Exhibit 8.4 shows what happens if they sell half of their portfolios to invest in either B or C. You can call these two (50,50) portfolios MB and MC, respectively. Start with MB. If your investors reallocate half their money from M into B, their portfolios would have the following rates of return:

	in S1 (♣)	in S2 (♦)	in S3 (♥)	in S4 (♠)	Reward	Risk
MB	1%	1%	6%	12%	5%	4.5%

The upper graph in Exhibit 8.4 plots the MB rates of return, plus the rates of return for both M and B by themselves. The averages are all close to both original rates of return. There is not much change in the risk of your portfolio in moving from a pure M portfolio to the MB portfolio. The risk shrinks slightly, from 5.0% to 4.5%.

The combination MC has much lower risk than M.

Now consider the combination of MC, which is the lower graph in Exhibit 8.4. By itself, C is a very risky investment (9% risk). It also has the single-worst outcome of any investment you have seen so far. However, if your investors instead reallocate half of their wealth from M into C, their overall portfolio would have the following rates of return:

	in S1 (♣)	in S2 (♦)	in S3 (♥)	in S4 (♠)	Reward	Risk
MC	7%	3%	8%	2%	5%	2.6%

The risk is much lower! Look again at the exhibit—the MC outcomes are bunched much more closely than either M or C alone. And MB, too, has a much wider range than the MC portfolio. The MC combination portfolio is simply much safer—even though C by itself is much riskier. In sum:

Portfolio	Reward	Risk	Note
M (=M) alone	4%	5.0%	Your investors' (market) portfolios
B alone	6%	5.0%	
C alone	6%	9.0%	C is riskier than B, if purchased by itself.
MB: half M, half B	5%	4.2%	Portfolio risk decreases less if B is added
MC: half M, half C	5%	2.6%	to M than when C is added to M!

The implication for your project choices as a corporate manager: Everything else equal, C could better reduce portfolio risk for your investors despite its higher own risk.

You now know that C's own high standard deviation compared to B's is not a good indication of whether C helps your investors reduce portfolio risk more or less than B. If your investors are primarily holding M, then a very risky project like C can allow them to build lower-risk portfolios. However, if your investors are not holding any assets other than C, they would not care about C's diversification benefits and only about its own risk. Thus, as a manager, you cannot determine whether your investors would prefer you to invest in B or C unless you know their entire portfolios. (Moreover, it could also depend on how your investors would like you to trade off more overall reward against more overall risk.)

<table>
<tr><td>A project's (own) standard deviation is not necessarily a good measure of how it influences the risk of your investors' portfolios. Indeed, it is possible that a project with a very high standard deviation by itself may actually help lower an investor's overall portfolio risk.</td></tr>
</table>

IMPORTANT

Q 8.7. Confirm the risk and reward calculations for the MB and MC portfolios in the table under Exhibit 8.4.

Asset Beta and Portfolio Risk Contribution

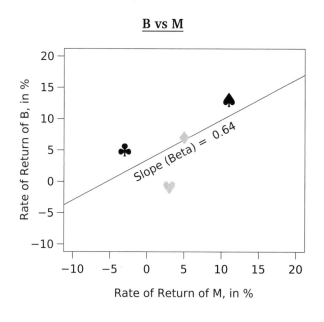
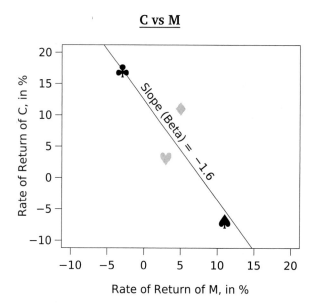

Exhibit 8.5: *Possible Outcomes: Rates of Return of C and D versus Rate of Return of M.* The four data points in each plot are taken from Exhibit 8.1 on page 178. They are the rates of return on the portfolios M, B, and C, quoted in percent. In the example, you know that these are the four true possible outcomes. In the real world, if the four points were not the true known outcomes, but just the historical outcomes (sample points), then the slope would not be the true unknown beta, but only the "estimated" beta.

C reduces M's risk because it tends to move in the opposite direction.

Why is the portfolio C so much better than portfolio B in reducing the overall risk when held in combination with the M portfolio? The reason is that C tends to go up when M tends to go down, and vice versa. The same cannot be said for B—it tends to move together with M. You could call this "synchronicity" or "comovement." It is why B does not help investors who are heavily invested in the overall market in their quests to reduce their portfolio risks.

Comovement can be measured by a line slope (beta). We want the M-beta, which means the asset's rate of return is on the y-axis and M's rate of return on the x-axis.

Exhibit 8.5 shows the comovement graphically. The rate of return on the market is on the x-axis; the rate of return on the asset is on the y-axis. Its slope is called the **market beta**. (It is common to write the formula for a line as $y = \alpha + \beta \cdot x$, which is where the Greek letter beta comes from.) A beta of 1 is a 45° diagonal line; a beta of 0 is a horizontal line. A positive beta slopes up; a negative beta slopes down. In statistics, you should have learned that you can find the beta by running a linear regression. If you don't remember, no worries: In Section 8.3, I will teach you again how to compute the beta. For now, take my word that the two best lines are

$$r_B \approx 3.4\% + (+0.64) \cdot r_M \tag{8.3}$$

$$r_C \approx 12.4\% + (-1.60) \cdot r_M$$

$$r_i = \alpha_{i,M} + \beta_{i,M} \cdot r_M$$

This formula is sometimes called the **market model**. The subscripts on the betas remind you what the variables on the x-axis and the y-axis are. The first subscript is always the variable on the y-axis, the second is the variable on the x-axis. Thus, $\beta_{B,M} \approx 0.64$ and $\beta_{C,M} \approx -1.60$. Market beta plays such an important role in finance that the name "beta" has itself become synonymous for "market beta," and the second subscript is usually omitted.

Market beta is a big deal in finance. It measures how your project covaries with the market.

The market model is the line that we care about in finance. As a corporate manager, you want to know how the rate of return on your own project comoves with that of the market. This is because you typically posit that your smart investors are on average holding the market portfolio. The best-fitting line between M and B slopes up. (It is also the same kind of line that you already saw in Section 7.1.) The positive slope means that B tends to be higher when M is higher. In contrast, the best-fitting line between M and C slopes down. The negative slope means that C tends to be lower when M is higher (and vice versa). Again, this market slope is a common measure of expected comovement or countermovement—how much diversification benefit an investor can obtain from adding a particular new project. A higher slope means more comovement and less diversification; a lower, or even negative, slope means less comovement and more diversification.

➤ Market beta of PepsiCo, Sect. 7.1, Pg. 161.

IMPORTANT

- Diversification works better if the new investment project tends to move in the opposite direction of the rest of the portfolio than if it tends to move in the same direction.

- It is often reasonable to assume that smart investors are already holding the market portfolio and are now considering investing into just a little of one additional asset—your firm's new project.

- If this new investment asset has a negative beta with respect to the market (its "market beta"), it means that it tends to go down when the market goes up, and vice versa. If this new investment asset has a positive beta with respect to the market, it means that it tends to move together with the market. If this new investment asset has a zero beta with respect to the market, it means that it moves independently of the market for all practical purposes.

- The market beta is a good measure of an investment asset's risk contribution for an investor who holds the market portfolio. The lower (or negative) the market beta, the more this investment helps reduce your investor's risk.

- The market beta of an asset can be interpreted as a line slope, where the rate of return on the market is on the x-axis and the rate of return on the new asset is on the y-axis. The line states how you expect the new asset to perform as a function of how the market will perform.

- You can think of market beta as a measure of "toxicity." In a reasonable equilibrium, holding everything else constant, risk-averse investors who are holding the market portfolio would agree to pay more for assets that have lower market betas. They would pay less for assets with higher market betas.

Before we conclude, some caveats are in order. From your perspective as the manager of a company, perhaps a publicly traded one, it is reasonable to assume that your investors are holding the market portfolio. It is also reasonable to assume that your new project is just a tiny new additional component of your investors' overall portfolios. We will staunchly maintain these assumptions, but you should be aware that they may not always be appropriate. If your investors are *not* holding something close to the market portfolio, then your project's market beta would *not* be a good measure of your projects' risk contributions. In the extreme, if your investors are holding *only* your project, market beta would not measure the project's risk contribution at all. This is often the case for entrepreneurs. They often have no choice but to put all their money into one egg in one basket. Such investors care only about the project's standard deviation, not the project's market beta.

Warning: All of this beta-related risk measuring is interesting only if your investors are holding (portfolios close to) the overall market.

When Beta? When Standard Deviation?

Do you care about your portfolio's beta or your portfolio's standard deviation? As CFO, do you care about your firm's beta or your firm's standard deviation? Make sure you understand the answer to these questions.

IMPORTANT

- As an investor, you usually care only about your portfolio's standard deviation (risk), and not about the risk of its individual ingredients.

- Typically, you do not care about the overall market beta of your portfolio. (The individual market-betas can help you design your overall portfolio.)

> • If you are the CFO of a firm that wants to get into the market portfolio, so that investors willingly buy your shares, then you should care about your own firm's market beta.
>
> • If you act purely in the interest of your diversified investors, you should not care about your firm's own standard deviation. Your investors can diversify away your firm's idiosyncratic risk. (If you care about your job or bonus, you might however take a different attitude towards risk. This is the subject of Chapter 24 (Companion).)

Portfolio Alpha

Alpha has meaning, too, even though you won't use it just yet.

Although we shall not use it further in this book, the alpha intercept in Formula 8.3 also plays an important role. Together, alpha and beta help determine how attractive an investment is. For example, if the rate of return on the market will be 10%, Formula 8.3 tells you that you would expect the rate of return on C to be

$$\mathscr{E}\left(r_C \mid \text{if } r_M = 10\%\right) \approx 12.4\% + (-1.60) \cdot 10\% \approx -3.6\%$$

The higher the alpha, the better the average performance of your investment given any particular rate of return on the market. Just as investment professionals often call the market beta just beta, they often call this specific intercept (here 12.4%) just alpha. (There is one small complication: They usually subtract the risk-free interest rate first from both r_C and r_M in their regressions. This usually does not make much difference.)

Computing Market Betas from Historical Rates of Return

➤ *Base Investment Assets, Exhibit 8.1, Pg. 178.*

You can compute the best-fit beta via a 4-step procedure.

So how can you actually compute beta? Let's return to the assets in Exhibit 8.1. What is the market beta of C? I have already told you that this slope is –1.6. To calculate it, I followed a tedious, but not mysterious, recipe. Here is what you have to do:

First, de-mean each rate of return. (How demeaning!)

➤ *Variance calculations, Sect. 6.1, Pg. 119.*

1. Just as you did for your variance calculations, first translate all returns into deviations from the mean. That is, for M and C, subtract their own means from every realization.

	In S1 (♣)	In S2 (♦)	In S3 (♥)	In S4 (♠)
Asset M Rate of Return	–3%	+3%	+5%	+11%
...in deviation from 4% mean	–7%	–1%	+1%	+7%
Asset C Rate of Return	+17%	+3%	+11%	–7%
...in deviation from 6% mean	+11%	–3%	+5%	–13%

➤ *Variance of M, Formula 8.1, Pg. 179.*

2. Compute the variance of the series on the X-axis. This is the variance of the rates of return on M. You have already done this in Formula 8.1: $\mathcal{V}ar(r_M) = 25\%\%$.

3. Now compute the probability-weighted average of the products of the two net-of-mean variables. In this case,

For covariances, multiply net-of-mean returns, then average.

$$\mathcal{C}ov(r_M, r_C) \quad = \quad \tfrac{1}{4} \cdot (-7\%) \cdot (+11\%) + \tfrac{1}{4} \cdot (-1\%) \cdot (-3\%) \tag{8.4}$$

$$+ \tfrac{1}{4} \cdot (+1\%) \cdot (+5\%) + \tfrac{1}{4} \cdot (+7\%) \cdot (-13\%) \quad = -40\%\%$$

$$= \text{Sum of (each probability times the returns' products)}$$

This statistic is called the **covariance**, here between the rates of return on M and C.

4. The beta of C with respect to the market M, formally $\beta_{C,M}$ but often abbreviated as β_C, is the ratio of these two quantities,

The beta is the covariance divided by the variance.

$$\beta_C \; = \; \beta_{C,M} \; = \; \frac{-40\%\%}{25\%\%} \quad \approx -1.6 \tag{8.5}$$

$$= \; \frac{\mathcal{C}ov(r_M, r_C)}{\mathcal{V}ar(r_M)}$$

This slope of -1.6 is exactly the market beta we drew in Exhibit 8.5. Many spreadsheets and all statistical programs can compute it for you: They call the routine that does this a **linear regression**.

You can confirm our calculations using a spreadsheet.

You should always think of an asset's beta with respect to a portfolio as a characteristic measure of your asset relative to an underlying base portfolio. The rate of return on portfolio P is on the x-axis; the rate of return on asset i is on the y-axis. As we stated earlier, most often—but not always—the portfolio P is the market portfolio, M, so $\beta_{i,M}$ is often just called the market beta of i, or just the beta of i (and the second subscript is omitted).

Think of market beta as the characteristic of an asset.

Now think for a moment. What is the average beta of a stock in the economy? Equivalently, what is the beta of the market portfolio? Replace C in Formula 8.5 with M:

The average beta of the market (all stocks) is 1, not 0.

$$\beta_M \; = \; \frac{\mathcal{C}ov(r_M, r_M)}{\mathcal{V}ar(r_M)}$$

If you look at the definition of covariance, you can see that the covariance of a variable with itself *is* the variance. (The covariance is a generalization of the variance concept from one to two variables.) Therefore, $\mathcal{C}ov(r_M, r_M) = \mathcal{V}ar(r_M)$, and the market beta of the market itself is 1. Graphically, if both the x-axis and the y-axis are plotting the same values, every point must lie on the diagonal. Economically, this should not be surprising, either: the market goes up one-to-one with the market.

Now that you know how to compute betas and covariances, you can consider scenarios for your project. For example, you might have a new project for which you would guess that it will have a rate of return of -5% if the market returns -10%; a rate of return of $+5\%$ if the market returns $+5\%$; and a rate of return of 30% if the market returns 10%. Knowing how to compute a market beta therefore makes it useful to think of such scenarios. (You can also use this technique to explore the relationship between your projects and some other factors. For example, you could determine how your projects covary with the price of oil to learn about your project's oil risk exposure.)

Why torture you with computations? So you can play with scenarios.

➤ An oil-price beta, Sect. App.9.C (Companion), Pg.≈61.

Real-World Market-Beta Estimation

Practical advice to help you estimate market beta in the real world: Use 3-5 years of daily observations and then adjust.

In the real world, you will sometimes think in terms of such scenarios. However, you will more often have to compute a market beta from historical rates of return, using overall stock market returns and your own project (or similar project) returns. Fortunately, as we noted up-front, the beta computations themselves are exactly the same. In effect, when you use historical data, you simply assume that each time period was one representative scenario and proceed from there. Nevertheless, there are some real-world complications you should think about:

1. Should you use daily, weekly, monthly, or annual rates of return? The answer is that the best market beta estimates come from daily or weekly data. Annual data should be avoided (except in a textbook in which space is limited). Monthly data can be used if need be.

2. How much data should you use? Most researchers tend to use three to five years of historical rate of return data. This reflects a trade-off between having enough data and not going too far back into ancient history, which may be less relevant. If you have daily data, three years works quite well.

3. Is the historical beta a good estimate of the future beta? It turns out that history can sometimes be deceptive, especially if your estimated historical beta is far away from the market's beta average of 1. Fortunately, there are at least two methods to help adjust historical betas so that you get better estimates of future betas:

   a) **Averaging:** You could rely not just on the historical beta computed from your own project's returns. Instead, you could use the average historical betas for many other projects that are similar to your own (for example, projects from the same industry or in the same size class). Such averages are usually less noisy.

   b) **Shrinking:** You could "shrink" your historical beta toward the overall market beta of 1. For example, in the simplest such shrinker, you would simply compute an average of the overall market beta of 1 and your historical market beta estimate. If you computed a historical market beta of 4 for your project, you would work with a prediction of future market beta of about $(4+1)/2 = 2.5$ for your project.

Many smart executives start with a statistical beta estimated from historical data (or they just look up the statistical beta on a website, such as **YAHOO!** FINANCE [finance.yahoo.com]) and then use their intuitive judgment to adjust it.

Q 8.8. Return to your computation of market beta of −1.6 in Formula 8.5. We called it $\beta_{C,M}$, or β_C for short. Is the order of the subscripts important? That is, is $\beta_{M,C}$ also −1.6?

Why Not Correlation or Covariance?

There is a close family relationship between covariance, beta, and correlation. The beta is the covariance divided by one of the variances. The correlation is the covariance divided by both standard deviations. The denominators are always positive. Thus, if the covariance is positive, so are the beta and the correlation; if the covariance is negative, so are the beta and the correlation; and if the covariance is zero, so are the beta and the correlation. The nice thing about the correlation, which makes it useful in many contexts outside finance, is that it has no scale and is always between −100% and +100%:

Covariance and beta (and correlation) always have the same sign.

- Two variables that always move perfectly in the same direction have a correlation of 100%.

- Two variables that always move perfectly in opposite directions have a correlation of −100%.

- Two variables that are independent have a correlation of 0%.

This makes correlations very easy to interpret. The not-so-nice thing about correlation is that it has no scale and is always between −100% and +100%. This means that two investments, the second being a million times bigger than the first (all project rates of return multiplied by a million), have the same correlation with the stock market. Yet, the second investment would go up or down with any slight tremor in the market by a million times more, which would of course mean that it would contribute much more risk. The correlation ignores this, which disqualifies it as a serious candidate for a project risk measure. Fortunately, beta takes care of scale—indeed, the beta for the second project would be a million times larger. This is why we prefer beta over correlation as a measure of risk contribution to a portfolio.

Spreadsheet Functions To Calculate Risk and Reward

Doing all these calculations by hand is tedious. We computed these statistics within the context of just four scenarios, so that you would understand the meanings of the calculations better. However, you can do this a lot faster in the real world. Usually, you would download reams of real historical rates of return data into a computer spreadsheet, like Excel or OpenOffice. Spreadsheets have all the functions you need already built in—and you now understand what their functions actually calculate. In practice, you would use the following functions in Excel:

In real life, you can do calculations faster with a spreadsheet.

average computes the average (rate of return) over a range of cells.

varp (or **var.p**) computes the (population) variance. If you worked with historical data instead of known scenarios, you would instead use the **var** (or **var.s**) function. (The latter divides by $N - 1$ rather than by N, which I will explain in a moment.)

stdevp (or **stdev.p**) computes the (population) standard deviation. If you used historical data instead of known scenarios, you would instead use the **stdev** (or **stdev.s**) function.

covar computes the population covariance between two series. (If Excel was consistent, this function should be called covarp rather than covar.) Unlike the earlier functions, this and the next two functions require two data cell ranges, not one.

correl computes the correlation between two series.

slope computes a beta. If *range-Y* contains the rates of return of an investment and *range-X* contains the rates of return on the market, then this function computes the market beta.

Statistical Nuances (Nuisances)

Is history a good guide?

➤ *Will history repeat itself?*, *Sect. 7.1*, *Pg. 164*.

In this chapter, we have continued to presume (just as we did in Section 7.1) that historical data gives us an unbiased guide to the future when it comes to means, variances, covariances, and betas. Of course, this is a simplification—and remember that it can be a problematic one. I already noted that this is less of a problem for covariances, variances, and betas than it is for means. Rely on historical means as predictors of future expected rates of return only at your own risk!

When working with a *sample*, the (co)variance formula divides by $N-1$. When working with the *population*, the (co)variance formula divides by N.

There is a second, smaller statistical issue of which you should be aware. Statisticians often use a covariance formula that divides by $N-1$, not N. Strictly speaking, dividing by $N-1$ is appropriate if you work with historical data. These are just sample draws and not the full population of possible outcomes. With a sample, you do not really know the true mean when you de-mean your observations. The division by a smaller number, $N-1$, gives a larger but unbiased covariance estimate. It is also often called the *sample covariance*. In contrast, dividing by N is appropriate if you work with "scenarios" that you know to be true and equally likely. In this case, the statistic is often called the *population covariance*. The difference rarely matters in finance, where you usually have a lot of observations—except in our book examples where you have only four scenarios. (For example, dividing by $N = 1,000$ and by $N = 1,001$ gives almost the same number.)

This is important to keep in mind if you use a spreadsheet to check your work.

The only reason why you even needed to know this is that if you use a program that has a built-in variance or standard deviation function, you should not be surprised if you get numbers different from those that you have computed in this chapter. In some programs, you can get both functions. In Excel, you can use the *varp* and *stdevp* population statistical functions to get the population statistics, not the *var* and *stdev* functions that would give you the sample statistics.

For market beta, the divisor cancels out and does not matter.

Beta is not affected by whether you divide the variance/covariance by N or $N-1$, because both numerator (covariance) and denominator (variance) are divided by the same number.

My fault: Our notation should have distinguished between true population and estimated sample statistics.

Furthermore, statisticians distinguish between underlying unknown statistics and statistics estimated from the data. For example, they might call the unknown true mean μ and the sample mean m (or $\bar{x}$). They might call the unknown true beta β^T and the estimated sample beta a beta with a little hat ($\hat{\beta}$). And so on. Our book is casual about the difference due to lack of space, but keep in mind that whenever you work with historical data, you are really just working with sample estimates.

8.4 Interpreting Some Typical Stock Market Betas

The market beta is the best measure of "diversification help" for an investor who holds the stock market portfolio and considers adding *just a little* of your firm's project. From your perspective as a manager seeking to attract investors, this is not a perfect, necessarily true assumption—but it is a reasonable one. Recall that we assume that investors are smart, so presumably they are holding highly diversified portfolios. To convince your market investors to like your $10 million project, you just need the average investor to want to buy $10 million divided by about $20 trillion (the stock market capitalization), which is 1/2,000,000 of their portfolios. For your investors, your corporate projects are just tiny additions to their market portfolios.

> Market beta works well when investors are holding the market and adding only a little of your project.

Company	Ticker	Cap[a]	Market Beta Yahoo	Market Beta Google	Company	Ticker	Cap[a]	Market Beta Yahoo	Market Beta Google
AMD	AMD	6	2.31	2.16	Boeing	BA	59	1.29	1.26
Coca-Cola	KO	154	0.60	0.59	Intel	INTC	126	1.07	1.13
Citigroup	C	129	2.62	2.52	PepsiCo	PEP	111	0.55	0.54
Goldman Sachs	GS	82	1.17	1.35	J.P. Morgan	JPM	180	1.17	1.14
IBM	IBM	206	0.72	0.73	Morgan Stanley	MS	39	1.23	1.34
Dell	DELL	31	1.41	1.42	Hewlett-Packard	HPQ	90	1.00	1.01
Apple Inc	AAPL	323	1.14	1.36	Sony	SNE	29	1.49	1.42
Google	GOOG	174	0.93	1.17	Yahoo	YHOO	24	0.93	0.88
Ford	F	57	2.40	2.37	General Motors	GM	47	NA	NA
Amer Airlines	AMR	2	1.47	1.45	Southwest	LUV	9.1	1.24	1.07
Exxon Mobil	XOM	411	0.41	0.49	Barrick Gold	ABX	48	0.53	0.40
Philip Morris	PM	122	0.85	0.85	Procter&Gamble	PG	183	0.52	0.53

Exhibit 8.6: *Some Market Betas and Market Capitalizations on May 11, 2011.* Table note [a]: "Cap" is the equity market value in billions of dollars. Yahoo explained its betas as follows: *The Beta is beta of equity. Beta is the monthly price change of a particular company relative to the monthly price change of the S&P 500. The time period for Beta is 5 years when available, and not less than 2.5 years. This value is updated monthly.* Note that **YAHOO!** FINANCE seems to ignore dividends, but this usually makes little difference. I could not find an explanation for the market betas provided by Google.

You can look up the market betas of publicly traded stocks on many financial websites. Exhibit 8.6 lists the betas of some randomly chosen companies in May 2011 from **YAHOO!** FINANCE and from Google's finance site. Most company betas are in the range of around 0 to about 2.5. A beta above 1 is considered risk-increasing for an investor holding the overall stock market (it is riskier than the stock market itself), while a beta below 1 is considered risk-reducing. Betas that are negative are quite rare. Gold is an asset that usually has a negative market-beta, but even Barrick Gold, whose

> Most financial websites publish market beta estimates.

fortunes are closely tied to the value of gold, did not have a negative beta in May 2011.

Beta can be viewed as the marginal change of your project with respect to the market.

Market beta has yet another nice intuitive interpretation: It is the degree to which the firm's value tends to change if the stock market changes. For example, Dell's market beta of approximately 1.4 says that if the stock market will return an extra 10% next year (above and beyond its expectations), Dell's stock will likely return an extra $1.4 \cdot 10\% = 14\%$ (above and beyond Dell's expectations). Of course, market beta is not a measure of how good an investment Dell is. (This measure is the aforementioned alpha

➤ Alpha, Pg. 192.

[which can be interpreted as an expected rate of return]. In the next section, you will learn a model that relates market beta to the expected rate of return by giving you a formula for alpha.) For now, let's say that the expected rate of return on the market is 7% and the expected rate of return on Dell is 9%. Then, if the market were to turn in –3% (10% less than its average), you would expect Dell to turn in $9\% + 1.4 \cdot (-10\%) = -5\%$. Conversely, if the market were to turn in 17% (10% more than its average), you would expect Dell to turn in $9\% + 1.4 \cdot (10\%) = 23\%$. Dell's high market beta is useful because it informs you that if you hold the stock market, adding Dell stock would not help you very much with diversifying your market risk. Holding Dell would amplify any market swings, not reduce them. But in any case, Dell's market beta does not tell you whether Dell is priced too high or too low on average, so that you should buy or avoid it in the first place.

Q 8.9. You estimate your project x to return –5% if the stock market returns –10%, and +5% if the stock market returns +10%. What would you use as the market beta estimate for your project?

Q 8.10. You estimate your project y to return +5% if the stock market returns –10%, and –5% if the stock market returns +10%. What would you use as the market beta estimate for your project?

8.5 Market Betas for Portfolios and Conglomerate Firms

Portfolios consist of multiple assets (themselves possibly portfolios). Definitions of value-weighted and equal-weighted portfolios.

Let's go back to your managerial perspective of figuring out the risk and return of your corporate projects. Many small projects are bundled together, so it is very common for managers to consider multiple projects already packaged together as one portfolio. For example, you can think of your firm as a collection of divisions that have been packaged together. If division B is worth $1 million and division C is worth $2 million, then a firm consisting of B and C is worth $3 million. B constitutes $1/3$ of the portfolio "Firm" and C constitutes $2/3$ of the portfolio "Firm." This kind of portfolio is called a **value-weighted portfolio** because the weights correspond to the market values of the components. (A portfolio that invests $100 in B and $200 in C would also be value-weighted. A portfolio that invests equal amounts in the constituents (for example, $500 in each) is called an **equal-weighted portfolio**.)

Thus, as a manager, you have to know how to work with a portfolio (firm) when you have all the information about all of its underlying component stocks (projects). If I tell you the expected rate of return and market beta of each project, can you tell me what the overall expected rate of return and overall market beta of your firm are? Let's try it. Use the B and C stocks from Exhibit 8.1 on Page 178, and call BCC the portfolio (or firm) that consists of $1/3$ investment in division B and $2/3$ investment in division C.

What are the expected rate of return and market beta of a portfolio?

Actually you already know that you can compute the returns in each scenario, and then the risk and reward.

You can average *actual* rates of return.

	In S1 (♣)	In S2 (♦)	In S3 (♥)	In S4 (♠)	Reward $\mathcal{E}(r)$	Variance[a] $\mathcal{V}\!ar(r)$	Risk $\mathcal{S}\!dv(r)$
Investment B	5%	−1%	7%	13%	6%	25%%	5%
Investment C	17%	3%	11%	−7%	6%	81%%	9%
Portfolio BCC	13%	1.67%	9.67%	−0.33%	6%	≈30%%	≈5.5%

It is also intuitive that *expected* rates of return can be averaged. In our example, B has an *expected* rate of return of 6%, and C has an *expected* rate of return of 6%. Consequently, your overall firm BCC has an expected rate of return of 6%, too. Check this.

You can average *expected* rates of return.

Unfortunately, you cannot compute value-weighted averages for all statistics. As the table shows, variances and standard deviations cannot be averaged ($1/3 \cdot 25\%\% + 2/3 \cdot 81\%\% \approx 62.3\%\%$, which is not the variance of 30%%; and $1/3 \cdot 5\% + 2/3 \cdot 9\% \approx 7.67\%$, which is not the standard deviation of 5.5%.)

(*But* you cannot average variances or standard deviations!)

But here is a remarkable and less intuitive fact: Market betas—that is, the projects' risk contributions to your investors' market portfolios—can be averaged, too. That is, I claim that the beta of BCC is the weighted average of the betas of B and C. You already computed the latter in Formula 8.3 as +0.64 and −1.60, respectively. Their value-weighted average is

News flash: You can also average market betas.

➤ *Market betas of B and C, Formula 8.3, Pg.190.*

$$\beta_{BCC} \;=\; 1/3 \cdot (+0.64) \;+\; 2/3 \cdot (-1.60) \;\approx\; -0.8533 \qquad (8.6)$$

$$\underbrace{w_B \cdot \beta_B} \quad + \quad \underbrace{w_C \cdot \beta_C}$$

You will be asked to confirm this in Q8.11.

IMPORTANT

- You can think of the firm as a weighted investment portfolio of components, such as individual divisions or projects. For example, if a firm named ab consists only of two divisions, a and b, then its rate of return is always

$$r_{ab} \;=\; w_a \cdot r_a + w_b \cdot r_b$$

  where the weights are the relative values of the two divisions. (You can also think of this one firm as a "subportfolio" within a larger overall portfolio, such as the market portfolio.)

- The expected rate of return ("reward") of a portfolio is the weighted average expected rate of return of its components,

$$\mathcal{E}(r_{ab}) = w_a \cdot \mathcal{E}(r_a) + w_b \cdot \mathcal{E}(r_b)$$

Therefore, the expected rate of return of a firm is the weighted average rate of return of its divisions.

- Like expected rates of return, market betas can be weighted and averaged. The beta of a firm—i.e., the firm's "risk contribution" to the overall market portfolio—is the weighted average of the betas of its components,

$$\beta_{ab} = w_a \cdot \beta_a + w_b \cdot \beta_b$$

The market beta of a firm is the weighted average market beta of its divisions.

- You cannot do analogous weighted averaging with variances or standard deviations.

A firm is a portfolio of debt and equity. Thus, the portfolio formulas apply to the firm (with debt and equity as its components), too!

You can think of the firm not only as consisting of divisions, but also as consisting of debt and equity. For example, say your $400 million firm is financed with debt worth $100 million and equity worth $300 million. If you own all debt and equity, you own the firm. What is the market beta of your firm's assets? Well, the beta of your overall firm must be the weighted average beta of its debt and equity. If your $100 million in debt has a market beta of, say, 0.4 and your $300 million of equity has a market beta of, say, 2.0, then your firm has a market beta of

$$
\underbrace{1/4 \cdot (0.4)}_{\left(\dfrac{\text{Debt value}}{\text{Firm value}}\right) \cdot \beta_{\text{Debt}}} + \underbrace{3/4 \cdot (2.0)}_{\left(\dfrac{\text{Equity value}}{\text{Firm value}}\right) \cdot \beta_{\text{Equity}}} = \underbrace{1.6}_{\beta_{\text{Firm}}} \qquad (8.7)
$$

This 1.6 is called the **asset beta** to distinguish it from the **equity beta** of 2.0 that financial websites report. Put differently, if your firm refinances itself to 100% equity (i.e., $400 million worth), then the reported market beta of your equity on **YAHOO!** FINANCE would fall to 1.6. The asset beta is the measure of your firm's projects' risk contribution to the portfolio of your investors. It determines the cost of capital that you should use as the hurdle rate for projects that are similar to the average project in your own firm.

Q 8.11. Let's check that the beta combination formula (Formula 8.6 on page 199) is correct. Start with the BCC line in the table on Page 199

1. Write down a table with the de-meaned market rate of return and de-meaned BCC rate of return in each of the four possible states.

2. Multiply the de-meaned rates of return in each scenario. This gives you four cross-products, each having units of %%.

3. Compute the average of these cross-products. This is the covariance between BCC and M.

4. Divide the covariance between BCC and M by the variance of the market.

5. Which is faster—this route or Formula 8.6? Which is faster if there are a hundred possible scenarios?

Q 8.12. Confirm that you cannot take a value-weighted average of component variances (and thus of standard deviations) the same way that you can take value-weighted average expected rates of return and value-weighted average market betas.

1. What is the value-weighted average variance of BCC?

2. What is the actual variance of BCC?

Q 8.13. Consider an investment of $2/3$ in B and $1/3$ in C. Call this new portfolio BBC. Compute the variance, standard deviation, and market beta of BBC. Do this two ways: first from the four individual scenario rates of return of BBC, and then from the statistical properties of B and C itself.

Q 8.14. Assume that a firm will always have enough money to pay off its bonds, so the beta of its bonds is 0. (Being risk free, the rate of return on the bonds is obviously independent of the rate of return on the stock market.) Assume that the beta of the underlying assets is 2. What would financial websites report for the beta of the firm's equity if it changes its current capital structure from all equity to half debt and half equity? To 90% debt and 10% equity?

Q 8.15. (Advanced) Does maintaining a value-weighted or an equal-weighted portfolio require more trading? (Hint: Make up a simple example.)

Summary

This chapter covered the following major points:

- The expected rate of return is a measure of expected reward:

$$\mathcal{E}(r_P) \;=\; \frac{\text{Sum over All Scenarios:}\left[\text{Return of Pfio P in each Scenario}\right]}{N}$$

- The variance is (roughly) the average squared deviation from the mean.

$$\mathcal{V}ar(r_P) \;=\; \frac{\text{Sum over All Scenarios:}\left\{\left[\text{Return of Pfio P in each Scenario}\right] - \mathcal{E}(r_P)\right\}^2}{\text{"N" or "N-1"}}$$

  If you work with known scenario probabilities, divide by N. If you work with a limited number of historical observations that you use to guestimate the future scenarios, then divide by N $-$ 1. (With a lot of historical data, N is very large and it really makes no difference what you divide by.) The variance is an intermediate input to the more interesting statistic, the standard deviation.

- The standard deviation is the square root of the variance. The standard deviation of a portfolio's rate of return is the common measure of its risk.

$$\mathcal{S}dv(r_P) = \sqrt{\mathcal{V}ar(r_P)}$$

- Diversification reduces the risk of a portfolio.

- Corporate executives typically assume that their investors are smart enough to hold widely diversified portfolios, which resemble the overall market portfolio. The reason is that diversified portfolios offer higher expected rates of return at lower risks than undiversified ones.

- An individual project's own risk *is not* a good measure of its risk contribution to an investor's portfolio.

- Market beta *is* a good measure of an individual asset's risk contribution for an investor who holds the market portfolio.

- Market betas for typical stocks range between 0 and 2.5.

- It requires straightforward plugging into formulas to compute beta, correlation, and covariance. These three measures of comovement are closely related and always share the same sign.

- Like expected rates of return, betas can be averaged (using proper value-weighting, of course). However, variances or standard deviations cannot be averaged.

Preview of the Chapter Appendix in the Companion

In the Appendix

The appendix to this chapter explains

- how risk and reward vary for different combination portfolios.

- how one can use the "matrix" of variances and covariances to quickly recompute the overall portfolio risk of different combinations.

- what optimal combination portfolios are. This is the efficient frontier, which you have already briefly encountered in this chapter. It is the cornerstone of modern investment theory.

- how the availability of a risk-free asset makes the optimal portfolio always a combination of this risk-free asset and some tangency portfolio. Thus, every rational investor would only purchase these two assets. The more risk-averse, the more an investor would allocate from the risk-free into the risky tangency asset.

- how market-beta coincidentally affects idiosyncratic risk, and how it influences market-conditional realized rates of return.

Keywords

Answers

Q 8.1 The average deviation from the mean is always 0.

Q 8.2 The mean of portfolio M was 4%. Adding 5% to each return will give you a mean of 9%, which is 5% higher. The variance and standard deviation remain at the same level, the latter being 5%. If you think of 5% as a constant $c = 5\%$, then you have just shown that $\mathcal{E}(r + c) = \mathcal{E}(r) + c$ and $\mathcal{S}dv(r + c) = \mathcal{S}dv(r)$.

Q 8.3 The reward of portfolio C is its expected rate of return, i.e., $[(17\%) + 3\% + 11\% + (-7\%)]/4 = 6\%$. (We can just divide by 4, rather than multiply each term by 1/4, because all outcomes are equally likely.) The variance of C is $[(11\%)^2 + (3\%)^2 + (5\%)^2 + (-13\%)^2]/4 = 81\%\%$. The standard deviation, which is our measure of risk, is $\sqrt{81\%\%} \approx 9\%$.

Q 8.4 The combination portfolio MA of 90% in M and 10% in A has rates of return of –2.4%, 3.8%, 4.2%, and 10.4%.

1. Thus, its mean rate of return is 4%. Its variance is 20.5%%. Its standard deviation is approximately 4.528%.

2. It would look more spread out, because it has higher standard deviation.

Q 8.5   1. The reward is $4 \cdot 10\% = 40\%$. The variance is $4 \cdot 400\%\% = 1,600\%\%$. Thus, the standard deviation (risk) is $\sqrt{1,600\%\%} = 40\%$. The Sharpe ratio is 1.

2. The reward is 90%. The risk is $\sqrt{9 \cdot 400\%\%} = 3 \cdot 20\% = 60\%$. The Sharpe ratio is 1.5

3. The reward is $T \cdot \mathcal{E}$. The standard deviation is $\sqrt{T} \cdot \mathcal{S}dv$. The Sharpe ratio is $(\sqrt{T} \cdot \mathcal{E})/\mathcal{S}dv$.

Q 8.6 Exhibit 8.3 shows that by combining M, A, B, and C, you get a risk-free rate of 3.6%; and investing in F alone gets you a risk-free rate of 1%. This means that you could borrow at 1% and invest at 3.67%, both risk-free—an arbitrage. The efficient frontier would be a vertical line at 0. Obviously, this could never be the case in the real world.

Q 8.7 For the MB portfolio, the portfolio combination rates of return in the four scenarios were on the bottom of Exhibit 8.4 on Page 187. Confirm them first:

In S1 (♣): $0.5 \cdot (-3\%) + 0.5 \cdot (5\%) = 1\%$

In S2 (♦): $0.5 \cdot (3\%) + 0.5 \cdot (-1\%) = 1\%$

In S3 (♥): $0.5 \cdot (5\%) + 0.5 \cdot (7\%) = 6\%$

In S4 (♠): $0.5 \cdot (11\%) + 0.5 \cdot (13\%) = 12\%$

The expected rate of return is

$$\mathcal{E}(r_{MB}) = \frac{1\% + 1\% + 6\% + 12\%}{4} = 5\%$$

The portfolio variance is

$$\mathcal{V}ar(r_{MB}) = [(1\% - 5\%)^2 + (1\% - 5\%)^2 + (6\% - 5\%)^2 + (12\% - 5\%)^2]/4$$

Therefore, $\mathcal{S}dv(MC) = \sqrt{20.5\%\%} \approx 4.52\%$.

For the MC portfolio,

In S1 (♣): $0.5 \cdot (-3\%) + 0.5 \cdot (17\%) = 7\%$

In S2 (♦): $0.5 \cdot (3\%) + 0.5 \cdot (3\%) = 3\%$

In S3 (♥): $0.5 \cdot (5\%) + 0.5 \cdot (11\%) = 8\%$

In S4 (♠): $0.5 \cdot (11\%) + 0.5 \cdot (-7\%) = 2\%$

The expected rate of return is

$$\mathcal{E}(r_{MC}) = \frac{7\% + 3\% + 8\% + 2\%}{4} = 5\%$$

The variance is $\mathcal{V}ar(MC) = [(7\%-5\%)2+(3\%-5\%)2+(8\%-5\%)2+(2\%-5\%)2]/4 = 26\%\%$ Therefore, $\mathcal{S}dv(MC) = \sqrt{26\%\%} \approx 2.55\%$.

Q 8.8 The order of subscripts on market beta is important. Algebraically, $\beta_{C,M} = [\text{cov}(r_C, r_M)]/[\text{var}(r_M)]$, while $\beta_{M,C} = [\text{cov}(r_C, r_M)]/[\text{var}(r_C)]$. The denominator is different. If you work this out, $\beta_{M,C} \approx -0.49$. Fortunately, you will never ever need to compute $\beta_{M,C}$. I only asked you to do this computation so that you realize that the subscript order is important.

Q 8.9 The market beta of this project is

$$\beta_{x,M} = \frac{r_{x,2} - r_{x,1}}{r_{M,2} - r_{M,1}} = \frac{(-5\%) - (+5\%)}{(-10\%) - (+10\%)} = +0.5$$

(This is not "half as volatile" because market beta is not a measure of volatility.)

Q 8.10 Using the same formula, the market beta of y is [(+5%) − (−5%)]/[(−10% − (+10%)] = −0.5.

Q 8.11 1. Start with our standard table:

	♣	♦	♥	♠	$\mathcal{E}(r)$	$\mathcal{V}\!ar(r)$	$\mathcal{S}\!dv(r)$
BCC	13%	1.67%	9.67%	−0.33%	6%	30%%	5.5%
…in dev	7%	−4.33%	3.67%	−6.33%			
M	−3%	+3%	+5%	+11%	4%	25%%	5%
…in dev	−7%	−1%	1%	+7%			

(Variances and standard deviations are rounded.)

2. The four cross-products are −49%%, 4.33%%, 3.67%%, and −44.33%%.

3. The average (covariance) is −21.33%%.

4. The beta is −21.33/25 ≈ −0.8533.

5. This is the more painful route—and it is more painful when there are more possible scenarios.

Q 8.12 Actually, this was already in the text. BCC has a variance of about 30%%, while the value-weighted average of the variances is about 62.3%%.

Q 8.13 The equivalent table is

	♣	♦	♥	♠	$\mathcal{E}(r)$	$\mathcal{V}\!ar(r)$	$\mathcal{S}\!dv(r)$
B	5%	−1%	7%	13%	6%	25%%	5%
C	17%	3%	11%	−7%	6%	81%%	9%
BBC	9%	0.33%	8.33%	6.33%	6%	11.67%%	3.4%

The market beta is easiest to compute as $2/3 \cdot \beta_B + 1/3 \cdot \beta_C \approx 2/3 \cdot (0.64) + 1/3 \cdot (-1.60) \approx -0.11$.

Q 8.14 For a firm whose debt is risk free, the overall firm beta is $\beta_{Firm} = 0.5 \cdot \beta_{Equity} + 0.5 \cdot \beta_{Debt}$. Thus, $0.5 \cdot \beta_{Equity} + 0.5 \cdot 0 = 2$. Solve for $\beta_{Equity} = \beta_{Firm}/0.5 = 4$. For the (90%, 10%) case, the equity beta jumps to $\beta_{Equity} = 2/0.1 = 20$.

Q 8.15 Value-weighted portfolios usually require no trading (unless there is a payout, like a dividend). For example, using the numbers from this section, if B triples from $1 million to $3 million and C halves from $2 million to $1 million, your original value-weighted portfolio or firm would become $3 + $1 = $4 million. You would still be exactly value-weighted. B would now constitute 75% of the firm and C 25% of the firm. In contrast, in an originally equal-weighted portfolio, your $1.5 million in B would become $4.5 million, your $1.5 million in C would become $0.75 million, and your portfolio would be worth $5.25 million. This means you would want to have $2.625 million invested in each. To maintain an equal-weighted portfolio, you would have to sell some stock in your past winner to buy some stock in your loser. Only a value-weighted portfolio requires no trading. Another interesting aspect is that if you do not trade, in the very long run, any portfolio will look more and more value-weighted, because those stocks that have had large returns will automatically garner a larger weight both in your portfolio and the economy.

End of Chapter Problems

Q 8.16. Multiply each rate of return for M by 2.0. This portfolio offers −6%, +6%, +10%, and +22%. Compute the expected rate of return and standard deviation of this new portfolio. How do they compare to those of the original portfolio M?

Q 8.17. The following table contains the closing year-end prices of the Japanese stock market index, the Nikkei-225. Assume that each historical rate of return was exactly one representative scenario (independent sample draw) that you can use to estimate the future. If a Japanese investor had purchased a mutual fund that imitated the Nikkei-225, what would her annual rates of return, compounded rate of return

(from the end of 1984 to the end of 2010), average rate of return, and risk have been?

Year	N-225	Year	N-225	Year	N-225
1984	11,474	1993	17,417	2002	8,579
1985	13,011	1994	19,723	2003	10,677
1986	18,821	1995	19,868	2004	11,489
1987	22,957	1996	19,361	2005	16,111
1988	29,698	1997	15,259	2006	17,225
1989	38,916	1998	13,842	2007	15,308
1990	24,120	1999	18,934	2008	8,860
1991	22,984	2000	13,786	2009	10,546
1992	16,925	2001	10,335	2010	10,229

Q 8.18. Compute the value-weighted average of $1/3$ of the standard deviation of B and $2/3$ of the standard deviation of C. Is it the same as the standard deviation of a BCC portfolio of $1/3$ B and $2/3$ C, in which your investment rate of return would be $1/3 \cdot r_B + 2/3 \cdot r_C$?

Q 8.19. What are the risk and reward of a combination portfolio that invests 40% in M and 60% in B?

Q 8.20. Consider the following five assets, which have rates of return in six equally likely scenarios:

	Awful	Poor	Med.	Okay	Good	Great
Asset P1	–2%	0%	2%	4%	6%	10%
Asset P2	–1%	2%	2%	2%	3%	3%
Asset P3	–6%	2%	2%	3%	3%	1%
Asset P4	–4%	2%	2%	2%	2%	20%
Asset P5	10%	6%	4%	2%	0%	–2%

1. Assume that you can only purchase one of these assets. What are their risks and rewards?

2. Supplement your previous risk-reward rankings of assets P1–P5 with those of combination portfolios that consist of half P1 and half of each of the other 4 portfolios, P2–P5. What are the risks and rewards of these four portfolios?

3. Assume that P1 is the market. Plot the rates of return for P1 on the x-axis and the return for each of the other stocks on their own y-axes. Then draw lines that you think best fit the points. Do not try to compute the beta—just use the force (and your eyes), Luke. If you had to buy just a little bit of one of these P2–P5 assets, and you wanted to lower your risk, which would be best?

Q 8.21. Assume that you have invested half of your wealth in a risk-free asset and half in a risky portfolio P. Is it theoretically possible to lower your portfolio risk if you move your risk-free asset holdings into another risky portfolio Q? In other words, can you ever reduce your risk more by buying a risky security than by buying a risk-free asset?

Q 8.22. Why is it so common to use historical financial data to estimate future market betas?

Q 8.23. Is it wise to rely on historical statistical distributions as our guide to the future?

Q 8.24. Look up the market betas of the companies in Exhibit 8.6. Have they changed dramatically since May 2011, or have they remained reasonably stable?

Q 8.25. You estimate your project to return –20% if the stock market returns –10%, and +5% if the stock market returns +10%. What would you use as the market beta estimate for your project?

Q 8.26. Go to **YAHOO!** FINANCE. Obtain two years' worth of weekly rates of return for PepsiCo and for the S&P 500 index. Use a spreadsheet to compute PepsiCo's market beta.

Q 8.27. Consider the following assets:

	Bad	Okay	Good
Market M	–5%	5%	15%
Asset X	–2%	–3%	25%
Asset Y	–4%	–6%	30%

1. Compute the market betas for assets X and Y.

2. Compute the correlations of X and Y with M.

3. Assume you were holding only M. You now are selling off 10% of your M portfolio to replace it with 10% of either X or Y. Would an M&X portfolio or an M&Y portfolio be riskier?

4. Is the correlation indicative of which of these two portfolios ended up riskier? Is the market beta indicative?

Q 8.28. Compute the expected rates of return and the portfolio betas for many possible portfolio combinations (i.e., different weights) of M and F from Exhibit 8.1 on Page 178. (Your weight in M is 1 minus your weight in F.) Plot the two against one another. What does your plot look like?

Q 8.29. The following represents the probability distribution for the rates of return for next month:

Probability	Pfio P	Market M
$1/6$	−20%	−5%
$2/6$	−5%	+5%
$2/6$	+10%	0%
$1/6$	+50%	+10%

Compute by hand (and show your work) for all the following questions.

1. What are the risks and rewards of P and M?

2. What is the correlation of M and P?

3. What is the market beta of P?

4. If you were to hold $1/3$ of your portfolio in the risk-free asset, and $2/3$ in portfolio P, what would its market beta be?

Q 8.30. Download the historical prices for the S&P 500 index and for VPACX (the *Vanguard Pacific Stock Index* mutual fund) from **YAHOO!** FINANCE, beginning January 1, 2004, and ending December 31 of last year. Load them into a spreadsheet and position them next to one another. Compute the historical rates of return. Compute the risk and reward. Compute VPACX's market beta with respect to the S&P 500 index. How do your estimates compare to the Fund Risk as noted by **YAHOO!** FINANCE?

Q 8.31. Download 5 years of historical monthly (dividend-adjusted) prices for Coca-Cola (KO) and the S&P 500 from **YAHOO!** FINANCE.

1. Compute the monthly rates of return.

2. Compute the average rate of return and risk of portfolios that combine KO and the S&P 500 in the following proportions: $(0.0, 1.0)$, $(0.2, 0.8)$, $(0.4, 0.6)$, $(0.6, 0.4)$, $(0.8, 0.2)$, $(1.0, 0.0)$. Then plot them against one another. What does the plot look like?

3. Compute the market beta of Coca-Cola.

Q 8.32. Are historical covariances or means more trustworthy as estimators of the future?

Q 8.33. Why do some statistical packages estimate covariances differently (and different from those we computed in this chapter)? Does the same problem also apply to expected rates of return (means) and betas?

The Capital Asset Pricing Model

Knowing how risk (market beta) and reward (expected rate of return) are measured, you are now ready to proceed to the punchline: a formula that tells you how much reward your investment projects have to offer to compensate your investors for their risks. If you can judge the risk of new corporate investment projects, you can then determine the appropriate costs of capital that you should use in your project's NPV calculations. Alas, like NPV, the formula may be simple, but the application is hard. The devil is in the details.

We will first briefly review what you already know. Then you will learn all about this new model—the CAPM. Finally, you will get to apply it.

One apology in advance: In this chapter, I do not fully explain where all the formulas come from. This is because it really takes a full investments course to derive them. (The appendix goes into more detail, but if you really want to learn about investments, you need to take a full course on the subject.)

9.1 What You Already Know and What You Want to Know

First, you already know the right train of thought for capital budgeting purposes: As a corporate manager, your task is to determine whether you should accept or reject a project. You make this decision with the NPV formula. To determine the discount factor in the NPV formula, you need to estimate an appropriate cost of capital—or, more precisely, the *opportunity* cost of capital for your investors. This means that you need to judge what a fair expected rate of return, $\mathcal{E}(r)$, for your project is, given your project's risk characteristics. If your project offers a lower expected return than what your investors can earn elsewhere in similarly risky projects, then you should not put your investors' money into your project but instead return it to them. If your project offers more expected return, then you should go ahead and invest their money into your project. Put differently, your goal is to learn what your investors, if asked, would have wanted you to invest in on their behalves.

You are still after an estimate for your opportunity cost of capital.

Second, the perfect market assumptions are not enough to proceed. We must assume that investors like overall portfolio reward (expected return) and dislike overall portfolio risk (variance or standard deviation of return). We also assume that investors are smart. Presumably, this means that they diversify appropriately, hopefully holding something reasonably close to the market portfolio. We assume that investors all have access to

Assume perfect markets, that investors dislike risk and like reward, and more.

207

exactly the same set of assets. (This means we are ignoring investments in people's own houses or education, for example.) And finally, mostly for convenience, we assume that they want to maximize their wealth in the market for only one period.

This allows you to figure out how they—and you—should measure project risk and reward.

Third, for investors with these preferences and who are therefore already holding the overall market portfolio, you can follow their trains of thought. You can infer how they view the risk and reward of your individual projects. Reward is the expected rate of return. Risk is *not* your project's own standard deviation risk, but the contribution of your project to your investors' overall portfolio risk. This can be measured by the market beta of your project—think of it as a measure of its "toxicity." A project that decreases in value when the market decreases in value, and increases when the market increases, has a positive market beta. It's toxic—investors don't like it. A project that increases in value when the market decreases in value, and vice versa, has a negative market beta. It's less toxic—investors like it more. That is, a project with a low market beta helps an investor who holds a portfolio similar to the market portfolio to reduce the overall investment risk.

This gives you a trade-off between risk and reward "in equilibrium."

You can also draw some additional conclusions without any math. In our assumed perfect world, you can guess that investors will have already snatched up the best projects—those that have low risk and high expected rates of return. In fact, anyone selling projects with lower risk contribution can ask for a higher price, which in turn immediately drives down their expected rates of return. Consequently, what is available for purchase in the real world must be subject to some trade-off: Projects that have more market-risk contribution must offer a higher expected rate of return if their sellers want to convince investors to purchase them. But what *exactly* does this relationship between risk and reward look like? This is the subject of this chapter—it is the domain of the capital asset pricing model, the CAPM.

Q 9.1. What are the assumptions underlying the CAPM? Are the perfect market assumptions among them? Are there more?

9.2 Using The Capital Asset Pricing Model (CAPM)

The CAPM gives you the cost of capital if you give it the risk-free rate, the expected rate of return on the market, and your project's market beta.

The **capital asset pricing model** (CAPM) is a model that gives you an appropriate expected rate of return (cost of capital) for each project if you give it the project's relevant risk characteristics. The model states that an investment's cost of capital is lower when it offers better diversification benefits for an investor who holds the overall market portfolio—less required reward for less risk contribution. Market beta is its measure. Projects contributing more risk (market beta) require a higher expected rate of return for you to want them; projects contributing less risk require a lower expected rate of return for you to want them. This is the precise relationship that the CAPM gives you.

IMPORTANT

To estimate the required expected rate of return for a project or firm—that is, the cost of capital—according to the CAPM, you need three inputs:

1. The risk-free rate of return, r_F

2. The expected rate of return on the overall market, $\mathcal{E}(r_M)$

3. A firm's or project's beta with respect to the market, β_i

The CAPM formula is

$$\mathcal{E}(r_i) = r_F + [\mathcal{E}(r_M) - r_F] \cdot \beta_i \qquad (9.1)$$

where i is the name of your project and $\mathcal{E}(r_i)$ is your project's expected rate of return.

The difference between the expected rate of return on the risky (stock) market and the risk-free investment, $[\mathcal{E}(r_M) - r_F]$, is called the **equity premium** or **market risk premium**, discussed in more detail later.

You need to memorize the CAPM formula.

Let's use the formula. If you believe that the risk-free rate is 3% and the expected rate of return on the market is 7%, then the CAPM states that

A first quick use of the CAPM formula.

$$\mathcal{E}(r_i) = 3\% + (7\% - 3\%) \cdot \beta_i = 3\% + 4\% \cdot \beta_i$$

$$\mathcal{E}(r_i) = r_F + [\mathcal{E}(r_M) - r_F] \cdot \beta_i$$

Therefore, a project with a beta of 0.5 should have a cost of capital of $3\% + 4\% \cdot 0.5 = 5\%$, and a project with a beta of 2.0 should have a cost of capital of $3\% + 4\% \cdot 2.0 = 11\%$. The CAPM gives an opportunity cost for your investors' capital: If the project with the beta of 2.0 cannot earn an expected rate of return of 11%, you should not take this project and instead return the money to your investors. Your project would add too much risk for its reward. Your investors have better opportunities elsewhere.

The CAPM is called an **asset-pricing model**, even though it is most often expressed in terms of a required expected rate of return rather than in terms of an appropriate project price. Fortunately, though messy, the two are equivalent—you can always work with the CAPM return first, and discount the expected cash flow into an appropriate price second. A given expected rate of return implies a given price. (If you do not know the fair price, you will however have to take two aspirins and work with a more difficult version of the CAPM formula. It is called **certainty equivalence** and explained in the chapter appendix.)

It is easier to work in required returns than in prices.

➤ *Certainty equivalence CAPM form,*
Sect. App.9.A (Companion), Pg. ≈49.

The CAPM specifically ignores the standard deviation of individual projects' rates of return. That is, the model posits that investors do not care about it, because they are smart enough to diversify away any idiosyncratic risk. The CAPM further posits that investors do care about the project market betas, because these measure the risk components that investors holding the market portfolio cannot diversify away.

The CAPM formula tells you what investors care about: comovement with the market.

The CAPM has three inputs. We will cover them in detail.

For the three CAPM inputs, as always, you are really interested in the future: the future expected rate of return on the market and the future beta of your firm/project with respect to the market. You really don't care about the past average rates of return or the past market betas. But, as usual, you often have no choice other than to rely on estimates that are based at least partly on historical data. In Section 9.4, you will learn how to estimate each CAPM input. But let's explore the model itself first, assuming that you know all the inputs.

➤ *Will history repeat itself?*, *Sect. 7.1*, *Pg.164*.

The Security Market Line (SML)

Examples of CAPM rates of return that individual securities should offer.

Let's apply the CAPM in a specific example. Assume that the risk-free rate is 3% per year and that the market offers an expected rate of return of 8% per year. The CAPM formula then states that a stock with a beta of 1 should offer an expected rate of return of $3\% + (8\% - 3\%) \cdot 1 = 8\%$ per year; that a stock with a beta of 0 should offer an expected rate of return of $3\% + (8\% - 3\%) \cdot 0 = 3\%$ per year; that a stock with a beta of $1/2$ should offer an expected rate of return of $3\% + (8\% - 3\%) \cdot 0.5 = 5.5\%$ per year; that a stock with a beta of 2 should offer an expected rate of return of $3\% + (8\% - 3\%) \cdot 2 = 13\%$ per year; and so on.

The SML is just a graphical representation of the CAPM formula.

The CAPM formula is often graphed as the **security market line** (**SML**), which shows the relationship between the expected rate of return of a project and its beta. Exhibit 9.1 draws a first security market line for seven assets. Each investment asset (such as a stock or a project) is a point in this coordinate system. Because all assets properly follow the CAPM formula in our example, they must lie on a straight line. In other words, the SML is just a graphical representation of the CAPM formula. The slope of this line is the equity premium, $\mathcal{E}(r_M) - r_F$, and the intercept is the risk-free rate, r_F.

If you know the inputs, the SML is a sharp line; if you estimate them, it is a scatterplot.

Alas, in the real world, even if the CAPM holds, you would not have the data to draw Exhibit 9.1. The reason is that you do not know true expected returns and true market betas. Exhibit 9.2 plots two graphs in a perfect CAPM world. The top graph repeats Exhibit 9.1 and falsely presumes that you know CAPM inputs—the true market betas and true expected rates of return. This line is perfectly straight. In the bottom graph, you have to rely only on observables—estimates of expected returns and betas, presumably based mostly on historical data averages. Now you can only fit an "estimated security market line," not the "true security market line." Of course, you hope that your historical data provides good, unbiased estimates of true market beta and true expected rates of return (and this is a big assumption), so that your fitted line will look at least approximately straight. A workable version of the CAPM thus can only state that there should roughly be a linear relationship between the data-estimated market betas and the data-estimated expected rates of return, just as drawn here.

Q 9.2. The risk-free rate is 4%. The expected rate of return on the market is 7%. What is the appropriate cost of capital for a project that has a beta of 3?

Q 9.3. The risk-free rate is 4%. The expected rate of return on the market is 12%. What is the appropriate cost of capital for a project that has a beta of 3?

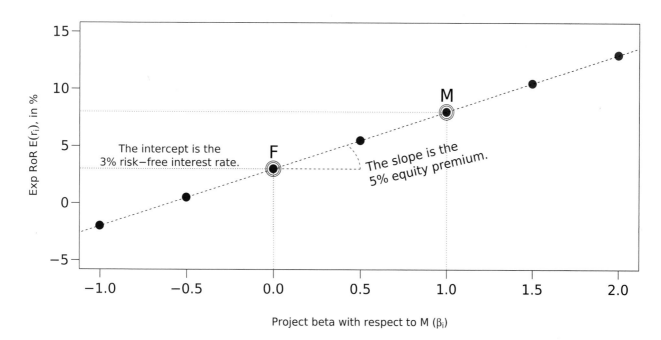

		Investment Asset						
		A	**B**	**F**	**C**	**M**	**D**	**E**
Market Beta	β_i	–1.0	-0.5	0.0	0.5	1.0	1.5	2.0
Expected Rate of Return	$\mathcal{E}(r_i)$	–2.0%	0.5%	3.0%	5.5%	8.0%	10.5%	13.0%

Exhibit 9.1: *The Security Market Line.* This graph plots the CAPM relation $\mathcal{E}(r_i) = r_F + [\mathcal{E}(r_M) - r_F] \cdot \beta_i = 3\% + (8\% - 3\%) \cdot \beta_i$, where β_i is the beta of an individual asset with respect to the market. In this graph, we assume that the risk-free rate is 3% and the equity premium is 5%. Each point is one asset (such as a stock, a project, or a mutual fund). The point M in this graph could also be any other security with a $\beta_i = 1$. F could be the risk-free asset or any other security with a $\beta_i = 0$.

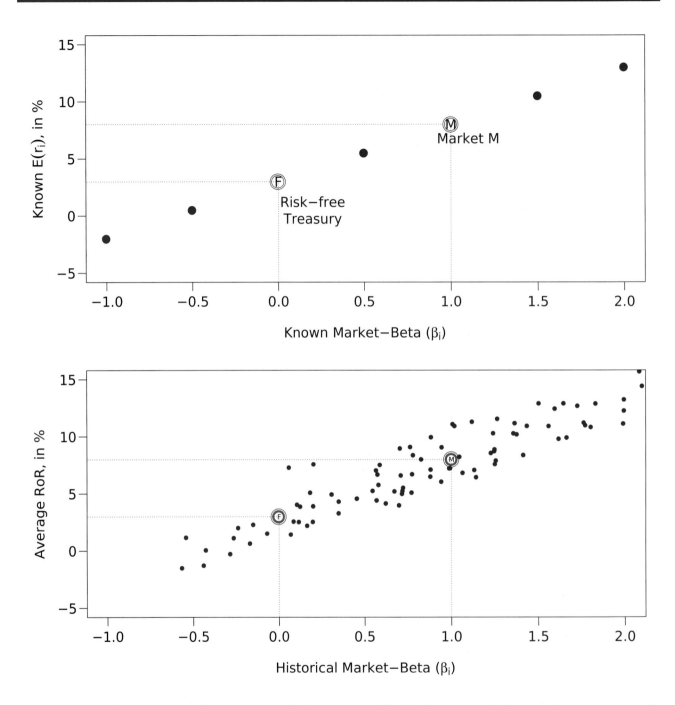

Exhibit 9.2: *The Security Market Line in an Ideal CAPM World.* The lower panel shows what we are usually confronted with: Historical average returns and historical betas are just estimates from the data. We hope that they are representative of the true underlying mean returns and true betas, which in turn would mean that they will also be representative of the future means and betas.

Q 9.4. The risk-free rate is 4%. The expected rate of return on the market is 12%. What is the appropriate cost of capital for a project that has a beta of –3? Does this make economic sense?

Q 9.5. Is the real-world security market line a line?

Q 9.6. The risk-free rate is 4%. The expected rate of return on the market is 7%. A corporation intends to issue publicly traded bonds that *promise* a rate of return of 6% and offer an *expected* rate of return of 5%. What is the implicit beta of the bonds?

Q 9.7. Draw the security market line if the risk-free rate is 5% and the equity premium is 9%.

Q 9.8. What is the equity premium, both mathematically and intuitively?

9.3 The CAPM Cost of Capital in the Present Value Formula

For a corporate manager, the CAPM is needed to get the denominator in the NPV formula, the opportunity cost of capital, $\mathcal{E}(r)$:

$$\text{NPV} = C_0 + \frac{\mathcal{E}(C_1)}{1 + \mathcal{E}(r_1)} + \frac{\mathcal{E}(C_2)}{1 + \mathcal{E}(r_2)} + \cdots$$

We usually use the CAPM output, the expected rate of return, as our discount rate.

Together, the CAPM and the NPV formulas tell you again that cash flows that correlate more with the overall market are of less value to your investors and therefore require higher expected rates of return ($\mathcal{E}(r)$) in order to pass muster (well, the hurdle rate).

Deconstructing Quoted Rates of Return— Risk Premiums

Let me return to the subject of Section 6.2. You learned that in a perfect and risk-neutral world, stated rates of return consist of a time premium and a default premium. On average, the default premium is zero, so the expected rate of return is just the time premium.

Reminder: Stated bond yields contain time and default premiums.

The CAPM extends the expected rate of return to a world in which investors are risk averse. It gives you an expected rate of return that adds a **risk premium** (as a reward for your willingness to absorb risk) to the time premium.

➤ *Time and default premiums, Sect. 6.2, Pg. 124.*

The CAPM gives you the time and risk premiums.

$$\text{Promised Rate of Return} \quad = \text{Time Premium} + \text{Default Premium} + \text{Risk Premium}$$

$$\text{Actual Earned Rate} \quad = \text{Time Premium} + \text{Default Realization} + \text{Risk Premium}$$

$$\underbrace{\text{Expected Rate of Return}}_{\text{provided by the CAPM}} = \text{Time Premium} + \text{Expected Risk Premium}$$

In the risk-neutral perfect world, there were no differences in *expected* rates of return across assets. There were only differences in *stated* rates of return. The CAPM changes all this—different assets can now also have different *expected* rates of return.

Important: *The CAPM totally ignores default risk and, thus, does not provide a default premium. You must take care of it yourself!*

However, the CAPM does *not* take default risk into account, much less give you an appropriate stated rate of return. You should therefore wonder: How do you find the appropriate quoted rate of return in the real world? After all, it is this stated rate of return that is usually publicly posted, not the expected rate of return. Put differently, how do you put the default risk and CAPM risk into one valuation?

Here is an example. Say you want to determine the PV of a corporate zero-bond that has a beta of 0.25 and promises to deliver $200 next year. This bond pays off 95% of the time, and 5% of the time it totally defaults. Assume that the risk-free rate of return is 6% per annum and that the expected rate of return on the market is 10%. Therefore, the CAPM states that the expected rate of return on your bond must be

A specific bond example: First compute the price necessary to make you "even" relative to the Treasury if you are risk-neutral. This price is based on the time premium and the default premium.

$$\mathcal{E}(r_{\text{Bond}}) \quad = 6\% + \quad 4\% \quad \cdot \ 0.25 \ = 7\%$$

$$= \ r_F \ + \ [\mathcal{E}(r_M) - r_F] \cdot \ \beta_{\text{Bond}}$$

This takes care of the time and risk premiums. To take the bond's default risk into account, you must still find the numerator. You cannot use the promised payment. You must adjust it for the probability of default. You expect to receive not $200, but

$$\mathcal{E}(C_{\text{Bond}}) \quad = \quad 95\% \quad \cdot \ \$200 \ + \quad 5\% \quad \cdot \quad 0 \quad = \$190$$

$$= \ \mathcal{P}\!rob(\text{No Default}) \cdot \text{Promise} + \mathcal{P}\!rob(\text{Default}) \cdot \text{Nothing}$$

Therefore, the present value formula states that the value of the bond is

$$\text{PV}_{\text{Bond}} \ = \ \frac{\mathcal{E}(C_{\text{Bond}})}{1 + \mathcal{E}(r_{\text{Bond}})} \ = \ \frac{\$190}{1 + 7\%} \ \approx \$177.57$$

Given this price, you can now compute the promised (or quoted) rate of return on this bond:

$$\frac{\$200 - \$177.57}{\$177.57} \qquad \approx \qquad 12.6\%$$

$$\frac{\text{Promised Cash Flow} - \text{PV}}{\text{PV}} = \text{Promised Rate of Return}$$

The risk premium is above and beyond the time and default premiums. On average, risky investments earn more than risk-free investments now.

You can now quantify the three components in this example. For this bond, the time premium of money is 6% per annum—it is the rate of return that an equivalent-term Treasury offers. The time premium plus the risk premium is provided by the CAPM, and it is 7% per annum. Therefore, 1% per annum is your "average" compensation for your willingness to hold this risky bond instead of the risk-free Treasury. The remaining $12.6\% - 7\% = 5.6\%$ per annum is the default premium: You do not expect to earn money from this default premium "on average." You only earn it if the bond does not default.

$$12.6\% \quad = \quad 6\% \quad + \quad 5.6\% \quad + \quad 1\%$$

Promised Interest Rate $=$ Time Premium $+$ Default Premium $+$ Risk Premium

In the real world, most bonds have fairly small market betas (often much smaller than 0.25) and thus fairly low risk premiums. Instead, most of the premium that ordinary corporate bonds quote above equivalent risk-free Treasury rates is not due to the risk premium, but due to the default premium. They simply won't pay as much as they promise, on average. However, for corporate projects and equity shares, the risk premium can be quite large. (Watch out—there are also some important imperfect market premiums that you will only learn in the next chapter.)

IMPORTANT

Never forget:

- The CAPM provides an expected rate of return.

- This return is not a stated (promised, quoted) rate of return, because it does not include a default premium.

- The probability of default must be handled in the NPV numerator (through the expected cash flow), and not in the NPV denominator (through the expected rate of return).

Q 9.9. A corporate bond with a beta of 0.2 will pay off next year with 99% probability. The risk-free rate is 3% per annum, and the equity premium is 5% per annum.

1. What is the price of this bond?

2. What is its promised rate of return?

3. Decompose the bond's quoted rate of return into its components.

Q 9.10. Going to your school has total additional and opportunity costs of $30,000 *this year and up-front*. With 90% probability, you are likely to graduate from your school. If you do not graduate, you have lost the entire sum. Graduating from the school will increase your 40-year lifetime annual salary by roughly $5,000 per year, but more so when the market rate of return is high than when it is low. For argument's sake, assume that your extra-income beta is 1.5. Assume the risk-free rate is 3%, and the equity premium is 5%. What is the value of your education?

9.4 Estimating the CAPM Inputs

How can you obtain reasonable estimates of the three inputs into the CAPM formula $\mathcal{E}(r_i) = r_F + [\mathcal{E}(r_M) - r_F] \cdot \beta_i$?

The Equity Premium

You must provide the CAPM with the equity premium. *Good luck!*

The input that is most difficult to estimate is the equity premium. It measures the extra expected rate of return that risky projects are offering above and beyond what risk-free projects are offering. Worse: Not only is the equity premium difficult to estimate, but the value you choose can also have a tremendous influence over your estimated cost of capital. Of course, the theoretical CAPM model assumes that you know the *expected* rate of return on the market perfectly, not that you have to estimate it. Yet, in real life, the equity premium is not posted anywhere, and *no one really knows the correct number*. There are a number of methods to guesstimate it—but, unfortunately, they do not tend to agree with one another. This leaves me with two choices: Either I can throw you one estimate and pretend it is the authoritative one, or I can tell you about the different methods that lead to different estimates. I prefer the latter, if only because the former would eventually leave you startled to discover that your boss is using some other number and has therefore come up with a completely different cost-of-capital estimate. I will explain the intuition behind five different methods and describe the estimates that their respective intuitions suggest. In this way, you can make up your own mind as to what you deem to be an appropriate equity premium estimate.

Method 1: Historical averages.

➤ *Morningstar,*
Exhibit 7.5, Pg. 158.

1. Historical averages I: The first guestimation method is to assume that whatever the equity premium was in the past will be the case in the future. Exhibit 7.5 gives Morningstar's historical statistics. The arithmetic average equity rate of return across large and small stocks was about 12%, either from 1926 to 2010 or from 1970 to 2010. If you use the 30-day Treasury as the risk-free rate, you should subtract about 3.6% or 5.6%. These two choices would leave you with an equity premium estimate of between 6% and 8%.

However, if you want to evaluate longer-term projects, maybe you should subtract the rates of return of longer-term government bonds instead. This would drop your equity premium estimate to around 3% to 6%. Further, you may then even want to use the geometric long-run buy-and-hold averages, in which case the range would be more like 2% to 5%.

➤ *Geometric versus arithmetic averages, Pg. 154.*

That's quite a range. 2% is defensible, as is 8%. So, which sample period and method should you choose? If you choose too few years, your sample average could be unreliable. It might just have been happenstance and not representative of the statistical process driving returns. Although your estimate can be more reliable if you use more years, you are then leaning more heavily on a brave assumption that the world has not changed. Is the world really still the same as it was in 1926? Is the United States really the right country to consider alone? (Maybe it just had an unusually lucky streak during the "American Century," which is unlikely to repeat. In this case, the average country's experience may be a better forecast for today's U.S., too.) No one knows the correct answers to these questions.

2. **Historical averages II:** The second method is to look at historical equity premiums in the opposite light. If stocks have become more desirable, perhaps this is because investors have become less risk averse, then more investors competed to own stocks, drove up the prices, and thereby lowered their future expected rates of return. High historical rates of return would then be indicative of low future expected rates of return.

   An even more extreme version of this argument suggests that high past equity returns could have been not just due to high ex-ante equity premiums, but due to historical "bubbles" in the stock market. The proponents of the bubble view usually cannot quantify the appropriate equity premium, but they do argue that it is lower after recent market run-ups—exactly the opposite of what proponents of the historical averages I method argue.

   However, you should be aware that not everyone agrees that there are bubbles in the market.

   Method 2: Inverse historical averages.

3. **Current predictive ratios:** The third method is to try to predict the stock market rate of return actively with historical dividend yields (i.e., the dividend payments received by stockholders). Higher dividend yields should make stocks more attractive and therefore predict higher future equity premiums. The equity premium estimation is usually done in two steps: First, you must estimate a statistical regression that predicts next year's equity premium with this year's dividend yield; then, you substitute the currently prevailing dividend yield into your estimated regression to get a prediction. Unfortunately, as of 2008, current dividend yields were so low that the predicted equity premium was negative—which would make no sense. Variations of this method have used interest rates or earnings yields, typically with similar results. In any case, the empirical evidence suggests that this method does not yield very solid predictions—for example, it predicted low equity premiums in the 1990s, which was a period of superb stock market performance.

   Method 3: Dividend or earnings yields.

4. **Philosophical prediction:** The fourth method is to wonder how much rate of return is required to entice reasonable investors to switch from bonds into stocks. Even with an equity premium as low as 3%, over 25 years, an equity investor would end up with more than twice the money of a bond investor. Naturally, in a perfect market, nothing should come for free, and the reward for risk-taking should be just about fair. Therefore, equity premiums of 6-8% just seem too high for the amount of risk observed in the stock market. This philosophical method generally suggests equity premiums of about **1%** to **3%**.

   Method 4: Introspection and philosophy.

5. **Consensus survey:** The fifth method is to ask investors or experts what they deem reasonable. The ranges can vary widely, and they seem to correlate with very recent stock market returns. For example, in late 2000, right after a huge run-up

   Method 5: Just ask!

Sidenote: A **bubble** is a runaway market, in which rationality has temporarily disappeared. There is a lot of debate as to whether bubbles in the stock market ever occurred. A strong case can be made that technology stocks experienced a bubble from around 1998 to 2000. It is often called the **dot-com bubble**, the **internet bubble**, or simply the **tech bubble**. There is no convincing explanation based on fundamentals that can explain *both* why the NASDAQ Index climbed from 2,280 in March 1999 to 5,000 by March 2000, *and* why it then dropped back to 1,640 by April 2001.

in the stock market, surveys by *Fortune* or *Gallup/Paine Webber* had investors expecting equity premiums as high as 15% per year. (They were acutely disappointed: The stock market dropped by as much as 30% over the following two years. Maybe they just got the sign wrong?!) The consulting firm McKinsey uses a standard of around 5% to 6%. The Social Security Administration settled on a standard of around 4%. A joint poll by Graham and Harvey (from Duke) and *CFO Magazine* found that the 2005 average equity premium estimate of CFOs was around 3% per annum. And in recent surveys of finance professors, the most common equity premium estimates were **5%** for a 1-year horizon and **6%** for a 30-year horizon.

Analysts' estimates are all over the map, too. Estimates between 2% and 6% per annum seem reasonable.

What to choose? Welcome to the club! No one knows the true equity premium. On Monday, February 28, 2005, the *Wall Street Journal* reported the following average *after-inflation* forecasts from then to 2050 (per annum):

Name	Organization	Stocks	Government Bonds	Corp . Bonds	Equity Premium
William Dudley	Goldman Sachs	5.0%	2.0%	2.5%	3.0%
Jeremy Siegel	Wharton	6.0%	1.8%	2.3%	4.2%
David Rosenberg	Merrill Lynch	4.0%	3.0%	4.0%	1.0%
Ethan Harris	Lehman Brothers	4.0%	3.5%	2.5%	0.5%
Robert Shiller	Yale	4.6%	2.2%	2.7%	2.4%
Robert LaVorgna	Deutsche Bank	6.5%	4.0%	5.0%	2.5%
Parul Jain	Nomura	4.5%	3.5%	4.0%	1.0%
John Lonski	Moody's	4.0%	2.0%	3.0%	2.0%
David Malpass	Bear Stearns	5.5%	3.5%	4.3%	2.0%
Jim Glassman	JP Morgan	4.0%	2.5%	3.5%	1.5%
				Average	2.0%

Incidentally, it does not matter that these numbers are inflation adjusted. Because the equity premium is a difference, inflation cancels out. However, it matters whether you quote the equity premium with respect to a short-term or a long-term interest rate. It is more common to use a short rate, because short-term bonds are typically safer and therefore closer to the risk-free asset that is in the spirit of the CAPM. This is why you may want to add another 1% to the equity premium estimates calculated in this table—the long-term government bonds used in the table usually carry higher interest rates than their short-term counterparts. On the other hand, if your project is longer term, you may want to adopt a risk-free bond whose duration is more similar to that of your project. You would then even prefer the equity premium estimates in this table. In addition, these are arithmetic rates of return. You already know that they are higher than geometric rates of return. (A +20% rate of return followed by a –20% rate of return gives you a 0% arithmetic average, but leaves you with a two-year loss of 4%.) Thus, if your project is long term, don't expect your project to offer geometric returns that can be compared to arithmetic returns on the market. It would be an unfair benchmark.

➤ *Duration,* <u>Pg. ≈17</u>.

➤ *Geometric versus arithmetic averages,* <u>Pg. 154</u>.

You now know that no one can tell you the authoritative number for the equity premium. It does not exist. Everyone is guessing, but there is no way around it—you have to take a stance on the equity premium. I cannot shield you from this problem. I could give you the arguments that you should contemplate when you are picking *your* number. Now I can also give you my own take: First, I have my doubts that equity premiums will return to the historical levels of 8% anytime soon. (The twentieth century was the "American Century" for a good reason: There were a lot of positive surprises for American investors.) I personally prefer equity premium estimates between **2%** and **4%**. (Incidentally, it is my impression that there is relatively less disagreement about equity premium forecasts today than there was just 5 to 10 years ago.) But realize that reasonable individuals can choose equity premium estimates as low as 1% or as high as 8%. Of course, I personally find their estimates less believable the farther they are from my own personal range. And I find anything outside this 1% to 8% range just too tough to swallow. Second, whatever equity premium you do choose, *be consistent.* Do not use 3% for investing in one project and 8% for investing in another. Being consistent can sometimes reduce your relative mistakes in choosing one project over another.

> Remain consistent: Don't use different equity premium estimates for different projects.

A N E C D O T E   Was the 20th Century Really the "American Century?"

The compound rate of return in the United States was about 8% per year from 1920 to 1995. Adjusted for inflation, it was about 6%. In contrast, an investor who had invested in Romania in 1937 experienced not only the German invasion and Soviet domination, but also a real annual capital appreciation of about −27% per annum over its 4 years of stock market existence (1937–1941). Similar fates befell many other Eastern European countries, but even countries not experiencing political disasters often proved to be less than stellar investments. For example, Argentina had a stock market from 1947 to 1965, even though its only function seems to have been to wipe out its investors. Peru tried three times: From 1941 to 1953 and from 1957 to 1977, its stock market investors lost *all* their money. But the third time was the charm: From 1988 to 1995, its investors earned a whopping 63% real rate of return. India's stock market started in 1940 and offered its investors a real rate of return of just about −1% per annum. Pakistan started in 1960 and offered about −0.1% per annum.

Even European countries with long stock market histories and no political trouble did not perform as well as the United States. For example, Switzerland and Denmark earned nominal rates of return of about 5% per annum from 1920 to 1995, while the United States earned about 8% per annum.

The United States stock market was indeed an unusual above-average performer in the twentieth century. Will the twenty-first century be the Chinese century? And do Chinese asset prices already reflect this? Or already reflect *too much* of this?

Goetzmann and Jorion (1999)

Yes, the equity premium may be difficult to estimate, but there is really no way around taking a stance. Even if you had never heard of the CAPM, you would still consider the equity premium to be one of the two most important numbers in finance (together with the risk-free rate, the other CAPM input). If you believe that the equity premium is high, you would want to allocate a lot of your personal assets to stocks. Otherwise, you would allocate more to bonds. You really do need it for basic investing purposes, too—no escape possible.

> The equity premium is an extremely important number, even without the CAPM.

The CAPM is about
relative pricing, not
absolute pricing.

In a corporate context, like every other corporate manager, you cannot let your limited knowledge of the equity premium stop you from making investment decisions. In order to use the CAPM, you do need to judge the appropriate reward for risky projects relative to risk-free projects. Indeed, you can think of the CAPM as telling you the *relative* expected rate of return for projects, not the *absolute* expected rate of return. Given *your* estimate of how much risky average stock market projects should earn relative to safe projects, the CAPM can tell you the costs of capital for projects of riskiness "beta." But the basic judgment of the appropriate spread between risky and safe projects is left up to you.

No way around it: You
must guesstimate the
equity premium.

Finally, I have been deliberately vague about the "market." In CAPM theory, the market should be all investable assets in the economy, including real estate, art, risky bonds, and so on. In practice, we typically use only a *stock* market index. And among stock market indexes, it often does not matter too much which index is used—whether it is the value-weighted stock market index, the **Dow Jones 30** (another popular market index consisting of 30 large stocks in different industries), or the S&P 500. The S&P 500 is perhaps the most often used stand-in for the stock market, because it's value-weighted and thus covers most of the public marketcap in the economy, and its historical performance is readily downloadable. From the perspective of a corporate executive, it is a reasonable simplification to use the S&P 500 as the market.

The S&P 500 is usually
used as an
approximation for the
market.

Q 9.11. What are appropriate equity premium estimates? What are not? What kind of reasoning are you relying on?

The Risk-Free Rate and Multiyear Considerations

Which risk-free rate?

The second input into the CAPM formula is the risk-free rate of return. It is relatively easy to obtain from U.S. Treasuries. There is one small issue, though—which Treasury? What if the yield curve is upward sloping and Treasuries yield 2% per year over one year, 4% per year over ten years, and 5% per year over thirty years? How would you use the CAPM? Which interest rate should you pick in a multiyear context?

➤ *US Treasuries,*
<u>Sect. 5.3, Pg. 95.</u>

Advice: Pick the
interest rate for a
Treasury that is "most
similar" to your
project.

➤ *Yield Curve,*
<u>Chapter 5, Pg. 83.</u>

Actually, the CAPM offers no guidance, because it has no concept of more than one single time period, and thus no concept of a yield curve. However, from a practical perspective, it makes sense to match projects and Treasuries:

To estimate one benchmark required expected rate of return (e.g., for benchmarking your project's one IRR), you should probably use the yield on Treasuries that seem to take similar time to come to fruition as your own project. A good rule of thumb is to pick the risk-free rate closest by some measure (e.g., maturity or duration) to your project. For example, to value a machine that operates for three years, it could make sense to use an average of the one-year, two-year, and three-year risk-free zero interest rates—perhaps 2.5% per annum. On the other hand, if you have a ten-year project, you would probably use the ten-year Treasury rate of 4% as your risk-free rate of return. You may think this is a pretty loose method to handle an important question (and it is), but it is also a very reasonable one. Think about the opportunity cost of capital for an investment with a beta of 0. If you are willing to commit your money for ten years, you could earn the ten-year Treasury rate of return. It would be your opportunity cost of capital. If you are willing to commit your money only for three months, you could earn only the three-month Treasury rate—usually a lower opportunity cost for your capital.

To estimate multiple required expected rates of return (e.g., for an NPV analysis with cash flows occurring at many different times), you should probably use different zero-bond rates, each corresponding to the timing of the cash flow in the numerator.

There is universal agreement that you should use a risk-free rate similar to the duration of your project in the first part of the CAPM formula (where it appears by itself). Thus, if your project has a beta of 0, you should expect to offer the same rate of return as the duration-equivalent risk-free Treasury. If your project takes longer to complete, and if the yield curve is upward sloping, then your project would have to offer a higher expected rate of return.

But should you also use a different risk-free rate in the second part of the formula (where the risk-free rate is part of the equity premium)? Your answer must depend on whether you believe that the expected rate of return on the market is higher for longer-term investments. This would be a reasonable conjecture—after all, if risk-averse Treasury investors can expect a higher rate of return if they buy longer-term claims, why would risk-averse equity investors not also expect a higher rate of return if they buy longer-term claims? If the expected rate of return on the market is higher for longer-term projects, too, then any premium for longer-term investments could cancel out in the equity premium, and you could use the same equity premium regardless of how long term your project is. Unfortunately, no one knows the answer. (After all, we don't know with great confidence even the short-term expected rate of return on the market.) My personal preference is to use the same (geometric) equity premium estimate, regardless of the duration of the project. Other CAPM users may come to a different conclusion.

A philosophical question of practical importance: Is the equity premium horizon-dependent?

Q 9.12. What is today's risk-free rate for a 1-year project? For a 10-year project?

Q 9.13. If you can use only one Treasury, which risk-free rate should you use for a project that will yield $5 million each year for 10 years?

Investment Projects' Market Betas

Finally, you must estimate your project's **market beta**. It measures how the rate of return of your project fluctuates with that of the overall market. Unlike the previous two inputs, which are the same for every project in the economy, the beta input depends on your specific project characteristics: Different investments have different betas.

Unlike the risk-free rate and the equity premium, beta is specific to each project.

The Implications of Beta for a Project's Risk and Reward

Projects with higher betas have more market risk, so their own idiosyncratic variances tend to be higher, too.

You already understand the role of market beta in determining the expected rate of return for an asset. This is the security market line—that is, the CAPM formula itself is an upward-sloping line when the expected rate of return is plotted against beta. But market beta also has implications for the standard deviation of assets. First, note that assets with a low beta are not very exposed to market risk. Thus, assets that have either a very high or a very low market beta tend to have higher standard deviation. Second, note that you can only learn much about an asset's market-beta in months in which the market does not turn in the same performance as the risk-free security. If the market and the risk-free asset turn in the same performance in a given month, then *any* asset's expected rate of return is just the risk-free rate, regardless of its market-beta.

Beta Estimation

Ways to estimate beta.

How do you find good beta estimates? Depending on the project, this can be easy or difficult.

If publicly traded, it's easy: Look it up or run regressions.

Market betas for publicly traded firms: For publicly traded stocks, finding a market beta is usually easy. Virtually every finance website publishes them.

➤ *Estimating betas from historical data, Sect. 8.3, Pg.192.*

Market betas from a regression: You could also run the market model regression yourself. There is no mystery: The betas published on financial websites are really just estimated from historical time-series regressions, too. They do exactly what we did in Section 8.3: They compute the covariance and divide it by the market variance. (They may do a little bit of shrinking, too, which in this context simply means that they report a weighted average of the regression coefficient and the number "1.")

Market betas from comparables: One problem with the simple regression method is that individual betas are often very noisy. (Shrinking helps a little, though.) For example, think of a pharmaceutical company whose product happened to be rejected by the FDA. This would cause a large negative rate of return in one particular month. This month would now become a "statistical outlier." If the market happened to go up (down) this particular month, the company would likely end up having a negative (positive) market beta estimate—and this beta estimate would likely be unrepresentative of the future market beta. In the long run, such announcements would appear randomly, so beta would still be the right estimate—but by the time the long run happens, you may already be dead. To reduce estimation noise in practice, it is common to estimate not just the beta of the firm in question but also the beta of a couple of similar firms (comparables similar in size and industry, perhaps), and then to use a beta that reflects some sort of average among them.

For private firms, use comparable, publicly traded stocks.

If your project has no historical rate of return experience—perhaps because it is only a division of a publicly traded company or because the company is not publicly traded—you may have no choice other than this method of estimating a beta from comparable firms. (However, recall that the CAPM is only meaningful to begin with if your investors hold most of their wealth in the market portfolio.) For example, if you believe your new soda company project is similar to PepsiCo, you could adopt the asset beta of PepsiCo and use it to compute the CAPM expected rate of return. Realizing that firms that are smaller than PepsiCo, such as your own, tend to have higher betas, you might increase your beta estimate.

Market betas based on economic intuition: If you really cannot think of a good publicly traded firm that you trust to be a good comparable, you may have to rely more heavily on your judgment. Think about how your project's rate of return is likely to covary with the market. If you can make such a judgment, you can rearrange the CAPM formula to obtain a beta estimate:

$$\mathcal{E}(r_i) = r_F + [\mathcal{E}(r_M) - r_F] \cdot \beta_i \iff \beta_i = \frac{\mathcal{E}(r_i) - r_F}{\mathcal{E}(r_M) - r_F}$$

The right side of this formula helps translate your intuition into a beta estimate. You can ask such questions as "What rate of return (above the risk-free rate) will your project have if the market were to have $+10\%$ or -10% rate of return (above the risk-free rate)?" Clearly, such guesswork is difficult and error-prone—but it can provide a beta estimate when no other is available.

Equity and Asset Betas Revisited

It is important that you always distinguish between asset betas and equity betas. Let me remind you with an example. Assume that the risk-free rate is 4% and the equity premium is 5%. You own a $100 million project with an asset beta of 2.0 that you can finance with $20 million of risk-free debt. By definition, risk-free debt has a beta of 0. To find your equity beta, write down the formula for your asset beta (firm beta):

Don't use the equity beta to estimate your project's hurdle rate. Use the asset beta instead.

➤ *Asset and equity betas, Formula 8.7, Pg.200.*

$$\beta_{\text{Firm}} = \underbrace{\left(\frac{\text{Debt value}}{\text{Firm value}}\right)}_{20\%} \cdot \underbrace{\beta_{\text{Debt}}}_{(0)} + \underbrace{\left(\frac{\text{Equity value}}{\text{Firm value}}\right)}_{80\%} \cdot \underbrace{\beta_{\text{Equity}}}_{(\beta_{\text{Equity}})} = 2.0$$

Solve this to find that your equity beta is 2.5. This is what you would find on **YAHOO!** FINANCE. You would not want to base the hurdle rate of your firm's typical average project on the equity beta: Such a mistake would recommend you use a hurdle rate of $\mathcal{E}(r_i) = r_F + [\mathcal{E}(r_M) - r_F] \cdot \beta_i = 4\% + 5\% \cdot 2.5 = 16.5\%$. This would be too high. Instead, you should require your average projects to return $\mathcal{E}(r_i) = 4\% + 5\% \cdot 2.0 = 14\%$.

➤ *Typical, average, and marginal betas, Sect. 12.3, Pg.327.*

Conversely, if your project is private, you may have to find its hurdle rate by looking at public comparables. Let's presume you find a similarly sized firm with a similar business that **YAHOO!** FINANCE lists with a beta of 4. Remember that financial websites always list only the equity beta. The CAPM tells you that the expected rate of return on the equity is $4\% + 5\% \cdot 4 = 24\%$. However, this is not necessarily the hurdle rate for your project. When you look further on **YAHOO!** FINANCE, you see that your comparable is financed with 90% debt and 10% equity. (If the comparable had very little debt, a debt beta of 0 might have been a good assumption, but, unfortunately, in this case it is not.) Corporate debt rarely has good historical return data that would allow you to estimate a debt beta. Consequently, practitioners often estimate the expected rate of return on debt via debt comparables based on the credit rating. Say your comparable's debt is rated BB and say that BB bonds have offered *expected* rates of return of 100 basis points

If you use comparables, first unlever them.

➤ *Credit ratings, Sect. 6.2, Pg.125.*

above the Treasury. (This might be 200 basis points *quoted* above the Treasury). With the Treasury standing at 4%, you would estimate the comparable's cost of capital on debt to be 5%. The rest is easy. The expected rate of return on your project should be

$$\mathcal{E}(r_{\text{Project}}) = 90\% \cdot 5\% + 10\% \cdot 24\% = 6.9\%$$
$$= w_{\text{Debt}} \cdot \mathcal{E}(r_{\text{Debt}}) + w_{\text{Equity}} \cdot \mathcal{E}(r_{\text{Equity}})$$

This would make a good hurdle rate estimate for your project.

Q 9.14. According to the CAPM formula, a zero-beta asset should have the same expected rate of return as the risk-free rate. Can a zero-beta asset still have a positive standard deviation? Does it make sense that such a risky asset would not offer a higher rate of return than a risk-free asset in a world in which investors are risk averse?

Q 9.15. A comparable firm (with comparable size and in a comparable business) has a **YAHOO!** FINANCE –listed equity beta of 2.5 and a debt/asset ratio of 2/3. Assume that the debt is risk free.

1. Estimate the equity beta for your firm if your projects have similar betas, but your firm will carry a debt/asset ratio of 1/3.

2. If the risk-free rate is 3% and the equity premium is 2%, then what should you use as your firm's hurdle rate?

3. What do investors demand as the expected rate of return on the comparable firm's equity and on your own equity?

Q 9.16. You own a stock portfolio that has a market beta of 2.4, but you are getting married to someone who has a portfolio with a market beta of 0.4. You are three times as wealthy as your future significant other. What is the beta of your joint portfolio?

9.5 Is the CAPM the Right Model?

The counterfactual. Now you know how securities should be priced in a perfect CAPM world. What evidence would lead you to conclude that the CAPM is *not* an accurate description of reality? And does the CAPM seem to hold or not?

The SML If the CAPM Does Not Work

Q: What happens if a stock offers too much or too little expected rate of return? A: Investor stampedes. What would happen from the CAPM's perspective if a stock offered more than its appropriate expected rate of return? Investors in the economy would want to buy more of the stock than would be available: Its price would be too low. It would be too good a deal. Investors would immediately flock to it, and because there would not be enough of this stock, investors would bid up its price and thereby lower its expected rate of return. The price of the stock would settle at the correct CAPM expected rate of return. Conversely, what would happen if a stock offered less than its due expected rate of return? Investors would not be willing to hold enough of the stock: The stock's price would be too high, and its price would fall.

Neither situation should happen in the real world—investors are just too smart. However, you must realize that if a stock were not to follow the CAPM formula, buying it would still be risky. Yes, such a stock would offer too high or too low an expected rate of return and thus be too good or too bad a deal, attracting too many or too few investors chasing a limited amount of value in this stock—but it would still remain a risky investment, and no investor could earn risk-free profit.

Assets not priced according to the CAPM do not allow you to make money for nothing. However, it could imply good deals.

Under what circumstances would you lose faith in the CAPM? Exhibit 9.3 shows what security market relations could look like if the CAPM did not work. In plot (A), there is simply no relation between beta and returns. The best-fitting line (dashed) is simply flat. How could this benefit you if you dislike risk? Let's assume you start out by holding the market portfolio. Because market beta is a measure of risk contribution to your portfolio, you should tilt your portfolio away from stocks with high market betas—given their rewards, their risk contributions to your portfolio are too high. You would tilt your portfolio more towards the low-beta stocks. Such a portfolio would offer more reward to you than what you would receive in a CAPM world. In plot (B), the security markets relation is even perversely negative. Now low-beta stocks are really looking like a steal. In plot (C), the relation is not linear, but an inverted U-shape. You would again want to tilt away from high-beta stocks, but now also tilt away from very low-beta stocks. You would want to tilt towards stocks with a beta around 1. They simply offer the highest expected rate of return for the money.

Some security market lines if the CAPM does not hold. First, relations that do not look positive and linear.

In plots (D) through (F), the problem is entirely different. Note that the slope through all points, the dashed line, is nicely upward sloping. But note also that something else matters for predicting stock returns—firm size. Yet, the CAPM says not only that market beta should matter, but also that *market beta is all that should matter*. This is violated in these plots. Of course, you have to be smart enough to realize that firm size can help explain returns! It is only your knowledge of the role of firm size that helps you realize that the relationship between beta and returns is not linearly increasing. In fact, in plots (E) and (F), beta does not matter positively *after you control for size*. How would you invest in a world in which firm size helps predict returns? You would tilt your portfolios towards the small firms with the lowest market-betas, and away from the large firms with the highest market-betas. Again, by doing so, your portfolio would earn a rate of return that beats the market.

More security market lines if the CAPM fails with respect to a specific better alternative. The CAPM is exclusive—in the snobbish sense.

But be warned: This role of firm size in predicting stock returns could also be a **spurious relation**. That is, it may have randomly explained returns in the past, but may not do so in the future. Remember that when you plot such figures with real-world historical data, you do not have the true betas or true expected rates of return. Even if your statistical procedures are sound, statistical noise makes this a hazardous venture. In particular, in real life, although you can estimate market betas pretty reliably, you can only roughly estimate expected rates of return from historical rates of return.

Historical patterns could be spurious.

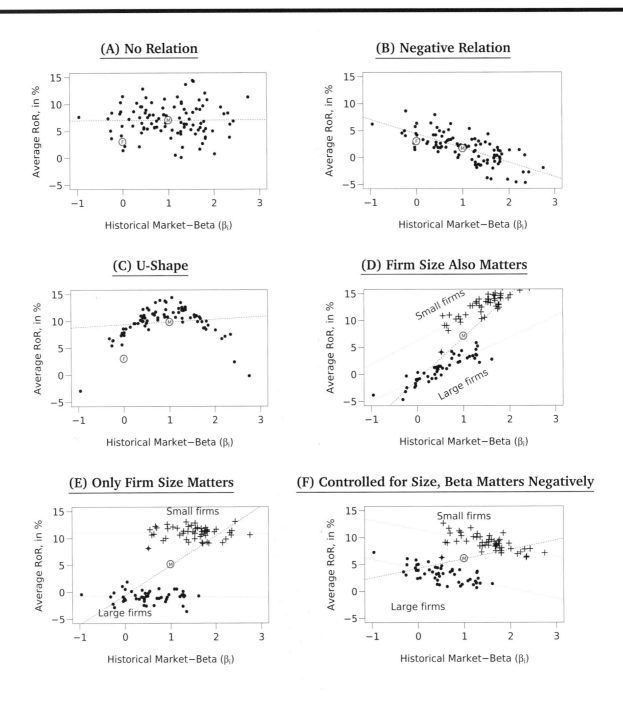

Exhibit 9.3: *The Security Market Line in Non-CAPM Worlds.* Each point is the historical beta and historical average rate of return on one asset. (The risk-free rate and the average market rate of return is noted with F and M, respectively.) The dashed line is from a regression predicting returns with market betas. The dotted lines are subset regressions. If these are not statistical mirages, then from the CAPM perspective, you can find "great deal" stocks that offer too much expected return given their risk contributions to your (market) portfolio, which you would therefore want to overemphasize; and "poor deal" stocks that offer too little expected return, given their risk contributions, which you would therefore want to underemphasize.

The Actual Historical Estimated CAPM (SML)

Before I let you in on the truth, please realize that a model is just a model—models are never perfect descriptions of reality. They can be useful within a certain domain, even if on closer examination they are rejected. For example, we do not live in a world of Newtonian gravity. Einstein's model of relativity is a better model—though it, too, is not capable of explaining everything. Yet no one would use Einstein's model to calculate how quickly objects fall. The Newtonian model is entirely appropriate and much easier to use. Similarly, planetary scientists use Einstein's model, even though we know it, too, fails to account for quantum effects—but it does well enough for the purposes at hand and there are as yet no better alternatives (even though string theory is trying hard).

> A model is just that—a model. It ain't always perfect.

The dark but open secret is that this latter situation is pretty much the situation in which corporations find themselves. The CAPM is not really correct. However, we have no good all-around alternatives that are clearly better for the purpose at hand—estimating reasonable costs of capital for corporate projects.

> The CAPM is *not* always correct.

The Empirical Evidence: Where It Works

Having apologized in advance, let me now explain where the CAPM works and where it fails. What does the security market line look like in real life? Exhibit 9.4 plots the relationships from 1970 to 2003. The typical stock with a beta of 0 earned a rate of return of about 0.6% per month (8% per annum), while the typical stock with a beta of 1 (e.g., the stock market itself) earned a rate of return of about 1.4% per month (18% per annum). Not drawn in the figure, the average stock with a beta of 2 earned about 2.2% per month (30% per annum), and the average stock with a beta of 3 earned about 3.5% per month (50% per annum). (These annual returns are arithmetic averages—the geometric annual rates of return would have been lower.) You can see that these 34 years were a very good period for risky financial investments! Most important, from the perspective of the CAPM, the historical relationship between average rates of return and betas seems to have been reasonably close to linear, just as the CAPM suggests. If we stopped now, I would have advised you to conclude that the CAPM is a pretty good model.

> This empirical relation looks reasonably linear and upward sloping: good for the CAPM.

The Empirical Evidence: Where It Fails

But look back at the six plots in Exhibit 9.3. The big problem of the CAPM is not so much that it fails in the sense of the first three plots, (A)-(C). Instead, the empirical evidence (hundreds of academic papers) show that the CAPM fails badly in the sense of the last three plots, (D)-(F): There are other classifications of stocks that matter for predicting stock returns. The most damaging such evidence may well be that firms classified as exciting "growth firms" (they have low sales and accounting values but high market values—the *Facebook*s and *Linked-In*s of this world) have generally underperformed boring "value firms" (the opposite—the *PepsiCo*s and *Proctor&Gamble*s of this world). Exhibit 9.5 illustrates roughly where these types of stocks have clustered in the plot of betas versus expected rates of return. The next-most damaging evidence comes from another classification—whether a stock was a recent winner or a recent loser over the last 12 months (excluding the most recent month and Januaries). Such recent winners

> But this is deceptive: The CAPM fails against specific better alternatives.

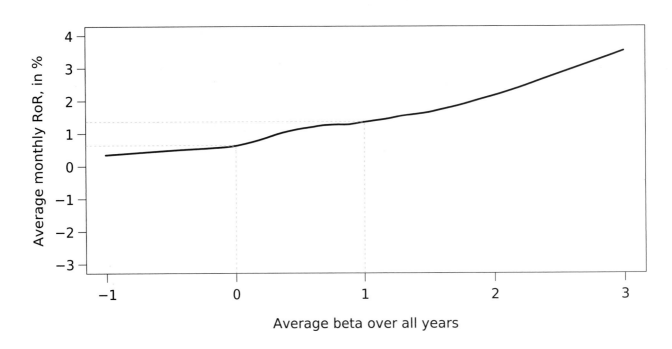

Exhibit 9.4: *Average Historical Rates of Return against Historical Market Betas, 1970-2003.* This is an estimated real-world empirical relationship between monthly betas and monthly average rates of return from 1970 to 2003. The betas are with respect to the value-weighted stock market. Extreme observations were truncated at –1 and +3 for beta, and at –3% and +4% for monthly returns. From the thousands of input points (each being a single firm), the fat plotted line here is "smoothed" version that fits these points locally, which is useful to allow it to show nonlinearities. The dotted blue lines indicate the approximate rate of return to securities with "beta = 0" (64 basis points per month, or about 8% per annum) and to securities with "beta = 1" (136 basis points per month, or about 18% per annum). Because these are arithmetic and not geometric averages, you would have earned less than this per year in a buy-and-hold strategy.

➤ *Other stock characteristics,*
Sect. App.9.C (Companion),
Pg.≈61.
What now?

have performed much better (though they did really poorly in the 2008-9 financial crisis). Moreover, the trading costs to exploit this **momentum** are quite high. In any case, after we take into account these other characteristics, market beta no longer seems to be too important, at all. That is, the world may be more like plot (D) than plot (C).

Unfortunately, although we can rationalize after the fact why these specific firm characteristics mattered for subsequent returns, we really know of no great reasons why they should have mattered in the first place. We also do not know whether these characteristics are themselves just stand-ins for something else that we have not yet found, or whether they matter in themselves. And not only do we finance experts not know for sure what characteristics should matter and why, but we also don't know how CFOs should operate in such a world. Should we advise managers to pretend that their firms are growth firms—because investors like this claim so much that they are willing

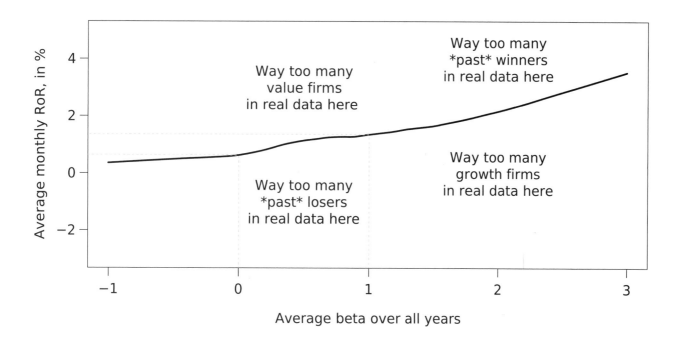

Exhibit 9.5: *Historical Firm Types Locations in Plot of Rates of Return against Historical Market Beta, 1970-2003.* Stocks that were past winners (north-east) tend to outperform past losers (south-west). Value stocks are "boring" firms with high sales and accounting values, but low market values—such as Procter&Gamble or RJR Nabisco (north-west). Growth firms are "exciting" firms with low sales, but high market values—such as Facebook or Linked-In (south-east).

to pay a lot for shares of such firms? And, as soon as they have their investors' money, should we then advise them to invest it as if they were value firms? We do not know yet. (On the plus side, it keeps ongoing academic finance research interesting.)

What Do You Do Now?

If the CAPM does not hold, why torture you with it? This is a much easier question to answer than how stocks are priced in the real world or what the best estimate of the appropriate hurdle rates for your project is.

Why CAPM?

Reasonable cost-of-capital estimates (often): Even though the CAPM is rejected, market beta is still often a useful cost-of-capital measure for a corporate finance manager.

Why? Look again at plot (E) in Exhibit 9.3. Let's presume it was just firm size that mattered to expected rates of return. If you have a beta of around 2, you are more than likely a small firm with an expected rate of return of 10%; if you have a beta of around 0, you are more than likely a large firm with an expected rate

Beta can also work as a proxy for firm size.

of return of 0%. Thus, beta would still provide you with a decent cost-of-capital estimate, even though it was not market beta itself that mattered, but whether your firm was large or small. (Market beta helped by indicating to you whether your firm was a big or a small firm.) Admittedly, using an incorrect model is not an ideal situation, but the cost-of-capital estimates are often reasonable enough that corporate managers generally can live with them for purposes of finding a hurdle rate.

However, please avoid the CAPM for extreme growth or value firms.

This logic does not always work. If your firm happens to be the very rare large outlier that had a market-beta of 3, then you would overestimate your cost of capital. In the real world, the logic also fails on extreme value and growth firms: Value firms with higher expected rates of return tend not to have higher betas. Thus, you should not use the CAPM as a proxy to compute expected rates of return for projects (stocks) that are extreme value or growth firms—for such firms, the CAPM cost-of-capital estimates could be far off. Don't rely on them.

The CAPM is based on the important concept of diversification.

Good intuition: The CAPM has impeccable intuition. It is a model that shines through its simplicity and focuses on what *should* matter—diversification. It thereby often helps you to sharpen your thinking about what your corporate projects should offer your investors.

And let's not forget—the CAPM is easy to use, at least relative to the potential alternatives that you can learn about in Section App.9.C (Companion).

There really is no better alternative to the CAPM.

➤ *CAPM alternatives, Sect.* App.9.C (Companion), Pg.≈61.

Alternatives—please stand up: The famous sociologist Lewin wrote that "there is nothing more practical than a good theory." If not the CAPM, then what else? If you cannot live with the fact that the CAPM is not correct, I really do not know what to recommend to you as a clearly better alternative. It takes a model to beat a model, and we really do not have an all-around good replacement for the CAPM.

For example, one alternative model is to use the size and value/growth firm characteristics that I just mentioned as proxies for appropriate expected rates of return. But it is not even clear whether the higher returns for value firms reflect appropriate rewards for risk-taking that investors require (and which therefore should flow into a hurdle rate), or whether these firms earned superior returns because the market was not perfect (and which therefore need not flow into a hurdle rate). Imperfect markets are the subject of our next chapters.

Important: Everyone expects you to know the CAPM!

Everyone uses it: Exhibit 9.6 shows that we are not alone: 73% of the CFOs reported that they always or almost always use the CAPM. (And use of the CAPM was even more common among large firms and among CFOs with an MBA.) No alternative method was used very often. Consequently, you have no choice but to understand the CAPM model well—*if you will work for a corporation, then the CAPM is the benchmark model that your future employer will likely use—and will expect you to understand well.* The CAPM is simply *the* standard. The CAPM is also used as a benchmark by many investors rating their (investment) managers, by government regulatory commissions, by courts in tort cases, and so on. It is literally the dominant, if not the only, universal model for the cost of capital.

Method	Usage Frequency	Usage Recommendation	Explained in
CAPM	▬▬▬▬▬▬ (73%)	With Caution	Chapter 9
Historical Average Returns	▬▬▬ (39%)	Rarely	Chapter 8
Modified CAPM	▬▬▬ (34%)	With Caution	Chapter 9
Backed Out from Gordon Model	▬ (16%)	Occasionally	Chapter 3
Whatever Investors Tell Us	▬ (14%)	Occasionally	Chapter 2

Exhibit 9.6: *CFO Valuation Techniques for the Cost of Capital.* Rarely means "usually no, and often used incorrectly." Not reported, use of the CAPM is more common among managers with an MBA—and in firms who rely on consultants who in turn use the CAPM. Original Source: John Graham and Campbell Harvey, 2001.

Let me infuse a bit more of my personal opinion now. Different academics draw different conclusions from the empirical evidence. Some recommend outright against using the CAPM, but most professors recommend "use with caution." I am among them. As a corporate executive, you will have to think about when you can reasonably use the CAPM. Think about whether it is useful for your own cost-of-capital estimates, or whether the CAPM errors seem too large to be useful for your particular needs. Of course, if the CAPM fails, I don't know what works better.

My personal opinion: Use the CAPM with caution in a corporate finance context for capital budgeting.

Here is what I would definitely warn against:

Caution!

Accuracy: The CAPM is a poor model if precision is of the essence. If you believe that CAPM expected rates of return should be calculated with any digits after the decimal point, then you are deluded. Please realize that, at best, the CAPM can only offer expected rates of return that are of the "right order of magnitude," plus or minus a few percentage points perhaps.

Don't expect accuracy and don't use it for financial investing.

Actually, if accuracy and precision are important, you are thoroughly in trouble. We do not have *any* models that offer great accuracy. (Fortunately, it is often less important to be accurate than to be *better* estimating value than your competitors. And always remember that valuation is as much an art as it is a science.)

Investment purposes: If you are not a corporate CFO looking for a project hurdle rate, but a financial investor looking for good investments from the universe of financial instruments, please do not use the CAPM. Although the CAPM offers the correct intuition that wide diversification needs to be an important part of *any* good investment strategy, there *are* still better investment strategies than just investing in the market index. Some are explained in Section App.9.C (Companion); more will be discussed in an advanced investments course.

Avoid using the CAPM for financial investment purposes.

And also please do not confuse the CAPM with the mean-variance framework discussed in the previous chapter. Mean-variance optimization is an asset-selection technique for your individual portfolio, and it works, regardless of whether or not the CAPM holds.

➤ *Mean-variance optimization,*
Sect. App.8.C (Companion),
Pg.≈34.

IMPORTANT

> - Be aware of the CAPM's strengths and weaknesses.
>
> - The empirical evidence suggests that the CAPM is not a great model for predicting expected rates of return. This is especially so for extreme-value and extreme-growth firms, or firms having recently experienced very high or very low rates of return.
>
> - The CAPM is still the benchmark model in the real world. Every corporation uses it—and every corporation expects you to know it.
>
> - The CAPM can offer reasonably good estimates for the cost of capital (hurdle rate) in many, but not all, corporate settings.
>
> - The CAPM never offers great accuracy.
>
> - The CAPM may be a decent model for corporate capital budgeting, but it is not a good model for a financial market investor. The CAPM speculates that the market portfolio is mean-variance efficient. In real life, you can optimize your portfolio and choose portfolios closer to the mean-variance frontier.
>
> - Mean-variance optimization (Section 8.2) works even if the CAPM does not.

Q 9.17. Does the empirical evidence suggest that the CAPM is correct?

Q 9.18. If the CAPM is wrong, why do you need to learn it?

How Bad Are Mistakes?

How Robust is the CAPM?

By now, you should realize that you will never perfectly know the required inputs for the CAPM. You can only make educated guesses. And even *after* the fact, you will never be sure—you observe only realized rates of return, never expected rates of return. Exactly how robust are CAPM estimates with respect to errors in its inputs? Well, it depends on the inputs.

The risk-free rate: Errors in the risk-free rate (r_F) are likely to be modest. The risk-free rate can be considered to be almost known for practical purposes. Just make sure to use Treasuries that match the timing of your project cash flows.

Market beta: Reasonable beta estimates typically have some uncertainty, but good comparables can often be found in the public market. If due care is exercised, a typical range of uncertainty about beta might be about plus or minus 0.4. For example, if the equity premium is 3% and if you believe your beta is 2, but it is really 1.6 instead, then you would overestimate the appropriate expected rate of return by $2 \cdot 3\% - 1.6 \cdot 3\% = 1.2\%$. Although this level of uncertainty is not insignificant, it is often tolerable in corporate practice.

Equity premium estimates: Reasonable equity premium estimates can range from about 1% per year to about 8% per year—a large range. *To date, there is no universally accepted method to estimate the expected rate of return on the market, so this disagreement cannot be easily settled with data and academic studies.* Unfortunately, reasonable differences of opinion in estimating the expected rate of return on the market can have a large influence on expected rate of return estimates. For example, assume the risk-free rate is 3%, and take a project with a beta of 2. The CAPM might advise this corporation that potential investors demand either an expected rate of return of 5% per year (equity premium estimate of 1%) or an expected rate of return of 19% per year (equity premium estimate of 8%), or anything in between. This is—to put it bluntly—a miserably large range of possible cost-of-capital estimates. (And this range does not even consider the fact that *actual* future project rates of return will necessarily differ from *expected rates of return*!) Of course, in the real world, managers who want to take a project will argue that the expected rate of return on the market is low. This means that their own project looks relatively more attractive. Potential project buyers will argue that the expected rate of return on the market is high. This means that they will claim to have great opportunities elsewhere, so that they can justify a lower price offer for this project.

Model errors: What about the CAPM as a model itself? This error is difficult to assess. Perhaps a reasonable approach is to use the CAPM in a corporate context unless the firm is unusual—an extreme value or growth or small firm, for example. Just remain aware that the model use itself introduces errors.

You will often use the CAPM expected rate of return as your cost of capital in an NPV calculation. Here, you combine errors and uncertainty about expected cash flows with your errors and uncertainty in CAPM estimates. What should you worry about? Recall that in Section 4.1 (errors in cash flows and discount rates), you learned the relative importance of correct inputs into the NPV formula. The basic conclusion was that for short-term projects, getting the cash flows right is more important than getting the expected rates of return right; for long-term projects, getting both right is important. We just discussed the relative importance of getting the equity premium and the project beta right. Now recall that your basic conclusion was that the CAPM formula is first and foremost exposed to errors in the market risk premium (equity premium), though it is also somewhat exposed to beta estimates. Putting these two insights together suggests that for short-term projects, worrying about exact beta estimates is less important than worrying about estimating cash flows first and the appropriate equity premium second. For long-term projects, the order of importance remains the same, but having good equity premium estimates now becomes relatively more important. In contrast, in most cases, honest mistakes in beta, *given reasonable care*, are relatively less problematic.

ANECDOTE   "Cost of Capital" Expert Witnessing

When Congress tried to force the "Baby Bells" (the split-up parts of the original AT&T) to open up their local telephone lines to competition, it decreed that the Baby Bells were entitled to a fair return on their infrastructure investment—with fair return to be measured by the CAPM. (The CAPM is either the de facto or legislated standard for measuring the cost of capital in many other regulated industries, too.) The estimated value of the telecommunication infrastructure in the United States is about $10 to $15 billion. A difference in the estimated equity premium of 1% may sound small, but even in as small an industry as local telecommunications, it meant about $100 to $150 million a year—enough to hire hordes of lawyers and valuation consultants opining in court on the appropriate equity premium. Some of my colleagues bought nice houses with the legal fees.

I did not get the call. I lack the ability to keep a straight face while stating that "the equity premium is exactly x point y percent," which was an important qualification for being such an expert. In an unrelated case in which I did testify, the opposing expert witness even explicitly criticized my statement that my cost-of-capital estimate was an imprecise range—unlike me, he could provide an exact estimate!   *Bradford Cornell, UCLA*

Q 9.19. Is the CAPM likely to be more accurate for a project where the beta is very high, one where it is very low, or one where it is zero?

Q 9.20. To value an ordinarily risky project, that is, a project with a beta in the vicinity of about 1, what is the relative contribution of your personal uncertainty (lack of knowledge) in (a) the risk-free rate, (b) the equity premium, (c) the beta, and (d) the expected cash flows? Consider both long-term and short-term investments. Where are the trouble spots?

Summary

This chapter covered the following major points:

- The CAPM provides an "opportunity cost of capital" for investors, which corporations can use as the cost of capital in the NPV formula. The CAPM formula is

$$\mathcal{E}(r_i) = r_F + \left[\mathcal{E}(r_M) - r_F\right] \cdot \beta_i$$

  Thus, there are three inputs: the risk-free rate of return (r_F), the expected rate of return on the market ($\mathcal{E}(r_M)$), and the project's or firm's market beta (β_i). Only the latter is project-specific.

- The line plotting expected rates of return against market beta is called the security market line (SML).

- The CAPM provides an expected rate of return, consisting of the time premium and the risk premium. It ignores the default premium. In the NPV formula, the default risk and default premium work through the expected cash flow in the numerator, not through the expected rate of return (cost of capital) in the denominator.

- The expected rate of return on the market is often a critical CAPM input, especially if market beta is high—but it is difficult to guess. There are at least five different common guesstimation methods, but no one really knows which one is best. Reasonable estimates for the equity premium ($\mathscr{E}(r_M) - r_F$) range from about 1% to 8% per annum. (As for me personally, I like 2% to 4%.)

- For r_F, you should use risk-free Treasuries that match the timing of your project's cash flows.

- There are a number of methods to estimate market beta. For publicly traded firms, it can be obtained from commercial data vendors (or self-computed). For private firms or projects, a similar publicly traded firm can often be found. Finally, managerial scenarios can be used to estimate market betas.

- The empirical SML from 1970 to 2003 has a reasonably CAPM-consistent upward slope, even though this is only true if other characteristics (such as growth/value) are not controlled for. Therefore, the CAPM is not a good model for investing purposes, although it often remains a reasonable model for capital budgeting purposes.

- The chapter appendix discusses certainty equivalence and CAPM alternatives (such as the APT and the Fama-French-Momentum model). You must use the certainty equivalence form of the CAPM when projects are purchased or sold for prices other than their fair market values. It is also often the only method if only underlying cash flows rather than value estimates are available.

Preview of the Chapter Appendix in the Companion

In the Appendix

The appendix to this chapter explains

- the "certainty equivalence value" (CEV) which allows you to use the CAPM for projects that you are not buying at the appropriate equilibrium price. For example, you need the CEV to work out how to value an inheritance that will be higher if your business fails. (Being free today does not mean that there is no value to such a promise.)

- how to use the CEV formula to estimate the value of a project for which you have historical cash flows, but no market value information.

- how the CAPM is derived from the fact that the optimal portfolio is always the combination of two portfolios, one of which may be the risk-free asset.

- what the CAPM alternatives are and how to use them. The first alternative is the APT (arbitrage pricing theory) and its relative, the Intertemporal CAPM. The second alternative are Fama-French value and momentum models. These seem to predict better than any alternatives, but are less grounded in theory (or, you may say, reason) than the former.

Keywords

Answers

Q 9.1 Yes, the perfect market is an assumption underlying the CAPM. In addition,

1. Investors are rational utility maximizers.

2. Investors care only about overall portfolio mean rate of return and risk at one given point in time.

3. All parameters are known (not discussed until later in the chapter).

4. All assets are traded. Every investor can purchase every asset.

Q 9.2 With $r_F = 4\%$ and $\mathcal{E}(r_M) = 7\%$, the cost of capital for a project with a beta of 3 is $\mathcal{E}(r) = r_F + [\mathcal{E}(r_M) - r_F] \cdot \beta_i = 4\% + (7\% - 4\%) \cdot 3 = 13\%$.

Q 9.3 With $r_F = 4\%$ and $\mathcal{E}(r_M) = 12\%$, the cost of capital for a project with a beta of 3 is $\mathcal{E}(r) = r_F + [\mathcal{E}(r_M) - r_F] \cdot \beta_i = 4\% + (12\% - 4\%) \cdot 3 = 28\%$.

Q 9.4 With $r_F = 4\%$ and $\mathcal{E}(r_M) = 12\%$, the cost of capital for a project with a beta of –3 is $\mathcal{E}(r) = r_F + [\mathcal{E}(r_M) - r_F] \cdot \beta_i = 4\% + (12\% - 4\%) \cdot (-3) = -20\%$. Yes, it does make sense that a project can offer a negative expected rate of return. Such projects are such great investments that you would be willing to expect losses on them, just because of the great insurance that they are offering.

Q 9.5 No—the real-world SML is based on historical data and not true expectations. It would be a scatterplot of historical risk and reward points. If the CAPM holds, a straight, upward-sloping line would fit them best.

Q 9.6 Write down the CAPM formula and solve $\mathcal{E}(r_i) = r_F + [\mathcal{E}(r_M) - r_F] \cdot \beta_i = 4\% + (7\% - 4\%) \cdot \beta_i = 5\%$. Therefore, $\beta_i = 1/3$. Note that we are ignoring the promised rate of return.

Q 9.7 The security market line is

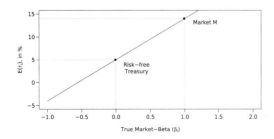

Q 9.8 The equity premium, $\mathcal{E}(r_M) - r_F$, is the premium that the market expects to offer on the risky market above and beyond what it offers on Treasuries.

Q 9.9 It does not matter what you choose as the per-unit payoff of the bond. If you choose $100, you expect it to return $99.

1. Thus, the price of the bond is PV = $99/(1 + [3\% + 5\% \cdot 0.2]) \approx$ $95.19.

2. Therefore, the promised rate of return on the bond is $100/$95.19 − 1 \approx 5.05\%$.

3. The risk-free rate is 3%, so this is the time premium (which contains any inflation premium). The (expected) risk premium is 1%. The remaining 1.05% is the default premium.

Q 9.10 The cost needs to be discounted with the current interest rate. Because payment is up-front, this cost is $30,000 now! The appropriate expected rate of return for cash flows (of your earnings) is $3\% + 5\% \cdot 1.5 = 10.5\%$. You can now use the annuity formula to determine the PV if you graduate:

$$\frac{\$5,000}{10.5\%} \cdot \left[1 - \left(\frac{1}{1 + 10.5\%} \right)^{40} \right] \approx \$47,619 \cdot 98.2\%$$
$$\approx \$46,741.46$$

With 90% probability, you will do so, which means that the appropriate risk-adjusted and discounted cash flow is about $42,067.32. The NPV of your education is therefore about $12,067.32.

Q 9.11 An estimate between 1% and 8% per year is reasonable. Anything below 0% and above 10% would seem unreasonable to me. For reasoning, please see the different methods in the chapter.

Q 9.12 Use the 1-year Treasury rate for the 1-year project, especially if the 1-year project produces most of its cash flows at the end of the year. If it produces constant cash flows throughout the year, a 6-month Treasury rate might be more appropriate. Because the 10-year project could have a duration of cash flows much shorter than 10 years, depending on use, you might choose a risk-free Treasury rate that is between 5 and 10 years. Of course, it would be even better if you match the individual project cash flows with individual Treasuries.

Q 9.13 The duration of this cash flow is around, or a little under, 5 years. Thus, a 5-year zero-coupon U.S. Treasury would be a reasonably good guess. You should not be using a 30-day or 30-year Treasury. A 10-year zero-coupon Treasury would be a better match for a project that yields cash only once at the end of 10 years. That is, for our project that has cash flows each year for 10 years, the 10-year Treasury as a benchmark would have too much of its payments as principal repayment at the end of its 10-year term.

Q 9.14 Yes, a zero-beta asset can still have its own idiosyncratic risk. And, yes, it is perfectly kosher for a zero-beta asset to offer the same expected rate of return as the risk-free asset. The reason is that investors hold gazillions of assets, so the idiosyncratic risk of the zero-beta asset will just diversify away.

Q 9.15 This is an asset beta versus equity beta question. Because the debt is almost risk free, we can use $\beta_{\text{Debt}} \approx 0$.

1. First, compute an unlevered asset beta for your comparable with its debt-to-asset ratio of 2 to 3. This is $\beta_{\text{Asset}} = w_{\text{Debt}} \cdot \beta_{\text{Debt}} + w_{\text{Equity}} \cdot \beta_{\text{Equity}} = (2/3) \cdot 0 + (1/3) \cdot 2.5 \approx 0.833$. Next, assume that your project has the same asset beta, but a smaller debt-to-asset ratio of 1 to 3, and compute your own equity beta: $\beta_{\text{Asset}} = w_{\text{Debt}} \cdot \beta_{\text{Debt}} + w_{\text{Equity}} \cdot \beta_{\text{Equity}} \Rightarrow 0.833 \approx (1/3) \cdot 0 + (2/3) \cdot \beta_{\text{Equity}} \Rightarrow \beta_{\text{Equity}} = 1.25$.

2. With an asset beta of 0.83, your firm's asset hurdle rate should be $\mathcal{E}(r_i) = 3\% + 2\% \cdot 0.83 \approx 4.7\%$.

3. Your comparable's equity expected rate of return would be $\mathcal{E}(r_{\text{Comps Equity}}) = 3\% + 2\% \cdot 2.5 = 8\%$. Your own equity's expected rate of return would be $\mathcal{E}(r_{\text{Your Equity}}) = 3\% + 2\% \cdot 1.25 = 5.5\%$

Q 9.16 Your combined happy-marriage beta would be $\beta_{\text{Combined}} = (3/4) \cdot 2.4 + (1/4) \cdot 0.4 = 1.9$.

Q 9.17 No, the empirical evidence suggests that the CAPM does not hold. The most important violation seems to be that value firms had market betas that were low, yet average returns that were high. The opposite was the case for growth firms.

Q 9.18 Even though the CAPM is empirically rejected, it remains the benchmark model that everyone uses in the real world. Moreover, even if you do not trust the CAPM itself, at the very least it suggests that covariance with the market could be an important factor.

Q 9.19 The CAPM should work very well if beta is about 0. The reason is that you do not even need to guess the equity premium if this is so.

Q 9.20 For short-term investments, the expected cash flows are most critical to estimate well (see Section 4.1 on Page 62). In this case, the trouble spot (d) is really all that matters. For long-term projects, the cost of capital becomes relatively more important to get right, too. The market betas and risk-free rates are usually relatively low maintenance (though not trouble free), having only modest degrees of uncertainty. The equity premium will be the most important problem factor in the cost-of-capital estimation. Thus, the trouble spots for long-term projects are (b) and (d).

End of Chapter Problems

Q 9.21. What are the assumptions underlying the CAPM? Are the perfect market assumptions among them? Are there more?

Q 9.22. If the CAPM holds, then what should you do as the manager if you cannot find projects that meet the hurdle rate suggested by the CAPM?

Q 9.23. In a perfect world and in the absence of externalities, should you take only the projects with the highest NPV?

Q 9.24. Write down the CAPM formula. Which are economy-wide inputs, and which are project-specific inputs?

Q 9.25. The risk-free rate is 6%. The expected rate of return on the stock market is 8%. What is the appropriate cost of capital for a project that has a beta of 2?

Q 9.26. The risk-free rate is 6%. The expected rate of return on the stock market is 10%. What is the appropriate cost of capital for a project that has a beta of –2? Does this make economic sense?

Q 9.27. Draw the SML if the true expected rate of return on the market is 6% per annum and the risk-free rate is 2% per annum. How would the figure look if you were not sure about the expected rate of return on the market?

Q 9.28. A junk bond with a beta of 0.4 will default with 20% probability. If it does, investors receive only 60% of what is due to them. The risk-free rate is 3% per annum and the risk premium is 5% per annum. What is the price of this bond, its promised rate of return, and its expected rate of return?

Q 9.29. What would it take for a bond to have a larger risk premium than default premium?

Q 9.30. A corporate zero-bond promises 7% in one year. Its market beta is 0.3. The equity premium is 4%; the equivalent Treasury rate is 3%. What is the appropriate bond price today?

Q 9.31. Explain the basic schools of thought when it comes to equity premium estimation.

Q 9.32. If you do not want to estimate the equity premium, what are your alternatives to finding a cost-of-capital estimate?

Q 9.33. Explain in 200 words or less: What are reasonable guesstimates for the market risk premium and why?

Q 9.34. Should you use the same risk-free rate of return both as the CAPM formula intercept and in the equity premium calculation, or should you assume an equity premium that is independent of investment horizon?

Q 9.35. Should a negative-beta asset offer a higher or a lower expected rate of return than the risk-free asset? Does this make sense?

Q 9.36. An unlevered firm has an asset market beta of 1.5. The risk-free rate is 3%. The equity premium is 4%.

1. What is the firm's cost of capital?

2. The firm refinances itself. It repurchases half of its stock with debt that it issues. Assume that this debt is risk free. What is the equity beta of the levered firm?

3. According to the CAPM, what rate of return does the firm have to offer to its *creditors*?

4. According to the CAPM, what rate of return does the firm have to offer to its *levered equity holders*?

5. Has the firm's weighted average cost of capital changed?

Q 9.37. Consider the following historical rate of return series:

Year	IBM	S&P 500	Year	IBM	S&P 500
1991	−0.175	0.263	2001	0.430	−0.130
1992	−0.400	0.045	2002	−0.355	−0.234
1993	0.156	0.071	2003	0.205	0.264
1994	0.322	−0.015	2004	0.072	0.090
1995	0.257	0.341	2005	−0.158	0.030
1996	0.676	0.203	2006	0.198	0.136
1997	0.393	0.310	2007	0.129	0.035
1998	0.775	0.267	2008	−0.208	−0.385
1999	0.175	0.195	2009	0.586	0.235
2000	−0.208	−0.101	2010	0.143	0.128

Assume that IBM had so little debt that it was practically risk-free.

1. What was IBM's equity beta over this sample period?

2. If IBM had a debt-equity ratio of 70%, what was its asset beta? (Hint: To determine a D/A ratio, make up an example in which a firm has a 70% D/E ratio.)

3. How important is the 1992 observation to your beta estimate?

4. If HP is similar to IBM in its business but has a debt-equity ratio of 10%, what would you expect HP's levered equity beta to be? (Hint: Use the same leverage conversion trick.)

Q 9.38. Look up betas on **YAHOO!** FINANCE today, and compare them to those in Exhibit 8.6 on Page 197.

1. How does the beta of Intel today compare to its earlier estimate from May 2008? Was its beta stable (over time)?

2. How does the beta of AMD today compare to its earlier estimate from May 2008? Was its beta stable?

3. AMD is a much smaller firm than Intel. How do their betas compare?

Q 9.39. A comparable firm (in a comparable business) has an equity beta of 2.5 and a debt-equity ratio of 2. The debt is almost risk free. Estimate the beta for your equity if projects have constant betas, but your firm will carry a debt-equity ratio of 1/2. (Hint: To translate a debt-equity ratio into a debt-asset ratio, make up an example.)

Q 9.40. A Fortune 100 firm is financed with $15 billion in debt and $5 billion in equity. Its historical equity beta has been 2. If the firm were to increase its leverage from $15 billion to $18 billion and use the cash to repurchase shares, what would you expect its levered equity beta to be?

Q 9.41. The prevailing risk-free rate is 5% per annum. A competitor to your own firm, though publicly traded, has been using an overall project cost of capital of 12% per annum. The competitor is financed by 1/3 debt and 2/3 equity. This firm has had an estimated equity beta of 1.5. What is it using as its equity premium estimate?

Q 9.42. Apply the CAPM. Assume the risk-free rate of return is the current yield on 5-year bonds. Assume that the market's expected rate of return is 3% per year above this. Download 5 years of daily rate of return data on four funds: NAESX, VLACX, VUVLX, and VWUSX.

- What were the historical average rates of return?

- What were the historical market betas?

- What were the historical market betas, adjusted (shrunk) toward 1 by averaging with 1?

- How do these estimates compare to the market beta estimates of the financial website from which you downloaded the data?

- Does it appear as if these funds followed a CAPM -like relationship?

Q 9.43. Draw some possible security markets relations that would not be consistent with the CAPM.

Q 9.44. Does the empirical evidence suggest that the CAPM is correct?

Q 9.45. Why do you need to understand the CAPM?

Q 9.46. Under what circumstances is the CAPM a good model to use? What are the main arguments in favor of using it? When is it not a good model?

Q 9.47. Explain the kinds of projects for which it is important to get accurate equity premium estimates.

Part III

Market Efficiency

...and Value in an Imperfect Market

You now understand the theory of finance in perfect markets. It is precisely the four perfect market assumptions that have allowed modern finance to become the "science" that it is today. Every important concept of finance has been derived in this perfect markets context first. In fact, with only a few exceptions, most finance formulas used in the real world today are still based on the (false) assumption that the world is perfect!

Fortunately, many financial markets are close to perfect, so the distance between theory and practice in finance is often small. However, it is almost never zero. The real world is definitely dirtier than our perfect one, and you can't just close your eyes and wish you were still in Kansas. Thus, the chapters in this part explain how you can navigate the troubled waters of the real world.

What You Want to Learn in this Part

- In Chapter 10, you will learn not only why the four perfect market assumptions are too good to be true, but also why they are so important. You will learn to think about what happens when individuals have different information, when financial markets are noncompetitive, and when investors or firms have to pay transaction costs and taxes. Sometimes you can adjust the perfect markets formulas explicitly to take market imperfections into account; sometimes you can only do so intuitively.

    Typical questions: What are typical transaction costs, and how do you work with them? How do taxes work? Why are capital gains better than ordinary income? If you have to pay 40% income taxes on interest receipts, the inflation rate is 2% per annum, and your investment promises 5% per annum, how much can you buy in goods tomorrow? Should you take this investment if you can earn 5% in taxable bonds and 3% in tax-exempt municipal bonds?

- In Chapter 11, you will learn about a concept that is not as strict as that of a perfect market: an efficient market. A market is said to be efficient if it uses all available information in the price setting. *All perfect markets are efficient (in equilibrium), but not all efficient markets are perfect.* Whether financial markets are efficient is the question that lies at the heart of "behavioral finance," a field of finance that asks whether individual investor irrationality—doubtlessly present—can be strong enough to influence financial market prices.

    Typical questions: Could it be that market efficiency is not absolute but

241

comes in different degrees? What exactly are the disagreements between classical finance and behavioral finance? What processes can stock prices reasonably follow? Do stock prices follow random walks? What is the signal-to-noise ratio in the context of financial markets? What is an arbitrage? What should you think of market gurus? What can you learn from stock price reactions to events?

10

Market Imperfections

Information/Opinions, Market Depth, Transaction Costs, and Taxes

So far, we have assumed no differences in opinions (and thus information), no transaction costs, no taxes, and a large market with many sellers and buyers—a "perfect market." Even when we covered uncertainty, risk, and the CAPM, we were still in the perfect market framework. In fact, most formulas in finance used in the real world today rely on the perfect markets assumptions. Without them, depending on the situation, they might be outright wrong.

Why is it that these perfect markets assumptions are so important? You will learn that it is because of what they have done for us: They have given us one unique, appropriate, expected rate of return—whether you want to borrow someone else's money to finance your projects or lend your money to someone else undertaking projects. Breaking these assumptions causes havoc in our models: Without a unique expected rate of return, project prices are no longer unique. Instead, they depend on the cash position of their owners. Without a unique price, what does "value" even mean in the first place?

Still, as wonderful as perfect markets are, they do not exist. They are conceptual, not real—although some financial markets come very close. You now have to leave this frictionless, utopian world and learn how to think about financial questions in "imperfect markets." Fortunately, many of your tools (and specifically NPV) will still work. But you need to apply them with a lot more caution and realize their limits.

10.1 Causes and Consequences of Imperfect Markets

So far, we have not distinguished between the cost of capital at which you can borrow money to finance your projects and the rate of return at which you can save money. In "perfect markets," these two rates are the same. Remarkably, the purpose of all four perfect markets assumptions is only to accomplish this one fact. It is the one fact on which everything else rests:

Perfect markets create an equality between borrowing and lending rates.

Without perfect markets, borrowing and lending rates are not equal.

Without equal
borrowing and lending
rates, project market
value is not unique.
When this is not the case, the implications are far-reaching. If these rates are not equal, then you cannot move in and out of an investment as often as you like. More fundamentally, even the value of a project stops being unique. Instead, a project may be worth any number in a whole range of possible values. Indeed, the whole concept of one project value may become meaningless. Value might depend on who owns the project, what the tastes of the individuals' relatives are, or even what time of day it is. We cannot even claim any longer that the value of a project is its PV. But let's take this one step at a time.

Q 10.1. What does the assumption of a perfect market buy you that would not be satisfied in an imperfect market?

Judging Market Perfection for PepsiCo Shares and Houses

For PepsiCo shares,
the perfect market
assumptions are not
perfectly true, but
they are not too far
from the truth.
Start by contemplating the four perfect markets assumptions for a stock like PepsiCo:

1. **No differences in opinion:** Recall that this assumption does not mean that there is no uncertainty, but that investors do not disagree about the uncertainty. Objective, rational traders with access to the same kind of information should come to similar conclusions about PepsiCo's value. They should agree on the distribution of prices that PepsiCo shares will likely sell at tomorrow, which in turn defines share value today. For the most part, it is unlikely that rational traders would disagree much about the value of PepsiCo shares—they should realize that it is not very likely that they can predict the price of PepsiCo much better than the market. Any disagreements would likely be minor. Of course, if some traders have insider information, then they could predict tomorrow's price better, and the perfect market would be no more—but trading on inside information is illegal.

2. **Infinitely many investors and firms:** On a typical day in 2006, around $250 million worth of PepsiCo shares changed hands. This is a lot of buyers and sellers. Thus, PepsiCo shares appear to trade in a competitive market, in which no single buyer or seller influences the price. There are lots of potential buyers willing to purchase the shares for the same price (or maybe just a tiny bit less), and lots of potential sellers willing to sell the shares for the same price (or maybe just a tiny bit more).

3. **No transaction costs:** Trading PepsiCo shares does incur transaction costs, but these are modest. A typical total round-trip transaction cost spread for PepsiCo is about 5 cents on a $50 share price, which is 10 basis points. An institutional trader may even be able to beat this. There are no searching costs for finding out the proper price of PepsiCo shares (it is posted by the NYSE), and there are very low costs to locating a buyer or seller.

4. **No taxes:** This may be the most problematic perfect market assumption in this context. Fortunately, we need this assumption of no taxes primarily for one purpose: The return to a seller owning PepsiCo shares should not be different from the same rate of return to a buyer. Here is what I mean.

Consider an extreme example in which PepsiCo starts out at $20 per share and happens to end up at $80 per share two years later. Assume that the capital gains tax rate is 20% and the risk-free discount rate is 5%. How much value is saved if you hold shares for two years versus if you sell them to me midway? If you keep the shares, the taxable capital gains would be on $80 - $20 = $60. At a 20% capital gains tax rate, Uncle Sam would collect $12. If you instead trade them to me at $50 after the first year, the capital gains consequences would be on $30 first for you ($20\% \cdot \$30 = \$6$), and then on $30 at the end for me ($6 again). This violates the perfect market assumption, because if you hold the shares for two years, the present value of the tax obligation at $\$12/1.05^2 \approx \$10.88$. If you sell them to me, it is $\$6/1.05 + \$6/1.05^2 \approx \$11.16$. Thus, shares are worth more if you hold them than if you trade them.

But the difference in how we value shares is really only in regard to the interest on the interim taxation. It is only 28 cents on a gain of $60. Moreover, this example is extreme not only in the 300% rate of return, but also in assuming a worst-case taxation scenario. This chapter later explains that many capital gains can be offset by capital losses and that investor tax timing discretion can further lower taxes. Furthermore, most shares are now held by institutions. Many of these are pension funds, which are entirely tax-exempt and therefore face no tax implications when trading.

In sum, the market for PepsiCo shares may indeed be reasonably close to perfect to allow you to use this as a first working assumption.

Unfortunately, not every good is traded in a perfect market. For example, think about selling your house—a pertinent question for many in the real estate slump of 2008. What is its value? What if your house is in a very remote part of the country, if potential buyers are sporadic, if alternative houses with the same characteristics are rare, or if the government imposes much higher property taxes on new owners (as, e.g., California does)? Intuitively, the value of your house could now depend on the luck of the draw (how many potential buyers are in the vicinity and see the ad, whether a potential buyer wants to live in exactly this kind of house, and so on); your urgency to sell (depending perhaps on whether you have the luxury to turn down a lowball first offer); or whether you need to sell at all (as current owner, you may be better off enjoying low property taxes, so your house may be worth a lot more to you than to a potential buyer). The value of such a house can be difficult to determine because the market can be far from perfect—and the house value may not even be one unique number.

The range in which possible values lie depends on the degree to which you believe the market is not perfect. For example, if you know that taxes or transaction costs can represent at most 2-3% of the project value, then you know that even if value is not absolutely unique, it is pretty close to unique—possible values sit in a fairly tight range. On the other hand, if you believe that there are few potential buyers for your house, but that some of these potential buyers would purchase the house at much higher prices than others, then it depends on your financial situation as to whether you should accept or decline a buyer's lowball offer.

For real estate, the market is not perfect. Thus, there may not be a unique value.

Use your judgment about market imperfections. Neither buyers nor sellers are assured of a fair price.

Many financial markets are not perfect either.

Not all financial markets are close to perfect either. Information differences, the unique power of large buyers or sellers in the market, transaction costs, or special taxes can sometimes play a role. For example, many corporate bonds are traded primarily over-the-counter. Just a small number of financial traders may make a market in them. If you want to buy or sell such a corporate bond, you must call their designated in-house desk trader. These traders are often your only market venue, and they will definitely try to gauge your expertise when negotiating a price with you. You could easily end up paying a lot more for a bond than what you could then sell it back for just 1 minute later. To repeat—no market, financial or otherwise, is ever "perfectly perfect." However, for some financial instruments, it is very close.

➤ *Over-the-counter, Sect. 7.2, Pg.167.*

IMPORTANT

> For many financial securities—for example, for large publicly traded stocks—the assumption that the market is perfect is reasonable. For other financial securities and many nonfinancial goods, this assumption is less accurate.

Q 10.2. What is the difference between a perfect market and a competitive market?

Q 10.3. Does a perfect capital market exist in the real world? What is the use of the perfect markets concept?

Perfect Market Assumptions and Violations

The four perfect market assumptions, and how their failures can drive wedges between borrowing and lending rates.

Now think more rigorously about what happens when each of the perfect market assumptions is violated:

1. **No differences in opinion (information):** This assumption means that everyone interprets all uncertainty in the same way in a perfect market. How could this assumption be violated? Here is an example. If your bank believes that there is a 50% chance that you will go bankrupt and default, and you believe that there is only a 10% chance, then your bank will lend you money only if you pay a much higher interest rate than what you will think appropriate. You will consider your borrowing rate to be too high. Of course, this also breaks the equality of one fair rate at which you can borrow and lend. Your expected rate of return is now lower when you lend than when you borrow.

   To avoid this, our perfect markets assumptions include one that posits *everyone has the same information and agrees on what it means.*

2. **Infinitely many investors and firms:** This really means that the market is very "deep." By itself, the assumption of the presence of many buyers and sellers defines a **competitive market**—one in which no buyer or seller has any market power. If buyers or sellers are heterogeneous, then this assumption must be slightly modified. It must be that you can easily find many of the most eager types of buyers and sellers. For example, say a truck is worth more if it is owned by a

truck driver. This assumption then states that there must be a large number of truck drivers.

How could this assumption be violated? If there is only one bank that you can do business with, then this bank will want to exploit its monopoly power. It will charge you a higher interest rate if you want to borrow money than it will pay you if you want to deposit money—and you will have no good alternative.

To avoid this, our perfect markets assumptions include one that posits *there are infinitely many buyers and sellers*.

3. **No transaction costs:** Transaction costs here are defined in a very broad sense, and they include indirect costs, such as your time and money to search for the best deal. In a perfect market, you can buy and sell without paying *any* such costs.

How could this assumption be violated? If it costs $1,000 to process the paperwork involved in a loan, you will incur this cost only if you need to borrow, but not if you want to save. Similarly, if it costs you 3 days of work to find the appropriate lender, it means that you will effectively have to pay more than just the borrowing rate. You will have to factor in your 3 days as a cost. Any such transaction costs make your effective borrowing interest rate higher than your effective savings interest rate.

To avoid this, our perfect markets assumptions include one that posits *there are zero transaction costs*.

4. **No taxes:** More accurately, this means that there is no distorting government interference (such as government regulation), and that there are no tax advantages or disadvantages to buying or selling securities. Specifically, neither trading of the good nor its possession by one particular owner should change the total tax consequences.

How could this assumption be violated? If you have to pay taxes on interest earned, but cannot deduct taxes on interest paid, your de facto savings rate will be lower than your borrowing rate. Similarly, if the total taxes paid are higher when shares are traded, they could be worth more if they were never traded to begin with. Another violation could be a government regulation requiring you to file lengthy legal documents with the SEC every time you have to sneeze—well, every time you have to execute some transaction.

To avoid this, our perfect markets assumptions include one that posits *there are no taxes*.

These four assumptions are actually "overkill," but if they hold, you are safe. Thinking about them helps you judge how close to perfect a given market actually is. However, the real usefulness of the perfect market is *not* that you should believe that it exists in the real world. Instead, its usefulness is that it gives you some simple first-order methods and tools that help you value goods. If these assumptions do not hold, borrowing and lending rates may or may not be similar enough to allow us to still use perfect market tools or variations thereon. (Almost all common finance formulas hope this is the case.)

If these assumptions are far from the situation in the real world, nothing will work anymore. In fact, markets may cease to function entirely. For example, if you fear that other parties you would be transacting with are *much* better informed than you, you

Let's hope the imperfections are not extreme—if they are, the entire market could even disappear.

could only lose—the other party would take full advantage of you, selling to you only if the price is too high. If you can avoid it, you should never trade. Such a market collapse may have happened in the market for corporate bonds *for retail investors*. These bonds are traded over-the-counter, which means that the Wall Street trader on the other side of the phone tries to gauge how much an ordinary retail investor actually knows about the correct value of these bonds. As a result, retail investors are so systematically disadvantaged that it makes no sense for them to buy corporate bonds directly. Instead, they are better off buying bond funds, where someone else who does not suffer a knowledge disadvantage (a bond mutual fund) buys and sells corporate bonds on their behalves. Similarly, if transaction costs are extremely high, there may be no market in which anyone could profitably buy or sell. Fortunately, such total market collapses tend to occur only if the perfect market violations are large. With modest violations, the benefits of transacting tend to outweigh the costs to buyers and sellers, and so markets can still function. This is the kind of situation that this chapter considers.

Q 10.4. Without looking back, what are the perfect market assumptions?

Ambiguous Value in Imperfect Markets

If savings and investment interest rates differ, the project's value (NPV) can depend on how wealthy the owner is—more generally, on *who* the owner is.

➤ *Investment consumption separation*, Sect. 4.1, Pg. 60.

An example of how project value can depend on your wealth. Consequently, a project's value may no longer be a single dollar figure, but any figure within a dollar range.

Why is an inequality between borrowing and lending rates so problematic? It is because it breaks the "unique value aspect" of projects. In a perfect market, project value depends *only* on the project, and not on you personally or on your cash position. You can think of this as a clean separation between the concepts of ownership and value. It also leads to the "separation of investments and financing decisions." Project owners can make investment choices based on the quality of the projects themselves, not based on their personal wealth or financing options. Indeed, the NPV formula does not have an input for your identity or current wealth—its only inputs are the project's cash flows and the rate of return on alternative investments.

For example, assume that you can lend (invest cash) and borrow money at the same 4% in a perfect market. What is the net present value of a project that invests $1,000 today and returns $1,050 next period? It is $9.62. It does not depend on whether you have money or not. If you do not have the $1,000 today, you borrow $1,009.62, invest $1,000, and hand the $1,050 to the lender next year. But if the financial market is imperfect and the borrowing and lending rates are *not* the same, then the value of the project does depend on you, because it depends on your cash holdings. For example, assume that you can lend money (invest cash) at 3% and borrow money (receive cash) at 7%. What is the net present value of a project that invests $1,000 today and returns $1,050 next period?

- If you have $1,000 and your alternative is to invest your money in the bank, you will only get $1,030 from the bank. You should take the project rather than invest in the bank so that you can earn $20 more.

- If you do not have the $1,000, you will have to borrow $1,000 from the bank to receive $1,050 from the project. But because you will have to pay the bank $1,070, you will lose $20 net. You should not take the project.

The value of the project and your best decision whether to take the project or not now depends on how much cash you have. Consequently, the separation between your project choice and your financial position breaks down. Having to take your current cash holdings into account when making investment choices makes capital budgeting decisions more difficult. In this example, it is fairly easy: If you have a lot of wealth, you should take the project. If you have no cash, you should not take it. But think about projects that have cash inflows and outflows in the future and how your decisions could interact with your own wealth positions in the future. This can become vexingly difficult. You can also see that the project value is no longer unique in imperfect markets. In our example, it could be anything between +$19.42 ($1,050 discounted at 3%) and −$18.69 ($1,050 discounted at 7%). The same ambiguity applies to ownership. Your capital budgeting decision can be different when you already own the project versus when you are just contemplating purchasing it. Again, your identity matters to the value of the project.

> If the market is not perfect, the separation of ownership and value breaks down. Therefore, project value is no longer unique. It can depend on who owns the project.

IMPORTANT

Do You Always Get What You Pay For?

Reflect a little on the insight that projects may not have unique values. You surely have heard the saying that "it's only worth what people are willing to pay for it" and the claim that some item "is worth much more than it is being sold for." Which is correct? Are there any good deals? The answer is that both are correct and neither is correct. The first claim is really meaningful only to the extent that markets are *perfect*: If a market is perfect, items are indeed worth exactly what buyers are willing to pay for them. The second claim is meaningful only to the extent that markets are *imperfect*: If a market is imperfect, items have no unique value. Different people can place different values on the item, and some third party may consider an item worth much more than what it was sold for.

Are there any good deals? Maybe—but how would one even define a good deal in an imperfect market?

In sum, when someone claims that a stock or firm is really worth more than he or she is selling it for, there are only a small number of explanations:

Salespeople may distort the truth and claim great deals.

1. There may be pure kindheartedness toward any buyer, or a desire by a seller to lose wealth. Not very likely.

2. The seller may not have access to a perfect market to sell the goods. This may make the seller accept a low amount of money for the good, so depending on how you look at it, the good may be sold for more or less than the seller thinks it is worth.

3. The market is perfect and the seller may be committing a conceptual mistake. The good is worth neither more nor less than what it is being sold for—it is worth exactly how much it is being sold for.

4. The seller may be lying and is using this claim as a sales tactic.

Q 10.5. Your borrowing rate is 10% per year. Your lending rate is 4% per year. Your project costs $1,000 and will have a rate of return of 8%. Assume you have $900 to invest.

1. Should you take the project?

2. You can think of the $900 as the amount of money that you are not consuming. Say your wealth is $2,000, but in the previous question, you wanted to consume $1,100. Could you still consume this much and take the project? How much could you consume and still want to take the project?

Social Value and Surplus

Buyers get what they pay for in a perfect market. They can "trust" market prices.

Perfect markets are not just privately useful but are also socially useful. If a market is perfect, buyers and sellers need not worry that one deal is better than another—that buying is better than selling, or vice versa. For example, consider gasoline and imagine that you do not yet know when and where on your road trip you will need to pump more gas. Unlike shares of stock, gas is not the same good everywhere: Gas in one location can be more valuable than gas in another location (as anyone who has ever run out of gas can testify). But in populated areas, the market for gasoline is pretty competitive and close to perfect—there are many buyers (drivers) and sellers (gas stations). This makes it very likely that the first gas station you see will have a reasonably fair price. If you drive by the first gas station and it advertises a price of $3 per gallon, it is unlikely that you will find another gas station offering the same gas for $2 per gallon or $4 per gallon within a couple of miles. Chances are that "the price is fair," or this particular gas station would probably have disappeared by now. (The same applies, of course, in many financial markets, such as those for large company stocks, Treasury bonds, or certain types of mortgages.) As long as the market is very competitive—or better yet, perfect—most deals are likely to be fair deals.

Perfect markets do not mean most buyers and sellers don't care: Perfect markets offer (maximum) surplus for average buyers and sellers.

There is an important conceptual twist here: If you are paying what an item is worth, it does not necessarily mean that you are paying what you *personally* value the good at. For example, if you are running out of gas and you are bad at pushing a 2-ton vehicle, you might very well be willing to pay $10 per gallon—but fortunately, all you need to pay in a competitive market is the market price. The difference between what you personally value a good for and what you pay for it is called your "surplus." Although everyone is paying what the good is worth in a perfect market, most buyers and sellers can come away being better off—only the marginal buyer and seller are indifferent.

Q 10.6. Evaluate the following statement: "In a perfect market, no one is getting a good deal. Thus, it would not matter from a social perspective if this market were not available."

10.2 Opinions, Disagreements, and Insider Information

You are now ready to learn how to handle violations of each perfect market assumption, one by one. You need to learn both how to judge the degree to which markets are imperfect and how to deal with them as a real-world investor or manager. (Even if there is no unique value, you can still learn how to think about maximizing your own wealth.) The remainder of the chapter thus explores the extent of market imperfections, what can mitigate them, and how you should work with them.

The rest of this chapter will hone in on the four individual imperfections.

We begin with the effects of disagreements, the violation of the first perfect market assumption that everyone has the same opinion. Like the other assumptions, this works well in some situations and poorly in others.

Information (opinions) is first.

Expected Return Differences or Promised Return Differences?

The assumption of no disagreement is only relevant in a world of uncertainty—it would be absurd to believe that differences in opinion could exist if there were no uncertainty. So what happens if the lender and borrower have different information or different judgments about the same information? Most prominently, they could disagree about the default risk. For example, if you have no credit history, then a lender who does not know you might be especially afraid of not receiving promised repayments from you—from the perspective of such a lender, you would be extremely high-risk. Your lender might estimate your appropriate default probability to be 30% and thus may demand an appropriate default premium from you of, say, 10%—an interest rate similar to what credit card vendors are charging. On the other hand, *you* may know that you will indeed return the lender's money, because you know that you will work hard and that you will have the money for sure. In your opinion, a fair and appropriate default premium should therefore be 0%.

Different opinions can lead to disagreements about what the project will pay.

When your potential lender and you have different opinions, you will face different expected interest rates depending on whether you want to save or borrow. You can use your knowledge from Chapter 6 to work an example to understand the difference between a perfect and an imperfect market scenario.

Expected rates of return for borrowing and lending now become different.

Perfect Markets: Assume that the bank and you agree that you have a 20% probability of default, in which case you will not repay anything. For simplicity, assume risk neutrality and that the appropriate interest rate is 5%. Solving $80\% \cdot r + 20\% \cdot (-100\%) = 5\%$ for the interest rate that you would have to promise yields $r = 31.25\%$. This gives the bank an expected rate of return of 5%. In contrast, the bank is government insured, so if you deposit your money with it, it would be default free.

Do not confuse different promised borrowing/lending rates in perfect markets...

	Promised	Expected
Your Savings Rate	5%	5%
Your Borrowing Rate	31.25%	5%

Although your quoted interest rate is higher by the credit spread, if you want to borrow, your cost of capital is still the same 5% either way.

➤ *Credit spreads, Sect. 6.2, Pg.124.*

Imperfect Markets: Now assume that the bank and you disagree about your default probability. The bank believes that it is 30%—it could be that it has experienced such a default rate for borrowers who seemed to look similar from the perspective of your bank. In contrast, you believe that your default probability is 10%. The bank will therefore quote you an interest rate of $70\% \cdot r + 30\% \cdot (-100\%) = 5\% \Longrightarrow r = 50\%$. Alas, you believe that the expected rate of return at the 50% quoted interest rate is $90\% \cdot 50\% + 10\% \cdot (-100\%) = 35\%$.

	Promised	Expected
Your Savings Rate	5%	5%
Your Borrowing Rate	50% from the bank's perspective	5%
Your Borrowing Rate	50% from your perspective	35%

The disagreements (information differences) are now causing differences in *expected* returns. The borrowing and lending *expected* rates of return are no longer the same. If the bank is wrong, your cost of capital now depends on whether you want to borrow or lend. And even if the bank is right, from your wrong perspective, you are still facing different borrowing and lending rates.

IMPORTANT

- The fact that credit spreads reflect a default premium—a difference between the *promised* rate of return and the *expected* rate of return—is not a market imperfection.

- The fact that credit spreads reflect differences in opinion between borrower and lender—a difference about the two assessed *expected* rates of return—is a market imperfection.

Q 10.7. Can there be a difference in the borrowing and lending rates quoted by the bank in perfect markets?

Q 10.8. "If the world is risk neutral and the market is perfect, then the promised and expected rates of return may be different, but the expected rate of return on all loans should be equal." Evaluate.

Q 10.9. A bond will pay off $100 with probability 99%, and nothing with probability 1% next year. The equivalent appropriate expected rate of return for risk-free bonds is 5%.

1. What is an appropriate promised yield on this bond today?

2. The borrower believes the probability of payoff is 100%. How much money does he believe he has to overpay today?

Covenants, Collateral, and Credit Rating Agencies

If you are an entrepreneur who wants to start a company, what can you do to reduce your cost of capital? The answer is that it is in your interest to disclose to the lender all the information you can—provided you are the type of entrepreneur who is likely to pay back the loan. You want to reduce the lender's doubt about future repayment. Unfortunately, this can be very difficult. The lender can neither peer into your brain nor give you a good lie detector test. Even after you have done everything possible to reduce the lender's doubts about you (provided your credit history, collateral, and so on), there will still be some residual information differences—they are just a fact of life. To the extent that you can reduce such information differences, your firm will be able to enjoy lower costs of capital. Also, if you as a borrower fail to give your best to convince the lender of your quality, then the lender should assume that you are not an average company but instead the very worst—or else you would have tried to communicate as much as possible.

Even when borrowers would love to convince their lenders, they may not be able to.

There are at least three important mechanisms that have evolved to alleviate such information differences. The first mechanism is **covenants**, which are contractual agreements that specify up-front what a debtor must do to maintain credit. They can include such requirements as the maintenance of insurance or a minimum corporate value. The second mechanism is **collateral**, which are assets that the creditor can repossess if payments are not made—anything that inflicts pain on the debtor will do. For example, if defaulting debtors were thrown into debtors' prison (as they often were until the nineteenth century), the promise to repay would be more credible and lenders would be more inclined to provide funding at lower rates. Of course, for the unlucky few who just happened to suffer incredibly bad luck ex-post, debtors' prison had some definite drawbacks.

Good borrowers want to convey credibly to the lender how good they are.

ANECDOTE   Sumerian Debt Contracts

Among the earliest known collateralized debt contracts is a tablet from Sumeria (Mesopotamia), which promised delivery of silver and gave as security the son of the borrower. (The tablet can be viewed at www.museumofmoney.org/babylon/index.html.) Such contracts are illegal today, but de facto "debt slavery" for debts not repaid is still common in many countries, according to the September 2003 issue of *National Geographic*.
                                                                  William Goetzmann, Yale University.

The third mechanism to alleviate repayment uncertainty is a credit rating, which is a history of past payments to help assess the probability of future default. This is why you need to give your Social Security number if you want to take out a substantial personal loan—the lender will check up on you. The same is true for large corporations. It may be easier to judge corporate default risk for large companies than personal default risk, but it is still not easy and it costs both time and money. You already learned about these credit ratings in Section 6.2.

Credit rating agencies help lenders estimate the probability of borrower default.

➤ *Credit ratings, Sect. 6.2, Pg. 125.*

Unfortunately, although bond rating agencies update their ratings if the condition of the firm changes, the empirical evidence suggests that these bond ratings are not very good in helping an investor earn superior rates of return. In fact, the ratings seem to respond more to drops in the value of the underlying bonds than vice versa. The

Incidentally, bond credit ratings have been historically useless for stock trading strategies.

bond rating agencies seem to be more reactive than proactive. (The low quality of debt ratings has also played a role in the credit crisis of 2008. Not surprisingly, it has become an important political issue how one might induce the ratings' providers to improve their products.)

Don't lose the big picture in the many little problems.

Let me close with a philosophical observation: Financial markets are truly amazing. People who would never lend their neighbors a few thousand dollars (fearing that they would not pay it back) have no second thoughts about lending total strangers in anonymous markets their entire lives' savings. It is the combination of the governance of repayments and risk-spreading that has allowed financial markets to develop even in the presence of great uncertainty.

Q 10.10. What mechanisms can borrowers use to assure lenders? If providing this information is not legally required, will they still volunteer to do so?

10.3 Market Depth and Transaction Costs

The assumption "no market power" is straightforward.

Our second perfect market assumption states that markets are very deep, consisting of many buyers and sellers. If there is only one lender, this lender will have market power over you. Of course, she will exploit her power by charging you a higher borrowing rate and offering you a lower deposit interest rate. Such an extreme form of market power is called a monopoly, but there are many milder forms of such power, too. For example, if you are already shopping in a grocery store, this store has a degree of market power over you. Even if the milk is 3 cents more expensive than in another store, you will still buy the milk where you are. Or say there is only one ATM close to you. In principle, you could get capital from any number of banks, but locally there is really only this one provider. Fortunately, such uniqueness of capital provision is rarely an important issue in the United States for corporations, especially large ones.

Transaction costs are this section's main topic.

So let's move on to the third perfect markets assumption: the role of transaction costs. Transaction costs drive a wedge between borrowing and lending rates. For example, if it is difficult and costly to administer loans, an investor must charge you a higher borrowing rate than deposit rate just to break even. This is the subject of this section, in which you will learn how corporations and individuals should handle transaction costs.

Typical Costs When Trading Real Goods—Real Estate

Real estate is an important market in itself. How perfect is it?

When you engage in transactions—that is, purchases or sales—you face costs to facilitate them. One way to think about the magnitude of transaction costs is to compute how much is lost if you decided that you have made a mistake the instant after a purchase, which you now want to undo by reselling. Real estate—most people's biggest asset—is a perfect example to illustrate transaction costs. What does selling or buying a house really cost?

Direct costs such as brokerage commissions: Housing transaction costs are so high and so important that they are worth a digression. In the United States, if a house is sold, the seller's broker typically receives 6% of the value of the house as commission (and splits this commission with the buyer's real-estate agent). Thus, if a real-estate agent sells your house for $300,000, her commission is $18,000. Put differently, without an agent, the buyer and seller could have split the $18,000 between themselves.

Direct transaction costs: a transfer of money.

Although only the seller pays the broker's cost, it makes sense to think of transaction costs in terms of **round-trip costs**—how much worse off you are if you buy and then immediately sell. You would be mistaken if you thought that when you buy a house, you have not incurred any transaction costs because the seller had to pay them—you have incurred an implicit transaction cost in the future when you need to resell your investment. Of course, you usually do not sell assets immediately, so you should not forget about the timing of your future selling transaction costs in your NPV calculations.

Think of transactions in "round-trip" form.

If you borrow to finance the investment, transaction costs may be higher than you think. The real-estate agent earns 6% of the house value, not 6% of the amount of money you put into the house. On a house purchase of $500,000, the typical loan is 80% of the purchase price, or $400,000, leaving you to put in $100,000 in equity. Selling the house the day after the purchase reduces your wealth of $100,000 by the commission of $30,000—for an investment rate of return of –30%. This is not a risk component; it is a pure and certain transaction cost.

House transaction costs are calculated based not on your equity but based on the whole house.

How good is your purchase if the house price decreases or increases by 10%? If house prices decline by 10% (or if you overpaid by 10%), the house can only be resold for $450,000, which leaves $423,000 after agent commissions. As the house owner, you are left with $23,000 on a $100,000 investment. A 10% decline in real estate values has reduced your net worth by 77%! In comparison, a 10% increase in real estate values increases the value of the house to $550,000, which means that $517,000 is left after real estate commissions. Your rate of return for the same up movement would thus be only 17%. If a 10% increase and a 10% decrease are equally likely, your instant expected loss is 30%!

Let's add some price volatility.

A N E C D O T E   Real Estate Agents: Who Works for Whom?

Real estate agents are conflicted. If they sell sooner, they can spend their time focusing on other properties. Thus, the typical seller's agent will try to get the seller to reduce the price in order to make a quicker sale. Similarly, the buyer's agent will try to get the buyer to increase the offer. In a financial sense, the buyer's agent is working on behalf of the seller, and the seller's agent is working on behalf of the buyer. Interestingly, Steve Levitt of *Freakonomics* found that when agents sell their own houses, their homes tend to stay on the market for about 10 days longer and sell for about 2% more.

Steve Levitt, University of Chicago.

In addition to direct agent commissions, there are also many other direct transaction costs. These can range from advertising, to insurance company payments, to house inspectors, to the local land registry, to postage—all of which cost the parties money.

Other direct costs.

Indirect costs such as opportunity costs: Then there is the seller's and buyer's time required to learn as much as possible about the value of the house, and the effort involved to help the agent sell the house. These may be significant costs, even if they

Indirect transaction costs are the loss of other opportunities.

involve no cash outlay. If the house cannot be sold immediately but stays empty for a while, the forgone rent is part of the transaction costs. The implicit cost of not having the house put to its best alternative use is called an **opportunity cost**—the cost of forgoing the next-best choice. Opportunity costs are just as real as direct cash costs.

Typical Costs When Trading Financial Goods—Stocks

Stock transactions also incur direct and indirect costs.

Transactions in financial markets also incur transaction costs. If an investor wants to buy or sell shares, the broker charges a fee, as does the stock exchange that facilitates the transaction. In addition, investors have to consider their time to communicate with the broker to initiate the purchase or sale of a stock as an opportunity cost.

The typical direct transaction costs for stocks are much, much lower.

Direct costs such as brokerage and market maker commissions: Still, the transaction costs for selling financial instruments are much lower than they are for most other goods. Let's look at a few reasons why. First, even if you want to buy (or sell) $1 million worth of stock, some Internet brokers now charge as little as $10 per transaction. Your round-trip transaction, which is a buy and a sale, costs only $20 in broker's commission. In addition, you have to pay the **spread** (the difference between the bid price and the ask price) to the stock exchange. For example, a large company stock like PepsiCo may have a publicly posted price of $50 per share. But you can neither buy nor sell at $50. Instead, the $50 is really just the average of two prices: the **bid price** of $49.92, at which another investor or the exchange's market maker is currently willing to buy shares and the **ask price** of $50.08, at which another investor or the exchange's market maker is currently willing to sell shares. Therefore, you can (probably) purchase shares at $50.08 and sell them at $49.92, a loss of "only" 16 cents, which amounts to round-trip transaction costs of $(\$49.92 - \$50.08)/\$50.08 \approx -0.32\%$. (Typical market spreads for PepsiCo shares are even lower.) You can compute the total costs of buying and selling 20,000 shares ($1,000,000 worth) of PepsiCo stock as follows:

Financial Round-Trip Transaction		
Purchase 20,000 Shares	Pay $50.08 · 20,000 = $1,001,600	
Add Broker Commission	+$10	= $1,001,610
Sell 20,000 Shares	Receive $49.92 · 20,000 = $998,400	
Subtract Broker Commission	−$10	= $998,390
	Net Round-Trip Transaction Costs	$3,220

This table is not *exactly* correct, though, because the bid and ask prices that the stock exchanges post are only valid for 100 shares. Moreover, some transactions can occur inside the bid-ask spread, but for most large round-trip orders, chances are that you may have to pay more than $50.08 or receive less than $49.92. So 0.32% is probably a bit too small. (In fact, if your trade is large enough, you may even move the publicly posted exchange price away from $50!) Your buy order may have to pay $50.20, and your sell may only get you $49.85. In real life, the true round-trip transaction cost on a $1 million position in PepsiCo shares may be on the order of magnitude of 50 basis points.

An example of how low transaction costs in stock can be is illustrated by an extremely large trade in a very liquid security that occurred on Thursday, November 30, 2006, at 12:12pm. Kirk Kerkorian, a billionaire investor, sold 5% of GM (a block of 28 million shares) at $29.25 per share (or about $820 million)—almost to the penny for the price that GM shares were trading at on the NYSE. Upon receiving the news, the GM stock price dropped to $28.49—but within 1 hour, it had recovered and even reached $29.50. Don't you find it remarkable how the sale of even very large blocks of shares seems to barely move the stock price?

An example of how stunningly low stock transaction costs can be.

Indirect costs such as opportunity costs: Investors do not need to spend a lot of time to find out the latest price of the stock: It is instantly available from many sources (e.g., from **YAHOO!** FINANCE). The information research costs are very low: Unlike a house, the value of a stock is immediately known. Finally, upon demand, a buyer can be found practically instantaneously, so search and waiting costs are also very low. In contrast, recall the often multimonth waiting periods if you want to sell your house.

The typical indirect transaction costs (opportunity costs) for stocks are also very low.

Comparing Stock Transaction Costs To Housing Transaction Costs

Let's compare the transaction costs in buying and selling financial securities to those of a house. Aside from the direct real estate broker fees of 6% (for the $100,000 equity investment in the $500,000 house, this comes to $30,000 for a round-trip transaction), you must add the other fees and waiting time. Chances are that you will be in for other transaction costs—say, another $10,000.

Compared to other economic assets...

Cost Type	Explanation	Real Estate (House)	Financial Security (Stock)
Direct	Typical round-trip commission, etc.	$\geq 6\%$	0-1%
Search/Research	Time to determine fair price	High	Zero
Search/Liquidity	Time waiting to find buyer	Variable	Zero

And houses are just one example: Many transactions of physical goods or labor services (but not all) can incur similarly high transaction costs.

In contrast, if you want to buy or sell 100 shares in, say, Microsoft stock, your transaction costs are relatively low. Because there are many buyers and many sellers, financial transaction costs are comparably tiny. Even for a $100,000 equity investment in a medium-sized firm's stock, the transaction costs are typically only about $300–$500. It may not be a perfectly correct assumption that the market for trading large stocks is perfect, but it is not far off. It certainly is convenient to assume that financial transaction costs are zero. For an individual buying and selling ordinary stocks only rarely (a **buy-and-hold** investor), a zero-transaction-cost assumption is often quite reasonable. But if you are a **day trader**—someone who buys and sells stocks daily—our perfect market assumption would be inappropriate.

...financial securities have such low transaction costs that they can be assumed to be almost zero for buy-and-hold investors.

Q 10.11. What would you guess are the transaction costs for a round-trip transaction of $10,000 in Dell Computer shares, in percentage and in absolute terms?

Q 10.12. List important transaction cost components, both direct and indirect.

Transaction Costs in Returns and Net Present Values

The ultimate rule.

As an investor, you usually care about rates of return *after* all transaction costs have been taken into account, not about pre-transaction-cost rates of return from quoted prices. Let's work out how you should take these transaction costs on both sides (buy and sell) into account.

Rates of return: Work with after-transaction-cost rates.

Return to our housing example. If you purchase a house for $1,000,000 and you sell it to the next buyer at $1,100,000 through a broker, your rate of return is not 10%. At selling time, the broker charges you a 6% commission. There are also some other costs that reduce the amount of money you receive, not to mention your many opportunity costs. Say these costs amount to $70,000 in total. In addition, even when you purchased the house, you most likely had to pay some extra costs (such as an escrow transfer fee) above and beyond the $1,000,000—say, $5,000. Your rate of return would therefore not be $1,100,000/$1,000,000 − 1 = 10%, but only

$$r = \frac{(\$1,100,000 - \$70,000) - (\$1,000,000 + \$5,000)}{(\$1,000,000 + \$5,000)} \approx 2.5\%$$

$$\text{Rate of Return} = \frac{\begin{array}{c}\text{Dollars Returned} \\ \text{after Transaction Costs}\end{array} - \begin{array}{c}\text{Dollars Invested} \\ \text{after Transaction Costs}\end{array}}{\text{Dollars Invested after Transaction Costs}}$$

Note how the $5,000 must be added to, not subtracted from, the price you originally paid. The price you paid was ultimately higher than $1,000,000. The $5,000 works against you. (Incidentally, in order to make their returns look more appealing, many professional fund managers quote their investors' rates of return before taking their own fees (transaction costs) into account. They add a footnote at the bottom that satisfies the lawyers so that you cannot sue the fund for having been misled—you are supposed to know how to adjust the returns to take these transaction costs into account.)

Net present value: Work with after-transaction-cost cash flows and with after-transaction opportunity costs of capital.

How do you take care of transaction costs in present value calculations? This is relatively straightforward. In the example, you put in $1,005,000 and receive $1,030,000—say, after one year:

$$\text{NPV} = -\$1,005,000 + \frac{\$1,030,000}{1 + \text{Opportunity Cost of Capital}}$$

The only thing you must still take care of is to quote your opportunity cost of capital also in after-transaction cost terms. You may not be able to get a 10% rate of return in comparable investments either, because you may also be required to pay a transaction cost on them. In this case, assume that your alternative investment with equal characteristics in the financial markets (not the housing markets) would earn an 8% per year rate of return, but with a 50-basis-point transaction cost. Your project would then have an appropriate NPV of

$$\text{NPV} = -\$1,005,000 + \frac{\$1,030,000}{1.075} \approx -\$46,860$$

Q 10.13. Compute your after-transaction-costs rate of return on purchasing a house for $1,000,000 if you have to pay 0.5% transaction fees up front (when you buy to cover various escrow fees) and pay a 6% broker's commission (plus 2% in waiting costs) at the end of one year when you sell (on the then house's selling price). Assume a $4,000/month effective dividend of enjoying living in the house. Assume that your opportunity cost of capital (not the bank quoted interest rate) is 7% per year. At what rate of capital appreciation would the NPV be zero if you resold the house after one year?

The Value of Liquidity

When *future* transaction costs influence your up-front willingness to purchase an asset, proper pricing gets even more interesting and complex. You might not want to purchase a house even if you *expect* to recoup your transaction costs, because you dislike the fact that you do not know whether it will be easy or hard to resell. After all, if you purchase a stock or bond instead, you know you can resell without much transaction cost whenever you want.

> Anticipating future transaction costs, buyers demand a higher rate of return for more illiquid investments.

What would make you want to take the risk of sitting on a house for months without being able to sell it? To get you to purchase a house would require the seller to compensate you. The seller would have to offer you a **liquidity premium**—an extra expected rate of return to compensate you for your willingness to hold an asset that you will find difficult to convert into cash if a need were to arise. The liquidity analogy comes from physics. The same way that physical movement is impeded by physical friction, economic transactions are impeded by transaction costs.

> "Liquidity" is a common analogy that finance has borrowed from physics.

Housing may be an extreme example, but liquidity effects appear to be important everywhere, even in financial markets with their low transaction costs. (Some financial markets are generally considered low-friction, or even close to frictionless.) Even finance professors and the best fund managers do not yet fully understand liquidity premiums, but we do know that they can be very important. Let us look at some examples of where liquidity premiums seem to play important roles.

> Liquidity (or lack thereof) is super-important in most markets, but we do not fully understand it yet.

Treasury Bonds

Believe it or not, even Treasuries have differences in liquidity. The most recently issued Treasury of a particular maturity is called **on-the-run**. The financial prominently reports its yield. Every bond trader who wants to trade a bond with roughly this maturity focuses on this particular bond. This makes it easier to buy and sell the on-the-run bond than a similar, but not identical, **off-the-run** bond. For example, in November 2000, the 10-year on-the-run Treasury bond traded for a yield-to-maturity of 5.6% per annum, while a bond that was just a couple of days off in terms of its maturity (and thus practically identical) traded at 5.75% per annum. In other words, you would have been able to purchase the off-the-run bond at a much lower price than the on-the-run bond.

> Even Treasuries have differences in liquidity: on-the-run and off-the-run bonds.

On-the-run is more
liquid.

The reason why you might want to purchase the on-the-run bond, even though it had a higher price, would be that you could resell it much more quickly and easily than the equivalent off-the-run bond. Of course, as the date approaches when this 10-year bond is about to lose its on-the-run designation and another bond is about to become the on-the-run 10-year bond, the old on-the-run bond drops in value.

Investors prefer
on-the-run bonds
because of their
immediate liquidity.

In a perfect world, there should be no difference between these two types of bonds. Yet, when a two-year bond is on-the-run, its bid-ask spread is on average about 1 basis point lower, and it offers on average 0.6 basis points less in yield. For a ten-year bond, both the bid-ask spread and the yield difference between the on-the-run and off-the-run Treasury are usually about 3 basis points. This can only be explained by an investor preference for the immediate liquidity of the current on-the-run bond.

Liquidity Provision As a Business: Market Making

Market = Liquidity
Provider.

You can think of a market maker on an exchange as someone who is providing liquidity. As a retail investor, you can sell your securities to the market maker in an instant, and it is up to the market maker to find some other investor who wants to hold it long term. To provide this liquidity, the market maker earns the bid-ask spread—a part of the liquidity premium.

Liquidity provision is a
common business.

The provision of liquidity in markets of any kind is a common business. For example, you can think of antique stores or used car dealerships as liquidity providers that try to buy cheap (being a standby buyer) and sell expensive (being a standby seller). Being a liquidity provider can require big risks and capital outlays. If it were easy, everyone could do it—and then there would be no more money in liquidity provision!

Liquidity Runs

Liquidity crises are
extremely interesting.

The most remarkable empirical regularity about liquidity, however, is that every few years, investors in all markets suddenly seem to prefer only the most liquid securities. This is called a **flight to quality** or **run on liquidity**. In such situations, the spreads on almost all bonds—regardless of whether they are Latin American, European, corporate, mortgage related, and so on—relative to Treasuries tend to widen all at the same time.

How the liquidity run
in 2008 spread.

In early 2008, the U.S. economy was facing just such a run on liquidity. It started in the mortgage sector, then spread to many other bonds. Every fund and bank was afraid that its investors would pull their lines of credit. Thus, they themselves were pulling lines of credit that they had extended to their clients (often other banks and funds). Many were selling even highly rated securities for low prices (sometimes fire-sale prices), just to avoid being caught themselves in an even worse liquidity run. There were many extremely curious pricing oddities during the 2008 liquidity run, but they were difficult to exploit by arbitrageurs (because no one would trust lending them the money to execute these arbitrages). For example, two-year bonds issued by a federal government agency, GNMA (not the same as the now-notorious FNMA), and thus fully backed by the federal government, traded at a full 200 basis points higher than the equivalent Treasuries.

If you are liquid in a
liquidity crisis, you can
earn a lot of money.

Selling liquidity in order to collect the liquidity premium is also a very common method for Wall Street firms and hedge funds to make money—perhaps even *the* most common. If you know you will not need liquidity at sudden notice or that you want to hold bonds to maturity, it can make sense to purchase less liquid securities to earn the liquidity premium. A sample strategy might be to buy illiquid corporate bonds, financed with cheaper borrowed money. Most of the time, this strategy makes modest amounts of money consistently—except when a flight to liquidity occurs and liquidity spreads widen. Exactly such a situation led to the collapse of a well-known hedge fund named Long-Term Capital Management (LTCM) in 1998. After Russia defaulted on its debt, the spreads on almost every bond widened—the average corporate bond spread in the United States rose from about 4% to about 8% in one week! LTCM simply could not find any buyers for its large holdings of non-Treasury bonds. On the other hand, those funds that could hold onto their positions throughout the crisis or who provided extra liquidity (buying securities that were now very cheap) did extremely well when liquidity returned to normal and their illiquid securities went back up in price. The same fate probably befell many financial firms in the 2008-9 crisis. Their own financiers demanded their money back quickly, but there was no liquid market to unwind them quickly.

Q 10.14. What is the difference between a liquidity premium and a transaction cost?

10.4 Taxes

The art of taxation consists in so plucking the goose as to get the most feathers with the least hissing.
Jean-Baptiste Colbert

Certainty? In this world nothing is certain but death and taxes.
Benjamin Franklin

Our fourth violation of market perfection is taxes. They are pervasive and are often an economically large component of project returns. The actual tax code itself is very complex, and its details change every year, but the basics have remained in place for a long time and are similar in most countries. Let me summarize briefly what you shall need to know for this book.

Only a sketch of the complex tax code.

The Basics of (Federal) Income Taxes

The **Internal Revenue Service** (**IRS**) taxes individuals and corporations similarly. (There are some differences, but we don't have the space to discuss them.) Gross income is adjusted by a set of allowable deductions into taxable income, and a (progressive) tax rate is applied. **Before-tax expenses** (deductions) are better for taxpayers than **after-tax expenses**. For example, if you earn $100,000 and there was only one 40% bracket, a $50,000 before-tax expense would leave you

The tax code basics have been simple and stable, but the details are complex and ever-changing.

$$(\$100,000 - \$50,000) \cdot (1 - 40\%) \quad = \quad \$30,000$$

$$\text{Before-Tax Net Return} \cdot (1 - \text{Tax Rate}) \quad = \quad \text{After-Tax Net Return}$$

while the same $50,000 as an after-tax expense would leave you with only

$$\$100{,}000 \cdot (1 - 40\%) - \$50{,}000 = \$10{,}000$$

Perhaps the most important deductible items for both corporations and individuals are interest payments, although individuals can deduct them only for mortgages. In addition, there are some other deductions such as pension contributions. There are also some nonprofit investors (such as pension funds) that are entirely tax-exempt.

➤ *Other tax shelters,*
Sect. 17.8, Pg. 558.

Among the four tax classes of income, dividends receipts and capital gains are the two best.

The tax code categorizes income into four different classes: ordinary income, interest income, dividend income, and capital gains. The tax rates on these classes differ, as does the ability to apply deductions on them to reduce the income tax burden.

Ordinary income applies to most income that is not derived from financial investments (such as wages). Individuals are allowed only very few deductions thereon, and the tax rate is the highest. The highest marginal ordinary federal income tax rate was about 35% in 2008.

Interest income is basically treated like ordinary income.

Dividend income from qualifying U.S. corporations is taxed at a significantly lower rate, often less than half that of ordinary income.

Capital gains on assets owned for one year or more (under the 2008 tax code) are also taxed at low rates similar to those at which dividends are taxed. (Assets held for less than one year are taxed essentially at the same rate as ordinary income.) In addition, unlike other income, which is taxed every year, both short-term and long-term capital gains are taxed only when realized, and losses can easily be deducted against gains.

From the perspective of an investor, capital gains are mildly preferable to dividend income, and both are greatly preferable to interest income.

The difference between marginal and average tax rates.

The **average tax rate** (the ratio of paid taxes to taxable income) is lower than the **marginal tax rate** (the rate on the last dollar of income), because lower marginal tax rates are applied to your first few dollars of income in the progressive U.S. tax system. For example, in 2008, the first $8,025 were taxed at 10%, the next $24,525 at 15%. Thus, ignoring a variety of subsequent adjustments, if you earned $20,000, you would have paid taxes of

$$\text{Tax} = 10\% \cdot \$8{,}025 + 15\% \cdot (\$20{,}000 - \$8{,}025) = \$2{,}598.75$$

Therefore, your marginal tax rate—the one applicable to your last dollar of income—was 15%, while your average tax rate was about 13.0%. Economists almost always work only with marginal tax rates, because they are relevant to your earning 1 dollar more or less. For large corporations, the distinction is often minor, because beginning at around $75,000 of income, the federal tax rate is about 34% (as of 2008). A corporation that earns or loses $10 million has an average tax rate that is, for all practical purposes, the same as its marginal tax rate.

The tax picture here is rather incomplete.

Of course, there are also other important taxes, such as state income taxes, Social Security and Medicare taxes, property taxes, sales taxes, and so on. In recent years, an alternative tax system, the **alternative minimum tax** (**AMT**), has become as important as the standard federal income tax system. Because the AMT categorizes most income the same way, we won't distinguish between the standard income tax and the alternative minimum tax. If you have to file in multiple states or even in multiple countries—although there are rules that try to avoid double taxation—the details can be hair-raisingly complex. (Professional athletes have to pay taxes in every state in which they have played a game, for example.) If you find yourself in such a situation, may the Force be with you!

IMPORTANT

- Remember that there are some tax-exempt investors, such as pension funds.

- You must understand how income taxes are computed (the principles, not the details), how to find the marginal tax rate, how to compute the average tax rate, and why the average tax rate is usually lower than the marginal tax rate.

- Expenses that can be paid from before-tax income are better than expenses that must be paid from after-tax income. Specifically, interest expenses are tax-deductible and thus better for the taxpayer.

- Capital gains (and secondarily dividend) income enjoys preferential tax treatment for the recipient, relative to interest and ordinary income.

Q 10.15. Is it better for the taxpayer to have a before-tax or an after-tax expense? Why?

Q 10.16. What types of income do taxpayers prefer? Why?

Q 10.17. Why is the marginal tax rate usually lower than the average tax rate?

The Effect of Taxes on Rates of Return

How does finance work if there are income taxes? Mechanically, taxes are similar to transaction costs—they take a "cut," which makes investments less profitable. One difference between them is that income taxes are higher on more profitable transactions, whereas plain transaction costs are the same whether you made or lost money. And, of course, taxes often have many more nuances. A second and perhaps more important difference is that taxes are often orders of magnitude bigger and thus more important than ordinary transaction costs—except in illustrative textbook examples. For many investors and corporations, tax planning is an issue of first-order importance.

Taxes are on profits, not on values or sales. Nevertheless, they are often much larger than transaction costs.

In the end, all investors should care about is after-tax returns, not before-tax returns. It should not matter whether you receive $100 that has to be taxed at 50% or whether you receive $50 that does not have to be taxed. This leads to a recommendation analogous to that for transaction costs—*work only in after-tax money*. For example, say you invest $100,000 in after-tax money to earn a return of $160,000. Your marginal tax rate is 25%. Taxes are on the net return of $60,000, so your after-tax net return is

Taxable investors (unlike tax-exempt investors) care about after-tax inflows and outflows.

$$75\% \cdot \$60{,}000 \qquad = \qquad \$45{,}000$$

$$(1 - \tau) \cdot \text{Before-Tax Net Return} = \text{After-Tax Net Return}$$

(The tax rate is commonly abbreviated with the Greek letter τ, tau.) In addition, you will receive your original investment back, so your after-tax rate of return is

$$r_{\text{after tax}} = \frac{\$145{,}000 - \$100{,}000}{\$100{,}000} = 45\%$$

Tax-Exempt Bonds and the Marginal Investor

State and municipal bonds' interest payments are legally exempt from (federal) income taxes.

In the United States, interest paid on bonds issued by smaller governmental entities is legally tax-exempt. (The Constitution's authors did not want to have the federal government burden states' or local governments' efforts to raise money.) If you own one of these bonds, you do not need to declare the interest on your federal income tax forms, and sometimes not even on your state's income tax form, either. (The arrangement differs from bond to bond.) The most prominent tax-exempt bonds are often just called **municipal bonds**, or even **munis** for short. As their name suggests, many are issued by municipalities such as the City of Los Angeles (CA) or the City of Canton (OH). State bonds are also categorized as muni bonds, because they are also exempt from federal income tax. Unfortunately, unlike the U.S. Treasury, municipalities can and have gone bankrupt, so their bonds may not fully repay. For example, Orange County (CA) prominently defaulted in December 1994.) Still, many muni bonds are fairly safe AAA credit. Tax-exempt bonds are often best compared to taxable corporate bonds with similar bond ratings. The difference between the prevailing interest rates on equally risky taxable and tax-exempt bonds allows us to determine the effective tax rate in the economy.

In March 2008, taxable bonds offered 133 basis points per annum above munis. An investor in the 35% tax bracket should have preferred the tax-exempt muni bond.

For example, on March 28, 2008, Bloomberg reported that tax-exempt AAA-rated 10-year muni bonds traded at a yield of 4.05%. Corporate 10-year AAA bonds traded at 5.38%. Which one would be a better investment *for you*? Well, it depends. If you invested $100 into munis at a 4.05% interest rate, you would receive $4.05 at year's end. Uncle Sam would get none of it. If you invested $100 in corporate bonds at a 5.38% interest rate, you would receive $5.38 at year's end. If your federal income tax rate is 0%, you would clearly prefer the $5.38 to the $4.05. However, if your marginal tax rate is 35%, Uncle Sam would collect $5.38 \cdot 35\% \approx \$1.88$ and leave you with $3.50. In terms of after-tax rate of return, this is

$$r_{\text{after tax}} = (1 - 35\%) \cdot 5.38\% \approx 3.50\%$$

$$r_{\text{after tax}} = (1 - \tau) \cdot r_{\text{before tax}}$$

With a 35% marginal federal income tax rate, you should prefer the 4.05% tax-exempt bond to the 5.38% taxable bond.

Investors above a critical tax rate should prefer the muni bond.

In economics, almost everything that is important is "on the margin." Thus, economists like to think about a hypothetical marginal investor. This is an investor whose marginal income tax rate is such that she would be exactly indifferent between buying the tax-exempt bond and the taxable bond. Using the previous formula, the marginal investor has a tax rate of

$$4.05\% = (1 - \tau_{\text{marginal}}) \cdot 5.38\% \quad \Leftrightarrow \quad \tau_{\text{marginal}} = 1 - \frac{4.05\%}{5.38\%} \approx 24.7\%$$

$$r_{\text{after tax}} = (1 - \tau_{\text{marginal}}) \cdot r_{\text{before tax}} \quad \Leftrightarrow \quad \tau_{\text{marginal}} = 1 - \frac{r_{\text{after tax}}}{r_{\text{before tax}}}$$

Any investor with a marginal income tax rate above 24.7% (such as a high-income retail investor) should prefer the tax-exempt bond. Any investor with a marginal income tax rate below 24.7% (such as a tax-exempt pension fund) should prefer the taxable bond. When economists think more generally about how assets are priced, they also use this tax rate as the effective economy-wide one.

Q 10.18. If your tax rate is 20%, what interest rate do you earn in after-tax terms if the before-tax interest rate is 6%?

Q 10.19. If the marginal investor's tax rate is 30% and taxable bonds offer a rate of return of 6%, what rate of return do equivalent muni bonds offer?

Q 10.20. On March 28, 2008, tax-exempt AAA-rated 5-year muni bonds traded at a yield of 3.04%. Corporate 5-year AAA bonds traded at 4.14%. What was the marginal investor's tax rate?

Taxes in Net Present Values

Again, as with transaction costs, you should take care to work only with cash in the same units—here, this means cash that you can use for consumption. Again, it should not matter whether you receive $100 that has to be taxed at 50% or whether you receive $50 that does not have to be taxed. As far as NPV is concerned, you should compute everything in after-tax dollars. This includes all cash flows, whether they occur today or tomorrow, and whether they are inflows or outflows.

> You should only care about your own after-tax cash flows.

IMPORTANT

Do all NPV calculations in *after-tax* money. This applies both to the expected cash flows and to the opportunity cost of capital.

Unfortunately, you cannot simply discount before-tax cash flows with the before-tax cost of capital (wrong!) and expect to come up with the same result as when you discount after-tax cash flows with after-tax costs of capital (right!).

> You must compute the after-tax opportunity cost of capital.

For example, consider a project that costs $10,000 and returns $13,000 next year. Your tax rate is 40%, and 1-year equivalently risky bonds return 25% if their income is taxable and 10% if their income is not taxable. First, you must decide what your opportunity cost of capital is. Section 10.4 showed that if you invest $100 into taxables, you will receive $125 but the IRS will confiscate ($125 – $100) · 40% = $10. You will thus own $115 in after-tax wealth. Tax-exempts grow only to $110, so you prefer the taxable bond—it is the taxable equally risky bond that determines your opportunity cost of capital. Your equivalent after-tax rate of return is therefore 15%. This 15% is your after-tax "opportunity" cost of capital—it is your best alternative use of capital elsewhere.

> Your opportunity cost of capital depends on your own tax rate.

You must discount your after-tax expected cash flows with your after-tax opportunity cost of capital.

Return to your $10,000 project now. You know that your taxable project returns 30% taxable ($3,000), while taxable bonds return 25% ($2,500), so NPV should tell you to take this project. Uncle Sam will confiscate 40% · $3,000 = $1,200, leaving you with $11,800. Therefore, the NPV of your project is

$$\text{NPV} = -\$10,000 + \frac{\$11,800}{1 + 15\%} \approx \$260.87 \quad \text{(after-tax cash flows and after-tax cost of capital)}$$

$$C_0 \quad + \quad \frac{\mathscr{E}(C_1)}{1 + \mathscr{E}(r_1)}$$

Here are incorrect shortcut attempts, working with before-tax cash flows and/or before-tax costs of capital.

It makes intuitive sense: If you had invested money into the bonds, you would have ended up with $11,500. Instead, you will end up with $11,800, the $300 difference occurring next year. Discounted, the $261 seems intuitively correct. Of course, there are an infinite number of ways of getting *incorrect* solutions, but recognize that none of the following calculations that use the before-tax expected cash flows (and try different discount rates) give the same correct result:

$$\text{NPV} \neq -\$10,000 + \frac{\$13,000}{1 + 25\%} = \$400 \quad \text{(taxable cash flows, taxable cost of capital)}$$

$$\text{NPV} \neq -\$10,000 + \frac{\$13,000}{1 + 15\%} \approx \$1,304.35 \quad \text{(taxable cash flows, after-tax cost)}$$

$$\text{NPV} \neq -\$10,000 + \frac{\$13,000}{1 + 10\%} \approx \$1,818.18 \quad \text{(taxable cash flows, muni-tax-exempt cost)}$$

You have no choice: To get the correct answer of $260.87, *you cannot work with before-tax expected cash flows.* Instead, you need to go through the exercise of carefully computing after-tax cash flows and discounting with your after-tax opportunity cost of capital.

In some, but not all, situations, you can compare two projects based on their before-tax NPVs.

You know that computing after-tax cash flows is a pain. Can you at least compare two *equally* taxable projects in terms of their before-tax NPV? If one project is better than the other in before-tax terms, is it also better in after-tax terms? If yes, then you could at least do relative capital budgeting with before-tax project cash flows. This may or may not work, and here is why. Compare project SAFE, which costs $1,000 and will provide $1,500 this evening; and project UNSAFE, which costs $1,000 and will provide either $500 or $2,500 this evening with equal probability. The expected payout is the same, and the cost of capital is practically 0% for 1 day. If you are in the 20% marginal tax bracket, project SAFE will leave you with $500 in *taxable* earnings. The IRS will collect 20% · ($1,500 – $1,000) = $100, leaving you with +$400 in after-tax net return. Project UNSAFE will either give you $1,500 or –$500 in *taxable* earnings.

- If the project succeeds, you would send $1,500 · 20% = $300 to the IRS. If the project fails, and if you can use the losses to offset gains from projects elsewhere, you would send $500 · 20% = $100 *less* to the IRS (because your taxable profits elsewhere would be reduced). In this case, projects SAFE and UNSAFE would have the same expected tax costs and after-tax cash flows: $1/2 \cdot \$300 + 1/2 \cdot (-\$100) = \$100$.

- If you drop into a different tax bracket, say, 25%, when your (additional) net income is $1,000 higher, then project UNSAFE becomes less desirable than project SAFE. For the $1,500 income, the first $500 would still cost you $100 in tax, but the remaining $1,000 would cost you $250. Thus, your project's marginal tax obligation would be either $350 or –$100, for an expected tax burden of $125. (The same logic applies if your losses would make you fall into a lower tax bracket—the UNSAFE project would become less desirable, because the tax reduction would be worth less.)

- If you have no capital gains elsewhere that you can reduce with the UNSAFE project capital loss, then the UNSAFE project would again be worth less. Corporations can ask for a tax refund on old gains, so the unrealized tax loss factor is less binding than it is for individuals, who may have to carry the capital loss forward until they have sufficient income again to use it—if ever.

Thus, whether you can compare projects on a before-tax basis depends on whether you have perfect symmetry in the applicable marginal tax rates across projects. If you do, then the project that is more profitable in after-tax terms is also more profitable in before-tax terms. This would allow you to simply compare projects by their before-tax NPVs. If gains and losses face different taxation—either because of tax bracket changes or because of your inability to use the tax losses elsewhere—then you cannot simply choose the project with the higher before-tax NPV. You will have to go through the entire after-tax NPV calculations and compare them.

IMPORTANT

> You can only compare projects on a before-tax NPV basis if the tax treatment is absolutely symmetric. This requires consideration of your overall tax situation.

You now know how to discount projects in the presence of income taxes. However, you do not yet know how to compute the proper discount rate for projects that are financed by debt and equity, because debt and equity face different tax consequences. Unfortunately, you will have to wait until Chapter 17 before we can do a good job discussing the two suitable methods—called APV and WACC—to handle differential taxation for different corporate securities.

Two more tax-adjusting corporate valuation methods, WACC and APV, unfortunately have to wait.

Q 10.21. You have a project that costs $50,000 and will return $80,000 in 3 years. Your marginal capital gains tax rate on the $30,000 gain will be 37.5%. Treasuries pay a rate of return of 8% per year; munis pay a rate of return of 3% per year. What is the NPV of your project?

Q 10.22. You are in the 33.3% tax bracket. A project will return $14,000 in 1 year for a $12,000 investment—a $2,000 net return. The equivalent tax-exempt bond yields 15%, and the equivalent taxable bond yields 20%. What is the NPV of this project?

Q 10.23. It is not uncommon for individuals to forget about taxes, especially when investments are small and payoffs are large but rare. Say you are in the 30% tax bracket. Is the NPV of a $1 lottery ticket that pays off taxable winnings of $10 million with a chance of 1 in 9 million positive or negative? How would it change if you could purchase the lottery ticket with before-tax money?

Tax Timing

It is often better if you are taxed only at the very end, rather than in the interim.

In many situations, the IRS does not allow reinvestment of funds generated by a project without an interim tax penalty. This can be important when you compare one long-term investment to multiple short-term investments that are otherwise identical. For example, consider a farmer in the 40% tax bracket who purchases grain (seed) that costs $300 and that triples in value every year.

- If the IRS considers this farm to be *one long-term two-year project*, the farmer can use the first harvest to reseed, so $300 seed turns into $900 in one year and then into a $2,700 harvest in two years. Uncle Sam considers the profit to be $2,400 and so collects taxes of $960. The farmer is left with an after-tax cash flow of $2,700 − $960 = $1,740.

- If the IRS considers this production to be *two consecutive 1-year projects*, then the farmer's after-tax profits are lower. He ends up with $900 at the end of the first year. Uncle Sam collects 40% · ($900 − $300) = $240, leaving the farmer with $660. Replanted, the $660 grows to $1,980, of which the IRS collects another 40% · ($1,980 − $660) = $528. The farmer is left with an after-tax cash flow of $1,980 − $528 = $1,452.

The discrepancy between $1,740 and $1,452 is due to the fact that the long-term project can avoid the interim taxation. Similar issues arise whenever an expense can be reclassified from "reinvested profits" (taxed, if not with some credit at reinvestment time) into "necessary maintenance."

Q 10.24. Assume that your marginal tax rate is 25%. Assume that the IRS would tax payments only when made. (Sorry, in real life, the IRS nowadays does tax zero-bonds even when they do not yet pay out anything.)

1. What is the future value of a 10-year zero-bond priced at a YTM of 10%? How much does the IRS get to keep?

2. What is the future value of a 10-year annual level-coupon bond priced at a YTM of 10%, assuming that coupons are immediately reinvested at the same 10%?

3. What would it be worth to you today to be taxed only at the end (via the zero-bond) and not in the interim (via the coupon bond)? Which is better?

10.5   Entrepreneurial Finance

Now that you understand how to work with market imperfections, for what types of firms do they matter most? Market imperfections are probably just mild for large, publicly traded corporations. These types of firms typically face only modest interest rate spreads between their (risky) borrowing and lending rates. Of course, their *promised* borrowing interest rates are a little higher than what they can receive investing their money in Treasury bonds. Yet, given that they still have some possibility of going bankrupt, large firms' required *expected* borrowing costs of capital are probably fairly close to the *expected* rates of return they could earn if they invested in bonds with characteristics similar to the bonds that they themselves have issued. Thus, large public corporations can often pretend to live in a reasonably perfect market. This also means that they have the luxury of separating their project choices from their financial needs.

In the world of individuals, entrepreneurs, and small companies, however, it is quite plausible that the costs of capital are often higher than equivalent expected savings interest rates. In fact, the most important difference between "ordinary corporate finance" and "entrepreneurial finance" is the degree to which their capital markets are perfect. Almost all entrepreneurs find it very difficult to convey credibly their intent and ability to pay back loans. And any credit that entrepreneurs receive is usually also very illiquid: Lenders cannot easily convert it into cash, should the need arise. Therefore, they demand a high liquidity spread, too. Many entrepreneurs even end up having to resort to financing projects with credit cards, which may charge 1,000 basis points or more above Treasury.

In sum, small firms often face extraordinarily high differentials between expected borrowing and lending rates. Entrepreneurs' high borrowing costs can thus prevent them from taking many projects that they would have undertaken if they had the money already on hand. Cash-on-hand can become a prime determinant of all their decisions. More established firms or wealthier entrepreneurs should optimally take more projects than poorer entrepreneurs. Yes, the world is not fair.

However, be careful in the real world before you believe the claims of entrepreneurs. Entrepreneurs also tend to have notoriously overoptimistic views of their prospects. Even venture capitalists, the financing vehicle for many high-tech entrepreneurial ventures, which advertise rates of return of 30% per year or more, seem to have managed to return only a couple of percentage points above the risk-free rate over the last 30 years. Adjusting for the correct default rates may actually mean that entrepreneurs face only high *promised* borrowing costs, not high *expected* borrowing costs. Thus, the large quoted spread between entrepreneurs' borrowing and lending rates, which is really all that you can easily observe, likely has a large component that is due not to information disagreements but simply to credit risk.

This issue of how to deal with market imperfections for small firms also arises frequently in the courts, where a cost-of-capital estimate is necessary to compute the value for an entrepreneurial enterprise—for example, for purposes of assessing the inheritance tax or resolving disputes among former business partners. (Such valuation services are an important revenue business for many finance professors and consulting firms.) It has become customary and legally acceptable to compute first the value of an equivalent publicly traded business or company as if it faced a perfect market, and then

For large companies, a perfect market assumption with equal borrowing and lending rates is reasonable.

➤ *Altman study of bond default rates, Sect. 6.2, Pg. 125.*

For entrepreneurs, a perfect market assumption is problematic.

The *expected* costs of capital are often very high for entrepreneurs needing capital.

➤ *Separation of Decisions, Sect. 4.1, Pg. 60.*

Be careful: Don't believe entrepreneurial claims! Often, high borrowing rates are just promised, not expected.

The courts apply an ad hoc discount to the values of entrepreneurial companies based on their limited access to capital.

to apply a **private discount** of around 10% to 30% of firm value in order to reflect the limited access to capital. The amount of this discount is ad hoc, but it is better than no attempt at all.

Q 10.25. What are the two possible reasons why entrepreneurs often have to finance their projects with credit cards, which can charge interest rates as high as 1,000 basis points above Treasury?

10.6 Deconstructing Quoted Rates of Return—Liquidity and Tax Premiums

➤ *Default Premium Deconstruction, Sect. 6.2, Pg. 124.*

Adding Market Imperfection Permia.

➤ *Risk Premium Deconstruction, Sect. 9.3, Pg. 213.*

In Sections 6.2 and 9.3, you learned that you could decompose quoted rates of return into a time premium, a default premium, and a risk premium. Market imperfections can create additional premiums.

$$\text{Promised Rate of Return} = \text{Time Premium} + \text{Default Premium}$$
$$+ \text{Risk Premium} + \text{Imperfect Market Premiums}$$

$$\text{Expected Rate of Return} = \underbrace{\text{Time Premium} + \text{Risk Premium}}_{\text{provided by the CAPM}}$$
$$+ \text{Imperfect Market Premiums}$$

Quantifying imperfect market premiums is not easy, but we will try anyway. Unfortunately, there is not much that can be said about one of the imperfect market premiums—the premium compensating for differences in opinion. The nature of information disagreements is that they are idiosyncratic. This does not mean that they are unimportant. As noted earlier, imperfections can be so large, even in financial markets, that they may destroy a financial market's viability. Fortunately, the other three imperfections—taxes, transaction costs, and shallow markets—create premiums that are often a little easier to quantify than the premium associated with information disagreements.

Tax premiums are usually similar within the same "asset class."

Tax differences are often modest across assets in the *same* class. However, when there are assets that are treated differently from a tax perspective, the one with the worse treatment has to offer a higher rate of return. For example, municipal bonds are excluded from federal taxation. Therefore, non-municipal bonds have to offer a higher rate of return relative to these tax-exempt bonds. Similarly, unlike federal Treasury bonds, the holders of corporate bonds are subject to state income taxes. This means that corporate bonds need to pay a premium relative to Treasuries—a **tax premium**.

Let me expand the imperfect market premium into its component premiums.

Transaction costs and deep markets also play important roles. The resulting premiums are often lumped under the general term "liquidity premiums." The idea is that, given a choice between a very liquid security that you can resell in an instant to many different investors in case you need money and a very illiquid security, you will demand an extra rate of return to buy the less liquid one. We can thus extend our earlier premiums analysis to the following:

Promised Rate of Return = Time Premium + Default Premium + Risk Premium

+ Liquidity Premium + Tax Premium

Actual Earned Rate = Time Premium + Default Realization + Risk Premium

+ Liquidity Premium + Tax Premium

Expected Rate of Return = Time Premium + Expected Risk Premium

+ Liquidity Premium + Tax Premium

Again, there could be other premiums that should go into this formula, such as information premiums or bond contract feature premiums. I omit them because I don't have empirical evidence to show you. In addition, our concept of a clean decomposition is a little problematic in itself, because these premiums overlap. For example, it is quite possible that there are covariance-risk aspects to liquidity. (In other words, it could be that liquidity spreads increase when the market goes down, which would mean that they have a positive market beta.) Thus, a part of the quoted spread could be considered either as a risk premium or as a liquidity premium. Nevertheless, the basic decomposition in the above formulas is useful.

➤ *Credit Ratings, Sect. 6.2, Pg. 125.*

Let's go back to corporate bonds. You already learned in Section 6.2 that many corporate bonds have significant default risk, which means that they have to offer a default premium (relative to Treasuries, of course). Let me now tell you that, depending on credit rating, they have market betas between about 0.1 (investment-grade bonds) and 0.5 (junk bonds). This means that junk bonds may have to offer a meaningfully large premium to compensate investors for market risk, but for investment-grade bonds, any beta premium would be trivial.

Corporate bonds: CAPM-type market covariance risk may matter for junk bonds but would be trivial for AAA-grade bonds.

However, many corporate bonds are difficult to resell quickly—most have to be traded over-the-counter, and not on an organized exchange. Therefore, they have to offer their buyers a liquidity premium. Finally, corporate bonds are subject to state income taxes. This means that they have to offer a tax premium.

Liquidity premiums could be high for all types of risky bonds. Tax premiums are probably similar among all taxable bonds.

In the Ed Altman study you first saw in Section 6.2, the historical average rates of return on corporate bonds from 1971 to 2003 were as follows:

The typical investment-grade bond promised about 200 basis points above the equivalent Treasury bond. However, investors ended up with only about 20-40 basis points above the Treasury. Thus, about 170 basis points was the default premium.

The typical junk bond promised a spread of about 500 basis points per annum above the 10-year Treasury bond. However, investors ended up with a spread of "only" about 220 basis points. The default premium was therefore about 280 basis points.

Differences in expected rates of return by credit rating suggest that riskier and less liquid bonds earn more than safer bonds—but not as much as it seems.

This suggests that the default premium is the most important premium in stated corporate bond yields. Only about 20-40 basis points for investment-grade and about 220 basis points for junk bonds still remain to be explained by the sum of the risk, liquidity, and other premiums.

Frank de Jong, a professor at the University of Amsterdam, produced a similar study on bonds from 1985 to 2003. Unlike Altman, he decomposed the *average* (expected) rates of return into a liquidity risk premium, a market risk premium, and a tax premium.

Exhibit **10.1** decomposes *expected* rates of return into market risk, liquidity premiums, and tax premiums.

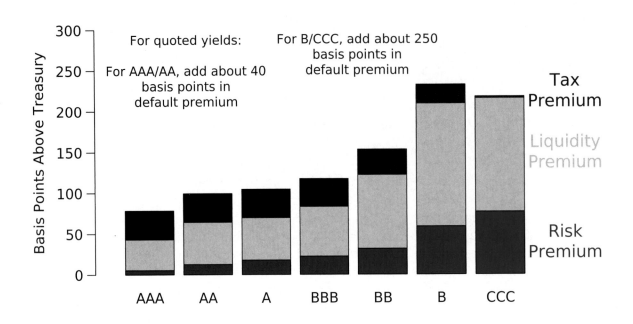

Exhibit 10.1: *The Components of Expected Rates of Return in Corporate Bonds, 1985-2003.* These are estimates of *expected* yield premiums for long-term corporate bonds. For highly rated bonds, the liquidity and tax premiums are much larger than the risk premium. For very low-rated bonds, the liquidity premium becomes relatively more important, followed by the risk premium and then the tax premium. To obtain stated (quoted) bond yields, you would have to add the default premium. The time premium has been taken out because all spreads are relative to the prevailing time-equivalent Treasury yield. For example, the average AAA bond would have quoted 7.2% when the average Treasury bond yielded 6%. The default premium would have added about 40 basis points, with the remaining 80 basis points having been compensation for risk, liquidity, and taxes. Original source: De Jong and Driessen, 2005.

Exhibit 10.1 shows that about 40 basis points for AAA and 250 basis points for CCC bonds were pure default premiums that you would not have earned on average. With betas of around 0.1, the market risk premium was negligibly small for AAA and AA bonds, but then was higher for CCC-rated bonds, accounting for as much as 1% yield per year. The liquidity premium was about 50 basis points for highly rated bonds, and 100-150 basis points for junk bonds. Incidentally, many institutional investors are only allowed to hold investment-grade bonds. Thus, dropping from investment grade to speculative grade incurs a large liquidity penalty. You can see this in the sudden and unusually steep rise in yield for BB and B bonds. Finally, the state income tax premium was about 20-30 basis points for all bonds, except for the CCC bonds (which may simply be a data glitch).

Q 10.26. An IBM bond promising to pay $100,000 costs $90,090. Time-equivalent Treasuries offer 8%.

1. Let's presume for a moment—just for this question—that the financial markets are neither risk-neutral nor perfect. What can you say about other premia in IBM's quoted interest rate? (These premiums will be explained in future chapters; they include the risk premium, the default premium, and the liquidity premium.)

2. Let's presume for a moment that the financial markets are now risk-neutral. What can you say about other premiums in IBM's quoted interest rate? (These premiums will be explained in future chapters; they include the risk premium, the default premium, and the liquidity premium.)

3. Assuming that the liquidity premium is 0.5%, what can you say about the risk premium, the default premium, and the liquidity premium?

Q 10.27. How important are the various premiums for investment-grade bonds and junk bonds? (Omit the time premium.)

10.7 Multiple Effects: How to Work Novel Problems

Of course, in the messy real world, you can suffer many problems (such as inflation, transaction costs, disagreements, sole potential buyers, and taxes) all at once, not just in isolation. In fact, there are so many possible real-world problems that no one can possibly give you a formula for each one. Thus, it is important that you approach the real world keeping a multitude of issues in mind.

Life is tough—it does not always offer simple solutions.

➤ *Inflation, Sect. 5.2, Pg. 90.*

1. Ask yourself in a given situation whether the assumption of a perfect market is reasonably appropriate. For example, in the case of large and possibly tax-exempt companies, you may consider it reasonable to get away with assuming a perfect market, and just work out the "perfect market" answer—a simple NPV, for example. Then think about the direction in which market imperfections would push you, judge the magnitude, and make an intuitive adjustment. You can thereby often work out a good answer without the enormous complications that the perfectly correct answer would require.

If you get lucky, you may get good estimates ignoring market inefficiencies altogether. Adjust a little maybe just intuitively.

2. If you conclude that you are a long way from home (i.e., from a perfect market), then you must first determine which market imperfections are most important. Then you must work out a good solution by yourself. If you had hoped for the one magic bullet that tells you how to solve every different kind of problem you might encounter, I have to disappoint you. There are just too many possibilities, and the task is often hard. Probably the best way to answer such new and thorny questions is to internalize the method of "thinking by numerical example." You really need to be able to work out formulas for yourself when you need them.

You must learn how to think for yourself. I can now only teach you the method, not the solution.

Solving a Problem with Inflation and Taxes

Now work an example of how both taxes and inflation could interact.

For example, let's see how you could approach a situation with both taxes and inflation. Always start by making up some numbers you find easy to work with. Let's say you are considering an investment of $100. Further, assume that you will earn a 10% rate of return on your $100 investment and Uncle Sam will take $\tau = 40\%$ (or $4 on your $10 return). Therefore, you get $110 before taxes but end up with only $106 in nominal terms. What you have just calculated is

$$\$100 \cdot [1 + 10\% \cdot (1 - 40\%)] \quad = \$106$$

$$C_0 \cdot \left[1 + r_{\text{nominal,before tax}} \cdot (1 - \tau)\right] \quad = \quad C_1$$

Now you need to determine what your $106 is really worth, so you must introduce inflation. Pick some round number, say, a rate of $\pi = 5\%$ per annum. Consequently, in purchasing power, the $106 is worth:

$$\frac{\$106}{1 + 5\%} \approx \$100.95$$

$$\frac{C_1}{1 + \pi} = P_0$$

Your after-tax, post-inflation, real rate of return is $\$100.95/\$100 - 1 = 0.95\%$. Knowing the numerical result, you need to translate your numbers into a formula. You computed

$$r_{\text{after tax, real}} = \frac{\$100.95 - \$100}{\$100} = \frac{\frac{\$100 \cdot [1 + 10\% \cdot (1 - 40\%)]}{1 + 5\%} - \$100}{\$100}$$

$$= \frac{10\% \cdot (1 - 40\%) - 5\%}{1 + 5\%} \approx 0.95\%$$

$$r_{\text{after tax, real}} = \frac{P_0 - C_0}{C_0} = \frac{\frac{C_0 \cdot [1 + r_{\text{nominal,before tax}} \cdot (1 - \tau)]}{1 + \pi} - C_0}{C_0}$$

$$= \frac{r_{\text{nominal,before tax}} \cdot (1 - \tau) - \pi}{1 + \pi} \tag{10.1}$$

This is, of course, not a formula that anyone remembers. However, it is a useful illustration of how you should approach and simplify complex questions—numerical example first, formula second.

Taxes on Nominal Returns?

If the real interest rate stays constant, does inflation hurt an investor? Yes, because taxes are assessed on *nominal* returns.

Here is an interesting question: If the real rate of return remains constant, does it help or hurt an investor if inflation goes up? Let's assume that the real rate of return is a constant 20%. If inflation is 50%, then the nominal rate of return is 80% (because $(1 + 50\%) \cdot (1 + 20\%) = 1 + 80\%$): You get $180 for a $100 investment. Now add income taxes to the tune of 40%. The IRS sees $80 in interest, taxes $32, and leaves you with $48. Your $148 will thus be worth $\$148/(1 + 50\%) \approx \$98.67$ in real value. Instead of a 20% increase in real purchasing power when you save money, you now suffer a $\$98.67/\$100 - 1 \approx -1.3\%$ change in real purchasing power. Despite a high real interest rate, Uncle Sam ended up with more, and you ended up with less purchasing power than you started with. The reason is that although Uncle Sam claims to tax only interest gains, you can actually lose in *real* terms because the interest tax is on *nominal* interest payments. Contrast this with the same scenario without inflation. In this case, if the real rate of return were still 20%, you would have earned $20, Uncle Sam would have taxed you $8, and you could have kept $112 in real value.

IMPORTANT

If real before-tax interest rates remain constant, because the IRS taxes nominal returns, not real returns, you get the following results:

- Higher inflation and interest rates hurt *taxable* savers.

- Higher inflation and interest rates help *taxable* borrowers.

(Economic forces of demand and supply for capital may therefore have to adjust, so that real rates of return increase when inflation increases.)

For much of postwar U.S. history, real rates of return on short-term government bonds have indeed been *negative* for taxed investors.

Yikes.

Q 10.28. Assume that you have both taxes and inflation. You are in the 20% tax bracket, and the inflation rate is 5% per year. A 1-year project offers you $3,000 return for a $20,000 investment. Taxable bonds offer a rate of return of 10% per year. What is the NPV of this project? Extra credit if you can derive the formula yourself!

Q 10.29. (Advanced) Assume that the inflation rate is 100% per year and the nominal rate of interest is 700% per year. (This was also our apples example from Section 5.2.) Now, assume that there is also a 25% default rate. That is, 1 in 4 apples are returned with worms inside and will therefore not be sellable (and be worth $0). What is your real rate of return? What is the formula?

Q 10.30. (Advanced) Assume there is a 10% nominal rate of return, a tax rate of 40%, and an inflation rate of 5%. (In the taxes-and-inflation example from Formula 10.1 we worked out that the post-inflation, after-tax rate of return was 0.95%.) Now, add a default rate, d, of 2%, where all money is lost (–100% return). What is the real, post-inflation, after-tax, post-default rate of return? (Hint: Losses are tax-deductible, too. Assume that the default rate reduces the nominal rate of return (on which taxes are charged) because you do not just take 1 such loan, but 1 million, which practically assures you of the exact default rate without any sampling variation.)

Q 10.31. If the private sector is a net saver (e.g., leaving the public sector as a net borrower), does Uncle Sam have an incentive to reduce or increase inflation?

Summary

This chapter covered the following major points:

- If markets are perfect, there are infinitely many buyers and sellers, no disagreements (opinions), no transaction costs, and no taxes.

- In perfect markets, *promised* borrowing and lending rates can be different, but *expected* borrowing and lending rates cannot. In imperfect markets, even *expected* borrowing and lending rates can be different.

- If markets are not perfect, capital budgeting decisions can then depend on the cash position of the project owner. NPV and interest rate computations can still be used, although you have to exert special care in working with correct and meaningful inputs (especially for the cost of capital). This is usually best done by thinking in terms of concrete examples first, then translating them into formulas later.

- Transaction costs can be direct (such as commissions) or indirect (such as search or waiting costs). It is often useful to think of round-trip transaction costs.

- Financial assets' transaction costs tend to be very low, so that it is reasonable in many (but not all) circumstances just to ignore them.

- In the real world, buyers often prefer more liquid investments. To induce them to purchase a less liquid investment may require offering them some additional expected rate of return.

- Many financial markets have such low transaction costs and are often so liquid that they are believed to be close to perfect—there are so many buyers and so many sellers that it is unlikely that you would pay too much or too little for an asset. Such assets are likely to be worth what you pay for them.

- The tax code is complex. For the most part, individuals and corporations are taxed similarly. You must understand the following:
    - How income taxes are computed (the principles, not the details)
    - The fact that expenses that can be paid from before-tax income are better than expenses that must be paid from after-tax income
    - How to compute the average tax rate
    - How to obtain the marginal tax rate
    - That capital gains enjoy preferential tax treatment
    - Why the average and marginal tax rates differ, and why the marginal tax rate is usually higher than the average tax rate

- Taxable interest rates can be converted into equivalent tax-exempt interest rates, given the appropriate marginal tax rate.

- Tax-exempt bonds are usually advantageous for investors in high-income tax brackets. You can compute the critical tax rate for the investor who is indifferent between the two.

- You should do all NPV calculations with after-transaction-cost and after-tax cash flows and costs of capital.

- Long-term projects often suffer less interim taxation than short-term ones.

- Entrepreneurial finance can be viewed as the finance of imperfect markets.

- Quoted rates of return on financial instruments contain a time premium, a default premium, a risk premium, and different imperfect market premiums. For many bonds, the imperfect market premiums are larger than the (CAPM-style) risk premium (compensating for covariance with the market).

- The IRS taxes nominal returns, not real returns. This means that higher inflation rates are bad for savers and good for borrowers.

Keywords

AMT, 262.   After-tax expense, 261.   Alternative minimum tax, 262.   Ask price, 256.   Average tax rate, 262.   Before-tax expense, 261.   Bid price, 256.   Buy-and-hold, 257.   Collateral, 253.   Competitive market, 246.   Covenants, 253.   Day trader, 257.   Flight to quality, 260.   IRS, 261.   Internal Revenue Service, 261.   Liquidity premium, 259.   Marginal tax rate, 262.   Muni, 264.   Municipal bond, 264. Off-the-run, 259.   On-the-run, 259.   Opportunity cost, 256.   Private discount, 270.   Round-trip costs, 255. Run on liquidity, 260.   Spread, 256.   Tax premium, 270.

Answers

Q 10.1 In a perfect market, borrowing and lending rates are identical. An important implication of equal borrowing and lending rates is that there is a unique price for which a product would be selling (which we can then call its value).

Q 10.2 A competitive market is only one of the four conditions of a perfect market.

Q 10.3 There is no perfect capital market in this world. However, the concept of a perfect market helps you evaluate what departures from a perfect market really mean—and even what kind of departures you should be thinking about.

Q 10.4 The perfect market assumptions are: (a) no differences in information, (b) no market power, (c) no transaction costs, and (d) no taxes.

Q 10.5 For the $1,000 cost project:

1. You would have to borrow $100 at an interest rate of 10% in order to take the project. If you take the project, you will therefore have $1,000 · 1.08 − $110 = $970 next period. If instead you invest $900 at the 4% savings rate, you will receive only $936. You should definitely take the project.

2. There is a trade-off between investing a smaller sum in the bank and a larger sum in the project now. Say you invest I.

If you put it into the bank, you receive I · (1 + 4%) = I · 1.04. If you put I into the project, you receive $1,000 · 1.08 from the project, borrow ($1,000 − I) at an interest rate of 10%. Therefore, you must solve

$$I \cdot 1.04 = \$1,000 \cdot 1.08 - (\$1,000 - I) \cdot 1.1$$

The solution is I ≈ $333.33, which means that if you want to consume more than $1,666.67, you should not take the project. Check: [1] If you consume $1,700, you have a remaining $300 to invest. The bank would pay $312 next year. The project would pay off $1,080, but you would have to borrow $700 and pay back $770, for a net of $310. You should not take the project. [2] If you consume $1,600, you have a remaining $400 to invest. The bank would pay $416 next year. The project would pay off $1,080, but you would have to borrow $600 and pay back $660, for a net of $420. You should take the project.

Q 10.6 False. A perfect market is still socially valuable, because sellers and buyers receive surpluses. The buyer surplus is the difference between the value that the good has to a particular buyer and the price at which this buyer can acquire it. (A similar argument applies to the seller—the nonmarginal producer can sell the good for a higher dollar amount than it costs to provide the good.) It is only the "marginal" buyer and seller that get no surplus. All inframarginal buyers and sellers are better off.

Q 10.7 Yes, banks can quote different borrowing and lending rates even in a perfect market! Stated interest rates include a default premium. A perfect market is about equality of *expected* rates, not about equality of *promised* rates.

Q 10.8 True. In a perfect and risk-neutral market, the default rates may be quite different, but the expected rates of return on all investments should be the same.

Q 10.9 For the bond that pays $100 99% of the time:

1. The expected payoff is $99. The discounted expected payoff is $99/1.05 \approx $94.286. The promised yield is therefore $100/$94.286 - 1 \approx 6.06\%$.

2. This borrower would believe the value to be $100/1.05 \approx $95.238. Therefore, the borrower believes he has to overpay by about 95 cents.

Q 10.10 Covenants, collateral, and credit ratings are all common mechanisms to aid the lender in determining the probability of default. Even if disclosure is not required, good borrowers would still want to do so. Therefore, no bank would trust a borrower who is not disclosing as much information as possible. To get credit, it is in the interest of the borrower to volunteer information.

Q 10.11 Dell is a large stock, just like PepsiCo. Therefore, a round-trip transaction would probably cost a bid-ask spread of between 0.1% and 0.3%. On a $10,000 investment, the bid-ask cost would be around $20, and broker fees would probably be around $10 to $30 with a discount broker. Thus, $50 (or 0.5%) is a reasonable estimate.

Q 10.12 Direct transaction cost components: broker costs, market maker or exchange costs (bid-ask spread), and other cash expenses (e.g., advertising costs and postage). Indirect transaction cost components: time taken to do research and/or searching for a buyer or seller, opportunity costs, anxiety, and so on.

Q 10.13 For this house transaction cost question, you first need to assume a proper discount rate for the $4,000/month rent. At a 7% effective interest rate per year, your true monthly rate is $1.07^{1/12} - 1 \approx 0.5654\%$ per month). A reasonable assumption to value the rent stream is as a 1-year annuity, whose value is $4,000/r \cdot [1 - 1/(1 + r)^{12}] \approx $46,281 today. Therefore,

$$- (\$1,000,000 + \$5,000) + \$46,281 + \frac{x \cdot (1 - 8\%)}{1.07} = 0$$

Solve this to $x \approx $1,115,031, so your capital appreciation must be 11.5% per annum for this project to be zero NPV for you.

Q 10.14 A liquidity premium is an up-front lower price to compensate you for transaction costs later on. This can allow you to earn a higher expected rate of return on the investment.

Q 10.15 A taxpayer prefers to have a before-tax expense, because it reduces the amount that Uncle Sam considers as income, which Uncle Sam would then want to tax.

Q 10.16 The first preference of taxpayers is to receive income in the form of capital gains (especially as long-term capital gains, which is usually under the control of the taxpayer). Their second preference is to receive income in the form of dividends. Both are much better forms of income than interest income or ordinary income. They are both taxed at lower rates under the U.S. tax code. (In 2008, their rates were about 15%, compared to 30% or more for interest and ordinary income). In addition, capital gains can most easily be offset by capital losses elsewhere, and there is no interim taxation before the capital gains realization.

Q 10.17 The marginal tax rate is usually *not* lower but higher. The average tax rate is usually lower, because the first few dollars of income are taxed at lower tax rates.

Q 10.18 For every $100, you receive $6. Uncle Sam takes 20% of $6, or $1.20. Your after-tax rate of return is $4.80/$100 = 4.8%. You could have also computed $(1 - 20\%) \cdot 6\% = 4.8\%$ directly.

Q 10.19 If the marginal investor's tax rate is 30% and taxable bonds offer a rate of return of 6%, then munis should offer $r = 70\% \cdot 6\% = 4.2\%$ to earn the marginal investor the same after-tax income.

Q 10.20 On March 28, 2008, 5-year AAA munis were offering $3.04\%/4.14\% \approx 73.43\%$ of the 5-year corporate AAA yields. Therefore, $(1 - \tau) \approx 0.7343$, which means that the marginal investor's tax rate was $\tau \approx 26.57\%$.

Q 10.21 First, you need to compute your best opportunity cost of capital if you do not take your project.

- The Treasury will pay $108 before tax. You could therefore earn $108 - 0.375 \cdot $8 = $105 after taxes. This is an after-tax rate of return of 5%.

- The muni will pay only $103 after taxes. This is an after-tax rate of return of 3%.

Comparing the two, your opportunity cost of capital—that is, your best investment opportunity elsewhere—is 5% *in after-tax terms*. Now, move on to your project. You will have to pay $11,250 in taxes on $30,000, so you will have $18,750 net return left after taxes, which comes to an after-tax amount of $80,000-$11,250 = $68,750. Your project NPV is therefore $-$50,000+$68,750/1.05^3 \approx +$9,389$. This is a great project!

Q 10.22 Your opportunity cost of capital is determined by the tax-exempt bond, because $66.67\% \cdot 20\% < 15\%$. Your project's $2,000 will turn into $66.67\% \cdot $2,000 \approx $1,334 after-tax earnings, or $13,334 after-tax cash flow. Therefore, your NPV is $-$12,000 + $13,334/(1 + 15\%) \approx -405.22. Check: The after-tax rate of return of the project's cash flow is $13,334/$12,000-1 \approx 11.11\%$. This is less than 15%. You are better off investing in tax-exempt bonds.

Q 10.23 The $1 is paid from after-tax income, so leave it as is. The $10 million is taxed, so you will only receive $7 million. With a 1 in 9 million chance of winning, the expected payoff is $7,000,000 \cdot 1/9,000,000 + $0 \cdot 8,999,999/9,000,000 \approx 78$ cents. Therefore, the NPV is negative for any cost of capital. If you could pay with before-tax money, the ticket would cost you only 70 cents in terms of after-tax money, so for interest rates below

$0.7778/\$0.70 - 1 \approx 11.1\%$ or so, the lottery would be a positive-NPV investment. (This assumes that you are risk neutral, on average, for such a small idiosyncratic investment.)

Q 10.24 For comparing the zero bonds and coupon bonds, assume that you start with $1,000 of money:

1. The 10% zero-bond would have a single before-tax payout of $1,000 \cdot 1.10^{10} \approx \$2,593.74$, for which the IRS would collect $1,593.74 \cdot 25\% \approx \$398.44$ in year 10. This means that you would keep an after-tax zero-bond payout of $2,195.30.

2. The 10% coupon bond has an after-tax rate of return of 7.5% per annum, because it is always taxed at 25% in the very same year. Reinvestment yields an after-tax rate of return of 7.5% ($75 in the first year on $1,000). After 10 years, you are left with $1,000 \cdot 1.075^{10} \approx \$2,061.03$.

3. The tax savings on the zero-bond are $134 in 10 years. Therefore, the zero-bond is better.

Q 10.25 Entrepreneurs pay interest rates as high as 1,000 basis points for one of two reasons: First, default rates are high. (This is not necessarily a difference in expected rates of return.) Second, market imperfections (especially information differences about default probabilities and liquidity premiums) are high. Banks cannot easily determine which entrepreneurs are for real and which ones will go bankrupt and take the bank's money with them. The entrepreneurs may or may not be better at knowing whether their inventions will work. (This can be a market imperfection.)

Q 10.26 For this IBM bond:

1. The total promised rate of return is $\$100,000/\$90,090 - 1 = 11\%$. The time premium is the Treasury yield of 8%, which leaves 3%. The sum of the three remaining premiums (risk, default, liquidity) would be 3%. You cannot deconstruct the three without more information.

2. Risk-neutrality means that the risk premium would be zero. Therefore, you now know the default premium and liquidity premium sum to 3%.

3. Risk-neutrality means that the risk premium would be zero. You now know the liquidity premium, too. This means that the default premium is 2.5%.

Q 10.27 From Altman's evidence: The default premium seems more important than the other non-time premiums. From de Jong's evidence, ranking the remaining premiums: For investment-grade bonds, the liquidity and tax premiums seem to explain most of the return above the Treasury. Risk premiums are very small. For junk bonds, liquidity and risk premiums can become large. The risk premium is typically still lower than the liquidity premium. The tax premium becomes relatively small.

Q 10.28 What is your after-tax rate of return on taxable bonds? $100 will grow to $110 at a 10% interest rate before tax, minus the 20% that Uncle Sam collects. Uncle Sam takes $1.1 \cdot \$100 = \$110$, subtracts $100, and then leaves you with only 80% thereof:

$$r_{\text{after tax}} = \frac{80\% \cdot (\$110 - \$100)}{\$100} = 8\%$$

$$r_{\text{after tax}} = \frac{(1 - \tau) \cdot (C_1 - C_0)}{C_0}$$

where τ is your tax rate of 20%. $(C_1 - C_0)/C_0$ is the before-tax rate of return, so this is just

$$r_{\text{after tax}} = 80\% \cdot 10\% = 8\%$$
$$= (1 - \tau) \cdot r_{\text{before tax}}$$

Now, in before-tax terms, your project offers a 15% rate of return. In after-tax terms, the project offers $80\% \cdot \$3,000 = \$2,400$ net return. On your investment of $20,000, this is a 12% after-tax rate of return. (On the same $20,000, the taxable bond would offer only $80\% \cdot (\$22,000 - \$20,000) = \$1,600$ net return (8%). So, you know that the NPV should be positive.) Therefore, the project NPV is

$$NPV = -\$20,000 + \frac{\$20,000 + 80\% \cdot (\$23,000 - \$20,000)}{1 + 8\%}$$

$$\approx \$740.74$$

$$NPV = C_0 + \frac{C_0 + (1 - \tau) \cdot (C_1 - C_0)}{1 + r_{\text{after tax}}}$$

You can now easily substitute any other cash flows or interest rates into these formulas to obtain the NPV. Note that everything is computed in nominal dollars, so you do not need the information about the inflation rate! (And you needed it in nominal, because taxes are computed based on nominal gains, not real gains.)

Q 10.29 First, a simple version of the answer: Your one real apple becomes eight nominal pseudoapples (at 700%), which is four real apples after 100% inflation. One goes bad, so you are left with three apples, i.e., a rate of return of 200%. Now, the more complete version: Your numeraire is one apple (1a) that costs $1. You will get $8 in nominal terms, next year $(a \cdot (1 + r_{\text{nominal,before tax}}) = a \cdot (1 + 700\%) = 8 \cdot a)$. This will purchase apples that cost $2 each $((1 + \pi) = (1 + 100\%) = \$2)$, that is, four apples $(a \cdot (1 + r_{\text{nominal,before tax}})/(1 + \pi) = 1a \cdot (1 + 700\%)/(1 + 100\%) = 4a)$. However, one of the apples $(d = 25\%)$ is bad, so you will get only three apples $(a_1 = a_0 \cdot (1 + r_{\text{nominal,before tax}})/(1 + \pi) \cdot (1 - d) = 1 \cdot a_0 \cdot (1 + 700\%)/(1 + 100\%) \cdot 75\% = 3 \cdot a_0)$. Therefore, the real rate of return is $(a_1 - a_0)/a_0$, or

$$r_{\text{real,after tax,post default}} = \frac{(1a \cdot \frac{1 + 700\%}{1 + 100\%} \cdot 75\%) - 1a}{1a}$$
$$= 300\% - 1 = 200\%$$

$$r_{\text{real,after tax,post default}} = \frac{[1a \cdot \frac{1 + r_{\text{nominal,before tax}}}{1 + \pi} \cdot (1 - d)] - 1a}{1a}$$

The "1a" of course cancels, because the formula applies to any number of apples or other goods.

Q 10.30 Instead of 10%, you earn only $98\% \cdot 10\% + 2\% \cdot (-100\%) = 7.8\%$. Translated into a formula, this is $(1 - d) \cdot r_{\text{nominal,before tax}} + d \cdot (-100\%) = r_{\text{nominal,before tax}} - d \cdot (1 + r_{\text{nominal,before tax}}) = 10\% - 2\% \cdot (1 + 10\%) = 7.8\%$. Now, using the formula from Page 274,

$$r_{\text{after tax, real, post default}} = \frac{V_0 - C_0}{C_0}$$

$$= \frac{\frac{C_0 \cdot \left[1 + r_{\text{nominal,before tax}} \cdot (1-\tau)\right]}{1+\pi} - C_0}{C_0}$$

$$= \frac{r_{\text{nominal,before tax}} \cdot (1 - \tau) - \pi}{1 + \pi}$$

$$r_{\substack{\text{post default,} \\ \text{after tax, real}}} = \frac{V_0 - C_0}{C_0}$$

$$= \frac{\frac{C_0 \cdot \left[1 + (r_{\text{nominal,before tax}} - d \cdot (1 + r_{\text{nominal,before tax}})) \cdot (1-\tau)\right]}{1+\pi} - C_0}{C_0}$$

$$= \frac{(r_{\text{nominal,before tax}} - d \cdot (1 + r_{\text{nominal,before tax}})) \cdot (1 - \tau) - \pi}{1 + \pi}$$

$$= \frac{7.8\% \cdot (1 - 40\%) - 5\%}{1 + 5\%} \approx -0.30\%$$

replace the nominal interest rate $r_{\text{nominal,before tax}}$ with the default reduced nominal rate $r_{\text{nominal,before tax}} - d \cdot (1 + r_{\text{nominal,before tax}})$, so the new formula is

Q 10.31 Uncle Sam would benefit from an increase in inflation, because he taxes nominal rates of return, not real rates of return. In the real world, interest rates would also have to rise to compensate private savers for this extra "tax" on money.

End of Chapter Problems

Q 10.32. Evaluate whether supermarkets operate in perfect markets.

Q 10.33. What are the perfect market assumptions?

Q 10.34. Your borrowing rate is 15% per year. Your lending rate is 10% per year. The project costs $5,000 and has a rate of return of 12%.

1. Should you take the project if you have $2,000 to invest?
2. If you have $3,000 to invest?
3. If you have $4,000 to invest?

Q 10.35. An entrepreneur is quoted a loan rate of 12% at the local bank, while the bank pays depositors 6% per annum.

1. If in bankruptcy the entrepreneur will not pay back anything, but otherwise everything will be repaid, then what does the bank believe the probability of failure to be?
2. What is the quoted default premium?
3. Compute the expected default premium. (Note that when you lose all your money plus the default premium, your rate of return can be below −100%. This is not only reasonable but necessary to get an average default premium that is what it should be.)

Q 10.36. "If the world is risk neutral, then the promised and expected rates of return may be different but the expected rates of return on all loans should be equal." Evaluate.

Q 10.37. Go to the Edgar page on the SEC's website. Look up the *El Torito* company (also *Real Mex Restaurants, Inc*) S-4 filing on 2004-06-09. Describe the covenants and requirements to which El Torito is obligated. (Note: This may take a while, but reading this S-4 will introduce you to how these agreements look in the real world.)

Q 10.38. The bid quote on a corporate bond is $212; the ask is $215. You expect this bond to return its promised 15% per annum for sure. In contrast, T-bonds offer only 6% per annum but have no spread. If you have to liquidate your position in 1 month, what would a $1 million investment be worth in either instrument? Which instrument should you purchase?

Q 10.39. Look up on a financial website what the cost of a round-trip transaction on $10,000 worth of shares in Dell would cost you today.

Q 10.40. You have discovered an investment strategy that can beat the market by 300 basis points per year. Assume that the stock market is expected to return 9% per annum. Unfortunately, to implement your strategy, you will have to turn over your portfolio three times a year. Think of this as rebalancing (selling and purchasing) 25% of your portfolio every month. You have very good traders, who can execute trades at a cost of only 7.5 cents per transaction (15 cents round-trip) on a $30 stock. Does this strategy make sense?

Q 10.41. A day trader has $10 million in assets. She buys and sells 30% of her portfolio every day. Assume that this day trader is very good and incurs single round-trip transaction costs of only 10 cents on a $30 stock. Roughly, by how much does this day trader's strategy have to beat the benchmark in order to make this a profitable activity? Assume that the trader could earn $200,000 in an equivalent alternative employment and that there are 252 trading days per year.

Q 10.42. Search online for the current federal income tax rates on the four different types of income for individual taxpayers and corporate taxpayers.

1. What are these rates?

2. Assume that a corporation has just earned $2 million in ordinary income, $1 million in interest income, and $3 million in realized long-term capital gains (net). Focusing only on the basics and ignoring deductions, what is its tax obligation? What are its marginal tax rates? What is its average tax rate?

3. Assume that you (an individual) have just earned $2 million in ordinary income, $1 million in interest income, and $3 million in realized long-term capital gains (net). Focusing only on the basics and ignoring deductions, what is your income tax obligation? What is your marginal tax rate? What is your average tax rate?

4. How much would your state income tax, Social Security, and Medicare add to your tax bill? Is your state income tax payment a before-tax or an after-tax expense?

Q 10.43. If your tax rate is 40%, what interest rate do you earn in after-tax terms if the before-tax interest rate is 6%?

Q 10.44. On September 28, 2007, tax-exempt AAA rated 10-year muni bonds traded at a yield of 3.99%. Corporate 10-year AAA bonds traded at 5.70%. What was the marginal investor's tax rate?

Q 10.45. Go to the Vanguard website and look up VWITX and VBIIX.

1. What is the current yield of a tax-exempt Vanguard bond fund?

2. What is your state income tax treatment?

3. How does it compare to the most similar Vanguard taxable bond fund?

4. What tax rate would an investor have to suffer in order to be indifferent between the two bond funds?

Q 10.46. Consider a real estate project that costs $1,000,000. Thereafter, it will produce $60,000 in taxable ordinary income before depreciation every year. Favorable tax treatment means that the project will produce $100,000 in tax depreciation write-offs each year for 10 years (nothing thereafter). For example, if you had $500,000 in ordinary income in year 2 without this project, you would now only have $400,000 in ordinary income instead. At the end of 10 years, you can sell this project for $800,000. All of this $800,000 will be fully taxable as write-up at your capital gains tax rate of 20%. If your ordinary income tax is 33% per annum, if taxable bonds offer a rate of return of 8% per annum, and tax-exempt munis offer a rate of 6% per annum, what would be the NPV of this project?

Q 10.47. You are in the 25% tax bracket. A project will return $20,000 next year for a $17,000 investment—a $3,000 net return. The equivalent tax-exempt bond yields 14%, and the equivalent taxable bond yields 20%. What is the NPV of this project?

Q 10.48. The lottery gives you a 1 in 14 million chance of winning the jackpot. It promises $20 million to the lucky winner. A ticket costs $1. Alas, the lottery forgot to mention that winnings are paid over 20 years (with the first $1 million payment occurring immediately), that inflation is 2% per year, and that winnings are taxable. Is the lottery a good investment? (Assume that you are in a 40% marginal income tax bracket and that the appropriate nominal discount rate is 10% per year.)

Perfect and Efficient Markets, and Classical and Behavioral Finance

How Trustworthy are Market Prices?

This chapter explains the concept of an efficient market, which is closely linked to that of a perfect market. A market is said to be efficient if it does not ignore available information. To illuminate perfect and efficient markets, this chapter also explains arbitrage, an essential concept of finance, without which no study of finance would be complete. We then discuss the consequences of the concepts: What do efficient and/or perfect markets mean for predicting stock performance? How should you interpret the success of famous investors? And how can you use the concept of efficient markets to run an event study to help assess the valuation impact of big corporate events?

11.1 Market Efficiency

A perfect market sets up stiff competition among many investors. This forces them to use all available information as well as they possibly can. This is called **market efficiency**: a situation in which prices reflect *all* available information. In a fully efficient market, you should not be able to use any available information to predict future returns better than the market can.

> Market efficiency means the market uses all available information in setting the price.

A price is called **efficient** if the market has set the price correctly using *all* available information.

> Warning: Market efficiency is a different concept from mean-variance efficiency (the efficient frontier), which was used in the context of portfolio optimization. Economists love "efficiency" and thus use the term in many contexts.

IMPORTANT

➤ *Mean-variance efficiency,* Sect. 8.2, Pg.183.

Exhibit 11.1 illustrates an efficient market. Suppose the market considers an expected rate of return of 10% on PepsiCo stock to be a fair rate of return, given PepsiCo's characteristics. This figure of 10% could come, for instance, from the CAPM. Market

> An example: PepsiCo's price today is based on the best estimate of future characteristics, obtained from a model like the CAPM.

efficiency then pins down the relation between the best estimate of the price next year and the price today. In our example, if the market expects PepsiCo to trade for $55 next year, it should set the price today at $50. The market would not be efficient if it set today's price at $49 or $51. You can turn this around, too. You should not be able to locate information that tells you today when/if/that the true expected value tomorrow is really $60 (for an expected rate of return of 20%) or $50 next year (for an expected rate of return of 0%). If you could find information telling you authoritatively that a better estimate of next year's price is $60 (or $50), then PepsiCo's stock would be mispriced. A market that has overlooked your information would not be efficient.

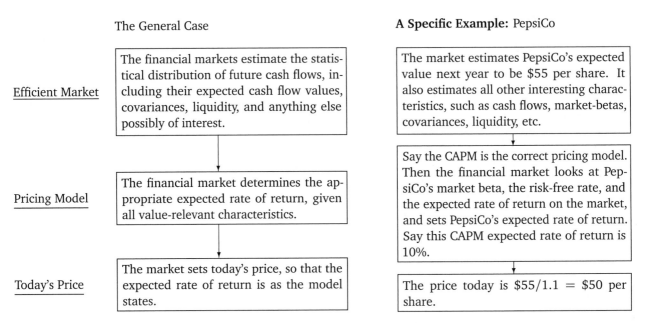

The General Case

A Specific Example: PepsiCo

Efficient Market — The financial markets estimate the statistical distribution of future cash flows, including their expected cash flow values, covariances, liquidity, and anything else possibly of interest.

The market estimates PepsiCo's expected value next year to be $55 per share. It also estimates all other interesting characteristics, such as cash flows, market-betas, covariances, liquidity, etc.

Pricing Model — The financial market determines the appropriate expected rate of return, given all value-relevant characteristics.

Say the CAPM is the correct pricing model. Then the financial market looks at PepsiCo's market beta, the risk-free rate, and the expected rate of return on the market, and sets PepsiCo's expected rate of return. Say this CAPM expected rate of return is 10%.

Today's Price — The market sets today's price, so that the expected rate of return is as the model states.

The price today is $55/1.1 = $50 per share.

Exhibit 11.1: *Market Efficiency and Pricing Model.* The critical question is *If you saw a price of, say, $45.83 today, what would you conclude has gone wrong?*

What is the model? What is the information set?

The practical use of the "efficient markets" concept begs two questions:

1. Where does the figure of 10% come from? It has to come from some model that tells you what rate of return PepsiCo should have to offer given its characteristics, such as risk, liquidity, and so on. The CAPM is such a model (though only a modestly successful one). Without a good model of what you should expect the rate of return to be, market efficiency is too vague a concept to be meaningful.

2. If the market is not perfect and different investors have different information, then exactly what information set are we talking about? If you are PepsiCo's CEO, then you may have more information than the public. You may know whether the SEC will open an investigation against you and whether you have the next new hit drink in the lab right now. You could know whether $50 today is too high or too

low. Put differently, the market may be efficient with respect to publicly available information, but it need not be efficient with respect to insider information.

What should you conclude if you can determine authoritatively that the expected rate of return is really 20%? (This can happen either if you determine that the expected payoff is $60, not $55, or if the expected payoff is $55, but today's price is $45.83.) You could now draw one of two conclusions:

If you find the expected rate of return is really 20%: (a) Your 10% model could be wrong; (b) the market was not efficient.

1. The CAPM is not the correct model. Instead, the market followed some other pricing model and wanted to set the expected rate of return for PepsiCo at 20% in the first place.

2. The stock market is not efficient.

Can you see why market efficiency is so difficult to prove or reject? If you wish to proclaim a belief in market efficiency, and if you then find empirically that prices are not what your model predicted, you would simply proclaim that it was your model for the appropriate expected returns in your financial market that was wrong, not that the market was inefficient. It was your fault, not the market's. You just have to go back and search more—possibly forever—until you find the right pricing model.

Is market efficiency so difficult to disprove that it becomes a "faith"?

Short-Term versus Long-Term Market Efficiency

Over long horizons (say, 1 year or longer), market efficiency is extremely difficult to disprove. The reason is that no one knows exactly what the correct model of pricing is—the CAPM may often be a reasonable model, but it is not infallible and its estimates are rarely accurate in practice. We are not sure whether a stock like PepsiCo should earn 10%, 20%, or 30% a year. This renders market efficiency a concept that in practice often evades empirical testing. It is also why market efficiency is sometimes (unfairly) disparaged as being more religion than science. Based on the existing long-run evidence, some reasonable analysts conclude that financial markets are generally efficient (and our [CAPM] pricing model is wrong); and other reasonable analysts conclude that financial markets are generally not efficient.

Practically useful? Rarely over very long horizons–efficiency is more a matter of faith.

Of course, in extreme circumstances, market efficiency can be a useful claim even on such long horizons. We know that no reasonable model of financial markets should give investors great bets like "+$1 million with 99% probability" and "–$1 with 1% probability." Expected returns this high would be way out of line with *any* reasonable pricing model. Even expected rates of return of 100% per year would surely be unreasonable for stocks such as PepsiCo. Of course, few people doubt that the stock market is, to such a first approximation, efficient—we all know that you just can't earn that much. But there is a large gray zone where it is difficult to distinguish between model error and market inefficiency. Because no one knows for sure what the correct model of expected stock returns is, no one can tell you affirmatively whether the stock market set the price of PepsiCo stock so as to offer investors an expected rate of return on PepsiCo of, say, 10% a year or 12% a year.

Okay, let me qualify this for long horizons.

However, over short horizons (say, a day or so), market efficiency is a surprisingly useful concept. The reason is that over a single day it does not matter as much whether you believe the expected rate of return on PepsiCo is 0%, 10%, or 20% per annum. Even on the high-end of 20% per annum, the expected rate of return is still only about 5 basis

Practically useful? Definitely yes over short horizons.

points per day. Roughly speaking, regardless of whether you believe in the CAPM or not, you should expect day-to-day returns to be just a tiny bit above 0%. You should attribute most daily price movement to random fluctuations, presumably caused by unpredictable news of changes in the economic environment. However, if you can predict day-to-day stock movements (and you have thousands of days of historical stock returns to work with), then chances are that you would not blame the pricing model. Instead, you would probably conclude that the market is not efficient.

IMPORTANT

> - Over short time intervals (say, days), market efficiency is a very powerful concept. The expected rate of return should be tiny. If it is different, the market is probably inefficient.
>
> - Over long time intervals (say, months or years), it is difficult to pin down what the appropriate expected rate of return is. This makes it difficult to disentangle errors in the pricing model from market inefficiency.

Relation to Perfect Market

Perfect market ⇒ efficient market.

Although the efficient market concept is different from the perfect market concept the two are intimately linked—in fact, so much so that they are often confused. The reason is that if a market is perfect, economic forces drive it instantly toward market efficiency. Put differently, if a market were perfect but inefficient, everyone would want to earn great returns and trade the same way. It would be too easy to become rich. Market prices would instantly adjust to prevent this. Therefore, if a market is perfect, it is inevitably also efficient.

Efficient market ⇏ perfect market.

The converse is not true, however. It is quite possible for an imperfect market—for example, one in which there are taxes or different opinions—to be efficient. You could even (crudely) think of market efficiency as the result of the trades of many investors with many different information sets (opinions). The market price is the outcome at which investors no longer wish to trade further. Appropriately weighted, one half believes the market price is too low; the other half believes it is too high. Of course, efficiency should be contemplated market by market. It is probable that some financial markets are efficient while others are not. The closer a market is to being perfect, the more likely it is to being efficient.

Transaction costs are often culprits in keeping prices from their efficient levels.

Perhaps the most important perfect market assumption driving prices toward efficiency is the absence of transaction costs. Without them, it is easy for you and other investors to trade on any information that the market has not yet incorporated in the stock price—and thereby earn an unusually good expected rate of return. However, the no-free-lunch axiom applies here, too. High transaction costs would make it more likely that you could expect to find violations of efficient markets. But if it is very expensive to trade and if the market is therefore not efficient and does not respond to news immediately, it would also be very difficult for you to take advantage of such inefficiencies.

Here is a practical example of how any market inefficiency would disappear quickly in a perfect market: What would you do if you learned that the market always goes down on rainy days and up on sunny ones? It is unlikely that the average investor requires extra return to hold stocks on sunny days—and, even if the average investor does, it is enough for you if you are not among them. You would never buy stocks when the weather forecast predicts that rain is coming. Instead, you would only buy stocks when the weather forecast predicts that the sun will shine. Investors like yourself—and there are of course many such investors in perfect markets—would rapidly bid up the prices before the sun shone, so that the prices would no longer systematically go up on sunny days. The end result is that if markets are efficient, then you should not be able to earn abnormally good sunny-day returns—at least not this easily. In a reasonable world, to earn higher expected rates of return, you must be willing to take on something that other investors are reluctant to take on—such as higher portfolio risk. Today's weather alone should not do it. (Interestingly, academics do disagree on whether the weather in New York City has a small influence on stock returns. Some papers claim it does, so that the market is inefficient. Others dispute this, claiming the historical correlation is spurious and disappears if the statistical tests are done correctly. All agree that the weather influence is small, however.)

Investor competition pushes markets toward efficiency.

Conversely, it is easier to believe that markets are *not* (or less) efficient if transaction costs are high. But even if the market is not perfect, market inefficiencies should still raise eyebrows. For example, let's say that the appropriate rate of return on PepsiCo was still 10% for an expected future price of $55—but when you look, you find that the current price today is already $58. (The true rate of return is thus –5.2%.) In a perfect market, many investors would immediately want to exploit this by selling PepsiCo short. This may not be possible if the market is so imperfect that the costs of going short are too high. However, this leaves the question of why investors who already own PepsiCo shares would not sell them ASAP. They would not incur the shorting transaction costs and would avoid the lower-than-appropriate rate of return. (Maybe they are asleep!?) Such "economic self-interested behavior" adds to the "third-party investor pressure" in driving markets toward efficient pricing, even in a market that is imperfect.

Prices should be generally efficient even in a nonperfect financial market. Who would be willing to hold overpriced stuff?

➤ *Shorting stocks, Pg.≈36.*

IMPORTANT

- If a market is perfect, market forces should drive it strongly and quickly toward efficiency.

- If a market is not perfect, self-interested individual behavior should still drive it toward efficiency. But this force is much weaker, and third-party traders may not be able to aid in the process.

Market Efficiency in Modern Financial Markets

You can reasonably assume that markets are efficient for large corporate stocks.

In the United States, the financial markets for Treasuries, for large corporate stocks, index mutual funds, currencies, and others, seem reasonably close to perfect and thus efficient. They are definitely very competitive. There are millions of buyers and sellers, thousands of tax-exempt investors, modest transaction costs, and it seems unlikely that some investors have real inside information. It is difficult to believe that you or I could outsmart the prices in such markets. After all, thousands of other traders are likely equally as smart. They would flock to good bargains and avoid bad bargains along with us. Of course, the smaller the firm, the less perfect and the less efficient the market in its stock is likely to be. Many small stocks on the NASDAQ exchange trade only rarely, and they can have large transaction costs:

- The bid-ask spread is often high.

➤ *Bid-ask spread,* Sect. 10.3, Pg.256.

- The posted bid-ask spread is only guaranteed for 100 shares—if you want to trade more shares, the price is likely to move against you.

- Commissions can be high.

- Shorting small stocks can be very costly when compared to the ideal of a perfect world in which you have full access to the proceeds (e.g., to earn interest).

In a round-trip transaction, you will face the first three issues once when you buy and once when you sell. Thus, it is unlikely that small stocks will immediately and fully reflect all information appropriately. The historical prices you see posted may be "stale" and may not even reflect the price that would have applied if you had wanted to trade. Market efficiency is never white or black, but always a shade of gray—just as it is for perfect markets. Large, liquid S&P 100 stocks are pretty close to efficient; small NASDAQ stocks may not be.

A N E C D O T E   **"Trading Places" and Citrus Futures**

The 1983 hit comedy *Trading Places*, starring Dan Akroyd and Eddie Murphy, centers around the trading of orange juice frozen concentrate **futures contracts**. (A future is a contract that specifies terms to buy or sell a commodity in the future—in this case, oranges.) If it is going to rain or if there is a frost, oranges will be scarcer and the futures price will rise. You can learn more about futures contracts at the website of the *Chicago Mercantile Exchange* at http://www.cme.com.

In a 1984 paper in the *American Economic Review*, Richard Roll found that these citrus futures contracts predict whether the U.S. Weather Service's forecast for central Florida temperatures is too high or too low. It is a great example of how financial markets help aggregate information better than the best nonfinancial institution. This should not surprise you. After all, there is a lot of money at stake!

The advantage of an efficient market: Prices can be trusted.

The fact that large-firm stock markets are pretty efficient means that, by and large, you can trust these financial markets to get asset values about right—at least within the limits of the typical transaction costs—and to get it right *immediately*. As an investor, would you not rather face an inefficient market? If it were inefficient, you might be able to find some good bets (opportunities that earn unusually high expected rates of return). But it would not all be gravy. In an inefficient market, you could not rely on market prices being fair—they could be inappropriately too high or too low. You would

➤ *Great bets,* Sect. 11.4, Pg.299.

never really know whether you are overpaying or underpaying. Investing would be a very messy business. You might have to spend a lot of time and money to determine whether prices are fair. The advantage of efficient markets is that if you hold a portfolio of many large and liquid stocks, you do not have to spend a lot of time and money to perform **due diligence** in order to determine whether stocks are fairly priced. All you need to do is to make sure you are appropriately diversified to meet your risk-reward preference. And you can probably accomplish this goal by purchasing just a few large index-mimicking mutual funds.

Q 11.1. What does it mean for a market to be efficient?

Q 11.2. As a believer in efficient markets, what would you likely answer when heretics claim that they can reject market efficiency because they have found assets that pay too much for their risk?

Q 11.3. Is market efficiency a more powerful concept over long or short horizons?

Q 11.4. How does an efficient market differ from a perfect market?

Q 11.5. Is it more or less likely for a financial market to be efficient when transaction costs are low?

Q 11.6. Would you expect the market for the dollar–euro exchange rate to be more or less perfect and efficient than the NYSE?

ANECDOTE How to Get Squeezed and Lose Money Even When You Are Right

Even in cases where it is probable that the market mispriced stocks, such as technology stocks during the famous "Internet bubble" at the turn of the millennium, it was almost impossible for an individual investor to take advantage of the market inefficiency. Believe me, I know.

In 1998, I shorted Netscape. I believed that Netscape's browser was about to be taken to the cleaners by Microsoft's Internet Explorer. I was right on my prediction—but in February 1999, AOL paid a lot of money to acquire Netscape. Not satisfied with one mistake, I proceeded to my next mistake. I believed Yahoo (YHOO) was worth less than what it was trading for. I speculated that it would go down. After I had lost more than three times my original investment, I realized that I had to either close my bet or risk going bankrupt. Consequently, I terminated my bet. Yes, I would have been right in the end and made a lot of money if I had held on longer, but I simply could not afford the risk (and mental anguish) any longer. I learned from this episode—after 15 years as a financial economist—that even if the stock market is irrational and even if it overvalues a stock by three times, it can also be irrational enough to overvalue it by yet another three times.

Later on, I found out that I was not alone. The most reprinted article in the history of *Fortune* magazine was "Mr. Buffett on the Stock Market," from November 22, 1999, in which famed financier Warren Buffett warned about the overvaluations of tech stocks and Internet stocks. Like me, Buffett had suffered from years of poor performance (and from yet another quarter of misery to follow), as Internet stocks reached ever higher.

Not everyone believes there was a bubble. The book's website has an impromptu email conversation between myself and Eugene Fama (perhaps the most famous finance professor alive and a strong defender of market efficiency). This will give you an authentic impression of the ongoing dialogue among finance professors.

11.2   Market Efficiency Beliefs and Behavioral Finance

Classical versus
behavioral finance.

A firm belief in efficient markets is what defines a school of thought known as **classical finance**, an outgrowth of the school of **rational economics**. This belief is that the evidence supports the **efficient market hypothesis**, or EMH, which holds that all securities are priced efficiently. In contrast, another school of thought often dubbed **behavioral finance** posits that markets sometimes do *not* use all available information. Depending on how strong a believer in classical finance versus behavioral finance you are, you may believe that there are no especially good trading opportunities, few trading opportunities, or plenty of trading opportunities. Both camps agree, however, that market perfection plays a crucial role in determining whether a particular market is efficient or not.

Many large financial
markets in the United
States are probably
close to efficient.

Almost all financial economists, regardless of camp, believe in basic market efficiency for large markets and liquid securities. No respectable economist believes that it is easy to get very rich trading on easily available information. Instead, the disagreement is, loosely, about whether stock markets are "99% efficient" or "97% efficient." Classical finance believes in the former, behavioral finance in the latter. Of course, you can trade millions of dollars in large-firm stocks or market indexes relatively easily and at low transaction costs. Thus, it does not require huge efficiency violations for behavioral finance economists to be right and for classical finance economists to be wrong. Exploiting just the tiny—say, $100\% - 97\% = 3\%$—violations from market efficiency could make you a star investor. (This is also not coincidentally why so many fund managers publicly proclaim their faith in behavioral finance.) However, don't take me too literally here—the 99% versus 97% is an analogy, and there is really a spectrum of beliefs in market efficiency among economists and fund managers. Now, although you should realize that any classification scheme really identifies just segments on a continuous line, you can still try to classify financial economists and investors by their faiths in efficiency. Let's look at some such classifications.

The Traditional Classification

The traditional
classification of
market efficiency is
about the type of
information needed to
beat the market.

The traditional definition of market efficiency focuses on information. In the traditional classification, market efficiency comes in three strengths: weak, semistrong, and strong.

Weak market efficiency says that all information in past prices is reflected in today's prices so that **technical analysis** (trading based solely on historical price patterns) cannot be used to beat the market. Put differently, the market is the best technical analyst.

Semistrong market efficiency says that all public information is reflected in today's stock prices, so that neither **fundamental trading** (based on underlying firm fundamentals, such as cash flows or discount rates) nor technical analysis can be used to beat the market. Put differently, the market is both the best technical and fundamental analyst.

Strong market efficiency says that all information, both public and private, is reflected in today's stock prices, so that nothing—not even private insider information—can be used to beat the market. Put differently, the market is the best analyst and cannot be beat.

In this traditional classification, all finance professors nowadays believe that most financial markets are not strong-form efficient: Insider trading may be illegal, but it works. However, arguments rage on as to which markets are semistrong-form efficient or even weak-form efficient, and even for large and liquid financial markets (such as large firms traded on the NYSE or NASDAQ, or some options on the CBOE). Finance professors regularly publish claims that some new rule would have outperformed reasonable average rates of return historically, often by large margins. Prominently among them are some particular forms of momentum strategies (buying stocks that have gone up and selling stocks that have gone down over the last year) and value strategies (buying boring old-economy stocks, selling glamorous high-growth new-economy stocks). These strategies would have offered "excess returns" as high as 1-2% per month.

Market efficiency champions quickly point out that many of these strategies' returns were **spurious**: They disappeared almost as quickly as they were discovered, and they probably were never real to begin with. Also, many of these trading strategies would have required such high transaction costs that they would not have been profitable in the real world. That is, even if prices had not incorporated all information, thus leaving the market inefficient, they may have been well within the bounds of transaction costs. Yet, some trading strategies, such as momentum or value, do seem to have produced large historical excess returns even after transaction costs. One good question is whether they will continue to work. (Personally, I am not claiming that they will or will not work in the future.) A second good question raised by EMH proponents is what part of these strategy returns was appropriate compensation for risk (not captured by the CAPM) and thus not excessive to begin with.

One conceptual question that had vexed academics for a long time was how markets could be efficient to begin with. After all, if there is no money to be made, why would anyone bother collecting information on firms? And if no one bothers to collect information on them, how can the market incorporate all information and thus be efficient? Eventually, a resolution to this puzzle was offered by Grossman and Stiglitz. They argued that markets can never be 100% efficient—they can only be, say, "99%" efficient. In equilibrium, good information collectors should earn just about enough trading profits to break even on their costs of information collecting. On the margin, the expected costs of learning and trading on more information are exactly equal to the expected trading profits. The informed investors earn this money trading against **noise traders**, who do not collect information and who may trade for idiosyncratic reasons (e.g., to pay for tuition).

Many finance professors no longer believe in *perfect* efficiency.

➤ *Momentum and value trading,*
Sect. App.9.C (Companion),
Pg.≈63.

Why do many trading strategies seem to have worked historically?

➤ *Value stocks,*
Sect. App.9.C (Companion),
Pg.≈63.

The returns to collecting information must be in "balance" with their costs.

Q 11.7. Which form of market efficiency do momentum trading strategies seem to violate?

The Fundamentals-Based Classification and Behavioral Finance

My preferred taxonomy of market efficiency is based on how much prices deviate from value.

I prefer an alternative classification of market efficiency, which grades economists based on their belief in whether prevailing market prices reflect underlying values:

A true believer would argue that financial prices always reflect the best net present value estimate of all future cash flows. This means that stock prices should change correctly if and only if news about fundamentals (cash flows or discount rates) appears.

A firm believer would argue that financial prices may sometimes deviate from the appropriate best estimate of future cash flows. However, transaction costs make it practically impossible for investors to find unusually good bets.

A mild believer would also argue that financial prices may sometimes deviate from the appropriate best estimate of future cash flows. However, unlike a firm believer, a mild believer would argue that there are occasions when it is possible to exploit this misvaluation. This would result in the occasional unusually good bet. Usually, the profitabilities of such bets should remain within economically reasonable magnitudes—a couple of percentage points a year on the high side. Mild believers thus think that smart fund managers can offer investors slightly better bets, but nothing more. There are no guarantees.

A nonbeliever would argue that financial prices regularly deviate from the appropriate value, and to an extent that allows investors to obtain great bets fairly routinely.

These classes are progressively weaker. For example, a firm believer need not be a true believer. Firm belief can be the right club to join if financial price changes are indeed unpredictable, but not because of news about fundamentals. There could be unrelated noise in stock price changes, especially in the short run. A mild believer need not be a firm believer: Transaction costs may be low enough to permit great trading strategies based on efficient markets violations. A nonbeliever need not be a mild believer: Financial markets may just beg to be exploited.

There is even some really weird but dramatic evidence against market efficiency.

Occasionally, there is evidence that refutes even the truest of believers—but this is rare. The most dramatic example occurred in 2000, when the network company 3COM spun off the PDA company Palm. Widely reported in the press at the time, 3COM retained 95% of Palm's stock—and announced that each shareholder of 3COM would soon receive 1.525 shares of Palm. After the IPO, Palm closed at $95.06 per share. Therefore, 3COM should have been worth at least $1.525 \cdot \$95.06 \approx \$145$. Instead, 3COM shares closed at $81.81. (It was impossible to exploit this discrepancy, because it was impossible to find Palm shares to short. Palm shares enjoyed an almost uninterrupted fall in price, down to less than $2 per share by 2003.)

This evidence as a whole suggests that the financial markets are usually somewhere between mildly and firmly efficient.

Where do most finance professors sit in this classification of beliefs? Virtually no academic is a perpetual nonbeliever, and only a very few remain in the "true believer" camp. Instead, most finance professors are somewhere between the "mild believer" camp (the center of behavioral finance) and the "firm believer" camp (the center of classical finance). The debates between the two more extreme sides of these camps—the more "classical rational economists" and the more "behavioral economists"—are intellectually exciting. After all, bringing new evidence to bear on these disagreements is the process by which we learn more.

Let me tell you my personal view. I sit right in the middle between the two schools of thought, somewhere in the firm-to-mild camp. In my view, most investors believe that they have more knowledge and control than they actually have. This is why I believe that trading in the stock market seems so (inexplicably) active. Many investors seem to believe that they can predict when stocks are going to go up or down. Some pundits like to call this "investor psychology." However, I also believe that an individual investor is unlikely to be able to find rate-of-return patterns in the stock market to earn high excess returns. A very few sophisticated funds may be able to earn systematically a few basis points extra per year. But these funds are scarce. Even after decades of academic research that has tried to identify better-performing funds, academics usually find that only about half of all funds outperform the market and half underperform the market—even before fund transaction costs.

> Buyer beware: Here is my own opinion.

Q 11.8. If you believe that market values do not always perfectly reflect underlying fundamental values, but that trading costs nevertheless prevent you from exploiting this profitably (in large scale), where would you classify yourself?

11.3   The Random Walk and the Signal-to-Noise Ratio

Why is the debate over market efficiency so tough to settle? It is the fact that the **signal-to-noise ratio** in financial returns is low. The signal-to-noise description draws on an analogy from physics—the **signal** (the appropriate expected price change) is small compared to the **noise** (the day-to-day price **volatility** that clouds our senses).

> The low signal-to-noise ratio allows our arguments about market efficiency to continue.

Let me explain. What are typical price change magnitudes? For example, October 4, 2007, was a fairly quiet and uneventful day on the financial markets. Ten-year Treasuries stood at 4.523%, down 2 basis points (–0.44%); 13-week T-bills traded at 3.84% (–0.13%); and 59% of NYSE stocks advanced, while 37% declined. The Dow Jones rose 6.26 (0.04%) to 13,974.31. The S&P 500 rose by +0.21%. On this day, the volume leaders (not the biggest price movers) were Level 3 Communications (+4.38%), Sun Microsystems (–1.56%), Cisco (–0.92%), and Ford Motor (+2.02%). (The 10 biggest price movers were smaller stocks, which gained between +116% and +20%.) Let me now pick two stocks randomly that had no big news on this day: PepsiCo gained 0.54% and IBM lost 0.61%. What can you learn from these magnitudes? Read on.

> Let me illustrate the signal-to-noise ratio with a stock's rate of return on a particular day.

The Signal

Let's first put your statistical and financial expertise to good use: *In a perfect market, if the shares of a company cost $50 today, what do you expect them to cost tomorrow?* What is a typical daily rate of return on a stock? Could you expect a reasonable model of market prices to predict that 1 day's stock price movement could be something on the order of ±1%? Think about it: If the expected rate of return on a stock were the same as the typical up or down movement of 1% per day, the rate of return on this stock over the 252 trading days in one year would be more than 1,000%. The $50 stock would be worth over $600 by next year. Who would want to sell such a stock? Who would

> You cannot expect a real-world trading signal to be as strong as 1% per day: It would amount to over 1,000% per year.

not want to bid a lot more than $50 for it right now? The same argument applies to a price decline of 1% per day. An investment strategy of holding onto such stocks would transform $50 into less than $5 by next year. Who would ever want to hold onto such stocks? The same logic would also apply to a signal that tells you on some days that one particular stock is expected to go up by 1% and on other days that some other particular stock is expected to go down by 1%. Each day, you would earn 1% by either going long or short in the relevant stock—according to your signal—and end up filthy rich. (The investors on the other side would end up poor.)

So what kind of average daily returns can you expect from the U.S. stock market? Say a reasonable range of rates of return is between 0% and 40% per year. For 252 trading days, absent complications, this gives you daily rates of return of between 0 basis points and about 15 basis points. The majority of stocks should allow you to earn expected rates of return of between 5 and 10 basis points a day. One basis point of signal per day is 3% per year. Thus, when you test for market efficiency with a reasonable model of stock pricing, about 5 to 10 basis points per day is what you would expect to find for most stocks. If your signal allows you to earn 1 bp extra per day, then your strategy will be better by about 3% per year.

ANECDOTE   Great Mathematicians and Gambling: The Origin of the Random Walk

In the 1700s, it was not beneath mathematicians to study how to gamble in order to gamble better. Jacob Bernoulli (1654–1705) and Abraham DeMoivre (1667–1754) studied the random walk of a gambler's stake in fair games.

Later reinventions and applications of the random-walk concept abound: Jan Ingenhausz (1730–1799), a physician and plant physiologist, placed charcoal powder on an alcohol film and observed that the grains moved randomly. The botanist Robert Brown (1773–1858) reported erratic dancing of small particles in fluids at rest. Albert Einstein (1879–1955) considered such fluids to be composed of discrete molecules, whose many collisions with a "Brownian particle" caused the particle to jump in random directions—a random walk. Einstein's analysis not only explained **Brownian motion**, which has itself become a building block of high-tech finance nowadays, but also bolstered the case for the existence of atoms, which was not yet universally accepted. The first recorded use of the phrase "random walk" was by Lord Raleigh (1842–1919) in 1899. (Raleigh made a connection between diffusive heat flow and random scattering and showed that a one-dimensional random walk could provide an approximate solution to a parabolic differential equation.) The name is believed to have originated with the description of a drunk who stands on a ladder. The drunk can walk up or down and does so in a random fashion—just like stocks.

Fortunately, in 1900, Louis Bachelier introduced the random-walk theory of financial market fluctuations (although Karl Pearson (1857–1936) introduced the term "random walk" only later, in 1905), finding that bond prices could diffuse in the same manner as heat. Unfortunately, this has only pointed out the obvious: It is not easy for an investor to outperform the market. The first rigorous and published investigation of the random-walk hypothesis was done by Alfred Cowles, an eclectic investor and economist at Yale in the 1930s and 1940s.   *Mostly Michael F. Schlesinger, Office of Naval Research,* Scienceweek.com, *2001.*

Over short intervals, the stock price should follow a mostly unpredictable random walk with practically no drift.

Let's make this into a formula. If your expected rate of return is a small constant m, that is, $\mathscr{E}(r) = [\mathscr{E}(P_1) - P_0]/P_0 = m$, then your best expectation of the price tomorrow (P_1) must be roughly the price today (P_0).

$$\text{Expected Price Tomorrow} = \text{Price Today} + \text{Tiny Drift} \qquad (11.1)$$

$$\mathcal{E}(P_1) \qquad = \qquad P_0 \quad + \quad \underbrace{m \cdot P_0}_{\text{Tiny Drift}}$$

This is customarily called a **random walk** with drift. As you just learned, depending on the stock, this tiny drift m may be around 5 to 10 basis points for most stocks. You should not be able to predict better than this drift, because this is your expected rate of return in an efficient perfect market.

Note that price behavior very close to a random walk is a necessary consequence of an efficient market, but you cannot conclude that a market is (truly) efficient just because stock prices follow roughly a random walk. For example, a market would be inefficient if you could find advance knowledge based on some other external signal— say, whether the sun is shining on a particular day—that would tell you whether the stock price will go up or down the following day. In this case, stock prices would still follow a random walk, but your signal would allow you to outperform the EMH. The random walk only states that the known lagged price can't be this signal.

Don't wag the tail: Market efficiency $\Rightarrow$ random walk. Random walk $\not\Rightarrow$ market efficiency.

A Complication—Transaction Costs

The important point of perfect markets (and market efficiency) is that, given today's information, no signal can be very accurate. It should not be possible to predict stock price movements accurately enough to earn, say, 1% on a given day. Of course, in the real world, financial markets are not perfect and there are financial transaction costs that would also prevent you from really exploiting misvaluations, especially short-lived ones that require a lot of trading to exploit. You would have to pay money to your broker to buy the shares, and again to sell them. (This is why financial markets are not exactly perfectly competitive, only approximately perfectly competitive.) Even small transaction costs can render trading strategies with very high turnover unprofitable. Even if the bid-ask spread is only 10 basis points, if incurred 252 trading days a year, you would only be left with $(1 - 0.1\%)^{252} = 0.999^{252} \approx 78\%$ of your original investment. For a *daily* trading strategy in which you have to pay the bid-ask spread every day, you need to have a signal that allows you to earn at least 23% per year before you break even—and few signals are that good.

Transaction costs destroy the profitability of many high turnover strategies.

➤ Transaction costs, Sect. 10.3, Pg.254.

In an imperfect market with transaction costs, you can view the efficient market hypothesis in one of two ways:

It may be best to think of the EMH in terms of after-transaction costs.

1. The EMH should hold if you work with post-transaction cost rates of return. 1% per day is still unreasonably large, because typical round-trip transaction costs should not exceed 10 to 30 basis points, depending on the stock and the size of the trade. A daily rate of return of 0.7% is still way too large.

2. The EMH could hold if you realize that certain investors have lower transaction costs. For example, a signal may tell you to purchase a stock today and sell it tomorrow. You would have to pay transaction costs. But the investor who was considering selling the stock anyway only needs to wait another day to take advantage of the misvaluation before selling it. This investor really incurs no additional transaction costs.

So the EMH won't hold perfectly in an imperfect market, but it should be a fairly reasonable description of reality—at least it is one that you can use to compute back-of-the-envelope magnitudes, and it is a hypothesis that can be tested.

Q 11.9. From memory, write down the formula for a random walk.

Q 11.10. What is the typical expected rate of return on a stock on an average trading day?

Q 11.11. What kind of rates of return does a strategy of trading stocks once a day have to offer in order for you to earn a positive rate of return? Assume typical real-world trading transaction costs are about 10 basis points.

The Noise

The daily noise in stock returns is much larger than the daily signal.

To put more emphasis on the noise, we can write our random walk with drift in terms of the stock prices that you will actually observe:

$$\text{Price Tomorrow} = \text{Price Today} + \text{Tiny Drift} + \text{Noise}$$

$$P_1 = P_0 + m \cdot P_0 + \epsilon$$

What do we know about reasonable typical standard deviations for the price noise of U.S. stocks? There is no particular theoretical reason why the day-to-day standard deviation of a particular stock could not be 10%, 50%, or even 100%. So it is best for us simply to rely on the empirical data. Historical averages suggest the following:

- The typical day-to-day standard deviation of individual stocks in the market is around 2-3% per day, of course depending on the firm. For well-diversified portfolios, like stock market indexes, the standard deviation is usually lower—perhaps 1-2% per day.

October 4, 2007, was on the low side in terms of volatility, but the typical noise movement of 200 to 300 basis points for individual stocks was clearly much higher than the 5 to 10 basis points that you would expect them to earn.

IMPORTANT

> In the financial market context, "random walk" refers to a process in which the *expected* value tomorrow is (almost) the same as the value today. Technically,
>
> $$\mathcal{E}(P_1) = P_0 + \underbrace{m \cdot P_0}_{\text{Tiny Drift}} \quad\Leftrightarrow\quad P_1 = P_0 + \underbrace{m \cdot P_0}_{\text{Tiny Drift}} + \underbrace{\epsilon_{0,1}}_{\text{Noise}}$$
>
> where m is a very small positive drift. (Another version of a random walk is $\mathcal{E}(P_1) = P_0 + m$; in practice, this version is almost indistinguishable from the one in the formula above.)
>
> Naturally, *actual* values tomorrow will likely be different from their values today. The empirical stock price evidence is highly favorable. Stock prices indeed tend to follow roughly a random walk, at least in the short run. This means that you cannot get rich trading based on past prices.

Q 11.12. What is the typical movement of a stock on an average day?

Q 11.13. If stocks follow a random walk, can the price tomorrow be different from the price today?

Detecting an Interesting Signal in the Noise

You now know that the tiny drift is typically around 5 to 10 basis points per day, and the noise is typically about 100 to 300 basis points per day for U.S. stocks and stock portfolios. How easy is it to determine whether you are facing a stock with 5 basis points' signal versus one with, say, 7 basis points' signal? Why 7 basis points? Because it is what you should be earning extra every day if you have a signal that allows you to earn an extra 5% per year in expected performance, above and beyond what your model of risk-adjusted returns says you should be earning. (A performance of 5% per year in risk-adjusted returns would be stellar for just about any fund.) Put differently, to determine whether your signal is real or illusory, you must be able to distinguish between an appropriate 5 basis points and an excessive 7 basis points for the average daily rate of return.

Detecting signal in a lot of noise is difficult.

How easy is it to detect an extra signal of 2 basis points when hidden in noise of about 200 basis points? Obviously, 1 daily return is not going to do it. If I tell you that your investment pick happened to earn 50 basis points today, you could not reliably conclude that it was your signal. In fact, if anything, you should believe it was primarily noise. Recall from your statistics course that the T-statistic is defined as the mean divided by the standard deviation, $\mathcal{E}(r)/\mathcal{S}dv(r)$. If your strategy performs as expected, your 1-day T-statistic would be only $2bp/200bp = 0.01$. To have good statistical confidence, you would want a T-statistic of around 2. Your expected 0.01 is a long way off.

You cannot conclude anything from just 1 day of return

To draw reliable conclusions, you need a lot more independent daily observations. Unfortunately, you cannot use the returns from many stocks from the same day as independent signals. First, your signal may only be for some particular stocks and not for all stocks. Second, all stocks tend to move together on a given day and are therefore not independent observations. (If all 100 oil stocks go up, and your signal suggested holding oil stocks, you do not have 100 independent observations confirming your signal's ability to predict.)

You cannot consider multiple returns from the same day as independent observations.

Fortunately, you can regard returns from different days as independent observations. You can therefore use sequential days of investment performance to investigate the quality of your signal. How many daily returns would you need to expect to be able to reliably detect a signal of an extra 2 basis points hidden in noise of 200 basis points? Let's ignore compounding and pretend that rates of return over time are just the simple sum of daily rates of return. In this case, your expected rate of return over N days is N times the expected rate of return over 1 day. Recall from Section 8.2 that the standard deviation of your rate of return over N days is $\sqrt{N}$ times the standard deviation over 1 day. Your T-statistic over N days is therefore

You can use consecutive days as independent observations. Here is how mean, standard deviation, and T-statistic accumulate over time.

➤ *How risk and reward grow over time, Sect. 8.2, Pg.183.*

$$\text{N-day T-Statistic} = \frac{\text{Excess Mean}}{\text{Standard Deviation}} = \frac{N \cdot \mathcal{E}(r)}{\sqrt{N} \cdot \mathcal{S}dv(r)} = \sqrt{N} \cdot \text{1-day T-Statistic}$$

Only diversified
strategies that
perform well for many
decades give us the
chance to learn
whether they are real.

How many trading days (N) do you need in order to expect a T-statistic of 2 if your 1-day T-statistic is 0.01? You need $200^2 = 40,000$ days to have such confidence. This is about 157 years worth of data. This is if your strategy performs as expected—if the world is not changing and your signal's forecasting ability is not deteriorating. If your signal is not about individual stocks but about large diversified ortfolios, then the noise is lower than 200 basis points. If it is, say, noise of 100 basis points per day, which may be the case for highly diversified portfolios, then you only need about $100^2 = 10,000$ days (39 years) of data. There are many signals for such diversified trading strategies, which can therefore be examined with real-world data. (I already described some of these, principally momentum and book/market value, although it is not perfectly clear whether their high historical average returns were due to risk or market inefficiencies.) Still, with the world and the signal always changing (after all, there may be more and more investors trying to profit from historical signals), the historical evidence alone may not always be entirely convincing.

➤ Momentum and
book/market,
Sect. App.9.C (Companion),
Pg. ≈63.

IMPORTANT

> - The quality of your inference about a strategy's performance increases roughly with the square root of time.
>
> - On an average day, the typical stock may easily move up or down by about 20 to 50 times as much as it offers in expected rate of return. Therefore, it takes at least many decades, if not centuries, of data to reliably conclude whether a signal-based strategy of picking individual stocks is real or illusory.

Q 11.14. To be a consistent superstar trader, by how many basis points should you be able to outperform the risk-adjusted financial market per typical day?

Q 11.15. Assume that the typical day-to-day noise (standard deviation) is about 100 basis points. Assume that you have the kind of stock-picking ability that earns you an extra 200 basis points per annum. Assume no transaction costs. Ignore compounding and assume that your rate of return is the sum of returns over trading days. Assume there are 252 trading days per year.

1. With only 1-day performance, how much extra do you expect to earn per day?

2. How bad is your noise over 1 day?

3. What is your expected T-statistic (the excess mean divided by the standard deviation)?

Recall from your statistics course that a T-statistic of 1.96 gives you good statistical confidence above the 95% level. In Section 8.2, you learned that the standard deviation grows with the square root of time.

4. With 252 trading days of performance, how much extra rate of return do you expect to earn per annum?

5. How bad is your noise over 252 days?

6. What is your expected T-statistic now?

7. Work out how many years you would expect to wait before you would obtain reliable statistical evidence that you have a positive ability to pick stocks.

11.4 True Arbitrage and Risk(y) Arbitrage

Measuring investment performance brushes on a closely related topic—what exactly is the financial concept of arbitrage? Intuitively, an arbitrage is a great investment opportunity, perhaps so great that you should not be able to find one. It is the desire of traders to exploit any arbitrage opportunity as soon as it appears that makes financial markets efficient. It is a matter of basic financial literacy for you to understand what arbitrage is.

Do you understand arbitrage?

The Definition of Arbitrage

First recall that the *law of one price* states that two identical items at the same time and location should have the same price. This is true in a perfect market, but even if the market is not perfect, it can be (and in fact usually is) still true. For example, even if all investors disagree about the future, even if there are taxes, even if there are transaction costs, and even if there is only one market maker, it should be, and usually still is, the case that one share of IBM costs the same as another. But in a perfect market, the law of one price does not just *usually* hold; it must *always* hold. If it were not to hold, you and the other infinitely many potential buyers could find arbitrage opportunities. The arbitrage concept is so important that you should understand it exactly, not just intuitively.

In a perfect market, the market will be efficient and the law of one price will hold.

➤ *Law of One Price, Sect. 1.1, Pg.2.*

- A **true arbitrage** is a business transaction

  – that offers positive net cash inflows in at least some scenarios,

  – and under no circumstance—either today or in the future—has a negative net cash flow. This means that it is risk free.

  An example: $5 for free.

- A **risk(y) arbitrage** is a business transaction that may not be risk free but that still offers an excessive expected rate of return given its (risk and other) characteristics. A good way to think of a risk(y) arbitrage is as a **great bet**. Admittedly, the term "risk(y) arbitrage" is an oxymoron. However, Wall Street uses the term "risk arbitrage" for a particular type of trading (most often in the context of M&A transactions) that is similar to the sense in which we shall be using it. Thus, we shall commit the same sin.

  An example: A chance to win $1,000,000 with 99% probability and to lose $1 with 1% probability.

IMPORTANT

Arbitrage is the "perpetual motion" of economics. It is defined in terms of (the possibility of) negative cash outlays.

➤ *Ex-ante fair bet, Sect. 6.1, Pg. 117.*

"Risk(y)" arbitrage ≈ great bet. Unlike a true arbitrage, a risk(y) arbitrage could possibly lose a little money.

Arbitrage is an ex-ante concept, not an ex-post concept—beforehand, not after the fact. For example, it does not mean that a lottery ticket that won was an arbitrage. Ex ante, a lottery ticket is not an arbitrage. Please also pay close attention to what the "no-negative-cash-flow" condition means in the definition of arbitrage:

1. Arbitrage is not the same as "earning money without risk." After all, Treasuries do just that, and they are not arbitrage. The reason is that you have to lay out cash to buy Treasuries. This is a negative net cash flow today.

2. Arbitrage is also not the same as "receiving money today without a clear obligation to repay": If you are willing to accept risk, you can often receive cash today. For example, insurance companies take money in exchange for the possibility that they may have to pay up in the future.

Now contemplate the difference between the examples of the true arbitrage and the risk(y) arbitrage in the definition. You can lose $1 with 1% probability in the risky arbitrage, so it is "just" a great bet and not a true arbitrage. One difference is conceptual: Every investor would want to take a true arbitrage opportunity, but an infinitely risk-averse investor would not take a risk(y) arbitrage. This does not mean that, given an either-or choice, a less risk-averse investor would necessarily prefer the small, true arbitrage opportunity. In our example, would you prefer the $5 true arbitrage, if it cannot be repeated, to the risk(y) arbitrage with an expected payout is close to $1 million? (If you could scale the true arbitrage opportunity to take it infinitely many times, the true arbitrage opportunity would dominate, of course.) Of course, this example of risk(y) arbitrage was extreme. More realistically, bets are never this great—"very good" is rare enough. And because there is still risk, you may not want to scale up good but risk(y) arbitrage bets in the same way you would always want to scale up true arbitrage bets as much as possible. Eventually, with enough investment in the risk(y) bet, your risk aversion would kick in and stop you from taking more of it.

There should be few arbitrages in competitive financial markets. Only this fact allows us to study and describe (sane) markets.

Most of all, unless financial markets are very imperfect, you should not expect to find many arbitrage opportunities of either type. If you agree with this assessment—basically that the world is sane and that money does not grow on trees—you can draw some surprisingly strong conclusions about how financial markets work. If you disagree, why are you still in this class? If you are right, you should be among the richest people in the world and there is little that this book can teach you.

Q 11.16. Is earning money without risk an arbitrage?

Q 11.17. Explain when and why you would prefer a risk(y) arbitrage to a true arbitrage opportunity.

More Hypothetical Arbitrage Examples

Of course, it is difficult to find real-world examples of arbitrage. Arbitrage is principally a concept. What would a hypothetical arbitrage opportunity look like? For example, if you can purchase an item for $1, borrow at an interest rate of 9% (all costs, including your time), and sell the item tomorrow for $1.10 for sure, you earn 1 cent for certain today without any possible negative net cash flows in the future. If you ever stumble upon such an opportunity, please take it—it is a positive-NPV project! More than this, it is a true arbitrage because you cannot lose money in any scenario; it is riskless. Yet it is obviously not a very important arbitrage by itself. Searching for 1-cent arbitrage opportunities in financial markets is potentially more lucrative, because they often allow transactions to be scaled up. If you could repeat this 1-cent arbitrage 1 billion times, then you could earn $10 million. Unfortunately, although you may find an arbitrage that works once for 1 cent, it is unlikely that you can find such an arbitrage opportunity that works for 1 billion items. After all, you are not the only one searching in the financial markets! True arbitrage opportunities are difficult or outright impossible to find in the real world, especially in very competitive financial markets.

In a sense, positive-NPV projects *under certainty* are arbitrage.

Small arbitrages matter only if they are scalable.

Another hypothetical example of arbitrage would involve stock prices that are out of sync on different stock exchanges. If PEP shares are quoted for $51 on the Frankfurt Stock Exchange, and for $50 on the New York Stock Exchange, you could theoretically buy one share in New York for $50 and sell it in Frankfurt for $51. You then pocket $1 today. If you can do this with 20,000 PEP shares worth $1 million, you earn $20,000 without effort or risk.

Arbitrage could conceivably occur between different financial markets.

But before you conclude that this is an arbitrage, you still have to make sure that you have not forgotten about costs or risks. The arbitrage may be a lot more limited than it seems—or may not even be present at all. Consider the following issues:

But be skeptical. There are many complications to take into account.

1. Could the price change in between the time you buy the shares in New York and the time you sell the shares in Frankfurt (even if it is only 3 seconds)? If such execution-timing risk exists, this is not pure arbitrage because there is a chance of a negative net cash flow. The real-world evidence suggests that price discrepancies between markets often disappear within a few seconds.

2. Did you account for the direct and indirect transaction costs? How much commission do you have to pay? Is $51 the Frankfurt bid price at which you can sell shares in a market, and $50 the NYSE ask price at which you can buy shares? Can you sell the share in Frankfurt and get it quickly enough from New York to Frankfurt to make the closing? Have you accounted for the value of your own time watching the screen for opportunities?

➤ *Bid and ask prices, Pg.256.*

3. Could the share prices move when you want to transact a significant amount of shares? Only the first 100 shares may be available for $50 for a net profit of $100. The next 900 shares may cost $50.50—perhaps still worthwhile, but less profitable. And purchasing the remaining 19,000 shares may cost you $51 or more.

4. Did you account for your fixed cost of setting up your business? If it costs you a million dollars to get offices and computers in order to "arbitrage" a few thousand

dollars, it is obviously not a real arbitrage. So you must account for how expensive it is to set up your operations.

It may be that small arbitrage opportunities occur from time to time, but large financial firms are constantly running automated computer trading programs that search for even tiny arbitrage opportunities in order to exploit them as soon as they appear—and thereby make them disappear.

Q 11.18. Before you dedicate your life to exploiting a seeming arbitrage between financial markets, what questions should you ask?

11.5   Investment Consequences

Is the past rate of return a good signal for the future rate of return?

How does the EMH matter to you if you are an investor? In an efficient market, there should be no obvious signals to outperform the risk-adjusted appropriate expected return to the tune of, say, 10 basis points a day above transaction costs. For sure, it should not be possible for you or anyone else to earn arbitrage returns. Let's consider two examples—technical analysis and investment fund management.

Weak-Form Efficiency and Technical Analysis

Could there be "cycles" in the market?

The main point of the traditional classification of market efficiency, specifically the "weak" version, is the claim that you should not become rich by trading a strategy that relies only on historical prices. So let me start with some trick questions. Look at the various graphs in Exhibit 11.2. Do they show what stock market patterns could look like? Perhaps. Does it make sense to think that all these patterns can predict the future? Absolutely not! Graphs (a) and (b) display a strong regular cycling pattern. If they indicated future returns, you should quickly become a wealthy technical analyst. You would purchase the stock only when it has "bottomed out"—a pattern that you can reasonably detect if you see a multimonth period of losses followed by about a quarter of stable returns. It need not be the kind of regular cycles in the figure: Any good predictable patterns (such as "every time the price hits $22, it drops by $2") would allow you to get rich. Now, if you look hard enough, can you find some stocks in the real world that have historically behaved like these graphs? Yes—because with over 10,000 stocks currently trading, by pure chance, maybe one or two could show a pattern that would look remarkably similar to a cycle pattern. But, despite assurances from some stock analysts that you could have made money if you had just trusted their cycle patterns and that you should trust them henceforth, the patterns would *not* represent the future—they would just be historical coincidence.

Cycles are not reasonably likely—although there are ups and downs in the market, too.

On the other hand, graphs (c) and (d) could actually be representative. On average, each price in the next month is just a little higher than the previous (i.e., the expected rate of return on stocks is positive), but the important aspect of (c) and (d) is that there is a lot of *noise*, up or down. Noise is by definition unpredictable, and stock prices must largely be unpredictable, or you could outsmart the stock market. Incidentally, one of these graphs is a real stock price that I picked at random, while the other is a simulated

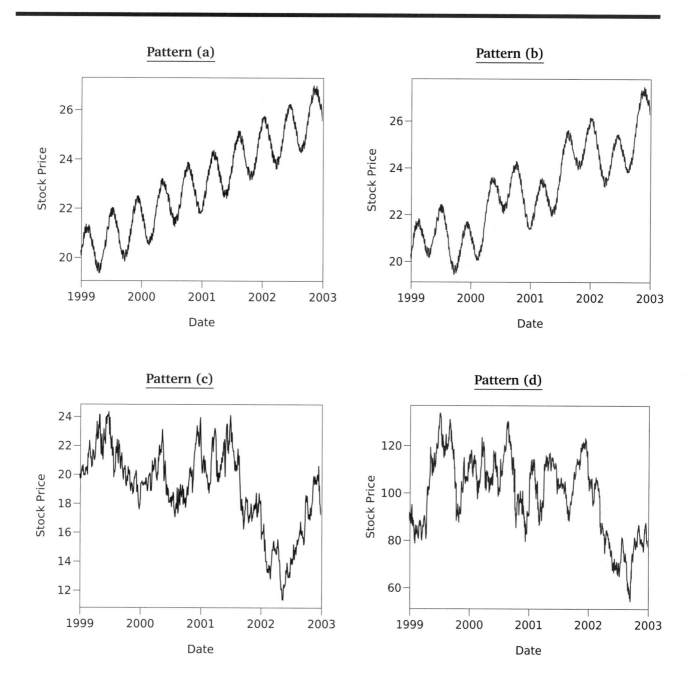

Exhibit 11.2: *Potential Stock Price Patterns.* If these patterns were systematic, some of them should make you rich. Which ones? And which is the real series?

random walk. Can you detect which one? I cannot! The real-world price series looks just like a simulation of patternless day-to-day random-walk changes. In fact, if you ever look at graphical representations of stock prices, most will look like graphs (c) and (d) and unlike graphs (a) and (b). (Solution: Graph (d) is an actual stock price series of IBM.)

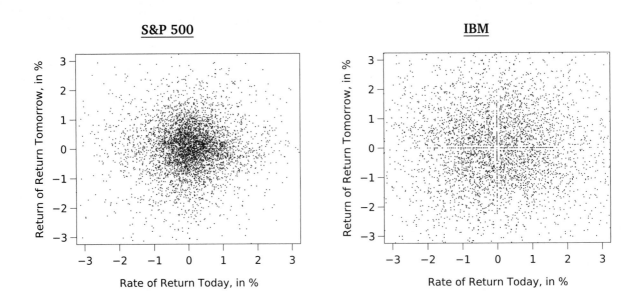

S&P 500   **IBM**

Exhibit 11.3: *The Relation between Lagged and Current Rates of Return.* Note: The figures chop off some outliers, especially the crash of 1987 and mini-crash of 1989, but even if they are included, there is no apparent predictability.

The Empirical Evidence

Predicting with past rates of return mostly appears to fail.

Traders have been trying all sorts of strategies in their efforts to become rich. So how well does technical analysis—which tries to find patterns in historical stock prices— typically do? For example, according to one version, stocks that rise one day are more likely to fall back the next day. Exhibit 11.3 shows tomorrow's rate of return on the S&P 500 and on IBM as a function of today's rate of return (from 1985 to 2003). The graphs show no pattern that would allow you to get rich quickly. There is definitely not much juice in trying to predict how a stock will perform tomorrow, given how it performed today. (Although difficult to spot here, there is a small day-to-day reversal in this data—a tiny negative slope. This is caused by the **bid-ask bounce**: If a stock's closing price is a [higher] ask price, on average it will fall back the next day when it will close with either a bid or an ask price with roughly equal probability. If the stock's closing price is a [lower] bid price, on average it will gain the next day. This is a data illusion and not exploitable.) Similar conclusions apply if you extend your use of historical price information beyond yesterday. You can even try out your own technical analysis at a number of financial websites, such as **YAHOO!** finance—look up any stock and choose "Charts," then "Technical Analysis"; it is fun, but unfortunately fairly useless.

However, over annual horizons, it appears as if stocks tend to continue their pattern just a little bit. This is the "momentum" effect mentioned earlier. It should be covered in more detail in an investments course. (Of course, as you already know from Section 11.1, it is very difficult to determine whether an extra few percent is an appropriate rate of return to compensate investors for some risk, or whether it is a market inefficiency.)

> Momentum: Firms that did well over the last year (with 1-month lag) continue to do well.
>
> ➤ *Momentum, Sect.* App.9.C (Companion), *Pg.* ≈63.

ANECDOTE Are Women Better Investors Than Men?

Analyzing 35,000 households from 1991 to 1997, Terry Odean and Brad Barber found that men trade 45% more than women. Apparently, men are overconfident in their trading prowess. (Men also have a higher propensity to suffer from compulsive gambling disorders.) On average, the men's investment rates of return were lower than women's by a little less than 1% per year. Much, but not all, of women's better returns could be attributed to the higher transaction costs that the men incurred for transactions that did not gain them higher returns. Despite strong evidence to the contrary, many investors still believe that stock prices do not follow random walks, as evidenced by the plethora of financial talk shows and investment newsletters. It would perhaps be better for the general public to watch more sports and cooking shows and fewer investment shows—especially for males like myself!

Odean and Barber, 2001

Investment Manager Performance Evaluation

What about all the televised stock analysts who explain which stocks are undervalued and which stocks are overvalued? And what about the aforementioned technical analysis, the art of seeing patterns (shoulders, price barriers, faces, etc.) in historical prices and using them to forecast future prices? And what about famous investors such as Warren Buffett, George Soros, and many others? Should you trust them?

> What about celebrity investors?

First, recall that the low signal-to-noise ratio means it is difficult to determine why a particular trading strategy has earned high returns:

> What could you conclude from their stellar past performances? These are three possibilities.

- Was it because it had a lucky outcome, which will not repeat (random luck)?

- Was it because it took on some risk that your appropriate return model forgot (your fault in measuring performance)?

- Or was it because the market was inefficient (you have a good signal, skill, and trading ability)?

This is not just a problem for academics. In fact, we finance professors are lucky: We can continue to write papers that argue one side or the other. The real conundrum is faced by every investor in the real world every day: How do you distinguish between a good and a bad signal—between skill and luck—when it comes to investing or to selecting a fund manager?

Here are possible objections to believing in their magical investment abilities (and in inefficient markets).

Why would they tell anyone?

➤ *Ascertaining superior performance,* Pg.297.

The industry standard of three years' performance is not driven by the need to get solid statistical inference.

Pure chance means that some investors succeed many years in a row.

➤ *Mutual funds,* Sect. 7.2, Pg.169.

Good past performers grow.

Why funds' average historical performance looks good to you as an investor *today*.

But the signal-to-noise ratio problem is not even the only problem that you need to consider when you pick an investment manager. If you believe that the market is inefficient so that your fund manager can make you money, consider the following:

Evidence? Of course, maybe there are some investors who *can* pick stocks. Unfortunately, they would not want anyone to learn how they do it. In fact, they may want to do so secretly and privately, never eager to appear on anyone's radar screen. This can make it difficult to find investors with superior ability and thus impossible to confirm their abilities.

Enough data? Recall our earlier conclusion that a strategy with great performance requires many decades before you can realistically conclude that it has worked. (This is assuming that the world is not changing.) Few strategies have such long track records.

Remarkably, the most common industry standard for evaluating funds is their most recent three years of investment performance. There is no disagreement that most of the 3-year performance of funds is noise. This means that many investors (and especially investors in hedge funds) shift their holdings often based on noise. Why? Either they do not understand how long it takes to determine reliably whether a strategy works (possible), or they do not care too much about reliability (more likely). If they believe that there are many other strategies that also have a close to 50-50 probability of success, then eliminating one strategy that had 3 bad years and therefore only a 49-51 probability of success may not be a costly choice.

Monkeys on keyboards? There are about 10,000 mutual funds today that invest money on their investors' behalf. How many of them are likely to outperform the overall stock market next year (at least before they collect fees) if none of them has any superior investing ability? About 5,000. How many of these outperform the year thereafter? About 2,500. Even if there is absolutely no ability, pure randomness means that about 10 funds outperform the market every year for 10 years in a row. With enough candidates, some funds will inevitably produce consistently positive long-run track records.

Who is still alive? What happens to the funds that have underperformed several years in a row? They disappear quietly. What happens to the funds that have outperformed several years in a row? They proudly announce their performances, advertise, boast, and collect more investments from outside investors. Their managers are supported by larger "research teams," appear better dressed and more "professional," and fly in executive jets. They are the ones that are most visible. Indeed, if you made money 10 years in a row in the stock market, would you not believe yourself that you have the ability to pick stocks?

Now put yourself in the shoes of an investor looking at the universe of mutual funds offered today. First, you won't notice funds that have performed poorly. They have already disappeared. Second, you will notice that the larger funds seem to have done better. On average, it will seem that currently available funds indeed can make you money—even if in the real world there is absolutely no ability. This phenomenon is called **survivorship bias**, because it means that you cannot consider the historical performance of existing funds to be a fair projection of their future performance.

Who gets the rents from trading ability? Even if the financial markets were inefficient and even if some fund managers could in fact systematically outperform the market, in a reasonable market, these fund managers would charge appropriately high fees to capture all the advantages that they provide to investors. After all, it is the fund manager who would have the scarce skill (picking stocks) and not the typical investor. Investors with money would compete to place money with such managers and accept higher and higher fund fees. In the end, it would be highly unlikely that uninformed investors could earn excess returns by investing in some manager's actively trading fund.

If there was superior fund performance, the fund manager—not the investor—would profit the most.

In sum, if you are looking for future performance, past performance may be your best guide. But always remember that recent past performance is still a very poor guide.

Obviously, picking the right investment manager is not an easy task. Many mutual funds earn fees regardless of whether they make you money or not. Would it be better to have them participate in the upside (as is the case for hedge funds)? Maybe, but consider this: I give you stock tips, and I ask for money only if you make money. In fact, I only want 10% of your winnings. "You have nothing to lose." I only get something if I help you make money. Sounds like a deal? Now, if I pick a stock randomly, I have a 50-50 chance of making money. If you gain, I get something. If you lose, I pay nothing. In effect, I am arbitraging you! Remember, next time someone gives you a great stock tip, regard it with some skepticism: It probably has a 50-50 chance of being right. (Maybe I should give you the advice to buy a stock, and your neighbor the advice to sell it. This way, I will surely make money from one of you.) My only mistake is that I have told you my plan.

Many hedge funds are compensated on the upside. This does not solve investors' problem, but the alternative is no better.

The Empirical Evidence

So what is the empirical evidence? In general, it suggests that fund managers' luck is far more important than their ability. Whenever academics (or the *Wall Street Journal*) have searched for better performance among analysts or professional fund managers who have outperformed in the past, they have found little or no exceptional forward-looking performance. (If some managers were truly capable of systematically earning better rates of return by picking stocks, you would expect those managers who have picked better in the past to pick better in the future also.) The evidence is that about 54% of mutual funds that have outperformed their benchmarks over the last 1-3 years tend to outperform their benchmarks over the following 1-3 years. This is better than 50%, but not by much. And if you subtract fund fees, the average performance drops significantly below 50%. As fund prospectuses aptly note, and as the evidence suggests, *past performance is no predictor of future performance.*

You must realize that even top investors can have at most mild predictive abilities.

➤ *Business of liquidity provision, Sect. 10.3, Pg. 257.*

There are, of course, other ways to make money: Warren Buffett's fund, *Berkshire Hathaway*, for example, runs many businesses (e.g., insurance and aircraft), too. These businesses make money. But it is money earned the old-fashioned way—through hard work, liquidity provision, and risk-taking. Writing insurance is risky business, and it deserves extra return. Warren Buffett himself would of course not attribute his own performance to luck, but to his ability. Still, even he acknowledges that the efficient

For the most part, it seems that old-fashioned work and insurance (or liquidity) provision work better in earning returns than stock picking.

ANECDOTE   The Three Top Investment Books of 1996

The three best-selling investment books of spring 1996 were David and Tom Gardner's *Motley Fool Investment Guide*, based on a popular investment website; Matt Seto's *The Whiz Kid of Wall Street's Investment Guide* (Matt Seto was 17 years of age at the time); and the *Beardstown Ladies' Common-Sense Investment Guide*, authored by septuagenarians whose first book mixed cooking recipes with investment advice. All touted "common-sense methods" to beat the market, earning 30% per year or more. Not a week went by without dozens of prominent radio and TV shows featuring their advice. Why does anyone need a Ph.D in finance? It is difficult to argue with performance!

Naturally, best-selling books are a great business. However, the stock performance of these three experts was not.

1. From 1996 to 2002, the *Motley Fool* recommended a number of hypothetical portfolios (now discontinued!). In 1997, they launched a real-money portfolio, called DRIP. From July 28, 1997, to July 31, 2002, it lost about 10%, while the S&P 500 lost 2.5% and NASDAQ lost 15%. One should not judge a fund by just 5 years of performance (and certainly not without risk adjustment), but it does appear that the *Motley Fool* has not exactly found the Holy Grail of investment opportunities.

2. Matt Seto stopped publishing his stock picking performance and decided to pursue a career as a student.

3. The Beardstown Ladies, five books richer, were found to have miscalculated their returns: Their returns were not 30%, but 9%—significantly lower than the 15% turned in by the S&P 500 stock market index during their investment period.

How disappointing: On average, about one of them should have continued beating the market, one should have done about the same as the market, and one should have underperformed it.   *Time Magazine, March 1998.*

---

markets hypothesis is the most natural benchmark. He is on record stating that "the professors who taught efficient market theory said that someone throwing darts at the stock tables could select stock portfolios having prospects just as good as ones selected by the brightest, most hard-working securities analyst. Observing correctly that the market was frequently efficient, they went on to conclude incorrectly that it was always efficient." Even Buffett is still a mild believer!

Where should the burden of proof be?

In sum, most finance professors nowadays would agree that when one particular investor earns an unusual amount of money, even over a few years, it is usually more likely due to luck than to ability. The burden of proof is with the side that is claiming superior signals and investing ability—and a number of former finance professors have taken up the challenge and started their own funds.

IMPORTANT

> Even in an efficient market, in which no one can pick stocks better than anybody else, with a very large number of investors, many will beat the market. A small number of investors will beat the market again and again.
>
> In the real world, there is little evidence that investors who did well picking stocks in the past are better at picking stocks in the future when compared to investors who did poorly.

Q 11.19. If you want to determine whether fund managers have an ability to outperform the stock market, given that many of them are likely to beat the market, does it make sense to look for these high-ability managers among the better historical performers?

Q 11.20. If a firm employs 10,000 analysts, how many of them are likely to issue forecasts that beat the market 10 years in a row *if* none of them has any special ability and there are no transaction costs?

Q 11.21. Explain what survivorship bias is and how it manifests itself in the mutual fund context.

11.6 Corporate Consequences

How does the EMH matter to you if you are a manager? Does it matter whether financial markets are perfect, efficient, or neither? Because a perfect market implies an efficient market, you need to think about three different cases:

When creating value for your firm, there are three different market scenarios to consider.

1. The market is efficient and perfect.

2. The market is efficient but not perfect.

3. The market is neither efficient nor perfect.

These cases help you organize your thoughts about what it takes to create value—which is *the* most important question if you are the CFO. Can you add value by changing your capital structure? Can you create value by splitting your shares, so that every share becomes two shares? Can you create value by paying out dividends next year rather than this year? Can you create value by changing how you present your earnings to investors? Can you create value by taking over other companies because/when they are priced too low if you do not have anything unique to add?

If the Financial Market is (Close to) Perfect

If the financial market is perfect, the answers to these questions are simple—they are always no. It does not matter how the firm communicates its earnings to investors, what its capital structure is, how many shares it has, how it pays out its dividends, and so on. In fact, you already know that the firm is worth the value of its underlying projects' present values. Everything else is irrelevant.

In perfect markets, all that counts are the firm's underlying projects.

Earnings reporting: For example, if you have previously reported your foreign division's earnings separately and now you consolidate them into your main earnings, you would indeed increase the firm's reported earnings. However, it would not create anything intrinsically valuable. Such a change should not add or subtract firm value. Your firm owned the subsidiaries' cash flows before and after its reporting change. Your investors can add or subtract the subsidiaries' numbers themselves, whether you include or exclude them in your overall report.

You cannot fool your investors by how you report your earnings.

➤ Do reported earnings matter?, Sect. 13.1, Pg.369.

There must be no value to changing capital structure.

➤ *Capital structure arbitrage, Sect. 16.3, Pg. 497.*

Capital structure: For example, say your firm is currently financed with equity only and worth $100, but if you had a 50-50 debt-equity ratio it would be worth $102. In this case, an arbitrageur could buy your firm, issue $51 in debt and $51 in equity, and pocket $2. With legions of entrepreneurs competing to do this, your firm value would instantly adjust to $102. Thus, a $100 price for your firm would be absurd.

Stock splits must be irrelevant, too.

➤ *Stock splits, Sect. 19.2, Pg. 614.*

Stock splits: In a stock split, each old share becomes multiple new shares. For example, if each share trading at $80 were to become two shares, the new shares should trade for $40 each in a perfect market. Nothing fundamental about your underlying projects would have changed. Splitting by itself cannot add value. If this were not the case—for example, if shares would be worth $41 each after the split—arbitrageurs would purchase the old shares for $80, and sell them an instant later for the equivalent of $2 \cdot \$41 = \$82$, pocketing $2.

Still trying to fool investors, this time with dividends? Fugeddaboutit.

➤ *Stock dividends, Sect. 19.2, Pg. 614.*

Dividends: The same argument applies to dividends. In a perfect market, a $100 firm that pays $10 in dividends should be worth $90 thereafter—no value is magically created or destroyed. Keeping the money for another year in the marginal zero-NPV investment (e.g., Treasuries) is as good as paying it out. Investors in a perfect market can borrow against this extra future money and use it today.

The lesson is simple: As a manager, you should forget about the smoke and mirrors and instead focus exclusively on finding and executing projects with positive net present values.

If the Financial Market is Not Perfect but At Least Efficient

An efficient market means "the price is right." Thus, you can learn from your own market price.

If markets are not perfect but efficient, the implications are not as profound. However, it means that you can still obtain valuable market intelligence. Your market price is the aggregate assessment of many investors who have put their money where their mouths are. The market price aggregates a whole lot of information that you as a corporate manager may not learn as easily yourself. For instance, if your stock price seems very high relative to current fundamentals, it probably means that the market sees great opportunities ahead for your firm and expects that you will take them. Thus, you should consider growing the business. Naturally, a high firm value allows you to raise more funds from the financial markets at favorable rates. On the other hand, if the stock price is very low, it probably means that the financial market anticipates your business to go down or expects you to waste the remaining money. In this case, you should think carefully about whether you should reinvest investors' money into the business or into repurchasing the (relatively cheap) stock.

You can also learn from other market prices.

In addition to learning from your own company's market price, you can also learn from all sorts of other market prices. You can find out how good your competitors' opportunities are, and whether you should get into the fray. Commodity price information can also be very helpful. If the price of oil in the forward market is $100/barrel, it probably does not make sense for you to plan ahead based on an oil price of $70/barrel. The financial market price for oil forwards is very large and efficient. It makes no sense for you to plan your business around much lower or higher oil prices in 6 months, simply because if you really knew this better, you could get rich easily without needing any of your current businesses—just start trading oil futures. This may sound obvious, but it is sometimes easy to overlook the obvious in the heat of the battle. For instance, a large conglomerate oil company in the 1990s planned to explore for more oil, based on a working assumption of doubling oil prices within two years. This company could just have purchased oil in the market instead of drilling. Why explore for oil if you can buy oil cheaper in the market? If you are a farmer planting, the futures exchanges provide you with forward prices for corn and wheat, and you can use this free price information to help you decide which crop to plant.

Let's consider a specific example of how you can learn from market prices in an efficient market. Put yourselves in the shoes of a smart and successful manager of an aircraft manufacturer. Every morning, you read the newspaper, and every morning you think that company X should really be worth a lot more. It makes no sense to you that X has annual earnings of $10/share but its shares are trading at only $50/share. X just seems undervalued. Should you go out and buy it? If the market is perfect, the answer is no. You would have no competitive advantage in owning X. The hordes of arbitrageurs could have accomplished it in an instant, and less expensively than you ever could. On the other hand, owning X would not do any harm either. But let's take away the perfect market assumption and leave only the efficient market one. This means that both your aircraft company's price and the price of X are correct. Buying X because you think that X is undervalued is likely to be wrong. After all, our working assumption is that the financial markets have used all available information to find the best possible price.

However, in the absence of perfect markets, the efficient market does not mean that you should never be able to create value by buying other companies. You can indeed sometimes create value. The trick is that you must be able to do something that investors cannot do for themselves, because the market is imperfect. Most likely, this would be related to your business's real operations. For example, if X is a supersonic aircraft parts supplier, you may have better information about the supplier's product. You may know that you will reward it with a huge contract soon. Or, by owning the patents of this supplier, you may make it more difficult for other aircraft companies to compete with you. Or you may find cost savings by cutting out the middleman in purchasing these parts, or improving X's products through your own intellectual capital, or by increasing the scale of operations. All of these can add value to the firm—value that outside arbitrageurs cannot accomplish without you. (This violates the infinitely many potential buyers assumption of a perfect market.)

But be careful: Market efficiency means that you cannot create value for your shareholders simply by your personal view that X is undervalued. Yes, you may be smart, but the financial markets are just as smart and presumably could recognize just as well whether X is undervalued—in fact, chances are that the target was rightly valued to begin with and it was you who got the target value wrong. For example, if X manufactures diapers, it is highly unlikely that you would create value for your shareholders, even if the firm is trading for only 5 times earnings and this makes no sense to you.

The same argument applies to all sorts of other corporate actions. You may be able to create value by reducing perfect market barriers. For example, you may be able to create value by reducing the costs with which investors can trade your shares (e.g., by listing on an exchange). Or you may be able to reduce the mistrust that your investors

Personal opinion alone (without synergies) is not a good argument for taking over other companies.

However, in an imperfect market, it is possible for an acquisition to add value...

...as long as you have more than just an opinion that the market got prices wrong.

In an imperfect market, you can also create value with financial transactions that reduce market imperfections.

have in your creditworthiness by hiring a good auditor or by reporting your earnings in a transparent fashion. Indeed, there is evidence that many corporate activities can create value by reducing the perfect market frictions, even in very efficient financial markets. For example, when firms split their shares 2-to-1, it is not necessarily the case that the two post-split shares are worth exactly half of the pre-split share of, say, $80. Instead, they tend to be worth a little more, say, around $40.20. The likely reason is that managers signal their confidence in the future by splitting shares today. This brings more information to the market.

➤ *Splits as signals,*
Sect. 19.4, Pg.626.

If the Financial Market is Not Even Efficient

Loosely speaking, financial markets tend to be reasonably, but not always perfectly, efficient. Perfect market efficiency is almost surely *not* a good description of reality. Even in a perfectly rational market, as an executive, you may know the firm value better than the market—for example, you may know that your company is about to sign a large contract, but this information cannot yet be disclosed. What should you do if you know that the stock price is not equal to the appropriate market value? The right way to conceptualize your problem is to consider what you would do if you were the sole owner of the firm. You would really care about firm value. (As its executive, you should want to maximize this value on behalf of the owners.)

If your shares are undervalued, you should recognize that your cost of capital is effectively too high, given the true characteristics of your project. The reason is that you cannot raise risky capital at fair prices—especially equity capital. The CAPM clearly is no longer the right model for the cost of capital.

For example, assume you know that your current projects will return $500 tomorrow. Also assume that you have no cash and that you can only raise financing through equity. Now assume you come across a new project that costs $100 and will return a terrific $200 tomorrow. The problem is that your investors do not believe that the firm will return $700, falsely believing that the combined firm will only be worth, say, $200. Thus, to raise $100, you would have to sell 50% of your firm, and keep only 50% of the true $700 return, for a true $350 share of it. You would therefore be better off passing up this new project and just taking the $500 from the old project. Put differently, the opportunity cost of new capital to fund this project is way too high for you.

You would definitely not want to raise cash at these "high" prices. Instead, you would want to do the opposite. The best use of corporate cash may now be to repurchase your own cheap, underpriced shares, for example, from other investors. However, there is an intrinsic paradox here: As an executive, you are supposed to act on behalf of your shareholders. Therefore, repurchasing underpriced shares from them at bargain prices would not be what would make the selling shareholders better off. (It would, however, make your remaining shareholders better off.)

If your shares are overvalued, your cost of capital would be very low. You should be tempted to take more projects. This is easiest to see if you again consider what you would do if you were the primary owner of this overpriced firm. You

What should you do if markets are not efficient?

➤ *Strong market efficiency, Sect. 11.2, Pg.290.*

If you are undervalued, sometimes it is better to pass up positive-NPV projects. . .

➤ *Separation of financing and investing, Sect. 10.1, Pg.248.*

. . . and use your cash to repurchase your own shares.

➤ *Share repurchases, Sect. 19.2, Pg.614.*

If you are overvalued, sometimes it is better just to issue more shares.

would want to sell more equity shares at higher prices and pay the money out in dividends to existing shareholders. (Alternatively, you can just invest in Treasury securities.) Here the paradox is, of course, that just one instant later, as CEO, you are now the representative of these new shareholders to whom you have just sold overpriced shares. They will not be happy campers. (Many researchers believe that this is exactly what happened when AOL purchased Time-Warner at the height of the Internet craze in the late 1990s. AOL used its overpriced shares to purchase Time-Warner's real assets.)

These are robust insights for CEO's who are not conflicted and wish to act on behalf of their existing shareholders.

IMPORTANT

When managers have superior information:

- If the firm is undervalued, CEOs should assume a relatively high cost of capital and consider repurchasing the firm's own shares.

- If the firm is overvalued, CEOs should assume a relatively low cost of capital and consider issuing more of the firm's own shares.

A good decision rule for managers is to take projects up to the point where the marginal costs and benefits of projects are the same as what they could obtain from repurchasing or issuing the firm's own shares.

(It can become a bit more complex if you see yourself as a representative of both new and old shareholders, though.) But be careful: Most executives are notorious for *always believing* that the financial markets do not fully reflect the value of their companies even if they have no inside information—as an executive, you should be wary of your own perceptions and biases!

➤ *Overconfidence, Sect. 12.7, Pg.352.*

Q 11.22. For convenience, assume a zero discount rate. You have no cash on hand and can only raise financing for new projects by issuing more equity. You know that your existing project will truly return $500 next year. Everyone knows that your second, newer project costs $200, but only you know that it will return only $180 next year. This newer project is the only one that investors think is in line with your current expertise—you cannot raise funds and deposit them elsewhere (or any new investors would smell a rat).

1. Does your second, newer project have a positive or negative NPV?

2. If your investors know both true projects' costs, but they also (incorrectly) believe that you have the magic touch and any of your expertise projects will earn a rate of return of 100%, what fraction of the firm would you have to sell to raise $200 to start the new project?

3. If you act on behalf of your existing investors, should you take this new project?

Comparison and Summary

A summary of the two market concepts and their consequences.

Here is a summary of the two conceptual classifications of how markets work:

Efficient versus inefficient markets: If the market is efficient, you can learn from financial market prices, because they accurately incorporate the information of financial market participants. This means that you cannot create value by taking over other companies just because you think that these companies are worth more than they are trading for.

If the market is inefficient, you may be able to identify underpriced firms that you can take over, or even create value by working on how information about your own company comes to the market.

Perfect versus imperfect markets: If the market is perfect, you can focus exclusively on your projects' net present values. You can forget about most financial choices, such as what your capital structure should be, how you should report earnings, and so on.

If the market is imperfect, you can create value, often by reducing the market imperfections themselves. For example, you could signal what you know about your company's prospects by reporting earnings sooner. On occasion, this can even become a dilemma: For example, what should you do if you know that a project has a positive NPV but the financial market does not believe you? If you take it, your stock price may go down. Now you have to think about the lesser of two evils—passing up on the project, or passing up on a higher stock price.

Don't be too dogmatic: Nothing is perfectly perfect or perfectly imperfect.

In the real world, financial markets are definitely not 100% perfect. For large firms, they are very close to efficient, but this is not necessarily so for small firms. Still, the economic magnitudes of deviations should be fairly modest. As a real-world manager of a publicly traded corporation, it is generally better for you to focus on underlying value creation than on actions that investors can accomplish for themselves without you. It makes sense for you to believe that market prices are almost always informative, but not to believe too slavishly that they are also always fully efficient—you may have better information than the market. Use it wisely when you have it.

11.7 Event Studies

Market reactions should be immediate and reflect all value changes.

The immediacy of price reactions in any efficient market offers a surprisingly useful real-world application: In some cases, market price reactions can allow you to estimate value consequences more easily than traditional NPV techniques, using a technique called an event study. An **event study** is an empirical analysis of the effect of a set of events on the price of assets. The idea of an event study is that if the public market is valuing projects appropriately, and if the value of an unexpected event or action is $1 million, then the stock price should increase by $1 million at the instant the event becomes publicly known. You can therefore (often) back out cash flow value changes from stock price changes. The details of how to conduct such a study are in the appendix.

Capital-Structure-Related and Other Event Study Results

Researchers have run event studies on all sorts of interesting events, ranging from new legislation, to corporate name changes, to analysts' opinions, to corporate earnings, to stock splits, to corporate dividends, to corporate debt and equity issuance and retirement, to deaths of the founder, and so on. Here are some of the more important findings. (You will see some more evidence obtained from event studies again in later chapters, especially in the chapters on capital structure and payout policies.) On the day of the announcement, firm values *increase* on average:

Event studies have been used on many different events. In finance, they often tell us whether corporate actions are good news.

- When firms announce increases in dividends, share repurchases, or stock splits (by about 0.1-1%; if you are interested, there is a longer explanation in Chapter 19).

- When firms are taken over by other firms (by about 10-30%).

- When firms announce earnings that significantly beat analysts' expectations.

- When drug firms announce that the FDA has approved one of their drugs.

- When the founding CEO dies (by about 3-4%).

Conversely, firm values *decrease* on average:

Bad news...

- When firms announce new stock sales (by about 1-3%; if you are interested, there is a longer explanation in Chapter 22 (Companion)).

- When firms overpay for other firms in acquisitions.

- When firms announce lower-than-expected earnings.

- When firms fend off an acquirer who has made a bid.

- When drug firms announce that the FDA has rejected one of their drugs.

Unfortunately, because we do not know the markets' probability assessments prior to these announcements (some of the effects would have already been anticipated and thus already incorporated in the stock price), these value estimates are conservative lower bounds.

Event studies have also informed us whether certain government regulations had a positive or negative impact on firms. For example, we know which firms were helped and hurt when the telecommunications, trucking, and airline markets were deregulated—or how the Treasury's rescue program of 2008 helped some banks, but not others.

Government Regulation—who benefits? who does not?

Q 11.23. In a perfect market, what kind of response ("unusual" stock price change and "unusual" rate of return) would you expect when your company announces that it has struck oil and plans to pay a special dividend next month? What reaction do you expect over this month? What reaction do you expect on the day that it pays the dividends?

Q 11.24. What kind of corporate events are greeted as good news by the financial markets? What events are greeted as bad news?

A N E C D O T E   The Effects of Sanctions on South Africa

South Africa's apartheid regime (1948–1994) rightly deserved to be overthrown. To accelerate its demise, the U.S. Congress imposed banking and tax-related sanctions on firms doing business with South Africa's apartheid regime.

We may all wish we could report success—that sanctions on South Africa's racist regime had been effective. Unfortunately, the event study evidence clearly shows that sanctions played no economic role. Upon the announcement of new sanctions or corporate divestments, neither prices of targeted U.S. companies nor of South African financial securities moved. One explanation is that there were too many loopholes and non-U.S. firms that were willing and able to evade the boycott.

Although we can conclude that, despite all its publicity, the boycott was largely ineffective economically, sanctions may still be appropriate on moral grounds regardless of their economic effectiveness. Whether to boycott socially objectionable behavior is a decision that policymakers should make, not economists. The role of the financial economist is only to inform policymakers of the ultimate effectiveness of their actions.

Teoh, Welch, and Wazzan, Journal of Business, *1999.*

Summary

This chapter covered the following major points:

- Market efficiency means that the market uses all available information in setting prices to offer "appropriate rates of return."

- In the short run, the appropriate expected rate of return on stocks must be small. Therefore, market efficiency prescribes that stocks roughly follow random walks.

- In the long run, it is rarely clear what this "appropriate rate of return" should be. Because noise makes it difficult to measure the average rate of return accurately, it is also difficult to test either models like the CAPM or long-run market efficiency.

- Beliefs in efficient markets come in different forms.

    - The standard efficient markets classification emphasizes what information it would take to beat the market: weak form (past stock price patterns are not enough to beat the market), semistrong form (other historical firm information is not enough to beat the market), and strong form (inside information is not enough to beat the market).

    - A more current efficient markets classification emphasizes the rationality of the stock market: true believer (stock prices always reflect underlying project NPVs), firm believer (small deviations between price and value, but difficult to take advantage of), mild believer (small deviations between price and value, and somewhat possible to take advantage of), or nonbeliever (arbitrage opportunities abound).

- The overall evidence suggests that it is not easy to become rich—a belief shared by most finance professors. The relative strength of their beliefs in market efficiency—the extent to which professors believe that market prices always reflect underlying value—separates finance professors into "rationalists" (or "classical" economists) and "behavioralists."

- In a perfect and efficient market, investors should not find arbitrage opportunities:
  - True arbitrage is a riskless bet with no negative net cash flows under any circumstances. Everyone would like to take all true arbitrage opportunities. When and if they appear, they are likely to be very small.
  - Risk(y) arbitrage is more like a great bet. An infinitely risk-averse investor would not want to take it, because there is a chance that risk(y) arbitrage will lose money.
  - Both true and risk(y) arbitrage opportunities should be very rare in the real world. An investor who is not too risk averse may or may not prefer taking one large, great bet to taking one tiny, true arbitrage.

- Given the millions of investors, many will beat the stock market by chance, and some investors will beat the stock market many years in a row. Market efficiency does not mean that there are not some investors who will beat the stock market 10 years in a row *ex post*; rather, it means that any one particular investor is unlikely to beat the stock market *ex ante* 10 years in a row.

- Managers can learn valuable information from market prices, both from their own share prices and from other prices. To improve corporate firm value, managers must create fundamental value—they must undertake positive-NPV projects. Simple activities such as purchasing a random firm to lower risk or splitting shares will not add value.

- Event studies allow you to ascertain the corporate value impact of sharp events, such as election results, legislative action (FDA rulings), or corporate events (dividend increases).

Preview of the Chapter Appendix in the Companion

The appendix illustrates a specific event study—the value relevance of the elections of 2006 for the overall market, health care stocks, and oil stocks. It explains the limitations of event studies, specifically how it is important to take out the *expected* events and focus only on the unexpected, i.e., the real news.

In the Appendix

Keywords

Behavioral finance, 290.   Bid-ask bounce, 304.   Brownian motion, 294.   Classical finance, 290.   Due diligence, 289.   EMH, 290.   Efficient market hypothesis, 290.   Efficient, 283.   Event study, 314. Fundamental trading, 290.   Futures contract, 288.   Great bet, 299.   Market efficiency, 283.   Noise trader, 291.   Noise, 293.   Random walk, 295.   Rational economics, 290.   Risk(y) arbitrage, 299. Semistrong market efficiency, 290.   Signal, 293.   Signal-to-noise ratio, 293.   Spurious, 291.   Strong market efficiency, 290.   Survivorship bias, 306.   Technical analysis, 290.   True arbitrage, 299.   Volatility, 293. Weak market efficiency, 290.

Answers

Q 11.1 The "efficient market" phrase is shorthand for "the market uses all available information in the setting of its price." There are further nuances about what "available" means, which creates different classifications of market efficiency.

Q 11.2 As a believer in market efficiency, you would point out that the heretics are wrong in how they measure the risk-reward trade-off (the model for what expected rates of return should be). Your second line of defense would be to ask the provocative question of why the heretics are not yet rich. (Of course, you would have to claim it was by pure chance if the heretic that you are talking to *is* rich.)

Q 11.3 Market efficiency is a much more powerful concept over short horizons, because the expected rate of return over a short horizon (say, a day) is very small (a few basis points) in virtually all reasonable models of market pricing.

Q 11.4 An efficient market is one in which the market uses all available information. In a perfect market, market pressures by arbitrageurs will make market efficiency come true, so a perfect market should be efficient. However, an efficient market need not be perfect. For example, stocks could be priced fairly even when there are taxes.

Q 11.5 Markets are more likely to be efficient when transaction costs are low, because this makes it easier for smart investors to compete away any unusual opportunities.

Q 11.6 The foreign currency market may well be the biggest market in the world, with the dollar and the euro both being the world's two main currencies. With so many smart investors trading on the exact same instrument, and with incredibly low transaction costs, we would expect arbitrageurs to take advantage of even the smallest inefficiency. Thus, it would seem likely that the foreign exchange market is much more efficient—and much closer to perfection.

Q 11.7 Momentum strategies seem to violate even weak-form market efficiency—unless you believe that their returns are just normal because they reflect some sort of normal compensation for risk.

Q 11.8 If you believe that market values do not always perfectly reflect underlying fundamental values, but that trading costs nevertheless prevent you from exploiting this profitably (in large scale), then you should classify yourself as a firm believer in market efficiency.

Q 11.9 The random-walk formula is on Page 295. It states that the expected price tomorrow is the price today plus a drift. The drift can be a small constant or a very small fraction of the price today.

Q 11.10 You should know that there are about 250 trading days per year. More accurately, it was 252. If a stock has an expected rate of return of 20% per year—which is definitely on the high side for most firms—the daily rate of return would be $1.2^{1/252} - 1 \approx 7.24$ basis points. If you computed the non-compounding $0.20/252 \approx 7.84$ basis points, or even used 365 calendar days instead of 252 trading days, you would still get a reasonable similar answer—the average daily rate of return is very small.

Q 11.11 A *daily* trading strategy would have to offer above 20% per annum in order to overcome typical transaction costs. The calculation in the text came to about 23% per annum.

Q 11.12 The typical movement (variation) of a stock is around plus or minus 2% to 3% a day. The average rate of return on a day is much lower. Thus, the signal-to-noise ratio is very low.

Q 11.13 Even if the stock price follows a random walk, its actual price can definitely—and most likely will be—different from today's. Only the *expected* price is the same as the price today.

Q 11.14 If you want to be a superstar trader who outperforms by, say, about 4% per year, you would have to earn an extra $\sqrt[252]{1.04} - 1 \approx 1.6$ basis points per day.

Q 11.15 With 100 basis points per day of noise and 200 basis points per year of excess performance:

1. With 1 day's performance, you would expect $200/252 \approx 0.794$ basis points per day.

2. The noise was given as 100 basis points per day.

3. The expected T-statistic is about $0.794/100 \approx 0.00794$.

4. Over 252 days, the performance was given as 200 basis points.

5. The noise would be $100 \cdot \sqrt{252} \approx 1,587$ basis points.

6. The expected T would be about $200/1,587 \approx 0.126$.

7. You need to solve $(0.79 \cdot N)/(100 \cdot \sqrt{N}) \geq 1.96$, or $0.0079 \cdot \sqrt{N} \geq 1.96$. The critical N is approximately 250 years.

Q 11.16 No! Treasuries earn money without risk, but they are not an arbitrage, because investing in them requires a negative net cash flow up-front.

Q 11.17 If the true arbitrage opportunity can only be done once and gains $10, it is probably worse than a risk(y) arbitrage that loses 1 cent with 1% probability, and gains $1,000,000 with 99% probability.

Q 11.18 Good topics to consider when thinking about how plausible an arbitrage is include: time and execution risk, direct and indirect transaction costs, price impact of trades, and fixed costs.

Q 11.19 Yes, it makes sense to look for high-ability managers among historical high performers. However, many high-ability managers will have underperformed historically, and many low-ability managers will have outperformed historically.

Q 11.20 If each of the 10,000 analysts has a 50-50 chance to beat the market in any given year, then the answer is that $10,000/2^{10} \approx 10$ analysts beat the market 10 years in a row.

Q 11.21 Survivorship bias means that you, as an investor, will only see the funds that were ex post successful. Most unsuccessful funds do not show up in the historical statistics of funds in existence today. Existing funds will therefore have had positive performances in the past.

Q 11.22   1. This project has a negative NPV, –$200 + $180 = –$20, at the zero interest rate. (A positive interest rate would make it even more negative.)

2. If you do take this second newer project, all your investors would believe that your firm would be worth ($500 + $200) · (1 + 100%) = $1,400. To raise $200 in funding, you would therefore have to sell $200/$1,400 ≈ 14.286% of your firm.

3. The true value of your firm will be ($500 + $180) = $680, and the 14.3% stake is worth only $97.14. Put differently, your old investors have just sold a $180 project for $97.14, giving them a net profit of $82.86. You can also compute this directly: Your old investors will therefore own (1 – 14.286%) · $680 ≈ $582.86. This is $82.86 more than the $500 that they would own if you did not take the new project. You should take it if you are acting on behalf of the existing investors.

Q 11.23 The immediate share price response to the news that you have struck oil would be positive. Over the following month, you would not expect any unusual upward or downward drift: It should be about zero. Finally, when your firm pays out the special dividend, the rate of return should be zero on average, too, because the market would have known that the dividend would be paid. Of course, its share price will have to drop by the amount of the dividend paid to keep the return around zero. Chapter 19 explains how this may not be the case in the presence of market imperfections, especially personal income taxes on dividend payouts.

Q 11.24 Good news: becoming an acquisition target; the announcement of new dividends, share repurchases, and stock splits; earnings significantly higher than analysts' projections; FDA approvals; and CEO deaths. Bad news: Acquiring other firms at too high a price; the issuance of new equity stock; earnings significantly lower than analysts' projections; declining an acquirer's bid; and FDA rejections.

End of Chapter Problems

Q 11.25. What kind of evidence would heretics against market efficiency ideally want to muster? If they fail to find this kind of evidence, does it mean that you should conclude that markets are efficient?

Q 11.26. Define "efficient market" and explain how it differs from a perfect market.

Q 11.27. Peter Lynch, a famous former fund manager for Fidelity, suggested that it is wise to invest in stocks based on "local knowledge"—you invest in the stock of your local supermarket if you notice that it does better than expected. In an efficient stock market, is this a wise recommendation?

Q 11.28. Evaluate the following statement: It does not matter what portfolio you are holding in a perfect and efficient stock market.

Q 11.29. A paper by Frieder and Zittrain looked at a large sample of spam email touting a particular stock. Such distributions increased the trading volume and resulted in a 4–5% gain over the 2 days following the spam release. Is this evidence against market efficiency?

Q 11.30. What are the three main categories in the traditional market efficiency classification? Give an example of what each excludes.

Q 11.31. Comment on the following statement: "An efficient market seems like an impossible concept. In an efficient market, no one can earn excess returns. Therefore, no one collects information. Therefore, prices do not contain information, and collecting information should earn excess returns."

Q 11.32. Describe the fundamentals-based classification of the strength of belief in market efficiency. Explain how one individual can be at one level but not in the level above or below.

Q 11.33. Does a random walk imply that the expected rate of return on a stock is zero?

Q 11.34. Assume that the typical day-to-day noise (standard deviation) is about 100 basis points. Assume that you have the kind of stock-picking ability that earns you an extra 400 basis points per annum. Assume no transaction costs. Ignore compounding and assume that your rate of return is the sum of returns over trading days. Assume there are 252 trading days per year.

1. With only 1 day of performance, how much extra do you expect to earn per day?

2. How bad is your noise over 1 day?

3. What is your expected T-statistic (the excess mean divided by the standard deviation)?

4. With 252 trading days of performance, how much extra do you expect to earn per annum?

5. How bad is your noise over 252 days?

6. What is your expected T-statistic now?

7. Work out how many years you would expect to wait before you would obtain statistically significant evidence to prove that you have a positive ability to pick stocks.

Q 11.35. Define arbitrage. How is it different from a great bet? Is one always better than the other?

Q 11.36. Would it make sense for a model of the financial world to assume that there is no arbitrage? Would it make sense for a model of the financial world to assume that there are no great bets?

Q 11.37. What kind of costs should you consider when evaluating whether an opportunity is an arbitrage?

Q 11.38. The typical hedge fund investor evaluates its fund based on the most recent three years of performance. What do you think of this practice?

Q 11.39. Why does the average mutual fund in the market today appear to have been a great performer? Does this evidence suggest that these funds will be good performers in the future, at least on average?

Q 11.40. Do you expect fund managers with high ability to prefer compensation that is more performance based? How good an "insurance" is this for fund investors?

Q 11.41. If a corporation acquires another firm, it can lower the firm's uncertainty. This should lower its cost of capital. This should create value. Is this correct?

Q 11.42. Give an example of how the cost of capital for taking a project can be too high if the market has undervalued your firm.

Q 11.43. For convenience, assume a zero discount rate. You know that your current projects cost $400 today and will truly return $500 next year—but your investors believe they will return only $400. In addition, you have no cash on hand and can only raise financing for new projects by issuing more equity. A new project costs $200 and will return $220 next year. Your investors mistakenly believe that your firm will earn an internal rate of return of 0%, either with or without this new project. Acting on behalf of your existing investors, should you take this project? Does it have a positive NPV?

Part IV

Real-World Applications

...Capital Budgeting, Financial Statements and Valuation, and Comparables

You now know *all* the important cost of capital and present value concepts. But you cannot yet appreciate all the nuances and difficulties of their application in a corporate environment. In the real world, valuation can prove to be quite difficult because firms do not exist merely in order to provide clean and convenient illustrations of the theoretical constructs! Thus, the next issue on the agenda is for you to learn (better) how to apply what you have learned in previous chapters.

By necessity, this part consists of a variety of subjects. First, you will learn about the many difficulties in applying the seemingly-so-simple capital budgeting concepts. NPV and IRR can have sharp teeth! Chapter 12 covers the various pitfalls that you are likely to encounter when using net present value in practice. Next, you will learn how to read the financial information that publicly traded companies provide. Let me just state that the net income is not the cash flow that you need as your direct input into your NPV analysis. Finally, you will learn about an alternative (and distant cousin) to classical NPV analysis: comparables. Sometimes, they are better than NPV, sometimes they are worse. Comparables are dangerous, though: They are exceptionally easy to misuse.

What You Want to Learn in This Part

The primary goal of this part is to show you the breadth of issues and problems that arise in the appli-cation of the concepts from the previous chapters, and especially in the application of net present values.

- Chapter 12 goes over many important issues that you should pay attention to when you have to make investment decisions.

    Typical questions: In valuing an ac-quisition target, should you use your own or the target's cost of capital? How should you think of projects that have side effects—for example, projects that pollute the air? How should you think of sunk costs? What is a "real option"? How do you value contingencies and your own flexibil-ity to change course in the future? How should your assessment of in-vestment value change if you know that someone else had to estimate the cash flows? Do people generally tend to misestimate future cash flows in systematically erroneous ways?

- Chapter 13 explains how you can extract cash flow estimates for a present value analysis from corporate financial statements. This is easiest to understand in the context of a hypothetical firm for which you construct the financials yourself. This makes it easy to translate them back into the economic cash flows that you need. At the end, you also get to extract the cash flows from a real financial statement.

Typical question: What are the economic cash flows in PepsiCo's financial statements that you would use to estimate the present value of PepsiCo?

- Chapter 14 shows how you can learn more information about your own firm, using publicly available information from comparable firms. It also explains a method of valuation that is both similar to, and different from, net present value.

Typical questions: How does "comparables-based" valuation differ from PV-based valuation? When is the P/E (price/earnings) ratio a good number to look at? What should the P/E ratio of your project be? How and when can you average P/E ratios? What can you learn from other financial ratios?

Capital Budgeting Applications and Pitfalls

Tips and Tricks

Applying the concepts of NPV and IRR in the real world can be very difficult. This chapter explains many of the nuances and pitfalls in their application. It will help you avoid many common mistakes that many companies commit almost every day—mistakes that cost them value.

12.1 So Many Returns: The Internal Rate of Return, the Cost of Capital, the Hurdle Rate, and the Expected Rate of Return

Before we begin, let us just recap the four commonly-used rates of return in finance: the *internal rate of return*, the *cost of capital*, the *expected rate of return*, and the *hurdle rate*.

In the real world, these four terms are often used casually and interchangeably.

Internal rate of return: The internal rate of return is a characteristic of project cash flows (hence "internal") and usually has nothing to do with capital markets (unless the project itself is a capital markets–related project). This is its big advantage—you can calculate it before you ever look at the capital markets. It is only later that you will compare the IRR to the prevailing rate of return in the economy. The IRR is the most different of these four rates. Be careful, though: You should not use promised cash flows to compute it. IRR requires *expected* cash flows, which are much harder to come by.

➤ *IRR, Sect. 4.2, Pg.64.*

Cost of capital: Always think of it as the *opportunity* cost of capital. It is the rate of return your investors could expect to receive by investing in similar projects elsewhere. It is determined by the prevailing required rates of return for projects of your type. Therefore, it is driven by the demand and supply for capital in the economy—the expected rate of return that your investors demand in order to give you money willingly. In perfect capital markets, with many lenders and borrowers, loans usually have zero net present values. (Otherwise the borrower or lender is giving away free money.) The cost of capital is sometimes called the "required expected rate of return." The CAPM is one perfect-market model that provides an estimate of the cost of capital. Finally, realize that the cost of capital is itself an expected value concept—you do not need to write the "expected cost of capital."

➤ *Cost of capital, Sect. 2.5, Pg.23.*

Expected rate of return: The expected rate of return is a generic term. It could mean your project's expected rate of return, or the cost of capital (the lender's expected rate of return). In most cases, if your project's actual expected rate of return is above its required expected rate of return (the cost of capital), then it is a positive-NPV project. If management makes smart decisions, projects' expected rates of return are above their costs of capital. The very last marginal project often has an expected rate of return just about the same as the cost of capital.

➤ *Expected rate of return, Sect. 8.1, Pg.179.*

Hurdle rate: The appropriate project hurdle rate is the expected rate of return above which management decides to accept and go forward with the project. It is set neither by the financial markets nor by the project, but by management. Bad management could choose any arbitrary, or even outright idiotic, hurdle rate. Good management should accept all projects that have positive net present values.

➤ *Hurdle rate, Sect. 4.2, Pg.69.*

Usually, this means that good managers should set a project's hurdle rate to be equal to the project's cost of capital, and management should then determine whether the project's IRR exceeds this hurdle rate. If management makes smart decisions, taking all positive-NPV projects, the "hurdle rate," "cost of capital," and "required expected rate of return" are all the same.

Warning: The IRR should be an expected return concept, but it is often misapplied to promised returns.

You already know that expected project returns are difficult to come by. Managers often incorrectly use promised rates of return. Because corporations are aware that claims based on expected project returns are regularly inflated, many of them have established hurdle rates high above a reasonable cost of capital for such projects. It is not uncommon to find corporations requiring projects to have hurdle rates of 15% or more, even when the cost of capital for such projects would seem to be on the order of only 10%. Venture capitalists even regularly employ project hurdle rates as high as 30%, knowing full well that this is far above the rate of return that their projects are *truly expected* to earn.

➤ *Agency problems, Sect. 12.8, Pg.354.*

The differences are sometimes subtle, and the terms are often used interchangeably—which is okay in many, but not all, situations.

Q 12.1. Can you compare a project's internal rate of return to its hurdle rate?

Q 12.2. Can you compare a project's cost of capital to its hurdle rate in a perfect market?

12.2 Promised, Expected, Typical, or Most Likely?

The simplest error—confusing promised and expected returns—is perhaps the worst.

By now, you know that you must distinguish between promised and expected numbers. In particular, the CAPM is a model of expected rates of return and simply does not tell you anything about credit risk. When you want to apply the present value formula, you must use the *expected* cash flows in the numerator (adjusted for credit risk), not the *promised* cash flows. Never discount promised cash flows with CAPM costs of capital!

Promised and Expected Returns

Let's recap this. Say you have a B-rated corporate zero-bond that promises $1,000 next year and has a beta of 0.2. Assuming you believe that the risk-free rate is 5% and the equity premium is 3%, you can still not compute the bond price as

Here is how users get it wrong most of the time.

$$PV \neq \frac{\$1,000}{1 + 5\% + 3\% \cdot 0.2} \approx \$946.97$$

$$PV \neq \frac{\text{Promised Cash Flow}}{1 + r_F + [\mathscr{E}(r_M) - r_F] \cdot \beta_i}$$

Yes, in a perfect CAPM world, the expected rate of return on this bond should be $5\% + 3\% \cdot 0.2 = 5.6\%$. (In an imperfect world, you would have to add the liquidity and tax premiums.) Yet, to determine the price, it is not enough for you to know the *promised* bond cash flow. You need the *expected* cash flow, a number that is always less than $1,000. The same problem arises, of course, not only in the context of bonds but also in the context of corporate projects. You cannot simply discount the "good-scenario" cash flows. You must discount the project's expected cash flows!

➤ *Imperfect market premiums, Sect. 10.6, Pg.270.*

The same mistake appears sometimes in another form when managers use the IRR capital budgeting rule. This rule says "accept the project if its IRR is above the hurdle rate." The common mistake here is that the cash flows from which the IRR must be computed are not the promised cash flows, but the expected cash flows. Of course, you can also compute a number from the promised cash flows, but you should probably call it the "promised IRR" to distinguish it clearly from the "expected IRR"—and you should never compare the promised IRR to a hurdle rate based on the expected rates of return of other projects in the economy when you want to determine whether you should accept the project or not. In fact, the promised IRR should not be used for capital budgeting purposes.

For capital budgeting (comparison to the cost of capital), an IRR must be computed from the project's expected (and not promised) cash flows.

Q 12.3. An Amazon.com bond quotes an internal rate of return of 8% per annum. Assuming the market is perfect, is this its cost of capital?

Expected, Typical, and Most Likely Scenarios

Managers often commit a related (but milder) error in applying NPV. They tend to confuse expected values with "typical" or "most likely." (Statistically speaking, this means that they confuse the mean with the median or the mode of a distribution.) If you do this, you will fail to consider low-probability events appropriately: a plane crash, a legal suit, an especially severe recession, or a terrific new client.

The NPV formula requires expected cash flows, not typical cash flows. (Do not ignore low-probability events.)

For example, your business may have the following payoffs:

An example: The statistical distribution has a left tail.

Event	Probability	Value
Good Business	46%	$1,200,000
Normal Business	44%	$1,000,000
Lawyers Sue for Punitive Damages	10%	−$10,000,000

The most likely payoff is $1,200,000. The median payoff is $1,000,000. The expected payoff, however, is only

$$\mathcal{E}(\text{Payoff}) \;=\; 46\% \cdot \$1,200,000 \;+\; 44\% \cdot \$1,000,000 \;+\; 10\% \cdot (-\$10,000,000)$$

$$=\qquad -\$8,000$$

An NPV analysis requires *this* expected payoff. If you run this business 100 times, you would receive $1.2 million 46 times, $1 million 44 times, and lose $10 million 10 times. Fortunately, if the statistical distribution is symmetric—as it is in the case of the normal bell-shaped distribution—then the center of the distribution is all three: mean, median, and mode. Unfortunately, few businesses are immune to low-probability shocks, often negative, so you need to think about whether the distinction between mean, median, and mode is applicable to your business.

Q 12.4. A zero-bond promises $100,000 and has a beta of 0.3. If the risk-free rate is 5%, and the equity premium is 3%, and the CAPM holds, then what is the bond's price?

Q 12.5. A machine that costs $910 is likely to break irreparably with 10% probability at the end of each year (assuming it has worked the previous year). (Many electric devices without moving parts have such breakdown characteristics.) However, the regulatory agency has phased out this machine, and so will neither allow you to replace it nor use it for more than five years. The machine can produce $300 in profit every year, beginning next year. The discount rate is 12% per annum. (Hints: This means that the machine will produce some value between $300/1.12 \approx $268 [if it breaks down immediately] and $1,081 [if it lasts for all years] in present value. First, work this out case by case for a two-year machine, then for a three-year machine. Think "DDDD," "WDDD," "WWDD," "WWWD," and "WWWWD," where W means working and D means dead.)

1. What is the most likely number of years that the machine will last? If this number were instead guaranteed to be the certain life of the machine in number of years (instead of just the most likely number of years), what would be the machine's value ?

2. What is the expected number of years that the machine will last? If this number were instead guaranteed to be the certain life of the machine in number of years (instead of just the expected number of years), what would be the machine's value ?

3. What is the correct present value of this machine?

12.3 Badly Blended Costs of Capital

One of your first lessons about NPVs was that you can add them if projects are independent. Yet, believe it or not, although most managers know that it is impossible to add
value by merely combining independent projects, in practice they often make exactly
this mistake. This error arises most commonly in contexts in which costs of capital need
to be blended across multiple projects. As always, the concept is straightforward, but
the devil is in the details. It is easy to overlook the forest in the trees. Let's make sure
you do not commit this mistake.

Independent projects should be considered based on their own costs of capital.

Does Risk Reduction Create Value?

In the 1960s and 1970s, many firms became **conglomerates**, that is, companies with
widely diversified and often unrelated holdings. Can firms add value through such
diversification? The answer is "usually no." Diversification indeed reduces the standard
deviation of the company's rate of return (diversified companies are less risky), but in a
perfect market, your investors can just as well diversify risk for themselves. They don't
need the firm to do it for them.

Diversification reduces risk, but does not create value.

For example, if your $900 million firm ABC (e.g., with a beta of 2 and a risk of 20%)
is planning to take over the $100 million firm DEF (e.g., with a beta of 1 and also a risk
of 20%), the resulting firm is worth $1 billion. ABC + DEF indeed has an idiosyncratic
risk lower than 20% if the two firms are not perfectly correlated, but your investors (or a
mutual fund) could just purchase 90% of ABC and 10% of DEF and thereby achieve the
very same diversification benefits. If anything, you have robbed investors of a degree of
freedom here: They no longer have the ability to purchase, say, 50% in ABC and 50% in
DEF. (In a CAPM world, this does not matter.) The CAPM makes it explicit that the cost
of capital does not change unduly. Say both firms follow the CAPM pricing formula, and
say that the risk-free rate is 3% and the equity premium is 5%,

A specific diversification example worked out for you, in which projects are priced fairly, and diversification neither creates nor destroys value.

$$\mathcal{E}(r_{ABC}) = 3\% + 5\% \cdot 2 = 13\%$$

$$\mathcal{E}(r_{ABC}) = r_F + [\mathcal{E}(r_M) - r_F] \cdot \beta_{ABC}$$

and

$$\mathcal{E}(r_{DEF}) = 3\% + 5\% \cdot 1 = 8\%$$

$$\mathcal{E}(r_{DEF}) = r_F + [\mathcal{E}(r_M) - r_F] \cdot \beta_{DEF}$$

The newly formed company will have an expected rate of return (cost of capital) of

$$\mathcal{E}(r_{ABC+DEF}) = 90\% \cdot 13\% + 10\% \cdot 8\% = 12.5\%$$

$$\mathcal{E}(r_{ABC+DEF}) = w_{ABC} \cdot \mathcal{E}(r_{ABC}) + w_{DEF} \cdot \mathcal{E}(r_{DEF})$$

➤ *Value-weighted portfolios, Sect. 8.5, Pg. 198.*

and a market beta of

$$\beta_{ABC+DEF} = 90\% \cdot 2 + 10\% \cdot 1 = 1.9$$

$$\beta_{ABC+DEF} = w_{ABC} \cdot \beta_{ABC} + w_{DEF} \cdot \beta_{DEF}$$

The merged company will still follow the CAPM,

$$\mathcal{E}(r_{ABC + DEF}) = 3\% + \quad 5\% \quad \cdot \quad 1.9 \quad = 12.5\%$$

$$\mathcal{E}(r_{ABC + DEF}) = r_F + [\mathcal{E}(r_M) - r_F] \cdot \beta_{ABC + DEF}$$

Its cost of capital has not unduly increased or declined. In an ideal CAPM world, no value has been added or destroyed—even though ABC + DEF has a risk lower than the 20% per annum that its two constituents had.

Synergies determine M&A value for shareholders; lower risk (diversification) does not. Managers, however, are conflicted: They like lower risk.

Of course, some mergers can add value due to synergies, which will be discussed in the next section. But these synergies are not a result of the plain diversification effect. Many researchers believe that the most common but unspoken rationale for mergers are not synergies but the fact that managers like to take over other firms. They prefer the reduced idiosyncratic firm uncertainty and higher salaries guaranteed by larger firms to the higher risk and lower salaries in sharply focused, smaller firms. To justify a merger, managers will want to argue for a lower cost of capital for the target any way they can—including incorrectly using the acquirer's cost of capital. (This is an example of an agency conflict, which will be explained later in this chapter.) There is also good evidence that in the real world, diversified firms often do not operate as efficiently as stand-alone firms (e.g., due to limited attention span of management or more bureaucratization). Many mergers actually *destroy* firm value.

A N E C D O T E   Risk and Conglomeration

In the 1970s, a lot of firms diversified to become conglomerates. Management argued that conglomerates tended to have lower risk, which created value for shareholders. This argument was, of course, total nonsense: Investors could diversify for themselves. It was the managers who liked lower risk, with less chance of losing their jobs and higher compensation packages that came from running a bigger company. Worse, because conglomerates often operated less efficiently than individual stand-alone, focused companies, diversification actually often destroyed firm value. In the 1980s, there were many "bust-up buyouts," which created value by purchasing conglomerates to sell off the pieces.

A good example of such a conglomerate was Gulf and Western. It was simultaneously involved in oil, movies (Paramount), recording (Stax), rocket engines, stereo components, finance, publishing (Simon and Schuster), auto parts, cigars, and on and on. It promptly crashed and split up in the 1980s. A more current example is Tyco, which has over 260,000 employees in 50 separate business lines, including electronics, undersea fiber optic cables, health care, adhesives, plastics, and alarm systems. (Its former executive, Dennis Kozlowski, became famous for his extravagant looting of Tyco's assets. With so many business lines, no wonder no one noticed for years!) The most interesting conglomerate, however, may be General Electric. It has hundreds of business lines, but unlike most other conglomerates, GE appears to have been running most of its divisions quite well.

Oligopoly Watch *and other sources*

Does Corporate Risk Management Create Value?

Hedging is a form of risk management.

➤ *Risk management and hedging, Sect.* 26.E *(Companion), Pg.* ≈336.

Although risk management is discussed in more detail in Chapter 26 (Companion), let me give you a brief preview. Firms can reduce their own overall risk by **hedging**. A hedge is an arrangement that reduces the firm's volatility. For example, a refinery could purchase crude oil today in order not to suffer if the future oil price were to increase.

Remarkably, a firm with a high market beta could even transform itself into a firm with a low market beta! (Hedge funds often do this.) The firm can hedge away market risk by selling the stock market itself. S&P 500 futures contracts make shorting the stock market exceptionally easy. Whenever the stock market goes up, the futures contract goes up in value. Being the seller, the hedging firm's side of the futures contract goes down in value. Put differently, the firm's hedge contract has a negative market beta. The hedged firm is now a bundle, consisting of the unhedged firm plus this contract. Therefore, the market beta of the hedged firm would be lower than the market beta of the unhedged one. If it wanted, the firm could even make its own market beta zero or negative. Usually, being hedged against market risk would also reduce the overall idiosyncratic risk of the firm. Many firms hedge against other risks. For example, Southwest Airlines purchases jet fuel far in advance (through futures contracts), which reduces its exposure to subsequent rises in the price of jet fuel.

Hedging against stock market risk can lower the market beta and risk of the firm. Hedging against jet fuel price increases can reduce risk exposure.
➤ *Shorting stocks, Sect. 7.2, Pg.167.*

But would this hedging contract create firm value in a perfect market? No. The firm has not given its investors a new positive-NPV project. If investors had wanted less exposure to the overall stock market, *they could have shorted the stock market themselves.* Alternatively, investors can simply undo a firm's hedging—they can buy the financial markets contracts that the firm has sold. This undoes any corporate hedge from the investors' perspectives. So, in itself, in a perfect market, trading fairly priced hedging contracts neither adds nor subtracts value. It is only if the market is imperfect that a hedge may allow a firm to operate more efficiently. For example, the extra cash from a hedge contract could help the firm to avoid running into a liquidity crunch in situations in which more funding would be difficult to raise. Or the firm may have inside information concerning what the future will hold and thus whether the hedged good is underpriced. In this case, risk management could add value.

Does hedging create value? Only in an imperfect market.

IMPORTANT

In a perfect market, the following holds:

- If two firms are independent, then combining them into a conglomerate usually reduces the overall firm risk, but does not create value for investors. Investors can easily diversify risk themselves.

- Adding independent projects to the firm cannot create value if these projects are not positive-NPV in themselves.

In an imperfect market, the value effects of hedging are complex. Hedges could indeed add (or subtract) value.

Q 12.6. When two unrelated firms with uncorrelated rates of return merge, is the resulting conglomerate riskier or safer? Does this add value?

How to Misuse the CAPM

A common misuse of CAPM is to use a uniform cost of capital for all projects.

This brings us to the most common abuse of the CAPM and NPV: managers forgetting that NPVs of independent projects are additive. Sounds obvious, but here is how it gets lost in the details: NPVs are only additive if you use the individual projects' own costs of capital. You cannot use the firm's overall cost of capital for its individual projects.

When Acquiring Another Company

Assume the firm uses the same overall cost of capital for all projects.

Here is a negative-NPV project. No sane firm should take it.

Assume the risk-free rate of return is 3% and the equity premium is 4%. Your old firm, cleverly named *old*, is worth $100 and has a market beta of 0.5. An acquisition target (or just a new project), cleverly named *new*, costs $10 and is expected to pay off $11 next year. (Its rate of return is therefore 10%.) The beta of this new project is 3.

The simplest method to compute the value of acquiring project *new* relies on the fact that the NPVs of independent projects are additive. You can value the new project using its own expected cash flows and its own cost of capital. *Who* owns *new* should matter little: The project is worth what it is worth. Therefore, *new* should offer an expected rate of return of

$$\text{Correct Cost of Capital:} \quad \mathcal{E}(r_{new}) \;=\; 3\% + \quad 4\% \quad \cdot \quad 3 \;=\; 15\%$$

$$\mathcal{E}(r_{new}) \;=\; r_F + [\mathcal{E}(r_M) - r_F] \cdot \beta_{new}$$

and the true NPV of project *new* is

$$\text{NPV}_{new} = -\$10 + \frac{\$11}{1 + 15\%} \approx -\$0.43$$

Therefore, if firm *old* adopts project *new*, *new*'s owners would be 43 cents poorer than they would be if their managers did not adopt it (i.e., $100 versus $99.57).

Bad company policy: Using its own cost of capital on this project, the firm would mistakenly take it.

Unfortunately, in many firms, it is standard policy to evaluate *all* projects by the firm's overall cost of capital. Would such a firm take the *new* project now? Evaluated with a market beta of 0.5, the hurdle rate for the project would be

$$\text{Incorrect Cost of Capital:} \quad \mathcal{E}(r_{old}) \;=\; 3\% + \quad 4\% \quad \cdot 0.5 \;=\; 5\%$$

$$\mathcal{E}(r_{old}) \;=\; r_F + [\mathcal{E}(r_M) - r_F] \cdot \beta_{old}$$

With its internal rate of return of $11/$10 − 1 = 10%, which is greater than the 5% incorrect cost of capital, a (bad) manager would indeed take this project.

The loss if the firm takes this project is exactly the negative NPV of the project.

If the *old* firm did take project *new*, how would its value change? With a beta of 0.5, the old firm had an expected rate of return of 3% + 4% · 0.5 = 5%. Its expected value next year would be $105. Using PV, we see that the present value of the combined firm would be

$$\text{PV}_{combined} \;=\; \frac{\$105}{1 + 5\%} + \frac{\$11}{1 + 15\%} \approx \$109.57$$

$$\text{PV}_{combined} \;=\; \text{PV}_{old} + \text{PV}_{new}$$

This is 43 cents less than the original value of $100 plus the $10 acquisition cost of the new project. Taking the project has made the *old* owners 43 cents poorer.

Of course, not all mergers are driven by such mistakes. Contrary to the perfect CAPM world, it is not always true in the real world that mergers *never* add value on the cost-of-capital side. If capital markets are not as efficient for small firms as they are for large firms, it would be possible for a large acquirer to create value. For example, if a target previously had no access to a perfect capital market, then the cost of capital to the target can change when it is acquired. The correct cost of capital for valuing the acquisition (the target), however, is still *neither* the cost of capital of the acquirer *nor* the blended post-acquisition cost of capital of the firm. Instead, the correct cost of capital then is the rate that is appropriate for the target's projects, given the "now ordinary" access to capital markets. For example, if an entrepreneur inventor of holographic displays previously had faced a cost of capital of, say, 303%, primarily due to access only to personal credit card and credit-shark financing, and if this inventor's business is purchased by IBM with its cost of capital of 6.5% (market beta of 1.5), the proper cost of capital is neither IBM's (market beta–based) cost nor a blended average between 303% and 6.5%. Instead, if part of IBM, the holographic project division should be evaluated at a cost of capital that is appropriate for projects of the market beta risk class "holographic display projects." This can add value relative to the 303% earlier cost of capital. (Of course, there are also many examples of large corporations that have destroyed all innovativeness and thereby all value in small companies that they had taken over.)

> Real-world exception: If the capital market for the target is inefficient, the act of acquisition can create value.

> ➤ *Entrepreneurial finance, Sect. 10.5, Pg.269.*

When Acquiring Another Project

It is important for you to realize that not only firms to be acquired, but also smaller projects themselves, consist of components with different market betas, which therefore have different costs of capital. For example, when firms keep cash on hand in Treasuries, such investments have a zero market beta, which is lower than the beta for the firms' other projects. These bonds should not need to earn the same expected rate of return as investments in the firm's risky projects. (The presence of this cash in the firm lowers the average beta of the firm and thus the average cost of capital for the firm by the just-appropriate amount.)

> Projects must be discounted by their own market betas.

Here is another application, which shows how you can decompose projects into categories with different costs of capital: Assume that you consider purchasing a rocket to launch a telecom satellite next year. It would take you 1 year to build the rocket, at which point you would have to pay $80 million. Then you launch it. If the rocket fails (50% chance), then your investment will be lost. If the rocket succeeds, the satellite will produce a revenue stream with an appropriate beta of 2, beginning immediately. (Telecom revenues tend to have a high covariance with the market.) The telecom's expected cash flows will be $20 million *forever*. Assume that the risk-free rate is 3% per year and the market equity premium is 5%.

> A project can have components that require one cost of capital, and other components (even contingent ones) that require another cost of capital.

The correct solution is to think of the rocket as one project and of the telecom revenues as another. The rocket project has only idiosyncratic risk; therefore, its beta is close to zero, and its discount factor is just about the risk-free rate of return of 3%. The rocket value (in millions of dollars today) is

> The solution to this multi-cost-of-capital problem.

$$PV_{rocket} = \frac{-\$80}{1 + 3\%} \approx -\$77.7$$

You can think of this as the cost of storing the $80 million in Treasuries until you are ready to proceed to your second project. The telecom revenues, however, are a risky perpetuity. With a beta of 2, their cash flows should be discounted at $3\% + 5\% \cdot 2 = 13\%$— and these flows appear with a 50-50 probability only. Therefore,

$$\text{PV}_{\text{telecom}} = \frac{\mathcal{E}(\text{ Telecom Cash Flows })}{\mathcal{E}(\text{ r}_{\text{telecom discount rate}})} = \frac{50\% \cdot \$20}{13\%} \approx \$76.9$$

Consequently, the combined project has an NPV of about –$1 million. If you had mistakenly discounted the rocket's $80 million cost by the same 13%, you would have mistakenly valued it at $-\$80/1.13 + \$76.9 \approx +\$6.1$ million.

Q 12.7. Some companies believe they can use the blended post-acquisition cost of capital as the appropriate discount rate. However, this also leads to incorrect decisions. Let's explore this in the context of the example in the text: The risk-free rate is 3%, the equity premium is 4%, and the old firm is worth $100 and has a market beta of 0.5. The new project costs $10, is expected to pay off $11 next year, and has a beta of 3.

1. What is the value of the new project, discounted at its true cost of capital, 15%?

2. What is the weight of the new project in the firm? (Assume that the combined firm value is around $109.48.)

3. What is the beta of the overall (combined) firm?

4. Use this beta to compute the combined cost of capital.

5. Will the firm take this project? (Use an IRR analysis.)

6. If the firm takes the project, what will the firm's value be?

Differential Costs of Capital—Theory and Practice

In practice, a good number of firms do not use project-specific costs of capital.

➤ *2001 CFO survey, Sect. 4.5, Pg. 76.*

It is indisputably the case that projects must be discounted by their project-specific costs of capital. Yet Graham and Harvey found in their 2001 survey that just about half of surveyed CFOs *always*—and *incorrectly*—used the firm's overall cost of capital rather than the project-specific cost of capital! And even fewer CFOs correctly discounted cash flows of different riskiness within projects. The easy conclusion is that CFOs are ignorant—and many CFOs may indeed use a uniform cost of capital simply because they are ignorant.

A possible reason: Finding project costs of capital may just be too difficult. Intuitive methods anchoring on the firm's cost of capital may work better than formal methods.

➤ *CAPM accuracy?, Sect. 9.5, Pg. 227.*

However, even some intelligent CFOs use the same discount rate quite deliberately on many different types of projects. Why? You already know that it can be difficult to estimate the appropriate cost of capital correctly. In theory, the CAPM works perfectly. In practice, it does not. In theory, you know the expected equity premium input. In practice, you are just guessing. In theory, you know the market beta of all your projects. In practice, you may not.

1. Even the historical betas of publicly traded corporations are not entirely reliable and indicative of the future. Different estimation methods can come up with different numbers. This is why you may want to use the average market betas of similar, publicly traded companies or the market beta of an entire industry. But many of your projects may be so idiosyncratic, so unusual, or in such far-away locales, that no comparable may seem particularly suitable.

2. You could try to estimate your own market beta. To do so, you would need a time series of historical project values, not just historical project cash flows. This is because you cannot rely on historical cash flow variation as a substitute for historical value variation. You already know that the market values themselves are the present discounted values of *all* future cash flows, not just the present discounted value of just one period's cash flow.

   Here is an example of how this can go awry. Consider a firm whose cash flows are perfectly known. Therefore, its appropriate true discount rate would be close to the risk-free rate. However, if its cash flows occur only every other month ($200, $0, $200,...), this firm would have infinite monthly cash flow volatility (–100% followed by +∞%). Its percent changes in cash flows would not be indicative of its value-based rates of return. Plus, almost surely, it would have an extreme market beta estimate, indicating a wrong cost of capital. In order to estimate your market beta, you would need to somehow obtain a time series of estimated market values from the known time series of cash flows. Of course, you already know that it is difficult to estimate one market value for your firm—but estimating a time series of how this market value changes every month is entirely beyond anyone's capability. (When only cash flows [but not market values] are known, your estimates must necessarily be less accurate. The best way to estimate an appropriate cost of capital relies on the certainty equivalence formula explained in Section App.9.A (Companion).)

3. Many firms may not have *any* historical experience that you can use, not just for market values, but even for cash flows. There would be nothing you could verifiably and credibly use to estimate in the first place.

➤ *Certainty equivalence,* Sect. App.9.A (Companion), *Pg.≈49.*

In addition, you have not even yet considered such issues as the influence of liquidity and tax premiums on your cost of capital. Quite simply, you must be aware of the painful reality that our methods for estimating the cost of capital are usually just not as robust as we would like them to be.

➤ *Imperfect markets premiums,* Sect. 10.6, *Pg.270.*

Together, your uncertainties distort not only your overall corporate cost-of-capital estimates, but also your relative cost of capital estimates across different projects. Consequently, the problem with assigning different costs of capital to different projects may now become one of disagreement. Division managers can argue endlessly about why their projects should be assigned a lower cost of capital. Is this how you want your division managers to spend their time? And do you want your managers to play revenue games? Managers could even shift revenues from weeks in which the stock market performed well into weeks in which the stock market performed poorly in order to produce a lower market beta. The cost-of-capital estimate itself then becomes a pawn in the game of agency conflict and response—all managers would like to convince themselves and others that a low cost of capital for their own divisions is best. What the

Flexible costs of capital can cause endless debate and worsen agency conflicts.

overall corporation would like to have in order to suppress such "gaming of the system" would be immutable good estimates of the cost of capital *for each division and potential project* that no one can argue about. In the reality of corporate politics, however, it may be easier to commit to one-and-the-same immutable cost of capital *for all projects* than it would be to have different costs of capital for each division and project. This is not to argue that this one cost of capital is necessarily a good system, but just that there are cases in which having *one* systemwide cost of capital may be a necessary evil.

How Bad Are Mistakes?

Do Projects Really Need Their Own Costs of Capital?

Does every project really need its own cost of capital? Let's not miss the forest here. Yes, in theory, each component must be discounted at its own discount rate if you want to get the value (and incentives) right. However, in practice, if you want to value each paper clip by its own cost of capital, you will never come up with a reasonable firm value—you will lose the forest among the trees. You need to keep your perspective as to what reasonable and unreasonable errors are. The question is one of magnitude: If you are acquiring a totally different company or project, with a vastly different cost of capital, and this project will be a significant fraction of the firm, then the choice of cost of capital matters and you should differentiate. However, if you are valuing a project that is uncertain, the project is relatively small, and its cost of capital is reasonably similar to your overall cost of capital, you can probably live with some error. It all depends—your mileage may vary!

IMPORTANT

- Theoretically, all projects must be discounted by their own costs of capital, and not by the firm's overall cost of capital.

- Practically, the effort involved and the "gaming" by division managers prevent you from discounting every project—every paper clip—by its own cost of capital.

It is up to you to determine when it is important to work with different costs of capital and when it is better to use just one cost of capital.

12.4 The Economics of Project Interactions

An example of projects whose cash flows are not independent. In fact, they "interact."

If projects are independent, you have the luxury to consider them in isolation. You can compute separately the costs and benefits necessary to make a decision whether to accept or reject each project. However, in the real world, projects are not always independent. Let's assume that you are the only person who can service a market and that you assess your potential profits in different states to be \$120,000 in NY, \$60,000 in CA and \$40,000 in RI *if* you enter only one of them. However, it may cost an extra \$70,000 to develop states on different coasts simultaneously, but the cost of developing two nearby markets may be sharable among neighboring states. For example, say that the potential profit is not $160,000 but $200,000 if you develop NY and RI. So, how do you select the best set of projects? (You could think about negative consequences, too. For example, if your best reseller in CT threatens to withdraw business if you develop either NY or RI [and even more if you develop both], you would have to figure this revenue loss into developing these two states.)

The ultimate project selection rule: Consider all possible project combinations and select the combination of projects that gives the highest overall NPV.

IMPORTANT

Optimal project selection is easier said than done. It is easy for the basic example with these three states (take NY and RI, skip CA), but this is rarely the case. For two projects at a time, there are usually only 2^2 options to consider: take neither, take one, take the other, or take both. But the complexity quickly explodes when there are more projects. For three projects, there are $2^3 = 8$ options. For four projects, there are 16 options. For 10 projects, there are about a thousand options. For 20 projects, there are over a million options. For 50 states, there are quadrillions. And even the simplest corporate projects can easily involve hundreds of decisions that have to be made. Mathematically, it is an impossible task to find the perfect combination.

There are too many possible action choices in the real world to evaluate (to compute NPV for). You need rules and heuristics!

To help you determine which projects to take, you need to find some rules that help you make a decision. Such rules of thumb are called **heuristics**–that is, rules that simplify your decisions even if they are not always correct. One common heuristic algorithm is to consider project combinations, one at a time. Start with the project combination that would give you the highest NPV if you were only allowed to take two projects (one pair from a set of many different projects). For example, start with the state that has the highest profit. There are only 50 of them. Now consider adding each state. There are only 49 possible choices. Then take this pair as fixed, that is, treat it as a single project. Now see which of the remaining 48 states adds the most value to your existing pair. Continue until adding the best remaining project no longer increases value. Computer scientists call this the greedy algorithm. It is a good heuristic, because it drastically cuts down the possible project combinations to consider and usually gives a pretty good set of projects. There are many possible enhancements to this algorithm, such as forward and backward iterations, in which one considers replacing one project at a time with every other option. Full-fledged algorithms and combinatorial enhancements that guarantee optimal choice are really the domain of computer science and operations research, not of finance. Yet many of these algorithms have been shown to require more time than the duration of the universe, unless you make simplifications that distort the business problem so much that the results are likely no longer trustworthy. Fortunately, finance is in the domain of economics, and economics can help simplify the project selection problem.

The "greedy" heuristic: Always take the next most profitable project.

Project Pairs

Project combinations can be classified into positive, zero, and negative interaction combinations.

Considering projects in pairs is not only common practice, but also clarifies many economic issues. With two projects, you can decompose the total net present value into three terms:

$$\text{Overall NPV} = \text{NPV Project 1} + \text{NPV Project 2} + \text{NPV Interactions}$$

For example, the original two state project (NY+RI) project choice yielded

$$\$200,000 \quad = \$120,000 \quad + \quad \$40,000 \quad + \quad (\$40,000)$$

NY+RI   NY   RI   NY RI Interaction

The final term reflects the interaction of the two projects. It suggests that you can classify project combinations into one of three different categories:

1. Projects with zero interactions

2. Projects with positive interactions

3. Projects with negative interactions

An **interaction** is also sometimes called an **externality** in economics, because one project has an external influence on another project—sometimes imposing external costs, and sometimes providing external benefits. Let's consider these three cases separately.

Zero Project Interactions

Project independence is the most common case. It allows the simplest decision making.

Most projects in this world are **independent**—they have no mutual interactions. For example, for Walmart, opening a mall in Japan probably has no effect on opening a warehouse in Canada. Independent project payoffs permit the separate evaluation of each project. This makes decision making much easier:

- Taking any positive-NPV project increases firm value.

- Taking a zero-NPV project leaves firm value unchanged.

- Taking any negative-NPV project decreases firm value.

If projects are independent, then the project interaction term is zero, and project NPVs are additive. Project independence makes decisions a lot easier: For 20 projects, only 20 independent decisions (accept or reject) have to be made, not a million.

IMPORTANT

> You can simply add the project NPVs of independent projects.

Positive Project Interactions

Positive interactions mean that the sum of the parts is worth more than the parts individually. If one project has a positive influence on the NPV of another project, you cannot value it without taking into account this positive influence. For example, think of a new product as one project and of an advertising campaign as another. The advertising campaign project is of lesser use without the product, and the product is of lesser use without the advertising campaign. You must consider creating a product and an advertising campaign together. Such positive externalities are even more plentiful in smaller decisions. For example, a computer keyboard is less useful without a computer, and a computer is less useful without a keyboard. In fact, some projects or products only make sense if purchased together. In this case, producers may bundle them together and/or purchasers may only buy them as bundles.

In many cases, what makes a project a project in the firm's mind is often the indivisibility of its components.

In the corporate context, investment in *infrastructure* is another classic example of positive project interactions. For example, building a road, hiring a security firm, or laying a fast Internet connection could enhance the values of many divisions simultaneously. The firm should factor in the increase in value to *all* divisions when deciding on how much infrastructure to add.

Infrastructure can benefit many different projects.

Don't take positive externalities too lightly: On a philosophical basis, positive project interactions are the reason why firms exist in the first place. If there were no cost savings to having all resources combined in the firm, all of us could work as individuals and dispense with firms altogether.

Positive externalities are why firms exist to begin with.

> When deciding whether to take a project, you must credit all positive interactions to the project. The overall NPV is higher than the individual project NPVs alone.

IMPORTANT

Internal conflict and cost allocation procedures (discussed further as "agency conflicts" below) often hinder corporations from taking advantage of many positive externalities. For example, in real life, your division managers might argue that they should not be charged for the Internet connection, because they did not request it and therefore do not really need it (even if it were to increase their divisions' values). After all, division managers would prefer getting the Internet for free from the company instead of paying for it out of their own divisional budgets.

Agency problems often prevent properly crediting projects with all their contributions.

Nowadays, managers who want to acquire other companies usually claim the presence of large positive externalities. **Synergies** are the managerial term for positive externalities between an acquirer and a potential acquisition target. It has become an important managerial buzzword. For example, in the 2001 acquisition of Compaq by Hewlett-Packard, HP touted synergies of $2.5 billion—most from cutting employees. Of course, whether enough synergies are ever realized to outweigh the acquisition costs is always another question.

Another name for positive externalities: synergies.

➤ *Mergers and acquisitions,* Sect. 23.C (Companion), Pg.≈205.

Negative Project Interactions

Negative interactions exist when taking one project decreases the value of another project.

Negative interactions mean that the sum of the parts is worth less than the parts individually. In this case, projects have negative influences on one another and thereby decrease one another's value. Economists sometimes call negative externalities **diseconomies of scale**. Here are a few examples.

Pollution and congestion: Think of an airline company with two divisions, but only one maintenance facility. One division handles cargo; the other handles passengers. If the cargo division wants to expand, it will use more of the maintenance capacity. This will leave the passenger division with longer service waiting times. In the extreme, the extra delays may cost the passenger division more than the extra profits that the expanded cargo operation adds.

Cannibalization: If a new Apple computer can produce $100,000 in NPV compared to an older Windows machine that only produces $70,000 in NPV, how should you credit the Apple machine? The answer is that the Apple would eliminate the positive cash flows produced by the existing Windows machine, so the cash flow of the project "replace Windows with Apple" is only $30,000: the $100,000 minus the $70,000 that the now-unused Windows machine would have produced. Be careful what you consider cannibalization, though. For example, in the 1970s, IBM did not produce personal computers, fearful of cannibalizing its mainframe computer business. IBM's mistake was that it did not realize that other computer manufacturers were able to step in and eat much of IBM's mainframe business for themselves. Put differently, IBM had not realized that the present value of its mainframe business's future cash flows had already changed with the advent of new technology in the competitive market that it was in.

Bureaucratization and internal conflict: If more projects are adopted, project management may find it increasingly difficult to make good decisions in a reasonable time frame. This may require more cumbersome bureaucracy and reduce cash flows for all other divisions. A good example of bureaucratic destruction of projects can be found on Moishe Lettvin's blog (Google is your friend). A programmer who worked for Microsoft for 7 years, he describes how it took between 24 and 43 people, separated by six layers of management, over a year just to talk about the Windows boot menu—and no one really knew who had the power to make the final decision.

Resource exhaustion: Perhaps the most common source of negative externalities—and one that is often underestimated—is **limited attention span**. Management can pay only so much attention to so many different issues. An extra project distracts from the attention previously received by existing projects. There are many anecdotal examples of overstretched attention spans. The most recent example of failed attention management may be the 2007 credit collapse, which left many investment banks with huge losses, and which ultimately cost the CEOs of Merrill Lynch, Citigroup, and others their jobs. Most of these CEOs did not even know what their firms' holdings and exposures were. They had to correct their own estimates multiple times, as they themselves learned only after the fact what their firms had actually invested in.

Although costs always include opportunity costs, in the case of negative project externalities these opportunity costs are more obvious. If your project cannibalizes another project or requires more attention, it's clearly an opportunity cost.

> When deciding whether to take a project, charge all negative interactions to the project. Because of these negative interactions, the overall NPV will be lower than the individual project NPVs alone.

IMPORTANT

Again, as in the case of positive externalities, agency problems and cost allocation systems often prevent proper accounting for negative externalities in the real world. Whatever division created the negative externality will argue that it is not its problem and that the complaining division overstates the problem. Clearly, companies that are better at overcoming these issues will end up being more profitable.

Again, agency problems often prevent properly crediting projects for all their detractions.

Q 12.8. Why is it so convenient to value projects that have zero externalities with one another?

Q 12.9. A company must decide if it should move division A to a new location. If division A moves, it will be housed in a new building that reduces its operating costs by $10,000 per year forever. The new building costs $120,000. Moving division A allows division B to expand within the old factory. This enables B to increase its profitability by $3,000 per year forever. If the discount rate is 10%, should division A move?

Q 12.10. A firm can purchase a new punch press for $10,000. The new press will allow the firm to enter the widget industry, thereby earning $2,000 per year in profits forever. However, the punch press will displace several screw machines that produce $1,500 per year in profits. If the interest rate is 10%, should the new punch press be purchased?

12.5 Evaluating Projects Incrementally

Usually, managers do not make the decision for all interacting projects simultaneously. Instead, many projects are already in place. Although existing projects should also constantly be evaluated in an ideal world, the manager often has to make a decision about adding or not adding a single new project (or project complex) in the real world. For practical purposes, the old projects are often present, given, and unalterable. The new project may have positive or negative externalities on other existing projects, and the question is how best to decide whether to take it or not. This simplifies the decision even further: The question is now only whether the new project adds or subtracts value from the total. In this case, economists use the concept of decision **on the margin**— holding the existing project structure as is, what is the *additional* contribution of the new project?

Capital budgeting rule for a scenario in which you can either take or not take one extra project. The rest stays in place.

You can come to the
right decision by using
the marginal method,
too.
Return to the U.S. state example. Let's work it via the method of contributions on the margin. Naturally, we should arrive at the same conclusion:

- If you have already committed to RI, you would earn only $40,000. Adding NY would get you to $200,000. Thus, entering NY would bring marginal benefits of $160,000 (and not $120,000).

- If you have already committed to NY, you would earn only $120,000. Adding RI would get you to $200,000. Thus, entering RI would bring marginal benefits of $80,000 (and not $40,000).

Note that having one of the states committed increases the marginal value of the other state that you should use in your calculations.

IMPORTANT

> - The decision on whether to take one additional project should be made based on the following rule:
>
> $$\text{Accept New Project If:} \quad \begin{array}{c}\text{Total Firm NPV with}\\\text{New Project}\end{array} > \begin{array}{c}\text{Total Firm NPV without}\\\text{New Project}\end{array}$$
>
> - This means that the single new project should be credited with any value increase or value decrease that it confers on other projects.
>
> - When considering a project on the margin (i.e., extra), credit/charge to this project all externalities that this project conveys onto the existing firm.
>
> - Everything else equal, projects with positive externalities on the rest of the firm have higher marginal benefits than do projects with negative externalities.

The big advantage of
the marginal method
is its solvability when
there are many, many
choices—possibly
infinitely many.
Although the marginal perspective on costs and benefits has also worked for our discrete "yes or no" projects, it becomes a lot more useful when you consider projects of which you can take a little more or a little less. (In fact, enumerating all possible combinations is no longer feasible.) Marginal thinking also helps you to understand economies of scale, sunk costs, overhead allocation, and space capacity. The marginal perspective on costs and benefits is particularly useful when it comes to projects that are not just "yes or no" but are projects of which you can take a varying amount—more or less of the project. With rare exceptions, the incremental way of thinking is the only way to make sense out of real-world complexity.

Q 12.11. A notebook computer costs $2,500; a desktop computer costs $1,500. If you buy either the notebook or the desktop, you can increase your productivity to $9,000. If you buy both, you can increase your productivity to $11,000. (There is no time-value dimension to your choice.) Assume there is no computer resale market or alternative use for a computer.

1. If you do not own either, should you buy the notebook, the desktop, both, or neither?

2. If you own the notebook, should you buy the desktop? What are the marginal costs and benefits?

3. If you own the desktop, should you buy the notebook? What are the marginal costs and benefits?

Economies of Scale

Consider an example in which there are **economies of scale**—the more airplanes you build, the lower your average per-airplane production cost will be (in millions):

$$\text{Average Cost per Airplane} = \$4 + \frac{\$10}{\text{Number of Airplanes} + 1}$$

An example in which your production function is continuous and exhibits economies of scale.

This states that it costs $\$4 + \$10/(1+1) = \$9$ million to produce 1 airplane. Producing 100 airplanes costs you $\$4 + \$10/(100+1) \approx \$4.10$ million per airplane. Again, let's assume that the interest rate is zero, so you do not need to discount.

Now say that you are currently selling 4 airplanes domestically, each for a price of $8 million. Your firm's net value is

Should you expand production?

$$\begin{array}{c}\text{Total Net Value} \\ \text{with 4 Airplanes}\end{array} = 4 \cdot \$8 - 4 \cdot \left[\$4 + \frac{\$10}{4+1}\right] = \$32 - \$24 = \$8 \quad (12.1)$$

Your big decision now is whether you should expand internationally. It would cost you $16 million to open a foreign sales office, but doing so would sell another 5 airplanes at the same $8 million per-airplane price. Should you expand?

With 9 airplanes in production, your average cost would fall to $\$4 + \$10/10 = \$5$ million per airplane. This means that 5 airplanes would cost only $25 million to build now, and bring in $5 \cdot \$8 = \$40$ million. The value of your foreign office would therefore be

An average cost calculation tells you not to expand.

$$\text{Value of Foreign Office} = 5 \cdot \$8 \quad - \quad 5 \cdot \$5 \quad - \quad \$16 \quad = \text{-}\$1$$

$$\text{Value} \qquad = \text{Gross Sales} - \text{Average Cost} - \text{Start-Up Cost}$$

This calculation suggests that you should not expand internationally.

Unfortunately, this calculation is wrong. To see this, compute your *total* net value if you open the foreign office. Your 9 airplanes generate sales of $72 million. Subtract your production costs of $9 \cdot \$5 = \$45$ million and your opening costs of $16 million. This means that your firm would be worth

Wrong! The reason is that the foreign sales office also lowers the cost of domestic production!

$$\text{Total Net Value with 9 Airplanes} = 9 \cdot \$8 - 9 \cdot \$5 - \$16 = \$11 \quad (12.2)$$

This is more than the $8 million that you earned without the foreign office. This is the correct calculation. It tells you that you should expand internationally, because this expansion will increase your net value by $3 million.

The difference between the right and the wrong calculation is that your foreign office has one additional marginal benefit that the first calculation overlooked: Foreign sales also reduce the average production cost of your domestic production. This cost reduction is a positive externality that you must credit to your foreign office. If you do not, you are throwing away $3 million.

You must credit the foreign office with any domestic cost reductions.

Thinking in terms of marginal costs exposes the economies of scale.

It is often more intuitive to think of projects such as airplanes in terms of marginal costs and benefits. The extra marginal cost of each airplane changes airplane by airplane—it is the difference in total costs of all airplanes:

Planes	Average	Total	Marginal	Planes	Average	Total	Marginal
1	$9.00	$9.00	$9.000	6	$5.43	$32.57	$4.238
2	$7.33	$14.67	$5.667	7	$5.25	$36.75	$4.179
3	$6.50	$19.50	$4.833	8	$5.11	$40.89	$4.139
4	$6.00	$24.00	$4.500	9	$5.00	$45.00	$4.111
5	$5.67	$28.33	$4.333	10	$4.91	$49.09	$4.091

If you go from 4 to 9 airplanes, your production creates extra marginal costs of $4.333 + $4.238 + $4.179 + $4.139 + $4.111 = 21 (million). There is an additional marginal cost of $16 million to open the foreign office. The total marginal cost is therefore $37 million. The marginal benefit of 5 extra airplanes is $40 million. Therefore, your foreign sales office creates marginal value of $40 - $37 = 3 million. This is exactly the difference between $8 million from Formula 12.1 and $11 million from Formula 12.2. Thinking in terms of marginal costs and benefits is just a different and sometimes more convenient way to compare overall project values.

Economies of scale are often responsible for the big corporate success stories of our time.

Economies of scale (decreasing marginal costs) are often responsible for the biggest corporate success stories. For example, Wal-Mart and Dell have managed not only to use their scales to negotiate considerable supplier discounts, but they have also created inventory and distribution systems that allow them to spread their fixed costs very efficiently over the large quantities of goods they sell. They have the lowest costs and highest industry inventory turnover rates—two factors that allow them to benefit tremendously from their economies of scale. Similarly, Microsoft enjoys economies of scale—with a large fixed cost and almost zero variable cost, Microsoft can swamp the planet with copies of Windows. No commercial alternative can compete—Microsoft can always drop its price low enough to drive its competitor out of business. The socially optimal number of operating-systems software companies is very small and may even be just one—it is what economists call a **natural monopoly**. If you think of the economy as one big firm, you would not want to incur the same huge fixed software-development cost twice. The same applies to utilities: You would not want two types of cable strung to everyone's house, two types of telephone lines, and two types of power lines. But companies with monopolies can also hurt the economy: They will want to charge higher prices to exploit their monopoly powers. Society has therefore often found it advantageous to regulate monopolists. Unfortunately, the regulatory agencies are themselves often "captured" by the companies that they are supposed to regulate, which can sometimes hurt the economy even more than the monopolies themselves. There are no easy and obvious solutions.

Negative economies of scale work alike.

Of course, there are also plenty of examples in which marginal costs are not decreasing, but increasing, with the number of items produced. In such cases, you must charge the diseconomies of scale to the new division you are adding. If you do not, you will be inclined to overexpand and thereby reduce your firm's overall value.

Q 12.12. The average production cost per good is estimated at $5 + $15/(x + 1)$. The firm can currently sell 10 units at $20 per unit.

1. What is the current total profit of the firm?

2. How much should the firm value the opportunity to sell one extra good (i.e., #11) to a new vendor? In other words, what is the marginal cost of selling one extra good?

3. A new vendor offers to pay $19 for one unit. However, your other existing vendors would find out and demand the same price. What is the marginal cost and benefit of signing up this new vendor now? Should you sign up this new vendor?

Q 12.13. A firm faces diseconomies of scale in both production and sales. It can produce goods for an average per-unit cost of $5 + (Q \cdot $1 + $20)/100$, where Q is the number of units. For example, to produce 10 goods would cost $10 \cdot ($5 + $30/100) = 53. The market price per good is $7 - Q \cdot $1/100$. So, sales of 10 goods would generate $10 \cdot ($7 - $10/100) = 69 in gross revenues. Use a spreadsheet to answer the following questions.

1. How many items should the firm produce?

2. What are the average per-unit gross sales at this point?

3. What is the average per-unit production cost at this point?

4. What are the average per-unit net sales (gross minus cost) at this point?

5. What are the marginal per-unit sales at this point?

6. What is the marginal per-unit cost at this point?

7. What is the marginal per-unit net change at this point?

8. If your average per unit net change at this point is positive, should you expand production? Why?

Sunk Costs

Sunk costs cannot be altered or reversed and thus should not enter into your current decisions.

An example of how first the capital investment becomes sunk, and then how the produced goods themselves become sunk.

Sunk costs are, in a sense, the opposite of marginal costs. A **sunk cost** is an incurred cost that cannot be altered or reversed. It is a done deal and therefore should not enter into your decisions today. It is what it is.

For example, consider circuit board production—a very competitive industry. If you have just completed a circuit board factory for $1 billion, it is a sunk cost. What matters now is *not* that you spent $1 billion, but how much the production of each circuit board costs. Having invested $1 billion is irrelevant. What remains relevant is that the presence of the factory makes the marginal cost of production of circuit boards very cheap. It is only this marginal cost that matters when you decide whether or not to produce circuit boards. If the marginal board production cost is $100 each, but you can only sell them for $90 each, then you should not build boards, regardless of how much you spent on the factory. Though tempting, the logic of "we have spent $1 billion, so we may as well put it to use" is just plain wrong. Now, assume that the market price for boards is $180, so you go ahead and manufacture 1 million boards at a cost of $100 each. Alas, your production run has just finished, and the price of boards—contrary to everyone's best expectations—has dropped from $180 each to $10 each. At this point, the board production cost is sunk, too. Whether the boards cost you $100 to manufacture or $1 to manufacture is irrelevant. The cost of the production run is sunk. If boards now sell at $10 each, assuming you cannot store them, you should sell them for $10 each. Virtually all supply costs eventually become sunk costs, and all that matters when you want to sell a completed product is the demand for the product.

Sunk costs are everywhere!

Sunk costs are everywhere. With the passage of time, virtually all decisions at some point become irrevocable and thus sunk. The examples are so abundant that you can even find whole books about them. Allan Teger's book *Too Much Invested to Quit* describes investments such as the continuing Concorde airplane development even after it had already become clear that it would never become profitable.

Time is a good proxy for what is sunk, but it may not be the deciding factor.

One more note—time itself often, but not always, decides on what is sunk or not. Contracts may allow you to undo things that happened in the past (thereby converting a sunk cost into a cost about which you still can make decisions), or they may bind you irrevocably to things that will happen in the future.

IMPORTANT

> A sunk cost has no cost contribution on the margin. It should therefore be ignored.

Exasperation—letting sunk costs frustrate you and misinterpret your marginal costs and benefits.

The flip side of not ignoring sunk costs and refusing to throw in the towel is "exasperation"—though it can come about through compartmentalization (explained in Section 12.7). It can occur when you think that you have already put too much money into the project, and rather than spend any more, you throw in the towel. You just consider your budget to be exhausted and you abandon the project, rather than doing the right thing (which would be to finish it).

Overhead Allocation

A closely related mistake is to forget that "overhead" is often a sunk cost. By definition, overhead is not a marginal cost but something that has been incurred already and is allocated to departments. For example, assume your firm has spent $500,000 on a computer that is currently idle half the time. It serves only one division. Assume that another division can take an additional project that produces $60,000 in net present value but will consume 20% of the computer's time. Should your firm take this project? If 20% of the cost of the computer is allocated to this new project (i.e., $20\% \cdot \$500,000 = \$100,000$), the net present value of the new project would appear to be −$40,000. But the correct decision process is not to allocate the existing overhead as a cost to divisions. The $500,000 on overhead has already been spent. The computer is a sunk cost—assuming that it really would sit idle otherwise and find no better purpose. It may seem unfair to have charged only the original division for the computer and exempt the other opportunistic divisions. Yet taking this additional project will produce $60,000 in profits without any additional cost—clearly, a good thing. Everyone who has worked in a corporation can recite plenty of examples in which overhead allocation has killed otherwise profitable projects.

Allocating already existing overhead budget to a project (i.e., adding it to the new project's cost) is a common real-world example of bad project valuation and decision making.

Real-World Dilemmas in Allocating Spare Capacity

Limited capacity is a subject that is closely related to overhead allocation. For example, consider building or buying corporate car garages that can park 300 cars for $1.5 million per garage. As CEO, you have to make choices about how many garages you want to have and how you should charge your corporate divisions for parking spots. Of course, having a garage makes owning corporate cars more profitable, because they will not deteriorate as much. A new garage offers a positive externality on the project "corporate cars."

If capacity is otherwise unusable, it should have a zero price.

Here is a bad solution to your problem: Charge users the average cost of building the garage. For example, you may calculate that about 150 cars from your corporate divisions would volunteer to use it, then divide the cost of $1.5 million by 150, and allow these divisions to buy spots at $10,000 each (which may be equivalent to, say, $60 rent per month). First, you may run into the standard overhead allocation problem. You may find that 75 of the 150 cars may not even take you up on the offer, and you may have to increase the rate to $120 per month. At this rate, more may jump ship, and you may end up with no cars wanting to go in. Second, even if you get all 150 cars to sign up, you still end up with another 150 empty spots—spots that could be used to park other, older corporate cars. You would never have built a garage just for them, but it would make sense to put them into the existing garage if it is otherwise empty. The marginal cost of adding one more old car would be zero. Is this how you should price parking spots?

Average cost allocation—an empty parking spot problem.

If you charge zero to the division for older cars, how would your other divisions with newer cars, who are still paying for their parking spots, feel? Should these divisions be charged then? After all, the marginal cost of their new cars, given that the garage is already built, is also zero. These are internal cost allocation issues that inevitably bring out the worst in discussions among corporate division managers. Everyone will claim

Should you charge your new division? Should you charge anyone?

Often you do not have easy, smooth margins. And you face more questions—these are difficult real-world dilemmas.

that it should be the other party that should pay more of the cost.

One reason why this is so difficult is that you can only add capacity in discrete chunks. And there is a time dimension, too. Should you really charge zero for parking corporate cars if you suspect that the unused capacity will not remain unused forever? What if another division comes along that wants to rent the 150 currently unused garage spaces in the future? Do you then kick out all the older cars that you gave spots to for free (or a very low price)? How should you charge this new division if it wants to rent 160 spaces? Should you give it the 150 remaining unused parking spots for free and build a new garage for the extra 10 cars? Presuming that garages can only be built in increments of 300 parking spots each, should you build another 300-car garage? Should this new division pay for the new garage, or should the divisions that held the original 150 spots pay a part of this or relinquish some of their original spots? If you ask the new division to pay, should it get a refund if some of the 290 spots are eventually rented out? Should you charge parking fees for these 290 spots? Tough questions.

Here is how to think about the parking allocation in terms of margins.

Usually, you should think in terms of the relevant marginal benefits and costs. But this does not work well if capacity can only be added in large discrete chunks. In that case, the extra cost of just one more parking spot is either zero or $1.5 million. If you charge marginal cost, demand also may not be marginal. At an internal price of zero, you will likely have a large number of users—more than the garage can accommodate. At a price of $1.5 million, no user will want to pay for the garage. You can think of less extreme schemes, but the basic problem is intrinsically the discreteness of capacity.

Advice: Use a market-pricing system if you can, to push the decision down to the divisions themselves. But do not try to maximize garage profits.

Remarkably, there are clear answers as to how you should solve your two dilemmas:

1. **Pricing of existing capacity:** You should use the magic of the market-price system to allocate your existing capacity. You should set the internal price of each parking spot so that those users who would value the garage the most will want to reserve exactly the 300 spots that are available. Do not set the parking spot price so that the garage generates maximum profits. (If you do, you may find yourself with parking rates that are too high, and cars that are parked on the street while the garage has some unfilled spots.) If there are more existing spots than cars that could benefit from a spot, then you should even set the parking spot price to zero. From an overall corporate perspective, it does not matter how or who you charge—just as long as you get the optimal capacity utilization. To the extent that cost allocation distorts optimal marginal decision making (i.e., that cars that should be in the garage end up not using the garage), it should be avoided.

2. **Building more capacity:** You should build more capacity when the marginal cost of adding the garage of $1.5 million is less than the marginal benefit of parking cars indoors. In principle, this is easy. In practice, this is difficult, because you need to forecast future parking needs.

Note that neither of these two decision rules requires the garage to generate profits by itself. In fact, your goal is to maximize the overall profit of the firm, which is achieved through optimal capacity allocation. It is irrelevant whether this increase comes about through a profitable garage or through more profitable divisions.

Managerial Gaming

Unfortunately, real life is not always so simple. Return to the earlier example of an Internet connection that has a positive influence on all divisions. You know that divisional managers will not want to pay for it if they can enjoy it for free—you cannot rely on them telling you correctly how much they will benefit. Would it solve your problem to charge only divisions that are voluntarily signing up for the Internet connection, and to forcibly exclude those that do not? If you do this, then you could solve the problem of everyone claiming that they do not need the Internet connection. However, you are then stuck with the problem that you may have a lot of unused network capacity that sits around, has zero marginal cost, and could be handed to the nonrequesters at zero cost. This would create more profit for the firm. Of course, if you do this, or even if it is suspected that you will do this, then no division would claim that they need the Internet to begin with, so that they will ultimately get it for free. For some projects, it is not clear whether financial incentives can solve even the first problems—if one of your top scientists has focused decades of her life on exploring Resveratrol as a potential longevity drug, do you really believe this scientist will now tell you if some of her preliminary findings now point towards a non-finding?

It becomes much harder if you do not know the right outcome, so you have to "play games" with your subordinate managers.

➤ *Internet connection example,* Pg.337.

In sum, what makes these problems so difficult in the real world is that as the boss, you often do not know the true marginal benefits and marginal costs, and you end up having to "play games" with your divisional managers to try to make the right decision. Such is real life! And in real life, more often than not, headquarters just mandates Internet usage and charges divisions for it, whether they like it or not. Hopefully, this is also the correct choice from a firmwide value-maximization perspective.

HQ often flies blind.

Q 12.14. A company rents 40,000 square feet of space and is using 30,000 square feet for its present operations. It wishes to add a new division that will use the remaining 10,000 square feet. If it adds the division, equipment will cost $210,000 once, and the operations will generate $50,000 in profits every year. Presently, the office staff costs $160,000 per year. However, the expansion requires a larger staff, bringing costs up to $180,000 per year. If the cost of capital $r = 10\%$, should the firm expand?

12.6 Real Options

There is another valuation issue that you have to consider. It can be even more important than externalities—and more difficult to work out. It is the fact that your ability to change course in the future, depending on the prevailing economic environment in the future, can itself create value. Such flexibility is called a **real option** (or sometimes a **strategic option**). In principle, the valuation of a real option is just a complex variant of the NPV problem. You have to assess all expected cash flows and their costs of capital correctly. In practice, the resulting complications can be so difficult that entire books have been written on this subject. Let me give you a taste of what real options are and how to value them.

A real option is the value of the flexibility to change course in the future.

A Specific Real Options Example

An example of a factory.

A factory costs $3 million to build. It can transform $2 million worth of inputs into 1 million gadgets. If demand is strong, gadgets will sell for $9 each. If demand is weak, gadgets will sell for $1 each. The discount rate is 10%. The expected value of the factory is therefore (in millions)

$$\text{NPV} = -\$3 + \frac{50\% \cdot (\$1 - \$2) + 50\% \cdot (\$9 - \$2)}{1.1} \approx -\$0.273$$

$$\text{NPV} = \text{Factory Cost} + \text{Present Value of Net Sales}$$

You should not undertake this project. Or should you?

Without the real option, you could have calculated the NPV using just the most likely (expected) pricing path.

Take a look at Exhibit 12.1. Without considering real options, there are two possible outcomes:

1. **Weak demand:** The running factory will yield –$1 million in net sales, which turns into –$3.909 million in total net present value.

2. **Strong demand:** The running factory will yield $7 million in net sales, which turns into +$3.364 million in total net present value.

Because both outcomes are equally likely, your loss is the $0.273 million already calculated.

With the real option, you can shut down the factory if there is no demand.

However, if you can shut down the factory when demand is weak, then your factory is worth more. You still get the upside (a full $3.364 million in present value), but you no longer suffer the full –$3.909 million downside. That is, you would still be out the up-front $3 million cost of the factory, but you would at least not produce an extra future loss of $1 million by running it. *With* the real option to shut down when demand is weak, your factory is worth about $50\% \cdot (-\$3) + 50\% \cdot (\$3.364) = +\$0.182$ million. (If you are really clever, you may detect that I am falsely assuming that your cost of capital is still 10%. This may no longer be the case. However, the contribution of your cost-of-capital uncertainty to your valuation is usually much more modest than the contribution of your cash flow uncertainty.)

Uncertainty usually makes real options more valuable!

Remarkably, real options are an instance in finance where you actually like uncertainty in the underlying economic environment. For example, how would you value the project if you could change the sales from the +$1 and +$9 million to $0 and +$10 million? In the bad state, it would not make a difference to you. You would still just shut down the factory and lose $3 million. However, in the good state, you would now earn $8 million next year, not $7 million. Your NPV would therefore go from $0.182 million to $50\% \cdot (-\$3) + 50\% \cdot (\$4.273) \approx +\$0.637$ million.

Family resemblance: This particular real option is like limited liability.

With its real option, this firm is a little similar to a contingent equity claim: *As owner, you can still get the upside, but you do not suffer the full downside.* However, it is not the limited liability that has created this payoff pattern. Instead, it is your managerial flexibility that increases the factory's expected cash flow. Your flexibility means that this factory is well worth building.

➤ *Limited liability, Sect. 6.4, Pg.134.*

Q 12.15. Your factory can either stamp 150,000 CDs at a cost of $5 per CD, or 500,000 CDs at a cost of $8 per CD. If your CD has a hit song, you can can sell it to retailers for $10 per CD. Otherwise, you can only charge $6 per CD. There is a 1-in-10 chance that

Prob	Component	Ignore Real Option Always Run Factory (Dumb NPV)	Recognize Real Option Shut Down if Optimal (Smart NPV)
50% Demand is Weak	Factory, Time 0	−$3 million	−$3 million
	Inputs, Time 1	−$2 million	$0 million
	Sales, Time 1	+$1 million	$0 million
	Net, Time 1	= −$1 million	= $0 million
	⇒ NPV at 10%, Time 0	**−$3.909 million**	**−$3 million**
50% Demand is Strong	Factory, Time 0	−$3 million	−$3 million
	Inputs, Time 1	−$2 million	−$2 million
	Sales, Time 1	+$9 million	+$9 million
	Net, Time 1	= $7 million	= $7 million
	⇒ NPV at 10%, Time 0	**+$3.364 million**	**+$3.364 million**
	Total Net Present Value	**−$0.273 million**	**+$0.182 million**

A. Ignore Real Option

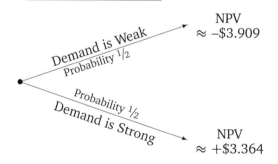

Expected Value: **−$0.273** million

B. Recognize Real Option

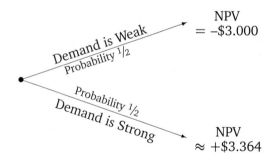

Expected Value: **+$0.182** million

Exhibit 12.1: *A State-Contingent Payoff Table for the Factory.*

your CD will be a hit. You will not find out whether you have a hit until next year, but fortunately this will be before you have to stamp CDs. Your cost of capital is 10% per year. You only have the lease of the factory for next year. There is no production this year.

1. What is the expected selling price per CD?

2. How many CDs should you produce at the expected selling price—that is, if you had to gear the factory for a particular production quantity today?

3. What is the value of your factory if you can decide next year?

4. What is the value of flexibility in this example?

Importance and Difficulty

You cannot work out the project value based on the expected input and output costs. You must work out a scenario analysis in a decision tree.

The reason why real options are so difficult to value is that you get the wrong answer if you are working out the value at the expected (or most likely) inputs. In our example, the expected gross sales were $(50\% \cdot \$9 + 50\% \cdot \$1) = \$5$ million. This was more than the $2 million cost of inputs. Thus, you would operate, which would give you $3 million in expected net sales *next year*. This is not enough to cover the $3 million in up-front factory costs *today*. You would therefore conclude that you should not undertake the factory—a mistake. In effect, in our example, working with the expected inputs is the same as assuming that you would always act the same way in the future, regardless of demand. Instead, the correct way to value a real option is first to consider all possible future demand scenarios, then to determine your own optimal behavior and the resulting cash flows in each scenario, and only finally to compute expectations over all possible scenarios. This is almost always easiest to do in a decision tree, like the one at the bottom of Exhibit 12.1. In management-speak, it is called **scenario analysis**.

IMPORTANT

- The expected value of a project is not the value of the project at its expected value or its expected inputs.

- This means that you cannot value a real option by computing project value in the expected (or most likely) scenario.

- Instead, you must first determine all possible scenarios, then figure out your own behavior and the cash flow this earns in each scenario, and only finally compute the expected net present values over all scenarios.

➤ *Sensitivity analysis, Pg.62.*

Here is what real-world managers tell us they do.

Sensitivity analysis is a close relative of scenario analysis. It means trying out different assumptions to see how sensitive the NPV is, and is usually done in a valuation spreadsheet. If it considers different managerial responses, it becomes in effect a form of scenario analysis. **Simulation analysis** (also called **Monte Carlo simulation**) can be an automated form of sensitivity or scenario analysis. It, too, is sometimes used to value real options. These methods can be simple or complex, and are generally beyond the scope of this book. (More real option valuation techniques are explained in a web chapter, which—you should be warned—is also a difficult chapter.) Valuing real options is so complex that it is not used as often as simpler NPV techniques, but it is also not obscure. In the same survey described in Section 4.5, 27% of surveyed CFOs explicitly value real options. About 52% perform sensitivity analyses and 14% perform simulation analyses.

➤ *CFO valuation method survey, Sect. 4.5, Pg.76.*

The ubiquity and economic importance of real options are unfortunately often matched by the difficulties that arise in estimating their values. They become both economically more important (and more difficult to value) when projects last longer and when there are many possible economic scenarios. You have to figure out what you would do in every possible *future* scenario. Sometimes, this is feasible. If there is only one variable that determines your optimal action, such as one prevailing product price, then the problem can often be broken down in a way that simplifies it. Sometimes, this is infeasible. If your decisions cannot be made based on just one variable, but instead depend in turn on the future or the past, then the complexities become vexing. For example, if it costs money to close and reopen your plant, then your decision to close the plant must also depend on your assessment of how quickly the product price can recover. If there is a good chance of recovery soon and if closing/reopening a factory is expensive, you may take your chances and continue operating your factory even if you incur a small loss. In turn, this means that you may find yourself with an operating or nonoperating plant, depending on the history of past demand, and this can influence what you decide to do in this period, too. With history dependence, even your optimal decision rule itself can be very difficult to work out. In any case, the current product price is no longer the only decision variable that you have to take into consideration, and this makes it a complex problem.

Real options are tough to value. If the optimal decision depends on the past history (and not just the current environment), then this problem becomes even harder.

A final complication is that the presence of a real option can have an influence not only on the expected cash flows but also on the cost of capital. For example, if this real option helps you to avoid losses when the stock market goes down, then your market beta, and with it your cost of capital, are lower, too. You already know that the cost of capital can have a strong value influence, especially for long-lived projects. However, compared to your headache of estimating the uncertainty about your cash flows and of assessing your own future flexibility, your headache about the right cost of capital is usually only a secondary malaise.

There are also cost-of-capital implications, but we have mostly ignored them.

➤ *Cost-of-capital errors, Sect. 4.1, Pg.62.*

Embedded Real Options

Most corporate projects teem with embedded real options. For example:

Here are some other examples of real options.

Expansion or contractions: If the future turns out better (or worse) than expected, firms can expand (or contract). In the extreme, firms may outright abandon a project.

Acceleration and delay: If the future turns out better (or worse) than expected, firms can speed up (or slow down) projects. This can often be done by hiring (or firing) additional consultants and contractors.

Switching: Different technologies may be best in different future scenarios—and some projects may be more amenable to multiple technology alternatives.

➤ *Real options,*
Sect. App.12.A (Companion),
Pg.≈*77*.

Spinoffs: If a technology makes a serendipitous discovery, firms can start entirely new businesses.

Section App.12.A (Companion) values some examples of these options.

Many projects are nothing except real options.

In fact, many projects are nothing but real options: For example, the value of unused land around cities is essentially the option that the city might expand enough to make building on the land economically worthwhile. Research and development often have no immediate usefulness, or even usefulness in the most likely scenario—but there is a chance that it might yield a highly profitable discovery. You have to consider this real option value in your expected cash flow computation, or you will underestimate your project's value.

Different projects contain different types of real options.

Real options become even more tantalizing when you consider not just the real options for one particular project but the fact that different projects come with different types of real options. For example, replacing workers with expensive, high-fixed-cost robots may be cheaper in the most likely scenario, but it effectively gives up on the real option to lay off workers if the future turns out worse than expected. Have you properly valued the project that has more real options?

It is most important to recognize the real options that you have.

Obviously, it would be best if you knew perfectly the types and exact values of all your real options. In practice, this is usually impossible. You should therefore focus on the most important real options. Strange as it may sound, the most common mistake that many managers commit when it comes to real options is that they just do not recognize that the real options are there. Once you recognize real options, even if you cannot fully value them, at least you can try to find an "intuitive" value adjustment. Fortunately, you have one further bit of knowledge that may help you here: The presence of a real option can only increase project value, because it is the value of *your* flexibility.

12.7 Behavioral Biases

Model inputs are usually not what they should be.

So far, we have neglected that you need accurate inputs and that you need to use them rationally if you want to make good decisions. But most cash flow and cost-of-capital estimates rely on human judgment, which is prone to all sorts of errors. We know that our brains tend to commit systematic decision errors. Managers who fail to recognize these biases will make poor decisions.

Innate human decision biases cause predictable valuation mistakes.

There are literally dozens of well-known behavioral errors, but limited space allows us to highlight just three: **overconfidence**, **relativism**, and **compartmentalization**.

1. **Overconfidence** is the tendency of people to believe that their own assessments are more accurate than they really are. In lab experiments, ordinary people are found to be dramatically overconfident. When asked to provide a 90% confidence interval—which is just a range within which they are confident that their true value will lie in 9 out of 10 times—most people end up being correct only 5 out of 10 times.

   It is difficult to document overconfidence empirically—after all, if it were easy, managers would recognize it themselves and avoid it. However, there is empirical evidence that many managers who are already heavily invested in their own

---

Deeper: This chapter's appendix escalates the depth of explanations for real options. The *Real Options* web chapter escalates it even further.

company tend to throw caution overboard and voluntarily invest much of their own money into the corporation—even in companies in rather shaky financial shape. There is also good empirical evidence that those of us who are most optimistic in overestimating our own life expectancy disproportionately will become entrepreneurs. Even if optimism is a disease, it seems to be a necessary one for entrepreneurs!

To understand overconfidence better, please fill out the self-testing questionnaire at the book website. Taking this quiz will make you realize the issue better than reading long paragraphs of commentary in this book ever could. (Incidentally, the only population segments who are known not to be systematically overconfident are weather forecasters and clinically depressed patients.)

The book website is at book.ivo-welch.info

ANECDOTE   Small Business Failures

In New York City, two out of every five new restaurants close within one year. Nationwide, the best estimates suggest that about 90% of all restaurants close within two years. If successful, the average restaurant earns a return of about 10% per year. Owners seem to lose money on average. So, why open yet another restaurant? I mentioned earlier that restaurateurs may just enjoy owning restaurants. But a more likely explanation is that restaurateurs are overly optimistic and just do not realize how tough it is to run a restaurant profitably.

More generally, a Small Business Administration study of small business failures from 1989 to 1992 found that 33% of businesses failed within 2 years, 50% within 4 years, and 66% within 6 years. Yet in a survey of about 3,000 entrepreneurs, 81% of entrepreneurs believed that their chances of success were at least 70%, and 33% believed that they had zero chance of failure!

San Diego Online (Jan 2002), Business Week (Apr 2001), WSJ (Oct 2002), and other sources

---

2. **Relativism** is the tendency of people to consider issues of relative scale when they should not. For example, most people are willing to drive 15 minutes to a store farther away to save $40 on the purchase of $80 worth of groceries, but they would not be willing to drive the 15 minutes to a car dealer farther away to save $100 on the purchase of a new $20,000 car. The savings appear to be less important in the context of the car purchase (0.5%) than in the context of a grocery purchase (50%). But this is flawed logic, similar to comparing IRRs while ignoring project scale. The marginal cost is driving 15 minutes extra, and the marginal benefit is a higher $100 in the context of the car than the $40 in the context of the groceries. Put differently, the problem is that humans tend to think in terms of percentages. The smaller the amount of money at stake, the more severe this problem often becomes. When a gas station advertises a price of $2 per gallon rather than $2.10, some customers drive for miles and wait in long lines—all to fill a 20-gallon gas tank at a total savings that amounts to a mere $2.

3. **Compartmentalization** is the tendency of people to categorize decisions. Most people are more inclined to spend more when the same category has produced an unexpected windfall earlier. For example, winning a lottery prize while attending a baseball game often makes winners more likely to purchase more baseball tickets, even though the project "baseball game" has not changed in profitability. Similarly, an unexpected loss may stop people from an otherwise profitable investment that

they should make. For example, say an individual likes to attend a particular baseball game. If she loses her baseball game ticket, she is less likely to purchase a replacement, even though the cost and benefit of purchasing the ticket are the same as they were when the original ticket was purchased. Compartmentalization can sometimes be the opposite of the sunk cost mistake. For example, Federal Express went through three venture capital funding rounds in the 1970s, the first two leading to rather disappointing operating profits. The investors that then compartmentalized—refusing to throw "good money after bad money"—lost everything. Only investors in the final venture capital round got rich.

Know thyself to avoid these errors!

Q 12.16. Is relativism a bigger problem when evaluating small or large projects?

Q 12.17. Describe how common mental decision biases can bias NPV calculations.

Q 12.18. Take the overconfidence quiz at book.ivo-welch.info.

12.8 Incentive Issues

Incentive problems arise when the information provider has incentives that are different from those of the project owner.

Mental biases are not the only source of bad choices. Another kind of bias arises when one individual has to act on behalf of others. This is called an **agency** problem or **moral hazard**. For example, it occurs in situations in which the owner of a project has to rely on information from someone else, who has divergent interests.

The essence of the problem.

A cynical synopsis of agency biases would be that "all people act and lie in their own self-interests." Now, although everyone does have incentives to lie—or at least to color the truth—not everyone does. Still, organizations are especially rife with such agency distortions. Of course, few people sit down and contemplate how to best and intentionally lie. Instead, they convince themselves that what is in their best interest is indeed the best route to take. Thus, mental biases often reinforce incentive problems: "Wishful thinking" is a disease from which we all suffer.

Some Examples of Moral Hazard

Conflict-of-interest dilemmas are pervasive and important in organizations.

Agency problems exist up and down the corporate ladder. The top management has to rely on division managers who have to rely on department managers who have to rely on their subordinates for information about what they should do and how profitable potential projects really are. You can take the fact that we have already had to mention agency problems repeatedly to indicate how important and pervasive they are. But, again, lack of space forces us to highlight just a few issues with some examples:

1. **Competition for capital:** Managers often compete for scarce resources. For example, division managers may want to obtain capital for their projects. A less optimistic but more accurate estimate of the project cash flows may induce headquarters to allocate capital to another division instead. Thus, division managers often end up in a race to make their potential projects appear in the most favorable and profitable lights.

2. **Employment concerns:** Managers and employees do not want to lose their jobs. For example, scientists may tend to highlight the potential and downplay the drawbacks of their areas of research. After all, not doing so may cut the project and thereby cost them their funding and then their jobs.

3. **Perks:** Managers do not like to give up perks. For example, division managers may like to have their own secretaries or even request private airplanes. Thus, they are likely to overstate the usefulness of the project "administrative assistance" or "private plane transportation."

4. **Power:** Managers typically love to build their own little "empires." For example, they may want to grow and control their departments because bigger departments convey more prestige and because they are a stepping stone to further promotion, either internally or externally. For the same reason, managers often prefer not to maximize profits, but instead focus on maximizing sales.

5. **Hidden slack:** Managers like to be able to cover up problems that may arise in the future. For example, division managers may want to hide the profitability of their divisions, fearing that headquarters may siphon off "their" profits into other divisions. They may prefer to hide the generated value (through legal accounting maneuvers discussed in the next chapter), believing that the cash they produced in good times "belongs" to them and that they are entitled to use it as "plaster" in bad times.

6. **Reluctance to take risk:** Managers may hesitate to take on risk. For example, they may not want to take a positive-NPV project because they may get fired if it fails—and may not be rewarded enough if it succeeds. A popular saying once was that "no one was ever fired for buying IBM," although these days Microsoft has taken over IBM's role.

7. **Direct theft:** Managers and employees have even been known to steal outright from the company. For example, a night club manager may not ring sales into the cash register. Or a sales agent may "forget" to charge her cousins. In some cases, this can be a fine line. Is taking a pad of paper from your company or answering a personal email on company computers really theft? In other cases, the theft is blatant. In September 2002, Dennis Kozlowski, former CEO of Tyco, was charged with looting $600 million. His primary defense was that he did so in broad daylight—with approval from the corporate board that he had helped put in place. (Dennis is now indisposed for the next 25 years.)

We do know where agency problems play bigger and lesser roles:

Agency problems are worse in certain (known) situations.

1. **Scale and owner engagement:** In a small company with one owner and one employee, agency conflicts are less important than they are in big corporations with their many layers of management and disengaged owners.

   Do you believe that professionally run companies really make the best decisions on behalf of their public shareholders? Remember that agency issues do not just arise between shareholders and management—they start with the lowest-level employee and bubble all the way up to the top-level CEO. Decision making is often based on a chain of miscommunications or even deceptions. It is a testament to the importance of sharing risks among many investors that large, publicly traded companies still manage to net-in-net create shareholder value!

2. **Project duration:** If the project is short term and/or comes with good interim progress points, it is easier to reward managers appropriately for success and punish them for failure than it is for longer-term projects. For example, think how you would judge and reward a manager who is (supposedly) working on an R&D project that is not likely to have visible results for decades. This is a difficult task. Agency problems for large and very-long-term projects may be so intrinsically high that they cannot be undertaken.

3. **External noise:** If good luck is an integral and important part of the project, it becomes more difficult to judge managerial performance, which in turn aggravates agency problems. For example, it is relatively easy to measure the productivity of a line worker in a factory; you know whether he works or slacks off. Therefore, agency problems matter less. In contrast, it is more difficult to determine if your sales agent worked hard but the customer just did not bite, or if your sales agent was to blame. Similarly, your night-watch security guard may or may not be working hard, and it could take years before you could learn (probably the hard way) whether she regularly stayed awake or just dozed off.

4. **Opaqueness:** If information is very difficult for outsiders to come by, agency problems will be worse. For example, if only your manager sees what projects are available, he can present only those that he would like to undertake. He can also not mention those that have higher NPVs but require skills he may not have or that require work he finds unpleasant.

Control Mechanisms

There are mechanisms that can help control agency problems.

Fortunately, the principals (i.e., the owners) are not helpless. There are a number of mechanisms that can help alleviate agency problems.

1. **Audits:** If the company runs independent assessments or **audits**, managers can make decisions based on better information, even if their employees are unwilling to provide it. However, many consultants suffer from the same disease as employees: They know that they are most likely to be rehired if they tell the manager what she wants to hear.

2. **Truth-telling incentives:** If managers can be rewarded for telling the truth, agency conflicts will become less important. For example, if your company has a research scientist who has expertise in alpha-proteins and works on an alpha-protein project, your goal as manager should be to allow this scientist to say, without suffering any negative consequences, "Do not waste your money putting any more research dollars into alpha-proteins." This means that the scientist's salary and promotion chances must remain the same regardless of the research outcome— even if this means that she no longer has a good alternative use for her time and effort. You might even offer a reward for any scientists who voluntarily cancel their projects due to lack of viability.

   Would you really be willing to carry through on such a promise? Would your research scientists believe you?

Some companies also undertake **post-audits**, which are designed to evaluate not only the quality of the financial numbers (like a usual audit) but also the quality of managers' up-front forecasts. Knowing that there will be such post-audits will strengthen managers' incentives to give accurate forecasts to begin with.

3. **Contingent compensation:** If managers are rewarded more for a successful project, agency conflicts will become less important. This is the carrot-and-stick approach. For example, if you pay your managers bonuses only when their projects succeed (or fire them when their projects fail), then your managers may work harder and choose projects that they believe are more likely to succeed.

   Of course, like any other mechanism to control agency problems, this control strategy has its costs, too: (1) Competent managers may not want to work for you if they get paid only if the firm succeeds; (2) Some risk-averse managers may not take positive-NPV risks in order to avoid a zero bonus; (3) Less risk-averse managers may take huge negative-NPV risks in order to gamble for a huge bonus.

4. **Reputation:** If managers can build a reputation for truth-telling and capable management, they are less likely to undertake bad projects. For example, agency concerns are likely to be a worse problem when it comes to secret one-shot projects, where your managers cannot build a track record that will help them with future projects. On the other hand, sometimes reputational considerations can themselves become the problem. Witness the many dysfunctional but beautifully artistic office buildings that are primarily monuments to some famous architectural firms.

5. **Capital rationing:** If nothing helps to restrain your managers from wasting money when they get it, just don't give it to them. Or give them only enough money to satisfy their most urgent needs, hoping that these needs will then more likely be positive-NPV projects.

6. **Selecting managers:** There are people out there who are more inclined to be honest and others who are not. If you can hire managers of high integrity, they may not abuse the firm, even when it is in their own self-interest.

There are no obvious and cheap solutions to moral hazard problems. You would not want to spend a million dollars in audit fees and complex control mechanisms to save a hundred dollars in theft. You would not want to hire a manager of the highest integrity who is utterly incompetent over another manager who may steal a small amount but will otherwise generate enormous value for shareholders. In the real world, you have to realize that all firms suffer from the fact that their employees act in their own—but not necessarily in the firm's—best interest. All you can do is to try to limit this intelligently. As a manager or principal, remain skeptical of your employees' estimates and judgments and take the biases and incentives of each information provider into account. My last word: Again, do not believe that agency problems are not too important because you have spent only a few pages on them—they are everywhere.

Some losses due to conflict of interest are unavoidable. The best "solution" is ample skepticism and common sense.

A N E C D O T E   Fiduciary Responsibility, or the Fox Guarding the Henhouse

On Wednesday, December 29, 2004, the *Wall Street Journal* reported on page 1:

In the biggest U.S. merger this year, JP Morgan Chase & Co. announced last January it would acquire Bank One Corp. To assure investors it was paying fair price, JP Morgan told them in a proxy filing that it had obtained an opinion from one of "the top five financial advisors in the world."
— *Itself.*
The in-house bankers at JP Morgan endorsed the $56.9 billion price—negotiated by their boss—as "fair."

Next to the main article was a sidebar called "Passing Muster," which explained:

A 'fairness' opinion tells a company's board that a deal's terms are fair to shareholders.
Purpose: Legal protection from an investor claim that a deal was done without due care.
Cost: A few hundred thousand dollars to a few million.
Potential Conflicts

- Bankers may have incentives to call a deal fair because most of their advisory fee is paid only if the deal closes.
- Bankers' fee is tied to the deal price.
- Bankers may support a deal where executives will personally profit, in hopes of securing future work.
- Bankers use financial data supplied by a client who wants the deal to go through.
- When the deal maker is a bank, its own bankers often write the fairness opinion.

Remember that everyone—in-house bankers, management, and corporate boards—are employed by the shareholders, to whom they owe fiduciary responsibility and whose interests they are supposed to represent. It is a clear agency conflict for an employee to provide a fairness opinion. But it would also be difficult for management to have these in-house bankers fired for doing them a personal favor—another agency conflict.
And there is also the original agency conflict: the incentive of acquiring managers to pay too high a price or of target managers to accept too low a price. Here is how the WSJ story continues:

But during the negotiations, Bank One Chief Jamie Dimon had suggested selling his bank for billions of dollars less if, among other conditions, he immediately became chief of the merged firm, according to a person familiar with the talks. That suggestion wasn't accepted by JP Morgan.

Obviously, Jamie Dimon did not offer to pay his own personal billions for the privilege of becoming CEO, but Bank One's shareholders' billions. Obviously, the JP Morgan management did not decline the billions on behalf of their own pockets, but on behalf of JP Morgan shareholders' pockets.
Still, there are of course the corporate boards that could have fired either the in-house bankers or their management teams. Neither happened. Instead, Jamie Dimon took over as head of JP Morgan, as scheduled, on December 31, 2005.

The Wall Street Journal

Corporate Governance

Corporate governance is how shareholders and creditors control the firm.

A very important aspect of managing moral hazard in firms is how firm owners (shareholders and creditors) deal with their firms—what rights they have. This is called **corporate governance**. If the top managers are not incentiviced to do the right thing, they will also not incentivice their subordinates to do the right thing, either. (The medieval proverb "the fish stinks from the head downward" very much applies.) How do shareholders and creditors get "their" managers to act in shareholders' interest—and not to buy themselves lavish airplanes, or take excessive gambles with investors' money? It's a tough problem.

Note that good management is not the same as good corporate governance. Governance matters only if management is bad. Apple's Steve Jobs was not only the best-performing executive in the world, but he also did not receive a lot of executive compensation. In contrast, corporate governance at Apple was poor. Jobs was almost in complete control of a board that was officially supposed to supervise him. This bad governance did not matter.

> Good management is *not* good governance.

Corporate governance works pretty badly for most large Fortune-100 firms with diffuse shareholders. A very self-interested CEO intent on gaining control of the board that supposedly supervises him or her will usually only take a few years to succeed. The best example of a complete collapse of corporate governance is the financial crisis of 2008-9. All financial corporations were set up with very little real incentives to control risk. (There was no more than lip service.) Thus, heads, the bonus payments made the executives rich. Tails, the firm went bankrupt. Almost all the executives who gambled and ultimately lost all the shareholders' money still walked away as super-rich individuals. (Of course, they would have ended up even richer if heads had come up more often. They did not *want* the financial crisis to happen.) You read it here first—this is also how the next financial crisis will happen. Nothing important has changed.

> Corporate governance in the U.S. is badly broken for many firms. It works well for smaller firms.

Fortunately, corporate governance works pretty well for small and growing firms— and especially in **private equity** firms, whose business it is to run their own portfolio firms under tight supervision. In fact, private-equity firms often pay their corporate managers more than publicly-traded firms pay theirs—but they also fire them more often.

> But it works well when there are concentrated owners.

The companion book contains a full chapter about corporate governance. It's my favorite. You should read it.

> Read all about it...

Q 12.19. Describe common agency problems and explain how they are likely to bias corporate NPV calculations.

12.9 An NPV Checklist

After reading this chapter, you probably understand now why professors think "theory is easy." The complications of real life make theory look like a child's game. Yes, the principles of capital budgeting theory are easy—only their application is hard. It is usually very difficult to estimate future cash flows (and even their appropriate interest rates), especially for far-in-the-future returns. It is usually more important and more difficult to avoid errors for the expected cash flow (the NPV numerator) than it is for the cost of capital (the NPV denominator). The NPV formula is less robust to cash flow errors than it is to cost-of-capital errors, and it is "easier" to commit dramatic errors in the cash flow estimation than in the cost-of-capital estimation.

> If you think academics like to make easy things difficult, you have it totally wrong. It is academics who try to avoid the difficult problems.

Here is an abbreviated list of issues to worry about when using NPV.

Here is an abbreviated checklist of items to consider when working out NPV estimates.

- **Appropriate (after-tax) dollars** (Pages 90, 94):

    – Have you quoted all relevant inputs and outputs in relevant-to-you after-tax dollars? This applies to both expected cash flows and to appropriate discount rates. (Corporate income taxes will be covered in more detail in Chapter 17.)

    – Have you properly included inflation? Preferably, have you performed all computations using nominal expected future cash flows and nominal costs of capital, with inflation used only to gross up nominal cash flows appropriately?

- **Interactions** (Pages 330, 334):

    – Have you credited all projects with their contributions, positive or negative, to the values of other projects (externalities)?

    – Have you judged all projects "on the margin," that is, without charging them for unalterable or previously made choices, such as sunk costs, overhead, and so on?

    – Have you used the cost of capital applicable to each project component, respectively, and not the (incorrect) overall average cost of capital? (Note: Some errors and simplifications here are unavoidable in the real world, because it is impossible to put different costs of capital on each paper clip.)

- **Real options and flexibility** (Page 347, Section App.12.A (Companion), Chapter 26 (Companion), Real Options web chapter):

    – Have you considered all possible future options (using scenario analyses) in order to find the correct *expected* cash flows, such as,

        1. your ability to extend a product into different markets,
        2. your ability to find product spinoffs,
        3. your ability to learn about future products,
        4. your ability to stop the project if conditions are bad,
        5. your ability to delay the project if conditions are bad,
        6. your ability to mothball the project if conditions are bad and to restart the project if conditions improve,
        7. your ability to accelerate the project if conditions are good,
        8. your ability to expand the project if conditions are good,

    and so on?

- **Accuracy** (Pages 62, 232, 352, 354):

    – How accurate are your estimated project cash flows?

    – If project success and project cash flows were estimated by someone else, what are the assessor's motives? How tainted can these estimates be? Does the estimator want the project accepted or rejected?

    – Is it possible to get another independent evaluation/audit of the project estimates?

– Can your cash flow estimates be improved by doing more research?

– Given unavoidable simplifications, assumptions, and errors, how sensitive/robust are your NPV calculations to changes therein?

- **Correct inputs** (Page 325):

    – Are your cash flows *expected* rather than *promised*? Are your interest rates *expected* rather than *promised*? (Recall: Expected interest rates are below promised interest rates due to default premiums, not just due to risk premiums.)

    – Are your expected cash flows the "average outcome" (correct), and not the "most likely outcome" (incorrect)?

    – Do your expected cash flow estimates include the correct weighted probabilities of low-probability events, especially for negative outcomes?

    – If you need to borrow money to execute the project, have you used the expected (not the promised) borrowing rate as your cost of capital? If capital is already available, are you using your expected lending (investments) rate as the appropriate cost of capital?

- **Corporate income taxes** (To be covered on Page 526f):

    – For use of WACC and APV, is the numerator in your NPV calculation the expected cash flow "as if all equity financed"? (This means that the company bears the full brunt of its corporate income tax load.)

➤ *WACC and APV, Sect. 17.2, Pg.526.*

    – In the weighted cost of capital, is your debt cost of capital the *expected* (not the promised) interest rate on debt? Is your numerator the *expected* cash flow, not the *promised* cash flow?

A final warning: Although many of these issues seem obvious in isolation, they are much harder to spot and take care of in complex real-world situations than in our highlighted expositions. Watch out! Another warning against the most common error is worth its own box:

Easy here. Tough in the jungle.

IMPORTANT

The most common NPV method is to estimate cash flows for the numerator, and to use an expected rate of return (cost of capital) from the CAPM formula (see Chapter 9).

- The default risk is handled only in the numerator, that is, in the computation of expected cash flows.

- The time premium and risk premium are handled only in the denominator. The CAPM formula provides an expected rate of return, which contains only these two components.

- Do not try to adjust the cash-flow numerator for the time or risk premium. Do not try to add a default premium to the rate of return in the denominator. (This would yield a promised, not an expected, rate of return on capital.) Do not believe that you have taken default risk into consideration merely by using the CAPM expected rate of return in the denominator.

Q 12.20. The CEO projects earnings of $100 million next year. List three reasons why this might not be a good input into an NPV valuation.

Summary

This chapter covered the following major points:

- You should never confuse promised and expected cash flows in the numerator, or promised and expected rates of return in the denominator. The *expected* cash flows are often not the *most likely* cash flows, either.

- Corporations can reduce their risk by diversification—but if investors can do so themselves as easily, diversification per se does not create value. As a manager, you can create value only by increasing cash flows or decreasing market beta (the cost of capital). Diversification for the sake of diversification does not add value.

- You should not use the cost of capital (and the market beta) applicable to the entire firm, but rather the cost of capital (and the market beta) applicable to this new project. However, because the effort involved can be enormous, it is reasonable to use individual, project-specific costs of capital only when it really makes a difference.

- When selecting projects, consider all possible project combinations and choose the combination that gives you the highest overall NPV.

- You should attribute to each project's NPV its influence on other projects, either positive or negative. If a project is independent from other projects, you can consider its NPV in isolation, and add it to the total.

- You should think about how you can take advantage of, or create, positive externalities among projects. If you cannot, there is no reason for the firm to exist in the first place.

- You should think "on the margin"—take all projects that contribute more marginal benefits than they create marginal costs.

- You should consider economies of scale, which can reduce average production costs and thus add to project value.

- You should ignore sunk costs.

- You should take real options into account. These are the value of your ability to change course depending on future conditions. They include your flexibility to delay or accelerate projects, and to expand or shut down projects.

- You should be aware of your own biases, such as overconfidence, relativism, compartmentalization, and others.

- You should realize that real-world implementation problems—which range from differences in short-term and long-term marginal costs, to political reasons and agency considerations inside corporations—often make taking the best set of projects difficult.

- You should design your operations to reduce agency conflicts when it is marginally profitable to do so.
- To make your task a little easier, refer to the NPV checklist in Section 12.9.

No doubt about it: Good capital budgeting is a difficult problem. Each subsection covered in this chapter can easily be expanded into a full chapter, or even a full book. There are pitfalls everywhere. In the end, capital budgeting is as much an art as it is a science. You have to rely as much on common sense and intuition as on the mechanics of valuation. The best analysis combines both.

Preview of the Chapter Appendix in the Companion

The appendix to this chapter shows how to value some specific real option scenarios with decision trees.

In the Appendix

Keywords

Agency, 354.   Audit, 356.   Compartmentalization, 352.   Conglomerate, 327.   Corporate governance, 358. Diseconomies of scale, 338.   Economies of scale, 341.   Externality, 336.   Hedging, 328.   Heuristic, 335. Independent, 336.   Interaction, 336.   Limited attention span, 338.   Limited capacity, 345.   Monte Carlo simulation, 672.   Moral hazard, 581.   Natural monopoly, 342.   Negative interaction, 338.   On the margin, 339.   Overconfidence, 595.   Positive interaction, 337.   Post-audit, 357.   Private equity, 583.   Real option, 347.   Relativism, 352.   Scenario analysis, 350.   Simulation analysis, 350.   Strategic option, 347. Sunk cost, 344.   Synergies, 337.

Answers

Q 12.1 Yes, it makes sense to compare the project's IRR to a hurdle rate. Indeed, if the hurdle rate is the cost of capital, the IRR rule tells you what you should do.

Q 12.2 Comparing a project's cost of capital to its hurdle rate would be silly, because your hurdle rate is just another name for your cost of capital in a perfect market.

Q 12.3 The Amazon.com bond's stated 8% is a promised rate of return. It is not the expected rate of return. Therefore, it is not the cost of capital.

Q 12.4 You cannot determine this, because you do not know the expected bond payoff.

Q 12.5 The probabilities of different outcomes are as follows:

Scenario	Probability	Y	PV
DDDD	$90\%^0 \cdot 10\% = 0.1000$	1	$268
WDDD	$90\%^1 \cdot 10\% = 0.0900$	2	$507
WWDD	$90\%^2 \cdot 10\% = 0.0810$	3	$721
WWWD	$90\%^3 \cdot 10\% = 0.0729$	4	$911
WWWW	$1 - \text{above} = 0.6561$	5	$1,081

1. The single most likely outcome (with 65.6% probability) is that the machine will operate for all 5 years (because there is only a 10% breakage probability each year). If this machine were guaranteed to work for exactly 5 years, then the present value would be PV = ($300/0.12) \cdot (1 - 1/1.12^5) \approx \$1,081$. The NPV would be $171.

2. The expected number of years that the machine will operate is $0.1 \cdot 1 + 0.09 \cdot 2 + 0.081 \cdot 3 + 0.0728 \cdot 4 + 0.6561 \cdot 5 \approx 4.1$. If this machine were guaranteed to work for exactly 4.1 years, then the present value would be PV $= (\$300,000/0.12) \cdot (1 - 1/1.12^{4.1}) \approx \$929$. The NPV would be $19.

3. The true expected value is $0.1 \cdot \$268 + 0.09 \cdot \$507 + 0.081 \cdot \$721 + 0.0728 \cdot \$911 + 0.6561 \cdot \$1,081 \approx \$906$. The NPV would be –$4. This number is lower than the $19, because the NPV at the expected outcome is not the same as the expected NPV. (The math name for this is Jensen's inequality.)

(As usual, because of rounding, your answers may be slightly off from those I report here.)

Q 12.6 The merged firm has a lower standard deviation (it is safer), but this adds no value.

Q 12.7 1. The new project's value is $11/1.15 \approx \$9.57$. At a cost of $10, the net present value is –$0.43.

2. The value today of the new project is $11/1.15 \approx \$9.57$. Therefore, the weight of the new project is $w_{new} = PV_{new}/PV_{combined} \approx \$9.57/\$109.48 \approx 8.74\%$.

3. The beta of the combined firm is $\beta_{combined} = w_{old} \cdot \beta_{old} + w_{new} \cdot \beta_{new} \approx 91.26\% \cdot 0.5 + 8.74\% \cdot 3 \approx 0.719$.

4. The combined cost of capital according to the CAPM is $\mathcal{E}(r_{combined}) \approx 3\% + 4\% \cdot 0.719 = 5.876\%$.

5. Yes! The IRR of *new* is 10%. (For IRR, see Chapter 5, Page 83.) 10% is above the blended cost of capital of 5.876%.

6. The firm value would be

$$PV = \frac{\mathcal{E}(C_{new}) + \mathcal{E}(C_{old})}{1 + \mathcal{E}(r_{combined})} \approx \frac{\$105 + \$11}{1 + 5.876\%} \approx \$109.57$$

Again, you conclude that the firm has destroyed $0.43.

Q 12.8 Zero externalities are convenient for valuation, because they allow you to add up NPVs. If there are nonzero externalities, the total NPV is larger or smaller than the sum of its part.

Q 12.9 Without taking the externality into account, the NPV of division A's move would be negative. The $120,000 of costs would be higher than the benefit of $10,000/10% = $100,000. However, the correct answer is "Yes, division A should move." Moving saves $10,000/10% = $100,000 in division A costs and $3,000/10%=$30,000 in division B costs. The total savings is therefore $130,000, which is $10,000 greater than the cost of the building.

Q 12.10 The firm should not purchase the press, because it earns $2,000/10% = $20,000. But the press costs $10,000 to purchase and eliminates $1,500/10% = $15,000 of profits from the screw machines. The total cost of the press, including the $15,000 in opportunity costs, is $25,000. The project's net present value is $20,000 – $25,000 = –$5,000.

Q 12.11 1. Either purchasing the desktop or the notebook would be a positive-NPV project. However, you should purchase the desktop, because it is cheaper (more bang for the buck).

2. You should still purchase the desktop. The marginal cost is $1,500. The marginal benefit is $11,000 – $9,000 = $2,000.

3. You should not purchase the notebook. The marginal cost is $2,500. The marginal benefit is $2,000.

Q 12.12 1. The profit of the firm is Profit$(x = 10) = 10 \cdot [\$20 - \$5 - \$15/(10 + 1)] \approx \$136.36$.

2. With 11 goods, the cost to produce is $5 + $15/(11 + 1) = $6.25. With 10 goods, it was $5 + $15/(10 + 1) \approx $6.3636. The marginal production cost is $6.25 \cdot 11 – $6.3636 \cdot 10 \approx $5.11.

3. The marginal cost would now be an additional $1 times 10 in rebates. It would therefore cost the firm $5.11 plus $10, or $15.11, assuming that the other clients also get the $1 discount ($19 price). Thus, because the marginal revenue of $19 exceeds the marginal cost of $15.11, the firm should still sign everyone up.

Q 12.13 Total sales and costs are

Units	Sales Price	Production Cost	Net
Q	$Q \cdot (7 - Q/100)$	$Q \cdot [5 + (Q + 20)/100]$	
1	$6.99	$5.21	$1.78
2	$13.96	$10.44	$3.52
⋮			
43	$282.51	$242.09	$40.42
44	$288.64	$248.16	$40.48
45	$294.75	$254.25	$40.50
46	$300.84	$260.36	$40.48
47	$306.91	$266.49	$40.42
⋮			

1. The table shows that the optimal production is 45 units.

2. The average per-unit gross sales at Q = 45 is $294.75/45 = $6.55.

3. The average per-unit production cost at Q = 45 is $254.25/45 = $5.65.

4. The net sales at Q = 45 are $40.50/45 = $0.90.

5. From 44 to 45, the marginal per-unit sales is $294.75 – $288.64 = $6.11. From 45 to 46, it is $6.09.

6. From 44 to 45, the marginal per-unit cost is $254.25 – $248.16 = $6.09. From 45 to 46, it is $6.11.

7. It is just about $0. (If you move from 44 to 45 units, or from 46 to 45 units, you gain 2 cents.) This is what it means to be at the optimal production level.

8. Your average per-unit net change at Q = 45 is still positive, but you should *not* expand production. If you do, you are ignoring the negative effects that unit number 46 would have on all your earlier units. This means that you would earn less money in total, not more.

Q 12.14 Yes, the firm should expand. The PV of the division's profits will be $50,000/10\% = \$500,000$. The division costs are $210,000 for new equipment and $20,000 per year in increased overhead. The PV of the increased overhead is $20,000/10\% = \$200,000$. The total PV cost of the new division is $210,000 + \$200,000 = \$410,000$, and the PV of the benefits is $500,000. Thus, bringing in the new division represents a project with an NPV of +$90,000.

Q 12.15   1. The expected per-CD selling price is $\$6 \cdot 90\% + \$10 \cdot 10\% = \$6.40$.

2. If $6.40 was the price, you would gear your factory to produce 150,000 CDs. Without flexibility, your factory would be worth $90\% \cdot [150,000 \cdot (\$6 - \$5)] + 10\% \cdot [150,000 \cdot (\$10 - \$5)] = 150,000 \cdot (\$6.40 - \$5) = \$210,000$.

3. With flexibility, you would expect to earn $90\% \cdot (150,000 \cdot [\$6 - \$5]) + 10\% \cdot (500,000 \cdot [\$10 - \$8]) = \$135,000 + \$100,000 = \$235,000$.

4. The value of flexibility is $\$235,000 - \$210,000 = \$25,000$.

Q 12.16 Relativism may induce you to make mistakes on both types of projects (and it is not clear which one is worse): For small projects, you may chase a large percentage increase too vigorously. For large projects, you may not realize that even a small rate of return can be a lot of money.

Q 12.17 Mental decision biases are the subject of Section 12.7. The text discussed overconfidence, relativism, and compartmentalization.

Q 12.18 The average student does not get one but five questions wrong.

Q 12.19 Agency problems are the subject of Section 12.8. The text discussed eagerness for capital, employment concerns, direct theft, and desire for perks, power, and laziness. The effects can be manifold, often resulting is misvaluation of projects.

Q 12.20 First, the CEO's projected figures probably represent the most likely outcome, not the expected outcome. It is probably more likely that the firm will go bankrupt due to totally unforeseen circumstances than that it will have a windfall. Second, the CEO has an incentive to distort the truth and report optimistic projections. This is an agency problem. Third, the CEO is probably subject to mental biases, too.

End of Chapter Problems

Q 12.21. Can you compare a project's internal rate of return to its expected rate of return?

Q 12.22. Does it make sense to distinguish between a promised and an expected internal rate of return? What do issuers provide? What do you usually need?

Q 12.23. A zero-bond has a stated rate of return of 8%. Its price today is $92,593. What is its expected payoff?

Q 12.24. A machine that costs $2,000 is likely to break irreparably with 20% probability at the end of each year (assuming it worked the previous year). You can neither replace it nor use it for more than 5 years. (Many electric devices without moving parts have such breakdown characteristics.) The machine can produce $1,000 in profit every year. The discount rate is 12% per annum.

1. What is the most likely operating time? If this comes true, what is the value?

2. What is the expected operating time? If this comes true, what is the value?

3. What is the true net present value of this machine? (Hint: First work this out case by case for a two-year machine, then for a three-year machine. Think "D," "WD," "WWD," "WWWD," and "WWWWD," where W means working and D means dead.)

Q 12.25. A $300 million firm has a beta of 2. The risk-free rate is 4%; the equity premium is 3%. Assume that the firm can easily tap a perfect capital market to obtain another $95 million. The firm can also easily tap the financial markets. So far, it has had a policy of only accepting projects with an IRR above the hurdle rate of 10%. Suddenly, one of its main suppliers (perhaps one facing credit constraints) has approached the firm for a 1-year loan. Assume that the loan is risk free for you—you hold more than enough sway over your supplier to ensure repayment. The supplier wants to borrow $100 million and pay back $106 million next year.

1. Without the new loan, what is the firm expected to earn per year?

2. What is the NPV of the loan?

3. If the firm changes its policy and extends the loan, how would its value change?

4. If the firm changes its policy and extends the loan, approximately how would its beta change?

5. If the firm changes its policy and extends the loan, approximately how would its cost of capital change?

6. If the firm changes its policy and extends the loan, can you compute the combined firm's NPV by dividing its expected cash flows (assets) by its combined cost of capital?

7. Should the firm change its policy?

Q 12.26. Assume that the risk-free rate is 5% and the equity premium is 2%. A $1 billion firm with a beta of 2 has just sold one of its divisions for a fair price of $200 million. The CEO is concerned that investors expect the firm to earn 9%, and so believes keeping the money in short-term Treasuries that only pay 5% would be a bad idea. Is it really a bad idea?

Q 12.27. What are the arguments for and against discounting every project by its own cost of capital?

Q 12.28. As the CEO of an expanding airlines cargo division, would you acknowledge that an increase in your operations would be harmful to the passenger division? Should you be charged for the increased use of shared maintenance facilities?

Q 12.29. What are the main sources of positive externalities? What are the main sources of negative externalities?

Q 12.30. As a manufacturer, you have to decide how many regional distributors to sign up. Serving a distributor costs more the farther away it is from the factory, and different distributors have different demand. By region, gross revenues and costs are (in millions of dollars) as follows:

Distributor	A	B	C	D	E	F	G
Gross Revenue	$5	$4	$4	$3	$2	$7	$1
Cost	$2	$2	$3	$4	$4	$5	$6

There is no "time value of money" dimension in this problem.

1. Is it feasible to work out all possible combinations of distributors you can service? Is it sensible?

2. Which regions should you deliver to?

3. What is the total profit for serving them?

4. What is the marginal benefit and cost of serving the least profitable of your serviced distributors?

5. What would be the marginal benefit and cost of serving one more distributor?

6. Now assume that to get into this business, you would also have to set up the factory. This would cost you a one-time up-front expense of $5 million. You can think of this as spreading the cost across distributors. How would this change your decision?

Q 12.31. A firm can produce goods for an average per-unit cost of $5 + $10/(Q \cdot $1 + 2)$. For example, to produce 10 goods would cost $10 \cdot ($5 + $10/12) \approx 58.33. The market price per good is $7 - Q \cdot $1/10$. So, you can fetch $10 \cdot ($7 - $10/10) = 60 for selling 10 goods. Use a spreadsheet to answer the following questions.

1. What is the break-even point where total gross revenues are equal to total cost?

2. What is the gross profit (revenues minus costs) at the break-even point?

3. What is the marginal gross profit at the break-even point?

4. How many items should the firm produce?

5. What is the average per-unit gross profit at this point?

6. What is the marginal gross profit at this point?

Q 12.32. Comment on, "It is best to allocate costs only to divisions that request a resource."

Q 12.33. Comment on, "It is best to allocate costs to divisions that benefit from a resource."

Q 12.34. A perpetual firm's headquarters consumes $1 million per year. It has six divisions of equal size, but not equal profitability. The annual profitabilities (in thousands of dollars) are as follows:

Project	A	B	C	D	E	F
Profitability	$180	$450	$900	$80	$130	$300

The cost of capital is r = 10%.

1. What is the firm's NPV?

2. If the firm adopts a rule whereby each division has to carry its fair (size-based) share of the headquarter overhead. (Assume that the total amount of overhead does not decrease unless the whole firm is closed, in which case the overhead is 0.) What is the firm's NPV?

Q 12.35. Your factory can either stamp 150,000 CDs at a cost of $5 per CD, or 500,000 CDs at a cost of $8 per CD. If your CD has a hit song, you can sell it to retailers for $10 per CD. If it is a moderate success, you can only charge $6 per CD. If it is a complete bomb, you cannot sell it at all. There is a 1-in-10 chance that your CD will be a hit, and a 3-in-10 chance that it will be a bomb. You will not find out whether you have a hit until next year, but fortunately this will be before you have to stamp CDs. Your cost of capital is 10% per year. You only have the lease of the factory for next year. There is no production this year.

1. What is the expected selling price per CD?

2. How many CDs should you produce at the expected selling price—that is, if you had to gear the factory for a particular production quantity today?

3. What is the value of your factory if you can decide next year?

4. What is the value of flexibility in this example?

Q 12.36. What are the types of real options that firms need to take into account in their project valuations?

Q 12.37. You have to purchase $600 worth of staples. You have just found out that the stationery store across from you charges $300 more than the warehouse outlet 20 miles away. Would you spend the 40 minutes to drive to the warehouse? Now, assume you are buying a Porsche that costs $100,000. You have just found out that the Porsche dealer also 40 minutes away offers the Porsche for $300 less. Assuming you can receive after-market service in both locations, would you drive 40 minutes to pay $99,700? What should you do from an economic perspective? Is this what you would be tempted to do?

Q 12.38. Explain how you can exploit human biases in attracting signups for your new health club.

Q 12.39. Describe a manifestation of an agency problem, where it is worse, and what can be done to remedy it.

Q 12.40. Are agency problems worse in upstart firms? Discuss.

Q 12.41. Should you suppress all agency conflicts? Discuss.

Q 12.42. Contrast Google and Wal-Mart. Which agency conflicts are likely to inflict Google worse than Wal-Mart, and vice versa? Discuss.

Q 12.43. Recall as many items from the NPV checklist as you can remember. Which are you most likely to forget?

From Financial Statements to Economic Cash Flows

Translating Accounting into Finance (Present Value Cash Flows)

Financial accounting is the "language of business." Although this book is not about financial statements, you must understand both their logic and their fundamentals. They contain information about the cash flows you need for an NPV analysis. Without understanding accounting, you also cannot understand corporate income taxes—a necessary NPV input.

This chapter begins with a simple hypothetical project. Its economics make computing NPV easy. The chapter then explains how accountants would describe the project in a financial statement. This makes it easy for you to see the correspondence between the finance and the accounting descriptions. Finally, the chapter applies the same analysis to the financial statements of a real corporation, PepsiCo (PEP).

This chapter also gently introduces some more details about corporate income taxes and capital structure. They will be explained in greater detail in Chapter 17.

13.1 Financial Statements

You already know that the value of a firm is determined by its underlying projects. These projects have cash flows that you use in an NPV analysis. Unfortunately, the accounting financials do not contain the kind of cash flows that you need for an NPV analysis. In addition to learning how to convert financials into cash flows, there are also many other good reasons why you should understand financial statements:

Isn't accounting just irrelevant numbers? Isn't what matters the project's actual cash flows, no matter how it is reported? (Yes and No.)

1. If you want to have an intelligent conversation about corporate finance and economics, you must understand the language of accounting. In particular, you must understand what earnings are—and what they are not.

2. Subsidiaries and corporations report financial statements, designed by accountants for accountants. It is true that they do not report the exact cash flows and cash flow projections that you need for PV discounting. But how can you make good decisions about which projects to take if you cannot understand the only information to which you may ever have access to?

3. Given that it may be all the information you ever get, you must be able to read what the company is willing to tell you if you want to get a glimpse of the operations of a publicly traded corporation or better understand its economics.

If you want to acquire a company, the corporate financials may be your primary source of information.

4. The IRS levies corporate income tax. This tax is computed from a tax-specific variant of the corporate income statement. It relies on the same accounting logic as the published financials. (The reported public and unreported tax statements are constructed using the same accounting principles. But there are differences that are mandated by the respective regulatory agencies.) Because income taxes are definite costs, you must be able to understand and construct financial statements that properly subtract taxes from the projected cash flows when you want to compute NPV. And, if you become a tax guru, you may even learn how to structure projects to minimize the tax obligations, although most of this is beyond the scope of a first finance course.

5. Many contracts are written on the basis of financials. For example, a bond covenant may require the company to maintain a current ratio greater than 1.5. Even if a change in accounting rules should not matter theoretically, such contracts can influence the reported financials on your projects' cash flows.

6. There is no doubt that managers care about their financial statements, if only because executive compensation is often linked to the numbers reported in them. Moreover, managers can engage in many maneuvers to manipulate their earnings *legally*. For example, firms can often increase their reported earnings by changing their depreciation policies (explained below). Companies are also known to actively lobby the accounting standards boards at great expense. For example, the accounting standards board adopted a mandatory rule in December 2004 that companies must value employee stock options when they are granted. Until then, firms' financial statements could treat these option grants as if they cost nothing. Although this new rule did not ask firms to change projects, it did reduce their *reported* net income (earnings), especially of technology firms. This rule was adopted despite extremely vigorous opposition by corporate lobbies, which was aimed at the accounting standards board and Congress.

Why should companies care about whether options costs have to be subtracted from reported earnings? After all, companies had disclosed enough information in the footnotes to allow investors to determine these costs themselves. This is a big question. Some behavioral finance researchers believe that the financial markets value companies *as if they do not fully understand corporate financials*. That is, not only do they share the common belief that firms "manage" their earnings, but they also believe that the market fails to see through even mechanical accounting computations.

Naturally, the presumption that the financial markets cannot understand accounting is a controversial hypothesis. If true, this could lead to all sorts of troublesome consequences. Value may no longer be just NPV, but instead be based partly on smoke and mirrors. For example, if the market cannot understand financials, you should realize that it could have real share-price consequences when managers (legally) manipulate their earnings. A firm would especially benefit from a higher share price when it wants to sell more of its shares to the public. In this case, managers could and should maneuver their financials (legally, of course) to increase their earnings just before the equity issue. There is good evidence that firms do this—and also that the financial markets are regularly disappointed by these firms' performances years after their equity issues.

Even more troublesome, there is also evidence that managers prefer not to take some positive-NPV projects if these projects would harm their earnings. Does this sound far-fetched? In fact, in a survey of 401 senior financial executives, Graham, Harvey, and Rajgopal found that 55% would delay starting a project and 80% would defer maintenance and research spending in order to meet earnings targets. Starting projects, doing maintenance, and conducting R&D are presumably the right kinds of (positive-NPV) projects, so not taking them decreases the underlying real value of the firm—even though it may increase the financial image of the firm's projects.

Of course, it is impossible for an introductory finance textbook to explain all the nuances of accounting. Instead, we focus here on only one issue of importance to a financier: How can you obtain the cash flows that you need for an NPV analysis, and why can you not use earnings? Accounting has, of course, more to offer than just this—and, fortunately, you can learn more about its broader scope in your accounting course.

Our chapter's accounting perspective: how to extract economic cash flows.

The Contents of Financials

Publicly traded companies report their financial results in **financial reports** to their shareholders and to the public. The standard rules that go into preparing the public financial statements are called **GAAP** (Generally Accepted Accounting Principles) and change rarely. They are set by a number of policymakers, most prominently **FASB** (Financial Accounting Standards Board). The most important financial report is the **annual report**, which is filed with the SEC in Form **10-K**. (There is also a much shorter required **quarterly report**, called a **10-Q**.) Almost all annual reports begin with a general description of the business and business developments, followed by the more formal presentation of the firm's financials. As a financier, you are most likely primarily interested in the financials. After all, you care more about *how much* money the firm makes than about *how* it makes it. Nevertheless, as much as you might like to keep the firm a black box, you rarely can: Knowledge of "how money is made" is usually necessary for good knowledge of "how much money is made" and "how more money can be made."

Companies communicate their internal operations through standardized financial reports.

If you have not seen an annual report (with financial statements), please spend some time reading one. Most large corporations publish their financials on their websites, so access is easy. If you own shares of stock in a publicly traded company, the annual report is also automatically mailed to you. Moreover, the SEC runs **EDGAR**—a comprehensive electronic repository of corporate financials, including annual and quarterly reports.

You must read some samples—please!

(in millions except per share amounts)	2001	2000
ASSETS		
Current Assets		
1 Cash and cash equivalents	$ 683	$ 1,038
2 Short-term investments, at cost	966	467
3	1,649	1,505
4 Accounts and notes receivable, net	2,142	2,129
5 Inventories	1,310	1,192
6 Prepaid expenses and other current assets	752	791
7 **Total Current Assets**	5,853	5,617
8 **Property, Plant and Equipment, net**	6,876	6,558
9 **Intangible Assets, net**	4,841	4,714
10 **Investments in Unconsolidated Affiliates**	2,871	2,979
11 **Other Assets**	1,254	889
12 **Total Assets**	$21,695	$20,757
LIABILITIES AND SHAREHOLDERS' EQUITY		
Current Liabilities		
13 Short-term borrowings	$ 354	$ 202
14 Accounts payable and other current liabilities	4,461	4,529
15 Income taxes payable	183	64
16 **Total Current Liabilities**	4,998	4,795
17 **Long-Term Debt**	2,651	3,009
18 **Other Liabilities**	3,876	3,960
19 **Deferred Income Taxes**	1,496	1,367
20 **Preferred Stock** no par value	26	49
21 **Deferred Compensation — preferred**	-	(27)
Common Shareholders' Equity		
22 Common stock par value $1\frac{2}{3}$ c per share	30	34
(issued 1,782 and 2,029 shares, respectively)		
23 Capital in excess of par value	13	375
24 Deferred compensation	-	(-21)
25 Retained earnings	11,519	16,510
26 Accumulated other comprehensive loss	(1,646)	(1,374)
27 Less: repurchased common stock, at cost	(1,268)	(7,920)
(26 and 280 shares, respectively)		
28 **Total Common Shareholders' Equity**	8,648	7,604
29 **Total Liabilities and Shareholders' Equity**	$21,695	$20,757

Exhibit 13.1: *PepsiCo's Consolidated Balance Sheet.* It contains figures for December 29, 2001, and December 30, 2000. In real life, it is accompanied by notes that explain more detail.

(in millions)	2001 Shares	2001 Amount	2000 Shares	2000 Amount	1999 Shares	1999 Amount
Common Stock						
Balance, beginning of year	2,029	$ 34	2,030	$ 34	2,037	34
Share repurchases	-	-	(9)	-	(13)	-
Stock option exercises	6	-	-	-	-	-
Quaker stock option exercises	3	-	8	-	6	-
Shares issued to effect merger	(256)	(4)	0	-	-	-
Balance, end of year	1,782	30	2,029	34	2,030	34
Capital in Excess of Par Value						
Balance, beginning of year		375		559		904
Share repurchases		-		(236)		(370)
Stock option exercises[a]		82		52		(21)
Reissued shares		150		-		-
Shares issued to effect merger		(595)		-		-
Other		1		-		46
Balance, end of year		13		375		559
Deferred Compensation						
Balance, beginning of year		(21)		(45)		(68)
Net activity		21		24		23
Balance, end of year		-		(21)		(45)
Retained Earnings						
Balance, beginning of year		16,510		14,921		13,356
Net income		2,662		2,543		2,505
Shares issued to effect merger		(6,644)		-		-
Cash dividends declared - common		(1,005)		(950)		(936)
Cash dividends declared - preferred		(4)		(4)		(4)
Balance, end of year		11,519		16,510		14,921
Accumulated Other Comprehensive Loss						
Balance, beginning of year		(1,374)		(1,085)		(1,139)
Currency translation adjustment (CTA)		(218)		(289)		(136)
CTA reclassification adjustment		-		-		175
Cash flow hedges, net of tax:						
Cumulative effect of accounting change		3		-		-
Derivative (losses)/gains, net		(21)		-		-
Minimum pension liability adjustment, net of tax		(38)		(2)		17
Other		2		2		(2)
Balance, end of year		(1,646)		(1,374)		(1,085)
Repurchased Common Stock						
Balance, beginning of year	(280)	(7,920)	(271)	(7,306)	(255)	(6,535)
Shares repurchased	(35)	(1,716)	(38)	(1,430)	(36)	(1,285)
Stock option exercises	20	751	29	816	20	514
Reissued shares	13	374	-	-	-	-
Shares issued to effect merger	256	7,243	-	-	-	-
Balance, end of year	(26)	(1,268)	(280)	(7,920)	(271)	(7,306)
Total Common Shareholders' Equity		$ 8,648		$ 7,604		$ 7,078

Exhibit 13.2: *PepsiCo's Consolidated Statement of Common Shareholders' Equity.* It contains figures for December 29, 2001, December 30, 2000, and December 25, 1999. In real life, it is accompanied by notes that explain more detail. They mention a closing stock price of $49.05/share, which indicates a market capitalization of $87.4 billion. Table note [a]: Includes total tax benefit of $212 in 2001, $177 in 2000 and $105 in 1999.

(in millions except per share amounts)	2001	2000	1999
NET SALES			
1 New PepsiCo	$ 26,935	$25,479	$22,970
2 Bottling Operations	–	–	2,123
3 Total Net Sales	26,935	25,479	25,093
COSTS AND EXPENSES			
4 Cost of sales	10,754	10,226	10,326
5 Selling, general and administrative expenses	11,608	11,104	11,018
6 Amortization of intangible assets	165	147	193
7 Merger-related costs	356	–	–
8 Other impairment and restructuring charges	31	184	73
9 Total Costs and Expenses	22,914	21,661	21,610
OPERATING PROFIT			
10 New PepsiCo	$ 4,021	$3,818	$3,430
11 Bottling Operations	–	–	2,123
12 Total Operating Profit	$ 4,021	$3,818	$3,483
13 Bottling equity income and transaction gains/(loss), net	160	130	1,083
14 Interest expense	(219)	(272)	(421)
15 Interest income	67	85	130
(net interest income is sum of preceding three items)	= 8	= –57	= 792
16 **INCOME BEFORE INCOME TAXES**	4,029	3,761	4,275
17 **PROVISION FOR INCOME TAXES**	1,367	1,218	1,770
18 **NET INCOME**	$ 2,662	$ 2,543	$ 2,505
NET INCOME PER COMMON SHARE			
19 Basic	$ 1.51	$ 1.45	$ 1.41
20 Diluted	$ 1.47	$ 1.42	$ 1.38

Exhibit 13.3: *PepsiCo's Consolidated Statement of Income.* It contains figures for December 29, 2001, December 30, 2000, and December 25, 1999. In real life, it is accompanied by notes that explain more detail.

in millions	52 Weeks Ending	53 Weeks Ending	52 Weeks Ending
	12/29/01	12/30/00	12/25/99
Cash Flows - Operating Activities			
1 Net income	$ 2,662	$ 2,543	$ 2,505
Adjustments to reconcile net income to net cash provided by operating activities			
2 Bottling equity income, net	(160)	(130)	(1,083)
3 Depreciation and amortization	1,082	1,093	1,156
4 Merger-related costs	356	–	–
5 Other impairment and restructuring charges	31	184	73
6 Cash payments for merger-related costs and restructuring charges	(273)	(38)	(98)
7 Deferred income taxes	162	33	73
8 Deferred compensation - ESOP	48	36	32
9 Other noncash charges and credits, net	209	303	368
Changes in operating working capital, excluding effects of acquisitions and dispositions			
10 Accounts and Notes Receivables	7	(52)	(141)
11 Inventories	(75)	(51)	(202)
12 Prepaid expenses and other current assets	(6)	(35)	(209)
13 Accounts payable and other current liabilities	(236)	219	357
14 Income taxes payable	394	335	274
15 Net change in operating working capital	84	416	79
16 **Net Cash Provided by Operating Activities**	4,201	4,440	3,605
Cash Flows - Investing Activities			
17 Capital spending	(1,324)	(1,352)	(1,341)
18 Acquisitions and investments in unconsolidated affiliates	(432)	(98)	(430)
19 Sales of businesses	–	33	513
20 Sales of property, plant & equipment	–	57	130
Short-term investments, by original maturity			
21 More than three months – purchases	(2,537)	(4,950)	(2,209)
22 More than three months – payments	2,078	4,585	2,220
23 Three months or less, net	(41)	(9)	12
24 Other, net	(381)	(262)	(67)
25 **Net Cash Used for Investing Activities**	(2,637)	(1,996)	(1,172)

Exhibit 13.4: *PepsiCo's Consolidated Statement of Cash Flows.* It contains figures for December 29, 2001, December 30, 2000, and December 25, 1999. In real life, it is accompanied by notes that explain more detail. (This table continues on the next page.)

in millions

		52 Weeks Ending 12/29/01	53 Weeks Ending 12/30/00	52 Weeks Ending 12/25/99
Cash Flows - Financing Activities				
26	Proceeds from issuances of long-term debt	324	130	3,480
27	Payments of long-term debt	(573)	(879)	(1,216)
	Short-term borrowings, by original maturity			
28	More than three months — proceeds	788	198	3,699
29	More than three months — payments	(483)	(155)	(2,758)
30	Three months or less, net — payments	(397)	1	(2,814)
31	Cash dividends paid	(994)	(949)	(935)
32	Share repurchases - common	(1,716)	(1,430)	(1,285)
33	Share repurchases - preferred	(10)	–	–
34	Quaker share repurchases	(5)	(254)	(382)
35	Proceeds from issuance of shares in conn. with Quaker merger	524	–	–
36	Proceeds from exercises of stock options	623	690	383
37	**Net Cash Used for Financing Activities**	(1,919)	(2,648)	(1,828)
38	Effect of Exchange Rate Changes on Cash and Cash Equivalents	–	(4)	3
39	**Net (Decrease)/Increase in Cash and Cash Equivalents**	(355)	(208)	(608)
40	**Cash and Cash Equivalents - Beginning of year**	1,038	1,246	638
41	**Cash and Cash Equivalents - End of period**	$ 683	$ 1,038	$ 1,246
	Supplemental Cash Flow Information			
42	Interest paid	$ 159	$ 226	$ 384
43	Income taxes paid	$ 857	$ 876	$ 689
44	Acquisitions			
45	Fair value of assets acquired	$ 604	$ 80	$ 717
46	Cash paid and debt issued	(432)	(98)	(438)
47	Liabilities Assumed	$ 172	$ (18)	$ 279

Exhibit 13.4: *Consolidated Statement of Cash Flows (continued).*

PepsiCo's Financials

Exhibits 13.1–13.4 contain the financial statements that PepsiCo reported in its 2001 annual report. (The entire annual report is available at http://www.pepsico.com/. I have tried to render the format of these PepsiCo tables just like the originals.) If you are wondering why we are using such old statements, there is a good reason. It will allow us to track in Chapter 20 what actually happened to PepsiCo in subsequent years. In any case, nothing major has changed in the accounting rules since 2001, so every principle in these statements remains applicable today.

We look at PepsiCo financials.

Every financial report has four main statements:

The balance sheet in Exhibit 13.1 provides a snapshot of the firm's assets and liabilities at a fixed point in time. (It is a measure of "stock," not of "flow" over an interval.)

Some assets (mostly cash and securities, accounts receivable, and inventories) are classified as **current assets**. The idea is that these assets will convert into cash within one year or less. They are thus short term in nature and are used by the firm to fund its day-to-day operations. They are also often (but not always) fairly easy to liquidate in case of distress. Current assets contrast with other assets such as plants or brand reputation (an intangible asset), which are expected to generate cash over more than one year. Noncurrent assets are often much harder to convert into cold, hard cash if the firm needs money quickly.

As in finance, accounting forces the sum total of all assets to be owned by creditors and shareholders. And, as with assets, some creditors are owed money over the short term. These are called **current liabilities**. Noncurrent liabilities include other debt that is more long term. And then there are obligations to our "friend," the IRS. The remainder—whatever assets are not accounted for by debt owed to creditors—is called equity. Therefore,

The financial statements: balance sheet, income statement, cash flow statement, and (the relatively less important) equity statement.

$$\text{Assets} = \text{Liabilities} + \text{Shareholders' Equity}$$

If all assets and liabilities were properly valued, then the accounting **book value** of shareholders' equity would be the market value, too. This is usually far from the truth. Difficulties in valuing assets and liabilities render many balance sheet numbers unreliable. *You have been warned!*

➤ *Warning about BV stock numbers, Sect. 13.7, Pg.405.*

The owners' equity statement (or "shareholders' equity statement") in Exhibit 13.2 explains the history of capital originally contributed to the firm, and of earnings that were retained (not paid out). We will not use this statement any further.

The income statement in Exhibit 13.3 reports the revenues and expenses of the company, resulting in earnings (also called net income) over the year. (Thus, it reports measures of "flows," not of "stocks.")

In the above three statements, accountants seek to "smooth out" temporary hiccups— which you will learn about in a moment. It is only in the fourth statement that this is not attempted:

The cash flow statement in Exhibit 13.4 reports the sources and uses of cash over the year. (It is a measure of "flow," not of "stock.")

You should stare at these four PepsiCo statements for a while. But however hard you look, you will not be able to find an item entitled "cash flow for an NPV analysis." And the cash flows on the cash flow statement look nothing like the earnings, which is what the world seems to consider important! Somehow, you must learn what these financials mean so that you can extract what you really need from them: a "cash flow for an NPV analysis" from the four financial statements.

The most important
statements are the
income and cash flow
statements, not the
two stock statements.

For the most part, U.S. GAAP rules focus more on the accuracy of the two flow statements than on the accuracy of the two stock statements. (The balance sheet does contain important information, but many of its entries are precarious.) Fortunately, this suits us well. We will be spending a lot of time explaining the income statement and cash flow statement. The upshot is that the cash flow statement comes closest to what you want. However, to understand why it is insufficient and where it comes from, you need to take a wider expedition into the logic of accounting (and, specifically, of net income), which is different from the logic of finance (and, specifically, of NPV cash flows). Your next step is to learn how to read, interpret, and transform financial statements into the cash flows that an NPV analysis demands. You also need this expedition to get a better understanding of earnings and financial statements in general.

Why Financiers and Accountants Think Differently

Earnings anticipate
future costs and
benefits (in some odd
sense).

Financiers try to understand the firm value by working with the exact timing of hard cash inflows and outflows over the entire project's lifetime. Like financiers, accountants are interested in firm value. (However, this is an oversimplification, because accounting estimates are also subject to a number of considerations that can trump their desire for accuracy—first and foremost, an explicit desire to remain conservative. For example, entries on the balance sheet are recorded at the lower of either cost or market value. Thus, even if an accountant knows that the value is higher than the cost, she may not want to use this information. We will mostly ignore conservatism, and focus on how we can use accounting information for our purposes.) Unlike financiers, accountants focus not just on economic cash flows but also on annual earnings (a flow variable). These earnings try to incorporate changes in the expected future immediately into the firm's net income today.

The difference
between income and
economic cash flows
is "accruals."

The main difference between these two concepts of income and cash flows is **accruals**, which are economic transactions that have delayed cash implications. For example, if I owe your firm $10,000 and have committed to paying you tomorrow, the accountant would record your current firm value to be $10,000 (perhaps time- and credit-risk adjusted). In contrast, the financier would consider this to be a zero cash-flow today—until tomorrow, when the payment actually occurs. The contrast is that the accountant (by and large) wants the financial statements to be a good (though also conservative) representation of the economic value of the firm *today* (i.e., you already own my commitment to pay), instead of a representation of the exact timing of inflows and outflows. The financier needs the timing of cash flows for the NPV discounting instead.

When financiers buy a
machine, they see one
big expense spike
up-front, followed by
years of no further
expenses.

Accruals can be classified into long-term and short-term accruals. The primary *long-term accrual* is **depreciation**, which is the spreading of asset-purchasing cost over a number of years. For example, when a financier purchases a maintenance-free machine, he sees a machine that costs a lot of cash today and produces cash flows in the future. If the machine needs to be replaced every 20 years, then the financier sees a sharp spike in cash outflows every 20 years, followed by no further expenditures (but hopefully many cash inflows).

The accountant, however, sees the machine as an asset that uses up a fraction of its value each year. An accountant would try to determine an amount by which the machine deteriorates in each year, and she would only consider this prorated deterioration to be the annual outflow (called an **expense**). The purchase of a $1 million machine would therefore not be an earnings reduction of $1 million in the first year, followed by $0 in the remaining 19 years. Instead, it would be an expense of, say, $50,000 in each of the 20 years. (This is a common method of depreciation and is called **straight-line depreciation**, here over 20 years. There are others.) Note also how neither the accounting nor the finance figure may be entirely accurate value-wise if you had to suddenly liquidate the machine after one year (e.g., if the firm went bankrupt). The machine could presumably be sold, but whether it could be sold for $950,000 or not at all would depend on the type of machine and prevailing market conditions.

> For this machine, accountants see depreciation: a little bit of use every year for many years.

To complicate matters further, accountants often use different standardized schedules over which particular assets are depreciated. These are called **impairment rules**, and you already know the straight-line rule. Residential investment properties (houses), for example, are commonly depreciated straight-line over 40 years (or 27.5 years for tax purposes)—often regardless of whether the house is constructed of straw or brick. The predetermined value schedule is usually not accurate. For example, if investors have recently developed a taste for old buildings, it could be that a building's value has doubled in line with prevailing real estate price increases, even though the financial statements might record this building to be worth nothing. (Even this is oversimplified. On occasion, accountants invoke procedures that allow them to adjust the value of an asset midway through its accounting life—but more often downward than upward.) Another common impairment rule is accelerated depreciation. (One form thereof is called MACRS, which is especially important in a tax context. But we are straying too far for the moment.)

> This "little bit of use" cost comes from standardized impairment schedules.

If the machine happens to continue working after 20 years, the financials that have just treated the machine as a $50,000 expense in year 20 will now treat it as a $0 expense in year 21. It remains worth $0 because it cannot depreciate any further—it has already been fully depreciated. The financier sees no difference between year 20 and year 21, just as long as the machine continues to work.

> There is usually inconsistency at the point when the machine has been fully depreciated.

Short-term accruals come in a variety of guises. To a financier, what matters is the timing of cash coming in and going out. A sale for credit is not cash *until* the company has collected the cash. To the accountant, if the firm sells $100 worth of goods on credit, the $100 is booked as revenue (which flows immediately into net income), even though no money has yet arrived. In the accounting view, the sale has been made. To reflect the delay in payment, accountants increase the **receivables (A/R)** by $100. (Sometimes, firms simultaneously establish an allowance for estimated nonpayments [bad debts].)

> For short-term accruals, such as receivables, accounting logic relies on predicted future cash inflows.

Another short-term accrual is **income tax**, which a financier considers to be an outflow only when it has to be paid—at least not until (the corporate equivalent of) April 15 of the following year. However, on the income statement, when a firm in the 40% corporate tax bracket makes $100 in profits, the income statement immediately

> The logic of finance relies exclusively on actual cash flows (or immediate values).

subtracts the corporate income tax of $40 (which will eventually have to be paid on the $100 in profits) and therefore records net income of only $60. To reflect the fact that the full $100 cash is still around, $40 is recorded as **taxes payable.**

Both approaches have their own advantages and disadvantages.

In sum, for a financier, the machine costs a lot of cash today (so it is an immediate negative), the accounts receivable are not yet cash inflows (so they are not yet positives), and the corporate income tax is not yet a cash outflow (so it is not yet a negative). For an accountant, the machine costs a prorated amount over a period of years, the accounts receivable are immediate positive earnings, and the corporate income tax is an immediate cost. There is a definite logic in the approaches of both accounting and finance: The accounting approach may be better in giving a snapshot impression of the firm's value; the finance approach is better in measuring the timing of the cash inflows and cash outflows for valuation purposes. Note that valuation leans much more heavily on the assumption that *all* future cash flows are fully considered. Today's cash flows alone would *not* usually make for a good snapshot of the firm's situation: The firm is not worth a negative amount just because it has recently purchased a machine that has caused a large negative cash flow this year.

ANECDOTE　　　Trashy Accounting at Waste Management

On December 14, 1998, Waste Management (WMX) settled a class action lawsuit by shareholders for $220 million, then the largest such settlement ever. The suit alleged that WMX had overstated its income by $1.32 billion over an 8-year period. From 1994 through 1997, about 47% of the company's reported income was fictitious.

One of WMX's dubious practices was that it had changed the accounting life of its waste containers from 12 to 18 years. Therefore, each year, it subtracted less depreciation, which increased its reported earnings by $1.7 billion. Of course, during that time, managers were handsomely rewarded for their superior earnings performance.

Q 13.1. What is the main difference between the depiction of a project in accounting (net income) and in finance (economic cash flows)?

Q 13.2. Is the firm's lifetime sum of net income roughly equal to the firm's lifetime sum of cash flows?

13.2　Long-Term Accruals (Depreciation)

This hypothetical project will illustrate the difference between an accounting and a finance perspective for depreciation.

Rather than starting off trying to understand a creature as complex as the PepsiCo financials, let's begin with a simple firm for which you know the cash flows. Your firm is basically just one machine, described in Exhibit 13.5. We shall construct hypothetical financials, and then we shall reverse-engineer them. The machine is rather unusual: It lasts 6 years, has no maintenance costs, requires capital expenditures not only in the first but also the second year, and produces full output even in year 1. It produces net sales (after taking costs into account) of $60 per year, and customers pay cash immediately. Your corporate income tax rate is 40%, and your cost of capital is 12% per year. With $50 of debt at 10% interest, the firm's annual interest payments are $5. (The debt interest is lower than the firm's average cost of capital, because investors are risk averse.) In this section, all sales and expenses are assumed to be cash transactions and not delayed.

➤ Risk aversion and cost of capital, Pg.139.

"Real Project"		Available Financing—Executed	
Real Physical Lifespan	6 years	Debt Capacity	$50
Capital Expenditure	$75, year 1 (Y1)	Debt Interest Rate	10%/year
	$75, year 2 (Y2)		(= $5/year)
Gross Output	$70/year		
– Input Costs (Cash)	$5/year	**Accounting Treatment**	
– Selling Costs (Cash)	$5/year	Project Life	3 years
= Net Output	$60/year		
Overall Cost of Capital	12%/year		
Corporate Tax Rate (τ)	40%/year		

Exhibit 13.5: *A Hypothetical Project. Sidenote:* This debt contract provides cash necessary in year 1, and requires a first interest payment in year 2. Both principal and interest are repaid in year 6.

Doing Accounting

For the public financials, GAAP requests that firms use their discretion to match reported depreciation to true depreciation, *although conservatively so.* (There are exceptions.) In real life, matching actual life to accounting life is almost impossible to accomplish, if only because it is often unclear up-front how long the assets will really last. (For this reason, many firms rely on standard depreciation schedules.) In contrast to the public statements, when it comes to tax accounting, the differences between actual and accounting life are even more pronounced. Depreciation rules for computing the corporate income tax are set by Congress. They are intentionally based on strict mechanical schedules, regardless of the true asset life, and change with tax laws—quite often. (Even states can have their own rules.) Although GAAP and IRS schedules are almost always different, for now just assume that both GAAP and the IRS have decreed that this particular machine should be depreciated over three years, even though it lasts longer. Consequently, $75 generates $25 in depreciation, three years in a row, beginning in the year of the capital expenditure, and none after the third year. How does depreciation affect the reported financials?

Depreciation schedules are not exact.

The income statement for this project is shown in Exhibit 13.6. (I use Y as an abbreviation for "Year.") In going down the leftmost column of any of these tables, you will notice that accounting has its own jargon, just like finance. **COGS** abbreviates *cost of goods sold.* **SG&A** abbreviates *selling, general & administrative expenses.* Both of

A standard project's income statement.

Income Statement

		Y1	Y2	Y3	Y4	Y5	Y6
	Sales (Revenues)	$70	$70	$70	$70	$70	$70
−	Cost of Goods Sold (COGS)	$5	$5	$5	$5	$5	$5
−	Selling, General & Administrative Expenses (SG&A)	$5	$5	$5	$5	$5	$5
=	EBITDA	$60	$60	$60	$60	$60	$60
−	Depreciation	$25	$50	$50	$25	$0	$0
=	EBIT (operating income)	$35	$10	$10	$35	$60	$60
−	Interest Expense	$0	$5	$5	$5	$5	$5
=	EAIBT (or EBT)	$35	$5	$5	$30	$55	$55
−	Corporate Income Tax (at 40%)	$14	$2	$2	$12	$22	$22
=	Net Income	$21	$3	$3	$18	$33	$33

Excerpts from the Cash Flow Statement

	Y1	Y2	Y3	Y4	Y5	Y6
Net Debt Issue	+$50					−$50
Capital Expenditures[a]	−$75	−$75				
Depreciation	+$25	+$50	+$50	+$25	$0	$0

Exhibit 13.6: *Income Statement and Excerpt of Cash Flow Statement of Hypothetical Machine.* Although I have broken depreciation out in this income statement, it is usually part of other components, most likely COGS or SG&A. Fortunately, depreciation is always fully broken out in the cash flow statement. This is why you need to look it up in the latter. Table note [a]: *Sign Warning:* The accounting convention is to record capital expenditures as a negative number, i.e., as −$75, on the cash flow statement. But beware: The same capital expenditures would be recorded as a positive asset on the balance sheet.

these are expenditures that have to be subtracted from **sales** (or **revenues**) to arrive at **EBITDA** (earnings before interest, taxes, depreciation, and amortization). Next, subtract out depreciation, which is a subject that deserves the long discussion below and that we will return to in a moment. Thus, you arrive at **operating income**, also called **EBIT** (earnings before interest and taxes). Finally, take out interest expense at a rate of 10% per year and corporate income tax (which you can compute from the firm's tax rate of 40%) and arrive at plain **earnings**, also called **net income**. Net income is often called the "bottom line" because of where it appears.

Note the similarity of this simple project's income statement to PepsiCo's income statement from Exhibit 13.3. In 2001, PepsiCo had $26,935 million in sales. COGS and SG&A (which included some depreciation) added up to $10,754 + $11,608 = $22,362 million. Amortization (another form of depreciation explained below) subtracted $165 million. Other expenses amounted to $387 million, leaving you with EBIT of $26,935 − $22,362 − $165 − $356 − $31 = $4,021 million. In PepsiCo's case, the combination of bottling equity income and transaction gains, interest expenses, and interest income was determined to be its net interest income of $8 million, perhaps better called net investment income here. Uncle Sam demanded $1,367 million, leaving shareholders with net income of $2,662 million. Yes, PepsiCo has a few extra items and changes some of the names around, but the broad similarity should be obvious.

Compare the similarity of our income statement to PepsiCo's.

You have already reported almost all the information of your project on the income statement. The two exceptions are the capital expenditures and the net debt issue. These do not go onto the income statement. Instead, they are reported on the cash flow statement (also in Exhibit 13.6). In this case, capital expenditures are $75 in year 1 and $75 in year 2, followed by $0 in all subsequent years. Net debt issuing is $50 in year 1, and the debt principal repayment of $50 occurs in year 6. (In addition, the cash flow statement also reports depreciation. I will soon explain why you should actually read depreciation off the cash flow statement—not off the income statement.)

Capital expenditures and debt issuing are recorded on the cash flow statement, not the income statement.

This is not to say that project capital expenditures and debt play no role in the income statement—they do, but not one-to-one. Specifically, capital expenditures reduce net income (in the income statement) only slowly through depreciation:

Here is how capital expenditures enter the income statement: depreciation.

Year Y1: The first $25 depreciation from the first year's $75 capital expenditures is accounted for.

Year Y2: The second $25 depreciation from the first year's $75 capital expenditures is accounted for, plus the first $25 depreciation from the second year's $75 capital expenditures is accounted for. Thus, a total of $50 is depreciated.

Year Y3: The third and final $25 remaining depreciation from the first year's $75 capital expenditures is accounted for, plus the second $25 depreciation from the second year's capital expenditures. Again, a total of $50 is depreciated.

Year Y4: There is no more depreciation from the first year's capital expenditures. You only have the third installment of the second year's capital expenditures left. Thus, depreciation is $25.

You can visualize this as follows:

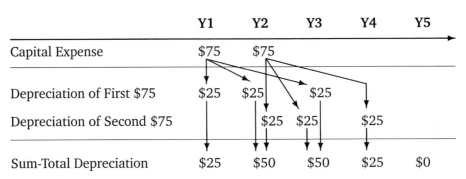

	Y1	Y2	Y3	Y4	Y5
Capital Expense	$75	$75			
Depreciation of First $75	$25	$25	$25		
Depreciation of Second $75		$25	$25	$25	
Sum-Total Depreciation	$25	$50	$50	$25	$0

The principal on the loan, either its funding or its repayment, plays no role on the income statement. However, the interest paid on the loan does go onto the income statement.

Doing Finance

Here is the difference between full ownership and levered ownership.

Now, forget accounting for a moment and instead value the machine from a finance perspective. The firm consists of three components: the machine itself, the tax obligation, and the loan.

$$\text{NPV Project} = \text{NPV Machine} - \text{NPV Taxes}$$

$$\text{NPV Levered Ownership} = \text{NPV Machine} - \text{NPV Taxes} + \text{NPV Loan}$$

Full project ownership is equivalent to holding both the debt (including all liabilities) and equity (the machine), and earning the cash flows due to both creditors and shareholders. Levered equity ownership adds the project "loan" to the package. As full project owner (debt plus equity), in the first year, you must originally supply $50 more in capital than if you are just a levered equity owner, but in subsequent years, as full owner, you then do not need to worry about paying back a lender.

Look only at inflows and outflows of the first component of the firm—the machine's actual cash flows, without taxes and loan.

First work out the actual cash flows of the first component, the machine itself. Without the taxes and the loan, the machine produces the following:

$$\text{NPV}_{\text{machine}} = \frac{\$60 - \$75}{(1 + 12\%)^1} + \frac{\$60 - \$75}{(1 + 12\%)^2} + \frac{\$60}{(1 + 12\%)^3}$$

$$+ \frac{\$60}{(1 + 12\%)^4} + \frac{\$60}{(1 + 12\%)^5} + \frac{\$60}{(1 + 12\%)^6} \approx \$119.93$$

$$\text{NPV}_{\text{machine}} = \frac{C_1}{1 + r_1} + \frac{C_2}{1 + r_2} + \frac{C_3}{1 + r_3}$$

$$+ \frac{C_4}{1 + r_4} + \frac{C_5}{1 + r_5} + \frac{C_6}{1 + r_6}$$

➤ *Income Statement, Exhibit 13.6, Pg.382.*

The tax obligation is a negative-NPV project, which must be valued.

Unfortunately, corporate income tax—the second component—is an actual cost that cannot be ignored. Looking at Exhibit 13.6, you see that Uncle Sam collects $14 in the first year, then $2 twice, then $12, and finally $22 twice. Assume that the stream of tax obligations has the same discount rate (12%) as that of the overall firm. (To value the future tax obligations, you need to know the appropriate discount factor. Unfortunately, we need to delay this issue until Chapter 17. It is both convenient and customary [if not exactly correct] to use the firm's overall cost of capital as the discount rate for its tax obligations.) With this cost-of-capital assumption, the net present cost of the tax liability is

➤ *Discount factor on tax obligations,* Sect. App.17.A (Companion), Pg.≈99.

$$\text{NPV}_{\text{tax liability}} = \frac{\$14}{1.12^1} + \frac{\$2}{1.12^2} + \frac{\$2}{1.12^3} + \frac{\$12}{1.12^4} + \frac{\$22}{1.12^5} + \frac{\$22}{1.12^6} \approx \$46.77$$

Put together,

The overall project NPV.

$$\text{NPV}_{\text{project}} \approx \$119.93 - \$46.77 = \$73.16$$

$$\text{NPV Project} = \text{NPV Machine} - \text{NPV Taxes}$$

Now consider the third component—the loan. Assume that you are not the "full project owner," but only the "residual levered equity owner," so you do not extend the loan yourself. Instead, you would obtain a loan from a (hopefully) perfect capital market. Let us assume that your company "got what it paid for," a fair deal—a reasonable assumption for most large corporations. Your loan that provides $50 and pays interest at a rate of 10% should thus be zero NPV. (This saves you the effort of having to compute the loan's NPV.)

The loan usually is a "zero-NPV" project, unless you can get an unusually great deal or suffer an unusually bad deal on the loan.

$$\text{NPV}_{\text{loan}} = \$0$$

Be my guest, though, and make the effort:

$$\text{NPV}_{\text{loan}} = \frac{+\$50}{1.10^1} + \frac{-\$5}{1.10^2} + \frac{-\$5}{1.10^3} + \frac{-\$5}{1.10^4} + \frac{-\$5}{1.10^5} + \frac{(-\$50) + (-\$5)}{1.10^6} = \$0$$

Therefore, the project NPV with the loan, that is, levered equity ownership, is the same as the project NPV without the loan. This makes sense: You are not generating or destroying any value by borrowing from one bank rather than another. Therefore,

$$\text{NPV}_{\text{levered ownership}} = \$119.93 - \$46.77 + \$0 = \$73.16$$

$$\text{NPV}_{\text{levered ownership}} = \text{NPV Machine} - \text{NPV Taxes} + \text{NPV Loan}$$

Although the NPV remains the same, the cash flows to levered equity ownership are different from the cash flows to the project. The cash flows (and net income) are shown in Exhibit 13.7. Note how different the cash flows and net income are. Net income is highest in years 5 and 6, but the levered cash flow in year 6 is negative. In contrast, in year 3—the year with the highest levered cash flow—net income is lowest.

Earnings and cash flows are often very different.

	Y1	Y2	Y3	Y4	Y5	Y6	Disc Rate	NPV
Cash Flow, Machine w/o Tax	−$15	−$15	+$60	+$60	+$60	+$60	12%	$119.93
+ Cash Flow, Uncle Sam	−$14	−$2	−$2	−$12	−$22	−$22	12%	−$46.77
= Cash Flow, **Project, After Tax**	−$29	−$17	+$58	+$48	+$38	+$38	12%	$73.16
+ Cash Flow, Loan	+$50	−$5	−$5	−$5	−$5	−$55	10%	$0.00
= **Levered Ownership**	+$21	−$22	+$53	+$43	+$33	−$17		$73.16
For Comparison, Net Income	$21	$3	$3	$18	$33	$33		

Exhibit 13.7: *Cash Flows and Net Income Summary.* Because investors are risk averse, the discount rate (also called the cost of capital or required expected rate of return) is higher for the machine than for the loan.

Reverse-Engineering Accounting into Finance

Discounting the net income would not give you the true project NPV.

If you did not know about the details of this machine but saw only the financials, could you compute the correct firm value by discounting the net income? Discounting net income with a cost of capital of 12% would yield

$$\text{A Incorrect NPV via net income} = \frac{\$21}{1.12^1} + \frac{\$3}{1.12^2} + \frac{\$3}{1.12^3} + \frac{\$18}{1.12^4} + \frac{\$33}{1.12\%^5} + \frac{\$33}{1.12^6} \approx \$70.16$$

which is definitely not the correct answer of $73.16. Neither would it be correct to discount the net income with a cost of capital of 10%,

$$\text{Incorrect NPV via net income} = \frac{\$21}{1.10^1} + \frac{\$3}{1.10^2} + \frac{\$3}{1.10^3} + \frac{\$18}{1.10^4} + \frac{\$33}{1.10^5} + \frac{\$33}{1.10^6} \approx \$75.24$$

Instead, you must reverse-engineer the economic cash flows from the corporate financials.

How can you reverse-engineer the correct cash flows for the NPV analysis from the financials? You first need to translate the financials back into the cash flows that NPV analysis can use. You just need to retrace your steps. You have both the income statement and cash flow statement at your disposal. First, to obtain the machine cash flow, you can apply the formula in the following table

		Y1	Y2	
	EBIT	+$35	+$10	
+	Depreciation	+$25	+$50	(13.1)
"+"	(−) Capital Expenditures	+(−$75)	+(−$75)	
=	Cash Flow, Project, Before Tax	−$15	−$15	

to the numbers from Exhibit 13.6. You add back the depreciation, because it *was not* an actual cash outflow, and you subtract the capital expenditures, because

➤ *Income Statement, Exhibit 13.6, Pg. 382.*

they *were* actual cash flows. I find the formula most intuitive if I think of the "depreciation + capital expenditures" terms as undoing the accountants' smoothing of the cost of machines over multiple periods.

IMPORTANT

> The main operation to take care of long-term accruals in the conversion from net income into cash flows is to undo the smoothing—add back the depreciation and subtract out the capital expense.

Now you need to subtract corporate income taxes (and, again, look at the numbers themselves to clarify the signs in your mind; income tax is sometimes quoted as a negative, sometimes as a positive). This gives you the following after-tax project cash flow:

Finish the reverse-engineering by subtracting off taxes.

		Y1	Y2
	EBIT	+$35	+$10
+	Depreciation	+$25	+$50
"+"	(–)Capital Expenditures	+(–$75)	+(–$75)
–	(+)Corporate Income Tax	–(+$14)	–(+$2)
=	Cash Flow, Project, After Tax	–$29	–$17

(13.2)

There is an alternative equivalent method to get these numbers. Net income already has corporate income tax subtracted out, but it also has interest expense subtracted out. You get the same cash flow if you start with net income instead of EBIT but add back the interest expense:

A different way to skin our cat—to reverse-engineer it.

		Y1	Y2
	Net Income	+$21	+$3
+	Depreciation	+$25	+$50
"+"	(–)Capital Expenditures	+(–$75)	+(–$75)
+	Interest Expense	+$0	+$5
=	Cash Flow, Project, After Tax	–$29	–$17

Investors (equity and debt together) must thus come up with $29 in the first year and $17 in the second year. (You can read the cash flows in later years from line 3 of Exhibit 13.7.)

Sidenote: The formula signs themselves seem ambiguous, because accountants use different sign conventions in different spots. For example, because capital expenditures are usually quoted as negative terms on the cash flow statement, in order to subtract capital expenditures, you just add the (negative) number. In the formula below, you want to subtract corporate income tax, which appears on the income statement (Exhibit 13.6) as a positive. Therefore, you have to subtract the positive. Sigh. . . I try to clarify the meaning (and to warn you) with the quotes around the + in the formulas themselves.

The cash flow to
levered equity
shareholders takes
care of money coming
in from and going out
to creditors.

If the project is financed partly by borrowing, then what part of the $29 and $17 can be financed by creditors, and what residual part must be financed by you? In the first year, your creditors provide $50; in the second year, creditors get back $5. Therefore, levered equity actually receives a positive net cash flow of $21 in the first year, and a negative cash flow of $22 in the second year. Therefore, with the loan financed from the outside, you must add all loan inflows (principal proceeds) and subtract all loan outflows (both principal and interest). Therefore, the cash flow for levered equity shareholders is as follows:

		Y1	Y2
	EBIT	+$35	+$10
+	Depreciation	+$25	+$50
"+"	(–)Capital Expenditures	+(–$75)	+(–$75)
–	Corporate Income Tax	–$14	–$2
=	Cash Flow, Project	–$29	–$17
+	Net Debt Issue	+$50	$0
–	Interest Expense	$0	–$5
=	Cash Flow, Levered Equity Ownership	+$21	–$22

A different way to skin
our cat.

Again, net income already has both corporate income tax and interest expense subtracted out, so the same result comes out if you instead use the following formula:

		Y1	Y2	
	Net Income	+$21	+$3	
+	Depreciation	+$25	+$50	
"+"	(–)Capital Expenditures	+(–$75)	+(–$75)	(13.3)
+	Net Debt Issue	+$50	$0	
=	Cash Flow, Levered Equity Ownership	+$21	–$22	

Q 13.3. Show that Formulas 13.1 through 13.3 yield the cash flows in years 3 through 6 in Exhibit 13.7.

Q 13.4. Using the same cash flows as in the NPV analysis in Exhibit 13.7, how would the project NPV change if you used a 10% cost of capital (instead of 12%) on the tax liability?

A N E C D O T E   Solid Financial Analysis

EBITDA was all the rage among consultants and Wall Street for many years, because it seems both closer to cash flows than EBIT and more impervious to managerial earnings manipulation through accruals. Sadly, discounting EBITDA can be worse than discounting EBIT *if* capital expenditures are not netted out—which EBITDA users rarely do. (Not subtracting either capital expenditures or depreciation is equivalent to assuming that production falls like manna from heaven. EBIT may spread capital expenditures over time periods in a strange way, but at least it does not totally forget it!) Sometimes, a little bit of knowledge is more dangerous than none.

In June 2003, a Bear Stearns analyst valued American Italian Pasta, a small NYSE-listed pasta maker. Unfortunately, Herb Greenberg from TheStreet.com discovered that he forgot to subtract capital expenditures—instead, he had added them. This mistake had increased the value of American Italian Pasta from $19 to $58.49 per share (then trading at $43.65). Bear Stearns admitted the mistake and came up with a new valuation in which Bear Stearns boosted the estimate of the company's operating cash flows and dropped its estimate of the cost of capital. Presto! The NPV of this company was suddenly $68 per share. How fortunate that Bear Stearns' estimates were so robust to basic errors. Incidentally, American Italian Pasta traded at $30 in mid-2004, just above $20 by the end of 2004, and at around $10 by the end of 2005.   *TheStreet.com*

Depreciation Nuances

I mentioned earlier that you should read depreciation off the cash flow statement, not the income statement. I now want to explain a little more about real-world accounting for depreciation.

Why you need to get the depreciation number from the cash flow statement.

Depreciation can come in three different forms: **depreciation**, **depletion**, and **amortization**. They are all "allocated expenses" and not actual cash outflows. The name differences come from the asset types to which they apply.

Depreciation comes in different forms with different names.

Depreciation applies to **tangible assets**, such as factories.

Depletion applies to **natural resources**, such as mines.

Amortization applies to **intangible assets**, such as patents, copyrights, licenses, franchises, and so on. As late as the 1970s, average intangible assets for publicly traded U.S. firms were below 10%. Today, it is these intangible assets that have become the overwhelming majority of public firms' assets. (The exact amortization rules are laid down in FASB Rule 142; they are complex and much beyond our scope.)

Because depreciation, depletion, and amortization are conceptually the same thing, they are often lumped together under the catch-all phrase "depreciation," a convention that we are following.

The reason why you need to use the cash flow statement to learn about depreciation is that the income statement does not report an exact equivalent for the depreciation that we wrote down for the machine on our hypothetical income statement. Instead, on the income statement, corporations can break out the depreciation (as we did) or decide to roll it into either "cost of goods sold" or "selling, general & administrative expenses." (Doing so does not affect reported net income.) For a machine, chances are that a real firm would not have reported it separately, but would have rolled it into COGS. In PepsiCo's case, most—but not all—depreciation was actually lumped into

In real life, do not use the depreciation and amortization on the income statement to extract economic cash flows.

SG&A. PepsiCo's amortization on the income statement contains only the depreciation of some nonphysical plant assets.

IMPORTANT

> - Do not use depreciation or amortization figures from the income statement to undo the accounting adjustments for capital expenses. These figures are incomplete. You must use the depreciation figures from the cash flow statement.
>
> - The most common use of the memorized rule *add depreciation to net income* has many users reading both net income and depreciation off of the same income statement. This is wrong.

Go to the cash flow statement for the depreciation number that is the equivalent of what we had in the machine example.

Therefore, the only complete picture of depreciation of all kinds, equivalent to our depreciation entries in our machine example, can be found on the cash flow statement. For PepsiCo, this is the $1,082 in line 3 of the cash flow statement in Exhibit 13.4. This number is the exact equivalent of the depreciation row ($25, $50, $50, $25, $0, $0) for the machine in Exhibit 13.6, not the $165 million amortization that PepsiCo reports on line 6 of its income statement in Exhibit 13.3.

Q 13.5. Rework the example (income statement, cash flow statement excerpts, cash flows, and NPV) with the following parameters:

Project		Available Financing—Executed	
Real Physical Lifespan	5 years	Debt Capacity	$100
Cost	$120, Y1	Debt Interest Rate	8%/year
Gross Output	$80/year		
– Input Costs	$6/year	**Accounting Treatment**	
– Selling Costs	$8/year	Depreciation Method	Linear
= Net Output	$66/year	Accounting Life	4 years
Overall Cost of Capital	8%/year		
Corporate Tax Rate (τ)	50%/year		

Assume that debt does not require any interest payment in the first year (the first payment of $8 occurs in the second year). The world is risk neutral, because the debt and the project require the same expected rate of return (cost of capital).

Q 13.6. For the machine example in the text, do both the financials and the cash flow analysis using monthly discounting. Assume that the loan is taken at the end of the first month (with an inflow of $50), and the first interest payment of $0.42 paid in the second month. (Thus, unlike in the previous question, interest is paid during the first year.) Assume most expenses and income occur pro rata. (Warning: Unless you are a masochist, do not solve this question by hand. Use a computer spreadsheet!)

13.3 Deferred Taxes

Our next real-world complication to attack is the fact that GAAP and the IRS require different depreciation schedules. To extract the economic cash flows, you need to learn how to undo the accounting for what the firm reports on its public financials and what the firm actually pays to the IRS.

The IRS depreciation schedules (and some other details) are not the same as those in the public financials.

Assume that the above example illustrated what GAAP requires the firm to disclose on its financial statements. The novelty is that we now assume that the IRS allows you to depreciate your plant in a different "accelerated fashion." Let's say the IRS depreciation schedule is not $25 each for three years (as reported in your public financials), but $60 in the first year and $15 in the second year.

In an example, we have the IRS allow for faster depreciation.

	Y1	Y2	Y3
Capital Expense	$75	$75	
Depreciation of First $75	$60	$15	
Depreciation of Second $75		$60	$15
Sum-Total Depreciation	$60	$75	$15

Consequently, although the accounting statement construction logic for the IRS is exactly the same as it is for your publicly reported financials, the numbers on your undisclosed IRS financials are necessarily different from those in your reported public financials:

Calculating Taxes.

IRS Income Statement (Not Disclosed)						
	Y1	Y2	Y3	Y4	Y5	Y6
Sales	$70	$70	$70	$70	$70	$70
− COGS	$5	$5	$5	$5	$5	$5
− SG&A	$5	$5	$5	$5	$5	$5
= EBITDA	$60	$60	$60	$60	$60	$60
− IRS Depreciation	$60	$75	$15	$0	$0	$0
= EBIT, IRS	$0	−$15	$45	$60	$60	$60
− Interest Expense, IRS	$0	$5	$5	$5	$5	$5
= EAIBT (or EBT), IRS	$0	−$20	$40	$55	$55	$55
− **Corporate Income Tax (at 40%)**	**$0**	**−$8**	**$16**	**$22**	**$22**	**$22**

(The IRS is not interested in a net income figure, so there is no reason to compute it.) Now compare the actual true taxes on your IRS financials against the GAAP allocated income taxes in Exhibit 13.6:

		Y1	Y2	Y3	Y4	Y5	Y6
Public Reported Income Statement	Pretend Tax	$14	$2	$2	$12	$22	$22
Undisclosed IRS Calculation	Actual Tax	$0	−$8	$16	$22	$22	$22

➤ Income Statement, Exhibit 13.6, Pg. 382.

Both lines contain $74 in total taxes, but your real IRS taxes are lower in the first two years and higher in the next two years. This is because the IRS permitted a faster depreciation schedule than GAAP did. (Good for you! The firm receives cash earlier.)

The deferred tax account on the balance sheet allows you to learn the real taxes paid.

Unfortunately, firms do not disclose their IRS financials, so you cannot work with them. Fortunately, publicly traded firms are required to report the differences between "IRS real taxes" and "GAAP pretend taxes." This is done in a "coded" fashion on the balance sheet and called accumulated **deferred taxes**. It is the "cumulated differences between GAAP and IRS taxes." To understand this better, think of a hypothetical annual flow number that would be the amount by which you have overreported taxes on your financials:

	Y1	Y2	Y3	Y4	Y5	Y6
"Deferred Tax" Annual Overreporting	$14	$10	-$14	-$10	$0	$0

This is still not reported. However, its cumulative sum is reported:

	Y1	Y2	Y3	Y4	Y5	Y6
Reported "Deferred Tax" Account	$14	$24	$10	$0	$0	$0

This deferred tax is reported as a liability on the balance sheet. An intuitive way to think of this number is as the amount by which your reported financial statements have overstated your real income taxes (and thus understated your real income) to date. Our example firm had overreported on the disclosed financials the taxes that it had paid by $24 by the end of year 2 ($14 in year 1 and $10 in year 2).

Here is how you work your way back to uncover the actual taxes paid to the IRS.

Your task is again reverse-engineering—how can you undo the fake income tax term and replace it with a real income tax? Here is the procedure:

1. Compute the annual overreporting of deferred tax from the reported deferred tax account. To do this, compute the change in this deferred tax account every year:

	Y1	Y2	Y3	Y4	Y5	Y6
Reported "Deferred Tax" Liability	$14	$24	$10	$0	$0	$0
Consecutive Annual Increase	$14	$10	-$14	-$10	$0	$0

2. To recover actual taxes paid, subtract the change from the GAAP-reported taxes paid:

		Y1	Y2	Y3	Y4	Y5	Y6
	Reported GAAP Taxes	$14	$2	$2	$12	$22	$22
−	Consecutive Annual Increase	$14	$10	-$14	-$10	$0	$0
=	Actual Taxes Paid to the IRS	$0	-$8	$16	$22	$22	$22

3. For financial figures that are before tax, subtract the actual taxes paid instead of the GAAP taxes paid. For example,

	Y1	Y2	Y3	Y4	Y5	Y6
Cash Flow, Machine w/o Tax	–$15	–$15	$60	$60	$60	$60
– True Taxes, IRS	$0	–$8	$16	$22	$22	$22
= Cash Flow, **Project**	–$15	–$7	$44	$38	$38	$38

For financial figures that are after tax, such as after-tax cash flows, first add back the GAAP taxes that your after-tax figure had already subtracted. Then subtract the actual IRS taxes paid instead. Or, simpler, just add increases in deferred tax. For example, add these changes to the after-tax cash flows that you computed in Exhibit 13.7 on Page 386:

	Y1	Y2	Y3	Y4	Y5	Y6
Earlier Formula, Cash Flow,						
Project, After Tax	–$29	–$17	$58	$48	$38	$38
+ Changes in Deferred Tax	$14	$10	–$14	–$10	$0	$0
= Better Formula for						
Cash Flows, **Project**	–$15	–$7	$44	$38	$38	$38

In sum, the new and improved formula to extract cash flows from financial statements is

Reverse-engineering: Add changes in deferred taxes to the cash flows from the earlier formula.

	Y1	Y2
EBIT	+$35	+$10
+ Depreciation	+$25	+$50
"+" (–)Capital Expenditures	+(–$75)	+(–$75)
– (+)Corporate Income Tax	–(+$14)	–(+$2)
= Cash Flow, Project, After Tax, GAAP Taxes	–$29	–$17
+ Changes in Deferred Taxes	+$14	+$10
= Cash Flows, Project, After Tax, Real	–$15	–$7

That's it. You have taken care of the differences between the GAAP and IRS taxes.

A final note—when you see "deferred taxes" on the cash flow statement, accountants really mean the "change in deferred taxes." (Otherwise, they could not add the numbers as cash flows to other cash flows.) You are supposed to be aware of this.

Deferred tax reporting.

Q 13.7. What are "deferred taxes"? On which of the four financial statements do they appear?

Q 13.8. Assume a firm reports the following information:

	2007	2006	2005
Deferred Tax Liability	$110	$332	$223

You have calculated the after-tax cash flows for a project based on GAAP to be $300 in 2007 and –$100 in 2006. What are the actual after-tax cash flows for the project?

13.4 Short-Term Accruals and Working Capital

More accruals are hidden in working capital.

In addition to long-term accruals and deferred taxes, you also need to learn how to undo short-term accruals. To run a business day to day requires cash. Firms must put money into cash registers (to make change), into inventories (to have something to sell), and into extending credit to buyers (to get them to bite). These current assets consist of **cash**, **accounts receivable**, and **inventories**. Current liabilities are **accounts payable**, **bank overdrafts**, **taxes payable**, and other soon-due bills. We will mostly work with current assets minus current liabilities, which is **net working capital**, often somewhat incorrectly just called **working capital**.

➤ *Current Assets and Liabilities, Pg. 377.*

$$\text{Net Working Capital} \quad = \quad \text{(Current Assets)} - \text{(Current Liabilities)}$$

$$= \quad \text{(Cash + Accounts Receivable + Inventories)}$$

$$- \text{(Accounts Payable + Bank Overdrafts + Taxes Payable)}$$

Net income books cash before it comes in, so accounts receivable need to be taken out.

The cash flow effects of working capital changes are best explained with an example. Say that a firm sells $100 of goods on credit at year 1. The firm books $100 as net income. But because the $100 is not yet available, the firm also books $100 into accounts receivable. To compute actual cash flows, recognize that the cash has not yet materialized: You need to subtract the $100 accounts receivable from the $100 net income.

		Y0	Y1	Y2	Y3
Finance	1. Sales (Net Income) Made, Payment Later	$0	$100	$300	$0
	2. Actual Cash Receipts (for NPV Cash Flow)	$0	$0	$100	$300
Accounting	3. Reported Net Income	$0	$100	$300	$0
	4. Reported Accounts Receivable	$0	$100	$300	$0

Exhibit 13.8: *Multiyear Working Capital.* I have made up the sales number in line 1. The actual cash receipts in line 2 arise because customers always pay one year later. Lines 3 and 4 show how accountants book these sales and payment patterns. (Ultimately, your task will be to translate accounting numbers back into cash receipts numbers.)

These differences between cash flows and net income are year-to-year changes in working capital.

This becomes more interesting if you consider multiple years. For example, the firm in Exhibit 13.8 always sells on credit and is always paid by its customers the following year. An NPV analysis requires the firm's actual cash receipts in line 2, but accountants have provided only the information in lines 3 and 4. How do you get back the information in line 2? Year 1 has already been discussed: You subtracted accounts receivable from net income to obtain the actual cash inflows of $0. Year 2 is more interesting: The firm previously had accounts receivable of $100, but now has accounts receivable of $300. It is the +$200 (= $300 – $100) *change* in accounts receivable that needs to be subtracted from the $300 in net income in order to infer the actual cash receipts of $100. In year 3, the firm no longer grows and is liquidated, so the remaining receivable turn into cash that can be recaptured from the business. Again, the formula to obtain the NPV cash flow (line 2) subtracts the change in working capital (accounts receivable) of $0 – $300 = –$300 from the $0 net income to conclude that you got a +$300 cash inflow. Exhibit 13.9 shows these calculations. (Incidentally, recall how you started this subsection with the year 1 computation: You subtracted $100 in accounts receivable from the $100 net income. This worked only because the accounts receivable was the same as the *change* in accounts receivable, because the original accounts receivable was zero.)

		Y0	Y1	Y2	Y3
Finance	1. Sales (Net Income) Made, Payment Later	$0	$100	$300	$0
	2. Actual Cash Receipts (for NPV Cash Flow)	$0	$0	$100	$300
Accounting	3. Reported Net Income	$0	$100	$300	$0
	4. Reported Accounts Receivable	$0	$100	$300	$0
Your Computations					
	5. Change in Accounts Receivable	$0	+$100	+$200	–$300
6. Net Income (line 3) – Change in Accounts Receivable (line 5)		$0	$0	+$100	+$300

Exhibit 13.9: *Multiyear Working Capital.* Line 6 recovers line 2 from the financials.

Other short-term accruals that are components of working capital work similarly. For example, although corporate income tax is deducted on the income statement for the year in which the earnings have occurred, firms do not have to immediately pay these taxes. Instead, they can often defer them—at least until (the corporate equivalent of) April 15 of the following year. To the extent that more taxes can be delayed, more cash is available than is suggested by net income. Therefore, delayed taxes must be added back to net income when computing finance cash flows. Of course, at some point in the future, these taxes payable will have to be paid, and they will then have to be counted as a cash outflow of the firm. But, for now, the permitted delay in payment is like a government loan at zero interest—and one that the accounting item *net income* ignores.

Working capital already contains other delayed payments, making our lives easier.

IMPORTANT

> To take care of short-term accruals in the conversion from net income into cash flows, undo the smoothing—subtract *changes* in net working capital. (Equivalently, you can add *decreases* in net working capital.)

Expand our valuation formula for another source of cash.

You can now expand our formulas to include changes in working capital:

Project Economic Cash Flow

$=$ EBIT

$+$ Depreciation $-$ Capital Expenditures   ← undoes long-term accruals

$-$ Corporate Income Tax $+$ Changes in Deferred Tax Account   ← undoes IRS tax timing

$-$ Increase in (Net) Working Capital   ← undoes advance booking

---

Sidenote: Alas, as with capital expenditures, the cash flow statement has its sign conventions. The change in cash, accounts receivable, and inventories is recorded as a negative. But accounts payable do not have the opposite sign from accounts receivable, though they are already an outflow (negative); they are left as is. As a result, to compute the firm's net working capital from its line items (accounts receivable, accounts payable, etc.), you do not subtract current liabilities (e.g., accounts payable) from current assets (e.g., accounts receivable), but add them together. Here is an example of the accounting sign conventions. Exhibit 13.4 (PepsiCo's cash flows) listed PepsiCo's changes in working capital as 84, 416, and 79 (in million dollars) for the years 2001, 2000, and 1999:

Cash Flow Statement	December		
	2001	2000	1999
Current Assets			
Accounts Receivable	+7	-52	–141
Inventories	-75	–51	–202
Prepaid Expenses, Etc.	–6	–35	–209
Current Liabilities			
Accounts Payable, Etc.	–236	+219	+357
Corporate Income Tax, Payable	+394	+335	+274
Adjustments for Change in Operating Working Capital	+84	+416	+79

This excludes the effects of acquisitions and dispositions. All figures are in millions of dollars.

Because these figures come from the cash flow statement, to obtain the adjustments for change in operating working capital, all figures are simply added up, not netted out! (The sign of current liabilities has already been reversed for you.) If you notice that these numbers cannot be inferred from other parts of the financial statements, this is because these numbers exclude the effects of acquisitions and dispositions, as well as nonoperating working capital (a catch-all category for a number of items).

Where would you find changes in cash (in the register) itself? These are *not* in the changes of working capital. Instead, they are what you find at the bottom of the cash flow statement. In other words, the very purpose of the cash flow statement is to tell you by how much the cash account on the balance sheet is changing year to year.

(In this formula, I am quoting the purchasing of assets in capital expenditures as a positive number. If you are using the negative number from the cash flow statement, don't subtract but add it.)

ANECDOTE   Working Capital Management

Entrepreneurs usually fail for one of two reasons, and both are common: The first is that the business is just not a good idea to begin with. (The best "cure" is to try to remain extra skeptical and careful.) The second is that the business is too good of an idea and the entrepreneur is not equipped to handle the success. The growth in sales consumes so much cash for increases in working capital that the firm fails to pay back its own loans: The cash is tied up in production, or in inventory, or in credit extended to customers (payment to be received), when instead it is needed to flow back to the bank. For growing firms, proper working capital management is an issue of first-order importance.

Q 13.9. A firm reports the following financials.

	Y0	Y1	Y2	Y3	Y4	Y5	Y6
Reported Sales (=Net Income)	$0	$100	$100	$300	$300	$100	$0
Reported Accounts Receivable	$0	$100	$120	$340	$320	$120	$0

Can you describe the firm's customer payment patterns? Extract the cash flows.

Q 13.10. Construct the financials for a firm that has quarterly sales and net income of $100, $200, $300, $200, and $100. Half of all customers pay immediately, while the other half always pay *two* quarters after purchase.

Q 13.11. (Advanced) Amazonia can pay suppliers after it has sold to customers. Amazonia has 25% margins and is reporting the following

Month	Jan	Feb	Mar	Apr	May
Reported Sales	$0	$100	$100	$400	$0
Reported Net Income	$0	$25	$25	$100	$0
Reported Accounts Payable	$0	$75	$75	$300	$0

What are Amazonia's actual cash flows?

13.5 Earnings Management

There is considerable
discretion in financial
reporting.
Even though the United States has the tightest accounting regulations of any country, managers still have a lot of discretion when it comes to financials. And there is often no clear line. The slope between an ethical and legal judgment call, and unethical and criminal manipulation can be a slippery one.

Not only
earnings—but also
cash flows—can be
managed.
You already know that managers must make many judgments when it comes to accrual accounting. For example, managers can judge overoptimistically how many products customers will return, how much debt will not be repaid, how much inventory will spoil, how long equipment will last, whether a payment is an expense (fully subtracted from earnings) or an investment (an asset that is depreciated over time), or how much of an expense is "unusual." However, manipulation is possible not only for earnings and accruals but also for cash flows—though doing so may be more difficult and costly. For example, if a firm designates some of its short-term securities as "trading instruments," their sale can then create extra cash—what was not cash before now counts as cash! Similarly, you already know that firms can reduce inventory, delay payments to suppliers, and lean on customers to accelerate payment—all of which will generate immediate cash, but doing so will also possibly anger suppliers and customers so much that it will hurt the business in the long run. Firms can also sell off their receivables at a discount, which may raise the immediate cash at hand but reduce the profit that the firm will ultimately receive. A particularly interesting form of earnings management occurs when a firm aggressively sells products on credit. The sales could be immediately booked as earnings, with the loans counting as investments. Of course, if the customers default, all the company has accomplished is giving away its product for free.

Comparing
(short-term) accruals
to those of similar
firms (industry, size,
and growth rate) can
sometimes give you
good warning signs.
One quick measure of comparing how aggressive or conservative financials are is to compare the firm to other similar firms on the basis of the ratio of its short-term accruals divided by its sales. It is important that "similar" here means firms that are not only in the same industry but also growing at roughly the same rate. The reason is that growing firms usually consume a lot of cash—an established firm will show higher cash flows than a growing firm. If the firm is unusual in having much higher accruals—especially short-term accruals—than comparable firms, it is a warning flag that this firm deserves more scrutiny. Managers who decide to manipulate their numbers to jack up their earnings more than likely will try to manage their accruals aggressively in order to create higher earnings, too. Of course, this does not mean that all managers who manage their accruals aggressively do so to deceive the market and will therefore underperform later on. A manager who is very optimistic about the future may treat accruals aggressively—believing in few returns, great sales, and a better future all around. Indeed, as noted earlier, the slope from managerial optimism to illegal earnings manipulation is slippery. Finally, another earnings warning sign for the wary investor is when a firm changes its fiscal year—this is sometimes done in order to make it more difficult to compare financials to past performance or to financials of other firms in the same industry.

Q 13.12. Are short-term or long-term accruals easier to manipulate?

Q 13.13. Give some examples of how a firm can depress the earnings that it currently reports in order to report higher earnings later.

13.6 Economic Cash Flows from PepsiCo's Financials

Now, if you take another look at the complete PepsiCo cash flow statement in Table 13.4 (remember that all numbers are in millions), you can immediately see the procedures that we have just discussed—starting with net income of $2,662 (line 1), adding back depreciation of $1,082 (line 3), subtracting capital spending of $1,324 (line 17), adding (changes in) deferred income taxes of $162 (line 7), and adding the decrease in net working capital of $84 (line 15).

The PepsiCo cash flow statement looks very much like our construction.

There are also some other items that have not been explained, so let's tie up these loose ends. There are two pieces of good news here. First, you now understand the main logic of what is going on. Second, you can now rely on the accountants to do most of the hard work for you. The logic of how to handle the remaining items in the cash flow statement is either similar to what we have already discussed and/or obvious from the name. For instance, you hopefully won't need an explanation from me for "bottling equity income, net" on line 2 in Exhibit 13.4, which is just below "net income." It is probably just another form of net income—even if I knew its meaning better than you, it would not help if I explained it to you, because every company has its own unique collection of named items in their financial statements. Like me, you will have to "wing it"—or, better, seek to understand the specific company you are analyzing.

Now "wing it" for PepsiCo —each firm does it a little differently.

There are two more common items on cash flow statements, which we have not discussed. One is called **investment in goodwill**. I have no idea who came up with this name, because it is a total misnomer. It actually has to do with cash laid out when our firm has acquired other firms. PepsiCo apparently had not made any large recent acquisitions, so it did not report goodwill. The other item is *miscellaneous increases in net other assets*. These consolidate a number of other items on the cash flow statement, for which we do not have a better category.

Here are two more potentially important items: goodwill and miscellany.

Putting short-term and long-term accruals and other sources/uses of cash together yields the complete formula in Exhibit 13.10. You can use it to estimate the cash flows for an NPV analysis from financial statements. Not surprisingly, when you take both long-term and short-term accruals into account, as well as a slew of other items, the formula begins to look almost like PepsiCo's own cash flow statement, though rearranged. It starts with *income before taxes and after interest* of $4,029 (from the income statement). To make this *income before taxes and before interest*, add back the interest expense. PepsiCo actually earned net interest of $8, so this becomes $4,021. This is *EBIT*. Now subtract reported income taxes of $1,367. This gets you to *net income after taxes before interest expense*, an amount of $2,654 that is called *net operating profit*. Now adjust for when taxes were really paid rather than accounted for, adding back *deferred taxes* of $162. Now undo the accruals. For long-term accruals, add back *depreciation* of $1,082 and subtract *capital expenditures* of $1,324. For short-term accruals, add the $84

Using our semi-complete cash flow formula to assess PepsiCo's project cash flows.

decrease in working capital. Next, there are a number of miscellaneous operating items, which differ from firm to firm: bottling equity of –$160, merger-related charges of $83 ($356 – $273), deferred ESOP compensation of $48, and other charges of $31 + $209. Together, these constituted a cash inflow of $211 (double negative). This left PepsiCo with $2,869 of cash from operations. Of this amount, $432 was used for net acquisitions, $500 went into more short-term investments (which are actually almost like cash), and $381 disappeared through other channels. This left PepsiCo's financial claimants—debt and equity together—with $1,556.

Now apportioning the PepsiCo cash flows to creditors and shareholders.

With $1,556 cash flows generated by PepsiCo's projects, all that is left is to apportion them between creditors and shareholders. Shareholders receive inflows from new debt issued, and pay interest and principal. New debt plus principal repayment is called "net issuance of debt." For PepsiCo, this amounted to –$341, which means that PepsiCo actually paid down debt. This left shareholders with $1,215. Shareholders also have to pay interest. In PepsiCo's case, shareholders actually earned $8 in interest. This left them with $1,223.

We have a suggestive cash flow formula, not a perfect catch-all one.

Please do not consider our cash flow formula to be the perfect, end-all formula to compute NPV cash flows. No formula can cover *all* items in *all* companies. Even for PepsiCo, we had to lump together some items and ignore others (such as foreign exchange effects). Again, every business operates and reports differently. Still, the formula in Exhibit 13.10 is a good start for estimating realized cash flows for an NPV analysis for most firms in the real world, and for understanding the link between earnings and cash flows.

IMPORTANT

> The easiest way to extract economic cash flows for a present value analysis is to rely on the accounting cash flow statement. We only need to take care of the fact that accountants consider interest a cost of doing business, whereas financiers consider it a payout to capital providers.
>
> **Project cash flows (CF)** are due to financial creditors and shareholders together and are computed as
>
> $$\text{Project Cash Flow} = \text{Cash Flow from Operating Activity} \qquad (13.4)$$
> $$+ \text{ Cash Flow from Investing Activity}$$
> $$+ \text{ Interest Expense}$$
>
> Net income, a component of cash flow from operating activity, has had interest expense subtracted out. But interest expense is cash that is being returned to (debt) investors. Thus, to obtain the total amount of cash flows generated by the project and available (paid out to) the sum total of both creditors and shareholders, the interest expense (from the income statement) must be added back.
>
> **Equity cash flows (CF)** are available only to levered equity (i.e., the company's shareholders):

		PepsiCo, 2001		**Financial Statement Source**
	Earnings after Interest before Taxes	$4,029		Income Statement (IS), L16
+	Interest Expense (&Bottling Equity Income)	+	($8)	IS, L13 + L14 + L15
=	Earnings before Interest and Taxes (EBIT)	=	$4,021	IS, L10
−	Corporate Income Tax	−	$1,367	IS, L17
=	Net Operating Profit	=	$2,654	(also Net Income − Interest Expense)
+	Changes in Deferred Taxes	+	$162	Cash Flow Statement (CFS), L7
+	Depreciation	+	$1,082	CFS, L3
=	Gross Cash Flow	=	$3,898	
−	Capital Expenditures	−	$1,324	CFS, L17
−	Changes in Working Capital (e.g., Payables)	−	($84)	CFS, L15
−	Investment in Goodwill			(usually CFS; PepsiCo reported none.)
−	Misc. Increases in Net Other Assets	−	($211)	CFS, L2 + L4 + L5 + L6 + L8 + L9
=	Free Cash Flow from Operations	=	$2,869	
−	Acquisitions and Divestitures	−	$432	CFS, L18 + L19 + L20
−	Short-Term Investments	−	$500	CFS, L21 + L22 + L23
−	Miscellaneous Investing	−	$381	CFS, L24
=	Total Project Firm Cash Flow to Financial Debt and Equity	=	$1,556	(also CFS L16 + L25 − (IS L13 + L14 + L15))
+	Net Issuance of Debt	+	($341)	CFS, L26 + L27 + L28 + L29 + L30
−	Interest Expense	−	($8)	IS, L13 + L14 + L15
=	Total Cash Flow to Levered Equity	=	$1,223	

Exhibit 13.10: *A Formula to Compute Cash Flows for a Present Value Analysis.* This table follows the accounting convention of reporting negative numbers in parentheses. Be careful—subtracting negative numbers yields positives. Keeping signs correct is often the most difficult aspect of this task.

$$\text{Equity Cash Flow} \quad = \qquad\qquad \text{Project Cash Flow} \qquad\qquad (13.5)$$

$$+ \text{ Net Issuance of Debt} - \text{ Interest Expense}$$

Equity receives all debt proceeds and pays all debt principal and interest. Substituting the first formula into the second formula shows that equity cash flows can also be computed as *Cash Flow from Operating Activity* plus *Cash Flow from Investing Activity* plus *Net Issuance of Debt*.

A common shortcut formula: "free cash flow."

On Wall Street, analysts also call the cash flow to financial debt and equity **free cash flow**. Sometimes, they work with an abbreviated formula:

$$\text{Free Cash Flow} \quad = \qquad\qquad \text{EBIT}$$

$$- \text{ Taxes}$$

$$+ \text{ Depletion \& Depreciation \& Amortization}$$

$$- \text{ Capital Expenditures}$$

$$- \text{ Increases in Working Capital}$$

The idea is to determine the following: If you were to take over the company, seize activities like acquisitions, and (to make your computation simpler) ignore items that are often not as large (like deferred taxes), how much cash could you wring out of the firm? For PepsiCo, this would have been $\$4{,}021 - \$1{,}367 + \$1{,}082 - \$1{,}324 - (-\$84) = \$2{,}496$.

Here is a much easier and foolproof method if you have the cash flow statement.

Fortunately, you can often avoid having to construct the cash flow with this long formula yourself. For a firm that has reported full financials, you can rely on the corporate **cash flow statement** itself. After all, it tries to construct most of the information for you. Its big categories, including some for which we just had a vague miscellaneous designation in our long formula, are *cash flows from operating activity* and *cash flows from investing activity*. You can use this sum instead of fiddling with the components. There is only one difference between what accountants consider cash flows and what financiers consider cash flows: interest payments. Accountants consider interest payments as a necessary expense to run the business. Financiers consider them a distribution to the firm's financiers. If you take care of this detail, you can then rely on our accounting friends.

PepsiCo's cash flow, the easy way.

Will these formulas give you the same result? Apply them to PepsiCo. Adding *total operating activity* of +$4,201 and *total investing activity* of –$2,637 gives $1,564 in *operating activity net of investing activity*. Finally, you need to add back any interest expense that was taken out from net income. (After all, the project generated these funds and they were paid out, just as dividends are paid out.) In PepsiCo's case, it is not an interest expense, but net interest income, so the cash flow that you would use in an NPV analysis of the business of PepsiCo for 2001 is

$$\text{Project Cash Flow} \quad = \quad \$4{,}201 \quad + \;(-\$2{,}637)\; + \qquad (-\$8) \qquad = \$1{,}556$$

$$\text{Project Cash Flow} \quad = \quad \text{Operating} \; + \; \text{Investing} \; + \; \text{Interest Expense}$$

(PepsiCo is the rare company that did not pay interest income, but rather earned interest income in 2001!) These are the cash flows accruing to all claimants together, debt and equity. You are still interested in the cash flow that is earned by PepsiCo's levered equity (without the creditors). You need to add cash obtained from *net issuance of debt* (the difference of debt principal that was raised and repaid, which you can read from the cash flow statement), and you need to subtract interest that was paid:

Equity Cash Flows $\quad=\quad$ \$1,556 $\quad+\quad$ (–\$341) $\quad-\quad$ (–\$8) $\quad=$ \$1,223

Equity Cash Flows $\quad=\quad$ Project Cash $+$ Net Issuance of Debt $-$ Interest Expense

Both numbers are identical to those in Exhibit 13.10. It must be noted that you might sometimes need the longer formula with its individual components, because the individual line items may need to be discounted by different interest rates. You will see more of this later.

PepsiCo showed an increase in net income from 1999 to 2001. Did it also have an increase in cash flows? The answer is no. In 1999, PepsiCo had NPV cash flows of \$3,605 – \$1,172 – \$792 = \$1,641; in 2000, it had cash flows of \$4,440 – \$1,996 + \$57 = \$2,501; and in 2001, it had NPV cash flows of \$4,201 – \$2,637 – \$8 = \$1,556. Yet, even in 2000, managers used *changes in working capital* to prevent PepsiCo's cash flows from dropping even further. It may be that PepsiCo did not show a stellar 3-year improvement after all. On the other hand, the cash was not discarded, but used. Naturally, judging whether these were profitable investment uses is a difficult matter.

> By how much did PepsiCo's earnings and cash flows differ?

The cash flow statement in Exhibit 13.4 also continues where we stopped. It proceeds to tell you what PepsiCo did with its projects' (post-interest) cash flows (all dollar figures are in millions):

> What PepsiCo did with the money.

Dividends: It used \$994 to pay dividends.

Equity: It repurchased \$1,716 in common stock plus \$10 in preferred stock, and \$5 of Quaker stock. It also received \$524 and \$623 as payment in exchange for shares. The net was a cash use of \$584.

Debt: It issued \$324 and paid off \$573 in long-term debt, issued \$788 in short-term debt, and repurchased \$483 and \$397. The net was a cash use of \$341.

In sum, PepsiCo had total capital market payout activities of \$1,919. In fact, this means it paid out more than it made in 2001 to the tune of \$1,919 – (\$1,556 + \$8) = \$355. (Presumably, PepsiCo still had cash lying around. Of course, this cash, too, was not generated in 1999, as PepsiCo also bled cash in 2000. It was in 1999 that PepsiCo produced the cash it consumed in 2000 and 2001.)

Your task is done—you can now look at a financial statement and obtain an estimate of the information it contains about cash flows that matter to your NPV analysis.

> The task is done!

Q 13.14. From memory, can you recall the main components of economic cash flows that are used in an NPV analysis? Do you understand the logic?

Q 13.15. A new firm reports the following financials (in million dollars):

Income Statement		December		
		2001	**2000**	**1999**
=	Revenue	200	162	150
	COGS	60	58	57
	+ SG&A	20	19	18
=	**Operating Income**	120	85	75
−	Net Interest Income (Gains & Losses)	35	35	35
=	**Income before Tax**	85	50	40
−	Corporate Income Tax (at 40%)	34	20	16
=	**Income after Tax**	51	30	24
−	Extraordinary Items	0	0	0
=	**Net Income**	51	30	24

The firm also reports:

Source	Item	2001	2000	1999
Cash Flow Statement	Capital Expenditures	0	30	200
Cash Flow Statement	Depreciation	25	23	20
Balance Sheet	Deferred Taxes	20	16	0
Balance Sheet	Accumulated Depreciation	68	43	20
Balance Sheet	Working Capital	35	25	20

(You will need to compute changes in deferred taxes, which are $20-$16 = $4 in 2001, as well as changes in working capital.) Can you compute an estimate of cash flows produced by this firm in these three years?

Q 13.16. What are the cash flows produced by PepsiCo's projects in 1999, 2000, and 2001? What are the cash flows available to residual equity shareholders in 1999, 2000, and 2001?

Q 13.17. Do a financial analysis for Microsoft. Obtain the past financial statements from a website of your choice (e.g., **YAHOO!** FINANCE or Microsoft's own website). Compute the cash flows that you would use for an NPV analysis of the firm value and the equity value, beginning in 2003 and ending in 2005.

13.7 What To Believe on the Balance Sheet

Generally, financial accounting in the U.S. is geared toward producing relatively accurate flow values on the income and cash flow statements, not accurate stock values on the balance sheet. There is one particular balance sheet item that is especially seductive: the **book value of equity** (BV of equity, or BVE). Unfortunately, it is also the least reliable value on the least reliable financial statement. Because of the way that depreciation and other rules work, after the accountants have completed all their bookkeeping, the book value of equity becomes what is required to equalize the left-hand side and right-hand side of the balance sheet. Put differently, the book value of equity is a "placeholder." On occasion, it can be entirely meaningless. For example, it can be negative—a negative value is not sensible for a claim that has limited liability. Firms in the same industry can have very different equity book values if they are of different age. For older firms, the book value of older assets is often just a fraction of the true market value, not because these assets are typically worthless, but because accountants have typically written them down to be of zero value.

The book value of equity is particularly tempting and problematic.

➤ Flow vs stock financials' accuracy, Pg.378.

Are other balance sheet items more reliable? It depends. Fortunately, unlike the book value of equity, the **book value of liabilities** tends to be more reliable, if only because it is harder for a firm to weasel out of its commitments to pay. Many of these commitments are relatively short-term, too. Even the **book value of financial debt** (a component of liabilities that can contain many long-term liabilities) is usually reasonably accurate, at least if interest rates have not changed dramatically since the debt's issue. Besides, you rarely have an alternative, because the *market* value of debt (or of total liabilities) is usually not available.

Don't confuse my statement: The book value of debt is often reasonable; only the book value of equity or the book value of assets are not.

Unfortunately, the **book value of assets** remains troublesome. It is the sum of the book value of equity, financial debt, and nonfinancial liabilities. Although the latter two are often reasonably accurate, the first is not. Thus, the accounting item "total assets" also generally misstates (often understates) the true values of (older) firms.

Total Assets have the same problem.

Balance sheet stock numbers are often inaccurate as measures of true values. This applies especially to the book value of equity, and, to a lesser extent, to the book value of assets.

IMPORTANT

Summary

This chapter covered the following major points:

- There are four required financial statements: the balance sheet, the income statement, the shareholders' equity statement, and the cash flow statement. Although every company reports its numbers a little differently, the major elements of these statements are fairly standard.

- Financial statements also serve more purposes than just NPV calculations, and are well worth studying in more detail—elsewhere.

- Earnings (net income) are *not* the cash flow inputs required in an NPV analysis.

- Accountants use "accruals" in their net income (earnings) computation, which you need to undo in order to extract actual cash flows.

- The primary long-term accrual is "depreciation," an allocation of capital expenditures. The prime operation to undo this is to add back depreciation and subtract out capital expenditures.

- Deferred taxes adjust for differences in the depreciation schedules that GAAP and the IRS prescribe.

- The primary short-term accrual is "changes in working capital," an allocation of soon-expected but not-yet-executed cash inflows and outflows. Examples are accounts payable, accounts receivable, and taxes payable. The prime operation to undo them is to subtract changes in working capital.

- If a cash flow statement is available, it conveniently handles most of the difficulties in undoing accruals for the NPV analysis. However, accountants believe interest expense to be a cost of operations, whereas financiers believe it to be a payout to financiers. Thus, interest expense requires special handling.

- Formula 13.4 shows how to compute cash flows that accrue to project financiers (the "owners," which, in the sense it is used here, are debt holders plus equity holders). It is *cash flow from operating activity*, plus *cash flow from investing equity*, plus *interest expense*.

- Formula 13.5 shows how to compute cash flows that accrue to levered equity owners (equity only). It is the cash flow that accrues to project owners, plus *net issuance of debt*, minus *interest expense*.

- Balance sheet values, especially the book value of equity and the book value of assets, tend to be unreliable measures of their true value equivalents.

A final observation: One common source of (avoidable) errors when analyzing financial statements is getting the accounting convention signs wrong.

Preview of the Chapter Appendix in the Companion

In the Appendix
The appendix to this chapter gives Coca-Cola's restated and unrestated financials in the same years, 1999-2001.

Keywords

Answers

Q 13.1 The main difference between how accountants see income and how financiers see cash flows is accruals. Examples are the treatment of depreciation (versus capital expenses) and the delayed payments/receipts.

Q 13.2 Basically yes: The lifetime sum of net income should be approximately equal to the firm's lifetime cash flows. Cash flows just have different timing. For example, a firm's capital expenditures are not booked immediately, but the sum of all lifetime depreciation should add up to the sum of all lifetime capital expenditures. This abstracts away from some discounting that accountants are doing, and many specific accounting cases that we have not covered, but the intent of earnings is that it should come out alike.

Q 13.3 The calculations in Exhibit 13.7 for years 1 and 2 are in the chapter text. Project cash flows thereafter are

Formula 13.1:	Y3	Y4	Y5	Y6
EBIT	$10	$35	$60	$60
+ Depreciation	$50	$25	$0	$0
– Capital Expenditures	$0	$0	$0	$0
= Cash Flow, Project, Pre Tax	$60	$60	$60	$60
Formula 13.2:				
– Corporate Income Tax	$2	$12	$22	$22
= Cash Flow, Project, Post Tax	$58	$48	$38	$38

Cash flows to levered equity are

Formula 13.1 or 13.3:	Y3	Y4	Y5	Y6
+ Net Debt Issue	$0	$0	$0	–$50
– Interest Expense	$5	$5	$5	$5
= Cash Flow, Levered Equity	$53	$43	$33	–$17

Alternatively,

	Y3	Y4	Y5	Y6
Net Income	$3	$18	$33	$33
+ Depreciation	$50	$25	$0	$0
– Capital Expenditures	0	0	0	0
+ Net Debt Issue	$0	$0	$0	–$50
= Cash Flow, Levered Equity	$53	$43	$33	–$17

Q 13.4 Analogous to the cash flows in Exhibit 13.7, a 10% instead of a 12% cost of capital on the tax liability would increase the NPV of the tax obligation from $46.77 to

$$\text{NPV}_{\text{tax liability}} = \frac{\$14}{1.1} + \frac{\$2}{1.1^2} + \frac{\$2}{1.1^3} + \frac{\$12}{1.1^4} + \frac{\$22}{1.1^5} + \frac{\$22}{1.1^6}$$

$$\approx \$50.16$$

Therefore, the project value would decrease by $3.39.

Q 13.5 The income statement is now as follows:

		Y1	Y2	Y3	Y4	Y5
	Sales (Revenues)	$80	$80	$80	$80	$80
–	COGS	$6	$6	$6	$6	$6
–	SG&A	$8	$8	$8	$8	$8
=	EBITDA	$66	$66	$66	$66	$66
–	Depreciation	$30	$30	$30	$30	$0
=	EBIT (Oper. Income)	$36	$36	$36	$36	$66

(continued)

=	EBIT (Oper. Income)	$36	$36	$36	$36	$66
–	Interest Expense	$0	$8	$8	$8	$8
=	EAIBT (or EBT)	$36	$28	$28	$28	$58
–	Income Tax (at 50%)	$18	$14	$14	$14	$29
=	Net Income	$18	$14	$14	$14	$29

The cash flow statement excerpt is now as follows:

	Y1	Y2	Y3	Y4	Y5
Capital Expenditures	–$120				
Net Debt Issue	+$100				–$100
Depreciation	$30	$30	$30	$30	$0

The cash flow formula is EBIT plus depreciation (or use EBITDA instead) minus capital expenditures, minus corporate income tax. For year 1, this is: $36 + $30 – $120 – $18 = –$72$. The first levered equity cash flows are $–$72 + $100 = +$28$.

Cash Flow	Rate	Y1	Y2	Y3	Y4	Y5	NPV
Machine	8%	–$54	$66	$66	$66	$66	$152.41
Uncle Sam	8%	–$18	–$14	–$14	–$14	–$29	–$69.81
Project	8%	–$72	+$52	+$52	+$52	+$37	$82.60
Loan	8%	+$100	–$8	–$8	–$8	–$108	$0
Lev. Eq.	8%	+$28	+$44	+$44	+$44	–$71	$82.60

Q 13.6 The (summarized) cash flows using monthly discounting (month is now abbreviated M) are as follows:

	M1	M2--M12	M13	M14--M36
EBIT	$2.92	$2.92	$0.83	$0.83
Depreciation	$2.08	$2.08	$4.17	$4.17
Cap.Exp.	–$75	0	–$75	0
Project CF, Pre Tax	–$70.00	$5.00	–$70.00	$5.00
Tax	$1.00	$1.00	$0.16	$0.16
Project CF, Post Tax	–$71.00	$4.00	–$70.16	$4.84
Loan	$50	–$0.42	–$0.42	–$0.42
Levered Cash Flow	–$21.00	$3.58	–$70.58	$4.42

Month	M37-M48	M49-M71	M72	PV
EBIT	$2.92	$5.00	$5.00	
Depreciation	$2.08	0	0	
Cap.Exp.	0	0	0	
Project CF, Pre Tax	$5.00	$5.00	$5.00	$115.59
Tax	$1.00	$1.83	$1.83	$46.25
Project CF, Post Tax	$4.00	$3.17	$3.17	$69.34
Loan	–$0.42	–$0.42	–$50.42	$0.00
Levered Cash Flow	$3.58	$2.75	–$47.25	$69.34

Tax is calculated as $40\% \cdot (\text{EBIT} - \text{Depreciation} - \text{Interest Expense})$. For discounting, this uses a 1% monthly rate for project cash flows and taxes, and an 0.83% rate for the loan.

Q 13.7 Deferred taxes is an account that represents the cumulated difference between taxes indicated on the firm's income statement and the (lower) amount of taxes that the firm has actually paid. They are the results of different accounting procedures that are used for reporting to shareholders and for reporting to Uncle Sam. (Note: Deferred taxes are *not* adjusted for the fact that taxes are typically paid the year after the income is earned.) They are reported on the balance sheet.

Q 13.8 The deferred tax account increased $109 from 2005 to 2006. This means that the cash outflow was not as large as the income statement would have you believe. Thus, we add that back to the GAAP cash flows. The 2006 real after-tax cash flow was $–$100 + $109 = 9. The deferred tax account decreased $222 from 2006 to 2007. This means that the firm paid out more than what the taxes on the income statement indicated, so this reduces the project cash flow. The 2007 real after-tax cash flow was $300 – $222 = 78.

Q 13.9 To find the cash flows, work out the change in accounts receivable each year. Then subtract these changes from the net income.

	Y1	Y2	Y3	Y4	Y5	Y6
Reported NI	$100	$100	$300	$300	$100	$0
Reported A/R	$100	$120	$340	$320	$120	$0
Change in A/R	$100	$20	$220	–$20	–$200	–$120
Cash Flows	$0	$80	$80	$320	$300	$120

The firm's customers did not all pay the next period. Therefore, the cash flows were delayed.

Q 13.10 The cash flows are as follows (Q is Quarter):

	Q1	Q2	Q3	Q4
Reported NI	$100	$200	$300	$200
Immediate CF	$50	$100	$150	$100
+ Delayed Cash Flow (CF)			+$50	+$100
$\Rightarrow$ = CF	=$50	=$100	=$200	=$200
$\Rightarrow$ Change in A/R	$50	$100	$100	$0
$\Rightarrow$ A/R	$50	$150	$250	$250

	Q5	Q6	Q7
Reported NI	$100	$0	$0
Immediate CF	$50	$0	$0
+ Delayed CF	+$150	+$100	+$50
$\Rightarrow$ = Cash Flow (CF)	=$200	=$100	=$50
$\Rightarrow$ Change in A/R	–$100	–$100	–$50
$\Rightarrow$ A/R	$150	$50	$0

It is easier to obtain the change in A/R first: You know that net income minus the change in A/R must add up to cash flows (change in A/R = net income – cash flows). And, knowing the change in A/R, calculating accounts receivable requires simple addition.

Q 13.11 In February, Amazonia has cash inflows of $100 ($25 net income plus $75 change in accounts payable). In March, Amazonia has another $100 in sales, but payables stay the same. (It has to pay its old suppliers $75, even though it gets to keep $75 from its new suppliers.) Amazonia gets cash inflows of $25 only. In April, Amazonia gets net income cash inflows of $100, plus the $225 change in payables, for cash inflows of $325. Finally, in May, Amazonia has cash outflows of $300. The pattern is as follows:

Month	Jan	Feb	Mar	Apr	May
Cash Flows	$0	$100	$25	$325	–$300

Note that Amazonia has total 5-month cash flows of $150, just as it has total 5-month net income of $150. The working capital has only influenced the timing attribution.

Q 13.12 Short-term accruals are easier to manipulate. To manipulate long-term accruals, you would have to manipulate the depreciation schedule, and though this may be possible a few times, if it is done often, it will most surely raise eyebrows.

Q 13.13 If a firm assumes that fewer of its customers will actually pay their bills in the future (i.e., more will default), then its earnings are (too) conservative. There are also many other ways in which a firm can do this that have not been discussed. For example, a firm can take out a reserve against a judgment in a pending lawsuit.

Q 13.14 The main components for a cash flow analysis are in Table 13.10. Start with EBIT. Then undo accruals for taxes: Subtract off corporate income tax and add changes in deferred taxes. Then undo long-term accruals: Subtract off capital expenditures and add back depreciation. Then take care of the other components, changes in working capital first. Don't forget goodwill and other miscellany—they are quite big in some firms.

Q 13.15 To compute the cash flows (in millions) produced by the firm (project), use the long formula in Exhibit 13.10:

		2001	2000	1999
EBIT		$120	$85	$75
– Income Tax	–	$34	$20	$16
+ Ch. in Deferred Taxes	+	$4[a]	$16[a]	N/A
= Net Operating Profit	=	$90	$81	N/A
+ Depreciation	+	$25	$23	$20[b]
= Gross Cash Flow	=	$115	$104	N/A
– Ch. in Working Capital	–	$10[a]	$5[a]	N/A
– Capital Expenditures	–	$0	$30	$200
= CF from Operations	=	$105	$69	N/A

Note [a]: The balance sheet gave the level of deferred taxes and the level of working capital, not the *changes* in these variables. You had to compute the differences yourself. [b]: Depreciation is only available from the cash flow statement, not from the balance sheet.

Q 13.16 The easiest ways to compute cash flows to residual equity shareholders are Formulas 13.4 and 13.5. PepsiCo's project cash flows, available for satisfaction of both creditors and shareholders, are as follows (in millions):

	2001	2000	1999
CF from Operating Activity	$4,201	$4,440	$3,605
+ CF from Investing Activity	–$2,637	–$1,996	–$1,172
+ Interest Expense	–$8	$57	–$792
= CF from Projects	$1,556	$2,501	$1,641

PepsiCo's shareholder cash flows are as follows (in millions):

	2001	2000	1999
CF from Operating Activity	$4,201	$4,440	$3,605
+ CF from Investing Activity	–$2,637	–$1,996	–$1,172
+ Net Issuance of Debt	–$341	–$705	$391
= Cash Flow to Equity	$1,223	$1,739	$2,824

Q 13.17 For Microsoft, the underlying project cash flows would have been as follows:

	2005	2004	2003
Operating CF	$16,605	$14,626	$15,797
+ Investing CF	$15,027	–$3,842	–$7,495
+ Interest Expense	$0	$0	$0
= Cash Flow to Project	$31,632	$11,284	$8,302

(The interest expense is from the Income Statement.) Microsoft has no debt, so all cash flows accrue to equity holders.

End of Chapter Problems

Q 13.18. Although accounting numbers are sometimes thought of as imaginary presentations, why is a firm not just a firm, and accounting numbers not just "funny numbers"? That is, what is the most important direct cash flow influence of accounting in most corporations?

Q 13.19. Which statements on the firm's financial reports are about flows, and which are about stocks?

Q 13.20. Use an appropriate website to find out how MACRS works. How would you depreciate $10,000 in computer equipment?

Q 13.21. What would be the most common accounting value of residential investment property that you purchased for $3 million in each of the next 50 years? (Hint: Use a straight line 40-year depreciation schedule.)

Q 13.22. What is an accrual? How do long-term and short-term accruals differ?

Q 13.23. Consider purchasing a $50,000 SUV that you expect to last for 10 years. The IRS uses an MACRS 5-year depreciation schedule on cars. It allows depreciating 20% in year 1, 32%, 19.2%, 11.52%, 11.52%, and 5.76% in the following years. You can finance this car yourself. You can produce income of $100,000 per year with it. Maintenance costs will be $5,000 per year. Your income tax rate is 30% per annum. Your cost of capital is 12% per annum.

1. What are the income and cash flow statements for this car?

2. What is the net present value of this car?

3. Show how you can infer the economic value of the car from the financials.

Q 13.24. Repeat the previous question, but assume that you finance the entire car with a loan that charges 10% interest per annum. (The net present value now is the bundle "loan plus car," of course.)

Q 13.25. PepsiCo's balance sheet lists its deferred income taxes as $1,367 million in 2000 and $1,496 million in 2001. Its net income statement further listed income tax payments of $1,367 million in 2001. How much did PepsiCo actually pay in income taxes in 2001?

Q 13.26. Construct the financials for a firm that has quarterly sales and net income of $100, $200, $300, $200, $100. One-quarter of all customers pay immediately, while the other three-quarters always pay *two* quarters after purchase.

Q 13.27. Consider the following project:

Project	
Real Physical Lifespan	6 years
Cost	$150
Gross Output	$50 in year 1
	$80 in year 2
	$90 in year 3
	$50 in year 4
	$25 in year 5
	$0 in year 6
– Input Costs (cash)	$5/year
– Selling Costs (cash)	$5/year
Overall Cost of Capital	12%/year
Corporate Tax Rate (τ)	40%/year
Available Financing	
Debt Capacity	$50
Debt Interest Rate	10%/year
Accounting Treatment	
Accounting Life	3 years
Depreciation Method	Linear

Assume customers pay one year after delivery. Construct (the relevant items of) the balance sheet, the income statement, and the cash flow statement. Compute the value of this firm, both from finance principles and from the financial statements. (Please note that this is a time-intensive question—almost a minicase.)

Q 13.28. PepsiCo reported the following information (in million dollars):

Income Statement

	1999	2000	2001
Net Income	$2,505	$2,543	$2,662

Balance Sheet

Year	1999	2000	2001
Accounts Receivable		$2,129	$2,142
Inventories		$1,192	$1,310
Prepaid Expenses		$791	$752
Accounts Payable		$4,529	$4,461
Income Tax, Payable		$64	$183

Ignoring all other accruals, how would you adjust PepsiCo's net income to be more cash-oriented, that is, reflective of short-term accruals?

Q 13.29. Coca-Cola reported the following information (in million dollars):

Income Statement

	2003	2004	2005
Net Income	$4,347	$4,847	$4,872

Balance Sheet

Year	2003	2004	2005
Accounts Receivable		$2,244	$2,281
Inventories		$1,420	$1,424
Prepaid Expenses		$1,849	$1,778
Accounts Payable		$4,403	$4,493
Loans Payable		$4,531	$4,518
Current Maturities of Long-Term Debt		$1,490	$28
Corporate Income Tax, Payable		$709	$797

Ignoring all other accruals, how would you adjust Coca-Cola's net income to be more cash-oriented, that is, reflective of short-term accruals?

Q 13.30. Give some examples of how a firm can depress the cash flows that it reports in order to report higher cash flows later.

Q 13.31. Explain why EBITDA is more difficult to manipulate than EBIT.

Q 13.32. Among PepsiCo's working capital items in 2001, which items allowed PepsiCo to pull cash out of the business, and which items forced PepsiCo to put more back into the business?

Q 13.33. Preferably answer this question from memory: If you have access to a firm's cash flow statement and net income statement, how would you compute the economic cash flows that accrue to shareholders?

Valuation from Comparables and Financial Ratios

A Practical Approach

You now know how to read financial statements, how to obtain cash flows from financial statements, and how to value them. You also know that forecasting cash flows is a very difficult task. Are there any shortcuts? Are there any good alternatives to NPV?

The answer is yes. "Valuation by comparables," or "comps" for short, is an alternative approach often resorted to by practitioners. Executed correctly, comps can give answers that are as good as those that you can obtain with a thorough NPV analysis. In practice, sometimes the NPV method gives a better value estimate, and sometimes the comparables method does.

The basic idea behind valuation by comparables is simple and best understood by analogy: Assume that you want to determine the value of five red marbles. If black marbles cost $2 apiece, and if you are willing to assume that red marbles are valued like black marbles, then you can compute that the value of your five red marbles should be $10. It is not necessary to forecast what value marbles will have in the future or what discount factor applies: The market price of black marbles has already taken all this information into account.

Of course, the more similar black marbles are to red marbles, the better this method works. If they are not similar, you can go spectacularly wrong. If black marbles are made from coal and red marbles are made from rubies, then your value estimate can be orders of magnitude off.

In sum, the method of comparables relies on three assumptions:

1. You can identify projects that are close comparables. In the example, it is "other marbles."

2. You can identify a measure that is value-relevant. Here it is "being a marble," not "being of red color" (in which case cherries or Ferraris would make better comparables than black marbles).

3. The market values comparable projects similarly. This is the law of one price.

14.1 Comparables and Net Present Value

An example application of comparables based on the P/E ratio.

Let's say you need to find a good market value for PepsiCo, perhaps because you own PepsiCo (fat chance) and are thinking of selling it. By the method of comparables, you first have to find another company that you deem to be similar. Let's assume you choose Coca-Cola as your comparable. Second, you have to decide on a particular value-relevant attribute as your benchmark. Let's say you use earnings. The most common valuation comparable, then, is the price-earnings ratio (P/E). In May 2011, **YAHOO!** FINANCE reported that Coca-Cola had a market cap of $156 billion, earnings of $11.9 billion, and thus a P/E ratio of 13.14. Each dollar of Coca-Cola earnings therefore translated into $13.14 of equity value. Third, you must assume that the financial markets value firms like PepsiCo and Coca-Cola at the same P/E ratio. Then, because PepsiCo had earnings of $5.9 billion, the method of comparables suggests

$$\underset{\text{Coca-Cola P/E} \,\cdot\, \text{PepsiCo Earnings (E)}}{\text{Value of PepsiCo Equity} \quad \approx \quad 13.14 \quad \cdot \quad \$5.9 \text{ billion} \quad \approx \quad \$77.5 \text{ billion}}$$

In reality, PepsiCo was worth about $111.5 billion, so this comparables-based value estimate was off by "only" $35 billion! This is not particularly good, but an error this large is unfortunately not an uncommon valuation error.

Comparables are seductively easy to compute.

The single biggest problem of comparables may well be that they are "seductive." They are so easy to compute that the temptation to use them badly is always there. Without good knowledge of the weaknesses of this method, you are getting only the dark side of the Force. But use comparables correctly, and you can get valuable information that is not easy to find by any other method.

The Law of One Price

Ultimately, NPV and comparables-based valuation are both applications of the law of one price—first cousins.

➤ *Law of one price, Sect. 1.1, Pg.2.*

Ultimately, the comparables method is really not that different from the "estimated NPV" method. Both methods seek to estimate a true net present value. Both methods want to do so by valuing your project *relative* to other projects. In an estimated NPV analysis, you compare your own project to a benchmark through the opportunity cost of capital (the discount rate). In comparables-based analysis, you compare your own project to a benchmark through a valuation ratio, such as P/E, for one or a number of similar firms. Although both estimated NPV and comparables are based on relative valuation, comparables lean more heavily on identification of immediately similar projects and on the assumption that the market has valued these particular projects correctly. NPV is a bit more forgiving, in that the opportunity cost of capital uses a more comprehensive set of alternatives than just a couple of similar-looking firms in an industry. (Think of NPV as effectively allowing you to use all investment opportunities in the economy as your benchmark.) But conceptually, either financial valuation method works the same way: through the law of one price.

> **IMPORTANT**
>
> It is the *law of one price* that ultimately gives you a present value estimate. This law states that companies with the same attributes should have the same value in a perfect market. In reality, it means that companies with similar attributes should have similar values.

Let me expand upon this. To find the true net present value of a project, you must choose one or more attributes upon which to base your valuation.

Both methods work with "attributes" of firms. (NPV values an estimated statistic.)

- One attribute can be your NPV *estimate*. You cannot use the *true* NPV, simply because you do not know it. In fact, if you knew it, you would be done.

- Another attribute can be the earnings for similar firms from the same industry. (You would then work with price-earnings ratios.)

There are also many other possible value-relevant attributes (e.g., cash flows or sales). However, the estimated NPV and earnings are the most prominent. In real life, you might even use multiple attributes. But multidimensional graphs are tough to draw, so we shall consider only single-attribute valuation techniques. Let us call a valuation attribute simply an "attribute" or a "measure." If you draw your attribute on the x-axis and the true firm value on the y-axis, you would hope that the relationship is close and accurate.

For example, look at graph (a) in Exhibit 14.1. Here the law of one price works well. All firms line up nicely, like ducks in a row. This suggests that your measure is value relevant, although it does not prove it. (It could merely be a lucky coincidence.) Now assume that you want to value a firm whose attribute (measure) is 60, which is indicated by a vertical line. You can easily identify similar firms, some with higher and some with lower measures. Your valuation is now simple and accurate. And it matters little whether your measure is estimated NPV, earnings, sales, or something else.

An example of a law-of-one-price valuation in which firms with similar attributes have similar values.

Graph (b) shows the situation in which you will usually find yourself. The values of all companies are surrounded by a good deal of uncertainty relative to your attribute measure. This is usually the case even if you use estimated NPV. Although theory tells you that true NPV would make the perfect measure, the fact that you had to estimate your NPV inputs usually renders your graph more like (b) than (a).

Unfortunately, this is not how it usually is in reality. Usually, there is more noise.

Graphs (c) and (d) illustrate two more problems that are common in the context of valuation by comparables. In (c), the attribute is basically irrelevant for valuation. It tells you nothing about the value of your firm. In (d), even if you know the right value attribute, you have no comparables that have a similar measure as your firm. Your earnings may be 60, but all comparables from your industry have earnings of around 15 to 25. How should you extrapolate? The graph draws two possible lines, and they come up with rather different values for your firm. In this case, analysts sometimes expand the set of firms they look at, so that they also find some firms with higher P/E ratios. Unfortunately, P/E ratios may mean something very different for firms drawn from a broader set of industries. So you might find yourself with a better value estimate, or you might end up with what you saw in (c) again—a measure that has very little or no relation to value.

Here are examples where the pricing method works poorly.

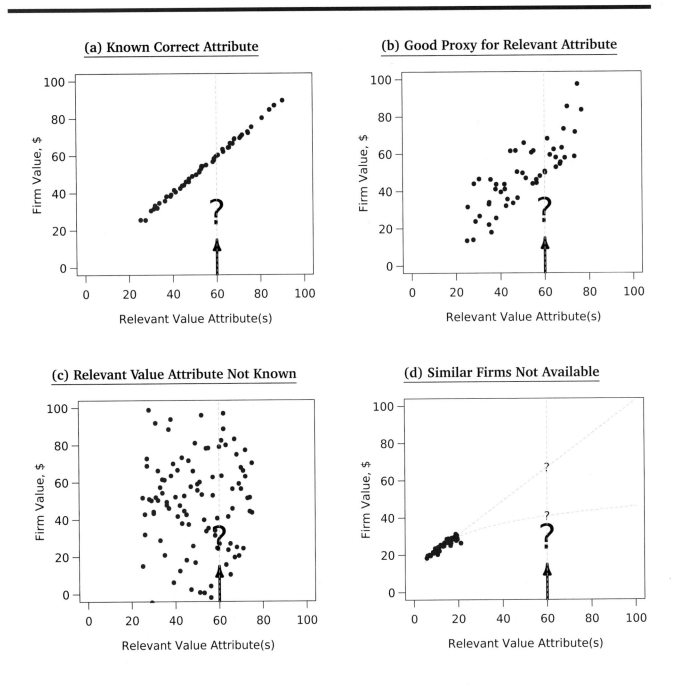

Exhibit 14.1: *Conceptual Issues with Attribute-Based Valuation by Comparables.* Your goal is to value a firm with some attribute of 60. You know the attributes and values of publicly-traded comparable firms, plotted as big dots here. In graph (a), an attribute-based comparables valuation for your firm would seem to work almost perfectly. In graph (b), there is a lot of uncertainty, but attribute-based valuation would still seem useful. In graph (c), the attribute is not relevant for valuation, and thus valuation by comparables would fail badly. In (a)–(c), similar firms with higher and lower attributes are readily available. In graph (d), even though the value attribute may be known, there are no similar firms available. Thus, it would be difficult to extrapolate a value, and attribute-based valuation would fail again.

In sum, the following are important for valuation:

The main conceptual requirements for using the law of one price.

1. You need to have a good value-relevant attribute. "Estimated NPV" and "earnings" (which then works through the P/E ratio) are among them, but there can be others.

2. You need to find other publicly traded companies that are similar to your own firm, so that you can believe that their price-to-attribute ratios should be similar. Preferably, you would have many such firms, some with measures higher, others with measures lower than your own firm. Preferably, your measure is relevant and accurate so that all comparables' market valuations line up nicely.

The law of one price gives you an accurate valuation only if these conditions are met.

Which Is Better?

Both estimated NPV and comparables are based on similar ideas. How do the two compare?

NPV has input estimation problems, but comparables are even more ad hoc in what the right input is. Comparables also often have a "no similar firms exist" problem.

Estimated NPV as a method has a lot of advantages. It has a beautiful theory ("true NPV") behind it. It identifies for you exactly what matters (the expected future cash flows) and how differently timed cash flows matter in different ways (through the discount rate). The theory even gives you the exact relationship between various estimated inputs and your final measures (the present value formula). To the extent that you can reach the ideals of the theory—finding good expected cash flow and discount rate estimates—you know that your valuation is accurate! (The theory even allows you to skip the time-consuming process of calibrating your measure to those of similar firms. If your inputs are accurate, then estimated NPV and true NPV have a one-to-one correspondence.) However, the estimated-NPV method also has two main disadvantages. First, your input estimates—especially your cash flow estimates—can be far off from the truth. Second, there is no objective standard for your estimates, and a third party cannot verify them. If you say the expected cash flows in 10 years will be $1 million, and I say that they will be $5 million, who is right?

Comparables as a method also has strengths and weaknesses. If there is a high correlation between the true NPV and your measure, then it can provide remarkably accurate value estimates. Its main disadvantage is that it is much more ad hoc: You have to make two important judgment calls. First, what is a good comparable firm? Second, what should you use as the appropriate valuation attribute? Again, earnings (through the P/E ratio) is a common measure, but it may not work well, and other attributes could fit better in your particular situation. Unlike estimated NPV, there is no one-to-one relationship between your measure and true NPV, so you must rely heavily on many firms in a graph such as those in Exhibit 14.1. Moreover, as with NPV, there are also numerous devils in the details, which you will soon learn more about. Yet one advantage of comparables is that the inputs can be more objective and more verifiable than those for NPV. Earnings and prices are known, so analysts can agree on precise numbers. Nevertheless, subjectivity comes back into play because analysts rarely agree on what firms are

Examples in which
one method is better
than the other.

appropriate comparables and what attribute fits best. Such disagreement can create dramatically different subjective estimates, too.

In sum, you trade off judgmental uncertainty about future expected cash flows and appropriate discount rates (in an NPV estimate) against judgmental uncertainty about how good your measure is and how similar your comparable firms are.

To be specific, consider an attempt to value an investment in PepsiCo shares. If your alternative is an investment in Treasury bonds, the method of comparables would fail miserably. T-bonds are so dissimilar that you should have no faith in any comps-based value estimate. You would prefer an NPV-based estimate. But if you have a close comparable, say, an investment in Coca-Cola, then you could easily end up preferring a comparables-based valuation. It probably approximates the true NPV better than any estimate of future expected cash flows you could ever come up with. You would in effect be better off free riding on the wonderfully accurate valuation (incorporating all the true expected future cash flows and appropriate discount rates) that has already been provided for you by the financial markets through Coca-Cola's market price.

Q 14.1. What is the law of one price?

Q 14.2. How do comparable projects enter the NPV formula?

14.2   The Price-Earnings (P/E) Ratio

For valuation, price
ratios (multiples) are
most convenient.

Now that you understand the general concept, let's dive into the details. The kind of ratios that you would be most interested in have a value in the numerator and an attribute in the denominator. The reason is that if you have a good price-ratio estimate, you merely need to multiply it by your project's or firm's attribute, and out comes an estimate of price:

$$\underbrace{\left(\frac{\text{Price}}{\text{Attribute}}\right)}_{\text{from Comparables}} \cdot \text{Attribute of Your Project} = \text{Price Estimate for Your Project}$$

We will spend a lot of time on the P/E ratio, and discuss other ratios thereafter. It will then become clear to you why the P/E ratio is the most popular comparables measure.

Definition

The price-earnings
ratio is price divided
by earnings. Dividing
a stock by a flow is a
bit odd.

The **price-earnings ratio** is often abbreviated as **P/E ratio**,

$$\underbrace{\left(\frac{\text{Price}}{\text{Earnings}}\right)}_{\text{from Comparables}} \cdot \text{Earnings of Your Project} = \text{Price Estimate for Your Project}$$

The price is a stock quantity (a snapshot), whereas the earnings, usually net income, is a flow measure (usually over a 1-year time period). This should raise one immediate caution that you should keep in the back of your mind: It is rare that apples divided by oranges gives you a meaningful number. In the case of the P/E ratio, the hope is that 1-year annual earnings are a good proxy for a stock value based on the entire set of all future discounted earnings flows. If 1-year earnings are not representative of many future earnings, the P/E ratio is most likely not a good measure.

It does not matter if you compute P/E firmwide or on a per-share basis. A firm worth $100 million with earnings of $5 million has a P/E ratio of 20. If it has 50 million shares outstanding, its price per share is $2, its earnings per share is 10 cents, and its P/E ratio computed from these quantities is still 20. Its shares sell for 20 times earnings.

It makes no difference whether you work with per-share or overall firmwide earnings.

In the real world, price-earnings ratios are often, *but not always,* quoted as the current market price divided by the analysts' consensus estimate of *next* year's earnings. (This is an *expected* quantity, known today.) The advantage is that these expected earnings focus more on the future—and valuation is forward looking, not backward looking. Moreover, an informal variant of the growing perpetuity formula, $P = C/(r - g)$, is often used. This variant, $\text{Price}_t = (\text{Expected Earnings}_{t+1})/ (\text{Cost of Capital} - \text{Expected Growth Rate of Earnings})$, relates today's price to next period's earnings. (In any case, this matters little: The intuition would remain the same if you used the most recently reported earnings instead.) This chapter keeps the notation on the perpetuity formula a bit loose—the underlying P/E theory is only an intuitive guide and not intended to be exact.

Earnings can be analysts' consensus forecast for next year, or current earnings. We keep the notation loose.

▶ *Growing perpetuities, Formula 3.1, Pg. 42.*

After a whole chapter about why you cannot use earnings instead of cash flows for an NPV valuation, is it not a step back to revert to earnings? Actually, no. The reason is that current earnings are often better representatives of future cash flows than current cash flows. At first glance, this may seem odd to you. However, it makes sense. Cash flows are usually "spikier" than earnings. When a firm makes a large capital expenditure or acquisition, it may have a large negative cash flow one year, followed by positive cash flows in the following years. This spikiness is not a problem in an NPV analysis, because the higher future cash flows also enter in the future terms. In contrast, earnings try to smooth inflows and outflows of large expenditures over many periods. It is a number that accountants have created for the very purpose you need here: a representative short-term stand-in for the long-term picture. For computing one representative ratio with just a single year's data, the current accounting earnings are usually more representative of the future than a current cash flow would be. On the negative side, earnings can vary tremendously from period to period, and managers can manipulate them more easily than they can manipulate cash flows.

Why use earnings and not cash flows in the ratio? Because accountants try to reflect more future in earnings.

Sometimes you may want to use the reciprocal of the P/E ratio, the earnings/price ratio, more commonly called the **earnings yield**:

The earnings yield, (E/P yield) is the inverse of the P/E ratio.

$$\text{Earnings Yield} = \frac{\text{Earnings}}{\text{Price}} = \frac{1}{\text{P/E Ratio}}$$

You can view the earnings yield as the percentage of price due to current earnings. The earnings yield has one big advantage over the price-earnings ratio. If the earnings are zero or negative, the price-earnings ratio is meaningless, and often indicated as not applicable (NA or N/A). If earnings are tiny, P/E ratios can be huge. In contrast, because a denominator price is always positive, the earnings yield is always meaningful, even if earnings are negative. If the earnings are positive, then a higher price-earnings ratio implies a lower earnings/price yield, and vice versa.

Why P/E Ratios Differ

The main question: What drives differences in firms' P/E ratios?

One way to think of the P/E ratio is that it attaches an implicit overall value to each dollar of earnings. At a P/E ratio of 20, you might say that each extra dollar of earnings translates into an extra $20 worth of valuation—the shares sell for 20 times earnings. But where do price-earnings ratios come from? What do they mean? Why do they differ across firms and industries?

One reason is that P/E ratios use current earnings as a proxy for all future earnings.

The reason is that today's earnings can mean different things for the future for different firms. If you believe that your firm will not produce any future earnings, then your value estimate per dollar of current earnings is just your earnings today. In contrast, if you believe that your firm will grow, then this year's earnings are just a shadow of your future earnings. Your value estimate per dollar of current earnings is a number greater than one.

IMPORTANT

> All else equal, the price-earnings ratio is higher for firms with more future growth.

This is easiest to understand with an example using the perpetuity formula.

In the growing perpetuity formula from Chapter 3, the relation between next year's single earnings number and the stream of future earnings is captured by one parameter: the expected growth rate. (In case you are curious, in the growing perpetuity formula, firms with lower costs of capital can also have higher P/E ratios, but this is rarely the main channel. Thus, we focus mostly on the growth channel.) Let's think about this.

Differences in Expected Earnings Growth Rates

Assume firms are growing perpetuities. Let's determine a sensible price-earnings ratio for a hypothetical firm.

Assume that your firm is expected to earn cash of $100 next year and that its appropriate cost of capital is 15%. This firm is a perpetuity whose income will grow by 5% per year forever. Also, assume that earnings are representative of cash flows. Adopting a variant of the growing perpetuity, Formula 3.1 ($P = C/(r-g)$), assume that the value of this firm is

$$\text{Value} \quad = \quad \$100/(15\% - 5\%) = \$1,000 \qquad (14.1)$$

$$\text{Value} = \text{Price} = \frac{\text{Expected Earnings}}{\text{Appropriate Interest Rate} - \text{Expected Growth Rate of Earnings}}$$

With a price of $1,000 and expected earnings of $100, the firm's price divided by expected earnings is its P/E ratio,

$$\frac{\text{Price}}{\text{Expected Earnings}} = \frac{\$1,000}{\$100} = \frac{1}{15\% - 5\%} = 10$$

$$\frac{\text{Price}}{\text{Expected Earnings}} = \frac{\left(\frac{\text{Expected Earnings}}{\text{Appropriate Interest Rate} - \text{Expected Growth Rate of Earnings}}\right)}{\text{Expected Earnings}}$$

$$= \frac{1}{\text{Appropriate Interest Rate} - \text{Expected Growth Rate of Earnings}}$$

What if this firm grew not by 5% but by 10% per year (forever)? Then its price/earnings ratio would be

$$\frac{\text{Price}}{\text{Expected Earnings}} = \frac{1}{15\% - 10\%} = 20$$

Faster-growing firms have higher price-earnings ratios.

This shows that the P/E ratio of this firm is higher if it has more future earnings growth.

What if the market expected this firm to shrink by 5% each year? Such a firm would have a price-earnings ratio of only

$$\frac{\text{Price}}{\text{Expected Earnings}} = \frac{1}{15\% - (-5\%)} = 5$$

Conversely, slower-growing firms have lower price-earnings ratios.

Cigarette producers, for example, may suffer from negative annual growth rates and as a result have low price-earnings ratios. For example, in May 2002, RJR Nabisco and Philip Morris (now Altria) had P/E ratios of about 12. Contrast this with high-growth firms such as AMGEN (a high-tech pharmaceutical), which had a P/E ratio of about 40, and Microsoft, which had a P/E ratio of about 45. In sum, you can conclude that high price-earnings ratios are at least partly a reflection of the market's expectations about how fast a firm's future earnings will grow (relative to its cost of capital).

Despite everything I have just stated, you can also find some companies that have performed poorly and even shrunk, but which still have high P/E ratios. For example, in October 2005, Sun Microsystems had a P/E ratio of 45—three times as high as Microsoft's P/E ratio at the time of 16. Does this mean that the theory is wrong? On the contrary! P/E is a value ratio relative to current earnings. Sun was generally believed to have experienced tough times from 2001 to 2005. Presumably, the market did not expect Sun's low earnings to indicate its more long-term earnings. Instead, it expected Sun's future earnings potential to be much higher than its distressed 2005 earnings. Relative to its 2005 earnings, Sun may indeed have been a growth company!

A paradox: High growth rates for shrinking companies?

Do you find it confusing that earnings can grow by only 5% but investors expect to receive a 15% rate of return? Shouldn't an investor's expected rate of return be the growth rate of earnings? No—not at all. (Indeed, the expected rate of return $[\mathcal{E}(r)]$ cannot be equal to the growth rate of earnings $[\mathcal{E}(g)]$, or the NPV would be infinite.) The reason is that *the price today already capitalizes all future earnings.* For example, take a firm whose appropriate cost of capital is 10% and that will produce $100 next year, $50 the next year, and $0 thereafter. There is no uncertainty. Clearly, the cash flows/earnings of the firm are shrinking dramatically. But the value of the firm today is $100/1.1 + \$50/1.1^2 \approx \$132.23$. Next year, the investor will receive $100 and hold a remaining project of $50/1.1^1 \approx \$45.45$, for a total wealth of $145.45. The (expected) rate of return, that is, the cost of capital, is $145.45/\$132.23 - 1 \approx +10\%$, even though the growth rate of earnings is –50%.

Remember that the growth rate of earnings is *not* the expected rate of return to investors.

➤ *Cash, Earnings, Dividend Growth,* Sect. 2.6, Pg.32.

The Present Value of Growth Opportunities (PVGO)

Another common way to express the same information—to give perspective to the meaning of the growth component in P/E ratios—comes from decomposing the cash flows of a firm into two components: the ratio of a different hypothetical firm that has

Practitioners often work with PVGO (present value of growth opportunities).

the same projected earnings as our company but has stopped growing, and the ratio of another hypothetical firm that has zero earnings right now but consists exclusively of growth opportunities. The latter component has its own name, the *present value of growth opportunities* (**PVGO**). You can split the market value of any company—regardless of its actual earnings—into these two components. You can label them the "steady" and "growth" components.

It comes from a hypothetical split of earnings into a "steady" part and a "growth" part.

For example, consider three eternal firms, all priced at $150 and all with an appropriate cost of capital of 10%. The first (stable) firm has expected earnings of $15, the second (growth) firm has expected earnings of $12, and the third (shrinking) firm has expected earnings of $20. What are their PVGOs? Decompose these firms' values into their two components:

1. **The stable firm** is worth

$$\$150 \;=\; \frac{\$15}{10\%} \;+\; ? \;=\; \$150 + ? \tag{14.2}$$

$$\text{Price} \;=\; \frac{\text{Expected Earnings}}{\text{Cost of Capital}} \;+\; \text{PVGO}$$

To be an equality, the question mark must stand for $0. The market has priced this firm exactly as if it had no expectation of any future growth. Thus, 100% of this firm's value comes from the "steady component," and 0% from the "growth component." Eventually, in the very long run, you would expect mature and stable companies to settle into this mode.

2. **The growing firm** is also trading at $150, but it earns only a constant $12 next year. Its constant steady component would only be worth $120:

$$\$150 \;=\; \frac{\$12}{10\%} \;+\; ? \;=\; \$120 + ?$$

$$\text{Price} \;=\; \frac{\text{Expected Earnings}}{\text{Cost of Capital}} \;+\; \text{PVGO}$$

With this firm's "steady component" worth $120, its growth opportunities must be worth PVGO = $30. Taking this further, you would say that $30/$150 = 20% of the firm's value is due to future growth opportunities, and 80% is due to its steady business.

3. **The shrinking firm** should have been worth $20/10% = $200 today if the market had expected it to earn its constant $20 forever. To justify its actual market value of $150, it must have negative growth in the future:

$$\$150 \;=\; \frac{\$20}{10\%} \;+\; ? \;=\; \$200 + ?$$

$$\text{Price} \;=\; \frac{\text{Expected Earnings}}{\text{Cost of Capital}} \;+\; \text{PVGO}$$

Specifically, the subtractive part is PVGO = –$50. This firm is not expected to maintain its business.

So, PVGO is aptly named: Firms that are stable have zero PVGO, those that are growing have positive PVGO, and those that are shrinking have negative PVGO.

Q 14.3. Why is it more common to compute a price-earnings ratio than a price/cash flow ratio?

Q 14.4. Which is likely to have a higher price-earnings ratio: Google or PepsiCo?

Q 14.5. A firm has earnings of $230 *this year*, grows by about 6% each year, and has a price-earnings ratio of 40. What would its price-earnings ratio be if it could grow by 7% each year instead? How much would its value increase?

Q 14.6. Rearrange Formula 14.2 into its price-earnings form. What does this say about the earnings/price yield for firms with no PVGO? About firms with positive PVGO? Negative PVGO?

Q 14.7. If PVGO is positive, is $\mathcal{E}(g)$ positive or negative?

Q 14.8. Consider a stable firm with a market value of $1,000 that produces cash of $100 per year forever. The prevailing cost of capital for the firm is 10%.

1. Assume that the firm is financed with 100% equity. What is the P/E ratio?

2. Assume that if the firm refinances to a capital structure where $500 is financed with debt and $500 is financed with equity, then its debt has a cost of capital of 7.5% and the equity has a cost of capital of 12.5%. (The numbers I chose make sense in a perfect market. The so-called weighted cost of capital ($500/$1,000 · 7.5% + $500/$1,000 · 12.5%) is still exactly 10%. The firm's cost of capital has not changed.) What is the firm's equity P/E ratio now?

3. Has the increase in debt increased or decreased the firm's P/E ratio?

14.3 Problems with Price-Earnings Ratios

You are now ready to learn more details about how to value individual firms from comparables—and what the pitfalls are.

Problems.

Exhibit 14.2 reproduces entries from the *Wall Street Journal* stock price columns on May 31, 2002. It shows that the price-earnings ratio was 35 for Coca-Cola, 34 for PepsiCo, and 21 for Cadbury. The (previous day's closing) price per share was $54.39 for Coca-Cola, $50.93 for PepsiCo and $29.20 for Cadbury. Using this information, you can back out Coca-Cola's earnings per share as

Here is a set of real-world earnings numbers.

YTD %CHG	52-Week HI	LO	STOCK (SYM)	DIV	YLD %	P/E	VOL 100s	CLOSE	NET CHG
13.5	31.91	23.55	Cadbury (CSG)	0.70g	2.4	21	475	29.20	–0.20
15.4	57.91	42.59	Coca-Cola (KO)	0.80	1.5	35	47,565	54.39	0.24
4.6	53.50	43.08	PepsiCo (PEP)	0.60f	1.2	34	26,539	50.93	0.00

Exhibit 14.2: *Excerpt from the* Wall Street Journal *Financials, for May 30, 2002.* The *Wall Street Journal's* explanation states that the P/E ratio is based on the closing price and on diluted per-share earnings ignoring extraordinary items, as available, for the most recent 4 quarters. Fully diluted earnings means that all common stock equivalents (convertible bonds, preferred stock, warrants, and rights) have been included. (Actually, the most convenient source of financial information on individual stocks may no longer be the newspaper. Websites like **YAHOO!** FINANCE make it even easier to find more comprehensive financial information.)

$$\frac{\$54.39}{\text{Earnings}_{KO}} = 35 \qquad \Leftrightarrow \text{Earnings}_{KO} = \left(\frac{\$54.39}{35}\right) \approx \$1.55$$

$$\left(\frac{\text{Price}_{KO}}{\text{Earnings}_{KO}}\right) = \left(\frac{\text{Price}}{\text{Earnings}}\right)_{KO} \qquad \Leftrightarrow \text{Earnings}_{KO} = \left(\frac{\text{Price}_{KO}}{\text{P/E}_{KO}}\right)$$

The task is to value PepsiCo based on Coca-Cola's P/E ratio.

Now do a valuation-by-comparables for PepsiCo. That is, pretend that you do not know PepsiCo's value but that you do know PepsiCo's internal financials (earnings). Your task is to value the shares of PepsiCo in light of the value of shares of Coca-Cola. To consider Coca-Cola to be a comparable company for PepsiCo requires the heroic assumption that the two are similar firms, at least in terms of earnings multiples. If you are willing to do so, you can apply Coca-Cola's P/E ratio of 35 to PepsiCo earnings of $50.93/34 \approx \$1.50$ per share:

$$\frac{\text{Price}_{PEP}}{\$1.50} = 35 \qquad \Leftrightarrow \text{Price}_{PEP} = 35 \cdot \$1.50 = \$52.50$$

$$\left(\frac{\text{Price}_{PEP}}{\text{Earnings}_{PEP}}\right) = \left(\frac{\text{Price}}{\text{Earnings}}\right)_{KO} \qquad \Leftrightarrow \text{Price}_{PEP} = \left(\frac{\text{Price}}{\text{Earnings}}\right)_{KO} \cdot \text{Earnings}_{PEP}$$

In PepsiCo's case, valuation-by-comps against Coca-Cola works well.

The valuation-by-comps method suggests that PepsiCo should have been worth $52.50. This was higher than the $50.93 that PepsiCo shares were actually trading for, but a difference of less than $2 (about 3%) is very small compared to your normal valuation uncertainty. Here the method of comparables has worked very well in predicting a correct market value for PepsiCo.

In Cadbury's case, valuation-by-comps against Coca-Cola does not work well.

Now, assume that you instead owned Cadbury (CSG), that it was not yet publicly traded, and that it had just earned $1.39 per share ($29.20/$21). Applying the Coca-Cola P/E ratio of 35 to Cadbury's earnings, you would have expected CSG to trade for

$$\frac{\text{Price}_{CSG}}{\$1.39} \quad = \quad 35 \qquad \Leftrightarrow \text{Price}_{CSG} \quad = \quad 35 \cdot \$1.39 = \$48.65$$

$$\left(\frac{\text{Price}_{CSG}}{\text{Earnings}_{CSG}}\right) = \left(\frac{\text{Price}}{\text{Earnings}}\right)_{KO} \quad \Leftrightarrow \text{Price}_{CSG} = \left(\frac{\text{Price}}{\text{Earnings}}\right)_{KO} \cdot \text{Earnings}_{CSG}$$

You would have been far off! The P/E ratios were not comparable: The value of Cadbury shares in the public markets was $29.20 per share, not $48.65 per share. The method of comparables would have misled you.

What could have gone wrong in the Cadbury comps-based valuation? There are basically two possible explanations. The first is that the law of one price has failed. The stock market valuations—of CSG, KO, or both—were just plain wrong. This is unlikely. If the market values were systematically wrong, you could presumably get rich if you purchased undervalued firms. Thus, let's assume that market misvaluation is not the principal reason. The second is that your assumption that the two firms were basically alike was incorrect. This is the more likely cause. There is a long litany of reasons why comparables are not really comparable, and why the technique failed you in valuing Cadbury. Here is an outline of possible problems:

If comparables are dissimilar, either the market or the comparable is wrong. Usually, it is the latter.

➤ *Getting rich "easily",*
Sect. 11.5, Pg.302.

Problems in selecting comparable firms: Comparing businesses is almost always problematic. Every firm is a unique combination of many different projects. Cadbury owns Dr. Pepper, 7-Up, A&W Root Beer, Canada Dry, Hawaiian Punch, Snapple, Mott's Apple products, Clamato juice, plus some confectionary brands. This may not be comparable to Coca-Cola, which owns Coca-Cola Bottling, Minute Maid, Odwalla, and some other drink companies. Each of these businesses has its own profitability, and each may deserve its own P/E ratio. Even for the cola business, as any soda connoisseur knows, not even Pepsi's and Coke's Cola are perfect substitutes. Different consumer tastes may cause different growth rates, especially in different countries.

Later in this section, we will examine the selection of comparable firms and discuss the aggregation of multiple P/E ratios into one measure.

Problems in comparing the ratio (accounting numbers): Not all accounting statements are prepared the same way. Here are a few possible reasons why valuing Coca-Colar in terms of Cadbury could have gone wrong:

- Maybe British firms like Cadbury use different accounting methods.
- Maybe Cadbury or Coca-Cola had an unusual year.
- Maybe Cadbury finished its annual statement 11 months before Coca-Cola, and comparing last year's Cadbury earnings to this year's Coca-Cola earnings is not a good idea (or vice versa). Below, you will learn how to adjust better for differences in the timing of reports.
- Maybe Cadbury and Coca-Cola have different debt ratios. I will soon explain how debt can distort P/E ratios.
- Maybe extraordinary items (which I excluded above) should have been included to make these firms more comparable. Section 14.5 will discuss some non-plain-earnings-based financial ratios.

Let's look at these problems in more detail.

Selection of Comparison Firms

Finding good comparables: On what dimension should comparables be similar?

Normally, the single biggest problem with valuation by the method of comparables is finding good comparable projects. For instance, assume that you own a little soda producer, called *Your Beverage Corporation* (YBC), with earnings of $10 million. Which of the 10,000 or so publicly traded companies are most comparable to your firm (or project)? Are firms more similar if they are similar in assets, in their business products and services, in their geographical coverage, in their age, or in their size and scale? Do they have to be similar in all respects? If so, chances are that not a single of the 10,000 firms will qualify!

Which alternative firm is the best comparable?

Let us assume that after extensive research and much agonizing, you have identified the (same) three companies: KO, PEP, and CSG. Which one is most similar? You know that depending on which firm you select, your valuation could be $210 million (Cadbury, P/E = 21), $340 million (PepsiCo, P/E = 34), or $350 million (Coca-Cola, P/E = 35). Which shall it be?

Different conclusions about the value of the same firm: Analyst errors and biases can create wide variations in valuations.

Selecting comparables depends both on the judgment and on the motives of the analyst. In the YBC case, one analyst may consider all three firms (KO, PEP, and CSG) to be similar, but CSG to be most similar because it is the smallest comparison firm. She may determine that a good P/E ratio would be 20. Another analyst might consider Coca-Cola and PepsiCo to be better comparables, because they tend to serve the same market as YBC. He may determine that a good P/E ratio would be 30. The owner of YBC may want to sell out and try to find a buyer willing to pay as much as possible, so she might claim Coca-Cola to be the only true comparable, leading to a P/E ratio of 35. The potential buyer of YBC may instead claim Cadbury to be the only comparable, and in fact attribute an extra discount to YBC: After all, YBC is a lot smaller than CSG, and the buyer may feel that YBC deserves only a P/E ratio of, say, only 10. There is no definitive right or wrong choice.

(Non-)Aggregation of Comparables

Betas and costs of capital combine nicely—you can take value-weighted averages. A merged company is worth the same as the sum of its parts. Is this true for P/E ratios? No!

Assume you are an analyst who relies on NPV for valuation. Your NPV analysis tells you that firm FMA is worth $1,000 and firm FMB is worth $5,000. If FMA and FMB merge and there are no synergies, what would your NPV analysis of the merged FMAB firm be? It would predict a $6,000 value, of course. (This is because your cost-of-capital averages can be value-weighted, and present values can be added.) Would this also be the case if you are an analyst who relies on comparables methods instead of net present value for your valuation? The answer is no—based on your analysis of the merged FMAB firm's price-earnings ratio, you would claim that its value was different from $6,000. Yikes!

You would want to average somehow. (Unfortunately, it has no underlying valid basis.)

The averaging property also has implications about how you value conglomerates and whether you can "average" P/E ratios for multiple comparable firms. You were probably tempted not to adopt either the CSG P/E ratio of 21 or the KO P/E ratio of 35 as your P/E ratio estimate for YBC, but rather to "split the difference." A reasonable P/E ratio that is better than either may thus be 28. With $10 million in earnings, this might mean YBC valuations of around $210 to $350 million, with $280 million a "golden" (or brassy) middle. Unfortunately, although some sort of averaging may be the easiest solution, it is not a correct one. In fact, it is also hazardous. Here is why: Companies are collections of many projects. How would you like it if your valuation method gave you a $1,000 estimate for FMA, a $5,000 estimate for FMB, and, say, a $12,750 estimate for a merged FMAB firm (even in the absence of synergies)? Probably not so much. So is the P/E ratio of a company the same as the weighted-average P/E ratio of its subsidiaries, so that you can seamlessly work with either individual subsidiary P/E ratios or with overall company P/E ratios? Unfortunately, the answer is no.

Consider two firms. Firm FMA has a 5% growth rate and earnings of $100 (next year). Firm FMB has a 14% growth rate and earnings of $50 (next year). Both have a 15% cost of capital. Their respective values should be

An example of why the average of individual P/E ratios is not the overall P/E ratio.

$$\text{Price}_{\text{FMA}} = \text{Value}_{\text{FMA}} = \frac{\$100}{15\% - 5\%} = \$1,000 \implies \text{P/E} = 10$$

$$\text{Price}_{\text{FMB}} = \text{Value}_{\text{FMB}} = \frac{\$50}{15\% - 14\%} = \$5,000 \implies \text{P/E} = 100$$

What would happen if these two firms merged into a single conglomerate, called FMAB? Assume FMAB does not operate any differently—the two firms would just report their financials jointly. FMAB must be worth $6,000—after all, nothing has changed, and you know that NPVs are additive. It would have earnings of $150. Thus, its P/E ratio would be $6,000/$150 = 40.

Correct but unknown
FMAB P/E Ratio:
$$\frac{\text{Price}_{\text{FMAB}}}{\text{Earnings}_{\text{FMAB}}} = 40 \implies \text{Price}_{\text{FMAB}} = 40 \cdot \text{Earnings}_{\text{FMAB}}$$

Your goal is to value FMAB. Fortunately, you just happen to know a perfectly comparable firm for division FMA (trading at about P/E = 10), and a perfectly comparable firm for division FMB (trading at about P/E = 100). You even have a good idea of the relative size of the divisions inside FMAB (1 to 5). Knowing the combined earnings of FMAB of $150, you want to estimate a value for FMAB, based on your two comparables. Unfortunately, neither the unweighted-average P/E ratio nor the weighted-average P/E ratio gives you the correct desired P/E ratio of 40:

Unweighted P/E Average
of FMA and FMB
$$\left(\frac{1}{2}\right) \cdot \left(\frac{\text{Price}_{\text{FMA}}}{\text{Earnings}_{\text{FMA}}}\right) + \left(\frac{1}{2}\right) \cdot \left(\frac{\text{Price}_{\text{FMB}}}{\text{Earnings}_{\text{FMB}}}\right) = 55$$

Weighted P/E Average
of FMA and FMB
$$\left(\frac{1}{6}\right) \cdot \left(\frac{\text{Price}_{\text{FMA}}}{\text{Earnings}_{\text{FMA}}}\right) + \left(\frac{5}{6}\right) \cdot \left(\frac{\text{Price}_{\text{FMB}}}{\text{Earnings}_{\text{FMB}}}\right) = 85$$

Applying either of these two P/E ratios to your $150 in earnings would result in a price assessment for FMAB that would be too high. With a P/E ratio of 55, FMAB would be worth $55 \cdot \$150 = \$8,250$. With a P/E ratio of 85, FMAB would be worth $85 \cdot \$150 = \$12,750$.

IMPORTANT

- Unlike market betas and costs of capital, price-earnings ratios should not be value-weighted and averaged.

- Mergers can change the P/E ratio even if they do not create value.

- However, in real life, analysts average anyway—not because it is a good way to do it, but because they have no better alternative.

Lack of sensible aggregation makes it difficult to value even well-defined firms, especially if the comparables are divisions inside of larger firms.

The inability to aggregate divisions' P/E ratios not only is an issue for the firm that is to be valued, but also makes it difficult to extract a single comparable ratio for a division from inside of a conglomerate firm. In our case, let's assume that you only wanted to value the U.S. Dr. Pepper division of CSG, and that the U.S. Minute Maid division of Coca-Cola is a perfect comparable for it. But how do you extract a P/E ratio for the Minute Maid division if all you know is the P/E ratio of the overall Coca-Cola company with its many components? You can't!

The consequences of the aggregation failure mean, strictly speaking, that only the most basic single-product firms should be compared.

There are no good methods to aggregate and disaggregate P/E ratios. Therefore, strictly speaking, you can only compare full firms that are similar. It also means that P/E ratios are likely to work well only for simple and well-defined companies, and not so well for complex conglomerates. In retrospect, it would have been a coincidence if the naïve attempts to apply the overall P/E ratio of Coca-Cola to Cadbury's overall earnings would have worked. Indeed, in retrospect, it was an amazing coincidence that PepsiCo and Coca-Cola had such similar P/E ratios. You lived for a brief moment in blissful ignorance.

How Bad Are Mistakes?

Averaging P/E Ratios and the 1/X Domain Problem

Unfortunately, averaging P/E ratios is not only formally wrong, it can also create huge problems by itself. The main problem is that ratios are not sensible if their denominator is tiny, zero, or negative. This is the case for the P/E ratio, because earnings can be (temporarily) zero or negative. This can totally mess up any P/E ratio analysis. The function 1/Earnings is both discontinuous and very steep when earnings are close to zero. For instance, if a firm with a price of $10 has projected earnings of 1 cent, it has a P/E ratio of 1,000; if its earnings fall by just one more cent, it has a P/E ratio that is undefined; if its earnings fall by yet another cent, its P/E ratio suddenly becomes −1,000. We shall call this the "1/X domain problem."

Consider the example where the choice of industry comparables for FMC is FMA.

	Value (Price)	Earnings (Earnings)		P/E Ratio	E/P Yield
Firm FMA	$20	−$5	$\Rightarrow$	−4	−25.0%
	Industry Average:			−4	−25.0%
Firm FMC	?	$2			

This would imply a negative value for Firm FMC,

$$\text{Value}_{FMC} = \text{Earnings}_{FMC} \cdot (\text{P/E ratio})_{FMA} = \$2 \cdot (-4) = -\$8$$

A value of −$8 for a firm with positive earnings and limited liability is not sensible. Luckily, this particular comparables-derived valuation is so far out that every analyst would notice it.

Yet, this problem is sometimes overlooked when an analyst uses a P/E *industry* average. For example, assume the analyst has one more comparable firm:

	Value (Price)	Earnings (Earnings)		P/E Ratio	E/P Yield
Firm FMA	$20	–$5	$\Rightarrow$	–4	–25.0%
Firm FMB	$1,000	+$50	$\Rightarrow$	20	5.0%
	Industry Average:			8	12.5%
Firm FMC	?	$2			

The average industry P/E ratio would be $[20 + (-4)]/2 = 8$. This is a reasonable-looking P/E ratio average that might not raise a red flag. A thoughtless analyst could end the analysis with the conclusion that Firm FMC should be worth $\text{Value}_{FMC} = \text{Earnings}_{FMC} \cdot (P_{FMB+FMA}/E_{FMB+FMA}) = \$2 \cdot 8 = \$16$.

Unfortunately, once you use a negative ratio in a P/E average, you are really working with garbage. Just consider what happens to the implied value of FMC if firm FMA's earnings had been just a little higher than –$5.

- If FMA had earnings of –$2 instead of –$5, the average P/E ratio would have been $[20 + (-10)]/2 = 5$, and your implied value for FMC would still have been a seemingly reasonable $10.

- If FMA had earnings of –$1, the average P/E ratio would have been $[20 + (-20)]/2 = 0$. Given limited liability, how can your firm be worth nothing?

- If FMA had earnings of –$0.10, the average P/E ratio would have been $[20 + (-200)]/2 = (-90)$, and your implied value would now be –$180. Huh?

- If FMA had earnings of +$0.10, the average P/E ratio would have been $[20 + (200)]/2 = 110$, and your implied value would be a positive $220. Yikes!

As you can see, small changes in earnings can produce either seemingly reasonable or unreasonable valuations. In other examples, even one comparable with earnings close to zero among a dozen comparables can totally mess up an average of many comparable P/E ratios.

Remedies for the 1/X Domain Problem

Ultimately, there is no entirely satisfactory method to remedy the 1/X domain problem, but there are common procedures that try to deal with it:

Here is a set of ad hoc methods to improve the averaging of P/E ratios. None are perfect. All are ad hoc.

1. **Use the median, not the mean:** The *mean* P/E ratio is often drastically changed by one outlier firm. In contrast, the *median* firm's P/E ratio is often not based on one negative earnings firm. Unfortunately, it also ignores potentially useful information: the P/E ratios of all firms above or below those of the median firm.

2. **Ignore nonpositive earnings firms:** One common industry practice is to drop out firms with nonpositive earnings from P/E averages. Unfortunately, this is not necessarily a good solution. First, you want an accurate valuation, and the stock market did value firm FMA at $20. You have no good reason to ignore firms with low earnings. Second, dropping out firms creates its own problem: A comparable firm could drop out of the P/E average if its earnings were –10 cents, but suddenly

drop back in if its earnings were +10 cents—and then exert enormous influence. (Sometimes, analysts even exclude firms with positive but low earnings.) In our example, if FMA had earnings of –10 cents, you would value FMC at a P/E ratio of 20 (i.e., Value$_{FMC}$ = $40), but if FMA had earnings of just +10 cents, you would value FMC at a P/E ratio of 110 (i.e., Value$_{FMC}$ = $220).

In sum, a small change in the earnings of just one comparable could still have a very large impact on your comparables valuation due to arbitrary inclusion/exclusion of comparables (rather than closeness of earnings to zero).

3. **Average E/P yields and invert:** The E/P yield is guaranteed to have a positive denominator. Therefore, it avoids the 1/X domain problem. In the example, the E/P yield of firm FMB is $50/$1,000 = 5%; the E/P yield of firm FMA if it earned –$0.10 is –$0.10/$20 = –0.5%. The average E/P yield is thus [5% + (–0.5%)]/2 = 2.25%. Inverting this back into a P/E ratio provides a halfway sensible value for the P/E ratio (1/2.25% ≈ 44).

4. **Work with sums:** Instead of averaging individual firms' P/E ratios, you can first add up all Ps and all Es before you divide them. In the example where FMA earned –$0.10, the total industry earnings would be $50.00 – $0.10 = $49.90, the entire industry market value would be $1,000 + $20 = $1,020, and the average P/E ratio would be $1,020/$49.90 ≈ 20.441. In this method, firms are effectively weighted by their relative market valuation. Large firms influence the outcome more than small ones. This may or may not be desirable. In the example, FMB would become the dominant determinant of your comparable valuation ratio.

These methods can sometimes provide reasonable estimates if only a very few among many firms in the industry have negative earnings. If this is not the case, it is better not to use the P/E ratio in the first place.

IMPORTANT

> - Formally, neither P/E ratios nor E/P yields can be averaged across projects or firms.
>
> - In real life, some sort of informal averaging is often called for. This is because it is often worse to rely on just one single comparable.
>
> - Simple averaging can lead to nonsensible estimates. There are ways to do it better: using the median, dropping firms with low earnings, averaging E/P yields, or dividing only aggregate price by aggregate earnings.
>
> Never take P/E ratio averages literally. Your goal is only to find an "intuitively good average P/E ratio equivalent" for your type of firm, derived from multiple comparables, not an exact number.

Q 14.9. Is the P/E ratio of a merged company with two divisions, A and B, the value-weighted or equal-weighted average of the P/E ratios of these divisions?

Q 14.10. A firm with a P/E ratio of 20 wants to take over a firm half its size with a P/E ratio of 50. What is the P/E ratio of the merged firm?

A N E C D O T E   **Which P/E Ratio to Believe?**

Exchange-traded funds (ETFs) are baskets of securities, often put together to mimic an index. You can think of ETFs as firms for which you know the value—and price-earnings ratio—of each and every division (stock component).

On March 13, 2006, the *Wall Street Journal* reported that Barclays Global Investors calculated the P/E ratio of its iShares S&P 500 ETF as 16.4 and that of its iShares Russell 2000 ETF as 19.1. The Russell 2000 includes many midmarket firms. It garnered nearly $7.5 billion from investors and was one of the fastest-growing funds in 2006. Do these two funds look comparable in terms of their valuation ratios?

If you had computed the weighted sum of the market value of all stocks in the Russell 2000 index and divided that figure by the companies' total earnings, you would have found that this ETF had a P/E ratio of 41, not 19.1. Why the difference? It is because BGI excludes all loss-making companies in its iShares ETF when computing its P/E ratio—thus there were many Russell 2000 components excluded. Karl Cheng, an iShares portfolio manager, said that investors don't normally look at negative P/E ratios for companies, so they don't include them in their average. He suggested that investors should consider other measures. Thanks, Karl!

The Wall Street Journal, March 13, 2006 (page C3).

Q 14.11. Why can it be most hazardous to work with P/E ratio averages? What would you call this problem (and where does it come from)?

Q 14.12. What can you do if only one among a dozen industry comparables has a negative P/E ratio?

Trailing 12-Month (TTM) Figures and Other Adjustments

There is one "small" mechanical detail remaining: timing. First, is it meaningful to use annual earnings for a firm if the last annual report was from 11 months ago? Or should you use just the most recent quarter's numbers? Second, some firms report earnings in June, others in December. You may not want to compare financials that are timed too differently, especially if the economy has changed in the second half of the year. For example, consider the following reports:

When comparable firms report annual statements in different months, the intrayear change in economic climate can introduce another problem.

	2001				2002		
	(Mar) Q1	(Jun) Q2	(Sep) Q3	(Dec) Q4	(Mar) Q1	(Jun) Q2	(Sep) Q3
Comparable Firm	$1	$2	$3	$9	$5	$6	$7
	⇒ 2001 Annual Earnings: $15						

Your own firm has closed its financial year with annual earnings of $12 in October 2002. What are the relevant comparable earnings? Should you compare your own annual earnings of $12 to the dated annual earnings of $15 from December 2001?

You could try to work directly with quarterly earnings, but this is usually not a good idea, either. Most firms do more business in December, and December can be the first or the last month in a quarter. Not only are different quarters difficult to compare across firms, but the December quarter may be difficult to compare even to the other quarters

Fortunately, this time difference can be relatively easily taken care of via "trailing 12-month" (TTM) figures.

of the same firm. Generally, the best method to adjust flows (such as earnings) into a "most recent annualized equivalent" is to use a **trailing 12-month (TTM)** adjustment. In the example, this means adding the earnings from Q4-2001 through Q3-2002:

$$\text{As if Annual in Sep. 2002} \quad = \quad \$9 \quad + \quad \$5 \quad + \quad \$6 \quad + \quad \$7 \quad = \$27$$

$$\text{TTM Earnings} \quad = \text{Q4/01} + \text{Q1/02} + \text{Q2/02} + \text{Q3/02}$$

Using the reported earnings, you can also compute this as follows:

$$\text{As if Annual} \quad = \quad \$15 \quad + \quad (\$5 - \$1) \quad + \quad (\$6 - \$2) \quad + \quad (\$7 - \$3) \quad = \$27$$

$$\text{TTM Earnings} = \text{Ann/01} + (\text{Q1/02} - \text{Q1/01}) + (\text{Q2/02} - \text{Q2/01}) + (\text{Q3/02} - \text{Q3/01})$$

TTM only works for "flow" numbers (such as income), not for stock numbers (such as assets).

There are three final caveats: First, TTM adjusts only "flow" numbers (such as earnings or sales), never "stock" numbers (such as corporate assets or liabilities). Stock numbers are whatever they have been reported as most recently. Second, firms sometimes account for 52-week years or 53-week years, even making consecutive-year comparisons problematic. Third, firms can, and occasionally do, change their fiscal year-ends—often to make it intentionally more difficult to compare numbers. In this case, you must exercise extra care.

Q 14.13. The following are quarterly earnings and assets for Coca-Cola and PepsiCo (in millions of dollars) from 2002 financial reports, including restated figures for 2001 (for PepsiCo):

Quarter Ending	Coca-Cola (KO)				PepsiCo (PEP)			
	Earnings		Assets		Earnings		Assets	
	Q	A	Q	A	Q	A	Q	A
6/2002	1,290		25,287		888		24,200	
3/2002	801[a]		23,689		651		22,611	
12/2001	914	3,979	22,417	22,417	667	2,662	21,695	21,695
9/2001	1,074		22,665		627		23,036	
6/2001	1,118		22,387		798		N/A[b]	
3/2001	873		22,248		570		N/A[b]	
12/2000	242	2,177	20,834	20,834	698	2,543	20,757	20,757

(a) A onetime cumulative accounting change dropped this to –125. (b) Because PepsiCo did not report quarterly assets when it restated its financials, these assets could not be found.

If it is now July 2002, what would be good comparable earnings and comparable assets for these two firms?

Debt Adjustments for P/E Ratios

As you already know, companies can be financed through a mix of debt and equity. Does the P/E ratio of a firm depend on this mix? If a firm with more debt in its capital structure has a different P/E ratio, then you cannot compare two otherwise identical companies, *because* they have different debt ratios. Put differently, your "just-perfect" comparable firm that does everything just like your own firm might have just evaporated, simply because it has a different capital structure.

Does leverage influence P/E ratios?

It turns out that debt indeed changes the P/E ratio, but not necessarily either positively or negatively. Roughly speaking:

Unfortunately, the answer is yes.

- For growth companies (with a high earnings growth rate), more debt tends to increase the P/E ratio.

- For value companies (with a zero or negative earnings growth rate), more debt tends to decrease the P/E ratio.

You will get to see this for yourself in the problems at the end of the chapter.

More importantly, how can you make your firms more comparable again? (If you don't, you should not compare them.) One sensible method to eliminate the influence of debt is to move from an equity-based to a firm-based P/E ratio, both for the firm to be valued and for its benchmarks. To do this, you must add the earnings-equivalent payments to creditors (i.e., interest payments) to the denominator, and add (financial) debt to the value of equity. Let's try this. Gather the relevant information from YAHOO! FINANCE (all quoted dollars are in billions):

Here are some sample inputs from YAHOO! FINANCE. We illustrate adjusting P/E ratios for different leverage ratios.

	Coca-Cola (KO)	PepsiCo (PEP)	Cadbury (CSG)
Interest Expense, Dec. 01	$0.244	$0.207	$0.155
Earnings, Dec. 01	$3.91	$2.74	$0.72
Equity Market Value, May 02	$136.85	$93.16	$15.12
Equity Book Value, Dec. 01	$11.37	$8.65	$4.12
Debt Book Value, Dec. 01	$5.12	$3.00	$2.00
Capital Book Value, Dec. 01	$16.48	$11.65	$6.12

It is easy to compute the standard, levered debt ratios. (I much prefer market-value based equity ratios to book-value based equity ratios, as you may remember.) They are also reported on many financial websites:

➤ *Warning on book-value based equity.*, *Sect.* 13.1, *Pg.377*.

	KO	PEP	CSG
Levered Reported P/E	35	34	21

What would happen if each company unlevered itself?

Think about how the P/E ratios of levered firms would change if they were unlevered.

1. All debt would become equity. We want to add the current market value (from May 2002) to the book value of debt from December 2001, simply because we do not have a market value of debt in December 2002.

2. All interest payments would become equity payments.

In a perfect market, this information is enough to compute the unlevered P/E ratio. In an imperfect market, a change in leverage could also change the total amount of cash flows. For example, if a firm could save on corporate income taxes by having more debt, the total amount of payments to debt and equity could increase. Let's ignore this for now, and focus on the perfect market scenario. In this case,

	KO	PEP	CSG
Interest + Earnings, Dec. 2001	$4.15	$2.95	$0.88
Capital Market Value, May 2002	$142.0	$96.2	$17.1
Unlevered Computed P/E	34.2	32.6	19.4

Unfortunately, in this case, after proper adjustment for leverage, the P/E ratios have become no more similar. (Doing it right would make our valuation inference worse.)

Does it appear as if Cadbury (the underlying unlevered company) is now a lot more like PepsiCo than levered Cadbury shares were to levered PepsiCo shares? Unfortunately, the answer is no. The P/E ratio of Cadbury is even more different from those of Coca-Cola and PepsiCo than it was before. You also have some more information to evaluate your earlier remarkable finding that PepsiCo could be accurately valued with the comparable of Coca-Cola. You chose Coca-Cola because you believed that the firm of Coca-Cola would be similar to PepsiCo, not because you believed that the equity shares of Coca-Cola would be similar to those of PepsiCo. But, in this case, the firms of Coca-Cola and PepsiCo are a little less similar than the equity shares of Coca-Cola and PepsiCo: Their unlevered P/E ratios are a little farther apart than their levered P/E ratios. If you had properly applied the valuation ratio of one firm to the other firm, you would have concluded that PepsiCo and Coca-Cola are not so similar after all. Nevertheless, unlevering in this case has not changed much, simply because these three firms did not have much debt (in market value). The unlevered KO and CSG were no more similar to the unlevered PEP than the levered KO and CSG were similar to the levered PEP. We did not get much mileage out of unlevering.

Q 14.14. A firm has a P/E ratio of 12 and a debt-equity ratio of 2:1 (66.7%). What would its unlevered P/E ratio (i.e., the P/E ratio of its underlying business) approximately be?

Q 14.15. On October 9, 2002, the seven auto manufacturers publicly traded in the United States were as follows:

Manufacturer	Mkt.Cap	Earnings	Manufacturer	Mkt.Cap	Earnings
Volvo (ADR)	$5.7	–$0.18	DaimlerChrysler	$32.3	$4.63
Ford	$14.1	–$5.30	Honda (ADR)	$37.7	$3.09
GM	$18.8	$1.83	Toyota (ADR)	$87.3	$4.51
Nissan (ADR)	$27.0	$2.55			

(All quoted dollars are in billions. Ignore debt. ADR means American Depositary Receipt, a method by which foreign companies can list on the New York Stock Exchange.) On the same day, Yahoo! Germany reported that Volkswagen AG had earnings of 3.8 billion euros. In terms of sales, Volkswagen was most similar to Volvo and Ford. What would you expect Volkswagen to be worth? What assumptions are you making?

14.4 The Empirical Evidence in 2011

Now let us look at the empirical data to assess how well earnings-based valuation by comparables works in practice. We will look at some snapshots taken in 2011 to learn about the relation between earnings, earnings growth, and price (value).

Statistics for Some Selected Firms

Start with a tasting sampler. Exhibit 14.3 presents price-earnings ratios and PVGO calculations for firms in four industries in May 2011—computers, retail stores, car companies, and financials. (In addition, I added our old friends, PepsiCo and Coca-Cola, both in 2004 and in 2011.) You can readily download data to create similar figures from **YAHOO!** FINANCE. Note how Baidu, the "Chinese Google," carried a much higher P/E ratio than Google itself. However, for the most part, large computer companies have P/E ratio between 10 and 20. (AOL has none, because it had negative earnings.) For PVGO inputs, I only had to guestimate a cost of capital, which I did using a simple CAPM and reported in the table. I then used Formula 14.2 to compute the PVGO, dividing it by the current market capitalization (in order to report it as a fraction of firm value). Apparently, in 2011, the market believed that the future lay with Baidu rather than Google; and with Toyota and Tata rather than Honda and GM. Over 84% of Baidu's value and 65% of Tata's value were their future opportunities!

Here is a sample of firms to illustrate the usefulness of PVGO.

Company	P/E	Beta	$\mathcal{E}(r)$	PVGO/P	Company	P/E	Beta	$\mathcal{E}(r)$	PVGO/P
Google	21	0.9	7%	29%	GM	7	–	–	NA
Baidu	72	1.5	8%	84%	Toyota	52	0.8	6%	70%
Yahoo	19	0.9	7%	21%	Honda	11	0.7	6%	–49%
AOL	∞	–	7%	–	Tata Motors	27	2.2	12%	65%
Apple	16	1.1	7%	14%	Citigroup	14	2.6	12%	39%
Intel	11	1.1	7%	–25%	Goldman Sachs	16	1.2	8%	18%
AMD	9	2.3	11%	–2%	JP Morgan	10	1.2	8%	–32%
Microsoft	10	1.0	7%	–43%	PepsiCo	19	0.6	6%	9%
Walmart	12	0.4	5%	–60%	Coca-Cola	13	0.6	6%	–33%
Costco	26	0.8	6%	40%	PepsiCo, *2004*	20	–	10%	50%
Target	13	1.0	7%	–10%	Coca-Cola, *2004*	20	–	6%	20%

Exhibit 14.3: *Various P/E Ratios in May 2011.* The P/E and betas were downloaded from **YAHOO!** FINANCE. I estimated the cost of capital as $\mathcal{E}(r_i) = 4\% + 3\% \cdot \beta_i$. I computed the ratio PVGO/Price from Formula 14.2, PVGO/Price $= 1 - 1/[\mathcal{E}(r) \cdot$ P/E ratio] with unrounded numbers. All reported figures are intentionally starkly rounded to reduce the illusion of accuracy. A dash means unknown. I also made no attempt to adjust for corporate debt ratios, which was explained in Section 14.3.

Earnings, Prices, and Price-Earnings Ratios

The conceptual figures in real life.

Individual firms are interesting, but it is usually more informative to look at the data more systematically. So, how useful was earnings-attribute-based valuation of publicly traded firms in late 2011?

Let's start with the simplest possible earnings-based valuation model: Do firms with the same expected earnings tend to have the same value? Asked differently, are their price-earnings ratio constant? In this naïve model, earnings growth rates are unimportant. To put this theory to the test, we need to draw the real-world equivalent of the conceptual plots in Exhibit 14.1. The valuation attribute are firms' earnings, as they were forecast by analysts standing in 2010 for the end of 2011. Prices are from 2010. If this simple model works, then the values (prices) should lie on a straight line.

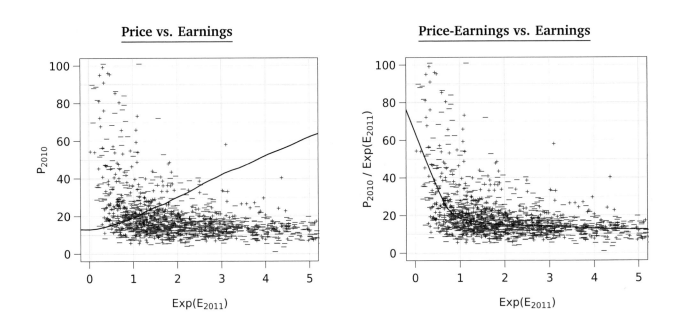

Exhibit 14.4: *Price-Earnings as Attribute-Based Valuation by Comparables.* This figure plots the prices and price-earnings ratios in Dec 2010 of 1,356 firms with more than $50 million in equity market capitalization against their prevailing analysts' forecast earnings for 2011. A "+" indicates a firm with more than 20% expected earnings growth from 2010 to 2011; a "−" indicates the opposite. The shape of the function was not assumed but fit by the data itself.

The relationship in December 2010 was beautifully linear on average...

First, the good news. Exhibit 14.4 shows that there was indeed a solid relationship between earnings and prices. Each "+" and "−" is one firm. ("+" is a firm with a forecast earnings growth rate above 20%; "−" is the opposite.) The left plot shows that firms with higher earnings had higher prices. Even better, for firms with more than $1/share in earnings, the relationship is roughly a line with a slope of 12: each dollar of forecast earnings translated into about $12 in value *on average*. In one sense, linearity should not come as a complete surprise—a firm with $1 million in earnings should be worth the same total amount (say, $12 million), regardless of whether it has 500 thousand shares (earnings of $2/share and a price of $24/share) or whether it has 1 million shares (earnings of $1/share and a price of $12/share). The relationship does break down for firms with less than $1 in earnings. If the relationship was perfectly linear, then firms with $0 in earnings should have been worth $0. Obviously, the theory should not work for them. (You would expect these firms to have earnings *eventually*.) The right graph translates the price into a price-earnings ratio. Firms with higher earnings had somewhat lower P/E ratios. Because of the non-linearity of the P/E ratio and variation in the denominator, the median price-earnings ratio is about 15 and not 12, suggesting that $1 in earnings translates into about $15, not $12. This discrepancy is because $\mathcal{E}(P) = b \cdot \mathcal{E}(E) \Leftrightarrow \mathcal{E}(P)/\mathcal{E}(E) = b$, but $\mathcal{E}(P)/\mathcal{E}(E) \neq \mathcal{E}(P/E)$. Plotting E/P ratios would have made more sense, but it would also have made for a less intuitive figure. Don't worry about the difference between $12 and $15 too much—there is worse to come.

➤ *Linear Operators and Expectations, Sect.* A, *Pg.697.*

So here is the bad news. Look at the wide distribution of prices for firms with the same forecast earnings. For example, some firms with earnings forecasts of around $1/share traded for $5/share, while others traded for around $50/share. This range is too large to be very useful. Even if you ignore all outliers, values between $10 and $20 are all still reasonable estimates. I have also made it easy to assess whether earnings-growth rates are primarily responsible for the poor fit. If you look hard, you will see that many of the low-priced firms had high expected earnings growth ("+") and many low-priced firms had low expected earnings growth ("–"). Knowing earnings-growth rates is useful, but it is not going to be able to explain the poor fit.

...but unfortunately the variability was very large.

Exhibit 14.4 should suggest to you that earnings-based attribute valuation (or, equivalently, price-earnings-based attribute valuation) is not a very accurate valuation method. Phrased in terms of Exhibit 14.1, the empirical reality in December 2010 fell somewhere between the "modestly useful" plot (b) and the "useless" plot (c). If you had hoped that attribute-based valuation was the panacea that would rescue you from NPV and CAPM calculations, you should be greatly disappointed.

Conclusion: It's useful information, but definitely not definitive. You cannot trust valuation by earnings-comparables.

Price-Earnings Ratios and Earnings Growth Rates

Although you already know that earnings-growth alone will not save the day, let's still look at the more sophisticated P/E ratio theory which says that firms with higher growth rates of earnings should have higher price-earnings ratios. To test it, we need two more assumptions: (a) the 1-year forecast growth rate of earnings is a proxy for the long-term growth rate of earnings, and (b) costs of capital are not too different.

Do high-growth firms in the real world have higher P/E ratios (lower E/P yields)?

Exhibit 14.5 plots the same analyst-forecast earnings-growth rates against the price-to-predicted-earnings ratios. Each dot is one firm. The figure shows that firms with higher growth rates had higher price-earnings ratios, just as the theory predicts. (The exception are firms with negative growth rates, but here the theory was unlikely to work anyway. Firms with negative earnings growth are unlikely to have negative earnings growth forever.)

The evidence supports the theory (with mild auxiliary assumptions): High-growth firms have higher P/E ratios.

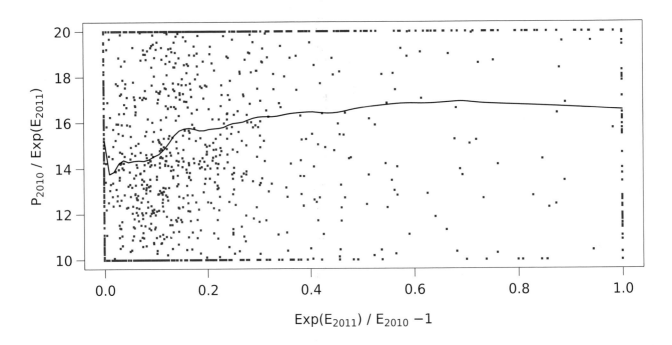

Exhibit 14.5: *The Relationship between 1-Year Analyst-Forecast Earnings Growth Rates and 1-Year Analyst-Forecast Price-Earnings Ratios, in December 2010.* The theory predicts that firms with higher earnings growth should have higher price-earnings ratios. Except for firms that had negative expected earnings growth (all of which were winsorized to zero earnings growth), this seemed to have roughly been the case in December 2010. However, the relationship between price and earnings growth is not strong. Original data sources: I/B/E/S provided analysts' earnings forecasts. CRSP provided stock prices. The graph plots data for 2,135 firms with a December 2010 fiscal year end, available earnings, and a median consensus earnings forecast for December 2011. P/E ratios were winsorized between 10 and 20 and earnings growth rates were winsorized between 0 and 100%.

The typical P/E ratio was about 15, with earnings growth giving you estimates between 14 and 16.

Eyeballing the figure, it seems that firms neither growing nor contracting tended to have price-earnings ratios of about 14, while firms growing by 50% or more tended to have price-earnings ratios of about 16. This is better than the unconditional price-earnings ratio of 15, but not greatly so. There is still tremendous variation across firms in their prices, given their earnings-growth rates. In terms of Exhibit 14.5, reality still falls somewhere between the "modestly useful" plot (b) and the "useless" plot (c).

Put the usefulness into perspective.

Why is even the sophisticated P/E model so bad? Perhaps it is because firms in different industries have different price-earnings ratio that are not completely captured by their earnings growth rates. Perhaps it is because our estimate of the expected rate of return was poor. Perhaps the theory is wrong. Well, the theory is useful, allowing you to assess value better than you would have if you had not considered earnings growth rates. For example, if you had been hired in 2010 to value a firm with $5 million in earnings but no expected earnings growth rate, an estimate of $70 million (P/E of 14) would have been better than an estimate of $80 (P/E of 16) million. But you should also acknowledge that some firms with such growth rates had values of $50 million while others had values of $100 million. To do much better, you would have to improve your valuation methods—perhaps restricting yourself to closer comparables and/or estimating present-value models for your firm.

Without telling you the details, let me close this section by saying that none of the pitfalls and corrections discussed in Section 14.3 would change your inference much. You would do a little bit better in assessing value, but there would still be a lot of residual valuation uncertainty. Valuation merely by comparables is bound to be very error-prone. You need to look at many different methods and form an opinion. Who said valuation was easy? Who said theory was harder than real life? It ain't so.

Out of space...

Stability

One warning: you cannot use this specific December 2010 figure to assess appropriate P/E ratios and thus firm values in future years. The reason is that during economic booms, earnings growth is high, and, although P/E ratios are high, too, they are not high enough for the eternal smooth-growth formula. After all, such earnings growth is unsustainable. Eventually, the boom must end. In contrast, during recessions, earnings growth can be negative. Yet P/E ratios remain relatively too high, because investors expect that earnings will eventually grow again. For example, in December 2000 corporate earnings grew at an average rate of +40%, which was clearly unsustainable. If you had relied on the growing perpetuity formulas, firms would have seemed to be undervalued. By December 2001, that is, post 9/11, the opposite had happened: The median earnings had fallen at a year-to-year rate of –40%. Investors would not have expected this malaise to last forever. If you had relied on the growing perpetuity formulas, firms would have appeared to be overvalued.

Unfortunately, the relation between earnings growth and price-earnings ratios (and thus the figure) changes over the business cycle, so you must use an up-to-date version for today's valuation.

IMPORTANT

The relation between earnings growth and earnings/price yields, especially using only 1-year-ahead earnings forecasts, is not stable over the business cycle. Therefore, to value firms, you must first plot the prevailing relation between earnings growth and earnings yields (the inverse of P/E ratios) before you can apply the theory.

Interpreting (Historical) P/E Ratios for the S&P 500

Finally, let's see how the P/E ratio model works in the overall stock market. This should be a lot easier than trying to explain the cross-sectional variation in values. We shall use the S&P 500 as a stand-in for the stock market. The upper plot in Exhibit 14.6 graphs the P/E ratio of the S&P 500. You should immediately notice the spikes in 2001 and 2008, when the P/E ratios exceeded 40. This meant that investors considered every $1 of corporate earnings to be the equivalent of $40 in value—much higher than was the case historically.

Use the theory on the S&P 500: the historical P/E ratio.

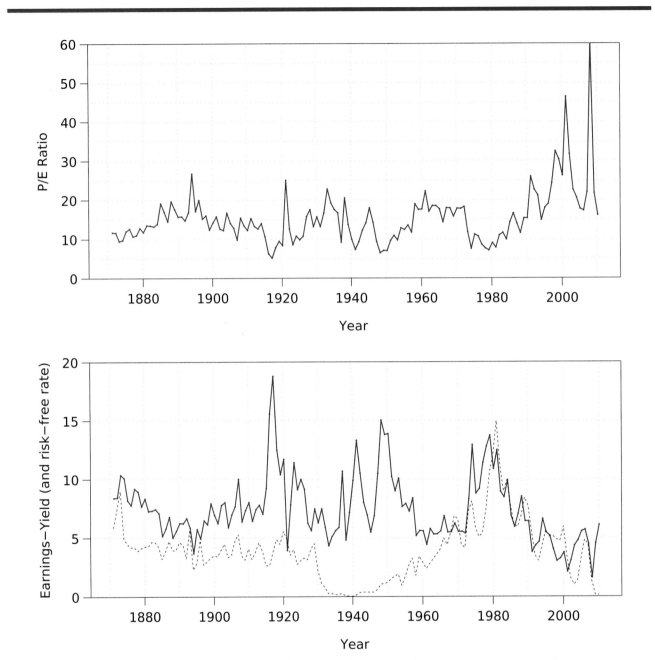

Exhibit 14.6: *The P/E Ratio and E/P Ratio of the S&P 500.* The upper plot shows the history of the price-earnings ratio for the S&P 500. It peaked first in 2001 and again in 2008. The lower plot (the earnings yield) is just the inverse, but it also plots the prevailing short-term risk-free interest rate. (The data is available from Amit Goyal's website at HEC Lausanne. His early data is originally from Robert Shiller's book *Irrational Exuberance*. Bob posts the (updated) original data on his website, http://aida.econ.yale.edu/~shiller/.)

How can you interpret spikes above 40? Start with our theory,

$$\text{Price Now} = \frac{\text{Expected Earnings Next Year}}{\text{Expected Rate of Return} - \text{Eternal Earnings Growth Rate}} \qquad (14.3)$$

You can rearrange this two ways:

Expected Rate of Return = Eternal Earnings Growth + Earnings Yield

Eternal Earnings Growth Rate = Expected Rate of Return − Earnings Yield

The 2000 spike should have been due to some combination of earnings growth and expected rates of return on the market.

where I have abbreviated the ratio "Expected Earnings Next Year/Price Now" as the earnings yield. Of course, a higher price-earnings ratio implies a lower earnings/price ratio for firms with positive earnings. Therefore, the first formula says that if your P/E ratio goes up, your expected rate of return goes down (if the growth rate of earnings is constant). The second formula says that if your P/E ratio goes up, your expected earnings growth rate also goes up (if the expected rate of return is constant). These are the only two possible explanations for high price-earnings ratios.

Let's put ourselves into investors' shoes at the turn of the millennium, and see how the numbers fit.

Do the numbers fit in 2000? Probably not. The P/E ratio was too high to justify high future stock returns, even given aggressive earnings growth.

1. **The earnings yield:** At a P/E ratio of 40, the earnings yield was about 2.5%. No guesswork needed.

2. **The earnings growth rate:** What would have been a reasonable estimate for the eternal growth rate of corporate earnings? Historically, the real (post-inflation) earnings growth rate was about 2%. In 2000, when prevailing inflation was about 1.5%, historical growth rates would have suggested nominal earnings growth rates of about 3.5%. Entertain a range from 3% to 5% for nominal earnings growth rates.

3. **The expected rate of return:** What would have been a reasonable estimate for the rate of return on the stock market? When surveyed in late 1999, investors claimed expected rates of return of 15-20% or more. After all, they had just experienced returns of above 25% per annum over several years in the late 1990s. Let's assume, conservatively, that most investors in early 2000 would have claimed expected rates of return of "only" about 12%, which was the long-run historical average rate of return on the stock market at the time.

4. **Plug it all in:** Pick the lowest expected rate of return on the stock market (12%), the highest corporate earnings growth rate (5%), and the P/E ratio of 40. Plug in these estimates:

   2.5%   ≠   12%   −   5%

   Earnings Yield = Expected Rate of Return − Eternal Earnings Growth Rate

It doesn't take a sophisticated financier to realize that these numbers do not add up. Something is wrong. Obviously, it isn't the P/E ratio. Thus, it must have been the case that (a) the expected rate of return was not 12%, but more like 7.5%; (b) the expected growth rate of corporate earnings was not 5%, but more like 9.5%; or (c) some combination of the two.

As for me, I conclude that expectations of future stock returns should have been lower in 2000.

We can actually narrow this down a little further. The highest *long-run* real growth rate of earnings (at the start of the Industrial Revolution) was no more than 4% per year. Add inflation, and you would estimate the nominal growth rate of earnings to be around 6%—and realize that this means that you would have predicted no less than the equivalent of a second industrial revolution. In fact, this was exactly what analysts at the time were touting to investors: It was the *new economy*, where old rules no longer applied. Even if you had bought into their argument, however, you should still have expected stock market returns of no more than 10% for the formula to add up. In fact, our earlier estimate in Section 9.4 was that a reasonable equity premium seems to be around 3-5%. To estimate the expected rate of return on the stock market, you must add back the Treasury bond yield, which stood at about 5% in 2000, for a reasonable range of 8-10%—just about right. Investors expecting rates of return above 10% must simply have been overoptimistic. This argument was most forcefully advanced by Professor Robert Shiller's best seller, *Irrational Exuberance*. It was published just before the stock market peaked in 2000—good timing, which transformed Bob into an instant market guru. (Bob also called the housing crash of 2007 years in advance. He deserves being called a guru.)

➤ *Equity premium estimates,* Sect. 9.4, Pg.216.

Q 14.16. Confirm the PVGO/price ratio for Google that is reported in Exhibit 14.3. (Use the formula in the caption.)

Q 14.17. Is the relation between earnings multiples and earnings growth rates usually positive or negative? Is it always so? If not, why not?

Q 14.18. If the P/E ratio on the S&P 500 is 20, given historical earnings growth patterns, what would be a reasonable estimate of long-run future expected rates of return on the stock market?

14.5　Other Financial Ratios

Let's look at financial ratios.

The P/E ratio is just one commonly used financial ratio. There are many others. Unfortunately, many users do not understand what these ratios really mean. (For some, neither do I nor anyone else!) As a result, they can lead to bad questions and wrong answers. However, sometimes they can be useful to understanding not only firm value but also other firm characteristics (such as risk or precariousness of the business). This section discusses two kinds of financial ratios. First, it covers other ratios that are primarily used for valuation. Second, it explains some ratios that measure profitability and debt burden. Their purpose is typically just to inform about the economics of the firm, not to advise you directly as to the appropriate value.

Valuation Ratios

A **valuation ratio** has price in its numerator and some measurable attribute in its denominator. The P/E ratio is the most common and typically best such ratio, although it is no magic bullet. Some other quantities regularly also appear as attributes in the denominator. Given a chosen valuation attribute, the analyst finds comparable firm(s) and multiplies the comparables' price/attribute ratios by the firm's own attribute to determine its value. This works well only if firms are similar enough. It is, of course, not possible to write down an exhaustive list of all other valuation ratios. Only the imagination limits the quantities that can be used in the denominator.

A valuation ratio has price in the numerator and something else in the denominator.

Earnings-Based Multiples

Your ultimate goal is to find a measure that is proportional to value. This means that you may want to use a different form of earnings. Earnings can be defined in a variety of ways: with or without extraordinary items, diluted, and so on. There is no right or wrong way for valuation purposes: Your goal is to find a ratio that makes your comparable firm appear to be as similar as possible to your own firm. You already saw one common alternative measure of earnings in Chapter 13, EBITDA (earnings before interest, taxes, depreciation, and amortization). Its rationale is that accounting depreciation is so fictional that it should not be subtracted out. But EBITDA has problems, too. It does not consider capital expenditures at all. Thus, this measure could suggest the same price-earnings multiple for a firm that reinvests all of its current earnings into capital expenditures (to produce higher future earnings) versus a firm that reinvests none. This is not a good thing.

You can use different flavors of earnings.

➤ *EBITDA Anecdote, Pg.388.*

In Chapter 13, you also learned that you can subtract off capital expenditures from EBITDA. This brings you close to a price/cash flow ratio. Yet such ratios can suffer from the shortcoming that cash flows can be very "lumpy" from year to year. (In a year when the firm makes a lot of fixed investments, the cash flows are often negative—and not reflective of the future.) This is why earnings-based multiples often (but not always) work better than cash flow–based multiples—and why the latter is therefore more common than the former.

You can use cash flows, although they are spikier.

You may also run across a **PEG ratio**, which is the P/E ratio divided by earnings growth. Interestingly, it uses basically the same ingredients as Formula 14.3. The idea behind both formulas is that firms with higher P/E ratios and lower growth rates of earnings are expensive and therefore will produce lower future returns. Unfortunately, the PEG ratio scrambles what it does with these inputs. For example, if the growth rate of earnings is very small, the PEG ratio pretty much produces nonsense. (Interestingly, empirically, low-growth firms are the firms that tend to produce higher average market rates of return, not lower rates of return.) My advice: Avoid the PEG ratio.

The PEG ratio is a common real-world statistic. It has the right inputs but puts them together incorrectly.

➤ $r = g + E/P$, *Formula 14.3, Pg.441.*

Multiples Based on Book Equity (And Book Assets)

The valuation measures so far have divided a market-based snapshot (the stock value) by an accounting flow, either from the income or cash flow statements. Some popular ratios do involve values from the balance sheet, even though balance sheets are known

Accounting is better at flow measures than stock measures.

➤ *Warning about BV
stock numbers,*
Sect. 13.7, *Pg.405.*

The book value of
equity is particularly
tempting and
problematic.

to be unreliable. Thus, if you choose a stock number from the balance sheet as your
valuation attribute, you need to be especially suspicious.

There is one particular balance sheet number that looks very attractive for ratio
analysis at first glance: the **book value of equity** (BV of equity, or BVE). Is this a great
attribute for the market value of equity, the number that you want? Unfortunately not.
As already explained, the book value is just a mechanical plug. (The fact that it can be
non-sensibly negative also means that if the book value of equity is in the denominator,
the market-to-book equity ratio can suffer from the 1/X domain problem.) The book
value of assets suffers from similar, though lesser problems. For older firms, book values
are often just a fraction of the true market values. This means that ratios dividing a flow
number by a book value often seem high, especially for older firms.

The BV versus MV
ratio. Older firms have
different book value
biases than young
firms, so don't
compare one to the
other.

With all these caveats, I can now tell you about an alternative to price-earnings or
price/cash flow ratios: the **market-equity-to-book-equity ratio**. Biased book values
in themselves are not a problem. For example, if all firms had book values that are
two-thirds of their market values, then the book-to-market ratio would be a perfect
valuation attribute. (The ratio method itself would undo the two-thirds bias.) The
problem is that different firms have different biases. My advice is this: If you do use a
multiple that relies on the book/equity attribute, hoping that similar firms have similar
market-to-book ratios, be careful to compare only similarly sized and similarly aged
firms. *Do not compare start-up firms to established publicly traded firms.* Of course,
non-comparability is a problem with other valuation ratios, too. Thus, a book-to-market
ratio can be a useful adjunct to other valuation measures.

Economic
interpretations?
Fuggedaboutit

Sometimes, the book value is interpreted as an estimate of physical replacement
value—a measure of what the firm is worth as a sum that is above and beyond its
individual pieces. This is a very precarious application of book values. My opinion is
that, at best, book value helps comparing two similarly aged firms in the same industry
with similar histories. If this is the case, then you might learn which of the two seems to
have more value than the sum of its parts.

More Esoteric or Specialized Multiples

Many biotech firms
have neither earnings
nor sales. What can
you use?

Sometimes you cannot use any of the above measures. You may have to value a firm
that does not have positive earnings, equity, or even sales. This is the case for many
research firms. They are primarily a bunch of real options.

➤ *Real options,*
Sect. 12.6, *Pg.347.*

P/S has no "negative
S" (1/X) domain
problem. It may work
when P/E fails. (Small
sales could still be a
problem.)

Price/sales (P/S) ratios: If the firm has negative earnings but positive sales, analysts
often resort to a price/sales ratio. Because sales are never negative, it largely
avoids the 1/X domain problem. The idea is that firms with higher sales should
be worth more. This ratio also has another advantage: sales may be more difficult
to manipulate than earnings, so it is sometimes used even for firms with positive
earnings.

Firms losing money
can have great sales.

The P/S ratio was especially popular during the tech bubble of 1998 to 2000,
when few Internet firms had positive earnings. At that time, many firms, such as
Amazon, sold merchandise at a loss. Naturally, it is relatively easy to sell $100
bills for $99! Nevertheless, to compare Internet firms, most of which had negative
earnings, many analysts indeed relied on a price/sales ratio. Consequently, the

more Amazon sold, the more money it lost—and the more valuable it appeared to be. This was perplexing, to say the least.

In sum, firms can increase sales and market share at the expense of profitability. If value is based on P/S, the implied value could be higher for firms that pursue bad pricing strategies.

Problems with price/sales ratio comparisons are also common in normal times. Some firms have intrinsically low sales, but high profitability. Compare Ford and Rolls-Royce in 2005. Quoting all dollars in billions (and equity in market value), we have

Rolls-Royce and Ford have similar valuation ratios based on P/E.

	Sales	Earnings	Debt	Equity	P/E Ratio
Rolls-Royce	$12	$0.64	$14	$6.5	10.2
Ford Motor	$170	$2.0	$150	$20	10.0

If you value Rolls-Royce with Ford's P/E ratio, or vice versa, you would come up with a reasonable valuation. Unfortunately, the same cannot be said for the price/sales ratio. Each dollar of Rolls-Royce sales translated into about 50 cents of equity. Each dollar of Ford sales translated into about 10 cents of equity.

They do not have similar price/sales ratio.

$$P/S_{\text{Rolls-Royce}} = \frac{\$6.5}{\$12} \approx 0.54$$

$$P/S_{\text{Ford}} = \frac{\$20}{\$170} \approx 0.12$$

Although both are in the same industry, Rolls-Royce specializes in low-volume, high-value-added niche products at high margins, while Ford follows the opposite strategy. If you mistakenly apply Rolls-Royce's P/S ratio of 0.54 to Ford, you would have overestimated Ford's value at $0.54 \cdot \$170 \approx \$92$ billion, which is off by a factor of four!

When firms do not have any sales yet, or when all firms' standard financials (earnings, sales, etc.) seem irrelevant to the eventual long-term profitability of the firm, analysts may use even stranger ratios. Here are a few:

Last-resort ratios.

Price/employees ratio: This ratio assumes that the employees at the comparable firm are as productive as the employees in the company to be valued. One problem is that this ratio induces firms to hire incompetent employees on the cheap in order to increase their valuations. After all, firms with more employees are presumably worth more.

Price/scientists ratio: As above.

Price/patent ratio: This ratio is another popular technology valuation ratio for scientific firms. Alas, one patent is not the same as another. U.S. Patent #174465 (March 1876) for the Bell telephone was worth a lot more than U.S. Patent #953212 (September 2004) for a "full body teleportation system: a pulsed gravitational wave wormhole generator system that teleports a human being through hyperspace from one location to another." Again, filing patents is cheap. Making meaningful discoveries is not.

Price/anything else: Your imagination is the limit.

If you can, avoid these ratios. Instead, it is better to think about the probability that the company will be successful—and its potential cash flows if it is.

Most other ratios cannot be used to value equity, only to value assets.

Most valuation ratios only make sense if you compute them for the entire value of the firm (that is, the value of all equity plus the value of all liabilities). The reason is that sales, employees, scientists, or patents are firmwide and independent of financing. However, the amount of equity is not. Here is what I mean: Let's assume that Rolls-Royce had been 100% equity financed, while Ford had remained as is. Rolls-Royce would have been worth about $14 + $6.5 \approx 20.5 billion. Each dollar of sales would have translated into equity of $1.71. Applying this ratio directly to Ford's sales would have made you think that Ford's equity should have been worth $1.71 \cdot $170 \approx 290 billion, not $20 billion. *A price/sales ratio in which the price is equity is garbage.* If you decide that you want to use a price/sales ratio, make sure that you only work with a full-firm-value-to-sales ratio, not an equity-value-to-sales ratio.

Firms with more debt have lower equity and lower earnings.

How does this situation compare with price-earnings ratios? Although P/E ratios also change with the debt ratio, the change is relatively mild. A simple sanity condition still applies: A firm with more debt financing has both a lower price of equity and lower earnings. Both the numerator and denominator change together.

Q 14.19. When would you use a price/sales ratio? Why?

Q 14.20. Why are price/sales ratios problematic?

Q 14.21. On July 28, 2003 (all quoted dollars are in billions):

Firm	Cash	Sales	Dividends	Value	D/E
CSG	N/A	$9.2	$0.4	$12.2	153%
KO	$3.6	$20.3	$2.2	$110.8	43%
PEP	$1.8	$25.9	$1.1	$81.0	22%

Hansen Natural had $210,000 in cash, $9.22 million in sales, zero dividends, and a debt-equity ratio of 10%. What would a price/cash ratio predict its value to be? A price/sales ratio? A price/dividend ratio? Elaborate on some shortcomings.

Nonvaluation Diagnostic Financial Ratios

Not all ratios are used to estimate firm value. Some ratios can help you assess a firm's financial health and profitability—or they can be merely interesting. They can assist you in the "art" of valuation if they can help you learn more about the economics of the firm. For example, a number of ratios are commonly used to judge proximity to bankruptcy and profitability. Like valuation multiples, many ratios are reasonably similar *within* an industry, but not *across* industries. They also often vary over the business cycle. Thus, they should only be compared to similar firms at the same time. Nevertheless, on occasion, ratios can be so extreme that they can raise a good warning flag. For example, if you find that the firm has 10 times its earnings in interest due, you might become somewhat concerned about the possibility of bankruptcy, regardless of what is standard in the industry at the time.

Many other ratios are commonly used for judging such factors as financial health and profitability.

First, a short recap of some important balance sheet numbers for PepsiCo:

Quick recap of the PepsiCo numbers.

| PepsiCo, 2001 | Book Value | | | | | Market Value |
	Total Assets	Common Equity	Total Liabilities	Financial Debt	Financial Capital	Common Equity
In millions	$21,695	$8,648	$13,021	$3,005	$11,653	$87,407

Sometimes, analysts use not just common equity, but all equity (including preferred equity). These days, few large firms issue preferred equity, so this rarely makes much difference. PepsiCo also had almost no preferred equity, so we will just use common equity. **Financial debt** is usually defined as the sum of long-term debt ($2,651) and debt in current liabilities ($354), which adds up to $3,005. Total liabilities are $4,998+$2,651+$3,876+$1,496 = $13,021; this can also be computed by subtracting equity from assets, $21,695 – $8,648 – $26 = $13,021. In addition to financial debt, total liabilities include such obligations as current liabilities, pension liabilities, and the like.

➤ *Preferred equity, Pg.472.*

Without further ado, here are some of the more interesting and common ratios. The sample calculations for PepsiCo in 2001 are based on the financials from Section 13.1. Be aware that many of these ratios exist in various flavors. The ratios are sorted, so that those in the beginning tend to reflect financial health and liquidity, while those at the end tend to reflect profitability. (Investopedia.com offers a nice reference for many of these ratios.)

You can now compute ratios for PepsiCo.

➤ *PepsiCo Financials, Sect. 13.1, Pg.377.*

Measures of Leverage and Financial Precariousness

We begin with ratios that reflect the firm's debt load. A firm that has high debt ratios (especially compared to its industry) must often be especially careful to manage its cash stock and cash flows well in order to avoid a credit crunch. Moreover, if it wants to borrow more money, then potential new creditors often use such ratios to judge whether the firm will default. They will often judge indebtedness relative to profitability, cash flow, and industry.

Debt-related (potentially distress-related) ratios.

The debt-equity ratio and liabilities-equity ratio come in many variations. For example, the long-term debt-equity ratio, defined in terms of market value of equity, is

$$\text{PepsiCo, 2001: } \frac{\text{Long-Term Debt}}{\text{Market Value (MV) of Equity}} = \frac{\$2,651}{\$87,407} \approx 3.0\%$$

The broader financial debt-equity ratio is

$$\text{PepsiCo, 2001: } \frac{\text{Financial Debt}}{\text{Market Value (MV) of Equity}} = \frac{\$3,005}{\$87,407} \approx 3.4\%$$

Even broader,

$$\text{PepsiCo, 2001: } \frac{\text{All Liabilities}}{\text{Market Value (MV) of Equity}} = \frac{\$13,021}{\$87,407} \approx 15\%$$

Some analysts use the book value of equity, which you can find on PepsiCo's balance sheet. For example,

$$\text{PepsiCo, 2001: } \frac{\text{Financial Debt}}{\text{Book Value (BV) of Equity}} = \frac{\$3,005}{\$8,648} \approx 35\%$$

You can also immediately notice how much higher the book-based ratio makes PepsiCo's debt ratio appear. I have already explained why I cannot recommend book value–based equity ratios. But intuitively, too, it is difficult to think of PepsiCo, a firm with an equity market cap of almost $90 billion, as having a 35% debt ratio, based on its (puny) $3.0 billion debt.

➤ *Warning about BV stock numbers, Sect. 13.7, Pg.405.*

Debt ratios add the value of debt to the denominator. Because market value of debt is rarely available, a common variant adds the book value of debt and the market value of equity. For example,

$$\text{PepsiCo, 2001: } \frac{\text{Long-Term Debt}}{\text{MV of Equity} + \text{BV of Debt}} = \frac{\$2,651}{\$87,407 + \$13,021} \approx 2.6\%$$

$$\text{PepsiCo, 2001: } \frac{\text{All Liabilities}}{\text{MV of Equity} + \text{BV of Debt}} = \frac{\$13,021}{\$87,407 + \$13,021} \approx 13\%$$

Some analysts divide by the book value of assets, which again tends to produce ratios that are too high. A better procedure is to subtract the book value of equity from the book value of assets and then add back the market value of equity.

Please avoid debt divided by assets as a measure of leverage.

You may also run into a definition for the firm's debt ratio that divides financial debt by total assets. (This is usually computed with book values. For PepsiCo, this would be ($2,651 + $354)/$21,695 ≈ 14%.) The intent is to compare firms based on how solid they are leverage-wise. Unfortunately, this is often wrong. Consider two simple firms:

	Financial Debt	Nonfinancial Liabilities	Book Equity	Debt Ratio
Firm A	$100	—	$100	50%
Firm B	$100	$300	$100	20%

Firm A has the same financial debt and equity as firm B. It is also clearly financially more solid and less indebted. Nevertheless, the financial-debt-to-asset ratio incorrectly shows a much *higher* debt ratio. (The underlying problem is that equity is not the opposite of financial liabilities; instead, equity and other financial liabilities together are the opposite.)

(Choosing the optimal leverage is the focus of the next part of the book. Thus, we will devote a whole section to the subject of measuring ratios in the special topics part.)

➤ *Leverage Measures, Sect.* 22.A (Companion), *Pg.≈149.*

Times interest earned (TIE) is often used to gauge long-term solvency. It is computed as earnings before interest (usually also before taxes) divided by the firm's interest. It is the inverse of interest coverage, so a lower number means the firm's debt burden is more precarious.

$$\text{PepsiCo, 2001:} \quad \frac{\text{Operating Income}}{\text{Interest Payments}} = \frac{\$4,021}{\$219} \approx 18$$

The definition of interest coverage can be ambiguous. The most common definition here is identical to TIE. (It is also occasionally defined as its inverse: the ratio of debt payments due, as a fraction of cash flows or EBIT.) Many variations exist: Debt payments can be only interest due, or include both principal and interest. Cash flows can be any of a number of choices. Popular choices are pure cash flows, operating cash flows, net income plus depreciation minus capital expenditures, and net income plus depreciation. Refer back to Exhibit 13.10 for PepsiCo's cash flows to compute, for example,

➤ *Cash Flow Calculations, Exhibit* 13.10, *Pg.401.*

$$\text{PepsiCo, 2001:} \quad \frac{\text{Interest Expense} - \text{Interest Income}}{\text{Operating Cash Flow}} = \frac{\$219 - 67}{\$4,201} \approx 3.6\%$$

The commonly used current ratio is the ratio of **current assets** (cash, accounts receivable, inventory, marketable securities, etc.) over **current liabilities** (soon-due interest, accounts payable, short-term loans payable, etc.). It is a measure of short-term liquidity.

➤ *PepsiCo's working capital, Pg.396.*

$$\text{PepsiCo, 2001:} \quad \frac{\text{Current Assets}}{\text{Current Liabilities}} = \frac{\$5,853}{\$4,998} \approx 1.2$$

The current ratio is often interpreted as "healthy" if it is greater than 1.5. This means that each \$1 of current liabilities is covered by \$1.5 in current assets. Do not read too much into this ratio. PepsiCo is very healthy, even though its current ratio is low. (For PepsiCo, it probably means that it runs its operations very leanly. For another company, such a low ratio might be more precarious.)

The quick ratio (or acid ratio) is similar to the current ratio but deletes inventories from current assets. The idea is that a firm with a high quick ratio can cover immediate expenses with immediate income. Inventory is subtracted, because unlike the other components of working capital, it still needs to be sold to turn into cash quickly.

$$\text{PepsiCo, 2001:} \quad \frac{\text{Current Assets} - \text{Inventories}}{\text{Current Liabilities}} = \frac{\$5,853 - \$1,310}{\$4,998} \approx 0.9$$

The acid ratio is often considered "healthy" if it is greater than 1.0. Again, for PepsiCo, this ratio is fairly unimportant. The **cash ratio** further eliminates receivables from current assets.

➤ *Duration,* *Pg.≈17.*
Duration and maturity are not indebtedness ratios, but they can be helpful.

Duration and maturity were explained in the bond context, but they can also be applied to projects and even to firms. They can measure whether the firm is making short-term or long-term investments. This is not an ordinary ratio, in that it requires projections of future cash flows.

Now come measures that are more profitability- and efficiency-based.

Many a turnover ratio divide sales by another number, usually a component of net working capital. (A variant uses "cost of goods sold" instead of sales as the numerator.)

- **Inventory turnover** measures how often your inventories translate into sales.

$$\text{PepsiCo, 2001:} \quad \frac{\text{Net Sales}}{\text{Inventories}} = \frac{\$26{,}935}{\$1{,}310} \approx 21 \text{ times (per year)}$$

  A high ratio usually means efficient inventory management. Most financials also provide the components of inventories, so you could further decompose this. (Of course, firms can also manipulate this ratio not by improving efficiency, but by selling their inventories at a discount.)

- **Receivables turnover** measures how quickly your customers are paying you.

$$\text{PepsiCo, 2001:} \quad \frac{\text{Net Sales}}{\text{Receivables}} = \frac{\$26{,}935}{\$2{,}142} \approx 13 \text{ times (per year)}$$

- **Payables turnover** measures how quickly you are paying your suppliers.

$$\text{PepsiCo, 2001:} \quad \frac{\text{Net Sales}}{\text{Payables}} = \frac{\$26{,}935}{\$4{,}461} \approx 6 \text{ times (per year)}$$

These measures are sometimes inverted (1 divided by the ratio) and multiplied by 365 to obtain a "number of days" measure. For example,

- **Days receivables outstanding (DRO)**, also called **days of sales outstanding (DSO)** or **average collection period**. To compute DRO, divide accounts receivable by total sales on credit and multiply by the number of days per year.

$$\text{PepsiCo, 2001:} \quad \frac{365 \text{ Days} \cdot \text{Receivables}}{\text{Net Sales}} = \frac{365 \text{ Days} \cdot \$2{,}142}{\$26{,}935} \approx 29 \text{ Days}$$

  PepsiCo collects its bills after about a month. A lengthening of this number often indicates that customers are running into financial difficulties. Such firms should probably reexamine their credit policies.

- **Days inventories outstanding** is inventory divided by total sales on credit, times number of days outstanding.

$$\text{PepsiCo, 2001:} \quad \frac{365 \text{ Days} \cdot \text{Inventories}}{\text{Net Sales}} = \frac{365 \text{ Days} \cdot \$1{,}310}{\$26{,}935} \approx 18 \text{ Days}$$

  PepsiCo turns over its inventory every 18 days.

- **Days payables outstanding (DPO)** is accounts payable divided by total sales on credit, times number of days outstanding.

$$\text{PepsiCo, 2001:} \quad \frac{365 \text{ Days} \cdot \text{Payables}}{\text{Net Sales}} = \frac{365 \text{ Days} \cdot \$4,461}{\$26,935} \approx 60 \text{ Days}$$

A lengthening of this number could mean that PepsiCo has difficulties coming up with cash to meet its financial obligations—or that it found a way to pay bills more efficiently (more slowly in this case).

There are also combined versions, such as the **cash conversion cycle**, which is the sum of the inventory-processing period and the number of days needed to collect receivables, minus the number of days the firm takes to pay its suppliers. For PepsiCo, this would be $18 + 29 - 60$, a negative number that is difficult to interpret intuitively.

Turnover ratios and their derivatives (below) are especially important for firms in the commodities and retail sectors, such as Wal-Mart. Good turnover control often allows firms to deploy economies of scale. In this sense, the above ratios measure corporate efficiency, which can help managers judge their own efficiency relative to that of their competition.

Measures of Profitability

Next are some accounting methods to compute margins or returns. The list.

The net profit margin (NPM) or return on sales (ROS) is the net income divided by sales.

$$\text{PepsiCo, 2001:} \quad \frac{\text{Net Income}}{\text{Sales}} = \frac{\$2,662}{\$26,935} \approx 10\%$$

PepsiCo could translate about 10 cents of every dollar sold into net income. Analysts also sometimes use other measures of income. For example, when they work with operating income instead of net income, the resulting measure would be called an **operating profit margin**. The gross profit margin uses gross income instead of net income.

Many growth firms have uninterpretable margins, because they may have practically no income and no sales.

The return on (book) assets (ROA) divides net income by the book value of assets.

$$\text{PepsiCo, 2001:} \quad \frac{\text{Net Income}}{\text{BV of Assets}} = \frac{\$2,662}{\$21,695} \approx 12\%$$

A variant of this measure that adds back interest expense is better, because it recognizes that assets pay out cash to both shareholders and creditors. Nevertheless, both measures are dubious, because the book value of assets contains the book value of equity and is therefore unreliable. You can think of the E/P yield as a better, market-based ROA measure.

➤ *Warning about BV stock numbers, Sect. 13.7, Pg.405.*

The return on (book) equity (ROE) divides net income by the book value of equity. You also know by now that I *really* do not like book equity–based measures.

$$\text{PepsiCo, 2001:} \ \frac{\text{Net Income}}{\text{BV of Equity}} = \frac{\$2,662}{\$8,648} \approx 31\%$$

Total asset turnover (TAT) measures how much assets are required to produce sales. Again, with book value of assets in the denominator, this is not a reliable ratio.

$$\text{PepsiCo, 2001:} \ \frac{\text{Sales}}{\text{BV of Assets}} = \frac{\$26,935}{\$21,695} \approx 1.2$$

Timing when stock
and flow measures are
both included.

For ratios in which both the numerator and the denominator are flows, such as the ROS ratio, we use the same time period for both. But for ratios with one flow and one stock, such as ROA and ROE, you have a choice. You can divide ROA (or ROE) by the assets (or equity) at the start of the period, at the end of the period, or even by an average of the two.

The DuPont model—a
legacy of a time
before modern
finance. It is still
commonly used,
although it explains a
measure that is not
very meaningful to
begin with.

The so-called **DuPont model** multiplies and divides a few more quantities into the definitions of ROA and ROE in an attempt to learn more about the drivers of value.

$$\text{ROE} = \frac{\text{Net Income}}{\text{BV of Equity}} = \underbrace{\frac{\text{Net Income}}{\text{Sales}}}_{\text{Profit Margin}} \cdot \underbrace{\frac{\text{Assets}}{\text{Book Equity}}}_{\text{BV of Multiplier}} \cdot \underbrace{\frac{\text{Sales}}{\text{Assets}}}_{\text{Asset Turnover}}$$

A similar operation can be applied to a variant of ROA:

$$\text{ROA} = \frac{\text{EBIAT}}{\text{Assets}} = \frac{\text{EBIAT}}{\text{Sales}} \cdot \frac{\text{Sales}}{\text{Assets}}$$

where EBIAT is earnings before interest after taxes. Your immediate question should be, "Why should you care about any decomposition of ROE or ROA in the first place?" Both measures are based on the book value of equity, which Section 13.7 pointed out as having severe problems. Your second question should be, "Can you trust the components of this decomposition, at least one of which also includes the book value of equity?" For both of these, hold your nose and hope that the error in your comparable firms' book values of equity is in the same direction as your own. In this case, the DuPont model may usefully inform you about what you can do to raise ROE or ROA. For example, everything else equal, if you can increase your asset turnover, it is likely that your ROE will increase. Your third question should be, "Why am I bothering you with this?" I can answer this one more easily: The individuals administering the CFA exam keep the DuPont model as one of their staples, and you may run into some corporate treasurers who still use it.

Measures Related to Stock Market Capitalization

Measures that are
more oriented toward
shareholders and the
stock market.

Let us now proceed to measures that are more oriented toward the stock market.

The book-to-market ratio is the inverse of the book equity–based valuation multiple. If you get very lucky (and don't count on it), the book value of assets hints at how much the assets would cost to replace. (By the way, your chances are better if the firm is very young.) If you are indeed lucky, then this book-equity-to-market-equity ratio can be interpreted as a measure of how much market value the firm has created via its unique growth opportunities.

$$\text{PepsiCo, 2001:} \quad \frac{\text{BV of Equity}}{\text{MV of Equity}} = \frac{\$8,648}{\$87,407} \approx 9.9\%$$

However, in PepsiCo's case, it is more likely that the book value of its equity is simply a number without much meaning. PepsiCo owns tangible and intangible assets—both accounted for by the accountants—that are worth far more than their book values.

The dividend payout ratio measures what percent of earnings is paid out as dividends. Holding everything else equal, the same firm that pays out more of its earnings today would pay out less in the future. (If it had retained earnings, it would have earned more cash for payout later.)

$$\text{PepsiCo, 2001:} \quad \frac{\text{Dividends}}{\text{Net Income}} = \frac{\$994}{\$2,662} \approx 37\%$$

PepsiCo's dividends here were those paid both to common and preferred equity (explained soon). The dividends here included both common and preferred dividends, because PepsiCo paid only $4 million to preferred equity (all of which was held in its employee stock option plan [ESOP]). More commonly, any dividend-based ratios are computed only for dividends paid to common equity.

The payout ratio expands the payout from only dividends to include share repurchases, or even net repurchases (i.e., share repurchases net of share issues).

$$\text{PepsiCo, 2001:} \quad \frac{\text{Dividends} + \text{Equity Repurchasing}}{\text{Net Income}} = \frac{\$2,725}{\$2,662} \approx 102\%$$

$$\text{PepsiCo, 2001:} \quad \frac{\text{Dividends} + \text{Equity Repurchasing} - \text{Equity Issuing}}{\text{Net Income}} = \frac{\$2,201}{\$2,662} \approx 83\%$$

PepsiCo distributed most of its earnings to shareholders.

The dividend yield is the amount of dividends divided by the share price. Dividends are a flow measure, whereas the stock price is a stock measure. Consequently, dividends can be measured relative to the price at the beginning or the end of the period. In the latter case, it is called the **dividend-price ratio**.

➤ *Dividend yield, Sect. 2.3, Pg.13.*

➤ *Equity payouts, Chapter 19, Pg.611.*

$$\text{PepsiCo, 2001:} \quad \frac{\text{Dividends}}{\text{MV of Equity}} = \frac{\$994}{\$87,407} \approx 1.1\%$$

Equity repurchases are also payouts to shareholders, so you can enlarge this measure to a payout/price ratio,

$$\text{PepsiCo, 2001:} \quad \frac{\text{Dividends} + \text{Equity Repurchasing}}{\text{MV of Equity}} = \frac{\$2,725}{\$87,407} \approx 3.1\%$$

An Earnings retention ratio is changes in retained earnings (i.e., this year's earnings that were not paid out), divided either by sales, assets, or income. All else equal, a firm that retains more earnings today should pay out more in the future. After all, the retained earnings should be reinvested, so such firms should have higher expected earnings growth. Retention ratios are usually calculated as 1 minus the dividend payout ratio, 1 minus the sum of dividends and equity repurchases divided by net income, or 1 minus the sum of dividends and net equity repurchases divided by net income. For example, PepsiCo paid out $994 in dividends and $1,731 in share repurchases. Thus,

$$\text{PepsiCo, 2001:} \quad \frac{\text{Net Income} - \text{Payout}}{\text{Net Income}} = \frac{\$2,662 - \$2,725}{\$2,662} \approx -2.4\%$$

PepsiCo also issued \$524 of shares in connection with the Quaker merger, so

$$\text{PepsiCo, 2001:} \quad \frac{\text{Net Income} - \text{Net Payout}}{\text{Net Income}} = \frac{\$2,662 - \$2,725 + \$524}{\$2,662} \approx 17.3\%$$

You can easily think of variations here, such as inclusion or exclusion of preferred stock payments, and so on.

The ratios can be useful, but please don't live by them.

How useful are these ratios? It depends on the situation, the industry, and the particular ratio for the particular firm—and what you expect to learn. If every firm in the industry has almost the same ratio—for example, days of receivables average somewhere between 25 and 32 days everywhere, but the firm in which you are considering investing reports 7 days—you should wonder about the economics of this shorter number. Is your firm better in obtaining money quickly? Does it do so by giving rebates to faster paying customers? Does it mostly work on a cash basis, while other firms in the industry work on credit? If so, why? Or is your firm simply cooking its books?

Q 14.22. How would you measure a financial-debt-equity ratio?

Q 14.23. What is the "current ratio"? Is a firm more or less precarious if this ratio is high?

Q 14.24. A firm has sales of \$30,000 and receivables of \$6,000. What is its receivables turnover? What is its DRO?

Q 14.25. What is the difference between the dividend-price ratio and the dividend payout ratio?

Summary

Use both comparables and estimated-NPV valuation methods, and use common sense to decide what you believe.

Should you estimate value based on comparables or net present value? In practice, comparables enjoy great popularity, primarily because their minimal application does not require much thought. Anyone can look up another firm's P/E ratio and multiply it by the earnings of the firm to be valued. In contrast, even a rough NPV analysis is quite involved. Of course, after reading this chapter, you should understand that both methods rely on inputs that you will almost surely never know perfectly. You will never have the perfect comparable, and you will never know the correct expected future cash flows. Fortunately, the cause of errors is different for these two methods. Therefore, if you use both, you can often get a better idea of where the true value lies. This does not mean that you should average the valuation estimates obtained from NPV and comparables. Instead, you should perform both analyses and then take a step back and make up your mind as to which combination of methods seems to make the most sense in your particular situation. Yes, valuation is as much an art as it is a science. It consists of the tools that you have learned *and* your ability to judge. If you can judge better than others, you will end up a rich person.

This chapter covered the following major points:

- Comparables can provide an alternative valuation of firms and projects. The comparables valuation techniques and estimated NPV have different weaknesses, which therefore often makes it worthwhile to contemplate both.

- A comparables analysis relies on three assumptions:

  - The identification of good value-relevant attribute(s)
  - The identification of good comparable firms with known market values
  - The law of one price

- The most common value attribute is earnings, making the P/E ratio the natural way to infer value. The P/E ratio divides the price of the firm by its earnings. This can be done with aggregate firm numbers or on a per-share basis.

  Often, earnings are not the current earnings but analysts' consensual earnings forecasts.

- All else equal, higher-growth firms have higher P/E ratios.

- Comparables suffer from many problems, some of which cannot be corrected. These problems can usually be traced back to the difficulty of finding good comparables.

- Never mechanically average P/E ratios. The 1/X domain problem can be toxic. Use one of the suggested techniques (such as using the median, ignoring firms with nonpositive earnings, averaging E/P ratios, or working with sums) to reduce its influence. Of course, none of the remedies are very attractive, so you may be better off avoiding P/E ratios altogether.

- There are also many other ratios that can be used to judge the profitability and the financial health of a company. As far as valuation is concerned, their primary purpose is often only to provide useful background information.

Keywords

Acid ratio, 449.   Average collection period, 450.   Book value of equity, 444.   Book-to-market ratio, 452. Cash conversion cycle, 451.   Cash ratio, 449.   Current assets, 449.   Current liabilities, 449.   Current ratio, 449.   DPO, 450.   DRO, 450.   DSO, 450.   Days inventories outstanding, 450.   Days of sales outstanding, 450.   Days payables outstanding, 450.   Days receivables outstanding, 450.   Debt-equity ratio, 447.   Dividend payout ratio, 453.   Dividend yield, 623.   Dividend-price ratio, 623.   DuPont model, 452.   Duration and maturity, 450.   Earnings retention ratio, 453.   Earnings yield, 419.   Financial debt, 447.   Interest coverage, 449.   Inventory turnover, 450.   Liabilities-equity ratio, 447.   Market-equity-to-book-equity ratio, 444.   NPM, 451.   Net profit margin, 451.   Operating profit margin, 451.   P/E ratio, 418.   PEG ratio, 443.   PVGO, 422.   Payables turnover, 450.   Payout ratio, 453.   Price-earnings ratio, 418.   Quick ratio, 449.   ROA, 451.   ROE, 451.   ROS, 451.   Receivables turnover, 450.   Return on (book) assets, 451.   Return on (book) equity, 451.   Return on sales, 451.   TIE, 449.   TTM, 432.   Times interest earned, 449.   Trailing 12-month, 432.   Turnover ratio, 450.   Valuation ratio, 443.

Answers

Q 14.1 The law of one price states that items with similar attributes should be priced similarly.

Q 14.2 Comparable projects enter the NPV formula through the (opportunity) cost of capital, also called the discount rate, usually abbreviated $\mathscr{E}(\mathrm{r})$.

Q 14.3 It is more common to compute a price-earnings ratio than a price/cash flow ratio because the earnings measure incorporates some forward-looking information, and is therefore less "spiky."

Q 14.4 Google is growing faster than PepsiCo, so it would have a higher P/E ratio.

Q 14.5 $\mathrm{E/P} = \mathscr{E}(\mathrm{r}) - \mathscr{E}(\mathrm{g}) \Rightarrow \mathscr{E}(\mathrm{r}) = \mathrm{E/P} + \mathscr{E}(\mathrm{g}) = 1/40 + 6\% = 8.5\%$. Therefore, $\mathrm{E/P} = 8.5\% - 7\% = 1.5\%$ and its P/E ratio would shoot from 40 to 66.7. The percentage change in value would therefore be $66.7/40 - 1 \approx 67\%$.

Q 14.6 Rearranging Formula 14.2,

$$\frac{\text{Price}}{\text{Expected Earnings}} = \frac{1}{\text{Cost of Capital}} + \frac{\text{PVGO}}{\text{Expected Earnings}}$$

It states that firms with zero PVGOs have E/P yields equal to their costs of capital. Firms that are growing have E/P yields below their costs of capital. Firms that are shrinking have E/P yields above their costs of capital.

Q 14.7 If PVGO is positive, $\mathscr{E}(\mathrm{g})$ is also positive.

Q 14.8 For the stable firm:

1. The P/E ratio is $1,000/100 = 10$.

2. The debt now has to receive $500 \cdot 7.5\% = \$37.50$ in interest every month. Therefore, there is $62.50 available to the equity. Therefore, the P/E ratio is $500/62.50 = 8$.

3. The increase in debt has decreased the firm's P/E ratio.

Q 14.9 The P/E ratio of the merged A and B company is neither the equal-weighted nor the value-weighted average! See Section 14.3.

Q 14.10 Let's do an example. The acquirer has value of $100, so it needs to have earnings of $5. The target has value of $50, so it needs to have earnings of $1. This means that the combined firm will have earnings of $6 and value of $150. Its P/E ratio will thus be 25.

Q 14.11 Averaging P/E ratios is very hazardous because it can easily lead to misleading estimates, as explained in Section 14.3. We called it the "1/X domain problem." The main problem is that earnings can be nonpositive or tiny.

Q 14.12 If only one among a dozen industry comps has a negative P/E ratio, you can ignore this firm with nonpositive earnings, you can use the median industry ratio, you can work with E/P yields and invert them, or you can work with sums of prices and sums of earnings—or all of the above.

Q 14.13 Earnings (in millions of dollars): The TTM earnings for KO is $3,979 + (801 - 873) + (1,290 - 1,118) = 4,079$. The TTM earnings for PEP is $2,662 + (651 - 570) + (888 - 798) = 2,833$. Assets (in millions of dollars): You would not compute a TTM, but instead use the most recent assets: 25,287 for Coca-Cola and 24,200 for PepsiCo, because these are "stock" numbers, not "flow" numbers.

Q 14.14 This question about the unlevered P/E ratio cannot be answered if you do not know the different costs of capital. For example, if the firm's cost of capital is equal to the debt cost of capital, the P/E ratio would not change at all!

Q 14.15 Yahoo! Germany reported an actual market value of $10.52 billion euros and an earnings yield of 36.9% (P/E of 27). The easy part is supplementing the table:

Manufacturer	Mkt Cap	Earnings	P/E Ratio	E/P Yield
Volvo (ADR)	$5.7	–$0.18	–31.7	–3.2%
Ford	$14.1	–$5.30	–2.7	–37.6%
GM	$18.8	$1.83	10.3	9.7%
Nissan (ADR)	$27.0	$2.55	10.6	9.4%
DaimlerChrysler	$32.3	$4.63	7.0	14.3%
Honda (ADR)	$37.7	$3.09	12.2	8.2%
Toyota (ADR)	$87.3	$4.51	19.4	5.2%
Sum	$222.9	$11.13	25.1	6.0%
Average	$31.8	$1.59	3.6	0.9%

The hard part is deciding on a suitable P/E comparable. Our first method (average E/P yield, then invert) suggests adopting the astronomical ratio of $1/0.9\% \approx 111$, due to Ford's enormous loss in terms of market capitalization (Ford had $85 billion in sales and a positive EBITDA of $4.8 billion. But Ford also has ongoing depreciation on the order of $15 billion per year, but capital and other expenditures on the order of $18 [2001] to $37 billion [2000 and 1999].) Our second method (sum up Es and Ps first) suggests $222.9/11.13 \approx 20$, but it weighs the larger (and Japanese) firms more highly. Nevertheless, in this case, the second method came closer to the actual Volkswagen P/E multiple of 27. Incidentally, by mid-2003, VW had introduced a couple of flops and its earnings had sagged to $2.5 billion, though its market capitalization had increased to $15 billion. This meant that Volkswagen's P/E multiple had shrunk from 27 to 6 in just 9 months! As to assumptions, they all fall into the category of "apples like apples." For example, you are assuming (hoping) that leverage ratios are similar, foreign earnings are comparable, timing is the same, and so on.

Q 14.16 Using the formula in Exhibit 14.3,

$$\frac{\text{PVGO}}{\text{Price}} = 1 - \frac{1}{\mathscr{E}(\mathrm{r}) \cdot \text{P/E ratio}} = 1 - \frac{1}{7\% \cdot 21} \approx 32\%$$

The reason why this is not 29% is that $\mathscr{E}(\mathrm{r})$ was rounded up from 6.7% to 7%.

Q 14.17 The relation between earnings multiples and earnings growth rates is usually negative. It is not always so, because it is not stable over the business cycle. During recessions, cash cow firms may actually trade at higher multiples than (precarious) growth firms. In a sense, as indicated by the formulas, economic recessions can transform what were previously growth firms in growing markets into dying firms!

Q 14.18 With a P/E ratio of 20 on the S&P 500, its E/P yield would be around 5%. The real earnings growth rate has been around 2%. Thus, the real stock market rate of return would be around 7%. Add inflation, and you get an estimate of the nominal rate of return on the stock market.

Q 14.19 You would use a price/sales ratio if earnings are negative and/or you believe that sales are more representative than earnings of the future value of the firm.

Q 14.20 Firms can increase sales at the expense of profitability. (Just sell goods for a very low price.) Moreover, you should never compute a P/S ratio for equity. Instead, you should only compute the P/S ratio for the entire firm.

Q 14.21 The price/cash ratio, price/sales ratio, and price/dividend ratio are usually calculated without debt adjustment—the equivalent of surgery without anesthesia. This is a huge problem, but it also makes this exercise relatively easy.

Firm	Value/Cash	Value/Sales	Value/Dividends
CSG	N/A	1.3	31
KO	31	5.5	50
PEP	45	3.1	74

- The cash-based ratio suggests a value between $6.5 million and $9.5 million. The cash-based ratio values all firms as if only current cash has any meaning, and the ongoing operations are irrelevant (except to the extent that they have influenced current cash).

- The sales-based ratio suggests a value between $12.0 million, $28.6 million, and $50.7 million. Because the smaller comparables have lower ratios, one might settle on a lower value. The sales-based ratio ignores that CSG's equity value is relatively low because more of its value is capitalized with debt than with equity.

- The dividend-based ratio suggests a zero value. Obviously, this is not a perfect estimate. Firms can choose different payout policies.

Hansen's actual value on this day was $51.4 million.

Q 14.22 A common financial-debt-equity ratio computes the sum of long-term debt plus debt in current liabilities, divided by the sum of the market value of the firm's equity.

Q 14.23 The current ratio is the ratio of current assets over current liabilities. A firm is less precarious if this ratio is high. (However, too high of a current ratio may mean that the firm is investing too much in short-term assets, which typically yield less.)

Q 14.24 Its receivables turnover is $30,000/$6,000 = 5 times per year. DRO is $365 \cdot \$6,000/\$30,000 = 73$ days.

Q 14.25 The dividend-price ratio divides dividends by price; the dividend payout divides dividends by net income.

End of Chapter Problems

Q 14.26. What are the three main requirements for a comps-based valuation?

Q 14.27. When negotiating house prices, would you value your next residence by the method of comparables or by the method of NPV? If comparables, what kind of ratio might you use?

Q 14.28. Is it better to compute a price-earnings ratio on a per-share or on an aggregate (total value) basis?

Q 14.29. Is it better to use cash flows or earnings in your valuation multiple? Why?

Q 14.30. Which is likely to have a higher price-earnings ratio: Google or Exxon?

Q 14.31. Consider a growing firm that is expected to produce earnings of $10 million next year. The firm's earnings growth rates are 15% per annum. The firm's cost of capital is 20%. Its tax rate is 0.

1. What is the market value of this firm?

2. What is the firm's P/E ratio if it has no debt?

3. Now assume that the cost of capital for debt of $100 million is 8%, while the cost of capital for the remaining levered equity is 32%. (Again, the weighted average cost of capital is $50\% \cdot 8\% + 50\% \cdot 32\% = 20\%$, so the firm's cost of capital has not changed.) Interest on the $100 million debt is paid out. What is the equity's P/E ratio now?

4. Has the increase in debt increased or decreased the firm's P/E ratio?

Q 14.32. Assume that the prevailing interest rate is 8% per year for value firms and 12% per year for growth firms. A growth firm with earnings of $100,000 has a market value of $100,000,000, while a value firm with earnings of $1,000,000 has a market value of $20,000,000.

1. What are the implicit growth rates?

2. What are the PVGOs?

Q 14.33. Pick 8 firms in the "department stores" sector. Using a financial website (e.g., **YAHOO!** FINANCE), graph next year's expected growth of earnings against the firms' earnings/price yield. Is there a relation?

Q 14.34. If the P/E ratio on the S&P 500 is 10, given historical earnings growth patterns, what would be a reasonable estimate of long-run future expected rates of return on the stock market? Assume a long-run inflation rate of 2.5% per annum.

Q 14.35. A firm has earnings of $200, and a price/earnings ratio of 20. What is its implied growth rate, if its cost of capital is about 10%?

Q 14.36. Redo Shiller's value analysis today. Find the current P/E ratio of the S&P 500 on the Web. Assume that the expected real growth rate of GDP is 2.5% per annum. What does the stock market suggest is the S&P 500's expected rate of return these days?

Q 14.37. Use Ford's P/E ratio to value General Motors today. If Ford still has negative earnings, then use Google to value Microsoft.

Q 14.38. A firm with a P/E ratio of 10 wants to take over a firm half its size with a P/E ratio of 25. What will be the P/E ratio of the merged firm?

Q 14.39. Compute a TTM earnings number for Microsoft.

Q 14.40. What are the main problems of comparables valuation? Give an example of each, preferably real-world or numeric examples.

Q 14.41. Is it reasonable to compare IBM's P/E ratio based on equity to the equivalent ratio at Microsoft? Is it more or less reasonable to compare IBM's P/E ratio based on total firm value to the equivalent ratio of Microsoft?

Q 14.42. Is there a problem with using a book value–based equity measure? If so, why, and when does it matter?

Q 14.43. How could you value a biotech start-up that has no sales or earnings?

Q 14.44. What is the "quick ratio"? Is a firm more or less precarious if this ratio is high?

Q 14.45. What ingredients are in the DuPont model? What are its problems?

Part V

Capital Structure and Payout Policy

How To Finance Projects

Although you now know how you should value projects and how you should think about your costs of capital, you do not yet know how firms can best get new investors to part with their cash. We just assumed that if you had a positive-NPV project, then the cash to start it would be there. However, in the real world, you must somehow get funds first. For example, you could use earnings that you do not pay out. Or you could borrow money. Or you could sell off your accounts receivable. Or you could issue more equity to new shareholders. In this part, we discuss both the types of claims that firms can sell to potential investors and the selling process itself.

To explain the concepts, we shall again start off with a perfect market. This illustrates the first-order determinants and explains how you should think about the problems. Then we layer on more complexity again—how real-world market imperfections alter some of the conclusions that you would draw in the idealized perfect market.

What You Want to Learn in this Part

The goal of this part of the book is to explain how firms finance projects with debt and equity, and how their mix of funding sources influences the firm's cost of capital.

- Chapter 15 describes the principal phenomenon that this part of the book is focused on—corporate capital structure. It explains how you should think of securities that firms sell (issue), and how these securities are sold into the financial markets. It then shows what IBM's capital structure looked like and how it evolved from 2001 to 2003. This helps you judge what the first-order aspects of capital structure are.

  Typical questions: What kind of claims can firms issue to raise money? What are cash flow and control rights? What claims have what rights? How can payoff diagrams help you think of firms' capital structures?

- Chapter 16 begins the theoretical analysis of what capital structure firms should choose *in a perfect financial market*. It shows that the value of the firm is the value of its underlying assets and does not depend on whether the firm is financed with debt or equity.

  Typical questions: Should firms maximize shareholder or firm value? What are the appropriate values, promised rates of return, and expected rates of return on different securities? What is the weighted average cost of capital, commonly called WACC?

459

- Chapter 17 moves on to an imperfect world, in which firms have to pay corporate income taxes. This market imperfection is important enough to deserve its own chapter. So how should firms make capital structure (and capital budgeting) decisions if they have to pay corporate income taxes? The chapter also explains why profitable firms with large corporate income tax obligations should prefer debt over equity.

  Typical questions: What is the firm's cost of capital and value if it finances itself with 50% debt and 50% equity, instead of with 100% equity? What exactly are tax-adjusted WACC, APV, and flow-to-equity?

- Chapter 18 shows how firms should make capital structure and capital budgeting decisions if there are market imperfections other than corporate income taxes. The chapter explains that some market imperfections should push the firm toward having more equity, others toward having more debt. In addition, it describes what conflicted managers like.

  Typical questions: Should different types of firms have different investor clienteles? Should a high-growth firm finance itself with more or less debt than a profitable value firm? What should investors be afraid of, and how can managers comfort investors? How do these factors influence the firm's cost of capital?

- Chapter 19 describes equity payout strategies: dividends and share repurchases.

  Typical questions: Are dividend payments better or worse than share repurchases? Does it matter? How do firms tend to pay out money they earn?

Chapters 21 (Companion)–24 (Companion) contain material that topically belong to this part but which few classes are likely to have the time to cover in the first course.

15

Corporate Claims

Who Owns What?

How should projects be financed? You have already encountered the two basic financing choices that firms have: Current firm owners can accept new limited partners, which they can accomplish by issuing equity (stock). Or they can borrow money, which they can accomplish by issuing debt (bonds), either to public lenders or private lenders (such as banks). However, there are also many other financial claims that firm owners can sell, most of which are hybrids between debt and equity. In addition, there are other claims that arise in the conduct of business, such as accounts payable, pension obligations, and income taxes due. The **capital structure** is the sum total of all claims on the assets of the firms. Together, the claims represent the rights that own all the firm's assets—they *are* the firm.

In the first part of this chapter, you will learn about firms' basic choices. It explains that you should think of a claim as a bundle of cash flow rights and control rights. The cash flow rights describe how much money the claims holders are supposed to receive. The control rights describe what claims holders can and cannot do, especially when they do not receive the cash flows originally promised to them.

In the second part of this chapter, you will see how IBM's capital structure evolved from 2001 to 2003. It will give you some intuition about how complex real-world capital structures can be and how they tend to evolve.

15.1 The Basic Building Blocks

The **corporate charter** is the document that lays down the basics of the firm. It specifies who formally holds decision power, how the firm can engage in further contracts, how the charter can be amended, and so on. The corporate charter also addresses how the firm may be governed in the future. Together with the legal and regulatory framework in which it operates—which is jurisdiction dependent—the charter facilitates the creation of financial and nonfinancial claims, each with its own cash flow rights and control rights. It is this nexus of implicit and explicit contracts that defines the firm broadly, and its financial structure specifically. Our interest in this chapter is this capital structure—which is the sum total of all the claims on the firm's assets. Of course, you have already encountered many features of financial claims, given how important they are and given that we are already more than halfway through the book.

The firm's charter sets up the governance of the firm.

Even real estate owners do not fully own properties. They have to accept certain obligations.

➤ *Mortgage and levered equity*, Sect. 6.3, Pg. 131.

The most basic aspects of capital structure were first explained in the building example in Chapter 6. If you finance your building with a mortgage, you own only the residual unmortgaged part as levered equity. This means that you really do not fully own the building. Although you can make a lot of decisions about the building, there are others you cannot make. For example, your mortgage covenants prevent you from demolishing the building or from selling it and keeping all the money. To do either, you must first repay the mortgage. And, of course, as a property owner, you must also satisfy other claims that do not arise financially but instead arise in the context of real ownership. For example, you must pay your county property tax obligation, or the county can repossess your building. And through legal ownership, you also have to accept other obligations. For example, you cannot simply convert your building into a liquor store without obtaining zoning permissions. In reality, any property owner is only part owner—the building is really owned by the (so-miscalled) property owner, plus the mortgage company, plus other claimants.

This is exactly how shareholders "own" corporations—only after other obligations are satisfied.

➤ *Limited liability*, Sect. 6.4, Pg. 134.

This is exactly how things work in the corporate context. The firm's assets are owned by multiple claimants. The basic building blocks of the firm's financial structure are **liabilities** (often called **leverage**) and **equity** (often called **stock**). To use our metaphor, the shareholders are the equivalent of the levered property owner (although with assured limited liability). They are usually in charge, but there are clear limits to what they are allowed to do. Such limits come from covenants that the shareholders accepted earlier—covenants that the firm took on when it borrowed money or when it acquired or operated its assets. For example, most corporate bond covenants prevent firms from destroying or not maintaining their assets, or from selling the assets and paying out the cash to shareholders. The set of all claims on the firm's future payoffs is called its capital structure.

Claims are often classified into financial and nonfinancial ones:

Firms are owned by financial claims (e.g., debt and equity) and nonfinancial claims (e.g., Uncle Sam, pension obligations, and vendor credit).

➤ *SEC*, Pg. 169.

- Financial claims are debt and equity. They are often loosely called **securities**, the name indicating registration with the *Securities and Exchange Commission*. However, the term has become so common that it is now used much more liberally. For example, neither foreign securities nor privately placed securities are necessarily registered with the SEC.

- Nonfinancial claims are such obligations as corporate income taxes due, pension obligations, and accounts payable.

By strict definition, to fully own the firm and be permitted to do whatever you wish, you must own *all claims* that the firm has issued. It is not enough for you to own only *all stock* or even all financial claims. In the most extreme perspective, you can never fully own any firm, because Uncle Sam always has some claim to future cash flows that you can never acquire.

Every meaningful claim has two important aspects:

Claims have two important features: cash flow rights and control rights.

Cash flow rights, which describe how firm-generated cash will be allocated.

Control rights, which allow the claim owners to enforce their cash flow rights. For example, creditors can force the firm into bankruptcy if the firm does not pay its obligations; and stockholders can appoint the corporate board, which in turn appoints management, which runs the firms.

Q 15.1. What is a control right? Give some examples.

Q 15.2. Is it ever possible for a private individual to fully own a firm?

Cash Flow Rights as Payoff Diagrams

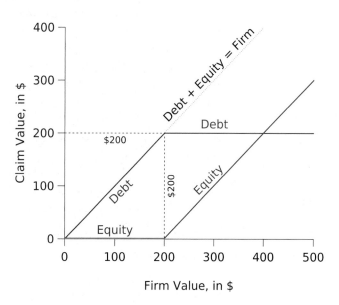

Firm Value	Bond Value	Stock Value
$0	$0	$0
$50	$50	$0
$100	$100	$0
$150	$150	$0
$200	$200	$0
$250	$200	$50
$300	$200	$100
$350	$200	$150
⋮	⋮	⋮

Exhibit 15.1: *Sample Bond and Stock Payoff Table and Diagram (at Maturity).* The bond in this example has a face value of $200. Thus, at maturity, if the firm is worth less than $200, the bond receives the entire firm. If the firm is worth more than $200, the bond receives $200 and the levered equity receives the rest. If you own both claims, you own the firm, which is the black diagonal line.

You have already learned the main tool for the analysis of *cash flow rights* in Chapter 6—payoff tables for contingent claims. Let's apply them in the corporate context. For example, consider a firm with a capital structure that consists of equity, a single bond that promises to pay $200 next year, and no other claims. The value of the corporation is the total value promised to bondholders and shareholders. How much each claims holder receives depends on the value of the firm. Exhibit 15.1 is a **payoff diagram**. It shows that if the firm is worth $100, bondholders receive $100 and shareholders receive nothing. If the firm is worth $200, bondholders receive $200 and shareholders receive nothing. If the firm is worth $300, bondholders receive $200 and shareholders receive $100. If the firm is worth $400, bondholders receive $200 and shareholders receive $200. And so on. This is the best way to think of the cash flow

Cash flow rights define payoff diagrams, which plot the claims' payoffs as a function of the underlying firm value at one fixed point in time.

➤ *Contingent claims payoffs, Exhibit 6.5, Pg. 137.*

rights of bonds, stocks, and most other financial claims. Because you can call the future value of the firm (the base asset) the underlying **state**, debt and equity are often called **state-contingent claims**: Their future values depend on the future state of the firm.

In a perfect market, the "firm terminates" aspect of the payoff diagram is not important.

Note that if the market is perfect, it is not important to the analysis whether the firm continues to exist after the bond comes due. You could imagine that the firm is then sold to new owners for its fair value first. The proceeds are then distributed to stockholders and bondholders according to their claims. Of course, stockholders and bondholders could use these proceeds to repurchase the firm immediately if they so desire.

Nevertheless, payoff diagrams cannot illustrate time-varying aspects of claims. They only illustrate firm-value varying aspects of claims.

Although payoff diagrams are very useful as conceptual aids, they do not convey all the information about a claim's cash flow rights. They work best for contracts that have only one payment at one fixed point in time. Our example above showed how easy they make it to understand a zero-bond. Unfortunately, payoff diagrams are not good at illustrating features that are themselves a function of time or many different points in time. It would be more difficult to use the payoff diagram to fully describe a coupon bond, because coupon bonds have many different payment dates. Payoff diagrams are even less useful to illustrate the value of a claim that receives randomly timed future payoffs. Nevertheless, even in such cases, there is usually a link between the value of the firm and the value of the financial claim—so thinking of financial claims as contingent claims in the context of payoff diagrams often remains a useful conceptual, if not entirely accurate, tool.

Q 15.3. Write down a payoff table for a stock and a zero-bond with a promised payoff of $300 million. What does the graph look like?

Q 15.4. Can you add payoff functions graphically in the payoff diagrams (if you own multiple claims), or do you first need to write down a revised payoff table? How? If so, what does the sum of all added claims look like?

Q 15.5. To gain some practice with payoff diagrams, assume your medical insurance pays 90% of your medical expenses, subject to a $500 deductible and an annual limit of $10,000 payout. Write down your insurance payoff table and graph an insurance payoff diagram, as a function of your medical expenses. What is the slope of the line at each segment?

Q 15.6. Can you draw a payoff diagram for a semiannual coupon bond with 15 remaining 10% coupon payments until maturity?

15.2 Liabilities

Firms' total liabilities are often classified into financial and nonfinancial claims.

Financial Claims (Debt)

You have already worked extensively with financial liabilities, such as bonds of all varieties in Part I. Still, let us review the rights of debt in the corporate context.

Bonds are loans to companies with specified obligations.

Cash flow rights: Bonds are just loans that promise specific payoffs at specific times in the future. The borrower (or issuer) receives cash up-front and contractually promises to pay cash in the future. The returned cash is commonly classified into interest payments (usually tax-deductible for the issuer) and repayment of principal. Most corporate bonds promise payments every 3 or 6 months and repay the remaining principal at **maturity**. In the event of liquidation, the law states that the **absolute priority rule** (APR) be applied. Bonds are senior securities, so their holders receive what they have been promised first, before more-junior claimants (such as equity) can receive anything. Different bonds from the same firm can themselves be classified into more-senior and less-senior claims, too. The more-senior bonds have first dibs when the firm's cash is distributed, and only after they are fully paid off do the junior bondholders receive anything.

➤ *Various bond features, Sect. 6.2, Pg. 125.*

Control rights: Unless the firm violates a bond covenant or is near financial distress (in which case, the law imparts managers with fiduciary responsibilities toward bondholders, too), bondholders typically do not have the right to participate in the decisions of the firm or the selection of its management. *But* if the firm misses a payment or violates a covenant that it has taken on to obtain the bond financing, then the bondholders have the right to force the firm into bankruptcy.

Bondholders have no control rights, unless the firm fails to pay what it promised or a bond covenant is violated.

ANECDOTE Judge Lifland and Eastern Airlines' Creditors

The absolute priority rule is the theory. In practice, bankruptcy courts can and sometimes do violate the pre-agreed priority rules in the bankruptcy process. In turn, because corporate managers can choose where to file for bankruptcy, they usually do so in the court where they expect to fare best.

Bankruptcy Judge Burton Lifland, of the Southern District of New York, was so notorious for violating creditors' rights that he attracted not only Eastern Airlines' bankruptcy, but also those of Manville, Orion Pictures, and LTV. But it was Eastern Airlines that was Judge Lifland's crowning achievement: When it went bankrupt in March 1989, it was fully solvent. Unsecured creditors would have likely been satisfied in full. Instead, Judge Lifland allowed Eastern to continue operating for 2 more years, partially on the basis that closing it would have disrupted Christmas travel. Eastern's ongoing operation evaporated about $1.5 billion through operating losses and another $100 million through legal fees. In the end, unsecured creditors received practically nothing of their $2.3 billion claim.

Despite such occasional spectacular examples of drastic APR violations, more commonly they are mild. (They may even be necessary. After all, society would not want to see lawyers starve!) These days, creditors are aware of expected violations and accumulating legal fees, and they therefore take them into account when they purchase bonds and stocks in the first place. Thus, the cost of legal wrangling primarily worsens corporations' borrowing terms up-front, and not the creditors' payoffs.

Cato.org

The U.S. Constitution has made bankruptcy a federal issue. The current *Federal Bankruptcy Code* allows for either corporate reorganization under **Chapter 11** or corporate liquidation under **Chapter 7**, named for their respective chapters. Both are supervised by a federal bankruptcy trustee under the supervision of a federal bankruptcy court. Either creditors or the firm itself can petition to enter bankruptcy.

In theory, bankruptcy allows bondholders to take over and thereby either keep the entire firm, or force it to pay what they were contractually promised. In practice, this is not as easy in the United States as it is, for example, in many European countries—but it does happen frequently enough. After the creditors' obligations are satisfied, any residual cash left over is paid to the more junior securities. In any case, no managers survive Chapter 7 (the firm is gone!), and few managers survive Chapter 11 bankruptcy. Not surprisingly, managers generally try to avoid missing bond payments like the plague.

In addition to bonds' universal right of repayment (through control in default), many borrowers grant their creditors additional control rights in the original lending agreement. These provisions are called **covenants**. For example, a loan agreement may specify that the firm must maintain a certain level of liquidity. If it does not, its loan can be declared to be in default, and it becomes due. If the firm fails to repay, creditors can petition the courts to force the firm into bankruptcy.

> Firms can contract any claim features they wish. Perfect markets offer fair pricing, but this does not mean that every bond feature is equally smart.

Bond features are not written in stone. Over time, firms have experimented and developed many variations and hybrids. Naturally, if any claim offers more features or protections that are of value to investors, then their buyers are willing to pay more for the claim up-front. In a perfect market, companies receive and investors pay the appropriate fair share (price), regardless of the features chosen by corporations offering claims for sale. The features described in this chapter are among those that have survived, evolved, and thrived over the years—those that increase value. Of course, corporations could issue claims that do not maximize value, even if they are fairly priced. For example, a claim might offer its owner the right to become CEO if it were to rain in Los Angeles next April 21. When sold, this claim would fetch an appropriate efficient and fair price in the market, but it would probably significantly lower the overall value of the firm.

> Par value is meaningless for equity. For bonds, par value helps to calculate the coupon payment schedule.

You may sometimes see the term **par value**. Although it is usually a vacuous concept when it comes to equity, it has a meaning for bonds. However, par is not really a value, but only a number that helps to quote coupon payment flow patterns. That is, coupon payout schedules at origination are described with reference to the bond's par value. (Issues that are sold below par are discount bonds, issues that are sold above par are premium bonds.) Principal and par value, and/or interest and coupon payment need not be identical, not even at the time of issue, much less later. But never think of par value as a real value.

> ➤ *Par value, Pg.51.*

Convertible Bonds

> Convertible bonds allow the bondholder to exchange the bond into something else, usually into equity.

A convertible bond is an example of how a bond can be more than plain vanilla. Convertible debt gives holders the right to convert this debt into equity at a predetermined price at predetermined dates. Thus, convertibles are hybrids with both debt and equity characteristics. Here is a simple example: A firm with 40 outstanding shares of equity has 20 outstanding convertible bonds that promise $10 thousand each in January 2050. Each such bond can be converted, at the bondholder's discretion, into three new shares of stock. This means that if all bondholders convert, they will own 60% of the firm. The original shareholders will own only 40% *but without an obligation to repay the debt.* The cost to shareholders will therefore no longer be the money that the firm has to pay to creditors, but a loss in ownership. This lessening of ownership is called **dilution**.

ANECDOTE   Are Convertibles Debt or Equity?

In a 2002 survey in which CFOs were asked to describe why they issue convertible debt, the most frequent answers alluded to the fact that convertibles are "equity in disguise": 58% of the managers answered that it is an inexpensive way to issue "delayed" common stock; 50% answered that they did so because they considered their own stock currently undervalued, which again could be interpreted as managers thinking of convertibles as equity in disguise.

Graham and Harvey, Duke, 2002

If you own these 20 bonds, what would you do if the value of the firm's assets in January 2050 were $200 thousand or less? Your 20 bonds would own the entire $200 thousand that the firm is worth. It would not be in your interest to exchange your bonds for shares. But what would you do if the value were $1 billion? You would make the following calculation: If you take advantage of the convertibility feature and exchange your 20 bonds for 60 shares, there will be 100 shares in total. Your shares will therefore own 60% of the firm, or $60 million—a whole lot more than the $200 thousand that you would receive if you did not convert. Therefore, you would definitely exercise your right to convert. Conversion makes sense only if the price is high.

> When a convertible comes due, its holders can decide whether they want to remain as such or become shareholders at the previously agreed-upon terms.

What is the firm value at which you would be indifferent between converting and not converting? It is where 60% of the firm would be equal to $200 thousand. This occurs when the firm value is equal to $200/0.6 ≈ $333 thousand. To summarize:

> Here is how to determine the firm value cutoff at which convertible bondholders prefer to convert.

- If the firm's value is below $200 thousand, the convertible bonds get everything.

- Between $200 and $333 thousand, the convertible bonds receive $200 thousand and the shareholders get the residual above $200 thousand.

- And above $333 thousand, both shareholders and bondholders benefit from higher values. The convertible bondholders own 60% of the firm's value; the shareholders own 40% of the firm's value.

The payoff diagram in Exhibit 15.2 shows the value of the claims.

Convertible bonds are popular, perhaps because they tend to align the interests of shareholders and bondholders. For example, if shareholders wanted to take a project that would help them but (accidentally or intentionally) hurt plain bondholders, the bondholders would usually try to fight the project. However, if the bonds were convertible, the bondholders could also profit from the resulting value increase and then not oppose such a project.

> Preview: Why is the conversion feature useful?
>
> ➤ *Bondholder expropriation, Sect. 18.4, Pg.583.*

One final question: Why would shareholders be willing to give bondholders this right to convert, which in effect deprives them of much upside? The answer must be that by doing so, bondholders are willing to pay more for the bond up-front. This means

> Firm owners are willing to give up the right to convert, because this feature increases the cash that creditors pay them up-front.

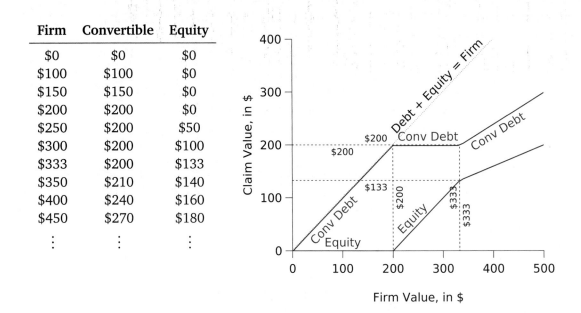

Firm	Convertible	Equity
$0	$0	$0
$100	$100	$0
$150	$150	$0
$200	$200	$0
$250	$200	$50
$300	$200	$100
$333	$200	$133
$350	$210	$140
$400	$240	$160
$450	$270	$180
⋮	⋮	⋮

Exhibit 15.2: *Sample Convertible Bond and Stock Payoff Table Diagram (at Maturity).* The convertible debt is indifferent between converting and not converting if the firm value is $333. The convertible's payoff slope beyond a firm value of $333 is 0.6; the equity's payoff slope is 0.4.

that the shareholders can negotiate for a lower interest rate. And, indeed, you know that if financial markets are perfect, bondholders get what they pay for.

Other Corporate Bond Features

Bonds come in a thousand varieties—and then some. Here are some common features.

If the bond claim includes more rights, then its interest rate is usually lower (equivalently, the value of the bond is higher). The issuer can choose what specific rights to offer to buyers and what rights to reserve for the firm. Among the more common bond features are the following:

A bond covenant specifies that the firm will keep certain promises, or else it will be forced to repurchase (*redeem*) the bond. Among the more common covenants are restrictions on what the firm can do with its assets, how much in dividends it may pay, how many and what kinds of other financial claims it may issue, what kinds of financial ratios (e.g., the debt-equity ratio) it needs to maintain, who the auditor is, what happens if the corporation defaults on any other bond, how much of its own bonds the firm will repurchase in each year, and so on. (This last feature is called a *sinking fund* provision and is common. See below.) Interestingly, the use of covenants varies over time. In good times, when plenty of credit is chasing investment opportunities, lenders are often less strict in their demands for specific covenants.

Bond seniority specifies exactly which bonds receive first dibs in case of bankruptcy and liquidation. A **senior bond** will have to be satisfied in full before a **subordinated bond** (or **junior bond**) may receive any money. In turn, equity receives its funds only after even the most junior bonds have been fully satisfied.

Collateral (or **security**) are specific corporate assets pledged to a specific bond in case of default. For example, mortgage bonds are collateralized by the value of the underlying real estate. If the issuer fails to pay, the bondholders may repossess the underlying real estate and use it to satisfy their claim. If the real estate is not enough to satisfy the claim of the **secured bond**, the remaining claim becomes an ordinary bond, waiting in line with other creditors for payment.

Convertibility, as you have seen, allows the bondholder to exchange the bond for shares.

Putability allows the bondholder to return the bond to the issuer, in exchange for a pre-agreed payment. This is like convertibility, except that the conversion is into cash, not into equity.

Callability allows the issuer (the firm) to "call in" the outstanding bond at a prespecified price. For example, a callable bond contract may state that the firm can redeem the bond by paying back principal plus 10% rate of interest in May 2020. Usually, callable bonds do not allow a call in the first 5 years. Callability is often present with convertibility, so that the call can be used to force bondholders to convert: The corporation calls the bonds, and the holder of the bond finds that it is in her interest to convert the bond into equity rather than to accept repayment.

While a convertible bond gives bondholders extra rights, callable bonds give the firm extra rights. Therefore, when a bond contains a call feature, it is less valuable than an otherwise identical bond. This means that issuers of bonds receive less money when they include a call feature. Put differently, the corporation must pay a higher interest rate up-front if it reserves a call feature. In effect, every mortgage in the United States is a callable bond, because the seller of the bond (the homeowner) can just pay back the remaining loan balance (the **principal**) and be absolved of all further obligations. Naturally, homeowners pay for this privilege with a higher interest rate up-front.

The call feature is a good example of where payoff diagrams do not capture the whole situation. The value of the callable bond is often more a function of the prevailing interest rate than it is a function of the firm value. Corporations tend to call bonds when the economy-wide interest rate has dropped so that replacement bonds have become much cheaper. (Similarly, homeowners tend to repay their mortgages and refinance when the mortgage interest rate has dropped.) But because the interest rate is not a one-to-one function of the firm value in the future, the payoff diagram against the firm value at a fixed point in time would not tell the whole story.

A **sinking fund** is a provision that the firm will repurchase a specified fraction (no more and no less) of the principal before maturity. Unlike the call feature, there is no optionality here. Thus, in one sense, it helps the purchaser by assuring that the firm pays back the money along the way. In another sense, it helps the firm, because it allows the firm to call a part of the bond early, often at a discount.

Other bond characteristics.

CFOs must also make decisions on the following corporate bond features. You already learned about them in Part I, because these features are shared by noncorporate bonds:

Bond maturity is the time to final payback. Indeed, borrowing may be very short term (as short as overnight!), or very long term (as long as forever). Bonds of different maturities may have different names. For example, **commercial paper** is short-term debt, often guaranteed by a bank's credit line (see below), and therefore is almost risk free to the lender. (To participate in this market, firms must have an investment-grade credit rating.) On the corporate balance sheet, **funded debt** is the term for debt that has a maturity of less than one year. **Unfunded debt** has a maturity of more than one year.

Again, payoff diagrams do not do bond maturity full justice. The reason is that maturity can sometimes be like "super-seniority." That is, a subordinated bond may be repaid before the more senior bonds come due, and, once paid, the money paid to the subordinated bond can often not be reclaimed to satisfy the senior creditor's higher-priority claims.

Bond duration is a measure of how soon payments are made.

➤ *Duration, Pg.≈17.*

Coupon bonds versus zero-bond:

➤ *Zero and coupon bonds, Sect. 5.3, Pg.102.*

Zero-bonds pay a fixed amount of money only at a final date. Coupon bonds make (interest) payments on a regular schedule, typically (but not always) twice a year, and the principal is repaid as a **balloon payment** at the end.

➤ *Units, Sect. 18.4, Pg.587.*

A **unit** is a bundle of multiple types of financial claims that are sold together. For example, one common type of unit bundles a bond with a warrant. (A **warrant** is a right to buy equity shares that the firm will then issue for a prespecified price at prespecified times in the future.) The purchaser can keep both types of claims or unbundle them and sell them separately.

Fixed-rate debt versus floating-rate debt: Fixed-rate bonds usually promise to pay a predetermined interest rate over the life of the bond. Floating-rate bonds offer a spread relative to some other interest rate, usually to *LIBOR* or to the *prime rate*. Highly reputable companies can typically borrow at interest rates that are about LIBOR. Riskier companies typically pay interest rates that are about 100-300 basis points (1-3%) above LIBOR. The interest rate on floating-rate debt is also often **capped** or **collared**—that is, the interest rate will never exceed a predetermined ceiling.

➤ *Prime rate and LIBOR, Bond Glossary, Sect. 27 (Companion), Pg.≈355.*

Here is an example of a less common bond feature.

There is no limit to the imagination as far as bond features are concerned. For example, the Russian carmaker Avtovaz issued Lada bonds in 1994, which allowed the holders to convert their bonds into Lada cars. Other bonds have had their payoffs linked to the price of commodities (such as oil), exchange rates, or other financial claims.

Concentrated Bank Debt or Diffuse Public Bonds?

Another important dimension along which loans differ is whether there is a relationship between the lender and the issuer. Firms can raise funds with a public debt issue, in which there is typically no relationship between the borrower and the many diffuse lenders, or with a private debt issue (e.g., a **bank loan**), in which there is often only one lender. The advantage of borrowing from the bank is that a single lender may get to know the firm, monitor it so that it acts appropriately in the future, and thereby grant better terms. The disadvantage is that there is less competition among banks for extending loans than there is among public bondholders. Bank loans can also take the form of a **credit line**. Credit lines are like instant debt, permitting borrowers to draw down money (and pay higher interest) only upon need. (Borrowers typically agree to pay a low interest rate even on the unused part of the credit line.) The opposite of a credit line is **negotiated debt**, in which both the bank and the firm commit to a fixed loan. Just as the lines between debt and equity are often blurry, so are the lines between bank loans, private debt, and public debt. There is now a large market for loans extended by syndicates of banks, in which multiple lenders can share the risk of a loan. It accounted for more than $1 trillion in new loans in 2006. On the other hand, many individual banks now routinely resell loans that they have made to firms. Then there are also vulture investors who purchase dispersed public debt in order to monitor the actions of the company, behaving much like a bank—as one fully coordinated lender. (And the liquidity crisis of 2008 has thrown these markets into general disarray, so it is not yet clear how they will look in years to come.)

> A public bond is usually owned by many diffuse creditors. A bank loan is usually owned by one (or just a few) banks. A bank loan can take the form of a credit line or of negotiated debt.

Q 15.7. A firm is financed with a senior bond that promises to pay $100, a junior bond that promises to pay $200 (of lower seniority but of equal maturity to the senior bond), and equity. Write down the payoff table and then draw the payoff diagrams when the two bonds are due.

Q 15.8. A convertible zero-bond that promises $10,000 can be converted into 50 shares of equity at its maturity date. If there are 2,000 such bonds and 300,000 shares outstanding, write down the payoff table. Describe how the payoff diagram for both bondholders and equity holders looks like?

Q 15.9. Write down all bond features (variations) that you remember.

Nonfinancial Liabilities

Although our book's focus is primarily on financial claims, most of the discussion also applies to nonfinancial claims. However, nonfinancial liabilities can vary widely in terms of both cash flow and control rights. They can have rights that are weaker or stronger than those of financial claims.

> For nonfinancial liabilities, cash flow and control rights can be weak or strong.

A nonfinancial liability with strong control rights: income tax obligations.

For example, Uncle Sam has cash flow rights that are specified in the tax code (i.e., computed according to tax laws and IRS rules). By law, corporate income tax obligations have priority before any other claim. The control rights that enforce this claim are similarly very powerful and even include criminal sanctions. If you evade corporate taxes, you can go to jail.

A nonfinancial liability with weak control rights: a customer who purchased a warranty from the firm.

On the other hand, your suppliers have fairly weak cash flow rights. They are supposed to be paid for the goods they have delivered to you. However, the cost of legally enforcing modest financial claims in the United States often exceeds the value of the claims. Thus, the best control right of your suppliers may be the threat to stop doing business with your firm if you do not pay. The same poor control rights often apply to customers, who may have purchased your products with a warranty. The customers may or may not have legal rights, but the enforcement costs are so high that they may not be worth the paper they are written on.

15.3 Equity (Stock)

➤ *Levered equity,* *Sect. 6.4, Pg.134.*

Stock = Equity. (Ordinary = Common.)

Stock is another name for equity, which you have already encountered in earlier chapters. If not further qualified, it refers to the most common flavor, which is called just this—**common stock** (or sometimes *ordinary stock*). Common stock, ordinary equity, and common equity are all the same thing. The terms *stockholders* and *shareholders* are just abbreviations for **stock shareholders**.

Shareholders usually have last dibs (i.e., money only after other obligations have been paid) but enjoy unlimited upside.

Cash flow rights: Stock receives whatever is left over *after* all liabilities have been honored. Thus, the bad news is that equity typically has the lowest priority in bankruptcy. If the firm does poorly, shareholders may get nothing. The good news is that the equity gets all the rest—potentially unlimited upside for the common equity. If shareholders are lucky, they receive dividend payments and capital appreciation.

Dividends have to be paid from *after-tax* earnings. Any paid-out dividends were thus taxed "at the source." Sometimes, other companies own these dividend-paying shares. The tax code intends to reduce a second round of tax for corporate owners on dividend income that was already taxed once at a source company. Thus, the **corporate dividend exclusion rule** has historically allowed corporations to pay a reduced tax rate on their dividend receipts. (However, this is subject to qualification—it can depend on whether the source firm was fully subject to income tax payments, on the type of firm paying the dividend, on the contractual ability of the issuer to call back the equity, and on the recipient's percent ownership.) In contrast to corporate investors, individual investors were historically subject to being taxed a second time at the full dividend personal income tax rate. This is called the **double taxation of dividends**, though it has been greatly reduced by the Bush tax cuts of 2003. (Similar arrangements have long been the norm in many other countries, such as in the United Kingdom.)

Shareholders elect the corporate board, which appoints and supervises management.

Control rights: Unlike creditors, shareholders cannot force the firm into bankruptcy if it refuses to pay dividends. Instead, shareholders' main control right is their right to elect the **corporate board**. The board is legally the principal of the firm and owns the control rights over the company itself. (The legal details to accomplish this delegation of power vary by corporate charter, by state, and by country.) The corporate board in turn appoints the managers, to whom they further delegate many, if not most, day-to-day control rights.

In addition to this contracted right, managers also have a legal **fiduciary responsibility** to shareholders, except if the firm is in financial distress, in which case this responsibility extends to both creditors and shareholders. There is some disagreement about whether dispersed shareholders in large, publicly traded corporations possess an effective control over the board (and in turn management) in real life, or whether it is more the other way around. The conflict between shareholders and managers is the focus of Chapter 24 (Companion) on corporate governance.

Most companies have only one type of common equity. A few firms have equity classes that differ in the number of votes each share carries. (Sometimes, they receive different amounts of dividends, too.) For example, when Rupert Murdoch purchased the Dow Jones company in 2007, he had to contend with the Bancroft founding family that owned only 24.7% of the total number of shares but controlled 64.2% of the votes. (Since the mid-1990s, the NYSE has refused to accept new firms that have such dual share classes.)

Nowadays in the United States, there is usually only one flavor of common equity.

In sum, although not perfectly correct, you can usually think of the equity holders as the corporate owners, though limited in power and protected by limited liability. There are also two other less common types of equity claims. They no longer play an important role in most large publicly traded firms, but they still have some use in small privately held companies. (Venture capitalists often use them.)

Generalizations.

Preferred equity is a claim with both debt and equity characteristics. Unlike ordinary equity, where dividends are declared annually at the discretion of management, preferred equity's dividends are specified at issuance (for example, $2.25 per calendar quarter per share). The preferred dividends are also usually higher than common dividends. In addition, the preferred equity covenants usually state that their dividend payments have priority over any dividend payments to common stock.

Preferred equity has some equity and some debt characteristics.

As equity, preferred is junior to any liabilities. However, the preferred covenants usually specify a higher priority relative to common equity in case of bankruptcy. Preferred equity also lacks the ability of creditors to force the firm into bankruptcy if the firm fails to pay the preferred dividends.

Preferred equity is often retired on a fixed schedule—even though many preferred equities have no formal maturity. Many preferred shares are redeemable, and if this is the case, investors receiving these dividends must treat them as interest income for tax purposes. As with common stock, some preferred stock is traded on public stock exchanges.

Naturally, many other features can be explicitly added by covenant. Indeed, the only context in which preferred equity is still commonly used nowadays is as **convertible preferred** in the context of nonpublic venture capital financing. These claims typically have covenants that provide explicitly for voting rights. The holders of such claims are usually themselves corporations—venture capitalists—who can write off the claims if the firm fails, or convert them into common equity if the firm succeeds.

We don't have time to cover warrants and options in detail here.

Warrants and options give their owners the right to purchase stock in the future at a predetermined price. If it is a warrant, the shares that the firm will provide are newly issued (and thus dilutive). Options and warrants are usually even more junior than common equity. They are often of value only if the firm experiences extraordinarily good times. In publicly traded corporations, they rarely have control rights—except for the right of the owner to convert them into equity. For more information on warrants and options, refer to Chapter 26 (Companion).

Q 15.10. Do shareholders enjoy limited liability?

Q 15.11. Did the Bush dividend tax cuts make corporate and individual holders of shares more similar or more dissimilar in their dividend income tax treatments?

Q 15.12. In what sense is preferred equity like bonds? In what sense is preferred equity like stocks?

15.4 Tracking IBM's Capital Structure From 2001 to 2003

You will learn a lot about capital structure by following a sample company (IBM) from 2001 to 2003.

You now have the conceptual understanding of how to think about different financial claims—their cash flow rights and control rights. In the real world, capital structure is highly complex. Perhaps the best way to understand what it *really* looks like is to examine the real-world capital structure of one company. We shall choose IBM, because it illustrates the many facets of capital structure quite nicely. And we'll look specifically at the period from 2001 to 2003, because this was a turbulent period at the end of the technology boom of the late 1990s. Exhibit 15.3 shows IBM's balance sheets from 2001 to 2003—you can download IBM's complete historical financials from IBM's corporate website. (Some numbers were restated in 2003, and thus not reported in 2001 and 2002 as I report them.) I added the "change" lines to the table to make it easier to see quickly what was happening. The top part of the table shows how IBM's liabilities evolved; the bottom part shows how IBM's equity evolved.

IBM's Liabilities

IBM had four nonzero liability components.

First look at the constituents of IBM's liabilities. A glance at Exhibit 15.3 tells you that there are four main categories of IBM's liabilities: long-term debt, short-term (or current) liabilities, pension liabilities, and other liabilities. Other firms may have two more components: minority interest of the business owned by third parties (which is therefore almost like equity) and negative goodwill (related to an accounting discount at which IBM might have purchased other companies). These two items rarely play large roles (except in companies that have been involved in large M&A activities), and they did not play any role in the case of IBM.

Liabilities	2001	Change	2002[r]	Change	2003	
Long-Term Debt	$15,963	+$4,023	$19,986	−$3,000	$16,986	(see Exhibit 15.4)
Short-Term Liabilities	$35,119	−$569	$34,550 ($34,220)	+$3,350	$37,900	(see Exhibit 15.5)
incl. Short-Term Financial Debt	$11,188	−$5,157	$6,031	+$615	$6,646	(see Exhibit 15.5)
Pension Liabilities	$10,308	+$2,907	$13,215	+$1,036	$14,251	
Other Liabilities	$5,465	+$486	$5,951 ($6,281)	+$1,175	$7,456	(see Exhibit 15.6)
Minority Interest	None		None		None	
Negative Goodwill	None		None		None	
Total Liabilities	$66,855	+$6,847	$73,702	+$2,891	$76,593	
Financial Debt	$27,151	−$1,134	$26,017	−$2,385	$23,632	

Equity	2001	Change	2002[r]	Change	2003
Number of Shares Outstanding	1,723.19	−0.82	1,722.37	−27.86	1,694.51
Book Price/Share	$13.61/s	−0.38/s	$13.23/s	+3.21/s	$16.44/s
Market Price/Share	$120.96/s	−43.46/s	$77.50/s	+15.18/s	$92.68/s
Stockholder's Equity (Book Value)	$23,448	−$666	$22,782	+$5,082	$27,864
Market Value of Equity	$208,437	−$74,953	$133,484	+$23,563	$157,047

Exhibit 15.3: *Major Components of Debt and Equity for IBM, 2001-2003 (dollars in millions, except share data).* Table note [r]: IBM revised its figures later, both in this and later tables.

More detail about a firm's capital structure usually has to be teased out of the financial footnotes.

If you want to learn more details about what all these claims are, you have to dive into the **financial footnotes** accompanying IBM's financial statements. These footnotes usually explain what the liabilities really are—and they are usually much longer than the financial statements themselves. Let me show you what I learned. It is not important for you to understand every little detail—IBM is just one company, and every company looks a little different. Your goal is to learn the basics and to be able to look up and interpret information when you need it.

Long-Term Debt

IBM's long-term debt consisted of many different securities. From 2001 to 2003, long-term debt increased and then decreased, mostly driven by IBM's notes.

Exhibit 15.4 shows *how* IBM's long-term debt first increased by $4 billion and then decreased by $3 billion. Like many other large Fortune 100 companies, IBM had a myriad of publicly traded long-term bonds outstanding. (Small firms tend to rely more on bank debt.)

Straight bonds: The top part of Exhibit 15.4 shows IBM's straight long-term bonds (debentures). (Note that one of IBM's bonds has about 90 years remaining to maturity! We can guess that these bonds do not appear to have an active call feature, or IBM would surely have retired its 8.375% bond due in 2019, given that it had considerably lower borrowing costs in 2003.) We can also guess that these bonds did not have an active sinking fund provision, because in most of these, the outstanding principal remained constant from 2001 to 2003. The only bond on which IBM retired any principal was its 6.5% bond, due in 2028. As to new debt, you can find deep in the footnotes that IBM issued a 5.875% bond for $600 million at 97.65 on October 1, 2003. (Par is 100, so this issue was below par. This bond was a discount bond, which means that its IRR was above 5.875%.)

Net-in-net, Exhibit 15.4 shows that IBM did not change its straight bond borrowing from 2001 to 2002, and increased it by only $219 million from 2002 to 2003.

Notes: There was more financing action in IBM's notes. **Notes** are in essence short-term bonds. They are also often callable. Together, these two features make it easy for a corporation to expand or contract debt, as needed.

➤ *Treasury notes, Sect. 5.3, Pg.95.*

IBM increased its medium-term notes by $3.5 billion from 2001 to 2002, and then decreased it by $2.4 billion from 2002 to 2003. (Relatively lower interest rates may help explain some of the shift from long-term into medium-term notes in 2002, but not in 2003. In any case, the two do not exactly offset one another.)

Net-in-net, $3.5 billion of IBM's $4 billion increase in long-term borrowing in 2002 and $2.4 billion of IBM's $3 billion decrease came from its medium-term notes. Other notes were used to offset some of this, but, nevertheless, IBM seems to have mostly used its notes program to expand or contract its long-term borrowing needs.

Hybrid financing: Note also that IBM had one hybrid debt-equity instrument—a convertible 3.43% note. It was issued by IBM to the partners of Pricewaterhouse Coopers Consulting (PwCC), a firm that IBM acquired in late 2002.

Foreign borrowing: Over this time period, IBM repurchased a good deal of euro debt. The euro appreciated in value from about 1.1 €/$ in 2001 to about 0.9 €/$

	Maturities	2001	Change	2002	Change	2003
U.S. Dollars						
Debentures:						
5.875%	2032	—		—		$600
6.22%	2027	$500		$500		$500
6.5%	2028	$700		$700		**$319**
7.0%	2025	$600		$600		$600
7.0%	2045	$150		$150		$150
7.125%	2096	$850		$850		$850
7.5%	2013	$550		$550		$550
8.375%	2019	$750		$750		$750
Change		$4,100	±$0	$4,100	+$219	$4,319
Conv. Notes: 3.43%[a]	2007	—		$328		$309
Notes: 6%, 5.9%[b]	2003-32	$2,772		$2,130		$3,034
Med.-Term Notes: 4%, 3.7%[b]	2003-18	$3,620		$7,113		$4,690
Other: 4.9%, 4.0%[b]	2003-09	$828		$610		$508
Change		$11,320	+$2,961	$14,281	−$1,421	$12,860
Other Currencies[c]						
Euros (5.4%, 5.3%)[b]	2003-09	$3,042		$2,111		$1,174
Yen (1.0%, 1.1%)[b]	2003-15	$4,749		$4,976		$4,363
Canadian (5.8%, 5.8%)[b]	2003-11	$441		$445		$201
Swiss (4.0%, 4.0%)[b]	2003	$151		$180		—
Other (6.6%, 6.0%)[b]	2003-14	$726		$730		$770
Change		$20,429	+$2,294	$22,723	−$3,355	$19,368
Unamort. (Prem.)/Disc.		$47		−$1		$15
SFAS #133 Fair Value Adj.[c]		$396		$978		$806
Change		$20,778	+$2,924	$23,702	−$3,543	$20,159
Less Current Maturities		$4,815		$3,716		$3,173
Total		$15,963		$19,986		$16,986
Change			+$4,023		−$3,000	

Exhibit 15.4: *IBM's Long-Term Liabilities (dollars in millions).* Table note [a]: These convertible notes were issued in the 2002 acquisition of PwCC to PwCC partners, and some began converting into equity in 2003. [b]: The first interest rate is the average from 2001 to 2002, the second from 2002 to 2003. [c]: This item "marks to market" the value of the debt instruments when interest rates change. IBM explained: *"In accordance with the requirements of SFAS No. 133, the portion of the company's fixed rate debt obligations that is hedged is reflected in the Consolidated Statement of Financial Position as an amount equal to the sum of the debt's carrying value plus a SFAS No. 133 fair value adjustment representing changes recorded in the fair value of the hedged debt obligations attributable to movements in market interest rates and applicable foreign currency exchange rates."*

by 2002, but the decline in the value of IBM's euro debt obligations was even steeper. IBM also reduced its Canadian debt and eliminated its Swiss franc debt. In contrast, IBM continues to rely heavily on financing in yen. Nevertheless, you cannot interpret these changes as speculation on exchange rates, because IBM described elsewhere in its financials how it hedged some of its currency risk. Moreover, not only IBM's obligations but also many of its assets were overseas, so the net exposure of IBM to foreign currency is not easy to determine.

➤ *Currency hedging, Sect.* 25.D *(Companion), Pg.≈295.*

Fair value adjustment: Usually, long-term debt is carried at historical value, not market value. However, some of IBM's debt was hedged against yield curve movements, too—that is, IBM had financial contracts that would change opposite in value to those of some or all of its bonds. From 2001 to 2003, short-term interest rates fell, while long-term interest rates remained around 5%. The fair value adjustment reflects the change in value of the hedged bonds. (Somewhere on the asset side of IBM's balance sheet will be an opposite item—an asset measuring the value change experienced by the hedge instruments.)

Current maturities: Some of IBM's long-term debt became current (had less than one year left before coming due) and therefore was reclassified into short-term liabilities. This could account for about $1.1 billion less in long-term borrowing in 2002, and $543 million less in 2003.

This stuff is complex.

In sum, there are many long-term financing instruments that can play a role. In IBM's case, the most important factor influencing changes in borrowing was the expansion and contraction of its medium-term notes program.

Current Liabilities

Note the many different short-term obligations—including many nonfinancial liabilities!

Exhibit 15.5 breaks out current (i.e., short-term) liabilities, which are due to be paid within one year. The CFO has more immediate influence over new issuing of more short-term financial debt (commercial paper and short-term loan borrowing) than almost any other claim. Exhibit 15.5 also shows you long-term debt (due in more than 1 year) that became short-term debt (with less than 1 year remaining) as the year went by. The remaining liabilities were not financial. They were incurred in the course of the firm's operations. IBM actively reduced its short-term borrowing from 2001 to 2002, and then expanded it from 2002 to 2003.

Other Liabilities

IBM's trends on other liabilities.

Exhibit 15.6 shows other liabilities that had an impact on the amount of corporate debt. IBM's other liabilities drifted upward from 2001 to 2003. Only changes in restructuring actions really mattered in 2002. In 2003, however, both changes in IBM's deferred taxes and deferred income increased somewhat. Nevertheless, other liabilities were also generally small (at around $5 to $7 billion) compared to IBM's total liabilities of $65 to $75 billion.

	2001	Change	2002^r	Change	2003
Short-Term Debt	$11,188	–$5,157	$6,031	+$615	$6,646
Commercial Paper	$4,809	–$3,507	$1,302	+$1047	$2,349
+ Short-Term Loans	$1,564	–$551	$1,013	+$111	$1,124
+ Long-Term Debt, Current	$4,815	–$1,099	$3,716	–$543	$3,173
Taxes	$4,644	+$832	$5,476	–$1	$5,475
Accounts Payable	$7,047	+$583	$7,630	+$830	$8,460
Comp. and Benefits	$3,796	–$72	$3,724	–$53	$3,671
Deferred Income	$4,223	+$1,053	$5,276^r ($4,946)	+$1,546	$6,492
Other Accrued Liabilities	$4,221	+$2,192	$6,413	+$743	$7,156
Total Current	$35,119	–$569	$34,550^r ($34,220)	+$3,680	$37,900

Exhibit 15.5: *IBM's Current (Short-Term) Liabilities (dollars in millions).* Table note [r]: This revision shifted $330 from deferred income into other liabilities, which can be seen in Exhibit 15.6.

	2001	Change	2002[r]	Change	2003
Deferred Taxes	$1,485	–$35	$1,450	+$384	$1,834
Deferred Income	$1,145	–$66	$1,079 ($1,409)[a]	+$433	$1,842
Exec. Comp. Accruals	$868	–$17	$851	+$185	$1,036
Restructuring Actions	$589	+$435	$1,024	–$153	$871
Postemployment, Preretirement	$493	+$80	$573 ($572)	+$7	$579
Disability Benefits	N/A	+$0	N/A ($304)[b]	+$45	$349
Environmental Accruals	$215	–$7	$208	+$6	$214
Other	$670	+$96	$766 ($463)[c]	+$268	$731
Total	$5,465	+$486	$5,951 ($6,281)	+$1,175	$7,456

Exhibit 15.6: *IBM's Other Liabilities (dollars in millions).* Table note [a]: This revision from $1,079 to $1,409 shifted $330 from deferred income into other liabilities, which can be seen in Exhibit 15.5. [b]: IBM broke out $304 million disability benefits in 2003, previously classified as "other." [c]: This is the net effect.

Other Observations and Discussion

Refer back to Exhibit 15.3. Just under 20% of IBM's obligations in 2003 were pension obligations to its more than 300,000 current and former employees. For many older and personnel-intensive firms, such as IBM, pensions are important liabilities. (These firms often have so-called defined benefit pension plans, in which the firm agrees to pay employees a pension that is based on a formula.) Firms do not need to fund *all* their future pension obligations, and indeed many firms fail to do so. Some firms, however, are more conservative and may even overfund their plans. (In the past, some of these firms have then found themselves the target of an external takeover attempt, in which the acquirer attempted to gain control of the excess pension assets in order to finance the acquisition itself.) The financial aspects of pensions are complex, but the financial footnotes contain a wealth of information about them. (IBM, in particular, had spent many years in court trying to change its [overfunded] pension plan into a cash plan. You can read more about this on IBM's website.) Unfortunately, it is almost impossibly difficult to discuss pensions adequately in less than a chapter (or less than a full book)—and it would lead you far away from the main topic—so we shall not discuss pensions any further.

Did you notice that Exhibit 15.3 shows that IBM shifted its obligations from short-term debt into medium-term and long-term debt in 2002? You can see this by dividing long-term debt by the sum of long-term debt plus financial debt in short-term liabilities from Exhibit 15.3:

$$2001: \quad \$15{,}963/(\$15{,}963 + \$11{,}188) \quad \approx 59\%$$

$$2002: \quad \$19{,}986/(\$19{,}986 + \$6{,}031) \quad \approx 77\%$$

$$2003: \quad \$16{,}986/(\$16{,}986 + \$6{,}646) \quad \approx 72\%$$

$$\text{Year:} \quad \text{Long-Term Debt}/(\text{Long-Term Debt} + \text{Short-Term Debt})$$

Incidentally, you could also see the same directions in borrowing trends within IBM's long-term liabilities, that is, in its arrangement between long-term and medium-term notes (Exhibit 15.4).

The passing of time itself also made outstanding obligations shorter term, so you might like to know how IBM's financial obligations for each year developed. If you dig deeper into the financial footnotes, you can discover the following aspect of IBM's capital structure:

| | **Term Structure of IBM's Liabilities Coming Due** | | | | | | | | |
	2001	**2002**	**2003**	**2004**	**2005**	**2006**	**2007**	**2008**	**2009**
As of 2001	$11,188	$5,186	$3,106	$1,501	$1,904	$2,261	$6,471	←	←
As of 2002		$6,031	$3,949	$3,613	$1,670	$2,705	$846+$9,940		←
As of 2003			$6,646	$4,072	$3,113	$2,760	$1,289+$225+$7,942		

This shows that IBM changed its capital structure dynamically. This was probably related to how economy-wide interest rates changed over this period:

Pension obligations are very important for some firms with many employees—for IBM, they were almost as important as its long-term debt.

➤ *Mergers and acquisitions, Sect. 23.C (Companion), Pg.≈204.*

The time dimension of IBM's obligations: IBM's debt became longer term from 2001 to 2003.

The prevailing yield curve probably influenced IBM's term structure, too.

	Maturity	2000	2001	2002	2003
U.S. Treasury, Short-Term	1 month	≈5%	2.47%	1.63%	1.02%
U.S. Treasury, Medium-Term	3 years	6.22%	4.09%	3.10%	2.10%
U.S. Treasury, Long-Term	20 years	6.23%	5.63%	5.43%	4.96%
Corporate, Short-Term	1 month	6.3%	3.8%	1.7%	1.1%
Aaa Bonds	Medium-Term	7.6%	7.1%	6.5%	5.7%

The footnotes further tell us about IBM's unused credit lines:

	2001	2002	2003
Unused Credit Lines	$16,121	$16,934	$15,883

To put them into perspective, realize that the unused credit lines were of a similar order of magnitude as IBM's long-term debt!

The financial footnotes also tell a little bit about IBM's interest payments:

	2001	2002	2003
Interest Paid and Accrued	$1,235	$815	$663

Again, to add a little more perspective, IBM earned $7.7 billion in 2001, $5.3 billion in 2002, and $7.6 billion in 2003. Somewhere, deep in the bowels of the 2003 financials, IBM also reported that its commercial paper (very, very short-term borrowing) had a weighted-average interest cost of 1%, while its short-term borrowings had a weighted-average interest cost of 2.5%. You could also try to estimate the average interest rate on all debt. With $663 million in interest on financial debt of $16,986 + $6,646 = $23,632 million, the average interest rate would have been around 2.8%.

IBM's Equity

Exhibit 15.7 illustrates the evolution of IBM's equity. You can see that preferred equity disappeared completely in fiscal year 2002. (The background is that in 1995 the IBM board had decided to repurchase all its remaining 7.5% callable preferred stock, and this was ultimately completed on May 18, 2001. This is not unusual—as already noted, preferred equity has largely disappeared from large publicly traded corporations.) Moving on to common equity, about 1.9 billion shares of IBM were officially issued. Of these, IBM itself held about 190 and 199 million shares in 2001 and 2002, respectively, and 243 million shares in 2003. (They are called **treasury shares**—not capitalized!) IBM therefore had 1.7 billion shares outstanding. If you had owned all of these 1.7 billion externally held shares, you would have owned all of IBM's common equity (although your ownership of the 200 million treasury shares would have been indirect through your ownership of the outstanding shares—after all, a firm cannot own itself). This number remained fairly constant, even though IBM actively repurchased its shares. Yet, although the dollar amount was large, it was only a small fraction of the company's outstanding stock. In addition, IBM then turned around and used these shares in other transactions, for example, to fund the PwCC acquisition or its employee stock option plans (**ESOP**). Consequently, although repurchases and net stock transactions were

The 10-K also gives some interest rate information.

Common equity: IBM did not change its number of shares by very much.

		2001	*Change*	**2002**	*Change*	**2003**
Preferred	Authorized	150,000,000		—		—
	Outstanding	2,546,011		—		—
Common	Authorized	4,687,500,000		4,687,500,000		4,687,500,000
	Issued	1,913,513,218	+7,444,554	1,920,957,772	+16,435,832	1,937,393,604
	Treasury	190,319,489	+8,271,387	198,590,876	+44,294,093	242,884,969
	Outstanding	1,723,193,729	−826,833	1,722,366,896	−27,858,261	1,694,508,635

Identifiable Changes

	2001	2002
PwCC Acquisition Issue, Restricted	−3,677,213	
To Pension Fund, from Treasury	−24,037,354	
Repurchase I	+48,481,100	+49,994,514
Repurchase II ESOP	+189,797	+291,921
Issue to ESOP, from Treasury	−979,246	−2,120,293
PwCC Acquisition Issue[a]	−$254	
Repurchase I	+$4,212	+$4,403
Repurchase II ESOP	+$18	+$24
To Pension Fund	−$1,871	

	2001	2002	2003
Retained Earnings	$30,142	$31,555	$37,525
Book Equity	$23,448	$22,782	$27,864

	2001	2002
Cash Dividends Paid	−$1,005	−$1,085
Common Stock Transactions	−$3,087	−$3,232
For Comparison: Interest Paid	−$831	−$853
For Perspective: Taxes Paid	−$1,707	−$1,841

	2001	2002	2003
Common Price/Share	$120.96	$77.50	$92.68
⇒ Common Market Value	$208,437	$133,484	$157,047

Exhibit 15.7: *IBM's Equity and Some Other Information (dollars in millions, except share data).* Table note [a]: An additional $30 million is recorded to be issued in the future.

larger than interest payments and dividend payments combined, the active issuing or repurchasing of shares ultimately did not play much of a role in changing IBM's capital structure.

However, IBM's stock price changed, which played a very large role in moving IBM's equity capitalization.

Instead, almost all the change in the value of equity came through one mechanism: changes in the price of each IBM share. From 2001 to 2002, shares dropped from $120.96 to $77.50, thereby losing about one-third of its market value. From 2002 to 2003, the market value bounced back again by about 20%. The effect was a drop in the equity value from $208 billion to $133 billion, followed by an increase back to $157 billion.

Observations on the Evolution of IBM's Capital Structure

Where did IBM's big capital structure changes come from?

You now understand how IBM's capital structure changed from 2001 to 2003. IBM's liabilities evolved fairly steadily. About one-quarter of its total liabilities consisted of pension and other unspecified liabilities. The pension obligations, in particular, marched upward fairly steadily. In terms of IBM's total liabilities increase of about $2.9 billion, the pension and other obligations accounted for one-half and three-quarters in 2002 and 2003, respectively. About another one-quarter of IBM's total liabilities (of about $70 billion) consisted of its long-term debt; the remaining one-half of total liabilities was short-term debt. In 2002, IBM ratcheted up its medium-term notes borrowing, accounting for a debt increase of $3.5 billion. In 2003, IBM mostly kept its borrowing at the same level, but shifted it from longer-term into shorter-term debt. These changes in the value of IBM's liabilities were dwarfed by the changes in the value of IBM's *equity*—and almost all of it came from changes in the per-share price, not from changes in the number of shares outstanding.

It is sometimes useful to think about the components of the capital structure as how easily they can be used as sources of funding.

This suggests that a useful perspective is to think about capital structure changes as being driven by three factors:

1. Claims that are for the most part outside the day-to-day control of the CFO—such as pension fund obligations.

2. Claims whose value is mostly determined by the performance of the company and the financial markets—such as common equity.

3. Claims that are for the most part under the day-to-day control of the CFO—such as the firm's financial claims. The obvious examples are (bank) debt and short-term notes. These are most interesting for us financiers, because they are often the primary source of marginal capital to fund new projects.

Total-liabilities-to-assets and financial-debt-to-capital are two good summary statistics that measure leverage.

We still need a summary measure to characterize a firm's indebtedness. There are two good common statistics:

1. **Total-liabilities-to-total-assets ratio:** In 2003, $76,593/$104,457 \approx 74\%$ of IBM's total *book-value-based* assets were financed with liabilities. However, though common, book assets clearly undervalue IBM's assets, primarily because book equity is less than market equity. If measured in market value, IBM's equity increases from $27,864 to $157,047 (i.e., by $129,183). This means that assets increase to $233,640. Thus, IBM's 2003 market-based liabilities-to-asset ratio was $76,593/$233,640 \approx 33\%$.

➤ *Warning about BV-Equity, Sect.* 13.7, *Pg.405*.

2. **Financial-debt-to-capital ratio:** Financial debt consists of two components: long-term debt and debt in current liabilities. IBM's financial debt was $23,632 in 2003. Financial capital consists of two components: financial debt and equity. (Capital therefore excludes the nonfinancial-liabilities component that is in assets). IBM's financial capital in 2003 was $23,632 + $27,864 = $51,496 in book value. Consequently, $23,632/$51,496 ≈ 46% of IBM's book-value-based capital was financial debt. If we measure equity in market value, capital was a higher $23,632 + $157,047 = $180,679, instead. Consequently, the market-value-based financial-debt-to-capital ratio was $23,632/$180,679 ≈ 13%.

These are just summary statistics. No single statistic can convey a full picture of IBM's complex capital structure. Depending on the context, you may find one or the other (or both) measures to be more suitable for your needs. Section 22.A (Companion) has a more detailed discussion of these and other measures of leverage. However, even without more detail, it seems pretty obvious that IBM was on solid financial footing. It was unlikely to suffer financial distress anytime soon.

➤ *How to measure leverage,* *Sect.* 22.A (Companion), *Pg.* ≈149.

Q 15.13. List some of the bigger categories that can go into the firm's capital structure.

Q 15.14. To take control of a firm, do you need to purchase all *outstanding* or all *issued* shares?

Q 15.15. From year to year, does the value of debt or equity tend to move around more?

Summary

This chapter covered the following major points:

- In the real world, firms are financed by a set of different financial claims. The same firm may have senior debt, junior debt (perhaps with a conversion feature), equity, and warrants. The right way to think about all these claims often involves the "magic" of the payoff table and the payoff diagram: If the firm ends up worth very little, only the senior debt is paid. If the firm is worth a little more, both the senior and the junior debt are paid. If the firm is worth even more, the equity becomes valuable and, finally, so do the warrant and/or the conversion feature.

- The two most basic building blocks of capital structure are debt and equity. These differ in their cash flow rights and in their control rights:

  - Debt has first rights to the distribution of cash flows. It is "senior." It can force the firm into bankruptcy if payments are not made.

  - Equity gets only what is leftover after debt has been satisfied. It is "junior." It is in control of the firm, unless the firm finds itself in financial distress.

- Payoff tables and payoff diagrams are often good ways to describe the cash flow rights of debt and equity. They are state-contingent claims, where the firm value is the state. But the plots are not perfect in summarizing all the important information about claims. They ignore factors that can influence security value other than the firm value at one point in time, such as the time pattern of multiple payouts, control rights, or economy-wide interest rates.

- Convertible bonds allow their owners to convert their bonds into shares. They can therefore often be considered as part debt, part equity.

- Preferred equity cannot force bankruptcy, but it receives its dividends before common equity does.

- Corporate borrowing comes in thousands of varieties. For example, it can be plain, convertible, callable, fixed-rate or floating-rate, short-term or long-term, and so on. Debt can also have detailed covenants of many kinds.

- The lines between different financial instruments are blurry. Issuers regularly introduce new kinds of securities that carry features traditionally associated only with either debt or equity. Nothing is written in stone. Debt and equity (or bank, private, and public debt) are nowadays better considered to be concepts rather than sharp categories.

- Equity is less colorful than debt. For many companies, it consists of only one class of common equity.

Looking at IBM in greater detail, you learned the following:

- Capital structure changes are influenced by factors under management's immediate control (primarily financial claims, such as debt issuing and share repurchasing), factors related to operations (primarily nonfinancial liabilities, such as pension obligations and working capital), and factors beyond the management's immediate control (such as discount rate changes and stock returns).

- The big liability categories (for IBM) were long-term debt, short-term liabilities, pension liabilities (details of which depend on the company), and the catch-all category called other liabilities. (Minority interest and negative goodwill are usually less important.)

- Financial debt is the sum of long-term debt plus the financial debt component of short-term liabilities.

- The financial footnotes give more details about firms' liabilities. Financial debt can contain many different types of borrowing simultaneously—bonds, notes, foreign credit, hybrid securities, credit-line–related borrowing, bank debt, and so on. Short-term debt contains financial debt, tax obligations soon due, accounts payable, compensation-related liabilities, and other items. Nonfinancial liabilities contain accounts payable and (usually) a large amount of specified or unspecified other liabilities. These other liabilities can contain such items as deferred taxes and deferred income, executive compensation, retirement-related items, disability benefits, environmental liabilities, and the like.

- Firms can, and often do, take the term structure of interest rates into account when they issue or retire debt. This means that their current capital structures are often history (interest-rate) dependent.

- The total-liabilities-to-assets ratio and the financial-debt-to-financial-capital ratio are two reasonable summary measures of indebtedness. Their value can be quite different, not only from one another but also depending on whether the equity component is measured in book or market value.

Keywords

APR, 465. Absolute priority rule, 465. Balloon payment, 470. Bank loan, 471. Bond covenant, 468. Bond duration, 470. Bond maturity, 470. Bond seniority, 469. Callability, 469. Capital structure, 461. Capped, 470. Chapter 11, 466. Chapter 7, 466. Collared, 470. Collateral, 469. Commercial paper, 470. Common stock, 472. Convertibility, 469. Convertible preferred, 473. Corporate board, 472. Corporate charter, 461. Corporate dividend exclusion rule, 472. Coupon bonds, 470. Covenant, 466. Credit line, 471. Dilution, 467. Double taxation of dividends, 472. ESOP, 482. Equity, 462. Fiduciary responsibility, 473. Financial footnote, 476. Fixed-rate debt, 470. Floating-rate debt, 470. Funded debt, 470. Junior bond, 469. Leverage, 462. Liabilities, 462. Maturity, 465. Negotiated debt, 471. Note, 476. Par value, 466. Payoff diagram, 463. Preferred equity, 473. Principal, 469. Putability, 469. Secured bond, 469. Securities, 462. Security, 469. Senior bond, 469. Sinking fund, 469. State, 464. State-contingent claim, 464. Stock shareholder, 472. Stock, 462. Subordinated bond, 469. Treasury share, 482. Unfunded debt, 470. Unit, 575. Warrant, 470. Zero-bond, 470.

Answers

Q 15.1 A control right is the right to influence decisions, specifically by changing management and/or the board.

Q 15.2 Individuals can never really own everything. The IRS and community have inalienable property rights over every firm in existence.

Q 15.3 The payoff table for the $300 million zero-bond is as follows (in million dollars):

Firm Value	Bond Value	Stock Value
$0	$0	$0
$100	$100	$0
$200	$200	$0
$300	$300	$0
$350	$300	$50
$400	$300	$100
⋮	⋮	⋮

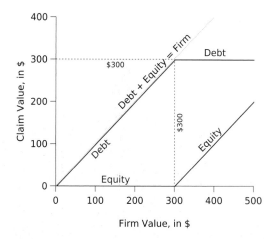

The bond is a diagonal line until firm value is $300, and then a horizontal line. The stock is a horizontal line at $0 until $300, and then a diagonal line.

Q 15.4 Yes, you can add up payoffs. It is basically stacking up lines. The sum total must be one diagonal line (i.e., slope of 1)—it is the value of the firm. Perhaps this is easiest to see if you draw it all, and then convince yourself that you can stack!

Q 15.5 For the medical insurance reimbursement example, consider another example. If you submit annual claims of $750, you first have to pay the deductible of $500 yourself. On the remaining $250, you get a reimbursement of 90%, that is, $90\% \cdot \$250 = \$225$. Doing this for more medical claims,

Medical Cost	Insurance Payout	Medical Cost	Insurance Payout
$0	$0	⋮	⋮
$250	$0	$11,500	$9,900
$500	$0	$11,600	$9,990
$750	$225	$11,611	$10,000
$1,000	$450	$11,700	$10,000
$2,000	$1,350	$12,000	$10,000
$3,000	$2,250	$13,000	$10,000
⋮	⋮	⋮	⋮

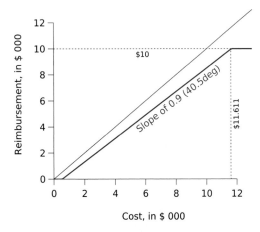

The "slope" is zero until $500 is reached, then 90% until $11,611.11 is reached (where the payout is $[\$11,611.11 – \$500] \cdot 0.9 = \$10,000$), and then zero again.

Q 15.6 No, you cannot draw a good payoff diagram for a coupon bond with so many remaining payments—at least not easily without making a lot of extra assumptions. Payoff diagrams only work well for a security's value at one given point in time.

Q 15.7 For the $100 senior bond, the $200 junior bond, and equity:

Firm	Senior	Junior	Equity
$0	$0	$0	$0
$50	$50	$0	$0
$100	$100	$0	$0
$150	$100	$50	$0
$200	$100	$100	$0
$250	$100	$150	$0
$300	$100	$200	$0
$350	$100	$200	$50
$400	$100	$200	$100
$450	$100	$200	$150
⋮	⋮	⋮	⋮

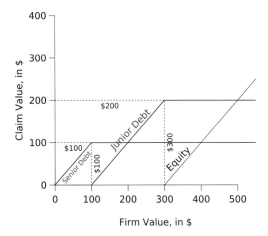

Q 15.8 For the 2,000 convertible $10,000 zero-bonds that can be converted into 50 shares of equity each (with 300,000 shares outstanding): If the firm is worth less than $2,000 \cdot \$10,000 = \$20$ million, the bondholders own the entire firm and shareholders receive nothing. If the bonds convert, they will be equivalent to one-quarter of all shares. At $80 million, bondholders are indifferent between converting and not converting, because $\$20,000,000/0.25 = \$80,000,000$. The payoff diagram for the debt is therefore a diagonal line (i.e., slope of 1) until $20 million, then a horizontal line until $80 million, and a line with a slope of 0.25 beyond $80 million. For equity, the line is horizontal until $20 million, then diagonal (i.e., slope of 1) until $80 million, and a line with a slope of 0.75 beyond $80 million.

Q 15.9 The various bond features are fully described in Section 15.2. Here is a short description: Most bonds make interest payments on a regular basis (e.g., semiannually or annually) and repay the principal of the bond at maturity. The interest rate (or coupon rate) may be either fixed or floating with some benchmark rate, (e.g., the prime rate). Bonds also come with covenants that are other requirements that a firm must abide by, such as a minimum level of liquidity, a maximum amount of debt, and/or a sinking fund requirement. Some bonds may be designated as senior to other bonds issued by the firm, which gives their holders a prior claim over the junior bond investors. Some bonds may also be collateralized, in which case the bond is backed by one or more of the firm's assets. In addition, a bond may be convertible, callable, or putable.

Q 15.10 Shareholders indeed enjoy limited liability, which is the fact that they can only lose their actual investment. They do not forfeit their personal possessions if the corporate managers act badly.

Q 15.11 The Bush dividend tax cuts reduced the double taxation of individuals. Because corporations always had some form thereof, they made corporations and individuals more similar.

Q 15.12 Preferred equity is like a bond in that it does not participate in the upside, and in that preferred equity is usually de facto senior to common equity. This applies both in bankruptcy and in respect to the dividends: Common shares do not get their dividends until preferred shareholders have received theirs. Preferred equity is like a stock in that its payments are not tax deductible by the issuer, and in that preferred shareholders have no ability to force the firm into bankruptcy if their dividends are not paid.

Q 15.13 Liabilities consist of long-term debt (bonds and notes), short-term debt (financial, taxes, payables, etc.), pension debt, and other debt. Equity consists of common and preferred stock.

Q 15.14 You cannot purchase all issued shares, because the firm holds treasury shares, which are a component of all issued shares. Instead, you need to purchase all outstanding shares. This gives you indirect control over the treasury shares, which the firm already holds itself.

Q 15.15 The value of equity moves around a lot more, primarily because it is a "levered value," which is more sensitive to changes in the value of the underlying firm. In contrast, debt changes drastically primarily when a firm issues or retires debt.

End of Chapter Problems

Q 15.16. What is a cash flow right? How does it differ from a control right?

Q 15.17. Write down the payoff table and graph the payoff diagram for an insurance contract with a deductible of $100,000, a coverage of 80% of the loss, and a maximum payout of $1,000,000.

Q 15.18. Draw a payoff diagram for a stock and a bond, where the bond promises to pay off $500 in one year.

Q 15.19. What can payoff diagrams illustrate well? Where do they fail?

Q 15.20. What are the two uses of the abbreviation "APR"?

Q 15.21. What are the main mechanisms through which creditors can increase the likelihood of being repaid? Give some examples.

Q 15.22. A convertible zero-bond that promises $20,000 can be converted into 100 shares of equity at its maturity date. If there are 8,000 such bonds and 1,200,000 shares outstanding, what would the payoff table and diagram for both bondholders and stockholders look like?

Q 15.23. Write down all bond features (variations) that you remember.

Q 15.24. What is the main control mechanism through which shareholders increase the likelihood of ever receiving cash?

Q 15.25. What are the main control rights for common equity, preferred equity, and debt?

Q 15.26. Is common stock or preferred stock more common? Does the name "preferred" mean it is better to own preferred stock than common stock?

Q 15.27. What are financial notes?

Q 15.28. What are the main categories of long-term liabilities?

Q 15.29. What is commercial paper?

Q 15.30. What are the main categories of short-term liabilities?

Q 15.31. Explain how the capital structure of IBM changed from 2008 to 2010.

Capital Structure in a Perfect Market

Should A Company Issue Stocks or Bonds?

How should entrepreneurs and managers think of the multitudes of instruments with which they can finance the firm? To understand how a firm should choose its capital structure, we start with the world that is easiest to understand and that you already know: the "perfect market" (no opinion differences, no transaction costs, no taxes, and no important buyers or sellers). This chapter shows (again) that the value of the firm's capital in a perfect market is determined by the present value of its projects, and not by whether the firm is financed with debt or equity. This is because in the perfect financial markets, someone would immediately step in to correct any mistakes managers could commit. As a result, the value of the firm's capital cannot depend on the claims a firm might choose to issue.

This chapter also explains the simplest version of the weighted average cost of capital formula (WACC). The next few chapters will then explain how financing in the real world differs from financing in this perfect-market world.

There are some small subtleties, however, when it comes to nonfinancial claims. Product markets are often not perfect. In these cases, the firm's average and marginal costs of capital can be different. Nevertheless, if the financial claims exist in a perfect market, then it is often still the case that the firm's marginal cost of capital—which is what managers ultimately want to know—is that of its financial claims. The financial claims' weighted average cost of capital would then still be the firm's marginal cost of capital. (However, this cost of capital would *not* be the firm's average cost of capital.)

16.1 Maximization of Equity Value or Firm Value?

Now that you understand the claims that firms *can* and *do* issue, let's focus on what they *should* issue. The best way to conceptualize an optimal firm structure is as follows: You are the entrepreneur who owns all of the firm. You want to sell it for the highest possible price. Your goal is to design your firm—including your corporate charter and capital structure—in a way that maximizes its total market value *today*. This value is the price that new investors are willing to pay to buy the firm from you. If your firm's charter or its capital structure allows or even induces you or your managers to take negative-NPV

You should think about an optimal capital structure from the perspective of an all-owning entrepreneur.

projects or steal from investors in the future, then who would want to buy your firm today? Thus, the better you design your firm today, the higher the price that you can get from outside investors. (The design of the firm will be an even more important subject in Chapter 24 (Companion), in which we will discuss corporate governance.)

Should our entrepreneur incentivize management to maximize shareholder value?

Let's first talk about what management will want to do in the future. Who does management represent (other than themselves)? Who *should* management represent? Does it make a difference whether management is representing just the shareholders or all the claimants on the firm? A popular view in the press is that the goal of managers should be **shareholder wealth maximization**. In the presence of other claims—such as financial debt, pension obligations, and accounts payable—this is not as simple as it may seem.

In the United States, managers primarily represent shareholders, although their duty may extend to creditors if the firm should go into distress.

Shareholders elect the corporate board of directors. Legally, this board is the principal of the firm. In turn, the board appoints management, which has a primary legal **fiduciary duty** only to shareholders. This is eminently sensible—management should negotiate on behalf of the residual equity owners for good terms with its suppliers, creditors, and so on, and not willingly pay such other claimants more than the firm has to. However, the legal situation changes when decisions made by management can threaten insolvency. In this case, management's legal fiduciary responsibility extends to other claimants, too. Again, this makes sense, because if the firm is underwater, it may ultimately belong to the creditors. These responsibilities can be different in other countries. For example, in German joint stock companies, limited liability companies, and cooperatives with more than 500 employees, one-third of the **supervisory board** must be employees. And in the case of companies in the iron, coal, and steel industry, shareholders and representatives of the workforce must be equally represented on the firm's supervisory board. German firms must also appoint one director who represents the employees and is responsible for "social affairs." In sum, German corporate boards are legally tasked with more than just shareholder wealth.

The dilemma—a situation in which shareholder maximization and firm value maximization are in conflict.

In practice, U.S. managers see themselves primarily as representatives of shareholders and not creditors. Yet, even if managers seek to maximize shareholder wealth, it is not necessarily clear how they should think and what they should do. Let me explain this. When both bondholders and shareholders benefit from a manager's actions, there is no problem. But what if there are situations in which optimizing the value of the equity is the opposite of optimizing the overall firm's value? For example, assume it is possible for managers to increase the value of equity by $1, but at a cost to the value of financial debt of $3. (You will later learn how easy it is to do exactly this.) This "expropriative" transaction would destroy $2 in the net value of the firm. Even in our perfect world, this is the type of situation that can create a dilemma for management: Should management maximize firm value or shareholder value? Recall that it is shareholders who ultimately vote managers into office and allow them to stay there. When the time comes, managers may find it in their interest to execute this dubious transaction because doing so raises the equity value—and with it their executive bonuses. Whether this transaction hurts creditors or destroys value may not even enter their minds.

➤ *Bondholder expropriation,* Sect. 18.4, Pg.583.

Rational bond buyers understand future conflicts of interest and assume the worst.

However, there is one hole in this logic. Put yourself in the shoes of the original entrepreneur today. You are trying to set up a corporate charter and capital structure that maximizes the value of your firm, that is, the price you could get if you sold it today. You want to find the best capital structure *today*. How can you attract new investors? How can you persuade them to part with their hard-earned cash? Clearly, any potential creditor contemplating purchasing your bonds will take into consideration what your managers may do to them in the future. If it looks as though managers will want to execute the aforementioned dubious transaction, your potential creditors would rationally demand much higher interest rates. If you do not commit the firm today *not* to undertake the $3-for-$1 transaction in the future, your prospective bond buyers will realize today (before the fact, or **ex ante**) that you or your management will have the incentive to execute it later (after the fact, or **ex post**), no matter what you tell them today.

If potential investors believe your firm will undertake this transaction in the future, what will your firm be worth today? The answer is "less than a firm that was committed not to destroy $2 of value in the future." Therefore, you have a choice:

To secure financing at a low cost of capital, entrepreneurs want to commit not to expropriate bond buyers in the future.

- You can avoid debt altogether, although this may hamper you for other reasons explained later.

- You can find a way to commit yourself today not to exploit bondholders in the future.

- You can sell the firm today for a lower net present value. This takes into account your value destruction tomorrow—because everyone realizes that you will be irresistibly tempted to destroy $2 of firm value.

It should be clear to you that you should want to do everything in your power to commit yourself visibly today not to exploit bondholders in the future. Committing yourself can optimize the value of your firm in the future, which in turn maximizes the value of your firm today.

This is one of the most important insights with respect to capital structure, and one worth repeating again and again: The cost of *ex-post* actions against claimants is not only borne by claimants tomorrow, but also internalized by the owners today. Thus, it is in owners' best interests today to commit themselves not to exploit future claimants tomorrow—especially if everyone knows that when the time comes, owners will want to change their minds. The advantage of a firm that is committed to maximizing firm value in the future is that it can obtain a better price for its claims (e.g., a lower interest rate for its bonds) today. Therefore, it is the firm itself that has the incentive to try to find ways to commit itself today (ex ante) to treating claimants well in the future (ex post).

The conceptual basis of capital structure theory: Future behavior and events impact corporate value and costs of capital today.

From a financial perspective, the ex-ante capital structure that results in the highest firm value today is the optimal capital structure. This entire argument is based on the implication that *caveat emptor* ("buyer beware") works: Bond and stock purchasers are forward looking. Moreover, they can only be hurt to the extent that future opportunistic actions by management are unforeseen surprises.

The entrepreneur's goal is to design a capital structure that will maximize firm value today.

In a perfect capital market, what will happen if your current management team cannot commit to avoid such bad future $3-for-$1 exchanges? In this case, another management team that has the ability to restrain itself would value the firm more highly than the current management team. It would purchase the firm and make an immediate profit. The competition among many management teams with this capability would push the firm toward the best capital structure. At the risk of sounding repetitive, the most important point of this chapter is that firms that can commit to doing "the right

Competition among management teams could pressure firms to improve capital structures.

thing" tomorrow (ex post) are worth more today (ex ante). *It is a direct consequence that entrepreneurs should maximize firm value and not just shareholder value.*

IMPORTANT

> - In deciding on an appropriate price to pay, the buyers of financial claims take into account what the firm is likely to do in the future.
>
> - The basis of **optimal capital structure** theory is the insight that entrepreneurs want to maximize the value of the firm in an up-front sale today, and not necessarily the value of equity today or in the future.

The conflict between shareholders and bondholders is usually dwarfed by the conflict between managers and owners.

In our theoretical perfect world, management should be committed to maximizing firm value, not shareholder value. In real life, even in existing companies, these two objectives differ only rarely (and usually only when firms are close to financial distress). Therefore the popular mantra of "shareholder value maximization" is most often synonymous with "total value maximization." The distinction then is useful more as a pedagogical tool: *The best capital structure is the one that maximizes overall value.* In the real world, however, managers are far less conflicted with respect to favoring shareholders at the expense of bondholders than they are conflicted with respect to their own welfare. (These are the agency conflicts that we first discussed in Section 12.8 and that we will take up again in great length in Chapter 24 (Companion)). In some cases, managers' own self-interests may even lead them to take projects that favor creditors over shareholders—a force that mitigates their incentives to expropriate creditors on behalf of the shareholders.

➤ *Agency conflicts, Sect. 12.8, Pg.354.*

Q 16.1. Explain the difference between ex ante and ex post, especially in the capital structure context. Give an example in which the two differ.

Q 16.2. Can an ex-post maximizing choice be bad from an ex-ante perspective? If you could, would you want to restrain yourself from acting in such a way later on?

Q 16.3. If a firm has just learned of a legal loophole that allows it to renege on its obligations to pay back its creditors, should it do so?

16.2 Modigliani and Miller: The Informal Way

A now-famous Miller presentation illustrates the main capital structure insights.

The famous **Modigliani-Miller** (**M&M**) propositions (honored with two Nobel Prizes) are a good start to understanding firms' capital structure decisions. Although the M&M theory involves some complex algebraic calculations, it is actually based on some surprisingly simple ideas. Merton Miller, who later received the Nobel prize in economics, explains them in the following (now famous) acceptance speech for an honorary doctorate at Louvain, Belgium, in 1986:

How difficult it is to summarize briefly the contribution of these papers was brought home to me very clearly last October after Franco Modigliani was awarded the Nobel Prize in Economics in part—but, of course, only in part—for the work in finance. The television camera crews from our local stations in Chicago immediately descended upon me. "We understand," they said, "that you worked with Modigliani some years back in developing these M&M theorems and we wonder if you could explain them briefly to our television viewers." "How briefly?" I asked. "Oh, take 10 seconds," was the reply.

Ten seconds to explain the work of a lifetime! Ten seconds to describe two carefully reasoned articles each running to more than 30 printed pages and each with 60 or so long footnotes! When they saw the look of dismay on my face, they said: "You don't have to go into details. Just give us the main points in simple, commonsense terms."

The main point of the first or cost-of-capital article was, in principle at least, simple enough to make. It said that in an economist's ideal world of complete and perfect capital markets and with full and symmetric information among all market participants, the total market value of all the securities issued by a firm was governed by the earning power and risk of its underlying real assets and was independent of how the mix of securities issued to finance it was divided between debt instruments and equity capital. Some corporate treasurers might well think that they could enhance total value by increasing the proportion of debt instruments because yields on debt instruments, given their lower risk, are, by and large, substantially below those on equity capital. But, under the ideal conditions assumed, the added risk to the shareholders from issuing more debt will raise required yields on the equity by just enough to offset the seeming gain from use of low-cost debt.

Such a summary would not only have been too long, but it relied on short-hand terms and concepts, like perfect capital markets, that are rich in connotations to economists, but hardly so to the general public. I thought, instead, of an analogy that we ourselves had invoked in the original paper. "Think of the firm," I said, "as a gigantic tub of whole milk. The farmer can sell the whole milk as is. Or he can separate out the cream and sell it at a considerably higher price than the whole milk would bring. (Selling cream is the analog of a firm selling low-yield and hence high-priced debt securities.) But, of course, what the farmer would have left would be skim milk, with low butterfat content and that would sell for much less than whole milk. Skim milk corresponds to the levered equity. The M&M proposition says that if there were no costs of separation (and, of course, no government dairy support programs), the cream plus the skim milk would bring the same price as the whole milk."

The television people conferred among themselves for a while. They informed me that it was still too long, too complicated and too academic. "Don't you have anything simpler?" they asked. I thought of another way that the M&M proposition is presented which emphasizes the notion of market completeness and stresses the role of securities as devices for "partitioning" a firm's payoffs in each possible state of the world among the group of its capital suppliers. "Think of the firm," I said, "as a gigantic pizza, divided into quarters. If now, you cut each quarter in half into eighths, the M&M proposition says that you will have more pieces, but not more pizza."

Again there was a whispered conference among the camera crew and the director came back and said: "Professor, we understand from the press release that there were two M&M propositions. Maybe we should try the other one."

He was referring, of course, to the dividend invariance proposition and I know from long experience that attempts at brief statements of that one always cause problems. The term "dividend" has acquired too great a halo of pleasant connotations for people to accept the notion that the more dividends the better might not always be true. Dividends, however, as we pointed out in our article, do not fall like manna from heaven. The funds to pay them have to come from somewhere—either from cutting back on real investments or from further sales (or reduced purchases) of financial instruments. The M&M dividend proposition offered no advice as to which source or how much to tap. It claimed, rather, that once the firm had made its real operating and investment decisions, its dividend policy would have no effect on shareholder value. Any seeming gain in wealth from raising the dividend and giving the shareholders more cash would be offset by the subtraction of that part of their interest in the firm sold off to provide the necessary funds. To convey that notion within my allotted 10 seconds I said: "The M&M dividend proposition amounts to saying that if you take money from your left-hand pocket and put it in your right-hand pocket, you are no better off."

Once again whispered conversation. This time, they shut the lights off. They folded up their equipment. They thanked me for my cooperation. They said they would get back to me. But I knew that I had somehow lost my chance to start a new career as a packager of economic wisdom for TV viewers in convenient 10-second sound bites. Some have the talent for it; and some just don't.

These simple, commonsense analogies certainly do less than full justice to the M&M propositions; crude caricatures or cartoons they may be but they do have some resemblance. So much, in fact, that looking back now after more than 25 years it is hard to understand why they were so strongly resisted at first. One writer—David Durand, the same critic who had so strongly attacked the Markowitz model—even checked out the prices for whole milk, skim milk and cream in his neighborhood supermarket. He found, of course, that the M&M propositions didn't hold exactly; but, of course, empirical relations never do.

Q 16.4. Explain the M&M argument to your 10-year-old sibling, using Merton Miller's analogies.

16.3 Modigliani and Miller: The Formal Way

The point that Modigliani and Miller argued is that under perfect conditions, the total value of all financial securities is the same, regardless of whether the firm is financed by equity or debt, or anything in between.

In a perfect financial market, no financial security adds or subtracts value.

> The Modigliani-Miller propositions state that in a perfect world, the value of a firm is independent of how it is financed. Instead, it is the underlying projects that determine the value of the firm.

IMPORTANT

Modigliani and Miller proved their argument by showing that there would be arbitrage opportunities if the value of the firm depended on how it is financed. Because there should be no arbitrage in real life, it follows that firms should be able to choose any mix of securities without impact on their values. This perfect world that M&M describe relies on the familiar perfect-market assumptions:

M&M must hold due to (lack of) arbitrage.

- There are no transaction costs. In this context, it excludes such frictions as deadweight losses before and in bankruptcy.

- Capital markets are perfectly competitive, with a large number of investors competing to buy and sell securities.

- There are no taxes.

- There are no differences in opinion and information.

You already know that these assumptions are the basics of any study of finance, even though they do not hold *perfectly* in the wild. However, once you understand how the M&M argument works, it becomes easier to understand what happens when these assumptions are violated—and to understand how important such violations can be. Indeed, the next few chapters are all about what happens if the world is *not* perfect.

➤ *Imperfect capital markets, Sect. 10.1, Pg. 243.*

How does the M&M proof work? For simplicity, take it as given that the firm has already decided on what projects to take. (M&M stated this as one of their necessary assumptions, but it turns out not to matter in a fully perfect market.) The firm now considers how to finance its projects. Because we all agree on all current and future projects' expected cash flows and proper discount rates, we agree on the present value of these projects today. Call the value of the projects under a hypothetical best capital structure "PV." (This is almost by definition the present value that the firm's projects can fetch in our perfect capital market, of course.) The M&M proposition says that the present value of the firm's projects must equal the present value of the firm's issued claims today. In other words, if the firm has no debt and issues 100% equity, the equity must sell for the PV of the projects. If the firm instead finances itself by 50% debt and 50% equity, the two together must sell for the same PV. If the firm issues x% debt and

M&M view #1: This is simple if we assume a fixed investment policy for the moment.

(1 – x%) equity, the two together must sell for PV. The capital structure cannot change the project PV.

Actually, this M&M argument should not come as a surprise to you. In Section 6.4, without calling it M&M, you already used it in the context of financing a building. You learned that neither the building value nor the weighted cost of capital were influenced by your debt versus equity mix: The building was worth what it was worth. This is M&M precisely. It is the very same argument.

Another way is to think of M&M financing as a decision that can be made independent of the underlying projects. In this case, net present values are additive. Thus,

$$\text{Firm Value} = \text{Project Value} + \text{Financing Value} \qquad (16.1)$$

The M&M proposition states that any method of financing in a perfect market has an NPV of $0. Neither debt nor equity, nor any combination of debt and equity, can change the present value contribution of financing. Any type of financing is obtained from perfectly competitive investors. For the M&M proposition to break down, it would have to be the case that some kind of financing scheme could add or subtract net present value.

This is so important that it is worthwhile to put this general but verbal-only proof into a more concrete scenario analysis. To accomplish this as simply as possible, let's work with a firm worth $100. Assume that all claims have to offer the same expected rate of return of 10%, which also means that investors are risk neutral. (You will work an example in a risk-averse world in Section 16.4. Risk neutrality is just for convenience, not because it makes any difference.) There are two ways to prove that it makes no difference whether the firm is financed with debt or equity:

The full restructuring (takeover) argument:

Assume that the managers could find—and actually did choose—a capital structure that makes the firm worth $1 less than its PV. For example, assume that the firm is worth PV = $100 under the optimal capital structure of 80% equity and 20% debt; and assume further that the firm is worth only $99 under the capital structure of 50% equity and 50% debt that the firm has actually chosen. Then, all you need to do to get rich is to purchase all old equity and all old debt, that is, the entire firm, for $99. Now issue claims duplicating the optimal capital structure (assumed to be 80% equity and 20% debt). These claims will sell for $100, and you pocket an instant arbitrage profit of $1.

Unfortunately, in a perfect market, you would not be the only one to find this opportunity. After all, all opinions are universally shared. Other arbitrageurs would compete, too. The only price at which no one will overbid you for the right to purchase the firm's current claims is $100. But notice what this means: the value of the old claims is instantly bid up to the firm value under the optimal capital structure. The logical conclusion is that, regardless of the financial structure that managers choose, they can sell their claims for $100, that is, the present value of their projects.

Exhibit 16.1 shows the only logical possibility for a firm whose project will be worth either $60 or $160. The expected future value is $110; the present value is $100. Under hypothetical capital structure LD ("less debt"), the firm issues debt with face value $55. Consequently, bondholders face no uncertainty, and they will pay $55/(1 + 10%) = $50. Equity holders will receive either $5 or $105, and they are thus prepared to pay $55/(1 + 10%) = $50. Simply adding the value of the firm's claims adds up to the same $100. Under hypothetical capital structure MD ("more debt"), the firm issues debt with face value $94. Consequently, bondholders will now receive either $60 or $94, and they are willing to pay $70 today. Equity holders will receive $0 or $66, and they are willing to pay $30 for this privilege. Again, the value of all claims adds to $100.

Any capital structure would be bid up to the value of the hypothetically best capital structure.

	Bad Luck	Good Luck	Future	Today's
Prob:	$1/2$	$1/2$	Expected Value	Present Value
Firm	$60	$160	$110	$100
Capital Structure "Less Debt (LD)": Bond with Face Value = $55				
Debt	$55	$55	$55	$50
Equity	$5	$105	$55	$50
Capital Structure "More Debt (MD)": Bond with Face Value = $94				
Debt	$60	$94	$77	$70
Equity	$0	$66	$33	$30

Exhibit 16.1: *Illustration of the M&M Proposition with Risk-Neutral Investors.* The cost of capital in this example is 10% for all claims. (This is equivalent to assuming the financial markets are risk neutral.) Later in this chapter, you will work out an example in which the cost of capital is higher for riskier projects. The table shows how the value of the firm remains the same, regardless of how it is financed—whether it is 100% equity financed, 50% equity financed, or 30% equity financed. This is because the world is perfect.

The homemade restructuring argument:

Ignoring control rights, here is a "partial purchase and sale" M&M proof.

A more surprising proof relies on the fact that you can relever the claims yourself—you do not need to own the entire firm to do it. The idea is that you do not buy 100% of the firm, but only 1% of the firm. If you buy 1% of all the firm's claims, you receive 1% of the projects' payoffs. You can then repackage and sell claims that imitate the payoffs under the presumably better capital structure for 1% of the firm's higher value, receiving an arbitrage profit of 1% of the value difference.

For example, assume that the firm has chosen capital structure LD, but you and other investors would really, really like capital structure MD. Perhaps you would really, really like to own a claim that pays $0.60 in the bad state and $0.94 in the good state. This would cost you 1% of the bond's $70 price, or $0.70. How can you purchase the existing LD claims to give you the MD-equivalent claim that you prefer *without* any cooperation by the LD-type firm?

You could sell synthetic MD securities if you can purchase worse LD securities.

First, work out what your claims are if you purchase d bonds and e stocks in the LD firm. You will receive payoffs of $d \cdot \$55 + e \cdot \$5$ in the bad scenario, and $d \cdot \$55 + e \cdot \$105$ in the good scenario. You want to end up with $0.60 in the bad scenario, and $0.94 in the good scenario—two equations, two unknowns:

$$\text{Bad Luck} \quad d \cdot \$55 + e \cdot \$5 \quad = \$0.60 \quad d \approx 0.0106$$

$$\text{Good Luck} \quad d \cdot \$55 + e \cdot \$105 \quad = \$0.94 \quad e \approx 0.0034$$

If you purchase 0.0106 LD bonds and 0.0034 of the LD equity, you will end up with $0.60 in the bad state, $0.94 in the good state—exactly the same as an MD firm would have given you! How much would you have to pay to get these payoffs? The cost today would be $d \cdot \$50 + e \cdot \$50 = 0.0106 \cdot \$50 + 0.0034 \cdot \$50 = \$0.70$, exactly the same as your desired payoffs would have cost you if the firm itself had chosen an MD capital structure.

In effect, you have manufactured the capital structure payoffs that you like without the cooperation of the firm itself. By repeating this exercise, you can replicate the payoffs of *any* financial claims in *any* kind of capital structure.

From here, it is an easy step to the M&M argument. If the value of the firm is higher under the MD capital structure than it is under the LD capital structure, you can yourself transform the lower-cost claims under the capital structure into the higher-value claims under a better capital structure. You could sell them, and thereby earn an arbitrage profit. This would contradict the conjecture that the firm value could depend on its capital structure—in a perfect world, this should not be possible.

Beware: This homemade restructuring argument ignores control rights.

However, there is an important caveat to this homemade restructuring proof: Homemade leverage only allows you to obtain the cash flow rights of claims under any different arbitrary, and presumably better, capital structure. *It does not give you the control rights!* It can fail, for example, if a better capital structure has more value *only* if you obtain majority voting control that allows you to fire the management and change policy to what the firm should really be doing.

There are two ways to take care of control rights.

Let me explain in more detail why the "full restructure" argument with control rights is more general. The "homemade restructuring" argument must assume the payoffs are not influenced by the capital structure. What happens if a firm finances itself with securities that are just bad—for example, with securities that have covenants requiring the firm to change management every week? How can a firm be worth as much under this awful capital structure as it would be if it had chosen more sensible securities? There are two ways to handle this issue.

Fixed projects means control rights cannot change project cash flows.

1. You can avoid all control rights–related issues by assuming that the projects and cash flows of the firm are already fixed. Thus, it does not matter whether the management changes every week. Control rights are irrelevant. Even if the firm changed its capital structure, its projects would still generate the same cash flows. This is the path that the M&M 1957 paper took—as we did above, too.

2. You can rely on the full restructuring (takeover) argument, discussed above. It leans more heavily on the perfect market assumption, because you must be able to freely buy and sell enough securities not just to restructure 1% of the firm's payoff promises, but enough securities to take full control of the firm. And this is also the real reason why the M&M argument worked: It assumes that if you own all the shares, you own all the control rights. This allows you to fire the old management and restructure the firm's capital structure optimally. (It also assumes you can undo any damage this bad management may have begun to set into action.) Thus, a firm with the bad capital structure that requires changing management every week could simply not exist.

Full market perfection with full control rights means that firms always take the best projects.

Again, you would not be the only one to recognize that this creates value. Therefore, in this perfect world, firms not only end up with the optimal capital structure but also with the optimal set of projects. They are always priced at exactly what they should be worth under the optimal operating and financing policy that they would indeed be pursuing.

The M&M implications are sometimes misunderstood. Yes, they do state that capital structure cannot influence value. But you should now realize why even an awful capital structure would be worth as much as a good capital structure. It is because the former would instantly disappear—competitive markets would bid to purchase all the (badly aligned) securities and restructure them into something better. Therefore, it is more accurate to think of the M&M proposition as stating not only that all capital structures are worth the same (which is true), but that bad capital structures are immediately eliminated and thus never observed in real life.

The bad capital structures would exist only for a short instant.

In Modigliani and Miller's world of perfect capital markets, arbitrage restrictions force the value of the firm's financial claims to be the same regardless of the firm's mix of debt and equity. A consequence of the perfect financial market assumption is that:

- Managers can make their real operations choices first without paying any attention to their debt and equity choices.

This can suffice for an M&M proof, in which project cash flows are fixed at whatever these real operations will generate. More interestingly, if arbitrageurs can undo what bad managers would otherwise want to commit, then the following holds true:

- Bad *capital structures* would be instantly eliminated by arbitrageurs and are thus never observed.

- Bad *project choices* would be instantly eliminated by arbitrageurs and are thus never observed.

Of course, if the world is *not* perfect, capital structure could matter to the value of the firm.

IMPORTANT

To the extent that the M&M proposition has some degree of realism, it is both good news and bad news. It is good news that you now know where to focus your efforts. You should try to increase the value of your firm's underlying projects—by increasing their expected cash flows, reducing their costs of capital, or both. It is bad news because

Know what and what not to care about!

you now know that you cannot add too much value by fiddling around with how you finance your projects if your financial markets are reasonably close to perfect.

Q 16.5. Under what assumptions does capital structure not matter?

Q 16.6. What does the assumption of risk neutrality "buy" in the M&M proof?

Q 16.7. In the example from Exhibit 16.1, how would you purchase the equivalent of 5% of the hypothetical MD firm's equity if all that was traded were the claims of the LD firm? (Hint: if you have d of the LD debt and e of the LD equity, you should end up with $0 in the bad-luck state and 5% of $66 in the good-luck state. How much d and e should you own? You need to solve two equations for two unknowns.)

Q 16.8. Is the "homemade leverage restructuring" a full proof of the M&M proposition that capital structure is irrelevant? If not, what is missing?

Q 16.9. Under M&M, if contracts cannot be renegotiated, could existing managers destroy shareholder value? Does this change the value of the firm?

16.4 The Weighted Average Cost of Capital (WACC)

Revisit the contingent claims example under risk aversion. Equity now requires a higher expected rate of return.

▶ *Splitting building payoffs into debt and equity, Sect. 6.4, Pg. 134.*

The value of the firm does not depend on the financing in a perfect market. This is equivalent to stating that the overall cost of capital to the firm does not depend on its debt ratio. To show that our example also works when the world is not risk neutral, let's repeat the building with mortgage example from Section 6.4. However, we now allow riskier claims to have higher expected rates of return. We can already draw on your knowledge of net present value, the capital asset pricing model, and capital structure concepts. Another reason why this example is important is that it reintroduces the "weighted average cost of capital" (WACC) in the corporate context. (The next chapter has a generalized WACC formula if corporations pay income tax.)

Risk Aversion and Higher Equity Cost of Capital

All tools learned in Section 6.4 still apply under risk aversion.

The payoff table example applies to firms just as it did to buildings.

When investors are risk averse, riskier claims have to offer higher expected rates of return. Nevertheless, our basic tools remain exactly the same as those in Section 6.4: payoff tables, promised rates of return, and expected rates of return.

From Chapter 15, you know that debt and equity are contingent claims on the underlying project. Although we continue calling this project a building (to keep correspondence with Section 6.4), we now extend the metaphor. Consider the corporation to be the same as an unlevered building, the mortgage the same as corporate debt, the levered building equity ownership the same as corporate equity, and the possibilities of sun and rain as future good or bad scenarios that the firm might face. There are no conceptual differences. However, we do take one shortcut: We ignore all nonfinancial liabilities and pretend that our firm is financed entirely by financial debt and equity.

The parameters of the problem are as follows:

Recap the example parameters.

- The probability of sun is $3/4$; the probability of a rain is $1/4$.

- If it is sunny, the project is worth \$100; if it is rainy the project is worth only \$60.

- The appropriate cost of capital (at which investors are willing to borrow or save) is 20% for the overall project. We retain this cost of capital for the overall project (though not for the debt and equity). You had also computed earlier that the building must then be worth \$75.

As before, the expected payoff on the project is $1/4 \cdot \$60 + 3/4 \cdot \$100 = \$90$, and the price today is $\$90/(1 + 20\%) = \$75$.

The novelty is that we now assume that Treasuries pay a lower *expected* rate of return. This is equivalent to assuming that investors are risk averse. The debt on the building is not exactly risk free, either. Let's assume that you want to raise \$65 today. Your investment banker tells you that you have to offer bond investors an interest rate of 16.92% if you want to raise so much. (Still, it's less than the 20% discount rate on the overall project.) If you do this, how much will you expect to get as the residual equity claimant? And what will be the firm's overall cost of capital? This will be just like a good crossword puzzle—seemingly difficult, but easy step-by-step.

Risk aversion causes *expected* interest rates on debt to be lower than *expected* rates of return on the project.

Step 0: Let's first collect all the inputs you have:

		Financing Scheme All Equity (AE)	Financing Scheme Debt and Equity (DE)	
			Bond promises 16.92%	Levered Equity after Bond
		100% Equity		
$\mathcal{P}rob\,(\text{Sun}) = 3/4$	\$100	\$100		
$\mathcal{P}rob\,(\text{Rain}) = 1/4$	\$60	\$60		
$\mathcal{E}$ Future Payoff		\$90		
Price P Now		\$75	\$65	
$\mathcal{E}$ Rate of Return		20%		

Step 1: Figure out how much the bond holders are really getting. At the 16.92% interest rate, they will get $\$65 \cdot (1 + 16.92\%) \approx \$76$—but only if it's sunny. Otherwise, they get what's left: \$60. Thus, their expected return is

$$\mathcal{E}(\text{Return}) = \underset{\text{Rain}}{1/4 \cdot \$60} + \underset{\text{Sun}}{3/4 \cdot \$76} = \$72$$

and their *expected* rate of return is

$$\mathscr{E}(\text{Rate of Return}) \ = \ \mathscr{E}(r) \ = \ \$72/\$65 - 1 \ \approx \ 10.77\%$$

Add all these figures into the table:

| | | Financing Scheme AE | Financing Scheme DE | |
| | | | Bond | Levered Equity |
		100% Equity	promises $76	after $76 Bond
$\mathscr{P}\!rob(\text{Sun})={}^3/_4$	$100	$100	$76	
$\mathscr{P}\!rob(\text{Rain})={}^1/_4$	$60	$60	$60	
$\mathscr{E}$ Future Payoff		$90	$72	
Price P Now		$75	$65	
$\mathscr{E}$ Rate of Return		20%	10.77%	

Step 2: How much is your levered equity going to get in each state? Here we invoke the perfect market assumptions. Everyone can buy or sell without transaction costs, taxes, or any other impediments. By "absence of arbitrage," the value of the building if financed by a bond plus levered equity must be the same as the value of the building if 100% equity financed. Put differently, if you own all of the bond and levered equity, you own the same thing as the building—and vice versa. Now use the arbitrage condition that the value of the levered equity plus the value of the bond should equal the total building value. The equity gets just what is left over, and the debt and equity together own the firm today. With the debt raising $65 today and the firm being worth $75, your equity must be worth $10. Write all these quantities into the table:

| | | Financing Scheme AE | Financing Scheme DE | |
| | | | Bond | Levered Equity |
		100% Equity	promises $76	after $76 Bond
$\mathscr{P}\!rob(\text{Sun})={}^3/_4$	$100	$100	$76	$24
$\mathscr{P}\!rob(\text{Rain})={}^1/_4$	$60	$60	$60	$0
$\mathscr{E}$ Future Payoff		$90	$72	$18
Price P Now		$75	$65	$10
$\mathscr{E}$ Rate of Return		20%	10.77%	

Step 3: What is the expected rate of return on equity? Easy! Your equity is worth $10 and expects to receive $18. Thus, its rate of return is $18/$10 − 1 = 80%.

| | | Financing Scheme AE | Financing Scheme DE | |
		100% Equity	Bond promises $76	Levered Equity after $76 Bond
$\mathscr{P}rob\,(\,\text{Sun}\,)=3/4$	$100	$100	$76	$24
$\mathscr{P}rob\,(\,\text{Rain}\,)=1/4$	$60	$60	$60	$0
$\mathscr{E}$ Future Payoff		$90	$72	$18
Price P Now		$75	$65	$10
$\mathscr{E}$ Rate of Return		20%	10.77%	**80%**

Given the prices of the two claims and their payoffs in each state, you can work out all the rates of return:

> Compute the riskiness of a dollar investment in each financial instrument.

| | Contingent Rate of Return | | Expected (Appropriate) |
	Rain	Sun	Rate of Return
Unlevered (100% Equity)	$\dfrac{\$60}{\$75}-1=-20\%$	$\dfrac{\$100}{\$75}-1\approx 33\%$	$\dfrac{\$90}{\$75}-1=20\%$
Loan (Bond)	$\dfrac{\$60}{\$65}-1\approx -7.69\%$	$\dfrac{\$70}{\$65}-1\approx 16.92\%$	$\dfrac{\$72}{\$65}-1\approx 10.77\%$
Shares (Levered Equity)	$\dfrac{\$0}{\$10}-1=-100.00\%$	$\dfrac{\$24}{\$10}-1=140\%$	$\dfrac{\$18}{\$10}-1=80\%$

Let's recap: You started knowing only the costs of capital for the firm (20%) and worked out the cost of capital of the firm's bond (10.77%). This allowed you to determine the cost of capital on the firm's levered equity (80%). Neat!

> ➤ *Risk-neutral investors, Exhibit 6.6, Pg. 138.*

As was also the case in the example with risk-neutral investors in Exhibit 6.6, the rates of return to levered equity are riskier (−100% or +140%) than those to unlevered ownership (−20% or +33%), which in turn are riskier than those to the corporate loan (−7.69% or +16.92%). But whereas these risk differences did not affect the expected rates of return in the risk-neutral world, they do in a risk-averse world. The **cost of capital** (the expected rate of return at which you, the owner, can obtain financing) is now higher for levered equity ownership than it is for unlevered ownership, which in turn is higher than it is for loan ownership. Moreover, you could work out *exactly* how high this expected rate of return on levered equity ownership must be. You only needed the "absence of arbitrage" argument in the perfect M&M world: Given the expected rate of return on the building and on the bond, you could determine the expected rate of return on levered equity ownership. (Alternatively, if you had known the appropriate expected rate of return on levered equity ownership and the rate of return on the

> Debt is less risky than unlevered ownership, which is less risky than levered equity ownership.

bond, you could have worked out the appropriate expected rate of return on unlevered ownership. Of course, the exact differences in expected rates of return should ultimately also be governed by some model like the CAPM.)

Q 16.10. In the text, we just stated that levered equity was riskier than ownership which was riskier than the bond. Let's confirm this. Work out the standard deviations of the rates of return for each of the three possible types of claims (full ownership, debt, and levered equity) in the building example in the text. What is their risk-ordering?

Q 16.11. If you can raise $60 in debt at an *expected* rate of return of 5%, what are the payoffs of debt and equity in rainy and sunny states, the appropriate expected rates of return, and the standard deviations?

Q 16.12. A firm can be worth $50 million, $150 million, or $400 million, each with equal probabilities. The firm is financed with one bond, promising to pay $100 million at an interest rate of 5%. If the firm's projects require an appropriate cost of capital of 10%, then what is the firm's equity cost of capital? What is the debt's expected payoff? What is the debt's promised rate of return?

Q 16.13. Assume that you have access to a project worth $100 that you cannot fully finance yourself. Moreover, you have only 20% of the project that you can finance and you need the money back next year, because you will have no other source of income. Can you fund the project?

The WACC Formula (without Taxes)

The WACC is independent of debt and equity distribution.

The **weighted average cost of capital** (**WACC**) is the value-weighted average cost of capital of all the firm's claims. Because the firm value is determined by the assets and is independent of how debt and equity are divided, the same independence should hold true for the cost of capital. Let's check, then, that if the perfect-market arbitrage condition holds—that is, if bonds and stocks together cost the same as the firm—then the cost of capital for the overall firm is the weighted cost of capital of stocks and bonds.

If you know any two costs of capital, you can deduce the third.

The constant WACC implies that the costs of capital of debt, equity, and the overall firm are directly linked. If you know the costs of capital for the debt and the equity, you can infer the cost of capital for the firm. Alternatively, if you know the cost of capital for the firm and the debt, you can infer the cost of capital for the equity. *If you know any two costs of capital, you can compute the third one.*

Here is a line-by-line derivation of the WACC formula.

Let's show this again to translate the numerical example into a formula for the WACC. In either state, the debt and equity together will own the firm:

$$\text{Sun } (^3/_4): \quad \$76 \; + \; \$24 \quad = \$100$$

$$\text{Rain } (^1/_4): \quad \$60 \; + \; \$0 \quad = \$60$$

$$\text{Debt } + \text{ Equity } = \text{ Firm}$$

(I am omitting the time subscripts to avoid clutter.) Therefore, the expected value of debt and equity together must be equal to the expected value of the firm.

$$\$72 \quad + \quad \$18 \quad = \quad \$90$$

$$\mathcal{E}(\,\text{Debt}\,) \;+\; \mathcal{E}(\,\text{Equity}\,) \;=\; \mathcal{E}(\,\text{Firm}\,)$$

Rewrite this in terms of today's values and expected rates of return ($\mathcal{E}(\text{r})$),

$$
\begin{array}{ccccc}
\$72 & + & \$18 & = & \$90 \\
\approx \;\; \$65 \cdot (1 + 10.77\%) & + & \$10 \cdot (1 + 80\%) & \approx & \$75 \cdot (1 + 20\%)
\end{array}
$$

$$
\begin{array}{ccccc}
\mathcal{E}(\,\text{Debt}\,) & + & \mathcal{E}(\,\text{Equity}\,) & = & \mathcal{E}(\,\text{Firm}\,) \\
= \;\text{Debt} \cdot \left[1 + \mathcal{E}(\text{r}_{\text{Debt}})\right] & + & \text{Equity} \cdot \left[1 + \mathcal{E}(\text{r}_{\text{Equity}})\right] & = & \text{Firm} \cdot \left[1 + \mathcal{E}(\text{r}_{\text{Firm}})\right]
\end{array}
$$

In the last row, debt, equity, and firm are now, and expected rates of return are from now to the future. Divide each term by the firm value today (Firm = $75) to express this formula in terms of percentages of firm value:

$$\frac{\$65}{\$75} \cdot (1 + 10.77\%) \quad + \quad \frac{\$10}{\$75} \cdot (1 + 80\%) \quad \approx \quad \frac{\$75}{\$75} \cdot (1 + 20\%)$$

$$\left(\frac{\text{Debt}}{\text{Firm}}\right) \cdot \left[1 + \mathcal{E}(\text{r}_{\text{Debt}})\right] + \left(\frac{\text{Equity}}{\text{Firm}}\right) \cdot \left[1 + \mathcal{E}(\text{r}_{\text{Equity}})\right] = \left[1 + \mathcal{E}(\text{r}_{\text{Firm}})\right]$$

Compute the fractions: Debt/Firm $\approx$ 86.7% and Equity/Firm $\approx$ 13.3%. These are the financing weights of the two securities in the firm *today*. Therefore, you can write this formula as

$$86.7\% \cdot (1 + 10.77\%) \quad + \quad 13.3\% \cdot (1 + 80\%) \quad \approx \quad 1 + 20\%$$

$$\text{w}_{\text{Debt}} \cdot \left[1 + \mathcal{E}(\text{r}_{\text{Debt}})\right] + \text{w}_{\text{Equity}} \cdot \left[1 + \mathcal{E}(\text{r}_{\text{Equity}})\right] = \left[1 + \mathcal{E}(\text{r}_{\text{Firm}})\right]$$

The "1+" cancels on both sides, because 86.7% + 13.3% = 100%. You have just discovered the perfect-market WACC formula:

$$\text{WACC} \;\approx\; 86.7\% \cdot 10.77\% \;+\; 16.7\% \cdot 80\% \;\approx\; 20\%$$

$$\text{WACC} \;=\; \text{w}_{\text{Debt}} \cdot \mathcal{E}(\text{r}_{\text{Debt}}) \;+\; \text{w}_{\text{Equity}} \cdot \mathcal{E}(\text{r}_{\text{Equity}}) \;=\; \mathcal{E}(\text{r}_{\text{Firm}})$$

No one bothers adding the expectation operator in front of the WACC, although this would be more accurate. The next two chapters will explain how WACC must be modified in the presence of corporate income taxes and other perfect-market distortions.

Leverage, Cost of Capital, and Quoted Interest Rates

You now understand how to compute costs of capital. But let's look at a few more trees to understand the forest better. How do shifts in capital structures generally influence individual securities' costs of capital? Return to the original debt-and-equity-only numerical example. In capital structure DE-0, the bond promises $36; in DE-1, it promises $76; and in DE-2, it promises $88. Everything included, we just worked out:

We want to consider different capital structures now.

Medium leverage.

		Financing Scheme AE	Financing Scheme DE-1	
		100% Equity	Bond promises $76	Levered Equity after $76 Bond
$\mathcal{P}rob$ (Sun)=3/4	$100	$100	$76	$24
$\mathcal{P}rob$ (Rain)=1/4	$60	$60	$60	$0
$\mathcal{E}$ Future Payoff		$90	$72	$18
Price P Now		$75	$65	$10
$\mathcal{E}$ Rate of Return		20%	10.77%	80%
Financing Weight		100%	$65/$75 ≈ 87%	$10/$75 ≈ 13%

To generalize, I need to describe how the debt cost of capital varies with leverage.

How would the promised rate of return, the expected rate of return, and the debt-equity ratio change if the firm changed the amount it borrowed? Let's say the firm has explored the capital markets and learned that in capital structure DE-2, a bond promising $88 in debt payments would raise $70 today. (Trust me that this is consistent with the same economy-wide risk-aversion that we used in the previous example.) The payoff table is now

		Scheme AE	Scheme DE-2	
		100% Equity	Bond promises $88	Levered Equity after $88
$\mathcal{P}rob$ (Sun)=3/4	$100	$100	$88	$12
$\mathcal{P}rob$ (Rain)=1/4	$60	$60	$60	$0
$\mathcal{E}$ Future Payoff		$90	$81	$9
Price P Now		$75	$70	$5
$\mathcal{E}$ Rate of Return		20%	15.71%	80%
Financing Weight		100%	93.3%	6.7%

Finally, let's determine what happens if debt promising $36 can be raised at a price of $35 today. This debt is risk free.

		Scheme AE	Scheme DE-0	
		100% Equity	Bond promises $36	Levered Equity after $36
$\mathcal{P}rob$ (Sun)=3/4	$100	$100	$36	$64
$\mathcal{P}rob$ (Rain)=1/4	$60	$60	$36	$24
$\mathcal{E}$ Future Payoff		$90	$36	$54
Price P Now		$75	$35	$40
$\mathcal{E}$ Rate of Return		20%	2.86%	35%
Financing Weight		100%	46.7%	53.3%

Putting this together, here are the capital-structure tradeoffs:

Many different leverages.

	Debt Promises		Expected Rate of Return			Weight	
	Payoff	Interest Rate	Debt	Equity	Firm	Debt	Equity
No Debt	$0	2.86%	2.86%	20%	20%	0.0%	100.0%
Low Debt	$36	2.86%	2.86%	35%	20%	46.7%	53.3%
Med Debt	$76	16.92%	10.77%	80%	20%	86.7%	13.3%
High Debt	$88	25.71%	15.71%	80%	20%	93.3%	6.7%
All Debt	$100	33.33%	20.00%	-	20%	100.0%	0.0%

I also added that when you borrow nothing, your marginal interest rate is still the risk-free rate; and if you promise $100, you expect to deliver $75—the debt *is* the firm.

How Bad Are Mistakes?

If all Securities are Riskier, is the Firm also Riskier?

Many practitioners commit a serious logical mistake. They argue as follows:

1. If the firm takes on more debt, the debt becomes riskier and the cost of capital for the debt ($\mathscr{E}(r_{Debt})$) increases.

2. If the firm takes on more debt, the equity becomes riskier and the cost of capital for the equity ($\mathscr{E}(r_{Equity})$) increases.

3. Because the firm consists of only debt and equity, the firm also becomes riskier when the firm takes on more debt, which must mean that the firm's cost of capital ($\mathscr{E}(r_{Firm})$) increases. A financier may even want to reduce the firm's debt in order to avoid such increases in volatility of the firm.

The first two statements are correct. With more debt, the cost of capital on debt increases because it becomes riskier: In corporate default, the debt is less likely to receive what it was promised. The equity also becomes riskier: The cost of capital on equity rises, because in financial default, which is now more likely to occur, more cash goes to the creditors before equity holders receive anything.

But the final conclusion—"the firm also becomes riskier"—is wrong. When the firm takes on more debt, the weight of the (safer) debt (w_{Debt}) increases and the weight of the (riskier) equity ($w_{Equity} = 1 - w_{Debt}$) decreases. Because the cost of capital for debt ($\mathscr{E}(r_{Debt})$) is lower than the cost of capital for equity ($\mathscr{E}(r_{Equity})$), the weighted sum remains the same. Confirm this:

$$\text{Low Debt}\quad 46.7\% \cdot 2.86\% \;+\; 53.5\% \cdot 35\% \;\approx\; 20\%$$

$$\text{Med Debt}\quad 86.7\% \cdot 10.77\% \;+\; 13.3\% \cdot 80\% \;\approx\; 20\%$$

$$\text{High Debt}\quad 93.3\% \cdot 15.71\% \;+\; 6.7\% \cdot 80\% \;\approx\; 20\%$$

Check that statements 1 and 2 are correct and that statement 3 is incorrect: The costs of capital for both debt and equity are (weakly) higher when the firm has more debt, but the overall cost of capital for the firm has not changed. In the perfect M&M world, the overall cost of capital is independent of the mix between debt and equity.

One more factoid: Expected (i.e., required) rates of return on equity can be very high if leverage is very high.

A final note—for high debt ratios, equity may well have to offer seemingly astronomical *expected* rates of returns. In our example, if the 20%-discount-rate firm raises $76 in debt, it has to offer 80% to the equity. This is common—for high leverage ratios, equity costs of capital often seem astronomical. This is not usury. It is simply fair. Coincidentally, when the equity *expected* rate of return is high, it is also often the case that the debt's *promised* [stated] interest rate is much higher than its expected interest rate.

Graphing Financing Schemes against Leverage Ratios

The binomial example "in pictures."

I have done the calculations for many more debt weights, and graphed the expected rates of return to both debt and equity in the upper graph in Exhibit 16.2. (This is the "forest" view I wanted to get to.) When leverage ratio is low, the debt is risk-free. Yet more debt still increases the risk of the equity and thus the equity's cost of capital. Eventually, with enough debt, the debt itself becomes risky, too. In this region, more debt means more risk for creditors, and thus a higher required rate of return on debt. (The promised rate of return is of course above the expected rate of return.)

A more normal example "in pictures."

In the real world, the plot can look a little different, because most projects do not have "binomial" but more "normally distributed" (bell-shaped) payoffs. This is the lower graph. In fact, it may well be possible that the firm may end up being worth nothing. Thus, it is impossible for the firm to issue truly risk-free debt. However, over a wide range, debt is "practically" risk-free, because the firm is very likely to be worth enough to pay its debt. Thus, the probability of default is tiny for modest debt loads. Eventually, as the debt-ratio of the firm increases ever more, the debt's expected rate of return must increase noticeably, too. And, again, the cost of equity rises with the fraction of debt of the firm over the whole domain. (Unlike the earlier graph, there is no sudden end to the riskiness of equity.) *Importantly, in both plots, the WACC is constant, regardless of the firm's mix of equity and debt.*

How Bad Are Mistakes?

Can the Equity's Cost of Capital be Lower than the Rate that the Firm is Paying to its Creditors?

You already know that the equity cost of capital is always higher than the debt cost of capital. So, can the equity's cost of capital be lower than the interest rate that the firm is paying on its debt?

Of course it can! Promised rate of returns have nothing to do with expected rate of returns. They can be anything. In the real world, the financially naïve often fixate on this promised rate of return and do not focus enough on the expected rate of return. They then make the logical mistake of comparing the equity expected rate of return (e.g., from the CAPM) to the interest *quoted* by the bank. This is bad mistake.

Q 16.14. Continue with Q 16.11, in which the firm raised $60 in debt by promising to pay $64. What are the debt and equity investment weights? Is the WACC 20% for this capital structure?

Binomial Payoffs (as in the text)

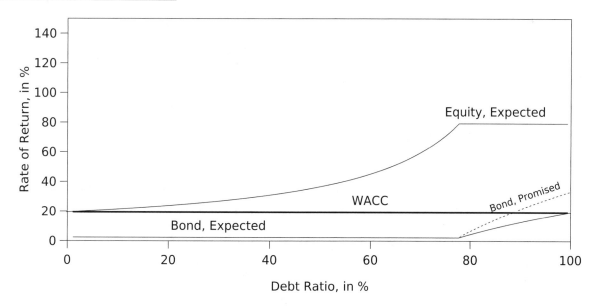

Normally Distributed Payoffs

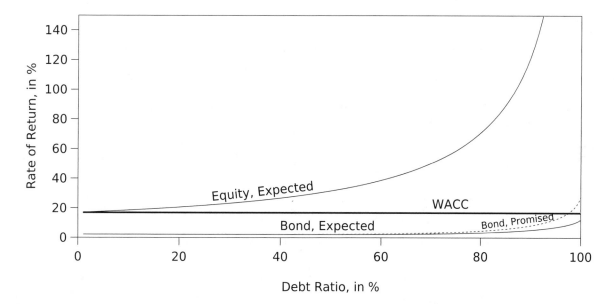

Exhibit 16.2: *The Cost of Capital in a Perfect World.* The top graph illustrates the binomial example worked out in the table in the text. Until the debt ratio reaches around 80% of the firm value, the debt is risk-free. However, more debt still increases the risk of equity, and therefore its expected rate of return. For debt ratios higher than 80%, the debt is risky and has to offer a higher promised and expected rate of return. The lower graph plots a similar figure for a firm that has normally distributed payoffs. In both cases, the WACC is *always* the same, regardless of the mix of debt and equity.

Q 16.15. In the sun/rain example, if the firm can raise $62.50 in debt by promising $70, show that the WACC is still 20%.

Q 16.16. Compared to hypothetical firm B, hypothetical firm A has both a higher cost of capital for its debt and a higher cost of capital for its equity. Does this necessarily imply that firm A has a higher overall cost of capital than firm B?

Leverage, Earnings Per Share, and Price/Earnings Ratios

EPS is meaningless.

What is the effect of debt on earnings per share (EPS)? This is a meaningless question, because EPS depends not on the firm but on the number of shares. The same capital structure can exist under different numbers of shares. Equity can be worth $7 million with 1 million shares valued at $7/share (an expected EPS of $0.70/share) or with 100,000 shares valued at $70/share (an expected EPS of $7/share). Any EPS figure is possible.

P/E is a more sensible ratio. It can go up or down. Ultimately, P/E is not important, though—only value is.

A more meaningful question is how leverage influences P/E ratios. I had already sneaked this into Section 14.3, but you had to trust me blindly that debt offers a lower expected rate of return than equity. The examples in that section satisfied the M&M constant WACC —and showed that more debt can sometimes cause lower P/E ratios (especially in value firms) and sometimes cause higher P/E ratios (especially in high-growth firms).

➤ *Debt adjustment for P/E ratios, Sect. 14.3, Pg. 433.*

16.5   The Big Picture: How to Think of Debt and Equity

IMPORTANT

> In a perfect M&M world with only financial debt and equity:
>
> **The Value of Claims**
> - The value of the firm is independent of cash flow or control rights, because arbitrageurs can—and always will—rearrange claims into an optimal structure.
> - An "absence of arbitrage" relationship ensures that the sum-total value of all its claims is equal to the total underlying project value.
> - Claims "partition" the firm's payoffs in future states of the world. For financial securities, this is often contractually arranged at inception.
>
> **The Risk of Claims**
> - Levered equity is the residual claim after the debt has been satisfied. It is riskier than full ownership, which in turn is riskier than the debt.
>
> **The Cost of Capital**
> - Riskier claims almost always have to offer higher expected rates of return. (The exceptions are pathological cases, in which the market beta is very negative.) Normally, levered equity has to offer a higher expected rate of return than outright ownership, which in turn has to offer a higher expected rate of return than debt and other liabilities.

- The *quoted* interest rate on financial debt can be not only much higher than its expected rate of return, but also much higher than the *expected* rate of return on equity.

- Assuming that the firm is financed only with debt and equity, the absence of arbitrage implies that the capitalization-weighted average expected rate of return (WACC) is:

$$\text{WACC} = w_{\text{Equity}} \cdot \mathcal{E}(r_{\text{Equity}}) + w_{\text{Debt}} \cdot \mathcal{E}(r_{\text{Debt}}) = \mathcal{E}(r_{\text{Firm}}) \quad (16.2)$$

  where the weights w_{Equity} and w_{Debt} are the values of equity and debt when quoted as a fraction of the overall firm value *today*.

- The project's WACC remains the same, no matter how the firm is financed. It is determined by the underlying projects.

Q 16.17. Is a firm making a mistake if it uses a weighted average cost of capital that is lower than the interest rate it has to pay to the bank?

Q 16.18. If a firm has a 5% cost of debt capital, a 10% cost of project capital, and a 20% cost of equity capital, what is its debt-equity ratio?

Q 16.19. How can it be possible for a firm with a positive cost of project capital to have a negative cost of equity capital? How high can the cost of project capital be in this case?

16.6 Nonfinancial Liabilities and the Cost of Capital

In Exhibit 15.3, you saw that IBM's total liabilities were about three times as large as its financial debt. This is typical for many U.S. companies. Does the M&M proposition—that firm value is not influenced by capital structure and thus that capital structure is irrelevant—still apply in the presence of nonfinancial claims?

Firms have many nonfinancial liabilities.

➤ *IBM, Exhibit 15.3, Pg. 475.*

Value Irrelevance

The argument is actually somewhat subtle. Start by recalling the logic of the M&M perfect-market argument: The value of the firm's financing does not depend on how it is divided between debt and equity. The proof was by contradiction. If a firm instituted a capital structure with a dumb debt covenant—that is, one that forced it to pay all its future cash flows to charity—could this firm be worth less than a more intelligently financed firm? No! A horde of arbitrageurs would immediately compete to purchase all these bad claims (at their presumably lower value) and undo the dumb capital structure. Therefore, this dumb capital structure could not trade for a lower price than the optimal capital structure. It would have the same value as the best capital structure, but it would

The logic of the perfect-market M&M proposition.

exist for only half an instant before it was undone. The perfect market provided two aspects important to the M&M argument:

1. The capital market is perfectly elastic. All financial claims that the firm could dream up would be snatched up by a perfect capital market at an appropriate price.

2. There is no link between the firm's operations and the financial claims that a firm is able to take on. (In the original M&M paper, the authors assumed that all operating decisions were already made.)

These two assumptions can fail on nonfinancial liabilities. Let me give you two respective examples:

1. Income tax liabilities: If you do not pay your taxes until April 15 (tax day), you can use your tax liability for your own investment purposes. Your effective cost of capital on these funds is zero. However, you cannot raise more funds at will at this same zero interest rate from Uncle Sam. You also cannot return this financing to the provider at a fair market cost of capital. If you prepay your taxes, Uncle Sam will not credit you with interest for early payment.

2. Trade credit: It is not uncommon for suppliers to give firms 0% financing as trade credit. This is *not* the perfect-market appropriate price for financing and you would want to take as much of this trade credit as possible. However, this trade credit is usually only available to you if you purchase more of the underlying good. Your supplier would not provide you more trade credit in order to pay your rent if you did not buy his goods. Consequently, if you were to buy your supplier's goods, a capital structure with more trade credit would be better than one without. Conversely, you may not even buy these goods without trade credit.

Now think back to how the value of your firm was determined by the net present values of your project. Formula 16.1 stated that

➤ *Firm=Project+Financing,*
Formula 16.1, Pg. 498.

$$\text{Firm Value} = \text{Project Value} + (\text{Trade Credit}) \text{ Financing Value}$$

Under M&M, the financing NPV was always zero. However, your trade credit in this example would be a positive-NPV project in itself. The consequence is that you might choose different real operations (purchasing the supplier's goods) if you were financed with rather than without trade credit. The separation between operations and financing has just broken. On the contrary, if trade credit is a bargain, it now makes sense to think of a bundle that includes the project and the project-specific financing that comes with it.

It is possible to put forth a perfect-market scenario for operations that unlinks their nonfinancial claims in order to get a full M&M proposition also for nonfinancial claims. However, this is not particularly useful for two reasons: First, we are interested primarily in finance, not in operations. Second, nonfinancial markets are generally far from perfect—much more so than financial markets—and many operational choices are irreversible once made. With such a large discrepancy between the necessary perfect-market conditions and reality, such a proposition would not be very helpful in thinking about real-world problems. But you do need to understand how to think of the firm's financing claims in a broader real-world perspective. Fortunately, this is easy.

Margin notes:

Nonfinancial financing can add value. Thus, M&M breaks down. In effect, its financing now takes on the characteristics of its nonfinancial market imperfections.

M&M for operations and nonfinancial liabilities would be less plausible and not very useful.

> **IMPORTANT**
>
> - The M&M proposition is helpful for thinking about the division of claims into debt and equity. This is because the markets for raising financing through these claims is fairly perfect, and the firm pays fair prices either way.
>
> - Thus, for financial claims, managers can think about financing and operational choices separately.
>
> - The M&M proposition is not helpful for thinking about the division of claims between financial and non-financial liabilities. This is because the markets for raising financing through non-financial liabilities are rarely perfect. Such financing, e.g., trade credit or delayed tax payments, often offer better deals but are available only together with certain project choices.
>
> - Thus, for non-financial claims, managers need to consider financing and operational choices together.

Q 16.20. In a world of perfect financial markets, is the value of the firm independent of how it is financed if there are also nonfinancial liabilities?

Q 16.21. In a world of perfect financial markets, is the value of the firm's financial claims independent of how it is financed?

The Marginal and Weighted Average Costs of Capital

There is one more important issue that you did not yet have to worry about in the M&M world. The **marginal cost of capital** applies to the next dollar of capital the firm would raise; the **average cost of capital** is the financing cost for all of the firm's existing projects. As a manager, you ultimately want to learn your projects' marginal costs of capital, because these rates are what you would compare to your projects' marginal rates of return. The firm's average cost of capital is really quite irrelevant. Fortunately, under M&M, the two are the same. Thus, if you compute the weighted average cost of capital, you know the marginal cost of capital for raising one more dollar.

Perfect world: The average cost of capital is the marginal cost of capital.

Unfortunately, in the real and imperfect world, the average and marginal costs of capital can be different. For example, it could be that the first dollar of financing obtained by the firm is internal (or trade credit) and thus cheaper than the billionth dollar of financing if the firm had to search for investors first. Thus, when you compute a WACC from a firm's existing capital providers (and published in the financial data), be aware that even if the project is typical for the firm, it may only be your average cost of capital—not the marginal cost of capital that you may need.

Real world: The two costs of capital can be different.

Now recall that the firm's weighted average cost of capital is

The natural definition of the firm's WACC with nonfinancial liabilities.

Firm's Average Cost of Capital = Sum of Value-Weighted Claims' Costs of Capital

In the context of a firm financed only with financial capital (debt and equity),

$$\text{Firm's Average Cost of Capital} = w_{\text{Debt}} \cdot \mathcal{E}(r_{\text{Debt}}) + w_{\text{Equity}} \cdot \mathcal{E}(r_{\text{Equity}})$$

➤ *WACC with nonfinancial liabilities, Sect. 22.A (Companion), Pg. ≈152.*

The original M&M proposition states that this cost of financial capital is not affected by shifting w_{Debt} to w_{Equity}. A convenient way to think about the cost of capital is that neither debt nor equity are positive-NPV or negative-NPV projects. Thus, shifting between them does not change the value of the firm.

Unfortunately, most nonfinancial liabilities are not zero NPV.

In the presence of nonfinancial liabilities (NFL), the definition of the firm's weighted average cost of capital expands into

$$\text{Firm's Average Cost of Capital} = w_{\text{NFL}} \cdot \mathcal{E}(r_{\text{NFL}}) + w_{\text{FL}} \cdot \mathcal{E}(r_{\text{FL}}) + w_{\text{Equity}} \cdot \mathcal{E}(r_{\text{Equity}})$$

where FL are the financial liabilities. Unfortunately, you cannot expand or contract the nonfinancial liabilities at will. Consequently, even if you finance and operate your projects optimally, you will probably not face the same risk-adjusted cost of capital on the margin for your nonfinancial liabilities as you will for your financial liabilities. Think about income tax liabilities. They have an interest rate of 0% if you delay paying before April 15 (the tax-due date). But you cannot expand the amount borrowed from Uncle Sam. Thus, you have a fixed and nonexpandable pool of financing at a cost of capital of 0% until you reach your tax liabilities, and an infinite cost of capital thereafter. Put differently, your average cost of capital would increase if you shifted financing from w_{NFL} to w_{Debt} or w_{Equity} by paying your taxes unnecessarily early.

Nonfinancial liabilities should be used until their costs of capital reach those of the financial claims.

The firm's best financing strategy now is to select the lowest-cost marginal source of financing.

Nonfinancial sources of funding tied to the firm: Step up the ladder.

- If your source of financing is tied to the firm (but not to particular projects), it may not influence your selection of projects. In this case, you should first finance projects with the lowest cost of capital (e.g., delay paying income taxes and/or pensions) before you proceed to more expensive sources of financing. Eventually, once you have gone up the ladder of financing costs, you reach the cost of financing via financial claims. Assuming debt and equity exist in a perfect capital market, you can then raise as much capital as you wish at their appropriate marginal costs of capital.

Nonfinancial sources of funding tied to the project: Potentially include NPV of nonfinancial funds in the project.

- If your cheapest source of financing is tied to a particular project, it may be best to include it in the costs and benefits of the project. For example, if a retail branch can be financed with trade credit from suppliers, and if this is cheaper than financial capital, then you could count the trade-credit NPV as part of the retail store project NPV. If trade credit is not cheaper, you would not use it and rely on the perfect capital market instead. (In the real world, it may also be difficult to measure the cost of capital. For example, what is your cost of capital for accounts payable, given that delaying payment can cost you goodwill among your suppliers?)

Note that in both cases, you use the cheapest nonfinancial sources of funds until you reach the cost of your financial capital. At this point, you rely solely on the perfect-market financial capital as your source of marginal funding. The financial cost of capital then becomes your firm's marginal cost of capital.

IMPORTANT

- If a source of low-cost (nonfinancial) financing is tied to a specific project, it is usually convenient to consider it as part of the project. You would include the financing's net present value in the project's return.

- If financing is not tied to specific projects, firms should first use up all sources of capital that are cheaper than what the financial capital markets are demanding.

- If the financial capital markets are perfect, and *after* the firm has already exhausted all cheaper sources of financing from the imperfect nonfinancial markets, then the firm's *marginal* cost of capital is determined by the cost of capital of debt and equity. In other words, for a firm that has optimized its nonfinancial sources of funding, the plain WACC formula holds,

$$\text{Optimized Firm's Marginal Cost of Capital} = \text{Firm's Cost of Financial Capital}$$

$$= w_{\text{Debt}} \cdot \mathcal{E}(r_{\text{Debt}}) + w_{\text{Equity}} \cdot \mathcal{E}(r_{\text{Equity}})$$

You would compare this marginal cost of financial capital to the rate of return of your marginal project.

- You can still use the original M&M proposition, but only within the context of financial claims—that is, the value of the firm's *financial* claims is indifferent to whether the firm is financed by debt or equity.

- This *marginal* cost of *financial* capital is also the *average* cost of *financial* capital in a perfect capital market. However, it is decidedly *not* the firm's *overall average* cost of capital. The firm's average cost of capital is lower, because the nonfinancial financing that the firm would accept would have to come with a lower cost of capital.

Again, don't get too carried away. The M&M propositions are helpful only for thinking about the subject of capital structure. They are not intended to be realistic. They are thought experiments. In the real world, capital structure can matter, and you have to think about how your cost of capital changes with different capital structures, whether it is financial or nonfinancial claims. This is the subject of the next chapters.

Don't think these propositions are too realistic.

Q 16.22. If you observe a firm with nonfinancial claims that have a zero marginal cost of capital (such as delayed income tax obligations), does it make sense to compute a cost of capital based only on the firm's financial capital (debt and equity)?

Summary

This chapter covered the following major points:

- Managers should want to maximize firm value, not shareholder value. If they do not, they would lose value. In a perfect market, managers who do not act in this way would be replaced with managers who do.

- Entrepreneurs have an incentive to set up a capital structure that maximizes firm value, not equity value. This is because capital providers know that entrepreneurs later would want to behave opportunistically.

- The Modigliani-Miller (M&M) capital structure proposition states that it makes no difference in a perfect market whether a firm finances itself with debt or equity.

    - Competitive arbitrageurs can buy all cash flow and control rights if they purchase all debt and equity.

    - Arbitrageurs can instantly eliminate and undo any bad capital structure choices (and/or any bad project choices).

    - Arbitrageurs would compete to bid up the value of any bad capital structure to the value of the firm under the optimal capital structure (and/or optimal operating policy).

    - The value of all claims under *any* capital structure is therefore that of the value under the *best* capital structure.

    - The firm's cost of capital is therefore invariant to the split between debt and equity. It is always equal to the same weighted average cost of capital (WACC).

An even simpler version assumes that project choices were already fixed and are now immutable. The M&M propositions are interesting not because they are realistic, but because they are benchmarks that point out when capital structure (and/or operating policy) would not matter.

- More debt does not imply that the overall cost of capital increases, even though both debt and equity become riskier.

- The bank may demand an interest rate that is higher than the expected cost of capital on the equity. This does not mean that the cost of debt capital is higher than the cost of equity capital.

- The CAPM is compatible with the M&M perfect-market point of view. It can provide costs of capital for financial debt and equity. However, it cannot provide costs of capital for other liabilities that do not originate in a perfectly competitive market, such as tax obligations. Such loans could even be interest-free.

- The marginal and average costs of capital are the same for claims that arise in a perfect market.

- Nonfinancial liabilities usually do not arise in a perfect capital market. Thus, their average costs of capital are often lower than their marginal costs of capital.

- When cheap financing (such as special trade credit) is tied to a particular project, it is often convenient to combine it with the project.

- If an optimizing firm has exhausted all its lower-cost nonfinancial sources of funding, then the infinitely elastic perfect capital markets' financial funding becomes the marginal source of capital.

Preview of the Chapter Appendix in the Companion

The appendix to this chapter is conceptual. It shows that the CAPM, WACC, and NPV all seamlessly fit together. There are no inconsistencies between them. (I used this when I made up the required costs of capital in the WACC example for different leverage ratios.)

In the Appendix

Keywords

Average cost of capital, 515.   Cost of capital, 505.   Ex ante, 493.   Ex post, 493.   Fiduciary duty, 492. M&M, 494.   Marginal cost of capital, 515.   Modigliani-Miller, 494.   Optimal capital structure, 494. Shareholder wealth maximization, 492.   Supervisory board, 492.   WACC, 506.   Weighted average cost of capital, 506.

Answers

Q 16.1 Ex ante means "before the fact"; ex post means "after the fact." To the extent that the original owner-entrepreneur can set up a situation (charter) that encourages best (i.e., from the perspective of the firm) ex-post behavior, the ex-ante value (for which the firm can be sold right now) is maximized. However, if the situation (charter) is such that the owner himself or his managers will later try to expropriate capital providers, or such that the managers will make bad decisions in the future, then the ex-ante value today for which the firm can be sold would be less.

Q 16.2 Yes, an ex-post maximizing choice can be bad from an ex-ante perspective. The example of the $3-for-$1 transaction in the text shows that you would want to restrain yourself.

Q 16.3 Clearly, managers in the future would not want to pay back debt if they can weasel out of it. However, such behavior could have repercussions for their future attempts to borrow money. The firm would have to weigh the gains from reneging on this particular loan (and the ethical implications of doing so!) against the costs of a lost creditor relationship and thus more expensive credit in the future.

Q 16.4 The idea is to explain it really simply. Milk, cream, pizza, and pockets are handy metaphors.

Q 16.5 Capital structure does not matter in a perfect market: No transaction costs, perfect competition, no taxes, and no differences in opinion and information.

Q 16.6 The risk-neutrality assumption really buys nothing. We do not need it. We only use it because it makes the tables simpler to compute.

Q 16.7 Work out the following:

$$\text{Bad Luck:} \qquad d \cdot \$55 + e \cdot \$5 = \$0 \cdot 5\%$$
$$\text{Good Luck:} \qquad d \cdot \$55 + e \cdot \$105 = \$66 \cdot 5\%$$
$$\text{(subtract)} \implies (\$105 - \$5) \cdot e = (\$66 - \$0) \cdot 5\%$$
$$\implies \qquad d = -0.003 \ , \ e = +0.033$$

You would purchase 3.3% of the LD equity and sell (issue) 0.3% of the equivalent of the LD debt. The equity would cost you $e \cdot \$50 = \$1.65$; the debt issue would give you $0.15 in proceeds. Your net cost would thus be $1.50—as it should be, because purchasing 5% of the MD equity would have cost you 5% of $30, which also comes to $1.50.

Q 16.8 The "homemade leverage restructuring" argument is not full proof, because it ignores the potentially important real-world aspect of control rights.

Q 16.9 Yes, they can destroy shareholder value. If existing management gives away debt claims at too low a price, creditors will own more of the firm having paid less money. New management cannot undo this, because the contract cannot be renegotiated. Giving away debt too cheaply would not change the value of the firm. It only changes who owns more or less of the firm.

Q 16.10 You need to recall the standard deviation formula (Formula 8.2) on Page 180. First compute the deviations from the mean, and their squares

| | Deviation | | Squared | |
	$1/4$	$3/4$	$1/4$	$3/4$
Own	−40%	+13%	1,600%%	169%%
Bond	−18.46%	+6.15%	340.8%%	37.82%%
Lev Eq	−180%	+60%	32,400%%	3,600%%

Thus, the standard deviations are

Own $\sqrt{1/4 \cdot 1{,}600\%\% + 3/4 \cdot 1{,}69\%\%}$ ≈ 23%

Bond $\sqrt{1/4 \cdot 340.8\%\% + 3/4 \cdot 37.82\%\%}$ ≈ 11%

Lev Eq $\sqrt{1/4 \cdot 32{,}400\%\% + 3/4 \cdot 3{,}600\%\%}$ ≈ 104%

The bond is safest, the levered equity is riskiest, and full ownership is in between.

Q 16.11 The solution is (the two new inputs are in blue):

| | | AE | DE | |
			Bond promises $64	Equity after $64
$\mathcal{P}rob$ (Sun)=$3/4$		$100	$64	$36
$\mathcal{P}rob$ (Rain)=$1/4$		$60	$60	$0
$\mathcal{E}$ Future Payoff		$90	$63	$27
Price P Now		$75	$60	$15
$\mathcal{E}(r)$		20%	5%	80%

The standard deviation of the rate of return on debt (either 0% with $1/4$ probability, or 6.67% with $3/4$ probability) is ≈ 2.9%. The standard deviation of the rate of return on equity (either −100% or +140%) is about ≈ 104%.

Q 16.12 To work out the firm's equity cost of capital and the debt's promised rate of return, imitate the payoff tables from the text (dollars are in millions):

| | | AE | DE | |
			Bond prom. $100m	Equity after $100m
$1/3$	$50	$50	$50	$0
$1/3$	$150	$150	$100	$50
$1/3$	$400	$400	$100	$300
$\mathcal{E}$ Future Payoff		$200	$83.33	$116.67
Price P Now		$181.82	$79.37	$102.45
$\mathcal{E}(r)$		10%	5%	13.88%

The debt's promised rate of return is $100/$79.37 − 1 ≈ 26%.

Q 16.13 Most likely, you can fund the project. In a perfect market, you can hold low-risk debt that has first dibs on all proceeds.

Q 16.14 The debt weight is $60/$75 = 80%, the equity weight is 20%. Recall that the debt had an expected rate of return of 5%, the equity of 80%. Thus, the WACC is 80% · 5% + 20% · 80% = 20%. Indeed, this is still the same.

Q 16.15 Debt that raises $62.50 and promises $70 offers a quoted rate of return of 12%. However, if it rains, the debt pays only $60, which is −4%. Thus, its expected rate of return is $1/4 \cdot$ (−4%) + $3/4 \cdot$ (12%) = 8%. Its weight in the capital structure is $62.50/$75 ≈ 83.3%. The equity receives $30 or $0, for an expected rate of return of 80%. Thus, it is worth $12.50 today, which is $12.50/$75 ≈ 16.7% of the firm value today. The WACC is 83.3% · 8% + 16.7% · 80% ≈ 20%.

Q 16.16 No. Firm A need not have a higher overall cost of capital than firm B. The example in the "How Bad Are Mistakes?" section illustrates this fallacy. The relative weights of debt and equity also change, therefore falsifying this claim.

Q 16.17 No! It is quite possible that the weighted average cost of capital is lower than the interest rate that it has to pay to the bank. After all, the bank rate is promised, not expected.

Q 16.18 In a perfect market, the cost of capital under a 100% equity financing strategy with cost 10% must be the same as it is under a mixed debt and equity strategy. Therefore, $w_{Debt} \cdot 0.05 + (1 − w_{Debt}) \cdot 0.2 = 0.1 \Longrightarrow w_{Debt} = 2/3$. This firm is 2 parts debt, 1 part equity, so the debt-equity ratio is 2.

Q 16.19 Though obscure, a firm with a very negative beta can indeed be in this situation. It must be the case then that the firm's project cost of capital is lower than the risk-free rate. (For example, a firm may have 90% debt at the risk-free rate of 5%, 10% equity at a rate of −1%, and a WACC of 4.4%—this is indeed less than the risk-free rate.)

Q 16.20 No, the value of the firm may be linked to its financing, because its financing is linked to its projects. You also need to break the link between nonfinancial liabilities and operations.

Q 16.21 Yes, the value of the firm's *financial* claims is independent of how the financial claims are arranged in an M&M world. This is because no financial security offers a positive or negative NPV—all financial securities are fairly priced.

Q 16.22 Yes, it may still make sense to compute a cost of capital based only on the firm's financial capital (debt and equity) if the firm has exhausted all its nonfinancial low-cost sources of capital. It is then an estimate of the marginal cost of another dollar of capital raised, which is now financial capital.

End of Chapter Problems

Q 16.23. Explain when "shareholder maximization" is the right goal and when it is the wrong goal for management.

Q 16.24. Comment on the following statement: "New shareholders would be worse off if management destroyed wealth by capturing the board and paying themselves much higher executive compensation without better performance."

Q 16.25. In a world that is not perfect but risk neutral, assume that the firm has projects worth $100 in the down-state, $500 in the up-state. The cost of capital for projects is 25%. However, if you could finance it with 50-50 debt, the cash flow rights alone are enough to make the cost of capital a lower 20%. Managers are intransigent and do not want to switch to this new capital structure. You only have $60 of capital and cannot borrow more to take over the firm. What can you do?

Q 16.26. A firm can be worth $100 million (with 20% probability), $200 million (with 60% probability), or $300 million (with 20% probability). The firm has one senior bond outstanding, promising to pay $80 million. It also has one junior bond outstanding, promising to pay $70 million. The senior bond promises an interest rate of 5%. The junior bond promises an interest rate of 26%. If the firm's projects require an appropriate cost of capital of 10%, then what is the firm's levered equity cost of capital?

Q 16.27. If a change in capital structure increases the risk both of the firm's equity and debt, and there are no other financial claims, does it imply that the firm's risk has increased?

Q 16.28. Work the example from Page 508 (sun [$100] with 3/4 probability, rain [$60] with 1/4 probability), if the debt promises $65 and offers an expected rate of 3%. What is the weight of equity in the capital structure?

Q 16.29. M&M states that, in a perfect market, although both debt and equity become riskier due to an increase in the firm's leverage, both the firm's value and risk remain exactly the same. Conceptually, what would it take for the firm to become worth more and/or be safer even when both debt and equity become riskier due to an increase in the firm's leverage?

Q 16.30. Compute a graph similar to Exhibit 16.2. Use a spreadsheet. Your firm will be worth either $50,000 or $100,000 with equal probabilities. The cost of capital on your debt is given by the formula $\mathscr{E}(r_{\text{Debt}}) = 5\% + 10\% \cdot \omega_{\text{Debt}}$—but only if the debt is risky. (Hint: The risk-free rate of return is 11.85%. What is the WACC of the firm if it is 100% debt financed?)

Q 16.31. Show how a firm can increase its cost of equity and cost of debt capital, yet still come out with an overall cost of capital that is unchanged.

Q 16.32. Does the standard M&M proposition apply to nonfinancial liabilities?

Q 16.33. In a world of perfect financial markets, is the cost of capital of the firm's financial claims independent of how it is financed?

Q 16.34. In a world of perfect financial markets (but not necessarily product markets), is the cost of capital of the firm independent of how it is operated and financed?

17

Taxes and Capital Structure

The Corporate Income Tax Advantage and Personal Income Disadvantage of Debt

Now that you understand how financing works in a perfect world, it is time to move on to the real and imperfect world. The presence of income taxes, both corporate and personal, is an important violation of the M&M perfect-market assumptions in the real world. This chapter shows how you can create value through an intelligent capital structure policy that reduces these taxes. There are even formulas that help you compute the explicit tax-value consequences for different leverage structures. The most popular are the adjusted present value (APV) formula and the tax-adjusted weighted average cost of capital (WACC) formula. These techniques are in such wide use that they deserve a lot of airtime. The next chapter will explain capital structure in the presence of market imperfections other than taxes (such as agency problems).

17.1 Relative Taxation of Debt and Equity

Let's assume you are running a simple firm with the following parameters:

A basic corporate example with equal taxation.

Investment Cost in Year 0	$200
Before-Tax Gross Return in Year 1	$280
Before-Tax Net Return from Year 0 to Year 1	$80
Corporate Income Tax Rate (τ)	30%
Appropriate Cost of Capital from 0 to 1	12%

(If you find it easier, think of your project as having 1-year depreciation, the before-tax gross return is EBITDA, and your before-tax net return as EBIT.) Your goal is to understand the value of your firm under different tax regimes. Until Section 17.7, just assume that all your investors are tax-exempt.

Hypothetical Equal Taxation and Capital Budgeting

This short section's
unrealistic tax code.

If the firm faces the same tax rate on debt and equity, no matter how it is financed, what is its value? In the real world, this assumption is entirely unrealistic. (Instead, only interest payments are tax deductible). This scenario is useful only to show that investors care about "after corporate income tax" returns, not about "before corporate income tax" returns.

Taxes mean that the
after-tax rate of return
is lower than the
before-tax rate of
return.

Under this tax regime, consider financing your firm entirely with equity. With $280 in before-tax earnings on the $200 investment, you have a before-tax internal rate of return of ($280 – $200)/$200 = 40%. But, with taxes to the tune of 30% on the net return of $80, Uncle Sam collects $24. Your firm's after-tax net rate of return is therefore only ($256 – $200)/$200 = 28%.

Investors receive an
after-corporate-
income-tax rate of
return from the
"black-box" firm.

Now hold your investors' other opportunities in the economy constant. What is the influence of a change in the corporate income tax that is applicable only to your firm? From the perspective of your firm, you are a "price-taker" when it comes to raising capital. This means that you are too small to make a difference. After all, you are competing with many other firms for the capital of many competitive investors. Ultimately, these investors care only about the cash that you will return to them. Let us assume that firms of your risk class (market beta) must offer an after-corporate-income-tax rate of return of $\mathcal{E}(r_{Firm}) = 12\%$ to attract investors. This 12% is the equivalent of a 17.14% before-tax rate of return, because $17.14\% \cdot (1 - 30\%) = 12\%$. Put differently, you can invest $100 in equally risky projects elsewhere, expect to receive back $117.14, pay Uncle Sam $5.14 in taxes on $17.14 in earnings, and keep $12. (In this chapter, we again omit time subscripts if there is little risk of confusion.) How exactly do taxes matter to the rate of return that your projects must generate?

Projects with more tax
liability must create
more value before
taxes to be on equal
footing after taxes.

Your investor-owners really do not care what happens inside the firm, only what your firm can pay them in the end. It is all the same to them if:

- your projects earn 12% before tax and you manage to avoid all corporate income taxes;

- your projects earn 24% but you have to pay half of it in corporate income taxes;

- your projects earn 600%, of which 98% is confiscated by the government ($600\% \cdot (1 - 98\%) = 12\%$); or

- your projects face a 30% corporate tax rate, and your own projects earn 17.14% in before-tax rate of return in order to generate for your investors 12% in actual rate of return. Of course, this is the same calculation we already made. Your investment of $200 turns into $234.28, you pay Uncle Sam 30% in taxes on income of $34.28 for a total income tax of $10.28, and you are left with $224 to return to your investors after the corporate income tax is paid.

Investors demand a
proper (risk-adjusted)
rate of return,
regardless of how the
firm gets there.

The NPV formula is well equipped to handle corporate income taxes. However, as already explained in Chapter 10, you must calculate the present value using after-tax quantities in both the numerator and denominator. For example, the "$280-before-corporate-income-tax" firm, with its 12% required after-corporate-income-tax cost of capital, has a PV of:

➤ *Taxes in NPV,*
Sect. 10.4, *Pg. 265.*

$$PV = \frac{\mathcal{E}(C_{after\text{-}corp\text{-}tax})}{1 + \mathcal{E}(r_{after\text{-}corp\text{-}tax})} = \frac{\$280 - \$80 \cdot 30\%}{1 + 12\%} = \frac{\$256}{1 + 12\%} \approx \$228.57$$

There are some simple mistakes you must avoid here. You cannot usually find the same result if you work with before-tax expected cash flows and before-tax required rates of return. And you would definitely get a very wrong result if you used after-tax expected cash flows and then compared them to a cost of capital obtained from investments that have not yet been taxed at the corporate level.

Q 17.1. Assume a 30% corporate income tax. Show that a project that returns 17% before-tax would have a negative NPV if it cost $100 today and if the appropriate after-tax cost of capital is 12%.

Realistic Differential Taxation of Debt and Equity

Let's move on to a model of a tax code that reflects reality better. In many countries—the United States included—individuals and corporations face similar tax treatments, tax schedules, and tax rates. Although tax code details vary from year to year, country to country, state to state, county to county, and even city to city, most tax codes are pretty similar in spirit. Thus, the tax concepts in this book apply relatively universally.

Tax codes worldwide violate the M&M no-tax assumption.

Section 10.4 described how the form of payout matters. Firms pay taxes on their earnings *net of interest payments*. That is, unlike dividend distributions or money used to repurchase shares or money reinvested, the IRS considers interest payments to be a cost of your operations. Therefore, it allows the payment of interest to be treated as a before-tax expense rather than as an after-tax distribution of earnings. The result is that a corporation saves on taxes when it distributes its earnings in the form of interest payments. For example, if PepsiCo's operations really produced $100, and if $100 in interest was owed to creditors, then Uncle Sam would get nothing and the creditors would get the entire $100. However, if not paid out in interest, Uncle Sam would first collect corporate income taxes, say, 30%. PepsiCo could only keep (or distribute) the $70 that would be left over. The point of this chapter is to show how an astute CFO can best exploit this difference in relative tax treatment.

Tax codes subsidize borrowing: Firms pay interest from before-tax income but pay dividends from after-tax income.

➤ *Introduction to taxes, Sect. 10.4, Pg. 261.*

You may be wondering why you would not always finance your firm with as much debt as possible. The short preview answer is that if you were in a world in which corporate income taxes were the only distortion, then having as much debt as possible would indeed be ideal. However, there is more going on. If you take on too much debt, eventually other forces raise the firm's cost of capital to the point where further increases in debt are no longer value-increasing. These forces are the subject of the next chapter. But you must first understand how managers should go about capital budgeting if there are only corporate income taxes, and no other taxes or perfect-market distortions.

Preview: With too much debt, other not-yet-explained forces may increase the cost of capital.

Q 17.2. A debt-equity hybrid security would like to pay out $500 to its holders. The firm is in the 33% corporate income tax bracket. How much would the firm have to earn if the IRS designates the payment an interest payment? How much would the firm have to earn if the IRS designates the payment a dividend distribution?

17.2   Firm Value Under Different Capital Structures

Introducing an interest tax subsidy leads to a corporate preference for debt.

In a perfect world, firms are indifferent between debt and equity. In the real world, Uncle Sam subsidizes firms that pay interest, relative to firms that retain earnings, pay dividends, or repurchase shares. Therefore, *on corporate tax grounds*, firms should have a preference for debt. What is the exact value of the firm in the presence of this tax subsidy for debt interest payments?

Debt can reduce money to the IRS.

To answer this question, begin with Exhibit 17.1. It works out the value of one hypothetical firm in two financing scenarios.

Both scenarios assume:

Investment Cost in Year 0	$200.00
Before-Tax Gross Return in Year 1	$280.00
Before-Tax Net Return from Year 0 to Year 1	$80.00
Corporate Income Tax Rate (τ)	30%
Appropriate Average Cost of Capital from 0 to 1[a]	12%

Scenario EF: 100% equity financing.

Taxable Profits Next Year	$80.00
Corporate Income Taxes Next Year (30% of $80)	$24.00
Owners Will Keep *Next Year*	$56.00

Scenario DF: $200 debt financing at 11%. The rest is levered equity.

Interest Payments	$22.00
Taxable Profits Next Year	$58.00
Corporate Income Taxes Next Year (30% of $58)	$17.40
Equity Owners Will Keep Next Year	$40.60
(Equity and Debt) Owners Will Keep *Next Year*	$22.00 + $40.60 = $62.60

Exhibit 17.1: *Two Financing Scenarios for a Safe 1-Year Firm.* Table note [a]: In order to clear its cost-of-capital hurdle rate of 12%, the firm's projects must earn a rate of return of 17.14% before the firm pays out corporate income tax. With a 30% corporate income tax rate, Uncle Sam would confiscate $30\% \cdot 17.14\% \approx 5.14\%$, from the firm itself and corporate investors would receive a rate of return of 12%.

An equity-financing (EF) scenario: In the all-equity scenario, the firm does not exploit the help of the IRS. It earns $280 on an investment of $200. At a 30% corporate income tax rate, it will pay corporate income taxes of $30\% \cdot \$80 = \$24$. It can then pay out the remaining $56 in dividends.

A debt-financing (DF) scenario: In the debt-financing scenario, the firm borrows $200 today at an interest rate of 11% for interest payments next year of $22. Therefore, its corporate profits will be $80 – $22 = $58, on which it would have to pay Uncle Sam $17.40. This permits owners (creditors and shareholders—and a person may be both) to receive $62.60, the sum of $22 for its creditors and $40.60 for its equity holders.

Relative to the 100% equity-financed case (in which owners keep $56.00), the debt-financed case (in which owners keep $62.60) increases the firm's after-tax cash flow by $6.60. A quicker way to compute the tax savings is to multiply the tax rate by the interest payments: If the IRS allows the firm to deduct $22 in interest payments, the firm will save $22 · 30% = $6.60 in corporate income taxes. This $6.60 in tax savings will occur next year, and it will therefore have to be discounted back. It is common (but not necessarily unique or even correct) to use the firm's cost of capital to discount the tax shelter for a growing firm. This chapter's appendix explains the appropriate discount rate in greater detail, but just realize that whether you discount the much smaller tax shelter of $6.60 by the low cost of capital on debt (11%) or by a higher one, say, 15% (the firm's cost of capital), it would only make a difference of $5.95 – $5.74 = $0.21. On a $280 expected cash flow, this is not big, especially compared to our other uncertainties in our cash flow estimate, our CAPM model use, our rate of return model estimate, and so on. We are done: Relative to the EF capital structure, the DF capital structure created just under $6 in present value.

A N E C D O T E   **The RJR Buyout Tax Loophole**

In a **leveraged buyout** (**LBO**), the firm's indebtedness can increase dramatically—and this can significantly reduce corporate income taxes. In 1988, First Boston's plan to take over RJR Nabisco relied on an esoteric tax loophole just about to be closed. By "monetizing" its food operations (a fancy way to increase indebtedness), the deferring of taxes would have saved an estimated $3–$4 billion of RJR's corporate income taxes—which would have increased the annual federal U.S. deficit by 2%! Ultimately, First Boston lost its bid, and this scenario did not come about.   *Barbarians at the Gate*

Q 17.3. A $1 million construction project is expected to return $1.2 million in one year. Your company is in a 45% combined federal and state marginal income tax bracket.

1. If you finance the project with cash, how much will you pay in taxes?

2. If you finance the project with an $800,000 mortgage at an interest rate of 5%, how much will you pay in taxes?

3. If the appropriate project interest rate is 8%, what is the present value of the tax savings from financing the project with a mortgage?

17.3 Formulaic Valuation Methods: APV and WACC

We need formulas that work for any intermediate debt ratios.

Are there formulas that allow you to compute the firm value today not only for the current financing arrangement but also for other debt ratios that you might contemplate? Yes. There are essentially three methods. This section explains two of them, the APV and WACC:

1. You can compute an **adjusted present value** (APV), which adds back the tax subsidy. (This is basically the calculation from the previous section.)

➤ *WACC, Sect.* 16.4, *Pg.502.*

2. You can generalize the *weighted average cost of capital* (*WACC*) formula to reflect the preferential treatment of debt by suitably lowering the cost of debt capital. It then becomes a **tax-adjusted WACC**.

Method #3 is called "flow-to-equity."

The next section explains a third method to value the tax benefits. This "flow-to-equity" method constructs the financials for the firm in the new hypothetical capital structure and then values the after-tax cash flows directly. (Without describing it as such, you have actually already done this in Chapter 13, and you will do it again in

➤ *Valuing after-tax cash flows, Sect.* 13.3, *Pg.391.*

Chapter 20, where you will have to create a pro forma.) Properly applied, all three methods should provide similar—though not necessarily the exact same—answers.

Keep our simplifications in perspective.

Before you get into the nitty-gritty, it is important for you to realize that the tax model is just that—a model. You are working out the debt-related tax savings for a company that faces a fixed marginal income tax rate. The model further ignores many other possibly important tax issues, such as delayed income tax payments, tax-loss carryforwards, recapture of past tax payments, different marginal corporate income tax rates at different income levels, the possibility of default on income tax payments, state taxes, foreign taxes, special tax incentives, transfer pricing, or even outright tax evasion and fraud. Most of the time, our model works fairly well, but do not get carried away with excessive accuracy after the decimal point.

Adjusted Present Value (APV): Theory

The main idea of APV: Value an all-equity firm, then add the tax subsidy.

APV decomposes the value of the firm into two components:

1. The value of the firm as if it were *all equity-financed and fully taxed*

2. An additional tax subsidy for each dollar that can be named "interest" rather than "dividend"

In our example from Exhibit 17.1, the expected cash flow of the firm if it is 100% equity-financed is $280 return minus $24 in corporate taxes for a net of $256. The APV method then adds the tax subsidy depending on the firm's debt ratio. For example:

Zero interest payments: If the firm is all equity-financed, the tax subsidy is zero.

High interest payments: If the firm has interest payments of $80, the IRS would believe that the firm had not earned a penny. Therefore, the owners could keep an extra $24 above the $256 all-equity scenario *next year*.

Normal interest payments: If the firm has interest payments of, say, $19, the IRS would see $280 − $19 = $261 in return minus $200 investment cost for a net return of $61. The IRS would therefore collect 30% · $61 = $18.30, which is $5.70 less than the $24 that the IRS would have collected if the firm had been 100%

equity-financed. Alternatively, you could have directly calculated the expected tax savings as $\tau \cdot (\mathcal{E}(r_{\text{Debt}}) \cdot \text{Debt}) = 30\% \cdot (\$19) = \$5.70$. This $5.70 is the APV tax subsidy next year.

We only need to make a formula out of this method. Your first step to a more general valuation formula in the presence of corporate income taxes is to relate the amount of debt today to the interest payments next year. Let's return to our example, in which you borrow $200 at an interest rate of 11%. The expected interest payment is now

Tax savings are the product of the tax rate and the interest paid (debt level times interest rate).

$$\text{Expected Interest Payment} \quad = \quad 11\% \quad \cdot \$200 \quad = \$22$$

$$\text{Expected Interest Payment} \quad = \quad \mathcal{E}(r_{\text{Debt}}) \quad \cdot \quad \text{Debt}$$

One important error to avoid is that you must use the *expected* debt interest rate (11%), not the *quoted* bank interest rate (which could be considerably higher than 11%). (This would not matter for large firms with little debt, but it could matter for smaller or more highly indebted firms.) Continuing, the future tax savings *relative to an all-equity-financed firm* is the amount of corporate income tax that the firm will *not* have to pay on the interest.

$$\text{Expected Tax Savings} \quad = \quad 30\% \cdot \quad [11\% \cdot \$200] \quad = \$6.60$$

$$\text{Expected Tax Savings} \quad = \quad \tau \quad \cdot [\mathcal{E}(r_{\text{Debt}}) \cdot \text{Debt}]$$

In words, Uncle Sam would expect to receive $6.60 less from the owners of the project, because $22 in profit repatriation is designated as "interest."

The $6.60 in tax savings still has to be discounted, because it will occur next year. The APV formula computes the discounted value of an all-equity-financed firm (with after-tax cash flows of $256 next year) and then adds back the *discounted* tax savings:

APV discounts these tax savings and adds them to an "all-equity type" hypothetical firm.

($200 debt at 11% interest, i.e., $22 interest payment discounted at 11%)
$$\text{APV} = \frac{\$256}{1 + 12\%} + \frac{30\% \cdot \$22}{1 + 11\%} \approx \$234.52$$

$$\text{APV} = \frac{\mathcal{E}(C)}{1 + \mathcal{E}(r_{\text{Firm}})} + \frac{\tau \cdot [\mathcal{E}(r_{\text{Debt}}) \cdot \text{Debt}]}{1 + \mathcal{E}(r_{\text{Debt}})}$$

$$\text{APV} = \begin{array}{c}\text{Value as} \\ \text{if 100\% Equity-} \\ \text{Financed}\end{array} + \begin{array}{c}\text{Tax Subsidy} \\ \text{from Interest} \\ \text{Payments}\end{array}$$

As described at length in the chapter appendix, you could also reasonably use the firm's cost of capital to discount the tax savings:

($200 debt at 11% interest, i.e., $22 interest payment discounted at 12%)
$$\text{APV} = \frac{\$256}{1 + 12\%} + \frac{30\% \cdot \$22}{1 + 12\%} \approx \$234.46$$

$$\text{APV} = \frac{\mathcal{E}(C)}{1 + \mathcal{E}(r_{\text{Firm}})} + \frac{\tau \cdot [\mathcal{E}(r_{\text{Debt}}) \cdot \text{Debt}]}{1 + \mathcal{E}(r_{\text{Firm}})}$$

$$\text{APV} = \begin{array}{c}\text{Value as} \\ \text{if 100\% Equity-} \\ \text{Financed}\end{array} + \begin{array}{c}\text{Tax Subsidy} \\ \text{from Interest} \\ \text{Payments}\end{array}$$

The difference of 6 cents is obviously trivial in any real-world application.

APV is easily
generalized to more
periods.

APV generalizes easily to multiple years: Just compute the tax savings for each year and add them up, the same way that you would add up present values. You will work such a multiperiod example in the next section.

IMPORTANT

> The adjusted present value (APV) formula computes an "as if all-equity-financed" PV (i.e., after corporate income tax) and then adds back the tax subsidy:
>
> $$\text{APV} = \begin{array}{c}\text{Value as if Firm is 100\%} \\ \text{Equity-Financed and Fully} \\ \text{Taxed}\end{array} + \begin{array}{c}\text{Tax Subsidies} \\ \text{from Interest} \\ \text{Payments}\end{array}$$
>
> If the project lasts for only one period, omitting tedious and obvious time subscripts, this translates into
>
> $$\text{APV Today} = \frac{\mathcal{E}(\text{FutureC})}{1 + \mathcal{E}(r_{\text{Firm}})} + \frac{\overbrace{\mathcal{E}(\tau \cdot \overbrace{r_{\text{Debt}} \cdot \text{Debt}}^{\text{Interest Payment}})}^{\text{Tax Shield}}}{1 + \mathcal{E}(r_{\text{Debt}})} \qquad (17.1)$$
>
> The $1 + \mathcal{E}(r_{\text{Debt}})$ cost of capital in the second term may or may not be correct. However, because the second term is small, it rarely makes much difference whether you discount with $\mathcal{E}(r_{\text{Firm}})$ or $\mathcal{E}(r_{\text{Debt}})$.

APV: Application to a 60/40 Debt-Financing Case

In the example, the firm with $200 debt is worth $234.46 today. This comes to a debt ratio of $200/\$234.46 \approx 85\%$. Now assume that the firm instead considers a new capital structure in which it would borrow only $139.16. The firm has determined that this lower-debt capital structure would reduce its debt cost of capital to 9% per annum—after all, at such low levels, the debt is risk free, so risk-averse investors would be willing to accept a lower *expected* rate of return. What would the firm's value then become?

According to the APV formula, you begin with the value of a 100%-equity firm, which is $256/1.12, and add back the tax subsidy. Interest payments on $139.16 of debt will be $9\% \cdot \$139.16 \approx \$12.52$ *next year*. Taxes saved will be $30\% \cdot \$12.52 \approx \$3.76$ *next year*. Discounted at 9%, this is worth $3.45 *today*. Therefore,

$$\begin{aligned}
\text{APV} &= \frac{\$256.00}{1 + 12\%} &+& \frac{30\% \cdot 9\% \cdot \$139.16}{1 + 9\%} \\[2mm]
&\approx \$228.57 &+& \$3.45 &= \$232.02
\end{aligned}$$

$$\begin{aligned}
\text{APV} &= \frac{\mathcal{E}(C)}{1 + \mathcal{E}(r_{\text{Firm}})} &+& \frac{\tau \cdot \mathcal{E}(r_{\text{Debt}}) \cdot \text{Debt}}{1 + \mathcal{E}(r_{\text{Debt}})} \\[2mm]
&= \text{"As if All-Equity-Financed" Firm} &+& \text{Tax Subsidy}
\end{aligned}$$

If you prefer discounting the expected tax shelter with the firm's cost of capital, use

$$\text{APV} = \frac{\$256.00}{1 + 12\%} + \frac{30\% \cdot 9\% \cdot \$139.16}{1 + 12\%} \qquad (17.2)$$

$$\approx \quad \$228.57 \quad + \quad \$3.36 \quad = \$231.93$$

$$\text{APV} = \frac{\mathscr{E}(\text{C})}{1 + \mathscr{E}(r_{\text{Firm}})} + \frac{\tau \cdot \mathscr{E}(r_{\text{Debt}}) \cdot \text{Debt}}{1 + \mathscr{E}(r_{\text{Firm}})}$$

$$= \text{"As if All-Equity-Financed" Firm} + \quad \text{Tax Subsidy}$$

(Again, the cost of capital on the tax shelter makes little difference, here only $3.45 - $3.36 = $0.09.) This is the APV answer: In the presence of corporate income taxes, a firm financed with $139.16 in debt would be worth about $232.

Tax-Adjusted Weighted Average Cost of Capital (WACC) Valuation: Theory

The second method for computing the value of the firm uses a tax-adjusted weighted average cost of capital formula. If you start with the APV formula and manipulate it, it will be apparent that the two methods can yield the same value, at least if you start from Formula 17.2. Therefore, stick with the same parameters: 60/40 debt-equity financing, a 30% corporate income tax rate, a 9% cost of debt capital, and $280 before-tax return ($256 after-tax return in the all-equity case). As before, the firm borrows $139.16 at a 9% interest rate for net interest payments of $12.52. The corporate income tax shield is 30% of $12.52, or $3.76. The APV formula (Formula 17.2) values the firm at

> To show that WACC and APV are similar, we derive the tax-adjusted WACC formula from the APV formula.

$$\text{PV} = \frac{\$256}{1 + 12\%} + \frac{30\% \cdot \overbrace{(9\% \cdot \$139.16)}^{\approx \$12.52}}{1 + 12\%} \approx \$231.93$$

where the top brace reads $\approx \$3.76$.

$$\text{PV} = \frac{\mathscr{E}(\text{C})}{1 + \mathscr{E}(r_{\text{Firm}})} + \frac{\tau \cdot [\mathscr{E}(r_{\text{Debt}}) \cdot \text{Debt}]}{1 + \mathscr{E}(r_{\text{Firm}})}$$

The main difference between APV and WACC is that whereas APV works with dollar values of debt and interest payments, the WACC method expresses debt as a ratio of firm value,

$$60\% \approx \$139.16/\$231.93 \qquad \$139.16 \approx 60\% \cdot \$231.93$$

$$w_{\text{Debt}} = \text{Debt/PV} \implies \text{Debt} = w_{\text{Debt}} \cdot \text{PV}$$

Substitute the debt expression into the APV formula,

$$\text{PV} = \frac{\$256}{1 + 12\%} + \frac{30\% \cdot [9\% \cdot (60\% \cdot \$231.93)]}{1 + 12\%} \approx \$231.93$$

$$\text{PV} = \frac{\mathscr{E}(\text{C})}{1 + \mathscr{E}(r_{\text{Firm}})} + \frac{\tau \cdot [\mathscr{E}(r_{\text{Debt}}) \cdot (w_{\text{Debt}} \cdot \text{PV})]}{1 + \mathscr{E}(r_{\text{Firm}})}$$

You now have PV on both sides of the equation, so you want to solve for PV. This requires a few algebraic steps.

1. Multiply both sides by $[1+\mathcal{E}(r_{\text{Firm}})] = (1+12\%) = 1.12$ to make the denominator disappear:

$$(1 + 12\%) \cdot \$231.93 \approx \$256 + 30\% \cdot [9\% \cdot (60\% \cdot \$231.93)]$$
$$[1 + \mathcal{E}(r_{\text{Firm}})] \cdot \text{PV} = \mathcal{E}(\text{C}) + \tau \cdot [\mathcal{E}(r_{\text{Debt}}) \cdot (w_{\text{Debt}} \cdot \text{PV})]$$

2. Move the second term on the right side over to the left side:

$$(1 + 12\%) \cdot \$231.93 - 30\% \cdot [9\% \cdot (60\% \cdot \$231.93)] \approx \$256$$
$$[1 + \mathcal{E}(r_{\text{Firm}})] \cdot \text{PV} - \tau \cdot [\mathcal{E}(r_{\text{Debt}}) \cdot (w_{\text{Debt}} \cdot \text{PV})] = \mathcal{E}(\text{C})$$

3. Pull out the PV:

$$\$231.93 \cdot [1 + 12\% - 30\% \cdot 9\% \cdot 60\%] \approx \$256$$
$$\text{PV} \cdot [1 + \mathcal{E}(r_{\text{Firm}}) - \tau \cdot \mathcal{E}(r_{\text{Debt}}) \cdot w_{\text{Debt}}] = \mathcal{E}(\text{C})$$

4. Divide both sides by the PV multiplier:

$$\$231.93 \approx \frac{\$256}{1 + 12\% - 30\% \cdot 9\% \cdot 60\%} \approx \frac{\$256}{1 + 10.38\%}$$
$$\text{PV} = \frac{\mathcal{E}(\text{C})}{1 + \mathcal{E}(r_{\text{Firm}}) - \tau \cdot [\mathcal{E}(r_{\text{Debt}}) \cdot w_{\text{Debt}}]} = \frac{\mathcal{E}(\text{C})}{1 + \text{WACC}} \quad (17.3)$$

My intuition for the WACC formula.

This is the tax-adjusted WACC valuation formula. Its big idea is to discount the "as if 100%-equity-financed and fully taxed" cash flows (of $\mathcal{E}(\text{C}) = \$256$), not with the plain cost of capital $\mathcal{E}(r_{\text{Firm}}) = 12\%$, but with a reduced interest rate that comes from the corporate income tax subsidy on interest payments. The term that does this— relative to our earlier no-tax WACC formula (Formula 16.2)—is $\tau \cdot w_{\text{Debt}} \cdot \mathcal{E}(r_{\text{Debt}}) = 30\% \cdot 60\% \cdot 9\% = 1.62\%$. Therefore, your revised discount rate is $1+12\%-30\% \cdot 9\% \cdot 60\% = 1 + 10.38\%$. The 10.38% is the (tax-adjusted) WACC —lower than your all-equity cost of capital of 12%.

➤ *Perfect-markets WACC, Formula 16.2, Pg.513.*

The more common form of WACC breaks out the equity cost of capital.

The WACC formula is often slightly rearranged. Split $\mathcal{E}(r_{\text{Firm}})$ into its cost of equity and cost of debt components, $\mathcal{E}(r_{\text{Firm}}) = w_{\text{Debt}} \cdot \mathcal{E}(r_{\text{Debt}}) + w_{\text{Equity}} \cdot \mathcal{E}(r_{\text{Equity}})$. In our example, to keep the weighted-average firm cost of capital at the constant $\mathcal{E}(r_{\text{Firm}}) = 12\%$, solve $\mathcal{E}(r_{\text{Firm}}) = w_{\text{Debt}} \cdot \mathcal{E}(r_{\text{Debt}}) + w_{\text{Equity}} \cdot \mathcal{E}(r_{\text{Equity}}) = 60\% \cdot 9\% + 40\% \cdot \mathcal{E}(r_{\text{Equity}}) = 12\%$, and find $\mathcal{E}(r_{\text{Equity}}) = 16.5\%$. Substitute this into Formula 17.3, and you get the more common version of the WACC formula,

$$\text{PV} = \frac{\$256}{1 + 10.38\%} = \frac{\$256}{1 + 40\% \cdot 16.5\% + (1 - 30\%) \cdot 60\% \cdot 9\%}$$
$$\text{PV} = \frac{\mathcal{E}(\text{C})}{1 + \text{WACC}} = \frac{\mathcal{E}(\text{C})}{1 + w_{\text{Equity}} \cdot \mathcal{E}(r_{\text{Equity}}) + (1 - \tau) \cdot w_{\text{Debt}} \cdot \mathcal{E}(r_{\text{Debt}})}$$

Your new WACC formula generalizes the old M&M WACC formula from the previous chapter. If the corporate tax rate τ is zero, the tax subsidy is useless, and the tax-adjusted WACC formula simplifies to your older and simpler WACC formula. This works for about half of all publicly traded firms in the United States, which indeed have a marginal tax rate of zero (e.g., due to tax-loss carryforwards or due to clever tax shelters). For these companies, the use of debt does not provide a useful tax shelter. They can use the simplified M&M version of the WACC formula, which ignores the tax subsidy of interest. But for highly taxed firms, you don't have a choice. You need the new WACC formula, which can also handle firms with positive corporate income tax rates.

The tax-adjusted WACC generalizes the perfect-market WACC from the previous chapter.

➤ *WACC in a perfect world,* Formula 16.2, *Pg.513*.

Unfortunately, you can only use the WACC formula in a multiperiod setting *if* the cost of capital, the firm's debt ratio, and the firm's tax rate all stay constant. In this case, a present value formula would look something like

Alas, in practical use—though convenient and intuitive—WACC is often difficult to apply.

$$
\text{PV} = \frac{\mathscr{E}(C_{\text{Time 1}})}{\{1 + [w_{\text{Equity}} \cdot r_{\text{Equity,Time 1}} + w_{\text{Debt}} \cdot \mathscr{E}(r_{\text{Debt,Time 1}}) \cdot (1-\tau)]\}^1} + (17.4)
$$

$$
\frac{\mathscr{E}(C_{\text{Time 2}})}{\{1 + [w_{\text{Equity}} \cdot r_{\text{Equity,Time 2}} + w_{\text{Debt}} \cdot \mathscr{E}(r_{\text{Debt,Time 2}}) \cdot (1-\tau)]\}^2} + \cdots
$$

If these quantities are not all constant, no one knows how to compute a proper WACC. It is not unusual for firms to plan on high debt financing up-front that they pay back later on. Unfortunately, this is a situation that the WACC formula cannot handle. Moreover, WACC is difficult to use if there are nonfinancial liabilities with marginal costs of capital that are different from those on financial liabilities. In general, the WACC formula is best applied in real life as a quick and useful approximation. The APV method is often more flexible than the WACC method.

➤ *WACC with nonfinancial liabilities,* Sect. 16.6, *Pg.515*.

IMPORTANT

- The (tax-adjusted) weighted average cost of capital (WACC) formula discounts future cash flows with a lower cost of capital that reflects the advantage of the corporate tax shelter for interest payments:

$$
\text{PV} = \frac{\mathscr{E}(C)}{1 + \text{WACC}} \tag{17.5}
$$

$$
\text{where} \quad \text{WACC} = \mathscr{E}(r_{\text{Firm}}) - \tau \cdot \mathscr{E}(r_{\text{Debt}}) \cdot w_{\text{Debt}}
$$

$$
= w_{\text{Equity}} \cdot \mathscr{E}(r_{\text{Equity}}) + w_{\text{Debt}} \cdot \mathscr{E}(r_{\text{Debt}}) \cdot (1-\tau)
$$

  The expected cash flows must be the cash flows "as if the firm were all-equity-financed and fully taxed."

- This formula is a generalization of the WACC formula from the perfect M&M world. Therefore, it is this formula that is usually called the WACC formula.

- It is not clear how to use the WACC formula in a multiperiod setting.

  The WACC formula is so common that it is worth memorizing.

The optimal capital
structure without
other forces is 100%
debt.
➤ *Cost of Capital,
Exhibit 16.2, Pg.511.*

Now recall Exhibit 16.2 from the previous chapter. It showed that the cost of capital remains the same 10%, regardless of the firm's capital structure. Is this still the case in the presence of corporate income taxes? No! Exhibit 17.2 shows that the tax subsidy pushes the firm's cost of capital down for high debt ratios. Indeed, if there were no other capital structure complications to consider, the optimal capital structure would be for the firm to take on as much debt as possible, a full 100%.

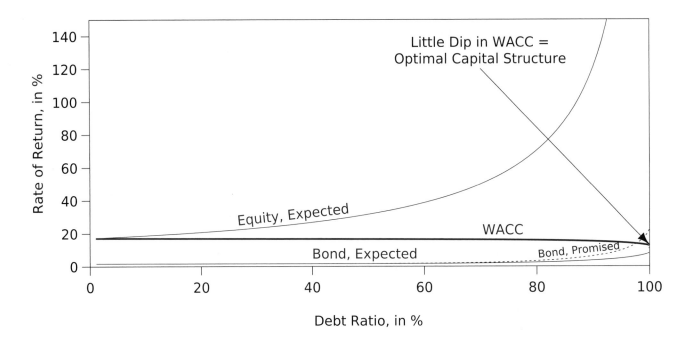

Exhibit 17.2: *The Cost of Capital in a World With Corporate Taxes.* This figure is the equivalent of Exhibit 16.2, except that debt now has a corporate income tax advantage. This means that the firm's overall cost of capital declines with the firm's debt ratio.

Q 17.4. Consider a 25/75 debt-equity financing case for your firm. As in the scenario in Exhibit 17.1 on page 526, your firm will produce a before-tax return of $280, the investment costs $200, the tax rate is 30%, the overall opportunity cost of capital (in other taxable projects) is 12%, and when the firm is 25% debt-financed, debt must offer an expected rate of return of 8%. (If you think of your opportunity cost of capital as the best your firm can achieve elsewhere, then these cost-of-capital numbers are your before-tax costs of capital from other projects before they would be taxed, too. If you think of your opportunity cost of capital as provided by your investors, who [like you] are also taxed, then it is the rate of return before their personal income taxes. The cost of capital for your personal investors is the subject of the next chapter.) First compute the WACC, then compute the debt as 25% of the WACC value, and show how the APV yields the same result.

Q 17.5. Consider financing your firm with $100 debt: The before-tax return is $280, the investment cost is $200, the tax rate is 30%, the overall cost of capital is 12%, and this debt must offer an expected rate of return of 8.7%. (These are again before-tax opportunity rates of return.) First compute the APV, then compute the capital structure in ratios, and finally show that the WACC yields the same result.

Q 17.6. If you are thinking of debt in terms of a (constant) fraction of firm value, would you prefer WACC or APV? If you are thinking of debt in terms of a (constant) dollar amount, would you prefer WACC or APV?

Q 17.7. From memory, draw the WACC of the firm as a function of its debt ratio if the only market imperfection is the corporate income taxes.

How Bad Are Mistakes?

Applying APV and WACC to the Current Cash Flows

Unfortunately, both WACC and APV are often used incorrectly. Analysts frequently forget that the correct expected cash flow in the present value numerator is the "as if fully-equity-financed and fully taxed" cash flow ($256 in our example). It is neither the before-tax project cash flow ($280 in our example), nor the after-tax cash flow under the current financing scheme (e.g., $280 − 9% · $139.16 ≈ $267.48). If you have worked through the examples in this chapter, you should understand why this would provide the wrong answer. Unlike errors in the discount rate applied to the tax shelter—which is a modest error—using the wrong cash flow is a big error.

IMPORTANT

WACC and APV operate with expected "as if 100%-equity-financed and after-corporate-income-tax" cash flows, not the firm's *current* cash flows (which depend on the *current* debt-equity financing).

Q 17.8. A firm in the 20% marginal tax bracket is currently financed with $500 debt and $1,000 equity. The debt carries an interest rate of 6%; the equity's cost of capital is 12%. The risk-free rate is 4%; the equity premium is 3%. What is the firm's beta? The firm is pondering a recapitalization to $1,000 debt, which would increase the debt's interest rate to 8%. The firm will exist for only 1 more year. What would the new equity be worth?

Sidenote: You may sometimes wish to adjust a firm's beta to reflect debt and corporate income taxes. This is done by the so-called Hamada Equation, $\beta_{\text{With Debt}} = \beta_{\text{Unlevered}} \cdot [1 + (1 - \tau) \cdot (\text{Debt/Equity})]$. We shall not use this formula any further.

Q 17.9. A firm in the 40% income tax bracket has an investment that costs $300 in year 0, and offers a before-tax return (cash flow) in year 1 of $500. Assume that the firm's before-tax opportunity cost of capital, as provided by the external capital markets, is approximately 20%. Its debt cost of capital is $\mathscr{E}(r_{Debt}) = 15\% + w_{Debt} \cdot 5\%$. Compute the APV, WACC, and a WACC-based value if the firm borrows $50 to finance it. Repeat if the firm borrows $100.

17.4 Sample Applications of Tax-Adjusted Valuation

Let's value a pro forma firm.

➤ *Machine,*
Exhibit 13.6, *Pg.382*.

Let's move on to a more realistic example. You are actually already familiar with it: It is the hypothetical machine from Chapter 13, Exhibit 13.6. To make the example more useful, add the following parameters:

- The appropriate debt interest rate is 20%, so a loan of $25 must offer an expected $5 in interest per annum.

- The appropriate overall cost of capital for the firm is 30%.

- The corporate income tax rate is 40%.

Exhibit 17.3 shows all you need to know. Shareholders invest $26 and receive a total of $137 in dividends. Bondholders invest $25 and receive $25 in total interest payments. (Your firm follows an odd capital distribution policy, but so be it.) What is it worth?

The Flow-to-Equity Direct Valuation from the Pro Forma Financials

The third valuation method is flow-to-equity.

The main point of the more involved example is to show you the third method to handle the tax subsidy. This **flow-to-equity** method works directly with a "pro forma." For now, think of a pro forma simply as a forward projection of the financial statements. (Pro formas will be discussed in detail in Chapter 20.) We will demonstrate all three methods now: flow-to-equity, APV, and WACC.

Method #1: Direct cash flows, already after-tax, from the financials.

➤ *Project cash flows,*
Formula 13.4, *Pg.400*.

The project cash flow formula (Formula 13.4) tells you that the project cash flows for your NPV valuation are:

Computing Project Cash Flows, $25 Debt Financing		Y1	Y2	Y3	Y4	Y5	Y6
	Total Operating Activity	$46	$53	$53	$43	$33	$33
+	Total Investing Activity	–$75	–$75				
+	Interest Expense		$5	$5	$5	$5	$5
=	**Project Cash Flows**	–$29	–$17	+$58	+$48	+$38	+$38

What is the discount rate for after-tax cash flows?

We need a discount factor for these after-tax cash flows. (This is very difficult to assess accurately, but fortunately the precise discount rate here does not matter too much. The chapter appendix explains this better.) We will be using the same 30% cost of capital for the firm. Now discount these cash flows on the overall firm:

The Income Statement

		Y1	Y2	Y3	Y4	Y5	Y6
	Gross Sales (Revenues)	$70	$70	$70	$70	$70	$70
−	Cost of Goods Sold (COGS)	$5	$5	$5	$5	$5	$5
−	Selling, General & Administrative Expenses (SG&A)	$5	$5	$5	$5	$5	$5
=	EBITDA (Net Sales)	$60	$60	$60	$60	$60	$60
−	Depreciation	$25	$50	$50	$25	$0	$0
=	EBIT (Operating Income)	$35	$10	$10	$35	$60	$60
−	Interest Expense	$0	$5	$5	$5	$5	$5
=	EAIBT (or EBT)	$35	$5	$5	$30	$55	$55
−	Corporate Income Tax (at 40%)	$14	$2	$2	$12	$22	$22
=	**Net Income**	$21	$3	$3	$18	$33	$33

Excerpts from the Cash Flow Statement

		Y1	Y2	Y3	Y4	Y5	Y6
	Net Income	$21	$3	$3	$18	$33	$33
+	Depreciation	$25	$50	$50	$25	$0	$0
=	**Total Operating Activity**	$46	$53	$53	$43	$33	$33
	Capital Expenditures	−$75	−$75				
=	**Total Investing Activity**	−$75	−$75				
+	Net Equity Issue	$26					
+	Dividends			−$53	−$43	−$33	−$8
+	Net Debt Issue	$25					−$25
=	**Total Financing Activity**	$51		−$53	−$43	−$33	−$33
	Net Change in Cash	+$22	−$22	$0	$0	$0	$0

Exhibit 17.3: *Financial Statements of Hypothetical Machine.*

$$\text{NPV} = \frac{-\$29}{1.30} + \frac{-\$17}{1.30^2} + \frac{+\$58}{1.30^3} + \frac{+\$48}{1.30^4} + \frac{+\$38}{1.30^5} + \frac{+\$38}{1.30^6} \approx \$28.95 \quad (17.6)$$

You would be willing to pay $28.95 *today* for the right to buy (and finance) the firm, which will initiate *next year* with this exact capital structure. But wait: Did you forget about the tax shelter that came with the debt? No, you did not! The pro forma itself had already incorporated the correct interest expense. The interest payments had already reduced the corporate income tax and thereby appropriately increased your project's cash flows.

APV

Method #2, APV, demands a detour: You must construct *as-if-100%-equity-financed* financials.

The second method to value this firm is APV. But be careful: The cash flows in Formula 17.6 are *not* the cash flows that you need for the APV analysis, because these are not the cash flows *as if 100% equity financed*. APV states that you can only add back the tax shield to the *as-if-100%-equity-financed* cash flows. If you used the cash flows in Formula 17.6 and then added the tax shield (due to the interest payment designation), you would mistakenly count the tax shield twice. You must therefore start over to find the correct expected cash flows as if the firm were fully equity-financed, in which case the tax obligation would be higher. By how much? You can intuit this even before you write down the full financials. In years 2-6, the taxable net income would be $5 more, so at your 40% corporate income tax rate you would have to pay not $2, but $4 in taxes. This means that you would have to pay an extra $2 in taxes each year.

Here are the 100%-equity-financed cash flows.

Check this intuition is correct. The financials of an all-equity-financed firm are:

Abbreviated Income Statement, 100% Equity-Financed

		Y1	Y2	Y3	Y4	Y5	Y6
=	EBIT (Operating Income)	$35	$10	$10	$35	$60	$60
−	Interest Expense	$0	$0	$0	$0	$0	$0
=	EAIBT (or EBT)	$35	$10	$10	$35	$60	$60
−	Corporate Income Tax (at 40%)	$14	$4	$4	$14	$24	$24
=	**Net Income**	$21	$6	$6	$21	$36	$36

(Note how the tax obligations are higher than they were when the firm had some debt financing.)

Abbreviated Cash Flow Statement, 100% Equity-Financed

		Y1	Y2	Y3	Y4	Y5	Y6
	Net Income	$21	$6	$6	$21	$36	$36
+	Depreciation	$25	$50	$50	$25	$0	$0
=	**Total Operating Activity**	$46	$56	$56	$46	$36	$36
	Capital Expenditures	−$75	−$75				
=	**Total Investing Activity**	−$75	−$75				

You can now reuse our present value cash flow formula on the 100%-equity-financed version of our firm:

Computing Project Cash Flows, 100% Equity-Financed						
	Y1	Y2	Y3	Y4	Y5	Y6
Total Operating Activity	$46	$56	$56	$46	$36	$36
+ Total Investing Activity	-$75	-$75				
+ Interest Expense	$0	$0	$0	$0	$0	$0
= **Project Cash Flows**	-$29	-$19	+$56	+$46	+$36	+$36

Comparing this to the equivalent table on Page 536, you can see that the project cash flows in your 100%-equity-financed firm have indeed lost the tax shelter of $2 in each of years 2-6. The intuition was correct!

Now discount these "as-if-100%-equity-financed" total project cash flows with the firm's appropriate cost of capital, which is assumed to be 30%. Standing at time 0, this gives you

Return to the main task: APV valuation.

$$\text{NPV}_{\substack{\text{Project, 100\%} \\ \text{Equity-Financed}}} = \frac{-\$29}{1.30} + \frac{-\$19}{1.30^2} + \frac{+\$56}{1.30^3} + \frac{+\$46}{1.30^4} + \frac{+\$36}{1.30^5} + \frac{+\$36}{1.30^6} \approx \$25.20$$

The APV formula states that you now need to add back the expected tax shield from the debt. The interest tax shields in years 2-6 are the interest payments ($5 per year) multiplied by the corporate tax rate (40%), or $2 per year. What is the value of this tax shelter?

$$\text{NPV}_{\text{Tax Shelter}} = \frac{\$0}{1.30} + \frac{+\$2}{1.30^2} + \frac{+\$2}{1.30^3} + \frac{+\$2}{1.30^4} + \frac{+\$2}{1.30^5} + \frac{+\$2}{1.30^6} \approx \$3.75$$

Therefore, the APV method tells you that the firm value is

$$\text{APV} \approx \$25.20 + \$3.75 = \$28.95$$

This is the same answer that you found in Formula 17.6.

WACC

The third method to value the firm is WACC. Start again with the firm's cash flows, as if 100% equity-financed.

Method #3: WACC. The debt is about 35% of the firm's financing.

Computing Project Cash Flows, 100% Equity-Financed						
	Y1	Y2	Y3	Y4	Y5	Y6
Project Cash Flows	-$29	-$19	+$56	+$46	+$36	+$36

The idea now is to use an appropriate tax-adjusted WACC to discount these cash flows. But there is another tricky issue: What is the firm's debt ratio? That is, WACC requires $w_{\text{Debt}} = (1 - w_{\text{Equity}})$ as an input. In the real world, you could just look up the current firm values. In our example, I am sparing you the details of working out that the debt is about 35% of the firm's value today. You know the other two remaining inputs that you need to compute WACC, which are the overall corporate cost of capital at 30%, and the debt cost of capital at 20%.

Return to the main
task: WACC valuation.

You can now compute the firm's weighted average cost of capital as

$$\text{WACC} = 30\% - 40\% \cdot 35\% \cdot 20\% = 27.2\%$$

$$\text{WACC} = \mathcal{E}(r_{\text{Firm}}) - \tau \cdot w_{\text{Debt}} \cdot \mathcal{E}(r_{\text{Debt}})$$

Under the incorrect but hopefully reasonable assumption that the debt ratio remains at 35%,

$$\text{NPV} = \frac{-\$29}{1.272} + \frac{-\$19}{1.272\%^2} + \frac{+\$56}{1.272\%^3} + \frac{+\$46}{1.272\%^4} + \frac{+\$36}{1.272\%^5} + \frac{+\$36}{1.272\%^6} \approx \$29.55$$

This is a (modest) 60 cents off the value of the APV formula. Most of the difference comes from the fact that the fraction of debt in the capital structure is 35% in the first year but a different proportion of the value in subsequent years. As noted on Page 533, the WACC method really does not apply in this case. However, in the real world, this error would be dwarfed by errors in what you have assumed about the tax code and by your uncertainty about the expected cash flows and costs of capital that such projects would carry.

Q 17.10. Construct a pro forma for the following firm: A 3-year project costs $150 in year 1 (not year 0) and produces $70 in year 1, $60 in year 2, and $55 in year 3. (All numbers are year-end.) Depreciation, both real and financial, is straight line over three years. Projects of this riskiness (and with this term structure of project payoffs) have an 18% before-tax opportunity cost of capital. The marginal corporate income tax rate is 40%.

1. Assume that the firm is 100% equity-financed. Construct the pro forma and compute expected project cash flows.

2. Compute the project IRR.

3. Compute the project NPV.

4. Assume that this firm expects to receive an extra tax-exempt bonus of $2 in years 2 and 3 from a benevolent donor. What would be the project's cash flows and IRR now?

For the remaining questions, assume that the firm instead has a capital structure financing $50 with debt raised in year 1 at a 10% (expected) interest rate. There is no interest paid in year 1, just in years 2 and 3. The principal is repaid in year 3.

5. Construct the pro forma now. What is the IRR of this project?

6. From the pro forma, what is the NPV of the debt-financed project?

7. Compute the NPV via the APV method.

8. Via the APV method, how much would firm value be if the firm would have taken on not $50, but $40, in debt (assuming the same debt interest rate of 10%)?

9. Does the debt ratio of the firm stay constant over time? Is this firm a good candidate for the WACC method?

17.5 The Tax Subsidy on PepsiCo's Financial Statement

Can you apply your newfound theoretical knowledge of how to handle corporate income taxes to a real-world firm—in fact, to the PepsiCo example from Chapter 13? What is the tax subsidy in PepsiCo's income statement, reproduced in Exhibit 17.4?

The application is easy.

Income Statement	Dec. 2000
= Revenue	$25,479
COGS	$10,226
+ SG&A	$11,104
+ Depreciation and Amortization	$147
+ Unusual Expenses	$184
− = **Total Operating Expenses**	$21,661
= **Operating Income**	$3,818
+ Net Interest Income	$ −57
= **Income before Tax**	$3,761
− Income Tax	$1,218
= **Income after Tax**	$2,543
− Extraordinary Items	$0
= **Net Income**	$2,543

Exhibit 17.4: *PepsiCo's Income Statement (Revisited), Dollars in Millions.*

In 2000, PepsiCo had $3.818 billion in operating income, but only had to pay income taxes on $3.761 billion. With income taxes of $1.218 billion, PepsiCo's average corporate income tax rate was about 32.4%. If PepsiCo had been purely equity-financed, it would have had to pay taxes on its operating income of $3.818 billion, or about $1.237 billion. Thus, by having $57 million in interest, relative to a hypothetical dividend payout of $57 million, PepsiCo enjoyed a tax shield in 2000 from its interest payments of

You can easily infer PepsiCo's tax subsidy from its corporate financial statements.

$$\text{PepsiCo's 2000 Debt Tax Shield} = 32.4\% \cdot \$57 \text{ million} \approx \$18.5 \text{ million}$$

$$\text{Tax Shield} = \tau \cdot \text{Interest Payments}$$

$18.5 million may not be a lot for a $50 billion company, but remember that this is risk-free cash for which no one at PepsiCo would have had to work hard—and it may well be enough to pay for the CFO office.

Why it's simple.   Note that you did not need to compute $\mathcal{E}(r_{\text{Debt}}) \cdot \text{Debt}$, because you could read the interest payments directly off the financials. The model's other assumption, that the marginal tax rate is fixed, probably works well in this case. For companies like PepsiCo with high income, the marginal and the average tax rates are practically the same, so you can assume that PepsiCo would have had to pay its average tax rate of 32.4% if it had paid out the $57 million interest in dividends instead. (Of course, the model here still ignores the many more complex tax issues, such as deferred taxes.)

Q 17.11. In 2001, Coca-Cola booked $1,691 million in corporate income taxes on $5,670 million in income. It also paid $289 million in interest to its creditors. How much did the corporate-income tax shelter save Coca-Cola's owners?

17.6 Contemplating Corporate Taxes

You now understand how managers should adjust to the presence of corporate income taxes. But there are a number of other tax-related issues that are still worth discussing, if only because you may wonder about them in the future.

Which Tax-Adjusted Valuation Method is Best?

None of the three methods always dominates. Estimated values should be similar.   Which of the three valuation methods is best: flow-to-equity, APV, or WACC? They are all in use because each has its advantages and disadvantages.

Of course, the three methods should usually come out with very similar results. As the example in Section 17.4 showed, if suitably applied, the differences are usually modest. This is especially true if you compare valuation-method differences to the errors that you will inevitably introduce in your assessments of future expected cash flows, your estimate for the appropriate costs of capital, and the necessary simplification of the tax code.

Compare the advantages and disadvantages of the methods.   Here is how I see the three methods:

Flow-to-equity: The advantage of the flow-to-equity method is that it is lucid and makes it less likely that you will use an incorrect expected cash flow. The disadvantage of the flow-to-equity method is that it requires a lot more effort (you have to construct full financials!), and that it does not break out the tax advantage of debt explicitly. This makes it more difficult to think about the tax-induced consequences of contemplated capital structure changes.

APV: The APV formula makes it relatively easy to determine how an extra dollar of debt increases firm value. When thinking of a specific addition or project with a specific cost, this may be the easiest formula to use.

WACC: The WACC formula makes it relatively easy to determine how an extra percentage in debt increases firm value. When thinking of a target ratio change in capital structure policy, this may be the easiest formula to use.

In many common cases, APV is easier to work with than WACC. For example, APV makes it much easier to think about projects that add debt capacity only at some stage in their lives. What drives project debt capacity? The simple answer is that more tangible (collateralizable) projects tend to add more debt capacity, because your bank will find it easier to repossess and resell tangible assets. A research and development (R&D) project may require an equity investment up-front, followed by the construction of a laboratory that can be debt-financed. The laboratory adds debt capacity, the R&D does not. APV makes it easy to add in the debt capacity only in later stages. APV also makes it easier to assign different discount factors to the firm's projects and tax shields.

My advice: APV is often simplest.

WACC is probably the most difficult method. No one knows how to do multiyear compounding with time-varying WACCs. Therefore, the method can only be applied if the firm's debt ratio remains roughly constant in future years. Of course, if you know that this is the case, WACC may be easier to use than APV. However, in all other cases, WACC usage errors could become important. The empirical evidence suggests that publicly traded corporations rarely keep constant debt ratios, often rendering WACC a less preferable method. On a more technical note, WACC also leans more heavily on the assumption that borrowing rates are competitive and thus zero NPV. Therefore, WACC works only in "normal" situations in which creditors are paid the appropriate cost of capital on the debt. WACC cannot deal with "below-market" or "above-market" unfairly priced loans—much like the plain version of the CAPM cannot. (You already know that you need to use a certainty equivalent form of the CAPM in this case.)

WACC is often most difficult for multiyear projects.

➤ *Certainty equivalence,* Sect. App.9.A (Companion), *Pg.≈49.*

Repeat: The One Important Mistake to Avoid

The one big mistake you should never commit is to use the wrong expected cash flows for APV or WACC. Using the wrong discount rate on the tax shelter or tax liability is forgivable (within bounds); using the wrong expected cash flows is not. Let's reemphasize what you must do. In the flow-to-equity method, you already have both the projected debt cash flows and the projected equity cash flows, so your life is simple. You can just use these pro forma cash flows, which already take the debt tax shield into account. In contrast, in both the APV and WACC methods, you must not use the expected cash flows of the firm under the current capital structure (much less the expected cash flows of the current equity), but the cash flows that would accrue if the firm were fully equity-financed.

Same warning again: Please don't ever adjust current non-100% equity cash flows via APV or WACC.

A Quick-and-Dirty Heuristic Tax-Savings Rule

Do not confuse the question of whether tax savings are important with whether the right discount factor for the tax savings is important. The former is much bigger than the latter. But aren't the tax savings too small to bother with altogether? Before you draw this conclusion, realize that the firm need not invent anything new or work extra hard to obtain the tax savings. In addition, tax savings materialize year after year after year. In fact, this constancy provides a nice back-of-the-envelope heuristic of what the firm can gain in value from one dollar extra in debt.

Why bother with such small 1-year tax savings?

Start with the APV formula. If a large firm today takes on and maintains an extra $1 billion in debt rather than an extra $1 billion in equity, the interest is on the order of

The tax savings will repeat. A rule of thumb: Each perpetual dollar of debt increases firm value by the corporate income tax rate.

about 6%, or $60 million per year. The tax rate for many corporations is about 40%, leading to a savings of $24 million—this can pay for a nice executive bonus. But this is only the first year. The $24 million per year savings is a perpetuity. If the cost of capital on the tax shelter is the cost of capital on the debt (6%), then you can compute the total value increase to the firm today to be $24/6% = $400 million.

$$\text{Value Increase} \approx \frac{40\% \cdot 6\% \cdot \$1\text{billion}}{6\%} = \$400 \text{ million}$$

$$\text{Value Increase} \approx \frac{\tau \cdot \mathcal{E}(r_{\text{Debt}}) \cdot \text{Debt}}{\mathcal{E}(r_{\text{Debt}})} \approx \tau \cdot \text{Debt}$$

This is a nice shortcut: For every dollar extra in eternal debt, the value of the firm increases by the tax rate of the firm. This formula is so easy that you can often compute it in your head. For example, compare financing a $1 million project with 50% debt (rather than all-equity), in which a firm in the 40% marginal tax bracket plans not to repay any of the debt principal or to take on new debt. The tax savings would be $40\% \cdot \$500,000 = \$200,000$.

Two small problems with this heuristic are the discount rate and the perpetuity assumptions.

It is important that you recognize that the $\tau \cdot \text{Debt}$ formula for the tax savings is not an exact calculation. It is only a heuristic—that is, a rule that gives you a good but not a perfect estimate very quickly. For example, it has made at least two assumptions that are never perfectly satisfied. The first is that the appropriate discount rate on the tax shelter is exactly the same as the cost of capital on debt. The second is that the debt and its tax shelter are truly perpetual, with constant cash flows and discount rates. Still, the formula is very useful to quickly get a handle on the long-term benefits of additional debt.

Are Investment and Financing Decisions Separate Now?

If the world is not perfect, projects with different financing options can offer different values. Thus, financing and investment decisions must be considered together, not separately.

In the perfect M&M world, investment and financing decisions can be made independently: Managers can focus on production choices and leave the financing to the nerds in the finance department. Unfortunately, if debt is tax advantaged, or if there are other market imperfections, this is no longer the case.

Real estate has more debt capacity, which may add value if debt has value.

For example, consider two projects with equal costs, equal payoffs, and equal costs of capital. (Alternatively, just consider their NPVs to be the same.) The first project is a research and development project; the second is a building. In the real world, it is difficult to find a bank to lend money for R&D: After all, if the firm fails to pay its interest payments, there is often little that the bank can collect and resell. Buildings, on the other hand, are easy to repossess. Therefore, the building offers more **debt capacity** (and income tax shelters) than the R&D project. This can make it more valuable than the otherwise equally promising R&D project. Managers cannot choose among projects without taking into consideration how each project aids the debt capacity of the firm.

IMPORTANT

> In an imperfect world, unlike the M&M world, managers cannot ignore or delay financing decisions when making real investment decisions. The two decisions are intertwined.

A second complication derives from the fact that the value of the debt capacity can depend on who the owner is. Although most profitable and older firms are in the same highest tax bracket, some younger, growing, and unprofitable firms are in lower tax brackets. To these younger firms, the debt capacity is worth a lot less than it is to a large firm like PepsiCo (which can immediately use the tax deduction).

The same complication you saw in Chapter 10 is at work here, too: The value depends on the owner's identity.

The Average and Marginal Cost of Capital

In Section 16.6, you already encountered the distinction between the average and the marginal costs of capital. Beware that in our current chapter, we have been computing only the *average* cost of capital. Unfortunately, as manager, you are often more interested in your *marginal* cost of capital on the next dollar of financing, because you want to compare it to the marginal rate of return on your next project. When the world is imperfect, the average cost of capital is usually lower than the marginal cost of capital. For example, your firm may have been able to finance its existing plants with tax-preferred debt, but lenders may not want to provide debt for the R&D that it wants to undertake now. Nevertheless, to help you estimate your marginal cost of capital, it is often still quite useful to learn your average cost of capital. If nothing else, it gives you a lower bound.

Different projects can have different financing.

➤ *Marginal versus average cost of capital, Sect.* 16.6, *Pg.515*.

Of course, the distinction between the two costs of capital does not change any of the calculations in this chapter. Our chapter is concerned with valuing the firm's tax shelter if you keep the same projects and have the ability to take on different levels of debt. The income tax shelter has an influence on the marginal cost of capital, just as it has on the average cost of capital.

Lesser Evils: Combining Tax-Adjusted WACC with the CAPM

Let me tie up one final loose end. Formally speaking, the CAPM is a perfect-market model and does not hold in an imperfect world. But the theoretical advice not to use it does not help you much in the real world. What can you use in the real world?

Formally, it is wrong to use the CAPM in a world of taxes.

One answer is that you can be a pragmatist and just use the CAPM anyway. You could combine the tax-adjusted WACC formula with a cost of equity capital estimated from the CAPM:

Informally, you often have no better alternative for the cost of equity capital.

$$\mathcal{E}(r_{Firm}) = w_{Equity} \cdot \mathcal{E}(r_{Equity}) + (1 - \tau) \cdot w_{Debt} \cdot \mathcal{E}(r_{Debt})$$

$$\approx w_{Equity} \cdot \left\{ r_F + [\mathcal{E}(r_M) - r_F] \cdot \beta_{Equity} \right\} + (1 - \tau) \cdot w_{Debt} \cdot \mathcal{E}(r_{Debt})$$

This use of the CAPM to estimate a cost of equity capital, $\mathcal{E}(r_{Equity})$, is widespread. After all, we do not have a much better model. The quality of this approximation depends on how good the CAPM is in our real and imperfect world—and it is imperfect not only with respect to corporate income taxes but also with respect to other distortions explained in the next chapter (such as personal income taxes). Users generally hope that the CAPM cost of capital reasonably reflects all these other market imperfections. For example, if Treasuries must also offer relatively higher rates of return to compensate investors for higher personal income taxes on interest receipts—say, 5% taxable instead of 3.5% tax-exempt—your firm and your CAPM risk-free parameter should use the 5%, too. Thus, the personal income tax has made it into the historical parameter estimates of your CAPM model. As a corporation, this extra compensation payable to investors is part of your cost of capital that you have to pay to your investors, too. After all, your investors also suffer this tax imperfection.

For the term on the right, the cost of debt capital, $\mathcal{E}(r_{\text{Debt}})$, practice is more varied. Again, you want to estimate your *expected* interest rate (cost of capital). Unfortunately, the CAPM may not be a good model for bond pricing. The risk premium that is the main subject of the CAPM is often modest for bonds. Instead, it is liquidity and other imperfect market premiums (also elaborated on in the next chapter) that can be quite important. You may have to be more pragmatic here. One common practice is to estimate the historical average realized spread over Treasury that was earned by bonds of similar credit ratings, and use it to adjust the interest rate that you are quoted by your bank.

Of course, you should never rely on such a *quoted* interest rate on corporate debt, either your own debt or for bonds of similar credit ratings—because doing so would ignore the default premium—even if some analysts mistakenly do so. Fortunately, if you commit this error for very large, publicly traded corporations, you are only making a modest error. They rarely default. Unfortunately, for small firms, this may not be the case.

Debt cost of capital: Maybe you can use historical average excess rates of return for bonds in the same rating category.

➤ *Components of expected rates of return on corporate bonds, Exhibit 10.1, Pg.272.*

Do not forget about the difference between expected and promised returns!

➤ *Expected versus promised yields, Sect. 6.2, Pg.124.*

Q 17.12. A firm has expected before-tax earnings of $20 per year forever, starting next year. The firm is in the 25% tax bracket.

1. If the firm is financed with half debt (risk-free, at 5% per year) and half equity (at 10% per year), and this is eternally maintained, then what is its NPV?

2. If this firm took on $50 in debt and maintained its debt load at $50 forever (i.e., not the 50/50 debt-equity ratio), then what would this firm's value be?

17.7 Personal Income Taxes and Clientele Effects

Firms can reduce their costs of capital if they can reduce their investors' taxable personal incomes.

So far, you could just assume that all your investors are tax-exempt. Now we need to change this. Uncle Sam also collects his share from investors' income. As a corporate manager, does this mean that you need to think about your investors' personal income taxes? Yes! In effect, your corporate owners pay both your corporate income tax and their own personal income taxes. Take an extreme hypothetical example in which personal taxes on interest are 99%, personal taxes on dividends are 0%, and corporate income taxes are 40%. As the corporate CFO, should you pay out earnings as interest or as dividends?

- You can pay out $100 in interest payments. This means that your company can avoid all corporate taxes and pay out the full $100 from before-tax earnings as interest. As the CFO, you have sheltered *all* corporate income from taxes. Congratulations?! No—you have failed your clients. Your investors would have to pay $99 in taxes and therefore be left with only $1 to consume.

- You can pay out $100 in dividend payments. This means that your company has to pay $40 in corporate taxes. Does this mean that you have failed in your job as CFO? No! Your investors would receive the dividends tax-free and therefore get to consume a full $60.

You would have done good by your investors in choosing the equity-based capital structure, in which payments become dividends, relative to the debt-based capital structure, in which payments become interest. Even though financing with debt would have saved your firm on corporate income taxes, it would have been a terrible overall financial strategy. (As you will learn later, your investors would demand a very high cost of debt capital under this tax code, which would make you, as the manager, determine that debt is not as good a method of financing as equity.)

As a CFO, you therefore need to understand how your investors' personal income taxes can influence the optimal corporate capital structure. There is a subtle interplay between personal and corporate taxes, which creates both investor and firm clienteles, each with different tax profiles and different strategies, all evolved to reduce the overall tax payment to Uncle Sam. In the real world, we should see the following:

Firm clienteles: Small-growth firms should have more equity in their capital structures than large, cash-rich firms.

Investor clienteles: Highly taxed individual investors should invest more in equity-financed firms, and tax-exempt investors should invest more in bonds.

Let me show you how this works.

Investor clienteles and firm clienteles play important roles.

Q 17.13. Why should a CFO be concerned with taxes that the firm itself is not paying?

Background: The Tax Code for Security Owners

➤ *Introduction to taxes, Sect. 10.4, Pg.261.*

First, let's review our investors' tax situations. Recall that investors care about the type of income they receive:

Ordinary income is taxed at relatively high ordinary income tax rates (up to 35% federal, plus state), and it is very difficult to shelter from taxes.

Interest income is basically taxed like ordinary income.

Dividend income is taxed at a lower rate. If a domestic corporation has already paid taxes on its earnings, its dividends are considered "qualified," which reduces the personal tax rate imposed on the dividend recipients. Individuals in the 10% and 15% ordinary income tax brackets pay a 5% dividend tax, while those in higher tax brackets pay 15%. Giving investors credit for dividends paid from already-taxed earnings is similar to how the United Kingdom and many other countries have taxed dividends for a long time. However, in the United States, a lower dividend tax rate (more similar to the long-term capital gains tax rate) was instituted in 2003.

Capital gains income is generally the most tax-advantaged form of income. Although short-term capital gains are taxed at the (high) ordinary income tax rate (where short-term usually means one year or less), long-term capital gains on financial

The type of income matters: Capital gains income is better than interest income for taxable investors.

securities are taxed at the same statutory rate as qualifying dividends (i.e., 15% for high-income tax investors). The tax advantage of capital gains is not limited only to its relatively low statutory tax rate, however. There are two more advantages: Capital gains are not incurred on an annual basis, but only when they are realized. And, unlike interest or dividend income, capital gains can be offset by capital losses. Therefore, the best form of income for investors remains long-term capital gains.

We are ignoring tax code details.

This perspective is simplistic. For example, the U.S. tax code contains many special rules that can apply to certain forms of income depending on the exact payor and recipient. For example, unlike individuals, corporations as security holders still pay a 35% capital gains tax rate. Furthermore, there are some very intricate tax rules on how capital gains income and interest income on bonds must be computed. Generally, these regulations are designed to prevent firms from paying out cash in a form that counts as interest payments for them and as capital gains for their investors. In addition, there are hundreds of special clauses in the tax code—some pure corporate subsidies, some targeted at only one qualifying company, and others penalizing particular situations. The tax code is not static, either, but changes every year! And all this ignores state and sometimes local taxes, Social Security and Medicare contributions, and the like.

You must understand the logic and principles, not the specifics.

The interplay between the tax treatment of financial securities and the reaction of corporations is an ongoing cat-and-mouse game. You must first learn how to think about taxes, before you learn how our specific tax code works at the moment. Any details will likely be outdated within 10 years—if not sooner. (In fact, as I am writing this in mid 2011, taxes are set to increase for 2011, but it is not yet clear how. The latest proposals have the highest ordinary income tax rate go up from 35% to 39.6%, the capital gains tax rate go up from 15% to 20%, and dividends be taxed like ordinary income.)

Q 17.14. What kinds of income do investors like and dislike from a tax perspective?

Q 17.15. Explain the (personal and corporate) tax treatments if a company pays out its operating cash flow through interest payments, repurchased shares, or dividend payments.

The Principle Should Be "Joint Tax Avoidance"

The owners do not care where taxes are paid (corporate or personal), just that as little as possible is paid in total.

The main point of this section is simple: If managers want to best represent their corporate owners, they should consider not only the corporate income taxes that they have to pay directly, but also other issues—specifically the personal taxes—affecting their investors. To understand the logic, pretend that you are the sole owner of a corner shop ("the corporation") and you are also its manager. Do you care whether the IRS taxes you right at the cash register of your corporate business or taxes you personally when you move the cash from the corporate register into your own pocket? Or do you care instead about how much you can ultimately put into your pocket and use to buy goods? The finance premise is that you care only about the money in your pocket that you have left over *after* Uncle Sam has had his dip from both. You want to reduce the net tax obligation both at the cash register (the corporate tax) and in your own pocket (the personal tax). Corporate investors are no different from your corner shop. They really should not care about the earnings of the corporation. They should only care about spendable after-tax personal income that these earnings ultimately translate into. It should not matter whether the corporation or they themselves paid taxes.

> **IMPORTANT**
>
> - Both avoided corporate and personal taxes are cash that the owners can keep.
> - Reducing the total taxes ultimately collected by Uncle Sam (now and in the future) at *either* the corporate *or* the personal level can increase the value of the firm to its owners.

Tax Clienteles

Your Problem: How Can You Minimize Total IRS Receipts?

As a manager acting on behalf of your corporate owners, your corporate goal should be to minimize overall taxes paid, not just corporate taxes paid. You can shift tax burdens from your company to your investors (and vice versa) through your corporate financing and payout policies. Recall that your investors cannot shelter interest income, can modestly shelter dividend income, and can easily shelter capital gains income. So you face a trade-off:

Distributions in interest help the paying firm, but not (taxable) recipient investors. Distributions in capital gains save investors tax money, but not firms.

- If you plan to pay out cash as interest income, you will save on your own corporate income tax—but your investors will receive cash as interest payments and thus face the full brunt of Uncle Sam. Thus, your bond investors should demand a relatively higher expected rate of return.

- If you plan to reinvest retained earnings, which means that your earnings will become capital gains for your investors, you will pay a lot more in corporate income taxes—but your investors will receive almost-untaxed capital gains instead of taxable interest. This allows them to avoid most personal income taxes. Thus, relative to the appropriate perfect-market rate of return, your equity investors should demand a relatively lower expected rate of return than your equivalent bond investors.

To make matters even more interesting, you have to be concerned that, in real life, not every investor faces the same tax rate. There are low-tax investors, like tax-exempt charities and pension funds, who pay low or no personal income taxes on anything. And there are high-tax investors, like most retail investors, who pay high taxes on interest income, medium-high taxes on dividends, and low taxes on capital gains. What should you do?

An important complication is that different investors face different personal tax rates.

The best way to understand your choices is to imagine that you are a puppeteer, controlling the private economy. Your opponent is the IRS. You have the following game pieces:

SimCity Live: Let's arrange firms and investors to minimize tax liabilities.

1. High-tax corporations—mostly mature value firms with high earnings that cannot avoid paying taxes. (For example, in this decade, PepsiCo and RJR Nabisco are bulging with earnings and thus tax liabilities.)

2. Low-tax corporations—mostly smaller and often high-growth firms. (You would not have heard of most of these companies, but let me give you an example, anyway. In 1985, *Itar* was a shell company that consisted of nothing except large tax-loss carryforwards on net operating losses. Therefore, any earnings it would create [e.g., after a merger with a profitable company] would not be taxed.)

3. High-tax investors—like retail investors earning over $100,000 per year.

4. Low-tax or tax-exempt investors—like pension funds or money in tax-advantaged 401K retirement accounts.

This is not a perfect classification, because even low-tax investors must eventually pay some taxes, and even low-tax corporations may run out of tax shelters (or they can immediately use up all their tax credits and thereby become high-tax companies!). But it serves us well in thinking about the problem. How would you arrange your pieces? Would you have the high-tax corporation finance itself with debt or equity? Would you have the low-tax investor own the high-tax corporation or the low-tax corporation?

Your Solution: Arrange Clienteles

Who should own what is only interesting if tax-exempt investors are not in practically unlimited supply—or else they would own everything.

Clearly, you would not face a difficult problem if 99% of all investors were tax exempt—you could make all taxed corporations issue lots of debt (and thereby avoid corporate income taxes). In this case, neither corporations nor the almost entirely tax-exempt investor sector would end up owing taxes. Corporations would not have to worry about, or compensate, their investors for their (nonexistent) personal income taxes. Corporations could offer bonds with the same yield as equivalently risky but tax-exempt entities.

In the real world, low-tax investors are not in infinite supply.

However, low-tax investors are not in unlimited supply. The NYSE's *Factbook* reports that there was $11 trillion in total equities outstanding in 2002, of which 49.8% was held by all institutional investors, 36% by retail investors, and 11% by foreign investors. Almost half of the institutional money—a total 21.5% of the equities market—were tax-exempt pension funds. Thus, tax-exempt institutions are indeed a force, although a limited one.

"Clientele effects": different firms attract different investors. This reduces Uncle Sam's take.

So what is your best strategy? As master puppeteer with a limited number of tax-exempt investors, and with the task of minimizing Uncle Sam's take and maximizing your private sector take, you should sort your pieces into the following clienteles:

High-tax, profitable firms should pay out via interest (thus, have debt).

High-tax, profitable firms: Make your "cash-cow" value firms in the highest tax bracket issue debt, so that their cash flows can be paid out as interest, thereby avoiding the high corporate income tax.

Low-tax investors should hold this debt.

Low-tax investors: Make your tax-exempt investors hold this corporate debt, so that the interest receipts remain untaxed at the recipient level. (If you instead made your high-tax investors hold this debt, Uncle Sam would be better off, and you and your investors would be worse off.)

Uncle Sam therefore sees little cash from either of these two. You still have low-tax firms and high-tax investors to allocate. What can you do with them?

High-tax investors should hold equity.

High-tax investors: Make your high-tax individual investors hold stocks instead of bonds. They will then either receive capital gains (taxed very little) or dividends (taxed just a little more). This way, your high-tax investors will suffer only fairly low tax penalties, too.

Low-tax firms: Make your growth firms and other firms in the lowest corporate tax bracket finance themselves with equity, not with debt. You need this arrangement to satisfy the demand for equity by your high-tax investors. You can make your low-tax firms use their cash flows to reinvest in the corporation, repurchase their shares, or pay dividends. In any case, it would allow these firms' predominantly high-tax investors not to suffer much in taxes. (If you instead made your low-tax firms finance themselves with debt, the firms would have little use for the corporate income tax shelter provided by debt, at least compared to high corporate tax firms—and your high-tax investors would have no equities to buy.)

Low-tax, unprofitable firms should pay out via share repurchases or dividends (thus, have equity).

Again, Uncle Sam therefore sees little cash from either of these two.

Exhibits 17.5 and 17.6 try to illustrate the best puppeteering choices for firms and investors—and Uncle Sam's consequent take. All the numbers and tax rates are illustrative only and not exact. For simplicity, let's assume that the world is risk neutral, so that you do not have to worry about higher costs of capital for equity than debt. Our tax rate assumptions roughly follow the U.S. tax code:

We make up some tax rates to illustrate our best clientele allocations.

- High-tax corporations can pay interest from before-tax earnings.

- High-tax corporations pay taxes at a rate of 40% on earnings. They can then use after-tax earnings to repurchase shares or pay dividends.

- High-tax corporations pay taxes at a rate of 20% on earnings *if the earnings are reinvested*. This is because they can designate some reinvestment as a cost of operations (advanced "maintenance") and/or because there are often investment tax credits of some form or another.

- Low-tax corporations pay one-tenth the effective corporate income tax as high-tax corporations (i.e., 4% on earnings and 2% on reinvested earnings). This reflects the fact that they may face positive tax rates in the distant future, after they have exhausted all their tax-loss carryforwards. That is, using up tax-loss carryforwards is not "free."

- High-tax investors pay a tax rate of 40% on interest receipts.

- High-tax investors pay a tax rate of 20% on dividend receipts.

- High-tax investors pay a tax rate of 10% on capital gains. This tax rate (which is lower than the dividend tax rate) sketches a situation in which capital gains are better than dividends, because capital gains can be deferred and offset by losses.

- Low-tax investors pay one-tenth the effective personal income tax as high-tax investors. This means tax rates of 4%, 2%, and 1% on interest, dividends, and capital gains, respectively. The tax rates are not zero, because not all low-tax investors are nonprofit organizations and pension funds.

Let's consider what happens if either type of firm has $100 at its disposal.

Exhibit 17.5 shows that the high-tax firm can pay debt from before-tax earnings without incurring any tax penalty. Investors would receive interest, on which they would have to pay the full 40% ordinary income tax rate that is also applicable to interest income. If the firm reinvests all cash, it would manage to get some maintenance or

Work out the high-tax firm first.

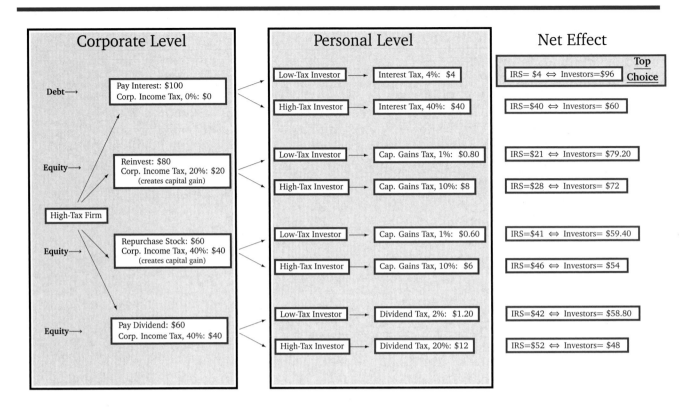

Exhibit 17.5: *Taxation Chain of a High-Tax Firm with $100 to Distribute.* A high-tax firm may be a value firm with lots of earnings and few deductions, such as RJR Nabisco. A high-tax investor may be a typical retail investor. A low-tax investor may be a tax-exempt pension fund. The low-tax investor is assumed to have an effective tax rate that is 1/10 that of a high-tax investor.

investment tax credits, so it would face a 20% effective corporate income tax rate. Investors would therefore get $80 in the form of capital gains (a higher value of their shares). If these are high-tax investors, they suffer only a 10% income tax rate on this gain, for a net personal tax obligation of $80 · 10% = $8. If the firm instead uses the money to repurchase shares or pay dividends, it would do so from after-corporate-income-tax cash. If the firm chose to repurchase shares, investors would pay 10% capital gains tax on $60 in share repurchases (i.e., $6) and twice this on dividends ($12). If you look at the last column ("net effect"), you can see that the best arrangement here is the top line—the clientele effect we discussed earlier, in which the IRS receives only $4.

Now work out the low-tax firm.

Exhibit 17.6 shows the low-tax firm. It can no longer use our low-tax investors—our economy has already used them up to help high-tax firms avoid corporate income taxes (in Exhibit 17.5). In addition, we still need to find our high-tax investors (like most ordinary retail investors) some investment opportunities. We therefore need to consider them only. If the low-tax firm pays interest, our high-tax investors would suffer a punitive $40 interest tax. Yikes! If the low-tax firm reinvests, it must pay $2 in corporate

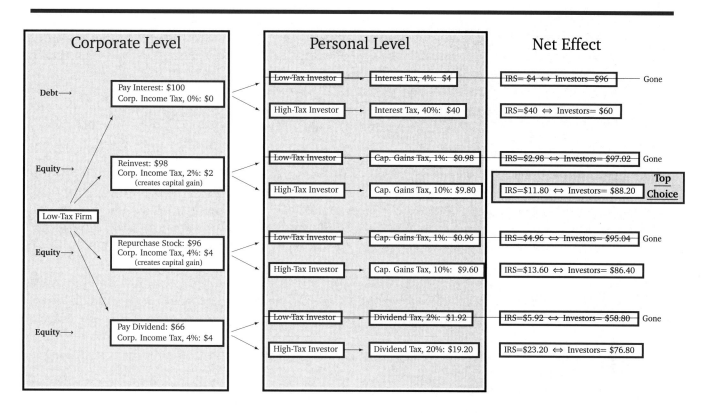

Exhibit 17.6: *Taxation Chain of a Low-Tax Firm with $100 to Distribute when Only High-Tax Investors Remain.* A low-tax firm may be a firm with a lot of tax-loss carryforwards or a growth firm that is unlikely to earn a profit for many years to come. The dark boxes in this figure (and "no longer available" lines) indicate that we have already used up our low-tax investors on high-tax firms, so that there are few or no low-tax investors left. *Side note:* A more realistic model would recognize that the Bush tax cuts of 2003 require the firm to have paid enough in tax, so that their investors qualify for the lower personal dividend tax rate. Because the low-tax firm here has not paid enough in taxes, investors may be taxed at the full rate of 40%. This 40% tax rate on $96 in income would result in a $38.40 dividend tax, on which the $4 of corporate income tax credit is applied. This means that the investor would have to pay a true dividend tax of $34.40, not $19.20.

income taxes. High-tax investors still suffer 10% as their effective personal income tax on capital gains, but this still leaves the IRS with only $11.80 and investors with $88.20. A choice that is just a little worse would be for the low-tax firm to repurchase its stock. The firm would pay a little more in corporate income tax ($4 instead of $2), and high-tax investors would still pay 10% ($9.60). Dividend payments still don't make much sense, because dividends are not as good as share repurchases for investors. (In fact, in the real world, because the low-tax firm has not paid enough in taxes, a special personal income tax rule applies, which taxes dividends at the ordinary income tax rate, instead of at the lower dividend tax rate.)

Can you do better? No.

Now put the two figures together. Our proposed solution leaves Uncle Sam with $4 + \$11.80 = \$15.80$ in receipts and the rest of the economy with $\$200 - \$15.80 = \$184.20$. Can you find a combination that is better? No! This is the best puppeteering that you can do!

Market Prices as Puppeteers

Extreme tax avoidance is interesting. But there is no puppeteer. Or is there?

But you are not a puppeteer, so why does any of the above matter? Is there a puppeteer in real life? Actually, there is. The puppeteer is the financial market! This is what capitalist markets are really good at—they allocate resources to their best uses, and the best use of capital here is where capital avoids paying taxes. The puppeteer's strings are the required costs of capital on debt and equity. They induce investors and firms to sort themselves to where the (tax-loss) frictions are the lowest. (If the market did not sort everything well, arbitrageurs could find a way to make money from rearranging firms and investors better to save on aggregate taxes.)

The puppeteer is the set of market prices that induce firms and investors to do the right thing.

Let me show you an example of how this might work. Let's work with the same example as before, in which $100 in before-tax cash is all that either type of firm has to decide on. However, to make it really simple, assume further that there is no uncertainty. What would happen if the financial market demanded a 10% interest rate as appropriate compensation for debt holders and a 7% capital gains rate as appropriate compensation for equity holders?

The high-tax (cash-cow) firm with $100 of income would realize that it had two options:

1. **Finance with equity:** After paying $40 in corporate income taxes, it would offer its investors a capital gain of $60, which would be worth $\$60/(1+7\%) \approx \$56.07$.

2. **Finance with debt:** Paying nothing in corporate income taxes, it would be worth $\$100/(1 + 10\%) \approx \$90.91$.

Value-maximizing managers of high-tax firms would therefore prefer to finance with debt.

The low-tax (growth) firm would realize that it had two options:

1. **Finance with equity:** After paying $2 in corporate income taxes, it would offer its investors a capital gain of $98, which would be worth $\$98/(1 + 7\%) \approx \$91.59$.

2. **Finance with debt:** Paying nothing in corporate income taxes, it would be worth $\$100/(1 + 10\%) \approx \$90.91$.

Value-maximizing managers of low-tax firms would therefore prefer to finance with equity.

High-tax (retail) investors could earn 7% in capital gains. After 10% in capital gains taxes, this would leave them with $7\% \cdot (1 - 10\%) = 6.3\%$ in after-personal-income-tax returns. Or they could earn 10% in interest income. After 40% in interest taxes, this would leave them with 6% in after-personal-income-tax returns. They will therefore prefer to invest in the equity of low-tax firms and not in the debt of high-tax firms.

Low-tax (pension fund) investors could also earn 7% in capital gains. This would leave them with a little under 7% in after-personal-income-tax returns. Or they could earn 10% in interest income. After 4% in interest taxes, this leaves them with $10\% \cdot (1 - 4\%) = 9.6\%$ in after-personal-income-tax returns. They will therefore prefer to invest in the debt of high-tax firms and not in the equity of low-tax firms.

As you can see, every party gravitated toward the choice that was most tax efficient—just as I claimed they would. It happened because I set the before-tax yields on interest above their perfect-market equivalents, and the before-tax yields on equity below their perfect-market equivalents. If there was uncertainty, then these required yields would of course also be affected by risk premiums.

You should now understand the tax rationale for how expected rates of return will sort firms and investors to minimize taxes. From your perspective as a corporate manager, the presence of personal income taxes has magically worked to increase your debt cost of capital relative to your equity cost of capital. However, relative to a nonclientele situation, clientele self-sorting has reduced the effective personal income tax penalty on debt. Clienteles mitigate your debt cost of capital.

Clienteles mitigate tax effects.

There is good empirical evidence that such tax-clientele ownership effects are important. For example, corporate bonds are overwhelmingly owned by tax-exempt institutions. Of course, in the real world, tax avoidance is just one (important) force at work, so the world is not as neat as our model. For instance, tax-exempt investors may want to diversify across many different companies, and not just hold exclusively the debt of high-tax, cash-cow corporations. The clientele net income tax reduction is not the only force at work.

The real world resembles this model sketch.

Q 17.16. Would Uncle Sam be better off if our puppeteer forced the low-tax firm to be financed with debt and the high-tax firm with (share-repurchasing) equity? Refer back to Exhibits 17.5 and 17.6.

Q 17.17. Would Uncle Sam be better off if our puppeteer forced low-tax investors to hold equity and high-tax investors to hold debt? Refer back to Exhibits 17.5 and 17.6.

Q 17.18. From a tax perspective, would you expect large, stable firms to be predominantly held by pension funds or by high-tax individuals? Would you expect young, growing firms to be predominantly held by pension funds or by high-tax individuals?

Q 17.19. Is it more critical for the high-tax firm or the low-tax firm to finance itself correctly?

Q 17.20. In a risk-neutral world, would a high-tax investor be satisfied with a lower rate of return on capital gains?

From the firm's perspective, tax-exempt investors (in the United States) reduce the cost of capital on debt.

➤ *WACC, Formula* 17.5, *Pg.533.*

➤ *APV, Formula* 17.1, *Pg.530.*

➤ *Another APV or WACC Formula?, Sect.* 18.9, *Pg.599.*

WACC and APV With Personal Taxes

Fortunately, you need no new formulas. WACC and APV remain the same. This will be explained in more detail in the next chapter. In brief, from a corporate CFO's perspective, the input figures will change with the taxes that are imposed on your investors, but not the formula. To the extent that retail investors have to pay more in taxes, they will demand higher expected rates of return. From your perspective, you can take the expected rates of return that they demand as given. (In contrast, you had to break out your own corporate income taxes in the APV and WACC formulas only because it was you yourself who had to pay corporate taxes on your net income.)

How to Think About Different Tax Codes

It is better to know how to analyze tax systems than to know just the current U.S. one.

Although this chapter has focused on the U.S. tax system, many other countries have similar tax codes, so the concepts remain universal. However, thinking about how taxes shape the optimal capital structure can help sharpen your understanding of the subject—and itself can be economically important. After all, there is no guarantee that the U.S. tax code won't be radically different in 10 years, or even that you will be working in the United States in 5 years. So let's consider the effects of two tax code changes:

1. Standing in 2002, what would you have expected the effect of the Bush tax cuts of 2003 to be? Recall that these tax changes lowered the effective tax rates on qualified dividends.

2. How should German firms behave, given that there are practically no tax-exempt investors?

How would either change your analysis?

Lower Individual Dividend Taxes: The Bush Tax Cuts of 2003

The Bush dividend tax cuts would have dropped the required rate of return on equity.

From an abstract capital structure perspective, you can think of lowering the dividend tax rate as the equivalent of lowering the effective personal income tax rate on equity. For argument's sake, assume an extreme perspective:

- Your investors demand an expected after-personal-income-tax rate of return of 6%.

- Ignore the fact that even before 2003 corporations often avoided all personal income taxes on dividends by repurchasing shares or by reinvesting earnings. Instead, assume that dividend tax cuts reduced the effective taxation from 50% to 25%.

Compared to 2002, at what rates were corporations expected to be able to finance projects in 2003?

Corporations should have taken on more equity in their capital structures, because they could now pay more in dividends with less of a tax penalty.

Before 2003, your investors would have held your shares only if the expected equity rate of return was $\mathcal{E}(r_{\text{Equity}}) = 12\%$, of which they got to keep 6%. At the newly lowered personal income tax rate, they should be equally pleased to hold your equity at the lower 8% before-personal income tax rate of return, because $(1-25\%) \cdot 8\% = 6\%$. Consequently, from the perspective of your corporation, the necessary and appropriate equity cost of capital, $\mathcal{E}(r_{\text{Equity}})$, in the valuation formulas would have dropped from

12% to 8%. (Of course, this is a simplification. The tax cuts may also have changed the economy and with it other alternatives available to investors. They could have attracted more firms and investors into this market, too, which could have forced an appropriate equilibrium after-tax expected rate of return on equity that was not exactly 6%.) For most firms, such a drop would mean that they should shift from debt financing to equity financing—and that they should take more projects, given the now lower cost of capital.

No Tax-Exempt Investors: Germany

Our second example of a different tax code is the situation in Germany, a country without tax-exempt investors. If the absence of such investors is the only difference, how would you advise the management of a German firm about its optimal capital structure?

Germany has no tax-exempt investors.

As just noted, personal taxes (and thus the absence of tax-exempt investors) would have an influence on the inputs in the APV and WACC formulas, but not on the formula itself. For example, if investors faced a higher tax rate, they would demand higher rates of return, especially when they buy corporate debt. See, the U.S. tax-clientele sorting had tax-exempt pension funds invest in corporate bonds and taxable retail investors invest in corporate stock. The presence of tax-exempt investors in the United States effectively reduced debt's cost of capital. Even though the previous section did not say so explicitly, this was the principal reason why high-tax corporations in the United States enjoyed net tax savings by issuing bonds—why the effective corporate income tax subsidy to debt financing was so high and the cost of capital to debt was so low. Tax-exempt investors kept the cost of debt capital, $\mathscr{E}(r_{\text{Debt}})$—and with it $(1-\tau) \cdot \mathscr{E}(r_{\text{Debt}})$—low relative to the cost of equity capital, $\mathscr{E}(r_{\text{Equity}})$. This favored debt financing over equity financing.

German corporations thus face higher costs of capital.

Without tax-exempt investors, financial market investors would demand a higher interest rate for corporate debt, $\mathscr{E}(r_{\text{Debt}})$. After all, taxable investors (which must also hold the corporate debt) care about their after-personal-tax rates of return, not their before-personal-tax rates of return. Investors would suffer especially high personal income taxes if they held corporate debt. Thus, they would demand a relatively higher $\mathscr{E}(r_{\text{Debt}})$. The result is that the overall corporate WACC in Germany, unlike in the United States, may not decline with w_{Debt}. It may even be that $\mathscr{E}(r_{\text{Debt}}) \cdot (1-\tau)$ is higher than $\mathscr{E}(r_{\text{Equity}})$ for even low corporate debt levels. Though algebraically correct, the tax-advantaged WACC formula would now be unimportant: The minimum WACC could even occur at a $w_{\text{Equity}} = 1$ if investors' personal taxes on received interest income are higher than the tax deductions that firms receive on paid interest.

Without tax-exempt investors, it could be that the optimal tax solution is for firms to be all-equity-financed (if interest income is sufficiently badly taxed for taxable investors).

Thinking more broadly about foreign tax codes, what should matter for the optimal capital structure is the relative effective tax rate of investors and corporations.

Our tax-shifting SimCity arrangements now depend more on the relative taxes that investors versus corporations would have to pay.

- If the effective tax rate is higher for individuals than for corporations, then the better tax arrangement is for corporations to pay the taxes—there would be no net tax advantage to debt. Corporate debt would not be subsidized, but rather penalized by the foreign tax code. Firms should be financed with equity, which allows investors to avoid tax liabilities.

- If the effective tax rate is higher for corporations than it is for individuals, then the better tax arrangement is for the investors to pay the taxes—there would be a net tax advantage to debt. Firms should now be financed heavily with debt, which forces the tax liability onto investors. This is conceptually similar to the U.S. solution, with a U.S.-style WACC formula, except that $\mathcal{E}(r_{\text{Debt}})$ could be fairly high.

Debt versus equity is still a mechanism to shift the tax liability, and low-tax firms should still finance with more equity than high-tax firms should.

However, even if corporate taxes are high and personal taxes are low, one feature of the U.S. situation would likely survive in other countries. Companies are heterogeneous, and debt remains a mechanism to shift tax liabilities from the firm to investors. Thus, there would still be some low-tax and some high-tax firms. Low-tax firms would find that their optimal capital structure would still be primarily equity, because they would not gain anything from the tax deductibility of interest. In contrast, high-tax firms would have to decide to finance with either debt or equity, and this decision would depend on their own marginal corporate income tax rates relative to the investors' marginal personal income tax rates. Their managers would obtain this information by looking at the relative costs of debt and equity financing offered to them in the financial markets. In sum, low-tax firms would want to keep the tax liability (by remaining equity-financed) rather than hand the tax liability to their investors. We cannot say what the optimal choice of high-tax firms would be. If the corporate income tax rate is lower than the personal income tax rate, then even high-tax firms may want to finance themselves with equity.

Q 17.21. In Atlantis, all firms are tax exempt. Only investors pay income taxes. How should firms be financed? How would the WACC formula work?

17.8 The U.S. Tax System

Some Other Corporate Tax Avoidance Schemes

There are too many tax avoidance schemes in existence to list in just one book. They are also changing all the time. Here are some examples.

Wall Street and Main Street employ armies of lobbyists and tax accountants and lawyers to help themselves and their clients avoid taxes, but this is really an arms race between the IRS (Congress) and investors. Investors and companies keep looking for or are actively lobbying Congress for new tax avoidance schemes; and the IRS (when it can) tries to close these new loopholes. There are a large number of both past (now closed) and current tax avoidance schemes. Some of the more noteworthy remaining tax reduction schemes are as follows:

- Sometimes, high-tax firms may be able to purchase low-tax firms, and thereby immediately use the acquired firm's existing **net operating losses** (**NOLs**).

  For example, the *Financial Times* reported on February 10, 1994, that the £2.5B GKN Corporation made a hostile bid for the £300M Westland Corporation, solely because GKN needed Westland's NOLs to reduce its own corporate taxes due.

- Compared to purchasing on credit, **leasing** can be a tax-advantageous arrangement. If the borrower does not have enough income to use the interest deduction efficiently, someone else should be the official owner of the asset and "lease" it to the borrower, thereby capturing the full benefit of the interest deductibility.

- Multinational corporations can shift difficult-to-value profitable assets from a high-tax to a low-tax country. For example, corporate income taxes in Switzerland (federal and canton) can be as low as 7.8% (for holding companies) and as high as 25%. This contrasts with state and federal corporate income tax rates as high as 45% in the United States. Now consider a company that has just developed a patent worth $10 million per year. If the U.S. branch owns the patent, the firm would retain only $(1 - 45\%) \cdot \$10 = \$5.5$ million per year. If the Swiss branch owns the patent, the firm would retain up to $(1 - 7.8\%) \cdot \$10 \approx \$9.2$ million per year. Why stop at $10 million? If the Swiss branch charges the U.S. branch $20 million per year, the firm's U.S. tax obligations (resulting from profits from other businesses) would decrease by $9 million per year ($45\% \cdot \$20$ million), but Swiss tax obligations would increase by $1.56 million per year ($7.8\% \cdot \$20$ million). Still, this is a healthy $7.4 million net gain per year (relative to a situation in which the Swiss branch would change nothing).

  This tax-efficient capital transfer can also be accomplished with capital structure. For example, if the Swiss branch lent funds to the U.S. branch at an interest rate of 36% per year, rather than 6% per year, the effect would be a reduction of the firm's tax liabilities. For every $1,000 in excess interest paid (at the 36% instead of the 6% rate), the company would retain an extra $(45\% - 7.8\% = 37.2\%)$ $372 in profits. Companies can play similar, but less drastic, tax games by choosing the U.S. state and municipality in which they are headquartered.

  The IRS is very much aware of these issues. For example, the *Wall Street Journal* reported on June 24, 2002, that the IRS is trying to prevent firms from shifting intellectual property, such as patents, to other countries in which corporations would have fewer taxes to pay. It's a tough cat-and-mouse game.

- Many firms move their headquarters to different states or even countries (to avoid most U.S. taxes on their worldwide income altogether).

A Sane Tax Code?

How good is the U.S. tax system? It's terrible. In fact, it can only be described as insane.

First, it costs a lot to administer, yet the U.S. collects very little from corporate income taxes. As of 2010, only about 1% of GDP was collected in corporate taxes, down from about 4.1% in 1965. (In Germany, it is similar. In Canada, it is about 3-5%.)

Among the reasons for this low tax take are the so-called *special income tax provisions* that Congress has enacted. These often apply to only one single company, usually a large political contributor and employer in a Congressional district or state. Together, the special income tax provisions amount to more than $1 trillion dollars a year. (For perspective, this is more than the total amount of federal discretionary spending.) The non-partisan GAO found that 72% of foreign corporations and 57% of U.S. corporations did not pay any taxes in at least one year between 1998 and 2005. More than 50% and 42% did not pay taxes for two or more years. Picking just the final year, 2005, about 25% of the largest U.S. companies paid no federal income taxes. It continues. In 2009, Exxon made $19 billion in profits, yet it *received* $156 million from the IRS. Bank of America made $4.4 billion in profits (having been bailed out by taxpayer funds), yet

It's insane.

The U.S. collects very little in corporate taxes.

Why so little? What does this mean for companies?

paid nothing. John Graham (from Duke University) reported that a large number of firms—but not all—are fully aware of how to manage their taxes effectively. In fiscal year 2001, about 6,000 firms had effective tax rates of 5% or less! Between 1,500 and 2,000 firms had tax rates between 5% and 30%. And about 4,000 firms had tax rates between 30% and 40%. As I write this in 2011, 160 high-powered corporate lobbyists are pressing for a tax holiday for more than $1.4 trillion in offshore profits, which their employers would then repatriate. The lobbyists include former chiefs of staff of the most important U.S. House and Senate members, both Democrat and Republican.

Should the government prevent corporate tax avoidance?

Before such corporate tax avoidance schemes outrage you too much, you should realize that you may even benefit when tax lawyers and Congress help many U.S. companies succeed in escaping some of their tax burdens. First, corporations are just vehicles owned by investors. Corporate income taxes are ultimately paid by the investors—often small dispersed investors like you, perhaps in your pension fund. Second, the United States has no monopoly on corporate locations. If U.S. taxes are too high, some corporations may just leave the United States; others may never come. Question: Where do you think Dell Computer is located? If you answered "Texas," you are wrong. Dell moved its worldwide headquarters to Singapore in January 2007. Question: Are Google world-wide sales primarily occurring in Silicon Valley? Nope. They occur mostly in Ireland, where Google pays a grand rate of 2.4%. Many financial services firms have already left, too. U.S. disclosure and tax laws and regulations have built strong financial service centers in places like the Bermudas, the Cayman Islands, and Switzerland. Some European countries have even stronger regulations than the United States, and many are in fact experiencing similar capital and corporate flight as the United States. (I do not have statistics, but I would guess that the tiny *Isle of Man* may have as many corporations today as the entire *United Kingdom* proper.)

Intra-U.S. State competition.

Tax reduction through relocation does not just apply to countries, but also to U.S. states. Question: Where does Microsoft sell its software from? If you answered "Seattle, Washington," you are wrong. Corporate software sales are located in Nevada, where there is no corporate income tax. This saves Microsoft over $50 million per year. Greenwich, Connecticut is the financial services center that the New York tax code built. These days, most hedge funds that remain in the United States (and all have foreign subsidiaries!) have located themselves not in New York City, but in Greenwich, CT, a small town just across the border from New York that was formerly a place for vacation homes. They did so to avoid N.Y. state and city taxes. (And, in a twist of irony, all these hedge fund managers now own vacation homes in New York City.)

But we get the worst of all worlds.

So, why am I upset? It is not because many corporations are paying low taxes. It is because of how this happens and its consequences. It would be wonderful if our low tax rate encouraged corporations to settle and operate in the United States. Unfortunately, it does not. The U.S. tax code actively does the opposite. The actual U.S. tax rates for established corporations with armies of good lobbyists, smart tax lawyers, and a global structure may be low, but the statutory tax rates for corporations that just want to come and operate in the U.S. is high. In fact, the situation is full of irony. It is not greed, but the legal fiduciary duty of U.S. executives to reduce their corporate taxes as much as they legally can. More often than not, this means locating their most valuable assets, their operations, and sometimes even their headquarters offshore. This is because foreign domiciles collect even less in incomes taxes when a corporation headquartered offshore then does business in the United States.

A N E C D O T E   **Stanley Works and Foreign Domiciles**

In mid-2002 Stanley Works, a 100-year-old prominent Connecticut-based global manufacturer of tools, was in the process of locating its headquarters to Bermuda. Relocating would have allowed Stanley's *foreign* subsidiaries to escape U.S. income taxes. (A U.S. corporation pays U.S. income taxes on all worldwide income. A foreign corporation pays U.S. income taxes only on its U.S. income.) In the end, unusually strong media attention, public outcries, and the threat of special legislation prevented Stanley's departure.   *The Wall Street Journal*

In sum, the United States has a system that not only offers incentives for companies to move out of the United States, but also collects very low corporate income tax receipts. So, why is Congress not fixing the matter? Simple—Congressmen depend on the financial contributions of corporate lobbyists, and usually become lobbyists after they retire. If Congress simply eliminated all corporate taxes and subsidies, there would be little reason for corporations to hire lobbyists and donate to reelection campaigns. It's not individuals that are corrupt; it's the system. It's all of us.

Don't blame individuals. It's the system.

Summary

This chapter covered the following major points:

- In the imperfect real world, the U.S. tax code favors debt over equity. Managers should take this corporate income tax advantage into account.

- The calculation of the income tax advantage can be done through the APV method, the tax-adjusted WACC method, or the flow-to-equity method (a full pro forma employing a financing scenario that subtracts the interest and thereafter corrects for the reduced tax burden).

- Both the APV and the WACC method begin with cash flows *as if fully equity-financed and fully taxed*, which is why they need to put back the tax advantage derived from the presence of debt.

  - APV does so by adding back the tax benefit:

$$\text{APV} = \frac{\mathscr{E}(C)}{1 + \mathscr{E}(r_{\text{Firm}})} + \frac{\overbrace{\tau \cdot \overbrace{\mathscr{E}(r_{\text{Debt}})}^{\text{Interest Payment}} \cdot \text{Debt}}^{\text{Tax Shield}}}{1 + \mathscr{E}(r)}$$

  For the discount rate $\mathscr{E}(r)$ applicable to the right term (the expected tax shelter), the following guidelines (explained in the appendix) may help: If the firm's debt ratio will decline over time, use the debt cost of capital. If it will remain constant, use the firm's overall cost of capital. If it will increase, use the equity cost of capital.

– WACC does so by lowering the cost of debt capital:

$$PV = \frac{\mathscr{E}(C)}{1 + WACC} \quad \text{and} \quad WACC = \mathscr{E}(r_{Firm}) - \tau \cdot \mathscr{E}(r_{Debt}) \cdot w_{Debt}$$

WACC can also be written as $w_{Equity} \cdot \mathscr{E}(r_{Equity}) + w_{Debt} \cdot \mathscr{E}(r_{Debt}) \cdot (1 - \tau)$.

• These methods usually arrive at similar but not exactly identical valuations. We are rarely sure about the appropriate discount rate that should be applied to the future tax benefits in the APV formula. The WACC formula cannot deal with changing costs of capital or debt ratios over time at all. However, the errors that an incorrect discount rate on the tax shield would cause are usually dwarfed by other simplifications and uncertainty in expected cash flows and discount rates.

• The one error you should never commit is to use the wrong expected cash flows. That is, never add the APV tax subsidy or lower tax-adjusted WACC cost of capital when the cash flows are not "as if fully equity-financed and after having been fully taxed."

• The following heuristic is often convenient: A constant extra dollar of debt *forever* increases the value of the firm by the firm's marginal income tax rate. For example, a $100 eternal debt increase will create $30 in value for a firm in the 30% marginal income tax bracket.

• In the imperfect real world, financing and investment decisions can no longer be separated: Projects that add more debt capacity may add value through the financing channel.

• In the imperfect real world, the WACC is not the marginal cost of capital.

• It is common and reasonable to combine the WACC formula or APV formula with the CAPM formula, even if this is not entirely correct.

• One managerial objective should be to minimize the overall tax burden—the sum of taxes paid by the corporation and its investors.

• Investor clientele effects arise because they reduce overall tax payments. These effects are illustrated below.

Choice	Low-Tax Investors (e.g., pension funds)	High-Tax Investors (e.g., high-income individuals)
Good	Hold bonds (or very-high-dividend stocks)	Hold (low-dividend) stocks with high capital gains
Bad	Hold (low-dividend) stocks with high capital gains	Hold bonds (or very-high-dividend stocks)

Choice	High-Tax Corporations (e.g., "cash cows")	Low-Tax Corporations (e.g., "growth firms")
Good	Finance with bonds	Finance with stocks (and pay out via share repurchases instead of via dividends)
Bad	Finance with stocks	Finance with bonds

It is the market prices for the cost of capital that incentivize smart firms and smart investors to arrange themselves in this clientele fashion to reduce overall taxes.

- There are numerous other tax-reduction schemes that firms can undertake—way too numerous to enumerate.

- The existing U.S. tax system is not only counterproductive, but outright insane.

Preview of the Chapter Appendix in the Companion

The appendix to this chapter explains how you should think of and select a good discount rate for the APV tax shelter. (If the debt ratio is likely to decline in future years, use the cost of capital on debt. If it is likely to remain stable, use the expected rate of return on the firm. If it is likely to increase, use the cost of capital on equity.)

In the Appendix

Keywords

APV, 528.   Adjusted present value, 528.   Debt capacity, 544.   Flow-to-equity, 536.   LBO, 527.   Leasing, 558. Leveraged buyout, 527.   NOL, 558.   Net operating losses, 558.   Tax-adjusted WACC, 528.

Answers

Q 17.1 This 17% and 12% scenario is the example in the text, slightly amplified: NPV $= -\$100 + (\$117.00 - \$17.00 \cdot 30\%)/1.12 \approx -\$0.09 < 0$.

Q 17.2 For this debt-equity hybrid, the firm has to earn $500 if the security is designated as debt with an interest payment. But if the security is designated as equity with a dividend distribution, then it would have to earn $\$500/(1-0.33) \approx \$746$, because only $500 of the $746 will be left after the firm has paid its corporate income taxes.

Q 17.3 For the $1 million construction project:

1. With a $200,000 return, Uncle Sam would receive $200,000 · 45% = $90,000 if you pay out cash.

2. If you finance with 80% debt, you will have $800,000 · 5% = $40,000 in interest to deduct from the $200,000 return. Thus, you would pay taxes only on $160,000. This lowers your tax bill to $160,000 · 45% = $72,000. (*Side advice:* If you borrow $800,000, you may have to invest your $800,000 elsewhere. If you do not choose tax-exempts, Uncle Sam may receive more taxes from your additional income on the $800,000.)

3. The net subsidy is $90,000 − $72,000 = $18,000 next year. At an appropriate cost of capital of 8%, this is a PV of $\$18,000/1.08 \approx \$16,667$.

Q 17.4 For the 25/75 debt-equity financing, the WACC valuation is

$$PV = \frac{\$256}{1 + 12\% - 25\% \cdot 30\% \cdot 8\%} \approx \$229.80$$

$$\frac{\mathcal{E}(C)}{1 + \mathcal{E}(r_{Firm}) - w_{Debt} \cdot \tau \cdot \mathcal{E}(r_{Debt})}$$

The firm has $229.80 · 25% = $57.45 of debt (and $172.35 in equity value today). Its APV is

$$APV = \frac{\$256}{1 + 12\%} + \frac{30\% \cdot 8\% \cdot \$57.45}{1 + 12\%} \approx \$229.80$$

$$APV = \frac{\mathcal{E}(C)}{1 + \mathcal{E}(r_{Firm})} + \frac{\tau \cdot \mathcal{E}(r_{Debt}) \cdot Debt}{1 + \mathcal{E}(r_{Firm})}$$

Q 17.5 For the $100 debt financing, the APV valuation is

$$\text{APV} = \frac{\$256}{1 + 12\%} + \frac{30\% \cdot 8.7\% \cdot \$100}{1 + 12\%} \approx \$230.90$$

$$\text{APV} = \frac{\mathcal{E}(C)}{1 + \mathcal{E}(r_{\text{Firm}})} + \frac{\tau \cdot \mathcal{E}(r_{\text{Debt}}) \cdot \text{Debt}}{1 + \mathcal{E}(r_{\text{Firm}})}$$

Therefore, the $100 debt is 43.3% of the firm's value today. The WACC-based valuation is

$$\text{PV} \approx \frac{\$256}{1 + 12\% - 43.3\% \cdot 30\% \cdot 8.7\%} \approx \$230.90$$

Q 17.6 You would prefer to use WACC if you follow a constant ratio-based debt target, and APV if you follow a dollar-based debt target. Look at the previous two questions. You cannot figure out the APV in the first question before you determine the WACC, and the opposite is true in the second question.

Q 17.7 Exhibit 17.2 draws the WACC as a function of the debt ratio with only corporate income tax distortions.

Q 17.8 The firm's overall cost of capital today is $6\% \cdot 1/3 + 12\% \cdot 2/3 = 10\%$. Because $4\% + 3\% \cdot \beta = 10\%$, the beta is 2. The easy way is to recognize that the firm is sheltering $500 \cdot 6\% = \$30$ through interest payments. If it refinanced with $1,000, it could now shelter $1,000 \cdot 8\% = \$80$. Uncle Sam would see an additional $50 less in income, which means that the firm would pay $50 \cdot 20\% = \$10$ less in income tax *next year*. Now you need to determine the appropriate discount rate for $10 in tax savings. For convenience, use the debt cost of capital: 8%. This means that our recapitalization increases firm value by $10/1.08 \approx \$9.26$. (If you prefer to use the overall firm cost of capital, you would obtain $9.09.) The question intentionally gave additional irrelevant information about the firm's future existence.

Q 17.9 Let's do this in steps:

- This project will offer $200 before-tax profit in year 1. Discounted back at the firm's cost of capital (don't worry if this is exact), the NPV without taxes is $-\$300 + \$500/1.2 \approx \$116.67$. But, if equity-financed, the IRS will declare taxes due on $200 of profit, or $80. Therefore, the NPV with taxes and all equity-financed is $-\$300 + \$420/1.2 = \$50$.

- Now, right after the investment, the firm has a value of $420/1.2 = \$350$. With debt of $50 ($100), the firm carries a debt load of around $\$50/\$350 \approx 14.3\%$ (28.6%). Let's round this to 15% (30%). The cost of debt capital formula given in the question suggests that $\mathcal{E}(r_{\text{Debt}}) = 15\% + 15\% \cdot 5\% = 15.75\%$ (16.5%). (Note: The question is a bit ambiguous in that it does not tell you what to use as firm value. The 15% and 30% debt ratios are reasonable values, though.)

- Interest payments on $50 ($100) at a cost of capital of 15.75% (16.5%) are $7.88 ($16.50) *next year*. Facing a tax rate of 40%, Uncle Sam would thereby subsidize the project to the tune of $40\% \cdot \$7.88 \approx \$3.15$ ($6.60), which in today's value would be worth around $\$3.15/1.2 \approx \$2.63$ ($5.50). Therefore, under APV, if financed with $50 in debt, the project is

worth $\$50 + \$2.63 = \$52.63$. (With $100 in debt, the APV is $\$50 + \$5.50 = \$55.50$).

- The equity cost of capital, if 15% of the firm is financed by debt at a rate of 15.75%, is the solution to $15\% \cdot 15.75\% + 85\% \cdot \mathcal{E}(r_{\text{Equity}}) = 20\% \Rightarrow \mathcal{E}(r_{\text{Equity}}) = 20.75\%$. Therefore, the WACC is given by the formula, $w_{\text{Equity}} \cdot \mathcal{E}(r_{\text{Equity}}) + w_{\text{Debt}} \cdot \mathcal{E}(r_{\text{Debt}}) \cdot (1 - \tau) = 85\% \cdot 20.75\% + 15\% \cdot 15.75\% \cdot (1 - 40\%) \approx 19.06\%$. Similarly, if $100 is borrowed, $\mathcal{E}(r_{\text{Equity}}) = 21.5\%$, and $\text{WACC} = w_{\text{Equity}} \cdot \mathcal{E}(r_{\text{Equity}}) + w_{\text{Debt}} \cdot \mathcal{E}(r_{\text{Debt}}) \cdot (1 - \tau) = 70\% \cdot 21.5\% + 30\% \cdot 16.5\% \cdot (1 - 40\%) \approx 18.02\%$. The WACC-based value with $50 in debt is thus $-\$300 + \$420/1.1906 \approx \$52.76$. (With $100 in debt, it is $-\$300 + \$420/1.1802 \approx \$55.87$.) Note that you have made enough little assumptions and approximations that it would make little sense to worry now about being off by a little in the APV and WACC computations ($52.76 and $52.63).

Q 17.10 For our 3-year project firm:

1. The pro forma for a 100% equity-financed firm is shown below.

Income Statement		Y1	Y2	Y3
	EBITDA (= Net Sales)	$70	$60	$55
−	Depreciation	$50	$50	$50
=	EBIT	$20	$10	$5
−	Interest Expense	$0	$0	$0
−	Income Tax (at 40%)	$8	$4	$2
=	**Net Income**	$12	$6	$3

Limited Cash Flow Statement		Y1	Y2	Y3
	Net Income	$12	$6	$3
+	Depreciation	$50	$50	$50
=	**Operating Cash Flow**	**$62**	**$56**	**$53**
	Capital Expenditures	−$150	$0	$0
=	**Investing Cash Flow**	**−$150**	**0**	**0**

Economic Project Cash Flows = (Operating CF + Investing CF + Interest)	Y1	Y2	Y3
Project Cash Flows	−$88	+$56	+$53

2. The IRR of our project solves

$$\frac{-\$88}{1 + \text{IRR}} + \frac{+\$56}{(1 + \text{IRR})^2} + \frac{+\$53}{(1 + \text{IRR})^3} = 0$$

Thus, the IRR of a purely equity-financed project is 15.69%.

3. The NPV of the purely equity-financed project is

$$NPV = \frac{-\$88}{1.18} + \frac{+\$56}{1.18^2} + \frac{+\$53}{1.18^3} \approx -\$2.10$$

This is in line with the fact that the project IRR of 15.69% is less than the 18% cost of capital.

4. The cash flows would increase to –$88, +$58, and +$55. The IRR would increase to 18.61%.

5. The debt-financed pro forma would now be as follows:

Income Statement

	Y1	Y2	Y3
EBITDA	$70	$60	$55
– Depreciation	$50	$50	$50
= EBIT	$20	$10	$5
– Interest Expense	**$0**	**$5**	**$5**
– Income Tax (40%)	$8	$2	$0
= **Net Income**	$12	$3	$0

(Limited) Cash Flow Statement

	Y1	Y2	Y3
Net Income	$12	$3	$0
+ Depreciation	$50	$50	$50
= **Operating CF**	**$62**	**$53**	**$50**
Capital Exp.	–$150	$0	$0
= **Investing CF**	**–$150**	**0**	**0**

Economic Project Cash Flows
=(Operating CF + Investing CF + Interest)

	Y1	Y2	Y3
Project CF	–$150 + $62	$53 + $5	$50 + $5
=	**–$88**	**+$58**	**+$55**

The Economics of Financing

	Y1	Y2	Y3
Debt Flow	+$50	–$5	–$55
Equity Flow	+$38	–$53	$0

Not surprisingly, these are the same as the aforementioned cash flows, with a $2 income tax subsidy in years 2 and 3. The IRR is again 18.61%.

6. The NPV of the debt-financed firm is

$$NPV = \frac{-\$88}{1.18} + \frac{+\$58}{1.18^2} + \frac{+\$55}{1.18^3} \approx +\$0.55$$

With the tax subsidy, this project becomes worthwhile.

7. The APV of this project would start with the as-if-100%-equity-financed value. This was computed above as

$$\frac{-\$88}{1.18} + \frac{+\$56}{1.18^2} + \frac{+\$53}{1.18^3} = -\$2.10$$

For APV, now add the discounted tax subsidies in years 2 and 3. These have a value of

$$Tax\ Subsidy = \frac{\$2}{1.18^2} + \frac{\$2}{1.18^3} \approx \$2.65$$

Therefore, the APV would be –$2.10 + $2.65 = $0.55.

8. By APV, the expected tax subsidy would shrink from $\tau \cdot \mathcal{E}(Interest\ Payment) = 40\% \cdot \$5 = \$2$ per year to $\tau \cdot \mathcal{E}(Interest\ Payment) = 40\% \cdot \$4 = \$1.60$ per year. The expected value of the tax subsidy would therefore be

$$Tax\ Subsidy = \frac{\$1.60}{1.18^2} + \frac{\$1.60}{1.18^3} \approx \$2.12$$

The net project value would be about $0.02.

9. You can see that after year 2 and before year 3, the debt is expected to be 100% of the capital structure. However, in year 1, with debt contributing $50, it is obviously not 0% of the firm. Thus, its weight in the capital structure is drastically changing. This firm is not at all a good candidate for using WACC.

P.S.: Please do not try to compute a weighted average cost of capital from the debt and equity internal rates of return (10% and 40%, respectively). If the debt would be at 57% of the firm's capital structure, then the appropriate rate of return of equity would have to be around 30% so that the weighted cost of capital would come out to $\mathcal{E}(r_{Firm}) = w_{Debt} \cdot \mathcal{E}(r_{Debt}) + w_{Equity} \cdot \mathcal{E}(r_{Equity}) = 18.6\%$. This is much lower than the equity IRR of 40% (which is the same as its expected rate of return from year 1 to year 2), because from year 2 to year 3, the equity becomes a much smaller part of the firm. What bites you in this case is the fact that you have a strong term structure of investment weights.

Q 17.11 With $1,691 million in taxes on $5,670 million income before the corporate income tax, Coca-Cola was paying around 30% income tax on average. Presumably, this was also close to its marginal tax rate. The $289 million that Coca-Cola paid in interest therefore cost Uncle Sam about $86.2 million in reduced taxes.

Q 17.12 For the $20 earnings firm in the 25% tax bracket:

1. The weighted average cost of capital is

$$WACC = 50\% \cdot 5\% \cdot (1 - 25\%) + 50\% \cdot 10\% = 6.875\%$$
$$WACC = w_{Dbt} \cdot \mathcal{E}(r_{Dbt}) \cdot (1 - \tau) + w_{Eqty} \cdot \mathcal{E}(r_{Eqty})$$

The numerator of the NPV calculation has to be after corporate income tax; therefore, it is $(1 - 25\%) \cdot \$20 = \$15$. This is an annuity, therefore the NPV is $PV = \$15/6.875\% \approx \$218.18$.

2. The cost of capital for a fully equity-financed firm without a tax subsidy would be 7.5%, because it had 50% debt at

5% and 50% equity at 10%. Therefore, the as-if-fully-equity-financed value is PV = $15/7.5% = $200.00. Now, you need to add back the tax subsidy. With $50 in risk-free debt and therefore with an interest rate of 5%, the interest payments would be $\mathscr{E}(r_{Debt}) \cdot Debt = \$2.50$ per year. The tax savings would be $\tau \cdot \$2.50 = \$0.625$, which is an eternal cash flow. At the interest rate of 5%, the value of the tax subsidy today is $\$0.625/0.05 = \$12.50$. Therefore, the value of this firm is $\$200 + \$12.50 = \$212.50$.

Q 17.13 A CFO should be concerned with the taxes that his investors are paying because he is supposed to act on behalf of the owners of the firm. This includes the task of minimizing any taxes that these owners are paying.

Q 17.14 Investors like capital gains best, then dividend income, then (equally) ordinary income and interest income.

Q 17.15 The firm must pay corporate income tax on cash used for repurchases and dividends, but it can use before-tax cash to pay interest. When the firm repurchases shares, investors receive the gains as capital gains (or, equivalently, an increase in the percentage of the firm that they own). Investors can easily shelter most of these payouts because they are capital gains, which face a lower statutory tax rate and can be delayed until opportune. In contrast, investors face the full brunt of Uncle Sam on cash that comes to them in the form of interest payments. Dividend payments receive a treatment that is in between the two (impossible to delay, but subject to a lower statutory tax rate).

Q 17.16 If the puppeteer forced low-tax firms to finance with debt, and high-tax firms to finance with equity:

- The IRS would collect no corporate income tax from the low-tax firm. Low-tax investors who do not mind interest receipts would preferentially sort themselves toward the low-tax firms. With a 4% tax on $100 interest receipts, the IRS would collect $4 from them.

- The IRS would collect a full $40 from the high-tax firm. High-tax investors who like equity gains would preferentially hold their shares. The $60 paid out to investors would face a 10% capital gains tax rate, for another IRS take of $6. In sum, Uncle Sam ends up with $46.

The total tax payment would therefore be $4 + $40 + $6 = $50. This is much higher than the $15.80 tax in our proposed best solution. So the answer to our original question is yes—Uncle Sam would be better off if he could eliminate the tax deduction of interest for high-tax firms.

Q 17.17 Assuming that the high-tax firm still borrows and pays out $100, and the low-tax firm still finances with equity and pays out $98 (the answer is qualitatively the same if you assume that they pay out $96), if the puppeteer forced low-tax investors to hold equity and high-tax investors to hold debt:

- The high-tax investors would receive $100 (from high-tax firms) but pay $40 for interest receipts to the IRS.

- The low-tax investors would receive $98 (from low-tax firms) and pay 1% ($0.98) in capital gains tax.

The net payment of $40 + $2 + $0.98 = $42.98 is higher than the $15.80 in our proposed solution. So the answer to our original question is yes—Uncle Sam would be better off if he could force interest receipts on high-tax investors.

Q 17.18 Old, stable firms typically have large profits and would issue debt to minimize their tax liabilities. Because pension funds are largely tax exempt, they like the interest receipts that they receive from bonds. Young, growing firms should use a lot of equity financing. The tax deductibility of interest payouts would be of little use to them. Thus, their investors would gain primarily from capital gains. This is of value primarily to high-tax individuals who want to avoid highly taxed inflows.

Q 17.19 It is usually more critical for the high-tax firm to do the right thing, because it has to try to avoid its own corporate income taxes.

Q 17.20 Yes—a high-tax investor would be willing to accept a lower rate of return on capital gains in a risk-neutral world. The alternative is to receive interest income, which would be too heavily taxed.

Q 17.21 In Atlantis, investors should never receive the tax liability. Firms should therefore be always fully equity-financed. In the WACC formula, τ would be equal to zero, and $\mathscr{E}(r_{Debt})$ would be relatively higher than $\mathscr{E}(r_{Equity})$, so $\mathscr{E}(r_{Firm})$ would increase with w_{Debt}.

End of Chapter Problems

Q 17.22. Assume a 20% corporate income tax. Does a project that returns 16% before-tax have a negative NPV if it costs $100 today and if the appropriate after-tax cost of capital is 11%?

Q 17.23. A firm will have before-tax cash flows of $3 million. It can invest in equally risky cash flows that earn a before-tax expected rate of return of 14%.

What assumption do you have to make to allow yourself to work with before-tax present values?

Q 17.24. If there are no market imperfections except for corporate income taxes, what should the firm's optimal capital structure be?

Q 17.25. Your firm is in a 40% combined federal and state marginal income tax bracket. Your annual income is $500,000 per year for two years. If you finance some project with a $1,300,000 mortgage at an interest rate of 8%, how much will Uncle Sam receive? If you finance the project with cash, how much will Uncle Sam receive? If other equivalent firms are offering investors expected rates of return of 10%, what is the PV of the tax savings from financing the project with a mortgage?

Q 17.26. You can take a $1 million project. However, this kind of project is ordinary income for you, and it will produce either nothing or $3 million next year, both with equal probabilities. Assume that your taxable opportunity cost of capital is 10% and your combined tax rate is 35%. Your after-tax cost of capital is thus 6.5%.

1. What is the project worth? Assume that you could fully use tax losses to offset other income taxed at 35%, too.

2. How would your answer change if you could not use the tax losses elsewhere?

Q 17.27. A firm will earn a taxable net return of $500 million next year. If it took on debt today, it would have to pay creditors $\mathscr{E}(r_{Debt}) = 5\% + 10\% \cdot w_{Debt}^2$. (The increasing cost of interest may be the case for different reasons, covered in the next chapter.) Thus, if the firm has 100% debt, the financial markets would demand 15% expected rate of return. Further, assume that the financial markets will lend the firm capital at this overall net cost of 15%, regardless of how the firm is financed. The firm is in the 25% marginal tax bracket.

1. If the firm is fully equity-financed, what is its value?

2. Using APV, if the firm is financed with equal amounts of debt and equity today, what is its value?

3. Using WACC, if the firm is financed with equal amounts of debt and equity today, what is its value?

4. Does this firm have an optimal capital structure? If so, what is its APV and WACC ?

Q 17.28. Go to the IRS website. Look up the highest marginal income tax rates for investors and corporations today on the different types of income that they might earn.

Q 17.29. What does a corporate manager have to do to assign high-tax investors to his equity securities and low tax investors to his debt securities?

Q 17.30. In Nirvana, all investors are tax exempt. Only firms pay income taxes. How should firms be financed? How would the WACC formula work?

Q 17.31. From a joint income tax perspective, how should a high-tax value firm be financed? How should a low-tax growth firm be financed?

Q 17.32. From an income tax perspective, what kind of investments should a high net-income investor hold? What should a tax-exempt pension fund hold?

Q 17.33. A multibillion-dollar corporation is undertaking an R&D project. It costs $1 million in R&D. Because it is risky, the appropriate cost of capital for R&D is 15%. Next year, if it succeeds (probability of 80%), the firm can build a factory for $10 million that can be financed with an $8 million mortgage, and it will earn $20 million the following year. It will have no risk, so the cost of capital will be only 6%.

1. Assume taxes in the economy do not exist. What is the value of this firm?

2. Assume there are taxes now. The firm is in the 33% tax bracket. The after-tax opportunity costs of capital are therefore 10% and 4%, respectively. The cash outflows of $1 million and $10 million are not tax deductible when they are incurred, but capital losses are fully tax deductible at the same corporate income rate. (Hint: What is the income that Uncle Sam works with in either case? What kind of effective tax credits does this mean from the perspective of the firm?) If the firm is fully equity-financed, what is the value of this project in the presence of taxes?

3. Using APV, what is the value of this project if the factory is fully financed with risk-free debt?

Q 17.34. Construct a pro forma for the following firm: A 4-year project costs $150 in year 1 (not year 0) and produces $70 in year 1, $60 in year 2, $50 in year 3, and $40 in year 4. (All numbers are year-end.) Depreciation, both real and financial, is straight line over 4 years. Projects of this riskiness (and with this term structure of project payoffs) have a 15% taxable cost of capital. The marginal corporate income tax rate is 33%.

1. Assume that the firm is 100% equity-financed. Construct the pro forma and compute expected project cash flows.

2. Compute the project IRR.

3. Compute the project NPV.

For the remaining questions, assume that the firm instead has a capital structure financing $100 with debt raised in year 1 at a 10% (expected) interest rate. Interest is paid out in each year. Principal and interest are paid out in the final year. Money in excess of interest payments is paid out as dividends.

4. Construct the pro forma now. What is the IRR of this project?

5. From the pro forma, what is the NPV of the debt-financed project?

6. Compute the NPV via the APV method.

7. Via the APV method, how much would firm value be if the firm would have taken on $40 (not $100) in debt (assuming the same interest rate of 10%)?

8. Does the debt ratio of the firm stay constant over time? Is this firm a good candidate for the WACC method?

Q 17.35. Chapter 13 Appendix on Page ≈91 contains the financials for Coca-Cola. What were the tax shields that debt provided in 2001, 2000, and 1999?

Q 17.36. Compute the 2005 tax shield for PepsiCo, using information from **YAHOO!** FINANCE.

Q 17.37. Estimate how PepsiCo's value would have changed in 2003 if it had announced that it planned to take on and maintain an additional $10 billion in debt in order to repurchase equity. Assume that corporate income taxes are the only market imperfection and that its marginal tax rate would not have been affected.

Q 17.38. Estimate how PepsiCo's value would have changed in 2003 if it had announced that it planned to increase its debt-to-asset target by an additional 5% and that it would use the generated funds to repurchase equity. Assume that corporate income taxes are the only market imperfection and that its marginal tax rate would not have been affected. (You can download PepsiCo's 2003 annual report from its website at http://www.pepsi.com.)

Q 17.39. Can you use the CAPM with the tax-adjusted WACC formula?

Q 17.40. A firm has a current debt-equity ratio of 2/3. It is worth $10 billion, of which $4 billion is debt. The firm's overall cost of capital is 12%, and its debt currently pays an (expected) interest rate of 5%. The firm estimates that its debt rating would deteriorate if it were to refinance to a 1/1 debt-equity ratio through a debt-for-equity exchange, so it would have to pay an expected interest rate of 5.5%. The firm is solidly in a 35% corporate income tax bracket. The firm reported net income of $500 million. On a corporate income tax basis only, ignoring all other capital structure–related effects, what would you estimate the value consequences for this firm to be? When would equity holders reap this benefit? That is, calculate the value the instant before it is known and the instant after it is known, and compute the percentage change in value.

Q 17.41. Is the negative effect of debt on the price/earnings ratio a force that pushes firms toward equity?

Q 17.42. Let's work a problem that shows how investors and firms sort themselves. Assume that taxable and tax-exempt firms each earn $1 of income. Assume that the financial markets offer 8% for tax-exempt income and 10% for taxable income. Assume that taxable firms and taxable investors are both taxed at 33.3%. Show what each type of firm and investors would do. Assume that capital gains are entirely untaxed. How would the arrangement change if the financial markets offered 9% for tax-exempt income?

More Imperfect-Market Capital Structure

Bankruptcy, information and agency costs, and biases

As a corporate manager, you should consider income taxes to be an important determinant of your capital structure—but not the only one. This chapter will show that you can increase firm value and lower the firm's cost of capital if you also optimize your firm's capital structure with respect to such factors as financial distress, agency considerations, and others.

The chapter ends with an overall perspective of capital structure, also taking into account the role of taxes that were discussed in the previous chapter.

18.1 What Really Matters?

What could prevent a firm from taking on too much debt to minimize its corporate income tax liabilities?

Investors should care only about value today.

Let's first think about a hypothetical firm in a Modigliani-Miller world without any market imperfections. It has $100 in value, must earn 10%, and indeed earns exactly this $10. Consider two capital structures:

What is really value relevant? (P/E ratios, for instance, are not.)

All-equity: The firm's price/earnings ratio is $100/$10 = 10.

$80 in 6% debt: With $80 in safer debt (which therefore has a lower interest rate), 6% · $80 = $4.80 will go to the creditors, and $5.20 will go to the equity. With $20 in equity and $5.20 in earnings, this firm's price/earnings ratio is 3.8.

Should the maintenance of a high price/earnings ratio therefore push the firm away from having debt? Obviously not. In an M&M world, structure does not matter. Therefore, whether the price/earnings ratio is 10 or 3.8 is not important. All that should matter to firm owners is value, and it is unchanged by the price/earnings ratio. Other factors that should be irrelevant to firm value include, for example, whether the debt or the equity is riskier or safer. In fact, you already know that with more debt, both debt and equity become riskier, but this need not be of any value consequence.

Look for real value-relevant causes, not incidental by-products.

Corporate income taxes alone would suggest that firms should be 100% debt-financed. To counteract this, there would have to be some value-relevant forces pulling the optimal capital structure toward equity. For example, if the firm were to get extra cash only if (and because) it is equity financed, then this would create an optimal capital structure that is not 100% debt. Any resulting changes to equity risk, earnings dilution, and all sorts of other financial ratios would be coincidental only. These changes would

Owners are smart
enough to care about
value, not P/E.
not in themselves influence what ultimately matters: the change in the overall value of the firm.

Fortunately, the capital markets are smart enough to know what really matters—money to investors. There is good empirical evidence that financial markets indeed appreciate money—such as money that comes from lower corporate or personal income taxes. Investors reward such managerial tax-reduction schemes with higher market values. (The cost of capital, being a measure of future cash flows relative to the value today, is often a one-to-one alternative measure of value. If a managerial action lowers the cost of capital, it usually raises the firm's present value.)

IMPORTANT

> Ultimately, specific capital structures have only two types of value consequences:
>
> 1. A financial structure may create more real costs than others.
>
> 2. A financial structure may lead managers not to take all positive-NPV projects and reject all negative-NPV projects.
>
> Value consequences also apply if such costs occur probabilistically in the future.

Value today is
influenced by future
payments and implied
future decision
making.

An example of the first type of value consequence is an equity-heavy capital structure that increases the corporate income tax obligations in the future. An example of the second type is a capital structure that is so debt-heavy and underwater that the manager would simply give up trying.

Q 18.1. Is the high debt risk and equity risk when the firm has too much debt a force away from debt and toward equity? Can this higher risk counterbalance the corporate income tax benefits of debt?

18.2   Operating Policy in Bad Times (Distress)

Too much debt can make it more likely that a firm will not be able to meet its repayment obligations and go bankrupt—creating a whole new can of worms. This means that firms may want to limit the amount of debt that they take on.

The Trade-off in the Presence of Financial Distress Costs

Start with the
perfect-market
example from
Exhibit 16.1 on
Page 499.
A firm that has debt in its capital structure is more likely to experience financial distress or even go bankrupt. Exhibit 18.1 shows how such financial distress can matter. If the firm has less debt, as in capital structure LD with its face value of $55, the firm can always fully meet its debt obligations. Consequently, we assume that it will not experience financial distress, and our LD scenario still matches our perfect world from Exhibit 16.1. However, if the firm has more debt, as in capital structure MD with its face value of $94, the firm may not pay creditors all it has promised. If the world were perfect, as it had been in Exhibit 16.1, this bankruptcy condition would merely change the payoff pattern. Everyone (including bondholders) would have known that the firm

➤ *Perfect-world house
payoffs, Exhibit 16.1,
Pg.499.*

		Bad Luck $\mathit{Prob} = 1/2$	Good Luck $\mathit{Prob} = 1/2$	Expected Value	Present Value $r = 10\%$
Project	Firm	$60	$160	$110	$100

Capital Structure LD: Bond with Face Value $55

Bond	Debt	$55	$55	$55	$50
Equity	Equity	$5	$105	$55	$50

Capital Structure MD: Bond with Face Value $94 and $10 Deadweight Costs When in Distress

		Distressed State			
Bond	Debt	$60 \boxed{-\$10} = \$50$	$94	$77 \boxed{-\$5} = \$72$	$70 \boxed{-\$4.55} = \$65.45$
Equity	Equity	$0	$66	$33	$30

Exhibit 18.1: *Illustration of Deadweight Costs in Financial Distress.* The cost of capital in this example is 10% for all securities, which is equivalent to assuming risk neutrality. Capital structure MD faces $10 financial distress costs in the bad luck state.

would be transferred to bondholders, who would liquidate a full $60. The firm value would not be impacted by the financial distress and would therefore still be $100.

However, bankruptcy matters if we introduce deadweight losses—such as legal fees—that are triggered in financial distress. In the lower part of Exhibit 18.1, we assume that these deadweight bankruptcy costs amount to $10. How does this matter?

Deadweight distress costs can make low-debt structures better.

- If you choose LD, you would borrow $50 and promise $55. Your cost of capital would be 10%. Your firm value would be $100 today.

- If you choose MD, you would borrow $65.45 and promise $94, for an interest rate of 43.6%. The expected rate of return to creditors would not change—it would still be 10%. (Every investment has to offer 10% in our risk-neutral world.) However, the deadweight bankruptcy cost increases *your* cost of capital. You are giving up what *should have been* $60 or $94 (because it is now only an expected value of $77) in exchange for a payment of $65.45. Thus, you could sell your firm only for $65.45 + $30 = $95.45, not for $50 + $50 = $100. Relative to its potential of $110, your cost of capital would have increased from $110/$100 − 1 = 10% to $110/$95.45 − 1 ≈ 15.2%!

From your perspective, capital structure MD is worse than capital structure LD, in which the firm could never go bankrupt. The important insight with respect to bankruptcy is that it is not bankruptcy per se that is the problem, but only the deadweight losses in and around financial distress that matter.

Owners may trade off debt's expected tax savings against its deadweight bankruptcy cost increases.

Who ultimately bears the cost of bankruptcy—you as the entrepreneur selling the firm, or the creditors providing capital? It would be you, because creditors demand fair compensation up-front. How would you want to structure your firm if you face both taxes and bankruptcy losses? You should now try to reduce not only the deadweight loss from taxes but also the deadweight losses from financial distress:

- Too little debt, and you lose too much in taxes.

- Too much debt, and you lose too much in bankruptcy costs.

Therefore, an amount of debt not too high and not too low maximizes the value of your firm today.

Deadweight distress costs can come in various forms.

The rest of this section describes other forms of deadweight losses in financial distress. These deadweight losses can be more important than any legal fees in formal bankruptcy. For example:

1. The firm may have to spend money to avoid formal bankruptcy.

2. Fear of bankruptcy may prevent the firm from taking a positive-NPV project. If the firm does not take otherwise optimal NPV projects, this would count as a deadweight loss.

3. Concern about bankruptcy may lead customers and suppliers to demand different terms.

The latter two issues are often called **indirect bankruptcy costs**, because they do not involve direct cash outlays. In any case, it does not matter whether the deadweight costs are direct or indirect. They all have the same effect in the end—they increase the firm's cost of capital and decrease the firm's value today. Note that the financial distress itself never needs to actually occur—the probability that it may occur in the future is enough to reduce the firm value today. The higher the probability of financial distress, the higher the costs.

IMPORTANT

> Financial distress costs usually favor equity over debt as a cheaper financing vehicle.

Q 18.2. Do deadweight bankruptcy costs favor debt or equity? Why?

Direct Losses of Firm Value

The Process

Chapter 7 liquidation and Chapter 11 reorganization. Firm owners internalize creditor costs.

Although the process and history of bankruptcy are fascinating, both in the United States and worldwide, the full legal details are beyond the scope of this book. In the United States, there are two legal forms of bankruptcy: **Chapter 7 liquidation** and **Chapter 11 reorganization**. Larger firms almost always petition to enter Chapter 11 (not Chapter 7), which gives them a stay from creditors trying to seize their vital assets. If the court determines that the business is still viable, the firm can reorganize its financial claims and emerge from bankruptcy if its creditors vote to agree to the reorganization.

Otherwise, the case is converted into Chapter 7 and the firm is liquidated. Both forms are supervised by a federal judge (and/or a federal bankruptcy trustee) and last on average about 2-3 years. In real life, creditors in Chapter 11 sometimes agree to modest violations from the absolute priority rule —which we have always used to construct our state-contingent tables—in order to reduce running bankruptcy costs. The firm typically has to pay for most of the legal fees of all creditor classes—but even if it does not, creditors will ask for compensation for their expected legal fees up-front. In one way or another, the firm's owners today have to carry the expected costs of bankruptcy in the future.

➤ *Absolute priority rule,*
Sect. 15.2, *Pg.465*.

Direct and Indirect Costs

The direct fees—the legal fees that the bankruptcy process consumes—are just the most obvious costs. There are also hours spent by management, employees, and experts to deal with the running process. But much of the cost of financial distress is indirect and on the real business side. For example, it may become more expensive to produce (e.g., because suppliers may charge more, fearing delayed or no payment), more difficult to focus (e.g., management may become distracted with bankruptcy and talented employees may leave), more expensive to sell products (e.g., customers may flee due to loss of confidence), and more expensive to sell assets (e.g., liquidation sales may mean low fire-auction prices). All these costs reduce the value of the firm, and they are real welfare losses caused by financial distress. These costs can also arise even before formal bankruptcy. Many of these costs originate from the fact that firms can shed promised claims in bankruptcy, even if they would like to commit themselves today (ex ante) to not shedding them in the future. This inability to commit causes a loss of value when future distress is possible. Consider the following examples:

Direct legal and administrative bankruptcy costs are easily visible. But bankruptcy also has non-cash-outlay costs.

- **When products require customer investments, customers may be reluctant to purchase the products and invest, knowing that their investments could turn out to be wasted if the firm were to disappear.** For example, the value of a computer is determined not only by its hardware but also by the manufacturer's continued provision of hardware and software support and development. End-of-life hardware or software, no matter how good, is often close to worthless. Even if the firm promises to continue development of faster hardware to preserve its customers' software investments, if the firm is liquidated, it would not be able to keep such a promise. The inability of the firm to commit to honoring its promises in the future hurts its sales to customers today—and may even cause the bankruptcy itself. An example were the consumer worries when the U.S. car companies were about to go bankrupt in 2009. These worries were such an important consideration that the government itself took the unusual step to guarantee all car warranties. (Of course, the government did not guarantee car resale value, and thus addressed consumer fears only partly.)

If a computer firm could disappear, customers become unwilling to purchase its computers—making this a self-fulfilling prophecy.

- **When product sales require promises of future contact, customers may be reluctant to purchase the product, given that the future promised rebate may fail to materialize.** For example, airlines depend on frequent flier plans to attract business travelers. When the promise of future free flights loses its credibility, an airline becomes severely handicapped. In effect, any firm whose products require warranties should weigh whether issuing debt might not alarm its customers. Such products may require future service, and customers may be reluctant to purchase the product, knowing that the service may become unobtainable in the future.

- **When product quality is difficult to judge, customers fear that companies may cut corners in order to avoid financial distress.**

Have you ever wondered whether an airline in financial distress cuts corners on airplane maintenance? (You should next time you are booking a ticket!) The capital structure influence here is not that maintenance would be cheaper but rather customers' fears that the firm may cut corners. Consequently, the price at which such an airline can sell tickets may be below that of a financially solid airline. Similarly, wholesalers will not deliver their goods to near-bankrupt retailers unless they are assured of payment. Because bankrupt retailers may no longer be able to purchase credit, the costs of their goods may increase—and their competitive advantage may erode.

Without trustworthy warranty programs, competing in some businesses is very difficult.

- **If suppliers fear that the retailer can go bankrupt, they may not extend trade credit.** Some businesses rely on **trade credit**, in which suppliers sell their goods to buyers in an open credit arrangement. (In effect, it is a credit line that is limited to the specific goods the supplier sells.) In some cases, not having access to trade credit can hamper business operations to the point where it can itself cause the onset of bankruptcy.

➤ *Trade credit, Pg.514.*

- **If buyers fear that the seller cannot provide service once bankrupt, they may not buy any goods to begin with.** When Aloha and ATA Airlines went bankrupt in early 2008, customers who believed they had purchased flights instead ended up owning only worthless pieces of paper. Even passengers who had already flown to their destination found themselves stranded without a return ticket. While this may not have been bad for Aloha and ATA (essentially owning passenger money without having had to provide service), many other airlines now face far more skeptical customers. Smaller airlines with more debt that are more likely to go bankrupt now may find customers hard to come by—and therefore go bankrupt.

Financial Distress Costs as Transaction Costs?

But there is a limit to the importance of bankruptcy costs. We can muster an argument similar in spirit to the M&M proof: If financial distress costs are too high, you could purchase all debt and equity—an action that would immediately eliminate any financial distress costs caused by too much debt. You would own an entire firm that suffers no more debt-caused distress costs. In the real world, if the transaction costs to purchase all securities are an extra $100, it must be that the value reduction caused by the financial distress costs is less than $100. Otherwise, you and every other arbitrageur around would clamor to take over the firm.

One upper limit to the importance of financial distress costs is the cost of turning debt back into equity.

So, how much extra (above the true value) could it possibly cost an arbitrageur to purchase all securities? Remarkably, this could be more than just the normal financial transaction costs. The reason is a **holdout** problem. Put yourself in the shoes of a single bondholder. Let's assume your bond promised to pay $100, but the firm is now worth so

Buying back debt and issuing equity should be cheap, but creditor holdout problems could imply that they are not.

ANECDOTE **Fear and Relief**

Here are some real-world examples of how companies in financial distress lose customers because they are in financial distress, which worsens their financial distress—a self-fulfilling prophecy. A capital structure with more equity and less debt would often have avoided such problems in the first place.

First, here is an example in which actual financial distress has reduced the value of the underlying operations. On March 3, 2008, the *Associated Press* reported how gift cards had become worthless when The Sharper Image filed for bankruptcy. The gift card business was among its most profitable operations, constituting about $32 million of outstanding credit. How many customers do you believe will buy gift cards from The Sharper Image in the future? One customer noted, "With the uncertainty today, I didn't want my aunt's gift to be only a card."

Second, here is an example in which merely the fear of financial distress has led to the de facto collapse of the entire firm. On Thursday, March 13, 2008, the 85-year-old Bear Stearns investment bank closed at $57.07 per share, a market value of about $8 billion. Half an hour after Friday's stock market opening, rumors emerged that some of Bear Stearns' sources of short-term capital were drying up. (These are the equivalent of suppliers in the financial services industry.) As a consequence, Bear Stearns had trouble not only finding other short-term capital suppliers but also in executing financial trades with counterparties (the equivalent of customers). Both suppliers and customers feared that Bear Stearns could go bankrupt. Bear Stearns' stock price fell to $31.54—a level that it maintained for the rest of Friday. However, these developments caused even more short-term capital providers and trading counterparties to jump ship. Over the weekend, the same withdrawal dynamic continued, and on Saturday morning, the Federal Reserve coopted JP Morgan for a bailout of Bear Stearns. JP Morgan announced that it had agreed to acquire Bear Stearns for—hold on to your hat—$2 per share. In September 2008, Lehman Bros, another heavily over-levered major investment bank, followed Bear Stearns into bankruptcy, where existing shareholders received nothing, and Barclays bought its best assets for a song. The Fed and U.S. Treasury then decided to save other financial services firms (such as Citibank) from the same fate. These are extreme examples of how a "run on the bank" can become self-fulfilling. Chances are that both suppliers and customers would not have jumped ship if they had not feared other suppliers and customers jumping ship. Capital structures with less debt, more equity, and more cash would have prevented such meltdowns.

little that your bond is worth only $50. Some arbitrageur has just offered you and every other bondholder a buyout for $55. Would you take this offer? You would if you held all the bonds. But if you are just a small bondholder among many, you could refuse to sell, hoping that the arbitrageur will be so exasperated that he will offer you the $100 just to get rid of you. The extra $45 won't make or break the offer, and your continued presence as a creditor (e.g., in the courts) could make the arbitrageur's life a nightmare. Unfortunately, every other little creditor would realize this, too, and would prefer to hold out and be bought off. Given such bargaining complications, the transaction costs of acquiring all the debt could be very high, which means the firm may end up running down the rest of its true economic value rather than being efficiently reorganized. (One justification for the U.S. Chapter 11 reorganization procedure is that it allows a judge to force all creditors to participate and thus eliminates the holdout problem.)

One attempt to reduce the transaction cost is for firms to bundle their financial claims into **units** (unit securities) of debt and equity. Each creditor would also be a shareholder. If the firm fails to pay interest in the future, creditors would be more inclined to compromise in order to avoid financial distress—after all, there is little

If all creditors are in the same creditor class and own equity, too, they would not hold out.

➤ *Unit securities, Pg.470.*

reason to force bankruptcy in order to collect assets from oneself.

Assessing the Magnitude of Direct Bankruptcy Costs

For most Fortune 500 companies, expected financial distress costs are small.

In small firms, future financial distress is always a possibility, and legal fees can quickly consume their assets. Managers of such firms need to be careful not to take on too many liabilities. But what about the average Fortune 500 company? What would be a good estimate for its expected direct bankruptcy costs? We can do some back-of-the-envelope calculations. Say you run a typical healthy Fortune 500 company today, worth $10 billion. Fewer than five Fortune 500 companies enter financial distress (either formal or informal) in a given year. Quadruple this number to get an estimate of 4% probability of bankruptcy at the outset of the year. To be among them, your company would have to drop by, say, about 70% of its market value. In other words, it is unlikely for you to run into real distress unless your firm value dropped to about $3 billion. (Year-to-year changes of plus or minus 30% [$3 billion] are common occurrences.) Finally, let's estimate the deadweight financial distress losses if you run into trouble. Assume that your bankruptcy costs would be 5% of the value of your distressed Fortune 500 company *when you enter bankruptcy*. Again quadruple this number to assume a 20% distress cost. For example, say you run a $10 billion company today. Say it has a 4% chance to drop to $3 billion in value, setting off financial distress and legal costs amounting to $20\% \cdot \$3\text{billion} = \$600$ million in distress costs. (Yes, $600 million in distress costs is a lot of money for bankruptcy lawyers to fight over *if* your firm goes bankrupt.) Yet, in expectation today, for your $10 billion firm this is only

$$\underset{\substack{\text{Distress} \\ \text{Probability}}}{4\%} \cdot \underset{\substack{\text{Value if} \\ \text{Distressed}}}{30\%} \cdot \underset{\substack{\text{Deadweight} \\ \text{Loss}}}{20\%} = \underset{\substack{\textit{High Expected Distress} \\ \textit{Costs Estimate}}}{24 \text{ basis points}}$$

or $24 million. This is not a whole lot when compared to the potential tax savings of debt if you are currently a healthy $10 billion firm in the 35% tax bracket and you are thinking about taking another loan. In sum, for the average healthy Fortune 500 firm today, bankruptcy costs do not seem large enough to prevent them from taking on more debt.

The fact that some firms used to go bankrupt "regularly" suggests that they had relatively low bankruptcy costs.

This argument does not, of course, apply to each and every firm. Which firms are likely to suffer high deadweight losses in bankruptcy? We know that many U.S. railroads have declared bankruptcy dozens of times, without interruption in service. Even large retailers, like Federated Department Stores (Macy's and Bloomingdales), have been in and out of bankruptcy several times. Airlines have some easily transferable and collateralizable assets (airplanes) and thus may have fewer deadweight losses—many airlines have ceased operations with their planes sold, repainted, and turned around for another carrier. Airlines' bankruptcy deadweight losses may be bearable. In contrast, firms with mostly intangible assets (such as reputation or name recognition) need to be more concerned with reducing the probability of future bankruptcy. For example, if Chanel were to go bankrupt, Chanel No. 5 might acquire the odor of death, rather than the odor of high style, and the entire business might disappear. Chanel should therefore choose a capital structure that is not too liability-heavy in order to avoid the loss of prestige that a bankruptcy could bring about.

The importance of bankruptcy costs as an important determinant of capital structure remains an empirical issue. The current academic consensus is that bankruptcy costs matter for some firms and some industries, particularly during recessions. They can easily be very large, but for most healthy Fortune 500 firms, the expected deadweight costs are probably small—some exceptions notwithstanding. (P.S. The Fortune 500 firms Enron and Arthur Andersen did not go bankrupt because they had too much debt.)

In sum, expected bankruptcy costs are probably small for healthy, large companies.

Q 18.3. What do U.S. managers usually mean by Chapter 11 and Chapter 7?

Q 18.4. Give examples of bankruptcy costs. Distinguish between direct and indirect costs.

Operational Distortions of Incentives

A second set of financial distress costs arises from the fact that shareholders' incentives diverge from bondholders' incentives if the firm gets close to financial distress. These are also our first examples of situations in which (debt-heavy) capital structures harm a firm ex ante, because they may lead it to pass up positive NPV projects. This distortion in its incentives can make such a firm worth less today.

➤ *Two types of value sources of capital structures., Pg.570.*

Underinvestment

The **underinvestment** problem is the bondholder concern that managers will not make necessary investments if the promised debt payments end up being too large. That is, owners may prefer to pay out cash to shareholders rather than spend their money on maintenance and repair (or other projects). This may be in their interest if the project proceeds would more than likely go to bondholders than to themselves. Ex ante, underinvestment reduces the payoffs bondholders expect to receive, which increases the price at which bond purchasers would be willing to lend money to the firm today.

When there is more debt than assets, equity holders may not take proper care of the assets.

For example, assume a firm has only $50 in cash and no projects. Worse, it owes creditors a promised $100 in a couple of years. Fortunately for the shareholders, in our simple example, the firm can pay $50 in dividends and leave the bondholders with nothing. Yet, suddenly, managers find an unexpected opportunity. They can pay the $50 to start a project that will yield either $60 or $160 by the time the debt is due. The firm should undertake this project, because it is a positive-NPV project. But would managers acting in the interest of shareholders be willing to do so?

Would "underwater" shareholders want to take all profitable projects?

Exhibit 18.2 shows that the answer is no. Managers would prefer to pay out $50 to shareholders rather than take this positive-NPV project. Most of the project's benefits would go to cover the "debt overhang," which is something that managers who act on behalf of shareholders would not care much about. Again, this "underinvestment problem" is a cost of debt to the firm. If the firm had chosen a zero-debt capital structure ex ante, such profitable future investments would not be ignored, which in turn would increase the value at which our hypothetical owner can sell the firm today.

Ex ante, entrepreneurs internalize the cost of future inefficient behavior.

Initial condition: The firm has $50 in cash, no projects, but has an outstanding bond with a $100 face value. It pays out $50 in cash to shareholders and waits.

		Bad Luck $\mathscr{P}rob = 1/2$	Good Luck $\mathscr{P}rob = 1/2$	Expected Value	Present Value $r = 10\%$
Project	Firm	$0	$0	$0	$0
Bond	Debt	$0	$0	$0	$0
Equity	After $50 dividend payout today	$0	$0	$0	$0

News Flash: Positive NPV Project Appears

New development: A positive-NPV project comes along that costs $50 and pays either $60 or $160.

Managerial choice #1: Pay $50 to shareholders today. Default on the debt that comes due in the future.

Managerial choice #2: Use the firm's $50 to take the project today. When the project finishes, the debt obligation with $100 face value is due, which the firm must then honor.

		Bad Luck $\mathscr{P}rob = 1/2$	Good Luck $\mathscr{P}rob = 1/2$	Expected Value	Present Value $r = 10\%$
Project	Firm	$60	$160	$110	$100
Bond	Debt	$60	$100	$80	$72.73
Equity	Equity	$0	$60	$30	$27.27

Exhibit 18.2: *Illustration of Underinvestment Distortions.* This firm is considering a positive-NPV project, which it should take. The management is assumed to act on behalf of shareholders, not on behalf of the overall firm. The cost of capital in this example is 10% for all securities. Will the managers take this project?

IMPORTANT

> Ex-post reluctance to do the right thing (such as additional maintenance investment) favors equity over debt as the cheaper financing vehicle.

Reluctance to Liquidate

Managers may not want to liquidate the firm, even if they should. If the firm is underwater, this can even hurt creditors.

A similar problem is **reluctance to liquidate**. Managers acting on behalf of equity holders may not always wish to liquidate the firm when it has fallen onto hard times, even if doing so would maximize firm value. Equity holders tend to prefer riskier payoffs because equity is essentially like an option. If there is even a small chance of improvement and even if deterioration is more likely, equity holders are better off to take their chances than to give up their options and liquidate. For example, assume that the $60 represents the liquidation value of the factory, and the MD debt is due in two years rather than in one. Further, assume that managers can continue running the factory, in which case it will be worth either $100 or $0 with equal probability. The optimal unconflicted behavior would be to liquidate the factory. Unfortunately, shareholders prefer to continue operating—they would get nothing in liquidation, but perhaps $6 if the factory were to be worth $100. In effect, equity holders have an option on the firm. They would often even make running interest and principal payments in order to keep their option alive! This inefficient behavior, caused by the presence of debt in the capital structure, reduces the value of a firm with both debt and equity *today*.

> Ex-post reluctance to liquidate *by managers not acting on behalf of the overall firm but on behalf of equity* can favor equity as the cheaper financing vehicle.

IMPORTANT

So far, we have assumed that management acts on behalf of shareholders. They indeed typically care more about equity than about debt, which we just argued may induce them to exploit the debt on behalf of equity. However, managers can also act on behalf of themselves, especially if shareholders would be best served by corporate liquidation, too. Managers may run down the firm's equity substance in order to keep their jobs instead of returning the money to the owners. To reduce the incidence of such behavior, firms may add debt to the capital structure. Debt can limit the ability of managers to run down the entire firm and force them to liquidate and disgorge some of the remaining assets. This can benefit both debt and equity.

However, reluctance to liquidate can also hurt equity.

> Ex-post reluctance to liquidate *by managers not acting on behalf of the overall firm but on behalf of themselves* can favor debt over equity as the cheaper financing vehicle.

IMPORTANT

We discuss agency problems between managers and owners in the next section (and in Chapter 24 (Companion)). They tend to be more dramatic in good times. But you should realize that conflicts of interest can occur in financial distress, too—in which case the presence of more debt could be a good remedy to discipline unwilling managers, just as it often is in good times.

Agency problems preview.

Q 18.5. Give an example of an underinvestment problem.

Q 18.6. What kinds of firms are most likely to be influenced by underinvestment costs when choosing a capital structure?

Q 18.7. Give an example of a reluctance-to-liquidate problem. Is this an issue that could hurt only the creditors, or only the shareholders?

Q 18.8. What kinds of firms are most likely to be influenced by possible reluctance-to-liquidate costs when choosing a capital structure?

Strategic Considerations

Debt can change the nature of the competition in the product market.

Finally, there are some theories in which debt is a strategic commitment device. This argument is perhaps easiest to understand by analogy. Consider playing a game of chicken (two cars driving toward one another; the first to "chicken out" and get out of the way loses). How can you make sure you win? If you can tie down your steering controls, remove the steering wheel, and throw it visibly out the window, any smart opponent would surely chicken out! The trick is to commit yourself visibly to not giving way. (Some people have suggested that driving an old, large, and apparently unstable Oldsmobile is the equivalent of throwing out the wheel; other cars will be in a hurry to get out of the way.)

This is an argument that debt can make firms more aggressive (commit to fight entrants), thereby making the firm itself better off.

➤ *Risk shifting,* *Sect.* 18.4, *Pg.584.*

The same argument has been made for debt—that by having debt, firms can commit to squash potential entrant competitors in their product markets. Assume for a moment that a monopolist has borrowed a lot of money. Consider the decision of a potential market entrant who knows this. The market entrant also knows that it is in the interest of the shareholders to increase risk—they will gain more of the upside than the downside. A price war is riskier than accommodation—so the monopolist's managers (acting on behalf of equity holders) may prefer the riskier strategy of a price war over accommodation. Consequently, the potential entrant may chicken out, and the monopolist may never have to start the price war. (Of course, if the market entrant is too stupid to understand the message, both players—the monopolist and the entrant—will be hurt badly. The two cars will end up crashing head-on.)

Empirically, the argument of intentional value-enhancing self-commitment seems not too important. On the contrary: Debt may make firms less competitive and worse off.

This argument is clever, but it may not be a first-order factor in the real world. We do know that industry matters—for example, financial services companies tend to rely on a lot of debt. However, it is not clear whether managers have strategic intent in mind when they pursue capital structure change. There is not much evidence that managers of companies with more debt have relatively more of a tendency to act in a more risk-seeking fashion in the product market. There is not much evidence that they choose a price war strategy. And there is even less evidence that they consciously increase their debt ex ante *in order to* commit themselves to a price war. Some empirical research has actually found that more debt tends to hurt firms in the product market. Owners tend to take on more debt when they are severely cash constrained, and this may prevent them from competing effectively. Indeed, there is some evidence that supermarkets that dramatically increased their leverage were systematically attacked by their competitors with price wars and failed to compete as effectively. In the aforementioned Sharper Image bankruptcy in 2008, the *Associated Press* writes, "Bankrupt businesses also face the risk that card holders left in the cold could defect to other stores just when struggling merchants need their customers the most... Sharper Image's rival, Brookstone, is capitalizing on the situation. It announced last week that it would exchange Sharper Image gift cards for 25 percent off any purchase, no matter the amount of the gift card or the cost of the item." To the extent that high leverage can cause weakness in the product markets, it would count as a direct cost of debt. The subject of product-market related strategic capital structure choice is still under active investigation, and the final word has not been spoken.

➤ *The Sharper Image,* *Pg.574.*

Competitive product-market environments could favor either equity or debt.

IMPORTANT

Q 18.9. Is debt always a strategic advantage? Describe the arguments on both sides.

18.3 Operating Policy in Good Times (Agency)

In most of the previous section, debt was usually worse than equity, because it made it more likely that the firm would enter financial distress. Just as too much debt can cause the firm to make poor operating decisions when financial distress looms, too little debt can also cause the firm to make poor operating decisions when the business is going well. Again, it is the fact that a particular capital structure—now one with too much equity—can make firms take projects that they really should not take. This reduces their values today. However, some agency costs are even more direct, with managers simply taking too much for themselves and giving too little to the owners. But I am getting ahead of myself.

Too much money can lead firms to take bad projects.

You already met agency conflicts in Chapter 12. A less academic name for an agency conflict is a **conflict of interest**. A more academic name is **moral hazard**, although this term is also common in the insurance industry. Agency conflicts play important roles in capital-structure theory:

Moral hazard is a gorilla in the room.

➤ *Corporate governance, Chapter* 24 (Companion), *Pg.≈223.*

Free cash flow: Managers usually prefer spending money internally on their pet projects instead of returning money to shareholders. For example, in the 1980s, many large oil companies continued exploring for oil even though it was well known that oil companies could be bought on the stock exchange for significantly less than the expected cost of finding equivalent oil reserves. Free cash flow issues are especially problematic in declining industries—faced with shrinking markets, managers often desperately search for alternative investing ventures that are not their competitive advantage, rather than returning the money to the rightful owners. How can capital structure counterweigh this tendency? Debt requires coupon payments, which force managers to perform. Managers who fail to generate enough income to pay the coupons are subject to bankruptcy and (as has been shown empirically) almost always lose their jobs. Therefore, managers who have more debt will spend less wastefully, which makes such firms worth more *today*.

Managers like building empires and receiving perks; debt restrains them.

Theft (and verification): Another important problem of too much equity instead of debt is implicit or explicit **theft**. If you are a passive partner, you are dependent on true and accurate reporting of what profits really are. The active partners or the managers, however, might try to avoid reporting large profits: They might rather use corporate cash to build more of an empire, to compensate themselves better, or just to outright steal it! Debt has the advantage that the creditor may

Managers might steal: Debt restrains their ability to do so without being discovered.

not even need to know what the profits are: If the agreed-upon payments are not made, the creditor can force bankruptcy.

Employees or other
critical stakeholders
may hold up the firm's
shareholders for more
of its money. Creditors
are much less
forgiving.

Stakeholder holdup: Higher potential hold-up costs are another important drawback of equity. When a company, especially a public company, rolls in cash, anyone who has the power to hold up the business will try to extort some of these profits. (This is called **rent seeking**.) For example, a supplier who delivers an important input, a wholesaler who is an important distributor, or any key employees who can bring production to a stop may want to pressure the firm to renegotiate their deals and gain more of the riches. Airlines, for example, suffer greatly from this problem. A strike by any one of its unions can render billions of dollars in airplanes useless and destroy much of the customer goodwill (though airlines have almost none these days). If the airline has the cash to afford it, it will have no choice but to give in. Yet if such a company is financed more via debt than equity, these third parties will recognize that there is less cash to expropriate. After all, if the company does not pay the debt, it can go bankrupt. Thus, in a company with more debt, the equity earnings (which parties can renegotiate) are smaller.

When management
owns more of the
levered equity,
possible only with a
lot of debt, then
management may be
less conflicted.

Higher effective managerial stake: More debt amplifies the effects of managerial equity holdings. For example, if managers have enough wealth to own $5 of a $100 firm, it would mean that they owned 5% of the firm. A decline in the value of projects from $100 to $80 would cost them $1. In contrast, if the firm were financed with $60 in debt, managers' $5 in shares would be a $5/$40 = 12.5% stake in the firm, and a drop from $100 to $80 would wipe out half of the value of their equity. Thus, managers would lose not $1 but $2.50. Chances are that with more debt, managers would be much less inclined to take bad projects that reduced firm value from $100 to $80.

IMPORTANT

> Free cash flow and agency problems favor debt over equity as the cheaper financing vehicle.

A more sinister view of
the corporation: Firms
have equity not
because it is
value-enhancing, but
because managers in
charge like it.

➤ *Do future capital needs
protect shareholders?*,
Sect. 24.B (Companion),
Pg. ≈230.

Agency conflicts are very important, especially in large, stalwart firms. But be careful: Just because these agency conflicts are important, and although it is true that the presence of debt helps control agency conflicts, it is not automatically true that real-world companies will have more debt. If managers have already taken effective control of the corporate board (by stacking it with insiders and friends), they become the "agents in charge." They will then act in their own interests and structure the firm to carry more equity and *not* more debt.

IMPORTANT

> Uncontrolled free cash flow and agency concerns can mean that firms have more equity than debt financing, even if this is not value maximizing.

Corporate governance
breakdown in many
large Fortune 500
companies could
explain excessive
equity in their
financing.

➤ *Governance,*
Chapter 24 (Companion),
Pg. ≈223.

In the real world, it comes down to how good the corporate governance of the firm is. A good independent board, a large external equity owner, or a set of potential external acquirers can sometimes exert enough pressure on management to issue more

---

ANECDOTE   Airlines, Unions, and Shareholders

In September 2002, American Airlines (AMR) operated over 1,000 airplanes and owned about half of them. It had assets valued at about $30 billion and debt valued at around $15 billion. Still, its equity market value was only $800 million—about the price of 3 of its 40 top-of-the-line Boeing 777 airplanes. And it is not clear if AMR was worth even this $800 million: Bankruptcy was imminent for all other major U.S. carriers (except Southwest).

In 2002, AMR lost a significant amount of money in its operations. If it is ever to make positive profits again, its unions will surely capture the lion's share. After all, it only takes one of its unions (pilots, flight attendants, or mechanics) to ground a fleet worth $30 billion and wreck customer loyalty. If there was only one union, it would ultimately make sure that shareholders would receive just enough for them not to kill the golden goose. Three unions, all trying to get the most for their members, may yet end up killing the goose. For AMR's owners, corporate debt is the only chance to resist union demands.

AMR's profit outlook continues to be negative. In the first edition of this book (2008), I wrote that I did not understand why AMR was worth $2.3 billion. As of October 2011, AMR's equity is worth $1 billion—and even this low a value may be too high. In my opinion, airlines should not exist as public corporations but be owned by their unions.

---

debt when it is optimal to do so. (Many economists argue that this is the role that **private equity** firms are playing—they take on more leverage that leads managers to cut wasteful projects and focus on creating value.) Unfortunately, strong corporate governance by shareholders over managers is the exception and not the rule in Fortune 500 firms. Thus, you should not be surprised that there are also many large blue-chip firms that could benefit substantially from exchanging their equity for more debt, but their management has chosen to keep the firm fairly unlevered.

Q 18.10. Give some examples of perks that management might have to give up if they work at a firm with more debt.

Q 18.11. Do managerial agency concerns induce firms to be more debt- or equity-financed?

18.4 Bondholder Expropriation

You already know that entrepreneurs should structure the firm *at the outset* (ex ante) so as to make it in their interest to optimize firm value in the future. In order to raise debt at an attractive interest rate, managers must also take into account that bondholders know that managers might later want to weasel out of their obligations. They would prefer to transfer value from bondholders to shareholders. After all, creditors realize that it is the shareholders who vote managers into office, not the bondholders. This section shows that managers can expropriate bondholders on behalf of shareholders in two ways:

If there is debt, equity shareholders may want management to expropriate these debtors. This has bad ex-ante value consequences.

1. They can increase the risk of the firm's projects (a change in operating policies).

2. They can issue more bonds of equal or higher priority. (Bonds that pay cash earlier are de facto higher priority.)

If potential bondholders believe that they can be expropriated, they will demand a higher cost of capital today. Let me explain this better.

Project Risk Changes

		Bad Luck $\mathscr{P}rob = 1/2$	Good Luck $\mathscr{P}rob = 1/2$	Expected Value	Present Value $r = 10\%$
Project	Firm	$60	$160	$110	$100

Capital Structure LD: Bond with Promised Payoff $55

Bond	Debt	$55	$55	$55	$50
Equity	Equity	$5	$105	$55	$50

News Flash: Negative-NPV Project Appears

Adding Risky Project "New"

		Probability				Expected Value	Present Value $r = 10\%$
		1/4	1/4	1/4	1/4		
Project	Old Firm	$60	$60	$160	$160	$110	$100.00
Project	New	$50	–$60	$50	–$60	–$5	–$4.55
Total Projects		$110	$0	$210	$100	$105	$95.45

Capital Structure LD: Bond with Face Value $55

Bond	Debt	$55	$0	$55	$55	$41.25	$37.50
Equity	Equity	$55	$0	$155	$45	$63.75	$57.95

Exhibit 18.3: *The Effect of Risk-Shifting on Debt and Equity Value.* The cost of capital in this example is 10% for all securities, which is equivalent to assuming risk neutrality.

Risk-shifting: Adding a risky, but negative, NPV project changes the state-contingent payoffs.

➤ *Deadweight Costs, Exhibit* **18.1**, *Pg.571*.

The first expropriation risk that creditors face is called "risk-shifting." Exhibit 18.3 returns to our firm with an LD capital structure from Exhibit 18.1 but allows managers to add project "New" after the original debt has been raised. The new project is independent of the old project and pays either +$50 or –$60 with equal probability.

It is a negative-NPV project, so it would not be too hard for managers to find such projects—any Las Vegas casino provides better investment opportunities. Why would a negative-NPV project matter? Would the managers not reject this negative-NPV project?

The lower half of the table shows that if the new negative-NPV project is taken, the value of the equity would increase from $50 to $57.95. If shareholders are in firm control of their managers and vote them into and out of office, managers would indeed take this project *despite the bad consequences for the firm overall*! In essence, the new project would eliminate $50 – $37.50 = $12.50 of bondholder value, waste $4.55, and hand $7.95 extra value to shareholders. The intuition is that this risky project gives existing shareholders relatively more of the upside and existing bondholders relatively more of the downside.

Everyone—managers, shareholders, and bondholders—recognizes that taking the project will be in the interest of the managers if a bond with a face value of $55 was originally sold. Although this is good for equity holders ex post, ex ante it is bad for them (and the firm). Skeptical creditors will assume that the debt payoff is only $41.25 (not $55) and thus pay no more than $37.50. The firm would have to pay a cost of capital of $55/$37.50 – 1 ≈ 46.7%, even if it wanted to finance itself with debt.

Note that the real problem is not that creditors receive less but that managers would have the incentive to destroy firm value in the process of reducing their liabilities in the future. If they did not destroy any value—if it were just reallocation of the payoffs in different states—both equity and creditors could simply recompute and pay the appropriate fair value of their contingent claims up-front, and the overall firm value today would be unaffected. As before, an ex-post problem has consequences ex ante.

If you now conclude that it is good for the corporation to commit itself not to take other projects, you would be wrong. This could backfire, too. If a new zero-cost project were to come along that either pays off –$60 or +$500, it would have a highly positive NPV. If creditors had negotiated a commitment at bond issue, they would insist that the project not be taken, because their wealth would still decline. But this would prevent the firm from taking great projects. Therefore, a wholesale ex-ante commitment not to take any more projects is not necessarily a good thing for the value of the overall firm.

If the shareholders can gamble with the bondholders' money, they may be better off.

Ex ante, entrepreneurs should prevent it to reduce their cost of debt capital.

Ex ante, the real problem is value reduction (taking negative-NPV projects)—not the state reallocation.

Unfortunately, committing not to shift risk could prevent positive-NPV projects—also costly.

Issuance of Bonds of Similar Priority

There are also other expropriation risks that creditors face. The first is the issuance of more bonds of equal or higher priority. (Paying out some cash before the original bond comes due is in effect higher priority.) Exhibit 18.4 shows an example, in which the firm issues another bond with a face value of $20 that has equal priority. In bankruptcy (the bad state), the old bond would have to share proceeds with the new bond of equal priority. Being equal, the "spoils" would often be allocated according to face value within bonds of the same priority. Because the $20 bond represents $20/($20 + $55) ≈ 27% of the debt claim, it would receive 27% · $60 ≈ $16; and the $55 bond would receive the remaining 73% · $60 ≈ $44. This means that when the firm announces the issuance of the new bond, the old bond would immediately drop by $50 – $45 = $5 in value. Would this be in the interest of the equity? It now receives nothing in the bad state and $85 in the good state—plus the one-time dividend of $16.36. In total, by issuing new

Managers can also exploit bondholders by issuing more debt of equal or higher priority.

debt of equal priority, equity holders would have increased their wealth from $50 to $38.64 + $16.36 = $55.

		Bad Luck $\mathcal{P}rob = 1/2$	Good Luck $\mathcal{P}rob = 1/2$	Expected Value	Present Value r = 10%
Project	Firm	$60	$160	$110	$100
Capital Structure LD: One Bond with Face Value $55					
Old Bond	Debt	$55	$55	$55	$50
Equity	Equity	$5	$105	$55	$50

News Flash: New Bond Issue, Equal Priority, $20 Face Value

		Bad Luck $\mathcal{P}rob = 1/2$	Good Luck $\mathcal{P}rob = 1/2$	Expected Value	Present Value r = 10%
Project	Firm	$60	$160	$110	$100
Capital Structure LD+: LS plus an equal-priority Bond					
Old Bond(Face Value $55)	Debt	73% · $60 ≈ $44	$55	$49.50	$45.00
New Bond(Face Value $20)	Debt	27% · $60 ≈ $16	$20	$18.00	$16.36
Equity	Equity	$0	$85	$42.50	$38.64
			plus extra payout of equity dividend	+$16.36 =	$55

Exhibit 18.4: *The Effect of Issuance of Equal-Seniority or Shorter-Term Bonds on Debt and Equity Values.* The cost of capital in this example is 10% for all securities, which is equivalent to assuming risk neutrality. 73% is the proportional allocation of the old debt, $55/($55 + $20) ≈ 73%.

Again, fearing expropriation, the entrepreneur has to pay a higher interest up-front to potential bondholders.

This expropriation is not as bad as our risk-shifting example, in that managers need not destroy firm value. But it can force a certain capital-structure dynamic on the firm. The first creditors will again assume that they will be expropriated, and therefore they will demand a higher interest rate today. They would demand a quoted interest rate of $55/$45 − 1 ≈ 22.2%. To recoup this higher interest rate, the managers will have no choice but to indeed issue more bonds that expropriate these first bond purchasers later. In effect, before deciding on any capital structure, the firm has two choices: Either issue no bonds or be dragged into a capital structure that will require expropriating existing debt more and more (by issuing more and more new debt).

A similar but even more benign form of creditor expropriation could be as follows: If creditors were always to receive x% of what they were promised, they would simply incorporate this into the interest rate they demand. The overall firm value would not change. This is actually quite relevant in the real world. In bankruptcy, the agreed-upon absolute priority rule (in which bondholders are supposed to be paid in full before equity holders receive anything) is often not followed. Fortunately, such deviations from promised absolute priority are expected and simply change the contingent payoffs and thus the effective values of the securities. They do not reduce the total value of the firm. Relative to a strict Absolute Priority Rule (APR), the equity value is higher by exactly the amount that the debt value is lower.

Again, the problem is that it requires contortion by the firm (negative-NPV projects) to expropriate creditors after the fact.

➤ *APR, Sect. 15.2, Pg.465.*

Q 18.12. Describe the two basic mechanisms whereby unprotected bondholders can be expropriated by shareholders. Can you illustrate your arguments with numerical examples?

Counteracting Forces against Expropriation

Bondholders demand a premium ex ante that they would not demand if the firm could commit to not expropriating them ex post. The premium may prevent the firm from raising debt at fair interest rates and thus tilt the optimal capital structure more toward equity. Even managers with the best intentions not to act against bondholders may not be able to shield themselves from the pressures of expropriating creditors later. Who ultimately loses? To the extent that smart bond investors anticipate their fate, they will demand and receive fair compensation. Ultimately, it is the firm that suffers. Its inability to commit to not expropriating creditors may prevent it from issuing debt at fair prices—which would mean it may have to forgo debt's other advantages (such as tax savings).

If the entrepreneur can commit to not expropriate creditors later, he can enjoy lower interest rates.

In the real world, there are a number of mechanisms that can help to reduce the fears of bondholders, thereby allowing the firm to issue debt at higher interest rates—which thereby often lowers the firm's overall cost of capital.

Mechanisms that help align managerial interests with those of prospective bondholders.

Managerial risk aversion: We noted earlier that shareholders like increases in project risk, because they help them at the expense of bondholders. However, it is not clear if managers really act on behalf of shareholders and thus like higher risk, too. After all, if the project fails and the firm enters financial distress, they might get fired themselves. Thus, managerial risk aversion is a natural counterbalance to the shareholders' incentives to increase risk.

Managers dislike going bankrupt, so they are probably not inclined to gamble unless the firm is already in terrible distress.

Bond covenants: A variety of bond covenants have developed to mitigate bondholder skepticism.

- Many bonds prohibit excessive dividend payouts.
- Many bonds prohibit large new debt issues, especially of shorter term and of equal priority.
- Many bonds require the maintenance of certain financial ratios. For example, covenants may mandate maximum debt-equity ratios, maximum payout

Bond covenants reduce exploitational opportunities in the future—but at a cost in flexibility.

➤ *Covenants, Sect. 10.2, Pg.253.*

ratios, minimum earnings retention ratios, minimum liquidity ratios, and so on. These ratio restrictions can all help prevent the firm from taking on riskier projects.

If the covenant is broken, creditors can sue or demand their money back. Covenants are never perfect. It is just impossible to enumerate all the things managers can do. In addition, if the firm enters Chapter 11 bankruptcy, the law says that any new debt issued will automatically receive higher priority, no matter what the covenants of the original bond stated.

Bonds with strong covenants often have a "call" feature that allows the firm to retire the bond before maturity at an agreed-upon price—and thereby free itself of the covenant requirements.

Corporate reputation: Covenants are inflexible, so they impose costs, too. For example, if the firm happens to come across a project with +$1 billion in NPV, the covenants could prevent the firm from taking it. Again, a firm that fails to take all profitable projects in the future is worth less today. One alternative to formal covenants is for firms to build a less formal "reputation." This is not easy to do, but firms may realize that it is in their interest not to exploit current bondholders because any future bondholders would henceforth definitely assume the worst behavior. Put differently, if managers were to take advantage of creditors today, then future financing costs would be so much higher that managers would rather not do so. Reputation is not perfect, though, especially if the advantage that can be taken of creditors today becomes very large. The most prominent example of broken reputation is possibly RJR Nabisco. In the 1980s, it was generally believed to be a safe investment for bondholders. However, when it was bought out in 1988 (in the largest leveraged buyout of its time), RJR tripled its debt overnight, its outstanding bonds went from investment grade to speculative grade, and bondholders experienced an announcement-month loss of 15%.

Convertible bonds or strip financing: Another mechanism is to try to allow creditors to partake in the upside of equity. The most common such financing vehicles are **convertible bonds**. Again, they can limit the ex-post expropriation of bondholders while still preserving the firm's option to accept new projects. Instead of straight bonds with strong covenants, "convertible bonds" with weak covenants allow creditors to participate if a great new project were to come along. This reduces the risk expropriation problem. **Strip financing**, in which individuals purchase debt and equity in equal units, is a similar idea—it eliminates the incentives of shareholders to exploit each other (i.e., themselves).

Units:

The same idea is behind the use of units. A unit is a combination of securities. It can consist of a debt security and an equity security. Thus, there is no difference in identity between shareholders and bondholders. However, if the firm pays interest, it shifts its tax burden to the unit owners. If the firm pays dividends, it shifts this tax burden to itself. More important, unless the buyers unbundle the units, it does not matter to them if the firm expropriates bondholders at the expense of shareholders. Every bondholder is a shareholder! Note that this also puts a stark

Sidenotes:

And, again, covenants reduce the flexibility of the firm to take advantage of other opportunities. Sometimes, reputation can substitute for covenants.

➤ *RJR Nabisco and other large LBOs, Sect. 23.A (Companion), Pg.≈193.*

Convertible bonds allow bondholders to participate in the upside, and reduce exploitational incentives in the future.

If shareholders are also the creditors, there would be little use for them to expropriate themselves.

➤ *Units of debt and equity, Sect. 18.2, Pg.572.*

limit on the amount that bondholder expropriation may possibly destroy. After all, if it were that important, someone could just purchase the securities and resell them as inseparable units. This cannot be too expensive, so ex-ante bondholder expropriation costs cannot be too much in equilibrium.

In the real world, firms have to undertake a delicate balancing act. When they issue debt, it can only be issued at favorable terms when the firm can promise not to exploit bondholders after the bonds are issued. Even if such promises can be credibly made, they cause a loss of flexibility, which can be expensive. This can mean that the firm cannot issue debt—and thus that it has to forgo some other beneficial effects of debt (such as tax advantages).

Recap: Entrepreneurs internalize the cost of future inefficient behavior.

IMPORTANT

> - Bondholders and other creditors can lose value if either of the following occurs:
>   - The firm later undertakes riskier projects.
>   - The firm adds more debt of equal or higher priority.
> - Creditors demand higher interest rates if they fear such expropriation. Thus, it is in the interest of the owners to assure creditors that they will not do so. The prime mechanisms to accomplish this are
>   - Loan covenants
>   - Reputation
>   - Bond convertibility

Q 18.13. Does managerial risk aversion mitigate or exacerbate the fear of creditors to be expropriated in favor of shareholders?

Q 18.14. In a market in which bond covenants are priced at what they are worth, can their presence still increase firm value? When could covenants reduce firm value?

Q 18.15. What is an advantage of adding a convertibility feature to a bond?

Q 18.16. Consider a project similar to the firm in Exhibit 18.3, but change the risk-neutral required interest rate to 0%. The firm is worth either $100 or $120. The bond promises $90. We shall consider two cases: one in which the bond is convertible into 75% of the firm's equity, and one in which it is not.

1. Work out the value of the firm. For the bond, create three rows for each state:
   a) If bondholders never convert (which is also the value for the nonconvertible bond);
   b) If bondholders always convert;
   c) If bondholders convert only if it is optimal for them (which is also the value for the convertible bond).

   Does the convertibility feature have any value?

590   More Imperfect-Market Capital Structure

2. Now a new and independent project "BAD" becomes available. It will pay off either +\$50 or –\$60 with equal probabilities.

   a) If the bond is not convertible, is it in the interest of shareholders to undertake "BAD"?

   b) If the bond is convertible (into 75% equity), is it in the interest of shareholders to undertake "BAD"? Would you expect to see many conversions if this were the case? How does frequency of actual conversion empirically relate to the value of convertibility?

18.5 Inside Information and Adverse Selection

New potential partners (shareholders) have less information than current managers and owners.

➤ *Two types of value sources of capital structures,* Pg.570.

If owners want partners rather than lenders, the project may not be as good.

Our next important determinant of capital structure is inside information. Typically, firm managers (acting on behalf of the old owners) have better information than new investors. If managers are acting on the behalf of their old investors, then new investors should be careful, so that they do not get exploited. As the old adage says, "Never bet with someone better informed than yourself." Again, to the extent that inside information concerns can prevent managers from taking the optimal set of projects, e.g., because they make it difficult to raise the necessary funding, some capital structures can create more value than others.

Consider this scenario: You are a potential investor in an oil well, and you know that the current owner/manager (who has to raise new capital) already knows whether or not there is oil. But you do not know. You have to ask yourself the following questions:

- What will you believe about the oil well if the present owner offers to make you a full partner who shares in all future profits?

- What will you believe about the oil well if the present owner asks you for a loan to be paid back that she is willing to collateralize with her present assets?

➤ *Winner's curse,* Sect. 21.G (Companion), Pg.≈135.

If you are offered partnership, you should be reluctant to believe that there is oil. If, however, the present owner wants to keep the profits and simply borrow, she probably knows that the project is profitable. This is sometimes called the **winner's curse**, **adverse selection**, or simply the **lemon problem**. If you receive the offer to become partner, it does not help you very much. (There won't be oil in the ground.) If you do not receive the offer to become partner, you would be better off if you had indeed received it. (There will be oil in the ground.) This analogy is directly transferable to capital structure. Sharing in the firm's equity is the equivalent of becoming a partner.

The basic scenario assumptions.

Let's assume that the firm still needs to raise \$25 to buy the rig, and if no money can be raised, there is no business. The firm's expected value is \$50 if it is bad and \$150 if it is good. Let's say that the effective time discount rate is zero. (This is merely to allow us to be lazy in our calculations.) Finally, we will assume that half of all firms that want to raise money are con artists, while the other half are "for real." Thus, for the average firm,

		Bad Luck $\mathscr{P}rob = 1/2$	Good Luck $\mathscr{P}rob = 1/2$	Expected Value
Project	Firm	\$50	\$150	\$100

Now let's say that firms can only be equity financed, and that there is no possibility whatsoever for any firm to get funds in any other way. In this case, both types of firms must raise equity financing if they want to operate. The fraction of the firm that you will demand in exchange for your $25 must depend on your assessment of whether the firm is good or bad. If you believe it is bad, and worth only $50, you would demand $25/$50 = 50% of the firm. On the other hand, if you believe it is good, and worth $150, you would demand only $25/$150 = $1/6$ of the firm. If you believe it's 50-50, you would demand $25/$100 = $1/4$ of the firm. Let's work out how much each type of firm will end up with, depending on what you believe.

No financing other than equity.

Outside Investors Believe Firm is		% Equity Sold To Raise $25	Bad Firm Keeps	Good Firm Keeps
Bad	$\Rightarrow \mathscr{E} = \$50$	$1/2$	$\$25 + 1/2 \cdot \$50 = \$50.00$	$\$25 + 1/2 \cdot \$150 = \$100.00$
50-50	$\Rightarrow \mathscr{E} = \$100$	$1/4$	$\$25 + 3/4 \cdot \$50 = \$62.50$	$\$25 + 3/4 \cdot \$150 = \$137.50$
Good	$\Rightarrow \mathscr{E} = \$150$	$1/6$	$\$25 + 5/6 \cdot \$50 = \$67.00$	$\$25 + 5/6 \cdot \$150 = \$150.00$

With both types of firms raising money, and with our assumption that half of the firms are really good, outside investors can believe that there is a 50-50 chance that a firm is good or bad. Its expected value is therefore $100. To raise $25 in equity, the entrepreneurs must promise outside investors 25% of their $100 firm. They keep the rest. The con artists end up with $62.50, and the good guys end up with $137.50. Note that the bad firm is better off claiming that it is a good firm, too, and the good firm suffers for it. Every dollar that the con artists skim off investors is in effect paid by the good guys.

The "only equity" equilibrium: You demand 25% of the firm.

Now assume that debt financing has suddenly become available. In this case, depending on your beliefs, a firm that sells debt will receive the following:

Now debt financing becomes available.

Outside Investors Believe Firm is		$ Debt Sold To Raise $25	Bad Firm Keeps	Good Firm Keeps
Bad	$\Rightarrow \mathscr{E} = \$50$	$25	$\$25 + (\$50 - \$25) = \$50$	$\$25 + (\$150 - \$25) = \$150$
50-50	$\Rightarrow \mathscr{E} = \$100$	$25	$\$25 + (\$50 - \$25) = \$50$	$\$25 + (\$150 - \$25) = \$150$
Good	$\Rightarrow \mathscr{E} = \$150$	$25	$\$25 + (\$50 - \$25) = \$50$	$\$25 + (\$150 - \$25) = \$150$

Pretty boring—you would always demand $25 and receive $25. But good firms are better off. If good firms can raise the $25 funding with debt, they end up with $150 in total. They simply pay back the loan after the oil comes out of the hole.

The "only debt" equilibrium: You demand $25 in debt.

However, the important insight of this example is altogether different. If debt financing is available, your outside investors' inference for a firm that asks you for an equity investment changes altogether. The reason is that it becomes irrational for you to believe that such a firm is not a con. Even if half of all firms in the pool are for real, not a single of these good firms would want to ask you for equity financing. Every single good firm is better off going with debt financing instead. As a result, there is only one possible inference for you: anyone who wants to raise equity financing must be a con artist!

The presence of debt financing renders equity financing a bad signal.

The "choose debt or equity" equilibrium: You demand either $25 in debt or 50% of the firm. (25% is no longer enough!)

Issuing more equity-like (partner-like) shares reveals bad news. Thus, new equity shares can only be sold at low prices.

You should now be convinced that unless entrepreneurs can credibly convince outside investors that they have raised as much funding from debt (and from themselves) as possible, outside investors will assume that entrepreneurial requests for equity financing signal that there is something wrong with the firm that they don't know. Thus, when existing owners announce a new equity offering, it releases information that the firm's projects are worse than generally believed, and the new equity can only be sold for a very low price. This is again an example of adverse selection—only companies fearing the future would want to share their prospects. In real life, we indeed observe that firms public equity value declines by about 10 cents when they announce that they plan to raise $1 in new equity.

This argument applies to all claims that are more junior, and leads to a "pecking order" of financing.

But this argument extends not only to equity but to other claims as well. The riskier the securities are that insiders want to sell rather than keep, the worse are their beliefs in their projects. Sharing in more junior (risky) bonds is the equivalent of the present owners making you a "little partner," when they are not willing to collateralize their loans. Consequently, the announcement of a risky junior security releases information that the firm's projects are not too great, but not too bad, either. In contrast, the new issue of a collateralized loan (or a risk-free senior bond) will indicate that the firm's projects are better than expected. The outcome is that the better the firm's projects are, the more senior the security the managers will offer for sale. This leads to a **pecking order** view of capital structure: The best projects are financed by the most senior debt, worse projects by junior debt, and the worst projects by equity.

Firms may want to avoid issuing equity to avoid signaling bad news.

What does this imply about the optimal capital structure? Consider a firm that cannot issue debt easily because it has little collateral or because additional debt would unduly increase expected bankruptcy costs. If it cannot issue equity because of these insider concerns, such a firm may have to pass up on some good (but perhaps not stellar) projects, simply because owners do not want to sell their projects at the price of the worst possible scenario. A publicly traded firm thus may take on too much debt (incurring financial distress costs) or ration its projects, failing to take at least some of its positive-NPV projects. And to the extent that adverse selection distorts the firm's otherwise optimal project choice, it lowers the firm value.

➤ Two types of value sources of capital structures, Pg. 570.

IMPORTANT

> The presence of inside information concerns (investors fearing the worst) favors debt over equity as the cheaper financing vehicle.

If managers can convey all they know, the adverse selection penalty would disappear.

When could a firm issue equity without an insider penalty?

- If there is a mechanism—for example, a detailed audit—by which insiders with good projects can credibly convey the true quality of the project, it would be in their interest to do so. Indeed, if such a mechanism is known to exist and owners do not undertake it, potential investors should immediately assume that current owners are not doing so because they know that the outcome will be bad.

- If current owners can convince potential investors that they have invested all of their own money, have maxed out their personal credit cards, and just cannot put any more personal capital at risk than they already have, then there is no bad inside information in the fact that they are trying to raise equity capital. In this case, external investors can assume that the project is not necessarily bad. Indeed, no venture capitalist will ever invest in a start-up in which the current owners do not have most of their personal wealth at stake.

The inside information and the free cash flow (agency) theories have a very close family relationship. The former says that when firms issue equity, managers signal a belief that the future will be worse. The latter says that when firms issue equity, managers will make the future worse—they will waste the money. In both cases, issuing equity sends signals to investors about bad futures. Therefore, both create pecking orders in which appropriate skepticism of investors should induce the ordinary manager to prefer issuing debt to equity. The main difference between the two theories is that the agency explanation is more causal than the inside information explanation.

> Agency costs and inside information are closely related—both create a pecking order.

Q 18.17. A house up for auction can be worth either $500,000 or $1,000,000 with 50-50 probability. The other bidders know the true value; you do not. If you bid for the house in an auction, what should you bid? If you bid $750,000, what is *your* expected rate of return?

Q 18.18. What is the pecking order? (Thinking question: In a real-world firm, will a pecking order lead to a **financing pyramid**, in which firms tend to be financed mostly by debt [the bottom of the pyramid] and by very little equity [the top of the pyramid]?)

Q 18.19. Does concern with inside information suggest that firms should issue debt or equity? Why?

Q 18.20. Go back to the oil rig example, which is worth either $50 or $150 with 50-50 probability. But now assume that there is an additional cost to issuing debt—perhaps because these types of firms are more likely to go bankrupt and incur the wrath (fees) of the legal profession.

1. If these fees are expected to be $10, how much will the good firms, the bad firms, and the lawyers get to keep?

2. If these fees are expected to be $15, how much will the good firms, the bad firms, and the lawyers get to keep? (You are not expected to get the answer right, but give it a stab.)

18.6　Transaction Costs and Behavioral Issues

Transaction costs are everywhere. They can definitely prevent optimal capital structure adjustment.

Transaction costs have played an important role in all capital structure examples above: If transaction costs had been zero, external pressures would force management to choose the best capital structure. But if transaction costs are high, managerial mistakes are difficult or impossible to correct for outsiders. It is not just enough for an outsider to purchase and sell shares. The appropriate corrective action requires accumulating enough shares to be able to influence management. Without external discipline, managers can act badly. They may take too much debt or too much equity, and the market may not be able to correct it.

The transaction costs of maintaining public equity can be quite large, especially for tiny firms. Equity-issuing costs are also expensive.

➤ *Sarbanes-Oxley, Sect.* 24.G (Companion), *Pg.≈265*.

➤ *Issuing Costs, Chapter* 21 (Companion), *Pg.≈115*.
Transaction costs could also prevent firms from issuing debt.
➤ *Issuing costs, Exhibit* 23.9 (Companion), *Pg.≈201*.

Transaction costs can also play a direct role. For example, the reporting requirements and liabilities imposed by the *1933 Securities Act* for publicly traded equity securities can be much larger than those for private borrowing. The recent *Sarbanes-Oxley Act* (explained in Chapter 24 (Companion)) has raised the costs of public equity even further. Other evidence further shows that issuing new equity has direct transaction costs of around 5-15% of the issue. For many small companies, these costs of equity may be large enough to warrant a capital structure consisting not of public equity but exclusively of private securities and bank debt.

Another example of how marketwide transaction costs may affect individual capital structures depends on the absence of certain markets. For example, many institutions are not allowed by law to hold securities with too low of a credit rating. Firms with a credit rating lower than BBB cannot tap the large commercial paper market. This could create a situation in which the cost of capital of debt is low only for low debt ratios (where the corporation can issue high-rated debt), but it rises dramatically if the firm takes on a lot of debt. On a more basic level, it is not cheap for retail investors to trade a specific company's corporate debt. If mutual funds cannot facilitate investor access, it could further raise the cost of issuing debt.

IMPORTANT

> Transaction cost considerations could favor either debt or equity.

Transaction costs "cause" behavioral finance concerns.

➤ *Behavioral finance, Sect.* 11.2, *Pg.290*.

Unfortunately, behavioral theory is often hard to use, perhaps because we are just getting started on it.

Section 11.2 has already explained the link between high transaction costs and behavioral finance. When transaction costs are high—which means that one cannot easily correct mistakes—then behavioral finance considerations are likely to play important roles. Such conditions are indeed common in corporate finance. It is simply too expensive to take over a firm in order to correct a capital structure that has, say, 10% too much or too little debt.

Behavioral considerations can explain a lot of managerial behavior, which is otherwise difficult to explain. For example, we know that managers like to imitate their peers, perhaps too much so. Unfortunately, on a vague level, without a further description of what the specific behavioral mistakes are, behavioral finance is less prescriptive than the earlier theories of capital structure optimality. That is, we do not yet fully understand the guidance that behavioral finance theory gives managers about the optimal capital structure in a world in which they, and others, can make all sorts of mistakes.

Behavioral finance is the most promising new direction in corporate finance. But it is probably still too early to tell where and how it will help us better understand the world. Some early insights suggest that certain behavioral mistakes are more common than others. For example, we now believe that **overconfidence** and **overoptimism** are common traits among both managers and investors. If managers are overoptimistic, it may aggravate agency concerns (they may take some negative-NPV projects) and reluctance-to-liquidate concerns, but alleviate underinvestment problems. If investors are overoptimistic, issuing equity may not be as disadvantageous as the inside information argument suggests. Investors may not necessarily believe the worst—and there is some evidence that such was the case during the Internet bubble at the turn of the millennium. Although it is less likely that markets rather than managers are committing mistakes, there is good evidence that financial markets may be imperfect, too. If markets indeed misvalue securities—either because they are irrational or imperfect—it would be rational for managers to try to find the best time to issue equity.

> Specific behavioral errors can have specific implications.

> ➤ *Behavioral biases, Sect. 12.7, Pg.352.*

| Behavioral considerations could favor either debt or equity. | **IMPORTANT** |

Q 18.21. Give an example of transaction costs that favor more equity in the capital structure. Give an example of transaction costs that favor more debt.

18.7 Static Capital Structure Summary

Exhibit 18.5 gives a summary of all capital structure effects discussed so far. The four major forces that pull the firm toward equity are uncontrolled agency problems (managers like equity, because it makes their lives easier and allows them to purchase other firms more easily), financial distress costs, personal income taxes, and debt expropriation—ordered by my assessment of their relative importance in many large firms. The three major forces that pull the firm toward debt are corporate income taxes, mitigating agency conflicts, and inside information issues—in my view, all very important and difficult to rank. Tugging against one another, these forces pull firms toward their capital structures. From a value maximization perspective:

> The static forces are summarized in Exhibit 18.5.

- Too much debt, and the firm would expect to lose too much in financial distress handling, impose too much in personal taxes on its owners, and suffer too many creditor trust issues.

- Too little debt, and the firm would pay too much in corporate income taxes, suffer from too much rent-seeking by management, employees, and possibly others, and not signal enough confidence about the future.

As noted, unmitigated agency conflicts can instead pull the firm toward having too much equity and too little debt, because managers in charge prefer it that way.

Managers Maximizing Their Own Welfare Pull the Firm Toward...

Unmitigated Agency Conflicts   Equity

Managers like shareholders' equity and the flexibility it provides, and they dislike debt and the discipline it imposes. Here, the presence of equity *reduces* the value of the firm.

Entrepreneurs Maximizing the Firm Value Pull the Firm Toward...

Financial Distress Costs   Equity (usually)

Include inefficient operations, underinvestment problems, supplier and customer incentives, failure to liquidate or sell at appropriate prices, predatory policies by competitors, and so on.

Personal Income Taxes   Equity

Interest receipts are tax-disadvantaged from investors' points of view.

Debt Expropriation   Equity

Includes costs arising from the interaction of borrower credibility and borrower flexibility. Includes complete contract specification costs. Possibly less important than other forces in this table.

Corporate Income Taxes   Debt

Interest payments are tax-deductible by the corporation.

Too Much Cash Flow (Mitigating Agency Conflicts)   Debt

Sometimes called moral hazard. Includes empire building, free cash flow, excessive managerial perks, verification, and so on.

Inside Information   Debt

Sometimes called adverse selection or even the lemon problem. (Sometimes, adverse selection is mistakenly called "pecking order"—inside information issues indeed create a pecking order, but so can other forces.)

Behavioral Finance   Situation-Dependent
Transaction Costs   Situation-Dependent

Exhibit 18.5: *Summary of Important Capital Structure Forces and Effects.* With the exception of the first effect, it is overall value maximization that should push firms toward financing themselves with the security that is described in the right column.

Q 18.22. List the main effects pulling capital structures toward equity. List the main effects pulling capital structures toward debt. Are all these forces working through the desire of entrepreneurs and managers to maximize firm value?

18.8 The Effect of Leverage on the Costs of Capital

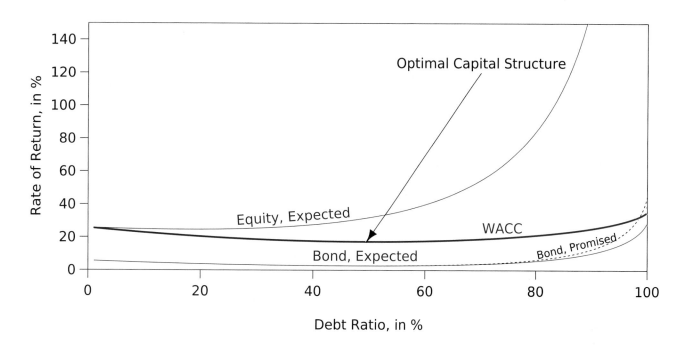

Exhibit 18.6: *The Cost of Capital in an Imperfect World.* This figure is the equivalent of Exhibits 16.2 and 17.2, except that both types of claims now have some drawbacks and some advantages. This results in an optimal leverage ratio for the firm (marked by the arrow).

This chapter described the effect of many forces on firm value and on optimal debt-equity financing. But how do these forces influence the firm's effective WACC? The firm value and the cost of capital are mirrors of one another, so higher costs of capital mean lower firm values, and vice versa. Just think of the value of the firm today as the expected future cash flows of given projects, divided by one plus the cost of capital. Holding expected cash flows (projects) constant, when the firm's cost of capital increases, its present value decreases, and vice versa. What does the firm's cost of capital look like as a function of its debt ratio? You have already seen it in a perfect world (Exhibit 16.2) and in a world with corporate taxes (Exhibit 17.2). Exhibit 18.6 shows how the figure would look like if there are multiple capital market imperfections, and

With more forces than just corporate income taxes, there could be an interior optimal debt ratio now.

➤ *Cost of capital in a perfect world,*
Exhibit 16.2, Pg. 511.

➤ *Cost of capital with corporate tax,*
Exhibit 17.2, Pg. 534.

the optimal capital structure balances many forces. The cost of equity capital and the cost of debt capital are now both influenced by these forces. As drawn in the graph, the resulting WACC function has a minimum at a debt ratio around 50%. It is also quite flat, so in this case the firm would not make a big mistake being off by, say, 10% in its ratio. Of course, this is not always the case. There are firms in which the effective cost of capital is considerably more curved, in which case a suboptimal capital structure would destroy a lot more value. So, make sure you focus on what the important first-order effects are for the specific company that you are involved with, not those minor effects that do not cause much curvature in the firm's cost of capital.

IMPORTANT

> - Capital structure can have dramatic value influences for firms that are (a) considering drastic changes in their capital structure (e.g., as in a private buyout); (b) close to financial distress; and (c) very highly levered. (For example, many banks routinely operate with liability-to-asset ratios above 95%. Any mishap can be catastrophic.)
>
> - For many other *large* publicly-traded firms, the capital-structure value function seems to be quite flat. That is, small deviations in their debt ratios from the optimum, one way or the other, do not seem to have large influences on firm value. (This does not mean that managers do not care; it means that even if they do, changes will not have much effect on firm value.)
>
> - When the value function is flat, and if there are high transaction costs to change debt into equity, or vice versa, taking no action may be the best choice, even when the firm is not at its otherwise best debt-equity ratio.

Q 18.23. If the firm is not in an M&M perfect-market situation, how will this be reflected in the relation between its cost of capital and its leverage?

18.9 Valuation Formulas with Many Market Imperfections

How should you think of corporate valuation formulas in the presence of market imperfections?

➤ *WACC/APV with personal taxes, Sect. 17.7, Pg.556.*

You now know that, as a corporate manager, you should care about your own corporate income taxes (and you have nice APV and WACC formulas to work with them), your investors' personal income taxes, about how corporate debt can raise your expected cost of bankruptcy, about how equity can lead managers to waste money on pet projects, and other issues related to your firm's capital structure. So how do you work out the net present value of your firm in the presence of these issues and in the presence of your ability to use capital structure to change them? How do all the capital market imperfections work together to determine the value of the firm and its capital structure? And do you need more complex APV or WACC formulas than those in Chapter 17?

First, recall that in an imperfect market the average cost of capital is not the marginal cost of capital that you would want to compare to your next project's internal rate of return. The cost of raising or retiring one more dollar in external financing can be substantially different from your cost of raising or retiring a billion dollars. The existing cost of capital that you can read from your balance sheet is just a historical number, and not what you need. Nevertheless, the average cost of capital can often be very useful to learn, if only because the same forces that influenced the average cost of capital in the past likely also influence the marginal cost of capital today. For many large firms, the average cost of capital may not be too far from the marginal cost of capital.

In an imperfect market, don't think the average and the marginal costs of capital are the same.

➤ *Marginal and average cost of capital,* Sect. 16.6, Pg.515.

Exhibit 18.7 illustrates how you can think about valuing your firm (or just your next project) from different perspectives. The firm's value would be $100 in a perfect market, but it is only $80 because of market imperfections. (The flow-to-equity approach works directly with cash flows and costs of capital that are reduced by the $20 worth of imperfections.) Although the tax shelter created by the tax deductibility of interest plays a special role in the algebraic formulation of APV (and WACC), the other factors can be just as important. This is shown in the last row, where $5 worth of corporate income tax mitigation is broken out. Yet, this is not because corporate income taxes were the only, or even the most important, factor. Only $5 of the $20 reduction is due to corporate income taxes. The remaining $15 of market imperfections is more important, but it enters value by flowing directly into the $75 present value of cash flows. Alternatively, you could think of an APV-type approach to other imperfections, too: You would work with $70 of value under extreme market imperfections if they remained totally unmitigated, and then you would add back the $10 in value that your clever capital structure has mitigated. This is rarely a useful method. Let me explain why.

Exhibit 18.7 is a conceptual graph that shows how different costs of debt and equity flow into the APV formula.

Do You Need Other Valuation (APV or WACC) Formulas?

Think back. In the previous chapter, you learned that you could handle corporate income taxes in one of the following ways:

APV and WACC are "as-if-bad but remedied." You can compute the exact corporate income tax remedy.
➤ *WACC and APV,* Sect. 17.3, Pg.528.

1. You could work with expected cash flows and costs of capital "as if fully taxed" and then add back the debt shelter-created remedy that reduces the corporate income tax. This was the principle behind the first two methods, WACC and APV.

2. You could work with expected cash flows that already reflect the actual corporate income taxes. This was the flow-to-equity method.

➤ *Flow-to-equity,* Sect. 17.4, Pg.536.

For corporate income taxes, any of these three methods work. The APV and WACC methods are especially useful because they make it easy to think about how a change in capital structure changes the firm's value. Moreover, as manager, you know the inputs (primarily your own corporate income tax rate), so you can compute the exact dollar value of both the as-if-fully-corporate-taxed value and the exact dollar value of the debt-induced tax shelter remedy.

Unfortunately, this is not the case for other capital structure influences. As the manager, you rarely have (or care about) this knowledge:

You do not have equivalent precise input values for other effects. You are thus better off just thinking about the costs themselves.

• It would be difficult for you to determine first the value of the firm if your investors received all payouts as interest and thus were fully taxed at the personal level, and then to adjust how equity financing would remedy their personal taxes. (In

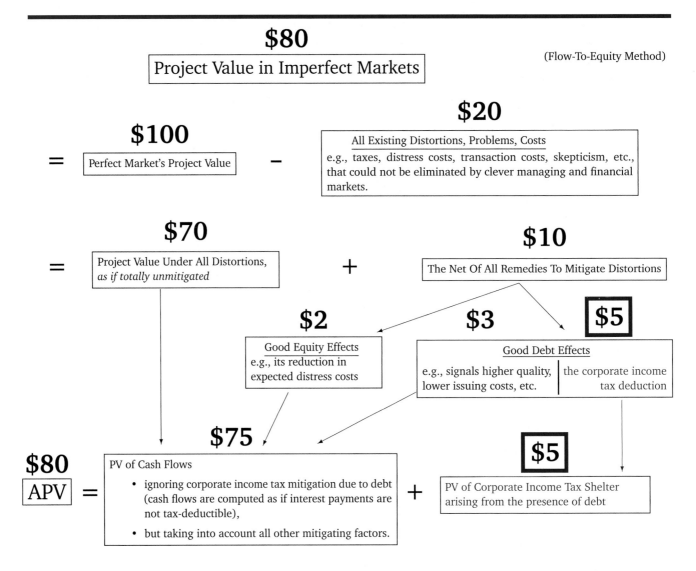

Exhibit 18.7: *Conceptual Framework for Capital Structure Effects and Formulas.* This figure provides a conceptual basis for thinking about capital structure in imperfect markets. All figures are made up to facilitate this explanation.

- Consider a project worth $100 in a perfect world. Market imperfections, such as corporate income taxes and financial distress costs that cannot be avoided, reduce this value to $80. This is the true imperfect-market value.

- You can think of this firm in another way, though. For example, consider a firm that has a capital structure that gets the worst of all worlds—it suffers market imperfections left and right, and does nothing to remedy it. This firm might be worth only $70. It follows that all imperfect market remedies together must save this firm $10.

- Now think about the potential remedies to market imperfections. There may be corporate taxes that can be avoided (e.g., by having debt and taking advantage of other tax loopholes). There may be ways to signal that the firm is worth more (e.g., by having more debt). There may be ways to reduce distress costs or to reduce personal income taxes (e.g., by having more equity). These increase the value of the firm relative to the $70 value.

- APV breaks out just one part of these remedies. It works with the value of the firm as if all noncorporate tax parts have been remedied as much as they can be remedied (here, $75), and then adds back the corporate tax shelter (here, $5).

- Note how in the real world, you still have to come up with the $75 number—the value of the firm assuming all other remedies. This includes all other net effects, such as personal income tax effects, financial distress costs, and so on. You must think about how debt and equity change this number.

fact, you do not even know with great accuracy what the correct marginal tax rates of your investors are.)

- It would be difficult for you to determine first the expected losses in bankruptcy if your firm were financed only with debt and then to adjust how equity financing would reduce these bankruptcy costs.

- It would be difficult for you to determine first how much money would be wasted on pet projects if the firm were financed only with equity and then to adjust how debt financing would reduce this pet-project waste.

Could you design new cost-of-capital formulas to handle each of these effects? In principle, you could. (In fact, there is a Miller formula that specifically incorporates personal income taxes.) In practice, without knowing the exact inputs to such novel formulas, they would be mostly useless.

But if these capital structure effects matter, then how should you value the firm under a given capital structure? The answer is that you are better off using the more direct equivalent that a flow-to-equity-like method provides. You would have to reflect all other capital structure influences in your inputs (expected cash flows and costs of capital).

The cost-of-capital inputs for debt and equity in the valuation formulas reflect the non-corporate-income-tax effects, not a new remedy term.

- If you can reduce your investors' personal income taxes on certain types of claims, then your own corporate cost of capital on these claims would be lower. The reason is that your investors will want to give you their money at lower expected rates of return. (You may want to ask your investment banker by how much.)

- If you can reduce your probability of bankruptcy, your expected cash flows would go up (and your cost of capital may go down).

- If you can reduce inefficient pet projects by adding more debt, again your expected cash flows would go up (and your cost of capital may go down).

And so on. In sum, all the non-corporate-income-tax factors enter your cost-of-capital formula, but they do so through their influence on your inputs in the existing formulas, not through a new term in a new formula. (In Exhibit 18.7, they flow into determining the $75.)

No formula does not mean less important or "no thinking required."

It is important for you to understand that just because you have no new formulas does not mean you can think less about other factors. On the contrary, personal income taxes, bankruptcy costs, and so on, are not any less important than corporate income taxes just because they do not have their own formulas. (Exhibit 18.7 gives you such an example.) As the CFO, you can create value for your investors and reduce your cost of capital not only by reducing your corporate income taxes but also by taking into account all the other effects. You must think about how your actions and your capital structure maximize firm value. More than likely, because you can rarely easily compute exact magnitudes of these market imperfections, you may have to spend more time to understand them, not less. In the end, as you learned in Section 17.6, if you can reduce market imperfections, your firm will ultimately enjoy lower costs of capital. From a managerial perspective, you can turn this around, too: If your capital structure is minimizing your expected costs of capital, you are choosing the best real-world tradeoffs, given the myriad of market imperfections in the background.

➤ *CAPM as a WACC input in an imperfect world, Sect. 17.6, Pg. 545.*

IMPORTANT

> - Corporate income taxes are just one factor influencing firm value.
>
> - Corporate income taxes are often handled through the specialized WACC and APV formulas presented in Chapter 17, because managers usually have the quantitative inputs readily available. (These two inputs are the value of the firm *as if it were fully taxed* and the value of the corporate tax shelter due to debt.)
>
> - Corporate income taxes could also be handled through a flow-to-equity approach, which relies on actual estimated costs of capital—not tax-adjusted costs of capital.
>
> - Other capital structure influences are better handled through a direct cost-of-capital estimate. This is analogous to the flow-to-equity method. Market imperfections enter the valuation through their influence on the expected cash flows and/or costs of capital. Deriving formula extensions, where these factors would receive their own formula terms, would rarely, if ever, be useful.
>
> - The fact that only corporate income tax has its own valuation formula and that other factors do not, does not mean that corporate income taxes are more important than other factors.
>
> - Good managers think about the value effects of other capital structures! They often use market intelligence to obtain good estimates of their after-all-effects expected cash flows and their after-all-effects costs of capital.
>
>   And don't forget—most large firms in non-finance industries have modest leverage ratios. Good project choice is much more value-relevant than good leverage choice (although this advice is not an excuse to get capital structure wrong).

Q 18.24. Does the lack of a personal income tax rate in the APV and WACC formula mean that the personal tax rate does not matter to the valuation of the firm?

18.10 Capital Structure Dynamics

Executing the value-optimizing strategy may not be possible. Of course, we have not covered *everything* about capital structure, but you now have a very good grasp of the most important factors to think about. Still, the real world is considerably more complex. First of all, the many forces are not as surgically isolated as they were presented above. Usually, many forces are pulling at the same time and in different directions. Second, the world is not static. In the description you have read, management looks at its projects and the forces determining the optimal capital structure, sets the capital structure once, and then everything goes its course. Alas, this is not realistic. Instead, managers are usually confronted with many issues, and not just this year but every year. This can raise altogether novel issues. The presence of one problem—or attempts to reduce it—often worsens others.

For example, there are often significant costs to move from a suboptimal to an optimal capital structure. Let us start with the simplest capital structure trade-off scenario: You own a firm in which you need to balance financial distress costs against the tax benefit of corporate debt. In a static scenario, you would choose an intermediate level of debt.

Should the firm trade off distress costs against tax benefits?

But why could you not optimize the capital structure dynamically? That is, instead of a medium debt-equity ratio, could you not keep a high debt ratio while the firm is healthy and lower it if and when bad news arrives? This way, your firm could take advantage of the tax deductions if it earns high profits, and avoid the financial distress costs if it does not. It would be the best of both worlds!

Why not get the best of both worlds?

In reality, this may not be so easy. It is true that if a firm is close to bankruptcy, issuing equity could avoid or reduce bankruptcy costs, which in turn would increase firm value. But the infusion of more equity may mostly benefit bondholders, so equity holders may not agree to put in more equity. Individual creditors might hold up a reorganization, too. Thus, even when a new start could install a better capital structure, you would still have to solve many problems to get there, given the current capital structure.

Conflict among different interest groups can prevent optimal solutions.

> **IMPORTANT**
>
> Interaction effects can make it difficult to adjust capital structure optimally in the future. Future adjustment costs can favor a more flexible capital structure (more equity and financial slack) today.

But what prevents the firm from arranging contracts ex ante, so that the optimal rearrangements happen automatically ex post? For example, an ex-ante bond covenant could force the firm to issue equity automatically, so there could be no reluctance by equity holders ex post. Or the firm could execute a simple tax arbitrage. It could give a major equity owner a bond in exchange for shares and simultaneously execute a forward contract that will reexchange the bond into the same number of shares in one year. The payments during the year to this equity (now bond) owner would now be called interest payments, and thus they would be tax deductible from the corporation's point of view. Nothing other than extra corporate tax savings (during the most likely healthy next year) would have occurred. Under both mechanisms, shareholders and bondholders would pay a fair price for their securities—but the sum total of these security values would be higher, because the firm has increased its tax savings without raising its financial distress costs. Yet few firms seem to engage in such practices.

Can we avoid the debt-or-equity dilemma by writing innovative dynamic contracts up-front?

Perhaps the reason is that our setup is not applicable to most firms. One premise was that we wanted to stave off financial distress, but equity infusions to stave off bankruptcy may not always be value maximizing. For example, equity infusions could allow the firm to continue burning its remaining assets instead of optimally liquidating them. Financial distress could also be the best or only mechanism for firing bad managers; and if managers could avoid financial distress at will, then debt would lose its function in the control of agency problems. Raising more equity to eliminate financial distress costs might thus facilitate the *wrong* managerial behavior.

Equity infusions may not always be so good, either.

Sometimes, owners are best off building a corporate reputation, which can help alleviate investor worries.

Another important issue that can come up in a repeated, multiperiod setting is reputation. It can lower financing costs, improve certain incentives, and increase firm value. Do you remember our earlier example in which the presence of an ex-post ability of managers to expropriate bondholders hurt the firm today? If managers had a reputation for not taking such bad projects, perhaps overly restrictive covenants could be avoided, in effect lowering financing costs ex ante. More importantly, the example assumed that everyone knew exactly what expropriation opportunities existed and what their probabilities were. But despite restrictive covenants, bondholders will always have the nagging suspicion that they may be expropriated, after all, when unforeseen opportunities appear. Thus, firms are often well advised to build trust and reputation to mitigate such suspicions.

To trust or not to trust!

Do investors trust managers? *Can* investors trust managers? *Should* investors trust managers? When is it worthwhile for a manager/firm to build such a reputation? How can this effectively be accomplished? These are difficult questions to answer empirically, but they are important in the real world.

Choosing the best capital structure is a combination of art and science.

Ultimately, the trick to being a good manager is to judge and weigh the plethora of marginal costs and marginal benefits of projects, of debt, and of equity, and to have sound judgment in deciding on a good combination thereof. Choosing a good capital structure is as much an "art" as a "science." This is good news for today's business students: Capital structure choices are unlikely to be taken over by a computer program anytime soon.

More background info is in the companion.

In the companion, there are two optional chapters that relate to the capital structure issues we just covered. Chapter 21 (Companion) explains the dynamic process that determines corporate capital structures (including the role of investment bankers and the role of mergers and acquisitions). Chapter 22 (Companion) explains the actual historical evidence describing corporate capital structures in the United States.

Q 18.25. A cash-cow firm, susceptible to agency problems, might hit short-term financial difficulties in a recession. What kind of financial security would maximize the firm's value?

Summary

This chapter covered the following major points:

- Capital structure can influence managerial behavior in good and in bad times. It can pull towards debt or equity.

- A specific capital structure can influence firm-value today because it can potentially impact firm value in the future. It can do so, by creating direct costs, or by inducing the firm to take suboptimal projects.

- Equity has an advantage in that it reduces the likelihood of financial distress, and with it deadweight bankruptcy costs in bad times. This includes both direct costs (such as legal fees) and indirect costs (such as underinvestment, reluctance to liquidate, and excessive risk taking).

- Debt has an advantage in that it imposes discipline on managers and thus reduces money wasting in good times. Managers and employees tend to work harder if poor performance can lead to bankruptcy.

- Equity has an advantage of not tempting managers to expropriate creditors. If bondholders fear expropriation from subsequent increases in corporate risk or from the issuance of more debt with earlier payments or payments that are equal or higher in priority, they demand a higher cost of capital.

- Debt has an advantage of signaling confidence. If owners—or managers acting on behalf of owners—prefer to sell partnership shares rather than debt, they probably believe that the project's true quality is worse. Thus, the cost of raising equity is high, because new partners will assume the worst.

- If agency conflicts are unmitigated, managers may not choose an optimal capital structure, but rather a relatively equity-heavy one.

- Section 18.7 summarizes the effects of different forces on firm value and cost of capital. It also summarizes how you should think of cost-of-capital formulas.

- Exhibit 18.7 illustrates how different forces enter valuation formulas.

- You do not need a more complex formula than WACC or APV from Chapter 17. The reason is that all market imperfections are better addressed with a flow-to-equity–like approach. That is, these factors should determine your expected cash flows and cost-of-capital inputs into the formula.

- Not needing a formula for other forces does not mean that these forces are any less important. You must think about (and often effectively estimate) how these forces influence your expected cash flows and costs of capital on both debt and equity.

Keywords

Adverse selection, 590.   Chapter 11 reorganization, 572.   Chapter 7 liquidation, 572.   Conflict of interest, 581.   Convertible bond, 588.   Financing pyramid, 593.   Holdout, 574.   Indirect bankruptcy cost, 572. Lemon problem, 590.   Moral hazard, 581.   Overconfidence, 595.   Overoptimism, 595.   Pecking order, 592. Private equity, 583.   Reluctance to liquidate, 578.   Rent seeking, 582.   Strip financing, 588.   Theft, 581. Trade credit, 574.   Underinvestment, 577.   Unit, 575.   Winner's curse, 590.

Answers

Q 18.1 Higher debt and equity risk when the firm is more levered is not necessarily a force against leverage. Even in an M&M world with unchanging firm value, debt and equity have higher risk when the firm takes on more risk. See Section 16.4 on Page 509. Consequently, higher risk in itself is usually not a counteracting force to the beneficial corporate income tax consequences of debt.

Q 18.2 Deadweight bankruptcy costs, both direct and indirect, favor equity: In the extreme, with no debt, the firm would never incur them.

Q 18.3 U.S. managers usually mean the chapters of the bankruptcy code: Reorganization is Chapter 11; liquidation is Chapter 7.

Q 18.4 Direct bankruptcy costs are legal fees and management time. Indirect costs are, for example, reluctance of customers to purchase goods from firms that could go bankrupt (e.g., if the good requires future contact or offers a warranty) and reluctance of suppliers to extend trade credit.

Q 18.5 As an example of an underinvestment problem, think of neglected maintenance that reduces the value of assets relative to the first-best behavior.

Q 18.6 To be influenced by underinvestment issues, assets must be very maintenance intensive (such as boats), and the firm must be reasonably likely to go bankrupt so that underinvestment considerations could come into play.

Q 18.7 Here are two examples of reluctance-to-liquidate problems:

- Entrenched managers may not want to sell off the remaining assets, because they would rather run down the firm and keep their jobs. This can hurt shareholders.
- Shareholders may not want to liquidate and sell the firm if it is "underwater," even if the offer is more than the firm is worth. The reason is that the benefits would go primarily to the creditors. The shareholders may prefer to gamble with the creditors' money on high-risk ventures instead. Note that this problem now helps shareholders, whereas in the previous case it hurt them.

Thus, this reluctance-to-liquidate issue is never good for creditors, but it can either hurt or help shareholders depending on the situation.

Q 18.8 Firms in declining industries are more likely to suffer reluctance-to-liquidate problems, especially if their managers are well entrenched.

Q 18.9 Debt is not always a strategic advantage. It could commit the firm to undertake riskier projects. In some cases, this could deter competitive entry into the firm's markets. However, debt could also make it more difficult for the management of a company to respond effectively.

Q 18.10 Management in firms with a lot of debt to service may have to forgo corporate airplanes, large headquarters, and/or large staff.

Q 18.11 It depends. If the firm is not yet under the firm control of management—for example, if it is under the control of a large value-maximizing shareholder-entrepreneur—then this entrepreneur would want the firm to be more debt-financed to keep management in check. However, if the firm is already under the firm control of conflicted management, then these managers will likely push to move away from debt and toward equity.

Q 18.12 First, shareholders can expropriate bondholders by issuing other claims that have an earlier or equal priority on the firm's cash flows in distress. This could be other bonds of equal or higher priority, or a straight-out dividend payment. Second, shareholders could induce the firm to take on riskier projects. Numerical examples illustrating these two mechanisms are in the text.

Q 18.13 Managerial risk aversion usually mitigates the fear of creditors that they will be expropriated by risk shifting because managers dislike the same kind of risk. After all, if the firm were to go bankrupt, these managers would lose their jobs.

Q 18.14 Bond covenants can help reduce the incentives of equity shareholders to expropriate bondholders. This can increase the firm value if it prevents managers from taking negative-NPV projects whose main purpose was to shift value from bondholders to shareholders. However, covenants can also decrease the firm value if they prevent managers from taking positive-NPV projects that would trigger the bond covenant.

Q 18.15 The convertibility feature can reduce the need for some bond covenants and thus give the firm more flexibility in case a great project were to appear suddenly. Bondholders would be happy because they would benefit, too. (Of course, bondholders get more if the firm does well, and shareholders get a lower interest rate, but this is just state reallocation. The important aspect here is that the net effect of the alignment of interests would be a reduction in the firm's overall cost of capital.)

Q 18.16   1. For the firm worth $100 or $120 with debt promising $90:

Project		Firm
Convertible Bond with Face Value $90		
(a) Bond is Never Converted		Debt···
(b) Always Converted (to 75% Equity)		Debt···
(c) If Optimal Conversion Choice		Debt···
		Equity···

	Prob		Exp
	1/2	1/2	Value
Firm	$100	$120	$110
Convertible Bond with Face Value $90			
(a) ···Debt	$90	$90	
(b) ···Debt	75%·$100 = $75	75%·$120 = $90	
(c) ···Debt	$90	$90	$90
···Equity	$10	$30	$20

With these project payoffs, it is optimal for bondholders never to convert. Therefore, the conversion feature has no value.

2. With the new project "BAD" (which pays +$50 or –$60 with equal probabilities, independent of the original project), the payoffs are:

Adding Risky Project "New"

		Prob				Exp
		1/4	1/4	1/4	1/4	Value
Project	Firm	$100	$100	$120	$120	$110
Project	BAD	$50	–$60	$50	–$60	–$5
Total Projects		$150	$40	$170	$60	$105

We can now consider the two scenarios:

a) In this case, the bond is nonconvertible.

Straight Bond with Face Value $90

		Prob				Exp
		1/4	1/4	1/4	1/4	Value
Total Projects		$150	$40	$170	$60	$105
Bond	Debt	$90	$40	$90	$60	$70
Equity	Equity	$60	$0	$80	$0	$35

Yes, in this case, the shareholders want this project to be undertaken, because $35 is more than $20.

b) In this case, the bond with $90 face value is convertible into 75% of the firm's equity.

(a) Firm	$150
(b) Bond	Debt
(c) If Conv. (75% Eq)	Debt
(d) If Optimal Conv	Debt
(e) Equity	Equity

		Prob			Exp
	1/4	1/4	1/4	1/4	Value
(a)	$170	$60	$105	$95.45	
(b)	$90	$40	$90	$60	
(c)	$30	$127.5	$45		
(d)	$40	$127.5	$60	$85	$77.27
(e)	$0	$42.5	$0	$20	$18.18

The shareholders are now no longer better off if project "BAD" is undertaken, because they now receive $18.18 either way. (If we made the debt convertible into 75.1% of the firm's equity, then the shareholders would be outright worse off.) Therefore, the convertibility adds value, even though we would never observe an actual conversion taking place. The convertibility would have deterred shareholders from taking bad projects in the first place.

Q 18.17 You should not bid anything above $500,000 for this house. If you bid $750,000, then you will get the house only if it is worth $500,000, and you would therefore earn $500,000/$750,000 − 1 = −33%. The other half of the time, you would not be the highest bidder so your rate of return would be 0%. Thus, your expected rate of return would be 50% · (−33%) + 50% · 0% = −16.7%.

Q 18.18 The "pecking order" refers to a scenario in which firms first issue as many senior securities (debt) as they can, before they issue more junior securities (equity). As to the thinking question, in a real-world firm, a pecking order may or may not lead to the firm being more debt-financed over time, however. The reason is that the projects of many firms are profitable, which increases the value of the equity of the firm over time, too.

Q 18.19 Firms that are concerned about inside information issues (i.e., that investors infer the quality of the projects from their behavior) should issue debt, because issuing equity would send a bad signal about the value of their projects.

Q 18.20   1. Good firms are still better off going with debt. Thus, they will still get to keep $140, the bad firms will go with equity and get to keep $50, and the lawyers expect to get $10 from half the firms (which you can count as $5).

2. It turns out that there are two equilibria now.

   - The first equilibrium has investors still assuming that all equity issuers are con artists. The good firms prefer $150-$15 (equity) to $100 (debt), and therefore all stick to debt. The bad firms prefer to raise funding with $50 equity. The outside investors are exactly correct—all equity issuers are scum, and all debt issuers are good. Lawyers expect to get $15 from half the firms (which you can count as $7.50).

   - The second equilibrium has investors assuming that all good firms prefer equity to debt, too. In this case, with both good and bad firms in the equity pool, outside investors can be satisfied with $1/4$ of the firm's equity. Good firms prefer the $137.50 from issuing equity to the $150–$15 from issuing debt. Thus, the outside investors are exactly correct, too—equity issuers can be either good or bad with equal probability. The lawyers get nothing.

(Economists often have elaborate arguments about which of these equilibria is more likely to be selected in the real world. They have a vague resemblance to arguments about how many angels can dance on the top of a pin.)

Q 18.21 An example of transaction costs favoring equity is market segmentation in the corporate debt market that might prevent selling corporate debt cheaply to many institutions and retail investors. An example of transaction costs favoring debt are high regulatory costs and exchange fees for listing the company's shares in the public market.

Q 18.22 See Exhibit 18.5 for these forces. Not all are value optimizing for the overall firm (e.g., unmitigated agency conflicts).

Q 18.23 In an imperfect market, the costs of debt and equity capital (and thus of the firm's capital) can be affected by the firm's leverage ratio. Thus, the WACC function is no longer a horizontal line.

Q 18.24 No, the personal income tax rate is still value relevant. However, it works through its influence on the cost of capital that enters the WACC formula, not through its own term.

Q 18.25 A cash-cow firm would best be financed by something that looks like a bond until a recession comes around. You could design a novel kind of bond that has the ability to cancel or delay bond payments *if, and only if,* the official GDP or unemployment numbers state that there is a recession. The presence of agency problems makes it better if the contract does not allow managers to delay payments at their own discretion under normal circumstances.

End of Chapter Problems

Q 18.26. When is financial distress neutral, with regard to capital structure? When is it not neutral?

Q 18.27. In what types of firms would you imagine financial distress costs to be high?

Q 18.28. Does it appear as if financial distress costs should be a significant determinant of Fortune 100 firms' capital structures? What about for small growth firms?

Q 18.29. A firm has debt with a face value of $100. Its projects will pay a safe $80 tomorrow. Managers care only about shareholders. A new quickie project comes along that costs $20, earns either $10 or $40 with equal probabilities, and does so by tomorrow.

1. Is this a positive-NPV project?

2. If the new project can only be financed with a new equity issue, would the shareholders vote for this? Would the creditors?

3. Assume the existing bond contract was written in a way that allows the new projects to be financed with first collateral (superseniority with respect to the existing creditors). New creditors can collect $20 from what the existing projects will surely pay. Would the existing creditors be better off?

4. What is the better arrangement from a firm-value perspective?

Assume that the time value of money is 0.

Q 18.30. Rent and watch the movie *Other People's Money*. Pay close attention to Danny DeVito's speech at the shareholders' meeting. What capital structure-related issue is he talking about? What kind of security would have reduced this problem?

Q 18.31. What kind of firms are most likely to be influenced by free cash flow issues when choosing a capital structure?

Q 18.32. A firm has debt with a face value of $100. Its projects will pay a safe $80 tomorrow. Managers care only about shareholders. A new quickie project comes along that costs $30, earns either $0 or $70 with equal probabilities, and does so by tomorrow. Assume that the time value of money is 0.

1. Is this a positive-NPV project?

2. If the new project can only be financed with a new equity issue, would the shareholders vote for this? Would the creditors?

3. Assume the existing bond contract was written in a way that allows the new projects to be financed with first collateral (superseniority with respect to the existing creditors). New creditors can collect $30 from what the existing projects will surely pay. Would the existing creditors be better off?

4. What is the better arrangement from a firm-value perspective if the old bondholders have veto power?

Q 18.33. What are the advantages and disadvantages of unit offering bundles?

Q 18.34. Are shareholders better off if they can expropriate bondholders?

Q 18.35. (Advanced) A firm has $100 in cash and debt of $80. Assume that the time value of money is zero. A novel project comes along that costs $60 and that will either deliver $0 or x with equal probabilities.

1. What is the value of debt and equity without the project?

2. What is the x value above which the project would be positive NPV? Call this xh.

3. What is the x value above which the shareholders want the firm to take the project? Call this xl.

4. Divide the possible regions into those below xl, those between xl and xh, and those above xh. More specifically, pick xl − $10, (xl + xh)/2, and xh + 10 as your returns in the good state. In these three cases:

a) If the debt can convert into 80% of the post-conversion equity, what would the debt and equity be worth? Would existing equity want to take the project?

b) If the debt can convert into 0% of the post-conversion equity (i.e., if it is not convertible), what would the debt and equity be worth? Would existing equity want to take the project?

c) If the debt can convert into 40% of the post-conversion equity, what would the debt and equity be worth? Would existing equity want to take the project?

5. Do you have all the information needed to recommend a conversion rate to maximize the value of the firm today?

Q 18.36. A stake in an oil field is for sale. It can be worth either $500 or $1,000 with equal probabilities. It costs $250 to develop. The seller knows the true value; you do not. The seller has no personal sources of funds. In an otherwise perfect market with no time value of money, what can the seller expect to raise and at what price?

Q 18.37. Repeat the last question but now assume that this seller has personal savings of $200. With this extra capital and bargaining power, what can the seller expect to raise and at what price?

Q 18.38. If investors are rational and managers are overoptimistic, how would the value of the firm change if management were to raise more money for new projects? Would it be worse if the firm raised equity?

Q 18.39. When private equity firms take over publicly traded firms, they usually increase the leverage tremendously. Discuss what effect this capital structure policy should have on the firm's value and why.

Q 18.40. Explain three forces that can make debt cheaper than equity for corporate financing.

Q 18.41. Explain three forces that can make equity cheaper than debt for corporate financing.

Q 18.42. If the firm maximizes its *value* in an imperfect financial market, how would this change its *cost of capital*?

Q 18.43. What forces can change the shape of the graph of cost of capital versus leverage?

Q 18.44. Where do agency considerations appear in the WACC formula? Do agency costs influence the firm's WACC ?

Q 18.45. If you could design a novel security at the inception of a growth firm that you expect to turn into a cash-generating value firm in 5 years, what would it look like?

Q 18.46. Is the ability of a firm to stave off financial distress always optimal from the firm-value perspective?

19

Equity Payouts: Dividends and Share Repurchases

Does Payout Policy Matter?

As a CFO, you can do four things with the money the corporation has earned: You can keep it in the company (spend or reinvest it), pay off liabilities, pay dividends, or repurchase shares. The latter two courses of action increase the debt-equity ratio and send money from inside of the firm to the outside, thereby shrinking firm size. They are the primary mechanisms by which equity shareholders receive a payback on their investment, and thus they are of interest in themselves. In addition, they are under the regular and easy discretion of management. The board can decide on these payouts almost every quarter. This is why they warrant their own chapter—although a short one.

19.1 Background

You have already seen cash dividends in previous chapters. Let me recap for you.

A short retrospective where you have seen dividends before.

In the context of perfect markets, you learned that as an investor, you can always sell your shares, thereby breaking the link between when the project generates cash and when you need it. Cash dividends do not destroy or generate value, because they do not fall like manna from heaven.

➤ *Separation of consumption and investment choices, Sect. 4.1, Pg.60.*

➤ *Tax clienteles and dividends, Sect. 17.7, Pg.546.*

In the context of imperfect markets, you learned that dividends are not a tax-efficient way to distribute cash, because investors cannot shelter dividend payments from the IRS as easily as they can shelter repurchase payouts or capital gains. However, vis-à-vis managers spending money on themselves, a dividend payout can reduce agency conflicts.

You can also think of equity payouts as the opposite of equity share issuing activity. In this sense, the arguments from all previous capital structure–related chapters apply just as well to equity payouts. An equity issue increases the firm size and decreases the debt-equity ratio. Both cash dividends and share repurchases reduce the firm size and increase the debt-equity ratio. However, the empirical evidence suggests that dividends and share repurchases are not very important in changing the debt-equity ratio in the typical publicly-traded U.S. company.

➤ *Issuing and firm size, Sect. 21.A (Companion), Pg.≈116.*

➤ *Debt-equity ratios and dividends, Sect. 22.C (Companion), Pg.≈161.*

Dividend Mechanics

The institutional
basics of ordinary and
special dividends.

A **dividend** is a distribution from the firm to its investors. If not qualified, this usually means a **cash dividend**. There are also regular and special dividends. In 2004, about one in four publicly traded companies (usually large earnings-rich stocks) paid a regular dividend, typically once per quarter. Special dividends are designated to be one-time payouts and can be considerably larger than ordinary dividends. Although the whole point of a special dividend is that investors should not expect it to be repeated, many companies repeat special dividends over and over anyway.

The two important
dates: the
announcement and
the cum-/ex-dividend
date.

There are two important dates when it comes to the execution of a dividend:

1. On the **declaration date**, the board of directors votes to pay a dividend on a particular date—usually a couple of weeks later. This is usually when the market first learns of the payment, although many dividends are so regular that investors practically know it in advance.

2. The **cum-dividend date** is the last date on which a share still has the right to receive the dividend. Shares traded the following day, the **ex-dividend date**, are without the payment of the dividend.

There are also two administrative bookkeeping dates: The *record date*, on which share ownership is ascertained (to determine where to send the check), and the *payment datem* on which the firm actually sends the money.

DRIPs—a tax liability
in the mail?!

One odd creature is the **dividend reinvestment plan** (DRIP). In a DRIP, participating shareholders agree to reinvest automatically any dividend payments into more shares of the company. Consequently, investors do not receive any cash. All that they receive is a tax obligation at the end of the year for the dividends that they presumably received. If the company had just kept all the money, its investors would not have received this obligation to pay personal income taxes on the dividend. To complicate matters further, if set up with the corporation itself rather than through a brokerage firm, many DRIPs reimburse investors with shares at a discount or at a rate that is not the current market value. (The average value over the most recent quarter is common.) In this case, the company effectively hands its investors a personal income tax liability, but compensates them for it. Thus, the firm pays much of the tax penalty itself (with the shareholders' money, of course).

Stock dividends and
splits are not payouts,
but changes in
numeraire.

A rarer type of dividend is the **stock dividend**. This is not an equity payout at all—no cash is involved. Instead, each share owner receives more shares. For example, if a $1 billion company whose shares are trading for $100 per share issues a 1-share stock dividend for every 10 outstanding shares, then its 10 million shares would just become 11 million shares. In a perfect market, each share would be worth $90.91. No money has changed hands, and all shareholders own the same fraction of the firm as they did before. A stock dividend is really more like a small **stock split**. An example of a 2-for-1 stock split is when the firm converts its 10 million shares, each worth $100, into 20 million shares, each worth $50. Again, there is no cash changing hands. Every shareholder owns exactly the same fraction of the company before and after. A **reverse stock split** is a similar exchange, but the number of shares declines and the price of the shares increases.

Q 19.1. What are the two important dates when it comes to dividends?

Q 19.2. What should be the stock market reaction to the announcement of a split in a perfect market?

Share Repurchase Mechanics

Share repurchases allow corporations to buy back their own stock. You can think of them as the opposite of equity issues. There are two main ways to repurchase stock:

The institutional basics of auction-based and open-market share repurchases.

Auction-based repurchase: In a typical auction-based repurchase program, shareholders receive an offer by the firm wanting to purchase a fixed number of shares at a fixed-price premium (typically around 15% to 20%) from its investors, or a notice that the firm wants to buy shares from those sellers willing to part with them at the lowest premium. If there is too much shareholder interest, the firm usually repurchases shares **pro rata** (i.e., in proportionally fair allocations).

Auction-based repurchases are fairly rare. In a typical year in the late 1990s, all publicly traded firms together announced only about $5 to $10 billion worth of auction-based repurchases. They are used primarily when a company wants to purchase large quantities of its shares quickly. This means that they usually occur when a firm faces a proxy fight or is targeted by outside hostile acquirers.

Rare but big.

➤ *Resistance to a hostile takeover,* *Sect.* 23.C (Companion), *Pg.*≈*210.*

Open-market repurchase: The more common way for firms to repurchase their shares is through open-market repurchases. Such a program is approved by the corporate board, and then must be disclosed publicly (because it is material news). However, the SEC imposes no filing requirements or progress disclosures. After its announcement, the firm can then purchase shares at its own discretion. There are no fixed limits on program size or duration. Typically, firms announce that they want to repurchase around 5% of their share base and that the repurchase program will last for two to three years.

Before 1982, repurchasing activity could violate the SEC rules against price manipulation (the well-known **Rule 10b-5**). Fortunately, in 1982, the SEC issued a clarification, (**Rule 10b-18**), which provides a **safe harbor**. (This safe harbor means that the SEC will not file price manipulation charges against companies repurchasing shares on the open market. Perhaps more important, because qualifying behavior is deemed reasonable by the SEC, it makes it harder for other investors to win a lawsuit against the firm for doing so, too.) Firms are in the clear if they use only one broker, do not execute the repurchase at market opening or during the last half hour of trading, do not pay unusual prices, and do not purchase more than 25% of average daily trading volume over the past 4 weeks. In addition, these limits do not apply to shares repurchased on behalf of an employee stock ownership plan (ESOP) and do not apply to negotiated off-market trades. And finally, the SEC has relaxed even these rules—for example, right after the 1987 stock market crash. Despite all these exceptions, it is common for firms to stay only within the spirit of Rule 10b-18, but not within the letter of the law.

Repurchases could face or avoid price manipulation charges.

Open-based
repurchases are very
common, but often
small.

Open-based repurchase programs are very common. In a typical year in the late 1990s, publicly traded firms together announced about $150 to $200 billion worth of such repurchasing. About 70% to 80% of S&P 500 firms had a share repurchase program going at any given point in time, and roughly one in four S&P 500 companies announced a new multiyear share repurchase program in a given year. The programs themselves are very flexible—firms may never purchase *any* shares if they so desire.

With no disclosure
requirements,
repurchase programs
are difficult to study.

Unfortunately, because firms also do not need to disclose the outcome, researchers can only guess what happens from bits and pieces of evidence that have surfaced informally. Our best estimates are that firms repurchase about three-quarters of their announced share repurchase target over a period of three years. (Of course, at the same time, corporations can issue many shares, e.g., in connection with ESOPs.) Nevertheless, in the aggregate, open-market announced repurchase programs are clearly much more important than auction-based programs.

Q 19.3. What are the two kinds of repurchase programs?

Q 19.4. Could a firm undertaking an open-market repurchase program be accused of manipulating its stock price?

19.2   Perfect-Market Irrelevance

In a perfect world à la
M&M, dividends
neither destroy nor
create value.

Corporate payout policy should not matter in a perfect-market setting. This is the second Modigliani-Miller proposition. From the corporate perspective, if managers pay $1 in dividends, this money has to come from somewhere. Dividends do not fall like manna from heaven, so no value is created or destroyed when firms pay dividends. Money that was previously owned by investors but held inside the corporate shell is just being moved to the same investors, so that it is now outside the corporate shell. The owners do not have any more or any less wealth because of the dividend payment. You can use an M&M arbitrage argument to give this statement more perspective. If managers undertook a dividend policy that destroyed value, then any investor could step in to purchase the firm, fire the management, institute the better dividend policy, and resell the firm for the difference. Therefore, the value of the firm cannot be a function of its dividend policy.

The M&M logic helps
us think about our
imperfect real world.

Like the point of the M&M capital structure proposition, the point of the M&M dividend proposition is not to argue that dividends do not matter. Instead, it is to point out what perfect-market violations must be in place for dividend policy to matter, and how much these violations can matter. For example, if it costs a round-trip premium of $10 million to purchase and then resell a firm, then it cannot be that the wrong dividend policy destroys more than $10 million. If it did, you could make money even in this specific imperfect world.

As of 2008, the average dividend yield of large firms was around 1% of firm value per year. This is probably so low that the real-world transaction costs are much larger than what you could earn by taking over a firm to correct a poor dividend policy. That is, if the optimal payout were actually 0% or 2% instead of 1%, the value gain is probably even less than this 1% value increase. You would not bother stepping in to correct it. As you will learn later in this chapter, there is good evidence that the M&M assumptions are indeed violated in this context: When firms announce dividend increases, their values usually go up; and when they announce dividend decreases, their values usually go down. Can you speculate which M&M assumption is most likely violated? Most finance professors believe that paying dividends sends a credible signal from management about the firm's future prospects and good managerial behavior (that managers will not waste the money on themselves). This violates the M&M assumption that everyone has the same information: In the real world, managers have inside information that investors do *not* have—even if it is only about how much money they may waste in the future.

The situation today: Dividend yields are generally low. Dividend increases are on average value-enhancing.

➤ *Dividend Yield, Sect. 2.3, Pg.13*.

Before we move on to a more realistic world, we can use perfect-market thinking to dispense with some naïve conceptions that are obviously wrong.

Some common fallacies to set straight. Dividends eat as much substance as share sales do!

1. **Dividends do not eat "investment substance," whereas selling shares does.**

   False. It makes no sense to argue that dividends are paid because investors "need" money or that share sales (repurchases by the firm) do not eat equal substance. It is true that if you hold 100 shares worth $4,000, and the company pays you a dividend of $200, you can use the dividends to spend if you so choose. You would have $3,800 worth of shares left. Yet, if the company reinvested the money instead of paying dividends, if you had sold 5 shares for $200 on the stock exchange, you would similarly have been left with $3,800 in shares and $200 in cash. Your "substance" (i.e., your remaining investment) would have been the same either way.

2. **Only tendering shareholders gain from share repurchases.** False. Share repurchases benefit not only shareholders who tender their shares into the repurchase, but all investors. This is the same situation as with dividends. When firms repurchase shares at a fair price in a perfect world, participating and nonparticipating investors prosper equally. Participating investors get cash; nonparticipating investors get to own a higher fraction of the firm. Here is an example. A firm with 100 shareholders, each owning $10 worth of shares, could pay $50 worth of dividends ($0.50 to each shareholder), and the firm would be worth $950. Each shareholder would have a share worth $9.50 and $0.50 in dividends. If the firm repurchased $50 worth of shares, the firm would be left with 95 shareholders, each owning $10 worth of shares. Both tendering and nontendering investors have neither gained nor lost.

   All investors gain from share repurchases.

   In sum, the following simple table illustrates some of what the firm can do with cash it has earned:

Reinvest cash	All investors receive (unrealized) capital gains
Repurchase shares	Some investors realize capital gains.
	Other investors own more of the firm.
Pay dividends	All investors receive taxable dividends.

Therefore, it also makes sense to compare dividends to the alternative of capital gains.

It is an important assumption in this example that the price paid for shares is fair. If it is not, then the remaining shareholders could be better off (if the firm repurchased the shares for less than their true value) or worse off (if the firm repurchased the shares for more than their true value). Indeed, the latter sometimes happens. In a **targeted repurchase**, management makes an offer to purchase shares at an above-market price only to specific shareholders. (For example, in the 1980s, it was common for management to "buy off" potential acquirers.) In this case, the stock value of the remaining shareholders goes down. Buying shares above fair value destroys value for the remaining shareholders.

➤ *Greenmail,*
Sect. 23.C *(Companion),*
Pg. ≈210.

3. Share repurchases increase EPS.

Share repurchases do not necessarily increase EPS. You should think of firm value rather than EPS.

False. It is correct that a repurchase reduces the number of shares outstanding. But the cash paid out also reduces the amount of money that is reinvested. Thus, it depends on whether the cash reinvested would have produced more or less earnings (in proportion). For example, if the firm pays out cash by selling its most profitable and riskiest projects, then its expected earnings per share should go down. As long as the price received is fair, this does not create or destroy value. Conversely, if the cash had been sitting in safe Treasuries and not in riskier projects with higher expected earnings, then the firm's expected EPS should go up. Of course, doing so does not generate value by itself. The firm's earnings will go up, but so will its risk. After all, Treasuries are zero-NPV projects.

More usefully, you should think of firm value (not EPS). In a share repurchase, value increases if the firm avoids taking negative-NPV projects that it would have otherwise undertaken.

In an imperfect world, very mild forms of the above fallacies could be true, though this is not likely.

To the extent that financial markets are close to perfect, real life should not be too different, so the above statements should hold more or less. Nevertheless, they do not need to hold perfectly. In an imperfect financial market, these statements may not necessarily be plain fallacies. However, to make this argument in an imperfect market requires a much more sophisticated train of thought. For example, retail investors receiving dividends who need spending money may save on transaction costs if they do not have to sell shares. Thus, a dividend may leave them with a little more substance than a share repurchase. This may not be plausible, but it is logically possible. For another example, a repurchase could increase a firm's EPS if it reduces agency conflicts and money wasting by managers.

Dividends and repurchase policy are irrelevant in the M&M world. Money can come from anywhere and go to anywhere.

In sum, in a perfect market, thinking about dividends and share repurchases is easy. They are irrelevant from a value perspective. *In the perfect M&M world, without taxes,* **all** *shareholders are equally well off with or without either a repurchase or a dividend payment.* It does not matter, either, where the funds for the payout come from. The firm could either raise new funds from new creditors or from new shareholders in order to pay out cash to existing shareholders (which many corporations do), or it could use its retained earnings, or it could sell some of its operations. What really matters instead is that the company takes all its projects with positive NPVs. The sum-total value of its projects is the value of the firm. If this were not the case, someone would take over the company and make it so.

The remainder of this chapter therefore focuses on the more interesting question of how dividends and share repurchases work in the real world—in an imperfect financial market.

Focus on the relevant aspects.

Q 19.5. In a perfect market, if a normal investor cannot participate in a share repurchase program, would she be better off with a dividend payout than with a share repurchase?

Q 19.6. Consider a firm with 80 shareholders, including yourself, who each own $10 worth of shares. In addition, I own 20 shares (for a firm total of 100 shares)—and I am trying to fire the management. To appease me, the management has offered to purchase my shares at $15 per share. How would this change the value of your shares?

Q 19.7. Under what circumstances do share repurchases increase the firm's EPS?

19.3 Dividends and Share Repurchases

You already know the answer to the question of whether paying out cash creates or destroys value in imperfect capital markets. There is nothing new here: The answer is based on exact analogs of the arguments in the capital structure section. Ultimately, it comes back to the question of whether, as CFO, you should put your investors' cash to use in your company or return it to them. If you pass up positive-NPV projects because you pay out cash, then you destroy value. If you pass up negative-NPV projects because you pay out cash, then you create value. The same market imperfections that determined capital structure are at play in determining payout policy, too. For example:

The "payout versus no payout" is the opposite of the "issue versus no issue" argument discussed in the previous chapters.

Corporate taxes: If you pay dividends or repurchase shares by issuing more debt, future payouts will be tax advantaged. In this case, equity payouts can create value.

➤ *How to invest if you know more than the market, Sect. 11.6, Pg.312.*

Personal taxes: If you pay dividends or repurchase shares, your investors will have a bigger tax liability on these receipts than if you reinvest the money. This can destroy value.

Financial distress: If you pay dividends or repurchase shares when the company is cash constrained, it can increase the probability that the firm will go bankrupt. This can impose direct and indirect bankruptcy costs, which can destroy value.

Agency and signaling: If you pay dividends or repurchase shares when the temptation is to use the cash on pet projects, empire building, or managerial perks—all of which are negative-NPV projects—you can create value.

And so on.

The more novel question concerns the decision of whether you should pay out cash in the form of dividends or share repurchases. The most obvious differences between dividend payments and share repurchases are those related to personal income tax treatment, so let's cover personal income taxes first.

Dividends or share repurchases as payout?

Q 19.8. Can you think of dividend payouts and equity share repurchases as the opposite of issuing equity shares? If so, do the forces from Exhibit 18.5 Page 596 apply here, too?

➤ *Tax clienteles, Sect. 17.7, Pg.546.*

Today, dividends are almost as good as capital gains from a tax perspective.

Personal Income Tax Differences and Investor Clienteles

The clientele diagrams in Section 17.7 illustrated a basic fact: From a personal income tax perspective, dividends are worse than share repurchases. Share repurchases remain the smarter way to pay out cash, even though the Bush dividend tax cut of 2003 has largely eliminated the differences in statutory personal income tax rates between capital gains and dividends. In a share repurchase, nonparticipating investors face no tax consequences, and participating investors face only potential capital gains taxes. The remaining advantages of repurchases, then, relate to the fact that dividends are taxed every year, whereas capital gains are only taxed when an investor realizes them.

➤ *Tax timing, Sect. 10.4, Pg.268.*

Accumulating taxation: For example, if a firm were to offer capital gains of 20% per year, then a $100 investment would earn you $100 \cdot 1.2 \cdot 1.2 = $144 over 2 years. (The same would apply if your benefit [from the repurchase] came not from a value increase but from each of your shares representing a larger fraction of the firm.) Assuming a 50% tax rate, you would keep $22. In contrast, if the $20 were dividend payments, then you would receive a 10% after-tax interest rate every year and thus keep only $100 \cdot 1.1 \cdot 1.1 - $100 = $21. The $1 difference between dividend and repurchase payments is due to the fact that Uncle Sam can earn interest on a part of your dividend receipts that were paid out after one year. The example is overstated, because the statutory tax rate is much lower than 50%—but over many years, the forgone return on intermediate taxes can accumulate and make a difference.

Capital loss offsets: Capital losses can be used to offset the benefits of any capital gains resulting from reinvestment or share repurchases. It is at the discretion of each investor to determine when she has enough capital losses elsewhere not to suffer capital gains taxes. In contrast, capital losses (mostly) cannot be used to offset dividend payments. Moreover, dividends are forced upon each and every investor, possibly in relatively inopportune years from a particular investor's perspective.

Clienteles: Repurchases allow retail clienteles to develop—a fact that helps to take some bite out of capital gains tax. Among retail investors, there will be some who purchased the stock at a high price and others who purchased it at a low price. When the firm repurchases shares, those investors with low accumulated capital gains (having purchased the stock at a relatively high price) can participate in the share repurchase without much of a capital gains consequence. This allows other investors with higher accumulated capital gains to delay/avoid realization and suffer no tax consequences.

Share repurchases are just a little better than dividends from a tax perspective nowadays.

Tax clienteles among retail investors with different unrealized capital gains are good at taking a bite out of the tax penalty on repurchases but not out of the tax penalty on dividends. However, other clienteles potentially can: Zero-tax retail investors or tax-exempt investors, such as pension funds or low-income investors, could take a bite even out of dividend taxes. They can not only hold bonds to shelter interest taxes, but also hold stocks to shelter dividend taxes. This is especially effective if it needs to occur only around the cum-/ex-dividend date (which determines whether an investor receives the dividend). However, the evidence suggests that low-tax investors are in short supply, and some IRS rules are making this special form of 1-day tax arbitrage illegal. Thus, dividend tax arbitrage is not perfect. The tax-exempt investor clienteles have only reduced the penalty of dividends relative to share repurchases—they have not eliminated it. Thus, the presence of pension funds cannot explain why firms pay dividends from a tax perspective: Share repurchases remain better, because they can de facto avoid almost *all* personal income taxes. From a tax perspective, share repurchases simply dominate dividends.

A N E C D O T E   **Pre-Bush Tax Cuts: Ralph Nader and Microsoft**

On January 4, 2002, Ralph Nader wrote an open letter to William H. Gates III, Chairman of Microsoft, that began as follows:

> We are writing to ask Microsoft to change its practice of not paying dividends to shareholders. Our reasons are as follows.
>
> 1. The quantitative failure to pay dividends year after year is an inappropriate and we believe unlawful device to shelter Microsoft earnings from federal income taxes.
>
> By not paying dividends, wealthy Microsoft shareholders such as yourself avoid paying the top marginal tax rate of 39.6 percent that would apply to income distributed as dividends. By taking earnings entirely through stock sales, wealthy shareholders lower their tax rate to the maximum 20 percent that applies to capital gains. According to the most recent SEC reports on insider trades, you personally sold more than $2.9 billion in Microsoft stock last year, benefiting enormously from the lower tax rate that applies to stock sales.

This letter does not even point out that 20% is an overstatement: Gates is taxed only on *realized* capital gains! If he does not sell his shares, he suffers zero taxes on increases in his wealth over the years. And, with the Republicans' elimination of the estate tax, his heirs may not suffer any taxes, either. In defense of Gates, most of his wealth has gone into a foundation that promotes global health.

The Bush tax reforms of 2003 have further significantly reduced the taxes on dividend payments. Microsoft promptly started paying dividends in 2003—many billions' worth.

Here is an interesting question: Is it the fault of Bill Gates (who is also a prolific political campaign donor) or is it the fault of the U.S. government that Gates has suffered only minimal tax obligations on his wealth gains over the last 20 years?

Ralph Nader

There may be one final minor wrinkle. The IRS could in principle declare a share repurchase as the equivalent of a dividend. However, enforcement of this provision has been weak or nonexistent in *publicly traded* corporations—in fact, I don't know of *any* recent instances. With some proper care to evade specific IRS tests, this is not a biting constraint for public firms.

An IRS rule against using share repurchases over dividends is largely irrelevant.

If you want to understand historical equity payout patterns, you need to know that dividends used to be treated much worse than repurchases from a tax perspective. Exhibit 19.1 plots the historical tax rates on dividends and capital gains. Until 2003, the

Empirical historical evidence about typical dividend yields and dividend changes. Repurchases and dividends are now approximately equally important.

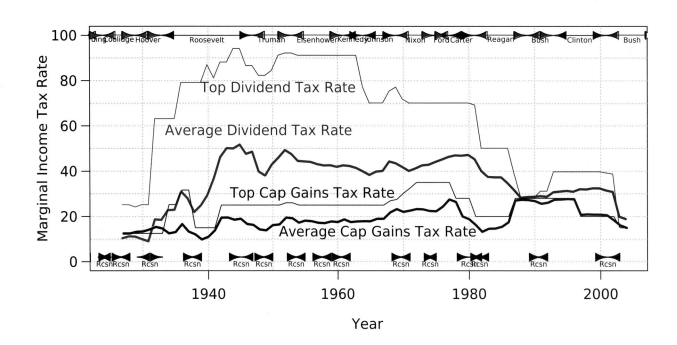

Exhibit 19.1: *Capital Gains and Dividend Tax Rates, 1927-2004.* The top lines show the marginal personal income tax rate on dividends for an investor in the top income bracket (thin) and for the average investor (thick). The lines below them are the equivalent capital gains tax rates. (The capital gains taxes are an overstatement, because they can be washed against capital losses and realized at the investor's discretion.) The arrows at the bottom indicate recessions. The arrows at the top indicate administrations. Original data source: Daniel Feenberg and Clemens Sialm, 2006.

tax rate on dividends was the same as the ordinary income tax rate (35% in 2002), not the 15% capital gains tax that it is in 2008. (The 35% still applies to foreign corporations' dividends and to some nonqualifying dividends if a domestic company has not paid appropriate income taxes.) Before the Reagan *Tax Reform Act of 1986*, it was yet worse again, because dividends suffered tax rates of 50% (just like ordinary income). Between World War II and 1965, the government practically confiscated dividend payments to investors in the top income bracket! You may find it difficult to understand why corporations pay out cash in dividends today—but it is merely a minor puzzle. Yet, 30 years ago, the academic community was really at a total loss trying to understand why any firm would want to pay dividends. Fortunately, education helped. A generation of business school–educated students eventually moved into corporate headquarters, and more and more companies followed the academics' advice, paying out more and more through share repurchases rather than through dividends. The empirical evidence shows that since the 1980s, many firms have been shifting away from dividend payments and toward share repurchases as a means to return money to shareholders. (It helped that other forces such as the 1982 10b-15 ruling and executive self-interest also pulled managers toward more share repurchases—discussed in more detail below.)

A good number of firms responded to the Bush dividend tax cut of 2003 in the logical way: They started paying dividends for the first time. The most prominent was Microsoft (MSFT). After the market closed on July 20, 2004, it announced a $32 billion special dividend, plus a $30 billion share repurchase, plus an increase in ordinary dividends from 16 cents to 32 cents per share (a yield increase from 0.56% to 1.12%). With a market capitalization of about $300 billion (a P/E ratio of about 20 [based on forward-looking earnings] or 37 [based on recent earnings], and a cash hoard of $56 billion), the total payout represented about 20% of Microsoft's market value. A few minutes after market opening on July 21, Microsoft's outstanding shares had jumped in value by a little over 3%. This means that for every dollar announced to change hands soon from investors' company pockets into their personal pockets, shareholders also felt $1 · 3%/20% = 15 cents happier! Interestingly, 2 days later, Microsoft announced quarterly earnings that fell short of expectations—and shares promptly fell back to where they had been before the payout announcement. It appears as if the payout announcement was a positive signal, and the failure to meet earnings expectations was a negative one. These two event effects just about canceled one another out.

> Microsoft's dividend initiation in 2003 is a good example of the effect of the 2003 dividend tax rate cut.

> ➤ *Event studies, Sect. 11.7, Pg.314.*

Q 19.9. Since the 2003 tax cuts, what is the most important remaining tax advantage that share repurchases enjoy over dividends?

Non-Tax Related Differences

With the reduction of the personal income tax differences, other differences between dividends and share repurchases have become relatively more important. Here they are, ranked by my assessment of their importance.

> There are still some nontax differences between dividends and share repurchases.

1. Dividend smoothing:

Many share repurchases used to be done fairly irregularly. In contrast, ordinary dividends informally obligate management to continue them. This was first noted in 1956 by John Lintner. He found that firms were reluctant to cut dividends, instead preferring to slowly increase them over time. This behavior is called **dividend smoothing**. It still holds today, though it is no longer as strong as it once was. In the mid-1990s, out of 100 firms that paid dividends, 10 would increase them every quarter, 89 would continue them, and 1 would cut them. (Lintner also documented a second fact: Companies had a target dividend-earnings payout ratio, to which they smoothly tried to adjust. This does not seem to be the case anymore.)

> Dividends are stickier.

This stickiness of dividends leads to a whole range of interesting behavior patterns. For example, there is an interesting signaling game that could ensue: Shareholders expect dividends to continue. This, in turn, may itself be the reason why managers tend to oblige. If they believe that an earnings shock is transitory, they would probably pay out cash via a share repurchase. They would use a dividend payment only if they believe it is permanent. The reason is that if they increased dividends because of a one-time positive shock to earnings, then they might have to cut their dividends in the future. This risks disappointment of the financial markets—and possibly their own jobs. A dividend increase therefore implies that managers signal more optimism about the future than they would signal with an equal share repurchase.

(The regularity difference is not perfect, though. Many companies have semiregular share repurchase programs, which make repurchases almost as regular as dividend payments. And many other companies pay "special dividends" [or bond dividends] that signal their one-time nature to investors. Such special dividends are as much "one-time" as share repurchases.)

Executives holding options prefer capital gains.

2. **Executive stock options:** Executives often receive **executive stock options** in the company, whose value depends on the share price. (You can find an estimate of their value in the financial statement footnotes. Chapter 26 (Companion) explains how this value is computed.) A dividend is bad for any call option owner, because the share price drops when it is paid. For example, if a manager of a $60 company has an option that allows her to purchase shares at $50, then the manager would be reluctant to pay $20 in dividends—after all, the share price would drop to about $40, making the right to purchase at $50 much less valuable. Therefore, managers with many options prefer repurchases to dividend payments.

Repurchases increase inside ownership.

3. **Executive ownership:** Executives and insiders are often not permitted to tender their shares in share repurchase offers. Thus, they will own relatively more of the company after a repurchase than after an equivalent dividend payment.

Some investors just like dividends.

4. **Investor preferences:** There is some "behavioral finance" evidence that small retail investors simply "like" dividends better than share repurchases—although it is a great mystery why this is so. You already know that the argument that investors like dividends "because they need cash" does not hold water. Selling a fraction of the shares in stocks that pay zero dividends provides physical cash, too—except that the investor would not have had to pay as much in personal income taxes. Indeed, personal tax considerations suggest that investors would likely end up with more if they sold shares. Still, it seems that many investors—especially less sophisticated ones—wrongly think only of share sales but not of dividend receipts as reductions in their "investment substance." Given the existence of such shareholders, companies may respond appropriately by paying dividends.

Fortunately, the tax penalty of dividends is lower today than it was in the past, so the mystery is smaller and less significant. The behavior of small investors is under active academic investigation. My guess is that the answer will likely be that these individual investor preference effects are real and irrational but that they are not universal, and ultimately not overly important.

Some funds cannot hold firms that pay no dividends.

5. **Fund charter exclusion clauses:** Some institutional shareholders are obliged by their charters to hold *only* dividend-paying stocks. This provision excludes them from holding stocks such as Microsoft prior to 2003, that is, before Microsoft initiated dividend payments.

Q 19.10. What are the differences, other than personal income tax differences, between a share repurchase and a dividend payment?

19.4 Empirical Evidence

You now know the factors at play when it comes to dividends and repurchases. But in what form, and how much, did firms actually pay cash to their shareholders historically?

Historical Payout Patterns

Dividend ratios: Exhibit 19.2 graphs the payout patterns over the last century. Graph (a) shows that S&P 500 firms paid out about half of their earnings in dividends. (This **dividend-earnings ratio** is sometimes just called the **dividend-payout ratio**.) This payout ratio has been fairly stable for large firms since World War II—well, except for an unusual spike in the financial crisis of 2008-9, when the S&P 500 dropped dramatically, but stocks kept their dividends fairly steady, nevertheless.

> Dividend-earnings ratios have been at a constant 50% for large firms.

Graph (b) shows that dividend payouts have become a smaller fraction of the share price (invested money), at least after 1980. (Since 2000, they have been slowly creeping up again.) Nowadays, S&P 500 corporations have **dividend yields** (or **dividend-price ratios**) that are below 2% of their stock market values. The two top graphs are consistent, because stock prices relative to earnings (P/E ratios) are higher today than they used to be.

> Dividend-price ratios have fallen.
>
> ➤ *Dividend yield, Sect. 2.3, Pg. 13.*

Total net payout (dividends, repurchases, and equity issues): As you already know, dividends are not the whole payout picture. Corporations can also repurchase and issue shares. You can think of the latter as the opposite of the former. Although graph (c) comes from a different set of firms (all NYSE firms, including smaller firms), chances are that this is not important. It appears that the overall net corporate payout has not changed much. Graph (c) shows that there was no clear trend in whether firms paid out more than they raised in equity. However, there are differences depending on the years. Until the 1980s, corporations paid out more than they raised. In the 1980s, firms began to raise equity capital much more aggressively, but by the 1990s the net-payout pattern had gone back to normal. The two big outliers were 1929 and 1930 (right after **Black Tuesday**—the stock market crash that began the *Great Depression*). In these two years, corporations paid out *much more* than they raised. (Although you cannot see this in the annual data, in the weeks after the October 1987 stock market crash, companies similarly repurchased their own shares aggressively.)

> For NYSE firms, net payout ratios have not changed much.

Dividends versus repurchases: A 2000 paper by Grullon and Michaely compared equity share repurchases and dividends for all publicly traded firms. They found that companies' expenditures on share repurchase programs increased from 4.8% of total earnings in 1980 to 50.1% in 1998. Furthermore, although share repurchase expenditures grew at an average annual rate of 28.3% from 1980 to

> Other evidence: Share repurchases have increased in importance.

(a) Percent of Earnings Paid Out As Dividends

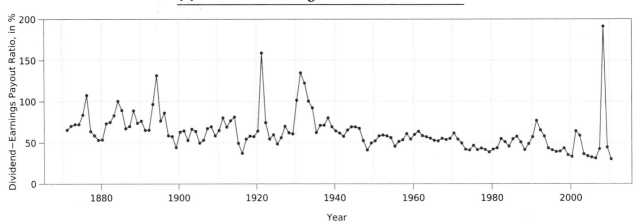

(b) Dividends as Percent of Stock Price

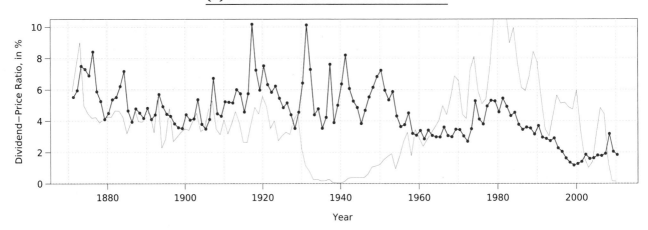

(c) Dividends Plus Share Repurchases Minus Share Issues, As Percent of Stock Price

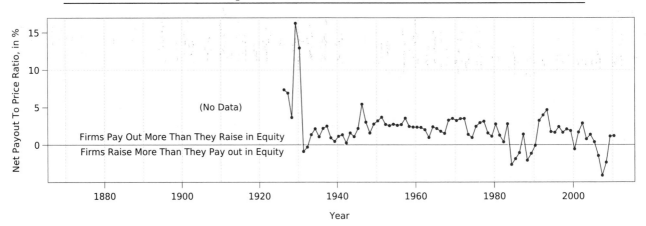

Exhibit 19.2: *Historical Dividend Payout Patterns, 1870-2004.* In (b), the interest rate is in black.

1998, dividends only grew at an average annual rate of 7.5%. As a consequence of these large differences in growth rates, share repurchases—which were only 13.1% of dividends in 1980—exceeded dividends by 1998. Specifically, industrial firms spent $181.8 billion on share repurchases versus $174.1 billion on dividend payments. However, be warned that many of these shares were just repurchased, not retired, so they may not have been true payouts that reduced firm size. Instead, they were immediately given out again in employee and/or executive compensation.

The Grullon and Michaely paper suggests that the main reason why firms increased their repurchases in the 1980s was not primarily the personal income tax penalty (though it mattered), but the 10b-18 SEC ruling. Before 1982, the risk of violating the antimanipulation provisions of the *Securities Exchange Act of 1934* simply deterred most corporations from repurchasing shares. Just one year after the approval of Rule 10b-18, the aggregate amount of cash spent on share repurchase programs tripled.

> Was the 1982 10b-18 SEC ruling a structural shock?

Disappearing dividends: Another 2000 paper by Fama and French documented that the fraction of firms paying dividends had declined from 67% in 1978 to 21% in 1999. That is, the decline in dividends was not just a phenomenon that firms paid lower dividends, but that fewer and fewer firms paid them at all. They attributed this development to two factors: There were more growth and tech firms, which traditionally do not pay dividends but instead reinvest their money; and firms of any characteristics, tech and nontech alike, had become less inclined to pay dividends. Their paper implied that the first component of this pattern would change as firms aged.

> Fewer and fewer firms were paying dividends until 2000...

The ink was not yet dry when the long-term declining pattern indeed started to reverse. Many start-up firms went bust, and the firms surviving the tech crash of 2000 had aged. Thus, they started to pay dividends—going from 17% of firms in 2000 to 25% of firms as of 2004. Interestingly, although the Bush dividend tax cut of 2003 provided a good push for firms to start paying dividends—to the tune of nearly 150 firms initiating dividend payments (of about $1.5 billion per year)—much of the reverse (with more companies paying dividends) had already begun three years earlier.

> ...but dividends have been making a comeback after 2000.

A 2004 paper by Baker and Wurgler tries to explain the year-by-year change in the fraction of firms paying dividends. They looked at how the stock market priced firms paying dividends relative to firms not paying dividends. They found that in years in which the former were trading at higher price multiples (recall Chapter 14), more firms began to join the party and pay dividends. But throughout the 1990s, firms that paid lower dividends seem to have been trading at higher multiples, so fewer firms were excited to start paying them. Indeed, this can even explain some of the reversal in 2000. Until then, tech and growth stocks paying no dividends were highly valued by the stock market. After the tech collapse of March 2000, investors much preferred value stocks with solid dividends, and companies started to oblige.

> More firms initiate dividends when dividend-paying stocks trade at higher multiples.

In sum, we have a fairly good idea of payout patterns. It seems that firms are now paying out more in total in terms of their earnings than historically, though most of the growth has been in repurchases. Dividends have not been cut, but also not raised. Firms' stock values have grown even more dramatically, perhaps to capitalize these additional future payouts.

Q 19.11. How do dividend-earnings payout ratios in the 2000s compare to those in the 1960s?

Q 19.12. How do dividend-price ratios in the 2000s compare to those in the 1960s?

Q 19.13. How do net-payout ratios in the 2000s compare to those in the 1960s?

Market Reactions

In addition to looking at how corporations pay cash to shareholders, we can also look at how the stock market responds to these payouts.

Announcement Response

Any reaction must
appear as soon as
investors learn of the
news. Usually, this is
on the *declaration*
date, not thereafter.
If an efficient stock market considers a dividend payment to be value-relevant news, any consequent reaction must occur when the market first learns about the dividend, that is, on or before the declaration date. *The reaction must not occur on the later cum- or ex-dividend date.* After all, every investor learns on the declaration date when the stock will go ex-dividend. Consequently, it should not be possible to use such dated information to earn excess profits. Similarly, you should not expect dividend continuation dates to be great news—most firms are expected to continue, so the news is only mild (that dividends are not lowered or raised). In contrast, because dividend initiations are far more difficult to forecast, we should expect them to be associated with considerably higher returns.

Exhibit 19.3 shows what happens when a firm declares a quarterly dividend. The graph represents over 13,000 ordinary dividend declarations, in which dividends did not decline. Importantly, the figure does not distinguish between continuations and initiations. (Initiations would have much higher responses.) The left graph shows that the share price increased by about 20 basis points around the declaration days. This is a large number. A typical firm with a dividend yield of 2% would only declare a quarterly dividend of about 50 basis points (0.5%). Thus, for every dollar that a firm declares in dividends, the value of shares increases by $20/0.5 = 40$ cents! (In addition, shareholders get the dollar of dividends later, too.) However, the right graph is a density plot (like a histogram) that shows that this 20 basis points is not the experience of any one given firm, just an average of many firms' announcement returns. Even though 20 basis points is a large increase, there are many firms that experience much higher or much lower returns. There are even many firms that declare a dividend and promptly drop by 200 basis points on the same day—often for entirely different reasons, though.

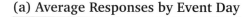

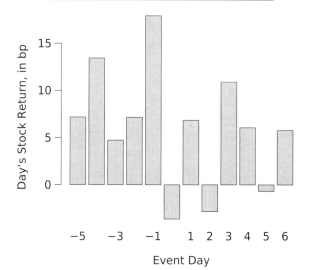

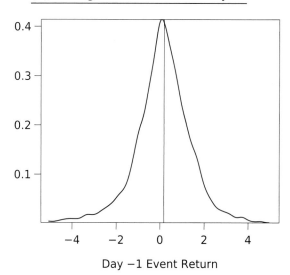

Exhibit 19.3: *Stock Price Responses to Non-Decreasing Dividend Declarations in 2010.* Stock returns are net of the S&P 500 return. Stocks must have at least $10 million in market cap to be included. The left graph shows average rates of return across all stocks on different trading days relative to each firm's aligned declaration date. Announcements typically occur the day before, so –1 is the event date. On a typical day in 2010, stocks earned an average 10 bp. On the dividend declaration date, they earned twice as much. This performance is highly statistically significant. Yet the right graph shows that individual firms may well have decreased rather than increased in value on the announcement day. The vertical line is the 20 basis point mean. It sits very close to zero, does it not?

Though not in these graphs, we can also look at how the market responded to different types of dividend announcements. When firms continue their dividends, their share price increases by only about 10 to 15 basis points. When firms meaningfully increase their dividends (10 or more basis points in the dividend yield increase), their stock price declaration response is a much larger 40 basis points. For new dividend initiations, the average increase is a much larger 200 to 400 basis points. We also know that large firms' share prices respond less than small firms. A dividend payment is even better news if the firm is small. However, be warned that you cannot interpret this to mean that you should pay dividends if you are the CFO for a small firm. The 37 basis points were for a particular set of small firms that considered paying dividends to be a good thing to do, perhaps because they did not have any good projects.

Dividend initiations have huge value effects.

This is so important that I need to repeat it. It is important that you do not draw causality inferences. It may well not have been dividend increases that lifted the stock price, but the news accompanying it. A firm that just looked at the empirical evidence and decided to increase its stock price without a good reason may not experience an

Don't draw causality inferences!

increased stock price. Here is an analogy: You observe that students who pulled all-nighters outperformed those who did not. Does this mean that you should pull one, too, if you wanted to increase your grade? Not necessarily! Students who pulled all-nighters may well have been those who study a lot more in general. They might have done better with a good night's sleep. Then again, all-nighters may have help them, after all. Without a better controlled experiment, you cannot conclude whether all-nighters (dividends) help grades (stock prices) or not.

Do dividends predict the future, or are they predictable history (which investors should already know)?

There is another intriguing and related puzzle brought up in a paper by Benartzi, Michaely, and Thaler about how we should interpret the announcement reaction. Do managers change their dividends when they suddenly anticipate a better future, or do they change them after they have experienced good times in the past? In other words, do dividends send a new signal of the future, or do they merely reflect the past? The answer is likely "both." We know that managers do not increase dividends unless they believe that the future will continue to be good. This means that they pay out earnings both when they have them and when they are confident that they will continue. (Another recent paper suggests that dividends signal not so much higher future earnings, but rather a lower market beta.) Finally, the market also learns from the declarations that managers are inclined to pay them, and continue to pay them—good news in itself.

Why would there be an announcement response if dividend changes contain no news?

The puzzle is not why firms pay dividends, but why they are such good news to the financial markets. They should only be good news if they tell investors something about the future (such as the permanence of good times). The fact that the market can infer from past good times that managers are likely to increase dividends should not matter. The financial markets should already have taken the latter into account; it should not have been news, and you should not have been able to trade profitably on it. Yet some evidence seems to suggest that the past is as, or more, important than the future in explaining why the stock market reacts so positively. However, because managerial dividend choices are so intertwined with both the past and the future, this is intrinsically not an easy question to answer. This question is still under active investigation—the jury is still out.

Tax Trading and the Cum-to-Ex Dividend Stock Response

In a perfect market, the cum-to-ex stock price drop should equal the dividend.

Although it is not news after the declaration date that a stock will soon trade without the dividend (i.e., the day on which the stock will go from *cum* into *ex* status is known in advance), there should still be a stock *price* reaction. Here is why. Consider a perfect market. The expected stock return should be just about zero (or only a few basis points). This means that the expected stock price change is not zero, because shares are worth more with the dividend. For example, if a $50 stock pays $1 in dividends, it should be trading for $49 on the following day. If shares fell only to $49.10, then you could earn a $0.10 profit: Buy at $50, earn the dividend of $1, and sell at $49.10. In sum, although the expected rate of return should be just about zero, the capital gain should be negative by just about the amount of the dividend payment.

> *Capital gains versus net returns, Sect.* 2.3, *Pg.13*.

Tax arbitrage if you have a low tax rate: Buy on the cum-date, sell on the ex-date.

In an imperfect world, the capital loss on the ex-date becomes more interesting: It should depend on investors' personal income tax rates. Consider again the $50 stock that pays a $1 dividend. If the drop is from $50 to $49, then the stock is priced as if investors suffer no personal income tax penalties. If the drop is from $50 to $49.50 instead, then the stock is priced as if investors faced a 50% personal income tax rate. Here is why. Ignore transaction costs, capital gains tax consequences, and IRS regulations for a moment. Concentrate only on the personal income tax rate consequences and the fact that an investor should not earn unusual rates of return overnight. Every investor with a tax rate below 50% should buy the stock on the afternoon of the last cum-day from investors with higher tax rates and then sell it on the morning of the following ex-day. For example, a tax-exempt institution could pay $50, receive $1 in dividends, and then resell at $49.50 for an instant profit of $0.50 per share. This would be an overnight rate of return of just about 1%. Do this every trading day of the year (there are 252 trading days in an typical year), and you end up with a rate of return of more than 1,000% per annum! An investor with a higher tax rate, say, 60%, should not hold onto the stock. Starting with $50, the investor gets to keep only $0.40 in dividends and $49.50 in stock—a perfectly predictable wealth loss of 10 cents. Such an investor should not want to hold the stock. Note that normal retail investors could even hold dividend-paying stocks for 248 out of 252 trading days of the year without paying any dividend taxes. They would just sell them to institutions on the cum-day, and repurchase them on the ex-day.

There is more than just one tax-exempt institution in the market. Consequently, these institutions should compete to bid up the cum-price from $50 to something more. This would mean that the effective income tax rate should come down to something more modest than 50%. In the real world, however, the tax arbitrage competition is limited by transaction costs, IRS rules, capital gains consequences, and overnight holding risk. If this were not the case, even the presence of a few smart tax-exempt investors would drive the cum-price to $50.50 and the effective tax rate to zero. In real life, some such tax arbitrage indeed happens. Tax-exempt funds compete to purchase these shares, driving up the share prices before the ex-dividend date. Such transactions are known as *bed-and-breakfast deals* for equity, and *bond-washing* for bonds—even though both the IRS and the Bank of England have specifically prohibited such tax arbitrage. The latter has imposed a 1-week holding period for tax-free institutions purchasing around dividend dates. Naturally, there is more tax arbitrage if the dividends are bigger (e.g., when it comes to large special one-time dividends).

Competition among (tax-exempt) investors for the best investment opportunities should bring down the *effective* tax rate.

➤ *Arbitrage, Sect.* 11.4, *Pg.299*.

Now return to our hypothetical drop from $50 to $49.50. As noted, it is only an investor with a tax rate of 50% who would be indifferent between buying and selling. Anyone with a higher tax rate should sell; anyone with a lower tax rate should buy. The formula to compute this marginal investor's **effective tax rate** is set by the fact that the overnight rate of return should be close to zero.

The price drop from the cum- to the ex-date allows us to infer the effective marginal income tax rate.

$$0 = \frac{\$49.50 - \$50 + (1-\tau) \cdot \$1}{\$50} \Leftrightarrow \tau = \frac{\$1 + \$49.50 - \$50}{\$1} = 50\%$$

$$r = \frac{P_{ex} - P_{cum} + (1-\tau) \cdot D}{P_{cum}} \Leftrightarrow \tau = \frac{D + P_{ex} - P_{cum}}{D}$$

With this formula, you can now use the capital loss to determine the marginal investor's tax rate for dividend-paying stocks on the dividend cum-/ex-days. For example, if the share price drop is from $50 to $49.25, the stock is priced as if the marginal investor suffered a $[\$1 + (\$49.25 - \$50)]/\$1 = 25\%$ tax rate.

The marginal tax rate measures a market imperfection: The inability of tax-exempt investors to exploit the tax arbitrage fully.

Although we know that some tax arbitrage does happen, the question is still how much. On a typical *quarterly* dividend day, a $50 stock with a 2% dividend yield would pay only $1/4 = $0.25. Subtract round-trip transaction costs, and take into account that the IRS won't look kindly on immediate purchases and sales by tax-exempt investors, that tax-exempts want to remain diversified, and that there are only a limited number of tax-exempt investors. Given all these complications, is the competition among tax-exempt investors—subject to transaction costs—enough to compete away the dividend tax penalty?

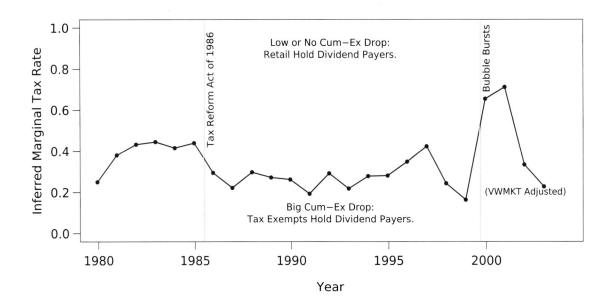

Exhibit 19.4: *Implied Tax Rates from the Cum-/Ex-Drop from Ordinary Dividends, 1980-2004.* If stocks drop from the cum- to the ex-date by exactly the amount of the dividend, we infer that the marginal investor does not care about personal taxes. If they drop by less, we infer a positive tax rate.

The empirical evidence suggests that the effective tax rate is close to the personal income tax rate. Tax-exempt investors seem to make little dent in eliminating the tax arbitrage.

Exhibit 19.4 shows that the answer is no. The marginal tax rate was historically closer to the prevailing personal income tax rate than it was to the tax-exempt rate of zero. The figure shows that in the early 1980s, it was around 50%. After the *Tax Reform Act of 1986,* it dropped to about 25%, from which it slowly crept up, roughly in line with the increase in personal income tax rates during the George H.W. Bush and early Clinton years. Interestingly, during the tech boom of the late 1990s, retail investors seem not to have held many dividend payers (Internet and similar stocks were "in"). And after the tech crash of 2000 (these stocks were "out"), retail investors were so eager to hold dividend payers that they practically ignored the tax penalty and put the same value on stocks cum-dividends and ex-dividends. The implied tax rate shot up to above 60%. An inferred tax rate this high—beyond all actual tax rates—also suggests that there is more going on than just tax effects. Most likely, with dividend yields very low, the transaction costs may have prevented ordinary investors from this tax arbitrage. Of course, this does not answer the question of who would have been willing to sell shares on the cum-date or buy shares on the ex-date, rather than vice versa. Fortunately, by 2003, the implied marginal tax rate had declined again to more normal levels, although 20%+ still seems high, given the Bush dividend tax cut.

Here is yet another financial mystery: There are countries in which dividends are not taxed, so the effective marginal tax rate should be zero. There should be a one-to-one drop of the share price with the dividends on the ex-date, or buying on the cum-date and selling on the ex-date would be a great trading strategy. Yet, even in these countries, there is a positive total rate of return on such days. Why would anyone sell such shares on the cum-date and why would anyone purchase such shares on the ex-date (rather than the cum-date)? It makes no sense. This evidence should caution us not to overinterpret the U.S. cum-to-ex price drop as purely a marginal tax effect. We may not understand this drop as well as we think.

> Maybe there is more going on than just taxes on the cum-/ex-drop?!

Other Important Empirical Evidence

Share repurchase announcements: Unfortunately, there is no clear announcement of how much firms will repurchase. They can announce that they plan to repurchase and then decide never to do so. This fuzziness makes empirical work much more challenging. Nevertheless, from what we know, it appears that the stock market response to a share repurchase seems roughly similar to that for a dividend payment *for similar amounts of cash involved*. This is remarkable (yet another mild puzzle), because share repurchases signal less permanence.

> Share repurchases tend to experience similar market responses as dividends do.

However, most open-market repurchase programs are larger than ordinary quarterly dividend announcements. Therefore, they tend to elicit stronger stock market responses. In addition, many auction repurchases are even larger, and so it should not be too surprising that the stock market responds much more positively to them. A typical announcement of an auction repurchase is greeted by an instant stock price jump of about 15%.

> Big repurchases naturally have bigger responses.

Stock splits and stock dividends: As explained at the outset, neither a stock split nor a stock dividend is a payout. In fact, neither event changes the firm's projects. Every investor owns the same fraction of the firm before and after the event, and no money changes hands. (It used to be that there were certain listing requirements and higher full-service brokerage commissions for stocks trading around $30 per share, but neither of these two factors is likely to be important nowadays.) Stock splits and stock dividends are good "null" benchmarks with which to compare dividend declarations and share repurchase announcements. We should expect just about a zero response to the announcement of either.

Alas, on average, investors seem to respond positively when firms announce a split, where the number of shares increases and the stock price drops. This suggests that the market considers a split to be good news—it must increase its assessment of the net present value of the firm's underlying project. Indeed, many firms that split often produce better earnings after the stock split. In a reverse split, the firm

> The market also responds to stock splits.

merges shares. For example, two shares each worth $5 become one share worth $10. Again, no money changes hands—and, again, the stock market responds. In this case, upon the announcement, the share price usually drops.

Long-term reaction: In an efficient market, we would expect stock prices to incorporate all relevant information at the announcement. There should be no slow long-term stock market reaction after the news has been released. However, there is evidence that there may indeed be a strategy that allows you to earn abnormal returns: Firms that pay out more in dividends and repurchases tend to perform better in the long run—not just in terms of their earnings (which you would expect) but also in terms of their financial market values (which you would not expect if the market had taken all available information into account as soon as it had the information). Firms that increased their dividends seemed to outperform those firms that decreased their dividends. The cumulative stock return difference was about 10% per year. Conversely, firms that issue equity tend to underperform over the following years.

However, before you invest all your money into firms that have recently raised their payout, be aware that long-term returns are quite difficult to measure reliably, and we do not know if the historical experience will continue in the future.

➤ *Relevance of empirical history, Sect. 7.1, Pg.164.*

Q 19.14. If the stock price is not expected to drop from the cum-day to the ex-day, what is the marginal income tax rate?

Q 19.15. What is the implied tax rate suggested by the real-world cum-/ex-drop?

Q 19.16. Should a stock split create value? Does it?

Q 19.17. Do stock price announcement responses to dividend initiations (or dividend eliminations) tend to be underreactions or overreactions?

19.5 Survey Evidence

What do the decision makers believe?

Instead of researching the data to determine what CFOs are actually doing, we can also just try to ask them. A 2004 paper by Brav, Graham, Harvey, and Michaely does exactly this, surveying 384 financial executives. This kind of evidence is not a substitute for, but a complement to, the empirical evidence. Managers may respond to immediate financial market pressures and incentives without fully realizing their underlying causes. The proverbial grain of salt is appropriate.

Here are their opinions that make sense.

The CFOs in this study have some very definite and interesting opinions:

- They state that they pay dividends because they are trapped by history. They do not want to cut existing dividends, but given the choice, they would not begin paying dividends in the first place. In fact, their desire not to cut dividends goes so far that they claim that they would not only raise more external capital, but even pass up positive-NPV projects to pay them. They claim not to care at all about investment opportunities when it comes to dividends.

- In contrast, CFOs do care about investment opportunities and residual cash left over when it comes to share repurchases. In fact, they seem to think of their own stock as an investment opportunity in that they try to earn money by attempting to "time" their own stock, buying more shares when the price seems low.

- 40% of these executives want to attract institutional investors with dividends—but they also believe that they can accomplish this with share repurchases.

- 40% of these executives target a dividend-per-share ratio (and 27% target changes therein), 28% target a dividend-to-earnings (payout) ratio, and 14% target a dividend-to-price ratio. When it comes to share repurchases, they tend to target a dollar value of repurchases, not any particular ratio.

- Repurchases are often related to option or stock compensation plans, providing the firm with the shares needed to satisfy their employee obligations.

- Repurchases offer a flexibility that dividends do not. Managers perceive this to be a good thing and would argue that it creates value for the company.

- However, managerial answers to surveys are in line with what one would expect if they were agency conflicted—that is, interested first in helping themselves. This is not to say that executives deliberately plot how to enrich themselves, but that over time their views tend to evolve toward what is in their own best interests. Although reinvestment increases the share price and firm size, payout only helps anonymous investors far away from the firm, who own less of the firm after the payout, and this diminishes the share price and firm size. Thus, payouts are less salient to managers.

➤ *CFO survey,*
Sect. 22.E (Companion),
Pg.≈*171*.

- It is further evidence of an agency conflict that dividend-paying financial executives answer that they would most like to use the money saved by a hypothetical dividend elimination not for a share repurchase (the obvious substitute) but for paying down debt. Avoiding bond-rating downgrades and retaining financial flexibility are important to CFOs. (Note again that high bond ratings and financial flexibility reduce external pressure on management, even if they do not create value.)

So far, so good. Now it becomes a bit stranger. Only one-third of the respondents contemplate personal income tax consequences, though 40% realize the relevant repurchase advantage. However, if they recognize it, they rarely consider their investors' personal income tax consequences to be important to their payout decisions. This finding may not be too strange, because differential tax consequences are rather modest today.

Here are their opinions that are more difficult to understand.

However, here is where it gets *truly* strange:

Here are their two opinions that seem incomprehensible.

- Many CFOs believe that repurchases automatically increase earnings per share, as if money paid out would not otherwise create more earnings. This is contrary to what you learned on Page 616.

- Clearly, dividends are related to the stability of future earnings, and CFOs recognize this fact. They also realize that they take future earnings into account when deciding on dividends. Alas, they then claim that there is no additional discipline imposed by dividend payments, and they claim that dividends and repurchases convey similar information. This is inconsistent. Moreover, they believe that it is unimportant that payouts, and especially dividends, convey information to the market. Again, this is odd, because they state that they pay out dividends depending on their opinions about the future. Why would the market not learn their inside perspectives from their dividend payout choices?

Q 19.18. Do CFOs feel more pressure to continue dividends or share repurchase programs?

Summary

What payout policy should a company choose? The most important recommendation is that a company should pay out cash when the alternative uses for it are not positive-NPV projects. Interestingly, Warren Buffett (from Berkshire Hathaway) has stated publicly something similar to this philosophy: "We will pay either large dividends or none at all if we can't obtain more money through reinvestment [of those funds]." Of course, many other managers do not like to hear this advice, or they assert that all of their projects are high NPV, whether this is true or not. They would rather govern large firms with much financial flexibility—firms that are unconstrained by debt or payout requirements. Compared to the question of whether the firm should or shoult not pay out, the question of whether the form of payout should be dividends or share repurchases is of secondary importance nowadays, given the small residual differences between them. Their differences mattered more in the past, before the double taxation of dividends was reduced in 2003. (Future tax-law changes may, of course, change this again.) Dividends signal more long-term confidence, but they cost investors more in personal income taxes.

This chapter covered the following major points:

- Equity payouts come in two forms: dividends and share repurchases. Share repurchases are either auction based or open market. Dividends are either ordinary or special. (Stock dividends are not payouts, but more like stock splits.)

- In a perfect market, it does not matter whether the firm pays out or reinvests, or how it pays out.

- Dividends and share repurchases have equal effects in terms of "eating substance" for investors.

- In a share repurchase, both tendering and nontendering shareholders benefit.

- Share repurchases do not necessarily raise EPS.

- An equity payout is the opposite of issuing. Thus, all factors discussed in the earlier capital structure chapters apply here, too.

- Share repurchases are better than dividends from a personal income tax perspective, but no longer greatly so.

- Unlike share repurchases, ordinary dividends are regular and steady. This behavior is called dividend smoothing. The financial market expects dividends to continue, which pushes managers to continue them, which in turn makes the market expect them.

- Executives with stock options benefit relatively more from a share repurchase than from a dividend payout.

- Since World War II, dividend-earnings ratios have held roughly stable at around 50%. The exception was the financial crisis of 2008-9, when dividends held steady but the S&P 500 dropped precipitously.

- Dividend-price ratios were volatile from 1920 to 1960, increased in the 1970s from 3% to 5%, trended smoothly down from 5% in 1980 to about 1.5% in 2000, and have since crept up again to about 2% in 2010.

- The net-payout ratio—dividends plus share repurchases minus share issuing—has not declined systematically over the last 20 years.

- Repurchases and dividends are about equally important today.

- In 1980, one in two firms paid dividends. Today, only one in four do so. However, as firms have matured, the trend is now back on the upswing. When the market places higher multiples on dividend payers, more firms seem to want to start paying dividends.

- Firms experience a positive stock price response when they declare a dividend. The effect of the initial dividend declaration is a stunning 2-4%.

- There is some evidence that the stock announcement response to a dividend payment and a repurchase, both for the same amount of cash, is roughly similar. If there is a difference, it is so small that it is easily lost in the ordinary stock-price noise.

- For special dividends and large (often auction-based) share repurchases, the value response can be very large–15% on average.

- The market response from the cum- to the ex-date allows us to infer the marginal investor's tax rate. For ordinary dividends, it tends to be fairly close to the tax rate of retail investors. This leaves room for tax-exempt investors to earn excess returns.

- When asked, financial executives feel trapped by their dividend history. They would rather not pay dividends but feel that they have to—even when paying dividends forces them to pass up good projects. They try to trade profitably on their own stock price when they repurchase. Their answers are broadly consistent with what is in their own best interests. Strangely, many believe incorrectly that repurchases always raise EPS, and they dispute that dividends carry useful information and/or discipline to the market.

Keywords

Auction-based repurchase, 613.   Black Tuesday, 623.   Cash dividend, 612.   Cum-dividend date, 612. DRIP, 612.   Declaration date, 612.   Dividend reinvestment plan, 612.   Dividend smoothing, 621.   Dividend yield, 623.   Dividend, 612.   Dividend-earnings ratio, 623.   Dividend-payout ratio, 623.   Dividend-price ratio, 623.   Effective tax rate, 629.   Ex-dividend date, 612.   Executive stock option, 622.   Open-market repurchase, 613.   Pro rata, 613.   Reverse stock split, 612.   Rule 10b-18, 613.   Rule 10b-5, 613.   Safe harbor, 613.   Share repurchase, 613.   Stock dividend, 612.   Stock split, 612.   Targeted repurchase, 616.

Answers

Q 19.1 The two important dividend dates are the declaration date (when the dividend payment is announced) and the cum- versus ex-dividend date (when the stock trades with versus without dividends).

Q 19.2 In a perfect market, a stock split should not change anything value-wise. It is merely a change in numeraire, which does not affect anything fundamental about the company (such as earnings, cash flows, etc.). Thus, the stock market response should be zero.

Q 19.3 The two kinds of programs are auction-based repurchases and open-market repurchases.

Q 19.4 Yes, a firm undertaking an open-market repurchase program could be accused of manipulating its stock price. This is why the SEC has laid down rules (i.e., Rule 10b-18) that allow firms to escape such lawsuits.

Q 19.5 No! Even a normal investor is as well off with a share repurchase as with a dividend payout in a perfect market. Neither a share repurchase nor a dividend payout changes the investor's wealth. (The "wealth increase" in a share repurchase comes from an increase in the fraction of the firm that each share now owns.)

Q 19.6 The firm was worth $1,000, so shares are currently worth $10 each. If the firm repurchases my shares, it pays out $20 \cdot \$15 = \$300$ and has $700 left, to be split among 80 shares. Thus, the remaining shares are now worth only $\$700/\$80 = \$8.75$ each. The moral of the story is that when a firm offers to purchase shares for more than they are worth, the nonparticipating shareholders suffer.

Q 19.7 If the firm uses money for share repurchases that previously was used to fund negative-NPV projects, then the firm's EPS should go up.

Q 19.8 Basically, yes: Dividends and share repurchases are indeed mostly the opposite of equity issuing. They reduce the equity investment in a firm—the opposite of what equity issues accomplish. Therefore, virtually all arguments made in Chapters 17 and 18 apply to dividends and repurchases in reverse.

Q 19.9 The remaining tax advantage of share repurchases comes from the fact that capital gains can be realized mostly by those investor clienteles who face low capital gains taxes, perhaps because they have low income and statutory rates, or perhaps because they have losses elsewhere. This allows the shareholders in the aggregate to escape most repurchase payout taxation. The remaining investors are not taxed in the interim—their money continues to bear fruit for them, and not for the IRS.

Q 19.10 The remaining differences are as follows: Dividends tend to be more regular than share repurchases; executives and insiders may often not tender into a repurchase, but they will enjoy the relatively higher share price from a repurchase through executive compensation that is linked to the share price; some retail investors like dividends; some funds cannot hold stocks that do not pay dividends.

Q 19.11 They are not much lower. D/E ratios in the 2000s are generally similar to what they were 40 years ago.

Q 19.12 D/P ratios in the 2000s are generally lower than they were in the 1960s. D/P ratios have declined to about 1-2%.

Q 19.13 Net-payout ratios are not very different in the 2000s than they were in the 1960s.

Q 19.14 If the stock price is the same on the cum-day and the ex-day, then the marginal income tax rate is $\tau = 100\%$, because every investor who would purchase the stock on the cum-day afternoon and sell it on the ex-day morning would get to keep "for free" whatever part of the dividend is not taxed. (I am ignoring the small daily upward drift of stock prices.)

Q 19.15 The tax rate implied by the average drop from the cum-date to the ex-date seems to be about 20%.

Q 19.16 A stock split should not create value in a perfect market. Logically, it is just a change in numeraire. It should make no difference to investors whether they own 1 stock worth $100 or 2 stocks worth $50 each. However, stock splits do seem to signal that the future is brighter, because the stock price usually responds positively to stock split announcements, and may therefore create value in the real world.

Q 19.17 The stock price does not seem to react fully to dividend initiations (or dividend eliminations), because the positive (negative) instant reaction is followed by more of the same, on average. Thus, they are underreactions.

Q 19.18 In a survey, CFOs indicated that they feel more pressure to continue dividends.

End of Chapter Problems

Q 19.19. Search the Web to find a company that has recently announced a stock split. What happened to its stock price on the day of the announcement?

Q 19.20. Use a financial website to identify the company with the highest dividend yield today. What is it?

Q 19.21. Use a financial website to identify three firms that are currently undertaking an auction-based repurchase program. What fraction of the shares are they repurchasing?

Q 19.22. Consider a firm in perfect market with 80 shareholders, including yourself, who each own 1 share worth $10. In addition, I own 20 shares (for a firm total of 100 shares), and I am trying to fire the management. To appease me, the management has offered to purchase my 20 shares at $9 per share. How would this change the value of your share?

Q 19.23. Can the firm's EPS go down if the firm takes on a positive-NPV project?

Q 19.24. How would the value change if a firm decides to increase its dividend payout, and if financial distress and agency/signaling costs are the only relevant concerns?

Q 19.25. Considering the differences other than personal income taxes, what companies should pay dividends rather than repurchase shares? How important is the right choice between the two?

Q 19.26. Think about the non-tax-related differences between share repurchases and dividends. Describe the firms in which each difference would be relatively more important.

Q 19.27. Do more or fewer firms pay dividends in the 2000s than in the 1970s? Is this a trend?

Q 19.28. In an efficient market, when should the stock price react to the value consequences of a dividend change? Discuss the effect both on the total return and on the capital gain. Which should be larger?

Q 19.29. Comparing the dividend announcement effect of 20 basis points to a typical daily standard deviation (60 basis points) and round-trip transaction costs (about 20 basis points) suggests that firms should not bother with dividends. Discuss.

Q 19.30. Would you expect trading volume to be higher for dividend-paying stocks on the declaration date or around the cum-date/ex-date?

Q 19.31. If the stock price drops on average by 0.65% from the cum-day to the ex-day when dividends of 1% of the firm are paid, then what is the marginal income tax rate?

Q 19.32. What are the dividend targets that different U.S. corporations seem to try to peg? If you cannot ask the executives, can you learn from the behavior of the firm what they peg their dividend targets to?

Q 19.33. How do managers view dividends and share repurchases differently? Which do they seem to prefer?

Q 19.34. Is there any survey evidence that suggests that there is an agency conflict between shareholders and managers when it comes to dividends? Can the answers be interpreted differently?

Part VI

Projecting the Future

...the "Business Way" with Pro Formas

In any formal setting, financial professionals propose new projects through pro formas—whether it is the expansion of a factory building within a corporation, or a new business for presentation to venture capitalists. A good pro forma is a combination of soft intuition and hard business and financial expertise.

Both art and science go into its construction. The book's synthesis chapter is the creation of such a pro forma. It combines all the ingredients from earlier chapters—capital budgeting, taxes, the cost of capital, capital structure, and so on.

Pro Forma Financial Statements

for Value, Financial Structure, and Corporate Strategy Analysis

According to Merriam-Webster, *pro forma* is a Latin term meaning "for form." Its use dates from around 1580. Pro forma has two definitions: "provided in advance to prescribe form or describe items;" and "made or carried out in a perfunctory manner or as a formality." In our context, a pro forma is a model of a hypothetical future scenario, and specifically the financial performance in this scenario. (Hopefully, your model will be more like the first definition in Merriam-Webster and less like the second.)

In a sense, pro formas are what much of corporate finance is all about—the standard business approach to contemplate financing or investing. For example, if you want to propose a new project to your boss, to the board of directors, or to an external venture capitalist, you will almost surely be asked to produce a business plan. The most critical part of this plan will have to be your "pro forma" financials. These financials will then be used as the baseline for discussion and evaluation of your proposed project.

Managers and entrepreneurs are not the only producers of pro formas. Analysts for major investment banks or for firms seeking acquisitions or mergers also have to produce pro formas to back up their analyses of corporate value. Their task is both easier and harder than that of the entrepreneur: Analysts can often rely on corporate history upon which to base their pro formas, but they also often lack the detailed knowledge of the business internals and corporate intentions that the internal managers and entrepreneurs would have.

Every business is different, and thus every pro forma is different. Still, this chapter tries to give you some guidance regarding the process of creating pro formas. Specifically, you will learn how to produce pro forma analyses of PepsiCo. These pro formas will be from a number of different perspectives—that of an analyst valuing it as if it were a privately traded company and had no market value, that of an investment banker proposing a capital structure change, and that of an economist who has the advantage of hindsight.

20.1 The Goal and Logic

Pro formas are more detailed than simple cash flow projections. This helps you think about the economics of business.

To repeat, a **pro forma** is a model of financial performance in a hypothetical future. Creating a pro forma is a challenge similar to what you encountered in earlier chapters, where you had to estimate a project's present value. There, you needed to understand a whole variety of issues—the expected cash flows (which requires knowledge of production, marketing, customers, etc.), appropriate costs of capital, corporate and capital structures, agency conflicts, and so on. The main novelty here is that you need to do this in the context of the financial statements rather than just in the context of isolated formulas. Creating a full pro forma is not an empty exercise: It will help impose some discipline and structure on your thinking about the design and value of your proposed project. It forces you to think about important "details," such as what you believe sales and costs will be, how you will manage working capital, how quickly earnings and cash flows will turn positive, whether taxes will be an important factor, and so on.

Forecasting pro formas is both hard and different from business to business.

No finance professor would dispute the importance of pro formas, but we are often reluctant to teach much about them. The cynical view is that constructing a pro forma is difficult and that we finance professors naturally prefer the "easy" tasks! The less cynical view is that there are at least three good reasons for our reluctance:

1. **Idiosyncrasy:** In contrast to the many beautifully simple, elegant, and universal theoretical concepts in finance (such as present value or the capital asset pricing model), financials and pro formas are messy and unique for each business. Forecasting the financials for a new cancer drug is different from forecasting the financials for a new toy fad, which is different from forecasting the financials for a retail store, which is different from forecasting the financials for aluminum mining, and so on. Many of the guidelines for creating good pro formas are necessarily less universal and more ad hoc.

2. **Relativity:** The difficulties in making good financial projections for a specific project are often tremendous. It is important that you realize the limits of what you can and cannot do. You should be able to do it better than your peers—a *relative* rather than an *absolute* standard. Looking in retrospect at what later actually happened in relation to what you predicted in your pro forma is often a great lesson in humility. You are not alone in this predicament.

3. **Learning by doing:** The best way to learn how to do a pro forma is to struggle with designing one. Such an active case-based approach is considerably more effective than a passive listening one. After reading this chapter, your next step in learning pro formas should be working through and critiquing many case studies—necessarily more of a trial-and-error-and-experience process than a tutorial process.

Still, this chapter seeks to prepare you at least a little. It will give you some general guidance, because, in the end, you must learn how to design good pro formas if you want to be an effective entrepreneur, manager, or analyst. You must be able to produce your own pro formas, and you must be able to analyze critically the financial pro formas of others.

Q 20.1. What does a full pro forma analysis force you to do that a simpler projection would not?

An External Analyst's View versus an Entrepreneur's View

There are two different types of users of pro formas. The first are outsiders, such as external analysts, who have to construct a pro forma for a privately-traded firm with an unknown market value. An outside perspective is also taken by analysts of private equity firms, who try to assess whether the market value of a publicly-traded company seems too low. If their own pro forma value estimates are much higher than the current market value, then the private-equity firm may take a closer look at the firm as a potential buyout candidate. This chapter mostly takes this perspective.

Pro formas put together by outsiders are often used to value the business—and potentially acquire it.

The second are insiders, such as entrepreneurs, who often create pro formas not only to assess value but also to help manage the firm. They often know the operational details of the proposed project in great detail. In contrast, external analysts rarely do. (This also often applies to venture capitalists considering funding start-up projects. For the PepsiCo pro forma that you will have to construct in this chapter, you don't know much of the internal operations, either.) However, insiders face some unique problems of their own:

Pro formas are often used by insiders to plan the business.

Working capital: Entrepreneurs usually must worry about working-capital projection and management for the sake of policy design. A small entrepreneurial firm could lose its entire business if it were to run out of cash, even if only temporarily and even if the underlying economics of its real business were sound. In contrast, working-capital projections to assure financial viability are fairly unimportant for PepsiCo. PepsiCo is so big, stable, and currently with so few liabilities and so little financial debt that it can easily borrow more capital if it were ever to need more. (Managing working capital well can be important even for large firms in the sense that better handling can cut costs. In this case, it is an operational-efficiency problem, not a forecasting problem to avoid financial distress.)

Start-up versus mature phase: Entrepreneurs usually do not have a long prior history of operations that can give good guidance. If everything goes according to plan, then their cash flows will often start with a sharp initial business growth curve, to be followed only later by a more stable period. As firms mature and grow, they become less likely to default. This later decline in credit risk allows their promised rates of return to decline. In addition to having to pay higher default premiums, many young, small firms also have to pay higher expected rates of return. The reasons are that they tend to be especially vulnerable to downturns in economy-wide conditions—which reflects itself in higher betas and higher costs of capital—and the fact that their capital markets are less perfect. In contrast, PepsiCo is an established company, and its projects have long prior histories.

➤ *Entrepreneurial finance, Sect. 10.5, Pg. 269.*

You will learn in a moment that the end of the start-up growth phase is often a natural break. It is often a good choice for T, the break of your pro forma into a detailed projection period and final market value. But PepsiCo is already in its mature, stable state and, as an outsider, you have no detailed knowledge of how the next year will be different from what will happen in 10 years. Therefore, you could even just work out a terminal value right now and dispense with the initial detailed-projection phase altogether. Nevertheless, we will work out the detailed projections to illustrate the process.

PepsiCo is an imperfect example, because it could be done a lot more simply.

We cannot illustrate all the issues discussed above in this chapter: PepsiCo will not run out of cash, we have no special knowledge of PepsiCo operations, and PepsiCo is mature. Moreover, we shall construct the pro forma as if we stand at the end of 2001. This will allow us later to use hindsight knowledge to "autopsy" how good or bad our forecasts turned out.

Q 20.2. What are usually the two most important projection goals for a pro forma analysis for an entrepreneur?

20.2 The Template

You decide on a detailed projection phase and a terminal value.

The standard method for creating a pro forma separates the future into a "detailed projection" time period, for which you forecast the financials in great detail, and a **terminal value**, which you can think of as the "then market value" of the business—a going-concern value of the business if you were to sell it at this point in the future. You have to decide for how many years you want to project financials in detail before capping your value analysis with your terminal value.

Here is the template of what you need to do.

➤ *PepsiCo's financials, Exhibits 13.1–, Exhibit 13.4, Pg.375.*

As our guinea pig, let's use PepsiCo, because you have already studied its historical financials in Chapter 13.   Your goal now is to construct a good pro forma as of December 2001 to estimate PepsiCo's market value, presuming you already know the 2001 financials. The construction template is in Exhibit 20.1. It shows the three big areas you must work on:

1. A choice of horizon T that separates the initial and terminal phases

2. The detailed financials during the initial projection phase, from time +1 (next year) to time T – 1

3. A terminal market value at time T – 1, which is a stand-in for the cash flows from time T to eternity

---

Q 20.3. What are the three main components of a pro forma that you need to work out?

	Pro Forma Income Statement							T is to be determined	Terminal Value
	Y_{-2}	Y_{-1}	Y_0	Y_1	Y_2	Y_3 $\cdots$	Y_T	
	1999	2000	2001	2002	2003	2004 $\cdots$		
Net Sales	$25,093	$25,479	$26,935	Projected each year from Y_1 to Y_T				
− COGS	$10,326	$10,226	$10,754	Projected each year from Y_1 to Y_T				
⋮	⋮	⋮	⋮	Projected each year from Y_1 to Y_T				
− Net Interest Expense	−$792	$57	−$8	Projected each year from Y_1 to Y_T				
⋮	⋮	⋮	⋮	Projected each year from Y_1 to Y_T				
= Net Income	$2,505	$2,543	$2,662	Projected each year from Y_1 to Y_T				

	Pro Forma Cash Flow Statement							
Net Income	$2,505	$2,543	$2,662	Projected each year from Y_1 to Y_T				
+ Depreciation	$1,156	$1,093	$1,082	Projected each year from Y_1 to Y_T				
⋮	⋮	⋮	⋮	Projected each year from Y_1 to Y_T				
= Operating Cash Flow	$3,605	$4,440	$4,201	Projected each year from Y_1 to Y_T				Wholesale PV Projection
⋮	⋮	⋮	⋮	Projected each year from Y_1 to Y_T				Wholesale PV Projection
Investing Cash Flow	−$1,172	−$1,996	−$2,637	Projected each year from Y_1 to Y_T				
= Economic Cash Flow	$1,641	$2,501	$1,556	Projected each year from Y_1 to Y_T				Wholesale PV Projection

Exhibit 20.1: *The Pro Forma Problem for PepsiCo.* The numbers for PepsiCo's income statement were taken from Exhibit 13.3 on Page 374. Economic cash flows can be computed from Formula 13.4 on Page 400. All net sales include bottling operations. The numbers for PepsiCo's cash flow statement were taken from Exhibit 13.4 on Page 375. (Small note: You may recall that PepsiCo actually earned interest in 1999 and 2001, which is rather unusual. Most corporations pay net interest.) Your goal will be to determine a good break for T, and to project future cash flows—T periods' worth of detailed financials—followed by a wholesale market value estimate of the remaining cash flows until eternity.

20.3 The Length of the Detailed Projection Period

How many years of
detailed financials
should you project?

Your first goal is to understand how to choose a suitable value for the horizon choice T in Exhibit 20.1. Remember that the horizon is the span of time up to which you project detailed financials and beyond which you substitute your "wholesale" terminal value estimate.

As an initial step, let us take a brief detour into forecasting. There are two surprising and key insights to note:

1. You may be able to project future cash flows in the very long term as accurately as in the intermediate term.

2. At some point, your cash flows are not very likely to grow that fast anymore. This is not to say that they won't grow at all—just that your expected value forecasts today no longer grow very steeply and/or reliably.

The very long run may
not be any more
daunting than the
intermediate run.
Although future cash
flows may be equally
uncertain, their
present values could
be less uncertain.

These issues imply that you would be able to estimate the *present* value of long-term cash flows *better* than that of intermediate-term cash flows. This is best explained by example.

An example of
"constant" uncertainty,
which does grow with
horizon.

If you have to forecast the temperature in 2 hours, your (short-term) forecast will be pretty good, and much better than your 6-month forecast. But how would your 6-month forecast compare to your 50-year forecast? Most likely, both your prediction and level of accuracy would be similar. For example, your temperature forecast for August of next year should probably be the same 80 degrees, plus or minus 10 degrees, as your forecast for August in 50 years. Thus, if the environment is stable, then your uncertainty is not likely to grow with your horizon after some point. (A stable environment is often a bigger assumption than you may realize—think about what global warming could do, for example.)

When you discount
the long-term
uncertainty, it may be
less problematic from
an NPV perspective.

Now say you want to value an ice cream store. How does your temperature forecast affect your store's estimated present value? The effect of temperature uncertainty for August of next year is less discounted and thus more important than the effect of temperature uncertainty in August in 50 years. If your store expects to earn $100,000, and a 10-degree temperature difference can cause you to earn anything between $75,000 and $125,000, then the temperature uncertainty for August of next year can cause a present value difference of about $50,000/1.15^1 \approx \$43,478$ at a 15% discount rate (cost of capital). But the same temperature uncertainty in 50 years causes only a present value difference of about $50,000/1.15^{50} \approx \$46$. Consequently, to estimate your store's value today, your intermediate-term uncertainty should worry you more than your long-term uncertainty.

Economics and
strategy: Scarce
resources create rents
for (existing)
shareholders!

The role of intermediate-term versus long-term uncertainty generalizes beyond ice cream stores, because knowledge of economics and strategy allows you to put reasonable bounds on long-term future profitability (in 20 or 50 years). At such far-out horizons, you should not expect businesses to still have unusually large growth rates and to earn **economic rents**, where economic rents are defined as investment rates of return that are much higher than the costs of capital. Economic rents can only be achieved when a firm has assets and capabilities that are scarce, valuable, and difficult to imitate. Examples of such scarce resources are the presence of a unique and excellent manager (e.g., Steve Jobs at Apple Computer), economies of scale (e.g., Microsoft's computer software or

Wal-Mart's mass logistics and buying power), unduplicable corporate reputation (e.g., Sony's brand name), legally protected intellectual property (e.g., Glaxo's retroviral drug patents or Disney's Mickey Mouse), or consumer switching costs (e.g., Comcast's cable television). In the long run (i.e., over decades) scarce resources tend to become less scarce as new technologies and consumers make old advantages obsolete. In 2004, I first wrote here that Wal-Mart seemed like an unbeatable juggernaut but that it would almost surely not remain such in 20 years. It surely would not have the scarce and unique resources that would allow its shareholder-owners to continue earning rates of return much above their investments' costs of capital. I had to wait less than I expected—as of 2008, Wal-Mart had already lost much of its glamour. Its share price had dropped from $60 in 2004 to below $50 in mid-2008. By 2011, it was still between $50 and $55.

To determine how long it might take before a product becomes a commodity and thus produces only normal profits, you need to apply economic thinking to your specific business knowledge. If the company owns few unique resources and there are few entry barriers, then it may only take a couple of years before unusually high corporate growth rates slow down and there are no more economic rents. For example, there are few entry barriers to flat-screen television technology today. Consequently, you can count on the industry that produces flat-screen televisions to earn few excess rents within 10 years. (If you do not believe this, think back to 1997, when the average DVD player sold for $800. Today, all entry barriers have disappeared, and you can purchase a DVD player for $20.) Other products, however, can enjoy more scarcity and entry barriers for longer periods of time. For example, if you can get a patent on an effective cancer drug, you will be able to earn economic rents for 15 to 25 years—although better competitors' drugs will eventually come onto the scene and your patent will eventually run out.

You should think about barriers to potential competition. The forces of economics have worked on products historically, too.

Your first reaction might be to dismiss such a long-term perspective. Google may just seem too good in 2008 for you to believe in its eventual slowdown or even demise. But like most of us, you are just letting your present-day experience color your long-term forecasts. Look back 50 years and ask yourself whether the fast-growing, exciting companies operating then are still the same. Or just look back 25 years. Can you even name the companies from the 1980s that still earn large economic rents? If you had picked two companies that looked similar in 1985, are both companies still around? For example, Dell may still be doing well, but Gateway looked just as good in 1985—and there are literally dozens of now-bankrupt mail-based computer retailers that looked no different then, either. Standing in 1985, you should not have expected to earn large economic rents if you had bet on any one computer hardware vendor then.

Don't get caught up in today's perspective.

The perspective of the economist lends insight into a good choice for T. The economics that helps you decide on when a firm is likely to settle into a lower economic growth rate is taught in great detail in business strategy courses and carries different labels (e.g., Porter's Five Forces). To determine when economic rents are likely to dry up, strategy suggests you ask questions such as:

The discipline of business strategy asks: What factors delay the erosion of economic rents?

- How long before your entry barriers will erode?

- How long before your success will be mimicked by the competition?

- How long before you will be squeezed by suppliers or customers?

The first consideration
for setting T: business
economics.

One good guideline for choosing your horizon T is to consider the underlying firm economics. It should be around the point when the company will earn only "ordinary profits." This is where long-run economic forces will have eroded most of the economic edge of the company—where growth will return from the initial but unsustainably high short-term rates to sustainable, ordinary long-term rates. At this point, a terminal value is relatively easy to forecast. Your goal, then, should be to capture the initially rapid and possibly unstable growth phase with detailed financial forecasts, and the stable period with the terminal value. Another way to say this is that a good T is the point in time when you expect the present value of growth opportunities (PVGO) to be low.

➤ *PVGO*, *Sect.* 14.2,
Pg.420.

The second
consideration for
setting T: discount
factors.

But there is also a second consideration to your choice of T. You want to pick a horizon such that the discount factor is high enough so that the precise choice of T would not matter *too* much. For example, at a 10% discount rate, $1 in 5 years is still worth 62 cents today. An incorrect terminal value would make a big difference to your NPV estimate. If you were to use 20 or even 30 years, $1 would be worth only about 15 or 6 cents in present value, respectively. Such high discount factors can help plaster over the errors that your terminal value estimate will inevitably commit. And when it comes to exit values on horizons that are so far away, the best you can hope for is a *halfway* reasonable estimate of market value, anyway.

Typical values for T: 5
to 10 years. We
"cheat" for PepsiCo
and use just 3 years.

For most businesses, you would pick a terminal phase about 3 to 20 years out, with 5 to 10 years being most common. Let's apply economic intuition to choose a T for PepsiCo. PepsiCo is a very stable company, so it is not necessary to project 20 years of financials in great detail. You can instead "lump" the value created in all future years into one terminal market value fairly soon. A short period is a relief—it saves you from guessing detailed numbers for many initial projection years about which you (as an outsider) have little clue. Thus, for expositional convenience, let us choose a horizon of T = 3 years. That is, you should try to project in detail from 2002 to 2004, and then summarize all cash flows from 2005 to eternity with one value estimate as of the end of 2004.

IMPORTANT

> The choice of break point T between a detailed projection period and a terminal market value is often dictated by two considerations:
>
> 1. A desire to distinguish between an up-front strong growth phase and a subsequent mature and stable phase
>
> 2. A desire to have a small discount factor on the terminal market value to reduce the present value importance of estimation errors
>
> In practice, most pro formas choose a T between 5 and 10 years.

Q 20.4. Is it usually easier to predict the growth rate of earnings (or cash flows) of new businesses in two years or in twenty years?

Q 20.5. What considerations would push you toward a longer detailed projection horizon?

20.4 The Detailed Projection Phase

You have now dealt with the first goal of choosing the horizon T. Your second goal is to determine your expected cash flows during the beginning growth period, from next year up to the year of your terminal forecast. The good news is that if you were an actual analyst, you would probably know your business quite well and thus be able to reasonably predict the immediate future. You could use PepsiCo's historical cash flows for some guidance about future cash flows. Of course, to do this well, you would still have to understand a lot about the underlying economics of the business, and you would still have to make many assumptions. In this process, you would want to use additional information that we have mostly ignored so far—such as the specific industry economics or the current and historical corporate balance sheets.

In real life, you must use all your economic knowledge to make a good projection.

Unfortunately, illustrating this process in a textbook is difficult. There are no clear rules that apply to all companies, and this book is not about PepsiCo or the soda industry. You probably do not know much about PepsiCo's business—and even if I could fully explain and analyze PepsiCo's many businesses for you, it would not help you elsewhere. Pharmaceutical drug research, aluminum mining, fad toys, and a new stamping machine each have their own unique business, financial, and accounting patterns. There is little generality here. In contrast to the terminal value, long-run economic forces are unlikely to bite forcefully in the projection-phase period.

Initial growth projections are highly product-specific.

Even though we lack specific information, we must not simply brush over the initial growth phase. Accurate, detailed forecasts have a significant impact on project wealth through two channels. First, these forecasts for the first three years have a direct contribution to today's present value. Second, the terminal value itself is (usually) estimated relative to a baseline expected cash flow from the last year of the initial phase. If your baseline is wrong, your terminal value will also be wrong.

IMPORTANT: Your detailed projections will also influence your terminal values.

We are going to have to make up some estimates to illustrate the process. Be warned: Our financial projections for PepsiCo are necessarily very naïve. Again, because you know very little about PepsiCo's business or the plans of its managers, accuracy is not the goal—illustration is.

Warning: Don't expect precision in any pro forma—especially in ours.

The two primary methods of projecting financials are explained in the next two subsections:

Projecting economic cash flows directly (almost a cheat) or indirectly (via detailed financials).

1. Direct extrapolation of the accounting component that you are interested in (i.e., the economic NPV cash flows for the project, though sometimes also the earnings)

2. Detailed financial modeling of all, or most, items in the financial statements

The first is a drastic shortcut, used by analysts only when time and knowledge are severely limited. We actually used this trick in the earlier parts of the book, where cash flow forecasts fell like manna from heaven. In real life, the second method is much more common. Incidentally, computer spreadsheets were originally invented primarily to facilitate the projections in pro formas. They make designing pro formas easier.

Q 20.6. Assume that it is easier in your business to forecast the long-run rather than the 5-year growth rate. Further, assume that 80% of the present value will sit in the terminal value. Is it still important to get good intermediate projections?

You could directly
project the final cash
flows themselves
forward. Here (and
probably often
elsewhere), it gives
bad results.

➤ *Economic cash flows,
Formula 13.4, Pg. 400.*

Faking It: Direct Extrapolation of Historical Cash Flows

The first method is really a "cheat": It is a shortcut that avoids having to do the full-blown financial pro forma analysis. It directly projects the historical cash flows forward, for example, by assuming a constant growth rate forever. By applying Formula 13.4 for project cash flows to PepsiCo from 1999 to 2001, you can compute the cash flows (from Exhibit 20.1) that accrued to both debt and equity:

$$\text{Asset Cash Flow}_{1999} = \$3,605 + (-\$1,172) + (-\$792) = \$1,641$$

$$\text{Asset Cash Flow}_{2000} = \$4,440 + (-\$1,996) + (+\$57) = \$2,501$$

$$\text{Asset Cash Flow}_{2001} = \$4,201 + (-\$2,637) + (-\$8) = \$1,556$$

$$\frac{\text{Economic Project}}{\text{Cash Flow}} = \frac{\text{Operating}}{\text{Cash Flow}} + \frac{\text{Investing}}{\text{Cash Flow}} + \frac{\text{Interest}}{\text{Expense}}$$

Warning: You really
need to understand
the business.
Mechanical
extrapolation rarely
works well.

➤ *PepsiCo Cash Flows,
Exhibit 13.4, Pg. 375.*

Over the three years, PepsiCo showed a cash flow decline of about $\$1,556/\$1,641 - 1 \approx -5.2\%$. This comes to an annual decline of about $(\$1,556/\$1,641)^{1/2} - 1 \approx -2.6\%$. Over the most recent 12 months, asset cash flows even dropped by one-third! You could assume that PepsiCo's cash flows will continue to decline at this rate forever. But does this make sense? If you investigate PepsiCo's cash flow statement in Exhibit 13.4 further, you can see that much of PepsiCo's decline was due to a heavy increase in (other) investing activity, not a decline in its business (sales). Some of it was due to the acquisition of Quaker, which PepsiCo hopes will eventually pay off in *more* cash, not less. This tells you how hazardous simplistic extrapolation of cash flows can be: You really need to know more about the business itself and the reasons behind the financial trends. Purely mechanical rather than economic models of the business usually just don't work well. Again, always remember that valuation requires much economic and common sense, and that it is as much an art as a science. For lack of a better estimate of cash flow growth due to higher investment spending, let us assume a growth rate of 10%. Exhibit 20.2 shows the cash flows if you adopt this projection.

You could project
earnings instead of
cash flows—which has
advantages (e.g.,
smoothness) and
disadvantages (e.g.,
not used for NPV).

Although it is not as much the case for PepsiCo, the typical lumpiness of cash flows when the firm makes acquisitions (such as when PepsiCo bought Quaker) often makes the forecasting of cash flows very difficult. But there is an alternative. In Chapter 14, you worked with earnings rather than cash flows, and for the same lumpiness-of-cash-flows reason. In the very long run, earnings and cash flows should be roughly equal—after all, earnings "just" shift the time-series accruals. The question here is whether historical net income growth or historical cash flow growth represents the present value of the future cash flow growth stream better, given that you have to work with time-truncated forecasts.

Net income (earnings): On the positive side, earnings are smoother than cash flows, because the accountants have reflected likely future cash flows in current earnings. On the negative side, the discount factors are wrong, because you are applying them not to actual cash flows but to earnings which may well be combinations of actual and future cash flows. Moreover, the human intervention also means historical net income could have been more easily manipulated than historical cash flows.

10% Growth Cash Flow Projections

	Known			"Detailed" Model Assumes Growth of 10%			Terminal Value (see next section)	
	Y_{-2}	Y_{-1}	Y_0	Y_1	Y_2	Y_3	Y_4	Y_4 **to** Y_∞
	1999	2000	2001	**2002**	**2003**	**2004**	**2005**	
Cash Flows	$1,641	$2,501	$1,556	$1,712	$1,883	$2,071	$2,278	?

3% Growth of Earnings Projections

	Known			"Detailed" Model Assumes Growth of 3%			Terminal Value (see next section)	
	Y_{-2}	Y_{-1}	Y_0	Y_1	Y_2	Y_3	Y_4	Y_4 **to** Y_∞
	1999	2000	2001	**2002**	**2003**	**2004**	**2005**	
Earnings	$2,505	$2,543	$2,662	$2,742	$2,824	$2,909	$2,996	?

Exhibit 20.2: *Pro Forma: Direct Projections (in millions).* In the top panel, we are simply projecting that cash flows will grow 10% per year, due to current investments, until at least 2005. In the bottom panel, we are simply extrapolating the two-year historical earnings growth rate of 3% into the future.

Cash flows: On the positive side, cash flows are the gold standard *if you can project them out accurately to infinity.* On the negative side, if you have to truncate your forecast in the future or rely on a finite number of cash flows as representative of the future, it is not clear whether or not your history paints an accurate picture of the future.

For example, if you have a plant that costs $20 million and produces $15 million that same year as well as the following year, the cash flow stream would suggest huge growth (from –$5 million to +$15 million). You could even be tempted to predict another $20 million in growth (i.e., $35 million) for the following year if you based your analysis on extrapolated historical cash flows. In contrast, with two-year linear depreciation, the earnings stream would be a more sensible $15 – $10 = $5 million of income followed by another $15 – $10 = $5 million of income the next year (suggesting a zero growth rate). At least, you would not predict the same runaway growth.

So let's also create a growth rate projection for earnings. PepsiCo had earnings of $2,662 million in 2001, having grown at rates of 1.5% and 4.7% over the 2 prior years. If PepsiCo were to grow its earnings by 3% per year, you would find the earnings trend at the bottom of Exhibit 20.2. As you can see, earnings would reach nearly $3 billion by 2005. This estimate is much higher than the equivalent cash flow projection for 2005.

Let's work a PepsiCo forecast based on earnings, not cash flows.

What should you use?
Earnings forecasting
tends to be better
than cash flow
forecasting.

In some cases, cash flow-based forecasting is better; in other cases, earnings-based forecasting is better. Academic research has shown that earnings-based terminal value projections are superior to pure cash flow-based terminal value projections *on average for publicly traded corporations*. You could also try other approaches. For example, you could try to distinguish between lower cash flows due to investment (which should create higher future cash flows) and lower cash flows due to lower sales or higher costs (which should not create higher future cash flows).

Q 20.7. If you do a direct projection, is it usually better to project cash flows or earnings based on the last three years of data?

The Real Thing: Detailed Financial Pro Forma Projections

The more
sophisticated method
attempts to model the
complete financial
statements, not just
the "end product of"
economic cash flows
(or earnings). (This is
the real pro forma
analysis.)

The second and more common method of projecting economic cash flows during the initial period is to project complete financial statements. This requires providing individual components for the economic cash flows you ultimately seek. Doing so is often (but not always) better than projecting economic cash flows directly for three reasons:

1. As just noted, neither cash flow nor earnings forecasts are particularly reliable. Cash flows are difficult to project directly, because they tend to be volatile and lumpy. Net income is smoother but contains many fictional accounting accruals that are not true cash. You are caught between the proverbial rock and hard place.

2. The full projection method can make it easier to incorporate your knowledge of the underlying business into the economic cash flow estimates. For example, you may happen to know that unusual expenses will be zero next year, or that a new payment system may speed the collection of receivables. By forecasting the individual items, you can integrate such economic knowledge into your cash flow estimates.

3. The full projection method can help you judge other important information—such as working capital availability, suitable debt-equity ratios, and your interest rate coverage. Especially for entrepreneurs who are often in danger of a liquidity crisis, such information can be just as important as the economic cash flows themselves. In fact, *all* ratio analyses, such as those exploring the financial health and profitability ratios, are often more useful for future pro forma financials than current financials. Ratio analysis can then help you judge whether the firm is on a sound or critical path.

➤ *Financial ratios,
Sect. 14.5, Pg.447.*

The Income Statement: Sales

The baseline for
detailed pro formas is
sales prediction.

The detailed projection method usually starts by forecasting future sales in the income statement. *Your sales forecast is the single most critical aspect of any pro forma,* because it becomes the baseline number from which many other financial item forecasts will follow. For example, in PepsiCo's case, you could use a mechanistic model that extrapolates sales growth from historical financials. Exhibit 20.3 allows you to compute that PepsiCo sales

Income Statement		1999	December 2000	2001	Estimated 2002	2003	...
=	Sales[a]	$25,093	$25,479	$26,935	$27,906	...	...
	COGS[b]	$10,326	$10,226	$10,754	$10,762	...	...
	+ SG&A[c]	$11,018	$11,104	$11,608	$12,279	...	...
	+ Deprec/Amort[d]	$193	$147	$165	$168	...	...
	+ Unusual Expenses[e]	$73	$184	$387	$279	...	...
−	= **Operating Expenses**[f]	$21,610	$21,661	$22,914	$23,486	...	...
=	**Operating Income**[g]	$3,483	$3,818	$4,021	$4,420	...	...
+	Net Interest Income[h]	$792	−$57	$8	$0	...	...
=	**Income Before Tax**[i]	$4,275	$3,761	$4,029	$4,420	...	...
−	Corporate Income Tax[j]	$1,770	$1,218	$1,367	$1,591	...	...
=	**Income After Tax**[k]	$2,505	$2,543	$2,662	$2,828	...	...
−	Extraordinary Items[l]	$0	$0	$0	$0	...	...
=	**Net Income** [m]	$2,505	$2,543	$2,662	$2,828	...	...

Exhibit 20.3: *A Possible PepsiCo Pro Forma Income Statement Model for 2002 (in millions).* Here are some explanations (notes) about how I guestimated the 2002 figures:

a. Grows by historical 3.6%	f. Sum the above, rounded	j. 36% · EBT
b. $3,506 + 26% · $\mathcal{E}$(sales)	g. Subtract the above	k. Subtract the above, rounded
c. 44% · $\mathcal{E}$(sales)	h. Ignorant and ad-hoc	l. Ignorant and ad-hoc
d. 3-year historical average	i. Sum the above	m. Subtract the above
e. 1% · $\mathcal{E}$(sales)		

grew at an annualized rate of $(\$26,935/\$25,093)^{1/2} - 1 \approx 3.61\%$ from 1999 to 2001. Let's assume that PepsiCo sales will continue in 2002 at the same growth rate. Therefore, you could project PepsiCo sales in 2002 to be $\$26,935 \cdot (\$26,935/\$25,093)^{1/2} \approx \$26,935 \cdot (1 + 3.61\%) \approx \$27,906$ million.

Like every other pro forma line item, the sales forecast should have a footnote (in Exhibit 20.3) to explain the basis behind the estimate. Admittedly, the footnotes in Exhibit 20.3 are mostly perfunctory. For example, note "a" does not even explain where the 3.6% came from. In the real world, you would carefully explain the background assumptions behind each and every critical component of your pro forma—sometimes with many paragraphs and additional tables.

Pro formas should explain all assumptions!

You can use more information and even subjective judgments!

Do not believe that sales forecasting is always as simple as this. You could, and should, use an economic model that uses detailed business intelligence. For example, as a real-world analyst, you might use your knowledge to determine

- whether PepsiCo is about to launch many exciting new products or whether it has few new projects in the pipeline;

- whether PepsiCo paid less in dividends in order to reinvest its earnings into operations, which eventually will turn into more sales or profitability;

- whether there is a recession or a boom on the horizon for 2002;

and so on. This would help you adjust your sales estimates for a more accurate projection. In a real pro forma where your money is on the line, it would be outright reckless to forecast sales through a mechanistic model without an economic model!

The Income Statement: Other Components

How to estimate other financial line items. You could extrapolate them by themselves, but the better way is often to project them in relation to (as a fraction of) sales.

You would then go down item by item on the income statement. Your next estimate would be for COGS. You have a whole range of options, including but not limited to a plain growth forecast (similar to what we used for sales). Here are five possible methods (and keep in mind that the following income statement figures are in millions):

1. **A plain growth forecast:** You could repeat the sales exercise with COGS: A pure growth model could take COGS' historical growth rate of $\sqrt{\$10,754/\$10,326}-1 \approx$ 2.05% and project that it will continue in 2002. If applied to the year 2001 COGS of $10,754, your 2002 COGS forecast would thus be $10,754 \cdot (1 + 2.05\%) \approx$ $10,975.

2. **A pure proportion of sales forecast:** You can forecast COGS not only relative to its own history but also relative to your already-projected sales of $27,906 for 2002. You also know the historical relationship between COGS and sales, which you can use to predict a relationship between 2002 sales and 2002 COGS. For example, PepsiCo's COGS was $10,326/$25,093 \approx 41.15\%$ of sales in 1999, 40.14% of sales in 2000, and 39.93% of sales in 2001. The simplest sales-based model might just project that COGS would be a slowly declining fraction of sales in 2002. In this case, your COGS forecast might be

$$\mathcal{E}(\text{COGS}_{2002}) \approx 0 + 39.5\% \cdot \mathcal{E}(\text{Sales}_{2002})$$
$$= 39.5\% \cdot \$27,906 \approx \$11,023$$

3. **An economies-of-scale forecast:** A more sophisticated model might pose economies of scale. In this case, COGS would not go up proportionally with sales. Instead, COGS would have both a "fixed component," whose cost would not change with sales (e.g., some necessary maintenance costs or salaries), and a "variable component," whose cost would increase with sales (e.g., the cola syrup) but at a rate of less than one to one. You might try to plot COGS against sales for 1999-2001 and determine visually that a good line fit would be

$$\mathcal{E}(\text{COGS}_{2002}) = \$3,500 + 25\% \cdot \mathcal{E}(\text{Sales}_{2002})$$
$$= a + b \cdot \mathcal{E}(\text{Sales}_{2002})$$

This says that $3,500 (remember we are working in millions) is an unalterable factory cost, but for each extra dollar of sales, you have to purchase only 25 cents of syrup. Substituting in our estimated 2002 sales of $27,906, you would project COGS for 2002 to be

$$\mathcal{E}(\text{COGS}_{2002}) \approx \$3,500 + 25\% \cdot \$27,906 \approx \$10,477$$

Or, you could use heavier statistical artillery and run a regression relating PepsiCo's COGS to sales over its most recent three years. (Don't worry if you do not know what this is.) Such a regression suggests that a better line fit would be

$$\mathcal{E}(\text{COGS}_{2002}) \approx \$3,506 + 26\% \cdot \mathcal{E}(\text{Sales}_{2002})$$

so your prediction would change to

$$\mathcal{E}(\text{COGS}_{2002}) \approx \$3,506 + 26\% \cdot \$27,906 \approx \$10,762 \qquad (20.1)$$

4. **An industry-based forecast:** You could draw on information from other firms, such as Coca-Cola. In 2001, Coca-Cola had COGS of $6,044 on sales of $20,092 (a ratio of 30%), which is much lower than PepsiCo's ratio. This may not only suggest that Coca-Cola's business is different but also that PepsiCo may be able to lower its COGS in the future to meet "better practice" standards. Thus, you might want to lower PepsiCo's COGS estimate from $10,762.

More sophisticated methods can use more information than just sales—for example, they can use industry benchmarks or the company's own depreciation.

5. **A disaggregated forecast:** If you were even more sophisticated, you could recognize that COGS contains some depreciation. Thus, the history of PepsiCo's past capital expenditures could also influence your COGS estimate. You could throw past capital expenditures into your statistical regression, too, to come up with a better predictive formula.

The sky—your economic and econometric background knowledge—is your limit. For illustration's sake, let's adopt $10,762 from Formula 20.1 as our predicted COGS in Exhibit 20.3.

You can repeat these forecasting processes to predict other income statement items. Again, you have many options. Like COGS, SG&A contains both fixed and variable expenses, as well as depreciation that relates to past investments. SG&A might thus be modeled as a combination of a fixed component, plus a sales-variable component, plus a past capital expenditure-based component. There is also no need to remain consistent across different items—you could use one method to estimate COGS and another to estimate SG&A (or any other financial statement item, for that matter). For example, you could relate net interest income to how much debt PepsiCo currently has and what you know current interest rates are and what you believe future interest rates will be. But because no money (only scarce book space) is at stake, for the rest of the income

Other financial line items in the table may follow other models.

statement, let's play it simple. The footnotes in Exhibit 20.3 describe the method of projection for each item. Clearly, if your money were at stake, you would want to know as much as possible about the business and use this knowledge to come up with better models for the relationships between PepsiCo's financial variables. Again, the limit is only your knowledge—and for our PepsiCo example, it is obviously very limited, indeed.

The Cash Flow Statement

Your cash flow statement model would rely on your income statement model.

Next, you would model the cash flow statement. Exhibit 20.4 is our attempt for PepsiCo. It starts by transferring the projected net income from the pro forma income statement model into the pro forma cash flow statement model. For the remaining cash flow items, our estimates remain perfunctory—after all, this is only an illustration. We really have no idea about PepsiCo's depreciation and depletion (or about PepsiCo's plants, for that matter), but a number on the order of $1,100 million looks "reasonably reasonable," given the stability of PepsiCo's prior history of depreciation and capital expenditures. (We also ignore the fact that some parts of depreciation have already been modeled into components of items in the income statement; you really should check the internal consistency of your forecasts—something we shall not do here.)

A quick rundown of other cash flow statement components.

Working down the cash flow statement, you must adopt a ratio for your model for deferred taxes that fits the history reasonably well—let's go with around 18% of PepsiCo's income taxes. You know nothing about noncash items, and PepsiCo's history does not suggest a clear pattern, so choose zero. Changes in working capital are more noteworthy, because their relation to sales contains interesting economics. We know that it is not the absolute level of sales but sales growth that determines the working capital consumed by the business—but not one to one. For example, you may have to carry more inventory to satisfy sales growth, although economies of scale may allow you to grow inventory less than one to one. Your receivables collection policies and technologies (and your willingness to sell to dubious customers) may influence how much your receivables should grow with sales. Your willingness to pay your suppliers may influence your payables, and so on. With a projected sales increase for 2002 of just under $1 billion, it would suggest that PepsiCo will need more working capital. Yet PepsiCo also grew in prior years, and it still managed to pull working capital out of the business rather than put it in! This is rather unusual and may hint at some interesting choices PepsiCo has made. We could dig further to find out; but without further knowledge, and after (not much pretend) analysis of the underlying business, just assume that PepsiCo will reverse its recent trend and put $200 million into the business to finance its sales growth. The outcome of all this hand waving is a forecast of operating cash flow of $4 billion. Finally, after equally long consideration of PepsiCo's business, and equally long interviews with PepsiCo management, let's assume that you determine PepsiCo is planning to invest $1.3 billion into capital expenditures, and

---

Sidenote: In the appendix to this chapter, there are similar formulas for many pro forma components estimated with data from the universe of publicly traded companies. These can be used "in a pinch"—or even to help you gain some intuition about how important the fixed and variable components are in a particular data item. However, the formulas there are mechanistic and therefore definitely not particularly reliable in any individual case—so be careful.

Cash Flow Statement		December			Estimated	
		1999	2000	2001	2002	⋯
	Net Income[a]	$2,505	$2,543	$2,662	$2,828	⋯
+	Depreciation and Depletion[b]	$1,156	$1,093	$1,082	$1,100	⋯
+	Deferred Taxes[c]	$573	$33	$162	$300	⋯
+	Noncash Items[d]	−$708	$355	$211	$0	⋯
+	Decreases in Working Capital[e]	$79	$416	$84	−$200	⋯
=	**Total Operating Activity**[f]	$3,605	$4,440	$4,201	$4,028	⋯
	Capital Expenditures[g]	−$1,341	−$1,352	−$1,324	−$1,300	⋯
+	Other Investing[h]	$169	−$644	−$1,313	$0	⋯
=	**Total Investing Activity**[i]	−$1,172	−$1,996	−$2,637	−$1,300	⋯
	Operating Plus Investing				$2,728	⋯

Exhibit 20.4: *A Possible PepsiCo Pro Forma Cash Flow Statement Model (in millions).* Explanations (notes) are applicable to the 2002 figures:

a. Transfer from IS (Table 20.3)	d. Ignorant and ad-hoc	g. Eyeballed
b. Eyeballed	e. ≈ −20% of revenue *increase*	h. Ignorant and ad-hoc
c. 15%-20% of corporate income tax, rounded	f. Sum of above	i. Sum the above, rounded.

Note that changes in working capital that contribute positively to the cash flows are decreases in the amount of net working capital on the balance sheet.

nothing into other activities. Thus, the outcome of operating plus investing cash flows is $2.7 billion.

Financing Policy, the Balance Sheet, and Linkages

One step that we have mostly bypassed is to think more about your financing policy. It would influence not only the remainder of your cash flow statement (the financing cash flows), but also your balance sheet (debt and equity positions), and even your income statement (interest payments). In fact, depending on what you assume, you may have to go back to the income statement and go through your forecasts again. Other linkages will arise, too. For example:

The four financial statements have other linkages, which we omit for lack of space.

- What you assume about financing cash flows will influence your end-of-period cash position on your balance sheet, because the cash position next year is the cash position this year plus the net of all cash flows.

- What you assume about how your technology will change your inventory or your collection abilities will influence both your current assets and current liabilities on your balance sheet, as well as your consumption of working capital on your cash flow statement.

Future years—more work and trouble.

Of course, you would also need to provide detailed projections for the remaining detailed projection period, 2003-2005. The principles are the same as they were for your projection of 2002. We will skip all these for lack of space.

Q 20.8. What financial statement line item plays the role of a "base forecast" off of which many other forecasts are often derived?

Q 20.9. How do economies of scale manifest themselves in line item forecasts?

Q 20.10. Are the income statement and the cash flow statement linked?

Ratio Calculations and Policy with Pro Formas

After you have also projected the other two financial statements—the balance sheet and the statement of owners' equity—up to the terminal value, T, what can you do with these numbers?

Economic Project Cash Flows

The projected cash flows for PepsiCo are now much higher, due to our "other investing" assumptions.

➤ *Economic cash flows, Formula 13.4, Pg. 400.*

➤ *Direct Valuation, Exhibit 20.2, Pg. 651.*

The first important use of the pro forma is project value analysis. Having guesstimated the components of the cash flow statement for 2002, you can now compute the economic cash flow for your NPV analysis, using the basic cash flow formula (Formula 13.4). Economic project cash flows for PepsiCo are the sum of operating cash flows and investing cash flows minus interest income (from Exhibit 20.3). Subtracting interest income is the same as adding interest expense. This comes to around $2,728 million— much higher than your $1,712 million direct projection in Exhibit 20.2. This is not because the forecasting technique is different but primarily because you now projected other investing activity to be zero. (It implicitly accounted for around $1 billion of consumed cash in 2001.) Without detailed knowledge of PepsiCo's business, you cannot resolve which of the two assumptions—investing activity at $0 or $1 billion—seems more reasonable.

Ratio and Soundness Analysis

Pro formas allow for ratio or financial health analyses.

➤ *Financial ratios, Sect. 14.5, Pg. 442.*

A second common use for detailed financial projections is forward-looking ratio analysis to judge whether the business remains viable and sound. Such an analysis can serve to check the reasonableness of your forecasts—and the viability of the firm in your scenario. For example, if a start-up firm were to end up with a very high debt-equity ratio and very little cash, the implied future interest coverage ratio should set off an alarm. Or, a growth path may have an interim negative cash position—which could doom an otherwise healthy firm. The firm may be on a collision course with reality, and management should change course to preserve cash before the entire firm evaporates. However, because most ratio analysis requires aspects of the financials that we do not have space to model—specifically, the financing policy on the cash flow statement and the full balance sheet—we will not discuss this any further. Once you have the full pro forma model, the ratio analysis principles and soundness principles remain exactly the same as they were in Chapter 14.

Corporate Policy Changes

Pro forma projections depend not only on external factors—for example, whether the economy is going into a recession—but also on many choices that managers make. For example, managers must make decisions about how quickly to pay or collect outstanding bills, how much to invest into new projects versus how much to pay out in dividends, how much to finance with debt versus how much to finance with equity, and so on. You have to be careful to realize that historical extrapolations may no longer work if either the external environment or the corporate policy is changing.

➤ *Other financial ratios, Sect.* 14.5, *Pg.* 442.

Historical projections work only if the economic environment is stable.

This is even more important to recognize when you are not an external analyst but a manager constructing a pro forma in order to contemplate a corporate policy change. For example, if you invest more in new factories, all sorts of relationships—some of them nonobvious—may change. For instance, the relationship between COGS and sales may change if the consumers of your product ask for more or less complementary products from other producers, which in turn may change the cost of raw materials that you require for production. Just be careful not to think too mechanistically about the effect of changes in one policy on other items in your financials.

If the firm is changing its own policy, then the world would likely no longer be stable—and history may no longer be a good guide for projecting.

Q 20.11. Does ratio analysis make sense in the context of a pro forma?

20.5 The Terminal Value

Your third goal is to determine the firm's terminal market value. Conceptually, the terminal value is your best estimate of what you believe the firm could be sold for at future time T. Practically, it is most commonly estimated with the growing perpetuity formula (Formula 3.1). You would start with your detailed estimated value of cash flows for time T, assume that it will grow forever at some sustainable long-term growth rate $\mathscr{E}(g)$, and discount it back:

After you have decided on T and the cash flows up to T, you can work on the terminal value.

➤ *Growing perpetuity, Formula* 3.1, *Pg.* 42.

$$\mathscr{E}\left(\text{Terminal Value}_{T=2004}\right) \;=\; \frac{\mathscr{E}\left(\text{Cash Flow}_{T=2005}\right)}{\mathscr{E}(r) - \mathscr{E}(g)}$$

For illustration's sake, the remainder of the chapter relies only on the direct cash flow forecasts from Exhibit 20.2 (i.e., $\mathscr{E}(\text{Cash Flow}_{T=2005}) = \$2{,}278$) in the numerator. You still need estimates for the eventual (stable and eternal) growth rate, $\mathscr{E}(g)$, and for the future cost of capital, $\mathscr{E}(r)$, or at least for the difference between them, $(\mathscr{E}(r) - \mathscr{E}(g))$. Let's look at the future cost of capital first.

➤ *Direct Valuation, Exhibit* 20.2, *Pg.* 651.

The Cost of Capital

Estimate an
appropriate expected
rate of return. You
might use the CAPM
on PepsiCo stock—or a
firm that is similar.

You would probably rely on the CAPM to determine the cost of capital for PepsiCo as of late 2001. Because PepsiCo was publicly traded, you could use its own historical return data. If the thought experiment is that PepsiCo is not yet publicly traded, then you could use information from one or more comparables, such as Coca-Cola, instead. Exhibit 20.5 gathers a couple of years of (dividend-adjusted) stock prices from **YAHOO!** FINANCE for the S&P 500, PepsiCo, and Coca-Cola.

Month	S&P 500	PEP	KO	Month	S&P 500	PEP	KO
Dec 97	970	$32.98	$60.64				
Jan 98	980	$32.86	$58.87	Jan 00	1,394	$31.94	$53.21
Feb 98	1,049	$33.20	$62.39	Feb 00	1,366	$30.07	$45.05
Mar98	1,102	$38.95	$70.56	Mar00	1,499	$32.79	$43.65
Apr 98	1,112	$36.22	$69.12	Apr 00	1,452	$34.49	$43.94
May98	1,091	$37.24	$71.40	May00	1,421	$38.25	$49.64
Jun 98	1,134	$37.70	$78.04	Jun 00	1,455	$41.92	$53.58
Jul 98	1,121	$35.64	$73.48	Jul 00	1,431	$43.22	$57.19
Aug98	957	$25.52	$59.44	Aug00	1,518	$40.23	$49.11
Sep 98	1,017	$27.06	$52.73	Sep 00	1,437	$43.54	$51.59
Oct 98	1,099	$31.02	$61.82	Oct 00	1,429	$45.85	$56.51
Nov98	1,164	$35.56	$64.24	Nov00	1,315	$42.95	$58.78
Dec 98	1,229	$37.70	$61.43	Dec 00	1,320	$47.06	$57.19
Jan 99	1,280	$35.97	$59.88	Jan 01	1,366	$41.84	$54.43
Feb 99	1,238	$34.64	$58.57	Feb 01	1,240	$43.75	$49.77
Mar99	1,286	$36.26	$56.42	Mar01	1,160	$41.86	$42.53
Apr 99	1,335	$34.18	$62.56	Apr 01	1,249	$41.59	$43.51
May99	1,302	$32.85	$62.97	May01	1,256	$42.63	$44.64
Jun 99	1,373	$35.94	$57.13	Jun 01	1,224	$42.23	$42.55
Jul 99	1,329	$36.17	$55.80	Jul 01	1,211	$44.55	$42.17
Aug99	1,320	$31.70	$55.11	Aug01	1,134	$44.91	$46.02
Sep 99	1,283	$28.44	$44.59	Sep 01	1,041	$46.48	$44.30
Oct 99	1,363	$32.35	$54.53	Oct 01	1,060	$46.68	$45.27
Nov99	1,389	$32.23	$62.36	Nov01	1,139	$46.61	$44.57
Dec 99	1,469	$32.99	$53.96	Dec 01	1,148	$46.80	$44.75

Exhibit 20.5: *Four Years of Historical Stock Prices.* Original data source: **YAHOO!** FINANCE prices from the last day of each month. They are adjusted for stock splits and dividends. It would have been better to compute a beta from daily stock returns, but there were too many to print them in a table here. For space reasons, S&P 500 quotes were rounded.

The PepsiCo example:
historical beta
estimates.

You could now compute historical rates of return from historical prices to obtain the following table:

Month	Prices			Rates of Return		
	S&P 500	**PEP**	**KO**	$r_{S\&P\ 500}$	r_{PEP}	r_{KO}
30-Jan-98	980.28	$32.86	$58.87	1.015%	−0.3639%	−2.919%
27-Feb-98	1,049.34	$33.20	$62.39	7.045%	1.0347%	5.979%
31-Mar-98	1,101.75	$38.95	$70.56	4.995%	17.3193%	13.095%
...						

(For example, $r = 1,101.75/1,049.34 - 1 \approx 4.995\%$). With these rates of return, you can compute (or trust me with) the relevant historical statistics:

Statistic	$r_{S\&P\ 500}$	r_{PEP}	r_{KO}
Mean	0.49%	1.08%	−0.21%
Variance	27.77%%	67.03%%	84.46%%
Standard Deviation	5.27%	8.19%	9.19%
$\mathcal{C}ov$ with S&P 500	27.77%%	19.30%%	12.76%%
$\mathcal{C}orr$ with S&P 500	100%	45%	26%

These statistics make it easy to calculate the historical equity beta of PepsiCo and Coca-Cola:

$$\beta_{PEP,S\&P\ 500} = \frac{\mathcal{C}ov(r_{PEP}, r_{S\&P\ 500})}{\mathcal{V}ar(r_{S\&P\ 500})} \approx \frac{0.001930}{0.002777} \approx 0.70$$

$$\beta_{KO,S\&P\ 500} = \frac{\mathcal{C}ov(r_{PEP}, r_{S\&P\ 500})}{\mathcal{V}ar(r_{S\&P\ 500})} \approx \frac{0.001276}{0.002777} \approx 0.46$$

(Of course, it would have been better to use a few years of daily stock returns.) What would be your best estimate of PepsiCo's future equity beta?

- You could just adopt PepsiCo's historical equity market beta of 0.7 (assuming you knew the historical return data for PepsiCo).

- You could assume that equity betas should be shrunk toward the average beta in the market, which is $\beta_{M,M} = 1$. In this case, you might want to choose a market beta of $\beta_{PEP,S\&P\ 500} = (0.7 + 1)/2 = 0.85$.

➤ *Beta shrinking, Pg.194.*

- You could compute an industry beta, which might be more reliable than even PepsiCo's own beta. After all, PepsiCo's data can be noisy because it relies on just one historical outcome for this single firm. (Well, you do not have industry information here, so let's skip this option.)

- You could assume that Coca-Cola is similar to PepsiCo, which gives you information about PEP's future market beta, too. You might then choose a market beta of 0.46, or an average between PepsiCo's and Coca-Cola's market betas. This would give you an equity beta estimate of around 0.6.

Let's say you adopt $\beta_{PEP,S\&P\ 500} = 0.7$ as your equity beta. But this is not the beta you need. You want to value PepsiCo's assets, not its equity. About 10% of PepsiCo's total market value was in financial and nonfinancial liabilities, which likely would have had market betas close to zero. Therefore, with an equity beta of 0.7, PepsiCo's asset beta would likely have been lower. Your asset beta estimate would be $\beta_{PEP\ (Firm)} \approx$

Convert the equity beta into the asset beta.

$90\% \cdot \beta_{\text{PEP (Equity)}} + 10\% \cdot \beta_{\text{PEP (Debt)}} \approx 90\% \cdot 0.7 + 10\% \cdot 0 \approx 0.6$. Henceforth, let us assume that your best asset beta estimate for PepsiCo is $\beta_{\text{PEP,S\&P 500}} = 0.6$. (For convenience, we omit subscripting the asset beta differently from the equity beta—the difference for PepsiCo is tiny.)

Estimate the other (economy-wide) CAPM inputs.

To use the CAPM, you also need estimates of the economy-wide risk-free rate and equity premium.

➤ *CAPM inputs, Sect. 9.4, Pg.216.*

The risk-free rate: At the end of 2001, the 5-year Treasury yield was about 4.4%, and the 20-year Treasury yield was about 5.7%, both holding pretty steady throughout 2001. Given that PepsiCo is likely to be around for a while, maybe a 10-year interest rate would be a good choice. You could choose a rate of around 5% per annum, perhaps plus or minus 1-2%.

(Oy vey.)

The equity premium: It is more difficult to settle on an appropriate equity premium. Pretend that the board of PepsiCo and the management team have unanimously declared that 3% per annum is the standardized estimate.

Okay, we now have a cost-of-capital estimate for PepsiCo.

Putting the three inputs (asset beta, risk-free rate, and equity premium) together yields a CAPM cost-of-capital estimate for PepsiCo—the firm (not the equity)—of

$$\text{Asset Cost of Capital:} \quad \mathcal{E}(r_{\text{PEP}}) \approx 5\% + \quad 3\% \quad \cdot \quad 0.6 \quad = 6.8\%$$

$$\mathcal{E}(r_{\text{PEP}}) = r_{\text{F}} + [\mathcal{E}(r_{\text{M}}) - r_{\text{F}}] \cdot \beta_{\text{PEP,S\&P 500}}$$

Let's just round this to 7%—the CAPM is not a model that has any accuracy after the decimal point. Reasonable variations on the estimate for PepsiCo's market beta, for the risk-free rate, and for the equity premium could easily justify other cost-of-capital estimates, say, between about 5% and 10%.

Q 20.12. When would you want to use asset betas, and when would you want to use equity betas?

Q 20.13. What is the most common model used to estimate the cost of capital in pro formas?

Q 20.14. You should always worry about something you have overlooked or that does not fit together. In Section 20.5 on Page 660, for example, PepsiCo's bonds were rated A+ in 2001. Such bonds carried an average interest rate of 7.5%.

1. Would it be better to use 7.5% in the CAPM formula to obtain PepsiCo's cost of capital?

2. Estimate PepsiCo's historical average interest rate. Use the income statement's interest expense and the balance sheet's debt (short-term and long-term). Is such an estimate in line with the prevailing interest rate on A+ bonds?

3. Does it make sense for bonds to have a higher cost of capital than equity? In light of the 7.5% interest rate on A+ bonds, should you change your 7% estimate for PepsiCo's cost of capital?

The Cost of Capital Minus the Growth Rate of Cash Flows

To compute your terminal value estimate with the perpetuity formula, you still need an estimate of the eternal expected growth rate of cash flows, $\mathcal{E}(g)$, or at least of the cost of capital, $\mathcal{E}(r)$, minus this growth rate. It is easy to come up with *high* upper bounds on sustainable growth rates. For example, $\mathcal{E}(g)$ cannot be above the firm's cost of capital, or PepsiCo's value would be infinite. You would also not expect $\mathcal{E}(g)$ to be much above the growth rates of GDP—you would not expect the economy to eventually consist of nothing but PepsiCo. In sum, a number like 5-6% is probably an upper bound on PepsiCo's $\mathcal{E}(g)$. You can also think of *low* lower bounds. Although it is not impossible to imagine PepsiCo fading away, this is unlikely to happen quickly, so you might want to choose an estimated growth rate of no less than, say, –1% per annum. Sometimes, it is more intuitive to think of such changes not in terms of nominal growth rates, but in terms of real growth rates. With an assumption of an inflation rate of 2% per annum, the –1% nominal growth rate would correspond to a real rate of about –3% per annum.

It is easy to come up with a (uselessly) wide range for $\mathcal{E}(g)$.

But you need to do better than these very wide limits. Otherwise, your valuation range would just be too wide to be useful. To improve on your eternal growth rate estimate, you can draw on information from two sources:

It is difficult to come up with a (usefully) narrow range for $\mathcal{E}(g)$. Subjective judgment is needed, yet again.

1. **Internal company information:** For example, you can assume that managers will not drastically overinvest or underinvest forever. This means you should be consistent in your choice of expected cash flows and the expected growth rate of your cash flows. Would you really want to assume that PepsiCo will invest 20% of its value each year forever, but that this investment will grow its cash flows by only 1% forever? Probably not.

   In PepsiCo's case, cash flow from investing activity was $2,637 million in 2001. This was a reinvestment rate of around 3% per annum. Admittedly, this required a peak at PepsiCo's asset market value of $100 billion to compute $2,637/$100,000 \approx 3\%$. But you could have instead used other base rates. For example, you could start with a reasonable growth rate, then use the value estimate that your pro forma produces, then check your reinvestment rate, then reestimate your value, and so on, until you end up with a consistent number. Consequently, a number in the 3% vicinity for $\mathcal{E}(g)$ would make sense.

2. **Industry or comparable firm information:** For example, you can analyze the publicly traded Coca-Cola to better understand PepsiCo. (Coca-Cola's financials are in Exhibits 13.1 (Companion) and 13.2 (Companion).) Coca-Cola's economic cash flows were described on Page ≈91. It had earnings (in millions) of $2,431 in 1999, $2,177 in 2000, and $3,969 in 2001. Its economic cash flows (in millions) were $799, $2,867, and $3,211, respectively—driving home yet again how lumpy cash flows are compared to earnings! Moreover, Coca-Cola was valued throughout 2001 at just about $100 billion.

   ➤ *Coca-Cola's financials and economic cash flows,* *Sect.* App.13.A (Companion), *Pg.* ≈91.

   If you think of Coca-Cola in 2000 or 2001 as comparable to a then-stable PepsiCo as of 2005, you can back out an estimate of $\mathcal{E}(r-g)$ from Coca-Cola's value of about $150 billion. For example,

$$\$150,000 \quad \approx \quad \frac{\$3,211}{\mathcal{E}(r-g)} \quad \Rightarrow \quad \mathcal{E}(r-g) \quad \approx 2.1\%$$

$$\text{Terminal Value}_{2000} \quad \approx \quad \frac{C_{2001}}{\mathcal{E}(r) - \mathcal{E}(g)}$$

➤ *Comparables with earnings versus cash flows, Sect. 14.2, Pg.418.*

This contains a small error: It is the estimate for 2000, not for 2001. However, this error is minor compared to the real problem: If you had computed this just two years earlier, the same calculation would have yielded not 2.1% but 0.8%! Clearly, the lumpiness of cash flows makes backing out eternal growth rates hazardous. This is why many analysts prefer to use the smoother earnings as a stand-in for cash flows, which is exactly analogous to why many analysts do comparables in terms of earnings rather than cash flows. Unfortunately, even Coca-Cola's earnings were lumpy, too. In 2000, they were only $2,177; in 2001, they were $3,969. Thus, alternative estimates for $\mathcal{E}(r-g)$ could be either 1.5% or 2.6%, respectively.

Wow—this is novel! We do not have too bad of a dilemma for PepsiCo with respect to the eternal growth rate.

Nevertheless, most of these estimates are not too different, suggesting that you should settle on an eternal growth rate of around 2-4% per annum. (Such agreement is, unfortunately, quite rare.) Moreover, this is about 1-2% above the inflation rate and roughly in line with generally predicted long-run real growth rates of GDP. This gives us some confidence in our estimates (or, more likely, overconfidence).

Still, you could have used other estimates.

You can now combine the estimate of your eternal growth rate with your estimate for the cost of capital. At an appropriate expected rate of return at 7%, you would expect $\mathcal{E}(r-g) = \mathcal{E}(r) - \mathcal{E}(g) = 7\% - 3\% = 4\%$ per annum. Your cash flow estimate for 2005 was $2,278 million (from Exhibit 20.2). All together, your estimate of the terminal value for all cash flows from 2005 to eternity could be a 2004 value of (according to Exhibit 20.6)

➤ *Direct Valuation, Exhibit 20.2, Pg.651.*

$$\text{Terminal Value}_{2004} \quad \approx \quad \frac{\$2,278}{\mathcal{E}(r) - \mathcal{E}(g)} \quad = \quad \frac{\$2,278}{4\%} \quad = \$56,950$$

$$\text{Terminal Value}_{T-1=2004} \quad \approx \quad \frac{C_{T=2005}}{\mathcal{E}(r) - \mathcal{E}(g)}$$

in millions of dollars, which rounds to about $57 billion. Again, this terminal value represents the 2004 value of all future cash flows that PepsiCo will create from 2005 to eternity—your assumed market value if you had to sell PepsiCo at the end of 2004. You still need to discount this back to 2001, of course. One issue we will not have to confront in PepsiCo's case is that of time-changing costs of capital. In start-up firms, the early discount rate would often be higher than the long-run discount rate (used in the growing perpetuity formula). The reason is that there is more uncertainty and market dependence before the firm reaches its more stable phase, causing a higher cost of capital early on. In contrast, for PepsiCo, the market risk is probably the same in 2001 as it is after 2005, so you can use the same discount rate. Therefore, you can just adopt the same $\mathcal{E}(r)$ for both early and late years. Discount the $57 billion in 2004 back to 2001 at the 7% cost of capital, and you find that PepsiCo's terminal value contributes about $\$57/1.07^3 \approx \$46.5$ billion in present value.

How Bad Are Mistakes?

How Robust Is Your Valuation?

Immediately after you have estimated your terminal value, you should wonder how robust it is. Recall that your cost-of-capital estimate could easily have been 10% instead of 7%, which would have implied $\mathscr{E}(r-g) = 10\% - 3\% = 7\%$ per annum on the high end; or it could have been 5%, which would have implied $\mathscr{E}(r-g) = 5\% - 3\% = 2\%$ or even $5\% - 4\% = 1\%$ per annum on the low end. Would it have made a difference if you had used a different cost of capital or a different eternal growth rate for earnings? Should you worry about it?

Unfortunately, the answer is yes. The uncertainty in your $\mathscr{E}(r-g)$ estimate is not only wide but also has a significant influence on your valuation. (This is often the case in the real world, too.) Table 20.5 shows the influence of your terminal value estimate on your overall present value if you vary the denominator.

			Value of Cash Flows from 2005 to ∞, in billions	
$\mathscr{E}(g)$	$\mathscr{E}(r)$	$\mathscr{E}(r-g)$	Terminal Value in 2004	Present Value in 2001
3%	4%	1%	$2.278/1\% \approx \$228$	$228/1.04^3 \approx \$203$
3%	5%	2%	$2.278/2\% \approx \$114$	$114/1.05^3 \approx \$98$
3%	6%	3%	$2.278/3\% \approx \$76$	$76/1.06^3 \approx \$64$
3%	7%	4%	$2.278/4\% \approx \$57$	$57/1.07^3 \approx \$46$
3%	8%	5%	$2.278/5\% \approx \$46$	$46/1.08^3 \approx \$36$
3%	9%	6%	$2.278/6\% \approx \$38$	$38/1.09^3 \approx \$29$
3%	10%	7%	$2.278/7\% \approx \$33$	$33/1.10^3 \approx \$24$

Thus, for reasonable $\mathscr{E}(r-g)$ estimates from 2% to 6% and $\mathscr{E}(r)$ estimates from 5% to 9%, you get present value estimates between $98 billion and $29 billion. Unfortunately, the discount factor has not worked miracles and plastered over differences in the denominator $\mathscr{E}(r-g)$; the value difference remains large.

You clearly face a problem. Your uncertainty about the difference between the cost of capital and the appropriate eternal growth rate has a big impact on your valuation. What should you do now? In real life, you would probably entertain a range of possible values, do more research, and pick estimates based on the purpose for which you wanted to use the pro forma. If you wanted to sell the company, you would pick a low discount and a high growth rate to make the value appear large. If you wanted to buy the company, you would want to claim a high discount and a low growth rate in your negotiations with the seller. Yes, you would probably choose whatever suits you. It's not all science!

Q 20.15. Are your present value estimates (usually) sensitive to your assumption about the eternal growth rate of earnings or cash flows, assuming that they are used only in the terminal value forecast?

20.6 Some Pro Formas

You now have the ingredients necessary to produce a pro forma with a market value: economic cash flow forecasts, a terminal value based on the cost of capital and the eternal growth rate, and discount factors. Let's put it all together.

An Unbiased Pro Forma

Y_{-1} 2000	Y_0 2001		Y_1 2002	Y_2 2003	Y_3 2004	Y_4 to Y_∞ 2005-
$2,501	$1,556	Projected Annual Asset CF's	$1,712	$1,883	$2,071	($2,278…)

Terminal Mkt Val in 2004 for CF's from 2005 to Eternity at $\mathscr{E}(g) = 3\%$: $\dfrac{\$2,278}{7\% - 3\%}$ $\approx \$57$ billion

		Total Cash Flows:	$1,712	$1,883	$\approx \$59$ billion	
		Discount Factor: $(\mathscr{E}(r) = 7\%)$	$1/1.07^1$	$1/1.07^2$	$1/1.07^3$	
		2001 Present Value of CF's:	$1.6 billion	$1.6 billion	$48 billion	

Total Present Value in 2001 of Asset CF's from 2002 to Eternity: $\boxed{\approx \$50 \text{ billion}}$

Exhibit 20.6: *An Unbiased Pro-Forma Cash Flow Statement, Based on Direct Economic Cash Flow Projections and Assuming Cash Flow Growth of 10% per Year.* This pro forma estimates the total firm value of PepsiCo (i.e., not merely value to shareholders) using the direct cash flow projections from Exhibit 20.2 The terminal value is obtained by assuming a 3% eternal growth rate and a 7% cost of capital. Final numbers are generously rounded to prevent giving the impression that there is much accuracy here. Unless noted as billions, dollar values are in millions.

Here is a first pro forma value estimate for PepsiCo. It is only $50 billion.

▶ *Direct Valuation, Exhibit 20.2, Pg. 651.*

Exhibit 20.6 uses one specific set of assumptions. It starts with the projected asset cash flows from Exhibit 20.2: $1,712, $1,883, $2,071, and $2,278 (million) from 2002 through 2005. Next, we adopt one particular terminal market value estimate based on an eternal cost of capital of 7%, an eternal growth rate of cash flows of 3%, starting from a 2005 base of $2,278 million. According to Table 20.5, this gives a terminal value for cash flows from 2005 to eternity of $57 billion as of 2004. Add to this the 2004 $2.1 billion in cash flows and you get a 2004 value of about $59 billion. Discount all cash flows (beginning in 2002) with a 7% cost of capital, and you find a present value of about $50 billion. Of course, this is not the only estimate that we could have produced. We could have reasonably relied on different forecasts and obtained possibly very different values.

A Calibrated Pro Forma

Now switch your perspective to someone who is analyzing not the hypothetical privately held company but the actual publicly traded PepsiCo. Why would you even want to create a pro forma for a firm for which you already have a public market value? You already know one such scenario—you are considering purchasing shares in PepsiCo and want to learn whether PepsiCo's market value is lower than its underlying fundamental value. But there is another common scenario: You may not just be a passive analyst but an investment banker who wants to suggest a capital structure change. Such a change might not only increase PepsiCo's value, but, more importantly, also generate investment banking fees for you if PepsiCo agrees. The pro forma is the language of proposing corporate capital structure changes.

As an investment banker, you need a pro forma to propose a capital structure change. If PepsiCo is public, then you can incorporate more information about its market value in your pro forma.

Because the firm is public, it is easy to check whether your pro forma value is in line with the actual market value. It turns out that PepsiCo's actual stock market value in 2001 was around $87.4 billion (plus about $3 billion of financial debt and another $10 billion in nonfinancial liabilities), yielding a total asset value of about $100 billion. This suggests that our pro forma value estimate of $50 billion would have been *way too low*. (In Section 20.9, we will look at PepsiCo's subsequent performance to try to find out why.)

Most important, compare our pro forma value and the market value.

➤ *Hindsight analysis of PepsiCo, Sect. 20.9, Pg. 676.*

Naturally, to propose a capital structure change, you will have to present our pro forma to PepsiCo's management. What would happen if you showed them our pro forma statement? PepsiCo's management would likely be so displeased with our low pro forma value estimate that they would not even listen to any of your proposals. Besides, it would also be silly for you to claim that PepsiCo is worth only $50 billion when it is trading for $100 billion.

Modify your pro forma to reflect the public market value information, or you will look silly.

Before you can go in front of management, you must come up with a pro forma with a value estimate that fits the actual market value of PepsiCo. You must find reasons why PepsiCo is worth more than what our original pro forma suggested. You must find reasons to change the inputs to your model. Although this could be called model "fudging," the technical term is model **calibration**.

You need to "calibrate" your model to the current market value. Calibrate = Fudge.

You basically have three tools at your disposal that can increase the pro forma value so that it will reach the market value: Change the cash flows, change the cost of capital, or change the growth rate.

You can tinker with all pro forma input numbers.

1. **Detailed projections:** You can depart from our current projected cash flow path. Our original pro forma relied on the direct-projection cash flows that assumed a growth rate of 10%. If you alter the cash flow growth rate, you get two important effects: You change both the initial-period cash flow projections and the 2005 cash flow projection of $2,278 million, on which your terminal value was based.

Change the growth rate of your cash flow estimates.

You can justify higher cash flows by arguing for higher sales, lower expenses, higher future cash flows, and the like. This can create a faster growth path for directly projected cash flows. For example, your calibrated model can assume that PepsiCo should be valued off of cash flows that grow faster than 10%—say, 15%:

Projected at 15% Growth	Y_0 2001	Y_1 2002	Y_2 2003	Y_3 2004	Y_4 2005
(Economic) Cash Flows	$1,556	$1,789	$2,058	$2,366	$2,721

➤ *Hypothetical Cash Flow Model, Exhibit* 20.4, *Pg.657.*

Try earnings forecasts instead.

Another way to increase value is to work off the detailed financials from Exhibit 20.4 rather than the direct projections, because the former were higher, reaching $2,728 million as early as 2002.

Yet another way is to shift your focus to earnings, either from the detailed financials or from the direct projection. You know that in the very long run, discounted earnings and discounted cash flows should be roughly equal—after all, earnings "just" shift the time-series accruals. You also know that earnings may be more suitable to a growing-perpetuity valuation, because they are less affected by temporary and possibly lumpy investment patterns. Perhaps PepsiCo accelerated its investments from 1999 to 2001, sacrificing immediate cash flows for higher future cash flows. Relying on earnings growing at 3% per annum, you have the following revised figures:

Projected at 3% Growth	Y_0 2001	Y_1 2002	Y_2 2003	Y_3 2004	Y_4 2005
Earnings (not cash flows)	$2,662	$2,742	$2,824	$2,909	$2,996

Or, you can rely on the detailed earnings projections in Exhibit 20.3, which were even higher, reaching $2,828 million as early as 2002.

➤ *Hypothetical Cash Flow Model, Exhibit* 20.3, *Pg.653.*

2. **Cost-of-capital projections:** You can reduce your estimate of PepsiCo's cost of capital from 7% to a lower number. This again has two effects: It makes future cash flows more valuable, and it increases your estimated terminal market value. The first effect is relatively unimportant—you already know that present values over short horizons are reasonably robust to modest changes in the cost of capital. It is the second effect that gives you a lot of valuation "bang for the buck." Referring back to the table on Page 20.5, you can see that reducing the cost of capital by just 1% can give you an extra $20 billion in present value. Reducing the cost of capital by 2% can give you an extra $50 billion in present value.

➤ *In-text Table, Pg.665.*

3. **Eternal earnings growth projections:** You can increase PepsiCo's eternal earnings growth rate estimate $\mathscr{E}(g)$, thereby changing its growth profile. Doing so would assume that PepsiCo has more of the characteristics of a growth firm than a value firm. Increasing the eternal growth rate is just as powerful as reducing the long-term cost of capital, because g and r enter only as a difference in the perpetuity formula.

Voila! With enough fudging, our pro forma value matches the market value.

In the real world, you would probably choose a combination of all three tools. Exhibit 20.7 contains one calibrated version of the PepsiCo pro forma that makes the following adjustments:

1. It increases the initial cash flow growth rate from 10% to 15%.

2. It reduces the cost of capital from 7% to 6%.

3. It increases the eternal growth rate of cash flows from 3% to 3.5%.

Together, these changes push the market value from $50 billion to $100 billion—and you could fudge our assumptions a little more to increase the value further. If you do this, PepsiCo's management will likely be pleased with our calibrated pro forma—it would indicate to them not only that their market value is justified but that even better

Y_0 2001		Y_1 2002	Y_2 2003	Y_3 2004	Y_4 to Y_∞ 2005-
$1,556	Projected Annual	$1,789	$2,058	$2,366	($2,721...)

$$\frac{\$2,721}{6\% - 3.5\%}$$

Terminal Mkt.Val. in 2004 for CF's, 2005-∞ at $\mathcal{E}(g) = 3.5\%$: $\approx \$109$ billion

	Y_1	Y_2	Y_3
Total CF's	$1,789	$2,058	$\approx \$111$ billion
Discount Factor ($\mathcal{E}(r) = 6\%$)	$1/1.06^1$	$1/1.06^2$	$1/1.06^3$
2001 Present Value of CF's	$1.7 billion	$1.8 billion	$93 billion

Total Present Value in 2001 of Asset CF's from 2002 to Eternity: $\boxed{\approx \$100 \text{ billion}}$

Exhibit 20.7: *A Calibrated Pro Forma Assuming Cash Flow Growth of 15% per Year, 3.5% Eternal Growth, and 6% Cost of Capital.* This repeats Exhibit 20.6, but with more aggressive assumptions that are intended to match the actual market value of around $100 billion of PepsiCo in 2000. Unless noted as billions, dollar values are in millions.

times may be ahead. (Of course, to keep them happy, you should not show them our original uncalibrated pro forma.)

What is most important here is that you remain conceptually clear about what you are doing when you are calibrating a pro forma: You are "fudging" input estimates to make the outcome fit a market value. You are adopting a "deus ex machina"—a number that is dropped on you from another part of the stage (the financial markets), even though you may not fully understand it. But don't be appalled: This is not so different from what we have always done. Calibration is the equivalent of conducting a *relative* valuation that accepts known market value as a good baseline. After all, every financial concept in this book is based on valuation relative to known market values—though usually only of comparable companies, not of the same company. Calibration is often a justifiable and reasonable procedure because the financial market value of PepsiCo is likely efficient and probably much better than our own pro forma estimate.

> Be cognizant of what you are doing when you are "calibrating" the inputs!

Finally, how would an investor in 2001, reading your analyst's report, have looked at our unbiased pro forma? He would have done an "intuitive" calibration. Most of his faith would have been in the market value of PepsiCo, not in our pro forma value analysis. He would not have trusted our ability to forecast the economics. However, if we had more knowledge of the underlying sales dynamics, our value analysis might have raised enough doubts in him to believe that PepsiCo might be a little overvalued. After all, any public market value is the clearing price where the bears and bulls on PepsiCo are in equilibrium—and our analysis would have led him to join the bears. But

> How should you look at our private attempt to come up with a pro forma value versus the actual value?

he would have kept it all in proper perspective—he would have found it unreasonable to believe that the pro forma value of $50 billion was the appropriate market price of PepsiCo when he could see that the market value was $100 billion. A reasonable synthesis of the PepsiCo value estimates would instead have concluded a value closer to the market value than to the pro forma value—say, a synthesis of $95 billion.

Q 20.16. What exactly does the technical term "calibration" mean in the context of a pro forma?

Q 20.17. What are your three main calibration tools?

20.7 Sensitivity and Scenario Analyses

Don't trust anyone.

What should you learn from this chapter? Perhaps most importantly, do not trust any single pro forma estimate. And when someone else is handing you a calibrated pro forma, be afraid—be very afraid.

You need sensitivity analysis—try different inputs.

In terms of your own pro formas, you should try to understand how robust your estimates actually are. Such analyses are usually easiest to perform in spreadsheets because they allow you to try out different assumptions and alternative scenarios relatively painlessly.

Fiddling with Individual Items

You want a best value estimate—not the simplest or most complex, easiest or hardest, or even most conceptually beautiful pro forma.

Always keep your ultimate goal in mind—you want to find the best value estimate for your business. Your goal is not an exercise in NPV analysis. It is not beauty or simplicity, either. Although both are nice to have, you cannot neglect important value drivers just because the outcome is messier. Use your imagination, your head, and your good common sense!

You can use ad hoc assumptions if you believe they offer better estimates.

You should always pay attention to other information—and even your personal intuition. For example, in the PepsiCo valuation, our estimated expected cash flow for 2005 was $2,278 million (or $2,996 million if you use earnings). If you had good reason to believe that this was a low estimate, you could adjust ("fudge") it. For example, if you believed that a new drink was going to hit the market and give cash flows a one-time upward value transition of $500 million, then you could use $2,800 million or even $3,500 million. Your estimate does not have to be based on formal, scientific forecasting. Of course, the consumer of your pro forma may not agree with your estimate, so you should be ready to mount a good and credible defense for your number.

You can also use alternative methods to estimate your terminal value.

Similarly, there are no laws that say that you have to use the growing perpetuity formula on cash flows to obtain your terminal market value. Instead of using the assumption that growth will remain eternally the same (say, 3% per year), you could develop another formula that assumes high growth rates for a few years (say, 5% next year), followed by growth-rate declines until the growth rate reaches the inflation rate (say, 2% per year). Or, you might deem it best if you avoided all formulas and instead assumed that you could find a buyer for PepsiCo who will be paying $200 billion in

2005—ultimately, it is this quantity that you seek to model with your terminal value. Again, you'd better be ready to argue why your $200 billion is the best estimate.

Modeling the pro forma as a spreadsheet also allows you to consider specific future scenarios. (Computer spreadsheets were invented precisely to make such analyses relatively easy.) For example, what would happen if the new product were to be wildly successful, or if it were to fall on hard times? What would happen in a recession, based on what has happened in past recessions? What would happen if sales were to decline by 5% next year rather than grow by 3.6% per year? What would happen if sales were to decline for a number of years, not just for one year? How bad would one, or many, inputs have to be for you to regret having bought into the project in the first place? And, of course, you can ask the venerable payback question: How long will it take before you get your money back? Admittedly, with more time, technology, and printing space, you should look at many different modified scenario analyses to understand our PepsiCo pro forma better. A detailed pro forma analysis of even one company, such as PepsiCo, could easily consume a few books all by itself. The sky is the limit. There is no point at which you know you have it perfectly nailed. More likely, at some point, you realize that you are not getting any more precise, so you might as well stop.

> Scenario analysis can help to determine expected (rather than just most likely) cash flows.

Q 20.18. What is the main computer tool for building pro formas?

Do Not Forget Failure

> ➤ *Typical versus expected values,* Sect. 12.2, Pg. 325.

The biggest problem in most pro formas, however, is not even in the details. It is the fact that a pro forma is just one particular scenario, and usually a reasonably optimistic one. Many pro formas model just a "typical" or median outcome (recall Section 12.2). This would not be dissimilar to an average outcome, *but it is conditional on the project not being aborted altogether.*

> The biggest problem: A pro forma is usually one scenario, not an expected value! Overall failure is often not considered.

Obviously, this is more important for entrepreneurial ventures or start-ups than it is for PepsiCo. For example, if someone pitches you a new magazine, most of the time the pro forma will project a mildly optimistic scenario—*on condition that the magazine succeeds.* It probably does not take into account the fact that 50% of all new magazines fold within a year. It is your task as the consumer of the pro forma to determine for yourself the probability of overall magazine failure, or you will end up misled. (Immediate death does not matter for our PepsiCo pro forma. PepsiCo is likely to stay around for a few more years.)

> Entrepreneurial ventures—especially tech ventures—often have almost all value in their terminal value estimates.

Q 20.19. What may be the biggest common mistake in contemplating most pro formas?

Assessing the Quality of a Pro Forma

Can you assess the robustness and quality of our pro forma?

By now, you should have realized that the question "Which PepsiCo pro forma is correct?" is not a good one. *No* pro forma is correct! A better question is, "Which PepsiCo pro forma is better?" This is not an easy question, either. Even if you know the ex-post outcome, you will still never know for sure what the best ex-ante pro forma would have been. Even a lousy pro forma forecast will occasionally beat a good pro forma forecast. (Even a stopped clock is correct twice a day.) It often remains a judgment issue, but there are clearly pro formas that rely on better assumptions, are better reasoned, and are more likely to come true than others. Perhaps the best question is, "How can I judge how good a pro forma is?" Or better, "How can I judge how good *my* pro forma is?" There is no easy answer, either. However, here are some relevant issues that you might contemplate.

An interesting diagnostic: What fraction of the value comes from the final value estimate?

➤ *Direct Pro Forma, Exhibit 20.6, Pg.666*.

➤ *Calibrated Pro Forma, Exhibit 20.7, Pg.669*.

You should definitely contemplate your uncertainty about each input. Often, the most influential source of uncertainty is the long-run value. For PepsiCo, it came into play in our terminal value. An interesting statistic is, therefore, what fraction of the value comes from the terminal value. In Exhibit 20.6, the present value estimate of $50 billion was driven mostly by the $57 billion in terminal value. In Exhibit 20.7, the present value estimate of $100 billion was driven mostly by the $111 billion in terminal value. So most of our PepsiCo pro forma value was buried in our terminal value estimate. To the extent that you do not trust our estimate of the present value embodied in the very-long-run future, you should be particularly careful. Of course, if you had stretched T, more value would have been part of the detailed period rather than in the terminal value—but this would not mean that our forecast would have had more reliability. Consequently, the fraction of terminal value in the overall value is only one interesting statistic. Often, this is just how it is, and there is little you can do about it. The terminal value is commonly large even for established companies. However, for start-up companies, it is often almost all of their values. The typical business plans that venture capitalists see have 80% to 95% of their present value (despite a high discount rate) in this "dark-gray box" called terminal value. Watch out!

Monte Carlo analysis may help, too.

Are there any tools that can help? Even though a spreadsheet is the right tool for presenting and playing with one pro forma at a time, it does not allow you to incorporate your uncertainty in a more systematic way. Your input into each cell of your pro forma spreadsheet should contain not just one number for your best estimate but also a second number that tells you how reliable you deem your best estimate to be. This requires an even more sophisticated method of analysis called **Monte Carlo simulation**. It allows you to associate your uncertainty with each cell in your pro forma spreadsheet. The Monte Carlo procedure then simulates a whole range of possible scenarios (NPV values) and gives you a distribution of outcomes. You can think of it as systematic, automated sensitivity analysis. But this is beyond the scope of a first textbook in finance. (However, Monte Carlo analysis is explained in the advanced web chapter on real options.)

➤ *Monte Carlo analysis, Pg.≈86*.

Q 20.20. If you produce a pro forma for a firm in which 60% of the value sits in the terminal value and one in which 90% of the value sits in the terminal value, which pro forma is more reliable?

20.8 Proposing Capital Structure Change

Return now to the scenario in which you are an investment banker seeking to propose a capital structure change. Equipped with our calibrated pro forma, you can now go in front of PepsiCo's management and present two capital structure scenarios—the current structure and your proposed change. Your exposition will rely on our calibrated pro forma. (It would have to include the full balance sheet and financing section on the cash flow statement, which I omit for space constraints in this textbook.)

Play investment banker to propose a capital structure change.

Let's begin by evaluating PepsiCo's current capital structure and tax liabilities. In 2001, its balance sheet shows that its asset market value of over $100 billion consisted of $87 billion in equity, $354 in short-term debt, $2,651 in long-term debt, and other liabilities and deferred income taxes of $5,372. Its income statement shows that it paid $219 in interest and $1,367 in corporate income taxes. With $4,029 in before-tax earnings, this is a 34% average tax rate.

The current capital structure situation.

➤ PepsiCo's balance sheet, Exhibit 13.1, Pg.372.

With so little financial debt, the only question of real interest (pun intended) is whether it would make sense for PepsiCo to take on more debt. To decide, you must weigh the various capital structure rationales from Chapters 17 and 18—and ask questions such as:

Judge the reasons for, and against, different capital structures.

- How much could PepsiCo save in corporate income taxes if it takes on more debt?

- How likely is PepsiCo to go into financial distress if it borrows more money?

- How important are agency-related free cash flow problems? Would more debt create more efficient operations, and if so, how much value would this add? What would investors infer about PepsiCo if the funds were used to repurchase shares or to finance other operations?

And so on.

In PepsiCo's case, many of these questions are relatively easy. For example, the probability that PepsiCo will experience financial distress if it took on a couple of billion dollars in extra debt is very low. Moody's rated PepsiCo's current debt an A1, Standard & Poor's rated it an A+. To pitch a new debt issue, you would have to inform PepsiCo what you believe its cost of debt would be if it took on more debt. You would probably begin by looking at the credit ratings of other companies. For example, Exhibit 20.8 gives some relevant statistics for firms with different credit ratings, debt ratios, and interest coverages. (These are not great statistics, but they were all I could find. Thus, we shall have to work with the same ratios.) In 2001, PepsiCo had a book value-based long-term debt/assets ratio of $3,005/$21,695 \approx 14\%$, and its EBIT/interest ratio was about 25. Looking at the table, PepsiCo seemed like an outlier—its S&P rating should have been AA, not just A+.

To sell a capital structure change to PepsiCo, you must estimate the cost of debt.

➤ Credit rating categories, Exhibit 6.2, Pg.126.

➤ Warning about BV-Equity, Sect. 13.7, Pg.405.

Exhibit 20.8 suggests that firms with long-term book debt ratios of about 33% and an EBIT/interest ratio of 5-7 still tended to rank as "investment grade," a category that many investment professionals consider an important break. How much more debt could PepsiCo take on and not get too close to the speculative-grade level? PepsiCo had a book value-based debt ratio of 37% on assets of $21,695 million. Its EBIT/interest ratio looked great, though. This suggests that it could take on another $1 billion and remain investment grade. Let's contemplate a debt-for-equity exchange in which PepsiCo issues $1 billion in debt and repurchases $1 billion in equity.

Let's speculate on debt interest rates under alternative capital structures.

		Investment Grade			Speculative Grade		
		AA	A	BBB	BB	B	C
Long-Term Debt / Book Assets	Mean	23%	26%	34%	43%	54%	62%
	Median	20%	26%	33%	42%	52%	56%
	Std. Dev.	15%	16%	16%	20%	26%	56%
	Quartile 1	11%	15%	23%	30%	36%	22%
	Quartile 3	32%	37%	44%	53%	67%	86%
EBIT / Interest	Mean	17	11	7	5	4	1
	Median	14	7	5	3	1	0
	Std. Dev.	15	15	11	14	25	4
	Quartile 1	6	4	3	2	0	-1
	Quartile 3	24	12	8	5	3	1

Exhibit 20.8: *Characteristics of Firms by S&P Bond Ratings, December 2001.* PepsiCo had an equivalent total long-term liabilities-to-assets ratio of ($8,023)/$21,695 ≈ 37%, and an equivalent operating income over interest ratio of $4,021/$219 ≈ 18. Assets are book value based. For an old firm such as PepsiCo, this book value method usually understates the true value of assets—often quite dramatically.

Here is a good estimate of our interest cost of capital.

With about $1 billion additional debt, and even if PepsiCo had to pay an 8% interest rate, it would still likely remain BBB rated. A quick look at prevailing interest rates on financial websites further reveals that AAA bonds promised to pay about 7% and BB bonds about 7.95% on average. Consequently, a PepsiCo with $3.5 billion in debt may have to promise an interest rate of about 7.7% (which seems high relative to our cost of capital, but this is a promised rate, not an expected rate). Of course, in order to convince PepsiCo, you should spend many more hours researching a good interest rate estimate for PepsiCo's new debt.

The point of releveraging is to produce long-term and short-term tax savings. Here is how big the savings could be.

You should advise management to weigh the potential benefits of more debt against these (and potentially other) costs of debt. What would the benefit of more debt be on PepsiCo's value? Fortunately, you even have formulas to help you assess the tax savings. For each extra dollar in debt rather than in equity financing *forever*, the corporate income tax avoided would be equivalent to a present value of $\tau \cdot$ Debt, or about 34% · $1billion ≈ $340 million. Computed in detail, with an interest rate of 7.7% on $1 billion of new debt, PepsiCo's interest payments would increase by $77 million. At its $\tau = 34\%$ tax rate, this would create a net present value of tax not paid to Uncle Sam of about $26 million in the first year alone—about 0.65% of net income. If PepsiCo maintained the $1 billion of extra debt in perpetuity, the present value of these tax savings would come to about $340 million—not bad for a day's work.

► *Tax savings rule, Sect. 17.6, Pg. 543.*

It is more difficult to judge the operational savings that more debt could bring. For example, PepsiCo's unions might see a seemingly less-profitable company (lower earnings), which might make them more willing to accept lower wages. Management might work harder, too—perhaps even cut a few corporate airplanes. In deciding whether it would make sense value-wise to relever, you would add these tax savings to any efficiency gains from debt and subtract any deadweight losses.

Other efficiency-related savings.

Another cost of a debt-for-equity exchange is that if the firm is overvalued, management should issue and not repurchase shares. After all, overvalued shares allow you to raise capital at very low expected rates of return. But to take advantage of the tax savings, the money would need to be returned to shareholders—or else PepsiCo would merely earn more taxable net income. It is not clear whether a share repurchase (or dividend payment) would truly be in the interest of existing shareholders. If you were the owner and manager, and you believed the firm was overvalued and underlevered, the right behavior would be clear: You should have the corporation borrow money and use it to repurchase your personal shares. But management may not want to do this. They have another conflict of interest—why would they want to help existing shareholders and then be saddled with shareholders who purchase the newly issued shares but will be unhappy later when the share price returns to its fundamental value?

You can return the cash to shareholders either as dividends or in a repurchase. This makes sense primarily if you do not believe that shares are already overvalued.

➤ *Optimal capital structure if overvalued, Sect. 11.6, Pg.312.*

This brings up your real problem. As a junior investment banker looking to create value for PepsiCo shareholders, how could you convince PepsiCo's management that more debt is good for *management* itself? Would it be enough to tell management that if they raised $1 billion in debt to repurchase $1 billion in equity, they would probably create an instant corporate value increase of, say, around $300 million—more than just one year's $26 million savings but less than the $340 million perpetuity income tax savings?

Will the management be convinced if all you argue about is "shareholder value"?

Unfortunately, this is unlikely to sway management. First, on an equity value of $87 billion, even $300 million in more value is only about 0.3% of PepsiCo's stock market value. (Later, you will find out not only that PepsiCo maintained its capital structure but also continued to incur tax obligations of around $1.4 billion every year.) Second, with more debt and less equity, management would have less ability to take over other companies, start new projects, purchase corporate airplanes, or build corporate empires. (They would probably explain it differently, though—something like: "More equity is good for PepsiCo, because it gives it the flexibility to take advantage of new opportunities. And it is good to have higher credit ratings.") In thinking about how to pitch to PepsiCo's management, you would have to ask yourself—what's in it for them?

Unfortunately, probably not. Management has its own interests.

➤ *Unmitigated agency conflicts and capital structure, Sect. 18.3, Pg.581.*

Clearly, as an investment banker hungry for business, you would have an uphill struggle on your hands, even though a debt-for-equity issue would just as clearly create shareholder value. Any productive answer for you would most likely have to lie in the compensation package of management. Managers tend to get higher compensation when they run larger firms. Consequently, you might want to identify other potential candidate firms that PepsiCo could take over—not only would this create issuing fees for debt necessary to finance the takeover, but it would also create additional M&A advisory fees! (And you may even find acquisitions that would create value for the acquirer, too!) In sum, your best shot may be to convince PepsiCo to take over another company and lever up in the process.

A common solution—suggest a merger that requires levering up!

Or, play the M&M
game: Take over the
firm, relever it,
capture the gain, and
resell it.

Your final alternative is less workable: You could try to convince a third party to take over PepsiCo and relever. Unfortunately, this is not very attractive in this case, because PepsiCo may already have been overvalued by the market, if you believe our original pro forma.

Q 20.21. Can capital structure issues affect the numbers in your pro forma?

Q 20.22. How can you estimate the required stated cost of capital on debt if you were to change the firm's leverage ratio?

20.9 Our Pro Forma in Hindsight

We analyzed PepsiCo
from a few years ago.
Thus, we can use
hindsight to do an
autopsy!

Let's now switch perspectives again. This time, you will get to look at your preceding analysis as an analyst. As a manager, it is always a good idea to look back and study your earlier analysis after the future has played out—how you ended up being right, wrong, or just plain lucky or unlucky. If you do not learn from your own past, you are destined to repeat your mistakes. With hindsight, why was this actual market value so much higher than our original unbiased pro forma estimate? Were the financial markets too optimistic, or were we too pessimistic?

You can learn from an
autopsy, but you can
never know for sure
what the best ex-ante
estimates would have
been, even with
perfect hindsight.

Before we delve into what happened to PepsiCo from 2002 to 2005, you should realize that the actual realized ex-post performance would not necessarily have been the best ex-ante forecast. The outcome contains subsequent and possibly unexpected developments. For example, if you had believed defense contractors to be poor investments in 2000, it might have been the right forecast, but the events of, and following, September 11, 2001 would have proven you wrong. (Knowing that you were right may, however, have been of little consolation if your bet had lost you a lot of money.) Nevertheless, on average, the best forecast is more likely to be borne out by the events of the future. Analyzing one realization of the subsequent events does not give you a perfect assessment of what you should have predicted—but it is informative. In our case, PepsiCo's actual 2002-2005 performance may indicate why the financial markets in 2001 were more optimistic than our pro forma was. An autopsy can therefore give you a guess—but not a perfect explanation—as to where our forecast went wrong.

Here is what you learn:
We may have been
pessimistic because
PepsiCo's actual
growth was faster
than our predicted
growth.

Our pro forma forecast would have been too low if our initial-period forecasts were too pessimistic. Unfortunately, there is a minor nuisance: You cannot directly compare the historical numbers to future numbers. PepsiCo sold its Quaker Foods division and two international Frito-Lay divisions, and made other accounting changes that affected the reporting of sales and COGS. This means that PepsiCo even revised its historical numbers for 2000 and 2001. Instead of looking at realized levels, you will therefore have to look at year-to-year changes. Exhibit 20.9, then, shows our predictions were generally too low.

Net sales: PepsiCo's sales actually increased from 2001 to 2002 by about $1,600 million. This is much more than the projected $971 million sales growth (from $26,935 million to $27,906 million) in our detailed pro forma forecast from Exhibit 20.1. Sales also grew generally faster than predicted in subsequent years.

► *Pro Forma Problem,
Exhibit* 20.1, *Pg.645.*

	Known			Actual or Estimated		
	1999	**2000**	**2001**	**2002**	**2003**	**2004**
Known Historical Sales	$25,093	$25,479	$26,935			
Sales, Direct Projection (Exhibit 20.3)				$27,906		
Change Therein				**+$971**		
Actual Sales, *Revised*		$22,337	$23,512	$25,112	$26,971	$29,261
Change Therein				**+$1,600**	**+$1,859**	**+$2,290**
Actual Economic Cash Flow	$1,641	$2,501	$1,556	$4,242	$2,169	$2,817
Projected, Direct (Exhibits 20.2 and 20.6)				$1,712	$1,883	$2,071
Projected, Detailed (Exhibit 20.4)				$2,728		
Actual Net Income	$2,505	$2,543	$2,662	$3,000	$3,568	$4,212
Projected, Direct (Exhibit 20.2)				$2,742	$2,824	$2,909
Projected, Detailed (Exhibit 20.3)				$2,828		

Exhibit 20.9: *Actual (Hindsight) versus Forecast Estimates of Sales, Cash Flows, and Earnings for PepsiCo (in millions).* The 2002 detailed projected cash flow of $2,728 omits interest paid and is therefore a little too low. Forecasts are in blue.

Cash flows: PepsiCo confirms what you already knew—cash flows are too lumpy to be well suited to direct projections. Selling off its subsidiaries, PepsiCo produced a one-time cash windfall. Added to ordinary cash flows, PepsiCo had over $4.2 billion in 2002, again much higher than our predicted $1.7 billion or $2.7 billion. However, in 2003, PepsiCo invested more than usual, and its cash flows dropped back to just above $2 billion. Still, our forecasts were generally too low.

Earnings: The PepsiCo earnings grew more smoothly than cash flows—but again much faster than what we had projected. By 2004, actual earnings were almost 50% higher than our direct forecast.

No wonder that our pro forma value estimate was too pessimistic: Almost all of PepsiCo's higher profits and earnings came from sales increases that were much higher than what we predicted. Our method of mechanistic projection models from past financial data is rarely very accurate, and the PepsiCo case was no exception. Unless we had known the business and market well enough to forecast sales this high, we would have stood no chance estimating the value as well as the financial market forecast it!

You can also autopsy the pro forma estimate of $\mathcal{E}(r-g)$. As of mid-2005, PepsiCo had an asset market cap of $100 billion ($87 billion in equity) on earnings of $4.3 billion, plus another $300 million in interest payments. Consequently, in mid 2005, it was capitalized at about $\mathcal{E}(r-g) = \mathcal{E}(CF)/PV = \$4.6/\$100 = 4.6\%$—in line with

Our cost-of-capital estimate was also too low, but our cost of capital minus the growth estimate looks okay.

our own forecasts. Next, autopsy the forecast for $\mathcal{E}(r)$, again as of 2005. PepsiCo had a lower beta of only about 0.35—closer to the optimistic historical 0.7 beta than the pessimistic, shrunk beta of 0.85. Interest rates also turned out to have remained low, so the 2005 cost-of-capital estimate might be

$$\mathcal{E}(r) = 5\% + 3\% \cdot 0.35 \approx 6\%$$

PepsiCo should have been an "easy" pro forma—and we were still off by a factor of two.

which is lower than our unbiased 7% cost-of-capital estimate. Together with the $\mathcal{E}(r-g) = 4.6\%$, this implies that PepsiCo is capitalized as if its earnings were to grow only by about 1.4% per year—not a very optimistic valuation, and indeed even lower than both the 2005 rate of inflation and the estimate in our unbiased pro forma. So, we did not do too badly on our $\mathcal{E}(r-g)$ forecast.

In sum, hindsight shows that the primary driver of PepsiCo's higher value was its higher sales from 2002 to 2005. Let this be a lesson in humility: Even for a large and established company with a solid history, valuation is difficult and suffers from plenty of uncertainties—though economic knowledge could have done much to improve our estimates. And for start-up projects, even more of the value is uncertain and lies far off in the future. Don't find the uncertainties too discouraging. Just as the CAPM is the premier model for the cost of capital, the pro forma is the premier model for writing business plans—*simply, there is no better alternative*. Forecasting the future is the tough job that economic value is all about. Fortunately, you do not even need to be able to forecast *well*. All that matters is that you can forecast *better* than the rest of us. If you can, you will become rich.

Q 20.23. Where did our forecast of PepsiCo's value go wrong?

20.10 Caution—The Emperor's New Clothes

Do not instinctively trust pro formas! They can look very professional, and still be utterly not credible.

➤ *Income Model, Exhibit* 20.3, *Pg.* 653.

➤ *Cash Flow Model, Exhibit* 20.4, *Pg.* 657.

Do not lose the forest and discuss only mini-details.

Did our projections seem arbitrary to you? They should have, because they *were* arbitrary—and this chapter made a point of telling you so throughout. But look back at our financial projections in Exhibits 20.3 and 20.4. If you did not round, but quoted a few more digits (for pseudo-accuracy), if you expanded the footnotes with some more mumbo jumbo, and if you added a few more columns of future years, a naïve reader might be fooled into thinking that you were a sophisticated analyst who knew what you were doing! A well-written pro forma can easily convey an image of professional knowledge even where there is none. (Form over content may work here!) It is important that you do not end up being such a naïve consumer of pro formas. In the case of pro formas, even the best emperor only wears a bathing suit.

Another danger for the unwary pro forma reader is falling into the trap of looking at the trees rather than the forest. You can easily get involved in endless discussions of a particular projected item in someone else's pro forma. In real life, most pro formas rely on plenty of heroic assumptions—in some cases, there are just one or two critical assumptions; in other cases, there may be many. You must look at the big picture as well as at the minor assumptions. There is devil in both the details and in the sum total.

I hope I have not been sounding dismissive of pro formas. On the contrary—again, you have *no* alternative. Forecasting the future is inherently a difficult, but important, task. The universal use of heroic assumptions does not mean that there is no difference between a good and a bad pro forma. You can distinguish a good one from a bad one. *On average*, if you do, you will come out ahead. A good pro forma pitched to a sophisticated audience must use solid economics and have detailed footnotes explaining and justifying just about every important line item. It is a starting point for a good discussion, not an end in itself.

With all the problems, a pro forma may still be the best tool you have at your disposal.

Ultimately, finance is about value, so it must revolve around projections, and pro formas are good tools to organize projections. Projecting is very hard. Remember how the book started? I told you then that valuation is both an art and a science. The formulas are easy; the application is hard. I trust that you believe me now. Welcome to the club of financiers!

Closing the circle—valuation is more art than science.

Q 20.24. How trustworthy are business pro formas?

Summary

This chapter covered the following major points:

- The purpose of pro formas is to project financials, which are then often used to compute a project's NPV today. You can also use pro formas to perform a ratio analysis to test the financial soundness of a business plan or to analyze a project's working capital requirement.

- Pro formas are usually split into a detailed forecast period and a terminal value.

- A good horizon choice for the detailed forecast period depends on the prevailing discount rate and the economics of the business. The detailed projection period is often applied to the initial strong-growth period, while the terminal value is often applied to the stable no-more-growth phase.

- A quick-and-dirty pro forma analysis may just project the line items of direct use. A more complete and detailed pro forma analysis can try to project many intermediate components.

- A useful distinction is to think of fixed versus sales-variable forecasts for individual components.

- Scenario analysis helps you to better understand the uncertainty in your pro forma.

- Calibration is the deliberate manipulation of inputs to meet the observed valuation in the financial markets.

- Pro formas are often idiosyncratic and not very reliable. But you have no better alternative. Use caution in constructing and interpreting pro formas.

Preview of the Chapter Appendix in the Companion

In the Appendix   The appendix to this chapter decomposes financial statement variables in historical firm data into fixed and variable cost components. These formulas can help in a pinch, although their use is not to be regarded as a particularly good idea.

Keywords

Calibration, 667.   Economic rent, 646.   Monte Carlo simulation, 672.   Pro forma, 642.   Terminal value, 644.

Answers

Q 20.1 A full pro forma analysis forces you to think more about the economics of your business, and about issues such as working capital and cash management.

Q 20.2 Entrepreneurs are inside analysts. They are often primarily interested in working capital management and secondarily in a present value analysis.

Q 20.3 The three components that you need to work out are your choice of horizon, your detailed financial projections, and your terminal market value estimate.

Q 20.4 The growth rate of earnings or cash flows is probably easier to predict in twenty years, when it is likely to be "normal." It is in the start-up phase (i.e., in two years) that most new businesses have unusual uncertainty. (Of course, if the business were to go bankrupt, your growth rate projection in twenty years is as good as any other—multiplying zero by your number will still give zero.)

Q 20.5 You would choose a longer detailed projection horizon if your growth phase is longer before you get to a stable business phase. You would also choose a longer horizon if your discount rate is smaller.

Q 20.6 The intermediate projections are still very important, because your terminal projection is based off of the intermediate projections.

Q 20.7 It is usually better to forecast earnings than cash flows, because earnings are smoother.

Q 20.8 The "base forecast" for pro formas is usually sales. It will in turn influence COGS, SG&A, and so on.

Q 20.9 Economies of scale manifest themselves in a coefficient that is not one to one with sales. For costs, (e.g., COGS) this means a smaller coefficient; for gains (e.g., earnings), this means a larger coefficient.

Q 20.10 Yes, the income statement and cash flow statement are linked. The latter even begins with net income. In addition, there can also be many other relevant linkages that you would expect a reasonable model for the firm to satisfy. For example, bill collection technologies could influence both cash management and earnings.

Q 20.11 Yes, ratio analysis does make sense—indeed, it may make *more* sense in a pro forma context than it does in a historical one.

Q 20.12 You would want to use asset betas if you are trying to determine the value of the firm. You would want to use equity betas if you are trying to determine the value of the equity. In turn, this depends on whether you care about (buying) the firm or the equity. For discounting the equity cash flows, use a cost of capital based on the equity beta; for discounting the asset cash flows, use one based on the asset beta.

Q 20.13 The most common model to estimate the cost of capital in pro formas is the CAPM.

Q 20.14   1. No, it would not be better to use PepsiCo's rate of 7.5% as the CAPM risk-free rate. The CAPM requires the risk-free rate, not PepsiCo's expected interest rate (and definitely not its promised interest rate, either).

2. PepsiCo had an interest expense of $219 in 2001 on balance sheet short-term borrowings of $354 and long-term debt of $2,651. This interest/debt ratio suggests a nominal interest rate of $219/($354 + $2,651) ≈ 7.3%. However. you do not know whether some of the interest expense went to pay for other liabilities, when PepsiCo contracted its debt, or what the interest rate would be if it could refinance in 2001. This rate is indeed reasonably in line with the 7.5% typical for A+ rated bonds.

3. Yes, it makes sense. Realize that PepsiCo's asset cost of capital also includes liabilities that are interest free (such as taxes

payable). More importantly, the 7.5% A+ bond yield is based on promised rates of return, not on expected rates of return. It contains a default premium, as well as a risk premium and a liquidity premium. So, 7% is not necessarily crazy as an overall cost of capital, but it definitely appears to be on the low side.

Q 20.15 Yes, unfortunately, present value estimates (usually) remain sensitive to the assumption about the eternal growth rate of earnings or cash flows.

Q 20.16 Calibration occurs in the context of publicly traded corporations. It means that you are changing your estimates to obtain a value that is in line with the actual observed market value.

Q 20.17 Your three main calibration tools are to change your three inputs of the pro forma analysis: the cash flow forecasts in the initial period (themselves based on sales and other items), the cost of capital, and the eternal growth rate.

Q 20.18 A computer spreadsheet is the main tool to help you build pro formas. If you are very sophisticated, you might consider a Monte Carlo simulator, too (explained in Section 20.7).

Q 20.19 The biggest common mistake in contemplating pro formas may be forgetting about the probability of total failure and business shutdown.

Q 20.20 You cannot infer from the percentage of the value that sits in the terminal value which of the two pro formas is more reliable! For instance, you can put more or less into the terminal value by stretching the number of years in the initial projection phase, but this does not mean that you have fed more information into your forecast.

Q 20.21 Yes, capital structure can influence the numbers in your pro forma. You need to take your capital structure into account when projecting the pro forma inputs, because the world is not a perfect M&M world. Therefore, your choice of capital structure affects your project's present value, most directly (but not only) through your corporate income taxes.

Q 20.22 You can estimate the required stated cost of capital on debt by relating variables such as interest coverage ratios to the firm's credit ratings, which in turn would give you a good estimate of the required interest rate.

Q 20.23 Our forecast of PepsiCo's value went wrong primarily in our sales forecasts that were not optimistic enough.

Q 20.24 Usually, pro formas are not very trustworthy. They may look professional, but no one has a true crystal ball for complex businesses.

End of Chapter Problems

Q 20.25. Are internal or external pro formas usually more accurate?

Q 20.26. What are common and reasonable detailed projection period horizons?

Q 20.27. What are the problems with a simple projection of historical sales growth rates?

Q 20.28. Look over a general income statement and balance sheet. Make a good guess and justify which financial statement items are likely to increase more than one to one with sales, which are likely to increase less than one to one with sales, and which are likely to move one to one with sales?

Q 20.29. What specific methods can you use to forecast individual financial statement items, such as SG&A? Discuss.

Q 20.30. In a detailed projection, does it make sense to project the cash flow statement before you project the income statement?

Q 20.31. How can you obtain a discount rate for use in your financial analysis?

Q 20.32. Can you compute the market beta of PepsiCo prevailing in early 2002 based on three years of daily stock returns? (You can download the data from YAHOO! FINANCE.) Would your beta estimate be different from the 0.70?

Q 20.33. If your course covered this: What would be the alternative to using the CAPM for determining the appropriate cost of capital? Look back at the appendix of Chapter 9. Can you compute the cost of capital with this alternative, following the recipe?

Q 20.34. When would you want to calibrate your pro forma model to available market data? Do you believe most pro formas are calibrated, whether they state it or not? Is caution advisable?

Q 20.35. When would you want to use only one of your three calibration tools? When would you want to use all three?

Q 20.36. Can agency problems affect the numbers in your pro formas?

Q 20.37. When would you believe pro formas in real life to be objective, and when would you believe them to be tailored to what the audience wants to hear?

Q 20.38. Come up with a pro forma for a company assigned by your instructor. (This makes a good final project for a corporate finance course.)

Q 20.39. Pick any publicly traded corporation today. Have yourself and a number of your friends work out three types of pro formas: one if you are a bidder for the corporation, one if you are the owner of the corporation, and an unbiased one. Compare the results. (Note: Often, the average value estimate is a good estimate. Who came closest?)

Back Matter

Congratulations! You have completed your first course in corporate finance. If you did your work, you should be well equipped to enter the real world now.

What's left?

- An epilog that muses about what you should expect from your business school education.
- A technical-background appendix.
- An index.

Epilogue

Afterthoughts and Opinions

You have traveled a long distance with me through this book. We have now reached the epilogue, where, by tradition, I am allowed to voice my own personal opinions—in effect, to pontificate. I want to leave you with some of my thoughts on finance theory versus practice, business and finance education, business school rankings, finance research, and what I hope you will take with you after having read this book.

Theory or Practice?

By nature, academic finance is very closely related to its practice. Quoting the famous sociologist Lewin,

There is nothing more practical than a good theory.

Finance theory and practice are ruled by the same ideas. As an academic myself, I am proud to claim that the majority of financial management ideas were either invented or developed in academia first *before* they crossed over into practice.

Academic Research—an Academic Question?

But finance research is not just for aspiring academics: Management consultants and economics consultants are basically researchers. Firms like McKinsey, Booze-Allen, or Boston Consulting Group (BCG) may have different audiences, production speeds, team systems, and publication and evaluation processes, but they research the same issues that academics do and with the same methods. Similarly, many proprietary trading and asset-management firms are really best characterized as "academic research departments in disguise." There is also much cross-fertilization: Many professors work regularly with major consulting or asset-investment firms—and some have even quit academia altogether to quadruple their pay. (If you want to become a management consultant or investment manager, my advice to you would be to try to work for a professor as a research assistant, paid or unpaid. Chances are you will learn as much or more from working on a research project as you have learned in your classes.)

Because finance is by nature such an applied discipline, after reading this book, you should not need anything else to understand finance research today. In an ideal world, you should be able to read the current state-of-the-art research right now. Unfortunately, there is one little problem: Academic finance journals love intimidating jargon. (They also prefer algebra to our numerical examples as the means for expressing ideas.) Thus, you may need some extra training in "language" if you want to read original-source academic papers. Nevertheless, if you were to decide to learn just a little bit more jargon, you would probably have the background to understand the most cutting-edge and interesting research ideas in finance journals today. Let me point you to some good initial sources to browse: Start with top academic journals (such as the *Journal of Finance*), top practitioners' journals (such as the *Financial Analysts Journal*), or good working-papers sites (such as www.SSRN.com). References in their articles can in turn direct you to other good journals and resources.

How Much Can We Really Know?

So, do we really understand finance? Certainly not fully. I have stated several times throughout the book that finance is as much an art as it is a science. All three parts of finance—valuation, investments, and financing—have simple conceptual underpinnings, but their applications in real life are difficult. And for all three of them, there is no alternative: Finding the proper value, the proper portfolio, and the proper capital structure may be tough, but this is what finance is all about.

Given our deficiencies—given that all our methods have their errors—what should you do? My best advice for you is to use common sense, to employ a number of different techniques to come up with a range of possible answers, and to then make a judgment at the end of the day as to what estimate appears most reasonable in light of different models. As I have noted many times, finance is art based on science.

If we research finance long enough, will we ever fully understand it? The answer is again no. It is the nature of the beast. Most financial economics is a social science. When there are no arbitrage conditions, then behavior and prices can and will deviate from the theory. On occasion, this leads some to conclude that finance is less worthy of study or even a lesser science than, say, physics. This is a mistake. Here is why:

- The questions are different. Finance is not interested in the Big Bang, and physics is not interested in the behavior of CFOs or investors. The study of one is not necessarily more or less worthy than the study of the other. We just have to bring the best tools to each question we want to study.

- Moreover, the perception that there is always more science and accuracy in physics is a misunderstanding, too: Some questions permit more precise answers than others. In physics, some systems (e.g., the weather or earthquakes) are by nature chaotic and difficult to predict, while others (e.g., Newtonian mechanics or planetary orbits) are more exact. It is the same in finance: Some questions are difficult to answer (e.g., the appropriate equilibrium rate of return on a stock), while others are relatively precise (e.g., option and fixed-income pricing).

- Economics and finance ask many questions to which the answers are more difficult and complex than those often pondered in mathematics and physics. For example, economic agents can react to economic forecasts, which makes predicting the stock market even harder than predicting the weather. Imagine how much more difficult it would be for meteorologists to forecast if the weather could read its own forecast and then change its behavior *because* it read the weather forecast!

- Physics and finance even share another property: Real-world constraints may prevent us from doing certain research. In physics, particle colliders have become so expensive that physicists can no longer study certain particles. In finance, our financial institutions have come to consider their data to be their proprietary competitive advantage. They also fear the legal liability that public disclosure and study could bring—and given the litigiousness of U.S. society, justly so. Sadly, as in physics, many interesting questions in finance may therefore no longer be researchable or answerable.

The fact that we do not have all the answers is both good news and bad news. The bad news is that we will never fully understand financial markets and individuals. The good news is that our knowledge will continue to improve and that there is plenty of space for new and exciting research in finance. For me, this means finance is still intellectually challenging enough to remain "fun." For you, if you go into practice, this means there is enough art involved so that computers will only help but never replace you.

Other Points

Before I end my monologue on research, let me mention that I have written about a number of other related issues, posted on my own website at www.ivo-welch.info:

- I wrote a description of what I think our profession has accomplished over the last few decades and what challenges lie ahead.

- I described alternative finance degree choices, such as undergraduate finance education or master's degrees. You could even consider getting a Ph.D. It is not as monastic as you may think—in fact, the starting salary for many finance professors is now around $200,000 per year. (However, because it takes more than 5 years on average to get a finance PhD, it is still not an NPV-maximizing choice.) I also explained how you should think of academic departments if you want to pursue a PhD program in financial economics.

- I explained why being a finance professor is a 60-hour-per-week job—the 20 hours of teaching that you see consumes only one-third of the time of a full-time finance professor, and the classroom time is only a fraction thereof, similar to the amount of time a lawyer would spend in a court room. The other two-thirds are consumed in roughly equal parts by research (to come up with the ideas that make it into books like mine), service to the university (to run the school), and service to the academic profession at large (to help weed out good ideas from bad ideas). Of course, part-time professors often have the luxury of focusing only on the teaching part.

  (My colleague, Bhagwan Chowdhry, has written an excellent piece about what it takes to publish an academic paper in the Huffington Post: huff.to/ocresc .)

Thoughts on Business and Finance Education

Let me move on to some thoughts about how we teach. I began teaching in 1989. Since then, I believe the gap between faculty and MBA students has slowly but steadily grown. First, I must admit that we faculty are at least partly to blame. We are often guilty in not selling our ideas to our students. Sometimes, we think that our ideas are too difficult to communicate, or we have simply not yet worked them out well enough for ourselves. Of course, the dense curriculum rarely leaves us much time to talk about current academic research in the classroom, too.

But allowing this to happen has been a mistake. After all, excitement about new knowledge and research is exactly what has drawn us academics to business schools rather than to practice—with the opportunity to convey our ideas to our students and to the world at large. If we do not incorporate our current academic research into the curriculum, too, then we should not be surprised if our students sometimes wonder about its value. *As a profession, we need to do better.*

I am as guilty of this as others. However, I have tried to take some steps in the right direction. In addition to sneaking in many novel ideas into this book, I have tried to find the time to give a special final lecture in my own classes: I pick five current working papers from my department and talk about the questions they address and the answers they provide. Every time, even those students who were dead bored of me in my other lectures woke up and started asking questions, often coming up with interesting and different interpretations themselves. This last class session has always been the most fun both for myself and for my students. Maybe you can suggest such a class session to your instructor.

Vocational Training?

Over the years, the common lack of exposure to (and thus appreciation for) research has made some students wonder what their education is all about. One view holds that business schools exist primarily to enhance job opportunities, and as such, they should provide a "vocational education." In this model, teachers ideally share plenty of war stories, vouch for the importance of their own teaching in their past business environments, and may even help some students to get jobs with their own or their friends' businesses. This model—teaching job-specific skills—is one that works for many community colleges. It is not a model that can work for a good business school. A good business school is a center of thought and research. If you expect primarily vocational training from your business school, your finance education will be a rather unrewarding experience.

Good business schools should provide a predominantly intellectual experience. Such an experience allows students to take a fresh look at the world, to explore other business areas for the first time, to learn how to think in economic and business terms, to consider the intellectual foundations of business, and to learn about the most novel ideas—those that have not yet permeated practice. Yes, real-world CFOs have a lot of knowledge and great skill that neither finance professors nor you possess. But do you really want to learn *only* what current CFOs know *today*? Chances are that many of their practices are based on what they learned in their own education *20 to 30 years ago*. Here is an example that should make this clear. In October 2003, the UK's City & Guilds Institution released its study of 405 random financial directors. One in seven needed help switching his or her computer on and off. One in five struggled to save a document. More than one in five needed assistance in printing. And a quarter could not understand spreadsheets—invented almost 25 years earlier for the purpose of financial analysis. You should not aspire to learn just what CFOs do know—instead, you should aspire to learn also what they do not know!

So what should business schools teach you? In my opinion, the answer is that we need to focus on subjects that we can teach better than practitioners can. If we do it right, you have to be patient: You should not receive much job-specific training from us. You should realize that this is not a problem. If you get a job in Goldman's fixed-income department, Goldman will explain in its own training program the specialized fixed-income and institutional knowledge that it will require. If you get a marketing job at Pfizer, its orientation program (and your partnered salespeople) will show you how to "market" Lipitor. I am not belittling sales. Selling products (or ideas) is a skill of first-order importance. However, even if we could teach such subjects in business schools, firms can simply teach them better and faster than we can. It's not what we in business schools do best. Rather, our job must be to provide businesses with students who are smart, flexible, open-minded, and suitably critical, with a solid understanding of fundamental ideas—of forests, not of trees. Table 1 is my perspective on who does what better. In closing, please do not expect to learn *everything* you need for success only from practice or only from school. If you do, you will be disappointed.

But, but, but. . . What about Finding a Job?

Naturally, like most students, you probably feel a great deal of anxiety about your first job prospects. Should you select your classes based on how "practical" you think they are? Is this not the "practical knowledge" that your recruiters expect?

Actually, the answer is mostly no. In my experience, recruiters are rarely looking for specific business practice knowledge. Employers first and foremost want to hire smart, curious, and enthusiastic individuals who are solid on the basic concepts *and who can think of how to apply them to new situations*. To quote Hannibal Lecter, what matters is, "First principles. Simplicity. Read Marcus Aurelius. Of each particular thing ask: What is it in itself? What is its nature?" If you can take a business scenario and simplify it—analyze it in the context of the theories that you have learned—you will do well. This process is really very similar to what this book has been trying to teach. I did not write my book as training for an interview—it is just that the skills that I consider to be important are also the skills that are important in the interview process. On the flip side, if you try to skip the basics in favor of more "applied classes," my guess is that you will fail your interviews.

Your value, as an MBA graduate—even to your first employer—is not your immediate business knowledge. Instead, your value is your intellectual ability and flexibility; your knowledge of the fundamentals, of the basic theories, of their application, and of cutting-edge ideas; your human skills, team skills, and sales skills; and so on. Some of these skills are innate, but most can be taught or at least improved upon by studying. In the end, it is your versatility and curiosity, your ability to generalize and synthesize, your

| Some Examples of: | |
What Business School Teaches Better Than Practice	What Practice Teaches Better Than Business School
General, universal knowledge	Job-specific knowledge
Concepts of business	The specific business
General tools (statistics, data, economics, etc.)	Specific tools (e.g., a particular accounting system)
Marketing methods	The company's specific product or service marketing
Method of thinking	Methods of *this* company's practice
Concepts of ideas for the next 20 years	Implementation of ideas from the last 10 years
Knowledge for a lifetime	Knowledge tailored to this year's business climate
Leadership principles and theories	Learning how to lead a particular set of people
Source of conflict	Conflict resolution with a specific person
Learning by study	Learning by doing
Reflection	Action
Selling principles	Selling the company's specific product or service
Negotiation principles	Negotiating with specific customers
"Forests"	"Trees"

Exhibit 1: *Advantages and Disadvantages of Business Schools over Business Practice.*

ability to apply theories to practice, and your talent for bringing a novel perspective to specific problems that will allow your MBA to be of value for you for many years to come.

Your First Finance Course and Student Heterogeneity

There is another issue in your introductory finance class that may initially make you unhappy—and it is important that you realize why this is so. Chances are that you will find yourself in a classroom with considerable heterogeneity in student preparation. Many students will find the tempo of the first finance course too slow, and other students will find it too fast. The reason is that as many as half the students in business school may come from a finance-related job background. Usually, their work experience will not have left them with knowledge solid enough that they can skip the finance core course. Still, their background makes it much easier for them to take in new finance-related teaching. Other students may not have seen an equation for many years in their work. It will be a challenge for such students simply to keep up. If you are one of them, you will initially feel overwhelmed by your class experience. (And you will likely not do as well on the early exams—the world is simply not fair.) But let me advise patience, practice, and reflection: Your new knowledge will eventually fall into place, and you can do well *in the end*. Some of my best and brightest students felt frustrated during the course, but they kept at it, studied twice as hard, and ended up at the top of their classes. Struggling and anxiety along the way are necessary, maybe even desirable, and in the end, unavoidable.

Before you blame your instructor for all your early frustrations, please contemplate how you would gear the introductory finance class toward the different kinds of students in your class. There are no easy solutions. It is generally agreed that teaching introductory finance in a business school is among the most difficult assignments an instructor can take on. There are different levels of student preparedness, and there is a large amount of material that absolutely cannot be skipped. Again, recruiters expect students to have a solid grasp of the finance basics and often ask questions that could go right onto the midterm or final. As an instructor, after having blamed the situation, let me not disavow our biggest responsibility: We must make the first finance course a surmountable challenge for *all* motivated students, regardless of background. Every unprepared student must be able to acquire a solid finance background; every prepared student must still find the class useful. It is not our duty to be entertaining or even to be liked. In fact, a recent study at the U.S. Air Force Academy has shown that students randomly enrolled in classes did better in subsequent courses if their first instructor was less generous in grading and less well liked.

The Business School Rankings

Now indulge me for a moment. If you are an MBA student, you are surely familiar with the biannual influential *Business Week* (*BW*) rankings, first published in 1998. This rankings issue has become one of *BW*'s top sellers. Unfortunately, the quality of the *BW* rankings is only mediocre. Worse, their influence on business education has been both enormous and negative.

The not-so-secret sauce in *BW* rankings is what they describe as "customer satisfaction" measures of students and recruiters. But do these measures really make sense for a ranking?

- Is student happiness really an appropriate measure of student education? For example, consider another prominent survey: *Playboy*'s party school rankings. How do you think students at a perennially top-rated school (California State University at Chico) would respond? They would probably rate their educational satisfaction very highly—but this does not necessarily make Cal State Chico a great school.

- Is recruiter evaluation the appropriate measure of student education? Most recruiters are themselves alums of *one* of the schools they are asked to rank. (They also see themselves reflected in the students from their own alma maters.) Most business school alums have never studied at any school other than their own—a fact that naturally makes them relatively ill-equipped to make comparisons. Because larger schools have more alums that are sampled, the size of the alum pool ends up being the primary predictor of "recruiter opinion" in the *BW* survey. The result is inevitable: The average recruiter ranks his or her own alma mater highest (or at least very highly). As a consequence, the correlation between the historical size of a school's graduating classes and its *BW* ranking is very high.

- Can *BW* expect truthful answers? It turns out that all schools, students, and alums are now catering to and manipulating the *BW* rankings. Students and alums now know that if they do not rank their own schools highly, the values of their degrees will go down. And at almost every school, some faculty member will explain this to those students who have not yet understood this basic fact.

At best, I would consider the *BW* rankings today to be measures of familiarity and size. But as a measure of educational quality, I can hardly imagine a worse methodology. Still, let's pretend for a moment that this is not the case. There is an even more fundamental error in these rankings: They treat education as if it were a consumption good sold by (business school) vendors. *It is not!* Instead, education is something that is coproduced by the school *and the student*.

See, the usefulness of the MBA degree is largely determined by the depth of student engagement. A student who coasts through classes that were selected to be easy and entertaining will learn little, no matter how good the school is. Yes, there are some quality differences, but the *BW* rankings do not fairly reflect them and they are not very large. Nowadays, most business schools teach similar curricula. In my opinion, my book is just as suitable to the #1-ranked school as it is to the #100-ranked school. My personal guess is that the educational quality difference (and average student quality difference) between the #1 school and the #10 school is quite small (as it would be between #10 and #30, or between #30 and #100). In contrast, there is great variation among students in the same school. *The variation in what any one individual gets out of a particular MBA program just swamps the average quality variations across schools.*

Ultimately, it is up to you to make your education top-ranked. Fortunately, although deciding on the right school is a tough problem, there are really many good choices to pick from. Many schools that never show up in these rankings offer excellent business educations today. Again, by selection of classes and instructors, you can easily get a better business education at the #100 school than many students get at the #1 school.

But not all is well. One worrisome trend is that in their quest to improve on their *Business Week* rankings, many schools have begun to make curriculum changes that I deem to be counterproductive. They are tempted to substitute happiness over content, at least at the margin—but good teaching is neither an entertainment nor a popularity contest. The material has to be tough and challenging, even if it makes the experience less fun. Perhaps as a result of curriculum changes over time, I have begun to hear complaints from more and more top recruiters these days that a good undergraduate or master of finance student can be as good at finance as the (twice-as-expensive) MBA counterpart. This needs to change. The answer must be to make the MBA curriculum tougher and more rigorous again. If MBA students want to get paid twice the money, they have to be twice as good! They can't have cake and eat it, too.

Bon Voyage

Our book has covered the principles of finance in some depth and breadth. You should be very well prepared now for the next steps in your finance/business education. You can probably choose your next courses á la carte: investments, derivatives, advanced corporate finance, fixed income, financial institutions, international finance, or something else. If you are still curious to learn more from or about me, then you can also visit the book's website at book.ivo-welch.info.

By now you should no longer be surprised by one of my quirkier obsessions. It was as important for me to try to teach you how to approach problems as it was to teach you finance. When you are confronted with a new problem, please think in terms of the easiest numerical example that you can come up with. Only gradually work your way up. That is, address your full problem only after you have understood simpler examples. Hey, you may not even have to remember any of the formulas in this book—given time, you should now be able to "reinvent" them. This would be my greatest victory.

I have enjoyed writing this book in the same way that I enjoy writing my academic research papers, and pretty much for the same reason: It has been like solving an intriguing puzzle that no one else has figured out in quite the same way—a particular way to see and explain finance. Of course, writing it has taken me far longer than I had anticipated—almost ten years by now.

But my effort will have been worth it if you have learned from this book. If you have studied it, you should now know about 90% of what I know about finance. Interestingly, there were a number of topics that I thought I had understood, but had not—and it was only my having to explain them to you that clarified them for me, too. And this brings me to a key point that I want to leave you with—never be afraid to ask questions, even about first principles. To do so is not a sign of stupidity—on the contrary, it is often a sign of deepening awareness and understanding.

I have no illusions: You will not remember all the fine details in this book as time passes—I know I won't. But more than the details, I hope that I will have left you with an appreciation for the big ideas, an arsenal of tools, a method for approaching novel problems, and a new perspective. You can now think like a financier.

Ivo Welch
UCLA
Fall 2011

Appendix Chapter. Technical Background

General Mathematical and Statistical Background

- Finding a base:

$$3^2 = 9 \qquad \Leftrightarrow \quad 3 = 9^{1/2}$$

$$x^a = b \quad \Leftrightarrow \quad x = b^{1/a}$$

  A power of $1/2$ is also equivalent to the square root operation.

- Finding an exponent:

$$3^2 = 9 \Leftrightarrow 2 = \frac{\ln(9)}{\ln(3)}$$

$$a^x = b \Leftrightarrow x = \frac{\ln(b)}{\ln(a)}$$

  (Instead of the natural log ln, you could use any other log, too.)

- Summation notation:

$$\sum_{i=1}^{N} f(i) = f(1) + f(2) + \cdots + f(N)$$

  This should be read as the "sum over all i from 1 to N." There are N terms in this sum. i is not a real variable: It is simply a dummy counter to abbreviate the notation. When 1 and N are omitted, it usually means "over all possible i."

- Summation rules:

$$\sum_{i=1}^{N} [a \cdot f(i) + b] = [a \cdot f(1) + b] + [a \cdot f(2) + b] + \cdots + [a \cdot f(N) + b]$$

$$= a \cdot \left[\sum_{i=1}^{N} f(i) \right] + N \cdot b$$

For example,

$$\sum_{i=1}^{3} \left[5 \cdot i^i + 2 \right] \quad = \quad [5 \cdot 1^1 + 2] + [5 \cdot 2^2 + 2] + [5 \cdot 3^3 + 2]$$

$$= 7 + 22 + 137 = 166$$

$$= 5 \cdot \left(\sum_{i=1}^{3} i^i \right) + 3 \cdot 2 = 5 \cdot \left(1^1 + 2^2 + 3^3 \right) + 6$$

$$= 5 \cdot 32 + 6 = 166$$

- Linear functions: A function $\mathscr{L}(\,\cdot\,)$ is called a linear function if and only if $\mathscr{L}(a + b \cdot x) = a + \mathscr{L}(b \cdot x) = a + b \cdot \mathscr{L}(x)$, where a and b are constants.

  Here is an illustration. The (weighted) average is a linear function. For example, start with (5, 10, 15) as a data series. The average is 10. Pick a = 2 and b = 3. For averaging to be a linear function, it must be that

$$\text{Average}(2 + 3 \cdot \text{Data}) = 2 + 3 \cdot \text{Average}(\text{Data})$$

  Let's try this—the left-hand side (LHS) would become the average of (17, 32, 47), which is 32. The right-hand side (RHS) would become $2 + 3 \cdot 10 = 32$. It works: Averaging indeed behaves like a linear function. In contrast, the square root is not a linear function, because $\sqrt{-2 + 3 \cdot 9} \neq -2 + 3 \cdot \sqrt{9}$. The LHS is 5, the RHS is 7. Linear functions are very important in financial economics:

  - Similar to averaging, expected values are linear functions. This is what has permitted us to interchange expectations and linear functions:

$$\mathscr{E}(a + b \cdot X) = a + b \cdot \mathscr{E}(X)$$

    This will be expounded in the next section.

  - The rate of return on a portfolio is also a linear function of the investment weights. For example, a portfolio rate of return may be $r(x) = 20\% \cdot r_x + 80\% \cdot r_y$, where r_x is the rate of return on the component into which you invested \$20. For $r(x)$ to be a linear function, we need

$$2 + 3 \cdot r(x) = r(2 + 3 \cdot x)$$
$$a + b \cdot r(x) = r(a + b \cdot x)$$

  Substitute in

$$2 + 3 \cdot (20\% \cdot r_x + 80\% \cdot r_y) = 20\% \cdot (2 + 3 \cdot r_x) + 80\% \cdot (2 + 3 \cdot r_y)$$

  Both sides simplify to $2 + 60\% \cdot r_x + 240\% \cdot r_y$, so our statement is true and a portfolio return is indeed a linear function.

  However, not all functions are linear. The variance is not a linear function, because

$$\mathscr{V}\!ar(a + b \cdot X) \neq a + b \cdot \mathscr{V}\!ar(X)$$

  You will confirm this in the next section.

Q A.1. If $(1+x)^{10} = (1+50\%) = 1.5$, what is x?

Q A.2. If $(1+10\%)^x = (1+50\%) = 1.5$, what is x?

Q A.3. Are $\displaystyle\sum_{i=1}^{N} x_i$ and $\displaystyle\sum_{s=1}^{N} x_s$ the same?

Q A.4. In $\displaystyle\sum_{x=a}^{b} f(x,y)$, what are the variables?

Q A.5. Write out and compute $\displaystyle\sum_{x=1}^{3}(3+5\cdot x)$. Is x a variable or just a placeholder to write the expression more conveniently?

Q A.6. Write out and compute $\left(\displaystyle\sum_{y=1}^{3} 3\right) + 5\cdot\left(\displaystyle\sum_{y=1}^{3} y\right)$. Compare the result to the previous expression.

Q A.7. Is $\displaystyle\sum_{i=1}^{3}(i\cdot i)$ the same as $\left(\displaystyle\sum_{i=1}^{3} i\right)\cdot\left(\displaystyle\sum_{i=1}^{3} i\right)$?

Laws of Probability, Portfolios, and Expectations

Let's go over the algebra of probabilities and portfolios, which you had to use in the investments chapters. It is presented in a more mathematical fashion than it was in the chapters, which you may find easier or harder, depending on your background. If you have a statistics background, realize that our book's notation is simplified, because we do not place tildes over random variables.

Single Random Variables

The **law of expectations** for single random variables are as follows:

- An expectation is defined as

$$\mathcal{E}(X) = \sum_{i=1}^{N} \mathcal{P}rob(i) \cdot [X = X(i)]$$

  It is basically a probability-weighted average.

- The expected value of a linear transformation (a and b are known constants):

$$\mathcal{E}(a \cdot X + b) = a \cdot \mathcal{E}(X) + b \tag{A.1}$$

To see this, consider a fair coin that can be either 1 or 2. Say $a = 4$ and $b = 10$. In this case, the LHS is $\mathcal{E}(a \cdot X + b) = \mathcal{E}(4 \cdot X + 10) = 0.5 \cdot (4 \cdot 1 + 10) + 0.5 \cdot (4 \cdot 2 + 10) = 0.5 \cdot 14 + 0.5 \cdot 18 = 16$. The RHS is $4 \cdot (0.5 \cdot 1 + 0.5 \cdot 2) + 10 = 16$. This all worked because expectation is a linear operator. (It is a fancy way of saying that it is a summation, which allows you to regroup the summation terms of the linear combination $a \cdot X + b$ inside the expectation, which is also a probability-weighted linear combination.) A little more generally, you could rename X as $f(X)$, so

$$\mathcal{E}(a \cdot f(x) + b) = a \cdot \mathcal{E}(f(x)) + b$$

However, you cannot always "pull" expectations in, so $\mathcal{E}(f(x))$ is not always $f(\mathcal{E}(X))$. For example, if $f(x) = x^2$, it is the case that

$$\mathcal{E}(X \cdot X) \neq \mathcal{E}(X) \cdot \mathcal{E}(X)$$

To see this, reconsider the fair "1 or 2" coin. The LHS is $\mathcal{E}(X^2) = 0.5 \cdot (1 \cdot 1) + 0.5 \cdot (2 \cdot 2) = 2.5$, but the RHS is $[\mathcal{E}(X)]^2 = (0.5 \cdot 1 + 0.5 \cdot 2)^2 = (1.5^2) = 2.25$.

- Definition of variance:

$$\mathcal{V}\!ar(X) = \mathcal{E}\left([X - \mathcal{E}(X)]^2 \right)$$

It is sometimes easier to rewrite this formula as $\mathcal{V}\!ar(X) = \mathcal{E}(X^2) - [\mathcal{E}(X)]^2$. Let me show you that this works. For our fair 1 or 2 coin example, the variance according to the main formula is $0.5 \cdot (1 - 1.5)^2 + 0.5 \cdot (2 - 1.5)^2 = 0.25$. For the second formula, we just computed $\mathcal{E}(X^2) = 2.5$ and $[\mathcal{E}(X)]^2 = 2.25$. Subtracting these terms yields the same 0.25.

- Definition of a standard deviation:

$$\mathcal{S}\!dv(X) = \sqrt{\mathcal{V}\!ar(X)}$$

- The variance of a linear combination (where a and b are known constants):

$$\mathcal{V}\!ar(a \cdot X + b) = a^2 \cdot \mathcal{V}\!ar(X) \tag{A.2}$$

For our fair 1 or 2 coin example, with $a = 4$ and $b = 10$, the LHS is $0.5 \cdot [(4 \cdot 1 + 10) - 16]^2 + 0.5 + 0.5 \cdot [(4 \cdot 2 + 10) - 16]^2 = 0.5 \cdot [-2]^2 + 0.5 \cdot [2]^2 = 4$. The RHS is $4^2 \cdot 0.25 = 4$.

Here is an extended illustration. A coin, whose outcome we call X, has 4 and 8 written on its two sides. These two outcomes can be written as $4 \cdot i$, where i is either 1 or 2. Therefore, the expected value of X is

$$\mathcal{E}(X) = \sum_{i=1}^{2} \mathcal{P}rob(X = (4 \cdot i)) \cdot (4 \cdot i)$$

$$= \mathcal{P}rob(X = 4) \cdot (4) + \mathcal{P}rob(X = 8) \cdot (8)$$

$$= 50\% \cdot 4 + 50\% \cdot 8 \qquad = 6$$

$$\mathcal{V}ar(X) = \sum_{i=1}^{2} \mathcal{P}rob(X = (4 \cdot i)) \cdot [(4 \cdot i) - 6]^2$$

$$= \mathcal{P}rob(X = 4) \cdot (4 - 6)^2 + \mathcal{P}rob(X = 8) \cdot (8 - 6)^2$$

$$= 50\% \cdot 4 + 50\% \cdot 4 \qquad = 4$$

The standard deviation is the square root of the variance, here 2.

$\mathcal{E}(X^2)$ is, of course, not the same as $[\mathcal{E}(X)]^2 = [3]^2 = 9$, because

$$\mathcal{E}(X^2) = \sum_{i=1}^{2} \mathcal{P}rob(X = (2 \cdot i)) \cdot (2 \cdot i)^2$$

$$= \mathcal{P}rob(X = 2) \cdot (2^2) + \mathcal{P}rob(X = 4) \cdot (4^2)$$

$$= 50\% \cdot 4 + 50\% \cdot 16 = 10$$

Now work with a linear transformation of the X, say, $Z = \$2.5 \cdot X + \$10$. This is a fundamental operation in finance, because the rates of return on portfolios are such linear transformations. For example, if you own 25% in A and 75% in B, you will earn $0.25 \cdot r_A + 0.75 \cdot r_B$. Thus,

$\mathcal{P}rob$	Coin	X	Z
$1/2$	Heads	4	$20
$1/2$	Tails	8	$30

You want to convince yourself that the expected value of Z, defined as $\$2.5 \cdot X + \$10$, is $\$2.5 \cdot \mathcal{E}(X) + \$10 = \$25$. First, compute by hand the expected value the long way from Z,

$$\mathcal{E}(Z) = \sum_{i=1}^{2} \mathcal{P}rob(X = (4 \cdot i), \text{ i.e., same as } Z = \$2.5 \cdot X + \$10) \cdot (Z_i)$$

$$= \mathcal{P}rob(X = 4, \text{ i.e., same as } Z = \$20) \cdot (\$20)$$

$$+ \mathcal{P}rob(X = 8, \text{ i.e., same as } Z = \$30) \cdot (\$30)$$

$$= 50\% \cdot \$20 + 50\% \cdot \$30 = \$25$$

Unlike the mean (the expected value), the variance is *not* a linear function. The variance of $Z = \$2.5 \cdot X + \$10$ is *not* $\$2.5 \cdot \mathcal{V}ar(X) + \$10 = \$2.5 \cdot 4 + \$10 = \$20$. Instead, $\mathcal{V}ar(Z) = \mathcal{V}ar(a \cdot X + b) = a^2 \cdot \mathcal{V}ar(X) = (\$2.5)^2 \cdot \mathcal{V}ar(X) = \$\$6.25 \cdot 4 = \$\$25$. You can confirm this working with Z directly:

$$\mathcal{V}ar(Z) \quad = \quad \sum_{i=1}^{2} \mathcal{P}rob(X = (4 \cdot i)) \cdot [(Z_i) - \mathcal{E}(Z)]^2$$

$$= \quad \mathcal{P}rob(X = 4 \text{ , i.e., same as } Z = \$20) \cdot (\$20 - \$25)^2$$

$$+ \quad \mathcal{P}rob(X = 8 \text{ , i.e., same as } Z = \$30) \cdot (\$30 - \$25)^2$$

$$= \quad 50\% \cdot (\$5)^2 + 50\% \cdot (\$5)^2 = \$\$25$$

The standard deviation of Z is therefore $\sqrt{\$\$25} = \$5$.

Let us quickly confirm Formula A.1 for $Z = \$2.5 \cdot X + \$10$:

$$\$25 \quad = \quad \mathcal{E}(\$2.5 \cdot X + \$10) \quad = \quad \$2.5 \cdot \mathcal{E}(X) + \$10 \quad = \quad \$2.5 \cdot 6 + \$10 \quad = \quad \$25$$

$$\mathcal{E}(Z) \quad = \quad \mathcal{E}(a \cdot X + b) \quad = \quad a \cdot \mathcal{E}(X) + b$$

Let us also quickly confirm Formula A.2:

$$\$\$25 \quad = \quad \mathcal{V}ar(\$2.5 \cdot X + \$10) \quad = \quad \$2.5^2 \cdot \mathcal{V}ar(X) \quad = \quad \$\$6.25 \cdot 4 \quad = \quad \$\$25$$

$$\mathcal{V}ar(Z) \quad = \quad \mathcal{V}ar(a \cdot X + b) \quad = \quad a^2 \cdot \mathcal{V}ar(X)$$

Q A.8. What is the expected value and standard deviation of a bet B that pays off the number of points on a fair die, squared? For example, if the die lands on 3, you receive $9.

Q A.9. Assume that you have to pay $30, but you receive twice the outcome of the bet B from Question A.8. This is a new bet, called C. That is, your payoff is $C = -\$30 + 2 \cdot B$. What is the expected payoff and risk of your position? (Suggestion: Make your life easy by working with your answers from Question A.8.)

Portfolios

A portfolio is a set of weights in possible investment assets. That is, for a set of assets i, each known investment is usually denoted as w_i. The rate of return on a portfolio is

$$r_P = \sum_i w_i \cdot r_i$$

where r_i is the security return on security i. Portfolio returns are the weighted sum of multiple random variables.

• Portfolio return expectations:

$$\mathcal{E}\left(\sum_i w_i \cdot r_i\right) = \sum_i w_i \cdot \mathcal{E}(r_i)$$

Although the weights are fixed and known constants, they cannot be pulled out of the summation, because they are indexed by i (each could be different from the others).

• Portfolio return riskiness:

$$\text{Var}\left(\sum_i w_i \cdot r_i\right) = \sum_{i=1}^{N}\left\{\sum_{j=1}^{N}\left[w_i \cdot w_j \cdot \text{Cov}(r_i, r_j)\right]\right\}$$

$$= \sum_{i=1}^{N}\sum_{j=1}^{N}\left[w_i \cdot w_j \cdot \text{Cov}(r_i, r_j)\right]$$

Of course, for intuition, one would often compute the standard deviation by taking the square-root of the variance.

Here is an illustration. A coin toss outcome is a random variable, T, and it will return either \$2 (heads) or \$4 (tails). You have to pay \$2 to receive this bet. This looks like a good bet: The mean rate of return on each coin toss, $\mathcal{E}(r_T)$, is 50%. The variance on *each* coin toss is

$$\text{Var}(r_T) = \tfrac{1}{2}\cdot(0\% - 50\%)^2 + \tfrac{1}{2}\cdot(100\% - 50\%)^2 = 2{,}500\%\% = 0.25$$

Therefore, the standard deviation of each coin toss is $\sqrt{2{,}500\%\%} = 50\%$.

Now, bet on two independent such coin toss outcomes. Say you invest \$10 on the first bet ($w_1 = \$10$) and \$20 on the second bet ($w_2 = \$20$). Your portfolio is $\{w_1, w_2\} = \{\$10, \$20\}$. You can also compute your portfolio's investment weights instead of its absolute investments.

$$w_1 = \frac{\$10}{\$30} \approx 0.33 \quad\text{and}\quad w_2 = (1 - w_1) = \frac{\$20}{\$30} \approx 0.67$$

Your overall portfolio rate of return is

$$r = \sum_{i=1}^{2} w_i \cdot r_i$$

We can now use the formulas to compute your expected rate of return ($\mathcal{E}(r)$) and risk ($\mathcal{S}dv(r)$). To compute your expected rate of return, use

$$\mathcal{E}(r) = \sum_{i=1}^{2} w_i \cdot \mathcal{E}(r_i) = w_1 \cdot \mathcal{E}(r_1) + w_2 \cdot \mathcal{E}(r_2)$$

$$= \tfrac{1}{3}\cdot(50\%) + \tfrac{2}{3}\cdot(50\%) = 50\%$$

(Recall that an expectation is a linear operator, that is, a summation. A portfolio is a summation, too. Because both are ultimately nothing but summations, you can regroup terms, which means that the above formula works.) To compute your variance, use

$$\text{Var}(r) = \sum_{i=1}^{2}\sum_{j=1}^{2} w_i \cdot w_j \cdot \text{Cov}(r_i, r_j)$$

$$= w_1 \cdot w_1 \cdot \text{Cov}(r_1, r_1) + w_1 \cdot w_2 \cdot \text{Cov}(r_1, r_2) + w_2 \cdot w_1 \cdot \text{Cov}(r_2, r_1) + w_2 \cdot w_2 \cdot \text{Cov}(r_2, r_2)$$

$$= w_1^2 \cdot \text{Cov}(r_1, r_1) + 2 \cdot w_1 \cdot w_2 \cdot \text{Cov}(r_1, r_2) + w_2^2 \cdot \text{Cov}(r_2, r_2)$$

$$= \quad w_1^2 \cdot Var(r_1) + 2 \cdot w_1 \cdot w_2 \cdot Cov(r_1, r_2) + w_2^2 \cdot Var(r_2)$$

$$= \quad (1/3)^2 \cdot Var(r_1) + 2 \cdot w_1 \cdot w_2 \cdot 0 + (2/3)^2 \cdot Var(r_2)$$

$$= \quad (1/9) \cdot Var(r_1) + (4/9) \cdot Var(r_2)$$

$$= \quad (1/9) \cdot 0.25 + (4/9) \cdot 0.25$$

$$\approx \quad 0.1389$$

The standard deviation is therefore $\sqrt{0.1389} \approx 37.3\%$. This is lower than the 50% that a single coin toss would provide you with.

Q A.10. Repeat the example, but assume that you invest \$15 into each coin toss rather than \$10 and \$20, respectively. Would you expect the risk to be higher or lower? (Hint: What happens if you choose a portfolio that invests more and more into just one of the two bets?)

Cumulative Normal Distribution Table

z	$\mathcal{N}(z)$	z	$\mathcal{N}(z)$	z	$\mathcal{N}(z)$	z	$\mathcal{N}(z)$	z	$\mathcal{N}(z)$	z	$\mathcal{N}(z)$
−4.0	0.00003										
−3.5	0.00023										
−3.0	0.0013	−2.0	0.0228	−1.0	0.1587	0.0	0.5000	1.0	0.8413	2.0	0.9772
−2.9	0.0019	−1.9	0.0287	−0.9	0.1841	0.1	0.5398	1.1	0.8643	2.1	0.9821
−2.8	0.0026	−1.8	0.0359	−0.8	0.2119	0.2	0.5793	1.2	0.8849	2.2	0.9861
−2.7	0.0035	−1.7	0.0446	−0.7	0.2420	0.3	0.6179	1.3	0.9032	2.3	0.9893
−2.6	0.0047	−1.6	0.0548	−0.6	0.2743	0.4	0.6554	1.4	0.9192	2.4	0.9918
−2.5	0.0062	−1.5	0.0668	−0.5	0.3085	0.5	0.6915	1.5	0.9332	2.5	0.9938
−2.4	0.0082	−1.4	0.0808	−0.4	0.3446	0.6	0.7257	1.6	0.9452	2.6	0.9953
−2.3	0.0107	−1.3	0.0968	−0.3	0.3821	0.7	0.7580	1.7	0.9554	2.7	0.9965
−2.2	0.0139	−1.2	0.1151	−0.2	0.4207	0.8	0.7881	1.8	0.9641	2.8	0.9974
−2.1	0.0179	−1.1	0.1357	−0.1	0.4602	0.9	0.8159	1.9	0.9713	2.9	0.9981
										3.5	0.99977
										4.0	0.99997

Exhibit 1: *Cumulative Normal Distribution Table.* Normal score (z) versus standardized normal cumulative distribution probability $\mathcal{N}(z)$

Exhibit 1 allows you to determine the probability that an outcome X will be less than a prespecified value x, when standardized into the score z, if X (and thus z follow a

normal distribution). For example, if the mean is 15 and the standard deviation is 5, an outcome of X = 10 is 1 standard deviation below the mean. This standardized score can be obtained by computing $z(x) = [x - \mathcal{E}(x)]/\mathcal{S}dv(x) = (x - 15)/5 = (10 - 15)/5 = (-1)$. This table then indicates that the probability that the outcome of X (i.e., drawn from this distribution with mean 15 and standard deviation 5) will be less than 10 (i.e., less than its score of z = −1) is 15.87%.

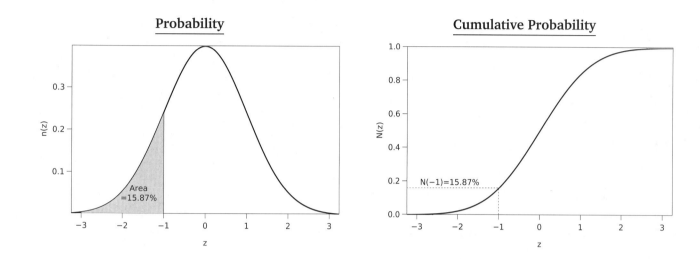

Exhibit 2: *The Normal Distribution.*

Exhibit 2 shows what the table represents. Exhibit 2(a) shows the classical bell curve. Recall that at z = −1, the table gives $\mathcal{N}(z = -1) = 15.87\%$. This 15.87% is the shaded area under the curve up to and including z = −1. Exhibit 2(b) just plots the values in the table itself, that is, the area under the graph to the left of each value from Exhibit 2(a).

If you ever need to approximate the cumulative normal distribution in a spreadsheet, you can use the built-in function **normsdist**.

Keywords

Law of expectation, 697.   Normal distribution, 703.

Answers

Q A.1 $x \approx 4.138\%$. Check: $(1 + 4.138\%)^{10} \approx 1.5$.

Q A.2 $x \approx 4.254$. Check: $1.1^{4.254} \approx 1.5$.

Q A.3 Yes! i and s are not variables, but notation!

Q A.4 x is not a variable, but simply a notation shortcut. Written out, the expression is $f(a, y) + f(a + 1, y) + \ldots + f(b - 1, y) + f(b, y)$, which makes it clear that a, y, and b are the variables.

Q A.5 The expression is

$$\sum_{x=1}^{3}(3 + 5 \cdot x) = (3 + 5 \cdot 1) + (3 + 5 \cdot 2) + (3 + 5 \cdot 3)$$

$$= 8 + 13 + 18 = 39$$

x is not a variable. It is simply a counter dummy used for writing convenience. It is not a part of the expression itself.

Q A.6 The expression is

$$\left(\sum_{y=1}^{3} 3\right) + 5 \cdot \left(\sum_{y=1}^{3} y\right) = (3 + 3 + 3) + 5 \cdot (1 + 2 + 3) = 39$$

The result is the same. This is an example of why $\sum_{i} a + b \cdot x = \left(\sum_{i} a\right) + b \cdot \sum_{i} x$.

Q A.7 No. The two expressions are

$$\sum_{i=1}^{3}(i \cdot i) = 1 + 4 + 9 = 14$$

$$\left(\sum_{i=1}^{3} i\right) \cdot \left(\sum_{i=1}^{3} i\right) = (1 + 2 + 3) \cdot (1 + 2 + 3) = 36$$

The two are not the same! Thus, be careful not to try to pull out multiplying i's! You can only pull out constants, not counters. Incidentally, this is also why $\mathcal{E}(X^2) \neq \mathcal{E}(X)^2$, as stated in the next section.

Q A.8 The expected value is

$$\mathcal{E}(B) = (1/6) \cdot \$1 + (1/6) \cdot \$4 + (1/6) \cdot \$9$$
$$+ (1/6) \cdot \$16 + (1/6) \cdot \$25 + (1/6) \cdot \$36 \approx \$15.17$$

The variance is

$$\begin{aligned}
\mathcal{V}\!ar(B) = \ & (1/6) \cdot (\$1 - \$15.17)^2 + (1/6) \cdot (\$4 - \$15.17)^2 \\
& + (1/6) \cdot (\$9 - \$15.17)^2 + (1/6) \cdot (\$16 - \$15.17)^2 \\
& + (1/6) \cdot (\$25 - \$15.17)^2 + (1/6) \cdot (\$36 - \$15.17)^2 \\
\approx\ & \$\$149.14
\end{aligned}$$

The standard deviation is therefore

$$\mathcal{S}\!dv(B) = \sqrt{\mathcal{V}\!ar(B)} \approx \sqrt{\$\$149.14} \approx \$12.21$$

Q A.9 You expect to receive

$$\begin{aligned}
\mathcal{E}(C) &= -\$30 + 2 \cdot \mathcal{E}(B) \approx -\$30 + 2 \cdot \$15.17 &\approx\ & \$0.34 \\
\mathcal{V}\!ar(C) &= 2^2 \cdot \mathcal{V}\!ar(B) \approx 4 \cdot \$\$149.14 &=\ & \$\$595.56 \\
\mathcal{S}\!dv(C) &= \sqrt{\mathcal{V}\!ar(C)} &\approx\ & \$24.42
\end{aligned}$$

Q A.10 Your investment weights are now $w_1 = w_2 = 0.5$. The mean rate of return remains the same 50%. The variance of the rate of return is computed similarly to the example in the text:

$$\mathcal{V}\!ar(r) = (1/2)^2 \cdot 0.25 + (1/2)^2 \cdot 0.25 = 0.125$$

Therefore, the risk (standard deviation) is 35.35%. This is lower than it was when you put more weight on one of the coin tosses. This makes sense: As you put more and more into one of the two coin tosses, you lose the benefit of diversification!

Index

A blue page number is the index where the term is defined as a keyword. Boldfaced entries contain the word unusually often.

If you were looking for a term that should have been in the index but which was not (or if an index entry did not point to the right page), please feel free to send the author an email to request a change for the next edition of the book.